The Literature of American History

AMERICAN CLASSICS

THE LITERATURE
OF AMERICAN HISTORY

A Bibliographical Guide

IN WHICH
THE SCOPE, CHARACTER,
AND COMPARATIVE WORTH OF BOOKS
IN SELECTED LISTS
ARE SET FORTH IN BRIEF NOTES
BY CRITICS OF AUTHORITY

Edited by
J. N. LARNED

FREDERICK UNGAR PUBLISHING CO.
NEW YORK

Republished 1966 in the American Classics series

Reprinted from the edition of 1902

Printed in the United States of America

Library of Congress Catalog Card No. 66-22990

INTRODUCTORY

ONLY those who have to do with the work of public libraries know how much there is of the desire for substantial knowledge among people who can satisfy it nowhere if not at those libraries, and how much such readers are misled towards books which are obsolete, or shoddy-made, or otherwise unprofitable, missing the ones that would instruct them most and inspire them best. All that librarians can do to light the way of the seeker to the worthiest literature is generally being done, with anxious and inventive zeal; but the utmost they are able to accomplish in their catalogues, without help from special students in a thousand different regions of knowledge, answers to the need of common students scarcely more than a railway map for travelers as compared with a Baedeker guide. The case is one that calls for information to be given with particularity and discrimination, by critics of recognized acumen and character, whose judgments are set forth with no claim to finality, but stand open to revision as error is detected or new truth disclosed.

An early perception of this need led the Society for Political Education, in New York, to publish in 1880 a list of books in political science recommended by Professor William G. Sumner, Mr. David A. Wells, and other special students in that department of knowledge. In 1891 this little bibliography was amplified, under the editorship of Messrs. R. R. Bowker and George Iles, who were assisted in the selection and annotation of titles by many well-known publicists and economists, including James Bryce, David A. Wells, Andrew Dickson White, Horace White, Professors Felix Adler, Davis R. Dewey, E. R. A. Seligman, Richmond Mayo Smith, and others. The work thus enlarged was published by the same society as "The Reader's Guide in Economic, Social, and Political Science," and proved to be a valuable and welcome aid.

With his understanding of the need of such "guides" much deepened by the experience obtained in this work, Mr. Iles brought the subject into discussion at a meeting of the American Library Association in 1892, by reading a paper on "The Evaluation of Literature," in which he urged the Association to undertake the organization and execution of some plan "which shall give an inquirer in any specialty of literature, at every public library, at all times, the services of the best informed and fairest adviser to be had in the Union." "A merchant or banker," said Mr. Iles, "when he has taken an inventory of his assets, is not content with a mere enumeration of them; he deems a bare list as of no worth whatever until each item has been carefully valued. So, I take it, the trustees of literature will enter upon a doubled usefulness when they can set before the public not catalogues merely, but also a judicious discrimination of the more from the less valuable stores in their keeping."

The suggestions of Mr. Iles were discussed with warm interest, and were referred to a special committee for more careful consideration; but the Association had many things to do with slender means, and it hesitated to enter on a project of labor and expense which showed no bounds. Then Mr. Iles began to give practical effect to the proposition he had advanced. Produced at his expense, and mostly by his own exertions, the American Library Association published in 1895 an exceedingly useful "List of Books for Girls and Women and their Clubs, with descriptive and critical notes and a list of periodicals, and hints for girls' and women's clubs; edited by Augusta H. Leypoldt and George Iles." This was followed in 1897 by an "Annotated Bibliography of Fine Art," in which a list of works on painting, sculpture, architecture, and arts of decoration and illustration, was selected and critically annotated by Mr.

iii

INTRODUCTORY

Russell Sturgis, and a list of works on music by Mr. Henry E. Krehbiel. Both of those gentlemen had been contributors to the "List of Books for Girls and Women"; in the Bibliography of Fine Art they expanded their two departments to a range which included about a thousand volumes. The work was edited by Mr. Iles, and published under the auspices and for the benefit of the Library Association, without cost to that body for the manuscripts.

Again addressing the Association, in September, 1896, on what he described as "The Appraisal of Literature," Mr. Iles placed the subject in a very impressive light. "One small class in the community," he said, "has the good fortune always to have the best reasons in reading and studying its books. The young men and women in our colleges and universities enjoy manifold advantages of training, discipline, and culture; among all these benefits one of the chief is their economy of time and attention through reading and studying only the best books. Thanks to the guidance of trustworthy judges, they can shun the output of the mere mechanic of the pen; one first-hand work of authority judiciously supplements another; the defects and errors chargeable even to the greatest writers are pointed out, and, where a subject is brought down to date in periodicals, the best of these are indicated. Popular education will receive an immense impulse when guidance of this kind is rendered the plain people, not only by the university professor, but by everybody else able and willing to give it."

Publication of the "Annotated Bibliography of Fine Art" was soon followed by proposals from Mr. Iles to the American Library Association which contemplated the undertaking of an "appraisal of literature" in the great and important field of American history, and provision was made by that gentleman, not only for the first execution of the work, but for continuing it in current notes of description and criticism on future historical writings as they appear, by a gift of ten thousand dollars. The work was begun in the spring of 1898; its completion has been delayed by various circumstances which could not well be controlled. My connection with it was consequent on the interest I have felt in the views of Mr. Iles, and my wish to see his plans carried out in so important a field as that of American history. I have not been a special student in that field, and therefore I lacked qualifications which ought to have been brought to the supervision of bibliographical work in it; but when no one with special equipments for the task seemed ready or free for it, I ventured myself in the undertaking, at the request of Mr. Iles. Fortune favored me; for the editorial function in this work has been minimized in importance to the last degree by a corps of contributors who brought counsel as well as labor, and zeal as well as knowledge, to ensure its success. Two who had eminence in that helpful company — General Jacob D. Cox, soldier, statesman, and man of letters, and Professor B. A. Hinsdale, the historian of "The Old Northwest" — have passed from life since they wrote what bears their names here.

In addition to the notes specially written for these pages, a considerable number have been drawn from books of critical authority, and from a few periodicals which are scrupulously careful to employ competent pens in the preparation of their book reviews. Permission for the quotation of such notes has been given with a kindness which claims hearty thanks. They are duly credited in each instance to their source.

At the outset, those who consult this work should understand that it is intended to be neither an exhaustive bibliography of American history, nor merely a selection of the *best* books in that department of literature, nor does it name merely curious books. The selective aim in its preparation has been to embrace the books of every character, good, bad, and indifferent, concerning which it seems to be important that readers of various classes should be told what their merit or demerit is. This takes in text-books for school-children as well as source-books for historians and treatises for statesmen; and it includes a considerable class of popular writings from past generations which have disappeared from the bookstores, but which survive on the shelves of public libraries, where lingering echoes of an old undeserved reputation help to carry them into unwary hands.

With the counsel and guidance to be found in the annotated lists given here, any person who has access to a public library in this land of free books may study any part of American history with thoroughness; for his study is not limited to the resources of a single library or a single town. The loaning of rare books from one library to another is now permitted to so great an extent that it is seldom impossible for an earnest student to obtain any book which he really needs to make his study complete. This is especially true in the State of New York, where any citizen, duly vouched for, may borrow books from the State Library at Albany on conditions that are simple and inexpensive in the extreme.

For guidance in purchasing books of primary importance in American history, the lists suggested on page 463 by Professor Edward Channing, of Harvard University, for small public libraries or for individual use, will be found of great value. They name the books in the order in which they may be most profitably read, and each title bears a section-number referring to its note in the body of this work. The note prefixed by Professor Channing to his lists contains sterling counsel to every young reader and student of American history, who cannot do better than to heed that counsel at the outset of his work.

The annotated lists in this volume include but few works issued from the press since the end of the year 1899. Arrangements have been made for continuing the "appraisal" of books produced from that date forward, on subjects connected with American history, under the editorship of Mr. Philip P. Wells, Librarian of the Yale Law School, New Haven, Conn., following in a general way the lines of classification and treatment adopted in this book. The supplement for 1900 and 1901, in pamphlet form, will be published either simultaneously with the present volume, or soon afterward. Subsequent issues will duly appear, and may from time to time include works published before the close of 1899. Enlarged by these issues, it is hoped that the present guide may be republished at suitable intervals in revised form.

On the work now made public my personal labor ended when the manuscript of titles and notes had been finished, classified, and arranged. From that point it was most painstakingly prepared for the press, and the type-setting and proof-reading supervised, by Mr. Franklin O. Poole, of the Boston Athenæum, with the aid of Mr. Iles, who has given his time and his care as liberally as he gave from his purse. The elaborate index has been prepared by Mrs. Mary E. Haines and Miss Mabel R. Haines, of Brooklyn, N. Y. Because many subjects are touched in more than one part of the classified bibliography, and the writings of many authors are noted in more than one place, the index is a feature of great importance and should be constantly used. To those unaccustomed to the use of a bibliography it may be said that, so far as could be ascertained, the books not priced were out of print when these pages were prepared. It has not been feasible to state the number of pages or the sizes of publications named.

It is the hope of the American Library Association that what Mr. Iles has enabled it to do for the literature of American History may be done hereafter, with help from other friends, for other departments of literature, until the whole domain of letters and learning is furnished with similar guides.

J. N. LARNED.

BUFFALO, N. Y., *January*, 1902.

It is proper to acknowledge here that Mr. Larned gave without fee or reward his labors as General Editor of this work.

GEORGE ILES.

NEW YORK, *January*, 1902.

CONTENTS

CONTENTS

CONTRIBUTORS

INITIALS PREFIXED TO NAMES

C. M. A. — Andrews, Charles McLean, Professor of History, Bryn Mawr College, Bryn Mawr, Pennsylvania.

J. B. — Bain, James, Jr., Librarian, Public Library, Toronto, Ontario, Canada.

E. G. B. — Bourne, Edward Gaylord, Professor of History, Yale University, New Haven, Connecticut.

C. S. B. — Brigham, Clarence Saunders, Librarian, Rhode Island Historical Society, Providence, Rhode Island.

R. C. H. C. — Catterall, Ralph Charles Henry, University of Chicago, Chicago, Illinois.

E. C. — Channing, Edward, Professor of History, Harvard University, Cambridge, Massachusetts.

C. W. C. — Colby, Charles William, Professor of History, McGill University, Montreal, Province of Quebec, Canada.

V. L. C. — Collins, Varnum Lansing. Library of Princeton University, Princeton, New Jersey.

J. D. C. — Cox, General Jacob Dolson, Soldier of the Civil War, Ex-Governor of Ohio (died August 4, 1900).

E. Cr. — Cruikshank, Lieutenant-Colonel Ernest, Fort Erie, Ontario, Canada.

W. M. D. — Davis, William Morris, Professor of Geology, Harvard University, Cambridge, Massachusetts.

D. R. D. — Dewey, Davis Rich, Professor of Economics and Statistics, Massachusetts Institute of Technology, Boston, Massachusetts.

S. A. D. — Drake, Colonel Samuel Adams, Care of Messrs. Little, Brown & Co., Boston, Massachusetts.

J. R. F. — Ficklen, John Rose, Professor of History and Political Science, Tulane University, New Orleans, Louisiana.

P. L. F. — Ford, Paul Leicester. 37 East 77th Street, New York City.

W. E. F. — Foster, William Eaton, Librarian, Public Library, Providence, Rhode Island.

G. P. G. — Garrison, George Pierce, Professor of History, University of Texas, Austin, Texas.

B. A. H. — Hinsdale, Burke Aaron, Late Professor of Pedagogy. University of Michigan, Ann Arbor, Michigan (died Nov. 29, 1900).

F. W. H. — Hodge, Frederick Webb, Bureau of American Ethnology, Washington, D. C.

J. K. H. — Hosmer, James Kendall, Librarian, Public Library, Minneapolis, Minnesota.

H. W. H. — Hulbert, Rev. Henry Woodward, Old Stone Church Study, Cleveland, Ohio.

S. M. J. — Jackson, Samuel Macauley, Professor of Church History, New York University, New York City.

G. K. — King, Grace, 2221 Prytania Street, New Orleans, Louisiana.

W. MacD. — MacDonald, William, Professor of History, Brown University, Providence, Rhode Island.

A. C. McL. — McLaughlin, Andrew Cunningham, Professor of American History, University of Michigan, Ann Arbor, Michigan.

W. McL. — McLennan, William, 1056 Dorchester Street, Montreal, Province of Quebec, Canada.

M. L. M. — Miller, Merton Leland, Walker Museum, Chicago, Illinois.

A. D. M. — Morse, Anson Daniel, Professor of History, Amherst College, Amherst, Massachusetts.

H. L. O. — Osgood, Herbert Levi, Professor of History, Columbia University, New York City.

B. J. R. — Ramage, Burr James, Professor of Law, University of the South, Sewanee, Tennessee.

E. C. R. — Richardson, Ernest Cushing, Librarian, Princeton University, Princeton, New Jersey.

F. H. S. — Severance, Frank Howard, 150 Jewett Avenue, Buffalo, New York.

F. J. S. — Shepard, Frederick Job, Public Library, Buffalo, New York.

C. H. S. — Shinn, Charles Howard, Niles, Alameda County, California.

E. E. S. — Sparks, Edwin Erle, Professor of American History, University of Chicago, Chicago, Illinois.

G. A. T. — Thayer, Rev. George Augustine, 304 Oak Street, Cincinnati, Ohio.

R. G. T. — Thwaites, Reuben Gold, Secretary, State Historical Society, Madison, Wisconsin.

S. B. W. — Weeks, Stephen Beauregard, Santa Fé, New Mexico.

G. P. W. — Winship, George Parker, Librarian, John Carter Brown Library, Providence, Rhode Island.

G. M. W. — Wrong, George McKinnon, Professor of Modern History, University of Toronto, Toronto, Ontario, Canada.

THE LITERATURE OF AMERICAN HISTORY

PART I. SOURCES

A SYLLABUS OF EXISTING MATERIALS FOR ORIGINAL STUDY OF AMERICAN HISTORY

By PAUL LEICESTER FORD

OF essential value to the historical student are classes of material not subject to analysis or appraisal. These may be divided roughly as follows : —

GENERAL
  Archives and Bibliographies
  Collected Documents
  Periodicals
  Publications of Societies and Clubs

PUBLICATIONS OF DIFFERENT GOVERNMENTS

Spanish	Swedish
Mexican	British
Portuguese	Canadian
Italian	United States
French	States in General
Dutch	States, Particular
German	

Necessarily the system involves a certain amount of duplication and cross-reference, as well as the inclusion of some volumes or series treated in a critical sense in another part of this work. As will be noted, wherever a satisfactory bibliography or index exists, a reference to it is given in lieu of any detailed description.[1]

GENERAL

Archives and Bibliographies

The Reports of the American Historical Manuscripts Commission, published in the Reports of the American Historical Association, are valuable, and include Printed Guides to, and Descriptions of Archives, etc. (Report for 1896, p. 483), and Items respecting Historical Manuscripts (Report for 1898, p. 573).[2] In Winsor's Narrative and Critical History of America (VIII, 414) is a description of manuscript ma-

[1] The reference numbers introduced in this matter are for convenient guidance from the author and subject index at the end of the volume.

terials for American history.[3] See, also, Lane and Bolton's Notes on Special Collections in American Libraries (Cambridge. 1892).[4] The Bulletins of the Department of State (Wash. 1893–1900. 10v.) are devoted to calendars and republications of the Department of State archives; for which see, also, Allen's The Historical Archives of the Department of State (Annual report of the American Historical Association for 1894, p. 281), and A List of Manuscript Volumes in the Department of State, containing the Records and Papers of the Revolution (American Historical Association Report for 1894, p. 554).[5] Friedenwald's Historical Manuscripts in the Library of Congress (American Historical Association Report for 1898, p. 35) and Hoar's Account of the Material for Historical Study now accessible in Washington (The American Antiquarian Society Proceedings, New Series, II, 118) describe government archives.[6] Other calendars of importance are those of the Arthur Lee Manuscripts (Cambridge. 1882), Winsor's Calendar of the Sparks Manuscripts (Cambridge. 1889), and the Calendar of the Emmet Papers (New York Public Library Bulletin, v. 1–3).[7]

In bibliography, Sabin and Eames's Dictionary of Books relating to America (N. Y. 1868–92. 19v.+), though unfinished, stands first, but of value is Rich's Bibliotheca Americana Nova (Lond. 1832–44. 3v.).[8] Of positive importance for special periods are Harrisse's Bibliotheca Americana Vetustissima (N. Y., Paris. 1866–72. 2v.), Bartlett's Bibliotheca Americana (Providence. 1870–82. 4v.) a catalogue of the John Carter Brown Library, and Leypoldt and Bowker's American Catalogue of Books in Print 1876 (N. Y. 1880–1. 2v. Supplements, 1885–1900. 4v.). A similar catalogue, for books printed 1800–76 is announced.[9] See, also,

Ford's Check List of Bibliographies, Catalogues, Reference-Lists, and Lists of Authorities of American Books and Subjects (Brooklyn. 1889).[10]

Collected Documents

Hazard's Historical Collections (Phil. 1792–94. 2v.) is the earliest collection of documents illustrating American history, and is still of value.[11] Brown's Genesis of the United States (Boston. 1890. 2v.) covers the foundations of the English influence in America, chiefly drawn from Spanish and English documents.[12] Force's Tracts (Wash. 1836–46. 4v.) contain many reprints of pamphlets relating to the early settlement of the British colonies.[13] Poore's Constitutions and Charters (Wash. 1877. 2v.) is a valuable collection of the governmental instruments and compacts of the colonies and states.[14] See, in this connection, the list of printed Commissions and Instructions to Royal Proprietary Governors in the English Colonies in North America (American Historical Review, III, 170).[15] Stevens's Facsimiles of Manuscripts in European Archives relating to America, 1773–1783 (Lond. 1889–98. 25v.), is a monumental piece of collecting and editing.[16] A vast storehouse of material for the years 1774–1776 is Force's American Archives (4th series, 6v.; 5th series, 3v.). A large mass of documents intended for the continuation of this work is in the Congressional Library.[17] The diplomatic correspondence has been edited, first in Sparks's Diplomatic Correspondence of the American Revolution (12v.), and better, in Wharton's The Revolutionary Diplomatic Correspondence (6v.). Supplementary to both is Diplomatic Correspondence of the U. S. 1783–89 (Wash. 1833–4. 7v.).[18] Next in importance on the American Revolution is Almon's Remembrancer (Lond. 1775–84. 17v.).[19] See, also, below, under French and British.

The Journal of the Federal Convention was printed (Bost. 1819), but is contained as well in the far more important Elliot's Debates (Wash. 1836–45. 5v.).[20] Appendices of documents relating to this period are given in Bancroft's History of the Formation of the Constitution, and the polemic literature is reprinted in The Federalist and in Ford's Pamphlets and Essays (Brooklyn. 1888, 1893). Cf. Ford's Bibliography of the Constitution, 1787–8 (Brooklyn. 1896).[21]

The national government has published two great series relating to the War of Secession : Official Records of the War of the Rebellion (Wash. 1880–1900. First series, 53v.; Second series, 8v.; Third series, 5v.; Fourth series, 3v.; General index), and Official Records of the Navies in the War of the Rebellion (Wash. 1894–9. 9v.+).[22] [See Part III, below, the introductory note by General J. D. Cox to the division, Period of Civil War.] Many contemporary government documents relate more or less directly to the rise and progress of this attempted division, of which the following are the more important : Proceedings of the Peace Conference (Wash. 1861), the Reports of the Joint Committee on the Conduct of the War (Wash. 1863–6. 8v.), the Diplomatic Correspondence [House Ex. Docs. Papers relating to Foreign Affairs] (Wash. 1863–8. 17v.), the Claims of the United States against Great Britain (Wash. 1869–70. 5v.), and the Treaty of Washington (Wash. 1872–4. 6v.).[23] Of essential importance are the reports of the state Adjutants-General, and scarcely less so are the many regimental histories which have been published.[24] A fairly complete list of the latter forms Abbot's Contributions towards a Bibliography of the Civil War (Phil. 1886).[25] Of a later period, though properly noticed here, is the Report of the Condition of Affairs in the Late Insurrectionary States (Wash. 1872. 13v.).[26] The papers of the Military Historical Society of Massachusetts relate entirely to this war, as do also the publications of the Military Order of the Loyal Legion, and of the Grand Army of the Republic.[27] See, also, under Societies and Periodicals, below. Anything like a bibliography of Secession is still a desideratum, but Bartlett's Literature of the Rebellion (Bost. 1866) is a step toward it.[28] See, also, the Military Literature in the War Department Library (Wash. 1897–8. 2v.).[29]

Two classes of books, while not strictly historical, are not negligible by the historian. These are the narratives of travellers in America, and the governmental explorations and surveys. The more important of the first division are analyzed in Tuckerman's America and her Commentators (N. Y. 1864).[30] See, also, Plympton's Travel in North America (N. Y. State Library Bulletin. Bibliography No. 3. Albany. 1897).[31] There is a complete list of the publications of the second class in Hasse's Reports of Explorations printed in the Documents of the United States Government (Wash. 1899).[32] In addition, there are a number of Government publications relating to disputed boundaries which are likewise of value.[33]

Periodicals

In the Bulletin of the Lenox Library (II, 120) is printed A List of Periodicals, Collections and Society Publications relating to American History and Genealogy, which is so full as to practically cover the whole field. A valuable supplement to this is the preliminary list printed in Griffin's Index of Articles upon American Local History (Bost. 1889–96. 2v.).[34] The most essential periodicals are the Historical Magazine (Bost. and N. Y. 1857–75. 23v.), the Magazine of American History (N. Y. 1877–93. 30v.), the American Historical Review (N. Y. 1895–. 7v.+), the Magazine of Western History (Cleveland. 1884–90. 14v.), the New England Historical and Genealogical Register (Bost. 1847–. 55v.+), the New York Genealogical and Biographical Record (N. Y. 1870–. 30v.+), the Pennsylvania Magazine of History and Biography (Phil. 1877–. 25v.+), Publications of the Southern History Association (Wash. 1897–. 5v.+), the Southern Bivouac (Louisville. 1884–87. 6v.), Papers of the Southern Historical Society (Richmond. 1876–. 29v.+), and Moore's Rebellion Record (N. Y. 1861–68. 11v. and supplt.).[35] Wherever a periodical specially relates to one state, it is mentioned in the lists of titles succeeding this. Though not limited to historical subjects, the historian cannot neglect Niles' Register (Balt. 1811–49. 76v.), the American Register, or General Repository of History, Politics and Science (Phil. 1807–1811. 7v.), the Historical Register of the United States (Wash. 1814. 4v.), the American Annual Register (N. Y. 1825–35. 8v.), the Southern Literary Messenger (Richmond. 1834–64. 38v.), and the Nation (N. Y. 1865–. 73v.+).[36] See, also, under British and French.

Societies and Clubs

The Proceedings and Collections of the various societies number many hundred volumes, a list of which, with the contents of each and an index, is given in Griffin's invaluable Bibliography of American Historical Societies (Wash. 1896).[37] The most important of these societies as regards published material are the American, the Massachusetts, New York, Pennsylvania, Virginia, and Wisconsin. In addi-

tion, there are many societies not absolutely historical which print historical material, the most important of which are the American Geographical Society, the American Philosophical Society, the American Antiquarian Society, the Johns Hopkins University in its Studies in Historical and Political Science, the Hakluyt Society, the various New England and Pilgrim societies, the Society of the Cincinnati, the Mayflower, Holland, Huguenot, Colonial Wars, and Colonial Dames societies, the Sons of the Revolution, the Sons of the American Revolution, the Daughters of the Revolution, the Daughters of the American Revolution, the Society of the War of 1812, the Aztec Club of 1847, the Loyal Legion, and the Grand Army of the Republic.[38]

Yet another class of publications are those of sectarian societies relating to their own history. The more important of these are: the Annual Reports of the American Baptist Historical Society (Phil. 1865–), the American Catholic Historical Researches (Phil. 1884–98. 15v.), the American Catholic Historical Society of Philadelphia Records (Phil. 1884–. 12v.+), the Proceedings of the United States Catholic Historical Society (published in New York, irregularly, beginning with 1885), Hawks's Contributions to the Ecclesiastical History of the United States of America (N. Y. 1836–39. 2v.), the Collections of the Protestant Episcopal Historical Society (N. Y. 1851–53. 2v.), Hawks and Perry's Documentary History of the Protestant Episcopal Church in Connecticut (N. Y. 1863–64. 2v.), Perry's Historical Collections relating to the American Colonial [Episcopal] Church (Hartford. 1870–78. 5v.), Perry's Historical Notes and Documents illustrating the Organization of the P. E. Church (Claremont. 1874), Facsimiles of Church Documents issued by the Historical Club of the American [Episcopal] Church (N. Y. 1874–9), the Papers of the American Society of Church History (N. Y. 1889–97. 8v.), the Reports of the Presbyterian Historical Society (Phil. 1852–99), and Dexter's Congregationalism of the Last Three Hundred Years as seen in its Literature (N. Y. 1880).[39]

Not easily divided from the foregoing are certain publications relating to special peoples, the lines of division of which nearly always have followed religious lines. The most important included in this division are the Proceedings of the Pennsylvania-German Society

(Lancaster. 1891–. 9v.+), Der Deutsche Pionier (Cin. 1869–87. 17v.), the Deutsch-Amerikanisches Magazin (Cin. 1887), the Proceedings of the Scotch-Irish Society of America (Phil. 1889–96. 8v.), the Journal of the American-Irish Historical Society (Bost. 1898–. v. 1+), the Proceedings (1884–. 3v.+) and Collections of the Huguenot Society of America (N. Y. 1836–), the Collections of the Holland Society of New York (1891–6. 3v.), and the Publications of the American-Jewish Historical Society (Balt. 1893–99. 7v.).[40]

Kindred to historical societies are certain clubs which have printed series of more or less value on American history, the publications of which are thoroughly treated in Growoll's American Book Clubs (N. Y. 1897).[41] The more valuable of these club publications are those printed by the Seventy-Six Society, the Bradford Club, the Prince Society, the Narragansett Club, and the Historical Printing Club.[42]

Spanish

Navarrete's Coleccion de los viages y déscubrimientos, que hicieron por mar los Españoles desde fines del siglo xv, con varios documentos inéditos concernientes á la historia de la marina castellana y de los establecimientos españoles en Indias (Madrid. 1825–37. 5v.), is the earliest Spanish collection.[43] Other series are : Ternaux's Voyages, relations et mémoires originaux pour servir à l'histoire de la découverte de l'Amérique (Paris. 1837–41. 2 series, 20v.), Cartas de Indias (Madrid. 1877), Zabalburu and Rayon's Nueva coleccion de documentos inéditos para la historia de España de sus Indias (Madrid. 1892–96. 6v.), Hinojosa's Materiales para la historia de España en el Archivo secreto de la Santa Sede (Madrid. 1896), Hinojosa's Los despachos de la diplomacia pontificia en España. Memoria de una misión oficial en el Archivo Secreto de la Santa Sede (Madrid. 1896), the Pacheco y Cárdenas Coleccion de documentos inéditos relativos al descubrimiento, conquista y colonizacion de las posesiones españolas en América y Occeanía, sacados, en su mayor parte, del Real archivo de Indias (Madrid. 1864–84. 42v.), the uncompleted fragment of Squier's Collections of Rare and Original Documents and Relations, concerning the Discovery and Conquest of America, chiefly from the Spanish Archives (N. Y. 1860), and the monu-

mental work of Navarrete, the Coleccion de documentos inéditos para la historia de España (Madrid. 1842–95. 112v.).[44] Of this latter series a List of Titles of Documents relating to America contained in Volumes I–CX has been compiled by G. P. Winship (reprinted from the Bulletin of the Public Library of the City of Boston for October, 1894).[45] The earliest edition of the Spanish laws governing the Indies has been reprinted under the title of New Laws of the Indies (Lond. 1893), and the collected statutes of Spain are given in Coleccion legislativa de España (Madrid. 1816–99. 150v.).[46] See Griffin's Bibliographical Sketch of Recopilacion de Indias, and other Collections of Spanish Laws relating to the Indies (Papers of Hist. Society of Southern California. Los Angeles. 1887).[47] Of some value are : Calendar of Letters, Despatches and State Papers relating to the Negotiations between England and Spain, preserved in the Archives of Simancas, 1485–1543 (Lond. 1862–99. 7v.), and Calendar of Letters and State Papers relating to English Affairs, preserved in the Archives of Simancas, 1558–86 (Lond. 1892–. 4v.+).[48]

Mexican

It is difficult to divide Spanish and Mexican material, but the following titles seem more properly to be classed under the latter heading : Icazbalceta's Colección de documentos para la historia de México (Mexico. 1858–66. 2v.), Icazbalceta's Historia eclesiástica indiana obra escrita á fines del siglo xvi (Mexico. 1870. 2v.), Icazbalceta's Nueva colección de documentos para la historia de México (Mexico. 1886–92. 5v.), Documentos para la historia de Mejico (Mexico. 1853–57. 4 series. 19v.), Boletin de la Sociedad mexicana de geografía y estadística (Mexico. 1839–1865. 15v.), Archivo mexicano (Mexico. 1852–3. 2v.), El archivo mexicana (Mexico. 1856–62. 6v.).[49] See, also, Beristain de Souza's Biblioteca hispano americana septentrional (Mexico. 1816), and Icazbalceta's Bibliografía mexicana del siglo xvi (Mexico. 1886).[50]

Portuguese

Collecáço de monumentos ineditos para la historia das conquistas dos Portuguezes em Africa, Asia e America, published by the Academia real das sciencias de Lisboa (Lisbon. 1858–98. 16v.), and Collecção de opusculos reimpressos relativos á historia das navigações, viagens, e conquistas dos Portuguezes (Lisbon. 1844–58).[51]

Italian

From the archives of the Vatican has been compiled Documenta selecta e tabulario secreto vaticano, quæ Romanorum pontificum erga Americæ populos curam ac studia tum ante tum paullo post insulas a Christophoro Columbo repertas testantur, phototypis descripta (Rome. 1893).[52] In connection with the Columbian celebration there was also printed Raccolta di documenti e studi ; pubblicati dalla R. commissione colombiana pel quarto centenario dalla scoperta dell' America (Rome. 1892–6. 14v.).[53] See, also, Winsor's America in Italian Libraries (The Nation, 53 : 9).[54]

French

The French government has published Inventaire analytique des archives du Ministère des affaires étrangères (Paris. 1885–94. 8v.+), and État sommaires des archives de la marine antérieures à la révolution (Paris. 1898).[55] Of considerable importance in an official sense is Le Mercure françois, 1605–44 (Paris. 1611–1648. 25v.), and the Ordonnances des rois de France (Paris. 1723–49. 21v.).[56] The Relations of the Jesuit priests are an important series. Some of these were printed in Lettres édifiantes et curieuses (Paris. 1717–76. 34v.).[57] Partial reprints have been made in Relations des Jesuites (Quebec. 1858. 3v.), in Shea's (25v.) and O'Callaghan's (8v.) series, and, with scholarly completeness, in Thwaites' The Jesuit Relations and Allied Documents (Cleveland. 1896–1901. 73v.).[58] Margry has edited Découvertes et établissements des Français dans l'ouest et dans le sud de l'Amérique septentrionale, 1614–1754 (Paris. 1879–86. 6v.), and Relations et mémoires inédits pour servir à l'histoire de la France dans les pays d'outre-mer (Paris. 1867).[59] See, also, Harrisse's Notes pour servir à l'histoire, à la bibliographie, et à la cartographie de la Nouvelle-France et des pays adjacents, 1545–1700 (Paris. 1872).[60] The part of France in the American Revolution is fully treated in Doniol's Histoire de la participation de la France à l'établissement des États-Unis d'Amérique (Paris. 1886–92. 5v.), and not to be neglected for the same epoch is the periodical Affaires de l'Angleterre et de l'Amérique (Paris. 1776–79. 17v.).[61] Some material is

contained in the Journal de la Société des Américanistes de Paris (Paris. 1896–. 2v.+).[62] See, also, Canadian, New York.

Dutch

Somewhat relating to the Dutch settlements in the New Netherlands is Wassenaer's Historisch Verhaal (Amst. 1622–35. 21v.).[63] See, also, G. M. Asher's Bibliographical Essay on Dutch Books relating to New Netherlands, the Dutch West India Company, Brazil, Angola, etc. (Amst. 1854–67), Jameson's Bibliography of Willem Usselinx (Papers of Am. Hist. Assoc. II, 349–368), and the Papers of the Holland Society.[64] See, also, under New York.

German

Of some importance are Samuel Urlsperger's Der ausführlichen Nachrichten van der königlichen grossbrittannischen Colonie salzburgischer Emigranten in America (Halle. 1735–52. 18 parts. Second series, Augsburg. 1754–67. 4v.).[65] For the American Revolution consult Schlözer's Briefwechsel meist historischen und politischen Inhalts (Göttingen. 1777–81. 10v.), which latter has been partly translated and reprinted in Stone's Letters of Brunswick and Hessian Officers during the American Revolution (Albany. 1891), Staats-Anzeigen gesammelt und zum Druck befördert von August Ludwig Schlözer (Göttingen. 1782–95. 19v.), and Remer's Amerikanisches Archiv (Brunswick. 1777–8. 3v.).[66]

Swedish

In the Pennsylvania Magazine of History and Biography (15 : 481) is an account of the Archivum americanum in the Consistory Court of the Archbishop of Upsal, by C. J. Stillé.[67] See, also, Jameson's Bibliography of Willem Usselinx (Papers of Am. Hist. Assoc. II, 349–368).[68]

British

A great mass of manuscript material relating to American history is in the State Paper Office in London. Of this the Office has printed for its own use, and not for sale, the briefest of check lists, in such limited editions as to make their consultation very difficult. Supplementary to these, and more valuable, are calendars of the various series (see Catalogue printed by Her Majesty's Stationery Office) now in course of publication. Many of these contain more or less material relating to America, but the only one of great importance is the Calendar of State Papers, Colonial Series (13v.+).[69] The collection is described in Sainsbury's British Public Record Office and the Material in it for Early American History (American Antiquarian Soc. 1893), and in Winsor's An Account of the London Archives of American History (Nation, 52 : 258).[70] In addition, the files of this office have furnished the bulk of the material contained in Brymner's Canadian Archives, and in several of the collections of documents printed by the various states, for which see New Hampshire, New York, New Jersey, Pennsylvania, Maryland, North Carolina, and South Carolina.[71] From this source, also, has been taken a material part of Stevens's Facsimiles of Manuscripts in European Archives.[72]

Only second in importance to the above collections are the reports of the Historical Manuscripts Commission (1–15+). A complete list of these is given in the Appendix to the 15th report, which includes a list of the collections examined but not yet reported upon. The most valuable for American history of those so far printed are the Townshend, Carlisle, Dartmouth, Lansdowne, and Sackville papers. A chronological and "colony" index is printed in the 3d Report of the American Historical Manuscripts Commission.[73]

Material is to be found in Cobbett's Parliamentary History of England from the Earliest Period to the Year 1803, and Hansard's Parliamentary Debates, as also in the Parliamentary Blue Books issued from time to time, bearing on such international questions as have arisen between the two countries since their separation.[74] For the period of the American Revolution, Almon's Parliamentary Register (1st series, 17v., 2d series, 18v.) not merely gives all the debates on the war, but, in the various appendices, prints many important papers laid before Parliament.[75] The Debates of the House of Commons, taken by Sir Henry Cavendish during the years 1768–74 (3v.), cover a period not included in Almon.[76]

The laws of Great Britain governing the colonies must be searched for in the mass of the Statutes at Large (Lond. 1762–1866. 109v.).[77] Most of the colonial charters are printed in Charters of the British Colonies (Lond. [1774]).[78] For the treaties, see Hertslet's Complete Collection of the Treaties and Conventions subsisting between Great Britain and Foreign Powers,

and of the Laws, Decrees, Orders in Council, etc., concerning the same (Lond. 1820–98. 20v.).[79]

Canadian

Brymner's Reports on Canadian Archives (Ottawa. 1884–. 18v.+) contains much material relating to the colonies and the United States ; see, also, in this connection Brymner's Description of the Canadian Archives in the Papers of the American Historical Association for the year 1889 (III, 149).[80] Of much importance are the publications of the Literary and Historical Society of Quebec, especially their series of Historical Documents, and Anderson's Archives of Canada (New Series, part 9).[81] In the Transactions for 1891 is Würtele's Index of Lectures, Papers and Historical Documents published by the Society, 1829–1891 ; this has also been separately published.[82] See Dennis' Sources of Northwestern History (Manitoba Historical and Scientific Society, Transactions, No. 6. 1883).[83] The Legislature of Quebec has published a Collection de manuscrits contenant lettres, mémoires, et autres documents historiques relatifs à la Nouvelle-France (Quebec. 1883–85. 4v.), and Jugements et délibérations du Conseil souverain de la Nouvelle France (Quebec. 1885–91. 6v.).[84] Faribault's Catalogue d'ouvrages sur l'histoire de l'Amérique et en particulier sur celle du Canada, de la Louisiane, de l'Acadie (Quebec. 1837), is of value, as is also Gagnon's Essai de bibliographie canadienne (Quebec. 1895). Under No. 145 of this latter are noted a number of reports on Canadian archives which should not be overlooked.[85] See, also, French, British.

United States

The documentary material relating to the government of the United States begins in 1774 with the meeting of the First Congress, everything prior thereto being of British or provincial origin. The official proceedings of the Continental Congress are contained in the Journals of Congress (13v.), and Secret Journals of Congress (4v.). A complete edition, including hitherto unprinted portions, and many official papers, edited by Worthington C. Ford, is announced for early publication.[86] The executive documents and miscellaneous publications of this period form a very rare class of material, for which see Ford's Bibliography of the Continental Congress.[87]

In 1789 the government of the United States was organized under the present constitution. The official proceedings of Congress are contained in Journals of the House of Representatives (Wash. 1826. 9v.) and Journal of the Senate (Wash. 1820–1. 5v.), supplemented by Journal of the Executive Proceedings of the Senate (Wash. 1829. 16v.).[88] The debates of the early period were collected from the newspapers and abridged in Gales's Debates and Proceedings in Congress, 1789–1824 (Wash. 1834–56. 42v.), continued in The Register of Debates in Congress (Wash. 1825–37. 14v., bd. in 29).[89] There are a number of minor publications covering various periods of this time which give the discussions at greater length. A convenient collection for this period is Benton's Abridgment of Debates of Congress from 1789–1856 (16v.).[90] The later period is contained in the Congressional Globe (46v.) and the Congressional Record (34v.+).[91]

The laws have been issued in innumerable forms, the most important being Statutes at Large (31v.+), and Revised Statutes of the United States (Wash. 1878–91. 2v.).[92] See, also, Index to the Laws, 1789–1827 (Wash. 1828).[93] Supplementary thereto are the United States Reports.[94] Related to these is Opinions of the Attorney-General of the United States (Wash. 1852–. 21v.+).[95] Cognate to the laws are Treaties and Conventions between the United States and other Powers, 1776–1887 (Wash. 1889).[96] See in this connection Wharton's Digest of the International Law of the U. S. (Wash. 1886. 3v.; 2d ed. 1887).[97] There have also been a number of special compilations, such as Laws respecting Public Lands, Navy and Marine Laws, Tariff Acts 1789–1897, Laws respecting Light Houses, Revolutionary Pension Laws, Acts of Congress relating to Coins and Currency, and Digest of the Revenue Laws.[98]

The executive documents of the United States government constitute a great mass, collections of the earlier part of which have been made : Wait's State Papers from 1789–1818 (12v.), and American State Papers, 1789–1837 (1st series, 21v., 2d series, 17v.).[99] There are several collections of the Messages and Papers of the Presidents, of which Richardson's (Wash. 1896–9. 10v.) is the latest and most inclusive.[100] See, also, Poore's Veto Messages of the Presidents of the United States (Wash. 1886).[101] Other government publica-

tions, more strictly historical than official, will be found above, under the first section.

During four years the Confederate government exercised sway over a material part of the United States, but its publications were few in number, and included little more than its laws and a few executive documents. See in this connection Sumner's Materials for the History of the Government of the Southern Confederacy (Papers of the American Historical Association, IV, 5). Many of its archives have, however, been printed in the Official Records of the War of the Rebellion, for which see sect. 22.[102]

There have been published many catalogues and bibliographies of government publications, the most valuable of which are Poore's Descriptive Catalogue of the Government Publications of the United States, 1775–1881 (Wash. 1885), and Crandall's Checklist of Public Documents, from the First to the Fifty-Third Congress (Wash. 1895. Second edition, revised and enlarged).[103] See, also, Index to the Subjects of Documents and Reports, and to the Committees, Senators and Representatives presenting them (Last edition, Fifty-Fifth Congress, 1898), and McKee's Index to the Reports of Committees (Wash. 1887. 2v.).[104] The earlier period is more fully treated in Greely's Public Documents of the Early Congresses (American Historical Association Report for 1896), and in the N. Y. Public Library Bulletin (III, 462).[105] The last few years are best given in Hickcox's Monthly Catalogue of Government Publications (Wash. 1885–94. 10v.), The Monthly Catalogue of the United States Documents (Nos. 1–83+), and the yearly lists contained in the Executive Documents.[106]

States, in General

Under each state is grouped the more important collections of historical material ; but as every state has issued certain publications, a brief résumé here will save needless repetition.

The beginning of a complete bibliography of all state official issues will be found in Bowker's State Publications, only one part of which, The New England States (N. Y. 1899), has been issued.[107] For the period covered, similar lists have been printed in The American Catalogue, 1884–1890 and 1890–1895.[108] Almost all the colonies and states have printed the journals of their respective Assemblies or Legislatures; a bibliography of these during the colonial period is given in the annual report of the American Historical Association for 1897 (p. 405).[109] In the interregnum between the suspension of the governments of the thirteen original colonies and the organization of state governments, various revolutionary conventions and committees carried on the government, and their proceedings were generally printed, and will be found reprinted in Force's American Archives.[110] The laws of each state were issued in the form of yearly session acts and occasional collections. For the colonial period, consult the Charlemagne Tower Collection of American Colonial Laws (Phil. 1890).[111] Not printed by the states, but of essential importance, are the Reports of decisions of their various courts.[112] From time to time each state has held conventions for the framing or revising of constitutions, most of which were printed.[113] In addition, the original thirteen states held conventions to consider the Federal Constitution, and a list of the Journals and Debates of each is given in Ford's Bibliography and Reference List relating to the Adoption of the Constitution of the United States (Brooklyn. 1896).[114] Many of these are reprinted in Elliot's Debates on the Federal Constitution (Phil. 1861. 5v.).[115] As a preliminary to the War of Secession, the southern states held other conventions to pass ordinances of secession, and to make such alterations in their constitutions as this involved, and the journals of most of these were printed.[116]

For the period of the War of Secession, the reports of the state Adjutants-General are of much value, as are the histories of the states during that war, and the histories of the various state regiments which have been published.[117]

Certain of the cities have printed material relating to their own history, the most important being the following : Reports of the Boston Record Commission (Bost. 1876–98. 28v.), and Early Records of the Town of Providence (Providence. 1892–9. 15v.); see, also, in this connection, the Bibliographical List of New England Town Records in the American Historical Review (I, 581, 771).[118] New York City has printed the Records of New Amsterdam (N. Y. 1897. 7v.), and the Manuals of the New York Common Council (N. Y. 1841–70. 28v.), which latter contains much relating to

the history of the city and state, and is analyzed in a Historical Index (N. Y. 1900).[119] Philadelphia has printed one volume, Minutes of the Common Council, 1704–76 (Phil. 1847). Charleston has issued for a number of years the Charleston City Year Book with documentary matter. Not strictly relating to local history, but appropriately mentioned here, are the Bulletins of the Boston Public Library, the Harvard College Library Bulletins, and the New York Public Library Bulletins, all of which contain historical material : see in this connection Newman's Index to Subject Bibliographies in Library Bulletins (New York State Library Bulletin. Bibliography No. 14. Albany. 1898).[120]

Maine

No systematic publication of the records has been made, but the following works have been issued : Bradbury's Transcript Copy of the Early Court Records and other Important Documents pertaining to the Settlement, 1636–1686 (Portland. 1843–5. 4v.), Sargent's Maine Wills, 1640–1760 (Portland. 1887), York Deeds, containing Ancient Land Grants in the Province of Maine (Portland. 1887–96. 11v.), and Hough's Papers relating to Pemaquid (Albany. 1856. Maine Hist. Soc. Coll., v. 5. 1857).[121] Of value are : Catalogue of Original Documents in the English Archives relating to the Early History of the State of Maine (N. Y. 1858), Drummond's Bibliographical Memorandum of the Laws of Maine (Maine Hist. Soc. Coll., 2d ser. II, 391), and Williamson's Bibliography of Maine (Portland. 1896. 2v.).[122] The Gorges Society publications relate chiefly to this state; likewise the Maine Genealogist and Biographer (Augusta. 1875–8. 3v.), the Maine Historical and Genealogical Recorder (Portland. 1884–98. 9v.), and the Bangor Historical Magazine (Bangor. 1885–92. 7v.), continued as Maine Historical Magazine (Bangor. 1893–95. 2v.).[123] [See, also, Maine Historical Society, sect. 275, below.]

New Hampshire

Under various editorships, the Provincial Papers and State Papers have been published (Concord. 1867–96. 27v.).[124] The state has also printed : Index of the Historical Matter contained in the New Hampshire Registers from 1772–1892, in the Political Manuals from 1857–1872, and in the People's Handbooks for

1874, 1876 and 1877 (Concord. 1891), List of Reports of Departments of the State of New Hampshire, and other Documental Matter, published in the Appendices of the Legislative Journals, and subsequently in the Annual Reports, 1822–1889 (Concord. 1890), Check List of New Hampshire Laws, 1789–1889 (n. p. 1889), Index to the Journals of the House of Representatives of New Hampshire, 1711–1784 (Concord. 1890–4. 2v.), and Index to the Records of the Council of New Hampshire, 1631–1784 (Concord. 1896).[125] Farmer's Collections, Topographical, Historical and Biographical (Concord. 1822–4. 3v.), is valuable, as are the New Hampshire Repository (Gilmanton. 1846–7. 2v.) and the Granite Monthly (Concord. 1877–. 27v.+).[126] The latter contains McClintock's Bibliography of New Hampshire (IV, 286).[127] See, also, Hoyt's Historical and Bibliographical Notes on the Laws of New Hampshire (Am. Antiquarian Society Proceedings, 1876).[128]

Vermont

The most important series on the history of the state is the Records of the Council of Safety and Governor and Council of Vermont (Montpelier. 1873–80. 8v.).[129] An earlier publication is Vermont State Papers, with the Journal of the Council of Safety, the Early Journals of the General Assembly, etc. (Middlebury. 1823).[130] There has been a reprint of the Laws of the State, 1782 (Wash. 1898).[131] In various numbers of the Argus and Patriot, M. D. Gilman has published an elaborate bibliography of Vermont, also published complete in one volume (Burlington. 1897), and a briefer list was printed in Norton's Literary Letter, 1860.[132] The Vermont Historical Gazetteer (Burlington. 1867–91. 5v.) is practically limited to the local history of various towns.[133]

Massachusetts

Under Shurtleff's editing have been issued Records of the Governor and Company of the Massachusetts Bay in New England, 1628–1686 (Bost. 1853–4. 5v. in 6 pts.), and Records of the Colony of New Plymouth (Bost. 1885–7. 12v.).[134] Goodale's reprints of the Acts and Resolves, with Historical and Explanatory Notes (Bost. 1869–. 8v.+), is now in course of publication.[135] The Acts and Resolves of 1780–1799 (Bost. 1890–7. 10v.) have been

printed.[136] The Laws of Massachusetts of 1660 and 1672, with Supplements thereto, have been reprinted under the editorship of W. H. Whitmore (Bost. 1887–89. 2v.).[137] Hutchinson's Collections of Original Papers relative to Massachusetts-Bay (Bost. 1769. Repr. Albany. 1865. 2v.), Hough's Papers relating to the Island of Nantucket (Albany. 1856), and Papers relating to the Public Events of Massachusetts preceding the Revolution (Phil. 1856) are important, as are also Journals of each Provincial Congress, 1774–5, and of the Committee of Safety, with other Documents, edited by Lincoln (Bost. 1838), and Bradford's Speeches of the Governors of Massachusetts, 1765–1775, and the Necessary Answers of the House of Representatives to the Same (Bost. 1818).[138] A Roll of Massachusetts Soldiers and Sailors of the Revolutionary War (Bost. 1896–. 8v.+) has been printed.[139] The state has published several reports on its archives, among which are Report to the Legislature of Massachusetts upon the Condition of Records, Files, Papers and Documents in the Secretary's Department (Bost. 1885), and Reports of the Commission of Public Records of Parishes, Towns and Counties on their Custody and Condition (Bost. 1885, 1889–1898. 11v.+).[140] Of value are Colburn's Bibliography of Local History of Massachusetts (Bost. 1871), and Green's and Paine's List of Early American Imprints (Cambridge. 1895; Worcester. 1896), which are really lists of Massachusetts publications prior to the year 1700.[141] Important magazines are: the New England Historical and Genealogical Register, and the Bay State Monthly, now continued as the New England Magazine.[142] It is scarcely necessary to call particular attention to the publications of the Massachusetts Historical Society, the Prince Society, the Essex Institute, the American Antiquarian Society, and the New England Historic and Genealogical Society, as well as to those of many minor societies.[143] [See, also, Historical Societies, sect. 227, 262, 284, 367, 387, below.]

Rhode Island

The Records of the Colony of Rhode Island were edited by J. R. Bartlett (Providence. 1856–65. 10v.). A necessary supplement to this is Staples' Rhode Island in the Continental Congress (Providence. 1870).[144] Another publication of the latter author is the Proceedings of the First General Assembly, and the Code of Laws adopted by that Assembly in 1647 (Providence. 1847).[145] Bartlett also issued An Index to the Acts and Resolves, 1758–1850 (Providence. 1856), supplementary volumes to which have been printed.[146] Sidney Rider has printed Laws and Acts, from the First Settlement in 1636, to 1705 (Providence. 1896), and Acts and Laws, with the Charters, 1719 (Providence. 1895), and his Rhode Island Historical Tracts are valuable.[147] The Early Records of the Town of Providence, 1636–1714, have been issued (Providence. 1892–8. 12v.).[148] Bartlett's Bibliography of Rhode Island was printed at Providence in 1864.[149] See, also, the Newport Historical Magazine, continued as the Rhode Island Historical Magazine (Newport. 1880–87. 7v.).[150]

Connecticut

The Colonial Records of Connecticut, edited by J. H. Trumbull and C. J. Hoadly, have been printed (Hartford. 1850–90. 15v.).[151] Supplementary to these are Hoadly's Records of the State of Connecticut (Hartford. 1894–5. 2v.).[152] Also consult Hoadly's Records of the Colony of New Haven, 1638–1665 (Hartford. 1857–8. 2v.).[153] Earlier publications are Hinman's Antiquities, or Letters from Charles II, James II, etc., to Governors of the Colony of Connecticut, with their Answers, and other Documents (Hartford. 1836), and his Historical Collection from Records, etc., of the Part sustained by Connecticut during the War of the Revolution (Hartford. 1842).[154] The Record of Connecticut Men in the War of the Revolution, War of 1812 and Mexican War was printed at Hartford in 1889.[155] Brinley reprinted the Book of General Laws, 1672 (Hartford. 1865); Andros, the Code of Laws established by the General Court, 1650 (New Haven. 1822); Hoadly, The New Haven Code of 1655 (Hartford. 1855), and this latter is also contained in Trumbull's Blue Laws (Hartford. 1876).[156]

New York

O'Callaghan's Documents relative to the Colonial History of New York (11v. including index) is a vast series of documents collected in Holland, England, and France. Subsequent to this, four supplementary volumes have been printed from material drawn from the state archives; see in this connection, Brodhead's Final Report to the Senate of New York (Al-

bany. 1845).[157] In addition the state has issued in two editions the Documentary History of the State of New York, edited by O'Callaghan (Albany. 1849–51. 4v.).[158] The state archives have been further treated in a Calendar of Historical Manuscripts in the Office of the Secretary of State (Albany. 1865–6. 2v.), a Calendar of Historical Manuscripts relating to the War of the Revolution (Albany. 1868. 2v.), a Calendar of New York Colonial Manuscripts, Indorsed Land Papers in the Office of the Secretary of State, 1643–1803 (Albany. 1864), O'Callaghan's Index to Vols. 1–3 of Translations of Dutch Manuscripts in the Office of the Secretary of State (Albany. 1870), and in a Catalogue of Historical Papers deposited in the New York State Library (Albany. 1849).[159] A complete republication of the laws to 1775 is included in the Colonial Laws of New York from 1664 to the Revolution (Albany. 1894. 5v.). Supplementary to these are Laws of the Colony of New York passed 1774–5 (Albany. 1888), and Laws of the State of New York passed 1777–1801 (Albany. 1886–7. 5v.). In this connection, see General Index to the Laws of the State from 1777–1865 (Albany. 1866), Index to the Journals of the House of Assembly of New York, 1777–95 (Albany. 1814), Index to the Journals of the Senate, 1777–99 (Albany. 1814), General Index of Documents and Laws of the State of New York (Albany. 1866), and General Index to the Legislative Documents of the State of New York (Albany. 1891).[160] Important republications are : Journal of the Votes and Proceedings of the General Assembly, 1691–1765 (N. Y. 1764–6. 2v.), Journal of the Proceedings of the General Assembly of the Colony of New York, 1766–76 (Albany. 1820), Journal of the Legislative Council, 1691–1775 (Albany. 1861. 2v.), Journal of the New York Provincial Congress, 1775–77 (Albany. 1842. 2v.), and Votes and Proceedings of the General Assembly, 1780 (Albany. 1859).[161] The Reports of the state historian for '96, '97, and '98 include two volumes, Colonial Series, and v. 1 of the Military Papers of Daniel D. Tompkins.[162] The University of the State of New York has published three History Bulletins, being Supplementary List of Marriage Licenses (Albany. 1898), Colonial Records, General Entries, v. 1, 1664–5 (Albany. 1899), and Annotated List of the Principal Manuscripts in the New York State Library (Albany. 1899).[163] It is needless to call attention to the value of the publications of the New York Historical Society and the New York Genealogical and Biographical Record (N. Y. 1870–. 30v.+ ; Index to v. 1–24).[164] O'Callaghan's Register of New Netherlands, 1626–1674 (Albany. 1865), his New York Colonial Tracts (Albany. 1866–72. 4v.), Hough's Papers relating to Pemaquid [Maine] (Albany. 1856. Repr. in Maine Hist. Soc. Coll., v. 5), his Papers relating to the Island of Nantucket (Albany. 1856), and Munsell's Historical Series (Albany. 1857–95. 23v.) cannot be omitted.[165] Hildeburn's List of the Issues of the Press of New York, 1693–1752 (Phil. 1889), with additions to the same in Old New York, is the only important piece of bibliography.[166] [See, also, New York Historical Society, etc., sect. 351, below.]

New Jersey

The Archives of the State of New Jersey (Newark. 1880–99. 21v. General Index to v. 1–10. Newark. 1888) are now in course of publication.[167] Supplementary thereto are : Journal of the Procedure of the Governor and Council, 1682–1703 (Jersey City. 1872), Journal and Votes of the House of Representatives of New Jersey, 1703–1709 (Jersey City. 1872), Journal of the Proceedings of the Provincial Congress of New Jersey, 1775 (Woodbury. 1835), Minutes of the Provincial Congress and Council of Safety, 1775–1776 (Trenton. 1879), Journal of the Votes and Proceedings of the Convention of New Jersey, 1776 (Trenton. 1831), Minutes of the Council of Safety of the State of New Jersey, 1777, 1778 (Jersey City. 1872), Minutes of the Provincial Congress and the Council of Safety (Trenton. 1879), the First Report of the Public Record Commission of New Jersey (Somerville. 1899), Stryker's Official Register of Officers and Men of the Revolutionary War (Trenton. 1872), and his Record of Officers and Men in the Civil War, 1861–5 (Trenton. 1876. 2v.).[168] Two important publications of the New Jersey Historical Society are Selections from the Correspondence of the Executive of New Jersey from 1776–1786 (Collections, v. 5. Newark. 1848), and Stevens' Analytical Index to the Colonial Documents of New Jersey in the State Paper Office in England, ed. by Whitehead (N. J. Hist. Soc. Collections, v. 5. N. Y. 1858); this latter contains a Catalogue of Books on New Jersey during the Colonial Period.[169] In this connec-

tion consult Nelson's Check List of the Issues of the Press of New Jersey, 1723, 1728, 1754–1800 (Paterson. 1899).[170]

Pennsylvania

A selection of Pennsylvania Archives (Phil. 1852–6. 12v.) has been supplemented by a second series (Harrisburg. 1874–93. 19v.) and a third series (1894–5. 4v.).[171] Kindred to this is Colonial Records, 1683–1790 (Phil. 1852. 16v.).[172] The Statutes at Large of Pennsylvania from 1682–1801 (Phil. 1896–. v. 2+) are now in course of publication. The Votes and Proceedings of the House of Representatives were collected and reprinted (Phil. 1752–76. 6v.).[173] The Proceedings relative to the Calling of the Conventions of 1776 and 1790, with View of Proceedings of the Council of Censors (Harrisburg. 1825) have been reprinted in one volume.[174] The Report of the Commission to locate the Site of the Frontier Forts of Pennsylvania (Harrisburg. 1896. 2v.) is an historical investigation authorized by the state.[175] The publications of the Historical Society of Pennsylvania form a series of much value, especially the Pennsylvania Magazine of History and Biography.[176] Other society publications and periodicals are Proceedings of the Pennsylvania German Society (Lancaster. 1891–. 8v.+), Egle's Notes and Queries (Harrisburg. Series 1–4. 8v.), and Hazard's Register of Pennsylvania (Phil. 1828–36. 16v.).[177] In calendars there have been published Report of the Select Committee on the Colonial Records of Pennsylvania (Phil. 1851), and a Catalogue of Papers relating to Pennsylvania and Delaware deposited at the State Paper Office, London (Phil. 1850).[178] Of essential importance is Hildeburn's Century of Printing : Issues of the Press of Pennsylvania, 1685–1784 (Phil. 1885–6. 2v.).[179] [See, also, Pennsylvania Historical Society, sect. 369, below.]

Delaware

The Minutes of the Council from 1776–1792 has been printed by the Delaware Historical Society (Papers, v. 6. Wilmington. 1887).[180] See, also, a Catalogue of Papers relating to Pennsylvania and Delaware, deposited at the State Paper Office, London (Phil. 1850).[181]

Maryland

The Archives of Maryland (Balt. 1883–. 21v.+) are, by authority of the state, in course of publication by the Maryland Historical Society.[182] Kindred thereto, of the publications of the same society, are Streeter's Papers relating to the Early History of Maryland (Fund publications, v. 9. Balt. 1876).[183] The General Public Statutory Law and Public Local Law from the Year 1692–1839, with a Copious Index, has been printed (Balt. 1840. 3v.).[184] In this connection see Indices to the Laws and Resolutions of Maryland, 1800–1845 (Annapolis. 1815–46. 4v.), Index to the Journals of the Senate and House of Delegates of Maryland (Annapolis. 1856–7. 3v.), Index to the Printed Bills of the House of Delegates of Maryland, 1824–49 (Annapolis. 1850), and Index to the Public Documents of the House of Delegates, 1834–44 (Annapolis. 1845).[185] The Proceedings of the Conventions of the Province of Maryland, 1774–6, was printed at Baltimore in 1836.[186] Publications on the state archives are: Alexander's Report of Certain Documents touching the Provincial History of Maryland (Balt. 1860), Ethan Allen's Report of the Condition of the Public Records (Annapolis. 1860), and Report of the Special Committee appointed for the Purpose of examining the Condition of the Public Records of this State (Annapolis. 1853).[187] In bibliography, see Lee's Hand List of Laws, Journals and Documents of Maryland, to 1800 (Balt. 1878), and the incomplete Bibliography of Maryland by J. G. Morris (Historical Magazine, n. s. 7: 240–328).[188]

Virginia

The Calendar of Virginia State Papers is now in process of publication (Richmond. 1875–. 11v.+).[189] Hening's Statutes at Large from 1619 was printed in various places (1819–1823. 13v.).[190] The Proceedings of the [Revolutionary] Convention [of 1775–6] (Richmond. 1816), the Journal of the Senate 1778–90 (Richmond. 1827–8. 9v.), and the Journal of the House of Delegates from 1776–1786 (Richmond. 1827–8. 4v.) have been printed.[191] The Virginia Historical Society has issued the Records of the Virginia Company (Publications, n. s., v. 7, 8. Richmond. 1888–9. 2v.), and other publications of this society are of importance, especially the Virginia Historical Register (Richmond. 1848–53. 6v.), the Virginia Historical Reporter (Richmond. 1854–60. 2v.), and the Virginia Magazine of History and Biography (Richmond. 1893–. 6v.+).[192] Another valuable magazine is the William and Mary College Quarterly (Williamsburg. 1892–. 7v.+).[193]

North Carolina

The Colonial Records of North Carolina have been printed (Raleigh. 1886–. 16v.+).[194] The state has issued Indexes to Documents relative to North Carolina during the Colonial Existence of said State, now on File in the Offices of the Board of Trade and State Paper Office in London (Raleigh. 1843), and Saunders' Abstracts of Records and Documents relating to the Colonial History of North Carolina (Raleigh. 1885).[195] Valuable publications are Weeks' Press in North Carolina (Brooklyn. 1891), which contains a list of books printed there to 1800, his Libraries and Literature of North Carolina in the Eighteenth Century (Wash. 1896), and his Bibliography of the Historical Literature of North Carolina (Cambridge. 1895).[196]

South Carolina

In the Collections of the South Carolina Historical Society (Vols. I and III) are printed Lists and Abstracts of Papers in the State Paper Office, London, relating to South Carolina, and the same society has recently issued a Report of the Committee in the Matter of Procuring Transcripts of the Colonial Records of this State from the London Record Office (Charleston. 1891); see, also, The Colonial Records of South Carolina (Magazine of American History, 26 : 388).[197] Of value are Carroll's Historical Collections of South Carolina (N. Y. 1836. 2v.), embracing many valuable and rare pamphlets and other documents relating to the history of the state, Weston's Documents connected with the History of South Carolina (Lond. 1856), Gibbes' Documentary History of the American Revolution, consisting of Letters and Papers relating to the Contest for Liberty, chiefly in South Carolina (N. Y. and Columbia. 1853–7. 3v.), and State Papers on Nullification (Bost. 1834).[198] The Statutes at Large from 1682 to 1838 have been printed (Columbia. 1836–73. 10v.), and subsequent volumes have been issued, covering the years 1839–1892 (v. 11–21+).[199] Whitney's Bibliography of the Colonial History of South Carolina is printed in the American Historical Association Report for 1894 (p. 563).[200] The Historical Society has just begun the publication of the South Carolina Historical and Genealogical Magazine.[201]

Florida

Buckingham Smith's Coleccion de varios documentos para la historia de la Florida y tierras adyacentes (Lond. 1857) is valuable.[202] In the Papers of the Southern History Association (I, 211) is a Bibliography of the Statute Law of Florida by T. L. Cole.[203] French's Historical Collections of Louisiana somewhat relates to Florida.[204] See, also, Alabama.

Alabama

In the American Historical Review (I, 380) is a reprint of part of the State Paper Office Calendars, Colonial Series, relating to West Florida.[205] A List of the Original Authorities on the History of the British Province of West Florida, in the Record Office, London, is printed in the publications of the Louisiana Historical Society (I, pt. 3, p. 31). In the American Historical Association Report for 1897 is printed Owen's Bibliography of Alabama, and the Bibliography of the Statute Law of the State, by T. L. Cole, is printed in the Papers of the Southern History Association (I, 61).[206]

Louisiana

French's Historical Collections of Louisiana (N. Y. 1846–75. 7v.) is of much importance, and includes an Analytical Index of all the Public Documents in Paris relating to the Discovery and Early Settlement of Louisiana, in the Archives de la departement de la marine et des colonies.[207] In this connection see Boimare's Notes bibliographiques et raisonnées sur les principaux ouvrages publiés sur la Floride et l'ancienne Louisiane (Paris. 1855).[208] See, also, French and Canadian above.

Tennessee

Journal of the Proceedings of the Legislative Council of the Territory of the United States south of the River Ohio, and the Journal of the General Assembly of the State of Tennessee for the Years 1794–6, were reprinted in Nashville in 1852.[209] The Tennessee Historical Society Papers (Nashville. 1884) contains a Bibliography of Tennessee.[210]

Ohio

The state has published no records, but of value are the issues of the Ohio State Archæological and Historical Society (Columbus. 1891–. 7v.+), the Ohio Valley Historical Series (Cin. 1868–71. 8v.), Howe's Historical Collections of Ohio (Columbus. 1889–91. 3v.), and Olden Time (Pittsburg. 1846–8. 2v.).[211] See Thomson's Bibliography of Ohio (Cin. 1880).[212]

The West

No systematic publication of archives, journals, or laws has been made throughout the balance of the United States, but a few passing notes may be of value. The State Historical Society of Wisconsin Reports and Collections (Madison. 1855–98. 14v.) are important, and only second thereto are the Iowa State Historical Society's Annals of Iowa (Iowa City. 1863–94. 16v.), supplemented by Documentary Material relating to the History of Iowa (Iowa City. 1895–6), and the Iowa Historical Record (Iowa City. 1885–. 15v.+).[213] A Bibliography of Arkansas Laws is given in the Papers of the Southern History Association (I, 113),[214] and other bibliographies are Yohn's Catalogue of Books relating to Indiana (Indianapolis. 1878),[215] Howe's Descriptive Catalogue of the Official Publications of the Territory and State of Indiana from 1800–1890 (Indiana Historical Society Pamphlets, No. 5. Indianapolis. 1890),[216] Williams' Bibliography of Minnesota (Minnesota Hist. Soc., v. 3, pt. 1, p. 13. St. Paul. 1870),[217] Durrie's Bibliography of Wisconsin (Historical Magazine, n. s., vol. 6),[218] Raines' Bibliography of Texas (Austin. 1896),[219] Williams' Bibliography of Dakota (Minnesota Hist. Soc., III, 37),[220] Foster's Bibliography of Oregon (Magazine of American History, VII, 461),[221] Taylor's Bibliografia Californica (Sacramento. 1863),[222] Shinn's Documents on California (Magazine of American History, XXV, 394), Shinn's Early Books and Magazines of California (Overland Monthly, n. s., XII, 337),[223] Silliman's Partial Reference List of United States Government Publications on Alaska (Monthly Catalogue of U. S. Pub. Doc., No. 37. Wash. 1898).[224]

13

THE more important documents and papers contained in the publications of such historical societies, printing clubs, etc., as have not restricted their collections to a limited field, are mentioned in the following notes. The publications of societies less general in the scope of their work are classed with the bibliography of the sections or divisions to which they pertain.

American Academy of Political and Social Science. Philadelphia, Pa. This society was organized in 1889, and has published *Annals of the American Academy*, 17 volumes, 1890–1901, with *Supplements*, 19 nos., 1891 to 1901 ; also a series of 318 numbered *Publications*, 1890 to 1901. [225

Among the *Publications* are the following: Canada and the U. S., by J. G. Bourinot: — Origin of Connecticut towns, by C. M. Andrews: — Constitution of Mexico, tr. by B. Moses: — Recent constitution-making in the U. S., by F. N. Thorpe: — Congress and the cabinet, by G. Bradford: — Constitution of Colombia, tr. by B. Moses: — First state constitutions, and sources of American Federalism, by W. C. Morey: — Nicaragua Canal and the Monroe doctrine, by L. M. Keasbey: — Growth of the French Canadian race in America, by J. Davidson: — First appointment of federal representatives in the U. S., by E. J. James: — State constitutions of the American Revolution, by W. C. Webster. [226

American Antiquarian Society. Worcester, Mass. The American Antiquarian Society was organized in 1812. At various dates from 1820 to 1885 it published 7 volumes of transactions and collections under the general title of *Archæologia Americana*. *Proceedings* of the society, from 1843 to 1880, were published in 64 numbers. In 1882 a new series of *Proceedings* was begun, of which 14 volumes had been published in 1901. [227

The most important contents of the *Archæologia Americana* are the following: —
V. 1: Accounts of the discovery of the Mississippi, by Lewis Hennepin. [228
V. 2: Synopsis of the Indian tribes of North America, by Albert Gallatin. [229
V. 3: Records of the Company of the Massachusetts Bay to the embarkation of Winthrop and his associates. [230
V. 4: Original documents from the State Paper Office,

London, and the British Museum, illustrating the history of Sir Walter Raleigh's first American colony and the colony at Jamestown: — A Discourse of Virginia, by E. M. Wingfield. [231
V. 5, 6: History of printing in America and an account of newspapers, by Isaiah Thomas. [232
In the new series of *Proceedings* the following are chiefly important: —
V. 1: Notes on the bibliography of Yucatan and Central America, by A. F. Bandelier: — Origin of the names of the states of the Union, by H. B. Staples. [233
V. 2: Notes on the history of witchcraft in Massachusetts, by G. H. Moore. [234
V. 3: The history of Connecticut, as illustrated by the names of her towns, by F. B. Dexter. [235
V. 4: The connection of Massachusetts with slavery and the slave trade, by Charles Deane: — Archæological research in Yucatan, by E. H. Thompson. [236
V. 5: Estimates of population in the American colonies, by F. B. Dexter: —King Philip's War, with special reference to the attack on Brookfield, by Grindall Reynolds: — The early African slave trade in New England, by W. B. Weeden: — Notes on the bibliography of witchcraft in Massachusetts, by G. H. Moore: — The legislative history of the Ordinance of 1787, by J. M. Merriam: — Naval history of the Revolution, by E. E. Hale. [237
V. 6: The navigation laws, by Edward Channing. [238
V. 7: Government in Canada and the U. S. compared, by G. F. Hoar: — The French Canadians in New England, by E. C. Smyth. [239
V. 8: Yucatan at the time of its discovery, by E. H. Thompson: — The British Public Record Office, and the materials in it for early American history, by W. N. Sainsbury. [240
V. 9: Edmund Burke, his services as Agent of the Province of New York, by C. Stebbins: — Concord, [Mass.], by J. McK. Merriam: — The rival claimants for North America, 1497-1755, by Justin Winsor. [241
Many of these articles have also been published separately.
Among the occasional publications of the Society are the following: Records of the Council for New England, in 3 parts, ed. by Charles Deane: — The Mathers and the witchcraft delusion, by S. F. Haven: — Lieut.-Gen. John Burgoyne and the Convention of Saratoga, by Charles Deane: — Massachusetts and Maine, their union and separation, by P. E. Aldrich: — The Katunes of Maya history, by P. J. J. Valentini: — Origin of New England towns, their powers and duties, by P. E. Aldrich. [242

American Historical Association. Washington, D. C. This association was organized in 1884. From 1885 to 1891 it published 5 volumes of *Papers*. The *Annual reports* with papers from 1889 to 1899 form 13 volumes. [243

The most important articles are the following: —
1891: The earliest Texas, by Mrs. L. C. Harby. [244
1893: The historical significance of the Missouri Compromise, by J. A. Woodburn: — The establishment of the first southern boundary of the U. S., by B. A. Hinsdale. [245
1894: The regulators of North Carolina, by J. S. Bassett. [246
1895: The surroundings and site of Raleigh's colony, by Talcott Williams: — Governor Edward Winslow, his place and part in Plymouth colony, by Rev. W. C. Winslow: — "Free burghs" in the U. S., by J. H. Blodgett: — Slavery in the Province of South Carolina (1670–1770), by Edward McCrady. [247
1896: Journal and papers of the Continental Congress, by Herbert Friedenwald: — The anti-rent episode in the State of New York, by David Murray: — The West as a field for historical study, by F. J. Turner: — Proposed amendments to the Constitution of the U. S. during the first century of its existence, by H. V. Ames. [248
1897: The diplomacy of the U. S. in regard to Cuba, by J. H. Latané: — The Protestant revolution in Maryland, by B. C. Steiner. [249
1898: The Society of Separatists of Zoar, Ohio, by G. B. Landis: — Diplomatic relations of the Confederate States with England, by J. M. Callahan. [250
Many articles in the *Reports* and *Papers* are also issued separately.

Bradford Club. New York. Organized in 1859. [251
Among other papers published are the following: Papers concerning the attack on Hatfield and Deerfield by a party of Indians, Sept. 19th, 1677: — The operations of the French fleet under the Count de Grasse, in 1781–82: — The northern invasion of October, 1780, papers relating to the expedition from Canada under Sir John Johnson: — The army correspondence of Col. John Laurens, 1777–78. [252

Columbia University. New York City. In 1891 the University began the publication of a series of *Studies in history, economics, and public law*, of which 13 volumes had been issued in 1901. [253
Among their contents are: —
V. 1: History of tariff administration in the U. S., by J. D. Goss: — Financial history of Massachusetts, by C. H. J. Douglas. [254
V. 3: History of elections in the American Colonies, by C. F. Bishop: — Commercial policy of England toward the American Colonies, by G. L. Beer. [255
V. 4: Financial history of Virginia, 1609–1776, by W. Z. Ripley. [256
V. 5: Double taxation in the U. S., by F. Walker. [257
V. 6: History of proprietary government in Pennsylvania, by W. R. Shepherd. [258
V. 7: History of the transition from provincial to commonwealth government in Massachusetts, by H. A. Cushing. [259

V. 8: Struggle between President Johnson and Congress over reconstruction, by C. E. Chadsey. [260
V. 10: Rhode Island and the formation of the Union, by F. G. Bates. [261

Harvard University. Cambridge, Mass. In 1890 and 1891 two volumes of *Harvard historical monographs* were published, and a series of *Harvard historical studies* was begun in 1896, of which 6 numbers have been issued. [262
The contents of the *Monographs* are: —
V. 1: The veto power in the U. S., by E. C. Mason. [263
V. 2: Introduction to the study of federal government, by A. B. Hart. [264
The *Studies* are: —
V. 1: The suppression of the African slave trade to the U. S. 1638–1870, by W. E. B. DuBois. [265
V. 2: The contest over the ratification of the Federal Constitution in Massachusetts, by S. B. Harding. [266
V. 3: A critical study of nullification in South Carolina, by D. F. Houston. [267
V. 4: Nominations for elective offices in the U. S., by F. W. Dallinger. [268
V. 5: A bibliography of British municipal history, including gilds and parliamentary representation, by Charles Gross. [269
V. 6: The Liberty and Free Soil Parties in the Northwest, by T. C. Smith. [270

Historical Printing Club. Brooklyn, N. Y. The Historical Printing Club was formed in 1876, and has published a considerable number of volumes and pamphlets on subjects relating to early American history, especially the Revolutionary period. [271
Among them are bibliographies of Alexander Hamilton and Benjamin Franklin, compiled by Paul Leicester Ford: — a collection of Pamphlets and of Essays on the Constitution of the U. S. published during the discussion by the people, 1787–1788, ed. by Mr. Ford: — Bibliography of the adoption of the Constitution of the U. S., by Mr. Ford. [272
There are also the following: Report of a Committee of the Lords of the Privy Council on the trade of Great Britain with the U. S., Jan. 1791: — The spurious letters attributed to Washington: — The U. S. and Spain in 1790, an episode in diplomacy, with an introduction by W. C. Ford: — The Washington-Duché letters: —Letters of William Lee, 1766–83. 3v. : — Prisoners of war (British and American), 1778, ed. by W. C. Ford. [273

Johns Hopkins University. Baltimore, Md. In 1883 the Johns Hopkins University began the publication of the *University studies in historical and political science*, of which 19 series and 19 extra volumes had been issued in 1901. The more important ones are separately noticed, in their proper places, hereafter. [274

Maine Historical Society. Portland, Me.

Organized in 1822, and from 1831 to 1891 published its 1st series of *Collections*, consisting of 10 volumes. The 2d series, called *Collections and proceedings*, from 1890 to 1901, contains 10 volumes. There is also a *Documentary series*, of which the 1st volume was issued in 1869, the 8th in 1901. All three series are devoted to subjects relating to the history of Maine.

[275

Among the most important articles in the 1st series are: —

V. 2: Briefe narration of the originall undertakings of the advancement of plantations into the parts of America, by Sir Ferdinando Gorges, London, 1658.

[276

V. 6: French neutrals in Maine, by Joseph Williamson.

[277

V. 7: Journal of the attack of the rebels on His Majesty's ships and troops, 24th July, 1779, in Penobscot Bay, from the Nova Scotia Gazette, Sept. 14, 1779: — Slavery in Maine, by Joseph Williamson. [278

In the 2d series is: —

V. 2. The capture of the Margaretta, the first naval battle of the Revolution, by G. F. Talbot. [279

On the contents of the *Documentary series*, Prof. H. L. Osgood writes as follows: —

" Vol. 1 contains J. G. Kohl's *History of the discovery of Maine*. This is an elaborate monograph, not simply on the voyages to the Maine coast, but on the entire work of discovery by Europeans along the North American coast from the time of the Northmen till, at the close of the 16th century, Raleigh initiated English colonization. It is an original work of the first importance and contains many of the most valuable among the early maps. [280

" Vol. 2 contains Richard Hakluyt's *Discourse concerning western planting*, edited, with notes by Charles Deane and introduction by Leonard Woods. [281

" In vol. 3 are *The Trelawny papers*, edited by J. P. Baxter. Robert Trelawny and Moses Goodyear secured from the New England Council in 1631 a patent for Richmond's Island and Cape Elizabeth, near Portland, Me. John Winter was sent over as agent, and a large trade was opened. Much of the correspondence here printed is between Trelawny and his agent. The rest of it chiefly concerns the controversy over the award in 1648, transferring Trelawny's plantation to Robert Jordan and his heirs. The papers throw much light on the early history of Maine. [282

" Vols. 4 and 5 contain the *Baxter manuscripts*, a miscellaneous collection of documents procured in part from the British Public Record Office. These relate to the history of the settlements along the Maine coast previous to 1700." [283

Massachusetts Historical Society, Boston, Mass. Organized in 1791, in 1900 this Society had published 61 volumes of *Collections*, and 36 volumes of *Proceedings*. [284

The *Collections* are divided into series of 10 vols. each — the tenth volume containing a consolidated index to the whole series. The first 20 volumes of the *Proceedings* form also a series with a consolidated index

in a separate volume. Several of the early volumes of the *Collections* have been reprinted. Innumerable papers, taken from the *Collections* and the *Proceedings*, have been separately printed, and many documents first printed by the society have since been published by individuals or by publishing houses. But, as many of these reprints have either been " privately printed " or published in " limited editions," the volumes of the Society's *Collections* and *Proceedings* remain the great storehouse to which the student must have recourse. The earlier volumes of the *Collections* contain masses of miscellaneous matter; but the later volumes have been devoted to single works or to classes of papers. Since 1858 the shorter disconnected pieces have been printed in the *Proceedings*. The following list is necessarily confined to an enumeration of the more important papers and volumes (the Society has in contemplation a working bibliography of its printed matter).

[285

COLLECTIONS

Francis Higginson's New England's plantation, 1629, describes events in the early history of Salem: — Examination of Dr. Benjamin Church: — New England's first fruits in respect to the progress of learning at Cambridge, 1643, the earliest account of Harvard College: — William Morrell's Account of New England, in verse. Ser. 1, v. 1. [286

Thomas Pemberton's Historical journal of the American war. Ser. 1, v. 2. [287

Roger Williams' Key to the language of North America. Ser. 1, v. 3. [288

Thomas Brattle's Witchcraft delusion, 1692: — William Bradford's Letter book [Extracts]: — [Hartwell, Blair, and Chilton], Present state of Virginia, 1696. Ser. 1, v. 5. [289

Review of the military operations, 1753–56 [and other papers relating to the same epoch]. Ser. 1, v. 7. [290

Edward Johnson's Wonder working Providence of Sion's Saviour in New England, an early account by one of the settlers. Ser. 2, v. 2–4, 7, 8. [291

J. Meigs' Journal of Arnold's expedition to Quebec. Ser. 2, v. 2. [292

New England's Jonas cast up in London, 1647. Ser. 2, v. 4. [293

William Hubbard's General history of New England, the earliest compiled history, now largely superseded owing to the discovery and printing of Bradford's and Winthrop's histories. Ser. 2, v. 5, 6. [294

Prince's Annals of New England, v. 2, nos. 1–3: — Rhode Island state papers (1638–1676). Ser. 2, v. 7.

[295

Massachusetts and the Commissioners, 1662–1666: — The new life of Virginia, 1612: — Capt. John Mason's Brief history of the Pequot war. Ser. 2, v. 8. [296

A perfect description of Virginia, 1649. Ser. 2, v. 9.

[297

Edward Winslow's New England's Salamander discovered: — Josiah Cotton's Vocabulary of the Massachusetts Indians. Ser. 3, v. 2. [298

John Smith's Advertisement for the unexperienced planters of New England: — Lechford's Plain dealing: — Josselyn's Two voyages to New England. Ser. 3, v. 3. [299

Tracts relating to the attempts to convert to Christianity the Indians of New England. Ser. 3, v. 4. [300

Journal of the Congress at Albany, 1754: — Journal of Christopher Gist, 1783: — Journal of a treaty with the Indians, 1793. Ser. 3, v. 5. [301

Underhill's History of the Pequot war, 1638: — Vincent's True relation [of the Pequot war]: — Sir Ferdinando Gorges's Description of New England: — A brief narration, etc., 1658: — Capt. John Smith's Description of New England, 1616. Ser. 3, v. 6. [302

Samuel Niles's History of the Indian and French wars. Ser. 3, v. 6; ser. 4, v. 5. [303

Documents relating to Gosnold's Voyage to New England, 1602: — Voyage made, 1605, by Capt. Waymouth: — Voyage into New England, 1623–24, by Christopher Levett: — Massachusetts' Body of liberties, 1641. Ser. 3, v. 8. [304

Winthrop papers. Ser. 3, v. 10; ser. 4, v. 6, 7; ser. 5, v. 1, 8; ser. 6, v. 3, 5. This mass of papers relates to the history of New England from 1630–1727, more particularly to that of Massachusetts and Connecticut. Many other papers from the Winthrop collection are scattered through the *Proceedings* and the earlier volumes of the *Collections*. For a partial enumeration of those in the *Proceedings*, see Coll., ser. 6, v. 9, preface. [305

Joseph Hunter's Collections concerning the early history of the founders of New Plymouth: — Strachey's Account of the Popham Colony and other papers relating to the same settlement: — Newell's Journal (Boston, 1775–76). Ser. 4, v. 1. [306

John Clark's Ill-newes from New England, 1652. Ser. 4, v. 2. [307

William Bradford's History of Plymouth Plantation, edited by Charles Deane, ser. 4, v. 3; still the most serviceable edition for the student. [308

Correspondence as to the relief of the sufferers by the Boston port bill. Ser. 4, v. 4. [309

Hinckley papers, ser. 4, v. 5; relate mainly to the affairs of New Plymouth Colony and Massachusetts from 1676 to 1690. [310

Mather papers, ser. 4, v. 8; relate to New England (1650–1725), especially to the period, 1670–1690. [311

Aspinwall papers. Ser. 4, v. 9, 10. Some of these papers relate to the earlier history of Virginia, but most of them have to do with the critical years, 1763–1775. [312

Belknap papers. Ser. 5, v. 2, 3; ser. 6, v. 4. These papers cover the years, 1766–1798; but the great mass of the material relates to the years after 1780. [313

Letters and documents relating to slavery in Massachusetts. Ser. 5, v. 3. [314

Centennial volume. Ser. 5, v. 4. It contains Washington's Letters to General Heath, John Adams's Correspondence with Professor Winthrop, and John Adams's Correspondence with Mrs. Mercy Warren. [315

Samuel Sewall's Diary, ser. 5, v. 5–7, and his Letter book, ser. 6, v. 1, 2, form an admirable exposition of New England life in the mid-colonial period. The diary is unique among American contemporaneous records. [316

Trumbull papers. Ser. 5, v. 9, 10. These papers relate to the colonial history of Connecticut and to the correspondence of Washington and Governor Trumbull. [317

Belcher papers, ser. 6, v. 6, 7, concern the history of New Hampshire, Massachusetts, and New Jersey, of which colonies Belcher was governor. Interesting also for the light they throw on social life at a later period than is covered by Sewall's Diary. [318

Historical index to the Pickering papers, ser. 6, v. 8, is a calendar of the papers of Timothy Pickering extending from 1769 to 1828. This collection numbers 57 bound manuscript volumes and is the largest collection of Federalist papers open to the public. The calendar is so constructed that the student can see at a glance what each paper contains. [319

Bowdoin and Temple papers. Ser. 6, v. 9. The papers printed in this volume extend from 1756 to 1782. Many of them are of great value. Among them are letters from Washington, George Grenville, Temple, Whately, Franklin, Bollan, Bowdoin, and Trumbull. [320

Pepperrell papers, ser. 6, v. 10, are an exceedingly valuable collection of official documents and private papers relating to the capture of Louisburg by the New Englanders in 1745. [321

Jefferson papers (1770–1826). Ser. 7, v. 1. These are personal papers, which throw light on Jefferson's character, a few important political letters, and a good deal of interesting material respecting the University of Virginia. [322

PROCEEDINGS

Diary of Thomas Newell at Boston, 1773–74. Ser. 1, v. 4. [323

George Livermore's The opinions of the founders of the Republic respecting negroes. Ser. 1, v. 6. [324

Samuel Sewall's The selling of Joseph, 1700. (Also in Coll., ser. 5, v. 6.) Reprint of a rare tract against negro slavery: — Ezekiel Price's Diary [siege of Boston]. Ser. 1, v. 7. [325

John Andrews's Letters, 1772–76. Ser. 1, v. 8. These relate to the period of the Revolution in Massachusetts. [326

Joel Parker's Origin of the towns of New England: — James Walker's Memoir of Josiah Quincy: — Bacon and Ingram's Rebellion [in Virginia]. A most valuable original account of this interesting movement: — T. C. Amory, Memory of General John Sullivan vindicated. Ser. 1, v. 9. [327

Charles Deane's The forms used in issuing Letters-Patent by the crown of England: — William Bradford's Dialogue between old men and young men. Ser. 1, v. 11. [328

Capt. John Smith's New England's trials [Lond. 1620]. Ser. 1, v. 12. [329

Papers relating to the Boston Tea Party: — Charles Deane, On the Massachusetts Bill of Rights. Ser. 1, v. 13. [330

Charles Deane, On Paul Revere's Signal. Ser. 1, v. 15. [331

Narrative of Jolley Allen, 1775–76 [a Boston Tory]. Ser. 1, v. 16. [332

Journal of Thomas Wallcut, to Marietta [and back in 1720]. Ser. 1, v. 17. [333

Papers relating to the Popham colony : — G. E. Ellis and J. G. Whittier on the latter's poem entitled The King's missive. Ser. 1, v. 18. [334

Journal of Dr. Belknap's journey to Oneida, 1796. Ser. 1, v. 19. [335

C. F. Adams' Sir Christopher Gardiner. Ser. 1, v. 20. [336

G. H. Moore and others on Witchcraft in Massachusetts: — Samuel Maverick's Account of New England in 1630: — Mellen Chamberlain's The authentication of the Declaration of Independence. Ser. 2, v. 1. [337

Wild's and Dearborn's Journals of Arnold's expedition to Quebec: — Perkins's Narrative of the insurrection in San Domingo, 1793: — Diaries and journals of Sullivan's Indian campaign, 1779. Ser. 2, v. 2. [338

Joseph Priestley's Letters, 1798–1800. Ser. 2, v. 3. [339

Josiah Quincy's Account of a journey through southern New England, 1801: — Report of the trial of Mrs. Anne Hutchinson, 1638. Ser. 2, v. 4. [340

Journals of the Canada expedition of 1760. Ser. 2, v. 4, 5. [341

Dr. Pierce's Notes on Harvard Commencements. Ser. 2, v. 5. This describes not merely the Commencement exercises, but many eminent persons who participated in them. [342

Ebenezer Wild's Journal, 1776–81: — H. M. Dexter's English exiles in Amsterdam, 1597–1625: — Inscriptions on the Cabot map. Ser. 2, v. 6. [343

C. F. Adams and others, Genesis of New England towns. Ser. 2, v. 7. [344

Francis Parkman's Autobiography. Ser. 2, v. 8. [345

Jabez Fitch's Journal [of the siege of Boston], Aug.-Dec. 1775: — Dr. Watts's Letters to New England correspondents. Ser. 2, v. 9. [346

John Rowe's Diary (Boston, 1764–1779): — E. L. Pierce's Recollection as a source of history. Ser. 2, v. 10. [347

Dudley Bradstreet's Diary at siege of Louisburg, 1745. Ser. 2, v. 11. [348

Amos Farnsworth's Diary (siege of Boston). Ser. 2, v. 12. [349

John T. Hassam's The Bahama Islands: — The Dudley records, cover the period of Dudley's presidency. Ser. 2, v. 13. [350

E. C.

New York Historical Society. New York City. This society was organized in 1804. Its *Collections* exist in three series, the 1st containing 5 volumes, the 2d 4 volumes, the 3d, or Fund series, containing 26 volumes. [351

The matter contained in the 1st series was prepared and issued in the earlier years of the Society's existence, and is naturally less abundant and less valuable than that to be found in its more recent volumes. The most valuable feature of the 1st series is an authoritative edition of William Smith's *History of New York*, in 2 volumes (vols. 4, 5). Next to that in importance is the reprint of the Easthampton MS. of *The Duke of York's laws*, to be found at the close of the 1st volume. The other volumes of the series contain reprints from Hakluyt and Purchas, and papers read before the Society in its earlier years. Among the reprints, the relation of Robert Juet concerning the third voyage of Henry Hudson, in which he discovered the Hudson River, is the most important. This is in volume 1. [352

The matter contained in the 2d series relates chiefly to the Dutch period and the early English period of New York history. It consists in large part of translations from Dutch and French sources concerning those times. We find here, for example, a translation of Verrazano's *Relation* of his voyage to the North American continent (vol. 1); a translation of Van der Donck's *Description of New Netherland, 1656* (vol. 1); a translation in full of De Vries' *Voyages from Holland to America, 1632–1644* (vol. 3); a translation of the narrative of the Marquis de Nonville's expedition against the Seneca Indians in 1687 (vol. 2); translations also of the *Representation of New Netherlands* (vol. 2), of Megapolensis' *Sketch of the Mohawk Indians* (vol. 3), of the *Broad advice*, and of the *Papers* of Father Jogues (vol. 3). The journal of the embassy of Father Druillettes from Canada to New England in 1650 also appears in vol. 3, while at the close of that volume are the *Proceedings of the First Assembly of Virginia, 1619*. Vol. 4 contains the only published catalogue of the library of the Society. [353

The material contained in the Fund series relates in the main to the history of the Revolution. Exceptions to this are the contents of the first three volumes, which embrace the continuation of Chalmer's *Political annals*; Colden's *Letters on Smith's History of New York*; a considerable array of documents relating to Leisler's rebellion; the *Clarendon papers* concerning New York and New England affairs soon after 1660; documents relating to the controversy over the New Hampshire grants; matter concerning local and family history of New York city in the eighteenth century. [354

In the volume for 1880 appear *The case of Chief Justice William Atwood, 1713*, and the *Journal of the Court of Lieutenancy at New York, 1686–1696*. [355

The volume for 1885 contains all the material available in the records of New York city and the archives at Albany, relating to great and small burgher rights in New Amsterdam, and to the admission of freemen by the city of New York, with full lists both of burghers and freemen, and a list of indentures of apprenticeship from Feb. 1694 to Jan. 1707. [356

The volume for 1891 is filled with the muster rolls of New York during the French and Indian war, while a part of the correspondence which appears in the other volumes relates also to that war. [357

The material in this series which concerns the Revolution begins with the *Papers of Gen. Charles Lee*, filling 4 volumes. The collection, much of which was left by General Lee to William Goddard, and was intrusted by one of his descendants, Mr. Samuel G. Goddard, to Mr. George H. Moore for publication, contains not only the correspondence, but the political and military writings of the General. The letters relate to the entire period of his active life, and every effort has been made to secure a complete collection. The 4th volume also contains reprints of three of the standard memoirs of General Lee, including that by Jared Sparks. That volume closes with a reprint of George H. Moore's *Treason of General Charles Lee*. [358

The volume for 1875 contains the letters of General James Pattison while he was an officer in the British artillery in the early part of 1779, and later while he was commandant in the city of New York (July, 1779 to Aug. 1780), also letters to General Lewis Morris, continuing through the Revolution and written from various quarters. [359

The volumes for 1876 and 1877 contain the *Colden papers*. These are the letter-books of Governor Cadwallader Colden, and extend from 1760, when, as President of the Council, he first became Acting Governor of the province, through his later terms of service till his death in 1775. The correspondence is voluminous, and it forms one of the most important sources of information concerning events in New York during the entire controversy which preceded the war of the Revolution. [360

The volumes for 1878, 1879, and 1880 form a sub-series, entitled *Revolutionary papers*. They contain the papers of Charles Thomson, secretary of the Congress of the Confederation, which relate especially to debates in that congress and to affairs in Pennsylvania during 1774 and 1775 ; letters of Colonel Armand, a French officer, relating in part to the siege of Yorktown; letters to Robert Morris; the proceedings of the courts-martial for the trials of General Schuyler (Oct. 1778), of General Robert Howe of North Carolina (Jan. 1782), and of General St. Clair (Aug. 1778); the journal of Commissary Rainsford of the British army, containing much matter concerning the employment by Great Britain of German auxiliaries for the war; a journal of occurrences at Quebec from Nov. 1775 to May, 1776, by an officer of the British garrison. [361

In 1881 the Society printed the *Montresor journals*. These are the diaries of two British engineers who were employed in the American service. The diary of Colonel James Montresor extends from 1757 to 1759, and thus relates wholly to the French and Indian war. That of his son, Captain John Montresor, extends from 1757 to 1778. [362

In 1882 the Society printed the letter-books of Lieutenant Von Krafft and Captain Alexander MacDonald, both officers on the British side during the Revolutionary war. [363

The volumes for 1883 and 1884 contain the *Kemble papers*. These are the journals of Colonel Stephen Kemble from 1773 to 1779, while he was Deputy Adjutant-General of the British army in America ; also during 1784–5 and 1788. This collection also includes a journal, order-books, and documents relating to an expedition in 1780–81 against Nicaragua, which was commanded by Kemble as Brigadier-General. In the first of these volumes (also from the *Kemble papers*) are the order-books of General Sir William Howe from Nov. 1775 to May, 1778, followed by some of the orders of Sir Henry Clinton. [364

In the volume for 1886 the Society began the publication of the *Papers of Silas Deane*, and these have been completed in 5 volumes (1886–1890). These letters and papers have been brought together both from printed and manuscript sources, and form as near as possible an exhaustive collection. They relate to the life of Mr. Deane as a member of the Continental Congress, to his labors as an American agent in France, and in great detail to the controversy which arose over his conduct in France, and to the justification of that conduct, to which Mr. Deane devoted much attention during his later years. [365

It will be noted that in the selection of material for this series the Society has drawn quite fully from British and loyalist sources. The contents of all the volumes have been carefully edited, and the series is amply provided with indexes. [366

H. L. O.

Old South Work, Directors of. Boston, Mass. This association was organized in 1881, and in 1883 began the publication of the *Old South leaflets,* of which 96 had been published in 1898. [367

The most important are the following: No. 7. Charter of Massachusetts Bay, 1629. No. 8. Fundamental orders of Connecticut, 1638. No. 9. Franklin's plan of union, 1754. No. 13. The ordinance of 1787. No. 14. The constitution of Ohio. No. 17. Verrazano's voyage. No. 21. Eliot's narrative, 1670. No. 22. Wheelock's narrative, 1762. No. 23. The petition of rights, 1628. No. 24. The grand remonstrance, 1641. No. 25. The Scottish national covenant, 1638. No. 26. The agreement of the people, 1648–9. No. 27. The instrument of government, 1653. No. 31. The voyages to Vinland, from the saga of Eric the Red. No. 37. Early notices of the voyages of the Cabots. No. 39. De Vaca's account of his journey to New Mexico, 1535. No. 40. Manasseh Cutler's description of Ohio, 1787. No. 41. Washington's journal of his tour to the Ohio, 1770. No. 44. Jefferson's life of Capt. Meriwether Lewis. No. 48. Bradford's memoir of Elder Brewster. No. 54. Letters of Roger Williams to Winthrop. No. 69. Description of the New Netherlands, by Adrian Van der Donck. No. 74. Hamilton's report on the coinage. No. 77. Cotton Mather's lives of Bradford and Winthrop. [368

Pennsylvania, Historical Society of. Philadelphia. This society, organized in 1825, has made extensive and valuable contributions to the history of the state. Its publications include 14 volumes of *Memoirs,* of which the 1st appeared in 1826 and the 14th in 1895, a *Bulletin,* of which 13 numbers were published in the years 1845, '6 and '7, one volume of *Collections,* 1853, and the *Pennsylvania magazine of history and biography,* a quarterly, which, begun in 1877, completed its 24th volume in 1901.

[369

The *Memoirs* contain much original material relative to the life of William Penn and the settlement of Pennsylvania. Articles deserving special notice are as follows: — [370

V. 1: Original letters of William Penn, and papers relating to them: — Notices of negro slavery as connected with Pennsylvania, by Edward Bettle. [371

V. 3, pt. 1: Short description of the province of New Sweden, now called by the English Pennsylvania, by T. C. Holm: — History of the University of Pennsylvania to 1827, by G. B. Wood: — Inedited letters of William Penn. [372

V. 3, pt. 2: Memoir on the history of the treaty made by William Penn with the Indians in 1682, by P. S. Du Ponceau and J. F. Fisher. [373

V. 5: History of an expedition against Fort Du Quesne in 1755, under Maj.-Gen. Edward Braddock, ed. from original manuscripts by Winthrop Sargent.

[374

V. 6: The insurrection of 1794 in the western counties of Pennsylvania, by Townsend Ward: The Acadian exiles, or French neutrals, in Pennsylvania, by W. B. Reed. [375

V. 7: A military journal kept by Maj. E. Denny, 1781 to 1795. [376

V. 8: Minutes of the Committee of Defence of Philadelphia, 1814–15. [377

V. 9 and 10: Correspondence between William Penn and James Logan, Secretary of the Province of Pennsylvania, and others, 1700–1750. [378

V. 11: History of New Sweden, by Isaac Acrelius. [379

V. 12: History, manners, and customs of the Indian nations who once inhabited Pennsylvania, by John Heckewelder. [380

V. 13: Life and times of John Dickinson, 1732–1808, by C. J. Stillé. [381

V. 14: Writings of John Dickinson, ed. by P. L. Ford. [382

Important articles in the *Bulletin* are: Journal of Isaac Senter on a secret expedition against Quebec, in September, 1775: — Letters from John Clark, Jr., to General Washington, during the occupation of Philadelphia by the British. [383

The *Collections* contain: Narrative and journals of Conrad Weiser: — General Muhlenberg's journals of 1776 and 1777: — Journal of the campaign to Amboy, &c., by B. Loxley: — Journal of William Feltman, 1781–82, embracing the siege of Yorktown. Many of these articles have also been printed separately. [384

The occasional publications of the Society are numerous, the following being specially notable: Life of John Heckewelder, by E. Rondthaler: — The Mormons, by T. L. Kane: — The history of Mason and Dixon's line, by J. H. B. Latrobe: — History of the Ordinance of 1787, by Edward Coles: — History of the consolidation of the city of Philadelphia, by Eli K. Price: — Historical map of Pennsylvania, ed. by P. W. Sheafer and others. [385

Prince Society. Boston, Mass. This soci-

ety was organized in 1858, and has published the following, which are separately noticed elsewhere. [386

The Hutchinson papers: — Wood's New England's prospect: — The Andros tracts, 3v. — Sir William Alexander and American colonization: — John Wheelwright, his writings: — Voyages of the Northmen to America, ed. by Rev. E. F. Slafter: — Voyages of Samuel de Champlain, tr. by C. P. Otis, 3v. — The New English Canaan of Thomas Morton: — Sir Walter Raleigh and his colony in America: — Voyages of Peter Esprit Radisson: — Capt. John Mason, the founder of New Hampshire: — Sir Ferdinando Gorges and his province of Maine, 3v. — Antinomianism in the colony of Massachusetts Bay, ed. by C. F. Adams: — John Checkley, or, The evolution of religious tolerance in Massachusetts Bay, 2v. [387

Scotch-Irish Society of America. Philadelphia, Pa. This society was organized in 1889, and from that year to 1896 published 8 volumes of proceedings at the annual congresses. [388

Wisconsin, University of. Madison, Wis. The University of Wisconsin was founded in 1848. In 1894 it issued the first number of a series of *Bulletins on economics, political science, and history*. Seven numbers had appeared up to Dec. 1901. [389

Their contents are : No. 1 : Geographical distribution of the vote of the thirteen states on the Federal constitution, 1787-8, by O. G. Libby. No. 2 : Finances of the U. S. from 1775 to 1789, with especial reference to the budget, by C. J. Bullock. [390

The reader should consult the index for further references.

PART II. AMERICA AT LARGE

GENERAL HISTORY

Adams, Charles Kendall. Manual of historical literature. N. Y.: Harper. 1882. New ed. $2.50. [391

One hundred pages, forming chapter XIV, are devoted to histories of the United States. Section VI of this chapter, entitled *Suggestions to students and readers*, contains many excellent helps. Later editions have some new matter. Too brief to be of much value to the student, but well suited to the needs of the general reader. E. C.

Annual register, 1758–. London. 1759–. [392

A record of events covering every year from 1758 down. Almost from the start the plan has been followed of reviewing the political history of the world in the first portion of each volume, and then recording the year's remarkable occurrences chronologically. The work contains many important state papers, reports of celebrated trials, and obituary sketches, and of late years there have been reviews of science, literature and art. Down to 1863, when the " new series " began, the English history — which is naturally much fuller than other history — consisted chiefly of a summary of parliamentary debates ; since then it has been put in narrative form as in the case of other countries. The *Register* was projected by Robert Dodsley, and for nearly 30 years Edmund Burke wrote the survey of events. Indexes have been published covering 1758–1780, 1781–1792, and 1758–1819, and beginning with 1820 each volume has been indexed. There are separate pagings for the political history and the chronology. F. J. S.

Bartlett, John Russell. Bibliotheca Americana. Catalogue of books relating to North and South America in the library of the late John Carter Brown of Providence, R. I. Part I. 1482–1601. Providence. 1875. Part II. 1600–1700. Second edition. Providence. 1882. Part III (in 2v.). 1701–1800. Providence. 1870–1. 4v. [393

During 25 years of rapidly increasing interest in early American history and of the continual publication of books on the subject, this catalogue of books printed in or about America before 1801 has retained its position as one of the most important reference books for Americana. This is due less to the rarity and the importance of the books which it describes than to the method adopted in the descriptions. Mr. Bartlett's collations are often inexact and his notes are often incorrect. His work falls far short of the

ideal standards of detailed accuracy which have been created by modern bibliographic science. But his method was the right one. The fact that it is an expensive method, in time, money, energy and knowledge, may explain why it has not yet been surpassed as a model of what such a catalogue should be.

Belknap, Jeremy. American biography. Boston. 1794–8. 2v. Enl. ed. N. Y. : Harper. 1851. 3v. [394

Contains thirty-one biographies of explorers and founders of colonies, as Columbus, Cartier, Bradford and Penn. A third volume would have dealt with eighteenth century characters, but was never printed. Based on the best sources attainable then ; but now useless. The edition of 1851 contains notes and some additional matter by the editor, F. M. Hubbard. Like the original work, it is now obsolete. E. C.

Boston, Public Library of the City of. America. (In Bulletins. 1890–91. v. 9, pp. 136, 137.) [395

A catalogue of bibliographies relating to America in the library.

Griffin, Appleton Prentiss Clark. Bibliography of American historical societies, the U. S. and Canada. Wash. : Govt. Prtg. Off. 1896. [396

Reprinted from the *Annual report* of the American Historical Association for 1895. It is a careful list of all the publications of the various historical societies, giving the contents of the various proceedings and furnished with an index of nearly 10,000 authors and subjects. It is a remarkably painstaking and indispensable instrument for the study of American history. E. C. R.

Hart, Albert Bushnell, *ed.* Source-book of American history ; ed. for schools and readers, with practical introductions. N. Y. : Macmillan. 1899. 60c. [397

" Is a volume that we have examined with close attention and can commend with confidence. In about 400 pages of text, it finds room for something like 150 examples of the original material of our history, ranging all the way from the voyages of Columbus to the Spanish-American war. The selections are judiciously made, edited, and annotated ; the introductory chapters for teachers are of the most helpful sort." *Dial* (Chicago), 27 : 80.

Holmes, Abiel. American annals. Cambridge. 1805. 2v.

—— Annals of America, 1492–1826. Cambridge. 1829. 2v. [398

"It is a book still to inspire confidence, and 'the first authoritative work from an American pen which covered the whole field of American history' [G. W. Greene in *Putnam's mag.*, 1870, p. 171]. Libraries in America were then scant, but the annalist traced where he could his facts to original sources." Justin Winsor, in *Narrative and critical hist. of Am.*, 5: 619.

"Few of the Spanish writers have been consulted, those few only in translation, and Herrera, the most important of all, in a very mutilated form. The author's collection of French authorities is equally incomplete ; and of the many important works which the ex-Jesuits have bequeathed to the world, as the legacy of their illustrious order, not one appears in his catalogue." R. Southey, in *Quarterly rev.*, 2 : 319 (1809).

Larned, J. N. History for ready reference, from the best historians, biographers, and specialists : their own words in a complete system of history. Springfield, Mass. Nichols. 1894-5. 5v. $25. [399

An extensive encyclopædia of history formed by selections from the better authorities in English on each of the various subjects. Texts are reproduced faithfully and abridgments are indicated. It contains among other things many important documents, charters, edicts, constitutions, etc. It is, in brief, a thesaurus of documents and extracts from secondary sources, arranged in most convenient form (alphabetical with chronological subdivisions). One of the most important features is an index or extensive system of cross references alphabetized with the regular headings, greatly simplifying the work of reference. The supplement contains a chronology of important events, a number of genealogical tables, a select bibliography, and a list of works quoted from. This latter is most suggestive of the character of the work, and contains an impressive list of good modern historical literature. While the authority cited is not in every instance the best, the average of the works cited is high. The proportions in the distribution of the material are on the whole surprisingly good, considering the fact that they are by quotation. The work is a unique, convenient and valuable book of reference for the general reader. It is indispensable for every public library, and even for special libraries of a more scientific kind. Its documents and its comprehensiveness make it extremely useful to every student. For work in secondary schools, and even in colleges, it is simply invaluable.　E. C. R.

—— *Same.* Revised and enlarged. Springfield, Mass.: Nichols. 1901. 6v. $30. [399a

For this edition the original 5 vols. have been considerably revised, and some new topics introduced, but their record of events still closes at about 1894-5. The added sixth vol. takes up the history of the world at that point, and fits the original edition, therefore, as well as the new. Its documentary history of the Spanish-American War and the sequels thereto, of the British-Boer controversies and war, and of events of recent years in China—to say nothing of other matters—is notably complete and authentic.　G. I.

Mackenzie, Robert. America: a history. Lond. and N. Y.: Nelson. 1882. New ed. 1889. $1. [400

"Mr. Mackenzie's 'America' is well planned to meet the needs of those Englishmen who wish a compendious history of all the American states; and it will not be unacceptable to Americans who desire to know something of the history of the other nations of North and South America." It is "all the more valuable as being from an English point of view. The book is to be commended in every way—in temper and spirit, in accuracy and fulness of knowledge, in graphic and interesting narrative. The first part, on the United States, contains 308 pages, rather more than half the work." *Nation*, 34: 152.

Muller, Frederik. Catalogue of books, maps, and plates on America. Amsterdam. 1872. [401

"Next in importance [to Asher's *Bibliographical and historical essay*] are the catalogues of Frederik Muller, of Amsterdam, particularly the series [entitled as above] begun in 1872, and which he calls an essay towards a Dutch-American bibliography. . . . Many of the larger notes in this catalogue were not repeated in the consolidated *Catalogue* . . . which Mr. Muller issued in 1877." J. Winsor, in *Narrative and critical hist. of Am.*, 4 : 439.

Payne, Edward John. History of the new world called America. Oxford: Clar. Press. 1892-99. 2v.+. 32s. [402

The first volume of this work is divided into two nearly equal parts. In the first part the author traces the development of geographical knowledge and the rise of the spirit of discovery, and gives an account of the principal voyages down to Verrazano, 1524. His point of view is suggestive and stimulating. His narrative, however, is in many places behind the present state of knowledge, and cannot be relied upon in its statements of fact. The second part is an investigation into the physical basis of primitive American culture, and accounts for its inferiority to and divergence from European culture by the nature of the food supply and the lack of useful domestic animals. The second volume (1899) continues this discussion, and is mainly devoted to the primitive culture and history of Mexico.　E. G. B.

Robertson, William. History of America. London. 1777. 2v. [403

This famous work, written late in the 18th century, is now entirely antiquated for the purposes of the student, with the exception of Book VIII, which gives one of the best accounts available in English of the Spanish colonial administration and commercial system.　E. G. B.

Winsor, Justin, *ed.* Narrative and critical history of America. Bost.: Houghton. 1886-89. 8v. Net $44. [404

Composed of critical essays by different writers covering American history in detail to the adoption of the Constitution and briefly to about 1850. The most valuable parts of the work are the critical essays on the sources and Mr. Winsor's notes, which together form an exhaustive and generally critical account of the printed and manuscript sources and of the secondary authorities on American history. The volumes are rich in facsimiles of maps, historical illustrations, and portraits. For the student it is the most useful and valuable work on American history that he can possess. E. G. B.

—— The rival claimants for North America, 1497-1755. See American Antiquarian Society, sect. 241. [405

GEOGRAPHY AND PHYSIO-GRAPHY

[Except as otherwise signed, the notes in this division have been prepared by Prof. W. M. Davis, of Harvard University, by whom the selection of works included in it has been made.] [406

Early Governmental Explorations and Surveys

The following list includes the titles of the more important reports of the governmental surveying expeditions in the western part of the United States. They contain a great amount of trustworthy information, and at the dates of their publication doubtless presented the best accounts available for their respective regions; but the older reports have now been largely superseded as far as their geographical and geological contents are concerned. It is chiefly as historical documents that they are valuable, recording conditions that have now entirely disappeared, particularly regarding the Indians. The illustrations in many of the volumes are lithographed from imperfect drawings that give incorrect and exaggerated ideas of western landscapes. [407

Emory, *Maj.* **William Helmsley.** Notes of a military reconnoissance from Fort Leavenworth, in Missouri, to San Diego, in California, including part of the Arkansas, Del Norte, and Gila Rivers. (U. S. 30th Cong., 1st sess., House ex. doc., no. 41.) Wash. 1848. [408

A narrative report by Emory and other officers of a journey through the Southwest, with a general account of topographical features and of various Indian tribes: to-day more interesting to the historian than to the geographer. W. M. D.
The journals of Lieut. J. W. Abert and Lieut.-Col. P. St. G. Cooke, and the uncompleted journal of Capt. A. R. Johnson form part of the same Congressional document. F. W. H.

—— Report on the United States and Mexican boundary survey, made under the direction of the Secretary of the Interior. (U. S. 34th Cong., 1st sess., House ex. doc., no. 135.) Wash. 1857. 3v. [409

The geographical chapters in this report are less of narrative form than is usually the case with the older western surveys, and therefore serve to give more easily a general idea of the region traversed. Much attention is as usual given to descriptions of Indians. Some of the outline illustrations are more truthful than the elaborated lithographs that illustrate most of the older reports.

Frémont, *Maj.-Gen.* **John Charles.** Report of the exploring expedition to the Rocky Mountains in 1842, and to Oregon and North California in 1843-4. (U. S. 28th Cong., 2d sess., House ex. doc., no. 166.) Wash. 1845. (Various editions of this report were published.) [410

Narrative of an adventurous overland expedition from the Mississippi to the Pacific, less valuable for its geographical descriptions, which are now superseded by much more accurate information, than for its account of the uncivilized condition of regions that are now traversed by railroads and well occupied.

Hasse, Adelaide Rosalia. Reports of explorations printed in the documents of the U. S. government. See in Syllabus of Materials, sect. 32. [411

Ives, *Lt.* **Joseph Christmas.** Report upon the Colorado River of the west, explored in 1857-8. (U. S. 36th Cong., 1st sess., House ex. doc., no. 90.) Wash. 1861. [412

An important and interesting report on the lower course of the Colorado River and of its canyon as seen from the plateaus on the south, by a party led by a lieutenant of engineers, U. S. Army. The geologist of the expedition was Newberry, by whom a clear statement was made of the origin of the canyon and of the cliffs on the plateau uplands by ordinary erosion. The steepness of the canyon walls is much exaggerated in the illustrations of this volume.

Lewis, *Capt.* **Meriwether,** *and Capt.* **William Clark.** History of the expedition under the command of Lewis and Clark to the sources of the Missouri River, thence across the Rocky Mountains and down the Columbia River to the Pacific Ocean, performed, 1804-5-6, by order of the government ; [ed.] by Elliott Coues. N. Y.: Harper. 1893. 4v. $12.50. [413

This edition of Lewis and Clark is in every respect commensurate with the literature of the subject and the importance of the expedition itself. It is reprinted from the authorized edition of 1814, and is accompanied by a copious critical commentary, prepared after examination of unpublished official papers, and many other sources of information, including a diligent study of the original manuscript journals and field notes of the explorers. There is also a biographical and bibliographical introduction, new maps and other illustrations, and a complete index. The information brought to the illustration of the text is remarkable for its amount, variety, minuteness and accuracy.   B. A. H.

Long, *Col.* **Stephen Harriman.** Account of an expedition from Pittsburgh to the Rocky Mountains, 1819-20, under command of Maj. S. H. Long; comp. from the notes of Maj. Long and other gentlemen of the party by Edwin James. London. 1823. 3v. Phil.: Carey. 1823. 2v.   [414

After a detailed narrative of the expedition through "a portion of our country which is daily becoming more interesting, but which is as yet imperfectly known," there are several supplementary chapters on scientific subjects, including geology and geography: but the chief interest attaches to the descriptions of the condition of the Mississippi valley and western plains and their Indian occupants in early days.

——— Narrative of an expedition to the source of St. Peter's River, Lake Winnepeek, Lake of the Woods, etc., in 1823 ; comp. from the notes of Maj. Long, Messrs. Say, Keating and Colhoun, by William H. Keating. London : Whittaker. 1825. 2v. Phil.: Carey. 1824. 2v.   [415

One of the earlier reports on the region of the upper Mississippi, more valuable for its account of the Indians than for its geographical descriptions, long ago superseded.

Marcy, *Capt.* **Randolph B.** Exploration of the Red River of Louisiana, in 1852. (U. S. 32d Cong., 2d sess., Sen. ex. doc. 54.) Wash. 1853.   [416

A narrative report of more than usual value for its geographical descriptions of the upper Red River and the region about the *Llano estacado.* The Appendix includes reports on geology by Hitchcock and Shumard.

Pike, *Brig.-Gen.* **Zebulon Montgomery.** The expeditions of Zebulon Montgomery Pike to headwaters of the Mississippi River, through Louisiana territory and in New Spain during the years 1805-6-7 ; [ed.] by Elliott Coues. N. Y.: F. P. Harper. 1895. 3v. $10 net. [417

In historical interest and importance, Pike's reports of his expeditions stand second only to the reports of Lewis and Clark. This new edition, reprinted from the original of 1810, with copious critical commentary, exhaustive memoir of Pike, new map, and other illustrations, and complete index, presents the explorer and his work in far better form than he presented himself in the original edition. The work is edited

on the same lines as Dr. Coues' Lewis and Clark, and shows an equal wealth of illustration.   B. A. H.

Simpson, *Brig.-Gen.* **James Hervey.** Journal of a military reconnaissance from Santa Fé, New Mexico, to the Navajo country, in 1849. (U. S. 31st Cong., 1st sess., Sen. ex. doc. 64, pp. 56–168.) Wash. 1850. Phil.: Lippincott. 1852.   [418

By an unusually careful explorer who, as a topographical engineer of the army, passed through a region of absorbing interest scientifically and historically. It contains valuable notes on the natives, including a comparative vocabulary of the tribes visited, as well as not altogether reliable reproductions of the early Spanish inscriptions on El Morro or Inscription Rock in New Mexico, recently effaced by vandals. Simpson's journal is still a valuable work of reference among students of the far southwest.   F. W. H.

——— Report of explorations across the great basin of the territory of Utah for a direct wagon-route from Camp Floyd to Genoa in Carson valley, in 1859. (U. S. Engineer Dept.) Wash. 1876.   [419

This report stands side by side in point of importance with the published accounts of Sitgreaves, Frémont, Ives, Emory, Stansbury, Marcy, Whipple, and other military explorers in the then almost unknown far west. As a contribution to the knowledge of the geography, ethnology, history, and natural history of the region traversed, it is important and for the greater part thoroughly reliable. Simpson's scientific collaborators were of high rank in their respective fields of work.   F. W. H.

Stansbury, *Capt.* **Howard.** Exploration and survey of the valley of the Great Salt Lake of Utah. Phil.: Lippincott. 1852. 1v. text, 1v. maps. $4.

——— *Same.* (U. S. 32d Cong., special sess., Sen. ex. doc. 3.)   [420

As an account of explorations from Fort Leavenworth to Great Salt Lake through a vast territory only vaguely known to the outside world, this report of a noteworthy military expedition is of value from many points of view. Stansbury was a careful observer and a thoroughly honest recorder of the physiographic features and the people of the country through which he passed or in which he sojourned. His liberal views of the Mormons, based on a year's intimate acquaintance and close study of them, but expressed at a time when only contrary opinions of the sect were elsewhere held, resulted in many unjust criticisms which seriously affected his sensitive nature, and probably hastened the termination of a useful life. The appendices to the report by various naturalists enhance its scientific value. A second edition appeared in 1855.   F. W. H.

United States. *War Department.* Reports of explorations and surveys, to ascertain the most practicable and economical route for a railroad from the Mississippi River to the Pacific Ocean, made under the direction of the Secretary of War, in 1853–4. (U. S. 33d Cong., 2d sess., Sen. ex. doc. 78; and 36th Cong., 1st sess., Sen. ex. doc. 56.) Wash. 1855–60. 12v. in 13.   [421

Narrative reports of many officers on various routes, giving much information concerning the western country, but in large part superseded by more recent surveys. The publication of the reports being chiefly in the form of original journals, kept day by day, gives them a certain accuracy that might have been lost had the writers more frequently indulged in general descriptions; yet the want of summaries by the very men best qualified to make them renders it difficult for the reader to gather all the results that these numerous expeditions might have afforded. The illustrations seem to have been elaborated from imperfect drawings, and when compared with photographs, they are often found to give very erroneous impressions. There are many scientific reports upon the collections brought home. Unfortunately there is no general table of contents.

Warren, *Maj.-Gen.* **Gouverneur Kemble.** Explorations in the Dacota country in 1855. (U. S. 34th Cong., 1st sess., Sen. ex. doc. 76.) Wash. 1856.

—— Preliminary report of explorations in Nebraska and Dakota in the years 1855, '56, '57. Wash. 1875.   [422

The geographical descriptions in these reports are excellent, including accounts of bad lands and sand-hill districts. As in all reports of early explorations, much information is given about Indian tribes.

Later Geological and Geographical Surveys

NATIONAL SURVEYS

The western exploring expeditions sent out by the Government through the first half of the 19th century were succeeded by more formally organized geological surveys. Several organizations of this kind were formed under different departments of the government between 1867 and 1876. In 1879 they were all discontinued, and a new organization, the United States Geological Survey, was established under the Interior Department; this action having been recommended by a special committee of the National Academy.   [423

The publications of these surveys contain much of geographical interest, essential to the understanding of our historical development and not accessible elsewhere, culminating in the unrivalled series of annual reports, mono-

graphs, etc., now in progress, which treat of the east as well as of the west. Brief indication of the results of the several surveys follows.   [424

Geological and geographical survey of the territories, F. V. Hayden in charge. Annual reports, 1–12, 1867–78. Wash. 1873–83. 12v.   [425

This survey, organized under the Department of the Interior, was directed by F. V. Hayden (hence commonly known as Hayden's survey) from 1867 to 1878. Twelve *Annual reports* and a number of *Bulletins* were issued, chiefly concerning Colorado, Wyoming and Montana. The first careful descriptions of many remarkable features in the Rocky Mountain region were published in these volumes. A detailed account of the Yellowstone Park is included in the 11th report. Many of the outline illustrations, from drawings by W. H. Holmes, are unexcelled. A geological atlas of Colorado accompanied these reports.

Geological exploration of the fortieth parallel, Clarence King in charge. [Report.] Wash. 1870–80. 7v. and atlas.   [426

This survey (commonly called the Fortieth Parallel survey) was under the direction of Clarence King, and reported to the Chief of Engineers, U. S. Army. Its field of exploration was a belt of country contiguous to the Union and Central Pacific railroads. The survey was begun in 1867, and about eleven years later seven volumes and a large topographical and geological atlas were published. The first and second volumes contain much original geographical information.

Geographical and geological explorations and surveys west of the 100th meridian, George M. Wheeler in charge. Reports. Wash. 1877–9. 7v. and 2 atlases.   [427

The United States geographical surveys west of the 100th meridian were in charge of Capt. G. M. Wheeler (hence known as Wheeler's survey), under the Chief of Engineers, U. S. Army. Seven volumes, one topographic atlas and one geologic atlas were published, embodying the results of expeditions chiefly in the southwestern territories from 1869 to 1879. The first volume of the series is devoted to geography, and contains much material of high value. App. F., vol. 1, is an account of the discovery and exploration of the western United States from 1500 to 1880, including an epitome of a memoir by G. K. Warren on explorations between 1800 and 1857. It is an invaluable aid to careful study of the western country. A brief abstract is given of various expeditions, with names of leaders, dates, routes, manner of publication, etc.

Geographical and geological survey of the Rocky Mountain region, J. W. Powell in charge. [Reports.]   [428

This survey was in charge of J. W. Powell, under the Department of the Interior. Its reports include among others the following volumes:— Powell, *Geology of the Uinta Mountains*, 1876:— Gilbert, *Geology of the Henry Mountains*, 1877:— Dutton, *Geology of the high plateaus of*

Utah, 1880. All of these reports contain abundant geographical material, much of which is of the very highest interest. Dutton's report in particular should be studied. Here may be mentioned Powell's *Report on the exploration of the Colorado River of the west and its tributaries* (Wash. 1875), which presents the results of four expeditions between 1869 and 1872, under the direction of the Smithsonian Institution. This report renewed the interest, first awakened by Newberry's account (*see* Ives, sect. 412), in the marvels of the Colorado canyon and the lofty plateaus through which it is eroded. The record of adventure during Powell's passage through the canyon in small boats is most thrilling. A more popular account of the expeditions is given by the same author in the *Canyons of the Colorado* (Meadville, Pa. 1895).

Geological survey. Annual reports, 1880–. Wash. 1880.

—— Monographs, v. 1+. Wash. 1882–.

—— Bulletins, no. 1+. Wash. 1883–.

—— Mineral resources of the U. S., 1882–. Wash. 1883–.

—— Water-supply and irrigation papers, no. 1+. Wash. 1896–.

—— Topographic atlas of the U. S. Sheets. Wash. 1882–.

—— *Same.* Physiographic types by H. Gannett, folio 1+. Wash. 1898–.

—— [Miscellaneous maps.]

—— Geologic atlas of the U. S., folio 1+. Wash. 1894–.   [429

The United States Geological Survey, under the successive directorships of King, Powell, and Walcott, issues a great variety of most valuable publications, a catalogue of which can be had, free, on application to the Director. The following deserve especial mention as affording the greatest proportion of geographical matter, presented by the most competent writers and well illustrated:—

ANNUAL REPORTS

2d: Dutton, Colorado Canyon :— Gilbert, Lake Bonneville (Utah).   [430

3d: Russell, Lake Lahontan (Nevada):— Chamberlin, Terminal moraines.   [431

4th: Russell, Southern Oregon.   [432

5th: Gilbert, Topographic features of lake shores:— Chamberlin, Artesian wells:— Russell, Glaciers of the U. S.   [433

6th: Chamberlin and Salisbury, Driftless area of upper Mississippi valley :— Shaler, Sea-coast swamps of eastern U. S.   [434

7th: McGee, Head of Chesapeake Bay.   [435

8th: Russell, Mono Lake, Cal.   [436

9th: Dutton, Charleston earthquake of 1886:— White, Northwestern Colorado.   [437

10th: Shaler, Dismal Swamp, Va.:— Irrigation report.   [438

11th: McGee, Northeastern Iowa:— Phinney, Natural gas of Indiana : — Hydrography and irrigation.   [439

12th: Shaler, Nature and origin of soils:— McGee, Lafayette formation (southern states): — Newell, Hydrography of the arid regions.   [440

13th: Russell, Expedition to Mt. St. Elias:— Shaler, Harbors.   [441

14th: Keith, Catoctin Belt (Va.):— Diller, Pacific coast.   [442

15th: Shaler, Common roads.   [443

16th: Reid, Glacier Bay (Alaska) :— Cross and Penrose, Cripple Creek, Colo.:— Newell, Public lands and their water supply :— Hay, Water resources of portion of great plains.   [444

17th: Diller, Northwestern Oregon:— Dall, Coal and lignite of Alaska:— Campbell and Mendenhall, New and Kanawha Rivers, W. Va.:— Gilbert, Arkansas Valley, E. Colo.:— Leverett, Water resources of Illinois.   [445

18th: Hill and Vaughan, Edwards Plateau, Texas:— Russell, Glaciers of Mt. Rainier:— Gilbert, Earth movement in the Great Lakes region:— Becker, Gold fields of southern Alaska:— Spurr and Goodrich, Yukon district:— Weed and Pierson, Judith Mountains, Montana:— Leverett, Water resources of Indiana and Ohio :— Darton, Well boring and irrigation in South Dakota.   [446

19th: Hayes, Chattanooga district:— Darton, Western Nebraska.   [447

MONOGRAPHS

1. Gilbert, Lake Bonneville (Utah).   [448
2. Dutton, Colorado Cañon district.   [449
11. Russell, Lake Lahontan (Nev.).   [450
25. Upham, Glacial Lake Agassiz (Minn. and N. D.).   [451
29. Emerson, Old Hampshire Co., Mass.   [452

BULLETINS

5, 76, 160. Successive editions of Gannett's Dictionary of altitudes of the United States.   [453

13. Gannett, Boundaries of United States, and of States and Territories: an authoritative historical account.   [454

39. Upham, Beaches and deltas of Glacial Lake Agassiz.   [455

40. Willis, Changes in river courses in Wash. Terr'y due to glaciation.   [456

44, 75, 91, 99, 135, 146, 149, 156. Successive bibliographies of N. A. geology, 1886 to 1897, by Darton and Weeks.   [457

53. Shaler, Geology of Nantucket.   [458

58. Wright, Glacial boundary in Ohio, etc.   [459

95. Holden, Earthquakes in Cal., 1890, '91. See also nos. 112, 114, 129, 147, 155.   [460

100. Warman, Bibliography and index to publications of U. S. Geol. Survey, 1879–1892.   [461

108. Russell, Reconnoissance in central Washington.   [462

115–118. Gannett, Geographic dictionaries of R. I., Mass., Conn., N. J.   [463

119. Eldridge, Northwest Wyoming.   [464

127. Darton, Catalogue of N. A. geology, 1782–1891. This bulletin is indispensable to every student. Its contents are arranged by authors, by states, and by geological formations.   [465

128. Darton, Artesian wells, Atlantic coastal plain. [466

144. Todd, Moraines of the Missouri coteau. [467

MINERAL RESOURCES OF THE U. S.

A series of annual statistical reports, from 1882 to 1893; after the latter date, these reports make a part of the *Annual reports* of the Survey. They contain the fullest and best summary of the product of our mineral resources. [468

WATER-SUPPLY AND IRRIGATION PAPERS

Similar to the *Bulletins* of the Survey; the most generally interesting is no. 4, Russell, Southeastern Washington. [469

TOPOGRAPHIC ATLAS SHEETS

The preparation of a geological map of the United States, one of the chief duties of the U. S. Geological Survey, has required the preparation of a topographical base map. Several of the states have coöperated with the national Survey in the necessary field work. The map is published in separate sheets, of which nearly 1000 have been issued for different parts of the country. The scale varies with the density of population: 1 : 62,500, 1 : 125,000, and 1 : 250,000 are mostly employed. The form of the surface is indicated by brown contour lines. Water is printed in blue. Many of the earlier sheets were of insufficient accuracy, and have been or are to be revised. Taken all together, these map sheets are indispensable in giving the best obtainable information concerning facts of position and relief. Their nominal cost (single copies, 5 cts.; 2 cts. each, if ordered by the hundred, payment in advance) places them within the reach of every library. [470

TOPOGRAPHIC ATLAS FOLIO

Two folios of a proposed *Topographic atlas* have been issued, in which a series of maps of typical' land forms is accompanied by an explanatory text by Gannett. [471

MISCELLANEOUS MAPS

Besides the ordinary map sheets, there are several maps of states or of the United States as a whole, which deserve to be widely known. The 3-sheet map of the United States, 1: 2,500,000, 1898, is to be especially recommended. [472

GEOLOGIC ATLAS

Each folio of the *Atlas* contains a topographic map, the same with geological coloring, the same with strongest colors and areas of economic importance, and generally a sheet showing structural sections. An explanatory text accompanies the maps from which much geographical information may be obtained. Over sixty folios have now been issued. [473

Coast and geodetic survey. The publications of this survey are of standard value, but for the most part technical. They are chiefly as follows : — [474

a. Annual reports of the Superintendent, separately published since 1844. These contain reports on progress of geodetic, topographic and hydrographic work, appendices treating various technical matters, and maps of the coast. [475

b. Coast pilots, containing descriptions of the coast and sailing directions for various sections of our seaboard. [476

c. Tide tables, giving data for the time of occurrence and range of tides at many points, calculated and published in advance. [477

d. Charts of the coast. These include Sailing charts, scale 1 : 1,200,000, showing a large extent of coast with off-shore soundings; — General charts, scale 1: 400,000 and 1: 200,000, to show general configuration of the coast; — Coast charts, scale 1: 80,000, for recognition of channels and other local features; — Harbor charts, on still larger scales, for details of local navigation. The coast charts are most generally serviceable. [478

e. Catalogue of charts and other publications (frequently revised ; to be had, free, on application to Superintendent). The location of all charts is here shown by rectangles on outline maps. [479

Mississippi River commission. Annual reports. [480

Missouri River commission. Annual reports. [481

These reports are included in the report of the Chief of Engineers, but are also published separately. They are chiefly occupied with technical details of engineering operations, but they also include occasional descriptions and illustrations of the great rivers not to be found elsewhere. The maps published by these commissions — especially by the first named — are of great value. One map of the alluvial valley of the Mississippi River in eight sheets should be more generally known.

STATE SURVEYS

Most of the states of the Union have, earlier or later, established local geological surveys for the purpose of developing their natural resources. Many of the reports contain, in one form or another, more or less geographical information. The reports of recent dates are in most cases to be preferred to those of 40 or 50 years ago. The list here given is by no means a complete index to state geological reports.

Alabama. The report for 1881–'82 gives a good general account of the agricultural and topographical features of the state. There are several special reports of later date on the coal fields and coastal plain. [482

Arkansas. Annual reports, 1888–1892 ; the volume on marbles describes the northern plateau ; that on novaculites (whetstones), the central mountain belt; that on Crowley's ridge, the Mississippi lowland. [483

California. A partial report was issued in 1865; the "Yosemite book" gives an elaborate account of the remarkable valley in the Sierra Nevada. [484

Georgia. The handbook of the state of Georgia, 1876, contains a brief general account of its physical features. [485

Illinois. A brief account of physical geography in vol. I, 1866. [486

Indiana. Little geographic information. [487

Iowa. Recent annual reports supersede the earlier volumes and contain many excellent descriptions of different counties. [488

Kansas. The reports of the University Geological Survey of this state include excellent accounts of its geographical features. [489

Kentucky. Many geological reports with little geographical information. [490

Maine. See W. Wells, sect. 545. [491

Maryland. Recent annual volumes contain much excellent geographical material, including an elaborate report on local cartography. The beautiful reports of the State Weather Service are the finest of their kind: vol. I contains an excellent essay on the physiography of the state. [492

Massachusetts. No official account of geographical features since the report on scenographical geology in vol. I, 1841. The Topographical Survey Commission, in coöperation with the U. S. Geological Survey, has issued an excellent atlas of Massachusetts in fifty-four sheets (Boston. 1890). The State Commission has in process of publication town boundary survey atlases. It is the intention to issue for each town and city in the Commonwealth an atlas, containing historical and descriptive accounts of the boundaries, with photographs of the boundary marks, also topographical, triangulation and position sheets giving all the details necessary for thorough general and geodetic information. In Dec. 1899 ten atlases had been issued, and it is planned to issue thirty-five or fifty each year. [493

Michigan. Little geographical material in various geological reports. [494

Minnesota. A long series of annual reports, and several volumes of final reports; much geographical material in special descriptions of counties. [495

Mississippi. Agriculture and geology are treated in the reports of 1854 and 1860. [496

Missouri. The tenth volume of the recent series is devoted to a well-prepared description of surface features. [497

Ohio. Reports of 1870–1880 contain something of physical geography, but more modern treatment is much needed. [498

New Hampshire. General description; the geographical treatment of features of glacial origin is better than the rest. [499

New Jersey. The general report of 1868, the later annual reports, and vols. I and V of the "final report" contain much geographical matter; the last-named volume includes a thorough discussion of local physical geography. Excellent relief maps of this state are published by the local Geological Survey. [500

New York. The early reports on the four districts of the state (184–) are not yet superseded by any modern official description. [501

North Carolina. The report of 1875 gives brief but effective geographical descriptions. The State Board of Agriculture has issued an attractive volume on the state and its resources (1896), the best source of geographical information. [502

Pennsylvania. The two large volumes of the "first survey" (1858) give much geographical information, not altogether superseded by the numerous county volumes of the "second survey" (1875–1895). Among the latter, a history of early geological surveys in the United States is given in vol. A; an account of terminal moraines in vol. Z; and a set of county geological maps with brief text in vol. X. A geological atlas of the state is also published. [503

South Carolina. The State Board of Agriculture has issued a useful volume on resources and population, institutions and industries (1888), the best source of geographical information. [504

Tennessee. The report of 1869 contains a general geographical description, not yet superseded. See also 10th U. S. Census, vol. I, pt. 1, pp. 381–464. [505

Texas. Occasional geographical pages in various reports. [506

Vermont. A chapter on physical geography in vol. II, 1861. [507

Wisconsin. A sketch of physical geography in vol. I, 1862; geographical descriptions associated with geological matter in the later reports, vols. I–IV, 1873–79, and in the several bulletins of the present survey. [508

Wisconsin, Iowa and Minnesota are treated together in a report by Owen in 1852, giving an early view of the Northwest. [509

Miscellaneous

Geographical Literature

American Geographical Society. Bulletin. N. Y. 1852-6. v. 1, 2.

—— Journal [each vol. comprising 5 nos. of Bulletin]. N. Y. 1859-. v. 1+.

—— Proceedings. N. Y. 1862-4. 2v. [510

The geographical publications of this society are the oldest of their kind in the United States, having been begun in 1852. The *Bulletin* contains for the most part records of foreign exploration and travel.

Appalachia. Boston. 1876-. v. 1+. [511

The journal of the Appalachian Mountain Club of Boston, first issued in 1876, and chiefly occupied with narratives of mountain ascents, in the United States and abroad.

Chittenden, Hiram Martin. The Yellowstone National Park : historical and descriptive. Cin.: Clarke. 1895. $1.50 net. [512

A useful account of a remarkable region, by a Captain of Engineers, U. S. Army, well illustrated, and preceded by a history of its discovery.

Davis, William Morris, C. F. King, *and* **G. L. Collie.** Report on governmental maps for use in schools ; prepared by a committee of the conference on geography, Chicago, Dec., 1892. N. Y.: Holt. 1894. 30c. [513

This report was prepared in pursuance of a recommendation by the Sub-committee on Geography of the Committee of Ten of the National Educational Association, in order to facilitate the selection of maps for practical use in schools. It contains specific directions about ordering maps, and descriptions of a large number of selected map sheets.

Dryer, C. R., *ed.* Studies in Indiana geography. Terre Haute, Ind. 1897. [514

Ten essays by six authors on the physical features of Indiana, of much service in giving a good picture of the state. One essay, "A century of changes in the aspects of nature," may be especially commended to the historian.

Foster, John Wells. The Mississippi valley ; its physical geography. Chicago: Griggs. 1869. [515

This is the first general account of the great river and its drainage basin that has any claim to scientific character. It is somewhat diffuse, including accounts of ancient fossils and of the atmospheric circulation ; certain theories here espoused are now antiquated : yet the work gives a good measure of "popular science" thirty years ago.

Glazier, Willard. Headwaters of the Mississippi. Chicago: Rand, McNally. 1893. [516

An account of a visit to a small lake, south of Lake Itasca, and previously recorded on the maps of the U. S. Land Office, which the author claims to have discovered and to which his name has been given, with many polemical pages regarding the rights of the subject. A large number of pages, with much trivial narrative, are given to a small matter.

Hall, James. The West ; its commerce and navigation. Cin.: Derby. 1848. [517

An interesting account of the Mississippi and its larger branches before the day of railroads, when rivers were the chief highways of travel and transportation.

Humphreys, Andrew Atkinson, *and* **H. L. Abbot.** Report upon the physics and hydraulics of the Mississippi River. (U. S. Eng. Corps.) Phil. 1861. Reprinted, Wash. 1867, and 1876 [with additions]. [518

A comprehensive and thorough report, universally regarded as one of the best pieces of scientific work produced by our government. The authors were officers in the Engineer Corps, U. S. Army. The report contains a general account of the Mississippi system, and elaborate measurements of the volume and sediments of the trunk river.

Jones, *Capt.* **William A.** Report upon the reconnoissance of northwestern Wyoming, including Yellowstone National Park, made in the summer of 1873. Wash. 1875. [519

Narrative and record of observations by a Captain of Engineers, U. S. Army, in a territory then little known, but much more fully described in the reports of later surveys. The numerous maps, like the text, are now superseded.

Journal of school geography. Boston : Hammett. 1897-. v. 1+. Ten numbers a year. $1. [520

This journal, founded in 1897, the only one of the kind in the United States, is edited by Prof. R. E. Dodge, Teachers' College, Columbia University, with the assistance of several associates. Its success may be judged from the fact that an English association of teachers of geography has made special arrangements to secure the *Journal* for its members. Among many articles of special use in teaching, mention may be made of descriptions of various states by local experts.

King, Clarence. Mountaineering in the Sierra Nevada. Boston : Osgood. 1872. [521

As member of the Geological Survey of California, King had frequent occasion to explore the mountains, which he here describes in most entertaining fashion. The book is decidedly among the best accounts of the Sierra Nevada.

Lesley, John Peter. Manual of coal and its topography. Phil. 1856. [522

Although treated from the standpoint of early geological theories, the descriptions of the Alleghanies here found are highly prized by geographers on account of their keen appreciation of mountain form and of the glowing style of their presentation.

Lyell, *Sir* Charles. Travels in North America, 1841–2 ; with geological observations on the United States, Canada and Nova Scotia. Lond. : Murray. 1845. 2v. N. Y. : Wiley. 1845. 2v:

—— Second visit to the United States. Lond. : Murray. 1849. 2v. N. Y. 1849. 2v.   [523

Pleasing narratives, descriptions and discussions by the eminent English geologist. The accounts of Niagara Falls and of the Mississippi are of especial interest. Few books of travel are better tempered than these.

MacCoun, Townsend. Historical geography of the United States. N. Y. : MacCoun. 1889. N. Y. : Silver. 1892. 90c. [524

"A most valuable aid to the study of American territorial history. The volume, a small quarto, contains forty-three maps, grouped in four divisions. The first, 'Discovery,' consists of six maps. . . . The second division is 'Colonial Period,' the third 'National Growth,' giving the successive changes in territorial possessions from the time of the French and Indian war to the purchase of Alaska. The fourth division, 'Development of the Commonwealth,' gives the divisions of territory — colonies, cessions, states, and territories — at successive epochs from the Revolution to the present day. The maps are followed by forty-four pages of 'Explanatory Text,' very compendious — perhaps too much so — but perspicuous and well arranged. The work is done with extreme care and accuracy. It is hardly possible that, in so varied and complicated a subject, and so comparatively new a field, there should not be errors; but we have not been able to detect any. . . . A copy of this work we must consider almost indispensable for any thorough study of the subject." *Nation*, 49 : 72.

Macfarlane, James. The coal regions of America : their topography, geology and development. N. Y. : Appleton. 1873. [525

A valuable and trustworthy account of our coal regions as developed 30 years ago, and still serving well as a general description of the chief coal fields east of the Mississippi.

Morse, Jedidiah. The American geography. Elizabethtown, N. J. 1789. New ed., rev:, corrected and enl. Lond. 1794. [526

The forerunner of American geographies, but united with American history. Many revised editions. Compiled from the author's observation as a clergyman in different states of the Union and from journeys expressly undertaken. Minute descriptions of the individual states, their topography, history, resources, inhabitants, etc. Numerous extracts from other writers unobtainable elsewhere. A storehouse of information, although not always exact. Two maps showing the United States in 1792.   E. E. S.

Muir, John. The mountains of California. N. Y. : Century Co. 1894. $1.50.   [527

A most enjoyable book by an enthusiastic lover of nature who has a close personal acquaintance with the

region he describes. The accounts of mountains and forest are admirable ; the geological portions of the book are less satisfactory.

National geographic magazine. Wash. 1889–. v. 1+.   [528

The organ of the National Geographic Society of Washington, founded in 1889, and since 1896 issued in monthly numbers. More than usual attention is given to the physical geography of the United States. Many articles are the best of their kind; for example, Hayes and Campbell, Geomorphology of the southern Appalachians: — McGee, Seriland: — Gilbert, Modification of the Great Lakes by earth movement : — Hayes, Physiography of Nicaragua Canal route: — Gannett, Lake Chelan. Maps and numerous illustrations accompany certain articles.

National geographic monographs. N. Y. : Am. Book Co. 1896. Single monographs, 20c. ea. ; 10 nos. pap. $1.88, in bound v. $2.50.
[529

A series of ten monographs prepared under the auspices of the National Geographic Society, giving serviceable descriptions of certain physical features of the United States by eight specialists. Physiographic regions of the United States, the northern Appalachians, the southern Appalachians, and Niagara Falls may be especially commended.

Philadelphia, Geographical Society of. Bulletin. Phil. 1893–. v. 1+.   [530

Articles on various geographical subjects, mostly beyond the limits of the United States.

Powell, *Maj.* John Wesley. Canyons of the Colorado. Meadville, Pa.: Flood. 1895.
[531

A more popular and extended account of the voyage down the Colorado canyon than was published in the official report (see U. S. Geol. Surveys, sect. 428). It is of much interest and value. Numerous and excellent illustrations are gathered from various sources, chiefly official reports.

Ratzel, Friedrich. Die Vereinigten Staaten von Nord-Amerika. Munich : Oldenbourg. 1878–80. 2v.   [532

The first volume of this valuable work is devoted to physical geography, treating in a comprehensive and studious manner the surface, drainage, climate, plants and animals. The second volume is devoted to population, aboriginal and immigrant, considered in its geographical rather than its historical relation. The author spent two years (1873–75) travelling in the United States, being at that time professor of geography in Munich (now in Leipzig), and one of the most serious and competent students of the subject in Germany. A second edition, entirely revised and rewritten, appeared in 1893.

Reclus, Jean Jacques Élisée. Nouvelle géographie universelle. Paris : Hachette. 1876–94. 19v.

—— The earth and its inhabitants : North

America. N. Y.: Appleton. 1890–3. 3v. $5 ea. [533

The sixteenth volume (published in 1893) of the original edition of this great work is devoted to the United States. It contains a great amount of information compiled from various sources, well illustrated with views and maps. More than usual attention is given to physical features. An English translation by A. H. Keane devotes three volumes to North America, of which the third covers the United States.

Russell, Israel Cook. Glaciers of North America. Boston: Ginn. 1897. $1.75.

—— Lakes of North America. Boston: Ginn. 1895. $1.50.

—— Rivers of North America. (Science series.) N. Y.: Putnam. 1898. $2.

—— Volcanoes of North America. N. Y.: Macmillan. 1897. $4. [534

Each of these four books carries the sub-title of "a reading lesson for students of geography and geology." They are the product of an experienced observer who as a member of the U. S. Geological Survey has travelled extensively, and who as professor of geology in the University of Michigan is an expert in presentation as well as in investigation. Each of the volumes contains a general discussion of its subject, followed by a special consideration of North American examples. The volume on rivers contains a larger proportion of general matters than the others. All are well illustrated and deserve wide reading.

Scaife, Walter Bell. America, its geographical history, 1492–1892. (Johns Hopkins Univ. studies, extra v. 13.) Balt. 1892. $1.50. [535

Six good lectures on the growth of information concerning America as illustrated by contemporaneous maps; on the location of national and state boundaries; and on the geographical work of the national government of the United States. Accompanied by photographic reproductions of ten ancient maps. E. E. S.

Shaler, Nathaniel Southgate. Nature and man in America. N. Y.: Scribner. 1891. $1.50. [536

"Particularly designed for beginners in the study of geology" (Preface). This is one of the best modern popular expositions of the relations of organic life to environment, full of suggestions for the maturest minds. The first four chapters are general; the last four take up the theme of the title. The racial, commercial and political bearing of these chapters is of the first importance. The style is simple, clear, winning. See *The Nation*, Jan. 14, 1892, p. 37.
H. W. H.

—— Story of our continent. Boston: Ginn. 1892. 75c. [537

The sub-title of this book, "a reader in the geography and geology of North America for the use of schools," sufficiently indicates its object. The sub-

jects treated include, among others, the geological development or growth of the continent, its present condition, and the effects of its form on its history. The style is pleasing and may well attract mature as well as young readers, and bring to their attention the correlation of many topics that are too generally considered apart.

Sierra Club. Bulletin. San Francisco. 1893–. v. 1+. [538

Narratives of excursions and ascents chiefly in the Sierra Nevada of California.

Stanford's compendium of geography and travel: North America; ed. and enl. by F. V. Hayden and A. R. C. Selwyn. Lond.: Stanford. 1883. 21s.

—— *Same*, new issue [rev. and in great part rewritten]. Lond.: Stanford. 1897–8. 2v. 15s. ea. V. 1. Canada and Newfoundland; by Samuel E. Dawson. V. 2. The United States; by Henry Gannett. [539

"No more competent editors could have been found than the Directors of the United States Geological Surveys. Dr. Hayden is at home in nearly every portion of the great Republic. . . . The same may be said of Dr. Selwyn so far as the Dominion is concerned. . . . In 636 pages a capital outline is given of the geography, natural history, government, and social polity of the New World, and what information the text fails to supply, the 48 wood-cuts and 16 admirable maps go far to furnish. In brief, though there are numerous works on America, some more pretentious and many more elaborate, there is none which affords a fairer idea of the continent than the present compact manual. It is, perhaps, not a popular work, and much of it is far from easy reading. . . . The title is a misnomer, for it is not a 'compendium' of 'travel' at all; and . . . it is not on 'North America,' but solely on Canada and the United States. . . . It is to be regretted that Hellwald's book was taken as the basis. In the original German it was of no authority whatever. . . . It would . . . have been better had an entirely new book been prepared by fresh authors, who would have gained full credit for their own work, without being hampered by the plan of the erudite Teuton. It is, however, all the more to the editors' credit that they have completed their task so well. . . . The maps are faultless [1883], and the cuts, . . . as a rule, good." Robert Brown in *Academy*, 23: 447.

Symons, *Lt.* Thomas W. Report of an examination of the upper Columbia River. (U. S. 47th Cong., 1st sess., Sen. ex. doc. 186.) Wash. 1882. [540

An exploration of the Columbia River east of the Cascade Mountains, with accounts of its rapids, branches, etc., and of the great lava plains of Washington, with some account of the Grand Coulée, Lake Chelan, and the neighboring mountain ranges. The descriptions of natural features are accurate, but the geological theories are sometimes superseded by those of later observers.

United States. *Mexican Boundary Com-*

mission. Report of the Boundary Commission upon the survey and remarking of the boundary between the United States and Mexico west of the Rio Grande, 1891–6. Wash. 1898. With atlas and album. [541

The brief descriptive text of this report gives an effective picture of the region traversed. The album containing a large number of plates illustrating boundary monuments, incidentally includes an unequalled series of landscape views of the arid country.

United States. *Northern Boundary Commission.* Reports upon the survey of the boundary between the territory of the United States and the possessions of Great Britain, from the Lake of the Woods to the summit of the Rocky Mountains. Archibald Campbell, Commissioner. Wash. 1878. [542

This report includes, among much astronomical matter, a narrative of the expedition across the northern plains and into the Rocky Mountains of Montana, with maps and illustrations.

Volney, Constantin Francois Chasseboeuf, *comte de.* View of the soil and climate of the United States of America ; tr. by C. B. Brown. Phil. 1804. Lond. 1804. [543

This is a translation from the French original, the account of an observant Frenchman, who travelled extensively in our country at the close of the 18th century; of value as giving an early picture of the physical geography of the eastern United States.

Warren, *Maj. Gen.* **Gouverneur Kemble.** See division of National Surveys, above, sect. 427. [544

Wells, Walter. The water-power of Maine. Augusta. 1869. [545

An official report on rivers and falls, with special relation to the use of water power in mills.

Whitney, Josiah Dwight. The United States : facts and figures illustrating the physical geography of the country and its natural resources. Bost.: Little. 1889.

—— Supplement 1: Population, immigration, irrigation. 1894. Net $2. [546

" In selecting Prof. J. D. Whitney to write the article upon the physical geography and statistics of the United States, for their new edition of the ' Encyclopædia Britannica,' the editors made a wise choice. Among the older geologists of the country he stands in the foremost rank, both in point of learning and of wide practical experience. Prof. Whitney's article was greatly cut down, whole topics being omitted in some cases, in others his matter so abridged that his meaning was, he claims, sometimes rendered unintelligible. He has published the whole article as a book. Prof. Whitney's work in general bears the impress of great erudition, both in a literary and a sci-

entific sense, and of a mind capable of broad and impartial generalization. Hence the occasional instances of a want of charity towards fellow-workers who may differ with him scientifically or personally are the more striking by contrast with the general tone of his writing." *Nation,* 48: 412.

Wright, George Frederick. The ice age in North America and its bearings upon the antiquity of man. N. Y.: Appleton. 1889. 3d ed. enl., with notes. 1891. $5.

—— Supplementary notes to 3d ed. 1891. [547

A general account of glacial action and its effects, especially in the northeastern United States. The chief criticism to be passed on this book is that it does not recognize the complexity of the glacial period, but represents it as consisting of a single invasion of an ice sheet from the Laurentian highlands across the Great Lakes, whereas at least three such invasions, separated by interglacial epochs of considerable duration, should be recognized.

ARCHÆOLOGY — ANTHROPOLOGY

Archæological Studies

Abbott, Charles Conrad. Primitive industry : or illustrations of the handiwork in stone, bone and clay, of the native races of the northern Atlantic seaboard of America. Salem : G. A. Bates. 1881. [548

This is a detailed description of axes, celts, knives, mortars, vessels and pipes made by the Indians, especially those of the eastern states. It gives a good idea of their work in the more durable materials. The view advanced in the chapter on palæolithic implements, that a people of ruder culture preceded the Indians in eastern America, has been discredited by more recent studies. Illustrations are numerous.
M. L. M.

—— Recent archæological explorations in the valley of the Delaware. (Univ. of Pennsylvania. Series in philology, etc., v. 2, no. 1.) Boston: Ginn. 1892. 75c. [549

A brief paper giving an account of a summer's field work. The author attempts to show from the evidence gathered that the Delaware valley was occupied as long ago as glacial times. He believes a palæolithic type of implement is as certainly found in this country as in Europe. His evidence has been strongly disputed, and at the present time the trend of opinion is against his theory.
M. L. M.

American antiquarian and oriental journal. Chicago. 1878-. v. 1+. [550

This periodical contains many important articles, many of ordinary merit, and some of little value. It is devoted mainly to American subjects — the ruins, relics, myths, religions and people of North America, with a little attention to South America.. What the specialist in anthropology has written is for the most part excellent, but some writers, either unused to the task or too much inclined to speculate, offer theories which have little to sustain them, especially in matters connected with myths and religions. Unfortunately it rests with the readers to determine what they may accept with confidence. Many editorial notes and a few articles are devoted to European archæology. M. L. M.

American journal of archæology. Balt. 1885-7. v. 1-3. Bost.: Ginn. 1888-96. v. 4-11. Ser. 2. N. Y.: Macmillan. 1897-. v. 1+ [o. s., v. 12+]. [551

A periodical devoted almost entirely to oriental and classical archæology. There are some original articles on North American archæology and a few reviews and notes pertaining to American subjects. M. L. M.

Archæological Institute of America. New York City. Organized in 1879, has published the *American journal of archæology* (see above), and a classical and an American series of *Papers*. [552

The contents of the latter are as follows: —
V. 1. Historical introduction to studies among the sedentary Indians of New Mexico. The ruins of the Pueblos of Pecos, by A. F. Bandelier. [553
V. 2. Archæological tour in Mexico in 1881, by A. F. Bandelier. [554
V. 3, 4, 5. Investigations among the Indians of the S. W. United States, by A. F. Bandelier. [555
Eminently fitted by reason of his scholarly attainments, thoroughly equipped for the work through years of arduous study among the Indians, as well as in the archives of Mexico and New Mexico, and with an unexcelled familiarity with all the early published sources, the author of these and other works on Southwestern history and historico-ethnology and archæology is the master of the field. Bandelier has probably done more toward solving the problems surrounding the Spanish discovery and colonization of New Mexico and Arizona, and the part the aborigines played therein, than all other investigators combined. His writings may be regarded as invaluable contributions to our knowledge of the region along these lines.
F. W. H. [556

Atwater, Caleb. Description of the antiquities discovered in Ohio and other western states. (In Am. Antiquarian Soc. Archæologia Americana, v. 1. Worcester. 1820.) [557

The value of this early account of the ancient earthworks of the Mississippi valley lies mainly in the fact that it was written when they were undisturbed by cultivation. The plans of the earthworks are among the earliest known. The descriptive part of the text is accurate, but the theories advanced to explain the purpose of the monuments and to establish the identity of the people who built them have for the most part been abandoned. M. L. M.

Baldwin, John Denison. Ancient America, in notes on American archæology. N. Y.: Harper. 1872. $2. [558

In its day this volume, prepared by a journalist with an arm-chair interest in the subject, was practically the only treatise on American archæology that ventured to cover the entire field. In the light of modern scientific research, there is almost nothing in the work to commend it to students. The general reader should leave it severely alone. Some of the illustrations are from authoritative sources. F. W. H.

Bandelier, Adolph Francis Alphonse. The gilded man (El Dorado), and other pictures of the Spanish occupancy of America. N. Y.: Appleton. 1893. $1.50. [559

In this succinct work Bandelier covers much ground. He clears away the mystery for centuries enveloping El Dorado, the land of the Amazons, the Seven Cities of Cibola, and the province of Quivira — all the result of personal familiarity with a vast body of documentary evidence, extensive travel, and careful ethnologic and historical study. From kindred sources he sheds much light on the massacre of Cholula in 1519, settles the question of the approximate date of the founding of Santa Fé, New Mexico, and renders important information regarding the expedition and betrayal of La Salle, thus supplementing Parkman's studies in this direction. Unfortunately the author was absent from the country when the work was passing through press, and the editorial labor was placed in incompetent hands. The result is a series of typographical blunders, many of them serious. See Archæological Institute of America, above, sect. 556. F. W. H.

Boston, Public Library of the City of. America before Columbus: Pre-Columbian visits ; Mexican civilization ; Peruvian civilization. (In Bulletins. 1875-78. v. 3, pp. 65-69.) [560

A sketch of the literature on this subject in the library, including magazine articles and maps, with critical estimates of their worth.

Brine, *Vice-Admiral* Lindesay. Travels amongst American Indians, their ancient earthworks and temples, including a journey in Guatemala, Mexico and Yucatan. Lond.: Low. 1894. N. Y.: Scribner. 1894. $5. [561

The book contains much that is trivial, and but little concerning the "American Indians, their ancient earthworks and temples," that is not found in previously published works of greater authority. As a narrative of adventures it is interesting ; it is not without literary merit, and in the main it is instructive to the general reader. F. W. H.

Carr, Lucien. Mounds of the Mississippi valley, historically considered. (Kentucky Geological Survey.) Cin.: Clarke. 1883. [562

The author attempts a clearly defined task, — to show

that the builders of the mounds were in the same stage of culture as the Indians, and that there is undoubted historic evidence that the Indians built mounds. He quotes freely from the writings of the early explorers, and reaches the conclusion that the mounds and earthworks of the United States were the work of the historic Indians or their immediate ancestors. The work is logically and critically done.   M. L. M.

Chapin, Frederick Hastings. The land of the cliff dwellers. Bost.: Appalachian Mt. Club. 1892.   [563

An excellent popular treatise of the region in southern Colorado in which the ruins of many ancient cliff dwellings abound. The descriptions are based on observations made during several extended visits to the ruins, supported by views previously expressed by more scientific writers. It contains an historical introduction from good sources, and is entertainingly written. The illustrations are excellent, but the map defining Coronado's route in 1540–41 is not in accord with more recent expert opinions.   F. W. H.

Charnay, Désiré. Ancient cities of the new world, being voyages and explorations in Mexico and Central America, 1857–82 ; tr. from the French by J. Gonino and Helen S. Conant. N. Y.: Harper. 1887. $6.   [564

The book is written somewhat in the form of a journal. The descriptions of modern Mexicans and Indians make it entertaining reading and do not detract from the value of the scientific part. The author has much to say about ancient Mexico and quotes frequently from the early Spanish writers. The important part of the book is the account of explorations among the famous ruins, as a result of which the theory of a Toltec civilization is strongly advocated. While it is hardly time to speak positively on this point, the author is supporting the weaker side.   M. L. M.

Congrès international des Américanistes. Compte-rendu. Paris. 1875–.   [565

The first article of the statutes declares that "The International Congress of Americanists has for its object to contribute to the progress of ethnographical, linguistic and historical studies relating to the two Americas, especially concerning the period anterior to Christopher Columbus, and to bring into communication with each other persons interested in such studies." *Magazine of Am. History*, 3: 65.

Dall, William Healey. On the remains of later pre-historic man obtained from caves in the Catherina Archipelago, Alaska. (In Smithsonian Inst. Contributions to knowledge, v. 22.) Wash. 1880.   [566

A brief paper of about thirty pages with ten plates. It contains a sketch of the life and customs of the Aleuts, especially of their burial customs. Bodies carefully prepared for burial have been found in the caves of the islands. These so-called mummies, together with the wrappings, and objects found with them, are described minutely. They give some idea of the earlier culture of the people.   M. L. M.

Domenech, Emmanuel, *abbé.* Seven years' residence in the great deserts of North America. Lond.: Longman. 1860. 2v.   [567

The Abbé Domenech (1825–1886), of questionable reputation for veracity, was private chaplain to Maximilian during the latter's residence in Mexico. About the time of the publication of his *Deserts* he issued, under the auspices of the French government, a *Manuscrit pictographique Américain, precédé d'une notice sur l'idéographie des Peaux Rouges*, with a facsimile of a manuscript in the archives of the Paris arsenal which he claimed related to the Indians; but its authenticity was strenuously denied by Julius Petzholdt, a German scholar. While the *Deserts* purports to be an account of the author's travels and labors in Texas, New Mexico, Arizona and California, his experience appears to have been confined solely to Mexico and Texas. The greater part of the two volumes is in reality a compilation from other works. The plates are prepared from reconstructed drawings of illustrations appearing in the books of others, and, like much of the text, are far from accurate.   F. W. H.

Force, *Maj.-Gen.* **Manning Ferguson.** Some early notices of the Indians of Ohio. To what race did the mound builders belong ? Cin.: Clarke. 1879. pap. net 50c.   [568

The first part of this too brief memoir gives much valuable information on the early aborigines of Ohio, derived from the best of the narratives of its first explorers, and presented in a manner that impresses the reader with the author's good judgment and familiarity with the early history of his state. The second part of the contribution, — that on the mounds and their builders, — although written more than twenty years ago, is thoroughly in consonance with modern scientific conclusions regarding the archæology of the Mississippi region. The presentation is commendable. General Force evidently inherited no small degree of the painstaking care and rare discrimination for which his illustrious father, Peter Force, was noted.   F. W. H.

Foster, John Wells. Pre-historic races of the United States of America. Chic.: Griggs. 1873.   [569

About one-fourth of the book is a résumé of the evidence for the antiquity of man in Europe and America. But its main purpose is to describe the mounds, shell-heaps, human bones and rude tools found throughout the United States. These the author believes are evidence that a race of mound builders preceded the Indians. He writes partly as an original observer, but mainly from the accounts of others. The descriptions are fairly satisfactory, but the several chapters on general anthropological subjects are of no especial value, and the theory of a race of mound builders distinct from the Indians has been almost entirely abandoned.   M. L. M.

Harvard University. *Peabody Museum of American Archæology and Ethnology.* Annual reports, 1–24, 1868–90. Cambridge. 1876–91. 4v. (Later reports printed with those of president and treasurer of Harvard College.)

—— Archæological and ethnological papers. Cambridge. 1888–. v. 1+.

—— Memoirs. Cambridge. 1896–. v. 1+.

[570

The various publications of the Peabody Museum, extending over more than thirty years, are of great importance to students of American ethnology and archæology. They contain various memoirs on special topics prepared by leading authorities in their special fields of work, and are extensively quoted by scientific men both in America and in Europe. F. W. H.

Haven, Samuel Foster. Archæology of the United States. (In Smithsonian Inst. Contributions to knowledge, v. 8.) Wash. 1856.

[57¹

This is a valuable chronological résumé of the opinions that have been held on the origin and culture of the aborigines of America from the time of the discovery. The survey is presented from three points of view — archæological, philological and physical. The last chapter, in which the author indicates the safe conclusions which had been reached and the points still in debate, is a careful and critical statement, and in the main is in close agreement with the scientific opinions of the present day. M. L. M.

Holmes, William Henry. Archæological studies among the ancient cities of Mexico. (Field Columbian Museum. Pubs. 8, 16.) Chicago. 1895–7. 2v.

[57²

Of prime importance, by a leading authority of wide experience and extensive scientific training in many fields. The accounts are based on personal observations, are presented in admirable style, and in the main are lucidly illustrated from sketches made by the many-sided author. Numerous writings by Holmes on archæologic and technologic subjects, of equally high merit, appear also in the publications of the Bureau of American Ethnology at Washington. His monograph on the archæology of the Potomac-Chesapeake tidewater region was awarded the first Loubat prize in 1898. F. W. H.

Humboldt, Alexander von. Researches concerning the institutions and monuments of the ancient inhabitants of America; tr. by Helen Maria Williams. Lond. : Longman. 1814. 2v.

[573

The original edition included a folio of sixty-nine plates, nineteen of which have been reproduced for this edition. In both editions the text is a series of descriptions of the plates, two-thirds of which are illustrations of ruins, sculptures, paintings and picture writings ; the other one-third are some remarkable views to be seen in South and Central America and in Mexico. The author's purpose was to show the origin and progress of the arts in America, and to point out analogies between them and the arts of the old world. Not all the opinions expressed are accepted to-day, but the work is entertaining and, with the plates, of great value. M. L. M.

Jones, Charles Colcock, Jr. Antiquities of the southern Indians, particularly of the Georgia tribes. N. Y. : Appleton. 1873. $6.

[574

The writer's object is to give a general account of the southern Indians, principally those of the Maskoki stock, at the time of the first coming of Europeans among them, and to interpret the relics found by reference to the early writers. A great number of objects is described, typical forms and mostly those in the author's possession. In the interpretation of some social and religious forms there are mistakes, but in general, as a picture of Indian life, the work is satisfactory. M. L. M.

Jones, Joseph. Explorations of the aboriginal remains of Tennessee. (In Smithsonian Inst. Contributions to knowledge, v. 22.) Wash. 1880.

[575

This is a study of Tennessee stone graves, with the skeletons and relics found in them, with a view to determining what people formerly lived in the region. Incidentally, other methods of burial in America are examined. The author believes these stone grave people were closely related to the people of Mexico and Central America. In this view he will find little support at the present time. But so long as he confines himself to a description of graves and to an examination of the historical data concerning the native population in Tennessee, his work stands to-day.

M. L. M.

Journal of American ethnology and archæology. Bost.: Houghton. 1891–4. 4v. $8.

[576

Most of the contributions to this journal are by its editor, Dr. J. Walter Fewkes, and contain the results of his researches in Arizona and New Mexico under the auspices of the Hemenway Archæological Expedition. Dr. Fewkes' papers in the first volume were prepared after only a brief season in a new field of research, and are therefore not comparable in importance with his later excellent work. The *Zuñi melodies* by Benj. Ives Gilman, also in the first volume, were based on phonographic records of native songs collected by Dr. Fewkes under somewhat unfavorable circumstances. They are not regarded as perfect reproductions of the native melodies, yet they afford a more than fair conception of the character of Zuñi vocal music. In the second and fourth volumes Dr. Fewkes has contributed largely to knowledge of the religious system of the Hopi or Moki Indians of Arizona. His *Snake ceremonials at Walpi* (with the assistance of A. M. Stephen and J. G. Owens, both now deceased) exhibit an enormous amount of painstaking observation and persistent energy. It is by far the best technical account of the celebrated "Moki Snake Dance," and sheds much light on primitive religious concepts.

Owens gives the results of his observations on the *Natal ceremonies of the Hopi Indians* in vol. 2, describing carefully, though briefly, interesting rites previously almost unknown among the Indians. Dr. Fewkes' reliable and well-illustrated account of Casa Grande ruin in southern Arizona appears also in vol. 2.

Vol. 3 is devoted largely to an extremely important

Outline of the documentary history of the Zuñi tribe by
Bandelier. Like all of this authority's contributions
to southwestern history, this is based mainly on documentary evidence gathered largely from obscure but
original sources. It is blemished by a few serious
typographical errors.

Dr. H. F. C. ten Kate, an anthropologist of note,
presents, in vol. 3, new and valuable material on the
physical anthropology of certain aborigines of New
Mexico and Arizona, both surviving and extinct.
                                        F. W. H.

Lapham, Increase Allen. The antiquities
of Wisconsin. (In Smithsonian Inst. Contributions to knowledge, v. 7.) Wash. 1855.   [577
The paper by Mr. Lapham occupies the greater part
of this volume. His object was to present surveys and
descriptions of the earthworks of Wisconsin, mainly
effigy mounds. He is cautious in offering explanations of the purpose of the mounds, but reaches the
probably correct conclusion, that they were required
by the ceremonies and beliefs of the builders, who
were themselves the ancestors of the present Indians.
Fifty-five plates, most of them from direct surveys by
the author, accompany the text.   M. L. M.

Mercer, Henry Chapman. Hill-caves of
Yucatan, a search for evidence of man's antiquity in the caverns of Central America.
Phil.: Lippincott. 1896. $2.   [578
The report that there were caves in a range of hills
in Central Yucatan led to an expedition to that country in 1894–95 to discover if possible whether a people
preceded the Maya Indians in the peninsula. This
little book is a record of the expedition, and gives a
careful, detailed account of the cave explorations
made. The conclusion was reached that the ancestors
of the present Mayas were the earliest inhabitants,
and that they came in comparatively recent times,
with their culture already developed.   M. L. M.

Moorehead, Warren King. Fort Ancient,
the great prehistoric earthwork of Warren Co.,
Ohio. Cin.: Clarke. 1890. $2.   [579
The writer's purpose in this little book was to describe in detail the famous earthwork and to throw
light on its history and purpose. The work is thoroughly done. The conclusion that Indians built it is
in all probability correct. But the wisdom of using
so many pages in describing a single rude earthwork
may be doubted.   M. L. M.

**Nadaillac, Jean François Albert du Pou-
get, *marquis de.*** Pre-historic America; tr.
by N. d'Anvers [Nancy Bell], ed. by W. H.
Dall. N. Y.: Putnam. 1884. $3.   [580
There is no question that the compiler amassed a
great deal of valuable material from many excellent
sources, but a considerable body of unauthoritative
matter is also included. It should therefore be read
with discriminating care.   F. W. H.

—— Prehistoric Americans. Pt. 1: The
mound builders. Pt. 2: The cliff dwellers.
(Catholic summer and winter school library.)
Chicago: McBride. 1896. 50c.   [581

A revision of two of the chapters in his *Pre-historic
America,* considerably improved by the incorporation
of later evidence.   F. W. H.

Peet, Stephen Denison. Pre-historic
America. Chicago: Am. Antiquarian. 1890–.
3v.+. V. 1: Mound builders. 1892. V. 2:
Emblematic mounds and animal effigies.
1890. V. 3: Cliff dwellers and pueblos. 1899.
$4.   [582
The books are made up largely of matter reprinted
from *The American antiquarian,* of which magazine the
author is the editor. The results of limited personal
field work, conducted at such times as the author's
ministerial duties permitted, are included, but in the
main the contents embrace the results of the researches of others (some of them of questionable authority), poorly digested and presented in unattractive
style. The books are not highly regarded by scientific
men.   F. W. H.

Pidgeon, William. Traditions of De-coo-
dah, and antiquarian researches: comprising
extensive explorations, surveys and excava-
tions of the wonderful and mysterious earthen
remains of the mound builders in America.
N. Y. 1858 [c. 1852].   [583
"The author was animated by an eager curiosity,
which unhappily was directed by no familiarity with
science. . . . The numerous plates afford very clear
illustrations of many remains of Indian structures."
T. W. Field, *Indian bibliography,* p. 311.

Priest, Josiah. American antiquities and
discoveries in the west. Albany. 1833.
                                          [584
Extensively read in its day, it did much toward in-
fusing erroneous notions regarding the American
aborigines. The book contains nothing to commend
it to students of the present time.   F. W. H.

**Rivero, Mariano Eduardo, *and* Johann
Jakob von Tschudi.** Peruvian antiquities;
tr. from the Spanish by Francis L. Hawks.
N. Y.: Putnam. 1853. Barnes. 1854.   [585
The purpose of the writers was to present an account
of Peruvian culture in the days of the Incas. It was
the result of extensive travels through the country and
examination of the early writers, and was written
primarily for the Peruvian people in the hope of interesting them more deeply in the past of their own country. Like so many other works on the natives of
America, it is fairly satisfactory in its descriptions of
the people, their government, ceremonies, arts and
architecture, but the interpretations of the various
forms, rites and traditions have been shown by later
studies to be inaccurate. Notes by the translator call
attention to some of these errors.   M. L. M.

Short, John Thomas. The North Americans of antiquity: their origin, migrations
and type of civilization considered. N. Y.:
Harper. 1880. $3.   [586

A survey of the culture attained by the mound builders, cliff dwellers, Pueblos, Mayas of Yucatan and Nahuas of Mexico. It is a comparative study, the ruins, sculptures, systems of writing and religions being considered with especial reference to the development shown by them, and to supposed analogies with the old world. The origin of the Indians from the standpoint of science, and as outlined in the traditions of the Mayas and Nahuas, is treated at length. In the main, the work is to be commended, indicating much careful research ; but the author's interest and enthusiasm seem at times to have led him to support some weak theories.   M. L. M.

Squier, Ephraim George. Aboriginal monuments of New York. (In Smithsonian Inst. Contributions to knowledge, v. 2.) Wash. 1851.   [587

The earthworks of New York are described by counties. Mr. Squier believes them to be defensive works of the Iroquois and of no great age. One hundred of the one hundred and eighty-eight pages in the article are devoted to an appendix, made up of brief papers treating of mounds and of defensive and sacred inclosures in other parts of America and of the world. Fourteen plates, mainly from the author's surveys, illustrate the text.   M. L. M.

Squier, Ephraim George, *and* **Edward Hamilton Davis.** Ancient monuments of the Mississippi valley. (In Smithsonian Inst. Contributions to knowledge, v. 1.) Wash. 1848.   [588

Attention is mainly given to the earth inclosures of the region. They are described with great accuracy and in great detail, almost entirely from original surveys. The mounds and the relics found in them are also described and illustrated. The theories offered in explanation of the purpose of the monuments and the view presented as to the people who built them have been corrected by later investigations, but the plates showing surveys and the descriptions must always remain the standard for reference.   M. L. M.

Stephens, John Lloyd. Incidents of travel in Central America, Chiapas and Yucatan. N. Y. : Harper. 1841. 2v.   [589

An entertaining account of travels in a country and among peoples little known at the time of Stephens's visit. It is especially valuable, too, for its accurate and detailed descriptions of the famous ruined cities. The author, while on a diplomatic errand in the country, was much interested in its early history, and visited most of the important ruins. He was accompanied by Mr. Catherwood, whose drawings of sculptures and buildings made on the spot add greatly to the value of the work. They will always be standard books of reference.   M. L. M.

—— Incidents of travel in Yucatan. N. Y. : Harper. 1843. 2v.   [590

Mr. Stephens's former journey in Mexico and Central America was cut short by the illness of his companion, Mr. Catherwood. Their second trip was confined to Yucatan, and is of equal interest with the first. The greater part of the two volumes is devoted to an accurate and interesting description of forty-four sites of ruins visited. To the student of Maya architecture, and to one interested in bright books of travel, they will always be entertaining and valuable. Mr. Catherwood's drawings, as in the former work, are indispensable.   M. L. M.

Thomas, Cyrus. Catalogue of prehistoric works east of the Rocky Mountains. (Smithsonian Inst., Bur. of Ethnology.) Wash. 1891.   [591

This is simply a catalogue of ancient mounds, graves, pictographs, ruins, etc. in the region indicated, grouped by states and counties and located as accurately as possible. References to descriptions of the works are given together with maps of various states and counties on which the different classes of works are indicated.   M. L. M.

—— The Cherokees in pre-Columbian times. N. Y. : N. D. C. Hodges. 1890.   [592

This little book is an attempt to trace back the history of an Indian tribe into pre-Columbian times. The migrations and tribal connections of the Cherokees, as indicated by traditions and references in the early writers, are outlined. Conclusive evidence from the mounds and from historic data that they were mound builders is presented. The work is valuable, in that it plainly shows that some Indians built mounds, and suggests the ready inference that there was no mysterious race of mound builders.   M. L. M.

—— The circular, square, and octagonal earthworks of Ohio. (Smithsonian Inst., Bur. of Ethnology.) Wash. 1889.   [593

The object of this brief paper is to give a summary of the results of a recent survey of the most noted mounds of central and southern Ohio, and to call attention to some mistakes of Squier and Davis in *Ancient monuments of the Mississippi valley.* The description of the new survey is minute, and is accompanied by many field notes, but adds little to our knowledge of the subject. The mistakes corrected are comparatively unimportant.   M. L. M.

—— Introduction to the study of North American archæology. Cin. : Clarke. 1898. $2.   [594

By an authority of wide experience in active field investigation. As an " Introduction " it is the best treatise on North American archæology thus far presented.   F. W. H.

—— Problem of the Ohio mounds. (Smithsonian Inst., Bur. of Ethnology.) Wash. 1889.   [595

An attempt to show that the mounds of the Mississippi valley were built by Indians, and to identify the Cherokees as one of the mound-building tribes. The historical evidence that some Indians built mounds is briefly presented, with a statement of the similarities in arts and customs of the mound builders and the Indians. The migrations of the Cherokees from Iowa to North Carolina are traced, and the tribe is shown to have built mounds in historic times. Mr. Thomas makes out a clear case. M. L. M.

—— Study of the MS. Troano. (In U. S. Geog. and Geol. Survey of the Rocky Mt. Region. Contributions to N. Am. ethnology, v. 5.) Wash. 1882. [596

Of the few Maya codices now in existence not all have been published. The MS. Troano was published at Paris in 1869. Mr. Brinton's introduction to this study gives an outline of the graphic system of the Mayas, with a brief statement of what is known of the codices. Mr. Thomas's paper is an attempted interpretation of parts of the MS. Troano. He believes it to consist of two parts — the first a religious calendar, and the second an illustration of the customs and employments of the people. The discussion of the complicated Maya calendar system is clear. The method of study followed — an examination of the MS. itself with comparison of other MSS., but without preconceived notions — is undoubtedly the right one. M. L. M.

Thruston, Gates Phillips. The antiquities of Tennessee and the adjacent states, and the state of aboriginal society in the scale of civilization represented by them. Cin.: Clarke. 1890. 2d ed. rev. 1897. $4 net. [597

The result of several years of intelligent study, based on active field investigation, careful inspection of many archæological objects, and thorough acquaintance with what other students have accomplished in solving the problems of prehistoric America. It is an important contribution not only to the archæology of the southern states, but to American archæology in general. F. W. H.

Valentini, Phillipp J. J. The Katunes of Maya history. See American Antiquarian Society, sect. 242. [598

Whittlesey, Charles. Description of ancient works in Ohio. (In Smithsonian Inst. Contributions to knowledge, v. 3.) Wash. 1852. [599

A brief paper of fifteen pages describing earthworks at eighteen localities in Ohio. It is supplementary to Squier and Davis's monograph on *Ancient monuments of the Mississippi valley*. Six plates showing surveys are appended. The author offers no theories in explanation of these monuments. M. L. M.

Aborigines

Adair, James. History of the American Indians. Lond. 1775. [600

"A work of great value, showing the relations of the English traders to the Indians, and is of much importance to the student of Indian customs." A. McF. Andrews, in *Narrative and critical hist. of Am.*, 5: 68.

American state papers: Indian affairs. Wash. 1832-34. 2v. [601

These volumes of nearly 1000 pages each contain legislative and executive documents relating to the Indians between 1789 and 1827, selected by the clerks of the Senate and House of Representatives, and include not only treaties, communications from the President, cabinet officers, and superintendents of Indian affairs, and reports of committees, but also speeches of Indians, memorials regarding their civilization, journals of explorers, and some scientific information. The first volume is indexed with special fulness and contains a tabulated statement of treaties made with Indians between 1789 and 1812. See *American state papers*, sect. 99. F. J. S.

Atwater, Caleb. Writings. Columbus. 1833. [602

"The zeal and industry of the author, stimulated by a thirst for the acquisition of knowledge regarding the mysterious people of whom these were the relics, have produced a work not much less valuable, because the author had little scientific training, to teach him what to search for." T. W. Field, *Indian bibliography*, p. 12.

Bancroft, Hubert Howe. Native races of the Pacific states of North America. N. Y.: Appleton. 1874-6. 5v. [603

In these volumes Mr. Bancroft realized the first part of his plan to systematize the contents of his great collection of 16,000 books, pamphlets and manuscripts relating to the Pacific slope, and publish the result.

"Indian archæology, mythology, and languages, European exploration and settlement, and American occupation, all had their part in this comprehensive scheme. And the boldness of the design is the more striking in view of the spirit of thoroughness in which it was undertaken. The treatment of each part of the subject was to be exhaustive.

[The work was] "written with the aid of a corps of fellow-laborers, who, judging from the results, were exceedingly well chosen. A knowledge of languages, ancient and modern, was indispensable, and several of the assistants were foreigners of scholastic training. All acted together in pursuance of plans determined by Mr. Bancroft, who followed them with critical supervision, testing their work by comparison with original sources, and giving form and character to the whole. If this method has its objections, it is certain that no one man could accomplish the proposed task by any other. . . . The book is a storehouse of facts, gathered with admirable industry and care, arranged with skill and judgment, and sustained, at all points, by copious reference to the sources whence they were drawn." Francis Parkman in *North American review*, 120: 34.

Bandelier, Adolph Francis Alphonse. The delight makers. N. Y. : Dodd. [c. 1890.] $1.25. [604

The title of the book is the English rendering of *Koshare*, a priesthood among the Pueblo Indians whose function, among other things, is to create merriment between and sometimes during the public religious dances. The author has adopted the plan of "clothing sober facts in the garb of romance." The plot alone is fiction; the details of the daily life of the participants, of their habits and customs, even of their food, clothing and architecture, are all the result of knowledge gleaned during several years of careful study of the Tewa and Queres Indians of New Mexico, and of the early Spanish records pertaining to them. The author has succeeded admirably in portraying Pueblo life as it existed before the advent of the white man in 1540. See, also, sect. 556, above.

F. W. H.

Beauchamp, William M. The Iroquois trail ; or Footprints of the Six Nations, in customs, traditions and history : in which are included David Cusick's Sketches of ancient history of the Six Nations. Fayetteville, N. Y.: H. C. Beauchamp. 1892. [605

A reprint of a curious pamphlet by a Tuscarora, which purports to throw light on the early history of the Six Nations, valuable as a chronicle of traditions, but absurd in its chronology. In elucidation of this pamphlet Mr. Beauchamp appends 112 pages of notes; some learned and acute, some shrewd guesses at truth, and others, it is to be feared, little more than a blind groping in the dark for interpretations of which, very likely, the Tuscarora chronicler had no conception. F. H. S.

Belknap, Jeremy. Journal of a visit to the Oneida Indians, 1796. See Massachusetts Historical Society, sect. 335. [606

Biart, Lucien. The Aztecs, their history, manners and customs ; from the French ; authorized translation by J. L. Garner. Chicago: McClurg. 1887 [1886]. $2. [607

Designed to portray the condition of the Aztec or Nahuatl Indians at the time of the conquest. It is a faithful account as based on the writings of the early Spanish historians, but, as is well known, these are, as a rule, very unreliable. The illustrations are chiefly from objects in the Trocadero museum of Paris.

F. W. H.

The plan of "repeating the accounts of the early writers without a word of explanation or a word of warning (except, perhaps, in one instance), seems to invite comment." Nothing could give a more false idea of the social and political condition of the ancient Mexicans than the accounts left by the Spanish conquerors, who interpreted and described what they saw in terms of old-world civilization, exaggerating for their own greater glory. The author has not profited by the studies of Morgan and Bandelier. See *Nation*, 44: 415.

Bourke, *Capt.* **John Gregory.** On the border with Crook. N. Y.: Scribner. 1891. $2.50. [608

By an army officer of wide experience among the Indians, especially those of New Mexico, Arizona and northern Mexico, and particularly the Apache tribes. Captain Bourke was a member of the staff of General Crook, and participated in many Indian campaigns. The book, which is entertainingly written, recounts personal experiences and observations during many years of frontier campaigning, and contains much information of ethnologic and recent historical value.

F. W. H.

—— The snake-dance of the Moquis of Arizona: being a narrative of a journey from Santa Fé, New Mexico, to the villages of the Moqui Indians of Arizona. N. Y.: Scribner. 1884. $5. [609

The recent and more complete writings of Dr. J. Walter Fewkes, who has witnessed the snake-dance a number of times at the various Moqui villages and become a member of one of the societies that participate in it, wholly replace Captain Bourke's description in ethnologic literature. (See sect. 576.) Captain Bourke's book, however, contains in popular form much information regarding the Pueblo Indians of Santo Domingo, in New Mexico, not found in any other work, as well as gleanings from recognized authorities regarding snake worship in general, and much that is interesting and amusing concerning life and custom in the far southwest. F. W. H.

Brett, William Henry. The Indian tribes of Guiana. N. Y. 1852. Lond.: Bell. 1868. [610

" All we know of the Aborigines who inhabit these deadly climes, is communicated by such fearless missionaries as Brett and Bernau." T. W. Field, *Indian bibliography*, p. 45.

Brinton, Daniel Garrison. The American race: a linguistic classification and ethnographic description of the native tribes of North and South America. N. Y.: Hodges. 1891. $2. New ed. in preparation. Phil.: McKay.

—— The books of Chilan Balam: the prophetic and historic records of the Mayas of Yucatan. Phil.: Stern. [1882.]

—— Essays of an Americanist. Phil.: Porter. 1890. $2.

—— The Lenâpé and their legends, with the complete text and symbols of the Walam Olum. Phil.: Author. 1885. $3.

—— Myths of the new world. N. Y. 1868. 3d ed. rev. Phil.: McKay. 1896. $2. [611

Forty years of continuous study of American ethnology have made the late Dr. Brinton's works as authoritative as his reputation is wide. His writings deal with almost every phase of American Indian life and thought, and his personal bibliography of the subject is doubtless more extensive than that of any other ethnologist. Although most of Dr. Brinton's studies were based on material gathered by other investigators, his writings occupy very high rank among those who have contributed largely to a scientific understanding of the American aborigines. *The American race* is the most comprehensive and accurate account of all the Indians of North and South America that has ever appeared, while it is difficult to overestimate the value of many other of his works. The literary treatment is commendable. F. W. H.

—— National legend of the Chahta-Muskokee tribes. Morrisania. N. Y. 1870. [612

" With the thoroughness which characterizes all of Mr. Brinton's literary labors, he has exhausted all the reservoirs of information relating to his subject. He takes no less pains to finish and illustrate it, when only a magazine article, than when it assumes the proportions of a volume." T. W. Field, *Indian bibliography*, p. 48.

—— *ed.* The Maya chronicles. Phil.: Brinton. 1882.   [613

Brinton, Daniel Garrison, *et al.* Culture status of the American Indian at the period of his discovery. (American archæologist [Columbus, O.], v. 2, pt. 2, Feb., 1898.)   [614

"The symposium on the culture status of the American Indian at the time of his discovery is an example of how eminent authorities can differ upon what at first sight seems a simple subject. According to Dr. Brinton, 'in the American race, at the time of the discovery, we see a race in its decline, drifting toward deeper savagery, toward degradation and degeneration.'" Mr. McGuire, Dr. Beauchamp and Prof. Abbott hold the opposite opinion. " There is very good reason to believe that at the epoch of the discovery the American Indians 'were on the threshold of a career that would have led in good time to the full utilization of the boundless resources of the country.' " — University of Toronto. *Review of hist. publications relating to Canada, 1898.*

Brooks, Elbridge Streeter. Story of the American Indian. Bost. : Lothrop. 1887. $1.50.   [615

For the greater part, the author has displayed the faculty of separating wheat from chaff in his use of the writings on American ethnology and archæology. His opening chapter on " The ancient American " contains so many errors of fact as to make it misleading to the layman ; but, while the remainder of the book is not free from blemish, it covers the scope for which it was designed in a manner calculated to warrant commendation. The book contains a list of what is called " The best hundred books on the American Indians," some of which, however, are bad or indifferent.   F. W. H.

Catlin, George. Illustrations of the manners, customs and condition of the North American Indians. Lond. 1841. 2v.

—— Letters and notes on the manners, customs and condition of the North American Indians, 1832–9. Lond. 1841. 2v. Am. ed. N. Y. 1841. 2v.

—— Manners, customs and condition of the North American Indians. Lond. 1841. 2v. [Reprint from original plates, 1892. 2v. Colored plates.]   [616

Mr. Catlin visited forty-eight tribes in the Mississippi and Missouri valleys and on the eastern slope of the Rocky Mountains during eight years' travels. His object was to paint portraits of men and women in every tribe, together with views of villages, games, etc. The two volumes are a series of fifty-eight letters written while the author was among the Indians. They form an unusually entertaining narrative of travels in an almost unknown region, and at the same time are of great value in their descriptions of Indian life. Over three hundred illustrations from Catlin's original paintings accompany the text.   M. L. M.

" A number of copies (often announced to have been but twelve) have the etchings colored. The first which were offered to the public were sold at a high price on account of the supposed rarity, but it is said that a large number of copies with colored etchings were found by Mr. Bohn in an out-house, and they have consequently become somewhat more common." T. W. Field, *Indian bibliography*, p. 63.

The 1857 Phil. ed. of the *Letters and notes* " is a reprint of the large work of Catlin, the title of which commences Illustrations. The plates of this are not so numerous as in the London edition, and are shaded instead of etched." T. W. Field, *Indian bibliography*, p. 64.

—— Last rambles amongst the Indians of the Rocky Mountains and the Andes. Lond. 1867. Edin. 1877.   [617

This is practically the second volume of *Life amongst the Indians*. It is a good book of adventure entertainingly written from the author's own experiences. It gives the story of his wanderings in South America and western North America. Information about the peoples of the countries visited is given incidentally.   M. L. M.

Chadwick, Edward Marion. People of the Long House. Toronto: Church of England Pub. Co. 1897.   [618

" Major Chadwick's book . . . is written in an interesting style, and contains much valuable information concerning the Canadian Iroquois, an Indian people in the midst of a white man's civilization. Not a little of the author's data seems to be derived from the older authorities, but Major Chadwick has made up for this by the novelty of some of his own contributions." University of Toronto, *Review of hist. publications relating to Canada, 1898.*

Charlevoix, Pierre François Xavier de. Letters to the Dutchess of Lesdiguieres. London. 1765.   [619

The author, a French Jesuit, well known for his monumental *History of New France*, spent four years in Canada from 1705, returning thither from France in 1720, when he ascended the St. Lawrence and reached the Mississippi by way of the Illinois River. He descended the Mississippi to New Orleans and returned again to France after an absence of two years. The journey was undertaken by order of the king, and this series of descriptive letters to the Duchess of Lesdiguières contain the results of his personal observations recorded at the time. Charlevoix was an acute observer. The letters are replete in valuable information regarding the Indian tribes and settlements visited, especially those of the lower Mississippi valley, many of which have since become extinct.   F. W. H.

Colden, Cadwallader. History of the five Indian nations of Canada, which are dependent on the province of New-York in America. N. Y. 1727. Enl. ed. London. 1747.

—— *Same*, reprinted from Bradford's ed., 1727, introd. and notes by J. G. Shea. N. Y. 1866. [620

Colden served as surveyor general and lieutenant governor of the colony of New York in behalf of the Crown ; he was an ardent royalist, and became eminent in several branches of science. The first edition of the above work (N. Y. 1727) is of great rarity; the editions of 1747, 1750 (the reprinted 1747 edition with a new title page), and 1755 were senselessly "enlarged" by English editors, thus depriving the work of much of its authenticity. A new edition, based on that of 1727, was prepared by John G. Shea and published in 1866, in which much space is devoted to a discussion of the changes made in the second and third editions. The 1727 and 1866 editions are of particular value, especially with respect to the political history of the Iroquois, and notably the relation of Indian affairs to commerce.   F. W. H.

Colton, Calvin. Tour of the American lakes, and among the Indians of the North-West Territory in 1830. London. 1833. 2v. [621

" More than half of the first volume is occupied with personal observations of aboriginal life, and statements made to him regarding it. The second volume is entirely filled with a collection of facts relating to their origin, wars, treaties, treatment by the governments of great Britain and the United States, and the result of missions among them." T. W. Field, *Indian bibliography*, p. 83.

Cotton, Josiah. Vocabulary of the Massachusetts Indians. See Massachusetts Historical Society, sect. 298.   [622

Cozzens, Samuel Woodworth. The marvellous country ; or Three years in Arizona and New Mexico, the Apaches' home. Boston : Shepard. 1873. $2.   [623

The author resided in New Mexico and Arizona between 1858 and 1860, serving in the latter year as a district judge. Much of his narrative, which purports to be a record of personal experience, is in reality derived from earlier publications, principally the reports of military reconnoissances. His references to the early history of the country treated are very unreliable, and his conclusions regarding the archæology and ethnology of the region are based on the inexpert observations of earlier writers. The illustrations in the main are sensational.   F. W. H.

Cremony, John C. Life among the Apaches. San Francisco : Roman. 1868.   [624

The late Colonel Cremony served with the U. S. Boundary Commission and with the California Volunteer Battalion. He had unusual opportunities for studying Indian and pioneer life in Arizona and New Mexico, at intervals from 1847 to 1862. This book gives a readable, popular account of the Apaches, Navajos, Comanches and other tribes, together with many curious frontier stories and personal adventures. Few

men of the period knew the Southwest so well, but carelessness and exaggeration mar his book and have obscured his really admirable powers of observation and description.   C. H. S.

Dall, William Healey. Tribes of the extreme Northwest. (U. S. Geog. and Geol. Survey of the Rocky Mt. Region. Contributions to N. Am. ethnology, v. 1. Wash. 1877.) [625

The first of three articles on Alaska outlines the distribution and gives the names of the native tribes ; the second is an interesting and careful account of the development of culture among the people of the Aleutian Islands and the time of occupation of the region as evidenced by the shell-heaps. In the third part, on the origin of the Innuit (Eskimo), the belief is expressed that they were at one time an inland people, forced later to the coast by the pressure of other tribes. This view is interesting, but the point is not yet proved. An appendix is devoted to a brief account of the native languages and lists of words. M. L. M.

De Forest, *Major* **John William.** History of the Indians of Connecticut. Pub. with the sanction of the Conn. Historical Soc. Hartford. [c. 1850.] Repr. Albany : Munsell. 1871. [626

The author made use of the best published and documentary material available, producing a book of value, especially in so far as it relates strictly to Indian history. The book still contains much material of ethnologic worth not found in any other book. It may be regarded as the best treatise on the aboriginal tribes of Connecticut.   F. W. H.

Dobrizhoffer, Martin. Account of the Abipones, an equestrian people of Paraguay ; from the Latin ; tr. by Sara Coleridge. London : Murray. 1822. 3v.   [627

" The author of this work was an Austrian Jesuit, who . . . in 1749 sailed from Lisbon for Buenos-Ayres, to enter upon the arduous duties of a missionary in Paraguay. There he remained till Spain, in an evil hour, expelled the Jesuits from its dominions. . . . In 1748 he published, under the title of a History of the Abipones, a full account of the remarkable people among whom he had been stationed, and of his own adventures in a wild country, among wild men. He wrote in Latin. . . . Perhaps there is no other [work] which gives so full and picturesque an account of savage life ; it has a liveliness, an originality, a freshness which makes even garrulity attractive." Robert Southey in *Quarterly rev.*, 26 : 277.

Dodge, *Col.* **Richard Irving.** Our wild Indians; with introd. by Gen. Sherman. Hartford : Worthington. 1882.   [628

During his extended experience among the Indians, particularly the plains tribes, General Dodge was enabled to make many observations of their character and customs that would not be possible in their present modified condition; hence his work contains data not found elsewhere. The book is presented in popular style, and relates many thrilling experiences of

41

army life in the Indian country. The narrative does not profess to be scientific, yet it contains much ethnologic matter, marred in some instances by unintentionally false statements.   F. W. H.

Donaldson, Thomas. Report on Indians taxed and Indians not taxed in the United States (except Alaska) at the 11th census, 1890. Wash. : Govt. Prtg. Off. 1894.   [629

The census of the Indians in 1890 was conducted under federal auspices by a man of considerable experience as a compiler of books pertaining to the Indians, but with no scientific ability. The census proper is doubtless as accurate as circumstances would permit, and the report would have been less misleading had it ended here. But Mr. Donaldson, the officer in charge of the work, introduced material of an historical and ethnological nature, compiled from various sources, regardless of their authenticity, or contributed by untrained and in some cases totally incompetent assistants. The result is a jumble of good, bad, and indifferent data that should be used only with discretion. The report is profusely illustrated, but comparatively few plates bear any reference to the text. The census officials improved the report by eliminating considerable useless matter ; to this the compiler protested ; a legal suit ensued, and it was decided that the Superintendent of the census was privileged to publish as much or as little of the report as he deemed fit. Mr. Donaldson consequently disclaimed its authorship, and it appeared anonymously.   F. W. H.

—— The Six Nations of New York. (U. S. Census, 1890. Extra bulletin.) Wash. 1892.   [630

Besides elaborate statistics fully illustrating the condition of the Iroquois in 1890 there is here a report by Gen. Henry B. Carrington, special agent, including an historical sketch of these Indians, maps and descriptions of each reservation, and much information regarding their government, religion, social life, traditions, etc., together with many photographs of individuals and reproductions of a 1723 map of New York province and of the Gov. Tryon map of 1771. This bulletin is considerably condensed as published in the census volume on the Indians.   F. J. S.

Drake, Francis Samuel. Indian history for young folks. N. Y.: Harper. 1885. $3.   [631

So much historical information drawn from the best sources and presented in popular and entertaining style had not previously been brought together for the use of the young. The first chapter, on " What we know about the American Indians," contrary to its title, contains more of what we do not know about them. In this chapter occur numerous misstatements. The historical part of the work, however, covers the ground quite fully, clearly, and as accurately as the writings of the best of the early authorities permit. It contains numerous illustrations from photographs, portraits, and early prints, a few of them being wrongly titled.   F. W. H.

Drake, Samuel Gardner. Biography and history of the Indians of North America. Bost.: Mussey. 1851.

—— Aboriginal races of North America. Phil. 1859. Rev. by H. L. Williams. N. Y.: J. W. O'Neill. 1880. $4.   [632

A fund of historical and biographical material pertaining to the aborigines of the U. S. The compiler (father of F. S. Drake) became an indefatigable student of the many books which he brought together from time to time at Boston in the first antiquarian bookstore established in this country. The sources of his historical studies were very extensive, and although his book betrays some lack of discrimination in the selection of material, it embodies a great many historical facts that would require untold labor to obtain in any other way. The list of " tribes and nations " is of course far from complete, and many names are duplicated through misprint or failure to identify variant forms. The work appeared in many editions and under various titles.   F. W. H.

Eickemeyer, Carl, *and* **Lilian Westcott.** Among the Pueblo Indians. N. Y. : Merriam. [c. 1895.] $1.75.   [633

Evidently without previous experience in the southwest, the authors saw four of the most frequently visited and widely exploited pueblos, and of these they say nothing that has not been told more authoritatively many times before. The volume is mechanically attractive, containing some photographic reproductions, but numerous misstatements practically deprive it of other value.   F. W. H.

Ellis, George Edward. The red man and the white man in North America. Boston : Little. 1882. $3.50.   [634

" Dr. Ellis does not concern himself with archæological questions. . . . His interest is not that of a scientist, but of a social and political philosopher, and his book appeals thus to the widest class. The method which Dr. Ellis uses is mainly topical, although in his arrangement of topics he follows as nearly as may be a chronological order. . . . He treats of the personal characteristics of the Indian, his condition, his resources and surroundings. . . . One of the strong points made by Dr. Ellis is in the substantial identity of the Indian seen by the first settlers and the Indian seen by the frontiersmen to-day ; the unimprovability of the savage when in contact with the white man is made to be one of the few facts established by history. . . . In two particulars only do we think the author falls short of his subject. The comparison of Romanist and Protestant missions is based almost exclusively upon a consideration of the Jesuits in Canada and of John Eliot in Massachusetts. . . . Again, there is a serious omission in a failure to recount the experiments of self-government in the Indian Territory. . . . Dr. Ellis, even in his last chapter, does not explicitly and deliberately outline an Indian policy. . . . He faces, fairly and squarely, the alternative of extermination and civilization. . . . But, in spite of the generations of failure which he has been obliged to record, he ranks himself with the undaunted but not blind adherents of the better way. . . . The soundness of his judgment has ordered a style which is refreshingly clear and direct." *Atlantic Monthly*, 50 : 560.

Field, Thomas Warren. Essay towards an Indian bibliography : being a catalogue of books relating to the American Indians in the library of Thomas W. Field. N. Y. : Scribner. 1873. [635

A list of 1708 works, relating wholly or in part to American Indians, with bibliographical and historical notes, and synopses of the contents of the least known works. Many of the notes are long and learned, but written with delightful spirit. Incomplete as a survey of literature relating to American Indians, but probably, for many years to come, incomparable in its field. F. H. S.

Finerty, John Frederick. War-path and bivouac; or The conquest of the Sioux. Chicago : Author. [c. 1890.] $2. [636

A clear account by a press correspondent of adventures with the U. S. forces in the campaign against the Sioux Indians in the Big Horn and Yellowstone regions in 1876, which resulted in the Custer massacre, and in the campaign on the Canadian border in 1879. The style is not of a high order. The narrator aims to adhere strictly to fact, and many of his statements are substantiated by official communications. It contains a very good map of the scene of operations, and several portraits (from photographs) of notable participants. F. W. H.

Fletcher, Alice Cunningham. Indian education and civilization : a report. (U. S. Bur. of Education. Special report.) Wash. 1888. [637

The original plan of the work was to give a history of every existing tribe from its first contact with the white people to the present time, with the special purpose of showing their progress toward civilization. The plan has been only in part realized. This book is a résumé of the relations between the Indians and the American colonists and a statement of the origin and development of the Indian policy of the U. S. government. It contains much information about the establishing of the Indian agencies and many statistics concerning the reservations. M. L. M.

Force, Manning Ferguson. Some early notices of the Indians of Ohio. To what race did the mound builders belong ? Cin. : Clarke. 1879. pap. 50c. [638

"The author has gathered together many statements, correct, false, and dubious, and quotations from writers of some and no authority, in generally undigested and sometimes indigestible masses. His essay upon the mound builders concludes that 'they were flourishing about a thousand years ago, and earlier and later,' which, though by no means incredible, is a rather vague result to reach after pages of patient reading. Neither is it unlikely that they were, as he asserts, of the same race as the tribes now living. But there are so many errors in the premises for all his deductions, that any opponent of his proposition is furnished with a full arsenal for successfully assaulting it. The title is somewhat misleading, as of 'the Indians of Ohio' attention is confined to the Eries and Shawnees." *Nation*, 28 : 357.

Gallatin, Albert. Synopsis of the Indian tribes within the United States east of the Rocky Mountains, and in the British and Russian possessions in North America. (In Am. Antiquarian Soc. Archæologia Americana, v. 2.) Cambridge, Mass. 1836. [639

The distribution and relations of the tribes in the area indicated, with the history of their contact with Europeans, are fully outlined. A brief section is devoted to the mode of life, degree and origin of culture of the people. More than half of the 420 pages are given over to a discussion of Indian languages in general and to grammatical notices of various linguistic families, besides vocabularies and phrases compiled from different sources. It is a valuable piece of work to every student of Indian linguistic relations. M. L. M.

Gatschet, Albert Samuel. A migration legend of the Creek Indians, with a linguistic, historic, and ethnographic introduction. V. 1. (Brinton's library of aboriginal Am. lit., no. 4.) Phil.: D. G. Brinton. 1884. $3. V. 2. (Acad. of Science of St. Louis. Transactions, v. 5.) St. Louis. 1888. [640

The author has spent many years in research among various Indian tribes, and much of our present accurate knowledge of the aborigines, and particularly of their languages, is due to his erudition and untiring zeal. He is one of the leading philologists and ethnologists in America, and his authority in his chosen fields is world-wide. The work above titled is of the utmost importance and displays the great familiarity of the author with the Creeks and other southern tribes. F. W. H.

Giddings, Joshua Reed. Exiles of Florida ; or The crimes committed by our government against the maroons who fled from South Carolina and other slave states, seeking protection under Spanish laws. Columbus, O. 1858. [641

"A glowing arraignment of the government of the United States for its complicity in the outrages perpetrated upon the Seminoles, in the interest of the slave-holders of Florida." T. W. Field, *Indian bibliography*, p. 148.

Gilman, S. C. Conquest of the Sioux. New rev. ed. Indianapolis : Carlon. 1897. $1. [642

A missionary book written from a Protestant standpoint (Congregationalist and Presbyterian). Anecdotes and personal observations gathered during summer visits among the missionary stations. Pleasantly told, emphasizing the work of Rev. Alfred L. Riggs, Rev. John P. Williamson, Dr. and Mrs. (Elaine Goodale) Chas. A. Eastman and Rev. James Garvie. Appendix on *The Indian question : a Christian point of view*, reprinted from *The story of a western claim*. H. W. H.

Gookin, Daniel. Historical account of the doings and sufferings of the Christian Indians of New England. (In Am. Antiquarian Soc. Archæologia Americana, v. 2.) Cambridge: 1836.   [643

A narrative of historico-ethnologic importance concerning the conditions existing in Massachusetts during the Indian wars in the latter part of the 17th century. Gookin was a man of learning, of high official position, of extreme piety, and of intimate acquaintance with the "praying Indians" of Massachusetts gained during 30 years' superintendency of all the aborigines who acknowledged the colonial government. The account was annotated principally by S. G. Drake.   F. W. H.

Grinnell, George Bird. Blackfoot lodge tales: the story of a prairie people. N. Y.: Scribner. 1892. $1.75.   [644

Mr. Grinnell knows the Indians, among whom he has been, and is in sympathy with them. He presents here thirty stories which treat of love and war, ancient customs and natural phenomena. They were taken down in Indian lodges from the Indian narrators themselves, and are told with admirable simplicity. About one half of the book is an account of the ancient Blackfoot history, their daily life and customs and a brief statement of their condition to-day.   M. L. M.

—— Pawnee hero stories and folk-tales, with notes on the origin, customs, and character of the Pawnee people. N. Y.: Forest and Stream. 1889. Enl. ed. N. Y.: Scribner. 1893. $1.75.   [645

These twenty-one stories are intended to show how Indians think and feel and especially to reveal the Pawnee character. Like the Blackfoot tales they were written in Indian camps from the words of Indian narrators. The second part does not profess to be a history, but merely notes gathered from the people themselves on the daily life, customs and beliefs in the old time and an account of their present condition and progess. The author's style is simple and pleasing.   M. L. M.

—— Story of the Indian. (Story of the west series.) N. Y.: Appleton. 1895. $1.50.   [646

The book is designed to picture the Indian as a man — how he wooed and fought, hunted and prayed, ate and slept. One who reads it will have neither a sentimental admiration for the red man nor a feeling of abhorrence of him, but will see him as he was. It is the Indians of the plains that Mr. Grinnell knows best, and it is of them mainly that he writes. There is perhaps no better book to give a picture of Indian life.   M. L. M.

Hale, Horatio, *ed.* Iroquois book of rites. Phil.: D. G. Brinton. 1883. $3.   [647

The editing of the rites used in the condoling council of the Iroquois gives occasion for presenting an account of the people themselves. In many visits to these Indians Mr. Hale learned about their traditions, customs and language. The first half of the book is devoted to a useful summary of this material. In the latter half the book of rites is given in the Iroquois tongue with a translation on opposite pages. Explanatory notes and a glossary are appended. M. L. M.

Harvey, Henry. History of the Shawnee Indians, 1681–1854. Cin. 1855.   [648

"The work is one of the most simple and veritable narrations of facts relating to the Indians ever printed." T. W. Field, *Indian bibliography*, p. 161.

Heckewelder, John. History, manners and customs of the Indian nations who once inhabited Pennsylvania and the neighbouring states. (In Am. Philosophical Soc. Trans. of hist. and lit. com., v. 1. 1819.)

—— *Same:* new and rev. ed., with introd. by Wm. C. Reichel. (Pennsylvania Hist. Soc. Memoirs, v. 12. Phil. 1876.)   [649

Mr. Heckewelder was a Moravian missionary among the Indians late in the 18th century. He wrote from personal knowledge of them and from information which they themselves gave him. His narrative is in the main a simple account of the daily life of the people, with some notice of their traditions and a very favorable estimate of the Indian character. For the tribes included one could not find a more simple, truthful picture of Indian manners and customs.   M. L. M.

—— Narrative of the mission of the United Brethren among the Delaware and Mohegan Indians, 1740–1808. Phil. 1820.   [650

A simple story of work among the Indians and a plain statement of the cruelty of the white settlers and the persecutions to which both missionaries and Christian Indians were subjected. The conduct of the latter through all this shows the milder side of the Indian character. The narrative is continuous, without division into chapters, and is written from personal knowledge.   M. L. M.

— Rondthaler, E. Life of John Heckewelder. See Pennsylvania, Historical Society of, sect. 385.   [651

Henry, Alexander. Travels and adventures in Canada and the Indian territories, 1760–76. N. Y.: Riley. 1809.   [652

"In Part I. the author relates the incidents of his life as a fur-trader among the Indians on the shores of the upper great lakes ; of the surprise and massacre of the garrison of Fort Michilimackinac, of his own narrow escape from the slaughter, and his capture. His narrative of the details of his long captivity is very interesting, and has been deemed the most authentic we have, relating to the domestic habits of the northern Indians. Part II. is a narrative journal of travels through the Indian countries." T. W. Field, *Indian bibliography*, p. 168.

Indian Rights Association. Annual reports of the executive committee, 1883–. Phil. 1884–.   [653

Contain much information regarding the treatment of the Indians by the whites, and especially on the policy of the government toward the aborigines. The reports are useful to students of the Indian question, but are not designed as contributions to ethnology.

F. W. H.

Irving, John Treat. Indian sketches taken during an expedition to the Pawnee tribes. Phil. 1835. 2v. New ed. N. Y.: Putnam. 1888. 1v. $1.50. [654

"The object of this expedition was of a higher humanitarian order than those which the government has usually organized for Indian affairs. . . . Mr. Irving accompanied the expedition, and his work affords us many interesting incidents of savage life. The work abounds in such fragments of the traditions, history and peculiarities of the Indian tribes as the opportunity offered the author." T. W. Field, *Indian bibliography*, p. 186.

Jackson, *Mrs.* **Helen Hunt.** A century of dishonor. N. Y.: Harper. 1881. New ed., enl. Boston : Roberts. 1885. $1.50. [655

The title is well chosen. The dealings of the U. S. government with the Indians have been at almost every turn dishonorable. The author shows in a series of sketches based on treaties and official reports what our treatment of the various tribes has been. An appendix tells of outrages committed on the Indians by the whites, and gives a variety of letters and reports showing the best side of the Indian character. Only one side of the case is presented, but it is the side little known. Mrs. Jackson was heart and soul in sympathy with the Indian. M. L. M.

Jemison, *Mrs.* **Mary.** SEAVER, JAMES E. Narrative of the life of Mrs. Mary Jemison. Canandaigua, N. Y. 1824. Rev. ed. Batavia, N. Y. 1842. 6th ed., with notes, etc., by Wm. P. Letchworth. N. Y.: Putnam. 1898. $1.25. [656

A book that has grown. Originally (1st ed., Canandaigua, 1824) Seaver's account of the life of Mary Jemison, as gathered from her own lips. She was captured by the Indians when a child (1755), and lived with them, mostly in the Genesee valley and at Buffalo, until her death in 1833. Unique in character, invaluable as a record of its period in western N. Y., the book has been edited, annotated and augmented with new chapters by able hands — Ebenezer Mix, Wm. Clement Bryant, Lewis H. Morgan and others ; the latest American editions (Buffalo, 1877, and New York, 1898) were edited by the Hon. Wm. P. Letchworth. F. H. S.

"The best résumé we have of incidents in the history and common life of the Seneca Indians. Its truthfulness is vouched for by such veracious testimony as that of Eli Parker, an educated chief of that nation." T. W. Field, *Indian bibliography*, p. 354.

Kingsley, John Sterling, *ed.* Standard natural history. V. 6: Natural history of man. Boston : Cassino. 1885.

—— *Same :* Riverside natural history. Boston: Houghton. [c. 1888.] 6v. $30. V. 6: Man. [657

The section of interest in the present connection is that devoted to The races of America. The chapter treating of palæolithic man is based on testimony now generally refuted by archæologists, and the Eskimo and the North American Indians are treated as distinct peoples in accordance with methods now considered to be obsolete. On the whole the treatise was good in its day, but American ethnology has advanced since the work was prepared. Many misprints of proper names display careless editing. F. W. H.

Kohl, Johann Georg. Kitchi-gami : wanderings round Lake Superior ; [tr. by L. Wraxall]. London: Chapman. 1860. [658

"Under this repellant name, suggestive of sensational or fictitious writing, the eminent German traveller, Mr. Kohl, has given one of the most exhaustive and valuable treatises on Indian life ever written. It is wholly the result of personal experience, and one which only the most fervent scientific zeal and earnest self-abnegation, as well as a very high order of intelligence, could produce." T. W. Field, *Indian bibliography*, p. 205.

Lafitau, Joseph François. Mœurs des sauvages amériquains comparées aux mœurs des premiers temps. Paris. 1724. 2v. [659

A Jesuit missionary among the Indians of Canada for many years, and later a professor of belles-lettres in France, Lafitau was well equipped for preparing a work of extreme value on the tribes with which he was so long in intimate contact. He succeeded in so far as his volumes are a record of the manners and customs of the lower Canadian tribes, but they are weakened in an endeavor to prove, by certain parallels in planes of culture, that the American aborigines are descendants of the primitive inhabitants of Greece. F. W. H.

McKenney, *Col.* **Thomas Lorraine.** Memoirs, official and personal. N. Y.: Paine. 1846. [660

McKenney was appointed, in 1816, superintendent of United States trade with the Indian tribes, and, in 1824, head of the Bureau of Indian Affairs, where he served until forced to retire by Jackson. He had great faith in the fundamental worth of the Indian, and has much to say in regard to the "abominable abuse of power" of the government with the Indians. In 1826 he made an extensive trip in order to negotiate a treaty with the Chippewa Indians at Fond du Lac. The author's observations and anecdotes are entertaining, although the volume is fragmentary. Stories are told in regard to political life at Washington during the administrations of Monroe, Adams, and Jackson which strikingly illustrate the corruption in governmental contracts and the workings of the spoils system under Jackson. The second volume represents lectures on the Indians. See, below, *History of the Indian tribes* by the author and James Hall. 3v. 1854. D. R. D.

McKenney, Col. Thomas Lorraine, *and* **James Hall.** History of the Indian tribes of North America, with 120 portraits from the Indian gallery at Washington. Phil. 1836–44. 3v. New ed. Phil.: F. Rice. 1854. 3v. [661

The principal value of this work, which has appeared in both folio and quarto editions, lies in the colored lithographic reproductions of many Indian portraits collected between 1825 and 1849 by the War Department, of which the Indian Office then formed a part. In the latter year the Indian Bureau was transferred to the Interior Department, while the paintings were deposited in the Smithsonian Institution. Most of the portraits were made from life by Charles B. King, but others were copies from originals by J. O. Lewis. The entire collection was destroyed in the burning of a portion of the Smithsonian Institution, Jan. 24, 1865, an unfortunate occurrence which made McKenney and Hall's volumes of permanent value. The various biographies forming part of the work are derived from authentic sources or from personal association with the living subjects. The *History of the North American Indians*, occupying part of the third volume, is unscientific and untrustworthy, although it contains many extracts from worthier publications. The text of the entire work was highly regarded in its day on account of the extended experience of McKenney, who was appointed superintendent of U. S. trade with the Indians in 1816, and was placed in charge of the Office of Indian Affairs on its establishment in 1824.

F. W. H.

Maclean, John. Canadian savage folk. Toronto: Wm. Briggs. 1896. $2.50. [662

The author has had wide experience as a missionary among the Indians of Canada, yet the greater part of his book is compiled from other writings. Mr. Maclean has shown commendable discrimination in the selection of his extracts and familiarity with the best ethnographic literature relating to his field of work; nevertheless some parts of the book are far behind modern scientific knowledge. It is entertainingly written.   F. W. H.

Marshall, Orsamus Holmes. Historical writings relating to the early history of the west; with introd. by William L. Stone. (Munsell's historical series, no. 15.) Albany: Munsell. 1887. $6. [663

Chiefly studies of the aborigines of western New York, and of the French explorers who visited the region, in good part based on the author's researches in French archives. Conspicuously conscientious work, accurate and thorough, the style not lacking literary grace. An " Index rerum," pp. 345-468, gives many hundreds of names local to the region, references to authorities, etc.   F. H. S.

Mason, Otis Tufton, *ed.* Miscellaneous papers relating to anthropology, from the Smithsonian report for 1881. Wash. 1883. [664

The first paper is a classified bibliography of anthropological literature published in 1881. The references are confined mainly to works on America or by Americans or republications in America of important works. This paper is followed by others on the mounds, relics, rock inscriptions, etc., mainly those in the Mississippi valley.   M. L. M.

Matthews, Dr. Washington. Ethnography and philology of the Hidatsa Indians. (U. S. Geol. and Geog. Survey. Misc. pubs., no. 7.) Wash. 1877.

—— Navaho legends, collected and tr., with introd., notes, etc. (Am. Folk-Lore Society. Memoirs, v. 5.) Boston: Houghton. 1897. $6 net. [665

With thirty-five years of intimate association among Indians, as an army surgeon, mainly during a period in which they had been little affected by civilizing influences; with unusual ability for ethnologic investigation, and a love of truth and accuracy of detail, Dr. Matthews has necessarily produced works only of the highest scientific value. His writings on the Hidatsa (or Minitari) and the Navaho are everywhere recognized as the leading authorities on those Indians and as standard works on American ethnology. The two books display not only the author's industry and knowledge, but his delightful familiarity with good English. The *Navaho legends* is generously illustrated.

F. W. H.

Megapolensis, Johannes. Sketch of the Mohawk Indians. See New York Historical Society, sect. 353. [666

Morgan, Lewis Henry. Houses and house-life of the American aborigines. (U. S. Geog. and Geol. Survey. Contributions to North American ethnology, v. 4.) Wash. 1881. [667

By the " Father of American Anthropology," who died in 1881. The work is of great interest and high importance. It embodied all the knowledge available at the time of publication, and even the subsequent advance made in the knowledge of the subject of which the book treats leaves little to be corrected.

F. W. H.

—— League of the Ho-dé-no-sau-nee, or Iroquois. Rochester: Sage. 1851. Rev. by H. M. Lloyd. N. Y.: Dodd. 1902. 2v. $15. [668

This was the first thoroughly scientific work on the Indians ever published, but the advance made since in ethnologic investigation has somewhat lessened its value. Its place in ethnologic literature has become occupied to a large extent by Horatio Hale's *Iroquois book of rites* (sect. 647), although Morgan's work still contains much data of both historical and ethnologic importance not found in any other work. Morgan was the leading American ethnologist of his time, and was the first to enter this field of research with a definite scientific appreciation of the problems which confronted him. He was adopted by the Senecas, and during his life among them gained the knowledge incorporated in the work here titled.   F. W. H.

Morse, Jedidiah. A report to the Secretary of War of the United States, on Indian affairs, comprising a narrative of a tour in the summer of 1820. New Haven. 1822. [**669**

The author, who was the father of S. F. B. Morse of telegraph fame, was distinguished as geographer, historian, and divine. Equipped with more than ordinary learning and keen sympathy for the red man, his official tour of the Indian country, within the limits of what was then the United States, was made for the purpose of ascertaining and reporting on the actual condition of the aborigines for the benefit of the federal authorities. This report contains far more information on the natives among whom he travelled than any work published up to that period, and it had great weight in the settlement of numerous Indian questions.   F. W. H.

New York State. *Assembly.* Report of special committee to investigate the Indian problem of the state of New York, appointed 1888. Albany. 1889. [**670**

The committee, of which J. S. Whipple was chairman, was appointed by an Assembly resolution of March 21, 1888, to investigate the social, moral and industrial condition of the Indians and their titles to the reservation lands. The report, transmitted to the Legislature Feb. 1, 1889, devotes 40 pages to a history of this people in New York with special reference to the complicated Ogden land claim. The remaining 39 pages of the report proper describe the conditions prevailing on the several reservations and are followed by appendices containing the full text of various national and state treaties with the New York Indians, land grants, legal decisions, and miscellaneous matter connected with the subject.   F. J. S.

Nordenskiöld, N. O. Gustaf. The cliff dwellers of the Mesa Verde, southwestern Colorado, their pottery and implements; tr. by D. Lloyd Morgan. Stockholm and Chicago: Nordstedt. [1893.] $20. [**671**

It is surprising that the late young author should have produced such a highly creditable work after only a single season's study of these remarkable cliff ruins, and yet his contribution to the literature of this interesting field of American archæology is one of the best that has ever been presented. In addition he has given a good summary of the characteristics of the Moki (Hopi) Indians of Arizona and of the condition of the Pueblos of New Mexico at the time they were first visited by whites in 1540 (quoting largely from the narratives of Coronado's great expedition), as well as a brief review of our present knowledge of the Pueblo tribes. A supplementary chapter on the human remains found by Nordenskiöld is contributed by Prof. G. Retzius. The volume is a large quarto, and as a piece of book-making has never been excelled by any work devoted to American archæology. Most of the illustrations are magnificent. The translation by Mr. Morgan was made from the author's manuscript before the latter's death; it has not been published in Swedish.   F. W. H.

Powers, Stephen. Tribes of California.

(U. S. Geog. and Geol. Survey of the Rocky Mt. Region. Contributions to N. Am. ethnology, v. 3.) Wash. 1877. [**672**

The Indians of California were divided into a great number of distinct tribes. Mr. Powers locates these tribes, points out their relation one to another, and describes their customs and mode of life. He gives also a great many myths and stories. The work is the result of months of living and travelling among the Indians. It is useful for reference, especially since many of the tribes no longer exist.   M. L. M.

Radisson, Pierre Esprit. Voyages, being an account of his travels and experiences among the North American Indians, 1652–84; with historical illustrations and introd. by Gideon D. Scull. Boston: Prince Soc. 1885. [**673**

An interesting portrayal of the Iroquoian and Algonquian tribes of Canada in the latter half of the 17th century, printed from transcriptions of the original manuscripts. It is a quaint record of personal experiences and observations by a scholarly Frenchman, containing much valuable historical and ethnological detail. As in all early writings of this kind, however, the author's conclusions cannot always be regarded as sound. The editor has performed his part well, although the notes are not so copious as they might have been.   F. W. H.

Rink, Hinrich Johannes. The Eskimo tribes; their distribution and characteristics, with a comparative vocabulary. (Meddelelser om Grönland, v. 11.) Copenhagen: C. A. Reitzel. London: Williams & Norgate. 1887. 4s. 6d.

——Tales and traditions of the Eskimo, with a sketch of their habits, religions, language, etc.; tr. from the Danish by the author, ed. by R. Brown. Edin.: Blackwood. 1875. [**674**

This eminent authority, recently deceased, held several prominent positions under the Danish government which necessitated residence in and travel about the shores of Greenland during sixteen winters and twenty-two summers up to the time of the publication of his *Tales and traditions.* He is the highest authority on the Greenland Eskimo, and his books are excellent reading.   F. W. H.

Ruttenber, Edward Manning. History of the Indian tribes of Hudson's River. Albany: Munsell. 1872. [**675**

Displays a great deal of careful, discriminating study of the early authorities, and the unusual ability of its author as an historian. It has received high praise from scientific students. The etymology of some of the Indian names is faulty. The literary feature is good.   F. W. H.

Schoolcraft, Henry Rowe. Historical and statistical information respecting the history, condition and prospects of the Indian tribes of the United States; prepared under the direction of the Bureau of Indian Affairs. Phil.: Lippincott. 1851–7. 6v.

—— Myth of Hiawatha, and other oral legends of the Indians. Phil.: Lippincott. 1856.

—— Notes on the Iroquois. Albany. 1847.

—— Oneóta; or Characteristics of the red race; from original notes and MSS. N. Y. 1844–5. 8 pts. [1v.]

—— Personal memoirs of a residence of 30 years with the Indian tribes on the American frontiers, 1812–42. Phil.: Lippincott. 1851.

—— Report to the Secretary of State, transmitting census returns in relation to the Indians: Census of the Iroquois. (N. Y. Senate.) Albany. 1846. [The official production of his Notes on the Iroquois, 1847. See above.] [676

In brief, the many writings of Schoolcraft may be regarded as of greater value to the advanced student of ethnology and archæology than to the general reader. Of wide experience among the Indians, particularly the Ojibwa and the Iroquois, with full acquaintance with the most reliable observations that had been made among various tribes, and with more or less general learning, Schoolcraft has written much that will prove of permanent value; but lacking in the scientific discrimination for which such students of his period as Albert Gallatin and Lewis H. Morgan were noted, Schoolcraft weakened many of his observations by false reasoning. Practically everything which he previously wrote on the Indians is embodied in his voluminous *Historical and statistical information*, etc., prepared under governmental auspices. These six volumes contain a vast body of data pertaining to almost every field of American ethnology. The material is badly arranged and poorly digested; but the compiler is scarcely to blame, since he was expected to produce at least a volume a year. The statistical information, drawn from many sources, occupies a large part of the work and is valuable. Material for a seventh volume had been gathered, but the necessary means for its publication were not afforded; the MS. is believed to be in the Library of Congress. In his Ojibwa studies Schoolcraft had the assistance of his first wife, an educated half-breed. Captain Eastman, U. S. A., of considerable Indian experience, prepared most of the illustrations for his largest production.

F. W. H.

The *Myth of Hiawatha* "is a reproduction of *Algic researches*, printed in 1839, with some additions. Mr. Schoolcraft was not the only claimant for the honor of bringing to Mr. Longfellow's notice the Indian legends, from which the poet derived the foundation of his beautiful poem. Mr. Clark traces its origin to the Onondagas, the central tribe of the Iroquois." T. W. Field, *Indian bibliography*, p. 352.

Oneóta " was originally published in numbers, subsequently in the above form, and afterwards rearranged and printed under the title of *The Indian in his wigwam*.

In his personal narrative, the author has told us precisely what no one cares to know, and omitted all that would possess any interest,— incidents of his personal intercourse with the Indians." T. W. Field, *Indian bibliography*, p. 352.

The *Report on the Iroquois* " is the most valuable of Mr. Schoolcraft's works, having been executed after personal examination in an official capacity of all the tribes inhabiting New York. There is an almost entire absence of the speculative and sentimental cogitations which so greatly marred his works." T. W. Field, *Indian bibliography*, p. 351.

Smet, Pierre Jean de. Letters and sketches, with a narrative of a year's residence among the Indian tribes of the Rocky Mountains. Phil. 1843. [677

Father de Smet spent many years among the Indians of the extreme northwest, among whom he seems to have become remarkably influential. His writings, shorn of their extreme religious bias, are of great interest and value. F. W. H.

Smithsonian Institution. *Bureau of Ethnology, John W. Powell, director.* Annual reports, 1879–. v. 1+. Wash. 1881–. [678

A series of volumes on American ethnology abundantly illustrated. Attention is given almost entirely to the natives of North America, their arts, architecture, customs, myths and rites. The object is to gather all possible information concerning our native tribes while it can be done. The sign language, pictography, burial mounds, religious rites, stone implements, etc., are described in the greatest detail. These papers are the result of original investigation and must always be one of the best sources of information on the subjects treated. Many of them are, however, far too long. Fewer words would convey the ideas and save the time and patience of the reader.

M. L. M.

Squier, Ephraim George. Historical and mythological traditions of the Algonquins, with a trans. of the "Walum-olum." (New York Hist. Soc.) [N. Y. 1848.] [679

Read before the N. Y. Historical Society in June, 1848; published in the *American review*, n. s., vol. III, N. Y., 1849. Reprinted in W. W. Beach's *Indian miscellany* (Albany. 1877), and in S. G. Drake's *Aboriginal races of North America* (N. Y. 1880). Superseded by D. G. Brinton's *The Lenape and their legends* (Phil. 1885), in which the complete text of the original "Walam Olum," with translation, appears. F. W. H.

Tanner, John. JAMES, EDWIN. Narrative of the captivity and adventures of John Tanner, U. S. interpreter at the Saut de Saint Marie, during 30 years' residence among the Indians, in the interior of North America. N. Y. 1830. [680

" Mr. James was a man of much information upon Indian affairs, and must have been able to discriminate between the probable and the uncertain portions of Tanner's narrative. The renegade himself (for he had during his long sojourn among the Indians become even more savage than they) was a person of retentive memory and fair intelligence. His relation of his life among the northern Indians is probably the most minute if not authentic detail of their habits, modes of living, and social customs, ever printed." T. W. Field, *Indian bibliography*, p. 189.

Thompson, Edward H. Archæological research in Yucatan. See American Antiquarian Society, sect. 236. [**681**

Tomo-Chi-Chi. JONES, CHARLES COLCOCK, JR. Historical sketch of Tomo-Chi-Chi, Mico of the Yamacraws. Albany. 1868. [**682**

"The large-minded and heroic Indian chief, who welcomed Oglethorpe to the lands of his nation, and fed and protected the infant colony during those early years when disease and the Spaniards threatened its existence, well deserved a biography. No hero of the colonies of North America, even the loud boasting Captain John Smith, the zealous yet humane Roger Williams, or the noble Oglethorpe himself, better deserved an enduring monument than Tomo-Chi-Chi. . . . Mr. Jones has done full justice to his subject by fortifying the facts of his biography with undoubted authorities." T. W. Field, *Indian bibliography*, p. 195.

Tracts relating to the attempts to convert to Christianity the Indians of New England. See Massachusetts Historical Society, sect. 300. [**683**

United States. *Congress.* Joint special committee [on the] condition of the Indian tribes; appointed under joint resolution of March 3d, 1865. Report, with an appendix. (U. S. 39th Cong., 2d sess., Senate report, no. 156.) Wash. 1867. [**684**

"This volume contains the evidence of the horrible massacre of unoffending Indians at Sand Creek. Nothing in Las Casas' relations of Spanish atrocities surpasses it." T. W. Field, *Indian bibliography*, p. 85.

United States. *Geographical and Geological Survey of the Rocky Mountain Region.* Contributions to North American ethnology. Wash. 1877–93. V. 1–7 and 9. [**685**

It is probable that no other volumes will be issued in this series. The papers relate to the natives of North America and include studies of stone carvings, house architecture, social customs in various tribes, myths and stories in the native tongues with interlinear translations, dictionaries, and a study of a Maya manuscript. More than half of the material is linguistic and is the more valuable as it is becoming increasingly difficult to gather. M. L. M.

Vetromile, Eugene. The Abnakis and their history; or historical notices on the aborigines of Acadia. N. Y. 1866. [**686**

Father Vetromile (1819–1880) had lived for 8 years as a missionary among the Indians of whom his little book treats, having been assigned to them in 1858. His

labors continued among the Abnaki for more than a quarter of a century, and he has been regarded as an authority on that tribe and its language; beyond the treatment of this tribe, however, he must be regarded with caution. Like many missionary writers, he displays extreme religious bias throughout. F. W. H.

Walker, *Brig.-Gen.* **Francis Amasa.** The Indian question. Boston: Osgood. 1874. [**687**

A scholarly treatise by a well-known statistician and economist, recently deceased. During 1870–71 General Walker was U. S. Commissioner of Indian Affairs, a position which afforded ample opportunity for studying the relations of the Indians with the Federal Government as they then existed. A section of the book is devoted to "Indian civilization," and another to "An account of the tribes"—the latter, mainly statistical, being compiled from official data. The book gives an excellent account of the policy of the United States toward the aborigines, and offers valuable suggestions. It contains a map showing the western reservations, tribal ranges, and areas of white population. F. W. H.

Wallace, *Mrs.* **Susan Elston.** The land of the pueblos. N. Y.: Alden. 1888. [**688**

By the wife of Gen. Lew Wallace who was Governor of New Mexico in 1878–81. The author's experience with the Pueblo Indians was evidently very limited, and her knowledge of the history of New Mexico even more so. The book contains so many glaring misstatements that it would prove misleading to any one in search of information regarding its subject. The style is light. F. W. H.

Washington, Anthropological Society of. American anthropologist. (Quarterly.) Wash. 1888–95. Illus., maps. 8v. $3 ea. (Monthly.) 1896–98. V. 9–11. $2 ea.

—— Transactions, 1879–85. Wash. 1882–5. 3v. $1 ea. Same, v. 1, 3. (In Smithsonian miscellaneous collections, v. 25, 34.)

—— Abstract of transactions, 1879–81. Wash. 1881. Same. (In Smithsonian miscellaneous collections, v. 25.) [**689**

The *Transactions* are devoted mainly to the proceedings of the Society, but they contain also a number of scientific papers by eminent authorities. The *American anthropologist*, first published as a quarterly, later as a monthly, is a storehouse of valuable information on anthropologic subjects, particularly the American Indians. No other periodical contains so many extended articles by leading scientific authorities on the topics to which the journal was devoted. It ceased publication at the close of vol. XI (1898), its place being taken by a larger quarterly bearing the same name, but with the addition of "new series." (N. Y.: Putnam. $4.) F. W. H.

Williams, Roger. Key to the language of America. See Massachusetts Historical Society, sect. 288. [**690**

Wilson, Daniel. The Huron-Iroquois of

Canada. (In Royal Soc. of Canada. Proceedings and transactions. Montreal. 1884.) [691

A study of this famous group of Indians is well suited to give a good conception of Indian life and culture. It is not a description of their customs, but a study of their history and migrations, mental characteristics, the development of their language, oratory and general culture. The fact is emphasized that, in spite of their progress in some lines, the Iroquois were typical barbarians.   M. L. M.

Wimer, James. Events in Indian history. Lancaster, Pa.: Hills. 1841.   [692

An attempt to write a history of the Indians as they have come in contact with the white man, chiefly in wars, beginning with the Plymouth settlement and closing with Revolutionary times. A second part is devoted to stories of whites in captivity, massacres, etc. Much of the material is taken from Drake, McClung, and other writers of Indian stories. These tales are more picturesque than reliable.   E. E. S.

EUROPEAN DISCOVERY AND EARLY EXPLORATION

General Accounts and Collections

A SELECT LIST OF SOURCES FOR THE HISTORY OF THE CENTURY OF DISCOVERY FROM PRINCE HENRY TO MAGELLAN WITH INDICATIONS OF SUCH ENGLISH TRANSLATIONS AS ARE ACCESSIBLE

Prepared by E. G. B.

a. THE PORTUGUESE SEARCH FOR A SEA ROUTE TO THE INDIES

Documents

Alguns documentos do Archivo nacional da torre do tombo, ácerca das navegações e conquistas portuguezas, publicados por ordem do governo de sua Majestada fidelissima ao celebrar-se a commemoração quadricentenaria do descobrimento da America; ed. by José Ramos-Coelho. Lisboa: Imprensa Nacional. 1892.   [693

Covers the period from 1416 to 1529, and gives excerpts, complete texts or résumés of contents, according to the importance or previous accessibility of the documents. Contains also several facsimiles of MSS., and autographs, and a full index of names and places.

Narratives

Azurara, Gomes Eannes de. Cronica do descobrimento e conquista de Guiné, etc. Paris. 1841.   [694

Notes by Santarem. Eng. trans. by Beazley and Prestage. Hakluyt Soc. 1896.

Gomez, Diogo. De prima inventione Gui-

neæ, ed. by Schmeller. (Abhandlungen der Königl. bayerischer Akademie. 4Bd. 1847.)   [695

Eng. trans. of Gomez's own voyages in Major's *Prince Henry* and Beazley's *Prince Henry*.

Cada Mosto, Aluise da. Navigatione. (In Ramusio's Navigationi et viaggi. New ed. Venice. 1837.)   [696

Eng. trans. in Kerr's *Voyages*, v. 2. Large extracts in Major's *Prince Henry* and Beazley's *Prince Henry*.

Gama, Vasco da. Roteiro da viagem que em descobrimento da India pelo cabo da Boa Esperança, fez Dom Vasco da Gama em 1497; ed. by Kopke and Paiva. Porto. 1838.   [697

Eng. trans. by Ravenstein. Hakluyt Soc. 1898.

Barros, João de. Da Asia. [Best ed.] Lisbon. 1778–88. 24v.   [698

Not a contemporary, nevertheless an important source and the one from which the history of the Portuguese discoveries has been drawn by all English writers except a few of the most recent. Barros' narrative down to 1502 was trans. into German by Dr. E. Feust. Nuremberg. 1844.

b. THE DISCOVERY OF THE NEW WORLD

Documents and Narratives

Raccolta di documenti e studi; pubblicati dalla Reale commissione colombiana pel quarto centenario dalla scoperta dell' America. Auspice il Ministero della pubblica istruzione. Roma. 1892–96. 6 parts in 14 v.   [699

The suggestion of this great memorial to Columbus came from Henry Harrisse. It comprises all of Columbus' writings arranged chronologically; all the documents relating to him and his family; all the references to him or to the discovery of America by contemporary Italians, excepting by Peter Martyr in his *Decades;* monographs on early Italian maps; the shipbuilding and seamanship of the time; a very elaborate *Life and times of Toscanelli* (by Uzielli, with notes, bibliog. and index, 745 folio pages); a monograph on Peter Martyr (by Pennesi); critical essays on Vespucci, Verrazano and Juan Bautista Genovese (by Hugues); John Cabot (by Bellenio) and Leone Pancaldo (by Peragallo); a critical edition of Pigafetta's account of Magellan's voyage and of Pigafetta's *Rules of navigation* (by Cada Mosto); critical essay by Allegri on Benzoni's *History of the new world;* and a complete bibliography of everything written or printed in Italy relating to Columbus, the discovery of America and Italian travels in America by Fumagalli.

For further details see notes on Lollis, Berchet, Belgrano and Staglieno, and Benzoni, sect. 763, 764, 768, 772, 773.

Navarrete, Don Martin Fernandez de. Coleccion de los viages y descubrimientos, que hicieron por mar los Españoles desde fines del siglo xv, *etc., etc.* Madrid. 1825–37. 5v. [700

In English mainly as follows: —
V. 1. In Major's *Letters of Columbus*, Markham's *Journal of Columbus* (Hakluyt Soc.), and Kettell's *Personal narrative of the first voyage.* Boston. 1827.
V. 2. In *Memorials of Columbus.* London. 1823.
V. 3. Partly in Markham's *Letters of Vespucci.* V. 3 is the basis of Irving's *Voyages of the companions of Columbus*, in which are translated many extracts.
An epoch-making work which bore immediate fruit in Humboldt's *Examen* and Irving's *Columbus.* It is thus the corner stone of modern critical knowledge of the discoveries. V. 1 has a critical introduction and is devoted mainly to the letters and narratives of Columbus; v. 2 mainly to his privileges and honors; v. 3 to the lesser voyages; v. 4 to Magellan and v. 5 to Loaysa's expedition to the Moluccas.

Spotorno, G. B., *tr.* Codice diplomatico colombo-americano. Genoa. 1823.   [701

In English as *Memorials of Columbus.* London. 1823. See note on Belgrano and Staglieno, sect. 773.

Coleccion de documentos inéditos para la historia de España. Madrid. 1842–1895. 112v.   [702

The material relating to America in the first 110 vols. is indexed by Mr. G. P. Winship. Boston Pub. Lib. Bulletin. Oct. '94. Las Casas' *Historia de las Indias*, and other Las Casas documents are among the most interesting.

Coleccion de documentos inéditos relativos al descubrimiento, conquista y colonizacion de las posessiones españolas en América y Oceanía, *etc.* Madrid. 1864–84. 42v.   [703

Although this collection is usually cited as ed. by Pacheco and Cardenas, the real editor was Luis Torres de Mendoza and his name appears alone on v. 5 and following. There is comparatively little in this series on Columbus that is not also in Navarrete. Its contents relate mainly to the 16th and 17th centuries. V. 7 is chiefly taken up with documents of Las Casas. As a whole the collection is badly arranged and uncritical. In v. 33 is a chronological table of contents of the vols. to date.

Coleccion de documentos ineditos relativos al descubrimiento, conquista y organización de las antiguas posessiones españolas de ultramar. Segunda serie. Madrid. 1885–98. 11v.   [704

This continuation of the Pacheco and Cardenas collection is arranged on a more systematic plan. Each vol. is devoted to a single country and the contents are presented in chronological order. There are so far 3 v. on the early administration of Cuba, 2 on Legaspi's expedition to the Philippines, 1 of descriptions of Yucatan, 2 on the pleas of Diego Colon in his suit against the crown, and 3 on the early legislation of the Indies coming down to 1540.

Histories

Martyr, Peter. De orbe novo. Compluti. 1530.   [705
See his name, sect. 761.

Bernáldez, Andrés. Historia de los reyes catolicos. Seville. 1870. 2v.   [706
Knew Columbus personally. Important for second voyage.

Oviedo, Gonzalo Fernandez de. Historia general y natural de las Indias, etc. [Best ed.] Madrid. 1851–5. 4v.   [707
Covers years 1492-1548. Oviedo had a wide experience in the new world. Views Columbus more impartially than Las Casas.

Las Casas, Bartolomé de. Historia de las Indias. Madrid. 1875–6. 5v.
—— Historia apologetica (selected chapters in last vol. of Historia).   [708
Written in Las Casas' old age but not published till above date. Used in MS. by Humboldt, Helps, Irving, Prescott and other scholars. All the important parts taken over by Herrera in his *Historia de las Indias*. Of independent value from 1492-1520. Earlier history of Columbus from Ferdinand Columbus. Portuguese matters from Barros. As a whole rather overloaded with irrelevant, classical and biblical illustration and discussion. The *Historia apologetica* is devoted to a description of the West Indies and the customs and life of the natives. Las Casas' discussion of Vespucci's voyages is translated in Markham's *Vespucci's letters.*

Herrera, Antonio de. Historia general de las Indias occidentales. Best ed. Madrid. 1728–30. 4v.   [709
Enormous index. [Eng. trans. by John Stevens. London. 1725-6. Very untrustworthy.] For Columbus, Herrera copied Las Casas. For the later history he used documents now lost. An important work but hastily and uncritically written. The stock source for the general historians of other countries.

The reader will find a penetrating criticism of these histories in the prologo to Muñoz' *Historia del nuevo mundo*, the first history of the new world to be written by an historical critic of a high order. (Madrid. 1793. Eng. trans. Lond. 1797. Fluent but lacks precision.) Their contributions to our knowledge of Columbus are examined in Harrisse's *Christophe Colomb*, I, 85–135. Their general characteristics are discussed in Markham's *Columbus*, pp. 328–334; and in Bancroft's *Central America*, I, 309–317.   E. G. B. [710

Behaim, Martin. GHILLANY, FRIEDRICH WILHELM. Geschichte des Seefahrers Ritter Martin Behaim nach den ältesten vorhandenen

Urkunden bearbeitet; eingeleitet durch eine Abhandlung: über die ältesten Karten des neuen Continents und den Namen Amerika von Alexander von Humboldt. Nürnberg. 1853.   [711

A highly important contribution to the history of the discoveries. Humboldt's essay is a succinct presentation of the results of his studies in the history of the earliest maps of the new world, which were to form the closing part of the third division of his *Examen de la géographie du nouveau continent*, but which were never published. Ghillany's monograph on the career of Martin Behaim is a masterly piece of investigation of all the materials printed and unprinted that could be collected in Germany and Portugal. In an appendix is a small collection of letters of Behaim and his family, a translation of essays on Behaim by two Portuguese scholars, Trigozo and Garção-Stockler. Behaim's globe is reproduced in two plane spheres of the actual size of the original with all the inscriptions legible.   E. G. B.

Boston, Public Library of the City of. Early explorations in America. (In Bulletins. 1875–78. V. 3, pp. 103–6, 136–41, 205–9, 241–4.)   [712

The main heads of this list are:—The Cabots, Juan de la Cosa, Americus Vespucius, Maps and explorations, America in the 16th century, Gomez, Verrazzano, Southern sea, Pizarro, Cartier, Notes of Americana, Early English explorations. It forms a sketch of the subject with bibliographical and critical notes on its literature. The works mentioned, with a few exceptions (mostly maps), are in the library.

Cronau, Rudolf. Amerika, die Geschichte seiner Entdeckung. Leipzig. 1892. 2v. M. 24.   [713

A richly illustrated work of a popular character by a German artist and newspaper correspondent. It begins with a sketch of prehistoric America, then follows an account, uncritical in character, of the pre-Columbian voyages. The ordinary range of contents of books in this field, Cronau has extended to include Polar expeditions and the exploration of the west. He has personally travelled over a very large part of the western hemisphere, and most of the illustrations of scenery are from his own drawings. A final chapter reviews the literature of American travel. These volumes are not the product of critical historical scholarship, but the author's extensive travels and readiness with pen and pencil have enabled him to write an attractive work for the general reader.   E. G. B.

Fiske, John. The discovery of America; with some account of ancient America and the Spanish conquest. Boston: Houghton. 1892. 2v. $4.   [714

A rare combination of thorough scholarship, well-balanced judgment and literary charm characterize this work. A distinctive feature is the thoroughgoing application of the theory of evolution to explain the features of primitive culture in America, which is

thereby correlated with the general evolution of human civilization. Mr. Fiske's defence of the authenticity of the first voyage of Amerigo Vespucci and his belief in the Zeni voyages are not in accord with the prevalent view of scholars, and his presentation of these questions is misleading as to the relative strength of the case for and against.   E. G. B.

Gaffarel, Paul. Histoire de la découverte de l'Amérique, depuis les origines jusqu'à la mort de Christophe Colomb. Paris: Rousseau. 1892. 2v. 18fr.   [715

The first volume of this work covers the field to which Humboldt devoted a large part of his *Examen de la géographie du nouveau continent* — the literary and archæological evidence advanced in favor of pre-Columbian voyages and the geographical ideas of the Middle Ages. Gaffarel's clear and orderly method of exposition and his abundant and systematic references to the literature of the subject make his book a very satisfactory guide. (The fullest treatment of this field for the English reader is in Winsor, I, pp. 1–132.) Gaffarel verges to the credulous at times in his attitude toward the evidence. Vol. 2 is devoted to the life of Columbus and to the discoveries down to his death. As in vol. 1 the narrative is clear and the references full and very serviceable. The shortcoming of Gaffarel's work is the lack of rigorous and penetrating criticism of evidence. Of this his acceptance of 1494 as the date of the first Cabot voyage is a good example.   E. G. B.

Hakluyt, Richard, *ed.* Divers voyages touching the discouerie of America and the ilands adiacent. London. 1582.

—— *Same;* ed. with notes and introd. by John Winter Jones. London: Hakluyt Soc. 1850.   [716

The earliest contribution of Hakluyt to the cause of English colonization, to promote which he devoted his life. The most important pieces are Robert Thorne's account of the Spanish and Portuguese discoveries (1527), the narrative of Verrazano's voyage, Ribault's *Discovery of Florida* (the original text is lost), the voyages of the Zeno brothers, some brief manuals of directions for voyages of discovery, and notes on the places where spices grow, prices of precious stones, etc. It was in this volume that the letters patent of Henry VII to John Cabot and his sons were first published. The editor gives in his introduction most of the comparatively little that is known of Hakluyt's life. The contents of the volume are included by Goldsmid in his new ed. of Hakluyt's *Principal navigations*.   E. G. B.

—— Principall navigations, voiages and discoveries of the English nation. London. 1589.
—— Principal navigations, voyages, traffiques and discoveries; ed. by Edmund Goldsmid. Edin.: E. and G. Goldsmid. 1884–90. 16v. Subs. V. 12–15: America. V. 16: Voyages of circumnavigation.   [717

Hakluyt's *Principal navigations* was the fruit of a life devoted to promoting the cause of English colonization and commerce by disseminating knowledge about, and stimulating interest in, all the less known or recently discovered parts of the world. This great repository of explorations, travels, and adventures "within the compass of these 1500 years" was aptly styled by Mr. Froude "the prose epic of the modern English nation." The earlier editions are scarce and expensive. In Goldsmid's edition the contents have been carefully rearranged according to a geographical classification, and Hakluyt's other works not originally included in his collection are incorporated.

The matter relating to America is in vols. 12–16. The range of this can be gathered from the fact that in the third vol. of the ed. of 1600 Hakluyt got together 243 narratives of voyages or travels in the new world. Goldsmid's edition is well provided with indexes and tables of contents, and is of more convenient size than the earlier ones. E. G. B.

—— [Selected papers.] See New-York Historical Society, sect. 352. [718

Harrisse, Henry. Diplomatic history of America; its first chapter, 1452–94. London: B. F. Stevens. 1897. N. Y.: Dodd. 1898. Net $2.50. [719

This first chapter of an extended discussion of the political relations in which the discovery of America involved the European powers is the most thorough and critical examination that we have of the Papal grants to Portugal in 1452 and later, of the demarcation Bulls of Alexander VI, 1493, and of the treaty of Tordesillas, 1494. Mr. Harrisse also gives a careful determination of the true location of the demarcation line. E. G. B.

—— Discovery of North America : a critical, documentary, and historic investigation, with an essay on the early cartography of the new world. London : H. Stevens. 1892. $27.50. [720

The first part of this monumental work, the greatest contribution to the history of American geography since Humboldt's *Examen*, is a concise, critically sifted presentation of the ascertained facts of the discovery and exploration of the coast of North America, down to 1525. The notes give the reader a clue to all the original sources and to the best modern discussions. The second and third parts on the early maps of the New World surpass in range and completeness all other treatises on the subject. In the fourth and fifth parts, — the chronological lists of voyages and the biographies of the pilots, — each notice is supplied with notes indicating the sources. For each phase of the history of the discoveries with which it deals, this work is an indispensable guide to the student and investigator. E. G. B.

Higginson, *Col.* Thomas Wentworth. A book of American explorers. Boston : Lee & S. 1877. $1.50.

—— Young folks' book of American explorers. N. Y.: Longmans. $1.20. [721

" He has rightly conceived that the narrative sources of history can be made as clear and as interesting to the youthful mind as ' Robinson Crusoe;' and happily the size of our continent, and the fact that three nationalities took a leading part in its discovery and settlement, combine to give a fascinating variety to the relations that are available, partly in the quaint English of the original, partly in that of Hakluyt and others, and partly in the sympathetic versions of modern scholars. Mr. Higginson's selections . . . have been made with great discrimination, and often with a more subtle purpose than children, not on the look-out for historical ' side-lights,' will discover on the first or on the twentieth reading. The field covered is surprisingly wide for the size of the volume. Columbus, the Cabots and Verrazano, Cabeza de Vaca, Cartier, De Soto, Ribaut and Laudonnière, Sir Humphrey Gilbert, Capt. John Smith, Champlain, Hudson, the Pilgrims and the Puritans, appear in chronological sequence, telling their own stories or celebrated by contemporaries and associates. Every book or chapter is introduced by a statement of the authorities quoted, and brief footnotes, not too numerous, explain the hard words and otherwise illustrate and correct the text. In short, the plan and the performance are admirable." *Nation*, 24 : 254.

Humboldt, Alexander von. Cosmos; tr. by E. C. Otté *et al.* London: Bohn. 1847–58. 5v. N. Y.: Harper. 1850–9. 5v. [722

The first six divisions of Part II of this great review of man's knowledge of the universe give a rapid survey of the progress of geographical discovery from the earliest times to the sixteenth century, and of the results of these discoveries in the development of the various phases of civilization. The quickening of the intellectual life and the extension of scientific knowledge that came from the great military and exploring expeditions in history is nowhere else so impressively displayed. E. G. B.

—— Examen critique de l'histoire de la géographie du nouveau continent, et des progrès de l'astronomie nautique aux quinzième et seizième siècles. Paris. 1836–8. 5v.

—— Kritische Untersuchungen über die historische Entwickelung der geographischen Kenntnisse von der neuen Welt, etc. ; aus dem Französischen übersetzt von J. L. Ideler. Berlin. 1852. 3v. [723

This pioneer and epoch-making book is the most important contribution of the century to the history of geographical ideas and knowledge relating to the discovery of America. According to Humboldt's design the work was to consist of four parts, but he completed only the first two (for the results collected for a portion of Part III, see Ghillany's Behaim, sect. 711), which take up the causes contributing to the discovery of America and the work of Columbus and Vespucci and the chronology of the discoveries. The most original part of the work was its revelation of the stock ideas about the world which formed the basis of Columbus's reasoning. Another striking contribution was the discovery of the origin of the name America, and the proof that Vespucci was in no way responsible for its being attached to the new world. The German edition is the best for use as it is provided with an index of 120 pages, while the French edition is a maze without a clue save the titles of the two parts. The English reader will find in the second volume of Humboldt's *Cosmos* some of the most important discussions of the *Examen*.   E. G. B.

Jacobs, Joseph. Story of geographical discovery. (Library of useful stories.) N. Y.: Appleton. 1899. 40c.   [724

A popular sketch on much the same scale as Keane's, and like that based on the common secondary authorities, but covering the history of exploration down to the present. The maps are less well executed than in Keane's book. A useful feature is the *Annals of discovery* — a chronological and a classified table of discoveries from the earliest times. The author has command of a more extensive literature in this field than Keane, but his references very inadequately represent even the best secondary authorities.
                                           E. G. B.

Keane, John. Evolution of geography: a sketch of the rise and progress of geographical knowledge, to the first circumnavigation of the globe. London: Stanford. 1899. 6s.
                                           [725

A popular survey of the same field reviewed by Kretschmer. The author was very inadequately equipped for the task, as is revealed by his text and his bibliography. His narrative is clear and readable and the facsimiles of the maps are well executed, but it would not be safe to rely upon his statements in regard to critical or doubtful questions.   E. G. B.

Kerr, Robert, *ed.* General history and collection of voyages and travels. Edin. 1811–24. 18v.   [726

This collection of voyages, like the earlier ones of Astley and Churchill and the later one of Pinkerton, contains a large number of narratives derived from Hakluyt. The student of American history will find in Kerr's collection the voyages of the Zeni (which the editor believes fictitious), Galvano's treatise on the discoveries (Hakluyt's version rewritten but not compared with the Portuguese), Cada Mosto's voyages, vol. 2, Ferdinand Columbus' life of his father, Herrera's account of Columbus, the voyages of Vespucci, trans. from the Latin as published by Grynæus, and in vol. 6 the early English voyages to America, mostly from Hakluyt.   E. G. B.

Kohl, Johann Georg. Popular history of the discovery of America, from Columbus to Franklin; tr. by R. R. Noel. London: Chapman. 1862. 2v.   [727

Besides the matter ordinarily to be found in histories of the discovery of America this work gives an account of the Russian explorations which resulted in the possession of Siberia and Alaska, and a review of Arctic exploration from 1572–1850. The final chapter entitled *Concluding observations on the results of the discovery of America to commerce, navigation, science, religion and politics*, is singularly rich in suggestion and instruction.   E. G. B.

Kretschmer, Konrad. Die Entdeckung Amerika's in ihrer Bedeutung für die Geschichte des Weltbildes. Berlin: Kühl. 1892. With atlas.   M. 75.   [728

A Columbian memorial of the German Geographical Society. An admirable history of the development of geographical knowledge and especially of the conceptions of the form of the world. The voyages of discovery from the earliest times are studied from this point of view, to determine what influence they had on the prevalent ideas about the shape of the world and its various parts. The accompanying atlas contains forty plates, twenty-four of which are maps from the Italian libraries published for the first time. These are accurately reproduced in outline, color and inscriptions. The sixteen other plates contain smaller reproductions. Maps from the atlases which were printed without color are simply colored to help the student. The chapters of the text are based on the best sources, are clear and interesting and, with the notes, place before the reader substantially the present state of knowledge. The author's judgment on doubtful questions is trustworthy.   E. G. B.

Peschel, Oscar Ferdinand. Geschichte der Erdkunde, bis auf A. v. Humboldt und C. Ritter. München: J. G. Cotta. 1865. 2te vermehrte Aufl., hrsg. von Sophus Ruge. München. 1877.   [729

About two thirds of this work is devoted to the period since the beginning of modern discovery, and a considerable portion of it relates to the discovery and coastal exploration of the new world. Brief reviews of the contemporary progress of astronomy, geology, and other allied natural sciences supplement the main narrative. Peschel's work is primarily the history of the progress of the general body of the geographical sciences, and is less full of material for the student of history proper than Vivien de St. Martin's *Histoire de la géographie et des découvertes géographiques.* There is an index. Like all of Peschel's work this history is marked by great learning, sound criticism and broad views.   E. G. B.

—— Geschichte des Zeitalters der Entdeckungen. Stuttgart. 1858. 2Aufl. [without changes]. 1877.   [730

A clear and admirable account of the discoveries based on a critical study of all the sources accessible forty years ago. Although a chapter here and there is now antiquated on account of the discovery of new materials, e. g., that on Sebastian Cabot, as a whole, owing to the author's accuracy, sound method, and absence of bias this work can fairly be called a classic in this field of research, and will long remain indispensable to the student. Peschel's footnotes will serve as very convenient clues to the original sources and to the most important critical discussions of them up to 1858.   E. G. B.

Pinkerton, John, *comp.* A general collection of voyages and travels. London. 1808–14. 17v.   [731

Pinkerton's *Voyages* is the best of the various collections published in England. He reprinted all of the previously published collections that he thought worth preservation. The last vol. contains a two column index of 472 pages and a bibliography of books of voyages and travels arranged chronologically by countries, which occupies 255 pages. Vols. XII, XIII, and XIV are devoted to America and contain Ferdinand Columbus' *Life of Columbus*, Frobisher's *Voyages*, Cartier's *Voyages*, the *Voyages to Virginia*, John Smith's *General history of Virginia* and the *Travels* of Lahontan, Kalm, and Burnaby. E. G. B.

Purchas, Samuel. Hakluytus posthumus; or Purchas, his pilgrimes, contayning a history of the world in sea voyages and lande-trauells, by Englishmen and others. London. 1625–6. 5v. [V. 5 bears title Purchas, his pilgrimage. 1st ed. pub. in 1613. This, the 4th, is best.] [732

Purchas took up the work of Hakluyt, but with unequal powers. His judgment was less sound as to the value of material, and he was not accurate in printing his texts. He inherited a mass of MSS. from Hakluyt, and these, with his own collections and a good many of Hakluyt's printed narratives, either complete or abridged, make up the contents of these volumes. Purchas preserved accounts of some voyages otherwise unrecorded, and this constitutes the basis of the value of his collection to-day to the student. His most important narratives, however, are now accessible in better editions. The contents of the *Pilgrims* may be found in the *Boston Athenæum catalogue*. Owing to its rarity, *Purchas, his pilgrimes* commands a very high price — about $100 a volume for good sets. A part of vol. III and vol. IV are devoted to America. The voyages to, and descriptions and early history of Virginia are fully represented. E. G. B.

—— [Selected papers.] See New-York Historical Society, sect. 352. [733

Ruge, Sophus. Geschichte des Zeitalters der Entdeckungen. Berlin : Grote. 1881. [734

This work is a clear and accurate history of the discoveries. It covers a somewhat wider field than Peschel and comes down to a later date. For example, the Portuguese conquests in India, the Spanish conquest of Mexico and of Peru, and the search for a northeast and northwest passage are included. The plan of the series to which the book belongs did not admit of many footnotes. Ruge's work, in consequence, is of less help to the investigator than Peschel's. In other respects, also, it is planned rather for the scholarly reader than for the special student, and admirably fulfils its purpose. The illustrations and maps are especially appropriate and finely executed.

E. G. B.

Smith, George Barnett. The United States, from the earliest times to the landing of the Pilgrim fathers. (Romance of colonization.) N. Y. : Dodd. 1897. $1.50.

—— *Same.* V. 2 : From the 17th century to the present day. London : Partridge. 1897. 2s. 6d. [735

This work deals with the colonization and develop-

ment of America. It is a compilation by a practiced hand and is in some ways skilfully done. It is, however, uncritical, and does not compare in charm of style with Fiske's *Discovery of America*. The evident purpose is to magnify the importance of the Anglo-Saxons, and as written in the interest of British readers has little value for the American student.

C. M. A.

Ternaux-Compans, Henri. Voyages, relations, et mémoires originaux pour servir à l'histoire de la découverte de l'Amérique. Paris. 1837–41. 20v. [736

Contains translations into French of most of the more important narratives and memoirs. Of some of these the Spanish original has disappeared. The translations are often inaccurate. Ternaux usually omitted altogether words and phrases that were difficult to decipher or to translate. The book therefore should never be used when Spanish texts can be obtained.

E. C.

Thacher, John Boyd. The continent of America, its discovery and its baptism: an essay on the nomenclature of the old continents, etc. N. Y. : W. E. Benjamin. 1896. [Limited ed.] $25. [737

This stately volume is the product of the enthusiasm of the amateur, rather than of the critical research of the scholar. The chief topics are the landfall of Columbus, that of Vespucci, Vespucci's first voyage and the naming of America. The author follows Varnhagen in regard to the interpretation of the first voyage. Of its inherent perplexities he seems hardly aware. The Italian and Latin texts of the voyage are given with Quaritch's translation. The naming of America is treated fully, but without adding anything to what is accessible elsewhere. A noteworthy feature of the book is the reproductions in actual size of fourteen early maps. For the discussion of these maps the student should resort to Harrisse. E. G. B.

Vivien de St. Martin, Louis. Histoire de la géographie et des découvertes géographiques ; accompagné d'un atlas historique. Paris : Hachette. 1873–4. 2v. [738

As compared with Peschel's *Geschichte der Erdkunde* this work is richer for the student of history and less adapted for the students of the science of geography. It devotes more attention than Peschel to ancient and mediæval geography, to the discoveries and to the inland explorations, and comes down to the date of publication. It gives relatively little attention to the progress of the auxiliary sciences to geography. The author was a most distinguished scholar in this field and his work is characterized by scientific impartiality and thoroughness. E. G. B.

Weise, Arthur James. The discoveries of America to the year 1525. N. Y. : Putnam. 1884. [739

The author of this work had the instincts and industry for sound historical work, but he lacked the training to deal with the difficulties of his theme. His work is based in the main on the original sources, but he has not subjected them to criticism and exact analysis, and he glides smoothly over the most perplexing problems. His work may be of service to the English reader for its extensive citations of the original sources in translation. Copies of parts of the maps of La Cosa and Maiollo are given in a cover pocket.

E. G. B.

Pre-Columbian Discovery

Anderson, Rasmus Björn. America not discovered by Columbus. Chicago: Griggs. 1874.

·—— *Same; also* Bibliography of the pre-Columbian discoveries of America, by P. B. Watson. 4th ed., enl. Chicago: Scott. $1.

[740

In this book "even the Skeleton in Armor is made to play a part. Excluding such vagaries, the book is not without use as displaying the excessive views entertained in some quarters on the subject. The author is, we believe, a Scandinavian, and shows the tendency of his race to a facility rather than felicity in accepting evidence on this subject." Justin Winsor, in *Narrative and critical history of America*, v. 1, p. 97.

The author believed the Welsh claim to the discovery of America to be not only possible but even probable. Twenty years later, he says: " After reading Mr. Stephens's exhaustive work [*Madoc*], with its overwhelming weight of argument, I am bound to revise my former opinion, and to say that he has not left a single shred of supposed evidence unrefuted. I believe no candid reader can rise from the perusal of *Madoc* with any other impression than that the story is not founded on facts." *Dial* (*Chicago*), 16: 138.

Beamish, North Ludlow. Discovery of America by the Northmen, in the 10th century ; with notices of the early settlements of the Irish in the western hemisphere. London. 1841.

[741

An adaptation of Rafn's *Antiquitates Americanæ* for English readers. The translations of the sagas and other Icelandic texts are from Rafn's Danish version. Rafn's discussion of the evidence and his account of the monuments and inscriptions of the Northmen is epitomized. The author also supplies a sketch of Icelandic literature based on that of Bishop Peter Erasmus Müller. Beamish accepted all Rafn's views, and his book may be resorted to as a clear and faithful presentation in English of Rafn's epoch-making book in this field.

E. G. B.

De Costa, Benjamin Franklin, *ed.* Pre-Columbian discovery of America by the Northmen, illustrated by translations from the Icelandic sagas. Albany: Munsell. 1868. New and enl. ed. 1889. $3.

[742

" The design of this volume is to present in an English dress to the historical student every portion of the Icelandic sagas relating to the pre-Columbian discovery of America by the Northmen. These sagas or narratives are translated, with the needful explana-

tions added in regard to persons and places. . . . The work has been well done, and affords general satisfaction as a useful addition to historical literature. The author, it is true, is still somewhat under the influence of the spell that lingers round the name of the Northmen, which dazzles his imagination and obscures his vision, preventing him from setting some facts in a clear light. . . . But he has one great merit seldom found among translators with strong prepossessions— he suppresses nothing and conceals nothing. He renders the old writings as they were first recorded, leaving the labor to the intelligent reader of separating the miraculous and incredible from the natural and credible." *Nation*, 8: 53.

Henry, *Prince, of Portugal.* BEAZLEY, CHARLES RAYMOND. Prince Henry the navigator, the hero of Portugal and of modern discovery, 1394–1460, A. D. (Heroes of the nations.) N. Y.: Putnam. 1895. $1.50. [743

The first 120 pages of this volume are taken up with a sketch of the progress of geographical knowledge and conceptions during the Middle Ages. The account, which follows, of the labors of Prince Henry to promote discoveries and commerce is one of the best that has been written and is adequate for ordinary purposes. There are fourteen reduced copies of mediæval maps. As a whole this work is one of the best brief introductions to the period of discoveries.

E. G. B.

—— MAJOR, RICHARD HENRY. Life of Prince Henry of Portugal, surnamed the Navigator, and its results, comprising the discovery, within one century, of half the world ; from authentic contemporary documents. London: Asher. 1868.

[744

A critical history of the geographical discoveries of the fifteenth century and the first part of the sixteenth. Prince Henry was the pioneer of modern scientific exploration, and the work done under his direction paved the way for Columbus and Magellan. Mr. Major in this volume discusses with wide learning and a keen critical spirit a great number of obscure and controverted questions relating to the early voyages of exploration. The second edition is a more popular and briefer treatment of the same general subject.

E. G. B.

Higginson, Thomas Wentworth. Tales of the enchanted islands of the Atlantic. N. Y.: Macmillan. 1898. $1.50. [745

" Colonel Higginson has had the happy thought of collecting for youthful readers some of those legends which are on the borderland of American history because they tell of sea expeditions which foreshadowed the discovery of America. From Plato to Ignatius Donnelly men have dreamed of the lost island Atlantis, and even in the seventeenth century the Dutch thought of it as a large island midway between Spain and America. . . . Colonel Higginson's selection includes tales connected with Norse explorations of America and with early Irish history. For these he has drawn largely on Lady Charlotte Guest's translation of *Mabinogion*, and on Joyce's *Ancient Celtic romances.* The result is a set of very pleasing stories, appropriately written, and likely to inspire an interest in Celtic literature. Mr. A. Herter's illustrations are pretty and well suited to the text." *Nation*, 67: 447.

Horsford, Eben Norton. Discovery of America by Northmen: address at the unveiling of the statue of Leif Eriksen, delivered in Faneuil Hall, Oct. 29, 1887. Boston: Houghton. 1888. Net $5.   [746

Prof. Horsford was an untiring advocate of the identity of Vinland with the immediate neighborhood of Boston. His linguistic arguments were fanciful and his other evidence has found little acceptance. This monograph contains his address reviewing the Norse voyages, facsimiles of early maps of America and Toulmin Smith's translation of the text of the sagas. The main contentions of Prof. Horsford's later monographs aiming to identify Vinland and to explain Norumbega are briefly summarized by Fiske, *Discovery of America*, I, 220.   E. G. B.

Leland, Charles Godfrey. Fusang; or The discovery of America by Chinese Buddhist priests in the 5th century. London: Trübner. 1875. N. Y.: J. W. Bouton. 1875.

[747

Mr. Leland " has translated into English a pamphlet on the subject by the late Professor Neumann, of Munich, with notes and comments of his own, and such quotations from other writers as bear on this hypothesis. The result is a volume slender in size and even slenderer in solid basis for so important a theory." *Atlantic monthly*, 37: 120. See, also, Vining, E. P., below, sect. 756.

Madoc, *or* Madoq, ab Owen Gwynedd. STEPHENS, THOMAS. Madoc: an essay on the discovery of America by Madoc ab Owen Gwynedd in the 12th century. N. Y.: Longmans. 1893. $2.50.   [748

Since Sir George Peckham in 1583 first based England's claim to America on the discoveries of Madoc, there has been a considerable body of literature devoted to this shadowy subject (cf. Winsor, I, 109–111). This work of Thomas Stephens is the definitive treatise on the question. The author was deeply versed in Welsh literature and history and an acute historical critic. He examines carefully all the historical evidence, the reports of travellers, the history of the Madoc legend, and the real history of Madoc so far as it can be discovered. His conclusions are convincingly destructive. The book was written in 1858 and published after the author's death.   E. G. B.

Neukomm, Edmond. Les dompteurs de la mer: les Normands en Amérique depuis le Xme jusqu'au XVme siècle. Paris: Hetzel. [1897.]

—— Rulers of the sea. Boston: Estes. 1896. $1.50.

—— Tamers of the sea; [tr.] by Mrs. Cashel Hoey. London: Low. 1897. 2s. 6d.   [749

" M. Neukomm has given us, in a very pleasant mixture of history, legend and fable, all the stories of the pre-Columbian discovery of America, so far as Normans had anything to do with it, and M. Gravier counts among Normans all the Scandinavian people, whether in Norway, Iceland, Greenland, or the northern isles. . . . M. Neukomm's book is interesting and, although it must not be taken as serious history, it may be useful in directing attention to the mass of legendary history concerning the opening up of the western world. It is well illustrated to interest young people." — University of Toronto. *Review of hist. publications relating to Canada, 1898.*

Rafn, Carl Christian. Antiquitates Americanæ, sive scriptores septentrionales rerum ante-Columbianarum in America; edidit Societas regia antiquariorum septentrionalium. Hafniæ. 1837.   [750

The pioneer and fundamental work on the Norse voyages to America, on which most of the subsequent literature has been based. (See Winsor, I, 87–107, for a history of the question.) This large folio contains the original text of the sagas in old Icelandic and translations into Danish and Latin followed by critical discussions in Latin; extracts from ancient Icelandic geographical writings, descriptions of European relics in Greenland; descriptions and discussions of supposed Norse relics in New England and an elaborate identification of localities. A summary of the evidence and conclusions is given in English. This summary was also separately published in French,— *Mémoire sur la découverte de l'Amérique au dixième siècle* (Copenhagen. 1843). Rafn was an enthusiast on this subject, and his enthusiasm made him over hasty and credulous in accepting the various alleged relics of the Northman and in pushing the identification of localities. His work was presented to English readers at the time by Beamish and Smith (sect. 741, 754).
                    E. G. B.

Reeves, Arthur Middleton. The finding of Wineland the good. London: Frowde. 1890. £2 10s. N. Y.: Macmillan. 1890. $11.
                    [751

Contains (1) phototypic reproductions of the important sagas relating to America with the printed text on the opposite page; (2) translations into English of these and other sagas; (3) elaborate notes and discussions; (4) a valuable introduction. The work of an accurate, painstaking American student. Reeves generally follows Storm (sect. 755). Taken altogether, this is by far the best work on the Norse discovery of America for all English-speaking students who cannot read the sagas in the original.   E. C.

Shipley, *Mrs.* Marie Adelaide Brown. Icelandic discoverers of America; or Honour to whom honour is due. London: Trübner. 1887. N. Y.: Alden. 1890.   [752

A special plea devoid of historical value. The author believes that the Norse discovery of America was known by the Catholic Church and the evidence suppressed, that the recognition of Columbus as the discoverer is one of the links in the chain which the

Papacy is forging to bind America, and that the rejection of the claim of Columbus and the recognition of the claim of the Norsemen is a patriotic duty and would be a second Declaration of Independence. In a pamphlet published in 1898 Mrs. Shipley contends that documents in the Vatican prove the colonization of Vinland, but the documents which she cites all refer to Greenland.   E. G. B.

Slafter, Edmund Farwell, *ed.* Voyages of the Northmen to America ; including extracts from the Icelandic sagas in an English translation by North Ludlow Beamish, opinion of Prof. Rafn, etc. (Prince Soc. Publications.) Boston. 1877.   [753

Substantially a republication slightly revised of Beamish's work which is out of print. Rafn's English summary of his researches (see note on Rafn, sect. 750) is also included. Mr. Slafter sketches a history of the question in his introduction and supplies a select bibliography of Scandinavian history and culture and of the literature of the voyages.

                         E. G. B.

Smith, Joshua Toulmin. Discovery of America by the Northmen in the 10th century ; comprising translations of all the most important original narratives. Boston. 1839. 2d ed. [corr.]. London. 1842.   [754

An attempt to put the materials and discussions published by Rafn in his *Antiquitates* before the English readers. The author unfortunately adopted the controversial dialogue as his method of presentation, and the average student cannot but be worn out and confused to the last degree by the discussions of Mr. Norset, Dr. Dubital and Mr. Cassall. Beamish's popularization of Rafn is every way preferable.

                         E. G. B.

Storm, Gustav. Studies on the Vineland voyages : extracts from Mémoires de la Société royale des antiquaires du nord, 1888. Copenhague. 1889.   [755

These ten brief studies are admirable specimens of historical criticism, and are one of the most important contributions to the subject since Rafn wrote. Storm, who is Professor of history in the University of Christiania, approaches his subject in a dispassionate and scientific spirit. The most original part of his work is the internal criticism of the saga narratives in no. IV. His conclusion, in brief, is that what is known commonly as Thorfinn Karlsefne's saga is the unabridged saga of Eric the Red, and is the oldest and most historical of these narratives, whereas the saga which in Rafn is called the saga of Eric the Red, and which is derived from the Flateyjarbók, is an alien narrative by an author ignorant of the earlier tradition of the Vineland voyages whose work later received interpolations from the real saga of Eric the Red. Storm would reject as questionable all the divergencies of the Flateyjarbók narratives from that of the real saga of Eric the Red. The number of Vineland voyages then drops from five to two. Storm finds Vineland in Nova Scotia.   E. G. B.

Vining, Edward P. An inglorious Columbus ; or Evidence that Hwui Shan and a party of Buddhist monks from Afghanistan discovered America in the 5th century, A. D. N. Y.: Appleton. 1885. $5.   [756

The question of the relation of American primitive civilization to that of Asia has been for generations a subject of speculation, and it is with this larger theme that this book really has to do. The author has collected together and published in full or in epitome all the most important memoirs of eminent orientalists on this subject, such as De Guignes, Klaproth, De Paravey, Neumann, D'Eichthal, Williams and others. These he has followed with the text of Ma Twin-lin's account of Fu-Sang with eight parallel translations by different scholars. The last half of the book is a commentary on this narrative and on the resemblances between Mexican and Asiatic culture. There is an extensive bibliography. More recently Professor Schlegel, Professor of Chinese at Leiden, has shown by an examination of Chinese literature, that the term Fu-Sang is not mysterious, but uniformly is applied to Saghalin (cf. his art. Problèmes géographiques, I, Fousang-Kono. T'oung Pao, pp. 3, 101).   E. G. B.

Voyages to Vinland, from the saga of Eric the Red. See Old South Work, sect. 368.

                         [757

Zeno, Nicolò *and* **Antonio.** Voyages of the Venetian brothers, Nicolò and Antonio Zeno, to the northern seas, in the 14th century ; tr. and ed. by Richard Henry Major. London: Hakluyt Soc. 1873.   [758

This volume contains the text of the Zeno narratives with an English translation. The editor in an introduction of 100 pages makes an heroic defence of the authenticity of the narratives and the map, directing his energies particularly against the destructive criticism of Admiral Zahrtmann (Journal of the Royal Geog. Soc., v. 5, 1836). For a time he stayed the tide of skepticism. During the last fifteen years, however, the drift of critical opinion has been steadily adverse to the authenticity of these voyages and very few of the present generation of scholars accept them. Major's argument is rather a special plea than a sound piece of historical criticism.   E. G. B.

—Lucas, Frederick W. Annals of the voyages of the brothers Nicolò and Antonio Zeno in the North Atlantic about the end of the 14th century, and the claim founded thereon to a Venetian discovery of America. London: H. Stevens. 1898. 42s.   [759

In this volume will be found most of the material necessary for an independent study of the Zeno voyages. There is a translation of the Zeno narratives, a facsimile of the original text, and of Hakluyt's translation, a table comparing the names on the Zeno map with the names on earlier or contemporary maps, a tabular view of the identifications of the Zeno names proposed by the leading writers on the subject, an extensive bibliography arranged chronologically with an index, and an exceptionally fine collection of facsimiles of early maps. Mr. Lucas himself is profoundly convinced of the spuriousness of the narratives of the voyages and makes out a very strong case. He has not, however, handled his material as effectively as one more expert in dealing with matters of internal criticism might have done.   E. G. B.

Spanish and Portuguese Discovery and Early Exploration

Andagoya, Pascual de. Narrative of the proceedings of Pedrarias Davila [1514–41] ; tr. and ed. by Clements R. Markham. London : Hakluyt Soc. 1865.   [760

An excellent translation of Andagoya's *Relacion de los sucesos de Pedrárias Dávila* printed in Navarrete's *Coleccion*, III, 393–456. The author was on good terms with the leading characters whose deeds are noted; he also had good means of observation. Narrative often indistinct and hard to follow; the editor has added extracts from valuable letters of Vasco Nuñez de Balboa.   E. C.

Anghiera, Pietro Martire d'. De rebus oceanicis et orbe novo decades tres. Compluti. 1530.
—— *Same* [8 decades] ; ed. by Hakluyt. Paris. 1587 [the only complete edition of eight decades].
—— Historie of the West Indies, containing the actes and adventures of the Spaniards which have conquered and peopled those countries, etc. ; tr. into English by M. Lok. London. *n. d.*
—— *Same.* (In Hakluyt, R. Principal navigations, etc. 1812 ed. V. 5, pp. 176–476.)   [761

The first history of America. Peter Martyr was an Italian who lived in Spain and was Chaplain to Queen Isabella and apostolic protonotary. He kept up a lively correspondence with prominent Italians and with Spaniards who were abroad detailing the news of the day. His collected letters were published in 1530 and 1670. All the passages relating to Columbus and the discoveries are in the *Raccolta colombiana*, part III, vol. II. (See sect. 699.) On the basis of his letters he wrote his *Decades* with more care and greater detail, still preserving the form of letters. In translation or abstract Peter Martyr's work was widely circulated in the sixteenth century, and is the foundation of contemporary knowledge of the new world. His official position, personal intercourse with Columbus and other discoverers and his efforts to gather material make his *Decades* an indispensable primary source for the history of the discoveries. Yet much of his work was hasty, and the obvious inaccuracies impair one's confidence where he cannot be checked, and enforce the necessity of careful criticism. The English translation is Eden's for the first three *Decades* and Lok's for the other five. This fifth vol. of Hakluyt was published separately in 1812.   E. G. B.

Azurara, Gomes Eannes de. Chronicle of the discovery and conquest of Guinea ; now first done into English by Charles Raymond Beazley and Edgar Prestage. London : Hakluyt Soc. 1896–9. 2v.   [762

The most important source of our knowledge of the Portuguese voyages of discovery down the coast of Africa till 1448. This contemporary and official narrative, after being lost to sight three hundred years, was discovered in Paris by F. Denis in 1837 and first printed there in 1841 with notes by Santarem. Prior to its discovery in 1837, Barros (circ. 1550) was the only historian who had seen it, and he only saw fragments, so that everything written earlier than 1841 on the Portuguese discoveries depended in the main on Barros. Besides being a priceless historical monument, Azurara's narrative is an interesting product of the revival of learning in Portugal. The English editors have incorporated most of Santarem's notes in their commentary, and Mr. Beazley's introduction to the second volume is the latest summary of the Portuguese discoveries of the fifteenth century. He also supplies brief studies of the maps and charts of that period. The footnotes serve as a guide to a large body of critical discussion.   E. G. B.

Benzoni, Girolamo. Historia del mondo nuovo. Venetia. 1565.
—— History of the new world, shewing his travels in America, 1541–56 ; tr. and ed. by W. H. Smyth. London : Hakluyt Soc. 1857.   [763

The wide popularity of this work, of whose author nothing is known except what he incidentally relates, is evinced by the many editions published in the 16th and 17th centuries. It was translated into Latin, French, German and Dutch, and epitomized by Purchas in English. No Spanish translation was ever made. Benzoni's narrative is not a systematic history, but a rambling, readable medley of history and travellers' observations and comment. He gives descriptions of the Spanish settlements in Hispaniola and Cumana, with accounts of slave hunts, of Las Casas' experience with his colony and of Peru, where Benzoni lived three years. He confirms Las Casas' picture of the cruelties to the Indians. The work has little independent value. Allegri has recently subjected it to a critical examination and found that a large part of its contents was derived from the third vol. of Ramusio's *Navigationi*. Through the medium of Ramusio, Peter Martyr is Benzoni's source for Columbus, and Gomara for the conquest of Peru. The natural history again is from Oviedo, and the manners and customs of the natives from Gomara. Benzoni's sole original contribution to the history of Columbus is the mythical egg story. His popularity Allegri attributes to the fact that his book is a readable compilation of the gist of more voluminous and less accessible works. Allegri's essay is in the *Raccolta colombiana*, pt. 5, vol. 3, pp. 137–154. (See sect. 699.) Benzoni's extensive borrowing from previous writers was noted by Muñoz in the prologo of his *Historia del nuevo mondo*, 1793.   E. G. B.

Berchet, Guglielmo. Fonti italiani per la storia della scoperta del nuovo mondo. I. Carteggi diplomatici. II. Narrazione sincrone

(Raccolta colombiana, pt. 3, v. 1–2; see sect. 699 above.)   Roma.   1893.   [764

The first of these volumes contains every reference to the discovery of the new world in Italian diplomatic correspondence down to 1536, comprising in all about 140 passages. Much of this material is new and printed for the first time. The most important single piece is the letter of Angelo Trevisan written in 1501 to Malipiero, which formed the basis of the famous *Libretto di tutta la navigazione de re di Spagna*, of which only a single copy is extant. This letter contains the oldest description of Columbus's personal appearance. In substance it is a translation several years before its publication of Peter Martyr's first *Decade*. The second volume comprises all the passages in books and MSS. by Italian writers down to 1550 which refer to Columbus or the discovery of America, excepting Peter Martyr's *Decades*, of which a full table of contents is given. Some of these books are extremely rare. The text of the unique copy of the *Libretto* (see above) is reprinted, as are all the relevant passages of Peter Martyr's letters, the letters of Vespucci, Giustiniani's sketch of Columbus's life, Verrazano's letter, etc. These volumes present more new material than any others of the *Raccolta* and make generally accessible much which, although known, was beyond the reach of all but the most favored scholars.   E. G. B.

Casas, Bartolomé de las.   Coleccion de las obras del obispo de Chiapa, ed. by J. A. Llorente.   Paris.   1822.   2v.   In Spanish and also in French, 2v.   [765

A useful reprint of the more important of Las Casas' publications (not including the *Historia*), with some pieces not before printed.

"Las Casas stands justly chargeable with enormous exaggerations of the number or estimate of the victims of Spanish cruelty. But I have not met with a single case in any contemporary writer, nor in the challengers and opponents of his pleadings at the Court of Spain, in which his hideous portrayal of the forms and methods of that cruelty, its dreadful and revolting tortures and mutilations, have been brought under question." G. E. Ellis, in *Narrative and critical hist. of America*, 2 : 313.

—— Historia de las Indias.   Madrid: Real academia de la historia, 1875–6.   5v.   [Also forms vols. 62–64 of Coleccion de documentos inéditos para la historia de España, sect. 702.]   [766

Brings the history of Spanish America to 1520. Largely written from personal observation. Otherwise based on documents many of which have since been lost. Written with prejudice against the conquerors, this work is the foundation of a large part of later accounts of the period.   E. C.
See, also, sect. 708.

— HELPS, *Sir* ARTHUR.   Life of Las Casas, "The apostle of the Indies."   Phil. : Lippincott.   1868.   [767

This "life," which was constructed mainly by the son of Arthur Helps out of *The Spanish conquest in America* by the father, is the most considerable account in

English. The larger work was written in a spirit readily appreciative of the character of Las Casas, and he is made such a centre of interest in it as easily to favor the excision of parts of it to form the lesser book. . . . The great friend of the Indian is mainly, however, to be drawn from his own writings." Justin Winsor, *Narrative and critical hist. of Am.*, 2 : 343.

Colombo, Cristoforo.   Scritti ; pubblicati ed illustrati da Cesare de Lollis.   (Raccolta colombiana, pt. 1.   See sect. 699.)   Roma. 1894.   [768

A critical edition of all the writings of Columbus, arranged chronologically, with elaborate introductions to each document. Where known writings have been lost, e. g. the journals of the second voyage, the editor prints texts which he believes faithful abstracts or transcripts : e. g. for the journal of the second voyage he prints in parallel columns the narratives of Fernando Colombo and Las Casas as immediately derived from it. All the quotations imbedded in the *Historie* and in Las Casas' *Historia de las Indias* are given in their proper order. The marginal notes that Columbus made in his copy of Cardinal d'Ailly's *Imago mundi* and in his *Marco Polo* are now made accessible to the student. The third volume is devoted to photographic fac-similes of every piece of writing known from the hand of Columbus excepting those printed in the *Autografas de Cristobal Colon*. The text of the new letters, etc., of Columbus in the *Autografas* Lollis was able to include. This great work must remain an indispensable source to the critical student of Columbus. Although not much of this material is strictly new, much of it has been relatively inaccessible from its being widely scattered.   E. G. B.

—— Select letters, with other original documents ; tr. and ed. by R. H. Major.   London : Hakluyt Soc.   1847.   2d ed.   1870.   [769

Contemporary narratives by Columbus or his companions of his four voyages to America, preceded by a critical review of the career of Columbus and the sources of his inspiration. The letters are printed in both the original Spanish and in a careful English version. There is also a bibliography of the fifteenth century editions of Columbus' first letter. The primary source of the larger part of our knowledge of Columbus' life and work.   E. G. B.

—— Writings descriptive of the discovery and occupation of the new world ; ed. by Paul Leicester Ford.   N. Y.: Webster.   1892. [770

A more comprehensive collection than that of Major, containing English translations only, which are by various hands. Besides letters the editor has included the will of Columbus, his deed of entail and the privileges of Columbus (1497 and 1501). These documents illustrate the beginnings of the Spanish colonial system.   E. G. B.

— ADAMS, CHARLES KENDALL.   Christopher Columbus, his life and his work.   (Makers of America.)   N. Y. : Dodd.   1892. $1.   [771

An excellent brief life, written in an impartial spirit. The author, although not a specialist in this period, has approached his material as an experiencod historical student and teacher, and has clearly discriminated in his narrative between the ascertained, the probable and the legendary elements of the body of fact and report that have come down to us as the life of Columbus. In general he has been guided by the results of Harrisse's researches. Too much significance is given to Cronau's study of the landfall and the actual resting-place of Columbus' remains.   E. G. B.

— BELGRANO, L. T., *e* M. STAGLIENO, *eds.* Documenti relativi a Cristoforo Colombo e alla sua famiglia. (Raccolta colombiana, pt. 2, v. 1.) Roma. 1896.   [772

This volume contains all the known documents of a non-public character which refer to Columbus, his family, his ancestors and his descendants, excepting such of his own writings as were included in the preceding vols. of the *Raccolta*. The critical introduction is by Staglieno on the basis of the labors of Belgrano. The larger part of the earlier documents from the notarial records of Savona and Genoa were discovered by Staglieno, and a considerable number are here published for the first time. Harrisse published a good many of those notarial records in the second vol. of his Christophe Colomb. The Spanish documents were, many of them, unearthed by Harrisse and published by him. There is a full index to this volume and a genealogical tree with dates recording succinctly the material in these records.   E. G. B.

— BELGRANO, L. T., *e* M. STAGLIENO, *eds.* Il codice dei privilegi di Cristoforo Colombo; edito secondo i manoscritti di Genova, di Parigi e di Providence. (Raccolta colombiana, pt. 2, v. 2.) Roma. 1894.

— SPOTORNO, G. B., *tr.*   Codice diplomatico colombo-americano, etc.   Genoa.   1823.

—— —— Memorials of Columbus; or A collection of authentic documents. London. 1823.
                                                [773
Columbus had several authenticated copies made of the royal documents which conferred upon him his official dignities and privileges relating to his voyages, discoveries and rights and duties as Admiral of the Indies. One of these copies came into the possession of the republic of Genoa in 1670, and was published in 1823. Spotorno prefixed a brief life of Columbus, which is in the English translation, and gave an Italian translation of the documents. Belgrano and Staglieno assure the student that they have reproduced the text of the MS. with scrupulous fidelity excepting as regards forms of letters like *u* and *v*, and affirm that Spotorno's text is in places incorrect. These documents were also published by Navarrete in the second vol. of his *Coleccion* from the MS. which Columbus retained and which went to his heirs.
                                                E. G. B.

— BOSTON, PUBLIC LIBRARY OF THE CITY OF. Columbus: a list of the writings of Christopher Columbus and of the works relating to him in the possession of the library. (In Bulletins. 1892–93. V. 11, pp. 221–33.)   [774

A list of his maps, letters and other writings, mainly in Spanish. The works about him concern his life, family, burial place, bibliography, portraits, etc., and include references to periodicals.

— COLOMBO, FERNANDO. Historie del S. D. Fernando Colombo; nelle quali s'ha particolare et vera relatione della vita, et de' fatti dell' Ammiraglio Christoforo Colombo, suo padre, etc. Venetia. 1571. [Several subsequent editions, the latest, London: Dulau. 1867.]

—— —— History of the life and actions of Admiral Christopher Columbus, etc., written by his own son. (In Churchill's Voyages, 2: 501–628; the same, ed. of 1744, 2: 481–604; Kerr's Voyages, 3: 1–242; Pinkerton's Voyages, 12: 1–155.)   [775

The source of the traditional accounts of Columbus and for the period before 1492 of most of the legendary matter rejected by Harrisse and other modern scholars. The Spanish original was never published and the MS. is not extant. The impossibility of reconciling the account of the earlier life of Columbus given in this biography with the facts established by documents discovered by himself and others, has led Harrisse to deny its authenticity. That Las Casas took over almost all of the earlier chapters into his *Historia de las Indias* is the strongest argument of the defenders of Ferdinand's authorship. The drift of present critical opinion is in favor of accepting the book as the work of Ferdinand. Its trustworthiness, however, for the period where it should be most useful, before 1492, is shattered. For a brief account of the controversial literature, see K. Haebler, *Historische Zeitschrift*, 57: 223–5; 74: 239–40. The Italian text of the London ed. of 1869 does not conform faithfully to that of the original edition of 1571. The English translation was originally prepared for Churchill's *Voyages*. It is a readable and tolerably faithful rendering. Pinkerton reprinted the Churchill text without change. For Kerr's *Voyages* the division into short chapters was dropped and the text revised, yet without consulting the original (!). The Spanish translation printed by Barcia in his *Historiadores primitivos* and reprinted in Madrid, 1892, is pronounced "malisima" by Muñoz.   E. G. B.

— HARRISSE, HENRY. Christophe Colomb devant l'histoire. Paris: Welter. 1892. 10fr.
                                                [776

The first part of this book is devoted to a sarcastic running commentary on some of the curiosities of the Columbian celebration, the fictitious relics, etc.; then follows a brief statement of the results of the author's investigations in regard to the disputed questions relating to Columbus' life, and an estimate of his work. In this last he defends Columbus from the disparagements of some recent biographers. The review of the ascertained facts is called forth by the superficial, uncritical, mistaken, and legendary character of much that was written about Columbus at the time of the celebration. There are full notes.   E. G. B.

— HARRISSE, HENRY. Christophe Colomb, son origine, sa vie, ses voyages, sa famille et ses descendants; d'après des documents inédits tirés des archives de Gênes, de Savone, de Séville et de Madrid : études d'histoire critique. Paris: Leroux. 1884–5. 2v. 100fr.   [777

The most important critical study ever devoted to the life of Columbus, and an indispensable guide to every student of the problems of his career. A most valuable feature is the elaborate critical discussion of all the known sources very systematically arranged. The title indicates clearly the scope of the body of the work. Footnotes provide the scholar with the materials for checking the author's results. The investigations in regard to Columbus' family have been especially exhaustive. A large number of hitherto unprinted documents are given in the Appendices. Besides this monumental work Harrisse has printed a large number of monographs and articles relating to Columbus and to his family. A chronological list is appended to his *Diplomatic history of America*. In Winsor, *Nar. and crit. hist.*, II, 88–92, the new material and conclusions of Harrisse are epitomized.   E. G. B.

— IRVING, WASHINGTON. Life and voyages of Christopher Columbus; to which are added those of his companions. N. Y.: Putnam. 1828. 4v. Various editions.   [778

"Washington Irving . . . being in Bordeaux in the winter of 1825–26, was informed by Alexander Everett, the United States Minister in Spain, that Navarrete was about to publish his famous *Collection of Documents*. Irving immediately planned a translation of it into English, and went to Madrid for the purpose. Upon his arrival, however, he changed his mind and wrote this fine *History of Christopher Columbus*, which, all in all, has never been equalled. . . . Irving studied with care almost all the documents relative to Columbus that were then known, and the genuineness of his research is proved by the frequent quotations from the histories of Las Casas, Oviedo, and Bernaldes, then unpublished and known to exist in only two or three copies. Irving's work has more than merely literary merit. It is a history written with judgment and impartiality which leaves far behind all the descriptions of the discovery of the New World published before or since." Henry Harrisse, in his *Christophe Colomb* (Paris. 1884), I, p. 136.

"Having the opportunity of examining excellent books and valuable manuscripts, of consulting specialists in this field, of using at every turn the authentic documents which we had just published, Irving has succeeded in giving his *History* a range and degree of impartiality and accuracy which place it far ahead of all writers who have preceded him." Navarrete, in the introduction to the third vol. of his *Coleccion de los viàges y descubrimientos*, pp. xiii–xiv.

The publication of Navarrete's third volume was closely followed by Irving's *Voyages of the companions of Columbus* which is closely based upon it. In addition to the contemporary verdict of Navarrete and to that of Harrisse it is only necessary to remark that the progress of critical scholarship and the publication of the sources since Irving's time have diminished the value of Irving's work for the student in the same way that they have diminished the value of Prescott's *Ferdinand and Isabella*. Irving, too, did not draw characters with the realistic fidelity now in favor. He smoothed his portrait of Columbus, and defects are passed over in silence or left obscure in the background.

— KAYSERLING, MEYER. Christopher Columbus and the participation of the Jews in the Spanish and Portuguese discoveries; tr. from author's MS. by Charles Gross. N. Y.: Longmans. 1895. $1.25.   [779

An interesting contribution to Jewish history and sidelight on the history of the discoveries. The author, after many years of study of the history of the Jews in Spain, undertook the special investigation of which this book is the result. It is based on an examination of a wide range of material. It is not, however, the work of a specialist in the history of the discoveries and is consequently not free from errors and hazardous conclusions. And it might further be said that if the author had been as well versed in the ancient history of Israel, as disclosed by modern criticism, as he is in the history of the Spanish Jews, he could not have treated so respectfully the idea that the aborigines of America might be descended from the "Lost Tribes" of Israel. In the appendix are about forty pages of hitherto unprinted documents from the Spanish Archives illustrating the relations of the Santangel family to the kings of Aragon and showing how the king met the expenses of Columbus' second voyage from the confiscated property of the Jews.   E. G. B.

— MARKHAM, *Sir* CLEMENTS ROBERT. Life of Christopher Columbus. London: Philip. 1892. 4s. 6d.   [780

Author a careful and conscientious student and translator of Spanish sources. The *Life* is impartial, readable, and accurate. The best brief account in English of the discovery of America.   E. C.

— ROSELLY DE LORGUES, ANTOINE FRANÇOIS FELIX. Christophe Colomb: histoire de sa vie et de ses voyages, d'après des documents authentiques tirés d'Espagne et d'Italie. Paris. 1856. 2v. 3e éd. 1886.

— —— Life of Christopher Columbus, from Spanish and Italian documents; comp. from the French of Roselly de Lorgues by J. J. Barry. Boston : Donahoe. 1870.   [781

An idealized picture of Columbus as a hero of the Church and deserving of sainthood. The author devoted himself to securing if possible the canonization of Columbus, and has become the accepted authority on Columbus of many of the Catholic religious writers. His forced interpretations, his ignoring counter evidence, and lack of sound criticism render this and the other works that he wrote in the same cause completely untrustworthy. Barry's *Life* is an abridgment and adaptation. Another presentation of Roselly's material in an engaging narrative is the *Life of Christopher Columbus* by Arthur George Knight. London. 1877.   E. G. B.

— TARDUCCI, FRANCESCO. Life of Christopher Columbus ; tr. from the Italian by H. F. Brownson.   Detroit : H. F. Brownson, 1890. 2v. $2.   [782

A very readable detailed narrative designed for the general public. Tarducci approaches his subject in the spirit of Irving. He is not a specialist in this field, and, in accordance with the aim in view, he does not discuss at any length the doubtful questions. In regard to some of them, in fact, he does not seem to be familiar with the latest investigations. It is strictly a life of Columbus, and little attention is given to the general history of the discoveries. There is no index.   E. G. B.

— WINSOR, JUSTIN. Christopher Columbus, and how he received and imparted the spirit of discovery. Boston : Houghton. 1891. $4.
                                            [783

Contains not only a detailed account of Columbus' achievements, but also a mass of bibliographical and cartographical detail of great value. Based on careful study of printed sources. Written in a spirit of hostility to Columbus. Style often hard to understand.

Eden, Richard.   The decades of the newe worlde or West India. London. 1555.
—— Decades 1–3. (In Arber, E., *ed.* First three English books on America. Birmingham. 1885. N. Y.: Macmillan. $6.50.)   [784

The first English collection of voyages and the main source of English knowledge of the new world before Hakluyt. The contents relating to America are the first three *Decades* of Peter Martyr (see sect. 761), a long extract from Oviedo's *Natural history of the West Indies* (manners and customs, flora, fauna and minerals), an epitome of Pigafetta's narrative of Magellan's voyage, a statement of the prices of precious stones and spices, Gomara's description of the conference at Badajos in 1524 to determine the demarcation line, and Gomara's account of Columbus and the earlier discoveries. Mr. Arber's introduction contains a very careful review of Eden's career. The *First* and *Second English books* are of more interest as literary and historical curiosities than as presenting primary sources to the English student. The *Second* is a translation by Eden from Sebastian Munster's *Cosmography*.
                                            E. G. B.

Herrera Tordesillas, Antonio de. Descripcion de las Indias ocidentales. Madrid. 1730. 4v.   [785

Original ed. 1601 and 1615. Best ed. by Barcia in 1730. Very poor translation of a portion, by John Stevens, in London in 6v. 1725–26. Various portions have been printed in translations, in collections of voyages, etc.
Describes the years 1492–1554. Herrera was second "Chronicler of the Indies." His work is a painstaking compilation. It is arranged chronologically. Based on Las Casas, on conversations with explorers and conquerors, and on documents, many of which have since disappeared. The best of the earlier Spanish compilations.

Magellan, Ferdinand. GUILLEMARD, FRANCIS HENRY HILL. Life of Ferdinand Magellan and the first circumnavigation of the globe, 1480–1521. London: Philip. 1891. 4s. 6d.
                                            [786
An admirable piece of work, based on a critical study of all the sources accessible, printed and unprinted. There are eight small facsimiles of the maps of Magellan's day, and in the appendices Magellan's genealogy, wills, a statement of the personnel of the fleet, a detailed statement of stock and equipment and the names of the crews that survived to circumnavigate the globe. The author's footnotes are a complete guide to his sources.   E. G. B.

— STANLEY OF ALDERLEY, HENRY EDWARD JOHN STANLEY, *3d baron, tr.* First voyage round the world, by Magellan; tr. from the accounts of Pigafetta and other contemporary writers; with documents, notes, etc. London: Hakluyt Soc. 1874.   [787
This volume contains all the contemporary narratives of Magellan's voyage and the first circumnavigation of the globe. The most important is that of Pigafetta. Of the other five, two are from the hands of pilots of the voyage and the third is a letter from Maximilianus Transylvanus, a secretary of Charles V., to the Cardinal of Salzburg, written a few weeks after the "Victoria" reached Spain. The introduction contains an excellent short life of Magellan and translations of the contracts that Magellan made with Charles V.   E. G. B.

Markham, *Sir* Clements Robert, *tr. and ed.* Journal of Christopher Columbus during his first voyage; and documents relating to the voyages of John Cabot and Gaspar Corte Real. London: Hakluyt Soc. 1893.   [788
This volume contains what has come to be considered as the recognized standard English rendering of the Cabot documents. These are reprinted in *American history leaflet,* no. 9. Mr. Markham's valuable introduction should be compared with his address on Cabot printed in the *Journal* of the Royal Geographical Society for June, 1897.   G. P. W.

Navarrete, Martin Fernandez de. Coleccion de los viages y descubrimientos, que hicieron por mar los Españoles desde fines del siglo xv. Madrid. 1825–37. 5v.   [789
Editor the most careful and successful of the Spanish compilers. These vols. contain five hundred of the most important documents relating to the period of discovery, 1400–1540. Vol. III comprises the *Viages menores* of which Irving's *Companions of Columbus* is scarcely more than a free translation. Supplementary works published after Navarrete's death give the results of his study of these documents and of other papers which were to form vols. V and VI.   E. C.

Oviedo y Valdés, Gonzalo Fernandez de. Historia general y natural de las Indias. [Complete edition, ed. by José Amados de los Rios.]

Madrid: Real academia de la historia. 1851–55. 4v.   [790

Comprises the history of the Spaniards in America to the end of the first third of the sixteenth century, and includes also the best memoir of Oviedo yet published. In later life Oviedo was the first "Chronicler of the Indies." He passed several years in Central America and West Indian Islands. He had ample knowledge from personal experience, from conversations with explorers and from access to official documents. Oftentimes prejudiced, and sometimes careless as to dates and sequence of events, his work is nevertheless a vast mine of information and indispensable to the student. It was only partly printed in the author's lifetime.

Pacheco, Joaquin Francisco, F. de Cardenas, *et al., eds.* Coleccion de documentos inéditos relativos al descubrimiento, conquista, y colonizacion de las posessiones españoles en America y Occeanía. Madrid. 1864–83. 42v.   [791

A vast repository of documentary evidence, badly edited and arranged. Vol. 33 is an index to the first 32 vols. This work is being continued as *Documentos inéditos . . . de ultramar. Series II.* No one can master the history of the Spanish conquest without a thorough knowledge of these volumes.

United States. *Commission to the Columbian historical exposition, Madrid, 1892–93.* Report. Wash. 1895.   [792

The exhibition was held in November and December, 1892, and January, 1893, under the auspices of the Spanish government, and was designed to exhibit American prehistoric remains, the characteristics of the American aborigines, and the results of European influence on America up to the middle of the 17th century. The United States Commission included Dr. George Brown Goode of the Smithsonian Institution. Its report, besides describing the exposition as a whole, gives catalogues of the anthropological, ethnological, and other exhibits sent from the United States, but its most interesting feature is an account of the 77 portraits of Columbus exhibited, reproductions of many of which are given, as well as pictures of numerous Columbus statues and monuments.

F. J. S.

Vespucci, Amerigo. First four voyages of Amerigo Vespucci; reproduced in facsimile with translation, introduction, etc. London: Quaritch. 1893. 3s.   [793

A very convenient edition of the Soderini letter with an excellent translation. The editor is favorable to the authenticity of all Vespucci's voyages, and believes this letter to be "the only genuine piece of sustained composition which Vespucci has left." Quaritch's translation of this Soderini letter is more exact than Markham's. This translation of the first voyage and Markham's translation of the third voyage are in *Old South leaflets,* nos. 34 and 90.

E. G. B.

— **Harrisse, Henry.** Americus Vespuccius: a critical and documentary review of two recent English books [Letters of Vespucci; tr. and ed. by Markham, *and* Voyage from Lisbon to India, 1505–6, by Albericus Vespuccius; tr. and ed. by Coote]. London: B. F. Stevens. 1895. 250 copies. 12s. [794

The main object of the first book "was to throw discredit on the arguments of Varnhagen and Fiske, adduced in support of the alleged voyage of 1497 to America. Harrisse, whose opinions have veered from time to time on this disputed question, now decides that 'the accounts which have reached us, whether in Italian or Latin, are all liable to grave objections, which we certainly do not pretend to be in a position to remove.' . . . It would seem, then, that Harrisse's present opinion is that Vespuccius could have made the disputed voyage, though there is not indisputable evidence that he did make it." The second book was "issued originally in Flemish at Antwerp in December, 1508, and reprinted in 1894 with annotations by C. H. Coote, accompanied by an argument to show that the author of it was Vespuccius." Mr. Harrisse concludes that the book was written by Balthazar Sprenger, who accompanied Almeida in 1505. The Antwerp publisher altered dates and text and published it under the name of Vespuccius. In the present aspect of the evidence Mr. Harrisse's views "must stand till some better solution of the enigma can be found. Mr. Coote has not certainly made out his case. Mr. Harrisse has come very near making one out." *Nation,* 61: 17.

— **Lester, Charles Edwards,** *and* **Andrew Foster.** Life and voyages of Americus Vespucius. N. Y.: Baker & Scribner. 1846.   [795

The author was attracted to his subject while consul at Genoa, but he lacked the critical training to produce a work abreast of the scholarship of his day. To-day the work is entirely out of date and would mislead and waste the time of any one beginning a study of the subject. It may still be serviceable, however, in a measure, from the translations which it contains of Vespucius's letters to one who cannot consult the work of Varnhagen, Markham, or Quaritch's *First four voyages.* To the more advanced student it is of some value as a compendium of the materials and views in the works of Bandini, Bartolozzi, and Canovai, who championed the cause of Vespucius in the last century. Canovai's famous eulogy is given in translation in an appendix. Another appendix gives Toscanelli's letters to Columbus. Bandini's *Life of Vespucci* has recently been republished with notes by Uzielli and a bibliography by Fumagalli. Florence. 1898.

E. G. B.

— **Markham,** *Sir* **Clements Robert,** *tr.* Letters of Amerigo Vespucci and other documents illustrative of his career; tr. with notes and an introd. London: Hakluyt Soc. 1894.   [796

This volume contains translations of Vespucci's two letters, of the most important documents in Navarrete respecting him, and Las Casas's detailed criticisms of Vespucci's claims. The last is new and important material for the English reader. Markham thoroughly distrusts Vespucci's narratives and in his introduction rejects without hesitation the first voyage. He attaches almost decisive importance to Las Casas's confutation and rejection of Vespucci's story as coming from an honest writer with ample opportunities of knowing the truth. Markham's translation is less exact than that of Quaritch in *The first four voyages*.   E. G. B.

— SANTAREM, MANOEL FRANCISCÓ DE BARROS Y SOUZA, *visconde de*. Researches respecting Americus Vespucius and his voyages; tr. by E. V. Childe. Boston: Little. 1850.   [797

This is a translation of *Recherches historiques, critiques et bibliographiques sur Améric Vespuce et ses voyages* (Paris. 1842). Viscount Santarem was a very eminent student of the history of geography. His little book is the most thoroughgoing of the attacks on the authenticity of the voyages of Vespucci. It is strongly biased against Vespucci on the conviction that either he or his friends had defrauded Columbus by attaching the name America to the New World. In Santarem's pages uncertain or ambiguous data are relentlessly turned against Vespucci as uniformly as they are interpreted in his favor by Varnhagen.   E. G. B.

— VARNHAGEN, FRANCISCO ADOLPHO DE. Amerigo Vespucci: son caractère, ses écrits, sa vie et ses navigations. Lima. 1865.   [798

Varnhagen was a distinguished Brazilian scholar, and is chiefly known for his *Historia geral do Brazil* (1854) and for his series of monographs on Vespucci (see Winsor, II, 156, for a list of them), which are among the most important contributions on this subject. Varnhagen was the first to print a critical edition of all the writings which have been attributed to Vespucci. These he divides into two classes, those published during his life and those published two or three centuries after his death. These texts form the first and second part of the monograph whose title is given above. The third part is a critical study of Vespucci's life. The later monographs are usually bound with this. The first is a critical investigation of the doubtful first voyage (pub. Vienna. 1869), which Varnhagen accepts and of which he gives explanations not generally adopted. A third essay, *Nouvelles recherches sur les derniers voyages du navigateur Florentin* (1869), is written in Portuguese, although the title is in French. In an appendix to it are the documents published by Navarrete which relate to Vespucci. In 1870 Varnhagen published a brief summary of the results of his investigations, entitled *Post face aux trois livraisons sur Amerigo Vespucci*. In 1874 in an essay in Portuguese he advanced new points in defence of his interpretation of the first voyage. The English reader will find in Fiske's *Discovery of America*, ch. VII, a presentation of Varnhagen's positions, of which Mr. Fiske is sometimes more confident than their author.   E. G. B.

Other Discoveries and Early Exploration

Bourne, Henry Richard Fox. English seamen under the Tudors. London : Bentley. 1868. 2v.   [799

A history of English exploration, merchant voyages and naval achievements during the sixteenth century. The author has constructed a very readable and comprehensive narrative on the basis of the material collected by Hakluyt and Purchas, supplemented by constant reference to the state papers. In regard to the naval history of this period, much new material has been brought to light since 1868 which the reader will find in Corbett's *Drake*. For the other aspects of his subject Mr. Bourne's work is still the most serviceable general account in English.   E. G. B.

Cabot, John *and* Sebastian. BEAZLEY, CHARLES RAYMOND. John and Sebastian Cabot : the discovery of North America. (Builders of greater Britain.) N. Y. : Longmans. 1898. $1.50.   [800

The most useful, and the most readable, volume upon the Cabots, for the purposes of the general reader. Like every other book devoted to these explorers, it is largely filled up with the original documents, which Mr. Beazley interprets with much care, conservatism and common sense.   G. P. W.

— BIDDLE, RICHARD. Memoir of Sebastian Cabot. Phil. and London. 1831.   [801

One of the earliest American works of serious historical scholarship, and important in the history of historical study and writing in America. A powerful argument advocating the achievements of the son, as more important than those of the father; the source from which nearly every article upon Cabot, during the succeeding forty years, derived both its inspiration and facts. Many of these facts, and most of the conclusions based upon them, have been overthrown by the discovery of documents unknown to Mr. Biddle.   G. P. W.

— DAWSON, SAMUEL EDWARD. The voyages of the Cabots. (In Royal Soc. of Canada. Transactions, v. 12. Montreal. 1894.)
— — The voyages: a sequel. (In Transactions, ser. 2, v. 2. Ottawa. 1896.)
— — The voyages : latest phases of the controversy. (In Transactions, ser. 2, v. 3. Ottawa. 1897.)   [802

These three papers contain the best discussion of the problem of Cabot's landfall in 1497. Dr. Dawson presents much stronger and more convincing arguments in favor of a landfall on Cape Breton than have been presented for any other locality. The three essays contain much valuable material upon all phases of the Cabot controversies.   G. P. W.

" Recent Cabot literature may be divided into three main sections, each corresponding to a subject of spirited debate. These are, firstly, the circumstances under which John Cabot came to England and made his voyage of 1497; secondly, the exact geographical site of the landfall, and, thirdly, the character of Sebastian Cabot. In Europe, as was natural, discussion has turned more on the first and third of the above topics, while in America the second has received the lion's share of attention." Dr. Dawson "is, we should think, the leading living advocate of a view once supported by Mr. Charles Deane and Dr. Winsor [the Cape Breton theory]. Mr. Harrisse in like manner stands for the pretensions of Labrador, and Judge Prowse for those of Newfoundland. Dr. Dawson now publishes in pamphlet form a long paper which he submitted to the Royal Society of Canada at its last meeting, and which is reprinted from its *Transactions*. The term 'latest phases' apparently relates to the landfall question alone. . . . Dr. Dawson believes that Cape Breton can lay claim to the honor of Cabot's landfall. . . . We should call attention to the large number of maps which are reproduced in support of Dr. Dawson's contentions. Much valuable material is also to be found in the appendices." *Nation*, 67: 96.

— DEANE, CHARLES. Voyages of the Cabots. (In Winsor, J. Narrative and critical history of America, v. 3. Boston. 1884.)   [803

This essay is the only thoroughly satisfactory, thoroughly sensible and well-proportioned statement of what is known and what may be surmised about the Cabots.   G. P. W.

— Early notices of the voyages of the Cabots. See Old South Work, sect. 368. [804

— HARRISSE, HENRY. Discovery of North America by John Cabot. 3d ed. enl. London: B. F. Stevens. 1897. 1s.   [805

An enlarged reprint of controversial periodical communications. It is an interesting presentation of the phases of the Cabotian history which seem most important to Mr. Harrisse, and which have absorbed a chief part of the attention of nearly every student of the Cabot discoveries.

Mr. Harrisse's later publications usually contain a list of his numerous writings in the magazines and elsewhere upon Cabotian problems.   G. P. W.

— HARRISSE, HENRY. John Cabot, the discoverer of North-America, and Sebastian his son. London: B. F. Stevens. 1896. 30s.   [806

An expansion, in English, of the narrative and argumentative portion of Harrisse's *Jean et Sébastien Cabot* (Paris. 1882). The French volume contains the most correct text Mr. Harrisse could secure of every important document which throws light upon the Cabots, and is the recognized source for reference to these texts. The English volume is "a laboratory manual, in which the student finds revealed each step of the processes through which the material of history has been forced, in order that it might be made to render up the truth which was contained within it."
G. P. W.

— Inscriptions on the Cabot map. See Massachusetts Historical Society, sect. 343.   [807

— NICHOLLS, JAMES FAWCKNER. Remark-

able life, adventures and discoveries of Sebastian Cabot. London: Low. 1869.   [808

A valueless eulogy, in which all the available evidence is interpreted so as to add to the glory of Sebastian as a native of England and of Bristol.   G. P. W.

— TARDUCCI, FRANCESCO. John and Sebastian Cabot; tr. from the Italian by Henry F. Brownson. Detroit: H. F. Brownson. 1893. $2.50.   [809

Useful as a presentation of what might be called the surviving legendary history of the Cabots. The author enthusiastically records whatever may add to the credit and glory of a son of Venice. A strong statement of the arguments of those who refuse to accept the destructive criticism of Harrisse, and who believe that Sebastian may have accomplished something, and may have possessed a creditable personality.
G. P. W.

— WEARE, G. E. Cabot's discovery of North America. Phil.: Lippincott. 1897. $3.50.   [810

A discursive narrative, possessing little critical value. The original texts, accurately printed and with English versions of all the Cabot documents, are embodied in the narrative, and may be compared here more conveniently than in any other single volume.
G. P. W.

Champlain, Samuel de. Narrative of a voyage to the West Indies and Mexico, 1599–1602; tr. with notes by Alice Wilmere. London: Hakluyt Soc. 1859.   [811

The original text of this narrative, the earliest product of Champlain's pen, was first printed by Laverdière in vol. I of his *Œuvres de Champlain* (Quebec. 1870). It is merely a sketch, occupying only thirty-six pages in the Hakluyt Soc. edition. It gives a glimpse of Porto Rico, San Domingo, Cuba, and a more detailed account of the city of Mexico. There are brief notes on the animals and products of the countries and on the administration of the Indians. The manuscript contains 62 quaint drawings, reproduced by Laverdière, of which the Hakluyt Society ed. contains twelve. The notes to this edition do not reveal any special scholarship. The long introduction on Champlain will not detain readers who have access to Laverdière, Parkman or Slafter.   E. G. B.

De Vries, David Peterson. Voyages from Holland to America, 1632–44; tr. by H. C. Murphy. (In New York Hist. Soc. Collections, ser. 2, v. 3. N. Y. 1857.)   [812

An interesting personal narrative throwing much light on the early history of New York, with glimpses of Virginia, New Haven and the Connecticut colony, and a somewhat more extended account of Guiana. De Vries was an energetic promoter of colonization, and gives expression to much candid criticism of the methods of Wouter van Twiller and Kieft. His account of the Indians is borrowed from that of Johannes Megapolensis which is given in the same volume of N. Y. Hist. Soc. Coll. In vol. I of the 2d ser. were published a series of extracts from De Vries. These extracts had been copied in MS. from the printed volume when no copy was to be found in this country. In some cases the narrative is condensed. Murphy's complete and superior translation entirely supersedes the earlier publication. E. G. B.

Drake, *Sir* Francis. CORBETT, JULIAN STAFFORD. Drake and the Tudor navy, with a history of the rise of England as a maritime power. N. Y.: Longmans. 1898. 2v. $5. [813

The best work on Drake and the rise of the English sea power. It is written in the light of the most recent researches in the English and foreign archives, and is especially useful to the student for its clear explanation of contemporary naval and marine terminology. The voyage of circumnavigation is fully treated (I, pp. 226–324), and an effort is made to present a solution of the mysterious case of Thomas Doughty. E. G. B.

— FLETCHER, FRANCIS. The world encompassed by Sir Francis Drake; ed. by W. S. W. Vaux. London: Hakluyt Soc. 1854. [814

This volume contains the original sources, so far as known in 1854, for Drake's voyage around the world. The main narrative *The world encompassed* was compiled from the notes of Drake's chaplain, Fletcher, and edited in Drake's interest. Fletcher's original notes, so far as extant, are given in running footnotes. The other narratives are those of Francis Pretty, the source of *The world encompassed* for the latter part of the voyage, that of John Cooke, unfriendly to Drake, and that of Nuno da Sylva, a Portuguese pilot, and Cliffe's account of the voyage of John Winter. The editor's analysis of his sources and discussion of their relative importance is unsatisfactory. For such a comparison and for the sources discovered since 1854 see Corbett's *Drake*, I, pp. 423–29. E. G. B.

Harrisse, Henry. Notes pour servir à l'histoire, à la bibliographie et à la cartographie de la Nouvelle France et des pays adjacents, 1545–1700. Paris: Tross. 1872. 15fr. [815

This book contains the titles of 187 publications printed between 1545 and 1700 relating to Canada and the valley of the Mississippi. It aims to be exhaustive and is based mainly upon the collections in the Bibliothèque Nationale at Paris. There are also descriptions of early maps, 76 unpublished and 111 engraved but not dated, and of 460 documents, such as letters patent, commissions, correspondence, etc., written between the above named dates but in many cases published later. The author sometimes gives the text of important documents and there are many historical and biographical notes. Mr. Harrisse has long devoted himself to the history of European discovery in America, and has studied the original material exhaustively. This work is scholarly, painstaking and indispensable as a record of the early editions of works like Champlain's *Voyages*, the Jesuits' *Relations*, etc. G. M. W.

Hudson, Henry. ASHER, GEORGE M., *ed.* Henry Hudson the navigator: the original

documents in which his career is recorded. London: Hakluyt Soc. 1860. [816

A collection of the original sources relating to Hudson's explorations with an introduction containing a critical account of these documents and a history of the attempts to find a northeast and a northwest passage. An appendix contains Dr. Cogswell's translation of the narrative of Verrazano's voyage and the original Italian, according to the MS. found in the Magliabecchian library, and a bibliography. Besides the original sources, the editor has included extracts from the contemporary Dutch historians, van Meteren, de Laet and Gerritz, from van der Donck's account of New Netherland, and from the modern writer Lambrechtsen van Ritthem. Of the contents of this volume, the *Divers voyages* and *Northerne discoveries*, derived from Purchas' *Pilgrims*, are to be found in *Collections* of the N. Y. Historical Soc., vol. I, 1811; and Juet's *Journal*, Verrazano's *Voyage*, and the extracts from van der Donck and de Laet, in vol. I, 2d ser., 1841. E. G. B.

— BARDSEN, IVAR. Sailing directions of Henry Hudson, prepared for his use in 1608; from the old Danish, with notes by B. F. De Costa. Albany: Munsell. 1869. [817

Bardsen, said to have been a functionary in Greenland, wrote, long before the days of Columbus, the fullest account we have of the Icelandic colonies in Greenland. This, which had been translated into Dutch in 1560, was retranslated into English in 1608 for Sir Henry Hudson. The text is here accompanied by explanatory notes and by a revised translation from the *Antiquitates Americanæ* of Rafn. The preface contains a dissertation on early voyages to America, with especial reference to the discovery of the Hudson River, and such information as exists regarding Hudson's career and character. F. J. S.

— JUET, ROBERT. Relation concerning the third voyage of Henry Hudson. See New York Historical Society, sect. 352. [818

— READ, JOHN MEREDITH, JR. Historical inquiry concerning Henry Hudson. Albany: Munsell. 1866. [819

This book "is a most scholarlike and admirable example of a species of investigation which lies at the base of all accurate and trustworthy history. Its subject is a discoverer who holds a conspicuous place in the early annals of this continent, but whose life has nevertheless been wrapped in an almost impenetrable obscurity. . . . Mr. Read traces the descent of the navigator Henry Hudson from the eminent merchant of the same name who was the founder of the Muscovy Company, and one of the leading spirits in that course of mercantile adventure which, in the sixteenth century, resulted in discoveries so glorious to the British name. . . . The most interesting part of the book is that which relates to the voyage of Hudson in the service of the Dutch East India Company." *Atlantic monthly*, 19: 764.

The *Nation* said, in 1866, that "we are rather inclined to believe than to doubt that the additions to the materials of history which Mr. Read's ingenuity and laborious research have given us are as correct and valuable as he thinks them." *Nation*, 2: 741.

Kohl, Johann Georg. History of the discovery of Maine; with an appx. on the voyages of the Cabots, by M. d'Avezac. (Willis, W., *ed.* Documentary history of Maine, v. 1. Maine Hist. Soc. Collections, documentary ser. 3, v. 1.) Portland. 1869. [820

Dr. Kohl was one of the most eminent students of the history of American geography, and this work until the publication of Harrisse's *Discovery of North America* was the most elaborate summary of the exploration of the eastern coast of North America down to 1525. It still remains such for the period 1525–1573. The narrative is illustrated by 22 reduced copies of early maps (mainly of the 16th century), each of which is the subject of a brief explanatory essay. Dr. Kohl inscribed on these copies the original legends in a readable form so that, although these copies are small, the clearness of outline and legibility of the names make them especially useful to the student. In using this book the reader must keep in mind that new light has been thrown on many points since Dr. Kohl wrote. This fact deprives the essay on the Cabots by d'Avezac in the appendix of much of its original value.

E. G. B.

Payne, Edward John. Voyages of the Elizabethan seamen to America: 13 original narratives from the collection of Hakluyt. London: De La Rue. 1880. New ed. Frowde. 1893. Ser. 1. 5s. Ser. 2, in press. [821

In view of the rarity or costliness of the editions of Hakluyt's voyages, this collection of the most important of the contemporary narratives illustrating the English explorations of Elizabeth's age is of especial service. Mr. Payne has supplied a suggestive introduction, and has modernized the spelling of Hakluyt's text. The narratives describe the voyages of Hawkins, Frobisher, Drake, Gilbert, Amadas and Barlow, Cavendish and Raleigh. The second edition contains only the voyages of Hawkins, Frobisher and Drake and is called " first series," but no continuation has as yet been published. E. G. B.

Raleigh, *Sir* **Walter.** Discovery of the large, rich and beautiful empire of Guiana, with a relation of the great and golden city of Manoa (which the Spaniards call El Dorado), etc., performed in 1595 by Sir Walter Ralegh. Reprinted from the edition of 1596, ed. with notes, etc., by Sir R. H. Schomburgk. London: Hakluyt Soc. 1848. [822

Sir Robert H. Schomburgk's memoir " is an admirable summary of what was then known of Raleigh, and the publication is a complete vindication of Raleigh's statements and conduct in reference to Guiana. The notes of the author are of the greatest value." W. W. Henry, in *Narrative and critical hist. of Am.*, 3 : 122.

Verrazano, Giovanni da. Relation of his voyage to the North American continent. See New York Historical Society, sect. 353. [823

— BREVOORT, JAMES CARSON. Verrazano the navigator; or Notes on Giovanni da Verrazano and on a planisphere of 1529 illustrating his American voyage in 1524. [Reprinted from Am. Geog. Soc. Rept., 1873.] N. Y. 1874. [824

A sketch of Verrazano's career followed by a running commentary on the narrative of his voyage identifying so far as practicable the places described with the help of the map of Girolamo da Verrazano which is given in reduced facsimile. Mr. Brevoort accepts the narrative of the voyage. An appendix contains an elaborate description of the map and a number of transcripts from MSS. and early printed books relating to Verrazano.

E. G. B.

— MURPHY, HENRY CRUSE. The voyage of Verrazzano: a chapter in the early history of maritime discovery in America. N. Y. Privately printed. 1875. [825

This monograph is an attempt to prove by the processes of external and internal criticism that the narrative of Verrazano's voyage of 1524 is a forgery based on the data supplied by the discoveries of Estevan Gomez recorded in the Ribero map of 1529. Mr. Murphy made out a strong case, but the drift of critical opinion has been in recent years in favor of the reality of Verrazano's voyage. A recent critical study of the question, which in the opinion of Sophus Ruge must finally remove all doubt, is that of Dr. Karl Lechner in *Globus*, 1890, pp. 114–116, 139–142, 153–156. Cf. also Harrisse's argument in his *Discovery of North America.* The appendix to Mr. Murphy's book includes Dr. Cogswell's translation of the Verrazano letter and translations of transcripts of documents about Verrazano as well as a facsimile of the Verrazano map. Dr. Cogswell's translation is also to be found in the N. Y. Hist. Soc. Coll., 2d ser., vol. I, with the Italian original, Asher's *Hudson*, and by itself in *Old South leaflets*, no. 17. E. G. B.

—— Verrazano's voyage. See Old South Work, sect. 368. [826

PART III. THE UNITED STATES

DIVISION 1: HISTORICAL PERIODS

1. Period of Colonial Settlement and Development. 1607–1760

THE COLONIES IN GENERAL

Albany, N. Y. Journal of the Congress at Albany, 1754. See Massachusetts Historical Society, sect. 301. [827

Alexander, *Sir* **William.** SLAFTER, EDMUND FARWELL, *ed.* Sir William Alexander and American colonization. With annotations and a memoir. (Prince Soc. Publications.) Boston. 1873. [828

"The episode of Sir William Alexander and his futile schemes of colonization is treated exhaustively." Mr. Slafter "reproduces all the original charters and other documents bearing on his inquiry, and apparently leaves nothing for any future gleaner in that field. But . . . it must be conceded that Mr. Slafter attaches more importance to Sir William Alexander's somewhat visionary plans than they really merit." Chas. C. Smith, in *Narrative and critical hist. of Am.*, 4:155.

Baird, Charles Washington. History of the Huguenot emigration to America. N. Y.: Dodd. 1885. 2v. $3.50. [829

A pioneer work of highest grade, giving illustrative details of earlier attempts at settlement in Brazil, Florida, Acadia, Canada, New Netherlands and the Antilles. The author analyzes the episode of the Revocation, the flight from various parts of France, the refuge in England, and the settlement in New England and adjacent parts, leaving accounts of other migrations to later volumes. A book more satisfactory to the genealogist than to the historian, though the meagre details at the author's command are handled with skill. A work stimulating to further research. Indispensable to the student of Am. history. See the *Nation*, May 28, 1885, p. 444. H. W. H.

Beer, George Louis. Commercial policy of England toward the American colonies. (Columbia College. Studies in history, etc., v. 3, no. 2.) N. Y. 1893. Pap. $1 net. [830

The author undertakes to prove that the colonial policy of England was not consciously tyrannical. "It was a policy of unconscious ignorance, not of conscious malice." A careful, though condensed account is given of the early English navigation acts

and a presentation of the forces and causes which led to colonization. This is followed by the history of some of the most important commercial products of the colonies ; also a statement of the restrictions placed upon commerce and manufactures. The investigation is thoroughly scholarly, and is based upon original state calendars and documents. It is a contribution to the rational method of regarding historical events as evolutionary. D. R. D.

Bradstreet, Dudley. Diary at siege of Louisburg, 1745. See Massachusetts Historical Society, sect. 348. [831

Burke, Edmund. Account of the European settlements in America. London. 1757. 2v. 2d ed., with improvements. 1758. 2v. [832

A very noteworthy account, not indeed written throughout by, but receiving its final revision from, one of the most eminent English men of letters. It describes the American colonies of six European nations from 1492 to about 1750; and was evidently undertaken in consequence of the Seven Years' War. It was compiled from a wide variety of sources, most of which are complained of in the preface, as unsatisfactory. In spite of this, the work shows wide knowledge, unusual judgment, a somewhat too slight tolerance for other nations than the English, and, here and there, Edmund Burke's resplendent English style, though not perhaps to such an extent as to draw the interest of the general reader. The work has no index nor illustrations, but has maps of North and South America. It was issued anonymously, and is not usually included in Burke's collected works. W. E. F.

Burnaby, Andrew. Travels through the middle settlements of North America, 1759–60. London. 1775. [833

"There is a pleasant tone, a wise and educated spirit in this record, which make ample amends for the obvious influences of the writer's religious and political views upon his impressions of the country and the people. The Rev. Andrew Burnaby was a native of Lancastershire, an élève of Westminster School, and a graduate of Queen's College, Cambridge. . . . His book on America was 'praised and valued' as a fair and agreeable report of 'the state of the colonies' then called the 'Middle Settlements.'" H. T. Tuckerman, *America and her commentators*, p. 173.

Bury, William Coutts Keppel, *Viscount.* Exodus of the western nations. London: Bentley. 1865. 2v. [834

The author is a scholarly English nobleman, and the period covered by the book is from 1492 to 1865. The work is less a study from original sources than a philosophic consideration of the principles of colonial development. It is intelligent, judicious, fair-minded, careful and eminently readable, but by no means an indispensable book to the student.   W. E. F.

Chalmers, George. Continuation of Political annals. (In New-York Historical Soc. Collections. Publication fund, v. 1. N. Y. 1868.)   [835

Three chapters of Book II of the work as planned by Chalmers are here printed. They contain the history of the colonies from the Revolution of 1689 to the establishment of the Board of Trade in 1696. Instead of treating each colony separately, as in Book I of the *Annals*, the author treats the colonies collectively as constituting a system ; though he adheres as closely as possible to the chronological order of events. The same qualities appear as in the earlier part of the work. [See sect. 354, above.]   H. L. O.

Coffin, Charles. Old times in the colonies. N. Y. : Harper. 1880. $2.   [836

An old style "juvenile" history of the American colonies to 1760 with especial reference to their inheritance from the old world of customs and principles of government. Attractive in its description of occurrences, but likely to be incomprehensible to a child's mind in its deductions. Also, likely to give erroneous impressions in its imaginary conversations between historical characters.   E. E. S.

Dexter, Franklin P. Estimates of population in the American colonies. See American Antiquarian Society, sect. 237.   [837

Douglass, William. Summary, historical and political, of the British settlements in North America. Boston. 1747–50. 2v. London. 1755. 2v.   [838

"A large part of the book relates to New England. It contains a good deal of valuable information from original sources, but it is put together without system or order." C. Deane, in *Narrative and critical hist. of Am.*, 3 : 346.

Doyle, John Andrew. The American colonies : Arnold prize essay. London : Rivingtons. 1869.   [839

An excellent brief sketch of the American colonies to the Declaration of Independence, discussing manners, religion, law and social customs, as well as politics. Almost one-half of the space is given to a study of the causes of the Revolution, justifying the colonists. The sources and secondary authorities have been carefully examined. The critical acumen so notable in Doyle's later work is in large part lacking. In judgment, temper and style, the book is a model of historical writing.   R. C. H. C.

—— English in America. V. 1 : Virginia, Maryland and the Carolinas. London : Longmans. 1882. N. Y.: Holt. 1882. $3.50. [For v. 2, see sect. 918.]   [840

Covers 17th century only. Based on printed sources and on documents in the British Record Office. Con-

tains some new facts. Oftentimes is necessarily very brief. Style dry and lacking in distinctive quality.   E. C.

Earle, *Mrs.* Alice Morse. Child life in colonial days. N. Y. : Macmillan. 1899. $2.50.

—— Colonial dames and goodwives. Boston: Houghton. 1895. $1.50.

—— Colonial days in old New York. N. Y. : Scribner. 1896. $1.25.

—— Costume of colonial times. N. Y. : Scribner. 1894. $1.25.

—— Curious punishments of bygone days. Chicago : Stone. 1896. $1.50.

—— Customs and fashions in old New England. N. Y.: Scribner. 1893. $1.25.

—— Home life in colonial days. N. Y. : Macmillan. 1898. $2.50.

—— In old Narragansett: romances and realities. (Ivory series.) N. Y. : Scribner. 1898. 75c.

—— Sabbath in Puritan New England. N. Y.: Scribner. 1891. $1.25.

—— *ed.* Diary of Anna Green Winslow, a Boston school girl of 1771. Boston : Houghton. 1894. $1.25.   [841

By means of a graphic and accurate account of dress, drinks, houses, furniture, home life, religious life, child life, etc., based on reliable sources of information, in print and manuscript, Mrs. Earle has succeeded in reconstructing the life, customs and manners of the New England colonists from the time of the earliest settlements to the Revolution. Much that she has done will appeal chiefly to the curious reader, but a great deal may demand the attention of the scholar, especially of him who studies social and economic history. In *Old Narragansett* the author gives a series of sketches of life in the lands occupied by the Narragansett Indians at the coming of the English ; and in *Colonial days in old New York* deals with the Dutch period. The books vary in merit ; Mrs. Earle is at her best in the *Sabbath in New England* and *Child life in colonial days;* and is not so good in *Costume of colonial times ;* but there is not one of her books that may not be cordially recommended for its accuracy and readableness.   C. M. A.

Eggleston, Edward. The beginners of a nation. N. Y.: Appleton. 1896. $1.50. [842

The first volume of what promises to be an extended work. Is devoted to the colonizing enterprises of the English on this continent prior to the middle of the 17th century. It adds little to positive knowledge of the subject, but is distinguished throughout by a broad and tolerant spirit and by keen criticism. Great care has been used in ascertaining and sifting facts. The book is written in a brilliant, sententious style, and contains some admirable characterizations of personalities. Roger Williams and that which he stood for seem to be special objects of the author's admiration.   H. L. O.

Entick, John, *et al.* General history of the

late war in Europe, Asia, Africa and America. London. 1763–4. 5v.   [843

Seven books in five volumes, dedicated to William Pitt, recite the causes leading up to the " Old French War," 1756–63, and, with unusual fulness, the events in America, Europe and the island possessions of France and Spain. Published in the year when peace was declared, it has the value of a contemporary record ; many letters, addresses and official papers are printed. The narrative of the American campaigns is fully and vigorously told ; it lacks the minuteness and accuracy of personal and technical knowledge to be found in Mante or Pouchot, but, better than they, it shows the relation of events to the general policy of the British empire. Its faults are those of a partisan who sees his king always in the right, the king's enemies always in the wrong ; and an antiquated style, little likely to attract the casual reader.   F. H. S.

Evelyn family. SCULL, GIDEON DELA-PHAINE, *comp.* The Evelyns in America, 1608–1805. Oxford: Privately printed. 1881.   [844

Compiled from family papers and other sources. Contains matter relating to early Maryland ; Plantagenet's *Description of New Albion; Memoir and letters* of Capt. W. G. Evelyn (1774–76) ; and an appendix of miscellaneous matter relating to the Revolutionary War. Most of the matter in the last two items is also printed separately. Editor's work unobtrusive. Contains much valuable material.   E. C.

Fernow, Berthold. The Ohio valley in colonial days. Albany: Munsell. 1890.   [845

Presents much valuable material concerning the discovery of the Ohio valley, the aborigines inhabiting it, and the struggle between the French and English for the supremacy. There is a brief chapter on the Indian wars following that struggle. The last two chapters give material concerning the earliest attempts at settlement both north and south of the Ohio before 1788. For the most part the book " is only an arrangement of already known facts."   H. W. H.

Fisher, George Park. The colonial era. (American history series.) N. Y.: Scribner. 1892. $1.25.   [846

An excellent book intended primarily for students. It covers the colonial period to 1756, treating the colonies separately and including brief discussions on " manners, customs and phases of intellectual progress." Three maps are given. Prof. Fisher is an able historical scholar, has consulted the sources, is temperate in judgment and accurate. An appendix contains a useful biographical note discussing briefly the chief secondary authorities in colonial history.   R. C. H. C.

Fisher, Sydney George. Men, women and manners in colonial times. Phil.: Lippincott. 1898. 2v. $3.   [847

Written by an acute historical student whose earlier published studies of the colonial period have been chiefly political in character. As compared with the

works of similar purpose by Mrs. Earle and Mrs. Wharton, this one is wider in scope, including something, at least, on all thirteen of the colonies (not, however, treated with equal fulness), and is rendered attractive by photogravures and other illustrations, chiefly of colonial architecture. The author's knowledge is wide, his judgment and temper fair, his method careful (though the reader is seldom allowed to verify his citations), and his style clear and interesting. There is a useful index. Emphatically a book for the general reader, rather than the special student.   W. E. F.

Force, Peter, *ed.* Tracts and other papers relating principally to the origin, settlement and progress of the colonies in North America. Wash. 1836–46. 4v.

—— *Same :* American colonial tracts, monthly. Rochester: G. P. Humphrey. 1897–. v. 1+. 25c. ea.   [848

This collection of tracts on early American history is indispensable to all students, whether of the north or the south, and by frequent reprints should be made accessible to all. The collection was made by Peter Force in order to supply his need for the possession of the writings it contains in accessible form as an aid to research. By far the larger number of the tracts concern the history of the south, but some of the most important have to do with New England. Among those of greatest value in the collection are Nova Brittania, and its second part, The new life of Virginia : — The beginning, progress and conclusion of Bacon's rebellion, by Thomas Matthews : — John Smith's New England's trials : — White's Planters' plea : — Virginia and Maryland, or Lord Baltimore's case uncased : — The simple cobbler of Agawam : — Leah and Rachel : — New England's Jonas cast up in London : — Gorton's Simplicities defence against seven-headed policy : — Father Andrew White's Relation of the Colony of the Lord Baron of Baltimore : — Byfield's Account of the late revolution in New England : — The revolution in New England justified.   H. L. O.

Franklin, Benjamin. Plan of union, 1754. See Old South Work, sect. 368.   [849

—— [Most works relating to Franklin are placed in the period next following.]

Grahame, James. History of the United States of North America, from the plantation of the British colonies to their revolt and declaration of Independence. London. 1836. 4v. 2d ed., enl. and amended. Phil. 1846. 2v.   [850

This edition of Mr. Graham's work comprises the revision of his *History of the United States till 1688,* which was first issued in 1827, and its extension to 1776. The author never visited this country, and relied wholly on such materials as he could collect in Great Britain or find in the library of the University of Göttingen. He does not seem to have made researches, at least to any extent, among the British archives. Pamphlet literature he does not seem to have extensively used. His materials, when compared with those at the command of the historian at the present time, were scanty. He wrote too under the influence of the extremely democratic ideas of 1830, and was not sparing in the use of strong expletives. The work then may be regarded as to a large extent superseded. Still it is written in an excellent style and contains passages of great suggestiveness.   H. L. O.

Great Britain. *Master of the Rolls.* Calendar of state papers, colonial series, 1574–1660, preserved in the State paper dept. of Public Record Office; ed. by W. Noël Sainsbury. London. 1860.

—— *Same;* colonial series: America and West Indies, 1661–80; ed. by W. Noël Sainsbury and J. W. Fortescue. London. 1880–96. 4v.   [851

These volumes are issued by the British government, under the immediate authority of the Master of the Rolls, and form a part of the great series in which the materials of modern British history are being given to the world. The volumes upon America and the West Indies contain, within the specified dates, carefully prepared outlines of every document in the Public Record Office relating to the western dependencies, all arranged in strict chronological order. Each volume has, in addition, an elaborate historical introduction by the editor, in which the period covered by its contents is discussed in the light of the new material made public in the calendar. This series is of the highest importance for all students of the British colonial system, and its value will increase with successive issues.   H. L. O.

While formal documents are very briefly described, the editors were instructed to adhere closely to the text in the case of secret or very rare information and when the papers were more than ordinarily obscure.
F. J. S.

Greene, Evarts Boutell. The provincial governor in the English colonies of North America. (Harvard historical studies, v. 7.) N. Y.: Longmans. 1898. $1.50.   [852

"The scope of this excellent monograph is somewhat narrower than its title indicates. It deals with the office of governor prior to 1763, but only in those royal and proprietary colonies which later became part of the United States. The forms of government these colonies gradually assumed, and the evolution of the executive office as such, constitute the subject-matter of the opening chapters. The precise powers attached to the office of governor and his relations with the various public bodies in the province — viz., the council, the judiciary and the assembly — are then discussed at length. Special attention is given to the conflict of mutually encroaching claims on the part of the governor and the assembly. From this conflict the popular body, strong in its control of the purse, came forth triumphant. A brief reference to the legal and political accountability of the governor concludes this very suggestive guide-book to the traveller in a new region of research. In the appendices are found several representative commissions and instructions, together with a list of others that have been elsewhere printed in full, and a complete bibliography. . . . The list of authorities shows almost complete dependence upon printed sources readily

accessible; and, with one exception, no use has been made of recent monographs." Wm. R. Shepherd, *Political science quarterly*, 14: 153.

Guerber, Helene Adeline. Story of the thirteen colonies. (Eclectic school readings.) N. Y.: Am. Book Co. [c. 1898.] 65c.   [853

Miss Guerber has added one more to her long list of compilations for young people. Her story of the colonies is pleasantly told.   C. M. A.

Hakluyt, Richard. Discourse on western planting, written in the year 1584 [first published, 1877]; with a preface and introd. by Leonard Woods, ed. with notes in the appendix, by Charles Deane. (Maine Hist. Soc. Coll., documentary ser., v. 2.) Cambridge. 1877.
[854

The most suggestive contemporary introduction to the study of English colonization. It was written at the request of Raleigh, to be laid before the Queen, and is a vivid revelation of the motives prompting the voyages and colonial undertakings of Elizabeth's reign. Hakluyt describes the resources of the new world and the opportunities for English commerce; Spain's possessions there are the sources of her strength in Europe, but her hold is really weak; her title by discovery to the Atlantic coast of North America is inferior to England's, and that by Papal Bull invalid; the Indies are the place to attack her and destroy her power, etc. Dr. Deane's notes translate the passages in the text in Latin and Italian, and supply explanations of Hakluyt's references. Goldsmid includes this *Discourse* in his new ed. of Hakluyt's *Principal navigations*.   E. G. B.

Haliburton, Thomas Chandler. The English in America. London. 1851. 2v.

—— Rule and misrule of the English in America. N. Y.: Harper. 1851.   [855

This work by the well-known "Sam Slick," a Nova Scotian statesman and judge, is a study in the spirit of Tocqueville of democracy in America. The author has an unbounded admiration for the United States as a republic, and thinks that the English colonies were practically republics long before their independence. On the other hand, he thinks that if Canada is to remain a part of the British Empire the authority of the mother country should be greater. The historical sketch of the English in America prior to 1783 forms the greater part of the work. The style is dignified and pleasing.   G. M. W.

Hazard, Ebenezer, *ed.* Historical collections: state papers and other authentic documents. Phil. 1792–4. 2v.   [856

This is the work of a pioneer among American collectors and editors of historical material. The first volume contains miscellaneous documents relating to the discovery and colonization of America prior to 1660. These have reference mainly to English enterprise, but that of the Spanish and French is not excluded. The documents are arranged in chronological order and are taken from strictly authoritative sources.

Many of these may now be found elsewhere, but some are still accessible only in this collection. The second volume consists mainly of the *Records of the United Colonies of New England*. A more perfect edition of these now exists in vols. IX and X of the *Plymouth Colony records*, and hence the second volume of Hazard's *Collections* has been largely superseded.   H. L. O.

Johnson, Rossiter. History of the French war, ending in the conquest of Canada ; with a preliminary account of the early attempts at colonization. (Minor wars of the U. S.) N.Y. : Dodd. [c. 1882.]   [857

Less than half the volume is devoted to the "Old French War," 1756–63, the first 200 pages containing a review of early voyages, French exploration, settlement and wars in America prior to the middle of the 18th century. The work is a compilation ; with no references to sources or authorities, the pages unincumbered with footnotes ; but it admirably fulfils the purpose for which it was written — to supply a popular narrative. Generally accurate, it well brings out the romantic features of the struggle for French dominion in America, while giving due recognition to the political forces which were operative. The style is animated and agreeable. There is an adequate index.   F. H. S.

Journals of the Canada expedition of 1760. See Massachusetts Historical Society, sect. 341.   [858

Kalm, Pehr. Travels into North America ; tr. by John Reinhold Forster. Warrington. 1770–71. 3v. London : Lowndes. 1772. 2v.   [859

The author was "Professor of Œconomy" in the University of Aobo, Swedish Finland. He set out from Sweden in February, 1748, accompanied by "a gardener well skilled in the knowledge of plants and mechanics," first studied husbandry and botany in England, and arrived at Philadelphia in September. He made a tour through the Middle Colonies, going as far west as Niagara, and returned to Stockholm in 1751. This English edition of the *Travels* omits his experiences in England, and abbreviates the journal of his trip to America, but otherwise practically gives the author's work in full. The translator contributes some notes of his own, and the publisher adds a map and several drawings of American birds and animals. Professor Kalm comments garrulously on all things American, especially in the department of natural history ; his observations upon manners and customs are informing, although sometimes amusing. Excellent for the student of American development, material and social.   R. G. T.

Knox, *Capt.* **John.** Historical journal of the campaigns in North America, 1757–60. London. 1769. 2v.   [860

A blunt, matter of fact record of events from day to day. It is absolutely candid and reliable and has furnished materials for all subsequent writers of any authority. The military and naval orders incorporated in this journal are singularly valuable for the light they throw upon the operations of war as they were

conducted at that time by the armies of two great nations.   E. Cr.

Leroy-Beaulieu, Pierre Paul. De la colonisation chez les peuples modernes. 4e éd. Paris: Guillaume. 1898. 12fr.   [861

This is a standard work upon the history and principles of colonization. The first part deals in detail with the colonial policy of the principal people of Europe and notes the different systems and their successive modifications from the discovery of America to the present time. The second part contains an exposition of the principles of the science of colonization, and deals in broad generalizations regarding the conditions under which colonization may be favorably carried on and the advantages other than material that will accrue to the people of the mother country. Successive editions have brought the historical portions down to date. The period from 1898 to 1901 will be covered by a fifth edition which is announced as soon to appear.   C. M. A.

Liberty bell leaflets ; ed. by Martin G. Brumbaugh and Joseph S. Walton. Phil. : Christopher Sower Co. 1899–. 5c. ea.   [862

1. Inducements offered by the States-General of Holland, 1614–26, to those merchants and navigators who would discover new countries ; together with the Charter of privileges granted to the Patroons.
2. The West Jersey constitution of 1677.
3. Penn's frame of government of 1682, and privileges and concessions of 1701.
4. Charter of the province of Pennsylvania, granted by Charles the Second to William Penn, January, 1682.

Lodge, Henry Cabot. Short history of the English colonies in America. N. Y. : Harper. 1881. Rev. ed. $3.   [863

This is a handbook of the history of the colonies. It contains political and social history combined. Each colony is treated separately, the author beginning with Virginia and working first southward and then northward. Three supplementary chapters on the Revolution conclude the volume. The book contains a large array of facts, and is written in a clear style. But its plan is wholly mechanical, and therefore it fails to bring out the spirit and meaning of the period. It is written from the ordinary American point of view.   H. L. O.

MacDonald, William, *ed.* Select charters and other documents illustrative of American history, 1606–1775 ; with notes. N. Y. : Macmillan. 1899. Net $2.   [864

"The period covered is 1606–1775, the series beginning with the first charter of Virginia and ending with the Prohibitory Act. One would expect to find in such a book as this many pieces taken from the 17th century, when all the most important colonies gained constitutional status, and so it is. For the period which lies before the peace of Ryswick, Prof. MacDonald is much more detailed than for the years 1697–1763. He gives 80 documents in all, and of these only eight are allotted to the 66 years which we have last indicated. . . . With the Peace of Paris he again becomes detailed, and traces distinctly each principal stage of the rupture between the colonies and the mother country. 26 documents relating to the last 12 years of the colonial era do not, however, constitute an undue proportion when one considers the interests at stake. Prof. MacDonald shows good judgment in his selections, and his book should materially assist the teaching of American history in colleges which are unfortunate enough to lack large libraries. More than this, it will be a great convenience everywhere." *Nation*, 69 : 429.

Mante, *Maj.* **Thomas.** History of the late war in North America, including the campaign of 1763-4 against His Majesty's Indian enemies. London. 1772.   [865

"Mante was an engineer officer in the service, but he did not share in the war till the last year of it. The book has eighteen large maps and plates. It has been praised by Bancroft and Sparks." Justin Winsor, in *Narrative and critical hist. of Am.*, 5 : 616.

Marshall, John. A compendious view of the colonies planted by the English on the continent of North America. (Life of Washington, v. 1. London and Phil. 1804. 5v.)
—— History of the colonies. Phil. 1824.   [866

In this volume the political history of the colonies till 1763 is reviewed. The author in its preparation made use of the standard works and sources accessible in his time, as Stith, Hutchinson, Smith, Chalmers. Occasionally, though not often, a statement appears which later investigations have shown to be improbable or unfounded. In general its accuracy, and in all parts its fairness, are unimpeachable. The view which the author took of Nathaniel Bacon may well be recommended to later historians. Still, except as evidence of the wide knowledge, clear style, and well-balanced judgment of the great jurist, the volume now possesses little importance for those who are acquainted with the later literature of the subject.   H. L. O.

Neill, Edward Duffield. The English colonization of America during the 17th century. London and N. Y.: Routledge. 1871.   [867

Rev. Mr. Neill was an assiduous and learned investigator, and one of the earliest critics of the beginnings of colonial history. In this work, as in his other writings, he has drawn largely from original manuscripts and documents, some of which have been since more fully and accurately printed. The narrative, which is badly proportioned and often disconnected and digressive, deals with the history of Virginia, Maryland and the Popham colony, and treats of Wingfield, Rolfe, Pocahontas, John Smith, of the Puritans in Virginia, of the services of Copeland, chaplain of the East India Company, of Calvert and Maryland to 1650, and of education and religion. Some of Mr. Neill's main contentions — such as his claim that Virginia was a penal colony and that religious toleration did not exist in Maryland — have not received the final stamp of approval. The chief value of the work to-day lies in its documents and notes.   C. M. A.

Niles, Samuel. History of the Indian and French wars. See Massachusetts Historical Society, sect. 303.   [868

Oldmixon, John. British empire in America. London. 1708. 2v.   [869

"The name of John Oldmixon . . . is signed to the dedication [of this book] and it passes under his name. A second corrected and amended edition appeared in 1741. Herman Moll made the maps which it contains . . . and some have supposed that he wrote the text. Dr. Hawks says of the book that it contains almost as many errors as pages, and unsupported is not to be trusted." Justin Winsor, in *Narrative and critical hist. of Am.*, 5 : 344.

Payne, Edward John. History of European colonies. (Historical course for schools, no. 7.) London: Macmillan. 1877. N. Y.: Macmillan. 1878. $1.10.   [870

This small volume is a manual of colonization and colonial development. It is not so much a narrative or a collection of facts as an analysis of the influences that have led to colonization, and a study of the conditions underlying commercial routes and colonial trade. The work needs revision in both text and maps, and to be of value should be brought up to date. Furthermore, the print is too fine and the book is deficient in bibliographical aids.   C. M. A.

Pemberton, Thomas. Historical journal of the American war, 1765-83. See Massachusetts Historical Society, sect. 287.   [871

Pouchot, *Capt.* Memoir upon the late war in North America, 1755-60 ; tr. and ed. by F. B. Hough. Roxbury, Mass.: Woodward. 1866. 2v.   [872

"In the study of the topography, so far as it was known, and of the geographical nomenclature of the frontier just previous to the outbreak of the Revolutionary War, the *Memoir* . . . by M. Pouchot will be found very useful." A. McF. Davis in *Narrative and critical hist. of Am.*, 6 : 660.

Pownall, Thomas. The administration of the colonies, wherein their rights and constitutions are discussed and stated. London. 1764-74. 2v. V. 1, 3d ed. enl. 1766. New ed. 1777. 2v.   [873

Pownall was governor of Massachusetts Bay Colony from 1757 to 1760, and knew intimately the needs of the colonies and the inefficiency of the British colonial administration. His work, which passed through five editions, was a plea for reorganization and reform. He treats of administration, commerce, taxation, justice, finance, Indian affairs, and the general importance of the colonies to the mother country. He was a man of unusual foresight and penetration, and his view of the form that the British colonial policy should take is far ahead of its time.   C. M. A.

Putnam, *Brig.-Gen.* **Rufus.** Journal kept in northern New York during four campaigns of the old French and Indian war, 1757-60 ;

with notes and biographical sketch by E. C. Dawes. Albany: Munsell. 1886. [874

A daily account of the author's life in the four campaigns, but gives little general information. Well annotated. In 1812 Putnam rewrote this diary in more general and connected terms and it is printed in Mary Cone's *Life of Rufus Putnam.* E. E. S.

Review of the military operations, 1753–56. See Massachusetts Historical Society, sect. 290. [875

Sainsbury, William Noël. The British Public Record Office and the materials in it for early American history. See American Antiquarian Society, sect. 240. [876

Sargent, Winthrop, *ed.* History of an expedition against Fort du Quesne, 1755, under Maj.-Gen. Edward Braddock; ed. from the original MSS. Phil.: Lippincott. 1856. (Pennsylvania Hist. Soc. Memoirs, v. 5. Phil. 1855.) [877

The contents include several journals of the expedition and other papers. "The introductory memoir goes over the whole ground of the rival territorial claims of France and England, and the whole narrative, including that of the battle itself, is given with care and judgment." Justin Winsor, in *Narrative and critical hist. of Am.*, 5: 575.

Seeley, *Sir* **John Robert.** Expansion of England. London: Macmillan. 1883. Boston: Roberts. 1883. Little. $1.75. [878

We have here two courses of lectures; one, dealing with the expansion of England in America, the other in India; and each the consequence of a "kind of second Hundred Years' War" with France. These lectures are noteworthy for breadth of view, simplicity and boldness in historical generalization, suggestiveness, and, despite a certain indifference to style, readableness. It would, for example, be difficult to find elsewhere in so few words so instructive a statement of the relations of England to India. A. D. M.

Slafter, Edmund Farwell. Sir William Alexander and American colonization. See Prince Society, sect. 387. [879

Smith, William. Historical account of Bouquet's expedition against the Ohio Indians, in 1764; with preface by Francis Parkman, and a translation of Dumas' Biographical sketch of General Bouquet. Cin.: Clarke. 1868. Net $3. [880

A reprint of an anonymous quarto published in Philadelphia and London in 1766, and now rare. The authorship was long ascribed to Thomas Hutchins, the geographer; but a letter in the Force Papers, in possession of the Library of Congress, shows that the credit belongs to Dr. William Smith, then provost of the College of Philadelphia. In addition to the account of this important and successful expedition for the relief of Fort Pitt, during the Pontiac Indian

uprising, the author gives us some *Reflections on the war with the savages of North America* — a careful study of frontier conditions, methods of forming new settlements, lists of towns, distances, and routes, and an attempt at a census of the fighting tribes. The reprint, invaluable to the student of the frontier history of the Middle West, contains a brief historical introduction by Francis Parkman, with C. G. F. Dumas' biography of Bouquet (translated from the French edition of the *Account*, published in 1769), and an index. Clarke's reprint is No. 1 of that publisher's important *Ohio valley historical series.* R. G. T.

Stockton, Frank Richard. Buccaneers and pirates of our coasts. N. Y.: Macmillan. 1898. $1.50. [881

"These characters have . . . spice in them, and their adventures give Mr. Stockton abundant excuse for the display of his peculiar and delightful talent. The effort to tell the truth about these artists in piracy has not prevented him from describing them gayly and with a kind of amused sympathy. The book is serious enough, but there are illuminating flashes of Mr. Stockton's dry humor. It is this quality in him which makes the work sane and wholesome. . . . The individuality of the book is reflected in the capital pictures by Mr. George Varian and Mr. B. West Clinedinst." *Dial* (Chicago), 25: 405.

Story, Thomas. Journal of life. Newcastle-upon-Tyne. 1747. [882

"First of importance among the published travels of this period is the narrative of an English Quaker, Thomas Story, who came over in 1697. From that time to 1708 he visited every part of the colonies from New Hampshire to Carolina, dwelling for much of the time, however, in Pennsylvania, where he became, under Penn's persuasion, a public official." Justin Winsor, in *Narrative and critical hist. of Am.*, 5: 243.

Thomas, Isaiah. History of printing in America, with a biography of printers. Worcester. 1810. 2v.

—— *Same.* 2d ed., with author's corrections and additions. (Am. Antiquarian Soc. Archæologia Americana, v. 5, 6.) Albany: Munsell. 1874. 2v. [883

The chief authority on the history of early American printing. Himself a printer, T. has produced a book which, although sometimes criticised for the disposition of material, is yet one of the classics of bibliography. E. C. R.

Thwaites, Reuben Gold. The colonies, 1492–1750. (Epochs of Am. hist.) N. Y.: Longmans. 1891. Rev. ed. 1897. $1.25. [884

The writer has succeeded well in his object, which was to produce a good text-book for schools, or a brief résumé for the use of the general reader. The style is clear; the most important facts in the history of the period have been correctly stated. Much information has been compressed within a limited space. A spirit of impartiality pervades the book. It does not appear that special use has been made of original materials. This indeed is not a fault, because it was quite sufficient for the purpose of the work that the accessible standard authorities should be judiciously used. The book contains useful bibliographies.

H. L. O.

Tyler, Moses Coit. History of American literature, 1607–1765. N. Y.: Putnam. 1878. 2v. Rev. ed. 1897. 2v. $2.50 ea. 1v. $3. [885

The names of the men and women great as writers in the time from the settlement of America to the Revolution are very few, but it is well worth while to have a thoroughly studied account of what was then written. Though in the case of the most illustrious their desert in other fields is greater than in literature,—as explorers, subduers of the forest, regulators of new societies, zealous preachers and teachers of the truth as they saw it—yet the world needs to know what they did with the pen. Professor Tyler's scholarship reaches deep and far. With picturesque felicity of touch, the grotesque quaintness, the pathetic shortcomings due to narrow surroundings, harsh intolerance, sturdy heroism in desperate crises, lurid beliefs, most forceful striving—things attractive and things repulsive are combined into a great portrayal.

J. K. H.

"The work is . . . unique in plan, as well as original in material, and occupies within its sphere a position of unapproached excellence. A feature of this work which is conspicuous alike for its novelty and its value is the space which is devoted to the arguments of the loyalists and the effort which is made to state their position fairly and fully." H. L. Osgood, in *Political science quarterly*, 13: 41.

Wallcut, Thomas. Journal, [journey] to Marietta [1720]. See Massachusetts Historical Society, sect. 333. [886

Washington, George. Journal of my journey over the mountains in 1747–48; ed. by J. M. Toner. Albany: Munsell. 1892. $3. [887

This work, claimed by its editor to be "the first systematic attempt to produce the writings of Washington with literal exactness as to abbreviations, the use of capitals, punctuation, spelling, etc.," is the initial volume of an intended complete collection of "all the writings of Washington," planned by the late Dr. J. M. Toner, "long engaged in collecting accurate copies of all the obtainable writings of this great man." Its chief interest centres in the fact that it is the earliest known composition of Washington, for the major part consists of surveying notes and records. The text is as literally printed as type can be made to reproduce script, but the insertion of numerous, and often over-long or irrelevant notes between the entries, instead of as footnotes, is a material piece of mis-editing, and another curious contradiction to the editor's claim of literal accuracy, is the inclusion of surveys, from "pen-tracings" instead of by photographic reproductions. P. L. F.

Weiser, Conrad. Narrative of a journey from Tulpehocken to Onondaga, 1737, and

Journal of proceedings in his journey to the Ohio, 1748. See Pennsylvania, Historical Society of, sect. 384. [888

Wharton, Anne Hollingsworth. Colonial days and dames. Phil.: Lippincott. 1895. $1.25.

——Martha Washington. (Women of Colonial and Revolutionary times.) N. Y.: Scribner. 1897. $1.25.

——Through colonial doorways. Phil.: Lippincott. 1893. $1.25. [889

A readable series on the general plan of choosing extracts from old letters and papers and connecting them by comments, conjectures and deductions. The first book describes colonial life under such topics as women, poetesses, old landmarks, and weddings and merry-makings. There is no order in the arrangement. The third book describes social life in the colonies, chiefly in Philadelphia and New York. The life of Mrs. Washington is necessarily made up of scanty material, eked out by contemporary description and events in the life of her husband. It is as good as anything of the kind that has been done.

E. E. S.

Wolfe, *Maj.-Gen.* James. WRIGHT, ROBERT. Life of Major-General James Wolfe. London: Chapman. 1864. [890

" In coming to the great victory which closed the war on the Heights of Abraham we can but be conscious of the domination which the character of Wolfe holds over all the recitals of its events, and the best source of that influence is in the letters which Wright has introduced into his life of Wolfe." Justin Winsor, in *Narrative and critical hist. of Am.*, 5: 602.

NEW ENGLAND COLONIES

Adams, Brooks. Emancipation of Massachusetts. Boston: Houghton. 1887. $1.50. [891

An account of the breaking of the bonds imposed by the theocracy instituted by Puritan ministers over Massachusetts in her colonial period. A work of learning, ability and courage; written, however, in a spirit far from judicial : the spirit is rather that of a prosecuting attorney determined upon a strong presentation of the side for which he is retained, leaving it to another to make the counter-plea. Mr. Adams has in his own veins the blood of some of the men whom he accuses, notably of John Norton, the foremost figure in the Quaker persecution, and of Thomas Shepherd of Cambridge. He ruthlessly uncovers the nakedness of his forefathers: he pulls from their niches some of the most conspicuous worthies of New England, to gibbet them as bigots, tyrants and hypocrites. While it is a book of absorbing interest and undoubted value, it gives the harshest emphasis to facts about which history has been reticent. There are two sides here.

J. K. H.

Adams, Charles Francis. Three episodes

of Massachusetts history : the settlement of Boston Bay, the Antinomian controversy, a study of church and town government. Boston: Houghton. 1892. 2v. $4.   [892

As to the settlement of Massachusetts Bay, Mr. Adams shows full knowledge of every extant source, reaching the essential truth with acuteness and stating it with a true Adams directness. Longer and more important than the other papers is a *Study of church and town government*, a detailed account of the town of Quincy, Mass., through two centuries and a half. An utter absence of glamour characterizes the narrative. With blunt plainness the shortcomings as well as the creditable things are unsparingly stated. In the realistic picture are traits to admire, to stand aghast at, to inspire loathing. While the reader will sometimes glow over the strength and worth of the generations concerned, he will be abundantly convinced that his own lot is cast in wiser and kinder times. No more trustworthy delineation of the life of a New England town has ever been drawn. J. K. H.

—— *ed.* Antinomianism in the Colony of Massachusetts Bay, 1636–38. (Prince Soc. Publications.) Boston. 1894.   [893

The important material reprinted in this volume is the *Short story of the rise, reign, and ruine of the Antinomians*, the examination of Mrs. Hutchinson before the general court at Newtown (reprinted from the appendix to Hutchinson's *History of Massachusetts*, v. 1), the trial of Mrs. Hutchinson before the church at Boston, and that part of Cotton's *Way of the churches cleared* which contains his account of Antinomianism. The object of the able introduction by the editor is to prove that the *Short story* was written, not by Rev. Th. Welde, but, excepting the introduction, by Gov. Winthrop ; also that it was sent at once and in manuscript to England. There it was kept till 1644, when the controversy over toleration between the Presbyterians and Independents had waxed hot. Then it was published in the interest of the Presbyterians, ultimately with the addition of prefatory matter by Mr. Welde.   H. L. O.

Adams, Hannah. Summary history of New-England. Dedham, Mass. 1799.   [894

"She does not profess to have done more than abridge the usual printed sources, as they were then understood, and to have made some use of MS. material, particularly respecting the history of Rhode Island." Justin Winsor, in *Narrative and critical hist. of Am.*, 5 : 159.

Andros, *Sir* **Edmund.** WHITMORE, W.·H., *ed.* Andros tracts ; with notes and memoir. (Prince Soc. Publications.) Boston. 1868–74. 3v.   [895

The first volume of this series contains Mr. Whitmore's *Memoir of Andros*, and pamphlets, with other material, which have directly to do with the uprising in Boston of April, 1689, and its causes. The second volume is devoted chiefly to the mission of Increase Mather to England, and contains his account of negotiations there and various writings which he issued in defence of the conduct of Massachusetts. The contents of the third volume are more miscellaneous, including papers relating to Andros' administration, a reprint of part of Cotton Mather's memoirs of Increase Mather, and papers relating to Edward Randolph. In these volumes is collected nearly all of the original material bearing on the revolution of 1689 in Massachusetts which is to be found outside the colonial archives.   H. L. O.

Mr. Whitmore's memoir has effected a great change of opinion regarding the character of Andros, an opinion for which the hostility of New England historians toward Andros is largely responsible. Mr. Whitmore has successfully refuted the old charges against Andros, and has relieved him of the stigma of being either a placeman or a tyrant.   C. M. A.

Arber, Edward, *ed.* Story of the Pilgrim fathers, 1606–23 A. D., as told by themselves, their friends and their enemies. Boston : Houghton. 1897. $2.   [896

Selections from contemporary narratives like those of Bradford and Winslow, the records in the English state papers, the city records in Leyden and Amsterdam, and those of Plymouth, etc., illustrating every phase of the history of the Pilgrim fathers down to 1624. An elaborate index, comprising over 90 columns, gives a complete clue to all the names mentioned in any of the extracts. The editor's work has been performed with great care and thoroughness. No other single volume contains so much varied contemporary and authentic information about the Pilgrims.   E. G. B.

Atwater, Edward Elias. History of the colony of New Haven to its absorption into Connecticut. New Haven: Author. 1881. [For sale by Edward P. Judd Co., New Haven, Conn. $5.]   [897

Arranged topically, e. g. : Foundations laid in church and state ; Domestic and social life, etc. Based on a careful study of the sources. Patriotic but fair. Covers only a limited period in a very detailed manner. Style suited to a work of reference. One of the best of the New England town histories.   E. C.

Baker, Charlotte Alice. True stories of New England captives carried to Canada during the old French and Indian wars. Cambridge, Mass. : Author. 1897. $3.50.   [898

No more picturesque stories can be found than those of some of the New England captives carried during King William's and Queen Anne's wars to Canada. Miss Baker, whose home is a house two centuries old, in the heart of old Deerfield, a house spared in Hertel de Rouville's raid, in 1704, seems to have imbibed from her surroundings her antiquarian zeal. With a most sympathetic touch, after having turned over in Canada many a parish and convent record, walking pityingly in tracks which the captives she celebrates trod with bare and bleeding feet, she tells of those by-gone sorrows.   J. K. H.

Bartlett, William Henry. Pilgrim fathers ; or Founders of New England in the reign of James the First. London. 1853. New ed. Edin.: Nelson. 1866.   [899

This work was written that the British public might be better informed regarding the early history of their kinsmen across the sea. It is a compilation put together in an anecdotal and gossipy fashion, calculated to interest its readers. Mr. Bartlett may lay claim to some originality in the attention he has given to topographical details, but taken as a whole he has shown little critical ability, and in all that relates to the Pilgrims in Holland and America has contributed nothing of value. C. M. A.

Baylies, Francis. Historical memoir of the colony of New Plymouth. Boston. 1830. 2v.

—— *Same ;* ed. by Samuel G. Drake. Boston: Wiggin. 1866. 2v. [900

Of the two editions of this work to which reference is here made the latter is the more valuable. It contains corrections and additions with a copious index, by S. G. Drake. Proof of the accuracy of the work is furnished by the fact that a scholar like Drake, after the lapse of thirty years, found so little to correct. Its chief defect, when viewed from the standpoint of present scholarship, arises from the fact that it was written before Bradford's *History* was recovered and published, and before the issue of the *Plymouth Colony records.* But it is still a book of such authority that the student cannot afford to neglect it. A part of it is devoted to the history of the towns of the Old Colony. It contains abstracts of the laws, and a very thorough treatment of King Philip's war. H. L. O.

Belcher papers. See Massachusetts Historical Society, sect. 318. [901

Boston. *Record Commissioners.* Reports. 1876–. Boston. 1876–. [902

These volumes contain, so far as printed, the records of the town of Boston. They have been carefully edited, and each is furnished with a brief introduction. The two principal series of records are those of the town meetings and those of the selectmen. Until 1700 these were kept in the same books, and so are printed together. But subsequent to that date they were separately kept, and are printed as two distinct series, *Boston town records* and *Selectmen's minutes.* Records of towns which are now a part of Boston — Charlestown, Dorchester, Roxbury — also appear in these volumes. The Roxbury church records (6th report) are especially interesting. A variety of miscellaneous matter has also been printed, as the " book of possessions," tax lists, deeds, lists of births, deaths and marriages, lists of admissions to the town. Of special interest are the " Gleaner " articles in the 5th Report. H. L. O.

Bradford, William. History of Plymouth plantation [ed. by Charles Deane]. (In Mass. Hist. Soc. Collections, ser. 4, v. 3.) Boston. 1856.

—— Bradford's history of Plimoth plantation ; from the original MS., with proceedings incident to the return of the MS. to Massachusetts ; printed by order of the General Court. Boston. 1898.

—— History of the Plimoth plantation, reproduced in fac-simile by photography of original MS. ; introd. by J. A. Doyle. Boston : Houghton. 1895. Net $25. [903

This ranks with Winthrop's *Journal* as one of the two most important works in early New England historical literature. It is as authoritative as Winthrop, and is superior to it in that it is not simply a diary or book of annals, but a history. It has, that is, plan, unity and a distinct literary form. It is a book which may be *read through* with pleasure. The author, after a part of the events occurred and as others were occurring, undertook to set them forth in a narrative, in such a way that their meaning might be interpreted to and by the reader. On the one side it is the careful record of an experiment in colonization, and in it may be read the account of the continuous struggle between planters and adventurers, i. e. between religion and state-building as motives, and profit as an incitement to activity. On the other side, however, the book is intensely idealistic. A fundamental thought underlying it is, that historical development is the result of the providential dealings of God with men, carrying his saints through to triumph and overwhelming their opponents with ruin. Bradford thought that the part played by the Pilgrims and New Plymouth in the great drama was not unimportant, and therefore he became the worthy historian of the colony.

The sumptuous fac-simile edition possesses value as a curiosity. It will enable those who desire to see how Gov. Bradford's handwriting and manuscript looked to be gratified without a journey to Boston, where it is now preserved. But to the ordinary reader or student the only value of the book is in the sketch of Bradford's life and writings which has been prepared for it by Mr. Doyle.

See, also, Jameson's *History of historical writing in America*, p. 13. H. L. O.

—— Letter-book. See Massachusetts Historical Society, sect. 289.

—— Mourt's Relation. See Mourt, George, beyond, sect. 990. [904

Brattle, Thomas. Witchcraft delusion, 1692. See Massachusetts Historical Society, sect. 289. [905

Brewster, William. STEELE, ASHBEL. Chief of the Pilgrims; or The life and time of William Brewster. Phil.: Lippincott. 1857. [906

This life of Elder Brewster was authorized by the Brewster family, and its execution placed in the hands of the Rev. Mr. Steele, already known as an authority on the subject. Mr. Steele had exceptional advantages in the way of obtaining information and his account is unbiased and fairly complete. The facts regarding Brewster's life are nowhere better given. The treatment is very subjective, the narrative being freely interspersed with personal comment. C. M. A.

Brown, John. The Pilgrim fathers of New

England and their Puritan successors. N. Y.: Revell. [c. 1895.] $1.50. [907

"Not a dull chapter in the book." A clear, strong account, written with special reference to Gov. Bradford's *History of Plymouth plantation* and having illustrations of high grade. Two thirds of the book are devoted to the Scrooby Company. The precursors of the Pilgrim fathers are dated back to 1165 A. D. A careful analysis of the writings of John Robinson is given. It is an English account of a great episode, unbiased and readable, but offering no new material. "Avoids controversy." "Conservative." See the *Nation*, Feb. 13, 1896, p. 144; *Amer. hist. rev.*, vol. I, Apr. 1896, pp. 541-2. H. W. H.

Byington, Ezra Hoyt. The Puritan as a colonist and reformer. Boston: Little. 1899. $2. [908

"Supplements the author's 'The Puritan in England and New England.' Chapters on the Pilgrim as a colonist, the Puritan as a colonist, John Eliot, the apostle to the Indians, Jonathan Edwards and the great awakening, and Shakespeare and the Puritans." *Publishers' weekly*, Dec. 16, 1899.

——The Puritan in England and New England; with introd. by Alexander McKenzie. Boston: Roberts. 1896. Little. $2. [909

Detached essays brought together into an attractive book. Written with a genial temper, which is in danger of lapsing "into mere apology." "Explains away the bigotry of the Puritan." A popular statement, written from secondary sources, largely. The arrangement is topical. The last three papers furnish the most valuable and original matter, especially the researches into the records of the Pyncheon family. See *Amer. hist. rev.*, Apr. 1897, p. 532; and the *Nation*, Jan. 14, 1897, p. 37. H. W. H.

Church, Benjamin. Entertaining passages relating to Philip's war. Boston. 1716.

——History of King Philip's war; [ed.] by Henry Martin Dexter. (Library of New Eng. history.) Boston: Wiggin. 1865. [910

This is not a history of King Philip's war, but of that part of it which was fought in southeastern New England. It is a carefully prepared edition of Col. Church's *Entertaining passages relating to Philip's war*. This is an account told by the Colonel himself, or prepared from his notes, chiefly of his own exploits in that struggle. It is one of the most interesting and realistic narratives of Indian warfare which has come down to us. The editor, Dr. Dexter, has corrected the text, has added notes which explain all points of topographical and genealogical interest, and has also furnished a chronological table which will be of material aid to the reader. H. L. O.

——History of the eastern expeditions of 1689, 1690, 1692, 1696, and 1704, against the Indians and French; [ed.] by Henry Martin Dexter. [Philip's war, pt. 2.] Boston: Wiggin. 1867. [911

This was originally issued with the *Entertaining passages*, though it concerns wholly different events. It

contains Col. Church's account of three expeditions led by him to Maine and two to Acadia. These were sent out during the first and second intercolonial wars. The last was the most important, and was a plundering expedition organized in retaliation for the destruction of Deerfield. (See Parkman, *A half century of conflict*, 1: 116.) The work is edited by the same hand and in the same manner as *King Philip's war*. The narrative is not so interesting or detailed as that of *King Philip's war*, but as a record of events the two are equally reliable. H. L. O.

Clark, John. Ill-newes from New England, 1652. See Massachusetts Historical Society, sect. 307. [912

Connecticut. Fundamental orders of Connecticut. See Old South Work, sect. 368. [913

Council for New England. Records; ed. by Charles Deane. See American Antiquarian Society, sect. 242. [914

Davis, William T. Ancient landmarks of Plymouth. Pt. 1: Historical sketch and titles of estates. Pt. 2: Genealogical register of Plymouth families. Boston: Williams. 1883. Damrell. $4.50. [915

Neither a history of the old colony nor a history of Plymouth. The result of long delving in the Plymouth records. Of local interest mainly. E. C.

Dexter, H. M. English exiles in Amsterdam, 1597–1625. See Massachusetts Historical Society, sect. 343. [916

Dexter, Morton. Story of the Pilgrims. Boston: Congregational Sunday-School and Pub. Soc. [c. 1894.] Pilgrim Press. Pap. 75c. [917

This volume was written by the son of the late Henry M. Dexter, the historian of Congregationalism, for the use of Scrooby clubs, which were formed in Congregational churches for the study of the history of the Congregationalists. Mr. Dexter is at his best in his treatment of the Pilgrims out of England, and his account of their life in Holland is valuable; but the work as a whole can be considered only moderately successful. The earlier chapters are marked by a tone of sectarianism, and the entire production is inferior, both in scholarship and in temper, to Walker's *Congregationalists*, which appeared in the same year (sect. 3104 a). C. M. A.

Doyle, John Andrew. English colonies in America. V. 2: The Puritan colonies. London: Longmans. 1887. 2v. N. Y.: Holt. 1887. 2v. $7. [For v. 1, see sect. 840.] [918

Covers the history of New England to near the close of Queen Anne's reign. Valuable as written by an English student from an English point of view. Based mainly on a study of some of the more important sources. Local records, as the *Reports* of the Boston Record Commission and serial publications as the *Proceedings* of the Massachusetts Historical Society were not used by the author. Bibliography poor and maps bad. Style heavy and indistinct. E. C.

Drake, Samuel Adams. Border wars of New England, commonly called King William's and Queen Anne's wars. N. Y.: Scribner. 1897. $1.50.   [919

Samuel G. Drake had collected a mass of materials for the history of these two French and Indian wars in New England, but he did not live to arrange them for publication. These materials and others his son has used in the preparation of this volume, and that with a beauty of style and arrangement to which the father could scarcely lay claim. The book is an original contribution to the history of the intercolonial wars, and has, at the same time, the popular charm which belongs to all the writings of this author. The views expressed concerning the essential conditions and issues of the struggle are believed to be sound.
H. L. O.

——The making of New England, 1580–1643. N. Y.: Scribner. 1886. $1.50.   [920

This book embodies the results of thorough scholarship, presented in attractive form. In it the history of New England is traced from the beginnings of discovery to the formation of the Confederacy in 1643. The part devoted to Massachusetts, New Hampshire and Maine is especially satisfactory. Connecticut and Rhode Island receive in comparison somewhat inadequate treatment. The purpose of the book being to interest youth and general readers in history, more attention is properly paid to social than to political development. It comes near to being a model of its kind, both as to matter and style.   H. L. O.

——On Plymouth Rock. Boston: Lee. 1897. 60c.   [921

Rehearses the Pilgrim story in a brief, attractive form. Well suited to school use.   E. C.

——The taking of Louisburg, 1745. (Decisive events in Am. history.) Boston: Lee. 1891. 50c.   [922

This is a brief story, popularly told, of the siege and capture of Louisburg in 1745. Mr. Drake has dealt with the topographical features of the fortress, its strategic importance, the composition and character of the besieging forces, and the incidents and results of the siege. The account is accurately and vividly presented.   C. M. A. ·

Drake, Samuel Gardner. Annals of witchcraft in New England: and elsewhere in the U. S. Boston. 1869.   [923

Earlier monographs deal almost exclusively with the well-known events of 1692. Mr. Drake here collects all the recorded cases of witchcraft, from the first settlement of New England to the culmination of the delusion. An opportunity for forming an impartial and independent judgment of the whole subject is thus made easily accessible to students, and much popular error refuted. More space is given to the earlier cases as being less familiar. Perhaps no writer has given the subject more thorough study. Ordinary students will find all they want in these *Annals*.
S. A. D.

——History and antiquities of Boston, 1630–1770. Boston. 1856 [c. 1852–6].   [924

Like all the writings of Mr. Drake, this shows exhaustive knowledge and scrupulous care. But it is the work of an antiquarian rather than an historian. The author failed to grasp the difference between a history of a town, or a municipality, and that of a colony. The larger part of the space is devoted to events which strictly concern the history of the colony. Municipal affairs proper are often referred to in notes rather than in the text.   H. L. O.

——The old Indian chronicle: being a collection of exceeding rare tracts written and published in the time of King Philip's war. Boston. 1836. S. A. Drake. 1867.   [925

The title of the work is suggestive of its exceeding importance as a contribution to the history and ethnology of Massachusetts in the latter part of the 17th century. It contains several tracts not appearing in the edition of 1836, and a map showing the places made memorable by King Philip's war.   F. W. H.

——Particular history of the five years' French and Indian war, 1744–49, sometimes called Gov. Shirley's war. Albany: Munsell. 1870.   [926

By "Particular history" the author means a detailed history. The book consists mainly of a "diary of the depredations" committed by French and Indians along the New England frontier between 1744 and 1749. The horrors of border warfare — what the French called *la petite guerre* — are brought out with clearness and force. Among the contemporary narratives used, the author mentions, with special praise, those of Rev. Benj. Doolittle of Northfield, Mass. In the valuable appendices Rev. John Norton's *Redeemed captive*, and a part of Rev. Th. Prince's thanksgiving sermon, preached after the fall of Louisburg, are reprinted. The author was one of the most painstaking students of Indian history, and here he lets the events, carefully collected and clearly presented, tell their own story.   H. L. O.

Dudley, Thomas. Jones, Augustine. Life and work of Thomas Dudley, the second governor of Massachusetts. Boston: Houghton. 1899. Net $5.   [927

"No one can deny that Mr. Augustine Jones, in his *Life and work of Thomas Dudley*, shows careful reading of his sources, and much zeal and patience in selecting and bringing together facts relating to that worthy. Not so much can be said for his literary method." *Dial* (Chicago), 27: 245.

Dudley records. See Massachusetts Historical Society, sect. 350.   [928

Dunton, John. Letters written from New-England, A. D. 1686; with notes by W. H. Whitmore. (Prince Soc. Publications.) Boston. 1867.   [929

An important and interesting account of New England, and particularly of Boston society, as it was near the close of the 17th century. The writer was a bookseller and editor, who visited New England in 1686, and who gives his impressions in letters which may, or may not, have been written in their present form to his friends in England. The writer is on the whole a sympathetic observer of Puritan society in its later and milder form. He borrows freely and without acknowledgment from other writers — Josselyn, Mather's *Magnalia*, and Williams' *Key to the Indian languages*. The long conversations which he reports must not be considered as verbally accurate reproductions.

H. L. O.

Eliot, John. Narrative, 1670. See Old South Work, sect. 368. [930

Elliott, Charles Wyllys. The New England history, A. D. 986–1776. N. Y.: Scribner. 1857. 2v. [931

The aim of the writer of these volumes was to give "a more simple, compact and picturesque re-presentation" of the history of the period than it had received. By the discussion of opinions, forms of general and local government, laws, manners and social life; by tracing the characters and careers of leading personalities, and by a judicious selection of events upon which to lay emphasis, the author sought to exhibit the real tendencies of the period. He frequently resorted to apt quotations to illustrate his views. But he did not produce a genuinely philosophical history. The work contains much that is suggestive, and the use made of material is often admirable. But the author exhibits the shallowness which is characteristic of 18th century writers, and his admiration for colonial democracy is of too pronounced a type to permit of his doing justice to aught save the independent tendencies of old Puritan New England. H. L. O.

Ellis, George Edward. Paper and letter on Mr. Whittier's poem, The king's missive, with letter of Mr. Whittier on the same. See Massachusetts Historical Society, sect. 334.

[932

—— Puritan age and rule in the colony of Massachusetts Bay, 1629–85. Boston: Houghton. 1888. $3.50. [933

An elaborate study of the sources, with a philosophical grasp of the essential elements of Puritanism. Impartial, critical. A portrayal of "the inner life of that strange period." The author's implied thesis is, — "No organic form of civil government can safely base itself on religion." He emphasizes the cordial reception given by the Puritans to the Jesuit Father Druillettes. See *Nation*, July 12, 1888, p. 35.

H. W. H.

Fassett, James Hiram. Colonial life in New Hampshire. Boston: Ginn. 1899. 60c.

[934

This book has been written to carry out the author's pedagogical theory : namely, that children should first be interested in local legends and tales, later in colonial history, and, finally, in state history. It is, therefore, a text-book for young New Hampshire students. It is admirably written and printed, and whether it be used as a text-book or not, it cannot fail to accomplish its purpose of interesting the young people for whom it is intended. C. M. A.

Felt, Joseph Barlow. Customs of New England. Boston. 1853. [935

Strictly speaking, this is more a catalogue of articles of domestic use, and of what the people of New England wore from infancy to old age, than of their customs 250 years ago. But from his standpoint Dr. Felt comes very near exhausting the subject. The correct stage-setting and costuming of a remote period have a recognized value to its history. These Dr. Felt gives us as no one else has done, describing the nature and uses of everything with painstaking fidelity.

S. A. D.

Ferguson, Henry. Essays in American history. N. Y.: Pott. [c. 1894.] $1.25. [936

This volume contains four essays, "The Quakers in New England," "The witches," "Sir Edmund Andros," and "The loyalists," written for the purpose of controverting the older views of such historians as Bancroft, Palfrey and others. Professor Ferguson presents a severe indictment of the Puritans for their treatment of the Quakers and the witches, yet treats the subject with calmness and impartiality, as well as with learning. In his defence of Andros and the loyalists he is more argumentative and assumes the attitude of a pleader. He cannot be said in either of these instances to be strictly impartial, though in relieving Andros and the loyalists of the reproach that has hitherto been cast upon them he has served the cause of truth and justice in history. C. M. A.

Fiske, John. Beginnings of New England ; or The Puritan theocracy in its relations to civil and religious liberty. Boston: Houghton. 1889. $2. [937

As the title indicates, this is not a formal history of New England, but an attempt to indicate the principles at work in its history down to the Revolution of 1689. The whole is considered as an illustration of the English method of nation-making, i. e., by incorporation with representation. The settlement of the Puritan colonies, the formation of the Confederacy and the overthrow of the Andros government are taken as the chief features of the period. But a good deal of extraneous matter is introduced, and the elements of the problem are not very clearly defined. The part played by the Gorges interest has been treated with scant justice. Though written in an interesting and suggestive style, it is not a well thought out book.

H. L. O.

Folsom, George. History of Saco and Biddeford, with notices of other early settlements. Saco. 1830. [938

"The best town history then written in New England, as it was also the best history of the Province of Maine." C. Deane, in *Narrative and critical hist. of Am.*, 3 : 365.

Foster, William Eaton, *ed.* Early attempts at Rhode Island history. See Rhode Island Historical Society. Coll., v. 7. 1885. [939

Gardiner, *Sir* Christopher. ADAMS, C. F. Sir Christopher Gardiner. See Massachusetts Historical Society, sect. 336. [940

Goodwin, John Abbott. The Pilgrim republic, an historical review of the colony of New Plymouth; with sketches of the rise of other New England settlements, the history of Congregationalism and the creeds of the period. Boston: Ticknor. 1888. Houghton. $4. [941

An elaborate and impartial study, based on a careful examination of original sources, not easily found. Written for popular reading, but "without much imagination and humor." The preface contains an estimate of the original and secondary authorities. There is considerable fulness of valuable detail as to local affairs at Plymouth. "Sombre." "Learned." See *Nation*, July 12, 1888, p. 35. H. W. H.

Gorges, *Sir* Ferdinando. Briefe narration of the originall undertakings of the advancement of plantations into the parts of America. See Maine Historical Society, sect. 276. [942

—— Description of New England. See Massachusetts Historical Society, sect. 302. [943

— BAXTER, JAMES P., *ed.* Sir Ferdinando Gorges and his province of Maine. (Prince Soc. Publications.) Boston. 1890. 3v. [944

Among the works issued by the Prince Society to illustrate the hitherto neglected side of New England history this occupies a prominent place. The first volume contains a careful memoir of Gorges by Mr. Baxter; also a critical reprint of Gorges' *Briefe relation.* In the second volume is a reprint of the *Briefe narration,* of the *Breefe answer* to charges against Gorges growing out of the Essex trial, of Gorges' will and other miscellaneous matter. The third volume, together with part of the second, contains the correspondence of Gorges. Here, edited with skill and accuracy, are all the accessible materials upon which to base a judgment concerning the character and objects of the Founder of Maine. H. L. O.

Gorton, Samuel. Simplicities defence. against seven-headed policy. See Rhode Island Historical Society. Coll., v. 2. 1835. [945

— JANES, LEWIS GEORGE. Samuell Gorton, a forgotten founder of our liberties, first settler of Warwick, R. I. (Rhode Island series, 3.) Providence: Preston. 1896. Net $1. [946

"Mr. Janes does not add much to our knowledge of Gorton (who is anything but 'forgotten'), but he makes plain the peculiar views of this uncomfortable neighbor to the Bay." *Nation*, 64: 114.

Gosnold, Bartholomew. Documents relating to his voyage to New England. See Massachusetts Historical Society, sect. 304. [947

Griffis, William Elliot. The Pilgrims in their three homes, England, Holland, America. Boston: Houghton. 1898. $1.25. (Riverside library for young people.) 75c. [948

A vigorous, rhetorical, popular account of the Pilgrim fathers. The closing chapters deal topically with the social, political and religious conditions obtaining in the early New England days. Polemic rather than historical.

Hall, Benjamin Homer. History of eastern Vermont to the close of the 18th century. N. Y.: 1858. Albany: Munsell. 1865. 2v. [949

This is emphatically an original work, the result of long research among the sources of Vermont history. The author himself states that the book was prepared from MS. materials found in the offices of the Secretaries of State of Vermont, New York, Massachusetts, New Hampshire and Connecticut. The Clinton papers at Albany proved a valuable source of information. Much detailed local history respecting the settlement of towns is incorporated into the work. It contains a very full and authentic history of the controversy over the New Hampshire grants. And yet this is imperfect, for it has reference chiefly to events which occurred in eastern Vermont. The account of that conflict merges into the history of the Revolution and of the organization of government in Vermont, which occupies more than one half of the work. It closes with the admission of Vermont into the Union. H. L. O.

Haven, Samuel F. The Mathers and the witchcraft delusion. See American Antiquarian Society, sect. 242. [950

Higginson, Francis. New England's plantation, 1629. See Massachusetts Historical Society, sect. 286. [951

Hinckley papers. See Massachusetts Historical Society, sect. 310. [952

Howe, Daniel Wait. The Puritan republic of the Massachusetts Bay in New England. Indianapolis: Bowen. [c. 1899.] $3.50. [953

This is an attempt to tell once more the story of the Puritans and the development of the government they established in America. Mr. Howe prejudices his reader against him at the outset by confounding Pilgrims with Puritans and so throwing doubt on his sense of historical accuracy. He has told his story with unnecessary dryness, and without an adequate appreciation of the needs of the general reader on one side or the demands of the student on the other. The book contains much information, but nothing that is either new or original. C. M. A.

Hoyt, Epaphras. Antiquarian researches: comprising a history of the Indian wars in the country bordering on the Connecticut River, to 1760. Greenfield, Mass. 1824. [954

"A systematic treatment of the whole subject." Justin Winsor, in *Narrative and critical hist. of Am.*, 5: 187.

Hubbard, William. General history of New England, to 1680. Boston : Mass. Hist. Soc. 1815.

—— *Same.* 2d ed. [rev.]. Boston: Mass. Hist. Soc. 1848.

—— *Same.* (Mass. Hist. Soc. Collections, ser. 2, v. 5–6.) Boston. 1848.   [955

James Savage, in a note to his edition of Winthrop's *History of New England*, I, 297 (old pagination), gave the following estimate of this work : " A small part of his (Hubbard's) volume was certainly compiled from several scarce tracts relative to the discovery of our coast and the early voyages to it; and for anything of date preceding 1630, his information is sometimes authentic, and often curious. A collation with Morton's *Memorial* will, however, prove the facility with which Hubbard transcribed whole pages in succession, even from a printed book. But from the time when Winthrop came to his aid, he generously relies on him, and deems the labor of copying sufficient; so that more than seven eighths of his volume, between 1630 and 1660, is borrowed, usually by specific extracts, occasionally with unimportant changes, from the text of the 'Father of Massachusetts.' It must be acknowledged, however, that sometimes he wisely abbreviates; though much more frequently he slides over circumstances, as dates or numbers, in which the chirography of the MS. would have given him too much trouble to be accurate." This judgment, while in the main correct, is a little too sweeping. Considerable matter about the smaller colonies of New England subsequent to 1630 will be found in Hubbard which is not in Winthrop, while purely ecclesiastical affairs are treated more at length. The value of Hubbard's *History* for the period following the death of Winthrop is not great.   H. L. O.

—— History of the Indian wars in New England to 1677. Rev. by Samuel G. Drake. Roxbury, Mass. : Woodward. 1865. 2v.   [956

This is Hubbard's best work; Drake calls it " valuable and popular." The latter it certainly was. It contains a detailed history of the so-called King Philip's war, in two parts. The subject of the first part is the war in southern New England; that of the second part is the war, or "troubles" from Piscataqua to Pemaquid. In addition the work contains a briefer review of earlier conflicts and difficulties with the Indians, especially the Pequot war. In his account of the latter, Hubbard made use of Capt. Mason's *History of the Pequod war*. Inaccuracies appear in the work; some declare that they are numerous. But Drake, whose notes are elaborate, and whose knowledge of the subject was unrivalled, makes few corrections, and they only in minor points.   H. L. O.

Hunter, Joseph. Collections concerning the early history of the founders of New Plymouth. See Massachusetts Historical Society, sect. 306.   [957

Hutchinson, *Mrs.* Anne. Report of her trial, 1638. See Massachusetts Historical Society, sect. 340.   [958

Hutchinson, Thomas. Collection of original papers relative to the history of the colony of Massachusetts-Bay. Boston. 1769.

—— Hutchinson papers. (Prince Soc. Publications.) Albany : Munsell. 1865. 2v.   [959

A miscellaneous collection of letters and other papers which was made by Hutchinson preparatory to the writing of the first volume of his *History of Massachusetts*. As the originals of many of them have been lost, the copies here are unique. Worthy of particular mention are documents illustrative of the Antinomian controversy, the record of the *quo warranto* proceedings against the Massachusetts charter in 1635, Winthrop's answer to the Ipswich letter about La Tour, the *Abstract of the lawes of New England* proposed by John Cotton, documents relating to the controversy with Robert Child and others (Presbyterians), and (in 2nd vol.) those relating to the controversy with the home government which culminated in the recall of the charter. Of special importance among these last are the letters and reports of Randolph. A collection of prime importance to the student and historian.   H. L. O.

—— Diary and letters, with an account of his administration; comp. from the original documents by P. O. Hutchinson. Boston : Houghton. 1884–86. 2v. $10, net.   [960

The story as narrated by himself of a man whose fate was perhaps as tragic as that of any figure in American history. Possessed of great abilities and high personal character, of the best New England stock, coming forward almost in youth into conspicuous position, an efficient public servant in a variety of places, — places thrust upon him rather than sought by him and in which he served for little or nothing, — selectman, representative, councillor, chief justice, governor, — the best financier, the ablest judge, the most capable administrator, the most conspicuous literary figure of his time, he yet was without democratic sympathies, and quite failed to see that the infringement by the British government of popular rights justified the breaking loose which resulted in the United States. For his shortcoming he was made to atone most bitterly. With his life in his hand he fought for his losing cause. Exiled at last, with his fortune confiscated, his sons ruined, his daughters dying broken-hearted, — with calamity overwhelming almost every being, almost every institution he cared for, he lived a pensioner until he sank into his welcome grave. The pathetic story is unrolled in these extracts, the editing of which leaves much to be desired. (See sect. 1371.)   J. K. H.

—— History of the colony of Massachusetts-Bay, 1628–91. Boston. 1764.

—— History of the province of Massachusetts-Bay, 1691–1750. Boston. 1767.

—— History of the province of Massachusetts Bay, 1749–74. London: Murray. 1828.   [961

A work of high importance as the first connected history of Massachusetts from its foundation to the beginning of the Revolution. Vols. I and II published in Boston, 1764, '67: vol. III not until 1828, nearly fifty years after the writer's death. Written in the intervals of a pressing public career; for the most part, as regards the first two vols. at least, it was the first thought that went to the printer, the writer finding no time for revision. The shortcomings are grave. There are unfortunate gaps, the historian failing to make note of important events which should have been considered. In the author's circumscribed view the relations of the story he is telling to the general world movement are imperfectly apprehended. The style is quite unrelieved by any picturesqueness. Hawthorne said of it that "a duller book never came from the brain of mortal." Making every deduction, however, it is a work of great value. Hutchinson had access to many documents which have since perished. He is in the main accurate, and when he reaches the period during which he himself was a great political figure, the calmness of his tone and his general candor are remarkable. The third volume has most interest. **J. K. H.**

Johnson, Edward. History of New England, 1628-52 [*running title*, The wonderworking Providence of Sion's Saviour in New England]. London. 1654.

——*Same.* (In Massachusetts Hist. Soc. Collections, v. 12, 14, 17, 18.) Boston. 1814-19. [962

"The London publisher saw fit to alter this upon the title-page to *The history of New England;* but in the head-lines of the pages the title chosen by the author is followed throughout. A history of New England the book is not, but rather a history of Massachusetts down to the year 1651. Among the New England histories it has the distinction of having been the first to appear in print, for it was printed in London in 1653 (dated 1654). It was printed anonymously, but its author is known to have been Captain Edward Johnson, selectman and town clerk of the town of Woburn in Massachusetts. . . . The hot zeal, the narrow partisanship, the confident dogmatism, which characterized so much of Puritanism, have in him a striking example. . . . While he gives much valuable information, especially as to the successive planting of new towns and churches in Massachusetts, he is not seldom inaccurate." J. F. Jameson, *The history of historical writing in Am.*, pp. 29-40.

Josselyn, John. Account of two voyages to New-England, 1638, 1663. London. 1674.

——*Same,* 2d ed. London. 1675.

——*Same.* (*In* Mass. Hist. Soc. Collections, ser. 3, v. 3.) Boston. 1833.

——*Same.* Boston : W. Veazie. 1865. [963

The only critical edition of the two voyages together is that published in 1865. Josselyn was chiefly an observer of nature (see his *New England's rarities*, in *Transactions* of Am. Antiquarian Soc. IV), and hence his narratives in this volume consist chiefly of accounts of the author's voyages across the ocean, of the weather, plants, animals, native inhabitants of

New England. He visited Boston and points on the Maine coast. The account of the first voyage is a very slight production; that of the second is much longer and more important. In this he devotes more space to the English settlers, describes Boston, comments unfavorably on the inhabitants of New England because of their independency in religion. "His history," says Ch. Deane, "is often erroneous." He returned home in 1671, "heartily weary."

H. L. O.

Knight, *Mrs.* **Sarah Kemble.** Journal, 1704-5, ed. by Theodore Dwight. N. Y. 1825. Albany. 1865. [964

"The *Journal* kept by Mistress Sarah Kemble Knight, a dame of Boston — buxom, blithe, and debonair — who in October, 1704, being then thirty-eight years of age, a wife and a mother, traveled on horseback from Boston through Rhode Island and southern Connecticut to New Haven, a journey of five days; thence in December, to New York, a journey of two days; returning home by the same route, and reaching Boston in March, 1705. In the pauses of her journey each day, she carefully jotted down her adventures and her own comments upon them, doing this with no little sprightliness and graphic power. . . . Her *Journal*, published for the first time in 1825, is an amusing little book, and has special value as a realistic picture of rural manners in New York and New England in the first decade of the eighteenth century." Moses Coit Tyler, *A history of American literature*, v. 2, p. 97.

Lechford, Thomas. Plain dealing ; or Newes from New-England : a short view of New-England's present government, both ecclesiasticall and civil, compared with the anciently-received and established government of England. London. 1642.

——*Same.* (*In* Massachusetts Hist. Soc. Collections, v. 23. 1833.)

——*Same ;* ed. with notes and introd. by J. Hammond Trumbull. Boston. 1867. [965

"Full of valuable information relating to the manners and customs of the colony, written by an able and impartial hand." C. Deane, in *Narrative and critical hist. of Am.*, 3 : 351.

Levett, Christopher. Voyage to New England. See Massachusetts Historical Society, sect. 304. [966

Love, W. DeLoss, Jr. Fast and thanksgiving days of New England. Boston: Houghton. 1895. $3. [967

A very thorough and exhaustive, but discriminating and interesting work. A culture-historical work of permanent value. **E. C. R.**

Lowell Institute, Boston. Lectures by members of the Massachusetts Historical Society on subjects relating to the early history of Massachusetts. Boston. 1869. [968

This volume contains a series of thirteen lectures delivered in 1869, and separately published by the Society. They concern the early institutions and policy of Massachusetts, chiefly under the first charter. Of special value are the lectures by Dr. Ellis, one on the *Aims and purposes of the founders of Massachusetts*, and the other on *The treatment of intruders and dissentients*. Out of these have grown his *Puritan age in Massachusetts*. In the *History of grants under the Great Council for New England*, S. F. Haven supplements and corrects the list of those grants given by Palfrey. *The first charter and early religious legislation*, by Joel Parker, is one of the most important monographs extant on the early policy of Massachusetts. The volume is one of great interest both to the student and general reader.   H. L. O.

McManus, Blanche (Mrs. M. F. Mansfield). Voyage of the Mayflower. (Colonial monographs, no. 1.) N. Y.: Herrick. 1897.   [969

The series of colonial monographs is intended to present terse but authoritative sketches of some of the most interesting, important, and decisive events that led up to the founding of the American republic. This volume contains only seventy-two pages, is cleverly illustrated, and gives an account of the movements of the Pilgrims from England to Holland, and from Holland to America. It is accurate and appreciative, and is more scholarly than are many more pretentious works.   C. M. A.

Mason, *Capt.* John. Brief history of the Pequot war. See Massachusetts Historical Society, sect. 296.   [970
— DEAN, JOHN WARD, *ed.* Capt. John Mason, the founder of New Hampshire: including his tract on Newfoundland, 1620, etc., with a memoir by Charles Wesley Tuttle. (Prince Soc. Publications.) Boston. 1887.
                                                  [971

This book is similar in plan to Baxter's *Gorges* (sect. 944). In the memoir is brought together all that is known about the European career of Mason. In this and other essays, particularly that on Mason's *Plantations on the Piscataqua*, his American projects are described. His charters and will are here printed, and also such correspondence of his as can be recovered. Of special importance is the light thrown on the history of the Laconia Company in the monograph on Mason's *Plantations*. The biographical and editorial work in this volume is thorough and exhaustive.   H. L. O.

Massachusetts and the Commissioners, 1662–66. See Massachusetts Historical Society, sect. 296.   [972
Massachusetts Bay, Company of the. Records to the embarkation of Winthrop and his associates. See American Antiquarian Society, sect. 230.   [973
Massachusetts Bay Colony. Charter, 1629. See Old South Work, sect. 368.   [974

Massachusetts. Body of Liberties. See Massachusetts Historical Society, sect. 304.
                                                  [975
Mather, Cotton. MARVIN, ABIJAH PERKINS. Life and times of Cotton Mather; or A Boston minister of two centuries ago. Boston: Congregational Sunday-School and Pub. Soc. [c. 1892.]   [976

This is a voluminous biography, dry, and conventional in treatment; a chronicle of the events of a busy man's life. Based on Mather's diary and other reliable sources, it is full of valuable facts. These facts are, however, badly arranged and without other nexus than that of time. No attempt is made to give Mather's place in New England history or theology, and consequently the work has neither historical background nor depth. It has, however, substantial merits in that it is accurate and full of details of Mather's public and domestic life. It is temperate and fairly impartial, though the author has great admiration for the subject of his biography and is anxious to relieve him of the charges brought against him, notably of superstition and belief in witchcraft.   C. M. A.

— POOLE, WILLIAM FREDERICK. Cotton Mather and Salem witchcraft. Boston. 1869.
                                                  [977

Mr. Poole here defends, vigorously and ably, Rev. Cotton Mather against the charge of having promoted the spread of the witchcraft craze, at Salem, Massachusetts, in 1692. Not only was Mr. Poole well equipped for the discussion, but he knew how to marshal his facts with telling effect. No stronger vindication of Mather has yet appeared, and no attempt to fix criminal responsibility upon him has been so ably controverted. Incidentally, some discrepancies in Calef's *More wonders* are noticed. Mr. Poole handles his opponents without gloves, but makes no loose or ill-grounded statements.   S. A. D.

Mather, Increase. Relation of the troubles which have hapned in New-England, by reason of the Indians there, 1614–75. Boston. 1677.
— Early history of New England; with introd. and notes by Samuel G. Drake. Boston : for editor. 1864.   [978

An elaborate edition of this famous source together with Mather's *Historical discourse concerning the prevalency of prayer, wherein is shown that N. England's late deliverance from the rage of the heathen is an eminent answer to prayer*. The text is reliable but introd. and notes crowded with affectations and of little or no value. See *Hist. mag.*, May, 1864, pp. 191, 192, for another view.
                                                  H. W. H.

Mather papers. See Massachusetts Historical Society, sect. 311.   [979
Maverick, Samuel. Account of New England in 1630. See Massachusetts Historical Society, sect. 337.   [980
Minot, George Richards. Continuation of

the history of the province of Massachusetts Bay, 1748–65; with introductory sketch of events from its original settlement. Published according to act of Congress. Boston. 1798–1803. 2v. [981

This is a continuation of Hutchinson's *History of Massachusetts Bay*, based on such material as could be found at that time in the state and dealing chiefly with the internal history. The work covers the administrations of Shirley, Phips, Pownal and Bernard. It was Judge Minot's intention to continue his history to 1775, but he died before he could do this, and the second volume, unfinished, was published posthumously. The work is inferior to that of Hutchinson both in plan and in arrangement, yet it contains much important information and comment and is written in a graceful and pleasing style. C. M. A.

This work, had its author lived to complete it, would have formed an introduction to the history of the Revolution in Massachusetts. It is written by a trained lawyer and judge, and is filled with sober and weighty discussion of political and constitutional questions. It, of course, is written from the American standpoint, but it does not betray that intensity of partisanship which some later writers have shown. It is one of the best of the older state histories. Its style is clear and concise. It may be read with profit in connection with the third volume of Hutchinson's *History of Massachusetts* and Bradford's *State papers*. H. L. O.

Moore, George Henry. Final notes on witchcraft in Massachusetts. Boston : Cupples. 1885. [982

Besides being Dr. Moore's final word in his discussion with Mr. Goodell, an Appendix deals with the legality of the court which tried the witchcraft cases. Dr. Moore emphatically denies its legality. There is also a history of the Massachusetts General Court records. Cotton Mather's agency in the witchcraft troubles is severely denounced. (Read with this Poole's vindication, sect. 977.) The discussion is chiefly important to that class of students who wish to leave no stone unturned, and for bringing out facts, in the form of citations and footnotes, that show exhaustive research. Dr. Moore argues with much force, and with thorough knowledge, though not always in a strictly judicial temper. S. A. D.

—— Notes on the bibliography of witchcraft in Massachusetts. See American Antiquarian Society, sect. 237. [983

—— Notes on the history of slavery in Massachusetts. N. Y.: Appleton. 1866. [984

This book was prepared to controvert the view, often expressed during the slavery controversy, that slavery was never legal in Massachusetts. The author shows by careful citation of facts and authorities that this view is false. He reviews thus the history of the enslavement of Indians, of their exchange in the West Indies for negroes, and of the direct trade in slaves carried on by provincial Massachusetts with Africa. The author also traces the growth of an anti-slavery sentiment in the colony, but finds no proof of its existence, except in the minds of individuals,

prior to the period of the American Revolution. No attempt is made to give literary form to the material in the book, but it is a most thorough and authoritative collection of data on the subject. H. L. O.

—— Notes on the history of witchcraft in Massachusetts. See American Antiquarian Society, sect. 234. [985

Moore, George Henry, *et al.* Witchcraft in Massachusetts. See Massachusetts Historical Society, sect. 337. [986

Morrell, William. Account of New England. See Massachusetts Historical Society, sect. 286. [987

Morton, Nathaniel. New-England's memoriall. Cambridge. 1669.

—— New England's memorial; [ed.] by John Davis. Boston. 1826.

—— *Same;* with [extracts from] Bradford's History, etc. Boston : Cong. Pub. Co. 1855. New ed. 1878. [988

This purports to be a history of New Plymouth from its settlement to 1669, with some account of the fortunes of the Leyden Separatists in Europe. The writer was for a long time Secretary of Plymouth Colony, and hence had a good opportunity to give original information. But the larger part of the book is, as Morton admitted in his preface, an outline of Bradford's *History*, to which he had access in manuscript. Some additional information was obtained from Winslow's writings. The only part of the book which has even any literary merit is that which has come from these sources. The rest possesses neither literary nor historical value. H. L. O.

Morton, Thomas. New English Canaan. London. 1632.

—— *Same;* [ed.] by Charles Francis Adams. (Prince Soc. Publications.) Boston. 1883. [989

The contents of this volume are an elaborate memoir of Thomas Morton by the editor, and a critical reprint, with notes, of Morton's *New English Canaan.* Morton was a royalist libertine transplanted into New England, who therefore speedily became an object of distrust and attack by the settlers in the neighborhood of Merrymount. He in turn labored against the Puritans both in England and in the colonies, so long as he had strength and opportunity. The book which he wrote and dedicated to the Commissioners of Plantations, at the head of whom was Archbishop Laud, is the production of an erratic mind, and contains a mixture of truth and error about New England, its aboriginal and English inhabitants. "It is," says the editor, " the author's sense of humor which gives to the *New Canaan* its only real distinction among the early works relating to New England." But its interest is such as to justify the able editing which it here receives. H. L. O.

Mourt, George. Relation or iournall of the beginning and proceedings of the English plantation at Plimoth. London. 1622.

——Mourt's Relation : or Journal of the plantation at Plymouth ; with introduction and notes by Henry Martyn Dexter. Boston : Wiggin. 1865. [990

This relation was edited with care by Alexander Young, and printed in his *Chronicles of the Pilgrims*, but Dexter's edition contains notes and a critical introduction by an antiquarian whose knowledge of the Old Colony has not been surpassed. In some minute points it improves upon Young's edition, and probably does for the *Relation* all that modern scholarship can accomplish. But in the preparation of the text — as in other instances of American bookmaking — antiquarianism has veritably run mad. So anxious were the editor and publishers to reproduce the original with exactness that they have been as careful to preserve the misprints as the genuine parts of the text. H. L. O.

Mourt's Relation, "a daily journal of the first twelve months (Sept., 1620, to Dec. 11, 1621), so called from the name, ' G. Mourt,' subscribed to the preface, but doubtless written by Bradford and Winslow. The standard edition is that of 1865, with notes by Dr. H. M. Dexter." Franklin B. Dexter, in *Narrative and critical hist. of Am.*, 3 : 290.

Neal, Daniel. History of New England, containing an impartial account of the civil and ecclesiastical affairs of the country to 1700 ; appendix containing present Charter, ecclesiastical discipline, and municipal laws. London. 1720. 2v. 2d ed. 1747. 2v. [991

Neal wrote in 1719, and brought his history down to the year 1700. His chief authorities were Winslow, Morton, Wood, Josselyn, Increase and Cotton Mather, and Hubbard, but he used also contemporary pamphlets and letters, and obtained by inquiry some private information. His work was, therefore, superior to anything of the kind that preceded it. He depended to a large extent on Mather's *Magnalia*, but his attitude is that of one who wishes to be impartial. This is shown in his condemnation of the Puritans for their treatment of the Quakers, and in his criticism of their attitude toward witchcraft. Though he deals chiefly with political, military, and religious questions, he has an interesting chapter, largely condensed from Josselyn, describing the state of New England ; and he has paid some attention to legislative history, as an abridgment of the laws and ordinances of New England, which is printed in his appendix, attests. His style is often sprightly and he displays a sense of humor. For some aspects of the revolution of 1688-9 his work is still useful. C. M. A.

Nevins, Winfield S. Witchcraft in Salem village in 1692. Boston: Lee. 1892. $1.25. [992

The author aimed at writing a popular book on the subject of witchcraft. He reviews the earlier cases, gives a good deal of the testimony, and adds brief sketches of the lives of the accused persons. So far the book meets the requirements of those who are looking for a condensed, yet fair, narrative. As regards the causes of this insolvable mystery, Mr. Nev-

ins advances a theory of his own which is interesting, if not convincing. He defends Cotton Mather. S. A. D.

New England primer : a reprint of the earliest known edition ; with many facsimiles and reproductions, and an historical introd. ed. by Paul Leicester Ford. N. Y. : Dodd. 1899. [c. 1897.] $1.50. [993

" Contains in a condensed form the essential features of the expensive illustrated edition of the New England primer edited by Mr. Ford and published in 1897. See notice, ' Weekly record,' P. W., October 16, '97." *Publisher's weekly*, 56 : 867.

New England's Jonas cast up in London, 1647. See Massachusetts Historical Society, sect. 293. [994

New Hampshire grants. Documents relating to the controversy. See New-York Historical Society, sect. 354. [995

New Hampshire province. Records and court papers, 1680–92. See New Hampshire Historical Society. Coll., v. 8. 1866. [996

Northend, William Dummer. The Bay Colony : a civil, religious and social history of the Massachusetts colony, 1624–50. Boston : Estes. 1896. $2. [997

" This is a well-written epitome of the story which has been told so many times in the larger histories. The introduction treats of Plymouth colony and the work antecedent to the foundation of Massachusetts Bay. . . . The settlements at Cape Ann led to the larger movement of the Bay Colony proper. . . . Of necessity, the story is founded on Winthrop's journal, and copious extracts are drawn from that masterly piece of history. If the general reader can be induced to read the original for himself, this book will have served a very useful purpose. . . . The book is interesting and agreeable, as much detail encumbering the larger histories is stripped off or avoided. It ends rather precipitately, with the death of Winthrop." *American historical review*, 2 : 534.

Oliver, Peter. The Puritan commonwealth : an historical review of the Puritan government in Massachusetts, to the abrogation of the first charter. Boston : Little. 1856. [998

An account of colonial Massachusetts from the point of view of an ardent churchman and upholder of aristocratic ideas. Peter Oliver was a descendant of the Olivers who at the time of the American Revolution stood stoutly with the Tories. He has no love for Puritanism. While the tone of Mr. Oliver is thus that of a belated cavalier and prelatist, he is well informed and able. The work has value as a counter-weight to the numerous presentments of New England Puritanism quite too partial. J. K. H.

Orr, Charles, *ed.* History of the Pequot war : the contemporary accounts of Mason, Underhill, Vincent and Gardener ; reprinted from the Collections of the Massachusetts Historical Society, with additional notes and an introd. Cleveland: Helman-Taylor. 1897. $2.50. [999

Contents : A brief history of the Pequot war . . . ; by Maj. John Mason, with introd. by Thomas Prince. Boston. 1736.—Newes from America; by Captaine John Underhill. London. 1638.—A true relation of the late battell fought in New-England, between the English and the Pequet salvages, by Philip Vincent. London. 1638.—Leift Lion Gardener his relation of the Pequot warres [extract].

Palfrey, John Gorham. Compendious history of New England to the first general congress of the Anglo-American colonies. Boston: Houghton. (c. 1873.) [v. 1–2 first pub. 1865.] 4v. $6. [1000

The character of these volumes can best be indicated by stating what parts of Mr. Palfrey's larger work they do not contain. All of the notes and references are omitted, as are the chapters in which Mr. Palfrey traced the progress of events in England during the 17th century. In some parts also the text of the original has been greatly cut down and merely the most important statements or passages retained. As the last two volumes of the original contain no special chapters on English history, those appear in the *Compendious history* with least change. Distinct headings have been supplied for the chapters throughout. To the serious reader the omission of the notes and references involves irreparable loss. He will not care to use the *Compendious history* if the original is accessible. H. L. O.

—— History of New England during the Stuart dynasty. Boston: Little. 1858–64. 3v. [1001

Mr. Palfrey was the leading representative of the so-called filio-pietistic school of New England historians. He was a thorough-going defender of Puritan Massachusetts. He seemed to think that the position which that colony sought to occupy within the British system was a normal one. He justified her ecclesiastical policy, as well as her attitude toward the home government. In these volumes may be found the facts and arguments upon which that view is based, and by which it is supported. It is a most thorough, painstaking work, indispensable to the student and serious reader. The notes are especially valuable. Rhode Island, New Hampshire, and Maine inadequately treated. H. L. O.

—— History of New England from the revolution of the 17th century to the revolution of the 18th. Boston: Little. 1875–90. 2v. (With preceding period, 5v., net $20.) [1002

The same point of view is held in these volumes as in their predecessors on the 17th century. Here may be found the colonial side of the controversies between the representatives and the royal governors in provincial Massachusetts, and of the discussions which immediately preceded the outbreak of the war for independence. These volumes also contain a good account

of the intercolonial wars, so far as they affected New England. A high degree of accuracy in the statement of facts is attained throughout. But we have by no means so exhaustive a treatment of the 18th as the earlier work furnishes of the 17th century. The MS. of the second volume was left incomplete at the author's death and was issued with some additions and corrections by his son. H. L. O.

Papers concerning the attack on Hatfield and Deerfield by Indians, Sept. 19, 1677. See Bradford Club, sect. 252. [1003

Penhallow, Samuel. History of the wars of New England with the eastern Indians, 1703–13, and 1722–25. Boston. 1726.

—— *Same* [with memoir and notes by W. Dodge]. Cin. 1859. [1004

" The chief English authority for Queen Anne's and Lovewell's wars is [Penhallow's *History*]. The author was an Englishman, who, in 1686, at 21, had come to America to perfect his learning in the college at Cambridge, designing to acquire the Indian tongue, and to serve the Society for the Propagation of the Gospel among the Indians. Trade and public office, however, diverted his attention, and he became a rich tradesman at Portsmouth. His book is of the first value to the historian, and the object of much quest to the collector, for it has become very rare. . . . It has been reprinted in the first volume of the N. H. Hist. Soc. *Collections*, and again in 1859 at Cincinnati." Justin Winsor, in *Narrative and critical hist. of Am.*, 5: 424.

Pepperrell, *Sir* **William.** PARSONS, USHER. Life of Sir William Pepperrell. Boston. 1855. [1005

Dr. Parsons, in his *Life of Pepperrell*, besides using the Pepperrell papers collected by Dr. Belknap for his *History of New Hampshire*, " sifted a mass of papers found in an old shed on the Pepperrell estate. This lot covered the years 1696–1759. . . . Unremitting research yielded gain to Dr. Parsons in other directions." Justin Winsor, in *Narrative and critical hist. of Am.*, 5: 436.

Pepperrell papers. See Massachusetts Historical Society, sect. 321. [1006

Peters, Samuel. General history of Connecticut; by a gentleman of the province. London. 1781.

—— *Same ;* with additions by Samuel J. McCormick. N. Y.: Appleton. 1877. $1.50. [1007

An entertaining but wholly untrustworthy account of Connecticut by an exiled and embittered Tory. Fiction and fact are so run together in the narrative that their separation is well-nigh impossible. The most famous part of the book is the alleged code of New Haven laws popularly called " Blue laws." Of the character and derivation of this " code " the most satisfactory discussion is that by W. F. Prince in the *Report* of the American Hist. Assoc. for 1898. E. G. B.

Pike, Robert. PIKE, JAMES SHEPHERD. The new Puritan. N. Y.: Harper. 1879. $1. [1008

This book contains an account of the life and opinions of a Puritan layman of the more liberal type, who lived in Massachusetts in the latter half of the 17th century. He freely criticised the policy of the General Court toward the Quakers and the attitude of the magistrates toward witchcraft at Salem. He was punished twice for his independence, but was not expelled from the colony. The book is chiefly important for the letters and documents which it contains and for the proof which it furnishes of the inadequate guarantees of personal liberty which existed in the American colonies. Its later chapters contain the record of Major Pike's share in the first intercolonial war.   H. L. O.

Popham colony, Papers relating to. See Massachusetts Historical Society, sect. 334. [1009

Prince, Thomas. Chronological history of New-England [to 1633]. [V. 1.] Boston. 1736. New ed. [complete]. Boston. 1826. [1010

For forty years Thomas Prince was pastor of the South Church, Boston. In the intervals of a busy life he collected, for the times, a large library of books and manuscripts on American history. With great diligence and care he prepared the material for his *Chronological history.* His aim was to present an epitome of history in the briefest and most accurate form. A strictly chronological arrangement and the simplest form of statement were chosen. As an introduction to the work he traced general chronology from the creation till the accession of James I. Then began the work proper — New England chronology. Of this only a part was completed, viz.: that from the accession of James I. till a few months subsequent to the landing of Winthrop and his colonists in Massachusetts Bay. Large use is made of Bradford's *History of New Plymouth.* Prince was one of the most accurate of compilers. He was intensely critical, though living a century before the art of criticism began generally to be applied to the preparation of historic material. The quaint statement given in his preface of what he considered to be his duty as an historian in the matter of accuracy and fairness is one of the gems of early New England literature.

                                        H. L. O.

"Even as a fragment, the *Chronological history of New England* is the most scholarly piece of literary work wrought in America during the colonial time." Moses Coit Tyler, *A history of American literature,* v. 2, p. 150.

Reynolds, Grindall. King Philip's war, with special reference to the attack on Brookfield. See American Antiquarian Society, sect. 237. [1011

Sewall, Rufus King. Ancient dominions of Maine. Bath, Me. 1859. [1012

Contains an account of the discovery and settlement of the region between the Kennebec and Penobscot Rivers and a narrative of the interminable Indian wars which characterize the history of that region.

The first part is now largely obsolete. The second part preserves the local traditions and also brings together extracts from records accessible when the book was compiled. Of interest only to the student of local history.   E. C.

Sewall, Samuel Edmund. Diary, 1674–1729. (Massachusetts Hist. Soc. Collections, ser. 5, v. 5–7.) Boston. 1878–82. 3v. [1013

A minute record of the daily doings of a prominent Bostonian who lived at about the middle of the Puritan period of Massachusetts history. In interest it ranks with the diaries of Evelyn and Pepys. For 36 years the author was a judge of the Superior Court, and during the last 10 of this period he was Chief Justice. The *Diary* throws some light on the political conflicts of the time, but is chiefly important for the material it contains which illustrates social life. All the events of the household, the neighborhood, the Church, the wider circle of acquaintances are set forth with perfect naturalness. Of course the leading feature is the religious devotion of the Puritan. The work is admirably edited.   H. L. O.

— CHAMBERLAIN, NATHAN HENRY. Samuel Sewall and the world he lived in. Boston: De Wolfe. 1897. $2. [1014

Based on a careful study of Sewall's *Diary* and *Letter-book.* Text largely made up of extracts from the *Diary.* Brings together in brief compass many of the most interesting events in Sewall's career. Generally readable.   E. C.

— TIFFANY, *Mrs.* NINA (MOORE). Samuel E. Sewall: a memoir. Boston: Houghton. 1898. $1.25. [1015

As a lawyer of high standing Mr. Sewall "rendered peculiar services to the cause in drafting anti-slavery measures or in helping rescue the fugitive; and this professional talent he concurrently applied to the amelioration of the laws affecting the status of women. . . . Mrs. Tiffany has found her material but scanty — no great store of letters even; and her additions to what was already accessible in print are chiefly in the province of the rights, not of man, but of woman." *Nation,* 67: 72.

Smith, *Capt.* **John.** Advertisement for the unexperienced planters of New England. See Massachusetts Historical Society, sect. 299. [1016

—— Description of New England, 1616. See Massachusetts Historical Society, sect. 302. [1017

—— New England's trials. See Massachusetts Historical Society, sect. 329. [1018

Standish, *Capt.* **Miles.** JOHNSON, HENRY. Exploits of Myles Standish. N. Y.: Appleton. 1897. $1.50. [1019

"The author of the following story has used the license of probability and inference to supply the deficiency of accredited facts" (*Preface*). The book is thoroughly uncritical and unreliable — slangy.

                                        H. W. H.

Strachey, William. Account of the Popham colony. See Massachusetts Historical Society, sect. 306. [1020

Tiffany, Mrs. Nina (Moore). Pilgrims and Puritans: the story of the planting of Plymouth and Boston. Boston: Ginn. 1888. 60c. [1021

This book is a compilation for the use of children, made from Bradford's *History of Plymouth*, Bradford and Winslow's *Journal*, the beginning of Winthrop's *Journal*, and a few of the other original authorities on the founding of the Old Colony and of Boston. Frequent quotations are made from the quaint and simple language of the originals, and thus the story is made more lifelike than otherwise would be possible. In style the book is well adapted for its purpose; but the story is not carried far enough to give an adequate picture of the founding of Plymouth or Boston. H. L. O.

Trelawny papers, and Baxter MSS. relating to the settlement of Maine. See Maine Historical Society, sect. 282, 283. [1022

Trumbull, Benjamin. Complete history of Connecticut, civil and ecclesiastical, to 1764. New Haven. 1818. 2v. New London: Utley. 1898. $5. subs. [1023

The reprint contains an index lacking in the original. Citations are usually made to the edition of 1818. Written from original sources. The standard history of Connecticut to 1764. An appendix to vol. I contains several valuable documents. E. C.

Trumbull, Henry. History of the Indian wars. Boston. 1841. New ed., rearranged, cor. and enl. Phil. 1854. [1024

This book appeared originally, without date, as a *History of the discovery of America . . .* by the Rev. James Steward, and has been republished, under different titles, many times. According to Dr. J. Hammond Trumbull, it was "written by Henry Trumbull, then of Norwich, when about seventeen years old." "It was vigorously denounced in Field's *Indian bibliography*. . . . Col. Peter Force is quoted as having said that he found twenty-two chronological errors on a single page." A. McF. Davis, in *Narrative and critical hist. of Am.*, 6: 651.

Trumbull, James Hammond, *ed.* The true-blue laws of Connecticut and New Haven and the false blue laws invented by the Rev. Samuel Peters; to which are added specimens of the laws and judicial proceedings of other colonies and some blue laws of England in the reign of James I. Hartford. 1876. [1025

This volume was compiled for the purpose of defending Connecticut and New Haven against the aspersions of the Rev. Samuel Peters in his *History of Connecticut* (1781); and at the time of its publication it served a useful end. It contains a learned introduction on the origin and history of "blue-laws," though the greater part of the volume is taken up with well-

known laws and codes of Connecticut, New Haven, and other colonies. The attitude of the author toward Peters is uncritically hostile. Dr. Trumbull's contention in chapter VIII that Peters forged the laws he prints has been disproved, though with unnecessary sarcasm, by Prince, *Report* of the American Historical Association, 1898, pp. 97–138. C. M. A.

Underhill, Capt. John. History of the Pequot war, 1638. See Massachusetts Historical Society, sect. 302. [1026

Upham, Charles Wentworth. Salem Witchcraft. Boston. 1867. 2v. [1027

Of this work no better description is possible than that given by Lowell in his learned essay on witchcraft: "He (Mr. Upham) has written not merely a history of the so-called Salem witchcraft, but has made it intelligible by a minute account of the place where the delusion took its rise, the persons concerned in it, whether as actors or sufferers, and the circumstances which led to it. . . . We are made partners in parish and village feuds, we share in the chimney corner gossip, and learn for the first time how many mean and merely human motives . . . gave impulse and intensity to the passions of the actors in that memorable tragedy. . . . Mr. Upham's minute details, which give us something like a photographic picture of the indoor and out-door scenery that surrounded the events he narrates, help us materially to understand their origin and the course they inevitably took. In this respect the book is original and full of new interest." The volumes "are in some respects a clinical lecture on human nature, as well as on the special and epidemical disease under which the patient is laboring." The account Mr. Upham has given of the phenomena of demoniacal possession, of the trials, of the conduct of the accused, of the reaction against the delusion, also contribute to make his book a notable contribution to the social history of New England. Upham lays heavy responsibility for the tragedy on the shoulders of Cotton Mather. A learned and able reply to this charge by W. F. Poole may be found in *North American review*, April, 1869. See sect. 976–7. H. L. O.

Vane, Sir Henry. HOSMER, JAMES KENDALL. Life of young Sir Henry Vane, Governor of Massachusetts Bay and leader of the Long Parliament. Boston: Houghton. 1888. $4. [1028

A thorough and critical biography. Treats of Vane in connection with the history of his times. The author sympathizes strongly with the political and religious views of Vane, but is not unduly partial. He uses original, as well as secondary sources, throughout. From the *Order books* of the Council of State under the English Commonwealth he throws new light on his subject's career. Vane's writings and the views which have been held concerning him are critically discussed. He is set forth as a connecting link between New and Old England, and a forerunner of the freedom and democracy which have come to prevail in both. H. L. O.

Vincent, P. True relation [of the Pequot war]. See Massachusetts Historical Society, sect. 302. [1029

Waymouth, *Capt.* **George.** ROSIER, JAMES. True relation of the voyage of Capt. George Waymouth. See Massachusetts Historical Society, sect. 304.   [1030

Wheelock, Eleazar. Narrative, 1762. See Old South Work, sect. 368.   [1031

Wheelwright, John. Writings, including his fast-day sermon, 1637, and his Mercurius Americanus; and a memoir by Charles H. Bell. (Prince Soc. Publications.) Boston. 1876.   [1032

The reader of this volume will turn with greatest interest to the *Memoir* of Wheelwright and to the famous *Fast Day sermon* which aroused such excitement in Massachusetts in 1637. If he is interested in Indian history and land claims, he will read the Wheelwright deed of 1629 and examine Mr. Bell's defence of its authenticity against the attacks of Mr. James Savage. The *Mercurius Americanus* is Wheelwright's defence of himself against the charges urged in the *Rise, reign and ruine of the Antinomians.* This pamphlet and the sermon are genuine specimens of Puritan polemic and argumentative literature. The editing is of the high character found in all the publications of the Prince Society.   H. L. O.

Williams, John. Biographical memoir of the Rev. John Williams; with papers relating to the early Indian wars in Deerfield. Greenfield, Mass. 1837.   [1033

" The narrative of the Rev. John Williams, who was taken captive to Canada, is the chief contemporary account " of the Indian attack on Deerfield in 1704. Justin Winsor, in *Narrative and critical hist. of Am.,* 5: 185.

Williams, Roger. Letters, 1632–82; ed. by John Russell Bartlett. (Narragansett Club. Publications, v. 6.) Providence. 1874. Providence. 1882. $6.50.   [1034

This is the standard edition of Williams' correspondence. Nearly all of the letters here brought together have appeared elsewhere in print, as in the *Winthrop papers,* Backus's *History of the Baptists,* and the various biographies of Williams, but here they may be seen together and in the order in which they were written. The collection is of the highest value, both to the student of New England history and to those who are interested in the career of Williams. Said J. R. Lowell, in his essay on *New England two centuries ago:* "There are two men above all others for whom our respect is heightened by their letters — the elder John Winthrop and Roger Williams. . . . Charity and tolerance flow so noticeably from the pen of Williams that it is plain they were in his heart."   H. L. O.

— ELTON, ROMEO. Life of Roger Williams. London. [1853.] Providence. 1853.   [1035

" Largely based on Knowles's *Memoir,* but contains some new matter, notably the *Sadlier correspondence.*" C. Deane, in *Narrative and critical hist. of Am.,* 3: 378.

— KNOWLES, JAMES DAVIS. Memoir of Roger Williams. Boston. 1834.   [1036

"A minute and conscientious biography; . . . but it is written with a strong bias in favor of Williams where he comes in collision with the authorities of Massachusetts." C. Deane, in *Narrative and critical hist. of Am.,* 3: 378.

— STRAUS, OSCAR SOLOMON. Roger Williams, the pioneer of religious liberty. N. Y.: Century Co. 1894. $1.25.   [1037

A reliable and trustworthy sketch of the life and opinions of the apostle of soul liberty. The author shows that he is familiar with the writings of Williams, with the material concerning him which is to be found in Masson's *Life and times of Milton,* in the works of John Cotton and of the other New England writers who treat of his career. On most important points he takes issue with Dr. Dexter and other writers who criticise Williams and defend the conduct of Massachusetts. His view of Williams is the one toward which opinion is now gravitating. The style in which the book is written is rather dull.   H. L. O.

Williams, Samuel. Natural and civil history of Vermont. Walpole, N. H. 1794. 2d ed., enl. and corr. Burlington, Vt. 1809. 2v.   [1038

This history was written more than a century ago by a clergyman who had been a close observer of the events he related, if not an actor among them. A large part of his work was devoted to the natural history of the region which became Vermont and to the Indians who inhabited it. The account of the French and Indian wars which appears in the second was not in the first edition. A clear, and so far as it goes, a trustworthy account of the controversy with New York follows. Letters and public documents are quoted at considerable length. After the history of the war of the Revolution along the northern frontier has been reviewed, the author returns to the internal affairs of the territory. An outline of the dealings with Congress, and with the neighboring states, accompanied by an account of the negotiations with the British, follows, which led up to the admission of Vermont as a state. The work is well written and holds an honorable place among the histories of the state.   H. L. O.

Winslow, Edward. New England's salamander discovered. See Massachusetts Historical Society, sect. 298.   [1039

— WINSLOW, *Rev.* WILLIAM C. Governor Edward Winslow, his place and part in Plymouth colony. See American Historical Association, sect. 247.   [1040

Winthrop, John. Journal of the transactions and occurrences in the settlement of Massachusetts and the other New England colonies. Hartford. 1790.

—— History of New England, 1630–49; from his original MSS., with notes by James Savage.

Boston. 1825–6. 2v. New ed. Little. 1853. 2v. [1041

The journal of John Winthrop, father and founder of the Colony of Massachusetts Bay, as a source for our early history is equalled in value only by the similar record of William Bradford, Governor of Plymouth. While Winthrop's name has sometimes suffered detraction, Mr. Brooks Adams, for instance, in the *Emancipation of Massachusetts*, painting him as the weak and culpable tool of tyrant priests, the only fair way is to regard him as a man of the most solid worth. In the struggles of his time, he was himself a combatant in the fore-front, always unassuming, brave and honest. The *Journal* (the first volume of which, preserved in Connecticut, was published in 1790; the second, found in the tower of the Old South, in Boston, at a later time) is quaint, not always clear, often short-sighted, — nevertheless the narrative of a wise, well-meaning man. The merits of the disputes are no more distorted in Winthrop's rendering than was inevitable. The antagonists whom he fought are not unworthily belittled or misrepresented; sometimes, the war being over and opportunity coming for a calm retrospect, the tone toward the rival, so far from being acrimonious, becomes magnanimous, even affectionate. This is especially to be noted in the later references to Henry Vane. James Savage, the best antiquarian of his day, has supplemented the *Journal* with notes of great value. J. K. H.

See, also, Jameson's *History of historical writing in America*, p. 25.

— TWICHELL, JOSEPH HOPKINS. John Winthrop, first Governor of the Massachusetts colony. (Makers of America.) N. Y.: Dodd. [c. 1891.] $1. [1042

Mr. Twichell has written a brief but delightful biography of the elder Winthrop. The work is based on well-known authorities, all readily accessible, and the author has dealt with the personal and private life of Winthrop, and not, so far as could be avoided, with the political history of the colony. No more attractive biography than this is to be found in the series. C. M. A.

— WINTHROP, ROBERT CHARLES. Life and letters of John Winthrop, Governor of the Massachusetts Bay Company. Boston: Ticknor. 1864–7. 2v. 2d ed., enl. Little. 1869. 2v. Net $7. [1043

This is one of the chief authorities for the life of the founder of Massachusetts. The first volume is one of the choicest examples of Puritan biography extant. It is made so by the extracts which are given from the early diaries and correspondence of Winthrop. It also contains material of the greatest importance for explaining the origin of the settlement of Massachusetts. The second volume closely follows Winthrop's *Journal*, but it also includes important state papers. The work is indispensable to the student of Puritanism, whether in Old or New England. H. L. O.

Winthrop, *Mrs.* Margaret (Tyndal). EARLE, *Mrs.* ALICE (MORSE). Margaret Winthrop. (Women of colonial and revolutionary times.) N. Y.: Scribner. 1895. $1.25. [1044

Mrs. Earle's appreciative biography of the wife of John Winthrop, the elder, is based in the main on the *Winthrop papers*, Winthrop's *Journal*, and Winthrop's *Life of Winthrop*, though the author has had access to manuscript materials also. The book gives a strikingly interesting picture of a woman's work and influence in Boston 250 years ago, and written, as it is, in a picturesque style, and being at the same time scholarly and reliable, it will appeal not only to the general reader for whom it is intended, but also to every student of the social and domestic life of the Massachusetts Bay colony. C. M. A.

Winthrop papers. See Massachusetts Historical Society, sect. 305. [1045

Wood, William. New England's prospect. See Prince Society, sect. 387. [1046

Young, Alexander. Chronicles of the first planters of the colony of Massachusetts Bay, 1623–36. Boston: Little. 1846. [1047

This volume contains a part of White's *Planters' plea*, the *Records* of the Massachusetts Company prior to its removal into New England, Higginson's *Journal*, and *New-England's plantation*, the *Humble request*, and a variety of other material relating to the founding of Massachusetts. Mr. Young was a learned antiquarian, and evidence of it appears in his notes and in the care with which the text of the documents has been edited. Though some of the material is now accessible elsewhere, this volume is still indispensable to the student of early Massachusetts history. H. L. O.

— Chronicles of the Pilgrim fathers, 1602–25. Boston: Little. 1841. [1048

This volume contains a reprint, of a part of Bradford's *History*, of Mourt's *Relation*, of Winslow's *Good newes from New England*, and of other less important sources relating to the founding of New Plymouth. They are edited with great care and learning by one of the best of the early Massachusetts antiquarians. In spite of the fact that Bradford's *History* has since been printed in full and Mourt's *Relation* has again been edited, Mr. Young's collection is still of great value both for its notes and for a part of its text. H. L. O.

MIDDLE COLONIES

Acrelius, Israel. History of New Sweden; tr. with introd. and notes by W. M. Reynolds. (Hist. Soc. of Pennsylvania. Memoirs, v. 11.) Phil. 1874. [1049

This is a careful translation, with notes, of the most important original work concerning New Sweden which has proceeded from any Swedish author. It reviews the history of the Swedish settlement on the Delaware, and follows the fortunes of that people till after the relations between Pennsylvania and the lower counties had been finally settled. The customs and secular pursuits of the Swedes also receive considerable attention. The last half, and more, of the book is devoted to the history of the Swedish churches along the Delaware and to their condition at the time the author wrote — middle of the 18th century. As the writer was provost over the Swedish congregations in America, and pastor of the church at Christina, he possessed ample opportunities for gaining information.   H. L. O.

Asher, Georg M. Bibliographical and historical essay on the Dutch books and pamphlets relating to New Netherland. Amsterdam. 1854–67.   [**1050**

"In the bibliography of New Netherland, the first place must be given to [Asher's *Essay*]. It embodies the results of work in the royal library and in the royal archives at the Hague ; at Leyden in the library of the University and in that of Dr. Bodel Nyenhuis, rich in maps, and particularly in the Thysiana Library, in which he found a rich field ; and at Amsterdam, among the extensive stock of Mr. Frederic Muller, without whose assistance, the author says, the book would not have been written. In his introduction he gives a succinct sketch of the history and geography of New Netherland." Justin Winsor, in *Narrative and critical hist. of Am.*, 4: 439.

Atwood, William. Case of Chief-Justice Atwood, 1713. See New-York Historical Society, sect. 355.   [**1051**

Bartram, John. Observations in travels from Pennsilvania to Onondaga, Oswego and the Lake Ontario ; [with] a curious account of the cataracts at Niagara, by Peter Kalm. London. 1751. Reprinted for G. P. Humphrey, Rochester. 1895. $1.50.   [**1052**

"Bartram was born in Pennsylvania, and made this journey in company with Conrad Weiser, the agent sent by Pennsylvania [1737] to hold friendly conference with the Iroquois. . . . Bartram's principal object was the study of the flora of the country, in which pursuit he acquired such a reputation as to attract the notice of Linnæus, but his record throws light upon the people which came in his way." Justin Winsor, in *Narrative and critical hist. of Am.*, 5: 244.

Broad advice to the United Netherland provinces. See New-York Historical Society, sect. 353.   [**1053**

Burgher rights in New Amsterdam. See New-York Historical Society, sect. 356. [**1054**

Clarendon papers concerning New York and New England affairs soon after 1660. See New-York Historical Society, sect. 354. [**1055**

Cobb, Sanford Hoadley. Story of the Palatines: an episode in colonial history. N. Y. : Putnam. 1897. $2.   [**1056**

The author has neglected the important German sources. His book "fulfills our expectations only as a sympathetic presentation of the *story* of the Palatines, and will do much to arouse popular interest in

the subject. The treatment of the early stage of the migration to England is superseded by the work of Mr. Diffenderffer [*Publications* of the Pennsylvania German Society, 1897]. . . . The *history* of the Palatines, however, written from the original sources and covering the entire migration, is yet to be written." M. D. Learned, in *American historical review*, 3: 553.

Colden, Cadwallader. Letters on Smith's "History of New York." See New-York Historical Society, sect. 354.   [**1057**

Dankers, Jasper, and Peter Sluyter. Journal of a voyage to New York, 1679–80 ; tr. and ed. by Henry C. Murphy. (Long Island Hist. Soc. Memoirs, v. 1. Brooklyn. 1867.) [**1058**

In 1679, "New York was visited and carefully described by two very keen and intelligent Dutch observers, the so-called Labadist emissaries, Jasper Dankers and Peter Sluyter. . . . The worthy brethren . . . left an interesting journal of their visit, which was discovered a few years ago ; and they made some quite artistic pencil sketches of the city withal, which are extremely precious as historical documents." John Fiske, in *Dutch and Quaker colonies*, 2: 61, 74.

Denton, Daniel. Brief description of New York ; new ed., with introd. and notes by Gabriel Furman. (Gowans' Bibliotheca Americana. 1.) N. Y.: Gowans. 1845. [**1059**

"Daniel Denton, the son of a minister in Connecticut, removed, in 1644, into the province of New York, where he rose to distinction both as a landowner and as a politician. In 1670, apparently with the view of attracting immigration to that province, he published, in London, *A brief description of New York*, — a book of twenty-two pages, uncommonly graphic and animated. He kept closely to the facts that had come under his own eyes." Moses Coit Tyler, in *A history of American literature*, v. 2, p. 207.

Donck, Adriaen van der. Description of New Netherland. See New-York Historical Society, sect. 353.   [**1060**

Dunlap, William. History of the New Netherlands, province of New York, and state of New York, to [1789]. N. Y. 1839–40. 2v.   [**1061**

See note under Lambrechtsen's *New Netherlands*, sect. 1078, beyond.

Du Ponceau, Peter Stephen, and J. Francis Fisher. Memoir on the history of the treaty made by William Penn with the Indians, 1682. See Pennsylvania, Historical Society of, sect. 373.   [**1062**

Easthampton MS. of the Duke of York's laws. See New-York Historical Society, sect. 352.   [**1063**

Ferris, Benjamin. History of the original settlements on the Delaware. Wilmington. 1846.   [**1064**

"Gives a very full account of New Sweden, extracted from works already published in English, and is interesting and valuable as identifying and describing many of the places mentioned." G. B. Keen, in *Narrative and critical hist. of Am.*, 4: 497.

Field, R. S. The provincial courts of New Jersey. See New Jersey Historical Society. Coll., v. 3. 1849. [1065

Fiske, John. The Dutch and Quaker colonies in America. Boston: Houghton. 1899. 2v. $4. [1066

"The latest addition to Mr. John Fiske's popular historical series is plainly marked by the well-known characteristics of its author — wide reading, affluence of interesting facts and ideas, firm grasp of materials, great literary skill, fondness for episodes, keen enjoyment of the picturesque, much ingenuity in hypothesis and explanation, proneness to generalization, ardent Americanism, and greater conformity to truth in the picture than in the single stroke. Still further, no subject that occurs in the series is better suited to his peculiar genius than the Dutch and Quaker colonies; perhaps no other is so well suited to it. Until recently, and even now in diminished degree, the larger sources of interest in our early history have been found in Virginia and New England, . . . but . . . from the point of view furnished by the word 'people,' Massachusetts and Connecticut, and even Virginia, are tame and monotonous compared with Pennsylvania or even with New York. . . . Such is Mr. Fiske's opportunity, and he makes the most of it. . . . The book is thoroughly characteristic of its author, and will be accounted one of the brilliant pieces of historical writing of its period." B. A. Hinsdale, in *Dial* (Chicago), 27: 357.

Gerard, James Watson. Old streets of New York under the Dutch. N. Y. 1874. [1067

This was presented as a paper before the New York Historical Society. It is one of the many topographical descriptions of New Amsterdam. In imagination a circuit is made of the old city, attention being called to the places where town life in its various phases centred. Some personal and social reminiscences are interwoven to give life to the picture. The literature relating to New York City abounds in essays of this character, which, without in any case being very valuable, doubtless serve to maintain an antiquarian interest in the subject. H. L. O.

Gordon, Thomas F. History of New Jersey, to the adoption of the federal constitution. Trenton: Fenton. 1834. [1068

In this volume the general facts of New Jersey history may be found clearly and concisely set forth. The most valuable part of the book is that which deals with the proprietary period, and with the land system as it was when New Jersey became a royal province. In the preparation of this original authorities were used, which cannot always be said of the later parts of the work. With the volume is bound up a topographical and statistical gazetteer of New Jersey in 1833. H. L. O.

—— History of Pennsylvania, to 1776. Phil. 1829. [1069

"It has never enjoyed much popularity. Its style is labored." F. D. Stone, in *Narrative and critical hist. of Am.*, 3: 508.

Hazard, Samuel. Annals of Pennsylvania, from the discovery of the Delaware, 1609–82. Phil. 1850. [1070

This is an elaborate and authoritative documentary history of the settlements on Delaware River and Bay from their origin till the founding of Pennsylvania. The title, therefore, is somewhat misleading, as the book forms rather an introduction to the history of Pennsylvania than the annals of that province itself. It is specifically concerned with the Dutch and Swedes on the Delaware. The materials have been collected from many sources and carefully sifted and edited. The book contains many extracts from original sources, as well as full reprints of valuable documents. The text binds these together in chronological order. The work is an authority of the highest value on the period of which it treats, though its importance has been somewhat diminished by more recent publications of New York and Pennsylvania documents. H. L. O.

Holm, Thomas Companius. Short description of the province of New Sweden, now called by the English, Pennsylvania. See Pennsylvania, Historical Society of, sect. 372. [1071

Horsmanden, Daniel. The New York conspiracy, 1741–2. N. Y. 1810.

—— The negro conspiracy; ed. by Wm. B. Wedgwood. N. Y. 1851. [1072

Originally published in 1744, as *Journal of the proceedings in the detection of the conspiracy, etc.* "The main printed source respecting the Negro plot of 1741." Justin Winsor, in *Narrative and critical hist. of Am.*, 5: 242.

Janvier, Thomas Allibone. In old New York. N. Y.: Harper. 1894. $1.75. [1073

New York writers on the history of their beloved city rarely go further than to treat of its topography and its social life. The streets, the Kissing Bridge, Love Lane, the Collect, the pleasure gardens of the olden time, and other similar localities chiefly awaken their interest. The genuine history of the city meantime lies buried and forgotten. Each writer contents himself with repeating the substance of what others have said before him, only attempting to make it, if possible, a little more agreeable to the popular taste. Mr. Janvier's book is one of the best of this class. H. L. O.

Jogues, Isaac. Narrative of a captivity among the Mohawk Indians, and a description of New Netherland in 1642–3; with a memoir of the holy missionary, by John Gilmary Shea. (In New-York Hist. Soc. Collections, ser. 2, v. 3.) N. Y. 1857. [1074

Father Jogues was a Jesuit missionary whom the Dutch rescued from captivity among the Mohawks. "The letters of this courageous and zealous servant of the Church to his superiors teem with information concerning the Indians, whom he endeavored to Christianize and at whose hands he died." B. Fernow, in *Narrative and critical hist. of Am.*, 4: 421.

Johnson, Sir William. GRIFFIS, WILLIAM ELLIOT. Sir William Johnson and the Six Nations. (Makers of America.) N. Y.: Dodd. [c. 1891.] $1.   [1075

Practically an Indian history of the Mohawk valley, the result of some local knowledge and tradition, and a certain amount of original study. In endeavoring to condense his abundant matter into the narrow limits of a "series" volume, the author has dwelt longest on the earlier and less generally known portion of Johnson's life, and given but a cursory review of his later and more active years, concerning which much has been written by others. This, of course, is unequal treatment; perhaps satisfying the reader who seeks entertainment, but sending the more serious student to other historians. Mr. Griffis' style is popular and picturesque; but frequently betrays haste and sometimes its free-and-easy tone becomes undignified.   R. G. T.

— STONE, WILLIAM LEETE, JR. Life and times of Sir William Johnson. Albany: Munsell. 1865. . 2v.   [1076

The subject of this extended biography was prominently connected with colonial affairs from 1746 till his death in 1774. He, more than any one else, opened up the Mohawk valley and central New York to English settlement. In these volumes Mr. Stone has described with accuracy and in detail the career of Sir William Johnson in all its relations. As his private life was less important than his public acts, the author has properly devoted much space to the history of his times. We have in this work the best and most thorough account of Indian relations in New York during the 18th century which has yet been published. But the method of treatment is rather mechanical, and the result is a book which in many parts is heavy and uninteresting. Not a sign appears in its pages of that insight and imaginative power which give such vividness to the narrative of Parkman. The reader will find outlines of the proceedings of interminable Indian conferences; but he will look in vain for a picture of what an Indian conference was. The political conflicts of Clinton's administration are described with evident approval of the Governor's course, but the traditional American view of the controversies preceding the Revolution is presented.   H. L. O.

Kapp, Friedrich. Die Deutschen im Staate New York während des achtzehnten Jahrhunderts. N. Y.: Steiger. 1884. [c. 1867, '84.] $1.   [1077

This volume appeared as the first of a series under the editorship of Carl Schurz, the object of which was to describe the life of Germans who had settled in America. It comprises the most interesting part of Kapp's *History of the Germans in the state of New York*, — a book long since out of print, — revised and improved. Its subject is the settlement of the Palatines on the Hudson and in the Mohawk valley, and the results which proceeded from it. Much information concerning local topography and family names and connections is given, and this is so used as to greatly enrich and enliven the narrative. In this book the distinguished author has given one of the best exhibitions of his style, and has produced one of the best social historical studies of which our literature can boast.   H. L. O.

Lambrechtsen van Ritthem, Nicolas Cornelis. Short description of the discovery and subsequent history of the New Netherlands [tr. from the Dutch]. (In New-York Hist. Soc. Collections, ser. 2, v. 1.) N. Y. 1841.   [1078

"Its value consists principally in the fact that the author had access to the papers of the West India Company, since lost, and that it instigated research and called attention to the history of their state among New Yorkers, several of whom now set to work writing histories. [*History of the state of New York*, by John V. N. Yates and Joseph W. Moulton, — only two parts published, 1824–26, covering 1609–1632; *Natural, statistical and civil history of the state of New York*, by James Macauley, 1829; *History of the state of New York*, by F. S. Eastman, 1833; *History of the New Netherlands, province of New York and state of New York*, by Wm. Dunlap, 1839.] Not one of them is of great value now, the documents procured in the archives of Europe having thrown more and frequently. different light on many facts. Many statements are given as based on tradition, others are absolutely incorrect." B. Fernow, in *Narrative and critical hist. of Am.*, 4: 431.

Leisler's rebellion, Papers on. See New-York Historical Society, sect. 354.   [1079

Miller, John. Description of the province and city of New York in 1695. (Gowans' Bibliotheca Americana, 3.) N. Y.: Gowans. 1862.   [1080

This little book constitutes No. 3 of Gowans' "Bibliotheca Americana," a series of reprints of rare pamphlets relating to America, which was started some forty years ago, but was discontinued after a few numbers had been issued. The volume is edited by J. G. Shea, who contributes an introduction and notes. The author was chaplain of the two companies of grenadiers stationed in New York, and acted in that capacity from 1693 to 1695. While here he collected many data about the province, including maps and plans of its chief cities, towns, forts and churches. But on his way home he was captured by a French privateer and had to throw his papers overboard. During his imprisonment, however, he wrote out, chiefly from memory, the account of the province here given. The text shows the bias of the clergyman, and is chiefly noteworthy for the low estimate it puts on the morals of the inhabitants, and the insistence of its author that a bishop should be sent over. The book also contains one of the most valuable of the early maps of New York City, as well as other maps and plans. In it the author also elaborates a plan for the conquest of Canada. Mr. Shea's notes contain valuable information on the status of the English Church in New York and on the Indians. The book, though small, contains one of the best general accounts we have of provincial New York.

H. L. O.

Morris, Lewis. Papers, 1738–46. See New Jersey Historical Society. Coll., v. 4. 1852.

[1081

Muster rolls of New York provincial troops, 1755–64. See New-York Historical Society, sect. 357.

[1082

New York City. Local and family history in the 18th century. See New-York Historical Society, sect. 354.

[1083

New York City and County. *Court of lieutenancy.* Journal, 1686–96. See New-York Historical Society, sect. 355.

[1084

New York State. Documentary history of the state of New York; arranged by E. B. O'Callaghan. Albany. 1849–51. 4v. [1085

A collection of miscellaneous documents, correspondence and other material relating to the colonial history of New York, published by the state after being collected and arranged by one of its leading archivists. Special attention may be called to the *Leisler papers* and *Johnson papers* in v. 2, to the various papers on ecclesiastical relations in v. 3, and to the *Papers relating to the Six Nations* in v. 4. This series is one of the chief storehouses of material on the history of colonial New York.

H. L. O.

—— Documents relating to the colonial history of the state of New York, procured by John R. Brodhead; v. 1–11 ed. by E. B. O'Callaghan, v. 12–15 by B. Fernow. Albany. 1853–83. 15v. [1086

A memorial from the New York Historical Society induced the Legislature of New York, in 1839, "to authorize the appointment of an agent who should procure from the archives of Europe the material [to fill gaps in the official records of colonial New York]. Mr. John Romeyn Brodhead, who, by a residence of two years at the Hague as Secretary of the American legation, seemed to be specially fitted for, and was already to some extent familiar with, the duties expected from him, was appointed such an agent in 1841, and, after four years of diligent search and labor, returned with 80 volumes of manuscript copies of documents procured in Holland, France, and England, which were published under his own and Dr. E. B. O'Callaghan's supervision . . . eleven volumes quarto, including index volume. The historical value of these documents, which the State procured at an expense of about $14,000, cannot be estimated too highly." B. Fernow, in *Narrative and critical hist. of Am.*, 4: 409.

V. 1–2, of the above named, contain Holland documents, 1603–1678; v. 3–8, London documents, 1614–1782; v. 9–10, Paris documents, 1631–1774; v. 11, Index. Under the editorship of Mr. Fernow, four more volumes have since been published, as follows: v. 12.

Documents, relating to Dutch and Swedish settlements on the Delaware River; v. 13. Documents, relating to towns on the Hudson and Mohawk Rivers; v. 14, Documents, relating to early colonial settlements principally on Long Island; v. 15 (v. 1 of a new series entitled "State Archives: New York in the Revolution") containing Proceedings of the Provincial Congress, the Committee of Safety, and Convention of N. Y. relating to military matters; with lists of soldiers in the N. Y. line of the Continental Army.

New York State. *Secretary of State.* Calendar of historical manuscripts in the office of the Secretary; ed. by E. B. O'Callaghan. Albany. 1865–6. 2v. [1087

The publication of these two volumes followed immediately on the issue of the *Calendar of land papers.* Mr. O'Callaghan was their editor, and the model followed was the first volume of the *Calendar of colonial papers* issued from the British Public Record Office under the editorship of Mr. Sainsbury. The entries are in most cases even briefer than those of Mr. Sainsbury, and experience has shown that the latter were too brief to relieve the student of the necessity of using the documents themselves. It may then be urged in this connection that, if the system of publishing calendars of documents shall be pursued further in this country, the entries be made considerably fuller. The documents in the 1st part of this work relate to the Dutch period, and those in the 2d part to the English period, closing with 1776. The documents calendared in the 1st part are those in the register of the Provincial Secretary's office, Council minutes, correspondence, ordinances, writs, Fort Orange records, Delaware papers, and land papers. Of these the ordinances, with additional ones, have been translated and printed in full by Mr. O'Callaghan in his *Laws and ordinances of New Netherland;* a few of the Fort Orange records have been printed in full in the *New York colonial documents,* v. 13; while most of the Delaware papers appear — with many others — in *New York colonial documents,* v. 12. Nearly all of the land papers here are of dates earlier than those calendared in the volume of land papers. Part second contains a calendar of the mass of original papers on which was based the action of the Governor and Council as an executive body, in matters both civil and military. They consist of letters, petitions, claims, accounts, etc., and were not entered on the minutes of the Council but were filed away for reference. They have been arranged in chronological order, and even the brief entries which appear in this volume indicate their great importance for the history of New York as an English province. Some — but not many, as compared with the whole number — have been printed in full in the *New York colonial documents.* The list of records in the office of the Secretary of State, given in the preface, is especially valuable.

H. L. O.

O'Callaghan, Edmund Burke. History of New Netherland; or New York under the Dutch. N. Y.: Appleton. 1846–8. 2v.

[1088

When this work was written, nothing of value, save original sources, existed on New Netherland history. Most people then derived their ideas concerning that period from Diedrich Knickerbocker. O'Callaghan's *History* came as a revelation, throwing a flood of light upon a period previously unknown. It is emphatically a work of original research, and still maintains its place as the leading authority upon the times of which it treats. Vol. 1 carries the reader to the close of Kieft's administration, and vol. 2 is devoted wholly to the career of Stuyvesant. Of special interest is the history of the encroachments of the English on New Netherland during the decade preceding its fall. The whole is written in a vigorous style, with copious citations and translations of documents, both in the text and the appendices.   H. L. O.

Pearson, Jonathan, *tr.* Early records of the city and county of Albany, 1656–75. Albany : Munsell. 1869. 1872. $10.   [1089

This volume contains the translation by Professor Pearson of two out of the seven volumes of early Dutch records which are preserved in the office of the clerk of Albany County, New York. The records which appear here set forth a part of the business which was done before the chief officials at Fort Orange, whether they went by the title of commissary, vice-director, deputy, or secretary. After the English conquest secretary became the regular title. The whole is valuable for the light it throws on Dutch procedure, especially in reference to transfers of property, and on phases of Dutch local government. The translation may be accepted as correct. The volume is supplied with a full index of names.
H. L. O.

Pearson, Jonathan, *et al.* History of the Schenectady patent in the Dutch and English times. Albany: Munsell. 1883.   [1090

This is a carefully prepared and valuable work. It was edited and published in the main from the papers of the late Professor Pearson of Union College, who was a very persistent investigator of the history of Albany (city and county) and of the lower Mohawk valley. The volume as a whole throws much light on the land system of New York in the colonial period ; it is a study of one of the large grants, made in Dutch times and confirmed by English governors, to trustees, to be managed for the benefit of the inhabitants upon the grant. In addition to the history of the patents Professor Pearson gives much material on the French wars, and an account of Indian trade at Schenectady. The material of the book is largely documentary and is of the highest authority.
H. L. O.

Penn, William. Letters. See Pennsylvania, Historical Society of, sect. 371.   [1091
— CLARKSON, THOMAS. Memoirs of the private and public life of William Penn. London. 1813. 2v. Phil. 1814. 2v.
— —— *Same;* new ed., with pref. by W. E. Forster. London. 1849.   [1092

This is one of the earlier, but yet one of the most valuable, of the lives of Penn. Its author — the famous English anti-slavery agitator — was not a Quaker, but he had a wide acquaintance among the sect, and was one of the best and most sympathetic

exponents of its views. (See his *Portraiture of Quakerism.*) His life of Penn is written, not from the standpoint of a critic, but of an admirer. But it is based on a thorough knowledge of Penn's writings and ideas, and it sets forth authoritatively and in agreeable style the Quaker view of his life and work. Proud supplied most of the material for Clarkson's account of the relations between Penn and his province. The work closes with an important and suggestive discussion of Penn as the Christian statesman. In London in 1849 a new edition of Clarkson's *Life* was published, with a preface by W. E. Forster, in which reply was made to the criticisms of Penn by Macaulay.   H. L. O.

— DIXON, WILLIAM HEPWORTH. William Penn: an historical biography. London. 1851.
— —— History of William Penn ; new ed. [rewritten]. London : Hurst. 1872.   [1093

" The most popular account that has appeared. Its style is agreeable, and it is full of interesting facts picturesquely grouped. In some cases, however, the authorities quoted do not support the inferences which have been drawn from them, and the historical value of the book has been sacrificed in order to add to its attractiveness." F. D. Stone, in *Narrative and critical hist. of Am.*, 3 : 506.

— FISHER, SYDNEY GEORGE. The true William Penn. Phil.: Lippincott. 1900 [1899]. $2.   [1094

" The volume takes its place with *The true Benjamin Franklin* by the same author, and *The true George Washington* by Mr. Paul Leicester Ford. In the case of William Penn, it was not possible to produce a very sensational story, because he has not been so idealized as have the two others. The value of the biography does not consist, therefore, in the dissipation of mists of error. . . . In place of this there is a very interesting description of the conditions of life in the time when Penn was growing up." *Dial* (Chicago), 28 : 91.

— JANNEY, SAMUEL M. Life of William Penn. Phil. 1852. 6th ed. Lippincott. 1882.   [1095

" A trustworthy book. All that was in print at the time it was written was used in its preparation, and it is to-day [1884], historically, the best work on the subject. . . . It treats . . . more of William Penn the Quaker than of William Penn the founder of Pennsylvania." F. D. Stone, in *Narrative and critical hist. of Am.*, 3 : 505.

Pennsylvania. *Commission to locate the Site of the Frontier Forts of Pennsylvania.* Report. Harrisburg. 1896. 2v.   [1096

" These volumes embody the result of the investigations of a commission appointed by the Governor under an Act of Assembly, passed in 1893, providing for ascertaining the sites of the provincial forts. . . . They are valuable not only because they tell us why the provincial map of the state along the Blue Mountains and on the frontier farther westward is dotted with fortified posts to secure each eligible position, and because they tell us what service these posts rendered, but also because they refute the commonly received opinion that the Quakers, who were supposed to have held a majority in the Assembly prior to the Revolution, refused to erect forts or raise troops for the defence of the inhabitants of the frontier against the hostile French and Indians. It is time that the truth in this matter should be known, and we may well forgive the poor printing and the still poorer binding" of this valuable report. "It would appear from these volumes that, so far from the province having been defenceless during the French and Indian wars, that there were erected during the campaigns of 1755–58, and that of 1763 (Pontiac's war), no less than 207 forts, large and small, on the frontier." *Pennsylvania magazine*, 20 : 257.

Porter, Peter Augustus. Champlain, not Cartier, made the first reference to Niagara Falls in literature. Niagara Falls, N. Y.: Author. 1899. $1.　　　　　　[1097

The author shows, by comparison of original texts, that the allusions to Niagara Falls in Lescarbot's *Histoire de la Nouvelle France* (1609), heretofore attributed to Jacques Cartier, are really quotations from Champlain's *Des sauvages*, published some five years before; and that there is no warrant for the oft-repeated statement that Cartier, in 1535, was the first white man to hear of these falls, that distinction passing to Champlain, who heard of them in 1603. Mr. Porter's citations are convincing; the typography, involving double columns of side-notes, is awkward.　　F. H. S.

Proud, Robert. History of Pennsylvania from 1681 till after the year 1742. Phil. 1797–98. 2v.　　　　　　　　　　[1098

Among the older histories of Pennsylvania this is the standard work; written from the Quaker standpoint. It contains an introduction on Quakerism and William Penn. The original documents and other material are much more valuable to the modern student than is the text. Judged by present standards, the text in all parts, but especially for the period subsequent to the death of William Penn, is inadequate. So far as it goes, however, it is accurate and authoritative. The style is heavy and uninteresting.
　　　　　　　　　　　　H. L. O.

Reed, William B. The Acadian exiles, or French neutrals, in Pennsylvania. See Pennsylvania Historical Society, sect. 375.　[1099

Representation of New Netherland. See New-York Historical Society, sect. 353.

　　　　　　　　　　　　　　[1100
Schuyler, *Mrs*. Catherine. GRANT, *Mrs.* ANNE. Memoirs of an American lady; with sketches of manners and scenery in America. London, Edin. 1808. Boston. 1809. 2v.

— —— *Same ;* with memoir by James Grant Wilson. Albany: Munsell. 1876.　[1101

The author, commonly known as "Mrs. Grant of Laggan," was the widow of a Scotch clergyman and came to be a somewhat prominent literary light of Edinburgh. The daughter of a British army officer,

she spent her early years in America, and was petted as a child by the subject of this book, Mrs. Philip Schuyler, aunt of Gen. Philip Schuyler. There is much in it of Albany customs, the country place of a well-to-do colonist, negro slavery, and the Indians. During a trip which the author took with her father through the woods to Oswego she saw the Mohawk chief Hendrick. While admiring the Schuylers and other New York leaders, she entertained a very poor opinion of the New Englanders, but the value of her recollections is greatly impaired by the fact that she left America at the age of thirteen and wrote this book almost forty years later. There are several editions, from that of 1808 to that of 1876, which has notes by Munsell and a memoir by James Grant Wilson.
　　　　　　　　　　　　F. J. S.

— HUMPHREYS, MARY GAY. Catherine Schuyler. (Women of colonial and revolutionary times.) N. Y.: Scribner. 1897. $1.25.
　　　　　　　　　　　　　　[1102

A kind of imaginary biography of the wife of General Philip Schuyler of Albany, New York. It makes the most of the very meagre information concerning her, and is much more of an interesting sketch of colonial and Revolutionary life in New York than a biography. There are many anecdotes and traditions, but no references. The author's comments and deductions connect much of the quoted matter.　　E. E. S.

"Mrs. Schuyler was the daughter of John Van Rensselaer, her mother was a Livingston, and she was in many respects a typical matron of her period — a period of which a very fair idea is given in this volume. . . . The chief value of the book lies in the glimpse it affords of family life and social customs among the colonial gentry and magnates in New York in the last half of the 18th century. . . . Life in the colonial period was as hard as circumstances could make it, and people in the position of the Schuylers had a sense of responsibility for those dependent on them now difficult to find anywhere." *Nation*, 67 : 78.

Schuyler, Philip. SCHUYLER, GEORGE WASHINGTON. Colonial New York: Philip Schuyler and his family. N. Y.: Scribner. 1885. 2v. $10 net.　　　　　[1103

This is a book of genealogy and family memoirs, with an abundant addition of history. The family whose career forms its subject is that of Philip Schuyler, Indian trader and grantee of large tracts of land, one of the founders of the prosperity of Albany in later Dutch and early English times. Under his son, Peter Schuyler, the influence of the family was greatly extended by long and distinguished service in war and Indian affairs, by increase of wealth, by civil office, and by intermarriages with several of the leading families of the province. The intermarriages give the author an opportunity to sketch the fortunes of the Van Cortlandts, Van Rensselaers, Livingstons and others. So closely were the Schuylers concerned with Indian affairs, that the author considers himself justified in recounting much of the history of relations with the Iroquois and the French during the colonial period. The Schuylers were Dutch, and that occasions a disquisition of nearly 200 pages on the history of

New Netherland. But the matter presented is reliable, and the book is a valuable commentary on many phases of social development in provincial New York. Taken all in all, it is the best book which exists on that subject. H. L. O.

Scot, George. The model of the government of East Jersey, in America. (In New Jersey Historical Society. Coll., v. 1.) [1104

Sharpless, Isaac. History of Quaker government in Pennsylvania. Phil.: Leach. 1898–99. 2v. $1.50 ea. (V. 1 originally pub. as A Quaker experiment in government. Phil.: Ferris. 1898. $1.50.) [1105

"The *Quaker experiment* of which President Sharpless treats in this little volume — a monograph it must fairly be called — is that endeavor to establish civil government on ethical principles which William Penn, in his letter to James Harrison August 25, 1681, termed 'an Holy experiment,' and which he ardently hoped he might then find room for in America, though not in England. The experience of seventy-five years, from the summer of 1681 . . . down to the summer of 1756, . . . this experience, it is, upon which President Sharpless has written this intelligent and fair-minded essay." Howard M. Jenkins, *American historical rev.,* 4: 165.

Shepherd, William Robert. History of proprietary government in Pennsylvania. (Columbia Univ. studies in history, etc., v. 6.) N. Y.: Macmillan. 1896. $4.50. [1106

Modestly announced by the author as an "outline," but in reality a detailed and thorough history of Pennsylvania, on its strictly political and governmental sides, during the period of proprietary control joined to an extended account of the land system of the colony. Liberal use has been made, and for the first time, of the Penn. MSS. in the possession of the Pennsylvania Historical Society. While not a general history of the colony, and hardly easy reading, the work has no equal in its field. W. MacD.

Simms, Jeptha Root. The frontiersmen of New York, showing customs of the Indians, vicissitudes of the pioneer white settlers, and border strife in two wars, with a great variety of romantic and thrilling stories never before published. Albany: Riggs. 1882. 2v. [1107

Originally published in 1845 as *History of Schoharie County and border wars of New York,* "both editions showing an industrious care to amass, with little skill in presentation." A. McF. Davis, in *Narrative and critical hist. of Am.,* 6: 659.

Smith, Samuel. History of the colony of Nova Cæsaria, or New Jersey, to 1721, with some particulars since. Burlington, N. J. 1765. 2d ed. Trenton. 1877. [1108

" Valuable to all examining the early history of the state, from the author's having had access to, and judiciously used, information obtained from sources not now accessible. He gives some interesting letters

from early settlers. . . . Although, as might naturally be expected, errors are occasionally found in it, Smith's *History of New Jersey* has ever been deservedly considered a standard work." W. A. Whitehead, in *Narrative and critical hist. of Am.,* 3: 454.

Smith, William. History of the late province of New-York, from its discovery to 1762. (New-York Hist. Soc. Collections, v. 4–5.) N. Y. 1829–30. 2v. [1109

This is still the best history of the province of New York. The author devoted little space to the Dutch and to the period of English proprietary government, and for those times he has been superseded by the detailed works of O'Callaghan and Brodhead. But within the period subsequent to the English Revolution, Smith is still without a successful rival. The father of the author was a prominent lawyer and orator, and played a part of some importance in public affairs subsequent to 1730. The author, a graduate of Yale, was one of the most cultured men who had then been reared in the colonies. He rose to higher rank than his father in the profession of the law, and also mingled actively in political life, ending his career as a loyalist exile. The second volume of his *History,* beginning with the administration of Gov. Cosby (1736), was not published during the author's life, because it dealt with events in which his father had been personally concerned. The material of the work throughout is drawn very largely from the journals of the Assembly and of the Legislative Council, principally from the former. It is strictly a political history, the narrative following a narrow channel, but one where the main current of provincial history may be found. The style is simple, concise, dry. The characterizations of men, parties and events are brief. So far as statement of fact is concerned, a high degree of accuracy is attained. The author sympathizes with the course of the Assembly [in its conflicts with the executive], but he does not make his preferences offensively prominent, statements of Cadwallader Colden (N. Y. Hist. Soc. Coll., 1868) to the contrary notwithstanding. This work ranks with Stith's *Virginia* and Hutchinson's *Massachusetts,* as one of the worthiest examples of historical literature produced in later colonial times. H. L. O.

Stevens, H., *comp.* Analytical index to the colonial documents of New Jersey in the state paper offices of England. (In New Jersey Historical Society. Coll., v. 5.) [1110

Stuyvesant, Peter. TUCKERMAN, BAYARD. Peter Stuyvesant. (Makers of America.) N. Y.: Dodd. 1893. $1. [1111

A useful and well-written account of the life of Stuyvesant and of the history of New Netherland during the last twenty years of its existence. The book also contains, in an introductory chapter, a sketch of the origin of the province and of its progress previous to the beginning of Stuyvesant's administration. The writer brings out clearly the absolutism of the executive, and the misuse which the Directors usually made of their unlimited power. The volume makes apparent the reasons for the failure of the Dutch at colonization here. One chapter contains a compact and valu-

able account of the topography and social condition of New Amsterdam just before the English conquest.
H. L. O.

Thomas, Gabriel. Historical and geographical account of the province and country of Pensilvania and of West-New-Jersey in America. London. 1698. Facsimile reprint for Henry A. Brady. N. Y. 1848. [**1112**

"In 1698 Gabriel Thomas published a small octavo of forty-six pages on West Jersey, in connection with a similar work on Pennsylvania, with a map of both colonies. He was then, it is thought, a resident of London, but he had resided in America about fifteen years, the information contained in the book being the result of his own experiences and observation. . . . The modes of life among the Indians, and the prevailing intercourse between them and the settlers were fully discussed, as well as the natural productions of the country and the improvements already introduced or in progress. . . . It was reprinted in lithographic facsimile in New York in 1848 for Henry Austin Brady." Wm. A. Whitehead, in *Narrative and critical hist. of Am.*, 3: 451.

Valentine, David Thomas. History of the city of New York. N. Y.: Putnam. 1853. [**1113**

Comes down only to 1750. Among the histories of the city published prior to 1884, this and Mrs. Lamb's "are of the most importance." Justin Winsor, in *Narrative and critical hist. of Am.*, 4: 440.

Van Rensselaer, Mrs. John King. The goede vrouw of Mana-ha-ta, at home and in society, 1609–1760. N. Y.: Scribner. 1898. $2. [**1114**

"Mrs. John King Van Rensselaer, by dint of patient ransacking of various collections of old family papers, has managed to piece together a rather readable picture of old Dutch and English-Dutch colonial home life. . . . Hitherto unexploited family papers furnish the basis of the book, but the authorities have not been neglected. As Mrs. Van Rensselaer's title implies, it is with the ways and doings of the matrons of Manhattan, rather than of their spouses, that her book is principally concerned." *Dial* (Chicago), 25: 353.

Vries, David Peterson de. Voyages from Holland to America, 1632–44. See New-York Historical Society, sect. 353. [**1115**

Whitehead, William Adee. East Jersey under the proprietary governments. (New Jersey Hist. Soc. Collections, v. 1.) 1846. 2d ed. enl. Newark. 1875. [**1116**

This book was first issued in 1846 as vol. 1 of the Collections of the New Jersey Hist. Soc. The edition to which reference is here made is a revision of its predecessor, into which has been incorporated material from the New York colonial documents and other sources. It is unsystematic, sketchy in parts, and written in poor style. But it is accurate, and is the work of one of the foremost students of New Jersey

history. It is the standard authority on the period of which it treats. In the notes and appendices it contains original material of considerable value ; also has valuable maps and plans. It is of great importance to the student of proprietary government. H. L. O.

—— *ed.* Documents relating to the colonial history of the state of New Jersey. 1631–1776. Newark. Patterson : State. 1880–99. 21v.
[**1117**

Wooley, Charles. A two years' journal in New York and part of its territories in America ; new ed. with introd. and notes by E. B. O'Callaghan. N. Y.: Gowans. 1860. [**1118**

The Rev. Charles Wooley or Wolley, a graduate of Emmanuel College, Cambridge, accompanied Sir Edmund Andros to New York in 1678 as his chaplain. Two years later he returned to England, and in 1701 he published in London this *Journal*, which describes the Indians whom he knew, but has little to say of the whites. It does, however, throw some light on the trade of New York, giving the prices of furs and other commodities. The notes contain sketches of many of the persons mentioned. F. J. S.

SOUTHERN COLONIES (ENGLISH)

Bacon's and Ingram's rebellion. See Massachusetts Historical Society, sect. 327. [**1119**

Baltimore, George *and* **Cecilius Calvert,** *barons.* BROWNE, WILLIAM HAND. George Calvert and Cecilius Calvert, Barons Baltimore of Baltimore. (Makers of America.) N. Y.: Dodd. [c. 1890.] $1. [**1120**

This work, which is seemingly a biography of the founders of Maryland, is in reality a history of the colony during the life of Cecilius Calvert. But two chapters are devoted exclusively to biographical details, and the remaining chapters have little to do with Calvert's personal history, though based upon the letters and official communications of the proprietor. The style lacks charm and the author is by no means always impartial in his judgment ; yet the work will serve as an introduction to the history of colonial Maryland from the point of view of the proprietors.
C. M. A.

Beverley, Robert. History of Virginia, in four parts ; with introd. by Charles Campbell. Richmond : Randolph. 1855. [**1121**

This work comes down to 1707, with a continuation to 1720. It was written primarily to correct Oldmixon, whose own account "was too faulty and too imperfect to be mended." Jefferson calls Beverley "concise and unsatisfactory," but this can apply only to the first book, which deals with the civil history and makes up only a third of the whole. The author had had experience in the public records of the colony, and the books treating the institutional life of the colony and the Indians are both full and satisfactory. The Indian section is particularly full, being based on Smith's and Hariot's accounts and illustrated by DeBry's engravings. The editor supplies a biographical introduction, and pronounces the style easy, unsophisticated and pleasing.   S. B. W.

Bozman, John Leeds. History of Maryland, 1633–60. Balt. 1837. 2v.   [**1122**

Written by a man who was thoroughly familiar with Maryland government and with the sources of her history. As a literary production the work is dull, but as a source of information for the student it is invaluable. The author in all cases used the original sources, and that with scrupulous care. He refers to all his authorities and prints many important documents in his appendices. The printing of the Maryland *Archives* since Bozman wrote has lessened the value of those appendices and of parts of the text, but the book as a whole has by no means been superseded. Viewed from the scientific standpoint it is one of the best of our state histories.   H. L. O.

Brown, Alexander. The first republic in America: an account of the origin of this nation, written from the records then (1624) concealed by the council, rather than from the histories then licensed by the crown. Boston: Houghton. 1898. $7.50 net.   [**1123**

A work of great importance, but difficult to read or use. Under a strict chronological arrangement, with hardly a trace of connected narrative form, are presented the important facts contained in the records of the Virginia Company, supplemented by others gleaned from the author's industrious researches, and interspersed with comment, correction and reflection. The disparagement of Capt. John Smith, abundantly shown in the author's *Genesis of the United States*, is here greatly intensified, while the plan of the work precludes extended discussion of the wider significance of events. The book contains invaluable material for history, but is itself annals rather than history.   W. MacD.

—— *ed.* Genesis of the United States: a narrative of the movement in England, 1605–16. Boston: Houghton. 1890. 2v. $15.   [**1124**

An invaluable collection of documents, the larger number previously unprinted, relating to the inception and first years of the Virginia colony. There is no narrative, but the documents are prefaced with necessary explanatory matter, and loosely connected by note or comment. The early history of Virginia here gains markedly in significance by being viewed, first, from the standpoint of previous attempts at colonization, and, after 1606, from the standpoint of influences and events in England. A feature of special value is an extended series of condensed biographies, filling half of vol. 2. The author is somewhat inclined to disparage the work of early writers on Virginia, and is particularly severe in his criticisms on Capt. John Smith, though not to such an extent as in his later volume, *The first republic in America.*   W. MacD.

Byrd, William. The Westover manuscripts; containing The history of the dividing line betwixt Virginia and North Carolina. Petersburg. 1841.

—— History of the dividing line, and other tracts, from the papers of William Byrd of Westover. Richmond: privately printed. 1866. 2v.   [**1125**

William Byrd of Westover was a Virginian of large fortune and English education, who took part, as one of the commissioners, in a survey of the dividing line between Virginia and North Carolina, in 1729. "Of the two expeditions that accomplished this labor, William Byrd kept a journal, which, after lying in manuscript upwards of a century, was first published in 1841, under the title given to it by its author—'The history of the dividing line.' In the peculiar qualities that distinguish this little book, it is almost unique in our colonial age; and it is without question, one of the most delightful of the literary legacies which that age has handed down to ours." Moses Coit Tyler, in *Hist. of Am. lit.*, p. 272.

Campbell, Charles. History of the colony and ancient dominion of Virginia. Phil. 1859.   [**1126**

This is the best general history of colonial Virginia for students' use. The narrative extends to 1781. The early portion is based on the now discredited publications of Capt. John Smith. Otherwise the work is sufficiently accurate.   E. C.

—— Introduction to the history of the colony and ancient dominion of Virginia. Richmond: B. B. Minor. 1847.   [**1127**

Based on insufficient materials and now to a great extent antiquated. Generally readable.

Carroll, B. R., *comp.* Historical collections of South Carolina. N. Y.: Harper. 1836. 2v.   [**1128**

Vol. 1 of this useful work contains a reprint, with notes and an introduction by the editor, of Hewatt's *Historical account of South Carolina.* Prior to the appearance of River's *Sketches*, Hewatt's was the best work extant on the colonial history of South Carolina. It still possesses value, owing to the special opportunities which the author enjoyed of obtaining original information. Vol. 2 contains 16 pamphlets, and extracts from works of the older writers, bearing on the early history of South Carolina. Of special importance among these are the *Description*, etc., by John Archdole; *The proceedings of the people . . . in 1719*, by F. Yonge; the *Description*, etc., attributed to Gov. Glen; and the text of the first set of *Fundamental constitutions.*   H. L. O.

Craig, Neville B. Washington's first campaign, death of Jumonville, and taking of Fort Necessity; also Braddock's defeat and the march of the unfortunate general explained by a civil engineer. Pittsburgh: Morse. 1848.   [**1129**

"Made up of papers from Mr. Craig's monthly publication, *The olden time*, published in Pittsburgh in 1846–1848, and reprinted in Cincinnati in 1876." Justin Winsor, in *Narrative and critical hist. of Am.*, 5: 576.

Drake, Samuel Adams. Making of Virginia and the middle colonies, 1578–1701. N.Y.: Scribner. 1893. $1.50. [1130

This book possesses much the same character as the author's *Making of New England*, though it shows a somewhat less intimate acquaintance with the subject than did his earlier volume. In this work he occasionally falls into error, as when, on p. 173, he implies that a trial of the claim of the Duke of York to West Jersey was held in England and a judgment rendered in the case, and when, on p. 178, he reports the tradition that Lord Delaware visited the bay which bears his name. His account also of the struggles in Pennsylvania which led to the issue of the Charter of Privileges in 1701 is so confused and inadequate as to be of no value. But in general the external events connected with the founding of Virginia and the middle colonies are correctly given, and the social traits of the settlers spiritedly depicted. The treatment of Long Island and of New York during the Dutch period is especially to be commended. It is a good book for the use of young people.   H. L. O.

Fiske, John. Old Virginia and her neighbours. N. Y.: Houghton. 1897. 2v. $4. [1131

Beginning with the movement which led to the colonization of Virginia, the author traces the settlement of the Southern colonies and their history until 1690. Two or three chapters in the second volume contain miscellaneous facts concerning this group of colonies in the 18th century. The materials used are well-known "relations," records, state histories and monographs, accessible in print. Secondary sources are not infrequently used where the originals were not difficult to procure. In the chapters on early Virginia the substantial accuracy of John Smith is warmly asserted. The cause of Virginia in its early controversy with Maryland is championed. Some new light is thrown on the later history of Maryland. A rapid sketch of Carolina history is given. The author writes in an interesting and popular style, but his treatment of the subject is unsystematic, and the work is not free from errors.   H. L. O.

Hariot, Thomas. Narrative of the first English plantation of Virginia ; first printed at London in 1588. London: Quaritch. 1893. [1132

The history of the unfortunate attempt of Sir Walter Raleigh to plant settlements on the coast of North Carolina, 1584–1590, is known from Hakluyt, who prints in his Collection the various official reports. One of the members of the first colony of 1585–86, who "remained to inhabit," was Thomas Hariot, whose *Narrative* was published by DeBry as the first part of his Voyages, accompanied by illustrations from the drawings of John White, also a colonist. These two authorities give us the first clear picture we have of the fauna and flora of eastern North Carolina and of the life and manners of the Indians. Later experience has verified most that had been written by these truthful and accurate observers. Their work has become the basis for modern accounts of the subjects treated by them.   S. B. W.

Hartwell, Blair, *and* **Chilton.** Present state of Virginia. 1696. See Massachusetts Historical Society, sect. 289. [1133

Hawks, Francis Lister. History of North Carolina. Fayetteville, N. C.: Hale. 1857–58. 3v. [1134

The first volume of Dr. Hawks deals entirely with the Roanoke Island settlements of 1584–91, and reproduces the original authorities from Hakluyt, with many annotations. Vol. 2 covers the proprietary period, 1663–1729, and contains many original documents. It deals largely with social phenomena : exploration and settlement, law and its administration, agriculture and manufactures, navigation and trade, religion and learning, civil and military history, manners and customs. Dr. Hawks was by far the most scholarly man who has ever undertaken a history of the state, as well as one of the most learned men of his day. In the matter of historical judgment and skill as a writer, he has had no competitor among the historians of North Carolina. The materials used were mostly original sources, and greater in extent than any previous writer had been able to command. But Dr. Hawks follows the lead of the English and Virginia Tories ; is at times both bigoted and partisan, and writes as an advocate of the conventional order and the Established Church rather than as an impartial judge. Notwithstanding these blemishes, his work is the fullest and best treatment which the proprietary period has ever received in a general history of the state.   S. B. W.

Hewatt, Alexander. Historical account of the rise and progress of the colonies of South Carolina and Georgia. London: Donaldson. 1779. 2v. [1135

"The earliest account of the history of South Carolina cast in a sustained retrospective spirit is the anonymous *Historical account* . . . which is known to have been prepared by Dr. Alexander Hewatt, — as his signature seems to fix the spelling of his name, though in the bibliographical records it appears under various forms. Carroll, in reprinting the book in the first volume of his *Historical collections*, added many emendations." Justin Winsor, in *Narrative and critical hist. of Am.*, 5 : 352.

See, also, sect. 1128.

Johnson, John. Old Maryland manors. (Johns Hopkins Univ. studies, ser. 1, no. 7.) Balt. 1883. [1136

Commended by Justin Winsor in *Narrative and critical hist. of Am.*, 5 : 271.

Jones, Charles Colcock, Jr. Dead towns of Georgia. (Georgia Hist. Soc. Coll., v. 4.) Savannah. 1878. [1137

A record of more than historical interest are these memorials of towns, that, once centres of vital interest in the development of a new colony, are now as silent, still and forgotten as the sleeping occupants of their own graveyards. Old and New Ebenezer and the faithful Saltsburgers ; Frederica and Oglethorpe ; Sunbury and the patriotic Liberty County ; Hardwicke, Petersburg, Jacksonborough, Francisville and the old tobacco trade,—the author tells their story with that inimitable effect that comes only from personal feeling and true knowledge, quoting his own gleanings from observation and tradition, as well as letters and reports from the English and American officials who played their part in the vicissitudes of the extinct corporations.   G. K.

Jones, Hugh. Present state of Virginia. London. 1724. (Sabin, J. Reprints, no. 5.) N. Y. 1865.   [**1138**

Jones was rector of Jamestown and a professor in the college at Williamsburg, and his book was a missionary enterprise to incite attention in the mother country to the necessities of the colony. " His book is one of solid facts and solid suggestions, written in a plain, positive style, just sufficiently tinctured with the gentlemanly egotism of a Virginian and a churchman." Moses Coit Tyler, *Hist. of Am. literature*, 2: 268.

Keith, *Sir* **William.** History of Virginia. London: Richardson. 1738.   [**1139**

"Sir William Keith's *History of Virginia* was undertaken at the instance of the Society for the Encouragement of Learning, as the beginning of a series of books on the English plantations; but no others followed. It was published in 1738 with two maps,—one of America, the other of Virginia,—and he depended almost entirely on Beverley, and brings the story down to 1723." R. A. Brock, in *Narrative and critical hist. of Am.*, 3 : 165.

Latané, John H. Early relations between Maryland and Virginia. (Johns Hopkins Univ. studies, ser. 13, nos. 3–4.) Balt. 1895. Pap. 50c.   [**1140**

The period covered by this monograph is that from 1632 to 1657. The first part of the work, which is largely political in character, deals with the Claiborne settlement on Kent Island and the controversies arising therefrom, and contains an excellent account of the mutiny against Governor Harvey of Virginia in 1634–5. The second part treats of the attitude of the two colonies towards the Puritans, and is largely religious in character. The most valuable portion of this part concerns the Puritans in Virginia. The essay is largely a narrative of facts, and is based upon reliable evidence ; but it is slight in treatment and but few conclusions are presented.   C. M. A.

Lawson, John. New voyage to Carolina; containing exact description and natural history of that country: together with the present state thereof and a journal of a thousand miles travel. London. 1709.

—— History of Carolina. London. 1711. 1714. 1718. Raleigh, N. C.: Strother. 1860.   [**1141**

This book is of importance as the first effort at an extensive review of the natural and Indian history of North Carolina since the days of Hariot. Lawson was a keen observer, no one had better opportunities to learn the country and the Indians than he, and no one had a more accurate knowledge of them. His work, while it contains errors in its natural history, is an uncommonly sprightly book and has been the basis of much published since, notably Brickell's *History of North Carolina* (Dublin. 1737). The civil and political life of the colony is not considered.   S. B. W.

McCrady, Edward. History of South Carolina under the proprietary government, 1670–1719. N. Y.: Macmillan. 1897. $3.50.

—— *Same*, under the royal government, 1719–76. N. Y.: Macmillan. 1899. $3.50.

—— *Same*, in the Revolution, 1775–80. N. Y.: Macmillan. 1901. $3.50.   [**1142**

This work, one of the best of the colonial histories, carries the narrative to the close of the year 1780, and in its final volume or volumes is expected to cover the national period also. It supplants the older works of Hewatt and Ramsey, and is not only interesting and readable, but, dealing as it does with the social, economic, and religious, as well as with the political and constitutional aspects of the history of the colony, is scholarly and fairly complete. Its chief defect is the strictly chronological arrangement of events, which has made a scientific treatment difficult, a fact that becomes most apparent in the author's discussion of constitutional questions. In this and other respects the second and third volumes are an improvement on the first. All things considered, the history is admirable, and emphasizes for almost the first time the importance of South Carolina as a factor in colonial and revolutionary history.   C. M. A.

The work [vol. 1] is mainly a political history, the social and economic side being but briefly treated. A controversial tone is also apparent, especially with reference to the Lords Proprietors. It is based on the very extensive printed and manuscript sources now available in South Carolina, and is beyond doubt the most complete and accurate book published on the period covered.   S. B. W.

—— Slavery in the province of South Carolina, 1670–1770. See American Historical Association, sect. 247.   [**1143**

Neill, Edward Duffield. History of the Virginia Company of London. Albany : Munsell. 1869.   [**1144**

This is the best work on the history of the South which the author has produced. The larger part of it consists of extracts from the MS. records of the London Company, a copy of which is preserved in the Congressional Library at Washington. These are supplemented by a variety of letters, documents and biographical notices brought together from other sources. Though the book is a collection of materials loosely arranged in chronological order, rather than a history, the compiler deserves much credit for having called attention so forcibly to the records of the Company, and for having shown to what an extent the colonization of Virginia was the result of a national effort in England. It follows from the point of view which Mr. Neill has chosen, that he should be a destructive critic of Capt. John Smith. The book has been of great service to historians, and will be superseded only when the records of the Company are printed in full.   H. L. O.

—— Terra Mariæ; or Threads of Maryland colonial history. Phil.: Lippincott. 1867. [1145

"A digressive account of the career of the first Lord Baltimore, with some notices of men more or less connected with the province in its early days. . . . What the volume contains relative to the internal affairs of the province is not always accurate." W. T. Brantly, in *Narrative and critical hist. of Am.*, 3: 560.

—— Virginia Carolorum: Virginia under the rule of Charles I. and II., 1625–85. Albany: Munsell. 1886. [1146

In this volume the writer aimed to do for Virginia between 1625 and 1685 what, in his *Virginia Company*, he did for the earlier period. But, owing to the comparative scarcity of records after the downfall of the Company, the compiler found it necessary to throw his material more into the form of a narrative. The book is valuable as a collection of material of miscellaneous sort, brought together without criticism save as to the reliability of the source whence it came. It is the work of an antiquarian, to whom facts of all sorts seem worth preserving. In parts it would not be uninteresting to the general reader; to the student of the period it is indispensable.   H. L. O.

—— Virginia vetusta, during the reign of James I. Albany: Munsell. 1885. [1147

This volume is filled with scraps of information collected and printed with the intention that they should supplement the author's *History of the Virginia Company*. The material is historical, biographical, genealogical—a few documents, some extracts from sermons preached before the Company, a few letters. It may be fairly described as an investigator's note-book put into print; a collection of miscellaneous facts strung together in the order of time. Of the making of books of this kind there may easily be no end, and it will require a goodly number of them to make a substantial addition to human knowledge.   H. L. O.

New life of Virginia, 1612. See Massachusetts Historical Society, sect. 296. [1148

Oglethorpe, Gen. James Edward. BRUCE, HENRY. Life of General Oglethorpe. (Makers of America.) N. Y.: Dodd. [c. 1890.] $1. [1149

A well-balanced sketch, treating briefly of Oglethorpe in England and largely of his colonial experiences. There is a chapter on the Wesleys in Georgia and the literary friends of Oglethorpe. This is the best brief biography of the subject.   E. E. S.

— HARRIS, THADDEUS MASON. Biographical memorials of James Oglethorpe, founder of the colony of Georgia. Boston. 1841.

— SPALDING, THOMAS. Sketch of the life of Gen. James Oglethorpe. (In Georgia Hist. Soc. Collections, v. 1. 1840.)

— WRIGHT, ROBERT. Memoir of Gen. James Oglethorpe. London. 1867. [1150

"The advantages enjoyed by Mr. Wright were exceptionally good, and until the appearance of his memoir that by Dr. Harris was justly regarded as the best." C. C. Jones, in *Narrative and critical hist. of Am.*, 5: 394.

Original documents from the State Paper Office, London, and the British Museum, illustrating the history of Sir Walter Raleigh's first American colony and the colony at Jamestown. See American Antiquarian Society, sect. 231. [1151

Perfect description of Virginia, 1649. See Massachusetts Historical Society, sect. 297. [1152

Raleigh, Sir Walter. CREIGHTON, LOUISE. Life of Sir Walter Ralegh. (Historical biographies.) London: Rivingtons. 1877.

—— —— Life of Sir Walter Ralegh. N. Y.: Dutton. 1877. N. Y.: Longmans. $1. [1153

In this volume, which is one of a series of historical biographies edited by the Rev. M. Creighton, late Bishop of London, Mrs. Creighton's object is to present clearly and vividly for young readers the life and times of Raleigh. While the five chapters devoted to Raleigh's voyages are particularly well written, the entire work is based on reliable evidence and is accurate and interesting. This little book is eminently suited to young readers.   C. M. A.

— EDWARDS, EDWARD. Life of Sir Walter Ralegh; with his letters. London: Macmillan. 1868. 2v. [1154

"The most valuable of all the biographies of Raleigh." W. W. Henry, in *Narrative and critical hist. of Am.*, 3: 122.

— HUME, Maj. MARTIN ANDREW SHARP. Sir Walter Ralegh: the British dominion of the west. (Builders of Greater Britain.) London: Unwin. N. Y.: Longmans. 1897. $1.50. [1155

This work, though intended to be popular, is in fact based throughout on documentary evidence, some of which is new. Major Hume has used Simancas and Madrid papers and aims to show that "Ralegh was a martyr to the cause of a greater colonial Britain, done to death by the basest king that ever sat on Britain's throne." At the same time his account of Raleigh's earlier career is far from flattering. The author's account is critical and trustworthy. It corrects and supplements the work of Stebbing.   C. M. A.

— ST. JOHN, JAMES AUGUSTUS. Life of Sir Walter Raleigh. London: Chapman. 1868. 2v. [1156

An "embodiment of the latest information, and is better adapted to the general reader than that of Edwards, and elucidates some points more fully."

W. W. Henry, in *Narrative and critical hist. of Am.*, 3: 122.

— SOUTHEY, ROBERT. Life of Sir Walter Raleigh. (In his Lives of the British admirals, Lardner's Cabinet cyclopædia: Biography, v. 4. London: Longmans. 1851.) [1157

" An excellent life. . . . The author's only addition to the knowledge afforded by previous writers was in reference to the Guiana expeditions, the additional information being drawn from Spanish sources." W. W. Henry, in *Narrative and critical hist. of Am.*, 3: 122.

— STEBBING, WILLIAM. Sir Walter Ralegh: a biography. London: Frowde. 1891. 1899. 6s. net. [1158

" It is not too much to say in praise of this biography that it brings Sir Walter Raleigh before us almost as vividly as though we saw him in the flesh. Students of the period may differ as to the correctness of Mr. Stebbing's treatment of this or that incident in Raleigh's career, and may, perhaps, consider that his conduct is sometimes defended by arguments not beyond question; they will not, we are sure, deny that we have in these pages a generally accurate picture of the man himself, and that the picture is full of interest. . . . Mr. Stebbing is stronger in criticism, whether of characters, events, or the opinions of other authors, than in telling a story; for, concise and well arranged as his narrative is, it lacks vigor and imagination. . . . He is weak in geography, a serious failing in a biographer of Raleigh." *Saturday review*, 72: 733.

— TARBOX, INCREASE NILES, *comp.* Sir Walter Ralegh and his colony in America. (Prince Soc. Publications.) Boston. 1884. [1159

This compilation, introduced by a memoir and portrait of Raleigh, covers exactly the same field as the first volume of Hawks's *History of North Carolina* (sect. 1134). It presents the charter of Elizabeth to Raleigh and the documents relating to the five voyages and attempts at settlement of Virginia, 1584–91 (the coast of the present North Carolina), and includes Hariot's *Narrative*. Tarbox makes a literal reprint from the original of Hakluyt, while that of Hawks is very slightly abridged, modernized in spelling and hence of less value. The notes of Tarbox are fewer in number, more general in character and of less topographical importance than those of Hawks.

S. B. W.

Randall, Daniel R. A Puritan colony in Maryland. (Johns Hopkins Univ. studies, ser. 4, no. 6.) Balt. 1886. Pap. 50c. [1160

This is a clear and readable account of the settlement of a body of Virginia Puritans at Providence (now Annapolis) in 1649. Dr. Randall outlines briefly the history of the Puritans in Virginia and the circumstances which induced the migration. His study is especially valuable for its local color and for its strong sympathy with the Puritan cause, though the

picture given is probably somewhat idealized. The work is deficient in references to authorities.

C. M. A.

Rivers, William James. Sketch of the history of South Carolina to the close of the proprietary government by the revolution of 1719. Charleston: McCarter. 1856. [1161

This work was continued by Prof. Rivers in *A chapter in the early history of South Carolina*, published at Charleston in 1874, "which largely consists of explanatory original documents." *Narrative and critical hist. of Am.*, 5: 356.

Smith, *Col.* James. Account of the remarkable occurrences in the life and travels of Col. James Smith during his captivity with the Indians, 1755–59; with notes by Wm. M. Darlington. Lexington, Ky. 1799. (Ohio valley hist. ser., no. 5.) Cin.: Clarke. 1870. [1162

The author, a Pennsylvanian, was a captive at Fort Duquesne at the time of Braddock's campaign. He was a witness of the French preparations for meeting that general's fatal expedition, and the jubilant return of the victors from the battle. The original edition of his book is very rare. " It was reprinted in Cincinnati, in 1870, ' with an appendix of illustrative notes by W. M. Darlington,' as No. 5 of the *Ohio valley historical series*. . . . It was reprinted at Philadelphia in 1831, since dated 1834. The author published an abstract of it in his *Treatise on the mode and manner of Indian war*, Paris, Ky., 1812. . . . Parkman calls the earlier book ' perhaps the best of all the numerous narratives of captives among the Indians.'" Justin Winsor, in *Narrative and critical hist. of Am.*, 5: 579.

Smith, *Capt.* John. Works, 1608–31; ed. by Edward Arber. Birmingham. 1884. N. Y.: Macmillan. 2v. $4. [1163

This is the standard edition of the works of Capt. John Smith; containing not only those which he himself wrote, but those which he edited. They are arranged in the order of publication. In the margins are cross references which enable the reader to compare statements about the same events which appear in the different writings. Mr. Arber, the editor, is an enthusiastic student and admirer of Smith, and has contributed valuable introductions both to the volume as a whole and to the separate writings which it contains. These, with the marginal references, furnish one of the strongest arguments yet advanced for the reliability of Smith. At the beginning of the volume a variety of letters and relations, e. g., Wingfield's *Discourse*, which throw light on Smith's career, are reprinted. The volume is an example of excellent editorial work. H. L. O.

See, also, Jameson's *History of historical writing in America*, p. 7.

Stith, William. History of the first discovery and settlement of Virginia. Williamsburg. 1747. London. 1753. N. Y.: Sabin. 1865. [1164

This is, and is always likely to be, one of the standard books on early Virginia history. As planned by the author, it is the first volume of an extended work; but it is the only installment which ever appeared. It covers the history of Virginia under the London Company. The author had access to the archives of the colony, to the papers of Sir John Randolph, to the Byrd library, to the *Records* of the London Company. He treats the writings of John Smith as reliable so far as they relate to events which occurred while he was in the country; considers Smith an honest man, but that his writings are very confused. The first part of Stith's volume is largely based on Smith, the latter part on the *Records* of the London Company. Defends the cause of the Company against the king. Written in dignified style, with thorough scholarship.

H. L. O.

Strachey, William. Historie of travaile into Virginia Britannia; ed. by R. H. Major. London: Hakluyt Soc. 1849. [**1165**

The author was a man of considerable learning. He became Secretary of Virginia under Lord Delaware in 1610, and returned to England during or before 1612. The *Historie* here printed consists of one book and part of another, which were introductory to an extended work on the history of early English colonization, but which the author failed to complete. The first book is devoted to topography and to the aborigines, and contains one of the best of the early accounts of the Virginia Indians. In the second book the history of English colonization is begun and is followed to the failure of the colony at Sagadahoc, 1608. The work is highly authoritative, the style dignified, though the treatment is occasionally pedantic. The editor contributes a valuable introduction.

H. L. O.

Trent, *Capt*. William. Journal, from Logstown to Pickawillany, 1752; ed. by Alfred T. Goodman. Cin.: Clarke. 1871. $1.50. [**1166**

Pickawillany was an English trading post established about 1750 on the Miami River at the mouth of Loramies Creek in the present state of Ohio. Trent was a Pennsylvania trader. The journal describes a journey made by him to the post to distribute presents to the Indians. The editor's notes and explanatory chapters with the journal make a valuable book on the French-English struggle for the Ohio valley.

E. E. S.

Virginia. *General Assembly.* Proceedings of the first Assembly of Virginia, 1619. See New-York Historical Society, sect. 353. [**1167**

Weeks, Stephen Beauregard. Libraries and literature in North Carolina in the 18th century. Wash.: Amer. Hist. Assoc. 1895. $1.

This paper, reprinted from the *Report* of the American Historical Association, is complementary and supplementary to *The press.*

—— The Press of North Carolina in the 18th century; with biographical sketches of printers, an account of the manufacture of paper, and bibliography of the issues. Brooklyn: Hist.

Printing Club. 1891. [For sale by the author, Santa Fé, N. M. $2.50.] [**1168**

"Dr. Weeks, in the preparation of this volume, has rendered a service to southern literature which only the specialist can appreciate. From Mason and Dixon's line southward the incunabula and early writers of the colonies are practically unknown quantities. . . . And with this careful study of North Carolina printers and printing naturally comes new light on its early publicists. One turns in vain to any of the ordinary works on American literature concerning the colonial papers and literature of this state. . . . The fullest and most satisfactory portion is that dealing with the laws of the colony and state." *Library journal*, 16: 151.

Weston, Plowden Charles Jennett, *comp.* Documents connected with the history of South Carolina. (S. Carolina Historical Soc.) London. 1856. (121 copies printed for private distribution.) [**1169**

This volume is made up of five original tracts, four of which deal with the history of South Carolina as follows: Land travels of David Ingram and others in 1568–9: — Letters of Capt. Thomas Young to Sir Francis Windebank with a brief relation of a voyage from Virginia to the northward in 1634; this tract has been hitherto unprinted, it does not concern South Carolina, but Virginia and Maryland: — Glen's Answers to the Board of Trade; written about 1748 and the original of A description of Carolina, 1761, reprinted in Carroll's Collections: — Letters of Richard Cumberland to Roger Pinckney, his deputy, in regard to the provost marshalship of South Carolina, 1764–1775: — the South Carolina part of the Philosophico-historico-hydrogeography of South Carolina, Georgia and East Florida by William Gerard DeBrahm. There is little in the volume by way of introduction, and few notes.

S. B. W.

Williamson, Hugh. History of North Carolina. Phil. 1812. 2v. [**1170**

This work stops with a scant narrative of the Regulation war and the battle of the Almance, 1766–71. There is no mention of the Revolution, nor a discussion of its causes. It is claimed to be based on manuscript documents, including legislative journals, letter books of governors, etc., since printed; but these materials have been used with little skill or judgment; for many of the facts are unimportant, and there is little historical perspective. The work is meagre, full of errors, and altogether unworthy of the subject.

S. B. W.

Wingfield, Edward Maria. A discourse of Virginia. See American Antiquarian Society, sect. 231. [**1171**

SOUTHERN AND WESTERN COLONIES AND SETTLEMENTS (FRENCH)

Bienville, Jean Baptiste le Moyne, *sieur* de. KING, GRACE. Jean Baptiste le Moyne, sieur de Bienville. (Makers of America.) N. Y.: Dodd. 1892. $1. [**1172**

Biography of the founder of New Orleans, called also " Father of Louisiana," one of the greatest of Canadian pioneers, who, coming in 1699, a boy, with his brother, the famous Iberville, to the discovery of the mouth of the Mississippi River, threw his life into the work of holding for France the vast territory acquired through success in this enterprise. And as his life, 1682–1769, was coextensive with the history of the province, from its naming by La Salle to its cession to Spain, his history is the history of the French possession of Louisiana and domination of the Mississippi River. Fresh sources of information, original local research and new handling of old material are the recommendations of the book to the student.

Catherwood, Mrs. Mary Hartwell. Heroes of the middle west : the French. Boston : Ginn. 1898. 50c. [1173

Five sketchy chapters " covering the French discovery and occupation of the middle west, from Marquette and Joliet to the pulling down of the French flag at Fort Chartres." Although avowedly written for school-children, the style is stiffly labored, and lacks life and color. The preface is curiously boastful of the author's historical knowledge, but the exhibition thereof smells of the lamp. Not calculated to assist in popularizing western history.

Chapman, Thomas Jefferson. The French in the Allegheny valley. Cleveland : Williams. [c. 1887.] [1174

Under this title the author has brought together a series of studies originally made, or at least written out, for publication in the historical magazines. The first one deals with Celoron's voyage down the Allegheny in 1749 ; the last one with the Virginia land claims in Pennsylvania ; while between them lie fourteen others having no historical centre of unity, but bound together somewhat loosely by geographical relations. The book is not a contribution to knowledge, but it may be commended as a contribution to popular information. B. A. H.

Falconer, Thomas. On the discovery of the Mississippi, and on the south-western, Oregon, and north-western boundary of the United States. London : Clarke. 1844. [1175

The first half is devoted to a sketch of La Salle's exploring expedition, based upon documents in the Archives of the Marine, at Paris. The second half consists of English translations of memoirs and letters of La Salle and Tonty, from the same archives. The author is a London lawyer, and the book a brief for the English contention in our northwest boundary dispute. The broad territorial acquisitions by La Salle and other French explorers who operated under Canadian auspices are considered to have included much of the western country, and to have been acquired by Great Britain upon the cession of New France. R. G. T.

Griffin, Appleton Prentiss Clark. Discovery of the Mississippi : a bibliographical account, reprinted from the Magazine of American history, March and April, 1883. N. Y.: Barnes. 1883. [1176

A bibliographical account of the travels of Nicolet, Alloüez, Marquette, Hennepin and La Salle in the Mississippi valley, and of La Salle's voyage to the Gulf, 1684–87. This critical list of the principal contemporary narratives of the first French explorations shows editions, reprints and translations, includes biographical accounts of the explorers and the arguments of their supporters, and also a list of later publications and periodical literature on the subject, arranged in chronological order, 1703–1882. The more important edited maps, bearing date previous to 1700, are included, with the printed works in which they may be found. The Joliet map, 1674, reproduced in facsimile, is the earliest which represents the Mississippi in connection with the Great Lakes.

Hebberd, Stephen Southwick. History of Wisconsin under the dominion of France. Madison : Midland Pub. Co. 1890. [1177

The author's principal thesis is, that the stubborn resistance to the French, made by the Fox Indians in Wisconsin, and their allies in the middle west, from about 1694–1763, was a primary cause of the downfall of New France. The conspirators weakened the chain of connection between Canada and Louisiana, thus sapping the life of the fur trade and jeopardizing military operations. Further, the Wisconsin Indians were the chief enemies of Pontiac ; and, overthrowing his plans, secured the English in possession of the continental interior. Therein Mr. Hebberd controverts the views of Parkman and many other writers. The book exhibits much research and historical acumen, but is not always convincing, and the tone sometimes is unnecessarily bitter. No index.

Hennepin, Louis. Description of Louisiana ; tr. from the ed. of 1683 by John Gilmary Shea. N. Y.: Shea. 1880. [1178

The relation of an exploration of the Illinois River and upper Mississippi by Hennepin, who accompanied La Salle as almoner on his expedition in the discovery of the Mississippi. Captured by the Sioux, and carried up beyond the Falls of St. Anthony which he named, Hennepin experienced the adventures which form one of the most interesting, as it is one of the most important relations of French pioneers in America. Unfortunately, Hennepin, after the death of La Salle, republished his narrative, changing it so as to contain an exploration of the mouth of the Mississippi, before ascending to its source, thus claiming the glory of La Salle's achievement. This was supported by plagiarized descriptions. Shea disputes the charges against Hennepin and publishes fairly all the versions of his relation. G. K.

—— New discovery of a vast country in America ; to which are added, several new discoveries in North-America [tr. from the French]. London. 1698.

—— New discovery of a large country in the northern America, extending above 4000 miles. — Account of Mr. La Salle's undertaking to discover the River Mississippi, by way of the

Gulph of Mexico. (In Am. Antiquarian Soc. Archæologia Americana, v. 1. 1820.) **[1179**

"'I here protest to you, before God,' he writes, addressing the reader, 'that my narrative is faithful and sincere, and that you may believe every thing related in it.' And yet, as we shall see, this reverend father was the most impudent of liars ; and the narrative of which he speaks is a rare monument of brazen mendacity. Hennepin, however, had seen and dared much: for among his many failings fear had no part; and, where his vanity or his spite was not involved, he often told the truth. His books have their value, with all their enormous fabrications. . . . It appears from his own later statements, as well as from those of Tonty, . . . that La Salle had instructed him to explore, not alone the Illinois, but also the upper Mississippi. That he actually did so, there is no reasonable doubt ; and, could he have contented himself with telling the truth, his name would have stood high as a bold and vigorous discoverer. But his vicious attempts to malign his commander, and plunder him of his laurels, have wrapped his genuine merit in a cloud. Hennepin's first book was published soon after his return from his travels, and while La Salle was still alive. In it, he relates the accomplishment of the instructions given him, without the smallest intimation that he did more. Fourteen years after, when La Salle was dead, he published another edition of his travels in which he advanced a new and surprising pretension. Reasons connected with his personal safety, he declares, before compelled him to remain silent ; but a time at length has come when the truth must be revealed. And he proceeds to affirm that, before ascending the Mississippi, he, with his two men, explored its whole course from the Illinois to the sea, thus anticipating the discovery which forms the crowning laurel of La Salle. . . . The story was distrusted from the first. Why had he not told it before? An excess of modesty, a lack of self-assertion, or a too sensitive reluctance to wound the susceptibilities of others, had never been found among his foibles. Yet some, perhaps, might have believed him. had he not, in the first edition of his book, gratuitously and distinctly declared that he did not make the voyage in question. . . . He ensnares himself in a hopeless confusion of dates. . . . Six years before Hennepin published his pretended discovery, his brother friar, Father Chrétien Le Clerc, published an account of the Récollet missions among the Indians, under the title of *Établissement de la foi*. This book, offensive to the Jesuits, is said to have been suppressed by order of government ; but a few copies fortunately survive. . . . It contains the journal of Father Zenobe Membré, on his descent of the Mississippi in 1681, in company with La Salle. The slightest comparison of his narrative with that of Hennepin is sufficient to show that the latter framed his own story out of incidents and descriptions furnished by his brother missionary, often using his very words, and sometimes copying entire pages." The earlier parts of Hennepin's book "square exceedingly well with contemporary records of undoubted authenticity. . . . He constantly, it is true, magnifies his own acts, . . . and yet, till he reaches the Mississippi, there can be no doubt that in the main he tells the truth." Francis Parkman, *La Salle and the discovery of the great west*, ch. 9, 17.

La Salle, Robert Cavelier de. BARTLETT, CHARLES H., *and* RICHARD H. LYON. La Salle in the valley of the St. Joseph. South Bend, Ind. : Tribune Prtg. Co. 1899. $1.25. **[1180**

The result of local investigation to secure materials for two historical paintings. It tries to locate the portage path used by La Salle from the St. Joseph to the Kankakee Rivers, in what is now northern Indiana, and the place where he held a treaty with the Miamis. The illustrations are reproductions of local photographs.   E. E. S.

LePage du Pratz. Histoire de la Louisiane. Paris. 1758. 3v.

—— History of Louisiana; tr. from the French. London: Becket. 1763. 2v. Abridged. 1774. 1v. **[1181**

One of the earliest and most useful authorities in the history of Louisiana. Coming to the colony in 1718 and remaining there sixteen years, part of the period as official physician to the royal plantation opposite New Orleans, the author had the time and opportunity to exercise his shrewd yet genial powers of observation, on the men and events about which he wrote on his return to Paris. If, when he dilates on his favorite theme, the Indians, particularly the Natchez tribe, his credulity, or his confidence in ours, appears at times excessive, and if naïve gossip too often passes with him for serious proof, his genuine intention to instruct and not to deceive is ever convincingly apparent to the reader.   G. K.

"The original edition [*Histoire de la Louisiane*] was published at Paris in 1758. . . . The presence of Le Page du Pratz in the colony for sixteen years (1718 to 1734) gives to his *Histoire de la Louisiane* a value which his manifest egotism and whimsical theories cannot entirely obscure. It was an authority in the boundary discussions." A. McF. Davis, in *Narrative and critical hist. of Am.*, 5: 65.

Margry, Pierre, *ed.* Découvertes et établissements des Français dans l'ouest et dans le sud de l'Amérique septentrionale, 1614–1698 : mémoires et documents inédits. Paris : Maisonneuve. 1879. 3v.

—— *Same*, 1614–1754: mémoires et documents originaux. Paris: Maisonneuve. 1881–88. 3v. **[1182**

" A collection of documents relating to La Salle . . . was in possession of M. Pierre Margry, director of the Archives of the Marine and Colonies at Paris, and was the result of more than thirty years of research. With rare assiduity and zeal, M. Margry had explored not only the vast depository with which he has been officially connected from youth, and of which he is now the chief, but also the other public archives of France, and many private collections in Paris and the provinces. The object of his search was to throw light on the career and achievements of French explorers, and, above all, of La Salle. A collection of extraordinary richness grew gradually upon his hands." In consequence of the efforts of Mr. Parkman and others, " Congress made an appropriation for the purchase of five hundred copies of the work, to be printed at Paris, under direction of M. Margry. . . . Of the papers contained in them" some of "the most interesting are the letters of La Salle, found in the original by M. Margry, among the immense accumulations of the Archives of the Marine and Colonies and the Bibliothèque Nationale. The narrative of La Salle's companion, Joutel, far more copious than the abstract printed in 1713, under the title of *Journal historique*, also deserves special mention. . . . The discovery of many of these documents is due to the indefatigable research of M. Pierre Margry. . . . In the department of American colonial history, these results have been invaluable ; for, besides several private collections made by him, he rendered important service in the collection of the French portion of the Brodhead documents, selected and arranged the two great series of colonial papers ordered by the Canadian government, and prepared with vast labor analytical indexes of these and of supplementary documents in the French archives, as well as a copious index of the mass of papers relating to Louisiana." Francis Parkman, *La Salle and the discovery of the great west*, prefaces to 1st and 11th editions.

" The severest criticism of Margry's publication has come from Dr. Shea, in a tract entitled *The bursting of Pierre Margry's bubble*, New York, 1879. . . . Margry is judged by his critic to have unwarrantably extended the collection by repeating what had already elsewhere been printed, sometimes at greater length. The ' bubble ' in question is the view long entertained by Margry that La Salle was the real discoverer of the Mississippi." Justin Winsor, in *Narrative and critical hist. of Am.*, 4 : 245.

Monette, John W. History of the discovery and settlement of the valley of the Mississippi. N. Y.: Harper. 1846. 2v. [1183

One of the old established standard works on the history of the Mississippi valley, extending in time from the first Spanish discoveries in Florida to the admission of Texas into the Union. Although, as to colonial records, superseded by a younger generation of books, whose authors have profited by subsequent researches in European and American archives, it is yet authoritative over an important field and period in American history; notably of the political and geographical complications following the Treaty of Paris, and the questions arising during the transitional period after the cession of Louisiana. The abundant notes given furnish a good bibliography on these subjects. G. K.

Nicolet, John. BUTTERFIELD, CONSUL WILLSHIRE. History of the discovery of the Northwest by John Nicolet in 1634, with a sketch of his life. Cin.: Clarke. 1881. $1. [1184

The author " has produced a meritorious monograph upon the first discoverer of the Northwest. John Nicolet had been so entirely forgotten that he is not even mentioned by Hildreth, and his expedition was first brought to light by Mr. Shea in 1852, who placed it in the year 1639 — the Jesuit relation having given no dates for it. Mr. Sulte, of Ottawa, found strong and almost conclusive reasons for referring it to 1634; and this date appears now to have been made certain by Mr. Butterfield's discovery of the mention, in 1635, of a treaty between the Winnebagoes and the Nez Percés, which could only have been negotiated by Nicolet. In this journey Nicolet went up the Fox River and crossed to the Wisconsin, being thus the first white man who visited the valley of the upper Mississippi, although he did not reach the river itself. The book is a complete and exhaustive account of the life and explorations of Nicolet, amply fortified by citations from the original authorities, and provided with a good index." *Nation*, 33: 421.

Parkman, Francis. Pioneers of France in the new world.
—— The Jesuits in North America.
—— La Salle and the discovery of the great west. [1185
See in Part V.

Pittman, *Capt*. Philip. Present state of the European settlements on the Mississippi, with a geographical description of that river ; illustrated by plans and draughts. London. 1770. [1186

" It is the earliest English account of those settlements, and, as an authority in early western history, is of the highest importance. He [Pittman] was a military engineer, and for five years was employed in surveying the Mississippi River and exploring the western country. The excellent plans [8] which accompany the work, artistically engraved on copper, add greatly to its value." W. F. Poole, in *Narrative and critical hist. of Am.*, 6: 702.

Shea, John Gilmary. Discovery and exploration of the Mississippi valley ; with the original narratives of Marquette, Allouez, Membré, Hennepin, and Anastase Douay. N. Y.: Redfield. 1852. (Hist. classic readings, no. 5.) N. Y.: Maynard. [1890.] Pap. 12c. [1187

Contains a facsimile of the newly discovered map of Marquette. A painstaking study of the above named sources, with introductions and biographical sketches, written with a Roman Catholic bias. Valuable for the translated text, edited with careful notes. The Marquette *Relation* is also given in the French. A fragmentary anticipation of Thwaite's *Jesuit relations*. H. W. H.

—— Early voyages up and down the Mississippi. Albany: Munsell. 1861. [1188
" Dr. Shea has collected, translated and annotated various relations concerning the voyages of Cavelier, De Montigny de Saint-Cosme, Le Sueur, Gravier and Guignas." *Narrative and critical hist. of Am.*, 5 : 67.

Tonty, Henri, *chevalier* de. LEGLER, HENRY E. Chevalier Henry de Tonty. (Parkman Club. Publications, v. 1, no. 3.) Milwaukee: Legler. 1896.
—— The man with the iron hand. Milwaukee: Haferkorn. 1896. [1189

Based largely on Tonty's memoir in Margry and references in New York colonial documents, Hennepin, La Potherie, and Parkman, with some independent research. A convenient narrative for reference; in the main accurate; but couched in "newspaper English."

SOUTHERN AND SOUTHWESTERN COLONIES AND SETTLEMENTS (SPANISH)

Anderson, Alexander D. The silver country; or The great Southwest. N. Y.: Putnam. 1877. [1190

Careful work has been done in this book, particularly in the compilation of chapter 5 on *The authorities,* which has interest for bibliophiles. The territory described from personal observation is that "former kingdom of New Spain, including Mexico, and the Mexican cession of 1848 and 1853." C. H. S.

Blackmar, Frank Wilson. Spanish colonization in the Southwest. (Johns Hopkins Univ. studies, ser. 8, no. 4.) Baltimore. 1890. Pap. 50c.
—— Spanish institutions of the Southwest. (Johns Hopkins Univ. studies, extra v. 10.) Baltimore. 1891. $2. [1191

The value of these books arises chiefly from the fact that their author, a young Californian, wrote from the Pacific coast standpoint, as modified by the methods and training of the Historical Seminar at Johns Hopkins University. The pamphlet upon Spanish colonization is merely a preliminary study to the larger book upon Spanish institutions. The latter should long maintain a respectable place, both as a book for popular reading, since its style is easy and attractive, and also for general reference. It does not claim to be a complete history, but is simply a University study of the missions, the colonial municipalities, the presidios and other Spanish-American institutions in California, Arizona, New Mexico and Texas. Its "local color" is excellent. C. H. S.

Davis, William Watts Hart. Spanish conquest of New Mexico. Doylestown, Pa. 1869. [1192

Equipped with more than ordinary ability for historical investigation, the author resided for several years in New Mexico as U. S. attorney and for a time as acting governor, becoming deeply interested in the history of the territory through the Spanish archives at Santa Fé to which he had access. The book was the first history of New Mexico published in English, and it far excelled any subsequent effort in that direction until Bandelier published the results of his own noteworthy researches. These latter shed light on many points concerning which Davis was either doubtful or in error — such, for example, as the location of Quivira, and the failure of Cabeza de Vaca to cross the present boundary of the territory. Considering General Davis's comparatively meagre facilities, his

book was far ahead of its time. It still contains much historical and ethnological information of value, presented in an entertaining manner. F. W. H.

Irving, Theodore. Conquest of Florida by Hernando de Soto. Phil.: Carey. 1835. 2v.
—— *Same, rev.;* History of De Soto's conquest of Florida. N. Y.: Putnam. 1857. $2. [1193

This work presents the early history of the country called Florida to the end of De Soto's invasion. It has generally been regarded as the standard work on this period. The author, a nephew of Washington Irving, studied in Spain the original authorities, De Vega, Biedma, etc., on which the early history of Florida should be based. His work enters somewhat more into details than the *De Soto in Florida* of Grace King (sect. 1197), and contains more critical notes on names and places. It is for the most part accurate; but the author, in tracing the route of De Vaca, unfortunately had to use the first edition of Buckingham Smith's work, which was corrected by Smith himself in 1871 (sect. 1195). The style is clear and simple; but not so vivid and attractive as that of Miss King. J. R. F.

Lummis, Charles Fletcher. The Spanish pioneers. Chicago: McClurg. 1893. $1.50. [1194

For a number of years Lummis was an intimate of Bandelier, both in New Mexico and Peru, and perhaps no higher compliment can be paid the authenticity of this book on the undertakings of the earliest makers of American history than to say that it was prepared under his guidance. The narratives are most interestingly related, and are illumined by sidelights reflected from personal experience in much of the territory which the Spanish pioneers trod. The book casts serious doubt on some of Prescott's writings. F. W. H.

Nuñez Cabeça de Vaca, Alvarez. Relation; tr. from the Spanish by Buckingham Smith. N. Y.: the estate of the author. 1871.
—— Journey to New Mexico, 1535–6; from [his] Relation. (Old South leaflets, no. 39.) [1195

"The narration of the unfortunate expedition of Cabeça de Vaca across the territory now occupied by the southern states from Florida to Texas in the year 1527, nearly three and a half centuries ago, is full of the most melancholy yet absorbing interest. Nine years of wanderings and captivity among the Indians elapsed before this ill-fated member of a still more unfortunate band escaped almost alone of all who set out so joyously with him. His narration has been received by all historians and antiquaries as veracious." T. W. Field, *Indian bibliography,* p. 55.

Rye, William B., *ed.* Discovery and conquest of Terra Florida, by Don Fernando de Soto; written by a gentleman of Elvas [1557]; tr. out of Portuguese by Richard Hakluyt. London: Hakluyt Soc. 1851. [1196

To promote interest in the new colony of Virginia, Hakluyt published this account of de Soto's exploration of Florida (equivalent in meaning to our "cotton states") in 1609 under the title: *Virginia richly valued*, etc. In 1611 the title was changed to *The worthye and famous history of the travailes . . . of that great continent of Terra Florida*, &c. His version was published again in the supplement to the 1809 ed. of his *Voyages*, in Force's *Tracts*, vol. 6, and in French's *Hist. Coll. of La.*, vol. 2. In 1866, Mr. Buckingham Smith published a new translation in the Bradford Club series. The narrative is a straightforward and trustworthy account by an eye-witness. It is one of the most important sources for the history of the southern Indians. This volume includes another briefer contemporary narrative by a Spanish soldier, Luys Hernandez de Biedma, translated by the editor, Mr. Rye, who has supplied an extended introduction. This narrative of the "Gentleman of Elvas" is included in Goldsmid's Hakluyt's *Principal navigations* under its original title, *Virginia richly valued*. The original was reprinted at Lisbon in 1844 and 1875 in the first vol. of the *Collecção de opusculos reimpresos relativos à historia das navegações, viagens e conquistas dos Portuguezes*, pp. 5–139.   E. G. B.

Soto, Fernando de. KING, GRACE. De Soto and his men in the land of Florida. N.Y.: Macmillan. 1898. $1.50.   [1197

The author had access to the best original authorities — especially Garcilaso de la Vega, Biedma, and the narrative of a "Gentleman of Elvas." All attempts to reconcile conflicting statements were avoided, the object being to produce an interesting rather than a critical work. The author has omitted as unsuitable for her work a portion of De la Vega's narrative, describing Indian customs, etc. The chief authority used is the original Spanish of De la Vega, with extracts here and there from a "Gentleman of Elvas." There are a few notes, identifying places through which De Soto passed. The story as told by Miss King is graphic and thrilling. It is destined to be the most popular account of De Soto's wanderings. The style is admirably suited to the matter; it is clear, simple, and vivid. There is no index.   J. R. F.

— WILMER, LAMBERT A. Life, travels and adventures of Ferdinand de Soto, discoverer of the Mississippi. Phil. 1859.   [1198

"Written in a style worthy of its subject. The story of De Soto's life is told with a vigor and nervous energy, characteristic of his restless career." T. W. Field, *Indian bibliography*, p. 425.

Venegas, Miguel. Natural and civil history of California; tr. from the original Spanish [Madrid. 1758]. London. 1759. 2v. [1199

The author was an erudite Jesuit missionary whose field of labor was in Mexico and California. While in the latter province he gathered much information from personal observation and even a greater body of data from the archives of the various missions. The volumes are replete with valuable historical, geographical, and ethnological material not found in other works, many of the sources of Venegas' knowledge never having been published. The work pertains as much to Lower California, southern Arizona, and northern Sonora as to California proper. Kino's map of 1702 formed the basis of Venegas' map.

F. W. H.

2. Period of Discontent, Revolt and Independence: 1760–1783

Abbatt, William. Crisis of the Revolution: being the story of Arnold and André. N. Y.: Abbatt. 1899. $20. Subs.   [1200

This volume is issued under the auspices of the Empire State Society, Sons of the American Revolution. Compiled from the sources and illustrated with excellent reproductions of original photographs. The story is well told. Altogether an excellent book.   E. C.

Adams, John. Works; with life, notes and illustrations by Charles Francis Adams. Boston: Little. 1850–6. 10v.   [1201

The famous grandson of John Adams was well-fitted to collect and order the vast mass of documents, the memorials of the long life-work of the second President. His cool judicial portrayal shows no trace of a tendency to exaggerate the merits of his subject: there is a marked abstention from filial partiality and family glorification. While many of the documents are invaluable, the world now and hereafter will probably most prize the letters and the diary. The character of John Adams is revealed in these in a most attractive light, — as frankly artless almost as Sewell, as abrupt and prejudiced as Dr. Johnson, — testy, full of foibles, self-conscious, but brave and honest to the very core; a brain of the finest power and a heart of oak.

J. K. H.

—— Correspondence with Professor Winthrop, and with Mrs. Mercy Warren. See Massachusetts Historical Society, sect. 315.

[1202

— ADAMS, CHARLES FRANCIS. Life of John Adams, begun by John Quincy Adams, completed by Charles Francis Adams; rev. and corrected. Phil.: Lippincott. 1871. 2v. $3.

[1203

A reprint in smaller form of the first volume of *The life and works of John Adams*, which appeared in 1856 (sect. 1201). The "revision" consists apparently in omitting the genealogical sketch, many of the footnotes, and the appendix.   E. E. S.

— CHAMBERLAIN, MELLEN. John Adams, the statesman of the American Revolution; with other essays and addresses. Boston: Houghton. 1898. $2.   [1204

"The initial essay on John Adams, the longest and most important piece in the volume, is a thoroughgoing examination of the causes of the Revolution and of the relation of Adams to the constitutional side of the struggle. No writer has set forth more clearly or instructively the nature of the influences which brought about the separation of the American colonies from the mother country. In Judge Chamberlain's view, writs of assistance, the Stamp Act, and the various revenue and coercive measures of Great Britain were the occasion, rather than the cause, of the Revolution. They were irritating and, from the standpoint of political expediency, indefensible, but they only hastened a crisis which, even without them, could not have been permanently averted. . . . It was the peculiar merit of John Adams that he was one of the first to see the constitutional significance of the contest, and that he led Massachusetts, and through her the other colonies, to a more or less discerning acceptance of his ideas." *Nation*, 68 : 115.

— MORSE, JOHN TORREY, JR. John Adams. (Am. statesmen.) Boston : Houghton. 1885. $1.25.   [1205

An interesting book, well conceived and well written, an excellent example of popular biography.
     E. C. R.

Adams, John *and* **Abigail.** Familiar letters during the Revolution ; [ed.] by Charles Francis Adams. Boston: Houghton. [c. 1875.] $2.   [1206

In 1764 Abigail Smith, just twenty years old, daughter of the minister of Weymouth, and having in her veins the blood of a score of the most noted Massachusetts worthies, married John Adams, son of a small farmer in Braintree, the undistinguished family of the bridegroom as well as the fact that he was a lawyer, a calling in those days scarcely deemed respectable, causing it to be regarded as a great come-down for the beautiful and well-born maid. John Adams achieved, through character and ability, the highest eminence ; and from the two has proceeded perhaps the most distinguished of American families. The letters of such a pair during the American Revolution naturally possess the utmost interest. The face of the time — the public trials, failures, triumphs — appears as in a perfect mirror. At the same time, as a revelation of noble manly and womanly worth, the correspondence has rarely, if ever, been surpassed.
     J. K. H.

Adams, Samuel. HOSMER, JAMES KENDALL. Samuel Adams. (American statesmen.) Boston: Houghton. 1885. $1.25.   [1207

This book sets forth the man, Samuel Adams, 1722–1803, in a brief and interesting manner. It is well conceived and well written, an admirable specimen of popular biography by a scholarly writer.   E. C. R.

— WELLS, WILLIAM V. Life and public services of Samuel Adams. Boston: Little. 1865. 3v.   [1208

A three-volumed work, filled with the most valuable materials, by the great-grandson of Samuel Adams, who had access to the manuscripts preserved in the family, one of the best of the Revolutionary collections, afterwards the possession of George Bancroft, and at present in the Lenox Library, New York. The defects of the book are that it is throughout eulogistic of its subject, and throughout condemnatory of the men against whom he strove. While to Samuel Adams rather than to Washington belongs the title "Father of America," a title accorded him by his contemporaries, Washington being rather the foster-father who protected and nurtured the child after it was born, the "man of the town-meeting" was after all a very human instrument. He was wily and narrow: his methods were to a large extent those of the "machine;" it is perhaps not too harsh to say he was the prototype of the "boss." Yet withal he was thoroughly sincere, self-forgetting and brave. The opponents of Samuel Adams were sometimes men of high character and courage, holding opinions susceptible of defence. The work of Wells is a treasury of important information ; but the reader must guard himself against being led by it into undiscriminating admiration of its hero, and into aversion just as undiscriminating as regards his adversaries.   J. K. H.

Adolphus, John. History of England from the accession of George III to 1783. London. 1805. 3v.

—— History of England from the accession to the decease of George III. London. 1840-45. 7v.   [1209

This history, by its elaborate defence of the government of George III and of the attitude of Parliament toward the American colonies, was designed to gratify British Tory sympathies, and was famous in its day. But, like all apologetic histories, it is vehemently one-sided, and worse still, in the portions dealing with the war of the Revolution is full of inaccurate statements and unjust conclusions. Some of the author's comments upon Washington and other leading Revolutionary leaders verge on the absurd. In general the work is heavy and dull, and any usefulness that it might have to-day is impaired by the absence of an index.   C. M. A.

Affaires de l'Angleterre et de l'Amérique. Anvers. [Paris.] 1776–[1779]. 15v. in 17.   [1210

This periodical, according to Barbier, was edited by Franklin, Court de Gebelin, Robinet, and others, with the purpose of placing before the French public the American side of the Revolutionary War; and for France it is what Almon's *Remembrancer* (sect. 1219) was for Great Britain. The plan of the work is threefold: First, to print in diary form a narrative of events. Second, to reprint from newspapers and pamphlets matter of special interest. Third, to give in what purported to be letters from a London banker, the inside political history and Parliamentary proceedings of Great Britain. Though edited to a certain extent in a partisan manner, and though containing many errors, it is of singular value for the history of the period covered; but, owing to its rarity, and to the extreme bibliographical confusion in its parts and volumes, it has been singularly neglected as historical material.   P. L. F.

Alden, George Henry. New governments west of the Alleghanies before 1780. (Univ. of Wisconsin. Bulletin, hist. ser., v. 2, no. 1.) Madison. 1897. 50c.   [1211

This monograph is a good example of a university

thesis submitted for the degree of Doctor of Philosophy. It throws new light upon its subject, or at least focalizes the light before scattered, and ranks as a useful addition to our political history.   B. A. H.

Allen, *Col.* Ethan.   Allen's captivity; being a narrative containing his voyages, travels, etc. Boston: Perkins. 1845.   [1212

This little narrative covers the capture of Ticonderoga, the Canadian expedition with Arnold, Allen's capture by the British, and his captivity for two years at Halifax and New York. It describes in strong language the treatment given the American prisoners. The narrative was first printed at Bennington in 1779 and has passed through many editions and forms. It has been used freely in all the lives of Allen.
                                E. E. S.

— HALL, HENRY. Ethan Allen, the Robin Hood of Vermont. N. Y.: Appleton. 1892. $1.   [1213

A biography of an interesting Revolutionary hero (1737–89), posthumously published. It seems less the result of an attempt to gain exact information than of the desire to write an entertaining narrative. It is fanciful rather than judicious (as instanced on the title-page), and uncritical in the extreme (as shown in the beginning of the 7th chapter). The book has neither index, maps, nor illustrations (beyond a vignette on the title-page).   W. E. F.

Allen, Jolley.   Narrative, 1775–76. See Massachusetts Historical Society, sect. 332.
                                [1214

Allen, Paul. History of the American Revolution. Balt. 1819. Balt.: Bell. 1822. 2v.   [1215

This is a work of but slight value, and has not even the merit of being composed throughout by the same "hack writer" who signs his initials to the preface. The "associates" whose names he omits to mention were John Neal and Tobias Watkins. It is one of the early instances of "book-making," pure and simple (to be paralleled, later, in numerous "Histories of the Rebellion," etc.), and possessing neither accuracy, judicial temper, nor an admirable literary style. It has no maps and no index.   W. E. F.

Almon, John, *comp.* Collection of political tracts, 1764–73. London. 1773. 4v.

—— Collection of scarce and interesting tracts, written by persons of eminence; upon the most important political and commercial subjects during the years 1763–70. London. 1787–88. 4v.

—— Collection of the most interesting tracts lately published in England and America on the subjects of taxing the American colonies and regulating their trade. London. 1766–79. 6v.   [1216

These are collections of tracts and pamphlets, the greater number of which had already been published either by Almon himself or by others. The gathering of them into the above volumes is not to be considered in the light of a regular publication, for there do not appear to have been many copies issued of any one of the Collections noted. The first contains tracts, mostly signed, but some anonymous, on political liberty and freedom of the press; the second deals with the trade, commerce, and taxation of America; and the third, which is of a much more general character, has to do with Tory administration in England, the trial of John Wilkes, the law of libel, and a few commercial topics. Pamphlets dealing with both sides of important questions are to be found here, though Almon was a strong Whig and a friend of John Wilkes. Most of the pamphlets exist in separate form.   C. M. A.

—— Parliamentary register. See in Part I: Sources, sect. 75.   [1217

—— [Prior documents]: A collection of interesting, authentic papers relative to the dispute between Great Britain and America, shewing the causes and progress of that misunderstanding, 1764–75. London. 1777.   [1218

This collection of documents is prefatory to Almon's larger work the *Remembrancer*, which opened with the commencement of hostilities in 1775. The prior documents are those which concern the earlier period from 1764 to 1775, and this collection of them was issued two years after the *Remembrancer* had first begun to appear. It includes acts, debates, resolves, messages, addresses, letters, petitions, and the like in England and America, such as were appearing in the newspapers of the day. Almon's collections have not lost their utility, and are still quoted.   C. M. A. Usually cited by the running title "Prior documents."

—— Remembrancer, The; or Impartial repository of public events. London: J. Almon. 1775–84. 17v.   [1219

Almon was a successful bookseller and journalist of liberal views, at the height of his career during our Revolutionary period. He was radical enough to be the ardent friend of John Wilkes, and sympathized fully with the contention of the Thirteen Colonies, which he helped with all his influence. His boldness brought him more than once under penalty of the law, and at one time he was driven into exile in France. Among his numerous writings and collections the *Remembrancer*, published monthly and running through the time of our war, from 1775 to 1781, has especial importance. Its plan was to select from the public prints accounts of the material public events, to issue them in octavo, and at the end of the volume to give a copious index. Almon throughout each year furnished, together with appropriate comments, a miscellany of news-jottings, state-papers, letters, documents of any kind likely to interest. Many important matters are here preserved, rare, or not at all to be found elsewhere. It is a fact worth noting that a man with a shrewd eye to business found his account in such a publication, there being many readers for it in the England of that day. The *Remembrancer* was supplemented by *Prior documents*, noteworthy papers preceding the outbreak. Indispensable to the student of the Revolution.   J. K. H.

American archives : a collection of authentic state papers [etc.], forming a documentary history of the North American colonies; [comp.] by Peter Force. Ser. 4, v. 1–6. Ser. 5, v. 1–3. Wash. 1837–53. 9v.   [**1220**]

Part of a projected great collection of documents, of which only 6 volumes of the 4th series (1774–1776), and 3 volumes of the 5th series (1776), were published. The contents include statutes, legislative and parliamentary proceedings, proceedings of local bodies, speeches, letters, etc. Though ill-arranged, the collection is invaluable for the study of the early Revolutionary period.   W. MacD.

Amory, T. C. Memory of General John Sullivan vindicated. See Massachusetts Historical Society, sect. 327.   [**1221**]

Anburey, Thomas. Travels through the interior parts of America. London : Lane. 1789. 2v.   [**1221 a**]

Anburey was an officer in Burgoyne's army, and many of his letters were written while he was a prisoner of war. " It is an agreeable surprise to find, with occasional asperity, much candid intelligence and interesting local information." H. T. Tuckerman, *America and her commentators,* p. 186.

André, *Maj.* **John.** DAWSON, HENRY B., *ed.* Papers concerning the capture and detention of Major John André. Yonkers, N. Y. 1866.   [**1222**]

" The most complete gathering of authentic material which has been made." Justin Winsor, in *Narrative and critical hist. of Am.,* 6: 464.

— SARGENT, WINTHROP. Life and career of Major John André. Boston : Ticknor. 1861. N. Y.: Appleton. 1871.   [**1223**]

This is the best biography of "the unfortunate André," written in the later spirit of regret which most Americans feel for his execution. The justice of the sentence is widely reviewed and various commentators quoted. The style of treatment is florid and the view-point extreme in André's favor. The appendix contains some information concerning the later life of Benedict Arnold.   E. E. S.

— SMITH, HORACE WEMYSS, *comp.* Andreana. Phil.: Smith. 1865.   [**1224**]

A collection of materials relating to André, made by Horace W. Smith. It embraces a reprint of the *Proceedings* of the Board of officers which tried André, the letters relating to a mitigation of his sentence, contemporary accounts of his execution, and a number of portraits and cartoons. There is no essay accompanying the collection, but the material has been gathered from many sources, some now inaccessible.   E. E. S.

Andrews, John. History of the war with America, France, Spain, and Holland, 1775–83. London. 1785–6. 4v.   [**1225**]

The period covered is from 1775 to 1783, and the narrative which has been herein embodied of the American struggle (scattered through all four of the volumes instead of being told separately), is one of the most detailed accounts written by any Englishman, and should be compared with the later work by Ludlow (sect. 1424). The work is frankly a compilation, but shows much effort to obtain the exact facts, is fairly judicial, and shows marked impartiality of temper in dealing with the motives of the American colonists, and a fair amount of care in preparation. It contains numerous portraits and 8 maps, with separate indexes to all four volumes at the end of the fourth volume. Its literary quality is not such as to commend it to the general reader of the present day, and it serves only as " materials for history." W. E. F.

— Letters, 1772–76. See Massachusetts Historical Society, sect. 326.   [**1226**]

Armand, *Col.* Letters, relating to the siege of Yorktown. See New-York Historical Society, sect. 361.   [**1227**]

Arnold, *Maj. - Gen.* **Benedict.** ARNOLD, ISAAC NEWTON. Life of Benedict Arnold. Chicago: McClurg. 1880. $2.50.   [**1228**]

The life of the celebrated general of the 18th century (1741–1801), whose treason is one of the Revolutionary episodes, written by a member of the same family, though not a descendant. The sources of information in the present volume are, in part, family papers. As the book is frankly an attempt to overcome the " universal prejudice " against Arnold, it loses somewhat in impartial treatment, though the desire of the author to be just and fair is everywhere evident. The book has an index and one portrait.   W. E. F.

— BARBÉ-MARBOIS, FRANÇOIS DE. Complot d'Arnold et de Sir Henry Clinton. Paris: Didot. 1816.   [**1229**]

" Marbois, the secretary of the French legation at Philadelphia at the time, wrote a *Complot d'Arnold et Clinton,* which was not published till 1816 at Paris. Sparks says, that what came under Marbois' personal observation is valuable ; but otherwise the book, as most students think, should be used with caution. . . . Marbois was translated by Walsh in the *Amer. register,* vol. 2." Justin Winsor, in *Narrative and critical hist. of Am.,* 6: 463, and note.

— SPARKS, JARED. Life and treason of Benedict Arnold. (Library of Am. biography, v. 3.) Boston : Harper. 1835.   [**1230**]

This was the most comprehensive life before the appearance of Arnold's Arnold (sect. 1228). It is devoted almost exclusively to Arnold's military career in the American Revolution from 1775 until his treasonable action in 1780. The periods of his earlier and later life are slightly treated. The general attitude toward Arnold is fair. A contrast is drawn between the case of André and that of Nathan Hale.
                E. E. S.

Arnold, Howard Payson. Historic sidelights. N. Y.: Harper. 1899. $2.50. [**1231**]

" Benjamin Franklin and his friends both in America and abroad are the central figures of a most entertaining collection of delightful gossip, personal anecdotes, and quaint and curious historical lore, gathered from those out-of-the-way corners which historians proper for many reasons neglect." *Publisher's weekly*, 56: 896.

Aspinwall papers. See Massachusetts Historical Society, sect. 312.   [1232

Balch, Thomas. The French in America during the war of independence, 1777–83; tr. by T. W., E. S., and E. W. Balch. Phil.: Porter. 1891–5. 2v. Phil.: Coates. 2v. $5.
                                             [1233

Originally printed as *Les Français en Amérique* (Paris. 1872). Vol. 1 contains a narrative of the doings of the French in America especially in the Yorktown campaign. Vol. 2 contains lists and descriptions of regiments and officers. A contribution to our knowledge of the Revolution.   E. C.

Barney, *Commodore* Joshua. Biographical memoir of the late Commodore Joshua Barney; ed. by Mary Barney. Boston: Gray. 1832.
                                             [1234

Compiled from "autographical notes" and journals in possession of his family and other authentic sources. In the form of a memoir with original material scattered here and there through the text, in notes, and in an appendix. Interesting, but full of prejudice.   E. C.

Bartram, William. Travels through North and South Carolina, Georgia, East and West Florida, etc. Phil.: James. 1791. London. 1792.   [1235

The author, a botanist, sailed from London for Charleston, S. C., in April, 1773, " at the request of Dr. Fothergill, of London, to search the Floridas, and the western parts of Carolina and Georgia, for the discovery of rare and useful productions in nature, chiefly in the vegetable kingdom." His path lay through the territories of the Creek, Cherokee and Choctaw tribes of Indians, as far west as the Mississippi River. He reached Philadelphia in January, 1778, here closing his narrative. While the author is largely concerned with natural history, the Indians and the white fur-traders interest him greatly, and his journal abounds in graphic descriptions of forest life and aboriginal manners. An appendix of 42 pp. specifically treats of "The persons, manners, customs and government of the" tribes visited. The work is of high value as an original authority upon our southern Indians, during the period of the Revolutionary War.   R. G. T.

Bassett, John S. The regulators of North Carolina. See American Historical Association, sect. 246.   [1236

Bean, Theodore W. Washington at Valley Forge one hundred years ago. Norristown, Pa.: Bean. 1876.   [1237
Handbook of the Pennsylvania campaign of 1777–78. Supplied with admirable maps. Covers the operations from Brandywine to the evacuation of Philadelphia by the British in 1778. Carefully written.   E. C.

Belknap papers. See Massachusetts Historical Society, sect. 313.   [1238
Beaumarchais, Pierre Augustin Caron, *called* de. LOMÉNIE, LOUIS LÉONARD DE. Beaumarchais and his times; tr. by Henry S. Edwards. London: Addey. 1856. 4v. N. Y. Harper. 1857. 1v.
—— —— *Same;* tr. with an introd. by F. Lyster. N. Y.: Drallop. 1895. $1.50. [1239
" It is not too much to say that the character of Beaumarchais — of whom M. de Loménie has ... written a charming biography — was one of the most extraordinary in an age of extraordinary characters. ... From a watch-maker's workshop he raised himself at one bound to a social intimacy with royal families : from suffering hardship for the want of a few francs, he passed suddenly into the ranks of the leading financiers of Europe, and as suddenly relapsed into poverty." He was " a merchant, a courtier, a diplomatist, a lawyer, a song-writer, an admiral, a contractor, an inventor, a banker, a politician, and the most successful dramatic author, next to Molière, that France ever produced. ... This extraordinary man — this French Alcibiades — was really the first man in Europe who saw the possibility of the independence of the United States, and labored practically to effect that great object. Nor does it diminish his claim on our sympathy to know that for forty years he and his heirs were unpaid creditors of this country." J. Bonner, in *Harper's magazine*, 14: 76.

Blanchard, Claude. Journal of Claude Blanchard, commissary of the French auxiliary army sent to the United States, 1780–83 ; tr. from a French MS. by William Duane ; ed. by Thomas Balch. Albany: Munsell. 1875.
                                             [1240
Notes made generally from day to day from the time the French army under Rochambeau left France in 1780 until its return in 1783. Contains little of importance as to military operations ; but gives an interesting picture of the country and people of New England, the middle states, and Virginia. Well translated and edited.   E. C.

Botta, Charles. History of the war of the independence of the United States ; tr. from the Italian by George A. Otis. Phil. 1820–21. 3v. 8th ed. New Haven : Brainard. 1840. 2v.   [1241
The most valuable of the earlier histories of the Revolution, and not yet considered antiquated. Military history predominates. The work closes with the retirement of Washington in 1783. The perspective of the history is bad in places, owing to its being based on European sources. It follows classical forms in putting imaginary speeches into the mouths of the chief actors. A lofty style adds to the heroic mold in which the forefathers of the republic are cast.
                                             E. E. S.

Boudinot, Elias. Journal ; or Historical recollections of American events during the

Revolutionary War; from his own original MS. Phil.: Bourquin. 1894. Trenton, N.J.: Traver. 1899. Limited ed. [1242

Literal and exact. Valuable source for Revolutionary history by one who took a prominent part in events, but miscellaneous and not very extensive.
E. C. R.

—— Life, public services, addresses, and letters; ed. by J. J. Boudinot. Boston: Houghton. 1896. 2v. $6 net. [1243

A well arranged but not critically edited publication of the private and public letters of Boudinot, with his "reminiscences" inserted at proper places. Several slips of memory appear in the latter. Many private letters to and from relatives are without public interest. Few of the public letters have not been printed heretofore; 175 pages of speeches are taken from the *Annals of Congress*. Valuable as a whole for the rise of the Revolution in New Jersey, Benedict Arnold, treatment of British prisoners, Yorktown, Continental Congress (1778, 1781-4), treaty of 1783, early Federal Congress, inauguration of Washington, and Philadelphia mint. E. E. S.

Bowdoin and Temple papers. See Massachusetts Historical Society, sect. 320. [1244

Brant, Joseph. EGGLESTON, EDWARD, *and Mrs.* ELIZABETH EGGLESTON SEELYE. Brant and Red Jacket. (Famous Am. Indians.) N. Y.: Dodd. [c. 1879.] $1. [1245

Disappointing and fragmentary. A book "for the general reader and especially young people." A hasty summary of the whole ground covered by Parkman. Title misleading. Brant and Red Jacket are merely incidental to the narrative. H. W. H.

—— STONE, WILLIAM LEETE. Life of Joseph Brant — Thayendanegea, including the border wars of the American Revolution, etc. N. Y. 1838. 2v. Albany: Munsell. 1865. 2v. [1246

A history of operations in the Indian country, particularly in New York and Pennsylvania, and on the Canadian border, during the Revolutionary War, with sketches of the Indian relations of the United States and Great Britain. The style of the author is clear and dignified, but is prolix and lacks imagination; the work is consequently not easy reading. These scholarly volumes abound in documentary material, for the author wrote from original sources and displays abundant topographical knowledge; the index also is ample. The point of view is that of strong sympathy with the aborigines, therein differing from most of the earlier historians of border warfare.
R. G. T.

Brooks, Elbridge Streeter. Century book of the American Revolution. N. Y.: Century Co. [c. 1897.] $1.50. [1247

A deservedly popular juvenile book, written as the story of a supposed visit by a party of young people to the Revolutionary battlefields. The arrangement is both chronological and geographical. The illustra-

tions are largely photographic reproductions and correspondingly valuable. This volume is akin to other "Century" juvenile books by the same author.
E. E. S.

Burgoyne, *Lt.-Gen.* John. A state of the expedition from Canada as laid before the House of Commons, and verified by evidence, with a collection of authentic documents. London: Almon. 1780. 2d ed. 1780. [1248

This defence of his campaign consists of Gen. Burgoyne's prefatory speech and narrative before a committee of the House, the evidence of his witnesses, his review of their testimony, and an appendix containing the written evidence. Included in this last is a return by Gen. Gates of the strength of his army Oct. 16, 1777, and there are several maps illustrating the campaign. F. J. S.

—— DEANE, CHARLES. Lieut.-Gen. John Burgoyne and the convention of Saratoga. See American Antiquarian Society, sect. 242.
[1249

—— FONBLANQUE, EDWARD BARRINGTON DE. Political and military episodes in the latter half of the 18th century; derived from the life and correspondence of the Right Hon. John Burgoyne. London: Macmillan. 1876.
[1250

Five of the ten chapters describe Burgoyne's services in the Revolutionary War as a British major-general from 1775 to 1779. The narrative is founded upon letters, reports, and records, and supplemented by the author's conclusions. These are extremely apologetic and explanatory in Burgoyne's behalf. The military mal-administration of England is the excuse. Some interesting papers are in the appendix. E. E. S.

Burke, Edmund. Conciliation with the colonies: speech; ed. by Robert Anderson. (Riverside lit. ser.) Boston: Houghton. [c. 1896.] 25c.

—— Speech on conciliation with America; ed. by Sidney C. Newsom. (Macmillan's pocket English classics.) N. Y.: Macmillan. 1899. 25c. net. [1251

The last is a useful pocket edition, well printed and well bound. The biographical introduction is good and contains a brief estimate of Burke as a statesman with an estimate of his literary position, which is limited to the statement of facts and ventures little criticism. The bibliography is a list of seven books that all libraries possess. The notes are of unequal value, and as a text-book the edition needs a synopsis of the speech. The only index is that of the notes.
V. L. C.

The first-named is also a convenient edition, with introduction and notes.

—— MORLEY, JOHN. Edmund Burke: a historical study. London: Macmillan. 1867. N. Y.: Macmillan. 1867. New ed. $1.50.

— MORLEY, JOHN. Burke. (English men of letters.) London : Macmillan. 1888. N. Y.: Harper. [1887.] 1892. 75c.   **[1252**

A different standpoint is adopted in each of these books. The first is philosophical and not in any sense biographical. Its six chapters treat of Burke's characteristics, the leading issues of his day, his attitude on the English constitution, on American independence, on political and economic reform for the British possessions and, lastly, on the French Revolution. The book remains the best estimate we have of Burke's political position. The style accords with the subject-matter. The "Men of letters" volume with its reprint is almost entirely biographical, taking up Burke's life by periods and giving a narrative of his career as a statesman, author, orator and as a figure in society. Well written and authoritative, it sadly needs an index and contains no bibliography. Together, these two books give all that the average reader or student needs in order to know Burke's place in English history and literature.   V. L. C.

— STEBBINS, C. Edmund Burke, his services as agent of the province of New York. See American Antiquarian Society, sect. 241.   **[1253**

Campbell, William W. Annals of Tryon County ; or, The border warfare of New-York, during the Revolution. N. Y.: Harper. 1831.   **[1254**

Tryon County included all of the province lying west of a longitudinal line running not far from the centre of Schoharie County. This region was long debatable land, and the scene of New York's principal border wars. Campbell's book attracted wide attention at the time of its appearance, and inspired many other frontier histories in New York and adjoining states. The author was a native of Cherry Valley, and wrote many of his chapters for a local historical society ; before publication, he widened his field to embrace all of Tryon County, but Cherry Valley remains the principal theatre of his investigations. A pioneer work in the annals of early western New York, it will always remain a standard authority, for it is compiled with judicious care, in good literary form, contains much which the author obtained from first sources, oral and documentary, and may be recommended as entertaining reading.   R. G. T.

Carrington, *Brig. - Gen.* **Henry Beebee.** Battles of the American Revolution. N. Y.: Barnes. 1876. $5. 2v. $6.   **[1255**

Covers only the military side of the Revolution. Based on a careful study of the leading sources. Abundantly supplied with good plans. An admirable book in conception and execution.   E. C.

Carroll, Charles. Journal during his visit to Canada in 1776 ; with memoir and notes by Brantz Mayer. (Maryland Hist. Soc. Publications.) Balt. 1845.   **[1256**

Carroll, with his brother John, Benjamin Franklin, and Chase, was sent by the Continental Congress to persuade the Canadians to join the rebellious colonies. The journal extends from April 2 to June 10, 1776, and is here edited with notes and an introductory memoir. Of interest as explaining why Canada did not join in the Revolution. The subject-matter has been made use of in the several lives of Carroll.   E. E. S.

— ROWLAND, KATE MASON. Life of Charles Carroll of Carrollton, 1737–1832. N. Y.: Putnam. 1898. 2v. $6.   **[1257**

Although associated with almost every public event from 1770 to 1800, Carroll habitually destroyed his correspondence. Hence this, his only worthy biography, finds its material largely in official records, publications of the Maryland Historical Society, the journal of William Maclay, and a few unpublished family letters. It is a mixture of his public and private life, but especially a Carroll family book. A point is stretched to prove him a strict constructionist and "states-rights" man, although a Federalist.   E. E. S.

Caruthers, E. W. Interesting Revolutionary incidents and sketches of character, chiefly in the "Old North State." Ser. 2. Phil. 1856. [Ser. 1: Revolutionary incidents, etc.]   **[1258**

"Much of this work seems to be based on good material ; but one should be especially careful to separate such portions from those founded on tradition, which must have misled Caruthers in several instances." E. Channing, in *Narrative and critical hist. of Am.*, 6: 514.

Carver, *Capt.* **Jonathan.** Travels through the interior parts of North-America, 1766–8. London. 1778.
—— Three years' travels, *etc.* Phil.: Cruikshank. 1784.   **[1259**

A narrative of a journey to the Mississippi River, in 1766–68, by a native of the New York Province, told with some skill but with an absence of critical insight, and showing an unscrupulous use of earlier narratives. The value of Carver's "Chippeway vocabulary," here included, is also impaired by the presence of the same defects.   W. E. F.

Cavendish, *Sir* **Henry.** Debates in Parliament, 1768–1774. See in Part I: Sources, sect. 76.   **[1260**

Chalmers, George. Introduction to the history of the revolt of the American colonies. London. 1782. Boston: Monroe. 1845. 2v.   **[1261**

One of the most suggestive works ever written on early American history. To be sure, it is only a sketch of a large subject ; it contains crude statements ; it shows lack of sympathy with much that was new and valuable in colonial development ; it exhibits the narrow spirit of English officialism. But it reveals, as does no other work, the essential unity of the period of which it treats. In it the correct point of view, viz., that the colonies were parts of a growing maritime empire, is chosen and maintained throughout. The conflict between the principle of imperial control on the one side, and that of local or colonial independence on the other, is shown to be the issue of profoundest significance in this period. It is that which gives unity to it, and it is not unlikely that the historians of the future will return to the fundamental thought of Chalmers, though it must be developed on broader and less partisan lines.

H. L. O.

—— Political annals of the present united colonies from their settlement to the peace of 1763. London. 1780.   [1262

Not strictly a book of annals, but a history of the English-American colonies prior to 1689. For his time Chalmers made good use of the materials in the British Public Record Office. He is an authority of the first importance on points of colonial public law. He is not sympathetic toward the Puritans or toward other early defenders of colonial independence. Still his temper is judicial, his knowledge — considering the time when he wrote — was adequate, his judgment sober. His style is clear, but without ornament. He cites authorities for all important statements.

H. L. O.

Chamberlain, Mellen. Authentication of the Declaration of Independence. See Massachusetts Historical Society, sect. 337.   [1263

Chastellux, François Jean, *marquis* de. Travels in North-America, 1780–82 ; tr. by J. Kent. London. 1787. 2v. N. Y.: White. 1827.   [1264

" Many important economical, social, and personal facts are gracefully recorded ; and the character of the country and of the men who directed the War of Independence and the formation of a free government are described ; there are some lively anecdotical episodes, and not a few acute speculations: the work is truly French in the constant alternation of a light vein of remark with serious observation, and warm sentiment with worldly wisdom." H. T. Tuckerman, *America and her commentators*, p. 60.

Chatham, William Pitt, *1st earl of.* Correspondence ; ed. by W. S. Taylor and J. H. Pringle. London : Murray. 1838–40. 4v. . [1265

These volumes are largely taken up with English political questions. The detailed correspondence practically begins in 1758 and continues to 1778 ; but for a large part of the time Chatham was either out of political life or was ill. On the whole the volumes are disappointing.   E. C.

— MACAULAY, THOMAS BABINGTON. Essays on William Pitt, Earl of Chatham. (In Edinburgh rev. Jan., 1834 ; Oct., 1844.)   [1266

Two of Lord Macaulay's most brilliant biographical essays. Devoted almost entirely to English politics. Only scanty allusions to American affairs — even to such episodes as the Stamp Act. May be most conveniently consulted in the editions of Macaulay's *Essays.*   E. C.

Chevalier, Édouard. Histoire de la marine française pendant la guerre de l'indépendance américaine ; précédée d'une étude sur la marine militaire de la France et sur ses institutions depuis le commencement du 17e siècle jusqu'à l'année 1777. Paris. 1877.

—— Histoire de la marine française sous la première République, faisant suite à l'Histoire de la marine française pendant la guerre de l'indépendance américaine. Paris. 1886.

—— Histoire de la marine française sous le Consulat et l'Empire, faisant suite à l'Histoire de la marine française sous la première République. Paris. 1886.   [1267

This history of the French navy covers the period from the beginning of the seventeenth century to the close of the Napoleonic empire. For the earlier period the reader must turn to the recent work of M. de la Roncière, for the later to single monographs dealing with special phases of the subject. Of the work before us only the first volume deals with American history, presenting fairly and clearly the share which the French fleet took in the war of the Revolution. In close connection with this, which is his main purpose, M. Chevalier attempts, and with considerable success, to relieve the fleet from charges of sloth and inactivity, and the officers, notably D'Estaing, from charges of disobedience and insubordination. The author has based his work upon the 133 manuscript volumes in the Archives de la Marine in Paris, and has given a clear, readable, and straightforward narrative.   C. M. A.

Chotteau, Léon. La guerre de l'indépendance, 1775–83 : les Français en Amérique ; avec une préface par Édouard Laboulaye. Paris. 1876. 3e éd. Paris. 1882.   [1268

Usually cited as Chotteau, Les Français, etc. Gives a French view of the Revolutionary War — with undue attention to the French participation. Not critical. Interesting merely from its point of view.

E. C.

Clark, *Brig.-Gen.* **George Rogers.** Col. George Rogers Clark's sketch of his campaign in the Illinois in 1778–9 ; with an introd. by Henry Pirtle. Cin.: Clarke. 1869. $2 net. [1269

" A very original and striking Revolutionary character is portrayed by himself. . . . The value of this campaign and of Col. Clark's services generally along the Ohio, in extending the domain of the United Colonies, and afterwards of the United States, is probably not exaggerated by Mr. Pirtle in his Introduction to the sketch. Clark's military capacity was certainly of a high order, and it is seldom one reads of a commander possessing such boldness, resource, and tact. He understood perfectly, for military purposes, the Indian nature, and how to exhibit at the right time courageous defiance and magnanimity. . . . Major Bowman's journal of the expedition against Vincennes is appended to Col. Clark's letter, and the notes of the editor of this volume add very much to its readableness and historical completeness." *Nation*, 9: 11.

" A little of the romance which belongs to all French colonial history hangs about Colonel Clark's unconscious page, and his sketch affords here and there a glimpse of the life of the *habitans* in the old seventeenth-century settlements of the French at Kaskaskia, Cahokia and St. Vincent ; but for the most part it is a plain and summary account of the military operations, and depends for its chief interest upon the view it affords of the character of as brave and shrewd a soldier, and as bad a speller, as ever lived. . . . The account of his campaign is in the form of a letter to the Hon. George Mason, of Gunston Hall, Virginia, and it is given with the most familiar frankness and with the greatest spirit. . . . The letter is now printed for the first time. We heartily commend it to all who love to taste history at its sources or who enjoy character." *Atlantic monthly*, 24: 641.

— ENGLISH, WILLIAM HAYDEN. Conquest of the country northwest of the River Ohio, 1778–83, and life of Gen. George Rogers Clark. Indianapolis : Bowen-Merrill Co. 1896. 2v. $6 net.   [1270

" The conquest of the Northwest of 1778–83 is only another name for the life and times of Clark, who first finds his adequate biographer in the author of this great work. The materials were copious ; their richness was almost embarrassing ; and Mr. English has utilized them all to the utmost advantage. The result is a noble historical and biographical work of permanent value, which at once takes first rank. The story is told with precision and in great detail ; it abounds in contemporaneous documentary material of the highest value, and is enriched with a great many facsimiles of letters and autographs, besides portraits, views, maps, and other illustrations. . . . The appendix to this volume contains a great variety of interesting matter, including in full Clark's account against the State of Virginia, and the strange history of the bill in chancery over his alleged will, filed May 6, 1835, and not dismissed till November 20, 1865." E. Coues, in *Nation*, 62: 102.

Clark, John, Jr. Letters to General Washington written during the occupation of Philadelphia by the British army. See Pennsylvania, Historical Society of, sect. 383.   [1271

Coffin, Charles Carleton. Boys of '76. N. Y.: Harper. [c. 1876.] $2.   [1272

One of a very popular juvenile historical series. It describes the events of the Revolution from the alarm after Lexington and Concord to the surrender of Cornwallis. There is no discrimination between the traditional and the authentic, but the stories are harmless. The style is well adapted to young readers. The illustrations are taken generally from Lossing's *Field-book of the Revolution.*   E. E. S.

Colden, Cadwallader. Papers. See New-York Historical Society, sect. 360.   [1273

Condorcet, Jean Antoine Nicolas Caritat, *marquis* de. De l'influence de la révolution de

l'Amérique sur l'Europe. (In Œuvres complètes, v. 11, pp. 237–395. Paris. 1847–49. 12v.)   [1274

A philosophical prophecy, on the probable influence of the American Revolution on Europe. Written about 1785. This edition contains a supplement of events since 1784, including the work of the Federal convention, the Constitution (in French) and a dissertation on the more important features of that great document. Interesting as a prophecy — among other enumerated advantages of the American Revolution is its effect on the preservation of peace in Europe.

E. C.

Conover, George S., *ed.* Journals of the military expedition of Major-General John Sullivan against the Six Nations of Indians in 1779; with records of centennial celebrations. Auburn, N. Y.: Knapp. 1887.   [1275

Prepared under direction of the New York Secretary of State, pursuant to a legislative statute of 1885. The volume contains the journals of twenty-six officers in Sullivan's expedition, with biographical notes by the editor ; the official reports of Sullivan ; and a roster of the officers engaged. Closely associated with this expedition were Van Shaick's Onondaga campaign and Brodhead's Allegheny campaign, in which some of the journalists were concerned ; Brodhead's own final report is also given. Care appears to have been exercised by the editor in literally reproducing the journals, where those were obtainable in the original MSS. ; but the MSS. of several are missing, and earlier publications, obviously "improved" by their editors, have been reprinted. An account of the centennial celebrations held in 1879 is also given. Numerous maps, plans and portraits embellish the volume, which may be accepted as an authoritative and exhaustive treatment of an important event in early New York history ; incidentally, the journals are of value to the student of Indians and frontier life.

R. G. T.

Cooke, William D., *ed.* Revolutionary history of North Carolina. Raleigh, N. C. : Cooke. N. Y.: Putnam. 1853.   [1276

The introductory sketch describes the " War of the Regulation" (Regulators) in 1771 and connects it with the Mecklenburg Declaration of Independence. The Declaration, the British invasion of 1776, of 1780 and of 1781, are treated in three lectures by different men. The result is a series of sketches rather than connected history. There are several illustrations and a facsimile of the Mecklenburg signatures.   E. E. S.

Cornwallis, Charles, *1st marquis.* Answer to that part of the narrative of Lieut.-Gen. Sir Henry Clinton which relates to the conduct of Lieut.-Gen. Earl Cornwallis during the campaign in North-America, 1781. London: Debrett. 1783. Phil.: J. Campbell. 1866. [1277

Following a brief introduction in which the author defends the conduct of his campaign, he prints the correspondence between himself and Clinton from January, 1781, down to his surrender, relative to his

North Carolina campaign, his march into Virginia, his operations therein, and his occupation and defense of Yorktown. The strength of his army on the first of each month from June to October is shown in detail by a table. F. J. S.

—— Correspondence; ed. with notes by Charles Ross. London: Murray. 1859. 3v. [1278

Letters often printed in extract without any indication of the fact that portions are omitted. Contains a few documents not to be found elsewhere. Editorial work poor and book uninteresting. E. C.

Correspondence as to the relief of the sufferers by the Boston port bill. See Massachusetts Historical Society, sect. 309. [1279

Cowell, Benjamin. Spirit of '76 in Rhode Island; or Sketches of the efforts of the government and people in the war of the Revolution. Boston. 1850. [1280

A collection of documents strung together by a brief narrative with traditions, reminiscences and biographical notices. Appendix A contains extracts from the *Journal* of Major Simeon Thayer, who took part in the Canadian expedition and in other operations of the war. A useful but heterogeneous collection of material. The book has neither table of contents nor index. E. C.

Cresap, *Capt.* Michael. JACOB, JOHN J. Biographical sketch of the life of Capt. Michael Cresap. Cumberland, Md. 1826. With notes and appendix. Cin.: Dodge. 1860. [1281

"With slight claim to literary merit, and much inaccuracy as to dates, it contains some important documents, and is an earnest vindication of Cresap's character." W. F. Poole, *Narrative and critical hist. of Am.*, 6: 712.

—— MAYER, BRANTZ. Tah-gah-jute; or Logan and Captain Michael Cresap: discourse before Maryland Hist. Soc. [Baltimore. 1851.]
—— —— *Same.* Albany: Munsell. 1867. [1282

This is a vindication of Capt. Michael Cresap from the charge made by Jefferson in his *Notes on Virginia* of massacring the Indian Logan's hunting party. The main evidence in behalf of Cresap consists of a letter written by George Rogers Clark in 1798, and Jefferson is incidentally accused of allowing his accusation to stand after being shown its injustice. The genuineness of Logan's famous speech is discussed at length with somewhat damaging effect. F. J. S.

Crevecœur, J. Hector St. John de. Letters from an American farmer. London: Davies. 1782. Phil.: Carey. 1793. [1283

"Somewhat like a prose idyl is this record; Hazlitt delighted in its naïve enthusiasm, and commended it to Charles Lamb as well as in the *Quarterly*, as giving 'an idea how American scenery and manners may be treated with a lively poetic interest.' . . . Hector St.

John Crevecœur was of noble birth, a native of Normandy, born in 1731; he was sent to England when but sixteen years old, which is the cause of his early and complete mastery of our language. In 1754 he came to New York, and settled on a farm in the adjacent region. . . . His 'Letters of an American farmer' were published in London in 1782. He translated them into his native tongue. They have a winsome flavor, and picture so delectably the independence, the resources, and the peace of an agricultural life, just before and after the Revolution, in the more settled states of America, that the reader of the present day cannot feel surprised that he beguiled many an emigrant from the Old World to the banks of the Ohio and the Delaware." H. T. Tuckerman, *America and her commentators*, p. 89.

Cruikshank, *Lt.-Col.* Ernest. Annals of Niagara. Niagara Falls South, Ont.: Lundy's Lane Hist. Soc. 1893. 75c. [1284

The author, a Canadian military officer, is one of the most competent of the several local historians of the Niagara frontier; perhaps the best of those dwelling upon the Canadian side. The monograph is written from original sources, and gives us apparently the last word upon an interesting region and period in midwestern history — Niagara during the Revolutionary War. Colonel Cruikshank's literary style lacks polish, but is clear and vigorous. R. G. T.

Curwen, Samuel. Journal and letters, 1775–84. N. Y.: Francis. 1842. [1285

Essential for an appreciation of the hardships incurred by those persons who chose the Loyalist (Tory) side in the American Revolution. Describes Curwen's flight from Salem, Massachusetts, to Philadelphia, and thence to England, and his daily life with the other refugees there. The information thus given can be obtained nowhere else. The 162 biographical sketches in the appendix, largely of his fellow Loyalists, are inferior to those given in a good biographical dictionary. E. E. S.

Cushing, Harry Alonzo. History of the transition from provincial to commonwealth government in Massachusetts. (Columbia Univ. studies in history, etc., v. 7, no. 1.) N. Y.: Macmillan. 1896. $2. [1286

A detailed and carefully written political history of Massachusetts from 1774 to 1780 — from the close of provincial government to the adoption of a state constitution. The end of provincial government, the administration of affairs by the provincial congress, the resumption of the charter, the rejected constitution of 1778, and the adoption of the constitution of 1780, are the topics treated. The work is based upon thorough study of primary authorities, and has attractiveness of style. W. MacD.

Dawson, Henry Barton. Sons of liberty in New York. N. Y. 1859. [1287

This is a paper which, in May, 1859, was read before the New York Historical Society. It contains a brief review of the development of government in the province of New York, showing how completely autocratic it was under Gov. Nicolls and his immediate successors. He outlines the resistance in New York to the stamp duty, and shows that this proceeded mainly from the common people, organized as Sons of Liberty. He claims that this was the only genuinely revolutionary element in the population, and that it had to contend not only with the crown officials, but against the self-interest and timidity of the aristocratic classes. The reader will find nothing in this monograph of special significance except the claim that New York led the way in organizing committees of correspondence.   H. L. O.

——— Westchester-County, New York, during the American Revolution. Morrisania: Author. 1886.   [1288

This monograph was published separately and also as a part of Scharf's *History of Westchester County*. It is a study of the conditions out of which the Revolution developed in the southern part of the province of New York, and contains a somewhat detailed account of the movement there, from the spring of 1774 till the close of 1776. Its author was one of the best known, and certainly one of the best informed, local historians of the region, and his work is in every respect a thorough, original study of the subject. His spirit and point of view are those of the moderate Loyalist; Isaac Wilkins is the leader of the times for whom he has the greatest respect. The great excellency of the book consists in the true picture which it presents of the contentment and political quietism of the farmers of Westchester County, and in the account which it gives of the process by which the county was revolutionized from without. The style is diffuse, labored and formal. Some extravagant views are expressed and implied. But, taken all in all, this, in my judgment, is the most suggestive book ever written concerning any phase of the American Revolution, and reveals a method of treatment which is likely to be greatly utilized in the future.   H. L. O.

Deane, Charles. On Paul Revere's signal. See Massachusetts Historical Society, sect. 331.   [1289
——— On the Massachusetts bill of rights. See Massachusetts Historical Society, sect. 330.   [1290
Deane, Silas. Correspondence of Silas Deane, delegate to the congress of Philadelphia, 1774–76. (In Connecticut Historical Society. Coll., v. 2. 1870.)   [1291
——— Papers, 1774–90. (New-York Hist. Soc. Collections, Publication fund series, v. 19–23.) N. Y. 1887–91. 5v.   [1292

The *Correspondence* is useful for the early history of the Revolution in Connecticut. The *Papers* is an invaluable collection of letters and documents to, from and about Deane, dating from 1774 to 1790, is ably edited and thoroughly indexed. It is indispensable as a source for the history of aid received from France in the Revolutionary War. Vol. 1 contains a succinct and favorable biographical notice of Deane by the editor, Mr. Charles Isham.   V. L. C.

Denny, *Maj.* **Ebenezer.** Military journal, 1781 to 1795. See Pennsylvania, Historical Society of, sect. 376.   [1293
Deux Ponts, Guillaume, comte de. My campaigns in America: a journal, 1780–81; tr. from the French MS., with notes, by Samuel Abbott Green. Boston.: Wiggin. 1868.   [1294

Deals mainly with the French at Newport and in the Yorktown campaign. The French text and the translation printed successively. An interesting view from the French standpoint.   E. C.

Dickinson, John. Writings; ed. by Paul Leicester Ford. V. 1. (Hist. Soc. of Pennsylvania. Memoirs, v. 14. 1895.)   [1295
Forms vol. 2 of the *Life and writings of Dickinson*, but vol. 1 of the *Writings* alone. Although not absolutely complete, it promises to be, when finished, the authoritative edition. Vol. 1 comes down to 1774, and includes, besides minor pieces, the *Declaration of rights* and *Petition to the King* of the Stamp Act Congress, the *Letters of a farmer*, and the *Letters to the inhabitants of the British Colonies*. The editor's notes are discriminating and valuable.   W. MacD.

——— STILLÉ, CHARLES JANEWAY. Life and times of John Dickinson, 1732–1808. Phil.: Lippincott. 1891.   [1296
——— *Same.* (Hist. Soc. of Pennsylvania. Memoirs, v. 13. Phil. 1891.)

A careful and thorough biography, by a competent scholar. The author naturally seeks to defend Dickinson from the charge of insincerity and political apostasy freely brought against him during his life, and goes with detail into the pamphlet and newspaper controversy of the time; he does not, however, bring out with clearness the singular "moral hesitancy" which determined much of Dickinson's wavering conduct.   W. MacD.

Doddridge, Joseph. Notes on the settlement and Indian wars of the western parts of Virginia and Pennsylvania, 1763–83, with a view of the state of society, and manners of the first settlers of the western country. Wellsburgh, Va. 1824.
——— *Same*, with a memoir of Doddridge by his daughter; ed. by Alfred Williams. Albany: Munsell. 1876.   [1297
"Doddridge was reprinted, with some transpositions, in Kercheval's *Hist. of the valley of Virginia*." *Narrative and critical hist. of Am.*, 5: 581.
See, also, note on Wither's *Chronicles of border warfare*, sect. 1579.

Doniol, Henri. Histoire de la participation de la France à l'établissement des Etats-Unis d'Amérique. Paris: Imprimerie nationale; Picard. 1886–1900. 5v. and supplt. 120fr.   [1298

A monumental work, being at once a diplomatic history and a collection of documents covering the events which led to the alliance between France and the United States in 1778, the coöperation of the two powers from that time till the close of the war, and the peace negotiations that followed. It has been prepared with great labor and scrupulous care. It is a thoroughly original work, a standard authority for all time to come.　　　　　　　　　　　H. L. O.

Drake, Francis Samuel, *ed.* Tea leaves: being a collection of letters and documents relating to the shipment of tea to the American colonies in 1773; with introd., notes, etc. Boston: Crane. 1884.　　　　　　　　[1299

The letters of the American consignees to the East India Company and accompanying documents form the most valuable portion of the book. The introduction running to 180 pages contains all the traditions and stories, including biographical notices, of those who are supposed to have taken part in the destruction of the tea. This part of the book is interesting but it is highly uncritical.　　　　　　　　　　E. C.

Drake, Samuel Adams. Burgoyne's invasion of 1777, with an outline sketch of the American invasion of Canada, 1775-76. (Decisive events in American history.) Boston: Lee. 1889. 50c.　　　　　　　　　[1300

A useful little book, compiled with intelligence and skill, on the basis of recent knowledge, and marked by judgment and fairness, and a good English style. It has an index, and a portrait, and one other illustration, but its most conspicuous merit lies in its lucid tracing of the military movements, enforced by about a dozen outline maps. Primarily for young readers, but interesting to the general reader, of any age.
　　　　　　　　　　　　　　　　W. E. F.

——Campaign of Trenton, 1776-77. (Decisive events in American history.) Boston: Lee. 1895. 50c.　　　　　　　　　[1301

Like the same author's account of the Burgoyne campaign, this is a book which has young readers chiefly in mind. It is intelligently compiled from trustworthy sources, and shows an effort to be accurate and fair in its statements. The story is told in a lucid manner, and is supplemented by four maps. There is a good index.　　　　　　　　W. E. F.

——*ed.* Bunker Hill: the story told in letters from the battlefield by British officers engaged; with introd. and sketch of the battle. Boston: Nichols. 1875.　　　　　　[1302

These 11 British narratives are preceded by Mr. Drake's brief introduction, in which Prescott is cited as the American commander, rather than Putnam. Mr. Drake belongs to a family of antiquaries, and his work is here marked by wide knowledge, fair temper, critical judgment, cautious method, and a direct style, yet the book is, on the whole, for the special student, rather than the general reader. There is no index.　　　　　　　　W. E. F.

Draper, Lyman Copeland. King's Mountain and its heroes. Cin.: Peter G. Thomson. 1881.　　　　　　　　　　　[1303

Dr. Draper's work covers operations in the southern states from the fall of Charleston, in May, 1780; presents sketches of the leaders, and reprints extracts from original sources, including the Campbell-Shelby controversy. It is based on traditional accounts, gathered from the descendants and connections of participants, and on many contemporary narratives and reports gathered by Dr. Draper during a long life, devoted, with infinite industry, to this subject. The work covers the whole subject minutely, and goes into great, almost oppressive, detail. It is a mine of information on that period, and gives vigorous sketches of the frontiersmen by whom the battle was won and a vivid account of the battle itself. While minor errors, arising from too much dependence on tradition, have been discovered, as an authority it has no rival in its field.　　　　　　　S. B. W.

Drayton, John. Memoirs of the American Revolution from its commencement to 1776 inclusive; as relating to the state of South Carolina. Charleston. 1821. 2v.　　　[1304

A concise description of the rise and progress of the American Revolution in South Carolina and neighboring states to the year mentioned. The material was gathered largely from the memoirs and papers of Chief Justice William Henry Drayton, a contemporary. The first volume gives the early political events and the second the early military movements in the South, especially the expedition against the Cherokees and the defence of Fort Moultrie.　　E. E. S.

Durand, John, *ed.* New materials for the history of the American Revolution; tr. from documents in the French archives. N. Y.: Holt. 1889. $1.75.　　　　　　[1305

This cannot rival, but may be used as supplementary to Doniol's monumental work (sect. 1298), since it translates in part many documents there published and adds others. As a reference book its value is seriously impaired by failure to cite the exact location of the documents used. There seems to be no reason, however, to entertain C. H. Lee's insinuation in *Vindication of Arthur Lee* (Richmond. 1894) that Durand drew at times from imaginary sources. The documents relate chiefly to Beaumarchais' services and misfortunes, four of the twelve sections of the book relating to him, while the appendix contains the 1822 appeal to Congress by his daughter. Selections from the correspondence of De Rayneval, 1778-79, and of De la Luzerne, 1779-81, form the principal residue and throw light on the secret debates of Congress and the cabal against Washington. The most important of the other documents are the memorials which led Louis XVI. to adopt the American cause. Deserving of special attention are Beaumarchais' letter of December, 1775, translated and published here for the first time; the Bonvouloir report on condition of the colonies in 1775; two unidentified reports of the same nature dated 1779 and 1780, and Thomas Paine's letter of May, 1793, to Danton on lessons for the young French republic, to be learned from the experience of the United States.
　　　　　　　　　　　　　　　　V. L. C.

Eddis, William. Letters from America, historical and descriptive, 1769–77. London. 1792.   [1306

" Forty letters, written between 1769 and 1777, by William Eddis, and published in London in 1792, contain numerous statistical and historical facts not elsewhere obtainable. The author's position as surveyor of the customs at Annapolis, in Maryland, gave him singular advantages as an observer ; and his letters are justly considered as the ' best account we have of the rise of Revolutionary principles in Maryland.' " H. T. Tuckerman, *America and her commentators*, p. 186.

Eelking, Max von. German allied troops in the North American war of independence, 1776–83 ; tr. and abridged by J. G. Rosengarten. (Munsell's Historical series, no. 19.) Albany. 1893. $5.   [1307

Though abridged from the German original (*Die deutschen Hülfstruppen*, published in 1863), this English version of Mr. Rosengarten is made more useful by an index and other welcome features, added by the editor. It remains the best source of information in this field, as regards knowledge and judgment, though parts of it are thought by Mr. E. J. Lowell to require acceptance with caution. The style is straightforward (and is well translated) ; and, to a reader who cares for the subject, the book is full of interest. It is scarcely a book for the general reader.   W. E. F.

Egerton, Hugh Edward. Short history of British colonial policy. London: Methuen. 1897. N. Y.: New Amsterdam Book Co. 1898. $4 net.   [1308

The first eight chapters of this fresh and suggestive essay concern the history of the British colonies in America and should be read by every student of American history. Mr. Egerton's attitude is impartial and critical ; he has made use of the papers in the Public Record Office and the reports of the Historical Manuscript Commission, and has produced practically the first work which attempts to view with frank impartiality colonial history from the standpoint of Great Britain. He concludes that, after all allowances have been made for special causes, the prime cause of the American Revolution was the burden of the mercantile system ; that Great Britain's conduct was not tyrannical, but incapable and weak ; and that British statesmen of the period of the Revolution were second-rate men and their statesmanship was full of blunders and mistakes. In view of the brevity of the work, American readers will regret the space that the author gives to familiar facts relating to the history of the colonies, while the special student will justly complain of Mr. Egerton's apparent unwillingness to give exact references to his authorities.   C. M. A.

Ellet, *Mrs*. Elizabeth Fries (Lummis). Domestic history of the American Revolution. N. Y.: Scribner. 1850.   [1309

The value of this book is chiefly due to the fact that no other writer has treated the same field with any

fulness. The bases for the statements here compiled were, in part, tradition (the writer having been born as late as 1818), and, in part, manuscript records. The book is not free from errors, but is marked by fair-mindedness and a not unattractive style. It has neither illustrations, maps, nor index. For the general reader.   W. E. F.

—— The women of the American Revolution. N. Y.: Baker. 1848. 2v.   [1310

Largely devoted to obscure women. Full of anecdotes — based on tradition. Not written in a critical spirit. Valuable for the light it throws on the everyday life of the time. Illustrated with many portraits mostly of slight value.   E. C.

Ellis, George Edward. History of the battle of Bunker's (Breed's) Hill, 1775. Boston: Lockwood. 1875. Boston : Lee. 50c.   [1311

A brief account, compiled in preparation for the one hundredth anniversary of the battle, by a well-known clergyman who had long resided in Charlestown. Dr. Ellis's point of view makes Prescott the commander, rather than Putnam. In respect to knowledge, judgment and temper, it is a well-constructed narrative, and its style is interesting. It has no index, but has one illustration and a map. For the general reader.   W. E. F.

Farnsworth, Amos. Diary (siege of Boston). See Massachusetts Historical Society, sect. 349.   [1312

Feltman, William. Journal, 1781–82, embracing the siege of Yorktown and the southern campaign. See Pennsylvania, Historical Society of, sect. 384.   [1313

Finlay, Hugh. Journal kept during his survey of the post-offices between Falmouth and Casco Bay in the province of Massachusetts and Savannah in Georgia, 1773–4. Brooklyn: Norton. 1867.   [1314

Finlay was appointed surveyor of post offices and post roads in America in 1772, and in February, 1774, he was appointed to succeed, as deputy postmaster-general in North America, Dr. Franklin, on account of the latter's act in revealing the Hutchinson correspondence. The editor of this journal, Frank H. Norton, suspects that the sending of Finlay to America was the first step towards Franklin's displacement. He contributes a documentary history of the colonial postal system down to 1775. The journal ends at York, Va., May 24, in spite of its title-page, indicating that the final part of it was never written out from the author's note-books. It is prefaced by an account of his journey from Quebec to Falmouth (Portland, Me.), and it contains many reflections upon the disaffection of the people in the country through which he passed, but is chiefly interesting as illustrating the postal system of the time.   F. J. S.

Fiske, John. The American Revolution. Boston : Houghton. 1891. 2v. $4.   [1315

" To those who have read any of the writings of John Fiske, it is needless to say that to an extraordinary degree he has succeeded in his endeavor to make plain the events of the American Revolution. His style is so transparent and limpid that it seems to disparage all claims to attention. Save as all language is largely metaphorical, there is scarcely a figure in the two volumes. There is no straining after effect, — nothing but the simplest narrative of events which are expected to be attractive in themselves and not to need the ornament of elaborate dressing-up. But the author sees all so clearly that the reader is forced to the same insight. The lucidity of his narration comes not only from a firm grasp of facts, but from a clear perception which enables him so completely to unravel the tangled skein that only he who has looked to other sources realizes at all that there were troubles to be overcome. Moreover, Mr. Fiske is a philosopher. The American Revolution has for him a place in the development of the world's history. . . . Mr. Fiske's book ought to be in every high school and college library in the country, and, indeed, bought and read by every one who can afford to buy books at all. There seems no human reason why it should not meet the coveted fate of Macaulay's history — that of supplanting for a week the latest novel from the circulating library on the dressing-table of the young woman of fashion, and it certainly merits the praise that Macaulay received ' for having written a history which workingmen can understand.'" A. C. McL., *Dial* (Chicago), 12: 135.

—— The war of independence. (Riverside school library.) Boston: Houghton. 1889. 75c. [**1316**]

As a historian, John Fiske, probably the most powerful intellectual force to-day in American literature, has been in some ways surpassed. He has not himself always delved deeply into sources, in manuscripts, newspapers, and the scrap-books of past times. Nor is his faculty that of the imaginative word-painter; nor yet is it the power to delineate with the touch of a Clarendon the characters of men. His peculiar gift lies in this, — to detect in the presence of a confused multitude of facts which the searchers have accumulated, the subtle relationships, and to crystallize the chaos at once into a perfect order. The result is set forth in a form so faultless that he may well be called our first master in the art of statement. Behind his presentment lies always his profound philosophic conception of man and life. As a writer for children Mr. Fiske is no less happy than as a writer for strong men. His language is simple and cheery; his illustrations from boyish sports and occupations; his whole manner so breezy and sympathetic that a bright boy or girl is sure to be captivated. J. K. H.

Fitch, Jabez. Journal [of the siege of Boston], Aug.-Dec. 1775. See Massachusetts Historical Society, sect. 346. [**1317**]

Ford, Paul Leicester. Some materials for a bibliography of the official publications of the Continental Congress, 1774–89. (In Boston Public Library Bulletins. 1887–92. v. 8, pp. 320–323; v. 9, pp. 299–304, 487–91; v. 10, pp. 87–92, 156–66.) [**1318**]

Mr. Ford states that the arrangement is strictly chronological, under the date of the introduction by the committee, or the adoption by the Congress. Those without date and collected publications are placed at the end of the year to which they belong.

Ford, Worthington Chauncey, *ed.* Prisoners of war (British and American), 1778. See Historical Printing Club, sect. 273. [**1319**]

Foster, William Eaton. Treaty of peace. (In Providence Public Library. Monthly reference lists, v. 3, no. 9, Sept., 1883, pp. 30–31.) [**1320**]

A brief bibliography of the Treaty of Paris, 1783.

Fox, Charles James. Memorials and correspondence; ed. by Lord John Russell. London: Bentley. 1853–7. 4v. [**1321**]

Compiled in succession by Lord Holland, Mr. Allen, and Lord John Russell — the whole being edited by the last named. Not a biography, but a collection of letters and anecdotes interspersed with comments of the three editors — each person's contribution being indicated. Extends from 1763 to 1792. A valuable and stimulating work although largely superseded by more formal collections and biographies. E. C.

Franklin, Benjamin. Complete works; ed. by John Bigelow. N. Y.: Putnam. 1887–9. 10v. [**1322**]

This latest, and, unfortunately, limited edition, supersedes all previous ones, not only because of its substitution of a chronological for a classical arrangement, but because, so far as possible, it gives the texts as Franklin wrote them, without the editorial suppressions, changes, and "improvements" made by William Temple Franklin and Jared Sparks in their editions. In addition, it includes some six hundred pieces not previously included in Franklin's *Works*, drawn for the most part from the Stevens' Franklin collection in the Department of State. It does not, however, include much that Franklin wrote, notably the *Dogood letters, Poor Richard's almanac* and the *Historical review*, and in this sense an edition of Franklin's writings is still a desideratum. P. L. F.

—— Life, written by himself; now first ed., from original MSS. and from his printed correspondence, by John Bigelow. 4th ed., rev. and cor. Phil.: Lippincott. 1888. 3v. $4.50. [**1322 a**]

It is to Mr. Bigelow, a descendant of Franklin, that we owe the recovery of the original manuscript of Franklin's autobiography, and the first printing of it, so as to correct some twelve hundred errors and alterations made in previous editions. To this correct version, which ends with the year 1757, and which fills little more than a half of the first volume, the editor has appended a selection of Franklin's letters and other pieces, so as to continue the narrative to the end of his life, in a partially autobiographical manner, with notes and comments to aid the reader; but the result more closely approximates to a selected and abridged collection of Franklin's writings than it does to a biography, such as the title leads one to expect. P. L. F.

—— Autobiography. (Riverside school library.) Boston: Houghton. 1896. 15c. [1323

A reprint of the Bigelow text, omitting the prefaces which separate the several parts of the work, and also one or two brief passages "not adapted to school use," and with inserted "chapter headings at natural breaks in the narrative," making this edition untrustworthy for use by any one but the popular reader. A few pages at the end complete the life of Franklin from the point where the autobiography ends.   P. L. F.

— BROOKS, ELBRIDGE STREETER. True story of Benjamin Franklin. (Children's lives of great men, no. 5.) Boston: Lothrop. [c. 1898.] $1.50.   [1324

"So familiar and conversational a style as his seems unnecessary even for very little children. Yet the story of Franklin cannot be told too early or too often, and this gossipy biography, with its many good pictures, may serve to introduce the man and his achievements to some children who would be bored by a more connected and rational account." *Dial* (Chicago), 25: 405.

— FISHER, SYDNEY GEORGE. The true Benjamin Franklin. Phil.: Lippincott. 1899. $3.   [1325

Useful, but overdone, and gives a false and rather mean impression, by accenting the faults and giving the benefit of the doubt in favor of the unfavorable.   E. C. R.

— FORD, PAUL LEICESTER, *comp.* Bibliography of Franklin. See Historical Printing Club, sect. 272.   [1326

— FORD, PAUL LEICESTER. The many-sided Franklin. N. Y.: Century Co. 1899. $3.   [1327

"Mr. Ford applies to our great diplomatist, politician, agitator, wit, moralist, inventor, and natural philosopher that same method of characterism he lately applied so successfully to Washington. . . . That is to say, he considers Franklin successively under all possible aspects in as many separate chapters." The merits of this method "are no less striking for artistic than for scientific purposes. It enables one to gain an intimate acquaintance with a great man that no chronological narrative of the events of his life could possibly confer. . . . The work, considered as conveying information and regardless of picturesqueness, is more a conveniently arranged assortment of facts to serve as a basis for a thorough study of Franklin, than an essay towards a clear and unitary conception of his mental constitution. . . . The volume contains portraits, . . . facsimiles, and other valuable illustrations. . . . The index is copious." *Nation*, 69: 355.

— HALE, EDWARD EVERETT *and* EDWARD E., JR. Franklin in France; from original documents, most of which are now published for the first time. Boston: Roberts. 1887–8. 2v. Little. 2v. $6.   [1328

In 1882 the United States government acquired from Mr. Henry Stevens of London a large mass of hitherto unprinted documents written by or relating to Benjamin Franklin, which had been bequeathed by Franklin to his son, Wm. Temple Franklin. From these papers Mr. Hale, assisted by his son, has compiled an account of Franklin's life in France during the nine years of his residence there (1776–85). The work has been done in a thoroughly impartial and scholarly manner, but has led to no revision of past judgments regarding Franklin's career in France, except in some minor matters of detail. The first volume closes with 1781; the second, which contains four valuable appendices, with 1785.   C. M. A.

— MACMASTER, JOHN BACH. Benjamin Franklin as a man of letters. (American men of letters.) Boston: Houghton. 1887. $1.25.   [1329

Written from the historical standpoint rather than the critical, in the author's brilliant allusive style. As Franklin wrote but little that may be called literature, the main subject is necessarily sometimes obscured by the interesting but secondary details. Sources have been consulted and many of the most important documents are quoted or alluded to. The closing chapter is a well-written account of the strange history of the Franklin MSS., ending with a judicious critical estimate. The only bibliography offered is merged into the index.   V. L. C.

— MORSE, JOHN TORREY, JR. Benjamin Franklin. (American statesmen.) Boston: Houghton. 1889. $1.25.   [1330

The author in effect confesses in his preface that he believes that Parton's *Life* "has left no place in English literature for another biography of this most illustrious of our countrymen," and that his own book is really written because the "'American statesmen series' without a life of Franklin . . . would have appeared as absurdly imperfect as a library of English fiction with Scott and Thackeray absent from the shelves." The *Life* does not pretend to be based on any original research (although the author uses Bigelow's edition of Franklin's *Writings*), being merely a well-told, popular account, not too careful as to exactness of fact, and without citation of authorities. Like all Mr. Morse's work, however, it is admirably written and most readable, and unquestionably ranks high among the minor biographies of Franklin. P. L. F.

— PARTON, JAMES. Life and times of Benjamin Franklin. N. Y.: Mason. 1864. 2v. Boston: Houghton. 2v. $5.   [1331

In this, as in his other books, Mr. Parton stands midway between the old-fashioned panegyrist of the Abbott type and the modern "critical" biographer. Much minute investigation is shown, and the result is entertainingly and graphically told. A lack of "authorities" and over-tendency to picturesque statement constitute the great faults of the book. Written before the recovery of the Stevens' Franklin collection, while access to the Franklin papers in the American Philosophical Society collection was impossible, and before the publication of Doniol's *Participation*, Stevens' *Facsimiles*, the *Reports* of the British Historical Manuscripts Commission, and of Bigelow's edition of Franklin's works, it is now thoroughly out of date, though still the longest and best balanced account of the great printer-diplomatist.   P. L. F.

— ROBINS, EDWARD. Benjamin Franklin, printer, statesman, philosopher, and practical citizen. (American men of energy.) N. Y.: Putnam. 1898. $1.50.   [1332

"The familiar story is told in an intimate and warm manner, with use of the phraseology and even slang of to-day. . . . The later pages are better done, for in them Mr. Robins invades no field held by the immortals of literature. Once free of his obligations to the *Autobiography*, he tells vividly of Franklin's services in England, France, and of the honors of the closing years. . . . In a book ostensibly addressed to younger minds errors of fact and speech become serious. . . . Something more of accuracy and less familiarity of style are commended, in a fair spirit, to Mr. Robins." *Nation*, 67: 136.

Friedenwald, Herbert. Journal and papers of the Continental Congress. See American Historical Association, sect. 248.   [1333

Frothingham, Richard. History of the siege of Boston, and of the battles of Lexington, Concord and Bunker Hill. Boston: Little. 1849. 4th ed. Boston: Little. 1873. $3.50.   [1334

Author a Charlestown antiquary. Work based on thorough study of materials accessible at the time. Well illustrated with plans. Well written though often dry. Somewhat laudatory and not always sound from a military point of view. The standard work on the subject.   E. C.

George III., *king of England.* Correspondence with Lord North, 1768–83; ed. by W. Bodham Donne. London: Murray. 1867. 2v.   [1335

These brief letters reveal the character and policy of George III, besides giving much information on the struggle between the King and Parliament, and on the American Revolution. The editor, Mr. Donne, has performed his task with extreme thoroughness, prefacing the collection with a valuable historical essay on the state of parties, and adding to the letters equally valuable explanatory notes.   R. C. H. C.

Gibbes, Robert Wilson, *ed.* Documentary history of the American Revolution, chiefly in South Carolina. N. Y.: Appleton. 1853–7. 3v.   [1336

The most valuable collection of documents in these volumes is the "Horry papers" which relate to Marion's career. Most of the other papers are of purely local interest, and the collection is less important than its title indicates.   E. C.

Gilmore, James Roberts. The rear-guard of the Revolution. N. Y.: Appleton. 1886. $1.50.

—— John Sevier as a commonwealth-builder. N. Y.: Appleton. 1887. $1.50.

—— The advance-guard of western civilization. N. Y.: Appleton. 1888. $1.50.   [1337

These three books are intended to form a continuous narrative of the settlement and growth of eastern and middle Tennessee up to the admission of the state into the Union. The central figures on the historical canvas are Sevier, Shelby and Robertson. These men are drawn in heroic proportions, and the author asserts in the preface to the *Advance guard* that "the three books will bear the closest scrutiny." Their historical value may be characterized in the words of Mr. Roosevelt, when he says (*Winning of the West*, III, 202): "In my first two volumes I have discussed once for all the worth of Gilmore's 'histories' of Sevier and Robertson and their times. It is unnecessary further to consider a single statement they contain." This estimate is borne out by the experience of the present writer, whose examinations of the sources show that nothing which crosses the pathway of Gilmore's heroes escapes a false presentation at his hands, even if sources have to be mutilated to that end.   S. B. W.

Girty family. BUTTERFIELD, CONSUL WILLSHIRE. History of the Girtys; a concise account of the Girty brothers, also of the part taken by them in Lord Dunmore's war, in the western border war of the Revolution, and in the Indian war of 1790–95; with a recital of the principal events in the West during these wars. Cin.: Clarke. 1890. $3.50.   [1338

Gathers from many obscure sources the thread of Simon Girty's renegade life, and the scarcely more reputable careers of others of the family, whose services, in aid of Indians and of British, made the name of "Girty" a terror along the western borders of Pennsylvania and Virginia. The author undertakes not merely to record the facts, but to show the falsity of a vast amount that has been published about the Girtys, some of it in works held in good repute. He finds Roosevelt's *Winning of the West* particularly open to assault. The work testifies to painstaking research, and a desire to do justice to a misunderstood character, bad enough at best. Around this unheroic hero the events of a tragically romantic period are woven into a chronicle of border warfare, so crowded with incident that the tale speeds best in plain phrases.   F. H. S.

Gist, Christopher. Journal, 1783. See Massachusetts Historical Society, sect. 301.   [1339

Goodloe, Daniel Reaves. Birth of the republic. Chicago: Belford. [c. 1889.]   [1340

There are many extracts in this work from the standard state histories, from proceedings of the continental and provincial congresses, and from the conventions, assemblies and committees of safety in all the colonies through which the gradual growth of the spirit of liberty is traced, up to the Declaration of Independence. In addition to the above, the states are taken separately, and the most important documents of the period in each are given in brief. A few of the well-known later documents are added, including the articles of confederation and the constitution. The sources from which these extracts are taken are not indicated, but they are well known and the transcripts are fairly accurate; the book will well serve as a handy manual for students who wish much of the sources in convenient compass.   S. B. W.

Gordon, William. History of the rise, progress and establishment of the independence of the United States of America. London. 1788. 4v. 3d Am. ed. N. Y.: Campbell. 1801. 3v.   [1341

Gordon was a dissenting minister in England, who like many of his class sympathized with the contention of the Thirteen Colonies. Going to America during the disturbances, and becoming pastor of the church at Jamaica Plain, now a district of Boston, he was throughout the Revolution a spectator close at hand of many important events, and the associate of many of the chief patriots. Returning to England he published his history, which has been held to be a source of value for more than a hundred years, but has been recently shown to be a plagiarism, in great part from the *Annual register*.   J. K. H.

Graham, William A. Address on the Mecklenburg Declaration of Independence of the 20th of May, 1775. N. Y.: Hale. 1875.   [1342

For this address, given preparatory to the centennial celebration, the author made a thorough investigation, and has presented the best claim yet made for the authenticity of the declaration and the date he champions. Much of the material was gathered from the descendants of the participants. A number of pertinent papers are added. This pamphlet is rare and worthy of reprinting.   E. E. S.

Graydon, Alexander. Memoirs of a life chiefly passed in Pennsylvania within the last sixty years. Harrisburg. 1811.

—— Memoirs of his own time; ed. by John Stockwell Littell. Phil.: Lindsay. 1846.   [1343

Revolutionary period in Philadelphia and in New York, where the author was a prisoner. Extremely interesting, gossipy memoir full of culture historical material. One of the earliest, best known and most used sources for the period, and places.   E. C. R.

Greene, George Washington. The German element in the war of American independence. N. Y.: Hurd. 1876.   [1344

The author disclaims in this book any original contributions to history. Its three popularly written chapters are based on Kapp's three volumes (1858, 1862, and 1864), relating respectively to Steuben, Kalb and the German mercenaries; and in the last named portion it needs to be supplemented by the later contributions of Max von Eelking, W. L. Stone and others. Mr. Greene's volume is not conspicuously impartial or judicial, but is a popularly written and readable narrative. It has no index.   W. E. F.

—— Historical view of the American Revolution. Boston: Houghton. 1865. $1.50.   [1345

Especially welcome as being a one-volume account of the struggle. The sequence of chapters does not follow the successive periods of the war, but treats of it in its various phases (as finances, diplomacy, literature, etc.). The book is based on extensive knowledge, excellent judgment, admirable temper, and a historical method which is usually cautious. These chapters were first written for delivery as lectures, and consequently the style is unusually attractive to the general reader.   W. E. F.

Greene, *Maj.-Gen.* **Nathanael.** GREENE, *Maj.-Gen.* FRANCIS VINTON. General Nathanael Greene. (Great commanders.) N. Y.: Appleton. 1893. $1.50.   [1346

Based on a careful study of the printed sources. Author a practical soldier as well as a military critic. The book is more moderate in tone than other lives of Greene. It is well supplied with clear and good maps and plans.   E. C.

—— GREENE, GEORGE WASHINGTON. Life of Nathanael Greene. N. Y.: Putnam. 1867–71. 3v. Boston: Houghton. 3v. $7.50.   [1347

Author grandson of the subject of the memoir. The volumes are extremely valuable on account of the documents contained in them which are here brought together for the first time. Work written in an uncritical spirit and greatly affected by the undisguised ancestor worship of the author.   E. C.

—— JOHNSON, WILLIAM. Sketches of the life and correspondence of Nathanael Greene. Charleston. 1822. 2v.   [1348

Based on original materials and valuable for the documents given with the text. It contains many good plans. Written in a spirit of fulsome flattery.   E. C.

Grenville, Richard *and* **George.** SMITH, WILLIAM JAMES, *ed.* The Grenville papers: being the correspondence of Richard Grenville, Earl Temple, and the Right Hon. George Grenville, their friends and contemporaries. London: Murray. 1852–3. 4v.   [1349

The papers are arranged chronologically. Vols. 2 and 3 cover the years 1762–66. The collection continues to the year 1777; but the chief interest is in the years 1764, 1765. Indispensable to students of the stamp act episode.   E. C.

Haas, Wills de. History of the early settlement and Indian wars of western Virginia. Wheeling: Hoblitzell. 1851.   [1350

"Wills de Haas ... has devoted one chapter to 'Land companies,' and another to the 'Employment of Indians as allies.' His treatment of these topics is brief, but the chapters contain much more information on the subjects than can generally be obtained from American histories." A. McF. Davis, in *Narrative and critical hist. of Am.*, 6: 649.

See, also, note to Wither's *Chronicles of border warfare*, sect. 1579.

Hadden, *Maj.-Gen.* **James Murray.** Journal kept in Canada and upon Burgoyne's campaign; [ed. by] Horatio Rogers. Albany: Munsell. 1884. [**1351**]

Hadden's *Journal* and *Orderly books* which are here printed together form one of the most important pieces of evidence of Burgoyne's expedition. Admirably edited by General Rogers. E. C.

Hale, Edward Everett. Naval history of the Revolution. See American Antiquarian Society, sect. 237. [**1352**]

—— One hundred years ago . how the war began. A series of sketches from original authorities. Boston: Lockwood. 1875. [**1353**]

This pamphlet is made up of extracts from newspapers, speeches, petitions and contemporary pamphlets, connected by a running explanatory commentary; and its object is "to bring before the reader such original descriptions of the eventful days of one hundred years ago as have not been often reprinted." The extracts are for the most part interesting and valuable and the commentary is entertaining and gossipy; but, taken as a whole, the collection adds little to historical knowledge. C. M. A.

Hale, John Peter. Trans-Allegheny pioneers: historical sketches of the first white settlements west of the Alleghenies, 1748 and after. Cin.: Cox. [c. 1886.] [**1354**]

Mr. Hale may be commended for some diligence and much enthusiasm in preparing his volume. His compilation may be accepted as a general picture of the first pioneer life west of the Alleghenies, but is often inaccurate in details. He patronizes the old stories about early western explorations made by Virginians, and finds the first over the mountain settlement in Draper's *Meadows on New River*, 1748. B. A. H.

Hale, *Capt.* **Nathan.** STUART, ISAAC WILLIAM. Life of Captain Nathan Hale. Hartford. 1856. [**1355**]

This short life of Nathan Hale, written for popular use, is of little value. Its chief defects are fulsome flattery of the subject of the biography, a rhetorical style that is wearisome and monotonous, and a wholly uncritical treatment of the many tales that have gathered about the name of Nathan Hale. It has been entirely superseded. C. M. A.

Hamilton, Stanislaus Murray, *ed.* Letters to Washington, and accompanying papers; published by the Society of the Colonial Dames of America. Boston: Houghton. 1898–. v. 1+. $5 ea. net. [**1356**]

"The Society of The Colonial Dames of America has issued the first volume of the *Letters to Washington*, and proposes to continue the series until the period of the Revolution is reached. It is to be hoped that no such limit will be maintained. Nothing that the society can do will better justify its existence, or prove more grateful to all interested in American history, than to publish the entire series of letters to Washington, now in the Department of State. The field is exceedingly rich, practically untouched, and is essential to a proper understanding of the man and of his time. We would go further, and collect all letters to Washington to be found in other collections. . . . The manner in which the volume has been edited by Mr. S. M. Hamilton calls for some comment, if only to serve as a note of warning. . . . He gives the impression of being a careful and most minute editor, even seeking to reproduce in type the little oddities of writing encountered. . . . The curiously close following of pen-points would lead one to expect that at least the words were correctly printed—as written; but this expectation is disappointed so often that serious doubt must apply to the entire text as printed. . . . The contents of the letters speak for themselves, and are full of touches of a personal and historical character. But the full value of these papers cannot be developed unless the editing is improved." Worthington Chauncey Ford, *Am. hist. rev.*, 4: 729.

Hancock, John. BROWN, ABRAM ENGLISH. John Hancock, his book. Boston: Lee. 1898. $2. [**1357**]

"Mr. Abram English Brown, an enthusiastic antiquary and genealogist, has given in *John Hancock, his book* a liberal selection from Hancock's commercial correspondence, as taken from his letter-book, the letters being strung together by the compiler on a slender thread of explanatory and biographical narrative. Mr. Brown does not pretend to call his book a life of Hancock, but merely a contribution to such a work." *Dial*, 26: 24.

Heath, William. Memoirs, containing anecdotes, details of skirmishes, battles and other military events during the American war; by himself. Pub. by act of Congress. Boston. 1798. [**1358**]

From the organization of the Massachusetts provincial troops in April, 1775, to December, 1783. Valuable for accounts of the retreat of the British from Lexington, battle of Bunker Hill, and the later engagements about New York. Also concerns the prisoners after Burgoyne's surrender and the coöperation with the French forces. This book is now out of print and very valuable. E. E. S.

Heitman, Francis B. Historical register of officers of the continental army during the war of the Revolution. 1775–1783. Wash.: Lowdermilk. 1893. $5. [**1359**]

Compiled from muster rolls and other records on file in the departments at Washington, gives date of rank in each grade, mentions all cases in which honors were conferred by Congress, gives date and place if killed, wounded, taken prisoner and exchanged, and in many cases the date of death after leaving the service, and furnishes a list of the French officers who served with the American army. Although no attempt was made to include all the militia officers, the names of many of them appear. F. J. S.

Henry, John Joseph. Account of Arnold's campaign against Quebec, 1775. Albany: Munsell. 1877. [**1360**

Better than the rare first edition (Lancaster, Pa. 1812) or other reprints because augmented with a map, memoir of the author, etc. Of the numerous narratives of this arduous and fruitless expedition, Henry's is the most minute and painstaking. He gives with particularity the details of the overland march, the assault on Quebec, and the incidents of Arnold's imprisonment until his arrival in New York, Sept. 11, 1776. The language is quaint and formal, but graphic. F. H. S.

Henry, Patrick. HENRY, WILLIAM WIRT. Patrick Henry: life, correspondence and speeches. N. Y.: Scribner. 1891. 3v. $12 net. [**1361**

Author a descendant of Patrick Henry. Had access to much new material. The "life" is written from a family standpoint. The documents given in these volumes, however, are of inestimable value and give a new and more correct view of Henry's great career. The standard work on the subject for students' use. E. C.

— TYLER, MOSES COIT. Patrick Henry. (American statesmen.) Boston: Houghton. 1887. $1.25. [**1362**

Written in a friendly spirit to the subject. Author a trained historian. Work based on materials later used in Henry's *Patrick Henry*. Style readable. The best short work on Patrick Henry. E. C.

— WIRT, WILLIAM. Sketches of the life and character of Patrick Henry. Phil.: Claxton. 1818. [**1363**

Based on inadequate materials. Often very unjust to Henry. Charmingly written but now antiquated and of no use to the student. E. C.

Hopkins, *Admiral* **Esek.** FIELD, EDWARD. Esek Hopkins, Commander-in-Chief of the continental navy during the American Revolution, 1775 to 1778, master mariner, politician, brigadier-general, naval officer and philanthropist. Providence: Preston. 1898. $3 [**1364**

"The author's work in the sources of the history of Rhode Island entitles him to attention. He now brings forward an interesting, illustrated biography of a man hardly known outside his native locality. Bancroft does not mention him, while Arnold treats the incidents of his career in their historic bearing justly but with meagre interest. The more famous brother Stephen played an important part in Congress and was the immediate cause of the appointment of Esek Hopkins to organize and lead our infant navy. . . . When the matter of a fleet came before Congress, Rhode Island led the way. . . . Esek Hopkins was appointed commander-in-chief and organized the little squadron of eight vessels. The first expedition to New Providence was thoroughly successful. . . . Unfortunately, Hopkins with his fleet was shut in Narragansett Bay, when the enemy occupied Newport. Sailors

were so scarce he could not man his ships to get out. . . . He had a great faculty for making enemies. Though he was a brave man and true patriot, he was at last deprived of his command. Mr. Field has made a needed addition to the literature of the Revolution, and one worth the attention of students." William B. Weeden, in *Am. historical review*, 5: 144.

Hopkins, Stephen. FOSTER, WILLIAM EATON. Stephen Hopkins, a Rhode Island statesman. (Rhode Island historical tracts, 19, 20.) Providence: Rider. 1884. [**1365**

A study in the political history of the 18th century grouped around the life of a distinguished man whose career included the Albany Congress and the 1st Continental Congress. Abundantly provided with notes. Well written and full of suggestion. E. C.

Hough, Franklin Benjamin, *ed.* The northern invasion of October, 1780, against the frontiers of New York, supposed to have connection with Arnold's treason. (Bradford Club series, no. 6.) N. Y. 1866. [**1366**

The editor's introduction, 47 pages, reviews the incidents of the two raids by the British upon the Mohawk valley in Oct., 1780, plausibly concluding that their purpose was to draw away troops from West Point, thus facilitating the surrender of that place, though the British Governor-General in Canada, Haldimand, may not have been a party to Arnold's treasonable plot. The correspondence here first published includes letters between Gen. Washington and Gov. Geo. Clinton, between Clinton and officers who led troops against the British, etc. It is valuable material, in the use of which the editor shows great carefulness, and the ability to set forth the salient points in compact and lucid language. F. H. S.

—— Siege of Savannah, by the American and French forces, 1779. Albany: Munsell. 1866. [**1367**

Contains a mass of documents relating to the siege — many of them to be found elsewhere — and an introduction. A useful work to the student of the siege, but not indispensable. E. C.

Howe, *Gen.* **Robert.** Proceedings of his court-martial. See New-York Historical Society, sect. 361. [**1368**

Howe, *Sir* **William.** Order-books. See New-York Historical Society, sect. 364.

[**1369**

Hunter, Cyrus L. Sketches of western North Carolina, historical and biographical. Raleigh: Raleigh News. 1877. [**1370**

This work presents a summary history of the Revolutionary War in the western and southwestern half of the state, particularly in Mecklenburg, Rowan, Iredell, Cleveland, Burke and adjoining counties, with some notices of the adjoining sections of South Carolina. It is made up in part of traditions and recollections, with some extracts from state and county archives, but it is fragmentary in character and has too many quotations from Wheeler's *History of North*

Carolina. There is a considerable amount of genealogy, and the history is written in a pleasant, gossipy style. 　　　　　　　　　　　　　　　S. B. W.

Hutchinson, Thomas. HOSMER, JAMES KENDALL. Life of Thomas Hutchinson, Royal Governor of the province of Massachusetts Bay. Boston: Houghton. 1896. $4. 　[**1371**

The new material which appears in this volume consists chiefly of extracts from Hutchinson's unpublished correspondence, which is preserved in the Massachusetts archives. The value of the book is further enhanced by the frank recognition on the part of the author of the large element of truth and justice which lay at the basis of the loyalist argument. The fact that the sympathetic biographer of Samuel Adams can do such ample justice to his chief opponent as is done in this volume proves the broad-mindedness of the writer, and indicates the extent to which the old-fashioned provincial views of early American history are being abandoned. 　　　　　　　　H. L. O.

Iredell, James. McREE, GRIFFITH JOHN, *ed.* Life and correspondence of James Iredell. N. Y.: Appleton. 1857–58. 2v. 　　[**1372**

Judge Iredell's life is told in his own letters and in those of his contemporaries, including most of the men who were prominent in North Carolina during the Revolutionary period. As he was in public life constantly from about 1775, the correspondence becomes fuller from that time and makes one of the few original sources we have for the social, political and intellectual life of the state, 1775–1800. Judge Iredell was a Federalist, but it is through his pages that we get most of our knowledge of his opponents who have left few memorials of their own. Many of his letters were written in the press of business, but they have an elegance and vivacity not always found in similar productions. 　　　　　　　　　　　　S. B. W.

Jay, John. (See in next following period.)
Jefferson, Thomas. Writings: collected and ed. by Paul Leicester Ford. N. Y.: Putnam. 1892–9. 10v. $50. 　　　[**1373**

The final and complete edition of Jefferson's *Works.* The arrangement is chronological, with the exception of Jefferson's *Autobiography* and the *Anas,* which are in the first volume. Each volume contains an itinerary and chronology. The editor has consulted new material in the French Foreign Office, the State archives, collections of historical societies, and the private papers of Washington, Adams, Madison, Monroe, Steuben and Gates. An introduction treating of Jefferson's work, his ideas, his character and his writings, is marked by acute critical sense, and much thought and study. Critical and explanatory footnotes are given throughout. This edition of Jefferson is indispensable to the future historian of the period. The mechanical details of the volumes are artistic and pleasing. 　　　　　　　　. R. C. H. C.

—— Notes on the state of Virginia. Paris. 1782.

—— *Same.* (In Writings; col. and ed. by Paul Leicester Ford. v. 3.) 　　　[**1374**

A comprehensive and very valuable description of the natural history, economic resources, and social condition of Virginia drawn up in the form of answers to queries presented by Barbé de Marbois, secretary of the French legation. Chiefly interesting to the student of history as an illustration of the range and versatility of Jefferson's intellectual interests. The answer to the 18th query contains his famous denunciation of slavery; that to the 17th his defense of liberty of conscience. 　　　　　　　　E. G. B.

—— Papers, 1770–1826. See Massachusetts Historical Society, sect. 322. 　　　[**1375**

— DWIGHT, THEODORE. Character of Thomas Jefferson as exhibited in his own writings. Boston.: Weeks. 1839. 　　[**1376**

"It was mainly given to setting forth the proofs, as he thought he found them in Jefferson's own words, of the allegations against Jefferson, which were the grounds of the Federal opposition to him; and, as summing up his opponents' allegations, the book is worth looking at." Justin Winsor, in *Narrative and critical hist. of Am.,* 7: 305.

— MORSE, JOHN TORREY, JR. Thomas Jefferson. (American statesmen.) Boston: Houghton. 1883. $1.25. 　　　　[**1377**

A brief popular biography based on Randall's *Life* and Jefferson's *Works.* Over two thirds of the book are devoted to Jefferson's official career after 1790, his relations to Washington, Hamilton, Randolph, Burr, to the Louisiana purchase, and to the embargo receiving particular attention. The author is fairly well informed, writes in a pleasant style, but rather carelessly, in too much of the spirit of the advocate, and with occasional inaccuracies. 　　　　R. C. H. C.

— PARTON, JAMES. Life of Thomas Jefferson. Boston: Houghton. 1874. $2.50. [**1378**

"Parton cannot commend the Jeffersonian ideas without expressing aversion to those opposed, and Adams and Hamilton were to him ideas incarnate, deserving of such aversion. His *Life of Thomas Jefferson* . . . is lively, easy reading, and generally unconvincing to the impartial student." Justin Winsor, in *Narrative and critical hist. of Am.,* 7 : 307.

— RANDALL, HENRY STEPHENS. Life of Thomas Jefferson. N. Y.: Derby. 1858. 3v. Phil.: Lippincott. 3v. $9. 　　[**1379**

The standard life of Jefferson, written from material much of which was accessible only to Randall. Unusual ability and careful scholarship are everywhere evident, but the tone is controversial, the temper unfair, and Randall is so partial that he degenerates into a special pleader. He is particularly unjust to Hamilton by suppression, by inference, by innuendo. The length of the book is excessive; the style is strong, but verbose and involved. 　　　　　　　　R. C. H. C.

— RANDOLPH, SARAH NICHOLAS. Domestic life of Thomas Jefferson. N. Y.: Harper. 1871. $2.50. 　　　　　　　[**1380**

When the great collection of Jefferson's manuscripts was sold to the United States government, there was reserved a mass of papers which were deemed to be of such a private nature as to possess no value in the national archives, and to belong more properly to the family. These eventually came into the possession of Jefferson's great-granddaughter, and they form the *raison d'être* of this book. It possesses the merits and demerits which might be expected, the documents being of positive value, and the family recollections and traditions of distinct interest; but the book is faulty in method, being both ill-proportioned and disjointed. It is, therefore, far more valuable to the maker than to the reader of history.   P. L. F.

— SCHOULER, JAMES. Thomas Jefferson. (Makers of America.) N. Y.: Dodd. 1893. $1.   [1381

Dr. Schouler " is well equipped for his task, alike by his historic studies and by sympathy for his subject, when Jefferson is regarded in the deeper relations which he bore to the politics of his time." He " sees clearly that all the intuitions of Jefferson, whether they are to be characterized for his justification or for his condemnation, were presageful of the nineteenth century, with its liberalism in politics and its liberality in religion. . . . Dr. Schouler is not blind to Jefferson's faults of character, and, after designating some of them, he expresses the opinion that the Virginian philosopher, in consequence of his residence and experiences in France, grew at length more French than English in his political methods and temperament as well as in his viands and cookery." *Nation*, 57 : 255.

— TUCKER, GEORGE. Life of Thomas Jefferson. Phil.: Carey. 1837. 2v.   [1382

Formerly the standard life of Jefferson, based largely on correspondence and papers, but written with a love of the subject which frequently leads to a strong bias. Eulogy often takes the place of critical judgment. Extracts from papers are written into the narrative without references.   E. E. S.

Johnson, *Sir* John. Orderly book during the Oriskany campaign, 1776–7; annotated by William L. Stone, with an historical introd. by J. Watts de Peyster, and some tracings from the footprints of the loyalists in America by Theodorus Bailey Myers. Albany: Munsell. 1882.   [1383

The orderly book, which was captured by Col. Marinus Willett during his sortie from Fort Stanwix while the battle of Oriskany was in progress, was printed in the *Magazine of American history* (6: 204, 283), but without most of the annotations which here appear. It shows the strength of St. Leger's force and otherwise throws some light on this part of Burgoyne's campaign. The contributions of De Peyster in telling the story of the Johnsons describe the battles of Oriskany and Fox's Mills from a loyalist point of view. Considerable information of a desultory sort regarding the course of the Revolution in New York is scattered through the book, much of which is written with a strong British bias.   F. J. S.

—— Papers relating to the expedition from Canada under Sir John Johnson, October, 1780. See Bradford Club, sect. 252.   [1384

Johnson, Joseph. Traditions and reminiscences, chiefly of the American Revolution in the South, particularly of the upper country. Charleston: Walker. 1851.   [1385

Recollections of an old man already conscious of failing memory as to recent events where its accuracy could be tested, but not as to events long past where there could be no such test. Often interesting and often important from the lack of better evidence.   E. C.

Johnston, Henry Phelps. Battle of Harlem Heights, September 16, 1776, with a review of the campaign. N. Y.: Macmillan, for Columbia Press. 1897. $2.   [1386

" In connection with the memorial celebration of the battle of Harlem Heights last fall, on the site of the battle, the present grounds of Columbia University, Professor Johnston has published the above careful and scholarly account of the campaign which led up to that skirmish, and of the results of the latter upon the succeeding movements of the British and American armies. The task could not have fallen to a more competent writer. . . . By a comparison of all the available original material, which is printed in full, and occupies just half the volume, Professor Johnston establishes once for all the exact site of the three successive skirmishes which constituted the battle." J. C. Schwab, *American historical review*, 3: 555.

—— Campaign of 1776 around New York and Brooklyn. (Long Island Historical Soc. Memoirs, v. 3.) Brooklyn. 1878.   [1387

This account includes the preparations for and the events of the Jersey campaign, up to and including the battle of Princeton. It is full of documents and has interesting maps and portraits. It is a mine of local information on the events of the campaign. Scholarly but interesting.   E. C. R.

—— Observations on Judge Jones' loyalist history of the American Revolution: how far is it an authority? N. Y.: Appleton. 1880.   [1388

Author one of the most careful students of the Revolution. Excellent in style and temper. A most interesting and useful critique.   E. C.

—— The Yorktown campaign and the surrender of Cornwallis, 1781. N. Y.: Harper. 1881. $2.   [1389

Based on careful study of the original sources. Accurate and impartial but not readable. Supplied with good plans. The best single work on the Yorktown campaign.   E. C.

Jones, Charles Henry. History of the campaign for the conquest of Canada in 1776. Phil.: Porter & Coates. 1882.   [1390

" Mr. Jones's book is a useful record of some of the most painful and least glorious events of the Revolutionary War. It is better worth reading than the bragging rhetoric which, masquerading in the guise of history, has been too apt to falsify or to ignore the less creditable aspects of that struggle; but his unattractive theme is not illuminated by any exceptional brilliancy of treatment. He tells, indeed, of little more than the retreat out of Canada. . . . But even this story might have been told either with graphic vivacity or with critical acuteness, or with philosophical insight, or, at least, with laborious research. None of these qualities are displayed in the work before us. What authorities the writer used there is no indication from the first page to the last. . . . A graver blemish upon the work, however, arises from the fact that it is frankly . . . a Tendenzschrift, for the special glorification of the Pennsylvania contingent in these operations. This purpose has seemed to the author to be most readily subserved . . . by frequent comparisons between the eastern and southern troops, to the great disadvantage of the former. . . . This volume is, in paper, type, and presswork, one of the handsomest of its class. The proof-reading is not always what it should be." *Nation*, 35: 185.

Jones, *Rear-Admiral* **John Paul.** MACKENZIE, ALEXANDER SLIDELL. Life of Paul Jones. Boston: Hilliard. 1841. 2v. [**1391**
"Was written at the instance of Jared Sparks, and its merit is that it has sifted all the existing material, making a more readable and better constructed narrative than the others,"—namely, a life by J. H. Sherburne, published in 1825, and anonymous memoirs, first published at Edinburgh, in 1830. Justin Winsor, in *Narrative and critical hist. of Am.*, 6: 590.

Jones, Thomas. History of New York during the Revolutionary War, and of the leading events in the other colonies at that period; ed. by E. F. De Lancey. N. Y.: New York Hist. Soc. 1879. 2v. [**1392**
This is the best account of the Revolution from the Loyalist standpoint, and the great number of notes and documents (about equal in bulk to the work itself) add much to the value. It is said that the information is all at second hand, as the author was on parole all the time, left the country in 1781 and had no share in the events; there are also a good many inaccuracies; but on the other hand it was written soon after the events (1783-8), and he was, until 1781, near N. Y. and likely to know about the matters under review. At least he represents the feelings of the Loyalists of the period—and rather caustically at times—and is fair enough, occasionally, even to give Washington his due. E. C. R.

Journal of occurrences at Quebec, from Nov. 1775 to May, 1776. See New-York Historical Society, sect. 361. [**1393**
Journal of the attack of the rebels on his Majesty's ships and troops, 24th July, 1779, in Penobscot Bay; from the Nova Scotia gazette, Sept. 14, 1779. See Maine Historical Society, sect. 278. [**1394**
Kalb, *Maj.-Gen.* **John.** KAPP, FRIEDRICH. Life of John Kalb, Major-General in the Revolutionary army. N. Y.: Holt. 1884. $1.75. [**1395**

A fair and unbiased account of the services of Kalb (de Kalb) in the Revolutionary War, considering both sides of each question and giving abundant references for the statements. The chief sources are his letters, several of which are reproduced in the original French in the appendix. The author's account of the early life of his subject differs widely from the accepted descriptions. E. E. S.

Kapp, Friedrich. Friedrich der Grosse und die Vereinigten Staaten von Amerika, mit einem Anhang; Die Vereinigten Staaten und das Seekriegsrecht. Leipzig. 1871. [**1396**
Author a careful student of the American Revolution; but uses little new material in this publication. Part 1 describes Arthur Lee's abortive negotiation with Prussia—including the episode of the theft of his papers. Part 2 deals with the negotiations preceding the treaty of 1784; the projects of the treaty as well as the treaty are given in the appendix. The article on maritime warfare has to do with the action of the United States on the Declaration of Paris of 1856. On the whole the book is interesting on account of its point of view; but is otherwise of little value. E. C.

Kemble, Stephen. Kemble papers. See New York Historical Society, sect. 364. [**1397**
Knox, *Maj.-Gen.* **Henry.** DRAKE, FRANCIS SAMUEL. Life and correspondence of Henry Knox. Boston. 1873. [**1398**
Covers Knox's whole life from 1750 to 1806. Consists of letters, mainly from Knox, loosely cemented with inadequate editorial comment. The original papers are valuable. E. C.

Krafft, *Lt.* **Johann Karl Philip von.** Journal, 1776–84. See New-York Historical Society, sect. 363. [**1399**
Lafayette, Marie Jean Paul Roch Yves Gilbert Motier, *marquis* **de.** Memoirs, correspondence and MSS.; pub. by his family. London: Saunders. 1837. 3v. [**1400**
Vol. I, 1776 to 1781; vol. II, 1782 to 1790; vol. III, 1790 to 1792. These "unaltered" memoirs cover the three voyages of Lafayette to America within the periods mentioned. They are invaluable for a proper conception of his actions and motives. They include his accounts of the various campaigns in the Revolutionary War. The letters were written to Washington and the other officers of the Revolutionary army. The last volume concerns only the French Revolution. E. E. S.

— BROOKS, ELBRIDGE STREETER. True story of Lafayette. Boston: Lothrop. [c. 1899.] $1.50. [**1401**
A juvenile sketch of the life of Lafayette, written in a pleasing and easy style. It employs all the old traditions and gives no authority for any statements. The illustrations are abundant, several being of historic places. The book is likely to prove pleasing to children. E. E. S.

— TOWER, CHARLEMAGNE, JR. The Marquis de La Fayette in the American Revolution. Phil.: Lippincott. 1895. 2v. $8.

[1402

Mr. Tower's account is most inclusive, careful, and satisfactory, full use having been made not merely of Doniol's *Participation* and Stevens' *Facsimiles*, but much hitherto unpublished material has been drawn from many other sources. It is not too much to say that he has quadrupled the amount of accessible material concerning Lafayette, relating to this period, and it is difficult to recall a biographical work in American history containing such a wealth of original material concerning the subject treated. For its accounts of the battles of Brandywine, Monmouth, and the campaign of 1781 in Virginia, it is unequaled; and scarcely less good is its outline of the French services to the United States during the Revolution. Mr. Tower writes clearly and interestingly, and has the additional advantage of being an admirable linguist; so his translations can be absolutely relied upon.
P. L. F.

— TUCKERMAN, BAYARD. Life of General Lafayette. N. Y.: Dodd. 1889. 2v. $3.

[1403

The first account of Lafayette founded on full modern critical apparatus. It is a thorough and careful work from the sources, interestingly and skilfully written, in an unpretentious but clear and well-considered style. For scientific purposes, fuller references to the sources that are used might be desirable, but as a good critical biography in small compass, whether for the scholar or for the general reader, it is excellent.
E. C. R.

Lamb, *Gen.* **John.** LEAKE, ISAAC Q. Memoir of the life and times of General John Lamb. Albany: Munsell. 1857. $2.50. [1404

Lamb was the leader of the Sons of Liberty in New York, beginning with the Stamp Act, and was connected with the most rabid spirits of the Revolution in that colony. Later, he was in the Canadian campaign, in command of West Point when Arnold tried to betray it, and was at the Yorktown surrender. His memoirs cover these topics, as well as the treatment of the Loyalists in New York, the adoption of the Constitution, and later New York politics. The eulogy of the subject is quite moderate for an old-time biography. References are generally to the Lamb papers in the N. Y. Hist. Soc. and to "family traditions."
E. E. S.

Laurens, *Col.* **John.** Army correspondence, 1777–8; with memoir by Wm. Gilmore Simms. (Bradford Club series, no. 7.) N. Y. 1867.

[1405

Written from the winter camp at Valley Forge and during the campaigns immediately preceding and following it, these family letters show the inner history of military life, the ambitions and jealousies of the officers, and the relations of Congress to the army. Washington, Lafayette and von Steuben appear in their private characters. The letters especially concern the Conway cabal, the French alliance and the battle of Monmouth.
E. E. S.

Lecky, William Edward Hartpole. The American Revolution, 1763–1783: being the chapters and passages relating to America from the author's History of England in the 18th century; arranged and ed. with historical and bibliographical notes by James Albert Woodburn. N. Y.: Appleton. [c. 1898.] $1.25.

[1406

"The chapters of Mr. Lecky's *History of England in the 18th century* which treat of the American Revolution, though forming one of the most instructive and judicious histories of the Revolution that has been written, have not hitherto been accessible except in the complete work. Now, under the editorship of Professor James Albert Woodburn, of Indiana University, these chapters and passages have been gathered together and published as a separate volume. . . . The editor has prefixed a brief bibliography of some of the important primary and secondary English and American authorities on the period. He has added also some fifteen pages of notes upon the text. . . . Taken as a whole the notes form a very useful addition to the book, though they seem to be distributed somewhat arbitrarily or accidentally. Excepting occasional suggestions to students the editor gives little comment of his own. Where pages and passages not bearing on American history have been omitted this has been mentioned in the notes, but it would seem that some mark of omission should also be found in the text." E. G. B., *Am. hist. rev.*, 4: 762.

—— History of England in the 18th century. London: Longmans. 1878–90. 8v. £7 4s. 12v. 6s. ea. N. Y.: Appleton. 1878–90. 8v. $20. 12v. (England, 7v., Ireland, 5v.) $1 ea.

[1407

It has been well said that Mr. Lecky is more truly an historical essayist than an historian, and that the subject which most interests him is the history of opinions and moral convictions. That is true of this work. His material is neither arranged nor treated systematically, in such a way as to show the steady growth of national life. With the exception of the last two volumes, it is not emphatically a work of original research. Printed secondary authorities are used with great freedom and in great profusion. In fact, the time has not yet come when it is possible to write on the 18th century a work of systematic and exhaustive research, such as Mr. Gardiner is writing on the first half of the 17th century. Those volumes of Mr. Lecky which treat of Ireland, and which occupy a disproportionately large space, approach nearer to that ideal than does any other part of the work. It consists in fact of two parallel, though connected histories, one of England to the outbreak of the war of the French Revolution in 1793, and the other the history of Ireland to the Union of 1801. If the part on England be read as a succession of studies or essays on the great social and political movements of the 18th century, it will be found to be a work of very great excellence. It is not only highly authoritative, but very interesting, and possesses as great value for the ordinary reader as for the student. The chapters on the American Revolution contain the most impartial treatment of that event which has yet been produced. H. L. O.

Lee, Arthur. LEE, CHARLES HENRY. Vindication of Arthur Lee. N. Y.: Randolph Co. 1894. [1408

Compiled to refute charges made by Franklin, Silas Deane, Beaumarchais or by their biographers. Contains few new facts. Written in a partisan spirit. Style readable. E. C.

— LEE, RICHARD HENRY. Life of Arthur Lee. Boston : Wells. 1829. 2v. [1409

The first 183 pages of this work are devoted to a valueless biography, in which is inserted, often without the slightest explanation or apparent reason, many letters from or to Lee, as well as other documents. The balance of the two volumes is filled with selections from the Lee papers, divided into eleven different groups, which nominally are the result of classification, but which as a fact can only be termed confusion. To neutralize their value still more, the texts are garbled, and parts are omitted, as the author-editor willed. As historical material, therefore, the work would be instantly dismissed from consideration, but for the fact that there is nothing better; and, in fact, it is the only book upon a man who, through the influence of his family, secured posts of such importance that his life and letters must receive consideration from all students of the history of that period. P. L. F.

Lee, Maj.-Gen. Charles. Papers. See New-York Historical Society, sect. 358. [1410

— LANGWORTHY, EDWARD. Memoirs of the life of Charles Lee. London : Jordan. 1792. N. Y. 1793. [1411

1731–82. Five sixths of the work is taken up by the letters and writings of Lee. The sketch of his life though brief is interesting, and the writings are often piquant. E. C. R.

— MOORE, GEORGE HENRY. Treason of Charles Lee. N. Y.: Scribner. 1860. [1412

First publication of the documents proving the treason of Lee, with a conclusive argument. A classic of the subject. E. C. R.

— SPARKS, JARED. Life of Charles Lee. (In his Library of Am. biography, ser. 2, v. 8. Boston: Little. 1846.) [1413

As favorable an estimate of Lee as this of Sparks is, since the publication of Moore's work, no longer possible. E. C. R.

Lee, Lt.-Col. Henry. 1756–1818. Memoirs of the war in the southern department of the United States. Phil.: Bradford. 1812. New ed., cor. Washington. 1827.

—— Same. New ed.; with revisions and biography by Robert E. Lee. N. Y.: University Pub. Co. 1869. [1414

"Light Horse Harry" Lee's account of the war in the South. Based on personal experience or on conversations with participants. Outspoken and usually impartial. The second ed. contains important additions. The memoir prefixed to the third ed. is the best memoir of Lee yet printed. Original work interesting and valuable. E. C.

Lee, Maj. Henry. 1787–1837. Campaign of 1781 in the Carolinas. Phil.: Little. 1824. [1415

Devoted mainly to what the title-page denominates "remarks, historical and critical, on Johnson's *Life of Greene* (sect. 1348)." The value of the volume consists (1) in the light thrown by these "remarks" on Greene's career; (2) in the fact that the author had access to papers now lost; and (3) in an appendix of documents most of which can now be found printed in other places. Style turgid and difficult to read continuously. E. C.

Lee, Richard Henry. LEE, RICHARD HENRY. Memoir of the life of Richard Henry Lee; by his grandson. Phil.: Carey. 1825. 2v. [1416

This life, written by the grandson of the man whose chief claim to fame is that he moved the resolution for independence in the Continental Congress, shows little knowledge on the part of the author as to what is needed in biography. Certain parts of Lee's life are treated with satisfactory fulness, but others are slurred, and in some cases entirely omitted, notably Lee's part in the local politics of Virginia during the Revolution, in which he was an important factor; and in the Conway cabal against Washington. As a biography, therefore, it can be dismissed with little attention, but the appendix of vol. 1, and the whole of vol. 2, print some hundred and fifty letters to and from Lee, which, in the absence of any collection of the Lee papers, make it a work of distinct value. It is to be noted, however, that there are traces of editing in the printing of these letters, the text not being wholly reliable. P. L. F.

Lee, William. Letters, 1766–83; ed. by Worthington Chauncey Ford. Brooklyn: Hist. Printing Club. 1892. 3v. [1417

These letters, written by a Virginia merchant residing in London, show the rise of the American Revolution as seen in England. Every phase of the changing political situations is touched upon. After 1776, when the writer engaged in diplomatic work for the United States, the letters are associated with the efforts of the American agents in Europe. The treaty with France, relations with Holland and Spain, the quarrels of the American representatives, and the progress toward peace are dealt with. Supplementary letters are introduced when necessary to the Lee letters, and, with the excellent footnotes, make the three volumes a general sketch of the early diplomatic history of the United States. E. E. S.

Livingston, William. SEDGWICK, THEODORE, JR. Memoir of the life of William Livingston ; with extracts from his correspondence. N. Y. : Harper. 1833.   [1418

Written from the original sources. Contains original papers of value and interest to the student of the years 1774 to 1789. The earlier part of the book has a purely personal interest. The compiler has done his work well.   E. C.

Lodge, Henry Cabot. Story of the Revolution. N. Y. : Scribner. 1898. 2v. $6.   [1419

" This work may be regarded as one of the latest contributions to the gratification of the prevailing taste in our country for military stories and pictures. . . One should not be surprised to find in the first volume . . . a list of illustrations covering six pages followed by a list of maps that does not take as many lines ; and in the second volume a three-page list of illustrations without any mention of a map. The second volume does, however, contain three maps. The work is devoid of any general map of the colonies or of the British possessions in North America. The illustrations are mostly works of the imagination or out of date. No references or authorities are given. Figures and dates are scarce. The reader will be charmed with the author's graphic and vigorous, often eloquent language. But he may be influenced by it to pass over unscanned or unquestioned statements of doubtful meaning or correctness." John Bigelow, Jr., *Am. hist. rev.*, 5: 362.

Lossing, Benson John. Pictorial fieldbook of the Revolution. N. Y. : Harper. 1851-2. 2v. Rev. ed. 1855. 2v. $7.   [1420

The result of a personal examination of the scenes described. Illustrations made from actual sketches. Replete with anecdotes derived from conversations with veterans or embodying local traditions. The principal drawback to its use is the fact that it is arranged according to the author's journeys and not according to sequence of events. A stimulating and useful work.   E. C.

—— The two spies, Nathan Hale and John André. N. Y. : Appleton. 1886. $2. [1421

Two Revolutionary sketches, turning about the dates 1776 and 1780. The one is based on Stuart's *Hale* and the other on Sargeant's *André*. The writer makes a strong presentation of André's courage, and a plea against the desecration of the monument erected to his memory by Mr. Field. The merit of the book lies in the illustrations drawn from nature by the author.   E. E. S.

Lowell, Edward Jackson. The Hessians, and the other German auxiliaries of Great Britain in the Revolutionary War. N. Y. : Harper. 1884.   [1422

A scholarly and sympathetic narrative based on contemporary diaries, letters, and other documents printed and unprinted. The experiences and observations of the intelligent German officers yield many vivid pictures of American life during the Revolutionary struggle. Much light is thrown on Burgoyne's march and capture, and on the experiences of the prisoners. A bibliography of the sources is added.   E. G. B.

Loxley, B. Journal of the campaign to Amboy and other parts of the Jerseys. See Pennsylvania, Historical Society of, sect. 384.   [1423

Ludlow, John Malcolm Forbes. War of American independence. (Epochs of modern history.) London, N. Y. : Longmans. 1876. $1.   [1424

The author is an intelligent Englishman who has written other works on American subjects. In about 250 pages this subject is very intelligently covered, with 4 useful maps, and an index. This work is a compilation, but it is skilfully made, and marked by judgment, by exceptional fair-mindedness, by a careful method, and by an attractive style. Ludlow's account may be compared with that of Andrews (sect. 1225), but it is far better adapted to the general reader.   W. E. F.

MacDonald, Alexander. Letter-books. See New-York Historical Society, sect. 363.   [1425

Mackay, Charles. Founders of the American Republic. Edin.: Blackwood. 1885.   [1426

Contains personal sketches of Washington, John Adams, Jefferson, Franklin, and Madison, " the principal founders of the independency of the United States." The author is a voluminous English writer. There is nothing new in the biographies, but the style is vivacious although sometimes wandering. A final chapter contains a sketch of the political history of the United States with a rehearsal of English fears for the future of democracy.

Marion, *Gen.* Francis. HORRY, *Brig.-Gen.* PETER, *and* MASON LOCKE WHEEMS [WEEMS]. Life of General Francis Marion. Phil.: Carey. 1816. N. Y.: Lovell. 1883. Phil.: Lippincott. $1.   [1427

Compiled largely from the Horry papers (see sect. 1336). Contains also stories gathered from local sources, or invented, or amplified by the authors. The original of the popular conception of Marion.   E. C.

— SIMMS, WILLIAM GILMORE. Life of Francis Marion. N. Y. 1844.   [1428

One of the Revolutionary biographies (1732-95), which is so preëminent in its interest (due to the author as well as the subject) as to be worn to pieces in the hands of northern as well as southern readers. Where it fails is in its uncritical method, and in the author's lack of the habits of a trained historian. In his preface Mr. Simms speaks somewhat admiringly of the celebrated romancist biographer, Weems, though censuring, indeed, his " loose " methods. W. E. F.

Marshall, Christopher. Passages from [his] remembrancer ; ed. by Wm. Duane. Phil. 1839.

—— Passages from diary. Phil. : Hazard. 1839–1849.

—— Extracts from diary, 1774–81 ; ed. by Wm. Duane. Albany : Munsell. 1877. $3. [1429

The standard authority for the Revolutionary events of 1774–1777 as seen in Philadelphia and Lancaster, Pa. Marshall was a retired business man of Philadelphia who had held many responsible positions, and his statements are accepted as reliable. The diary has been printed in various forms, but has never been fully annotated. The appendixes of the different editions contain valuable matter on the signing of the Declaration of Independence, etc. The last edition contains all of the diary that is of interest or importance at the present day. E. E. S.

Martin, *Gen.* **Joseph.** WEEKS, STEPHEN B. General Joseph Martin and the war of the Revolution in the West. (In Am. Hist. Assoc. Annual report, 1893.) Repr. Baltimore : Johns Hopkins Press. $1. Pap. [1430

General Martin (1740–1808) was the agent of Virginia among the Cherokees. By his address and diplomacy he was able to keep them quiet during the autumn of 1780, and so made it possible for the over-mountain men to leave their homes and strike a blow at the British and Tories at King's Mountain, thus turning the tide of war in the South in favor of the Americans. General Martin's services in negotiating the treaty of Hopewell, his opposition to the state of Franklin, and subsequent service, are also told.

Massey, William. History of England during the reign of George III. London : Parker. 1855–63. 4v. 2d ed., rev. and cor. London : Longmans. 1865–6. 4v. [1431

Massey was, in the middle of the century, a political figure of some importance, sitting much in Parliament, and connected at one time with the Government of India. His reputation was that of a man of ability, who, however, was handicapped by indolence and lack of ambition, — a reputation well borne out by his principal literary work, his history, which, while creditable, was left unfinished. The work is sensible and good-tempered : while criticising sharply the British policy during the American Revolution, and speaking appreciatively of Washington and of much that was done in America, he yet does not take the American view. J. K. H.

Meigs, J. Journal of Arnold's expedition to Quebec. See Massachusetts Historical Society, sect. 292. [1432

Montresor, James *and* **John.** Journals. See New-York Historical Society, sect. 362. [1433

Moore, Frank, *ed.* Diary of the American Revolution, from newspapers and original documents. N. Y. : Scribner. 1860. [c. 1858.] 2v. [1434

The editor, who later accomplished a similar service in the compilation of the " Rebellion record," was fortunate in gaining access to very copious Revolutionary materials, as well as in his habits of accuracy and careful citation of authorities. The extracts included are from both sides, and are here printed without comment by the editor. The work has an excellent index, and several portraits, and contemporary maps and plans ; and it has a basis of usefulness for both the special student and the general reader. W. E. F.

—— Songs and ballads of the American Revolution. N. Y. : Appleton. 1856. [1435

The editor performed an invaluable service in rescuing the more than 90 poems here collected. This subject may also be studied in Tyler's *Literary history of the American Revolution.* In Moore's collection there are illustrative notes, and a somewhat unsatisfactory index. W. E. F.

Morgan, *Maj. - Gen.* **Daniel.** GRAHAM, JAMES. Life of General Daniel Morgan of the Virginia line. N. Y. : Derby. 1856. [1436

Author had access to Morgan's papers and possessed a full knowledge of North Carolina traditions. Book contains many valuable documents not elsewhere in print. E. C.

—— McCONKEY, REBECCA. The hero of Cowpens. N. Y. : Barnes. [c. 1881.] Rev. ed. N. Y. : Funk. 1885. $1. [1437

An avowed thesis to prove that on the Quebec expedition and the movements against Burgoyne, Morgan deserves the credit generally ascribed to Benedict Arnold. The subsequent career of Morgan in the southern campaign completes the book. The chief merit is in calling attention to the services of one of the lesser known officers, but the whole is far from scholarly. E. E. S.

Morris, Lewis. Letters to General Morris. See New-York Historical Society, sect. 359. [1438

Morris, Robert. Letters to Robert Morris. See New-York Historical Society, sect. 361. [1439

Morse, Jedidiah. Annals of the American Revolution. Hartford. 1824. [1440

A " compilation " of the chief events in the history of America, beginning with its discovery and ending with the close of the Revolutionary War. The " Military operations of the Revolutionary War " occupies the bulk of the book, the " Origin of the American Revolution " a smaller portion, while the first one hundred pages are devoted to the years prior to 1763. This was for many years the standard book on the Revolution, but its facts have been worked over in more presentable shapes. An appendix contains biographies of the most prominent military officers of the war. These are composed largely of anecdotes and traditions which have been set aright by later investigations. They are of little value save as curiosities. E. E. S.

Moultrie, *Maj.-Gen.* **William.** Memoirs of the American Revolution, so far as it related to the states of North and South Carolina and Georgia. N. Y. 1802. 2v.   [**1441**

Contains account of the Revolutionary history of Charleston from personal observation. Very outspoken and often prejudiced. One of the most interesting of the Revolutionary narratives.   E. C.

Muhlenberg, *Maj.-Gen.* **Peter.** Journals of 1776 and 1777, relating to military events. See Pennsylvania, Historical Society of, sect. 384.
[**1442**

— MUHLENBERG, HENRY AUGUSTUS. Life of Major-General Peter Muhlenberg of the Revolutionary army. Phil.: Carey. 1849.
[**1443**

Written by a relative with notes giving authority for statements. The only book on this subject. Not as painstaking as modern biographical writing, but free from much of the old-time eulogy. In the notes is a short but valuable journal of H. M. Muhlenberg written in 1777 during the battle of Germantown. The appendix contains the correspondence of General Muhlenberg and his very valuable journal of a trip to the Falls of the Ohio (Louisville, Kentucky) as a superintendent to locate the Virginia Military lands.
E. E. S.

Murray, James. Impartial history of the present war in America. Newcastle-upon-Tyne. 1780. 2v.   [**1444**

This work is seldom found in complete form as it was published in parts, probably at irregular intervals. It bears a strong resemblance to *An impartial history etc.* (London. 1780). Both books were largely copied with little attempt at concealment from the *Annual register*, the historical portions of which were at this time probably written by Edmund Burke. So far as thus copied they are valuable.   E. C.

Neilson, Charles. An original, compiled and corrected account of Burgoyne's campaign and the memorable battles of Bemis's Heights. Albany: Munsell. 1844.   [**1445**

A naïve sketch "in the plain and simple language of a humble *farmer*," according to the preface. The material was derived largely from the father of the writer, who resided at Bemis's Heights during the war. The authentic is mingled with the legendary, and the whole is interspersed with anecdotes, often told in the vernacular. Some of these stories concern General Burgoyne, Generals Clinton, Stark, Gates and Arnold, and the Baron and Baroness Riedesel. The work is more curious than instructive.   E. E. S.

Newell, Thomas. Diary at Boston, 1773–74. See Massachusetts Historical Society, sect. 323.   [**1446**

Newell, Timothy. Journal, Boston, 1775–76. See Massachusetts Historical Society, sect. 306.   [**1447**

Niles, Hezekiah. Principles and acts of the Revolution in America. Balt.: Niles. 1822. N. Y.: Barnes. 1876. $2.50.   [**1448**

A miscellaneous collection of patriotic orations, addresses, proclamations, letters, documents both public and private, relating to the Revolution. The collection was made and published by the editor of the famous *Weekly register*, which was issued at Baltimore during the first half of the 19th century. The material was first published without effort at arrangement, but, in the edition of 1876, it was arranged chronologically by states. The volume is the result of an early effort, not only to preserve historical documents, but by that means to keep alive the "spirit of '76." The material it contains is fragmentary, and much of it can better be consulted now in other works. The most valuable single portion is the *Journal* of the Stamp Act Congress.   H. L. O.

Norton, A. Tiffany. History of Sullivan's campaign against the Iroquois. Lima, N. Y.: Author. 1879.   [**1449**

A thorough study of the expedition made against the Six Nations in central New York in 1779 by Sullivan and 3,800 men. The details of the campaign are carefully worked out. The author gains the confidence of the reader by his careful statements and his numerous references. He defends Sullivan against the charges of not completing his task, of injudicious ceremonies on the advance, and of wanton cruelty in destroying Indian property.   E. E. S.

Operations of the French fleet under the Count de Grasse, 1781–82. See Bradford Club, sect. 252.   [**1450**

Otis, James. TUDOR, WILLIAM. Life of James Otis; containing notices of contemporary characters and events, 1760–1775. Boston: Wells. 1823.   [**1451**

James Otis was a chief among the leaders in Massachusetts who, in the decade and a half before war broke out, made it impossible that the breach opening between motherland and colonies should be reconciled. The term meteoric fits Otis more aptly than any other figure of our early history. His power, though fitful, was very brilliant; and by personal magnetism he subdued men as completely as did Chatham, a statesman and orator with whom it is not absurd to compare him. A morbid quality in his nature, early manifest, developing into insanity, caused his early retirement to a remote farm, where his career was dramatically ended by a stroke of lightning. While opposing independence, Otis strove for redress of grievances, more than any other man, making that half-forgotten principle of English liberty, no taxation without representation, the war-cry of America. Tudor remembered men who had known Otis well. He wrote his book at a time when no justice could be done to the losing side. With that drawback, it may rightly be called a fair-minded account of a picturesque and noble figure; and incidentally much valuable light is thrown on the contemporaries of Otis.   J. K. H.

Paine, Thomas. Writings; collected and

ed. by Moncure D. Conway. N. Y.: Putnam. 1894–6. 4v. $10.   [1452

Few writers have exerted a more powerful influence than Paine, since the world began, if the claim set forth at the time and never refuted be just, that his *Common sense* made possible the Declaration of Independence and therefore the United States of America. Certain it is that down almost to the spring of 1775 the colonies were throughout indifferent or quite opposed to the idea of independence ; and no other influence can be pointed out so potent as that of Paine's memorable pamphlet, in swinging the land into the new position. If gratitude and honor are denied to him as having been irreligious, there are many others among the fathers who should also suffer — notably Franklin, John Adams, Jefferson and Ethan Allen. Paine probably differed from these men mainly in being more outspoken in his free-thinking, holding fast, however, as they did, to belief in God, immortality and the moral law. In this collection an ardent admirer has tried to include everything important of Paine's. *Common sense* and the *Age of reason* are given scrupulously as they came from the hand of the author: while with them are included tracts which, in the editor's judgment, establish the fact that he was skilful in practical affairs ; that in financial and economic science his conceptions entitle him to a place among the wisest ; and that he was the first of American abolitionists.   J. K. H.

—— Letter addressed to the Abbé Raynal on the affairs of North America, in which the mistakes in the Abbé's account of the Revolution in America are corrected and cleared up. Phil.: Aitken. 1782. Boston: Edes. 1782. [Several other reprints.]   [1453

Written to correct certain statements made in the *Revolution of America* by the Abbé Raynal and to convict the Abbé of plagiarism. Of slight interest or value at the present time.   E. C.

— CONWAY, MONCURE DANIEL. Life of Thomas Paine [1737–1809]; to which is added a sketch of Paine by Wm. Cobbett. N. Y.: Putnam. 1892. 2v. $5.   [1454

By the editor of Paine's *Writings*, subsequently published. The unique and invaluable character of this work, among the published accounts of Paine, may be seen, in part, from the instances cited in the author's Preface. The work is the result of unwearied efforts to secure the exact facts, and also to state each point fairly and accurately, though avowedly in defence of him ; and it is marked by an English style whose vivacity and interest never flag. The book has an index, a list of writings and portraits.   W. E. F.

— SEDGWICK, ELLERY. Thomas Paine. (Beacon biographies.) Boston: Small. 1899. 75c.   [1455

" The writer brings to his task a more judicious temper than that manifested by any of Paine's better-known biographers heretofore. 'It is difficult,' he says, 'to write of Paine without enthusiasm,' and

fortunately he does not succeed in doing so ; but he gives us no rhapsodies. Neither have we any of those impossible theories and explanations which disfigured the elaborate apology for Paine to which Mr. M. D. Conway devoted so much patient zeal. . . . The rapid movement necessitated by Mr. Sedgwick's restricted space heightens the interest of his narrative." *Nation*, 70: 185.

Papers relating to the Boston Tea-Party. See Massachusetts Historical Society, sect. 330.   [1456

Paterson, *Maj. - Gen.* **John.** EGLESTON, THOMAS. Life of John Paterson ; by his great-grandson. N. Y.: Putnam. 1894. 2d ed., rev. and enl. 1898. $3.50.   [1457

Of the new edition the *Nation* said: " A large part of the new matter is derived from the correspondence of Generals Heath and Knox, and is of good quality. . . . Prof. Egleston has been very industrious in searching for mention of Gen. Paterson in orderly books, diaries and newspapers ; and this enables him to record much that is too trivial to find a place in a formal history, yet possessed of enough personal interest not to be entirely passed over. The value of the work has thus been greatly increased, and cannot be neglected by any historian of the Revolution."

Pattison, James. Letters, 1779 and 1780. See New-York Historical Society, sect. 359.   [1458

Pausch, *Capt.* **Georg.** Journal during the Burgoyne campaign [1776–7] ; tr. and annotated by Wm. L. Stone ; introd. by Edward J. Lowell. (Munsell's hist. series, no. 14.) Albany. 1886. $2.   [1459

Since the author of the original journal, in German, was a Hessian officer in Burgoyne's army, his information is at first hand. Mr. Stone's translation into English is supplied with intelligent and helpful notes, and an index. For the special student, rather than the general reader.   W. E. F.

Pitkin, Timothy. Political and civil history of the United States. New Haven: Howe. 1828. 2v.   [1460

These volumes cover the period from 1763 to 1797, and are devoted to the political events of the time. Pitkin was an industrious, careful scholar who wrote from original sources. His work is marked by accuracy, judicial temper, excellent judgment and exhaustive research ; is still useful, though largely superseded by later histories built upon material then inaccessible. The style is dry and uninteresting. Valuable appendices are found in both volumes, including among other documents, the New England Articles of Confederation, 1643 ; the Plan of Union, 1754 ; the Stamp Act ; the Declaration of Right by the Stamp Act Congress ; the Circular Letter of the Massachusetts House of Representatives, 1768 ; Address to the People of Great Britain by Congress, 1774 ; the Last Appeal to the King, 1775, and a letter to the President of Congress by the British Commissioners, June 10, 1778.   R. C. H. C.

Pontgibaud, Charles Albert de Moré, *chevalier* de. A French volunteer of the war of independence; tr. and ed. by Robert B. Douglas. N. Y.: Appleton. 1898. $1.50.   [1461

An exceedingly bright and interesting little book of reminiscence. American experience begins in 1778. Not much light on the military history of the Revolution, but gossip concerning Lafayette, Talleyrand, Washington, the French emigrés, and Philadelphia after the close of the war.   E. E. S.

Price, Ezekiel. Diary [siege of Boston]. See Massachusetts Historical Society, sect. 325.   [1462

Price, Richard. Observations on the importance of the American Revolution. London: Cadell. 1784. Boston. 1784.   [1463

Price was ardently interested in the welfare of the British colonies and repeatedly expressed his confidence in their future after they achieved independence. This essay is dedicated to the people of the United States as a testimony of good will. It briefly considers the measures necessary to promote human improvement and happiness in the United States through the perpetuation of peace, liberty of conscience, and education. The essay is not long. The style is stilted, and at the present time the work has but little interest save for the special student.   D. R. D.

—— Observations on the nature of civil liberty, the principles of government, and the justice and policy of the war with America. London: Cadell. 1776.   [1464

A celebrated tract by a somewhat famous philosopher and economist against the justice and policy of the British government's course toward the colonies. It is said that the encouragement it gave had no inconsiderable share in bringing about the Declaration of Independence, and it gained for its author great repute. There is an appendix on the state of the British national debt and the income and expenditures of the government since the French war.   F. J. S.

Putnam, *Maj.-Gen.* **Israel.** HUMPHREYS, *Col.* DAVID. Essay on the life of the Honorable Major-General Israel Putnam: addressed to the State Society of the Cincinnati in Connecticut. Hartford. 1788. Enl. ed. Boston: Avery. 1818.   [1465

This address, by a former officer on Putnam's staff, was delivered during Putnam's lifetime to a society, many of whose members had served under Putnam in the war of the Revolution. It is, therefore, inevitably more or less of an eulogy. But it is interesting and so proved to the readers of that time ; it is also accurate and corrects many errors of Peters and others. It is full of anecdotes about Putnam, and its style, though somewhat poetic and rhetorical, is pleasing.   C. M. A.

—— TARBOX, INCREASE NILES. Life of Israel

Putnam ("Old Put"). Boston: Lockwood. 1876. Lothrop. [1884.] $1.   [1466

This is an honest attempt to write an authoritative life of Putnam by a biographer of the old school. The work is, however, not so much a life of Putnam as an elaborate discussion of Putnam's connection with the battle of Bunker Hill. Two hundred out of 331 pages deal with the history of but two months of Putnam's career. Dr. Tarbox is a special pleader, though, apart from his defence of Putnam's leadership at Bunker Hill, he does not appear to be actuated by undue admiration. The work does not display any exceptional critical ability, and the style is dry and hard. It is, however, probably the best source of information regarding Putnam, for Dr. Tarbox has used good material unknown to either Humphreys or Sparks.   C. M. A.

Quincy, Josiah. *1744–75.* QUINCY, JOSIAH. *1772–1864.* Memoir of the life of Josiah Quincy, Jr., of Massachusetts Bay, 1744–75. Boston: Cummings. 1825, 2d ed. Boston: Wilson. 1874.   [1467

Invaluable observations on life of the colonists recorded during a journey through the Atlantic coast cities in 1773, and a journal kept whilst the author was in England in the service of the rebellious colonies. It contains reminiscences of Franklin and of English statesmen. Letters written to Quincy show the progress of the revolution in the different colonies. The volume also contains extracts from his defence of Captain Preston (Boston massacre) and from his political writings.   E. E. S.

Rainsford, Charles. Journal as commissary of the British army. See New-York Historical Society, sect. 361.   [1468

Ramsay, David. History of the American Revolution. Phil.: Aitken. 1789. Trenton: Wilson. 1811. 2v.   [1469

David Ramsay, born in Pennsylvania, educated in Princeton, N. J., where he became son-in-law of the Whig Witherspoon, President of the College, settled as a physician in Charleston, S. C. At the outbreak of the Revolution he took service as a surgeon, but was more marked as a legislator than in professional work. He served in the Continental Congress, and was long President of the So. Carolina Senate in our critical period. His second wife was daughter of Henry Laurens. He appears to have conceived early the idea of writing a history of the Revolution, for from the first he was a diligent collector of documents. His memory was tenacious, his disposition impartial, his acquaintance among the great men of the time wide and intimate, connected as he was with important figures, himself a man of prominence. His history has the faults and merits of a contemporary record. As the work of an alert and sturdy eye-witness, it is a source of value.   J. K. H.

—— History of the Revolution of South Carolina from a British colony to an independent state. Trenton: Collins. 1785. 2v.   [1470

Author a resident of Charleston and of South Carolina during the greater part of the Revolution. Work based on personal observation or on conversations with participants. Reflects contemporary southern opinion. Style uninteresting.   E. C.

Raynal, Guillaume Thomas François, *l'abbé.* Révolution de l'Amérique. London: Lockyer. 1781.

—— Revolution of America. London: Lockyer. 1781. Phil.: Bell. 1782. Salem: Hall. 1782. [Numerous other reprints.]   [**1471**

The work of a philosophical French writer on political science. States in brief form the leading facts from 1763 to 1778. Discusses, after the manner of the time, the claims of both parties. Interesting from its point of view.   E. C.

Read, George. READ, WILLIAM THOMPSON. Life and correspondence of George Read, a signer of the Declaration of Independence; with notices of some of his contemporaries. Phil.: Lippincott. 1870.   [**1472**

Treats mainly of the years 1769 to 1791. Contains many original letters and other documents. The text is written in a spirit of filial piety. Especially valuable are the footnotes and the supplementary notes appended to the several chapters. An uninteresting but useful book.   E. C.

Reed, *Mrs.* Esther (De Berdt). REED, WILLIAM BRADFORD. Life of Esther De Berdt, afterwards Esther Reed of Pennsylvania. Phil.: privately printed. 1853.   [**1473**

Esther De Berdt Reed, daughter of the London merchant Dennis De Berdt, and wife of Joseph Reed, President of Pennsylvania, was born in 1747 and died in 1780. This simply written story by her grandson is valuable for the insight afforded into the situation in London just before the Revolution and for the description of life in the American middle colonies during the struggle. The story is told mainly by contemporary letters, for the most part to or from Mrs. Reed.   V. L. C.

Reed, Joseph. REED, WILLIAM B. Life and correspondence of Joseph Reed. Phil.: Lindsay. 1847. 2v.   [**1474**

1741–1785. Revolutionary officer, Aide to Washington and President of Pennsylvania. The author was grandson of General Reed. The work is extremely able, written from the sources in an excellent method, interesting and illuminating.   E. C. R.

Revere, *Col.* Paul. GOSS, ELBRIDGE HENRY. Life of Colonel Paul Revere. Boston: Cupples. 1891. 2v.   [**1475**

This is the only worthy biography of Revere. It is scholarly and thorough. There are numerous illustrations, some of them reproductions of Revere's engravings. The chapters treat of the services of Revere as a cartoonist in the Revolution; as an express rider, especially the April rides to Lexington; as an officer in the Revolutionary War; on the unfortunate Penobscot expedition; in connection with the adoption of the Federal Constitution in Massachusetts; as a Mason, and in private business relations. Quotations from Revere's diary and letters are numerous. An appendix contains valuable papers, including a sketch of Dawes, Revere's fellow rider to Lexington.   E. E. S.

Rhode Island Revolutionary correspondence, 1775–82. See Rhode Island Historical Society. Collections, v. 6, 1867.   [**1476**

Riedesel, Friederike Charlotte Louise von Massow, *Freiin* von. Letters and journals relating to the war of the American Revolution; tr. from the German by Wm. L. Stone. Albany: Munsell. 1867.   [**1477**

These invaluable memoranda record the observations of an eye-witness of the Burgoyne campaign (born 1746; died 1808). She is frankly anti-American in her sympathies, but her notes are pervaded by an admirable temper, and a genuineness and directness of style which retain even the general reader's interest. Mr. Stone's editorial work is performed with intelligent care and critical judgment; and his translation is a competent one. The book has an index, a portrait and illustrations.   W. E. F.

Riedesel, Friedrich Adolph, *Freiherr* von. EELKING, MAX VON. Memoirs, and letters and journals of Major-General Riedesel; tr. by Wm. L. Stone. Albany: Munsell. 1868. 2v.   [**1478**

This careful account, by an eye-witness (born 1738; died 1800), is the basis of our later and more accurate knowledge of the Burgoyne campaign (1777), in which Riedesel commanded Burgoyne's Brunswick allies. Mr. Stone has added, in his serviceable English translation, explanatory notes, an index, and illustrations, but no maps. Not for the general reader. W. E. F.

Rochambeau, Jean Baptiste Donatien de Vimeur, *comte* de. Memoirs relative to the war of independence of the United States; tr. by M. W. E. Wright. Paris. 1838. [**1479**

"Count Rochambeau describes at length the military operations of which he was a witness in America, and looks at the country, for the most part, with the eyes of a soldier. He repudiates all idea of writing in the character of a professed author, and both the style and substance of his autobiography are those of a military memoir. Still he records many significant facts, geographical and economical." H. T. Tuckerman, in *America and her commentators*, p. 111.

Rockingham, Charles Watson Wentworth, *2d marquis of.* ALBEMARLE, GEORGE THOMAS KEPPEL, *6th earl of.* Memoirs of the Marquis of Rockingham and his contemporaries; with original documents. London: Bentley. 1852. 2v.   [**1480**

Vol. 1 contains papers relating to the Stamp Act episode, including letters from George III. The second volume has documents of the years 1766–1782.

Every careful student of the Revolutionary era must use these volumes, but they are less interesting than might be expected.   E. C.

Rogers, *Maj*. Robert. Concise account of North America. London. 1765.

—— Journals. London. 1765.

—— *Same;* with introd. and notes by Franklin B. Hough. Albany : Munsell. 1883. $3.
[1481

" Rogers was a native of New Hampshire. He commanded a body of provincial rangers, and stood in high repute as a partisan officer. Putnam and Stark were his associates. . . . His mind, naturally active, was by no means uncultivated ; and his books and unpublished letters bear witness that his style as a writer was not contemptible. But his vain, restless, and grasping spirit, and more than doubtful honesty, proved the ruin of an enviable reputation. . . . At the opening of the war of independence, he returned to his native country, where he made professions of patriotism, but was strongly suspected by many, including Washington himself, of acting the part of a spy. In fact, he soon openly espoused the British cause, and received a colonel's commission from the crown. His services, however, proved of little consequence. In 1778 he was proscribed and banished. . . . Although Rogers, especially where his pecuniary interest was concerned, was far from scrupulous, I have no hesitation in following his account of the expedition up the lakes. The incidents of each day are minuted down in a dry, unambitious style, bearing the clear impress of truth. . . . Rogers' published works consist of the *Journals* of his ranging service and his *Concise account of North America*, a small volume containing much valuable information. Both appeared in London in 1765." Francis Parkman, in *Conspiracy of Pontiac*, ch. 6 (v. 1).

Rowe, John. Diary [Boston, 1764–1779]. See Massachusetts Historical Society, sect. 347.   [1482

Rumford, *Sir* Benjamin Thompson, *count*. ELLIS, GEORGE EDWARD. Memoir of Sir Benjamin Thompson, Count Rumford. Boston and Phil. 1871. London : Macmillan. 1876.
[1483

Describes the early life of Count Rumford ; but devotes most attention to his later career in Europe. The controversies as to his Revolutionary career are lightly passed over, or not mentioned at all. The only large life of Count Rumford.   E. C.

Ryerson, Egerton. Loyalists of America, 1620–1816. Toronto: Briggs. 1880. 2v.
[1484

The author, son of a Tory exile from New Jersey, who filled the important office of Superintendent of Education for Upper Canada from 1844 to 1876, writes his two volumes from the point of view of a " United Empire Loyalist," in a tone throughout temperate and scholarly. He sketches the colonial history at length, supplying many documents, giving a presentment in which the dealings of the Stuarts with Amer-

ica are more favorably regarded than is usual. Having narrated the French and Indian wars, the author considers the troubles out of which came the Declaration of Independence with an earnest sympathy for the Americans and strong condemnation of British policy. With the passing of the Declaration of Independence, however, his approval of the American course ceases. That was a mistake calamitous to the whole English-speaking race. The years of war following were years of disgrace to both sides, — the expatriation of the Tories at last foolish and infamous inhumanity. The fortunes of the descendants of the Tories, the United Empire Loyalists, are followed into the 19th century. Received American opinions are often contradicted, but the views are worth weighing. It is a profitable book for an American to read.   J. K. H.

Sabine, Lorenzo. Biographical sketches of Loyalists of the American Revolution ; with an historical essay. Boston : Little. 1864. 2v. $7.   [1485

Lorenzo Sabine, in his latter years a respected citizen of Massachusetts, and once a representative in Congress, passed much of his life on the Maine frontier adjoining New Brunswick. Coming there into close connection with the descendants of the exiled Tories, he dared to compile sketches of a number of these, speaking of them in a way quite in contrast with the execration which up to that time, 1847, had been the usual tone. The world wondered at the boldness of author and publishers who dared attempt the rescue from oblivion or obliquy of the men who in our Revolution took the losing side. The work, however, found readers, a new edition appearing after an interval. It was a path-breaker in a new class of historical writing, and has contributed in an important way to produce a more just and humane estimate of the men who went down in '76. Mr. Sabine's candor, industry, and excellent sense appear in all the numerous sketches. Though many of the sketches are brief, all have value.   J. K. H.

Saffell, William Thomas Roberts. Records of the Revolutionary War. N. Y.: Pudney. 1858. 3d ed. Balt. : Saffell. 1894.
[1486

A compilation of the names of Revolutionary officers and privates, arranged by regiments or companies ; of distinguished prisoners of war ; of the officers of the Society of the Cincinnati; of the officers entitled to land pay ; of foreign officers; and of officers receiving land warrants. These lists are valuable for genealogical purposes. A number of letters from paymasters and other officers is added, together with legislation on military land warrants. These serve the purpose of those who are tracing Revolutionary claims.
E. E. S.

Sanderson, John. Biography of the signers to the Declaration of Independence. Phil. 1820–7. 9v. 2d ed., rev. and enl. Phil.: Brown. 1828. 5v.   [1487

Written from the best source available at the time. Vol. I contains: Introduction; A view of the British colonies . . . from their origin to their independence.

141

It occupies 226 pages and when written was a valuable concise sketch of the colonial and Revolutionary eras. The whole work is now out of date as to all the important men whose lives it records. Written in a monotonous style. E. C.

Sargent, Winthrop, *ed.* Loyalist poetry of the Revolution. Albany. 1860. [**1488**

A collection of 43 poems, mostly doggerel, privately printed (only 99 copies). It opens with a tedious satire in three parts, "The American times," followed by a few rollicking ballads. One entitled "Hot stuff" by Edw. Botswood, sergeant, 1759, is of merit, worthy of place in Kiplingiana. "The Tenth Regiment's voyage to Quebec" (1767) contains details valuable for the historian. The introduction and notes are fair-minded. See *Hist. mag.,* June, 1858, pp. 164–5. H. W. H.

Schenck, David. North Carolina, 1780–81. Raleigh, N. C.: Edwards. 1889. [**1489**

The history of the invasion of the Carolinas by Cornwallis in 1780–81 is here traced, beginning with the siege of Charleston and ending with Eutaw Springs. Its particular design is to show the part borne by North Carolina in that campaign, and to correct some of the errors into which Lee, Johnson and other historians have fallen in regard to the state, especially in the conduct of her militia at Guilford Court House. It is made up from well-known printed sources, from which many extracts are reproduced. The arrangement is good. S. B. W.

Schuyler, *Maj.-Gen.* **Philip John.** Lossing, Benson John. Life and times of Philip Schuyler. N. Y.: Sheldon. 1860–73. 2v. Holt. 1884. 2v. $3.50. [**1490**

The life of one of the American Revolutionary generals (1733–1804), constructed chiefly on the basis of Schuyler's meagre papers which are preserved; and written by an author who had made himself somewhat familiar with the campaigns described. In point of information, Lossing's materials leave much to be desired, nor was he so much a writer of rigidly historical methods as a practised purveyor to the general reader, yet the story is not only entertainingly but skilfully told. The work has an index and portraits, but no maps. W. E. F.

—— Proceedings of his court-martial. See New-York Historical Society, sect. 361. [**1491**

Scudder, Horace Elisha, *ed.* Men and manners in America one hundred years ago. N. Y.: Scribner. 1876; 1887. $1.25. [**1492**

Pictures of life during the Revolution in the words of contemporary observers. From diaries, letters, autobiographies, recollections, and travels of Englishmen, Frenchmen, Hessians and Americans have been culled vivid and entertaining descriptions of almost every phase of life in New England, the Middle States and the South. The best single volume from which to derive a just idea of the life of the time. E. G. B.

Senter, Isaac. Journal on a secret expedition against Quebec in September, 1775. See Pennsylvania, Historical Society of, sect. 383. [**1493**

Seventy-Six Society. Philadelphia, Pa. This society was organized in 1854. Its publications are as follows: — [**1494**

Papers in relation to the case against Silas Deane; ed. by E. D. Ingraham. — The examination of Joseph Galloway, Esq., by a committee of the House of Commons, ed. by Thomas Balch. — Papers relating to public events in Massachusetts preceding the American Revolution. — Papers relating chiefly to the Maryland line during the Revolution; ed. by T. Balch.

Shelburne, William Petty Fitzmaurice, *2d earl of.* Fitzmaurice, Edmond George Petty, *lord.* Life of William, Earl of Shelburne, afterwards first marquess of Lansdowne; with extracts from his papers and correspondence. London and N. Y.: Macmillan. 1875–6. 3v. [**1495**

A dull long-drawn-out book upon a subject worthy of better handling. Shelburne, at a later time the first Marquis of Lansdowne, was a statesman of liberal views, who, coming into public life at the time of the Stamp Act, stood with Pitt and Camden in resisting the policy of the government. He later stood with the Earl of Chatham, the two alone among the officers of the government, in resisting coercive measures against America, and was the only man in the cabinet opposed to the expulsion from Parliament of John Wilkes. With his intimate friend Barré, Shelburne fought the policy of the King and his friends to the close, although he no more than Chatham could endure the thought of American independence. After Chatham's death, he became the leader of Chatham's adherents, but was hampered by great unpopularity, partly due to lack of a conciliatory spirit, but largely to his advanced views. In several ways he was before his time. He warmly advocated parliamentary and economic reform, Catholic emancipation and complete tolerance; and anticipated Cobden as to free trade. Disraeli called him the first great minister to comprehend the rising importance of the middle class. He was possessed of unusual boldness and independence, and was pronounced by Camden second only to Chatham in the House of Lords as an orator. J. K. H.

Shelburne papers, pt. 2. (In Great Britain, Royal Commission on Historical Manuscripts. 5th report. London. 1876.) [**1496**

"The *Shelburne papers,* belonging to the Marquis of Lansdowne, which make up a large part of the 5th report [of the English Historical Manuscripts Commission], while of most interest in connection with the American Revolution, reveal not a little concerning the colonial history of the earlier part of the 17th century." Justin Winsor, in *Narrative and critical hist. of Am.,* 5: 164.

Sikes, Enoch Walter. Transition of North Carolina from colony to commonwealth. (Johns Hopkins Univ. studies, ser. 16, nos. 10–11.) Balt. 1898. Pap. 50c. [**1497**

This account of the downfall of the royal government in North Carolina and the establishment of the state government in 1776 is based on material which is drawn almost entirely from volumes nine and ten of the *North Carolina colonial records*, 1770–1776. The author presents clearly the last stages in the quarrel between governor and assembly in North Carolina, and his work is chiefly of value in disclosing the conditions under which the constitution of 1776 was drafted.   C. M. A.

Simcoe, *Lt.-Col.* **John Graves.** Journal of the operations of the Queen's Rangers. Exeter. 1787.

—— Military journal: a history of the operations of a partisan corps called the Queen's Rangers; with memoir of author, etc. N. Y.: Bartlett. 1844.   [**1498**

"Simcoe's narrative is even more egotistical than Tarleton's. But his details may be relied upon if one constantly remembers that events are related without any regard to their real importance." E. Channing, in *Narrative and critical hist. of Am.*, 6: 518.

Simms, **Jeptha Root.** Trappers of New York. Albany: Munsell. 1850.   [**1499**

This book contains a biography of Nicholas Stoner and of Nathaniel Foster, two well-known trappers and frontiersmen of western New York in the latter part of the eighteenth century. Some account is also given of Sir William Johnson and his life at Johnson Hall. The material in the book was derived largely from the conversation of Stoner (who had been a famous Indian fighter), and after it was written out it was submitted to him and received his corrections. Though error could not be excluded by such a course, yet the book may be accepted as fairly accurate. Though not a work of great importance, it gives some personal details which are of value in helping the reader to form a picture of the conditions of frontier life at and subsequent to the period of the Revolution. The style is agreeable.   H. L. O.

Sloane, **William Milligan.** The French war and the Revolution. (American history series.) N. Y.: Scribner. 1893. $1.25.
    [**1500**

A compendious account, covering the period 1756–83. The conditions do not admit of much new matter or striking originality of treatment; but the state of the French and English colonies at the outbreak of the last French and Indian war, the causes of the Revolution, and the connection between the Revolution and changing American political ideas, are well brought out. The style is agreeable.   W. MacD.

Smyth, **John Ferdinand D.** A tour in the United States. London. 1784. 2v.   [**1501**

" Though replete with falsehood and calumny, it contains the truest picture of the state of society and manners in Virginia (such as it was about half a century ago) that is extant. Traces of the same manners could be found some years subsequent to the adoption of the federal constitution, say to the end of the century." John Randolph (in 1822); quoted in *Narrative and critical hist. of Am.*, 5: 284.

Soulés, **François.** Histoire des troubles de l'Amérique anglaise. Paris. 1787. 4v. Zurich (in German). 1788.   [**1502**

Supposed to have been inspired by Rochambeau. Covers the whole field of the Revolution from 1774 to 1783 — especially of the French and Spanish participation in the war. Includes also an account of the struggle between the English and the French in India and some interesting matter on the financial and social condition of the United States in 1783. There are also documents and letters, such as Washington's letter to the Governors. The text is generally accurate, but contains little that is not to be found in English. There are a few maps. Altogether the book is rather a curiosity than an authority.   E. C.

Sparks, **Jared,** *ed.* Correspondence of the American Revolution. Boston: Little. 1853. 4v.   [**1503**

These volumes should be used in connection with the standard editions of the *Writings of Washington*, whether by Sparks or Ford (sect. 1538, 1539). They contain the letters written to Washington which Mr. Sparks collected while editing the correspondence of that commander. The collection is not exhaustive, but consists of letters selected by the editor. Especially important and numerous are the letters of Greene, Lafayette, Schuyler, Knox, Lincoln, George Clinton, Rochambeau, Hancock and Jonathan Trumbull. Many by Hamilton, Jefferson, G. Morris and Madison also appear. Appendices contain correspondence respecting the operations in Canada in 1775 and 1776, operations in Virginia in 1776, and against Burgoyne and along the Hudson River in 1777. About three fourths of the collection relates to the Revolution, and the rest to the later events of Washington's career.   H. L. O.

—— Diplomatic correspondence of the American Revolution. Boston. 1829–30. 12v.
    [**1504**

Sparks had access to the papers of the Department of State, and made here the first authoritative collection of the Revolutionary diplomatic correspondence. The letters and other papers are grouped under the names of the persons by or to whom they were written, the arrangement within each group being chronological. The writers of the volumes are: 1. Silas Deane, and the American Commissioners to France. 2. Arthur Lee, Wm. Lee, Ralph Izard, Henry Laurens. 3. Franklin. 4. Franklin, John Adams. 5, 6. John Adams. 7. John Adams, John Jay. 8. Jay, Francis Dana. 9. Wm. Carmichael, John Laurens, C. W. F. Dumas. 10. Lafayette, the Peace Commissioners of 1781-3, C. A. Gerald, C. A. de la Luzerne. 11. Luzerne, Robert R. Livingston, Robert Morris. 12. Robert Morris. Sparks's method of editing has now fallen into disrepute: he printed only such documents as he thought of importance, and did not hesitate to omit or alter passages containing what he considered irrelevant or objectionable matter. His texts, accordingly, cannot be relied upon. For most purposes, the collection has now been superseded by Wharton's *Revolutionary diplomatic correspondence* (sect. 1574).   W. MacD.

Stanhope, **Philip Henry Stanhope,** *5th earl, viscount* **Mahon.** History of England from

143

the peace of Utrecht to the peace of Versailles, 1713–83. London: Murray. 1836–54. 7v. Rev. ed. 7v. 5s. ea. [**1505**

A book written from original sources by a competent scholar, whose knowledge of the period is unusually large. The author possessed a judicial temper, sound judgment, and was desirous of being absolutely just. His work, therefore, commands and deserves the reader's confidence. The book is well-proportioned, the narrative is clear, and the English is choice. Valuable excerpts from original documents used by the historian are appended to each volume.

R. C. H. C.

Stark, *Maj.-Gen.* John. STARK, CALEB. Memoir and official correspondence of Gen. John Stark. Concord, N. H.: Eastman. 1860. [**1506**

1728–1822. About half of this work is taken up with correspondence which is full of good documentary material. This fact, together with the relationship of the author, makes the book an excellent source, although less suited for popular use, perhaps, than Everett's. E. C. R.

Stedman, Charles. History of the origin, progress, and termination of the American war. London. 1794. 2v. [**1507**

Author was a "commissary" in the British army during the Revolutionary War. Work reflects opinions of British officers. Sometimes very candid. Contains many excellent maps and plans. Best contemporary account of the war from the British side. E. C.

Steuben, *Gen.* Frederick William von. KAPP, FRIEDRICH. Life of Frederick William von Steuben; with introd. by George Bancroft. N. Y.: Mason. 1859. [**1508**

"Steuben was a young soldier under Frederick the Great. He gained reputation in many a field, and was in years of peace leading a very easy life as a sort of head-chamberlain at a little German court, when the French government secretly engaged him to cross to America, and teach the undisciplined levies of the insurgent patriots to overthrow the rule of the English sovereign. . . . Steuben performed his mission well. . . . A large German population in the States . . . were determined that the memory of Steuben should not die. Mr. Kapp took the matter in hand. On all sides, but one, he met with ready assistance. Family papers, letters, documents from Germany, France, England . . . were liberally placed at his disposal. To make his story perfect, Mr. Kapp only required to consult the state archives at Washington, but there he was 'ignominiously repulsed.' . . . Despite this opposition . . . Mr. Kapp has accomplished his task satisfactorily." *Littell's living age*, 64: 126.

Stevens, Benjamin Franklin, *ed.* Campaign in Virginia, 1781: an exact reprint of six rare pamphlets on the Clinton-Cornwallis controversy, with very numerous important unpublished manuscript notes by Sir Henry Clinton; with a supplement containing extracts from the journals of the House of Lords, etc. London. 1888. 2v. [**1509**

Contains practically everything concerning the controversy between Clinton and Cornwallis as to which was responsible for the fortification of Yorktown. The pamphlets here reprinted are in some of our larger libraries, but the notes, the letters and some of the papers printed in the second volume as a supplement are to be found nowhere else and give the volume its great value to students of the Virginia campaign of 1781. Admirably indexed. E. C.

—— Facsimiles of manuscripts in European archives relating to America, 1773–83; with descriptions, editorial notes, collations, references and translations. London. 1889–98. 25v. £100. [**1510**

It is not too much to characterize this work as monumental. For some thirty years, Mr. Stevens took notes of all the material he could find relating to the period of the American Revolution, and in this vast collection embodies 2107 documents, reproduced in facsimile, chiefly from the Public Record Office, the Royal (Military) Institution, the Tower of London, and the British Museum, in England, the French Bureau des Affaires des Étrangères, in France, and the private collections of the Marquis of Abergavenny, the Earl of Carlisle, the Earl of Dartmouth, Lord Auckland, and of Mr. Stevens; and the editor does not exaggerate the value of the result when he asserts that "it is like taking up a whole collection of the State Paper Office of London or Paris, and transferring it to an American library." A condition made by the Public Record Office in London, in giving access to all papers, "whether general, confidential, secret, or most secret," was, Mr. Stevens states, "that I should take the whole, or leave the whole of each individual document, and that I should garble none, as had been done by two most eminent historians;" and a little experimentation with printed texts convinced him that it was impossible to obtain accurate printing. "In this dilemma I conceived the notion of attempting to solve the difficulty by substituting the art of photography, with its incontrovertible and recognized accuracy, as the mode of making my further copies of original manuscripts. Each document is an absolute facsimile, without any editorial words or explanation to alter its appearance as compared with the original, except an identifying mark and number for reference; but annexed to it is a separate statement, or title-page, with corresponding mark and number, indicating its endorsements, enclosures, seals, memoranda, etc., with various notes and references, the location of its original, its duplicates, triplicates, etc., if any, and if printed, where. There is also added in a note in a legible handwriting, a translation into English, when the document originated in another language. . . . The translations are intended to be literal rather than literary. They are given upon the advice of some of the best known students." So well has the work been done, that the editor's claim that his facsimiles, "for all practical purposes, are the originals themselves," is no exaggeration. Indeed, in his initial experiments in reproducing them, he states that he was "both complimented and grieved to find that some facsimiles were taken to be originals, and some originals were pronounced to be facsimiles," leading him to have special paper manufactured for the book. Necessarily, in so vast a publication, objects of criticism can be found. The collection does not pretend to be in any sense complete, the facsimiles being limited almost wholly to unpublished manuscripts; and, in addition, the editor has excluded the peace transcripts, including the Gérard and Luzerne correspondence, secured by him for the Department of State at Washington, and all the letters printed in his volume on the Clinton-Cornwallis controversy. The arrangement, too, which is practically without chronology or classification, and almost haphazard, is extremely faulty and bewildering; though liberal cross references, and a most admirable index, go far to remedy the confusion.

P. L. F.

See, also, in Part I: Sources, sect. 72.

Stirling, William Alexander, *6th earl of* (?). DUER, WILLIAM ALEXANDER. Life of William Alexander, Earl of Stirling. (New Jersey Historical Soc. Collections, v. 2.) N. Y. 1847. [1511

The life of one of Washington's generals (1726–83). Though it is written by Stirling's grandson, there is a manifest effort to avoid bias, and to secure accuracy; yet the book's value is impaired by the disappearance (pp. xiii–xiv) of some of the most valuable of the family letters. It has an index and a portrait, and five maps. Alexander's claim to the earlship was never allowed by the Lords' committee on privileges.   W. E. F.

Stone, Edwin Martin. Invasion of Canada in 1775: including the journal of Captain Simeon Thayer, describing the army under Colonel Benedict Arnold, in its march to Quebec; with notes. (In Rhode Island Hist. Soc. Collections, v. 6. Providence. 1867.) [1512

The editor gives a full, carefully written account of the ill-starred expedition, and the assault on Quebec under Montgomery and Arnold. Thayer's *Journal* is somewhat illiterate, but has the prime value of recording important details, perhaps otherwise lost. Of particular value, to the student of this episode, are the copious and careful notes, and biographical sketches of the principal persons in Arnold's command.

F. H. S.

—— Our French allies in the great war of the American Revolution, 1778–82. Providence: Prov. Press Co. 1883. [1513

A mass of information, but undigested and ill-edited. A portion of the book was prepared for the centennial celebrations at Yorktown and at Providence, R. I. A number of the illustrations possess some historic value.

E. E. S.

Stone, William Leete. *1792–1844.* Border wars of the American Revolution. N. Y. 1843. 2v. [1514

"This work is composed principally of the narratives and incidents of adventure with the Indians,

which are found in the two large volumes of the *Life of Brant*" (sect. 1246). T. W. Field, *Indian bibliography*, p. 382.

Stone, William Leete. *1835–.* Campaign of Lieut.-Gen. John Burgoyne, and expedition of Lieut.-Col. Barry St. Leger. Albany: Munsell. 1877. [1515

The St. Leger portion of Mr. Stone's volume (1777), avowedly reproduced from his father's life of Brant; and the Burgoyne portion, also in 1777 (chiefly based on Riedesel and Eelking), are serviceable, as the first connected English account founded on latest information. There is an elaborate appendix occupying about one half of the book. It is frankly a compilation, but it is the work of a historian who has made this field of investigation his own, in a half dozen other historical studies of the Burgoyne campaign, and is usually marked by fair judgment and temper. The book has an index, illustrations, and maps. Intended for the general reader.   W. E. F.

—— *ed.* Ballads and poems relating to the Burgoyne campaign. Albany: Munsell. 1893. [1516

Among these ballads are included recent compositions as well as those contemporaneous with the events they describe, and they have for their subjects the death of Jane McCrea and the battles of Oriskany and Bennington as well as incidents more closely connected with the British general. Footnotes and appendices convey much information of a personal nature regarding the campaign.   F. J. S.

—— *tr.* Letters of Brunswick and Hessian officers during the American Revolution. Albany: Munsell. 1891. [1517

These were published in a monthly magazine established in 1776 by Prof. August Ludwig Schlözer of the University of Göttingen for the purpose of printing private letters from German officers in all parts of the world. Most of those contained in this volume were written by officers of Burgoyne's army, and they describe their expedition and their captivity in a very interesting way. The story of the engagements at Saratoga is told by an eye-witness, and we learn how many of the American officers looked and how the American soldiers were clad as well as something of the home life of the country. Among the letters is one from Gen. Steuben.   F. J. S.

Stryker, William Scudder. Battles of Trenton and Princeton. Boston: Houghton. 1898. $4. [1518

Covers the period from the beginning of the retreat through the Jerseys until after the battle of Princeton. Part I (pp. 1–307) contains the narrative, illustrated with more than a hundred maps, portraits, etc. Part II contains 122 original documents, being the chief sources of the work, followed by a list of books used. The author uses many documents never before laid under contribution, especially German records of the Hessian soldiers.   E. C. R.

Sullivan, *Maj.-Gen.* **John.** Centennial celebration of General Sullivan's campaign against

145

the Iroquois in 1779; prepared by Diedrich Willers, Jr. Waterloo, N. Y. 1880. **[1519**

"Contains a carefully prepared and clearly written historical address by the Rev. David Craft, which the editor calls 'the most complete and accurate history of General Sullivan's campaign which has yet been given to the public.' The diligence of Craft in his search for the sources of authority for the campaign is shown in his *List of journals, narratives, etc., of the western expedition*, 1779 (*Mag. of Amer. hist.*, 3: 673)." A. McF. Davis, in *Narrative and critical hist. of Am.*, 6: 670.

—— Diaries and journals of Sullivan's Indian campaign, 1779. See Massachusetts Historical Society, sect. 338. **[1520**

Talbot, George F. The capture of the Margaretta, the first naval battle of the Revolution. See Maine Historical Society, sect. 279. **[1521**

Tancock, Osborne William. England during the American and European wars, 1765–1820. (Epochs of English history.) London: Longmans. 1878. (Harper's half-hour series.) N. Y.: Harper. 1878. N. Y.: Longmans. 30c. **[1522**

Since the "American" portion of the wars here included (1775–82) comprises less than 40 pages, its only value is as supplying a briefer English view of the American struggle than those by Andrews and Ludlow. The author is an Oxford man, with many years' experience in teaching, of sound capacity, excellent judgment, fair temper, and careful historical methods. The work has an index, and also 5 maps which, however, are of no great value. Professedly a compilation, and for the general reader. W. E. F.

Tarleton, *Lt.-Col. Sir* Banastre. History of the campaigns of 1780 and 1781 in the southern provinces of North America. London. 1787. **[1523**

Hardly a "history" but a bit of special pleading. Supplied with some good maps and many valuable documents not easily found elsewhere. Tarleton's unjust attacks on others brought out *Strictures on Lt.-Col. Tarleton's History*, by Roderick Mackenzie: By using both books one may gather a few valuable facts. E. C.

Thacher, James. Military journal during the American Revolutionary War, 1775–83. Boston. 1823. 2d ed., rev. 1827. **[1524**

Dr. Thacher (1754–1844) served as a surgeon in the American army, and his journal has the great value of first-hand knowledge of the events. It is the work of a fair-minded man, and, while apologized for in the author's preface as embodying "crude fragments," is seldom conspicuously partisan or careless in its statements; and, had it not been too narrowly revised and diluted, would have had the literary merits of directness and vivid narration which make it still of interest to the general reader. W. E. F.

Thomson, Charles. Papers of Charles Thomson, Secretary of the Continental Congress. (New York Hist. Soc. Collections, 1878.) N. Y. 1879. **[1525**

These consist of 62 pages of correspondence between Thomson and Franklin, Jay, R. R. Livingston, and others during the years 1765–82, the greater part of them conveying information from Thomson to his correspondents; a report of the debates of the Continental Congress from July 22 to Sept. 20, 1780; 100 pages of further correspondence between 1783 and 1787, chiefly personal letters to and from Jefferson, but including an important one to David Ramsay supplying facts for his history; and, finally, a paper entitled *Joseph Reed's narrative* and a letter to W. H. Drayton, both presenting pictures of the state of affairs in Pennsylvania in 1774–5 and supposed to have been contributions to projected histories of the Revolution. F. J. S.

Trescot, William Henry. Diplomacy of the Revolution. N. Y. 1852. **[1526**

Founded mainly on Sparks's *Diplomatic correspondence of the Revolution*. An essay and not a history. Now antiquated. E. C.

Trevelyan, *Sir* George Otto. The American Revolution. N. Y.: Longmans. 1899–. v. 1+. v. 1, $3. **[1527**

"Sir George Trevelyan's history is in the highest degree panegyrical, and in that respect resembles the American histories of former days, though it escapes their grandiloquence. American historians have greatly advanced in impartiality as well as in research. They now admit that there were two sides to the question, and endeavor to do justice to the Royalists. The change is marked in the school histories, which are still supposed to be the great source of American feeling against England. In reading Sir George Trevelyan's panegyric, and comparing it with recent treatment of the subject, we have a sense of relapse." Goldwin Smith, *Literature*, May 5, 1899. "It is delightful reading. . . . Perhaps the chatty sidelights on the careers and characters of the soldiers and statesmen who fought out the opening period of the Revolution are the most characteristic features of the author's treatment. . . . Occasional overstatements are perhaps due to this love of the striking." F. J. Turner, in *American hist. rev.*, 5: 141.

Trumbull, Jonathan. STUART, ISAAC WILLIAM. Life of Jonathan Trumbull, Sen., Governor of Connecticut. Boston. 1859. **[1528**

This work, though marred by serious defects, is possessed of many merits. It is based on reliable data, consisting of information furnished by papers, memoirs, and the like, which have been gathered with great industry. Though flattering to Trumbull, it is not excessively so, and it is the only biography that has been written of a man whose career deserves greater recognition; and it is, moreover, the best work that Stuart ever wrote. But padded as it is with the American bombast characteristic of many historical works written in the middle of the century, it is twice as long as it ought to be; and the material, valuable and important as much of it is, is neither well sifted nor well arranged.   C. M. A.

Trumbull papers. See Massachusetts Historical Society, sect. 317.   [1529

Tyler, Moses Coit. Literary history of the American Revolution, 1763–1783. N. Y.: Putnam. 1897. 2v. $3 ea.   [1530

After an interval of a score of years Professor Tyler continues his *Colonial literature* into the great period of the nation's birth. The tireless research, the picturesque touch, the fine sympathy of the preceding record are preserved to the full in this. Very noticeable, too, in the present work is the calm, broadminded candor capable of doing justice to men widely sundered in their ideas — the combatants in the fierce struggle out of which the new nation was about to emerge. Among the fathers and founders many a neglected figure receives adequate illustration. In the case of the Tory champions, the American now learns for almost the first time that there were men of conscience, ability, manly courage and persistency, however mistaken. Such were Boucher, Seabury, Galloway, Dulany, Jonathan Sewall, Daniel Leonard, and Thomas Hutchinson. As regards the poets of the period, perhaps the work of Tyler has a still greater value. The world will think better henceforth of Hopkinson, Trumbull, and Freneau, — and of the Tories Stansbury and Odell, after the illustration of them given here.   J. K. H.

United States. *Continental Congress.* Journal of the proceedings of the congress held at Philadelphia, Sept. 5, 1774; containing the bill of rights, a list of grievances, occasional resolves, the association, an address to the people of Gt. Britain, a memorial to the inhabitants of the British American colonies, an address to the inhabitants of the province of Quebec, an authentic copy of the petition to the king. London: Dilly. 1775.   [1531

The latter half of this small volume containing the documents cited above, except the petition to the king, was printed in 1774. Later the proceedings and the petition were prefixed, so that we have here what purports to be "the entire journal of the proceedings" of the 1st Continental Congress. The most important contents, besides the papers already cited, are the credentials showing how the members were chosen and the resolutions and the address to Gen. Gage of the Suffolk, Mass., towns adopted Sept. 6 and 9.
                                                  F. J. S.

Van Schaack, Peter. VAN SCHAACK, HENRY CRUGER. Life of Peter Van Schaack. N. Y.: Appleton. 1842.   [1532

Peter Van Schaack "spoke and acted in sympathy with the Whigs till the crisis when independence was declared, and recourse was had to arms, when he withstood further action, and sought to maintain a position of quiet neutrality in his native village. This was not allowed him. His brother-in-law, Henry Cruger, Jr., a New Yorker, was then a merchant in Bristol,

Eng., and represented the town in the House of Commons. Van Schaack furnished Cruger, in his letters, materials and arguments for effective speeches in Parliament against the unwise and mischievous measures and the oppressive acts of the mother country, but a final rupture with her Van Schaack would not contemplate for a moment; and though, after his return from his six years of exile, he was an honored and serviceable citizen of New York, he seems never to have become in heart and conscience reconciled to the result of the Revolution. . . . New York passed a banishment act in June, 1778, and in the next year a confiscation act. The latter was so harsh in its terms as to be condemned by Jay and other Whigs, and was subsequently softened. Van Schaack sailed for England in October, 1778, and returned home in July, 1785, where he was reunited to his three young children. He was wholly unmolested, and was kindly received by old friends, but was never chosen to office, occupying himself with the law and the training of many pupils." G. E. Ellis, in *Narrative and critical hist. of Am.*, 7: 201.

Walker, Francis Amasa. Making of the nation, 1783–1817. (American history series.) N. Y.: Scribner. 1895. $1.25.   [1533

A well-written, compact narrative, standing chronologically between Sloane's *French war and the Revolution* and Burgess's *Middle period*. Without novel or striking features, its characteristics are its skill in presenting essential facts, and the healthy balance of its inferences and judgments.
                                                  W. MacD.

Walpole, Horace. Journal of the reign of King George III., 1771–83; ed. by John Doran. London: Bentley. 1859. 2v.   [1534

Usually cited from its running title as "Last journals of Horace Walpole." Vol. I ends with the year 1775. Contains much interesting matter in connection with American affairs — though mainly devoted to English politics. An interesting and useful work.
                                                  E. C.

Walworth, *Mrs*. Ellen Hardin. Battles of Saratoga, 1777. The Saratoga Monument Association, 1856–91. Albany: Munsell. [c. 1891.] $2.   [1535

Contains a sketch of the campaign; a History of the Monument Association; Guide to the battleground; a [supposed] Visit to the battle-ground; and a Visitors' guide to Saratoga Springs. Illustrated with maps, photographs of the monument, of stones marking battle-sites and of the officers of the Association — including Mrs. Walworth. Forms a useful guide-book to the traditional spots.   E. C.

Warren, Joseph. FROTHINGHAM, RICHARD. Life and times of Joseph Warren. Boston: Little. 1865.   [1536

An admirable biography of the eminent Revolutionary leader (1741-75), by the author of *The rise of the republic*, all of whose historical studies had given him the best of qualifications for this task. The book is characterized by fulness of knowledge, uncommon judgment, an admirable temper, rigid accuracy of statement and a fitting literary style. It has an index and a portrait. It will hold the interest of the general reader, while meeting the wants of the special student. W. E. F.

Warren, *Mrs.* **Mercy (Otis).** History of the rise, progress, and termination of the American Revolution. Boston. 1805. 3v. [**1537**

The eminent author, as the sister of James Otis and wife of James Warren, had uncommon facilities for information relating to certain phases of the Revolutionary movement. The work is not of equal value in this respect, throughout; and it is certainly not conspicuous for impartiality nor for a rigid historical method. The literary style of the book (published at the age of 77) is not to be commended, being " interspersed with biographical, political, and moral observations." It is now of interest only to the special student, as being one of the earliest connected narratives of the struggle. W. E. F.

Washington, George. Writings; coll. and ed. by Worthington Chauncey Ford. N. Y.: Putnam. 1889–93. 14v. [Ed. limited.] $70. [**1538**

The reader has not even yet the entire body of Washington's writings, collected in any one place, as will be seen from the list of " Letters printed in Sparks's edition omitted in these volumes," printed at pp. 470–79 of Ford's 14th volume; but otherwise this version of the letters and other writings should supersede that of Sparks, as being a rigidly accurate reproduction of the text. Mr. Ford's editorial work has been done on the basis of long familiarity with the subject, as well as of fullest knowledge (except in the case of certain papers refused him, v. 1, p. xxiv), exceptional judgment and critical discernment, and a fair-minded spirit; and it is marked by painstaking accuracy, and lucidity of language. He has reproduced many invaluable maps and plans from Winsor's *Narrative and critical history of America*, and supplied a comprehensive index of 58 pages, at the end of the 14th volume. W. E. F.

—— Writings; [ed.] with life by Jared Sparks. Boston: Am. Stationers' Co. 1837. 12v. [**1539**

The first volume contains a life of Washington, sometimes printed separately; vol. 2, letters before the Revolution; vols. 3–8, Revolutionary correspondence and papers; vol. 9, from the peace of 1783 to his inauguration as president; vols. 10 and 11, from his inauguration to the end of his life; vol. 12, public speeches and papers.

This was for years the standard set of Washington's works, but it has to a certain extent been superseded by Ford's *Writings of George Washington*. Sparks followed the copies of Washington's letters as they were found in his letter-book. Discrepancies between the copies and the originals as preserved caused charges that the editor had made wilful alterations in addition to " editing " the letters. He explains his method in the preface to the second volume. On the ensuing controversy, see pamphlets by Sparks, Lord Mahon, and William Reed. E. E. S.

—— Letters to General Heath. See Massachusetts Historical Society, sect. 315. [**1540**

—— Spurious letters attributed to Washington. See Historical Printing Club, sect. 273. [**1541**

—— Washington-Crawford letters; the correspondence between George Washington and William Crawford, 1767–81, concerning western lands; [ed.] by C. W. Butterfield. Cin.: Clarke. 1877. $1. [**1542**

Crawford was a surveyor and trader living in southwestern Pennsylvania who acted as agent in locating and disposing of Washington's western lands. Several letters from Crawford's brother are added. All give valuable information concerning Washington's business habits, life in the " back country," indentured servants, and troubles with the Indians. E. E. S.

—— Washington Duché letters. See Historical Printing Club, sect. 273. [**1543**

— BAKER, WILLIAM SPOHN. Bibliotheca Washingtoniana. Phil.: Lindsay. 1889. $4. [**1544**

A descriptive list of the biographies and biographical sketches of Washington in the order of their publication. It begins with an eight-page sketch written in 1777 and closes with Lodge's life (American statesmen, 1889). The various editions are carefully designated and further information given in footnotes. This catalogue of 502 titles is the most exhaustive yet made on this subject. E. E. S.

— BAKER, WILLIAM SPOHN, *ed.* Early sketches of George Washington. Phil.: Lippincott. 1893. $2. [**1545**

A reprint of personal descriptions of Washington by his contemporaries, with notes on the writers of the descriptions. These sketches were written between 1760 and 1795. They gratify curiosity to see the early opinions concerning Washington rather than serve any historic purpose. E. E. S.

— BAKER, WILLIAM SPOHN. Itinerary of General Washington, from June 15, 1775, to December 23, 1783. Phil.: Lippincott. 1892. $2.50. [**1546**

Extracts from the diary or correspondence of Washington, from the public records or from newspapers or books in which Washington is mentioned, are set down for each day in each year. This chronological arrangement makes it possible to follow him and ascertain his employment, surroundings and companions almost every day of the period embraced in the book. The notes are full and clear, identifying all persons and locating all places. The work is invaluable for students as a ready reference. In connection with the author's *Early sketches of Washington* (sect. 1545), and his *Washington after the Revolution* (sect. 1703), it makes a continuous record of Washington's life. E. E. S.

— BROOKS, ELBRIDGE STREETER. True

story of George Washington, called the Father of his country. Boston : Lothrop. [c. 1895.] $1.50. [1547

Printed in large type, for young readers, with more than 100 illustrations, some of which are wholly fanciful. The book is not preëminent for accuracy, judicial temper, nor critical discrimination. A "familiar" English style is aimed at, but not always with very happy results. There is no index. W. E. F.

— CARRINGTON, *Brig.-Gen.* HENRY BEEBEE. Washington the soldier. Boston: Lamson. 1898. N. Y.: Scribner. 1899. $2. [1548

" *Washington the soldier*, by Gen. H. B. Carrington, is, in the main, an abridgment of the valuable work by the same author, *Battles of the Revolution* (sect. 1255). The maps of battlefields are the same, and for authenticity and completeness are among the very best that are accessible. They were carefully compiled and drawn by the author himself. In the briefer form, recast and made more distinctly biographical, the book will be welcome to a large class of readers to whom the larger work is not easily within reach." J. D. Cox, in *Nation*, 68: 126.

— CUSTIS, GEORGE WASHINGTON PARKE. Recollections and private memoirs of Washington, by his adopted son ; with memoir by his daughter and notes by B. J. Lossing. N. Y.: Derby. 1860. Phil. 1861. [1549

These reminiscences of Washington were written by Mrs. Washington's grandson, who was adopted by George Washington at six months of age. He was nineteen years old when Washington died. The recollections were contributed for the most part to newspapers at various times for twenty years, but are here collected for the first time. They form the storehouse for the usual traditions about Washington, accepted but largely unproven. To the recollections are added a memoir of the writer, the correspondence between Washington and himself while a student at Princeton, and that between Washington and the father of the writer. The topical rather than chronological arrangement causes occasional reduplication. E. E. S.

— EVERETT, EDWARD. Life of George Washington. N. Y.: Sheldon. 1860. [1550

This sketch was written for an edition (1860) of the Encyclopædia Britannica and shows the marks of haste. It avowedly follows the Sparks's life, is well proportioned, but has no special merit. The appendixes contain a professional review of the medical treatment given Washington in his last illness, an inventory of his personal property as made by the appraisers after his death, and the will of Martha Washington. E. E. S.

— FORD, PAUL LEICESTER. The true George Washington. Phil.: Lippincott. 1896. $2. [1551

The writer's aim, very successfully attained, is to make Washington "a man rather than a historical figure." Few writers have used more abundant historical resources, or made better use of them. The book has an index, and also portraits, and other illustrations. For the general reader. W. E. F.

— HALE, EDWARD EVERETT. Life of George Washington, studied anew. N. Y.: Putnam. 1888. $1.75. [1552

Characterized by the author as a study of "the human Washington," and emphasizing the domestic rather than the public side of his life. In its compilation, the diaries and private letter-books have been more fully used than the public papers ; and the book is characterized by much fulness of knowledge in this field, judicious selection of materials, the inclusion of 25 illustrations and 2 maps, and a vivacious style which at all times retains the interest of the general reader. W. E. F.

— HEADLEY, JOEL TYLER. Washington and his generals. N. Y.: Baker. 1847. 2v. Scribner. 2v. $2.50. [1553

The uncritical point of view of this compiler will be inferred from his complacent remark in the preface, that earlier writers in this field had saved him "a world of trouble." It is difficult to see what excuse such a work now has for existing, except for the few instances of generals not included in Sparks's biographies, or in separate biographies, or in the recent series of "Great commanders." W. E. F.

— HOUGH, FRANKLIN BENJAMIN, *ed.* Washingtoniana ; or Memorials of the death of George Washington. Roxbury, Mass.: Woodward. 1865. 2v. [1554

A collection of the descriptions of Washington's death and funeral, the proceedings of the various public bodies, and the eulogies and poems brought out by this event. The collection is not confined to America. An incomplete bibliography of books and pamphlets on Washington is added. The value of the volumes will be measured by individual need of this material. A similar collection, bearing this title, was printed by Sower in Baltimore in 1800, another in Lancaster, Pa., in 1802, and a third in Virginia, having no date. E. E. S.

— IRVING, WASHINGTON. Life of George Washington. N. Y.: Putnam. 1855-9. 5v. $3.75. [1555

Coming twenty years later than Sparks's life, and fifty years after Marshall's, this admirable biography, by one of the most eminent of American authors, at once took its place among the three standard biographies of Washington. The chief hindrance to its wider use by readers at present is the fact that it is not a one-volume work ; and this lack has been met, to some extent, by Mr. Fiske's abridgment of it (sect. 1556). It is written on the basis of extended knowledge, though Mr. Irving's mental equipment for historical investigation would not now be called an ideal one, and is expressed with fair judgment and temper, and much care, though completed in too great haste. It is preëminent in its literary style. It has an index of 56 double-column pages, many portraits, and very useful maps. For the general reader. W. E. F.

— IRVING, WASHINGTON. Washington and

his country; abridged for schools, with a brief outline of United States history, by John Fiske. (Classics for children.) Boston: Ginn. 1887. 80c. [1556

The abridgment from Irving occupies pp. 55-506, or more than three quarters of the whole. Mr. Fiske's part of the work shows a competent knowledge, judgment, fairness, and painstaking care, especially in the treatment of the military campaigns, but is partly superseded by his own later separately published histories. The book has no illustrations, but has 15 maps and an index.   W. E. F.

— JOHNSON, BRADLEY TYLER. General Washington. (Great commanders.) N. Y.: Appleton. 1894. $1.50.   [1557

Few of the lives of Washington exceed this in serviceableness to the military student, written as it is by one of the most eminent of the Confederate generals in the Civil War; and yet it is to be regretted that the few and inadequate maps in the book had not been replaced by a more liberal equipment. The book shows intelligent acquaintance with the subject, and a fair temper, but its style is not attractive. It has an index, and a portrait.   W. E. F.

— JOHNSTON, ELIZABETH BRYANT. George Washington day by day. N. Y.: Baker & T. 1895. $2.50.   [1558

Very much upon the plan of Baker's *Itinerary of Washington* (sect. 1546), but unfortunate in selecting a daily instead of a yearly arrangement. This makes it impossible to follow Washington's movements day by day. The descriptions of his whereabouts and employments, together with extracts from his correspondence, are fairly well chosen. But the editing, in the way of explanatory notes and the filling of blanks, is insufficient. Much space is occupied with valueless extracts from eulogies. There are several fine and accurate illustrations of historic places. The volume would be of some value were it not for the kindred and superior work of Baker.   E. E. S.

— KING, *Lt.-Col.* CHARLES COOPER. George Washington. London: Chapman. 1894. N. Y.: Scribner. 1894.   [1559

A study of Washington's career by an officer in the English army. Interesting from its point of view. Style clear, simple and cogent.   E. C.

— LODGE, HENRY CABOT. George Washington. (American statesmen.) Boston: Houghton. 1889. 2v. $2.50.   [1560

Were it not in two volumes, instead of one, this might be designated the ideal life of Washington. Even as it is, it is written on the basis of abundant knowledge, and embodies excellent judgment and temper, a strong desire to be accurate in its statements and a good English style. It has an index, but no illustrations; and yet few works have held so well the interest of the general reader.   W. E. F.

— MARSHALL, JOHN. Life of George Washington. Phil.: Wayne. 1804-7. 5v. and at-

las. 2d ed. rev. Phil.: Crissy. 1832. 2v. and atlas.   [1561

Written by an eminent Virginian contemporary of Washington, and based on the Bushrod Washington manuscripts. The first three volumes appeared within five years after Washington's death; and, though the haste with which it was prepared is deprecated in the author's preface, its nearness to the events, together with several other notable qualities, make it one of the three most famous lives of Washington. Marshall served as Chief Justice of the United States Supreme Court from 1801 until his death in 1835, and he carried his eminently judicial temper into the composition of this book; yet he did not wholly avoid giving it a bias which has caused it to be regarded as a "Federalist narrative." Included in a separate quarto "atlas" are the 10 maps which accompany his account of Washington's military campaigns. Marshall's style was almost wholly lacking in literary quality, and his work has no charms for the general reader. It is now chiefly serviceable as "materials for history," merely. The 1st volume was reissued, with additions and other changes, in 1824, under the title of "A history of the colonies," etc.   W. E. F.

— PAULDING, JAMES KIRKE. Life of Washington. N. Y.: Harper. 1835. 2v. [1562

Two small volumes written for children and appearing originally as part of a "Family library." In addition to the official information concerning Washington, the volumes contain many anecdotes which the author gained from contemporaries of his subject. The descriptions of places are marked by a familiarity gained in personal observation. The value of the book for historical purposes is somewhat impaired by later investigations and by the total lack of references, but its delightful style gives it a lasting charm as a literary essay. The sketch of Washington, in the last chapter, is generally accepted as unexcelled.   E. E. S.

— RAMSAY, DAVID. Life of George Washington. N. Y. 1807.   [1563

A small book dedicated to the youth of the United States. Of the thirteen chapters, seven are devoted to the campaigns of the Revolutionary War. The personal element is altogether lost in the official life of the general and president. The appendix contains the Newburgh address, Washington's farewell to the army, and his will. No index. Between 1807 and 1832, five editions were printed in English, one in French and two in Spanish. As a juvenile book, it has been supplanted by later authors who write in a less lofty style.   E. E. S.

— RUSH, RICHARD. Washington in domestic life. Phil.: Lippincott. 1857.   [1564

A score of letters written by Washington to Col. Lear, his secretary, between 1790 and 1798, are here printed. Unfortunately the editor has rewritten or described them instead of preserving the original form. Only too frequently names of persons are struck out. These letters concern the furnishing of the President's residence in Philadelphia and other private matters. Hence the title. The famous anecdote about the ungovernable passion of Washington upon the news of St. Clair's defeat is here told as coming from Lear. Also an interesting extract from Lear's diary quoting Washington on the treason of Arnold.   E. E. S.

— SCUDDER, HORACE ELISHA.   George Washington. (Riverside library for young people.) Boston : Houghton. 1889. 75c. (Riverside school library.) Net 60c. (Riverside lit. ser.) Net 40c.   [1565

The writer has been widely known as editor of the *Atlantic monthly.* Though it has only 8 illustrations, this book has been recognized for more than ten years past as one of the best of the lives of Washington for young readers, and among the best of the one-volume lives of Washington for readers of any age. It embodies no original work, but is judicious, fair, cautious, and of admirable literary quality.
                                             W. E. F.

— WEEMS, MASON L.   Life of George Washington. Georgetown. 1800. Phil.: Lippincott. 1891. $1.   [1566

This *Life,* from which the letter *f* might be justly omitted, achieved its early success from the announcement on its title-page that its author was "formerly Rector of Mt. Vernon Parish," the inference being that he was Washington's clergyman. The facts are, that he preached occasionally at Pohick Church after it had ceased to have a regular incumbent, and long after Washington had ceased attending service there ; but he never had any acquaintance with the man of whom he wrote. The first edition (Georgetown. 1800) appeared only a few months after the death of Washington, and is a curious piece of writing ; but it was for the fifth edition (Augusta. 1806), when the author rewrote it, that the hatchet and other stories, or, as the title expressed it, "curious anecdotes equally honorable to himself and exemplary to his young countrymen," were invented, and it became a standard book for Sunday schools, the last of over seventy editions having been printed by J. B. Lippincott in Philadelphia in 1891. The author's aim is told in a letter concerning his life of Marion, in which he wrote his fellow author : "You have no doubt constantly kept in memory, that I told you I must write it in my own way, and, knowing the passion of the times for novels, I have endeavoured to throw your facts and ideas about Gen. Marion into the garb and dress of a military romance."   P. L. F.

— WILSON, WOODROW.   George Washington. N. Y. : Harper. 1897. $3.   [1567

This is one of the latest of the biographies of Washington. Mr. Wilson, while not ignoring the "everyday" character of Washington's services, yet lays no such emphasis on this phase of the subject as Ford does. The author's knowledge is wide, his judgment and temper excellent, his desire for accuracy great, and his style eminently readable. Few books will appeal more strongly to the general reader. The book has an index, and very numerous illustrations.
                                             W. E. F.

Washington, *Mrs.* Martha (Dandridge). WHARTON, ANNE HOLLINGSWORTH.   Martha Washington. (Women of colonial and Revo-

lutionary times.)   N. Y. : Scribner.   1897. $1.25.   [1568

To some extent biographical, but based as much on tradition as on established fact. The scanty information is stretched out by many imaginings and suppositions.   E. E. S.
See note under Wharton, *Colonial days and dames,* sect. 889.

Washington, *Mrs.* Martha (Dandridge), *and Mrs.* Mary (Ball).   LOSSING, BENSON JOHN. Mary and Martha, the mother and the wife of George Washington.   N. Y. : Harper.   1886.
                                             [1569

Belongs to the better class of popular writing, yet unimportant to the student of history. Preserves the current traditions of the two women. Entertaining to the general reader. Remarkably free from the gushing style commonly affecting this class of composition.   E. E. S.

Washington, *Mrs.* Mary (Ball).   HARLAND, MARION, *pseud.* of *Mrs.* M. V. (HAWES) TERHUNE.   Story of Mary Washington.   Boston : Houghton. 1892. $1.   [1570

A harmless compound of tradition and hearsay, but not history. Repeats the pleasant fictions of Walter and others. Creates an ideal heroine, but far removed from the querulous though lovable mother of Washington. Tries to explain away every friction between the two which would make them human. Written in a bright style and for the laudable purpose of calling attention to the uncompleted monument to Mary Washington.   E. E. S.

Watson, Elkanah.   Men and times of the Revolution : memoirs ; ed. by Winslow C. Watson.   N. Y.   1856.   [1571

The record of an eye-witness, yet in many respects uncritical and prejudiced. The memoirs are clumsily written, and show little evidence of editing; and the book has neither index, illustrations nor maps. Its almost sole value is as embodying the record of several isolated episodes (as the Gaspé episode of 1772).
                                             W. E. F.

Wayne, *Maj.-Gen.* Anthony.   STILLÉ, CHARLES JANEWAY.   Major-General Anthony Wayne and the Pennsylvania line in the continental army.   Phil. : Lippincott.   1893.
                                             [1572

Relates to Ticonderoga, Germantown, Monmouth, Stony Point, the Virginia and Georgia campaigns and the campaign against the northwestern Indians. It shows Gen. Wayne as not merely a dashing leader but an able general. The work is from the sources, by a thorough student, and written in scholarly but not pedantic style.   E. C. R.

Webb, Samuel Blachley.   Correspondence and journals ; coll. and ed. by Worthington C. Ford.   N. Y. : Burnett.   1894.   3v.
                                             [1573

Most of the papers in the three volumes relate to the years 1774–1789. A biographical sketch by the compiler occupies pp. 251–396 of vol. 3. The original material in these volumes is interesting and important, the biographical sketch well written and adequate.

                                    E. C.

Wharton, Francis, *ed.* Revolutionary diplomatic correspondence of the United States; ed. under the direction of Congress, with notes. Wash.: Govt. Prtg. Off. 1889. 6v.   [**1574**

This work was authorized by an Act of Congress, August 13, 1888, and was designed to correct, complete, and enlarge the *Diplomatic correspondence of the Revolution* by Jared Sparks, 1829–1830 (sect. 1504). It is a mine of wealth to the student of the diplomatic history of the Revolution, for it contains papers from published memoirs, family archives, and the records of the Department of State, all edited with scrupulous care. The period covered is that from 1775 to 1785. Volume first is entirely taken up with an elaborate table of contents, a life of Dr. Wharton (d. 1889) by Professor John Bassett Moore, and an introduction, long, discursive and ponderous, by the editor on the development of diplomacy and the careers of the diplomats of the United States during the period covered.   C. M. A.

Wild, Ebenezer. Journal, 1776–81. See Massachusetts Historical Society, sect. 343.

                                         [**1575**

Wild, Ebenezer, *and Lt.-Col.* **Henry Dearborn.** Journals of Arnold's expedition to Quebec. See Massachusetts Historical Society, sect. 338.   [**1576**

Wilson, Samuel Farmer. History of the American Revolution. Balt.: Kelly. 1834. New ed. 1869.   [**1577**

A civil and military history of the period 1763 to 1783, with an introductory chapter on the colonists. No recognition of the Tory side of the controversy. Each event is due to a special Providence, rather than the outcome of natural laws. The work is based on good authorities, and was at one time an acceptable history; but it is discredited in many particulars by later investigation and supplanted by less generalized writings; e. g., Frothingham's *Rise of the republic*, Fiske's *American Revolution*, and Carrington's *Battles of the American Revolution* (sect. 1315, 1255, 2734).   E. E. S.

Winsor, Justin. Reader's handbook of the American Revolution, 1761–83. Boston: Houghton. 1880. $1.25.   [**1578**

A popular bibliography, still of great value for a detailed study of the period. It is supplemented, but not superseded, by the bibliographical notes in the same editor's *Narrative and critical history* (sect. 404). The arrangement is topical, and the nature and worth of the authorities are exhibited.   W. MacD.

Withers, Alexander Scott. Chronicles of border warfare; or A history of the settlement by the whites of northwestern Virginia and of the Indian wars and massacres in that section of the state. Clarksburgh, Va. 1831.

—— *Same.* New edition, ed. and annotated by Reuben Gold Thwaites. Cin.: Clarke. 1895. $2.50.   [**1579**

"Withers' *Chronicles* is one of the number of books which have a great value because they preserve the traditions of the border about the Indian fighting of the second half of the eighteenth century in the West. They tell what the settlers themselves thought of the deeds done by the rough backwoodsman of the Alleghanies and the upper Ohio in the ceaseless warfare of the white man against the red ; they contain valuable sidelights on the ways of life and the habits of thought of the backwoodsmen ; but, as a record of facts, each of them must be used with extreme caution. Withers, like De Haas and Doddridge, both of whom covered much of the ground that he did, gathered some of his material from the pioneers themselves in their old age ; but more often he adopted what the children of the pioneers told him, or what their successors reported as having been done. Thus what he relied on was really little more than family or local tradition. . . . Rather curiously these border annalists are more trustworthy when they deal with small events than when they deal with the larger facts of western history." The author's "account of St. Clair's defeat is valueless, and is followed by what is probably the wildest fabrication to be found in any book of border annals. . . . However, in spite of some looseness in matters of fact, the book has great value, and must be consulted by every student of early western history. Mr. Reuben Gold Thwaites is an ideal editor for such a work; a trained student and scholar. . . . The editorial work of this edition of the *Chronicles* is excellent throughout." Theodore Roosevelt, in *American historical review*, 1 : 170.

3. Period of Federal Union and Consolidation, 1783–1828.

Adams, Henry. History of the United States of America [during the administrations of Jefferson and Madison]. N. Y.: Scribner. 1889–91. 9v. $18.   [**1580**

The most valuable history of this important period, remarkable alike for its research, its penetrating analysis of character and political tendencies, and for the flood of light which it throws upon every phase of the foreign relations of the country. The student of Napoleon will find in it a critical and detailed study of episodes in his career that have been cursorily passed over by other historians, e. g., the retrocession of Louisiana by Spain to France and the attempted subjugation of the negroes in San Domingo. Mr. Adams is at his best in unravelling the complications of diplomacy, and in analyzing the mind and feeling of the different sections of the country. For the former task he discovered masses of unutilized material in foreign archives ; in the latter he combines intellectual insight in interpretation with critical poise in exposition. He stands aloof from both parties ; according due recognition to the work of the Federalists and sympathizing with the aspirations of the Republicans. E. G. B.

—— *ed.* Documents relating to New England federalism, 1800–15. Boston: Little. 1878. [**1581**

A collection of documents, mainly letters, and without narrative comment, but of high importance for the light they shed on the political movements of the period, and on the opposition to the administration which resulted in the Hartford Convention. The most important document is J. Q. Adams's *Reply to the appeal of the Massachusetts Federalists.* An appendix contains a number of brief letters, mainly from the Pickering papers in the possession of the Massachusetts Historical Society. W. MacD.

"The *Reply* was written under the disappointments of Adams when driven from the presidency, and with a natural bitterness; and the editor finds it prudent to omit some passages respecting H. G. Otis." Justin Winsor, in *Narrative and critical hist. of Am.*, 7: 313.

Adams, John. WOOD, JOHN. The suppressed history of the administration of John Adams; republished, with notes, by John Henry Sherburne. Phil. 1846. [**1582**

A virulent party attack, prepared by the hired pen of an English writer, John Wood, for use in the presidential campaign of 1800. Aaron Burr, fearing that it would do injury to his own party, is said to have bought off the publisher and secured the suppression of the book until after the election was passed. When it did appear, in 1802, "a large part of the first issues was burnt up; but some copies escaped." It was reprinted in 1846 with the title given above. Justin Winsor, in *Narrative and critical hist. of Am.*, 7: 334.

— See also in preceding period, sect. 1201–06.

Adams, John Quincy. Memoirs, comprising portions of his diary from 1795 to 1848; ed. by Charles Francis Adams. Phil.: Lippincott. 1874–7. 12v. [**1583**

The most elaborate and valuable of the journals of American statesmen. The author kept a full daily record of events, accompanied with criticisms, reflections and expressions, often pointed, of personal opinion. The volumes, accordingly, shed light upon nearly every political incident of importance in the period which they cover. Vol. 12 has a full index to the series. W. MacD.

— MORSE, JOHN TORREY. John Quincy Adams. (American statesmen.) Boston: Houghton. 1882. $1.25. [**1584**

One of the most successful volumes in the American statesmen series. It is written in the easy graceful style of which the author is a master. Trustworthy in details, its chief merit lies in its comprehension of the essential character of Adams and its sympathetic interpretation of the man and his work. A. C. McL.

— QUINCY, JOSIAH. Memoir of the life of John Quincy Adams. Boston: Phillips. 1858. [**1585**

This has been called "a valuable and creditable work, though written on the ancient principle of presenting the public with a perfect man." It must be said that few statesmen are such fit subjects for hero-worship as is Adams, and the tendency to present him in a favorable light does not greatly detract from the value of the volume. The author made use of good material including unpublished sources, and gives many excerpts from Adams' speeches and writings, which add to the usefulness of the book and give it vitality and interest, for these extracts, well worded and strong, help us to come into contact with the spirit of a fearless, honest, able statesman. One will get, however, a better idea of Adams' place in history from the life written by Morse. A. C. McL.

— SEWARD, WILLIAM HENRY. Life and public services of John Quincy Adams. Auburn: Derby. 1849. Phil.: Porter. 1886. Coates. 75c. [**1586**

This biography was undertaken, but not completed by Seward. Indeed the book seems to be in large measure the work of the writer whose "literary assistance" the publishers acknowledge in a prefatory note. Still the political views and the reverent attitude towards Adams everywhere maintained are characteristic of Seward himself. As a political biography the matter is reasonably full; but the treatment is not graphic. Appended to the *Life* is Seward's striking *Address* on John Quincy Adams before the legislature of New York. A. D. M.

Ames, Fisher. Works, with a selection from his speeches and correspondence; ed. by his son, Seth Ames. Boston: Little. 1854. 2v. [**1587**

The 2d volume, chiefly political, has the wider interest and value, as representing the point of view of a Federalist leader, at the end of the 18th century. The two volumes are edited with a fair amount of care, but with slight critical judgment or literary skill, and they are valuable chiefly as materials for history. W. E. F.

Ashe, Thomas. Travels in America in 1806, for the purpose of exploring the rivers Alleghany, Monongahela, Ohio and Mississippi. London: Phillips. 1808. [**1588**

"A curious mixture of critical disparagement, quite too general to be accurate, and of romantic and extravagant episodes." H. T. Tuckerman, *America and her commentators*, p. 203.

Barlow, Joel. TODD, CHARLES BURR. Life and letters of Joel Barlow. N. Y.: Putnam. 1886. [**1589**

The life of a once noted poet, compiled largely from Barlow's papers. Todd is hardly a competent biographer. His materials are not well digested, he lacks sense of proportion, is inaccurate in details, exalts Barlow unduly and fails to explain facts derogatory to his hero. There is little new, though much scattered information is brought together. There is material relating to the Scioto Land Company, to Fulton and his steamboat, to our affairs with the Barbary powers (1795–97) and with France (1811–12), to Connecticut literary and social life at and after the Revolution, and to the views of prominent Americans regarding the French Revolution. R. C. H. C.

The account of the Scioto Company, whose agent Barlow was in France, is too meagre to be satisfactory. B. A. H.

Bates, Frank Greene. Rhode Island and the formation of the Union. (Columbia Univ. studies in history, etc., v. 10, no. 2.) N. Y.: Macmillan. 1898. $1.50. [**1590**

This is an admirable study of the attitude of Rhode Island toward federal union and the Constitution in the period from 1781 to 1791. Mr. Bates has considered with full appreciation of their importance the agricultural, commercial, and financial aspects of Rhode Island's history; and has brought out clearly the strength of the conservative and particularistic elements, the grounds of their hostility to the Constitution, the ignorance, suspicion, and prejudice that characterized their actions, and the nature of the long struggle that preceded ratification. The monograph is a valuable contribution to the history both of Rhode Island and of the federal Constitution.
C. M. A.

Beltrami, Giacomo Constantino. Pilgrimage in Europe and America, leading to the discovery of the sources of the Mississippi and Bloody River; with a description of the whole course of the former, and of the Ohio. London: Hunt. 1828. 2v. [**1591**

"Beltrami must have moved in a gigantic world, if he saw external objects through the same media with which he viewed his own person and accomplishments." T. W. Field, *Indian bibliography*, p. 28.

Bernard, John. Retrospections of America, 1797–1811. N. Y.: Harper. 1887. $1.75.
[**1592**

Bernard was an English actor, whose experiences were gained during his professional visits to this country. His travels extended up and down the Atlantic coast from Canada to the Carolinas and westwardly to the Ohio River. The historical investigator will find a mass of anecdotes and incidents of the drama, and scattered through it a few glimpses of Washington, Jefferson, John Adams, and others, although some of the stories must be taken with allowance. Of more value are the glimpses of the life of the people, the cities, dress, and customs. The portraits and footnotes are confined to actors and actresses. E. E. S.

Biddle, Charles. Autobiography, 1745–1821. Phil.: Claxton. 1883. [**1593**

Valuable for political and social life in America, especially Pennsylvania, before, during and after the Revolution. It contains also letters of Burr and Truxtun throwing some light on Burr's character, plans and duel with Hamilton. Biddle wrote from memory, in some cases years after the events narrated, a fact which detracts from the value of his relation. He tells what he saw and what he himself did in a plain,

unpretentious style. He was a man of more than average ability, of clear intellect, excellent judgment and few prejudices. An appendix contains the Biddle pedigree. R. C. H. C.

Bradford, Alden. History of the federal government, 1789–1839. Boston: Simpkins. 1840. [**1594**

Covers the period 1789–1839. The author professes to aim at a brief narrative account adapted to general use, and free from political speculation and partisan bias; but the style is formal and rather heavy, and the Federalist and anti-Democratic sympathies of the writer are not concealed. The work has no longer particular importance. W. MacD.

Brissot de Warville, Jean Pierre. New travels in the United States of America, performed in 1788; tr. from the French. London: Jordan. 1792. [**1595**

The author, a Frenchman, restlessly interested in politics, afterwards a prominent character in the French Revolution, came to America in 1788 "to study men who had just acquired their liberty." The work was published in Paris in 1791 as useful in supporting the Revolution. Brissot's journey, covering a period of six months, extended from Boston through the Atlantic states to Virginia. Although many of his observations are naïve and superficial, his sketches of life and manners are entertaining and are frequently quoted by historians. He had a considerable interest in the economic institutions of the country. A second volume, included in the English edition, written in 1787, is an essay on the commerce of America with Europe. Brissot at that time had not visited America, and this discussion has but little value.
D. R. D.

Burges, Tristam. BOWEN, HENRY L. Memoir of Tristam Burges; with selections from his speeches and occasional writings. Providence: Marshall. 1835. [**1596**

The speeches occupy nearly one half of the volume. The *Memoir* is also copiously interlarded with extracts from other speeches by Mr. Burges. Occasionally the book throws an interesting sidelight on social and political conditions at Providence and Washington in the first third of the century. Style painfully dull.
E. C.

Burr, Aaron. Private journal during his residence of four years in Europe, with selections from his correspondence; ed. by Matthew L. Davis. N. Y.: Harper. 1838. 2v.
[**1597**

Gives an interesting glimpse into the daily life and thought of an enigmatical man. Has little to do with America. Well edited. Interesting but inconsequential. E. C.

— DAVIS, MATTHEW L. Memoirs of Aaron Burr; with miscellaneous selections from his correspondence. N. Y.: Harper. 1836–7. 2v. [**1598**

Written from original sources and from notes of conversations with Burr. Has all the disadvantages of using recollections of an old man as a source of history. Well written and replete with interesting letters and parts of letters. E. C.

— KNAPP, *Col.* SAMUEL LORENZO. Life of Aaron Burr. N. Y.: Wiley. 1835. [1599

" Published the year before his [Burr's] death, and of not much value, except as reflecting current opinion." Justin Winsor, in *Narrative and critical hist. of Am.*, 7: 316.

— MERWIN, HENRY CHILDS. Aaron Burr. (Beacon biographies.) Boston: Small. 1899. 75c. [1600

" A pleasantly written sketch . . . in which the immorality of that extraordinary life is lightly touched, and some of its grosser faults in part condoned. Burr's eventful course as a free lance in politics and a pagan in social relations is, on the whole, sufficiently well set forth, though with less attention to the political side of his career than is usually given. The portrait frontispiece is well executed." *Nation*, 70: 92.

— PARTON, JAMES. Life and times of Aaron Burr. N. Y.: Mason. 1858. Boston: Osgood. 1874. 2v. Enl. ed. Houghton. 2v. $5. [1601

This brilliantly written and popular work has been criticised as uncritical, too favorable and persuasive, but it adds something of real value to our knowledge of Burr and did show clearly that he had been unjustly judged in many particulars. It is a fascinating piece of biographical writing. E. C. R.

Cabot, George. LODGE, HENRY CABOT. Life and letters of George Cabot. Boston: Little. 1877. Net $3.50. [1602

Cabot was a leading Massachusetts Federalist, and president of the Hartford Convention. Aside from its general value as an authoritative biography, the volume has special importance for its publication of Cabot's letters, and its exhibition of the attitude of the New England Federalists towards the national government in the time of the war of 1812. W. MacD.

Campbell, P. Travels in the interior inhabited parts of North America, 1791–2. Edin.: Guthrie. 1793. [1603

The author, formerly an officer in the 42d Highlanders, arrived at St. John, New Brunswick, on 27th August, 1791. After visiting the new settlements in that province he travelled overland on foot to Quebec; thence to Niagara and the Six Nations' tract on the Grand River, visiting all the loyalist settlements on the St. Lawrence and Lake Ontario on his way. He then went to Albany by the Genesee and Mohawk valley route and down the Hudson to New York. He was a careful and competent observer, and his book is specially valuable for the information it contains on the social life and commercial activity of the people. There is a circumstantial account of St. Clair's defeat derived from Indians who were in the battle and from Lieut. Turner, an American officer taken prisoner. The style is concise and unpretentious and the matter generally accurate. E. Cr.

Carey, Mathew. The olive branch ; or Faults on both sides. Phil. 1814. 10th ed. improved. Phil. 1830. [1604

A review of the history of the United States with the object of showing both Federalists and Republicans their faults and errors, and so drawing the parties together for the salvation of the Union, which seemed to be on the verge of dissolution. It contains some valuable original documents ; impartially scourges both parties, and bitterly attacks the Hartford Convention. Carey was a conscientious, industrious, narrow-minded man, who wrote with care, but was too near the subjects he discusses to be either fair or accurate. As literature the book is worthless. R. C. H. C.

Chateaubriand, François Auguste René, *vicomte* **de.** Travels in America and Italy. London: Colburn. 1828. 2v. [1605

" All of the first volume, from p. 196 to p. 356, and all of vol. 2, from p. 1 to p. 142, are devoted to the relation of the history and customs of the aborigines, or an examination of their antiquities." T. W. Field, *Indian bibliography*, p. 72.

Cobb, Joseph B. Leisure labors ; or Miscellanies, historical, literary, and political. N. Y.: Appleton. 1858. [1606

The historical and political essays relate to Jefferson, W. H. Crawford, slave trade in the District of Columbia, and the " true issue between parties in the South for union or disunion." The author is a states-rights southerner and writes from that standpoint. The review of Randolph's *Life of Jefferson* is a detailed survey in 130 pages of Jefferson's political career. It is discriminating, and notes the defects in Jefferson's character. D. R. D.

Cobbett, William. Porcupine's works : a faithful picture of the United States of America, their governments, laws, politics and resources, 1783–1801. London: Cobbett. 1801. 12v. [1607

Of importance to the historian of the early politics of the United States. The volumes include Cobbett's accounts of contemporary events, and controversial articles on the men and measures of the day. At the time of writing Cobbett hated the United States ; despised the men and principles of the Revolution, and delighted especially in assaulting the anti-Federalists. He was the most able and scurrilous pamphleteer in the country ; an impudent slanderer, extremely prejudiced and intemperate, and master of a vigorous, cutting style. R. C. H. C.

—— A year's residence in the United States of America (1817–18). London : Sherwood. 1818–19. 3 pts. [1608

The year consisted of ten months in Long Island and two in Eastern Pennsylvania, and was spent in farming. Cobbett wrote with the particular object of describing the United States as a country for farmers, giving, however, some space to customs, manners, political and religious institutions. The third part of his book contains Hulme's *Journal of a tour in the West* (Ohio, Indiana and Illinois), and a criticism of Birkbeck's *Writings on America*. Cobbett was a shrewd observer, and wrote in a far better temper and more judicial mood than was common with him.

R. C. H. C.

— SMITH, EDWARD. William Cobbett: a biography. London: Low. 1878. 2v. [1609

A study from the sources of the career of Cobbett. Written from a sympathetic standpoint. Style clear and readable. Vol. I contains Cobbett's American experiences. E. C.

Coe, Charles H. Red patriots: the story of the Seminoles. Cin.: Editor Pub. Co. 1898. $1.50. [1610

A history of the Seminole Indians of Florida, and their contests with the encroaching white man. The author was for some time a resident of Florida, and in his researches became convinced that the " wronged and despised Seminole fought in no less sacred a cause than did our forefathers in the days of '76." The charge that the Indians held slaves is denied. Authorities are given. An extensive bibliography and a list of forts erected in Florida during the war are added. E. E. S.

Coffin, Charles Carleton. Building the nation; from the Revolution to the beginning of the war between the states. N. Y.: Harper. 1883. $2. [1611

A very popular relation of events between 1783 and 1860, to show the expansion of territory, spread of civilization, changes in social life, and the fruits of art and invention. Political and constitutional elements minimized. Meagre evidences of investigation. Purely narrative, without deductions or conclusions. The peculiar value of the book is in the large number of reproductions and facsimiles of old pictures and documents. E. E. S.

Cooper, Thomas. Consolidation: an account of parties from 1787. 2d ed. Columbia, S. C. 1830. [1612

An "ultra southern view" of states-rights. Justin Winsor, in *Narrative and critical hist. of Am.*, 7 : 323.

Davis, John. Travels of four years and a-half in the United States, 1798–1802. London. 1803. [1613

" A visitor whose narrow means obliged him often to travel on foot and rely on casual hospitality, and whose acquirements enabled him to subsist as a tutor in a southern family, for several months, would challenge our respect for his independence and self-reliance, were it not for an egotistical claim to the rank of a practical and philosophical traveller, which obtrudes itself on every page of his journal. Some descriptive sketches, however, atone for the amiable weakness of John Davis, whose record includes the period between 1798 and 1802, during which he roamed over many sections of the country, and observed various phases of American life." H. T. Tuckerman, *America and her commentators*, p. 200.

Dwight, Theodore. History of the Hartford Convention. N. Y.: White. 1833. [1614

A dull narrative of the political events and conditions which bred the Hartford Convention of 1814–15. The report of the convention is the only feature of the book of permanent interest. W. MacD.

Dwight, Timothy. Travels in New-England and New-York. New Haven. 1821–2. 4v. [1615

These volumes contain accounts of seven journeys in New England and of six in New York made in the years 1796–1815. President Dwight was a careful and intelligent observer of the people and their customs, as well as of the scenery and the phenomena of nature. The narratives of these journeys were composed from notes taken at the time, and present a complete and trustworthy picture of New England and New York one hundred years ago. In the fourth volume President Dwight reviews in detail the learning, morals, and religion of New England and the characteristics of the people. As a whole, Dwight's *Travels* ranks among the most valuable of its class of historical sources. E. G. B.

Fiske, John. Critical period of American history, 1783–89. Boston: Houghton. 1888. $2. [1616

The " critical period " is the period from 1783 to 1789. The work thus follows, in point of time, the same author's *American Revolution* (sect. 1315). The state of the country at the close of the war with Great Britain, the development of the states and the westward expansion, the imperfect working and gradual breakdown of the Articles of Confederation, and the formation and adoption of the Constitution are the topics treated. The work has the clearness and literary grace which characterize all the author's writings, and while not an exhaustive history of the time, is the best comprehensive account of the period. W. MacD.

Ford, Worthington Chauncey, *ed.* The United States and Spain in 1790: an episode in diplomacy; with an introd. See Historical Printing Club, sect. 273. [1617

Gallatin, Albert. Writings; ed. by Henry Adams. Phil.: Lippincott. 1879. 3v. [1618

This collection is of primary importance to the student of the early political, economic and financial history of the United States. The correspondence throws much light upon the administrations of Jefferson and Madison; and to a less extent upon those of Monroe and Adams. Vol. 3 contains a speech made during the Whiskey Rebellion, a sketch of the finances of the United States in 1796, two essays on finance and banking in the United States (1830 and 1841), and discussions on the Oregon question and the peace with Mexico. The editor's work is most thorough. R. C. H. C.

— ADAMS, HENRY. Life of Albert Gallatin. Phil.: Lippincott. 1879. [1619

This biography was published in the same year that the author issued his edition of the writings of Gallatin in three large volumes. Mr. Adams had unusual access to the private papers left by Gallatin, and adds much from the government archives not hitherto published. Several series of letters written to party leaders have also been rescued. As Gallatin's papers are fairly voluminous, the volume forms an important original source of history. Particularly is this so in the politics of Jefferson's and Madison's administrations. The typography and mechanical execution of the volume are defective and do not do justice to the editing, which is sound. The reader is obliged to be watchful to distinguish between Gallatin's writing and that of Mr. Adams. It is too large a biography for the reader with limited time — Stevens' being preferable; but for the special student it is indispensable.   D. R. D.

— STEVENS, JOHN AUSTIN. Albert Gallatin. (American statesmen.) Boston: Houghton. 1884. $1.25.   [1620

This is an excellent volume in the American statesmen series. It is clear and well arranged, although the division into chapters is not strictly chronological. The author by inheritance and occupation was well equipped to describe the life of a public financier. While admiration is expressed for Gallatin, there is no eulogy. The volume serves as a political history of the United States, 1790–1816. Chapter 6, devoted to Gallatin's administration of the Treasury, is a useful monograph on the financial history of the period.   D. R. D.

Gerry, Elbridge. AUSTIN, JAMES TRECOTHICK. Life of Elbridge Gerry. Boston: Wells. 1828–9. 2v.   [1621

The life of one of the most prominent Anti-Federalist party leaders (1744–1814), by his son-in-law, also a pronounced Anti-Federalist. Its value is due chiefly to the great number of contemporary letters embodied in it. It is marked by a fairly judicial temper, in spite of the author's relationship; and also by care in preparation. It contains one portrait, one facsimile and no index. It is not a book for the general reader.   W. E. F.

Goodrich, Samuel Griswold (Peter Parley, *pseud.*). Recollections of a lifetime. N. Y. 1851. 2v.   [1622

The author, Peter Parley, describes the "homely country life in which I was born and bred." His birth was in 1793, and he lived in Ridgefield, Conn., until 1808. Of interest is the description of household customs, domestic habits, food, clothing, furniture, travelling, school-teaching, and religious opinion. He lived in Hartford, Conn., during the war of 1812, and gives interesting notes in regard to the Hartford Convention. In 1826, he removed to Boston, and engaged in literary work. One chapter is devoted to reminiscences of Washington life.   D. R. D.

Hall, *Capt.* **Basil.** Travels in North America in the years 1827–28. Edin.: Cadell. 1829. 3v.   [1623

"Captain Hall has not only punctiliously abstained from offensive personalities, but he professes throughout, and, we doubt not, sincerely, a great degree of personal good will and kind feeling toward the Americans, with whom he became acquainted on his tour." The tone of his book, however, is far from cordial. "With a few insulated exceptions, nothing is well; the whole system and spirit are bad. Captain Hall seems to have had a misgiving that the extent and accuracy of his observation would be questioned; and is constantly trying to be beforehand with his answer, by insinuating the unreasonableness of the Americans in exacting unqualified praise." His observations are strangely inaccurate, and he has a passion for generalizing from single facts, often ill understood. His style "errs in the extreme of plainness. It is frequently slovenly, and still more frequently incorrect." E. Everett, in *North American review*, 29: 522.

Hamilton, Alexander. Complete works; ed. by Henry Cabot Lodge. N. Y.: Putnam. 1885–86. 9v.   [1624

This is the most extensive edition of Hamilton's writings. It includes the Federalist eliminated from J. C. Hamilton's edition, and all letters to Hamilton with one or two exceptions. Only a small number of Hamilton's writings have been omitted, such as revenue circulars, statements of accounts, etc., and a list of these is given in vol. 9. There is also included the Reynolds pamphlet, vol. 6. The writings with the exception of the private correspondence are arranged by subjects. There are but few notes, for the editor believes that "Hamilton is not a writer who requires much annotation." The mechanical execution of this edition is exceptionally fine. Volumes 2 and 3 are devoted to finance and volume 8 contains the general index.   D. R. D.

— FORD, PAUL LEICESTER, *comp.* Bibliography. See Historical Printing Club, sect. 272.   [1625

— HAMILTON, JOHN CHURCH. Life of Alexander Hamilton, by his son. N. Y.: Appleton. 1834–40. 2v.   [1626

This is the unfinished life of Hamilton by his son. It closes abruptly with the adjournment of the Federal Convention in 1787. The material was largely used in the author's *History of the republic of the United States* (1857), which see, sect. 1630, beyond.   E. E. S.

— LODGE, HENRY CABOT. Alexander Hamilton. (American statesmen.) Boston: Houghton. 1882. $1.25.   [1627

A biography of fascinating interest. Mr. Lodge has been exceptionally successful in this work in bringing into strong relief the salient features of Hamilton's character and work. The author, although strongly in sympathy with Hamilton's political position, maintains a more temperate and judicial attitude than he does in some of his later writings. Few books are so well adapted as this life of Hamilton to kindle an intelligent interest in American history.   E. G. B.

— MORSE, JOHN TORREY, JR. Life of Alexander Hamilton. Boston: Little. 1876. 2v. $4.50.   [1628

This book presents what is probably one of the fairest views of Hamilton that has yet appeared; the writer's appreciation and praise of the Federalist leader, while hearty, are, in general, discriminating and not excessive; but in the account of the Adams-Hamilton quarrel, Mr. Morse seems not fully considerate towards Adams, and quite unduly charitable towards Hamilton and the secretaries who conspired with Hamilton against the President. Many will reject as untrue the decidedly sinister portrait of Jefferson. As a whole the book is more successful in portraying Hamilton than his adversaries.

A. D. M.

— SUMNER, WILLIAM GRAHAM. Alexander Hamilton. (Makers of America.) N. Y.: Dodd. 1890. $1. [1629

This volume is not strictly a biography, but is "undertaken to show how, and in what sense, Alexander Hamilton was one of the makers of this American state." It is in no sense a summary of other biographies, but is an independent and vigorous study, in which the author makes no attempt to conceal his own political and economic philosophy. The special merit of the work is that Hamilton is brought into close relationship with the circumstances and forces of his time. Hamilton is considered as a hero in the contest with anarchy and repudiation at the end of the last century. A hundred pages are devoted to an exposition of the defects and faults of American public life between 1765 and 1780. Unfortunately there is not sufficient care given to portray the sterling qualities of the American people at that time. The author makes a special and original study of Hamilton's opinions on financial matters, and believes that his attainments in this domain have been greatly exaggerated. This work is more critical and scholarly than the biography by Lodge. The reader must, however, note that Prof. Sumner, in making judgments, is apt to impose present standards upon a more immature past. D. R. D.

Hamilton, James Alexander. Reminiscences; or Men and events during three quarters of a century. N. Y.: Scribner. 1869. [1630

This volume contains original material useful for the study of national affairs from 1800 to 1866, particularly dealing with Alexander Hamilton's party affiliations and Jackson's administration, and to a less extent with the administrations of Harrison and Lincoln. It includes many letters to and from prominent politicians. Hamilton participated actively in some of the measures of Jackson's presidency, but neglects to speak fully of the Jackson-Calhoun quarrel, which he was instrumental in precipitating. Much space is given to foreign experiences. The book is chaotic in construction, and Hamilton shows excusable prejudice against his father's opponents and all secession movements. R. C. H. C.

Hamilton, John Church. History of the republic of the United States, as traced in the writings of Alexander Hamilton and of his contemporaries. N. Y. Appleton. 1857–64. 7v. 4th ed. Boston: Houghton. 1879. 7v. [1631

"This work was sharply attacked for its criticisms of Jefferson, the Adamses, Madison, and Joseph Reed, and [the author] gave much offence by his inordinate claims for Hamilton's having been the author of a large number of Washington's letters, which he wrote as secretary. He says that he found over a thousand of such letters in Hamilton's handwriting. In the preface to his second volume he attempted a defence of his claims for them to have been Hamilton's proper work. The book is, nevertheless, the essential storehouse for the student of Hamilton." Justin Winsor, in *Narrative and critical hist. of Am.*, 7: 307.

Hamilton Club. New York. This club was organized in 1865 and has published: [1632

The life of Alexander Hamilton, by John Williams (Anthony Pasquin). — Observations on certain documents in "The history of the United States for 1796," by Alexander Hamilton. — The Hamiltoniad, by John Williams (Anthony Pasquin). — Letters to Alexander Hamilton, king of the Feds.

Hart, Albert Bushnell. Formation of the Union, 1750–1829. (Epochs of Am. history.) N. Y.: Longmans. 1892. Rev. ed. 1897. $1.25. [1633

An admirably constructed book, well provided with maps and classified lists of books for further reading. The narrative is confined mainly to political history, only brief attention being given to the military events. The treatment is scientific and devoid of partisan bias, and in the choice and presentation of the subject-matter is abreast of the best scholarship of the day. E. G. B.

Hazen, Charles Downer. Contemporary American opinion of the French Revolution. (Johns Hopkins Univ. studies, extra v. 16.) Balt. 1897. $2. [1634

The scattered opinions of Americans upon the French Revolution are here conscientiously brought together. The sources have been carefully explored. The comment on the extracts given and the conclusion drawn therefrom are scholarly, just and accurate. One notable service rendered is the clear evidence given of the powerful influence of the Revolution upon the formation of American parties, and upon American political and social ideas. R. C. H. C.

Ingersoll, Charles Jared. MEIGS, WILLIAM M. Life of Charles Jared Ingersoll; by his grandson. Phil.: Lippincott. 1897. $1.50. [1635

Written from Ingersoll's papers, and of value in relation to politics from 1812 to 1850. Ingersoll was a Philadelphia lawyer, a Democrat who supported the war of 1812, Jackson's attack on the Bank, the Mexican war and southern interests. The events of his life are here presented in a satisfactory manner, with accuracy, in judicious proportion and in a pleasant and correct style. R. C. H. C.

Jackson, Andrew. PARTON, JAMES. General Jackson. (Great commanders.) N. Y.: Appleton. 1893. $1.50. [1636

"In accordance with the plan of the series, Jackson's military career is here given with all the fulness that could be desired. . . . The author's criticism of Jackson's faults, both personal and political, is frank and explicit. . . . His political career is briefly given, but the outline is a distinct one, and while the volume professedly deals with his military life as its principal topic, it is quite likely to be found sufficiently full in other respects to become the popular biography of a remarkable and picturesque character." *Nation*, 56: 427.

— REID, JOHN, *and* JOHN HENRY EATON. Life of Andrew Jackson. Phil. 1817. 1824. [1637

"The first four chapters, carrying the narrative partly through the Creek war, were written by Major John Reid, U. S. A., who was an eye-witness of the events related." J. R. Soley, in *Narrative and critical hist. of Am.*, 7: 436.

— (Works relating to Jackson are mostly placed in the next following period.)

Jay, John, *chief-justice.* Correspondence and public papers; ed. by Henry P. Johnston. N. Y.: Putnam. 1890–93. 4v. $20. [1638

It is doubtful if the reader will get a better idea of the character and services of Jay from these volumes than from the biographies mentioned below. The editor has, naturally, not sought to give in his own words any account of Jay's career, but has confined his editorial work to selecting material and adding occasional notes to disclose the circumstances under which letters or documents were written. The books are useful to the specialist, inasmuch as they contain a greater amount of original material from the Jay manuscripts than can be found elsewhere in print; but unfortunately they do not include everything which an investigator would hope to find.
A. C. McL.

— JAY, WILLIAM. Life of John Jay, with selections from his correspondence and miscellaneous papers. N. Y.: Harper. 1833. 2v. [1639

As unprejudiced as a son's life of his father is likely to be. The *Life* occupies Vol. 1. It is composed of letters patched together with what are scarcely more than editorial notes. Vol. 2 is devoted to "miscellaneous correspondence." The original papers contained in this work give it great value to the close student.
E. C.

— PELLEW, GEORGE. John Jay. (American statesmen.) Boston: Houghton. 1890. $1.25. [1640

A thoughtful and judicious account of the life of one of the best and ablest of the old Federalist statesmen. Although not so interesting as some of the other volumes in the series to which it belongs, it is far from dull. It abounds in excerpts from Jay's correspondence, and gives an unusually clear picture of

the Revolutionary period and the two succeeding decades. The author was able to use some material to which others do not seem to have had access, and this volume is therefore the most satisfactory life of Jay that has been published.
A. C. McL.

— WHITELOCK, WILLIAM. Life and times of John Jay. N. Y.: Dodd. 1887. [1641

An historical sketch of the history of the United States during the years 1774 to 1800, with Jay as the central figure. Based on the ordinary materials. Very favorable to Jay. Style clear and readable. E. C.

Jefferson, Thomas. (See preceding period, sect. 1373–1382.)

Journal of a treaty with the Indians, 1793. See Massachusetts Historical Society, sect. 301. [1642

Kendall, Edward Augustus. Travels through the northern parts of the United States, 1807–8. N. Y.: Riley. 1809. 3v. [1643

"No previous work on this country so fully explains the state polity and organization of New England, and the social facts connected therewith. . . . He analyzes the municipal system and the social development with so much knowledge and fairness, that the political and economical student will find more data and detail in his work than, at that period, were elsewhere obtainable. It still serves as an authentic memorial of the region of country described at that transition era." H. T. Tuckerman, *America and her commentators*, p. 206.

Kent, James. KENT, WILLIAM. Memoirs and letters of James Kent. Boston: Little. 1898. $2.50. [1644

"Kent's Life has never before been written. His son, Judge William Kent, was to have brought it out, but died, leaving some materials which his greatgrandson has now put together in an agreeable sketch. . . . During his judicial career his greatness never seems to have been questioned by his contemporaries. They saw that he was a great judge; we see that he was a legal giant. . . . But when we read his life, and perceive his simplicity and modesty, and his unfailing refusal to trust to anything but industry and minute accuracy and research, we feel that, wonderful as his powers were, he earned his fame by labor as unusual, and hence the record of his achievements inspires in us, as it did in his contemporaries, less envy than a sort of affectionate veneration." *Nation*, Aug. 4, 1898.

King, Rufus. KING, CHARLES R., *ed.* Life and correspondence of Rufus King. N. Y.: Putnam. 1894–1900. 6v. $30. [1645

A valuable contribution to American political history. Concerns the later sessions of the Continental Congress, the formation and adoption of the Federal Constitution, the first United States Senate, the Jay treaty, and especially relations with England from 1796 to 1803. Also embraces the admission of Missouri and many political questions to 1827. Many of the letters have been unpublished hitherto. Very worthy editing, giving only absolutely necessary explanations and connection. E. E. S.

Lafayette, Marie Jean Paul Roch Yves Gilbert de Motier, *marquis* **de.** LEVAS-SEUR, A. Lafayette in America in 1824 and 1825; or Journal of Travels in the United States. N. Y.: White. 1829. 2v. [1646

A detailed account of Lafayette's visit to the U. S., written by his private secretary, who accompanied him. Contains not only a history of all the general's movements, but also many descriptive, historical and statistical notes concerning the U. S. of that day.

La Rochefoucauld-Liancourt, François Alexandre Frédéric, *duc* **de.** Travels through the United States, the country of the Iroquois and Upper Canada, 1795–7. London. 1799. 2v. [1647

"There is little of novel information to an American reader in his voluminous work, except the record of local features and social facts, which are now altogether things of the past; yet the fairness and minute knowledge displayed account for the value and interest attached to this work for many years after its appearance. . . . He occupied himself chiefly with economical investigations, especially those connected with agriculture. . . . The Duke was a philosophical traveller, content to journey on horseback, making himself as much at home with the laborer at the wayside as with the gentleman of the manor; and seeking information with frankness and patience wherever and however it could be properly acquired." H. T. Tuckerman. *America and her commentators,* p. 94.

An original source of the first class for American history at the close of the 18th century. Full of keen, fair-minded observation regarding every variety of detail of life in America as this exiled French nobleman found it, told in a readable style, not without an occasional touch of humor. An 18th century anticipation of Bryce's *American commonwealth.*

H. W. H.

Livingston, Edward. HUNT, CHARLES HAVENS. Life of Edward Livingston; with introd. by George Bancroft. N. Y.: Appleton. 1864. [1648

Edward Livingston was a member of the New York state bar in the last part of the 18th century and the first of the 19th, a member of Congress from 1794 to 1800, and for a brief period after that, mayor of New York. He then removed to New Orleans, where he followed his profession for many years, until, in 1822, he was once more elected to the House of Representatives, where he served for six years. He was then elected senator and became secretary of state under President Jackson. In 1832 he was appointed minister to France. Livingston's life is of special interest because of his preparation of a penal code for Louisiana which gave him great reputation, not only in this country but in Europe. He was also closely identified with President Jackson's administration, and, it is generally understood, had much to do with the preparation of Jackson's important papers. The biography is clear, though not particularly interesting. The editor had access to all of the papers left by Mr. Livingston at his death.

D. R. D.

Lyman, Theodore. Diplomacy of the United States, 1778–1814. Boston: Wells. 1826. [1649

Another edition in 1828 brings the story down to 1826. Arranged by treaties and countries — not chronologically. Good table of contents, but no index. A creditable work when published. Now out of date.

E. C.

Maclay, William. Sketches of debate in the first Senate of the United States, 1789–91; ed. by George W. Harris. Harrisburg. [c. 1880.] N. Y.: Brown. 1882.

—— [*Same,* enl.] Journal, 1789–91; ed. by Edgar S. Maclay. N. Y.: Appleton. 1890. $2.25. [1650

The only continuous and detailed account of the debates in the Senate during the first Congress. Maclay was the leader of the opposition to the Federalist programme, and his diary reveals without restraint the temper and motives of that opposition. His anti-Federalist feeling was so strong as to make him credulous of every evil report of the party in power. Consequently his narrative is to be used with critical caution. There are many interesting glimpses of New York social life in 1789–91.

E. G. B.

Madison, *Mrs.* **Dorothy (Payne).** Memoirs and letters of Dolly Madison. Boston: Houghton. 1886. $1.25. [1651

Letters written by the wife of the fourth president, a bright intelligent woman who took a lively interest in what was passing about her. All of them are sprightly and entertaining; some of them give valuable accounts of important historical events. Short narrative statements by the editor serve to connect the letters and to explain their allusions.

A. C. McL.

Madison, James. Letters and other writings. Phil.: Lippincott. 1865. 4v.

—— Papers: being his correspondence and reports of debates during the Congress of the Confederation, and his reports of debates in the Federal Convention; pub. under the superintendence of Henry D. Gilpin. Wash.: Langtree. 1840. 3v. N. Y. 1841. 3v. [1652

A new and complete edition of Madison's letters and works is announced under the editorship of Gaillard Hunt. The letters in Gilpin's *Madison papers* relate to the years 1782–1787, while the correspondence in the *Letters* extends over the years 1769–1836 and constitutes an invaluable source of historical knowledge, especially for the period of Madison's political service. The *Writings* include Madison's constitutional papers, except the contributions to *The Federalist.* Of the material besides letters in Gilpin's collection, the debates of the Congress of the Confederation are especially to be noted, as they have not been reprinted elsewhere, as the debates of the Federal Convention have been.

E. G. B.

—— ADAMS, JOHN QUINCY. Lives of James

Madison and James Monroe, with historical notices of their administrations. Buffalo. 1850. [1653

Eulogies rather than critical biographies, but valuable as the estimates of the character and services of these statesmen made by a contemporary who knew them well and who had himself taken a large part in the events whereof he writes. They were written to be delivered as public addresses, and are somewhat formal in style and oratorical in method.
A. C. McL.

Adams places a high estimate on the character and public services of both Monroe and Madison, anticipating in this the judgment of the most recent writers. Of great value, too, is the distinguished author's luminous interpretation of that long and important period of American history in which Madison and Monroe lived and acted. A. D. M.

— GAY, SYDNEY HOWARD. James Madison. (American statesmen.) Boston: Houghton. 1884. $1.25. [1654

Viewed from a Federalist (and later non-" states-rights ") standpoint. Severe, if not unsympathetic. The author thinks Madison possessed of great powers in ordinary affairs, but lacking purpose in crises ; deplores his defection from the Hamiltonians; belittles the War of 1812, and sustains the attitude of New England. Nevertheless it is the best brief biography of Madison extant. Especially full on the origin of the Federal Convention. E. E. S.

— RIVES, WILLIAM CABELL. History of the life and times of James Madison. Boston: Little. 1859–68. 3v. [1655

This work was intended to form 4 vols., but, on account of the death of Mr. Rives, only three were completed. The author was a long-time and intimate acquaintance of Madison and had access to all the manuscript material. It is therefore a contribution which will always have value, although it is to be hoped that it will some time be superseded by a more complete life, giving perhaps more of life and less of times. E. C. R.

Mansfield, Edward Deering. Personal memories, with sketches of many noted people, 1803–43. Cin.: Clarke. 1879. $1.50. [1656

Mr. Mansfield was educated at West Point and in Connecticut. In 1825 he moved to Ohio to practice law. The early chapters are devoted to life as cadet at West Point in 1815 ; to reminiscences of Princeton, 1820 ; and life at Litchfield, Conn., in attendance upon the law school. His father was a professor at West Point, 1814–1820, where the young man enjoyed the opportunities of the best society, and the book gives many anecdotes and speeches of men of note, both in science and politics. There is considerable information in regard to the early condition of scientific learning in this country. There are sketches of Ohio society, theatres, and of famous western characters as Clay and Corwin. There is no index. There are many slips in spelling and in dates. There is not very much absolutely new in the book for the general reader.
D. R. D.

Marshall, John. MAGRUDER, ALLAN B. John Marshall. (American statesmen.) Boston: Houghton. 1885. $1.25. [1657

" Only a month previous to the inauguration of Mr. Jefferson, Mr. Marshall, then Secretary of State and a pronounced Federalist, became Chief-Justice ; and during his long leadership the current of decision was distinctively upon the Federal line of governmental theory," that the Constitution should receive a latitudinarian construction, and that the Government should be made as powerful in the internal administration of the whole country as in the management of its foreign affairs. " This book presents in a succinct and compendious form the life and character of this eminent man and the elements which went to make up his greatness. We see him in the discharge of all the duties of exalted office and in the walks of private life, and the author is particularly felicitous in the representation of his buoyancy of spirits, his kind and playful temperament, the zest with which he enjoyed the pleasures of the table or the club. Numerous personal incidents are narrated in illustration of the simplicity of his character." Melville W. Fuller, in *Dial* (Chicago), 9 : 128.

Mason, George. ROWLAND, KATE MASON. Life of George Mason, 1725–92; including his speeches, public papers and correspondence. N. Y.: Putnam. 1892. 2v. $8. [1658

The biography of an eminent Virginian, by one of his descendants. The work is the result of great industry, of access to the necessary materials, and of constant efforts to secure accuracy, but is not so strong in judicious selection and sense of proportion. Mason's individuality would have made the book of much interest to a wider circle of readers if it could have been condensed within briefer limits. The work has an index, a portrait, and one facsimile. Scarcely a book for the general reader. W. E. F.

Minot, George Richards. History of the insurrection in Massachusetts in 1786, and the rebellion consequent thereon. Worcester. 1788. 2d ed. Boston: Burdett. 1810. [1659

In this work one finds an analysis of the causes and circumstances of Shays' rebellion in Massachusetts. Judge Minot was well known to his contemporaries as a participant in the political events of his time, and as the author, not only of the work in question, but also of a continuation of Hutchinson's *History of Massachusetts Bay*. Although his sympathies are unmistakably with the Commonwealth, the *History of the insurrection* is written on the whole in a dignified and temperate spirit. It contains many documents illustrative of the text, and shows the author's familiarity with the views of the leading men of the time. C. M. A.

Monroe, James. Writings, including a collection of his public and private papers and correspondence, now for the first time printed ; ed. by Stanislaus Murray Hamilton. N. Y.: Putnam. 1898–. 4v.+. $5 ea. subs. (To be 7v.) [1660

"No collection of the writings of Monroe until now had ever appeared. . . . The reproach, whatever the cause may have been, is about to be removed; we have the first two volumes of an edition of Monroe that promises to be all that our historical scholars and public men could reasonably expect. The materials to draw upon, the editor thus describes: 'Monroe has left material in the shape of notes, together with a large collection of letters from and to the most distinguished men of this and other countries. . . . The greater part of this collection was acquired by Congress from Monroe's heirs, under an appropriation of $20,000 by Act approved March 3, 1849. These manuscripts are now deposited in the Bureau of Rolls and Library of the Department of State, handsomely mounted and bound and calendared; others are in our greater libraries and familiar archives, and many yet remain in the hands of individual owners. From the greater collection this edition is substantially drawn, but generous and cordial responses from other sources have enabled me to include many of the scattered papers.'" B. A. Hinsdale, in *Dial* (Chicago), 26: 333.

—— View of the conduct of the Executive in the foreign affairs of the United States connected with the mission to the French republic, 1794–6. Phil.: Bache. 1797. [1661

An attack on Washington's management of foreign affairs. Gives Monroe's account of his diplomatic mission in France in 1795–6. It reveals the man's mediocrity; and convicts him of the offences charged against him by his enemies. It is an ill-written performance; little skill and less judgment are apparent, and the whole is decidedly unfair and ill tempered. The appendix contains many useful documents, and gives Monroe's letters expressing his opinions of the state of France in 1795–6. R. C. H. C.

— GILMAN, DANIEL COIT. James Monroe. (American statesmen.) Boston: Houghton. 1883. $1.25. [1662

A short and simple account of the most important events in Monroe's life. When the book was written the Monroe manuscripts at Washington, while not inaccessible, were not easily handled: they are now being printed in large part. Although the author used these materials, he was far, he tells us in his preface, "from having exhausted these rich mines." The publication of these papers may show the desirability of a more extended biography; but probably the general judgments of this book will not be overthrown. A thorough bibliography of Monroe and the Monroe doctrine materially adds to the value of the volume. A. C. McL.

Morris, Gouverneur. Diary and letters; ed. by Anne Cary Morris. N. Y.: Scribner. 1888. 2v. $7.50. [1663

The diary was used to some extent in Sparks's *Life of Morris* (see below, sect. 1665), but here it is given almost entire and unmodified. It begins with Morris's arrival in France, and its constant use by writers upon the French Revolution attests its value. The later letters have reference to American politics and public life to 1815. The editing in these volumes is most judicious, limiting the comments to a simple framework for the diary and letters. E. E. S.

— ROOSEVELT, THEODORE. Gouverneur Morris. (American statesmen.) Boston: Houghton. 1888. $1.25. [1664

Everything which Mr. Roosevelt writes has a certain dash and spirit, and in the portrayal of this energetic and brilliant statesman he found a congenial task. Occasionally the author indulges in flippant comments, or in exaggerated praise or blame; but on the whole his method and temper are commendable. The life of Morris in Paris during the days of the French Revolution is entertainingly described. Extracts from the writings of Morris, who was a master of good English, add charm and interest to the book. A. C. McL.

— SPARKS, JARED. Life of Gouverneur Morris. Boston. 1832. 3v. [1665

The early standard life of Morris. The first volume contains a biography into which are woven extracts from his correspondence and diary, conscientiously expurgated and revised according to the Sparks method. The remaining volumes contain Morris's correspondence, miscellaneous writings and addresses. This work has been supplanted to a certain extent as a biography by Roosevelt's *Morris* (see above), and the diary and later letters have been printed with fewer alterations by Anne C. Morris (see above, sect. 1663). E. E. S.

Noah, Mordecai Manuel. Travels in England, France, Spain and the Barbary states, 1813–15. N. Y. 1819. [1666

"Col. M. M. Noah was consul of the U. S. at Tunis during the Algerine war, and his *Travels in England, France, Spain and the Barbary states* gives a minute picture of the condition of the affairs at this time in northern Africa, and recounts fully the circumstances of Decatur's negotiations at Tunis." Justin Winsor, in *Narrative and critical hist. of Am.*, 7: 438.

Palmer, T. H., ed. Historical register of the United States, 1812–14. Phil. 1814–16. 4v. [1667

The purpose of the publication was to give a detailed account of proceedings of Congress beginning with the second session of the 12th Congress. This is presented in chronological order with no classification of topics. Reprints of important state papers are added. The last three volumes deal particularly with the War of 1812. Save as a slight index of contemporary judgment and weight given to current events, the work is of little value to the student to-day. D. R. D.

Paulding, James Kirke. Letters from the South. N. Y.: Eastburn. 1817. 2v. [1668

A charming account of an excursion made into Virginia, in the summer of 1816, with bright, refreshing descriptions of the country and the people. The opening letter contains the confession: "The first thing that strikes a northern man, who flounders into Virginia, or either of the more southern states, loaded with a pack of prejudices larger than a pedler's, is, that he has all his life long been under a very mistaken notion of their manners." The last letter closes with the genial conviction, that sounds like a heartening benediction across the lapse of time: "I am satisfied that nothing but ignorance of each other causes those stupid misconceptions, unfounded aspersions, and ridiculous antipathies, that still subsist between the different sections of the country." G. K.

Perkins, Samuel. Historical sketches of the United States, from the peace of 1815 to 1830. N. Y.: Converse. 1830. [**1669**

A continuation of Perkins's *History of the late war* [of 1812]. An accurate and painstaking chronicle of the Era of Good Feeling by the hand of a contemporary. Dull but useful. E. C.

Philadelphia. *Committee of defence of Philadelphia, 1814–15.* Minutes. See Pennsylvania, Historical Society of, sect. 377. [**1670**

Pickering, Timothy. PICKERING, OCTAVIUS, *and* CHARLES W. UPHAM. Life of Timothy Pickering. Boston: Little. 1867–73. 4v. [**1671**

This work covers Pickering's career as a student of Harvard College, officer in the Revolution, Postmaster-General, Secretary of State, Chief-Justice of Massachusetts, Senator, Representative. It is very full of the best historical material. Begun by his son and finished by Mr. Upham, it is competently and sympathetically written. E. C. R.

Pickering papers. Historical index to the Pickering papers. See Massachusetts Historical Society, sect. 319. [**1672**

Pinckney, *General* Thomas. PINCKNEY, CHARLES COTESWORTH. Life of General Thomas Pinckney; by his grandson. Boston: Houghton. 1895. $1.50. [**1673**

"Thomas Pinckney . . . was born in 1750, and his death in 1828 closed a career characterized by ability, discretion, and a high ideal of political duty. He served as an officer in the Revolution, and as a general in the War of 1812. He was Governor of South Carolina from 1787 to 1789, and presided over the convention which ratified the Federal Constitution. He was, for four years, American Minister to Great Britain, was the Federalist candidate for Vice-President in 1796, and served two terms as a member of Congress. He also performed the important and delicate task of negotiating the treaty of 1795 with Spain. The brief biography by his grandson gives an intelligent account of Mr. Pinckney's public services, and a pleasing picture of his private life. In general, the volume follows the beaten track,—except in its lack of an index,—and the extracts from family correspondence and papers do not add materially to our knowledge of the period. . . . An unpleasant feature of the book is the frequent reference to the Civil War and the note of contrast between North and South." Charles H. Haskins, in *American historical review*, 1: 169.

Pinkney, William. PINKNEY, WILLIAM.

Life of William Pinkney; by his nephew. N. Y.: Appleton. 1853. [**1674**

"One of those overdone performances [by a nephew of the subject] that make the unsympathetic regret." Justin Winsor, in *Narrative and critical hist. of Am.*, 7: 317.

— WHEATON, HENRY. Some account of the life, writings, and speeches of William Pinkney. N. Y. 1826. [**1675**

Part I contains the memoir, private correspondence, etc.; Part II contains official papers and speeches, and correspondence with Madison. The memoir is well written. It was later condensed into a life for Sparks's *American biography*, vol. 6. E. C.

Plumer, William. PLUMER, WILLIAM, JR. Life of William Plumer; ed. by A. P. Peabody. Boston: Phillips. 1856. [**1676**

Plumer made excellent use of his father's papers and produced a well-written, temperate and judicious biography. He presents a careful summary of the secession movement in New England, with remarks on such movements elsewhere throughout the Union. The elder Plumer was Governor of New Hampshire and Senator of the United States. Originally a Federalist, he became a Republican about 1812. His public life began before the Revolution and extended to 1820. R. C. H. C.

Poole, William Frederick. Anti-slavery opinions before the year 1800. Cin.: Clarke. 1887. $1.25. Pap. 75c. [**1677**

"Mr. William F. Poole's essay on *Anti-slavery opinions before the year 1800* has been converted into a handsome book, . . . enriched by copious notes and addenda, and a facsimile reprint of Dr. George Buchanan's anti-slavery oration of 1791, of which a copy, it will be remembered, was preserved in Washington's library and led to Mr. Poole's researches. In its present form this essay gives perhaps not a complete, but certainly a just view of the state of public opinion on the subject of slavery at the close of the last century especially at the South, among men prominent in laying the foundations of the Federal Government." *Nation*, 16: 182.

Porter, *Commodore* David. PORTER, *Admiral* DAVID DIXON. Memoir of Commodore David Porter. Albany, N. Y.: Munsell. 1875. [**1678**

Traces Porter's connection with the United States navy during the latter part of the Revolutionary War; through the "French war" of 1798; the Tripolitan war, in which he was captured; the War of 1812; the suppression of West India piracy; complication with the Spanish authorities; and resignation after a court-martial. The biography is largely a vindication of Porter and a criticism of the management of the navy. The author is a son of the subject. E. E. S.

Preble, *Commodore* Edward. SABINE, LORENZO. Life of Edward Preble. (In Sparks, J., *ed.* Library of Am. biog., ser. 2, v. 12. Boston. c. 1844.) [**1679**

"An invaluable book, by far the largest part of which is taken up with a full and satisfactory examination of Preble's Tripoli campaign." J. R. Soley, in *Narrative and critical hist. of Am.*, 7: 419.

Priestley, Joseph. Letters, 1798–1800. See Massachusetts Historical Society, sect. 339.

[1680

Quincy, Josiah. *1772–1864.* Speeches delivered in the Congress of the United States; ed. by Edmund Quincy. Boston: Little. 1874. Net $3. [1681

Josiah Quincy was a member of the national House of Representatives from 1805 to 1813, i. e., from the beginning of our serious troubles with Napoleon and England to their culmination in the War of 1812. The fourteen well-edited speeches here presented are of great value to the student of that stormy period in American politics and party history. Of the Federalist leaders then serving in Congress Mr. Quincy was one of the ablest, and without question the foremost orator. His famous speech on the admission of Louisiana, delivered in 1811, is a classic among Northern utterances in support of state sovereignty.

A. D. M.

— QUINCY, EDMUND. Life of Josiah Quincy, by his son. Boston: Ticknor. 1867.

[1682

An admirable and judicious presentation of the letters and occasional journals of a fiery and radical Federalist and a member of the "Essex junto." Contains his views as member of Congress from 1805 to 1812, his opposition to the acquisition and admission of Louisiana, and his attitude toward the War of 1812. Especially valuable for the history of Harvard College during Quincy's presidency from 1829 to 1845.

E. E. S.

Quincy, Josiah. *1802–82.* Figures of the past from leaves of old journals. Boston: Roberts. 1883. Little. $1.50. [1683

A delightful book of political and social reminiscence, covering roughly the period 1820–1845. The accounts of John Adams in old age, of the visits of Lafayette and Jackson to Boston, and of life in Washington in 1826, are well known. The author was a son of President Josiah Quincy of Harvard College.

W. MacD.

Randolph, Edmund. CONWAY, MONCURE DANIEL. Omitted chapters of history disclosed in the life and papers of Edmund Randolph. N. Y.: Putnam. 1888. $3. [1684

"The services of Randolph in the constitutional development of the United States are clearly set forth. . . . The main purpose of Mr. Conway's volume is to disperse [the] cloud of obloquy that has so long shrouded the name of Edmund Randolph. In his labor of love and justice, Mr. Conway has been successful. So far as Randolph's integrity is concerned, Mr. Conway has shown, by documents in French, British, and American archives, how baseless is the imputation that Randolph sought, in secret collusion with the French minister, to thwart the policy of the administration he served. He has also conclusively disposed of the fiction by which he is made to appear on the books of the United States Treasury as a defaulter. From the fresh materials gathered Mr. Conway has painted a new portrait wholly unlike the traditional one drawn by Jefferson. . . . Mr. Conway has rendered a service to students of American history by his arduous and fruitful labors in a field largely untilled. He has made a protracted search among unpublished manuscripts, state archives and family papers, previously unexamined or inaccessible. He has elucidated these papers in a style dignified, forcible and at times dramatic." Edward P. Smith, in *Political science quarterly*, 4: 321.

Randolph, John. ADAMS, HENRY. John Randolph. (American statesmen.) Boston: Houghton. 1882. $1.25. [1685

The best brief biography of John Randolph; written from original sources by a scientific historian who is scrupulously accurate, and possessed of excellent judgment. Adams has, however, little sympathy with the personality or the views of Randolph. The style is clear and scholarly. R. C. H. C.

— GARLAND, HUGH A. Life of John Randolph. N. Y.: Appleton. 1850. 2v. $2.

[1686

"The main account of Randolph." Justin Winsor, in *Narrative and critical hist. of Am.*, 7: 317.

Rosenthal, Lewis. America and France: the influence of the United States on France in the 18th century. N. Y.: Holt. 1882. $1.75.

[1687

An exceptionally interesting and suggestive monograph. The author by a very thorough study of the literature of political discussion and speculation in France from 1775 to 1790 shows the lines on which the American Revolution prepared the way for and influenced the course of the French Revolution. It illustrates the international significance of the struggle for independence and the sensitive susceptibility of the French mind at that time to the inspiration of new political ideals. E. G. B.

Rush, Richard. Residence at the court of London, 1817–25. Phil.: Carey. London: Bentley. 1833. 3d ed. Phil.: Lippincott. 1872. [2d ed. rev. (Phil. 1833) was entitled Memoranda of a residence at the court of London.] [1688

Relates chiefly to the year 1818. Rush, during his long residence as the American representative in London, helped to strengthen the tradition of ability and courtesy in our representatives there, and was *persona grata* in society everywhere. Of the English reviews of the time, some criticise the publication of personal matters in this work, and others praise its judgment and taste in this regard; but all agree as to its being a faithful and interesting account of the times. E. C. R.

Sargent, Nathan. Public men and events, 1817-53. Phil.: Lippincott. 1875. 2v. [1689

A superficial book, written by a Washington newspaper correspondent, who was an "old line Whig;" presents character sketches of notable men, together with a variety of information, sometimes weighty, sometimes trivial, on political measures. The book is vividly written, is not accurate, and is decidedly though not violently partisan. R. C. H. C.

Seybert, Adam. Statistical annals; embracing views of the population, commerce, navigation, fisheries, public lands, post-office establishment, revenues, mint, military and naval establishments, expenditures, public debt and sinking fund of the United States of America; founded on official documents, 1789-1818. Phil.: Dobson. 1818. [1690

The title sufficiently indicates the scope and contents of this extremely valuable compilation. Seybert was thoroughly competent, and his statistics and statements are full, accurate and conveniently arranged. His book is well-nigh indispensable for the student of early American financial history.

R. C. H. C.

Sherman, Roger. BOUTELL, LEWIS HENRY. Life of Roger Sherman. Chicago: McClurg. 1896. $2. [1691

Prepared from the materials collected by Senator George F. Hoar. The loss of the larger part of Roger Sherman's papers has made impossible as complete a biography as has fallen to the lot of his distinguished contemporaries. Mr. Boutell's work includes all the private letters that are extant and a careful study of Roger Sherman's activity in the Federal Convention. It is a painstaking and trustworthy narrative.

E. G. B.

Stephen, James. War in disguise; or The frauds of the neutral flags. Lond. 1805. N. Y. 1806. [1692

Written to rouse public feeling and move the ministry to attack American commerce. Few political tracts have had greater direct influence. Style admirably suited to the purpose. E. C.

Story, Joseph. STORY, WILLIAM W., ed. Life and letters of Joseph Story. Boston: Little. 1851. 2v. [1693

The best life of Story, being written by his son. Covers politics of Massachusetts and United States from 1805 to 1811; the Republican party and the embargo. Concerns the Supreme Court of the United States from 1811 to 1848 and is valuable for many of the cases decided within that period. Gives many anecdotes of Chief-Justice Marshall and the other justices. Also valuable for history of Harvard Law School. Treatment biased in favor of subject. Slightly marred by intrusion of author's personality.

E. E. S.

Sullivan, James. AMORY, THOMAS COFFIN.

Life of James Sullivan, with selections from his writings. Boston: Phillips. 1859. 2v. [1694

Sullivan was an active politician for forty years, embracing the period of the Revolution, and was Attorney-General, judge, and twice Governor of his state. As a leader of the Jeffersonian Republicans in Massachusetts, he was the object of the frantic hate and detestation of the Federalists. Amory, his grandson, bases his life upon Sullivan's papers and letters, quoting these at great length. The extracts exhibit the principles of New England Republicanism in the clearest and best light. Amory's task is performed with sympathy, candor and impartiality, but he is too diffuse, shows lack of historical training and writes in a monotonous, heavy style. R. C. H. C.

Sullivan, William. Familiar letters on public characters and public events, 1783-1815. Boston. 1834.

—— Public men of the revolution. 2d ed. enl. Phil.: Carey. 1847. [1695

Sullivan was a pessimistic and irreconcilable Federalist, and his work is extremely biased. It contains interesting and often accurate sketches of men and events, but frequently want of knowledge is apparent. He is particularly hostile and unfair to Jefferson, though he supports his characterization by quoting copiously from Jefferson's *Writings*. He develops in a clear manner and pleasant style the principles for which Federalists stood. R. C. H. C.

Thomas, Ebenezer Smith. Reminiscences of the last sixty-five years. Hartford. 1840. 2v. [1696

The first volume contains a collection of sketches upon various subjects: battle of Lexington, Washington, travels in the United States, biographical sketches, and descriptions of American cities. Being written from observation, the biographies possess some value, if taken with allowances. The second volume contains the author's experience as a bookseller and editor in South Carolina and Ohio from 1798 to 1840. The comments on political and social life are interesting and the style quite unique. E. E. S.

Trescot, William Henry. Diplomatic history of the administrations of Washington and Adams. Boston. 1857. [1697

A clear, well-proportioned narrative of American diplomacy during the critical period 1783 to 1789, and the scarcely less critical period from 1789 to 1800. Jay's treaty and the convention made with Bonaparte in 1800, each an event of the first importance in our domestic politics as well as foreign relations, are treated with considerable fulness and in a judicial spirit. Indeed the writer is exceptionally temperate and fairminded. A. D. M.

United States. *Congress.* State papers and publick documents of the United States, from the accession of George Washington to the Presidency, exhibiting a complete view of our foreign relations since that time. 2d ed. Bos-

165

ton : Wait. 1817. 10v. 3d ed. Boston. 1819.
12v.   [1698

Contains the most important public documents on foreign affairs from 1789 to 1818. The folio edition of the state papers [Gales and Seaton ed.] is preferable to this edition, inasmuch as the former covers a longer period and gives some material not to be found in these volumes. This collection is, however, convenient and useful where the folio edition is not obtainable. Probably in the great majority of instances, when reference is made in historical writings to the state papers, the folio edition is the one referred to.   A. C. McL.

United States. *State Department.* Report of the Secretary of State relative to the papers on file in the Department of State concerning the unpaid claims of citizens of the United States against France for spoliations prior to July 31, 1801, etc. (49th Cong., 1st sess., Sen. ex. doc. 102.) Wash. 1886.   [1699

This consists of three lists: (1) an alphabetical list of claimants against France on account of the capture of American vessels, showing the names of the vessel and master, disposition of the vessel and of the claim, etc. ; (2) an alphabetical list of the vessels, with references to the first list ; (3) a list of names incidentally mentioned in the other two lists, with references thereto. The first list indicates whether or not evidence exists in support of each claim. A list is also given of contemporary memoranda and official reports concerning French spoliations on file in the Department of State.   F. J. S.

Ward, Townsend. Insurrection of 1794 in the western counties of Pennsylvania. See Pennsylvania, Historical Society of, sect. 375.
                                                [1700

Warden, David Baillie. A statistical, political, and historical account of the United States of North America. Edin. 1819. 3v.
                                                [1701

The author of this work was Consul of the United States at Paris. His work was chiefly a compilation, but gives a good account of the country for its time. It was also published in French translation.
                                                W. M. D.

Warfield, Ethelbert Dudley. The Kentucky Resolutions of 1798. N. Y.: Putnam. 1887. 2d ed. $1.25.   [1702

In this study of the causes that led to the adoption of the Kentucky Resolutions of 1798, President Warfield has made an examination of the condition of Kentucky at the time, and reaches the conclusion that no mere chance assigned to that state the important rôle it played, but " a manifest destiny long in preparing." He believes that to understand Kentucky's action it is necessary to know thoroughly the history of the state, and the prevalence there of a radical democratic spirit. He defends Jefferson's authorship of the Resolutions, and explains in detail the place and influence of Breckenridge, who introduced them. The

monograph is an admirable one, and its value is but little impaired by the author's bias toward Kentucky.
                                                C. M. A.

Washington, George. BAKER, WILLIAM SPOHN. Washington after the Revolution, 1784–99. Phil. : Lippincott. 1898. $2.50.
                                                [1703

A calendar showing the whereabouts and occupation of Washington each day as gathered from his writings, correspondence, and the newspapers. The constant reference to persons and places demands a familiarity with Washington not possessed by the average reader. To the history student the compilation is invaluable. The domestic life of the Washington family is shown better than in any other writing, and suggestive material for investigation abounds on every page. The statement of facts is unmarred by comments. The footnotes are excellent.   E. E. S.

— (Works relating to Washington are mostly placed in the preceding period, sect. 1538–1567.)

Weld, Isaac. Travels through the states of North America and the provinces of Upper and Lower Canada, 1795–7. London. 1799. 2v.
                                                [1704

The author visited Philadelphia, Baltimore, New York, and many parts of Pennsylvania, New Jersey, and Virginia. From New York he ascended the Hudson to Albany and entered Canada by way of Lake Champlain. After remaining for several months at Montreal and Quebec he passed up the St. Lawrence and Lake Ontario to Niagara, and eventually made his way as far west as Detroit. Returning down Lake Erie to Buffalo, he visited the settlements on the Genesee River and went by canoe from Newtown, N. Y. (Elmira), to Wilkesbarre and thence across the mountains on horseback to Philadelphia. Travelling in a leisurely manner and being a careful and generally unprejudiced observer, he produced a work of much value, which is concise and readable and remarkably accurate in detail.   E. Cr.

" Scarcely any contemporary writer of American travels was more quoted and popular, sixty years ago, than Isaac Weld, whom the troubles in Ireland, in '95, induced to visit this country. . . . He expatiates on the beauties of the landscape with the perception of an artist, and is one of the few early travellers who enriched his journal with authentic sketches of picturesque and famous localities. The French translation of Weld's Travels in America is thus illustrated." H. T. Tuckerman, *America and her commentators,* p. 207.

Wharton, Francis. State trials of the United States during the administrations of Washington and Adams ; with references, historical and professional, and preliminary notes on the politics of the times. Phil.: Carey. 1849.   [1705

A valuable collection of original material of considerable significance in our political and constitutional history. It includes the trial of the western insurgents [1795] ; the impeachment of Senator Blount ; and the trials of Cobbett, Lyon, Cooper, and a great deal of other matter not easily obtainable elsewhere. The excuse for the passage of the Alien and Sedition Laws, as well as the method and consequences of the enforcement of the latter act, may best be studied in such material as this. A. C. McL.

Wilkinson, Gen. James. Memoirs of my own times. Phil. 1816. 3v. and atlas. [1706

1757–1825. Valuable for the history of the Revolution and the Burr conspiracy. Vols. 2 and 3 are chiefly taken up with the various investigations, courts-martial, etc., of Gen. Wilkinson. The extra volume of diagrams and plans is both valuable and rare. The fact that he was a competent military critic and himself took part in the events gives great interest and value ; but the Revolutionary events were written down many years after they happened, and his memory of them is not always trustworthy. Its method is disproportionate and somewhat desultory, and it is to be used with caution, but yet used. For the matters mixed up with his own later tribulations it is a primary source. [See sect. 1824.] E. C. R.

Wirt, William. KENNEDY, JOHN PENDLETON. Memoirs of the life of William Wirt. Phil.: Lea. 1849. 2v. New rev. ed. 1850. 2v. N. Y. 1872. [1707

Valuable for history of the practice of the law rather than of statesmanship. Concerns early Virginia politics, the cabinets of Monroe, Adams and Jackson, but especially the bar of the Supreme Court from 1814 to 1834. Also the rise of the Anti-Masonic party. Especially full on the trial of Aaron Burr. E. E. S.

Wolcott, Oliver. Memoirs of the administrations of Washington and John Adams ; ed. from the papers of Oliver Wolcott, Secretary of the Treasury, by George Gibbs. N. Y. 1846. 2v. [1708

A source of primary importance for the history of the Federalist party, consisting mainly of letters to and from Wolcott. The editor's narrative connecting and summarizing the original papers is clear and accurate, but his judgments are strongly biased against the Republicans. Wolcott's correspondence throws a full light on the ideas and purposes of the Federalists, the beginnings of party organization, and upon the practical work of putting the new government under the Constitution into operation. E. G. B.

THE WAR OF 1812

Adams, John Quincy. The duplicate letters, the fisheries and the Mississippi: documents relating to transactions at the negotiation of Ghent. Wash.: Davis. 1822. 2d ed. Louisville. 1823. [1709

While Adams was Secretary of State, he had a peppery dispute with Jonathan Russell, one of his col-

leagues in the negotiation of the treaty of Ghent, over a proposition at one time made by a majority of the American commissioners to continue to permit the British navigation of the Mississippi in return for the continued use of the Atlantic fisheries. Adams here charges Russell with misrepresenting the latter's position seven years earlier and defends his own course, but prints Russell's statement as well as his own. The book therefore supplies a detailed account of the Ghent negotiations and an elaborate dissertation on the right of the United States to the fisheries and on the value to them of the same. F. J. S.

Armstrong, Maj.-Gen. John. Notices of the War of 1812. N. Y. 1836–40. 2v. [1710

The first volume is confined to the operations on the frontier; vol. 2 embraces those on the seaboard. The author (Major-General and Secretary of War) did not hesitate to combine with his narrative much personal criticism, reflecting on the gallantry or judgment of commanding officers. Appendices, giving correspondence, official reports, etc., in some cases fortify his conclusions ; but the work cannot be recommended for its impartiality. F. H. S.

Auchinleck, G. War of 1812. Toronto. 1855. [1711

Written in 1855 for serial publication, it is unduly lengthened by the insertion of long dispatches and orders, principally introduced to expose the misstatements of previous American writers. All the documents quoted were already in print. At the time it was written it was the best presentation of the British conduct of the war, but the question has since been restated in the light of the Canadian and American archives by historians on both sides. J. B.

Bancroft, George. History of the battle of Lake Erie, and miscellaneous papers ; [with] life and writings of George Bancroft, by Oliver Dyer. N. Y.: Bonner. 1891. $1. [1712

Sixty pages devoted to the battle of Lake Erie give a clear account of that engagement, wholly favorable to Perry. Lack of foresight on the part of the Secretary of War, and of gallant coöperation by Elliott, are shown in dispassionate language, in marked contrast to most of the earlier literature on the Perry-Elliott quarrel. This, and other essays in the book (" A day with Lord Byron," " Edward Everett," " Washington's birthday," " His monument ") were originally contributed to the New York *Ledger*. Oliver Dyer's sketch of the historian (pp. 1-128) recites briefly the principal events in his life. F. H. S.

Barnes, James. Naval actions of the War of 1812. N. Y.: Harper. 1896. $4.50. [1713

A book for uncritical readers, who are sufficiently pleased if the story of war is "patriotically" told. The introduction shows but moderate knowledge of the causes of the war.

Brackenridge, Henry Marie. History of the late war between the United States and Great Britain. Baltimore: Cushing. 1817. [6th ed.] Phil. 1839. [1714

Long esteemed one of the best histories of this war, and probably most popular of all, with many editions in several languages. Free from the acrimony that embitters many of the early records of this war, it gives credit where due and for the most part refrains from censure. It is not a discursive history of the times, but a concise narrative of the naval and military events, told in plain, unpretentious but agreeable style.   F. H. S.

Brannan, John, *ed.*   Official letters of the military and naval officers of the United States, 1812-15.   Wash.   1823.   [**1715**

"One of the most valuable and comprehensive collections of official despatches on the American side. . . . The papers are printed verbatim, without comment, and comprise all the more important reports." J. R. Soley, in *Narrative and critical hist. of Am.*, 7: 420.

Brock, *Sir* Isaac. Tupper, Ferdinand Brock, *ed.* Life and correspondence of Major-General Sir Isaac Brock. London : Simpkin. 1845.   [**1716**

Written by a nephew, and based largely on family papers. The second edition, 1847, is preferable to that of 1845 by reason of greater documentary fulness. Brock's personality is not very clearly depicted by his biographer, but shines out in his letters — which are also highly valuable in connection with the War of 1812.   C. W. C.

Burges, Tristam. Battle of Lake Erie; with notices of Commodore Elliot's [Elliott's] conduct in that engagement.   Providence: Brown.   Phil.: Marshall.   1839.   [**1717**

A lecture, delivered 22 years after the battle, and 14 years after Perry died, to refute the claims, made in *A biographical notice of Commodore Jesse D. Elliott*, in behalf of that officer. The value of the narrative is lessened by the obvious desire to make out as bad a case for Elliott as possible. Many documents in the Appendix testify to Elliott's failure promptly to come to Perry's relief, during the battle. Burges is ridiculed by J. Fenimore Cooper (see *Battle of Lake Erie*, sect. 1721). As history, it has the faults inherent in all special pleas ; as literature, it lacks distinction.
                                       F. H. S.

Butler, Nicholas Murray. Effect of the War of 1812 upon the consolidation of the Union. (Johns Hopkins Univ. studies, ser. 5, no. 7.)   Balt.   1887.   Pap. 25c.   [**1718**

An argument is presented in a brief essay of thirty pages to prove that particularism was ruined by the War of 1812 and nationalism, or national unity, was given invigorating life. "Patriotism and national pride had conquered sectionalism and personal selfishness." It constitutes a useful résumé of the contending forces of federalism and state sovereignty. The author relies largely upon and is evidently much influenced by Von Holst.   D. R. D.

Coffin, *Lt.-Col.* William F. 1812: the war

and its moral : a Canadian chronicle.   Montreal.   1864.   [**1719**

The author, as an official of the Canadian government, enjoyed unusual facilities for collecting materials, but many of the details based on reminiscences accepted by him without hesitation are quite untrustworthy. It is faulty in judgment and intemperate in tone. There are numerous errors in proper names. The style is rhetorical and diffuse, and much trivial and irrelevant matter is introduced. The narrative ends in November, 1813. Altogether the book has little worth.   E. Cr.

Coggeshall, *Capt.* George. History of the American privateers and letters-of-marque, during our war with England, 1812, '13 and '14. 2d ed., rev. and enl., with additional notes.   N. Y.: Author.   1856.   [**1720**

A collection of narratives of the irregular sea-fights of the War of 1812; plainly, often baldly, told, but trustworthy and readable withal ; most so when Capt. Coggeshall writes of the exploits of the David Porter and the Leo, which he commanded. The work profits by its author's nautical knowledge, but falls far short of being an adequate history of the subject. For wellnigh half a century practically the only work on the exploits of American privateers, it is now (1900) supplemented by Maclay's more comprehensive history.
                                       F. H. S.

Cooper, James Fenimore. Battle of Lake Erie; or Answers to Messrs. Burges, Duer and Mackenzie.   Cooperstown: Phinney.   1843.
                                       [**1721**

An exposition of disputed points in the battle of Lake Erie, intended not only to clear Capt. Elliott from charges reflecting upon his conduct, but to defend Cooper's *History of the War of 1812* against many hostile critics. The manœuvres of the two fleets, and especially of the Niagara, are given with great particularity, assisted by diagrams. Less an account of the battle than a rancorously combative cross-examination of authors who had written of it. Sharp and hot-tempered, it is a revelation of Cooper at the climax of the controversial period of his career.
                                       F. H. S.

See, also, sect. 1717.

Cruikshank, *Lt.-Col.* Ernest. Battle of Lundy's Lane. 3d ed., rev. Niagara Falls South, Ont.: Lundy's Lane Hist. Soc. 1895. 25c.

—— Battle of Queenston Heights. 2d ed. rev. Niagara Falls South, Ont.: Lundy's Lane Hist. Soc. 1891. 25c.

—— Drummond's winter campaign, 1813. 2d ed. Niagara Falls South, Ont.: Lundy's Lane Hist. Soc. 1899. 15c.

—— Fight in the beechwoods. 2d ed. Niagara Falls South, Ont.: Lundy's Lane Hist. Soc. 1895. 25c.   [**1722**

The most conscientious and painstaking of special studies, the author supplementing his patient study of many publications by the use of important new material and by intimate knowledge of military duty and the topography of the Niagara peninsula. These and other pamphlets from Lt.-Col. Cruikshank's pen are models of dispassionate research. Although pro-British sympathies are occasionally disclosed, there is always evident a desire to recognize and state the truth. The style is engaging, seldom ornate, but always natural and forceful.   F. H. S.

—— Battle-fields of the Niagara peninsula during the war, 1812–15. (In Canadian Military Institute. Transactions, 1890–1; also Selected papers. Toronto.)   [1723

A lecture delivered before the Canadian Military Institute in which he deals with the history of the war in its military aspects. The accounts of the battles are in the main condensations of his monographs on *Queenston Heights, Beechwoods, Fort Erie*, and *Lundy's Lane* in the *Lundy's Lane Hist. Soc. Col.* These are based principally on documents in the Canadian archives, and take the British, in preference to the American, view. No previous writer has gone into the consideration of the movements with the same minuteness.   J. B.

See, also, note above.

—— *comp.* Documentary history of the campaign upon the Niagara frontier in the years 1812–14; collected and ed. for the Lundy's Lane Historical Soc. Welland. 1897–1900. Pts. 1–4. Niagara Falls South, Ont. $2.75.   [1724–5

"The despatches and reports of each side are arranged chronologically, and the student is able to follow closely the course of events, the changing intentions of either side, the fears and the hopes which alternately depressed and stimulated the British and the American forces. The secrets of the respective generals are laid bare, and the deficiencies of the two armies revealed." University of Toronto. *Review of historical publications relating to Canada*, 1899.

The first part contains the most of the important papers to be found in the Canadian archives, relating to the conflict in 1812–14. The second part, in addition to the British despatches, contains a large number of American, taken from official and non-official publications. Many letters from the papers of the Hon. P. A. Porter are, for the first time, printed, together with extracts from the report of the Loyal and Patriotic Society of Upper Canada. The collection is invaluable for a study of that portion of the war.   J. B.

Cullum, *Maj.-Gen.* **George Washington.** Campaigns of the war of 1812–15, against Great Britain, sketched and criticised; with brief biographies of the American engineers. N. Y.: Miller. 1879.   [1726

Not a minute history of the war, but studies of the chief operations in their tactical and strategical aspects. An admirable attempt to bring out clearly the truth on many disputed points, and to bestow praise where it rightfully belongs. Especially valuable are

the copious biographical data, and the *Journal of the northwestern campaign of 1812–13, under Maj.-Gen. Wm. H. Harrison*, by Bvt. Lt.-Col. Eleazer D. Wood, here first published.   F. H. S.

Decatur, *Commodore* **Stephen.** MACKENZIE, ALEXANDER SLIDELL. Life of Stephen Decatur. Boston: Little. 1846.

—— *Same.* (Sparks, J., ed. Library of Am. biog., ser. 2, v. 11. Boston. 1864.)   [1727

Compiled from manuscript material furnished by the Decatur family and from printed matter available at the time of writing. Written in the high-flown style of the first half of the 19th century. The standard memoir of Commodore Decatur.   E. C.

Gleig, George Robert. Narrative of the campaigns of the British army at Washington and New Orleans, 1814–15. By an officer who served in the expedition. London: Murray. 1821.

—— *Same*, at Washington, Baltimore and New Orleans. Phil.: Carey. 1821.

—— Campaigns of the British army at Washington and New Orleans, 1814–15. 4th ed., corr. and rev. London: Murray. 1861.   [1728

"The author served in the British army (subsequently chaplain of H. M. forces), and his narrative of the Washington campaign, based upon his journal, is exceedingly temperate and valuable. Although not without inaccuracies, its tone is judicial, and the author evidently intends to be fair." J. R. Soley, in *Narrative and critical hist. of Am.*, 7: 435.

Great Britain. *Admiralty.* Papers relating to the war with America. London. 1815.   [1729

Give returns of the British armaments on the lakes, the vessels captured and destroyed by the Americans, returns of Americans taken prisoners, and American vessels captured.

Halbert, H. S., *and* **T. H. Ball.** The Creek war of 1813–14. Chicago: Donohue. 1895.   [1730

Describes in detail the earlier portion of the war. Compiled from all available material — original, secondary, and traditional. Often prejudiced, but indispensable to an understanding of the events described. Poorly illustrated.   E. C.

Hatch, *Col.* **William Stanley.** A chapter of the history of the War of 1812 in the northwest; with biographical sketch of the celebrated Indian chief Tecumseh. Cin.: Clarke. 1872. $1.25.   [1731

An account of Hull's surrender of Detroit, Aug. 16, 1812, and related events, by the acting Asst. Quartermaster-General in that campaign. Hull's conduct is attributed to connivance with the British general, Brock, a theory to which Hatch's allegations lend color, though inadequate as proof. A soldier's, not a scholar's narrative; crude, unliterary, but of value because of its first-hand information, much of it not elsewhere given; feeble in generalizations beyond the author's personal knowledge.   F. H. S.

Headley, Joel Tyler. Second war with England. N. Y.: Scribner. 1853. 2v. [**1732**
Pleasantly written, but animated throughout by an intensely anti-British feeling. The book is based largely on contemporary newspaper accounts, and reproduces all the misconceptions and misrepresentations of the war period. It refuses to see any good in those who were fighting for their homes and country. For history it substitutes that inflation, and that denial of the rights of others, which we now associate with yellow journalism.   J. B.

Hull, *Brig.-Gen.* **William.** CAMPBELL, *Mrs.* MARIA (HULL). Revolutionary services and civil life of General William Hull. N. Y.: Appleton. 1848.   [**1733**
1753–1825. The work includes also the separately titled but continuously paged *History of the campaign of 1812, and the surrender of Detroit,* for which Hull was court-martialled. The first part is by his daughter on the basis of an autobiography, and the latter part by his grandson, James Freeman Clarke. The second work is of course vindicatory and appreciative, but its results are on the whole accepted.   E. C. R.

Ingersoll, Charles Jared. Historical sketch of the second war between the United States and Great Britain. Phil.: Lea. 1845–9. 2v.
—— History of the second war. Ser. 2. Phil.: Lippincott. 1852. 2v.   [**1734**
Ingersoll wrote from personal knowledge, being a member of Congress during the war, and on " intimate and confidential terms " with most of the administration. He was a Republican, a violent partisan, dogmatic and deeply prejudiced, particularly against the Federalists. He has many shrewd and profound observations on the political measures of the time, and his character sketches are frequently just, sometimes unfair, always striking. He digresses occasionally, as in the case of the Second Bank of the United States, of which he gives a complete sketch. His work possesses great value, though much in relation to the war is now known which was hidden from contemporaries. The reader will find the book entertaining.   R. C. H. C.

Jackson, *Maj.-Gen.* **Andrew.** WALKER, ALEXANDER. Life of Andrew Jackson: the achievements of the American army at New Orleans, 1814–15. Phil.: Evans. 1860. [**1735**
This book is misnamed. It is in fact an intensive study of the battle of New Orleans, with only a preliminary chapter on the early life of Jackson. It closes with the end of the battle. The author seems to have visited the places about which he writes. The style is lively and the book entertaining, but without references for its statements.   E. E. S.

James, William. Full and correct account

of the chief naval occurrences of the late war between Great Britain and the United States. London. 1817.   [**1736**
Much of the substance of this volume appeared in the *Naval chronicle* during the years 1813 and 1814, and was subsequently published at Halifax, N. S., as a pamphlet in March, 1816, entitled *An inquiry into the merits of the principal naval actions between Great Britain and the United States of America during the late war.* In a condensed and revised form it has been virtually incorporated with the sixth volume of his best-known work, the *Naval history of Great Britain,* which has been reprinted four times since its publication in 1823. In spite of an uncouth style and bitterly controversial and biased tone, James still remains the standard British authority on this subject; as a rule his statements have been unhesitatingly accepted and reiterated by later writers of his own nationality.   E. Cr.

—— Full and correct account of the military occurrences of the late war between Great Britain and the United States. London. 1818. 2v.   [**1737**
"The companion piece to the *Naval occurrences.* Its tone is equally offensive, and its comments are of the same scurrilous character. When dealing with the enemies of his country, James is nothing if not vituperative. The War of 1812, with its absurd generals and its farcical strategy, affords a fine opportunity for caustic humor, but James only makes it the occasion of a tirade of vulgar abuse. The value of the book consists chiefly in the official reports and documents which it contains." J. R. Soley, in *Narrative and crit. hist. of Am.,* 7: 425.

—— Naval history of Great Britain, 1793– 1820. London. 1822. 5v. and 2v. Tables.
—— *Same;* [ed. by Capt. F. Chamier]. London. 1837. 6v.
—— *Same;* epitomised by Robert O'Byrne. London : Allen. 1888.   [**1738**
"Vol. 6 treats principally of the naval operations during the American war. The book shows much careful and even minute investigation, but its partisan reasoning is carried to the furthest limit of special pleading. . . . In dealing with matters exclusively British, James will generally be found a safe guide, but in his volume on the American war he has lost or sunk all sense of fairness or candor." J. R. Soley, in *Narrative and crit. hist. of Am.,* 7 : 422.

Johnson, Rossiter. History of the war of 1812–'15. (Minor wars of the U. S.) N. Y.: Dodd. [c. 1882.] $1.   [**1739**
A description of the land and naval battles, with chapters on the causes of the war, and the Hartford convention, by a voluminous writer. The style is easy and the book readable, but shows no evidence of investigation or new matter.   E. E. S.

Latour, *Maj.* **Arsène Lacarrière.** Historical memoir of the war in West Florida and Louisiana in 1814–15; tr. [from the French] by H. P. Nugent. Phil: Conrad. 1816. [**1740**

A succinct and graphic account of the campaign that culminated in the battle of New Orleans. The first appearance of the British fleet in the Gulf; the attempt before Mobile; Barrataria; Lafitte's gallant attitude; Jackson; the marshalling of his forces, and means for defence of New Orleans; the final and glorious victory of the 8th January,—are described in pages that still glow with the freshness of their first writing. An appendix contains copies of the official documents relating to the campaign, and a series of maps shows the military points involved in it.

G. K.

"Latour [who was Gen. Jackson's chief engineer] is the only trustworthy contemporary American historian of this war, and even he at times absurdly exaggerates the British forces and loss." Theodore Roosevelt, *Naval war of 1812*, p. 483, note.

Lossing, Benson John. Pictorial field-book of the War of 1812. N. Y.: Harper. 1868.

[**1741**

"This is a noteworthy work, partaking of the nature of what the French call *mémoires pour servir à l'histoire*, and a rich archæological collection, with its . . . sketches, views, plans, monuments, portraits, caricatures, autographs, medals, arms, remarkable houses, and scraps of contemporaneous poetry. Not only is the history of the campaigning of 1812-14 attempted, but also that of the civil administration and leading political events of the period extending from the Revolution to the treaty of Ghent. To these are added personal sketches and biographies. . . . Note-book and pencil in hand, the author has travelled more than ten thousand miles between the Great Lakes and the Gulf of Mexico, visiting nearly all the scenes of the incidents recorded, receiving accounts from survivors, and sketching scenery, battle-fields, and notable localities. . . . Criticism of the book as a history of the War of 1812, or of the civil and political events of the period, is disarmed by its title. So much diversified material enters into its composition that the unity and sequence of a strictly historical narrative must necessarily suffer. Omissions, contradictions, and confusion of detail necessarily occur. . . . The military operations are well described for popular reading, and many of the battles, particularly the naval engagements, are admirably painted in words." *Nation*, 9 : 569.

McAfee, Robert B. History of the late war in the western country, comprising a full account of all the transactions in that quarter, from the commencement of hostilities at Tippecanoe, to the termination of the contest at New Orleans on the return of peace. Lexington: Worsley. 1816.

[**1742**

"The author of this now scarce work sought and obtained a large amount of information, regarding the Indian wars of the western frontier, from the actors engaged in them. His narrative, therefore, contains much material, which later histories either do not possess, or only copy from his pages." T. W. Field, *Indian bibliography*, p. 251.

Martineau, Harriet. History of England, 1800-15; being an introduction to the history of the peace. London: Bell. 1878. [**1743**

Miss Martineau treats of social as well as political history. She had a strong, active intellect, was liberal-minded, and possessed keen insight into character and events. She diligently searched through a great part of the material then accessible to the historian in England (1850), and has written a useful, interesting and fairly accurate book. R. C. H. C.

Morris, *Commodore* Charles. Autobiography; [pref. by J. R. Soley]. Boston: Williams. 1880. [**1744**

"Unique. It is the only narrative published by a naval officer of the older period, giving in his own words the story of his own life. It begins with Morris's entry into the service in 1799, and ends in 1840." J. R. Soley, in *Narrative and critical hist. of Am.*, 7 : 417.

Perkins, Samuel. History of the political and military events of the late war between the United States and Great Britain. New Haven. 1825. [**1745**

One of the best histories of the War of 1812. It narrates with sufficient fulness the land and naval operations; brings out clearly the points of controversy which led to the war, the national questions involved and the effect on party spirit and the character of the people. Although like all American histories of its period, it is strongly partisan, it takes due recognition of the claims of both parties to the conflict, and obviously aims to present the truth with judicial impartiality. The work is not free from errors, mostly typographical. The diction is concise, lucid and agreeable. F. H. S.

Perry, *Commodore* Oliver Hazard. BARNES, JAMES. The hero of Erie. (Young heroes of our navy.) N. Y.: Appleton. 1898. $1.

[**1746**

A biography of Commodore Perry, written for the young in an animated style which sometimes slips into poor English. Slight typographical inaccuracies occur in the account of operations on Lake Erie and the Niagara; but as a whole the sketch is admirably planned to teach American history and strengthen the manliness, self-reliance and patriotism of the young American. F. H. S.

Red Jacket. HUBBARD, J. NILES. Account of Sa-go-ye-wat-ha; or Red Jacket and his people, 1750-1830. (Munsell's historical series, no. 13.) Albany: Munsell. 1886. [**1747**

A futile attempt to do greater justice to Red Jacket than Wm. L. Stone had done, years before (see below). It offers no new information of importance, and presents few facts which may not be found better stated elsewhere. The author unduly exalts the character of the "orator of the Senecas," and overestimates his influence. The style is sometimes ornate, grandiose, but oftener barren. F. H. S.

— STONE, WILLIAM LEETE. Life and times

of Sa-go-ye-wat-ha, or Red Jacket. N. Y. 1841. Albany: Munsell. 1866. [1748

"Col. Stone has connected, in a very happy manner, with the life of Red Jacket, a number of anecdotes and sketches, particularly of our war of 1812 with England, which add greatly to the interest and value of his work. His narration of many facts and movements on the northern frontier during that war; his account of the battle of Chippewa and its effects; of the principles and conduct of the Indians in our contest with Great Britain; of several Indian treaties, and sales of their lands; and of a number of the interviews of Red Jacket with distinguished men, both foreigners and native Americans, render his volume as entertaining as a novel." S. Miller, in *Princeton review*, 14: 194.

Richardson, *Maj.* John. War of 1812. 1st series; containing a full and detailed narrative of the operations of the right division of the Canadian army. Brockville. 1842. [1749

Much of the text was originally published in the *London monthly magazine* in 1826–7 under the title of "A Canadian campaign by a British officer." Amplified in some respects and curtailed in others, it next appeared in weekly parts in the *New era or Canadian chronicle*, at Brockville, Upper Canada, and finally in book form as above. The author served during the campaigns in the vicinity of Detroit, which he undertakes to describe as a volunteer attached to the 41st Regiment, depending on his recollections, with the help of a few official documents. The narrative is generally fluent and vivid, but in many instances inaccurate in detail and intemperate in judgment. It abounds, however, in local color and deserves attention as the statement of an eye-witness. E. Cr.

Roosevelt, Theodore. The naval war of 1812. N. Y.: Putnam. 1882. $2.50. [1750

A history of the navy during this war from good, often original sources. The appendix includes a brief "Previous history of the U. S. Navy." Impartial, reliable, and scientific, without being dry. It is incidentally a source for the naval history of 1898, as giving a key to Assistant Secretary Roosevelt's preparations. E. C. R.

Russell, J., Jr. History of the war between the United States and Great-Britain, compiled chiefly from public documents. Hartford: Russell. 1815. [1751

Contains a list of vessels captured from Great Britain during the war.

Thomson, John Lewis. History of the war of the United States with Great Britain in 1812; with additions and corrections. Phil.: Lippincott. 1887. [1752

Early editions published in 1816 and 1818. "Contains much detail, but is of doubtful value." J. R. Soley, in *Narrative and critical hist of Am.*, 7: 422.

Van Rensselaer, Solomon. Narrative of the affair of Queenston: in the War of 1812. N. Y. 1836. [1753

Far from adequate as a history of the battle of Queenston (Oct. 11, 1812), but more than adequate as a vindication of the conduct and discretion of Maj.-Gen. Stephen Van Rensselaer, as presented in Armstrong's *Notices of the War of 1812*. Lt.-Col. Solomon Van Rensselaer, nephew of the general, was an aide on his staff, and shared in the battle. The soldier's honest account of what he saw and experienced is supplemented by rancorous rebuttal of Armstrong's strictures. The "Narrative" informs the student of to-day not only of events of a battle, but of the bitter enmities and controversies that grew out of it.
F. H. S.

WESTWARD EXPANSION: 1783–1828

(See sect. 2016–2077, also, in Part IV)

Adams, Herbert Baxter. Maryland's influence upon land cessions to the United States. (Johns Hopkins Univ. studies, ser. 3, no. 1.) Balt. 1885. 75c. [1754

Commended by Justin Winsor, in *Narrative and critical hist. of Am.*, 5: 271.

Annals of the west, to 1845; comp. by James H. Perkins. Cin.: J. R. Albach. 1846. —— *Same*, to 1850. 2d ed.; rev. and enlarged by J. M. Peck. St. Louis: J. R. Albach. 1850. —— *Same*, to 1856; comp. from the most authentic sources and published by James R. Albach. Pittsburg: W. S. Haven. 1856. [1755

"James Handasyd Perkins was a careful student of the early history of the country, and contributed many articles to the periodical literature of his day on the subject of Indian history and border warfare, which have been collected," in the *Memoir and writings of James Handasyd Perkins*, edited by William Henry Channing, and published in 2 vols. at Boston, in 1851. Andrew McFarland Davis, in *Narrative and critical hist. of Am.*, 6: 648.

Barbé-Marbois, François, *marquis* de. History of Louisiana; tr. from the French. Phil.: Carey. 1830. [1756

The true intention of the author is set forth in his sub-title: "Particularly of the cession of the colony to the United States." The history that precedes the account of this transaction is a mere summary to explain and justify the political necessity of it to his countrymen, for whose enlightenment upon the subject he avowedly wrote. As the commissioner appointed by Bonaparte to represent France in the preliminary negotiations with the United States, Barbé-Marbois was well qualified to be the historian of the event; and his book has proved the general source of information about it. The vividness of its style quickens the usual tedium of diplomatic negotiations into a real dramatic interest, which culminates in the cession as a climax rather than as a result.

G. K.

Barker, Jacob. Incidents in life of Jacob Barker, of New Orleans. Wash. 1855. [**1757**

A curious and interesting collection of incidents and documents illustrative of the financial and political career of a man of much note in his day. Published to further a claim against the Government, for money loaned during the War of 1812; and from material of the claimant's own furnishing, the volume represents but a fragmentary value. The second volume, promised in the Introduction, which would have dealt with the more interesting period of Mr. Barker's life, and political and financial experiences in New Orleans before and during the Civil War, has never been published.   G. K.

Barrett, Jay Amos. Evolution of the Ordinance of 1787. (Univ. of Nebraska. Depts. of History and Economics. Seminary papers.) N. Y.: Putnam. 1891.   [**1758**

An admirably clear and methodical history of the Ordinance of 1787 up to its adoption. Mr. Barrett treats impartially and judicially the rival claimants for the honor of having shaped the tenor of the Ordinance. There are full references to the sources, bibliographical notes preceding each chapter and finally an alphabetical list of authorities.   E. G. B.

Birkbeck, Morris. Letters from Illinois. Phil.: Carey. 1818.   [**1759**

The author, an English communist, in 1817 purchased 16,000 acres on English Prairie, Illinois, founding thereon the town of New Albion, which was settled by English immigrants. The volume consists of letters written to persons in England, in reply to questions relative to economic and social conditions in the West. It is an intelligent, discriminating statement by a foreigner who soon came to understand his adopted country, and did much to inspire and wisely direct English emigration into Illinois. The *Letters* contains two maps — one, showing Birkbeck's journey (1817) from Virginia to Illinois; the other, of English Prairie and adjacent country.

R. G. T.

—— Notes on a journey in America. London: Ridgway. 1818. Phil.: Richardson. 1817.   [**1760**

This is a brief and intelligent account of the journey of an English farmer travelling from Virginia to Illinois Territory, then a frontier settlement. Birkbeck was a radical both in politics and religion, and his judgments show a slight bias. He had a keen eye for a suitable place for future settlement and, in agricultural matters, showed practical knowledge. The book gives a vivid picture of the difficulties attending pioneer settlement. It passed through several editions in England.   D. R. D.

Blanchard, Rufus. Discovery and conquests of the northwest. Chicago: Cushing. 1880.

[**1761**

"Chicago is the oldest Indian town in the west of which the original name is retained. Its history naturally involves an account of the three conquests of the country in which it is situated. The first of the six parts covers the history of the French conquest from the exploration of the St. Lawrence by Jacques Cartier, and closes with a narrative of Bouquet's expedition, from an account printed by T. Jefferies, London, in 1766. This covers a period of great historical interest, concerning many of the details of which there has been controversy. Day by day, however, materials to control individual statements are being brought to light. Mr. Blanchard has made use of the best materials and put them together in an attractive way. We hesitate to question the correctness of the origin of the name given, but we refer Mr. Blanchard to La Salle's account of the rivers and peoples discovered by him in 1681-2 (*Mag. of Am. hist.*, 2: 619), in which he will find the word Chucugoa, which means 'the Great River.' This seems conclusive." *Magazine of American history*, 4: 318.

Blennerhassett, Harman. SAFFORD, WILLIAM HARRISON. The Blennerhassett papers; embodying the private journal of Harman Blennerhassett, and the hitherto unpublished correspondence of Burr, Alston, and others, developing the purposes and aims of those engaged in the attempted Wilkinson and Burr revolution; 'also the first account of the "Spanish Association of Kentucky," and a memoir of Blennerhassett. Cin.: Clarke. 1864. $3.

[**1762**

The author published a small life of Blennerhassett in 1850, but having secured the papers in the possession of the Blennerhassett family, he issued this work, the changes and additions in which were so numerous that, he says, it may be regarded as a separate and independent publication. It narrates the story of the Burr conspiracy with much fullness and contains Blennerhassett's journal (Aug. 4 to Nov. 20, 1807), covering the entire trial at Richmond, but there is lack of literary skill, the account of Wilkinson's Spanish intrigue being given in two widely separated chapters, the 5th and 15th.   F. J. S.

Boone, *Col.* Daniel. ELLIS, EDWARD SYLVESTER. Life and times of Col. Daniel Boone with sketches of other leaders in the settlement of the West. Phil.: Porter; Coates. [c. 1884.] 75c.   [**1763**

A popular account of a notable life, written in a pleasing style, occasionally rhetorical. A boys' book.   H. W. H.

See, also, Filson, John, sect. 1777.

Breese, Sidney. Early history of Illinois, 1673–1763, including the narrative of Marquette's discovery of the Mississippi; ed. by Thomas Hoyne. Chicago: Meyers. 1884. Net $3.   [**1764**

A scholarly sketch of the French occupation of the Illinois country from its discovery to 1763. Written by a resident of Kaskaskia (Illinois) and from sources to be found there. It seems to be a portion of a projected history of the state. The book contains also a biographical sketch of Judge Breese, with an appendix of translations of pertinent French documents, and facsimiles of Marquette's maps. E. E. S.

Brown, John Mason. Political beginnings of Kentucky. (Filson Club. Publications, no. 6.) Louisville: Morton. 1889. Net $2.50. [1765

A valuable contribution to an interesting subject; but written primarily to clear the memory of the author's ancestor, John Brown, one of the foremost men of his time west of the Alleghany Mountains, of the charge of complicity in the plan to separate Kentucky from the Union and unite it with the Spanish Government of Louisiana. See Green, *The Spanish conspiracy*, sect. 1784. B. A. H.

Burnet, Jacob. Notes on the early settlement of the north-western territory. Cin.: Derby. 1847. [1766

A valuable original contribution to the early history of the Northwest and particularly of Ohio. The author, educated at Nassau Hall and bred to the law in New Jersey, made his home in Cincinnati in 1796 and died in that city in 1853. He rode the circuit with the territorial judges; filled numerous important offices; was an active participant in many of the events which he relates; a strong Federalist, but very sensible of the faults of Governor Arthur St. Clair. The book is not to be implicitly trusted, although perfectly sincere and aiming to be impartial. The author depended too much upon his memory, which he did not sufficiently refresh by reference to authorities. B. A. H.

Cass, Lewis, *et al.* Historical and scientific sketches of Michigan. Detroit. 1834. [1767

These sketches and discourses, delivered by Governor Cass, H. R. Schoolcraft, Henry Whiting, and John Biddle, are interesting and valuable because they belong to the early literature of Michigan. For the rest, they deal instructively with the more salient facts of Michigan and northwestern history, and to a less extent with scientific observation of nature. B. A. H.

Coles, Edward. History of the Ordinance of 1787. See Pennsylvania, Historical Society of, sect. 385. [1768

Craig, Neville B., *ed.* The olden time. Pittsburg. 1846–8. 2v. New ed. Cin.: Clarke. 1876. 2v. $6. [1769

A mixture of original journals, reminiscences, and records, with many reprints from papers of Washington, Franklin and others, descriptive of the early history of western Pennsylvania and eastern Ohio. A large portion can be found in the Pennsylvania Archives. Has articles on the various Pennsylvania boundary disputes, the French in Ohio, Mason and Dixon line, etc. Of local value for the region named. E. E. S.

Cutler, Ephraim. CUTLER, JULIA PERKINS. Life and times of Ephraim Cutler; prepared from his journals and correspondence, by his daughter, with biographical sketches of Jervis Cutler and William Parker Cutler. Cin.: Clarke. 1890. $2.50. [1770

The subject of this book, a son of Dr. Manasseh Cutler, made his home in Ohio, 1795, and died there in 1853. He was active in the affairs of the state as well as in private life. He served many years in the General Assembly, where he interested himself especially in education, taxation, and internal improvements. The book throws light upon these and other questions relating to the growth of Ohio; it contains much documentary material. B. A. H.

Cutler, Manasseh. CUTLER, WILLIAM PARKER *and* JULIA PERKINS. Life, journals, and correspondence of Rev. Manasseh Cutler. Cin.: Clarke. 1888. 2v. Net $5. [1771

The most complete account ever published of the beginnings of the colonial system of the United States, in the first settlement and civil organization of the region beyond the Ohio River, grouped around the personality of one of the most prominent actors in the events themselves. The theory first brought forward prominently by the late Dr. W. F. Poole (see sect. 1807), that Dr. Cutler was the real author of the most characteristic features of the Ordinance of 1787, is pushed to its extreme limit, and sometimes supported by arguments that cannot be considered valid. Much of the matter is documentary, and the book does not show much literary skill. B. A. H.

Cutler, William Parker. The Ordinance of July 13, 1787, for the government of the territory northwest of the River Ohio. Marietta, O.: E. R. Alderman. 1887. [1772

A valuable study of the Ordinance from the historical point of view, by an admiring descendant of the pioneers. Prepared as a paper for reading before the Ohio State Hist. and Archæol. Soc. Feb. 23, 1887. The Appendices discuss the Origin of the Ohio Co. (with names of petitioners to Congress): — The character of Marietta pioneers — in memoriam: — Services of the Ohio Co. in defending the U. S. frontier from invasion: — and the Soc. of the Cincinnati. A useful monograph. H. W. H.

Denny, Ebenezer. Military journal of an officer in the Revolutionary and Indian wars; with an introductory memoir by W. H. Denny. (In Hist. Soc. of Pennsylvania. Publications, v. 7.) Phil.: Lippincott. 1860. [1773

Maj. Denny, who had seen service on an American privateer and who lived to be the first mayor of Pittsburg, joined a Pennsylvania regiment as an ensign in 1781, participated in the siege of Yorktown, and was the adjutant of Harmar and an aide-de-camp of St. Clair during the disastrous Indian campaigns of 1790–1, bringing the news of St. Clair's defeat to Philadelphia. The journal extends from May 1, 1781, to May 31, 1795, with a gap from 1792 to 1794. There are diagrams illustrating the campaigns of Harmar and St. Clair, and a number of Harmar's letters and vocabularies of Delaware and Shawanee words are appended.   F. J. S.

Dodge, Jacob Richards. Red men of the Ohio valley, 1650–1795. Springfield, O.: Ruralist Pub. Co. 1860.   [**1774**

"Embracing notable facts and thrilling incidents in the settlement by the whites of the states of Kentucky, Ohio, Indiana, and Illinois." The author was editor of *The American ruralist*, at Springfield; he frankly confesses that his book is largely a compilation, "hastily prepared" from such works as Jefferson's *Notes on Virginia* (1787), Boone's *Life* (1823), McDonald's *Biographical sketches of . . . early settlers in the western country* (1838), Bradford's *Notes on the Northwest* (1847), Burnet's *Notes on the North-western Territory* (1847), and Taylor's *Ohio* (1854). It is one of a large class of similarly constructed popular books on frontier life in the middle West. It is useful as a compilation, but has the ill-digested character of a scrapbook, and cannot be cited as authority.
                    R. G. T.

Dunn, Jacob Piat, Jr. Indiana: a redemption from slavery. (Am. commonwealths.) Boston: Houghton. 1888. $1.25.   [**1775**

This book gives a general view of Indiana from the time when the first French explorers entered the country to the admission of the state to the Union. The interest, however, centres in the sub-title. The attempt to break down the prohibition of slavery incorporated in the Ordinance of 1787 was vigorous and persistent, though not in the end successful, and this work gives the best accessible account of the struggle.
                    B. A. H.

Ellicott, Andrew. Journal of Andrew Ellicott, late commissioner on behalf of the United States, 1796–1800, for determining the boundary between the United States and the possessions of his most catholic majesty in America, etc. Phil. 1814.   [**1776**

Ellicott, who had been Surveyor-General of the United States, went down the Ohio and Mississippi Rivers in flat-boats, noting everything that caught his trained scientific eye on the route. He had among his companions a part of the way the famous Philip Nolan, who was afterwards killed by the Spaniards in Texas. Ellicott was detained over a year at Natchez by the unwillingness of the Spanish authorities to carry out the treaty of San Lorenzo el Real by joining him in running the boundary line, and this delay enables him to give a long account of the political troubles of the Mississippi territory and of British intrigues there. Ultimately the boundary line was surveyed from the Mississippi River to the Atlantic Ocean, Mr. Ellicott returning north in a sailing vessel. Chapter 4 contains an interesting description of the Mississippi River, and a footnote supplies a translation of Louis XV's order giving up Louisiana to Spain.
                    F. J. S.

Filson, John. Discovery, settlement and present state of Kentucke. Wilmington. 1784.

— **DURRETT, R. T.** John Filson; the first historian of Kentucky: account of his life and writings. (Filson Club. Publications, no. 1.) Louisville: Morton. 1884.   [**1777**

"Filson's book was issued in French, at Paris, in 1785, and reprinted in English in Imlay's *Topographical description of North America* (London, 1793 and 1797), in conjunction with Imlay; again by Campbell in New York, in 1793. Filson first presented to the world the story of the adventures of Daniel Boone in the appendix of his book, and from that it has been copied and assigned to Boone himself. . . . The life of Boone embodies much of the history of the pioneer days of Kentucky. His subsequent biographers . . . have depended upon Filson." W. F. Poole, *Narrative and critical hist. of America*, 6: 708.

"Principally interesting on account of its map and for the personal reminiscences of Daniel Boone. It laid the foundations of Boone's enduring reputation as a hero of western life." N. S. Shaler, *Kentucky*, v. 1.

Flint, Timothy. Condensed geography and history of the western states, or the Mississippi valley. Cin.: Flint. 1828. 2v.

—— History and geography of the Mississippi valley, [with] a physical geography of the whole American continent. 2d ed. Cin.: Flint. 1832. 2v.   [**1778**

"Timothy Flint was extensively read and widely beloved. A native of Massachusetts, and by profession a clergyman, he entered on a missionary life in the valley of the Mississippi in 1815; sojourning in Ohio, Indiana, Kentucky, Missouri, Arkansas, and Louisiana, now as a teacher and now as a preacher; at home in the wilderness, a favorite in society. . . . The peculiar value of Timothy Flint's account of the remarkable region of whose history and aspect he wrote consists in the fact that it is not the result of a cursory survey or rapid tour, but of years of residence, intimate contact with nature and man, and patient observation. The record thus prepared is one which will often be consulted by subsequent writers." H. T. Tuckerman, in *America and her commentators*, p. 402.

Flower, Richard. Letters from Lexington and the Illinois. London. 1819.   [**1779**

A few letters written whilst the author was travelling from Lexington, Kentucky, through the communistic settlement at New Harmony, Indiana, to the English colony at Albion, Illinois. Valuable chiefly because of the rarity of contemporary accounts of English colonization in the Mississippi valley. Supplemented by the writer's *Letters from the Illinois*. (See next title.)   E. E. S.

—— Letters from the Illinois, 1820–1. London: Ridgway. 1822.   [**1780**

Describing the condition and environment of Birkbeck's English colony at Albion, Illinois, southwest of Vincennes, Indiana. Written to encourage migration and to refute the charges against the region made by William Cobbett in his *Weekly political register* during the year 1821. On same topic see Morris Birkbeck's *Notes on a journey*, etc. (sect. 1760), and the first volume of the Chicago Historical Society's *Collections*.   E. E. S.

Ford, Worthington Chauncey, *comp.* The United States and Spain in 1790. (Historical Printing Club. Winnowings in American history. Diplomatic ser., no. 1.) Brooklyn. 1890.   [**1781**

An Introduction of 42 pp. describes the first question in diplomacy after the inauguration of the government under the Constitution. Then comes about 60 pp. of documents, some printed for the first time. Valuable, well-written and interesting.   E. C.

Franchère, Gabriel. Narrative of a voyage to the northwest coast of America, 1811–14; or The first American settlement on the Pacific; tr. and ed. by J. V. Huntington. N. Y.: Redfield. 1854.   [**1782**

This is an English translation made by J. V. Huntington, from the Montreal edition of 1819. Monsieur Franchère, a young French Canadian, was employed in 1810 by John Jacob Astor, to help in founding Astoria. His modest little book was quoted from by Senator Benton in the boundary dispute of 1846 and was liberally drawn upon by Washington Irving. Franchère's narrative of the famous and unfortunate voyage of the Tonquin, on which vessel he was one of the clerks, should always be read in connection with Irving's more brilliant but less accurate *Astoria*. Franchère's narrative is a very unpretending and fair-minded book. The translator justly speaks of the "clerkly minuteness of details," and their accuracy is manifest in every line. There is an abiding literary charm about the story. It would justify a modern dress, with illustrations, if the latter were really historical, and with notes, if some one like the late Dr. Coues could be found to undertake them.   C. H. S.

Giddings, Joshua Reed. Exiles of Florida. Columbus, O.: Follett. 1858.   [**1783**

The "exiles" are the fugitive Indian and negro slaves who fled from the Carolinas and Georgia to Spanish protection in the Floridas. In this connection the author treats of the Seminole Indian wars, the troubles between the Seminoles and Creeks, and the final flight of the remnant of the "exiles" to Mexico. The author, being an ardent anti-slavery agitator, writes from that view-point. The latter portion of the book has no official basis. See the *Atlantic monthly*, September, 1858.   E. E. S.

Green, Thomas Marshall. The Spanish conspiracy: a review of early Spanish movements in the south-west. Cin.: Clarke. 1891.   [**1784**

This work deals with an important but keenly controverted subject in an acutely controversial spirit. Family feeling in Kentucky has entered deeply into the matter, and the author may be said to hold the brief of one side to the quarrel. The book is a reply to John Mason Brown's *The political beginnings of Kentucky* (sect. 1765), and will be valuable to the student of the general subject.   B. A. H.

Hale, Will T. The backward trail: stories of the Indians and Tennessee pioneers. Nashville: Cumberland Press. 1899. 75c. [**1785**

"This book is a series of sketches of early Tennessee history, ranging, in a way, over the period from the earliest discovery of the soil to 1800. While the book concerns itself principally with the picturesque features of pioneer life, particularly with incidents of heroism, there is also an outline of the history of the time, but this outline is apparently constructed mainly to serve as a framework for the stories, and, such as it is, after a few chapters it fairly fades away. The stories are culled from the older writers, and even in the telling of them there is little that is new." Edmund C. Burnett, *Am. hist. rev.*, 5: 400.

Hall, James. Letters from the West. London: Colburn. 1828.   [**1786**

Descriptions of travels along the Ohio River and adjacent states, originally printed in the *Portfolio* (Phil.). Describes the Cumberland Road, Burr's expedition, Boone and the Kentucky frontiersmen, routes and means of travel, border superstition, etc. Extremely verbose. Useful for its view of the development of the middle West.   E. E. S.

—— Romance of western history. Cin.: Applegate. 1857. Cin.: Clarke. 1869. $1.25.   [**1787**

This is a book manufactured out of the same author's *Sketches of history* (see title below), with the first and last parts omitted, and valueless border tales and legends added. The earlier book is stripped of nearly all that was of any historic import.   E. E. S.

—— Sketches of history, life and manners in the West. Phil.: Hall. 1835. 2v. [**1788**

A mingled traditional and authoritative account of the early settlers in the Ohio and Mississippi valleys. Shows their intercourse with the Indians, the disappearance of the French element, and the civil and military progress of the territories and states northwest of the Ohio River. The book gives a popular account of the Revolutionary state of Transylvania, and other relations of Kentucky to Virginia. The style of composition may be called diffuse.   E. E. S.

Harrison, *Maj.-Gen.* **William Henry.** DAWSON, MOSES. Historical narrative of the civil and military services of Major-General Harrison, and a vindication of his character and conduct as a statesman, a citizen, and a soldier; with a detail of his negotiations and wars with the Indians. Cin.: Dawson. 1824.   [**1789**

"One of the most thorough, complete, and authentic treatises, relating to the border wars, ever printed." T. W. Field, *Indian bibliography*, p. 96.

Henry, Alexander, *and* **David Thompson.** New light on the early history of the greater northwest: the MS. journals of Alexander Henry, fur trader, of the Northwest Company, and of David Thompson, official geographer and explorer of the same company, 1799–1814;

ed. with copious critical commentary by Elliott Coues. N. Y.: F. P. Harper. 1897. 3v. Net $10.   [**1790**

These journals of exploration and adventure among the Indians on the Red, Saskatchewan, Missouri, and Columbia rivers had never been published until taken in hand by Dr. Coues. He has not printed them in full, but has used his judgment in abridgment and selection. While much of the action lies on our side of the northwestern boundary, the work is perhaps most valuable for the light that it throws on exploration and adventure north of that line and beyond the head of the Great Lakes. The editing is of the same kind as that shown in the Lewis and Clark by the same hand, only some kinds of material are less abundant.
B. A. H.

Hermann, Binger. The Louisiana purchase and our title west of the Rocky Mountains; with a review of annexation by the United States. Washington: Govt. Prtg. Off. 1898.   [**1791**

Hermann argues the hardly disputed thesis that the Louisiana cession did not include the Oregon territory. He presents a brief history of American expansion and sketches of men prominent in the movement, also five maps, one by Franquelin (1684) and one by Moll (1710) deserving mention. He has explored no unfamiliar sources and gives no evidence of sound scholarship, while he is inaccurate in details. His dull style is occasionally enlivened by cheap rhetorical outbursts.   R. C. H. C.

Hildreth, Samuel Prescott. Biographical and historical memoirs of the early pioneer settlers of Ohio. Cin.: Derby. 1852.   [**1792**

This work is a supplement to the same author's *Pioneer history* (see following title). Its value consists in the fact that it is made up of a series of well-written biographical notices, forty in number, of the pioneers of Ohio and the Northwest, some of them men of great note in their day. These notices were prepared soon after the pioneers passed away by a competent writer who lived on the ground where these men made their first beginning, knew the traditions that lived in the community they established, and was in communication with their descendants and representatives.   B. A. H.

—— Pioneer history : first examinations of the Ohio valley and early settlement of the northwest territory. Cin.: Derby. N. Y.: Barnes. 1848.   [**1793**

After a chapter devoted to French exploration, the author enters upon his story with the first adventuring of English-speaking men into the Ohio valley, about 1740. The interest culminates in the colony [Marietta] planted by the Ohio Company in 1788. The author made large use of original manuscripts, and the work embodies considerable documentary material.   B. A. H.

Hough, Franklin Benjamin, *ed.* Diary of the siege of Detroit in the war with Pontiac ;

also, a narrative of the principal events of the siege, by Major Robert Rogers ; a plan for conducting Indian affairs, by Col. Bradstreet ; and other authentick documents never before printed. Albany: Munsell. 1860.   [**1794**

A valuable collection of documents relating to an interesting period, and especially to an interesting event, in American history. The documents are edited with judgment, including the necessary introductions and explanatory notes.   B. A. H.

Howe, Henry. Historical collections of Ohio. Cin.: Derby. 1847.
—— *Same* [enl.]. Ohio centennial ed. Columbus, O.: Howe. 1889-91. [c. 1888.] 2v.   [**1795**

An invaluable treasure house of materials relating to the history of Ohio, particularly of the first half century. The author was one of the first and best practitioners of the art of making state historical collections. He gathered the materials for his first division mainly by travelling over the state on foot and horseback, at a time when many of the pioneers were still living. This edition made Mr. Howe's name a household word in Ohio. The book has the characteristics of its class. The value of the Centennial edition was much enhanced by the addition of a considerable number of monographs by specialists on interesting phases of the general subject. B. A. H.

Howells, William Cooper. Recollections of life in Ohio, 1813-40. Cin. : Clarke. 1895. $2.   [**1796**

A pleasant picture of life in southeastern and southwestern Ohio in the period named. The many interesting facts are enlivened by wise reflection, good feeling, and strokes of humor. In politics the author was an anti-slavery Whig ; in religion his views were liberal and tolerant, not favorable to orthodoxy. His son, William Dean Howells, contributes an Introduction and Conclusion.   B. A. H.

Imlay, *Capt.* **Gilbert.** Topographical description of the western territory of North America. London : Debrett. 1792. 3d ed. 1797.   [**1797**

"Captain Imlay, of the American army, is considered the best of the early authorities in regard to the topography of the western country. The original London edition of his *Topographical description of the western territory of North America* is the result of observations made between 1792 and 1797. The third edition is much enhanced in value as a reference, by including the works of Filson, Hutchins, and other kindred material." H. T. Tuckerman, *America and her commentators*, p. 390.

Jesuit relations and allied documents, 1610-1791 : with English translations and notes ; ed. by Reuben Gold Thwaites. Cleveland : Burrows. 1896-. V. 1+. Net $3.50 ea. [**1798**
See in Part IV.

Kinzie, Juliette A. (*Mrs.* **John H.**). Waubun: the "early day" in the north-west. N. Y.: Derby. 1856. Phil.: Lippincott. 1873. [**1799**

Descriptive of a journey to the Indian agency at Fort Winnebago (Wisconsin), life among the Indians and French half-breeds, and a journey to Chicago in 1831, with details of the appearance of Chicago at that time. It contains the best account of the "Chicago (Indian) massacre" of 1812, as related by survivors. Because writings on these points are so few, this book becomes of some historic value, although it is burdened with a mass of trifling domestic details.

E. E. S.

Lanman, James H. History of Michigan, civil and topographical, in a compendious form, with a view of the surrounding lakes. N. Y.: French. 1839. [**1800**

"A minute narration of the early dealings of the whites with the aborigines of the territory, the Jesuit missions, and border wars, is given in the first ten chapters of the work." T. W. Field, *Indian bibliography*, p. 211.

M'Clung, John A. Sketches of western adventure connected with the settlement of the West, 1755–94. Maysville, Ky.: Collins. 1832. Covington, Ky. 1872. [**1801**

"A monograph of interest." *Narrative and critical hist. of Am.*, 5: 581.

Massie, Nathaniel. MASSIE, DAVID MEADE. Nathaniel Massie, a pioneer of Ohio: a sketch of his life and selections from his correspondence. Cin.: Clarke. 1896. $2. [**1802**

A bare matter of fact narrative of events in the life of a distinguished actor in early Ohio history. General Massie was a Virginian, lived some time in Kentucky, and first entered the country beyond the Ohio River in 1788, the year that civil government was organized; died at Chillicothe in 1813. He was a surveyor, land speculator, founder of towns, and politician. He was a pronounced Jeffersonian, and one of the most prominent opponents of Governor St. Clair, and an active advocate of the early admission of Ohio to the Union. Historically, the main interest of the book is found in the original documents relating to this event.

B. A. H.

May, *Col.* **John.** Journal and letters relative to two journeys to the Ohio country, in 1788 and '89; with biog. sketch by Rev. Richard S. Edes, and illustrative notes by Wm. M. Darlington. Cin.: Clarke. 1873. Net $2. [**1803**

The author, a Revolutionary officer, and a business man of venturesome habits, left Boston in April, 1788, proceeding overland on horseback, by way of Philadelphia, Baltimore, and the Laurel Hills, to Pittsburg, there taking a flat-boat for Marietta, where he had landed interests, and arrived the last week of May. Early in August, he returned to Boston by a somewhat different route. Next year he made a second

trip to the Ohio country, this time on a trading venture, going as far as Maysville, Ky. There is no journal for this tour, but the editor supplies several of the author's descriptive letters to friends. The journal of 1788 and the letters of 1789 together furnish an interesting picture of frontier conditions, modes of life and business, and difficulties of inter-communication. The tone is sprightly, the author observant, so that aside from being a source of information, the book makes agreeable reading.

R. G. T.

Michaux, François André. Travels to the westward of the Allegany Mountains, in the states of the Ohio, Kentucky, and Tennessee, and return to Charlestown, through the upper Carolinas, 1802: tr. from the French by S. Lambert. London: Mawman. 1805. [**1804**

Michaux was a careful observer and discriminating writer. He gives clear and trustworthy descriptions of the states named in the title, — their inhabitants and products, and the occupations of the people. His book is free from Indian legends and border stories, which constitute so large a part of the average "frontier" writing.

E. E. S.

Pattie, James Ohio. Personal narrative during an expedition from St. Louis through the vast regions between that place and the Pacific Ocean, thence back through the city of Mexico to Vera Cruz; ed. by Timothy Flint. Cin.: Flint. 1833. [**1805**

"The narrative of Pattie's expedition and captivity has more than the ordinary interest and value which attaches to the stories of adventurers. He crossed the continent of America on a route which his party were the first to pursue. He encountered tribes of Indians who then saw a white man for the first time, and his narrative has the merit of being given in a candid, unexaggerated style, which impresses us with its veracity. The story of the perilous expedition, the frightful extremities to which his party were reduced, the fights with the savages, and his final capture, are all narrated with spirit and candor." T. W. Field, *Indian bibliography*, p. 304.

Pickett, Albert James. History of Alabama and incidentally of Georgia and Mississippi from the earliest period. Charleston: Walker. 1851. 2v. New ed. enl. Birmingham, Ala.: Webb Bk. Co. 1900. 2v. $2.50. [**1806**

Pickett's work is founded in part on original printed authorities and in part on the interviews of the author with Indian chiefs and white pioneers during the first half of the 19th century. It is far above the average state history in the author's grasp of his subject, has been accepted as an authority on the subjects of which it treats and is invaluable to students, but it comes no later than the admission of the state to the Union in 1819 and is filled with many details of small historical importance. A fourth edition was published in 1896 and a fifth in 1900, which has been greatly increased in value by the addition of the *Annals of Alabama, 1819–1900*, by Thomas M. Owen, a brief general history of the state during that time with additional chapters on the literary history, bibliography and state officers, and an index wanting in all previous editions. It is well supplemented by Brewer.   S. B. W.

Poole, William Frederick. The Ordinance of 1787 and Dr. Manasseh Cutler as an agent in its formation. Cambridge, Mass. : Welch. 1876.   [1807

A small monograph defending the claim of Cutler to the authorship of the ordinance governing the Northwest territory as against the claim of Nathan Dane. See Edward Coles's *History of the Ordinance of 1787* (sect. 385) and numerous periodical articles.   E. E. S.

Putnam, *Brig.-Gen.* **Rufus.** CONE, MARY. Life of Rufus Putnam, with extracts from his journal and an account of the first settlement in Ohio. Cleveland: Williams. 1886. [1808

The first part contains the rewritten journal of Putnam (see *Journal* of Rufus Putnam, sect. 874) and a sketch of his life as an engineer in the Revolutionary War and as Surveyor-General in the Northwest Territory. They are based on his letters and journal, but very poorly arranged and unedited. A disappointing work, considering the importance of Putnam's official positions and the length of time the papers were held before being printed. The second part consists of an irrelevant sketch of the founding of Marietta, Ohio. Printed from small type.   E. E. S.

Ramsey, James Gattys McGregor. Annals of Tennessee. Charleston: John Russell. 1853.   [1809

This work covers the history of the Watauga Association and of the other settlements from which came the state of Tennessee, and follows the state itself down to 1800. The author says that he had examined all the public records relating to his subject and had had many of the papers of leading pioneers in his hands. It is largely documentary, for there are many extracts from original records, but the groundwork is Haywood, whom he follows almost blindly at times.   S. B. W.

Reynolds, John. Pioneer history of Illinois, 1673-1818. Belleville, Ill. : Randall. 1852. Chicago: Fergus. 1887.   [1810

From the Indians of Illinois to the organization of the state in 1818. Describes the government of the region by the French and by the English, the introduction of religious organizations, the development of industries, and the growth of political divisions. The work lacks historic judgment; much irrelevant matter is introduced; but it preserves local color in describing the life of early settlers. Probably its greatest service is in numerous short biographies of prominent pioneers, easily found from the index.   E. E. S.

Rice, Harvey. Incidents of pioneer life in the early settlement of the Connecticut western reserve. Cleveland: Cobb. 1881.

—— Pioneers of the Western Reserve. Boston : Lee. 1883.

—— Sketches of western life. Boston: Lee. 1886.   [1811

The general character of these books is well shown by their titles. Their author came at an early day to Cleveland, where he was long a prominent citizen, and where, in his last years, he wrote the chapters and papers that make up the two volumes. Much of the history that he writes he had seen and some of it he had been. A few miscellaneous papers have been added to fill out the second book. The works have a value as serving to keep alive in men's minds the pioneer days.   B. A. H.

Roosevelt, *Col.* **Theodore.** The winning of the West. N. Y. : Putnam. 1889-96. v. 1-4. $10.   [1812

Mr. Roosevelt "has rescued a whole movement in American development from the hands of unskilful annalists ; he has made use of widely scattered original sources, not heretofore exploited ; and with graphic vigor he has portrayed the advance of the pioneer into the wastes of the continent. He has considered his subject broadly, in its relations to world-history, not in the spirit of the local historian. This is an admirable thing to do ; and Mr. Roosevelt's appreciative sympathy with the frontiersman, due in part to his own western experiences, has enabled him to depict the movement as probably no other man of his time could have done. The difficult question of the relations between the Indian and the pioneer he has handled in a courageous and virile way. . . . He has brought into prominence an important, but much-neglected, subject by unfolding our relations with Spain and England respecting the frontier, and has given a valuable treatment of the tortuous intrigues of western leaders with the Spaniards and the French. These are some of the strong features of Mr. Roosevelt's work. . . . It is the dramatic and picturesque aspects of the period that most interest him, — the Indian fighting, the intrigues with Spain, and the exploration of the far West. He handles the subject with dash and lightness of touch ; and sometimes this facility shows itself in a readiness to pass over institutional development with a comment of praise or blame, instead of information that the reader has a right to expect. . . . Taken as a whole, the volumes will be to the general reader a revelation in American history. But the special student must regret that Mr. Roosevelt does not find it possible to regard history as a more jealous mistress, and to give more time, greater thoroughness of investigation, particularly in foreign archives, and more sobriety of judgment to his work." Frederick J. Turner, in *Am. hist. rev.*, 2: 171.

Rupp, Isaac Daniel. Early history of western Pennsylvania and of the west and of western expeditions and campaigns, 1754-1833. Pittsburg: Kauffman. 1846.   [1813

A peculiar compilation of fact and legend concerning the trans-Alleghenian region. It begins with the discovery of America, describes the expulsion of the French, the Indian wars, the War of 1812, and ends with the Black Hawk war in 1832. The only real merit of the book lies in the reprint of journals and memoranda of Indian treaties. A few "histories" of individual counties in western Pennsylvania close the volume.　　　　　　　　　　　　　　　　E. E. S.

St. Clair, *Maj.-Gen.* **Arthur.** Narrative of the manner in which the campaign against the Indians, 1791, was conducted, under the command of Maj.-Gen. St. Clair; and reports taken from the files of the House of Representatives. Phil. 1812.　　　　　　　　　　　　　　[**1814**]

St. Clair's own story of his disastrous campaign, with documents. Written long after the event and the work of a disappointed man. Of value only to the close student.　　　　　　　　　　　　　　　E. C.

—— Proceedings at his court-martial. See New York Historical Society, sect. 361. [**1815**]
— SMITH, WILLIAM H., *ed.* The St. Clair papers: life and public services of Arthur St. Clair, with his correspondence and papers. Cin.: Clarke. 1882. 2v. $6.　　　　[**1816**]

"The existence in Kansas of a mass of papers in the handwriting of Arthur St. Clair, the first Governor of the Northwestern Territory, was made known to the state of Ohio in 1869 by a memorial presented to the Legislature by the Western Reserve Historical Society. . . . The General Assembly voted an appropriation the following year for the purchase of the St. Clair manuscripts, which were finally secured for the State Library," and are now made public. "The first volume contains the editor's own study of the 'Life and public services of Arthur St. Clair,' occupying 256 pages, and more than one-third of the *St. Clair papers.* . . . The second volume is devoted entirely to papers touching the government and defence of the Northwestern Territory. Valuable as were St. Clair's military services in connection with the French and Indian wars and as an adviser of Washington during the Revolution, it is chiefly for his subsequent merits as the pioneer of law and institutions in the Northwest that he ought to be known; and it is perhaps the chief merit of Mr. Smith's work that he has laid special stress upon the above introduction of government by St. Clair under the Ordinance of 1787. . . . St. Clair is perhaps best known, not as the founder and civic organizer of the Northwest, but as an unfortunate general under whom the western army suffered a terrible defeat by Indian savages. . . . Congress investigated the whole matter, and reported that it was simple justice to St. Clair to acknowledge that 'the failure of the late expedition can in no respect be imputed to his conduct, either at any time before or during the action.'" *Nation,* 34: 383.

Sheldon, *Mrs.* **Electra M.** Early history of Michigan, to 1815. N. Y.: Barnes. Detroit: Kerr. 1856.　　　　　　　　　　　　　[**1817**]

Five sixths of this work are given to the French period of Michigan history, while the amount of space devoted to Cadillac is also quite disproportionate to the rest of the book. The explanation is that the writer, in preparing the work, had the use of original material relating to this division of the subject, obtained in Paris by Hon. Lewis Cass. The Michigan

story down to 1815 is told in its essential features, at times with much detail, and in a pleasing manner.
　　　　　　　　　　　　　　　　　　　B. A. H.

Taylor, James W. History of the state of Ohio: first period, 1650–1787. Cin. 1854.
　　　　　　　　　　　　　　　　　　[**1818**]

"The early Jesuit missions, the wars of the Eries and the Iroquois, the border warfare which was waging for nearly a quarter of a century, between the Scotch-Irish inhabitants of Pennsylvania and the Delawares, Shawanese, and Wyandots, are the subjects which nearly fill the volume. The appendix contains other and more minute particulars of the various Indian tribes which once inhabited the state. . . . The work is a very judicious and interesting collection of material already printed in one form or another, not always accessible to the student, even in great libraries." T. W. Field, *Indian bibliography,* p. 388.

Tecumseh. DRAKE, BENJAMIN. Life of Tecumseh and of his brother the prophet; with a historical sketch of the Shawanoe Indians. Cin.: Morgan. 1841.　　[**1819**]

Founded largely on Harrison's letters (1808–13), and on material furnished by other participants in the events described. Contains also a good deal of traditional information of doubtful value. Style clear and unadorned.　　　　　　　　　　　　　　E. C.

— EGGLESTON, EDWARD, *and Mrs.* ELIZABETH EGGLESTON SEELYE. Tecumseh and the Shawnee prophet. (Famous Am. Indians.) N. Y.: Dodd. [c. 1878.] $1.　　　　[**1820**]

A series of narratives of border warfare in the Northwest Territory grouped about Tecumseh. A popular account for the general reader, especially for boys. Uncritical, occasionally disconnected, but generally interesting. A vivid picture, not over-drawn, of the great Indian orator, statesman and warrior. Appendix on authorities for the life of Tecumseh.　　　　　　　　　　　　　H. W. H.

Thwaites, Reuben Gold. Afloat on the Ohio: an historical pilgrimage of a thousand miles in a skiff, from Redstone to Cairo. Chicago: Way. 1897. $1.50.　　　　　[**1821**]

The author of this pleasantly told story of a family trip down the Monongahela and Ohio is an authority on the early history of the west, and he explains the historic interest of every point along the route, except that he is silent regarding the Civil War. The journey was, indeed, undertaken to gather "local color" for work in history. One appendix is an historical outline of Ohio valley settlement, and the other is a list of journals of previous travelers down the Ohio.　　　　　　　　　　　　F. J. S.

United States. *Congress.* [Ordinance of 1787.] See Old South Work, sect. 368. [**1822**]

Wallace, Joseph. History of Illinois and Louisiana under the French rule, embracing a general view of the French dominion in North

America, with some account of the English occupation of Illinois. Cin.: Clarke. 1893. Net $2.50.   [**1823**

A clear and correct but prosaic presentation of the subject; no advantage is taken by the writer of its picturesque features; well arranged; largely but not wholly drawn from secondary sources.   B. A. H.

Wilkinson, *Maj.-Gen.* **James.** CLARK, DANIEL. Proofs of the corruption of General James Wilkinson, and of his connexion with Aaron Burr. Phil. 1809.   [**1824**

The evidence here presented is based upon documents given in the appendix. Clark strives to prove that Wilkinson was a pensioner of Spain from 1794 to 1803; and an accomplice of Burr in treasonably plotting a separation of the states. The case is clearly and forcibly put and is a strong one. The accompanying documents, consisting of state papers, letters and affidavits, also give information about Jefferson's administration of the West, and reveal the causes there working towards a secession in the early years of the Republic. [See sect. 1706.]   R. C. H. C.

Winsor, Justin. The Mississippi basin, 1697–1763; with full cartographical illustrations from contemporary sources. Boston: Houghton. 1895. $4.   [**1825**

This section of the author's continuous story, covering a very important period, closes with the final triumph of England over France in North America in 1763, and leaves the reader well equipped for the succeeding period, in which the American people, in their own right, appear distinctly upon the scene. The volume has the qualities of the series to which it belongs. [See Winsor's *Cartier to Frontenac.* Boston: Houghton. 1894. $4.]   B. A. H.

—— The westward movement: the colonies and the republic west of the Alleghanies, 1763–98; with full cartographical illustrations from contemporary sources. Boston: Houghton. 1897. $4.   [**1826**

This book "is monumental in its erudition and is a work of the highest importance to students of the beginnings of the West. . . . Never before has the whole field been surveyed with more minute care." Mr. Winsor "loved an abundance of facts, and he knew the uses of the card catalogue. He lacked the artistic instinct, he was wanting in that historical imagination which fuses the separate elements of historical knowledge into a single and pleasing presentation; his classified cards are always in sight. The result is that Mr. Winsor's work is a thesaurus of events for the student, rather than a history for the general reader. His work is essentially monographic, and yet, by a most regrettable policy, Mr. Winsor . . . has omitted, except in the rarest cases, to cite the authorities for his statements. . . . The work gives some indications that the author's final revision, of style particularly, was not as complete as he no doubt would have wished to make it. . . . When all minor criticisms on detail have been made — and in a work so abounding in statements of fact it is remarkable

how few such criticisms must be — the book remains a splendid proof of the immense research of its author, of his skill and fairness in dealing with a multiplicity of detail, and of the continental breadth of his view." Frederick J. Turner, in *Am. hist. rev.*, 3: 556.

4. Period of the Slavery Question: 1828–1860

Abdy, Edward Strutt. Journal of a residence and tour in the United States, 1833–4. London: Murray. 1835. 3v.   [**1827**

The author, fellow of Jesus College, Cambridge, devoted much attention in his travels in this country to charitable and philanthropic institutions. He gives accounts of many visits to prisons, schools, insane asylums, and institutions for defectives. There is much in regard to the condition of negroes, and the state of public sentiment in the North concerning their treatment. The author is pronounced in his opinions against schemes of colonization, and his sympathies are anti-slavery. His tour embraced New York, Connecticut, Massachusetts, Rhode Island, and Toronto. He did not go farther south than Virginia and Kentucky. There is considerable information in regard to prices of provisions, cost of living, and wages. The work is free from hyper-criticism, and is a helpful record of American institutions for the period described.   D. R. D.

Ampère, Jean Jacques Antoine. Promenade en Amérique. Paris. 1855. 2v. [**1828**

"Ampère's record of his American tour is singularly unpretending. It resembles in tone and method the best conversation. The style is pure and animated, and the thoughts naturally suggested. He describes what he sees with candor and geniality, criticises without the slightest acrimony, and commends with graceful zeal. . . . He has that catholic taste and temper so essential to a good traveller. He takes an interest in whatever relates to humanity." H. T. Tuckerman, *America and her commentators*, p. 143.

Bacourt, Adolphe Fourier, *chevalier* de. Souvenirs of a diplomat: private letters from America during the administrations of Van Buren, Harrison and Tyler; tr. from the French. N. Y.: Holt. 1885. $1.50. [**1829**

These private letters begin in June, 1840, and end in July, 1842. The Chevalier de Bacourt was the French minister in Washington, and his letters are full of lively descriptions, mingled with trenchant comment, of the political and social life of those days. Homesickness sharpened his pen, but he was honest and not indisposed to be friendly. Vivid realistic sketches of the public men that he met abound in these pages. As an historical source, these private letters, not intended for publication, rank distinctly higher than most of the travels of this period.   E. G. B.

Bassett, John Spencer. Slavery in the state of North Carolina. (Johns Hopkins Univ. studies, ser. 17, no. 7–8.) Balt. 1899. Pap. 75c.   [**1830**

"No. southern historical monographs are, to our mind, more useful or more interesting than those essays of recent years, beginning with Dr. J. R. Brackett's *Negro in Maryland* (sect. 1837), in which the attempt is made to set forth, from trustworthy original sources, the actual facts of slavery as a concrete institution. Among such attempts Professor Bassett's modest and judicious performance has an important place. Its spirit is admirable, and, though its style is sometimes inelegant, in other respects its workmanship is careful. . . . Perhaps the most interesting sections are those on the religious and social position of the negroes in North Carolina." *Am. hist. rev.*, 5: 168.

Bennett, James Gordon. PRAY, ISAAC CLARK. Memoirs of James Gordon Bennett and his times; by a journalist. N. Y.: Stringer. 1855. [1831

Mr. Bennett was a prominent figure in New York journalism, beginning with about the year 1825. He founded the *New York Herald* in 1835, and aroused intense opposition, especially during the earlier part of his career, by publishing articles then regarded as sensational, and tending to degrade the press. The author does not entirely excuse Bennett, but is, on the whole, sympathetic in his treatment. He asserts that he has not consulted Mr. Bennett or any one connected with him. While the volume is diffuse (about 500 pages), it is of value in tracing the development of the American press, and throwing light on the tone of political and social sentiment. Incidentally the author describes many of the episodes of the day, theatrical, financial, and political. The table of contents is sufficiently full to enable the reader to extract information quickly on any particular point. D. R. D.

Benton, Thomas Hart. Thirty years' view; or A history of the working of the American government, 1820–50, chiefly taken from the Congress debates, private papers of General Jackson and speeches of Senator Benton. N. Y.: Appleton. 1854–6. 2v. $8. [1832

A work of the first importance in the field of political reminiscence and reflection. The author was a member of the Senate during the period of which he writes, and had access to primary sources of information, including the papers of Jackson. In a succession of short chapters, he has commented on nearly every important political event and political leader of the time, personal opinion being reinforced by extended quotations from the author's speeches. Bearing in mind Benton's positive views, the personal estimates of contemporaries of opposing politics is notable for its fairness. W. MacD.

— ROOSEVELT, THEODORE. Thomas Hart Benton. (American statesmen.) Boston: Houghton. 1887. $1.25. [1833

The author understands Benton and sympathizes with him. He points out his merits and demerits as a statesman, noting particularly his ignorance of the great financial questions of the day, upon which, however, Roosevelt is himself insufficiently informed. The book is written mostly from secondary sources, is dogmatic in temper and imbued with the writer's political prejudices. The style is forcible but careless and slovenly. R. C. H. C.

Bettle, Edward. Notices of negro slavery as connected with Pennsylvania. See Pennsylvania, Historical Society of, sect. 371. [1834

Birney, James Gillespie. BIRNEY, WILLIAM. James G. Birney and his times. N. Y.: Appleton. 1890. [1835

James G. Birney occupied an unique position in the development of the anti-slavery movement. A Kentuckian by birth, of the richer class, well educated for that day, lawyer and planter in Alabama, an owner of slaves, he was gradually converted to the idea that civil liberty and slavery were incompatible. It was not merely a question of negro bondage, but also a vital struggle for the whites. He freed his slaves, published an anti-slavery paper, and became corresponding secretary of the Anti-Slavery Society in New York. In 1840 and 1844 he was the presidential candidate of the Liberty Party. His life, therefore, constitutes an essential part in the anti-slavery struggle, 1830–1845. This biography by his son is unfortunately characterized by a bitter rancor displayed toward the Garrison family, in the apparent fear that the father's reputation may suffer with posterity. Apart from this glaring defect, the book contains much of value in regard to southern thought on slavery before 1828 and deepens the impression that the anti-slavery movement had its origin and growth from many sources. Those who desire to follow the Garrison controversy should read the review in the *Nation*, vol. 50, p. 206. D. R. D.

Blake, William O. History of slavery and the slave trade, ancient and modern. Columbus, O.: Miller. 1858. [1836

A vast compilation of facts connected with the history of slavery, beginning with the ancient Hebrews, and coming down to the John Brown insurrection at Harper's Ferry. About one half of the book is given to slavery in the United States. It forms a kind of compendium or storehouse of facts, but is of little value otherwise. E. E. S.

Brackett, Jeffrey R. The negro in Maryland. (Johns Hopkins Univ. studies, extra v. 6.) Balt. 1889. $2. [1837

Describes the condition of slaves in Maryland from 1642 to the Civil War. Has a preliminary chapter on white and Indian servants and two supplementary chapters on "Manumission" and "The free negro." The latter treats of colonization and other schemes. The book is carefully written, frequent references being given, and the marks of scholarship are everywhere shown. E. E. S.

Brothers, Thomas. The United States of North America as they are; not as they are generally described: being a cure for radicalism. London: Longmans. 1840. [1838

Brothers, an Englishman by birth and training and a radical in his youth, lived for 15 years in America, and on his return to England, having become a thorough-going conservative, wrote this amazing book to demonstrate the dangers of democratic government. There is probably not a word in the whole volume that is not condemnatory of this country, some of the special objects of the author's attacks being the Pennsylvania prisons, the American system of banking, the ballot, Stephen Girard, universal suffrage and the treatment of the Indians. The appendix of nearly 300 pages is made up chiefly of newspaper accounts of crime. The fact that the book contains the full text of Stephen Girard's will may make it of more value than it would otherwise be.   F. J. S.

Brown, *Capt.* **John.** BROWN, G. W. Reminiscences of old John Brown. Rockford, Ill. Boston: Lee. 1880.   [**1839**

A pamphlet written by the editor of the first Free Soil newspaper established in Kansas and for eleven years a resident of that state. Its object is to bring the "hero" down to his merited level. It claims to tell the exact truth about Brown's Kansas campaign. It contains many letters from contemporaries in verification of the author's statements.   E. E. S.

— CHAMBERLIN, JOSEPH EDGAR. John Brown. (Beacon biographies.) Boston: Small. 1899. 75c.   [**1840**

This biography "is distinguished for nothing so much as for the frontispiece portrait from a daguerreotype of the beardless Kansas partisan. It may well be compared with that of the same era in R. D. Webb's life, but it is more symptomatic of the unhumorous and unbalanced mind which was at once the weakness and the strength of the man of Harper's Ferry." *Nation*, 69: 447.

— HINTON, RICHARD JOSIAH. John Brown and his men. (American reformers.) N. Y.: Funk. 1894. $1.50.   [**1841**

"His memoir of John Brown is by far the fullest treatment of the subject yet [1895] printed, except that of Mr. Sanborn (sect. 1845). It perhaps falls short of this last work in arrangement, but surpasses it in directness and simplicity; shows less profuse details of historical investigation; but more of personal intimacy, at least during the Kansas period. The author went first to Kansas in 1856. . . . He knew most of Brown's men, and traces their career more thoroughly, in some respects, than has hitherto been done. Incidentally he makes clear the utter preposterousness of the view taken in Nicolay and Hay's *Lincoln* . . . that these men were largely a set of impecunious hangers-on, attracted to Brown by the prospect of support. . . . Perhaps the most eminent service rendered by Mr. Hinton's book is in exploding, even more thoroughly than Mr. Sanborn's, the curious theory urged of late years in some quarters, and embodied in Prof. Spring's volume on Kansas in 'American Commonwealths,' to the effect that there was a distinct division in that Territory, during its period of struggle, between the advocates of diplomacy and those of armed resistance. . . . He throws, from his own memory and the correspondence of others, many side-lights on the man and his times." *Nation*, 60: 225.

— HOLST, HERMANN VON. John Brown. Boston: Cupples. 1889.   [**1842**

An essay originally contributed to the *Preussische Jahrbücher* (vol. 41). Of interest as a study of the significance of John Brown's career by a foreign historian who was making a profound study of the influence of slavery on American politics. The editor, Frank Preston Stearns, has supplied an introduction on Von Holst and an appendix discussing the various recent judgments of John Brown.   E. G. B.

— REDPATH, JAMES. Public life of Capt. John Brown. Boston: Thayer. 1860.   [**1843**

Written by a newspaper reporter, for many years an Abolitionist, and one in touch with the friends of Brown. The work is affectionately if not skilfully done. Many original papers are used. The details of Brown's Kansas campaign, Virginia insurrection, trial and execution are fully told. Sanborn derived much of his material from this work.   E. E. S.

— RICHMAN, IRVING B. John Brown among the Quakers, and other sketches. Des Moines: Historical Dept. of Iowa. 1894.   [**1844**

The author "has gathered into a small volume a half-dozen unpretending essays in the history of Iowa and the neighboring regions. . . . The essay which gives title to the volume deals with an episode in John Brown's life, his sojourn in Iowa from August, 1857, to April, 1858, and from February to March, 1859, first at Tabor and afterward at Springdale. . . . The letters and other data here first published cast light on the character of Brown's companions and on his relations to them at a time when his final expedition was already resolved upon, and exhibit impressively their spirit and motives. An essay on Nauvoo and the Prophet deals with the present aspects of that town and with its history as, for a brief period, the capital of the Mormon organization. The other studies in the book are of episodes in the history of the early relations of the white man to the Indian in or near Iowa, and are less interesting." *Am. hist. rev.*, 2: 575.

— SANBORN, FRANKLIN BENJAMIN, *ed.* Life and letters of John Brown. Boston: Roberts. 1885. Little. $2.   [**1845**

The most elaborate life of John Brown, and the fullest collection of his letters and papers. The style is somewhat loose, and the size of the volume is swelled by the inclusion of some irrelevant matter; but details of all sorts have been painstakingly gathered. The editor, himself an actor in some of the earlier scenes, is a hero-worshipper, and goes to some lengths in attempting to explain and justify the Pottawatomie massacre. As a whole, the book is indispensable material for a concise and readable biography.   W. MacD.

Buchanan, James. Mr. Buchanan's administration on the eve of the Rebellion. N. Y.: Appleton. 1865.   [**1846**

Buchanan intended this to be a triumphant defense of his administration. In that respect, it is a failure. Sources are used and quoted, but the account of very important events (for instance, the Kansas question) is inadequate and one-sided. The book reveals clearly the limitations of Buchanan, and especially makes plain that he never perceived the moral side of the slavery struggle. It is temperate, argumentative, and written in a labored, dull style. **R. C. H. C.**

— CURTIS, GEORGE TICKNOR. Life of James Buchanan. N. Y.: Harper. 1883. 2v. $6.
[**1847**

The author, well known for his *Life of Daniel Webster* and his *Treatise on law*, was selected by the executors and relatives of Buchanan to write the life of the ex-President. He was not personally acquainted with Buchanan, and this *Life* is in no sense an official eulogy, nor an attempt to vindicate Buchanan or his party. Mr. Curtis asserts a desire to be independent and impartial. He believes that injustice has been done Buchanan. He was entrusted with Buchanan's private papers, of which there was a large amount, as Buchanan made a practice of preserving notes of important conversations, and the work includes generous extracts of such. The second volume contains a valuable review of the Clayton-Bulwer treaty, and deals particularly with the critical events of 1860–61. The author's style throughout is temperate. The standpoint, therefore, is that of a lawyer interpreting the situation legally, but with a lack of appreciation of the social and moral changes rapidly developing in the period 1830–60. **D. R. D.**

Buckingham, James Silk. America, historical, statistic, and descriptive [1837–38]. London: Fisher. 3v. N. Y.: Harper. 1841. 2v.
[**1848**

These volumes, with those devoted to the eastern, western, and slave states, make a large work of eight volumes, constituting a record of three years' travel through the United States between 1837 and 1840. The author, an Englishman, had some reputation in his own country as a traveller in the East and as a reformer especially interested in the cause of temperance. While travelling in this country he delivered many courses of lectures which brought him a valuable acquaintance. This accounts in a measure for the general correctness of his narrative. The writer is candid and endeavors to be impartial. His style is dignified though touched by self-complacency. Of special value are his comments on education, benevolent institutions and the treatment of the Indians. In this series, the first volume describes his journeying in New York, Baltimore, and Washington; the second, Philadelphia and a trip through the state of New York; and the third, New England. **D. R. D.**

—— Slave states of America. London: Fisher. 1842. 2v.
[**1849**

The author, an ex-member of the British Parliament, travelled through the southern states in 1839, and delivered lectures on his travels in the Orient. At the same time he took copious and valuable notes on the manners of the people, the products of the states, and on the fauna, flora, and antiquities. A violent prohibitionist and abolitionist, he delivers many sermons in his book on the evils of drinking and slaveholding. The use of tobacco was as hateful to him as to James I. Meeting the best people of the South, he

was able to obtain valuable information on the slavery question, but his prejudices were so strong as often to affect his judgment. He finds much to praise, but more to blame in southern morals. He was a keen and careful observer; but in his historical sketches, he lacks accuracy. The work is too long for the modern reader, but well written and very entertaining. No index. **J. R. F.**

Burgess, John William. The middle period, 1817–58. (American history series.) N. Y.: Scribner. 1897. $1.75.
[**1850**

Portrays the struggle between the national and states-rights theories, tracing their growth from the Missouri Compromise. The Mexican cessions and their political consequences are discussed at disproportionate length. Mr. Burgess possesses keen logical power; has written from the sources; holds pronounced views and is not unbiased, though he usually states both sides fairly and moderately. In considering the Mexican war he surrenders this attitude, justifying the United States at all points. A stimulating book. **R. C. H. C.**

Byrdsall, F. History of the Loco-foco or Equal Rights party. N. Y.: Clement. 1842.
[**1851**

About 1830 there were various social reform movements in the United States. Among these was a political movement, originated in New York city in 1835, "to bring back the Democratic party to the principles upon which it was originally founded," and expounded by Jefferson. Adherents to this movement, because of an incident at a political caucus, were termed Loco-focos. Its followers were hostile to monopolies; opposed banks of every kind; favored hard money; and in part supported other radical measures. The party had little success in elections, but undoubtedly secured the more serious discussion and agitation of reform, and did something to modify the platforms of the two great parties. The author of this little work was recording secretary of the Loco-foco organization during nearly all the time of the existence of the body. This careful record is indispensable to the student of the detailed politics of New York. There are brief sketches of many men connected with the movement. **D. R. D.**

Cairnes, John Elliot. The slave power. London: Parker. 1862. 2d ed. enl. London: Macmillan. 1863.
[**1852**

This little volume, written just at the outbreak of the Civil War and published in this country the following year, is an able and interesting discussion of slavery. It deals with the economic basis of slavery and the moral and industrial fruits of the system, as well as with the general purposes of southern leaders and the meaning of the Civil War. The writer, a professor of jurisprudence and political economy, seems to have studied the subject with scientific calmness; but his sympathies as well as his scientific conclusions are strongly opposed to slavery and its advocates. **A. C. McL.**

Calhoun, John Caldwell. Works; [ed. by Richard K. Crallé]. Charleston, S. C. 1851. N. Y.: Appleton. 1853–5. 6v. $15. [**1853**

V. 1. Disquisition on government, and a discourse on the constitution and government of the United States.

V. 2-4. Speeches in Congress : 2, 1811-37 ; 3, 1837-41 ; 4, 1841-50.

V. 5. Reports in Congress and as Secretary of War: — Public letters.

V. 6. Reports and public letters ; including South Carolina exposition: — Relation of state and federal governments : — Address to the people of South Carolina:—Address to the people of the United States:— Letter to Governor Hamilton. An appendix contains correspondence relating to the breach between Jackson and Calhoun in 1830.

Subjects principally treated: — Tariff: — Internal improvements: — Currency: — Banking: — Sub-Treasury: — Surplus revenue: — Powers of the President: — Nature of the Constitution : — States-rights: — Nullification: — Slavery. A study of these volumes is essential to a thorough understanding of Calhoun, his ideas and policy. On constitutional questions, no one has so profoundly argued the ultra states-rights theory ; while as to slavery, Calhoun's insight was preternaturally keen. On financial questions, his grasp was not so assured.   R. C. H. C.

— HOLST, HERMANN VON. John C. Calhoun. (American statesmen.) Boston : Houghton. 1882. $1.25.   [1854

A study of Calhoun as the leader and philosopher of the slave-holding interest. Embodying the view of the political aspects and influence of slavery which is set forth in so elaborate and detailed a form in the author's *Constitutional history*. Von Holst is strongly nationalist and anti-slavery in feeling, but he writes of Calhoun the man with sympathy and appreciation.   E. G. B.

— JENKINS, JOHN STILWELL. Life of John Caldwell Calhoun. Auburn : Alden. 1850.   [1855

The author also wrote lives of Polk, Silas Wright, and Jackson, all of which are in the nature of hack work. The style is rhetorical, and the author is warm in his praise of Calhoun. Some extracts of speeches and letters are given, and there is a clear statement of Calhoun's position in reference to nullification.   D. R. D.

Cass, Lewis. MCLAUGHLIN, ANDREW CUNNINGHAM. Lewis Cass. (American statesmen.) Boston : Houghton. 1891. $1.25.   [1856

" By far the most attractive and the most fruitful part of his [Cass's] life was the earlier period when, as Colonel in the War of 1812, and as Governor of the Territory of Michigan, he showed a manly vigor and an intelligent initiative in affairs that warranted the high reputation which he brought into national politics when he entered the cabinet of Jackson in 1831. . . . In spite of all ingenious efforts to magnify the importance of his national career, Cass must remain one of that unhappy class of northern politicians who were not able to forecast the future of the country, and who were chained, by fetters which they could not break, to a cause inevitably doomed. . . .

Professor McLaughlin's own sympathies are so strongly with the cause that triumphed that, in reading his pages, one feels his apologies and his glosses to be labored. The sympathy he feels for a man of considerable ability, of honorable and successful private life, of kindly and hospitable nature, disarms his criticism, and he glides, perhaps unconsciously, into the rôle of the advocate pleading for a favorable judgment." *Nation*, 53 : 204.

Chambers, William. American slavery and colour. London : Chambers. 1857. N. Y.: Dix. 1857.   [1857

The result of a Scotchman's study of the history and aspects of the peculiar institution. Slavery at the Revolution, the Missouri Compromise, the struggle in Kansas, the outrage on Mr. Sumner, and black laws and usages are some of the chapter titles. The appendix describes a number of distressing incidents characteristic of slavery.   F. J. S.

Channing, William Ellery. Slavery. Boston : Munroe. 1835. 2d ed. rev. 1836.   [1858

Eight chapters on such topics as " Slaves as property," the " Scriptures on slavery," " Abolitionism," " Means of removing slavery," etc. Advocates amelioration of the condition of the slave by his owner. Gave great offence to the radical Abolitionists. The essays are entirely abstract.   E. E. S.

Chase, Lucien B. History of the Polk administration. N. Y.: Putnam. 1850.   [1859

The author was a member of Congress from Tennessee during the period described, which is characterized as an age of progress and reform, with evidences of chivalry and military enthusiasm. In spite of a somewhat undue extravagance of admiration for Polk, the work is valuable. It treats of the settlement of the boundary between the United States and Great Britain ; recognizes Polk's blunder in connection with the Oregon question ; gives a sketch of Mexican and Texan history previous to the war ; furnishes a reprint of Iturbide's statement of 1824 ; and gives many notes on official papers. The political and military events of the Mexican war are described, with an account of the disputes between Polk, Taylor and Scott. The relations of the Pacific coast to the Oriental trade are discussed. There is a full abstract of the debates on the tariff of 1846, with a discussion by the author adverse to protection. In the appendix is Scott's letter of February 24, 1848, to the Secretary of War, with the reply of the latter under date of April 25.   D. R. D.

Chase, Salmon Portland (see in the Period next following).

Chevalier, Michel. Society, manners, and politics in the United States: being a series of letters on North America [1834-35]; tr. from 3d Paris ed. Boston : Weeks. 1839.   [1860

Chevalier was a Frenchman sent to this country in 1834 under a government appointment to inspect the public works of the United States. Much interested in political and social organization, he spent two years in further observation. " His letters give the results of his observations, the impressions made on his mind, the speculations in regard to the future destiny of our institutions, rather than a detailed narrative of facts and even events." A considerable part of the book is devoted to an account of banking questions. There are chapters on railroads in the United States; the city of Lowell and its factory girls; Fitchburg; Cincinnati; western steamboats; speculation; progress of society; social reform; middle classes; aristocracy, and democracy. Chevalier was a trained observer and a careful writer, who afterwards established a reputation as an author on money and other economic subjects.   D. R. D.

Choate, Rufus. Works; with a memoir of his life by S. G. Brown. Boston: Little. 1862. 2v. $2.25 ea.   [**1861**

The memoir of Choate is of moderate merit, somewhat superficial and helped out by long quotations from memorial addresses. It is, however, fair and accurate, and written in good plain English. Choate's speeches are of much more interest and deal fully and thoroughly with many subjects, notably with the McLeod case; Protection; the Oregon question; the Annexation of Texas; Webster; Slavery, and Judicial tenure. The point of view is always that of a Webster Whig.   R. C. H. C.

Christy, David. Cotton is king; by an American. Cin.: Moore. 1855.   [**1862**

After reviewing the development of the cotton trade, the author concludes that slavery is the energizing influence of nearly all the industrial interests of America and Great Britain, and that it is impracticable, in the existing condition of the world, to overthrow the system. He regrets the failure to support the American Colonization Society, criticises the Abolitionists, and has much to say of the relations of free trade to slavery. In the appendix the growth of the cotton trade is shown by years. The author's name appears in a revised and enlarged edition (N. Y. 1857), but not in this.   F. J. S.

Clarke, James Freeman. Anti-slavery days: a sketch of the struggle which ended in the abolition of slavery. N. Y.: Worthington. 1884.   [**1863**

The author hoped, he said, in these chapters — originally given as lectures — only to call attention to a few important events and characters of the struggle against slavery. He naturally dwelt mostly on the events with which he was personally familiar and the persons with whom he happened to be best acquainted, that is, occurrences in Massachusetts and in which New England men participated. The literary charm of the book is, also naturally, very great.   F. J. S.

Clay, Henry. Works; ed. [with life] by Calvin Colton. N. Y.: Barnes. 1857. 6v. Contents: v. 1–3. Life and times; by Colton [1844. 2v. Rev. ed. c. 1856. 3v.]:— v. 4. Private correspondence. [1855.]:— v. 5–6. Speeches.

—— *Same ;* with introd. by Thomas B. Reed, and history of tariff legislation, 1812–96,

by Wm. McKinley. N. Y.: Henry Clay Pub. Co. 1898. 7v.   [**1864**

In Colton's original edition of six volumes, the speeches cover his whole political career, 1810–1851. Clay was prominently identified with the advocacy of the war with England in 1812, the promotion of domestic manufactures by tariffs, federal aid for internal improvements, open though not aggressive sympathy with the South American colonies for liberty, the colonization of negroes in Africa, the public land policy, the settlement of southern disputes through the Missouri Compromise and the important compromise measures of 1850. On all these, as well as on other topics, Clay's speeches are part of the history of the United States. The first two volumes of the *Life* were written at an earlier period than the third and bring Clay's career down to 1845; the third volume deals with the last seven years of Clay's life, contains in particular the speeches on the Compromise of 1850, the eulogies after his death, and correspondence 1843–51. Colton's biography is eulogistic, but on the whole well done. The author was engaged on this work for years, and in the correspondence made his selections from more than three thousand documents. Down to the Treaty of Ghent there were few letters to be obtained. The editor includes some letters written to Clay. The edition of 1897 is a reprint of Colton's with the addition of an Introduction by Thomas B. Reed and a History of tariff legislation, 1812–1896, by William McKinley. These additions were apparently perfunctory tasks and non-critical, and the latter is scrappy. Neither can be relied upon by the careful student. Mr. Reed furnishes a useful bibliography on Clay, vol. 1, pp. 34–38.   D. R. D.

—— Schurz, Carl. Life of Henry Clay. (American statesmen.) Boston: Houghton. 1887. 2v. $2.50.   [**1865**

This is one of the best of the biographical American statesmen series, and as Clay occupies a large space in public affairs from the war of 1812 until the middle of the century, it constitutes an important contribution to narrative American history. The full significance of Clay's life is recognized in assigning two volumes to its treatment. The work has literary as well as biographic character. In narrating the political struggles and changes of Clay's period, the author shows a full recognition of the significance of movements of popular feeling which so frequently upset the balance of politicians. The work is also a real biography. The personality of Clay is constantly brought to the front. His weakness as well as strength is fully recognized.   D. R. D.

Clayton, Mrs. Victoria Virginia. White and black under the old régime; with introd. by Frederic Cook Morehouse. Milwaukee: Young Churchman Co. [c. 1899.] Net $1.   [**1866**

" In this little book we have the reminiscences of the widow of General Henry D. Clayton of the Confederate army. . . . It is a simple, straightforward account of the home of a southern girl and woman, on an Alabama plantation, from 1835 to 1886. . . . The second half of the book describes the Civil War, and its effects upon the quiet plantation life. The period of reconstruction is treated with simple dignity and with a strong sense of justice. . . . The book is written in an unpretending, at times almost school-girlish, style, and is strongly religious in tone. Slave-holding is justified by numerous citations from the Scriptures." *Am. hist. rev.*, 5: 401.

Clingman, Thomas Lanier. Selections from speeches and writings; with notes. Raleigh, N. C.: Nichols. 1877.   [1867

A collection of addresses and periodical contributions on various literary and scientific subjects. There are also many political speeches made while Clingman was a member of Congress between 1843 and 1861. He was first a Whig, then a Democrat, and withdrew from Congress when his state seceded.   E. E. S.

Cobb, Howell. Scriptural examination of the institution of slavery in the United States. [Perry], Ga.: Author. 1856.   [1868

The institution of slavery is held to rest upon two propositions: (1) African slavery is a punishment inflicted upon the enslaved for their wickedness; (2) slavery, as it exists in the United States, is the providentially arranged means by which Africa is to be lifted from her deep degradation to a state of civil and religious liberty. The Bible is taken as the authority. By repudiating slavery, England and the northern states declined the objects, present and ultimate, of the institution, and withdrew from this great providential enterprise. Abolitionism is regarded not as a political question, but as a religious delusion. The work, apart from the curious interpretation of Biblical authority, is marred by vulgar abuse of Abolitionists. The historical portion, relating to the importation of slaves, begins with chapter 3. Chapter 4 treats of the laws of the states; and chapter 5, of colonization.   D. R. D.

Cobb, Thomas R. R. Historical sketch of slavery from the earliest periods. Phil.: Johnson. Savannah: Williams. 1858.   [1869

The introduction and two chapters are taken from *The law of slavery* by the same author. The volume treats of slavery from the time of the Jews to about 1845. The freed negro is said to return to barbarism. The efforts of the Abolitionists are deplored. Colonization is claimed to be the only remedy.   E. E. S.

Coffin, Levi. Reminiscences. Cin.: Western Tract Soc. [c. 1876.] 2d ed. with app. Cin.: Clarke. 1880. $1.50.   [1870

Coffin was a member of the Society of Friends; resided in youth in North Carolina; and removed in early manhood (1822) to Indiana. Successful in business, he devoted time and money to the help of escaping slaves, — several thousand, it is estimated, in number. Because of his activity he was termed by some the president of the underground railroad. This volume of his reminiscences is a simple but thrilling record of the escapes with which the author was associated. It is one of the few books on the subject, and, owing to the fact that the work of aid had to be done in secrecy and without many written records, it is likely to remain a principal authority. The author kept diaries which are drawn upon for these memories, written in his 78th year.   D. R. D.

Congdon, Charles Taber. Reminiscences of a journalist. Boston: Osgood. 1880. [1871

These reminiscences begin with 1830. The author was reared in New Bedford. There is interesting information in regard to the Quakers, and the clergy of the day. The author afterwards became editor of the *Atlas* newspaper in Boston, and advocated the nomination of Harrison instead of Webster. Chapter 8 is devoted to an account of the Dorr rebellion. The author joined the staff of the New York *Tribune* in 1857. In the latter portion of the work there are many anecdotes of the stage and of literary characters, as Margaret Fuller, and Willis.   D. R. D.

Corwin, Thomas. MORROW, JOSIAH, *ed.* Life and speeches of Thomas Corwin. Cin.: W. H. Anderson. 1896. $3.50.   [1872

The best life of Corwin. It is accurate and impartial, but rather superficial. There is no thorough research, and too little discrimination in the use of material. The speeches are well edited, and are of value in the study of the history of the Union. Corwin was a Whig, and bitterly hostile to the Mexican war. His great speech on that topic deserves careful reading, as does also his noteworthy speech in the House on the eve of the Rebellion.   R. C. H. C.

— RUSSELL, ADDISON PEALE. Thomas Corwin; a sketch. Cin.: Clarke. 1881. $1.
    [1873

This sketch throws some light upon Corwin's character and career. It is full of anecdotes and gives some information upon social matters in Ohio. It is written in a loose, rhetorical style, and is of slight value.   R. C. H. C.

Crittenden, John Jordan. COLEMAN, *Mrs.* ANN MARY. Life of John J. Crittenden; with selections from his correspondence and speeches. Phil.: Lippincott. 1871. 2v. [1874

Crittenden, an able lawyer in Kentucky, was a member of the United States Senate 1817–19, 1835–41, 1842–48, and 1855–61; U. S. Attorney-General, 1841–42, during Harrison's brief administration, and also, 1850–53. This life is not a continuous narrative, but is made up of explanatory paragraphs, a large number of letters written to Crittenden and by him, and some of his speeches, pleas at the bar in criminal trials, and his somewhat famous argument while Attorney-General in favor of the constitutionality of the fugitive slave law. The work is of importance for the understanding of the inside politics which controlled the election of Harrison, and especially of Taylor in 1848. Much of this correspondence is of an intimate political character. There are nearly a score of letters from Henry Clay, fifteen from General Scott, three from General Taylor, four from Corwin, and nearly forty from Governor Letcher, of Kentucky. Light is thrown upon the rivalries of Jackson and Clay; the influences which led President Tyler in the veto of the bank bill; and Clay's presidential campaign in 1843–45. There is an important letter of Daniel Webster, October 23,

1843, defending his course in remaining in the Cabinet. The position of General Scott in the Mexican war and the Democratic plots against him are brought out in Scott's letters.   D. R. D.

Dabney, Thomas Smith Gregory. SMEDES, *Mrs.* SUSAN DABNEY. Memorials of a southern planter. Balt.: Cushings. 1887.
—— A southern planter. 4th ed. N. Y.: J. Pott. 1890. $1.25.   [1875

Mr. Thomas Dabney, born 1808, died 1886, resided the greater portion of his life in Mississippi. His daughter designed these memorials originally for the family, but was prevailed upon to publish them for a wider circulation. They are intensely interesting, vivid, and valuable as a portraiture of a southern planter of wealth and intelligence, who treated his slaves with patriarchal dignity and affection. The writer wishes the reader to know that all slave-owners were not wicked. Mr. Dabney lost nearly everything during the Rebellion, and the volume gives an account of the deprivations undergone during this period. The book is of less value for the reconstruction period. This work is of great importance, not merely as a biography, but as a contribution to social history.
    D. R. D.

Davis, Reuben. Recollections of Mississippi and Mississippians. Boston: Houghton. 1889. $3.   [1876

The work of a Mississippi "fire-eater," who was prominent in state politics for many years before the Civil War and member of Congress from 1857 to 1861 ; primarily of value for the social and political history of Mississippi, secondarily for national history, especially during Davis's congressional career ; evidently written from memory, however, and hence not always trustworthy. The author has little method, but a dispassionate temper, sound judgment and entertaining style.   R. C. H. C.

Dickens, Charles. American notes for general circulation. London: Chapman. 1842. 2v. [Many reprints.]   [1877

A superficial book, written as the result of a residence of six months in the United States. Dickens visited New England, the Middle States and the West, spending a few days also in Washington and Richmond. While sincere and fair, he had little insight into the conditions underlying American society. The furore caused by his book rather surprises the reader, for it is on thê whole favorable to America, though it violently attacks slavery and American manners.
    R. C. H. C.

Dix, John Adams. Speeches and occasional addresses. N. Y.: Appleton. 1865. 2v. $7.   [1878

The claims of the United States to Oregon are here forcibly and exhaustively presented. Other speeches deal in a scholarly and accurate manner with the French spoliation claims; the Mexican question, and the disputes growing out of the Mexican cessions. Dix was a Union Democrat. The volumes include papers on the New York militia system (1832), and on the New York system of education for teachers (1834).   R. C. H. C.

Douglas, Stephen Arnold. FLINT, H. M. Life of Stephen A. Douglas, by a member of the western bar. N. Y.: Derby. 1860. [1879

This was a campaign life of Douglas, written by the editor of a Chicago newspaper and published anonymously just prior to the Democratic Convention at Charleston in 1860. It is made up almost entirely of extracts from Douglas's speeches and from various resolutions and platforms. It is of little value.
    E. E. S.

—— SHEAHAN, JAMES W. Life of Stephen A. Douglas. N. Y.: Harper. 1860. [1880

No worthy life of Douglas exists. This one (written to secure for him the presidential nomination in 1860) is the best. Although fully as biased as Flint's (sect. 1879), it is more logical and better proportioned. Nor is it composed so largely of extracts from Douglas's speeches. Extremely eulogistic.   E. E. S.

Douglass, Frederick. Life and times; by himself. Hartford: Park Pub. Co. 1881. New rev. ed. Boston : De Wolfe. 1893. $2.50.   [1881

A highly interesting and instructive narrative. The account of slavery as it appeared to a slave is invaluable, and no other single source gives us such a strong and effective picture. The later portions, dealing with the author's life after the Civil War, are not of so much importance as are the earlier portions; but the whole volume is well written and worth reading.
    A. C. McL.

Du Bois, W. E. Burghardt. Suppression of the African slave trade to the United States. (Harvard historical studies, no. 1.) N. Y. : Longmans. 1896. Net $1.50.   [1882

This is a laborious and careful compilation of provincial, state and federal enactments in relation to the suppression of the slave trade. It shows great industry in the collection of facts and the examination of sources ; while there is little literary ability, it is written in a judicial spirit. The appendixes, including a typical list of cases of vessels engaged in the slave trade and a bibliography, occupy nearly a third of the whole volume and reproduce in brief the materials on which the narrative itself is based.
    S. B. W.

Dyer, Oliver. Great Senators of the United States forty years ago. N. Y. : Bonner. 1889. $1.   [1883

Chatty, entertaining, inaccurate and of little value. Dyer was a Washington newspaper correspondent, acquainted with the subjects of his sketches. He gives striking pictures of Clay, Webster, Calhoun, Benton, and others, which are by no means true, though hitting off disproportionately the most salient features of these men. There is no insight, and much exaggeration. There is some information about the nomination of Taylor.   R. C. H. C.

Everett, Edward. Orations and speeches on various occasions. Boston : Little. 1850–68. 4v. Net $16.   [1884

The only extended collection of Everett's addresses. The general arrangement is chronological. The author was sought for as the orator upon many great occasions during his public career, both at home and abroad ; and his orations and addresses, consequently, cover a remarkably wide range. Political addresses and speeches in Congress are not included in this collection.   W. MacD.

Fillmore, Millard. CHAMBERLAIN, IVORY. Biography of Millard Fillmore.   Buffalo : Thomas. 1856.   [1885

Published 18 years before Mr. Fillmore's death, it pays little heed, in any part of his career, to the purely personal elements ; yet fairly portrays the characteristics of the man. Nearly one half the book is devoted to the events of Mr. Fillmore's administration. His course on the compromise measures, especially the Fugitive Slave Act of 1850, is defended on constitutional grounds. An unpretentious but worthy work.   F. H. S.

Foote, *Rear-Admiral* **Andrew Hull.** Africa and the American flag. N. Y. : Appleton. 1854.   [1886

Lieut. Foote commanded the U. S. brig Perry, 1850–51, on the coast of Africa, with orders to break up the slave trade carried on in vessels flying the American flag. The first few chapters, devoted to a narrative of discoveries in Africa, the character of native tribes, commercial products, establishment of foreign trading agencies, the development of slave trade, are at the present time antiquated and unsatisfactory. Of value is the sketch of the foundation and early history of Liberia. The last half of the book is practically a copy of the log of the ship during the cruise to capture slavers. The narrative is clear, concise, and includes many thrilling incidents.   D. R. D.

Fowler, William Chauncey. The sectional controversy. N. Y.: Scribner. 1862. New ed. 1868.   [1887

" An outline history of parties in their territorial relations." Justin Winsor, in *Narrative and critical hist. of Am.*, 7: 298.

Fremont, *Mrs.* **Jessie (Benton.)** Souvenirs of my time. Boston : Lothrop. 1887. $1.50.   [1888

Mrs. Fremont does not believe in relating the defects of any one. Consequently, her chatty and interesting little book is almost worthless in regard to politics and politicians. It has value, however, as a picture of social life in Washington and the South prior to the War, as well as for some details in the life of Senator Benton. One half of the space is devoted to foreign memories.   R. C. H. C.

Garrison, William Lloyd. GARRISON, WENDELL P. *and* FRANCIS J. William Lloyd Garrison, 1805–79 : the story of his life told by his children. N. Y. : Century Co. 1885–9. 4v. New ed. Boston : Houghton. 1894. 4v. $8.   [1889

On the publication of the first two volumes, James Bryce wrote : " Although the treatise . . . is primarily a biography, and a very full and minute one, and although it is written with the reverential admiration of children rather than from the point of view of a dispassionate and critical historian, it is also virtually a history of the anti-slavery struggle. Seldom has a cause and a contest been more closely associated with the life of one man than in the case of abolition and Garrison. . . . All that need be now done is to call attention to the mass of valuable materials which the biographers of Garrison have provided for historical inquirers. These consist partly of extracts from his speeches and articles in the various journals which he edited, documents which have become so rare or so difficult of access as to be practically unavailable to a European reader, partly of his own letters and those of various friends or opponents to him. . . . The singular mental ferment which produced transcendentalism, the beginnings of the movement to obtain equal rights for women, the position of the New England clergy, are all brought out from a point of view new to most Englishmen, as well as the vehement intolerance which made it so difficult to advocate abolition even in the northern states." *English historical review*, 1: 185.

The *Atlantic* says that the book " might well bear the motto of the old Antislavery Standard, 'without concealment, without compromise.' The sons believe too completely and absolutely in their father to keep anything back." They are " so entirely truthful and so sure of their own case that, however much they may err, they will never be found withholding anything through unfair motives." Garrison's biographers " give from his own words a long series of self-revelations, which not only account for the triumphs of his life, but for its antagonisms and its troubles." *Atlantic*, 57: 120.

— SMITH, GOLDWIN. The moral crusader, William Lloyd Garrison : a biographical essay founded on The story of Garrison's life told by his children. N. Y. : Funk. 1892. $1. [1890

Few Americans have been so worthy of a biography as Garrison, dauntless hero that he was, however narrow and fanatical. The four-volumed work of his children, treating with fulness the incidents of his manly career, is a work which the world cannot at all spare, although few can spare time to read it throughout. Goldwin Smith rendered a service when, having in view the needs of busy men, he gave the pith of the four volumes in a little book of two hundred pages. Here at a glance it is possible to get a view of this most memorable life. Goldwin Smith, while writing with sympathy and admiration, yet uses a tone cool and discriminating. It is a résumé, put with the clearness and power of one of our first masters of English, of the career of one of our purest and strongest men.   J. K. H.

Giddings, Joshua Reed. JULIAN, GEORGE

WASHINGTON. Life of Joshua R. Giddings. Chicago: McClurg. 1892. [1891

Giddings entered Congress from the Western Reserve in Ohio in 1838, and from that time until the Civil War was one of the most determined anti-slavery agitators. He stood by John Quincy Adams in the long struggle for the right of petition. He believed in the principle of federal non-intervention with slavery. He declined to act with the Republican party in its early days, and was devoted to Henry Clay. He was, however, independent of party connection in his career. During his first session in Congress he kept a diary, much of which is reprinted, pages 47–72. His letters to Sumner, 1846–51, were also preserved, and are reprinted in part. The diary was recommenced in 1849. This work is invaluable for treatment of questions concerning the annexation of Texas, Oregon, and the long Kansas-Nebraska struggle. In the appendix is a series of essays published in 1842 over the signature of Pacificus. The biographer, his son-in-law, has done the work extremely well. The book ranks among the first of the political biographies for the period immediately preceding the Civil War. D. R. D.

Gobright, Louis A. Recollections of men and things at Washington during the third of a century. Phil.: Claxton. 1869. [1892

The author was an editor, correspondent, and Congressional reporter. The volume is exceedingly scrappy. The recollections begin with Jackson's administration. There are many anecdotes of Congressional and official life, but little of value that cannot be found elsewhere. D. R. D.

Greeley, Horace. History of the struggle for slavery extension or restriction in the United States. N. Y.: Dix. 1856. [1893

The title further says that it is mainly compiled from the journals of Congress and other official records, and that it shows the votes by yeas and nays on the most important divisions in either house. It is purely a history of action by Congress, and over 90 of the 164 pages are devoted to the Kansas-Nebraska struggle, including committee reports, texts of bills and of the Topeka constitution, and Seward's speech of March 3, 1854. The earlier contests in Congress, especially those over Missouri and the compromise of 1850, are also treated at length, abstracts of many of the speeches being given as well as the text of memorials, bills, etc. F. J. S.

—— Recollections of a busy life. N. Y.: Ford. 1868. New ed. ; with memoir. N. Y. Tribune. 1873. [1894

The larger part of these recollections was first published in the *New York ledger*. They are a frank revelation of the forces which influenced the author's life and thought, and are intended to represent convictions which, as he states, were a part of his being. The book is indispensable, not only for the understanding of the character of the most influential journalist in the United States 1840–1870, but also for throwing light upon certain phases of social and industrial development in regard to which there is none too much material. Here may be noted his accounts of pioneer settlement in western Vermont and Pennsylvania, the early condition of journalism in New York; the data as to earnings of artisans, the amount of pauperism and beggary, the condition of farming in the West, and the beginnings of the temperance movement. Mr. Greeley was interested in social reform movements. He was a supporter of the National Bank and a protective tariff, and had much to do with the early fortunes of the Republican party. Greeley's judgments are not well balanced, and an historical narrative by him demands further examination. D. R. D.

Grund, Francis Joseph. The Americans in their moral, social, and political relations. London: Longmans. 1837. 2v. Boston. 1837. 1v. [1895

The author, born in Bohemia (1806), emigrated to the United States and engaged in journalism. This work is written for the English people, "not as the observations of a tourist, but as the results of the experience of one who has resided in America many years." An attempt is made to give an impartial account of the present conditions of the United States, and to delineate the features which distinguish the American from the different nations of Europe. The author regarded the Americans as grossly misrepresented by several travellers and writers, such as Mrs. Trollope, Hamilton, and Basil Hall, who emphasized the superficial and anomalous features of society. This work is a serious discussion of American manners, the attitude of the United States toward foreign immigration, theatre and the arts, literature, journalism, education, religion, temperance, settlement of the west, commerce, travel, militia, and slavery. The tone is philosophic although the style is labored. The volume is one of the best aids in the study of the fundamental characteristics of the United States in the period 1830–1840. D. R. D.

Harris, Alexander. Review of the political conflict in America, from the commencement of the anti-slavery agitation. N. Y.: Pollock. 1876. [1896

"A compact book." Justin Winsor, in *Narrative and critical hist. of Am.*, 7: 323.

Helper, Hinton Rowan. The impending crisis of the South: how to meet it. N. Y.: Burdick. 1857. [1897

This book, written by a North Carolinian, created a tremendous sensation forty years ago. Its thesis is that slavery has ruined the South, in the interest of the slave-holders at the expense of the non-slaveholders. This is established by statistics illustrating southern inferiority as compared with the North, in agriculture, manufactures, commerce, wealth, population, education and literature. The statistics, though accurate, are unfair because incomplete. The book is written in the most violent anti-slavery temper, appealing as much to the passions as to the intellects of its readers. As a literary performance it is without merit. R. C. H. C.

Hildreth, Richard. Despotism in America, an inquiry into the nature, results, and legal basis of the slave-holding system in the United States. Boston : Whipple. 1840. Jewett. 1854. [1898

Written to prove that while the northern states were advancing toward democracy the southern states were growing into aristocracy. It considers, without concrete examples, the relation of the master and slave, the political, economical and personal results of the system, and the legal basis for slavery in the United States. The several chapters or essays are carefully written, but they set forth nothing novel even at the time they were written, except in the last chapter. The appendix contains an arraignment of Daniel Webster for his seventh of March speech.   E. E. S.

Hodgson, Joseph. Cradle of the Confederacy ; or The times of Troup, Quitman and Yancey. Mobile, Ala.: Hodgson. 1876. [1899

An historical sketch of the " cotton belt " states, with their grievances against the Federal government (alien and sedition laws, internal improvements, tariff, removal of Indians, etc.), closing with the successful attempt of Yancey to bring about the secession of Alabama. Written to prove that " the majority of the people of the South were opposed to secession, but were driven into it by northern enemies, rather than persuaded into it by southern leaders." Valuable as showing the attitude of parties in the south and the growth of secession feeling between 1850 and 1860. No index.   E. E. S.

Hoffman, Frederick L. Race traits and tendencies of the American negro. (Am. Economic Assoc. Publications, v. 11, nos. 1–3.) N. Y.: Macmillan. 1896. $2. [1900

This is by far the most intensive study of the negro race in America. Separate chapters deal with vital statistics, anthropometry, race amalgamation, and social and economic conditions and tendencies. The author, being of foreign birth, believes that he is free from personal bias. The statistical method is followed, and yet there is an abundance of descriptive text to make the book readable. The work is written from the standpoint that racial traits largely determine the form of social problems and their solutions. The conclusions are extremely depressing.   D. R. D.

Hone, Philip. Diary, 1828–51 ; ed. by Bayard Tuckerman. N. Y.: Dodd. 1889. 2v. $7.50. [1901

Philip Hone was born in New York in 1780 and was identified until his death in 1851 with the business, social, and in a slight measure the political life of his native city. His range of acquaintance in New York, Boston, and Baltimore was large. In 1826 he was chosen mayor of New York. The diary was begun in 1828 as a record chiefly of events of a business and personal character for convenience of reference; it soon became more elaborate, and the author " devoted an hour or more daily to chronicling events of interest, to comments on politics, literature, art, drama, or industrial subjects." This was without any view to publication. Large omissions are made in editing, and only about one fourth of the manuscript diary is published in these two volumes. The diary is inter-

esting in particular to the New Yorker and the student of the ceremonial life of society. Mr. Hone was an ardent Whig and enjoyed the friendship of many party statesmen, in particular that of Webster. There are convenient side headings and a fairly serviceable index.   D. R. D.

Houston, David Franklin. Critical study of nullification in South Carolina. (Harvard historical studies, 3.) N. Y.: Longmans. 1896. $1.25. [1902

A concise, scholarly work, dealing at first hand with a limited field. The early history of nullification in South Carolina, and its connection with the politics of the state and tariff legislation of the United States, have nowhere been so accurately exhibited. Especially important is the discussion of Calhoun's attitude, and his claim to leadership in the movement. An appendix gives a few relevant documents.   W. MacD.

Hurd, John Codman. Law of freedom and bondage in the United States. Boston: Little. 1858–62. 2v. [1903

The authority on this subject. An exhaustive classified abstract of national and local legislation and judicial decisions touching upon the question of slavery. The arrangement is chronological. Special attention is given to celebrated cases, such as Prigg *vs.* Pennsylvania, and Dred Scott. The volumes are too profound for the general reader.   E. E. S.

Jackson, *Gen.* **Andrew.** PARTON, JAMES. Life of Andrew Jackson. N. Y.: Mason. 1860. 3v. [1904

These volumes contain much valuable information, drawn from materials accessible only to Parton. He had not, however, the training of a scientific historian, or a clear perception of the causes of events. Moreover, he does not hesitate to draw conclusions unwarranted by the facts, sometimes contrary to the facts. He is, therefore, untrustworthy. There is much gossip, much elaborate writing for effect in an entertaining, diffusive style.   R. C. H. C.

— SUMNER, WILLIAM GRAHAM. Andrew Jackson. (American statesmen.) Boston : Houghton. 1882. Rev. ed. 1898. $1.25. [1905

A very able and critical treatment of the political and financial history of the years 1824–1840. The same aspects of the history of the preceding quarter of a century are discussed in a suggestive way in the earlier chapters. Prof. Sumner writes as an expounder of the processes of democratic government and a vigorous critic of financial theories and practice, rather than as the biographer of Jackson. The book is one of the most instructive on this period. It is written in a trenchant style and is compact with information.   E. G. B.

—— (See, also, in the preceding Period, sect. 1735.)

Jay, William. Miscellaneous writings on slavery. Boston : Jewett. 1853. [1906

Jay most skilfully and effectively presented the anti-slavery argument from the moral, social and political points of view, employing material drawn from public speeches, judicial decisions, the writings of slavery defenders and the newspapers. He was accurate, laborious and careful, and possessed great literary skill, a remarkable command of language, and a keen logical mind. He had no sympathy with the southern position. The book is the best of its kind. It savagely attacks the Colonization Society and all half-way measures; discussing also the action of the federal government in behalf of slavery; the right of petition; the question of territorial government in New Mexico and California; the Compromise of 1850 (particularly the fugitive slave clause) and the attitude of the Episcopal Church towards slavery.

R. C. H. C.

— TUCKERMAN, BAYARD. William Jay and the constitutional movement for the abolition of slavery; with pref. by John Jay. N. Y.: Dodd. 1893. $3.50. [1907

"A study of Judge Jay in a single phase of his career was well worth making. Something more than this, though less than a full life, is to be found in Mr. Tuckerman's narrative and Mr. John Jay's summary; but in the main we have to do with the relations of the subject of this memoir to the abolition societies and the political anti-slavery parties. . . . So far as Jay is allowed to speak in his own words, the book is a substantial addition to the sources of anti-slavery history; how much more so might it have been made if the store of MS. material implied on pp. 158–159 as available had been printed even without link or comment." *Nation*, 58: 16.

Jones, William D. Mirror of modern Democracy: a history of the Democratic party, 1825–61; [with] sketch of the old Federal and Republican parties. N. Y.: Miller. 1864.

[1908

The title fairly indicates the partisan spirit of the work, which is a non-critical arraignment of the Democratic party. The Democratic party and the institution of slavery are treated as identical. The several chapters treat of the Congressional acts during successive presidential administrations. The style, as well as the printing, is slovenly. The work has no value at the present time. D. R. D. ·

Julian, George Washington. Political recollections, 1840–72. Chicago: Jansen, McClurg & Co. 1884. [1909

The author was one of the most able public men of Indiana. He began political life as a Whig in the campaign of 1840, joined the Free-Soil party in 1848, and was a prominent anti-slavery man thereafter. He entered Congress in 1849 from the 4th Indiana district, when O. P. Morton was a Democratic leader. A natural antipathy between these men marked the course of both their lives. In 1872 Mr. Julian supported Greeley for the Presidency, and usually acted with the Democratic party thereafter, but with no abatement of his radicalism in everything growing out of the anti-slavery movement. He was son-in-law of Joshua

R. Giddings and intimate with the original anti-slavery men. He was an honest, aggressive, and independent leader, most vigorous in combat. His book is very valuable as a comment on and illumination of current events from his standpoint. He was also author of the *Life of Joshua R. Giddings* (sect. 1891), and of a volume of *Later speeches*. J. D. C.

Kemble, *Mrs.* Frances Anne. Journal of a residence on a Georgia plantation in 1838–39. London: Longmans. 1863. N. Y.: Harper. 1863. [1910

"The book is a permanent and most valuable chapter in our history. . . . It is a journal, kept from day to day, of the actual ordinary life of the plantation, where the slaves belonged to educated, intelligent, and what are called the most respectable people. . . . It is the journal of a hearty, generous, clear-sighted woman, who went to the plantation, loving the master, and believing that, though slavery might be sad, it might also be mitigated, and the slave might be content. It is the record of ghastly undeceiving. . . . There is no writing for effect. There is not a single 'sensational' passage. . . . As the mistress of the plantation, she was brought into constant intercourse with the slave-women; and no other account of this class is so thorough and plainly stated. . . . A sadder book the human hand never wrote." *Atlantic monthly*, 12: 260.

Kendall, Amos. Autobiography; ed. by William Stickney. Boston: Lee. 1872. $3. [1911

Not actually an autobiography, but written from Kendall's notes by his son-in-law. As Kendall was extremely able, and was most intimate and influential with Jackson, the work is of value as an original source especially for the years 1829–1840, during which the author held office under the government; but it is disappointing for its omissions, and not altogether trustworthy, since Kendall, though puritanically honest, was violently partisan. The style is bad, and wearisome. R. C. H. C.

King, Horatio. Turning on the light: a dispassionate survey of President Buchanan's administration from 1860 to its close. Phil.: Lippincott. 1895. [1912

The author of this book was Assistant Postmaster-General under President Buchanan, and Acting Postmaster-General after Mr. Holt's appointment as Secretary of War. About half the contents are an unsuccessful attempt to defend the administrative acts of President Buchanan dealing with secession, during the few months preceding the Civil War; but leaving much essential evidence entirely out of view. A number of letters are, however, printed which are worth examination by readers who wish to make an exhaustive study of the political history of that period. Only a small portion of the book bears directly upon the principal topic; it includes a biography of the author; original poems; essays on Webster, Raleigh, the Trent affair, Lincoln's Gettysburg address and many other subjects. The book is really a series of newspaper and magazine articles, the chapters having no logical connection, the whole possessing little literary merit, but written in a fair and impartial temper. R. C. H. C.

Lanman, Charles. Letters from the Alleghany Mountains. N. Y.: Putnam. 1848.   [1913

An interesting account of visits to the southern Appalachians, mostly in North Carolina, at a time when Dahlonega, Ga., was "reputed to be the wealthiest gold region in the United States." W. M. D.

Lawrence, Abbott. HILL, HAMILTON ANDREWS. Memoir of Abbott Lawrence. Boston: Little. 1883.   [1914

Lawrence was a Clay Whig, prominent as a New England manufacturer, philanthropist and politician. His biographer's abilities are moderate, and he fails to present Lawrence's position on slavery. Otherwise, he has done sufficient justice to his subject, the work being accurate, painstaking and valuable from the political and social points of view. It is a dull book. There is an appendix containing six letters from Lawrence to Rives, of Virginia, discussing the tariff and Virginia's economic conditions. R. C. H. C.

Leggett, William. Collection of political writings; [ed.] by Theodore Sedgwick, Jr. N. Y.: Taylor. 1840. 2v.   [1915

These volumes are collections of leading editorials appearing in the *New York evening post* and the *New York plaindealer*, from March, 1834, to July, 1837. They contain a variety of information, and materially assist in the comprehension of public opinion on Slavery; Abolition; Currency; the Sub-Treasury system; the Tariff and other vital questions of the day. Leggett was a Jackson Democrat, of strong natural parts, but imperfectly educated, with violent prejudices, savage temper, and erring judgment, but absolutely honest and open to conviction. His writings show strong argumentative and logical talents, supported by a plain and vigorous style. R. C. H. C.

Letters and documents relating to slavery in Massachusetts. See Massachusetts Historical Society, sect. 314.   [1916

Lieber, Francis. PERRY, THOMAS SERGEANT, *ed.* Life and letters of Francis Lieber. Boston: Osgood. 1882. Boston: Houghton. $3.   [1917

This is a very valuable book for a student of conditions in the United States from 1827 to 1872. Lieber dwelt for twenty-one years in South Carolina, but his sympathies in the slavery controversy were with the North. His criticisms and comments are always eminently fair and unprejudiced, and reveal his remarkable insight and correctness of judgment. Here, in letters to prominent Americans, are discussions of many political topics, particularly slavery, the McLeod case, the right of search, and the Kansas-Nebraska question, along with much information about the leaders of the nation, especially those in New England. R. C. H. C.

Lincoln, Abraham, *and* **Stephen Arnold Douglas.** Political debates in the campaign of 1858 in Illinois; including the preceding speeches of each, at Chicago, Springfield, etc.; also the two great speeches of Lincoln in Ohio, in 1859. Columbus: Follett. 1860. Cleveland: O. S. Hubbell. 1895. New ed. Burrows. 1898. Net $3.50.   [1918

This book, with a slightly different arrangement of the speeches, and with the addition of an index, was republished in 1895 by O. S. Hubbell & Co. of Cleveland. There were seven joint debates, and five other speeches by Lincoln and two by Douglas are included. F. J. S.

Livermore, George. On the opinions of the founders of the republic respecting negroes. See Massachusetts Historical Society, sect. 324.   [1919

Lovejoy, Elijah Parish. TANNER, HENRY. The martyrdom of Lovejoy: life of Rev. Elijah P. Lovejoy, who was killed by a pro-slavery mob at Alton, Ill., 1837. Chicago: Fergus Prtg. Co. 1881.   [1920

Mr. Tanner was not only an eye-witness of the killing, but, rifle in hand, was one of the twenty defenders of the building which contained Lovejoy's press, the destruction of which was the principal object of the mob. His statement is accompanied by that of another of the defenders, and the book contains also the address of Dr. Channing to the citizens of Boston regarding the Lovejoy killing and the memorable maiden speech of Wendell Phillips in Faneuil Hall Dec. 8, 1837, at a meeting held to take action regarding the Alton outrage. F. J. S.

Lowell, James Russell. The Biglow papers. Cambridge. 1848. Boston: Houghton. 1890. $1.   [1921

The first series, published originally in the *Boston courier*, 1846–1848, gave a most telling expression to the New England anti-slavery feeling in opposition to the Mexican War. As such they are an historical document throbbing with life and of the highest value. The second series, published in the *Atlantic monthly*, similarly gives utterance to the Unionist feeling during the Civil War in regard to the South and the attitude of England. In the Introduction to the second series the author gives an account of the origin of the first series. The *Biglow papers* are by far the most powerful political satire that has been produced in America. E. G. B.

Lunt, George. Origin of the late war; traced from the beginning of the Constitution. N. Y.: Appleton. 1866.   [1922

The author was the editor, in connection with George Hillard, of the democratic *Boston courier* prior to and during the Civil War. His point of view is that of the northern pro-slavery man, and his thesis is that the anti-slavery agitation was factitious in its origin and character, so far as its positively efficient agents pursued it, and was the fruit of a struggle for political power, instead of a moral or philanthropical demonstration. The aggression of the anti-slavery men is treated as the cause of the war, and slavery, if not actually defended, is palliated as a good thing for the country and perhaps even for the slaves, as shown by their submissiveness. The view taken of Lincoln's character in chap. 20 illustrates the opinion of him held by his contemporary opponents. F. J. S.

McDougall, Marion Gleason. Fugitive slaves, 1619–1865. (Fay House monographs, no. 3.) Boston : Ginn. 1891. [1923

A scholarly investigation of the legal and social history of runaway slaves in the United States from 1619 to 1865. It includes the national legislation to secure the return of slaves, the personal liberty laws, the underground railway, the various emancipation steps, and the final repeal of the fugitive slave acts. The references are voluminous. Appendixes contain a summary of all laws bearing on the subject and a good bibliography. Published as one of the Fay House monographs of the Harvard Annex. E. E. S.

Marryat, *Capt.* Frederick. Diary in America. London : Longmans. 1839. 6v. [1924

Captain Marryat visited the United States in 1837 after Miss Martineau had greatly irritated the American people with her book on the United States. Marryat considered himself much handicapped by this prejudice and thought it inadvisable, even if there had been an opportunity, to seek introductions which would admit him to social privileges. He travelled quite generally, and his book is made up of numerous anecdotes and not very profound observations in regard to the scenes that he passed through. He is, however, keen in his analysis of human character, and in distinguishing between the many types of American character. The book is characterized by a reckless humor, with a large stock of anecdotes. The last volume is devoted to Canada. D. R. D.

Martineau, Harriet. Retrospect of western travel. London : Saunders. 1838. 3v. N. Y.: Harper. 1838. 2v. [1925

A description of a voyage from England to America and a tour through the latter country made in 1834. The tour included the Hudson, Niagara, Washington, New Orleans, the Mississippi, Cincinnati, and New England. The descriptions of social life are the most valuable, but are not always reliable. The strictures on slavery were ill received when first published. There are side chapters on Aaron Burr, Channing, and a Harvard Commencement. See *Society in America* by the same author, below. E. E. S.

—— Society in America. London : Saunders. 1837. 3v. N. Y. 1837. 2v. [1926

Miss Martineau's object was to give an account of her travels, and to compare "the existing state of society in America with the principles on which it is proposedly founded." She was in the country from the 19th of September, 1834, to the 1st of August, 1836 ; visited all sections, and met the leading men and women. She discusses politics, economic life, civilization and religion. Possessing extensive knowledge, natural quickness to acquire, sound judgment and a keen intellect, her opinions are of much value, and are presented in a clear, incisive and entertaining manner. R. C. H. C.

May, Samuel Joseph. Some recollections of our antislavery conflict. Boston : Fields. 1869. [1927

Mr. May "was one of the earliest disciples that gathered around Mr. Garrison when he first rallied the movement which marched forward during thirty years through an unbelieving and resisting world to its final triumph. . . . The ferocity of the pro-slavery papers of thirty years since can hardly be conceived of by the generation that has grown up since then. . . . Mr. May was spectator and part of all this passage of history, and we think his tale of what he witnessed and underwent while a minister in Connecticut and as General Agent of the Massachusetts Anti-Slavery Society will seem hardly credible to the present generation. And yet it is but a plain, unvarnished tale of unexaggerated facts. Mr. May does not profess to write a history of the anti-slavery movement, but merely to relate his own experiences in connection with it. . . . His sketches of the men and women who took part in it, especially in its early days, are generally good, though perhaps a little undiscriminating in point of praise. Although always an ardent and active Abolitionist in whatever sphere of other duty he might find himself, he was not directly connected with the operations of the movement after he ceased to be the agent of the Massachusetts Society." *Nation*, 9: 343.

—— Mumford, Thomas J., *ed.* Memoir of Samuel Joseph May. Boston : Roberts. 1873. New ed. Boston : Am. Unitarian Assoc. 1882. 75c. [1928

A considerable portion of this memoir is autobiographical, another portion is made up of extracts from a diary, while the rest consists of chapters contributed by various writers, friends of Mr. May. The volume is an appreciative and beautiful tribute to a singularly noble life. B. A. H.

Monroe, James. Oberlin Thursday lectures, addresses and essays. Oberlin, O.: Goodrich. 1897. $1.25. [1929

An early associate in the lecture field with Garrison, Phillips, and Douglass, U. S. Consul at Rio de Janeiro during the Civil War, Member of Congress for ten years, and the rest of his life Professor of History and International Law, Mr. Monroe has garnered in these papers most valuable recollections of the early abolitionists, of the causes of the war, of Mr. Seward and Lincoln's Department of State, of our naval officers on foreign station, and outside views of our great conflict. For matter, for wisdom of appreciative comment, and for attractive style, alike, the book is important in its field and period. J. D. C.

Mott, James *and* Lucretia. Hallowell, Anna Davis, *ed.* James and Lucretia Mott : life and letters. Boston : Houghton. 1884. $2. [1930

Among the few biographies relating to the Friends (Quakers). Of service in studying the abolition movement, the anti-slavery societies, and fugitive slaves and "the underground railroad" in the state of Pennsylvania. Introduces Garrison, Phillips, Parker and others. Judicious although sympathetic editing.

E. E. S.

Nichols, Thomas L. Forty years of American life. London: Maxwell. 1864. 2v. 2d ed. 1v. Longmans. 1875. [**1931**

The author was a northerner who, on the outbreak of the rebellion, took refuge in England. He regarded the action of the government as unconstitutional, and yet he could not fight against the union. While in exile, he wrote the work as a description of America, to show what was most distinctive in its institutions and people. It includes a survey of the customs, militia system, country schools, state of religion and morals. Chapter 9 describes the mobbing of Garrison in Boston; chapter 10, factory life in Lowell. Other chapters describe Buffalo and life on the Great Lakes, early visits to the West about the period 1840, New Orleans in 1845, social experiments, spiritualism, foreign elements in the population, Roman Catholic Church, etc. Vol. 2, pages 227–347, is devoted to slavery and the cause of the war. The work is clearly and attractively written, and, while not important, is interesting in its portraiture.

D. R. D.

Olmsted, Frederick Law. The cotton kingdom ; a traveller's observations on cotton and slavery in the American slave states. N. Y.: Mason. 1861. 2v. [**1932**

Based upon three previous books by the author, namely, *A journey in the seaboard slave states* (1856); *A journey through Texas* (1857); *A journey in the back country* (1860). "The actual economical results of slave labor upon the value of property, the comfort and the dignity of life and manners, mind, domestic economy, education, religion, social welfare, tone and tendency, may there be found, copious, specific, and authentic." H. T. Tuckerman, *America and her commentators*, p. 417.

—— Journey in the seaboard slave states. N. Y.: Dix. 1856. [**1933**

This work, contributed in the form of letters to the *New York daily times*, deals almost entirely with economic life in the South. The author, an ardent abolitionist, sees everything from that standpoint. He makes slavery responsible for all its ills, and has a remarkable faculty for seeing the worst side of southern society. But this is not to be wondered at when his great ability in reporting the small talk picked up from negroes and the lower class of whites is considered. The work abounds in bitterness, prejudice, misrepresentation and contradictions. Still, the author was a close observer, and there is much in the way of descriptions of country that is reliable.

S. B. W.

Ormsby, Robert McKinley. History of the Whig party. Boston: Crosby. 1859. [**1934**

This work, at the present time, is of little consequence to the general reader, save as an example of a work written by an ardent supporter of the Whig party strongly criticising the abolition movement in the North. He has much to say in regard to the hypo-

crisy of England and the publication of anti-slavery misrepresentations in America by British gold. Chapters 22–24 are devoted to the tariff and nullification questions. The author again refers to the use of British gold to defeat the election of Mr. Clay in 1844. Mr. Seward is regarded as an unsafe counsellor, and altogether too radical on the slavery question. Webster's seventh of March speech is commended.

D. R. D.

Parker, Theodore. Trial of Theodore Parker for the "misdemeanor" of a speech in Faneuil Hall against kidnapping, before the Circuit Court of the United States, at Boston, April 3, 1855 ; with the defence by Theodore Parker. Boston: Author. 1855. N. Y.: Appleton. 1864. [**1935**

While the return of Anthony Burns to slavery was under consideration by the federal court in Boston, Mr. Parker was one of the speakers at a Faneuil Hall meeting held to protest against this enforcement of the fugitive slave law. At the same time a riot occurred at the court house in which one of the United States Marshal's men was killed. On the theory that Parker's speech led to this affair he was indicted as having wilfully obstructed, resisted, and opposed the Marshal. The indictment was ultimately quashed on a technicality, but Parker published in August this defence as if it were a speech to the jury in his case. It is largely a review of past judicial tyranny in England and America and a vindication of the right of juries to disregard instructions, while the federal officials who sought to enforce the fugitive slave law are scored with withering severity.

F. J. S.

—— FROTHINGHAM, OCTAVIUS BROOKS. Theodore Parker. Boston : Osgood. 1874. N. Y.: Putnam. $2. [**1936**

In this life of Theodore Parker Mr. Frothingham has given us an exceptionally good biography of a great American of the New England type. Parker's inherited traits and gifts, his home and student life, his career as preacher, philosopher, heretic, reformer, philanthropist and patriotic citizen, are set forth in a way that makes him an attractive and impressive personality. The story is told with sympathy and great delicacy, with hearty appreciation and yet with unfailing candor. The space given to John Brown seems disproportionate ; but the matter is interesting.

A. D. M.

Paulding, James Kirke. Slavery in the United States. N. Y.: Harper. 1836. [**1937**

A defence of slavery on the ground that it is necessary to have a laboring class, that the negro is better off in civilized slavery than savage freedom, and that the condition of the slave in America compares favorably with that of the common laborer in Europe. The argument is in the abstract, without examples. Numerous stories of the atrocities and superstition of the blacks are added.

E. E. S.

Peck, Charles Henry. The Jacksonian epoch. N. Y.: Harper. 1899. $2.50. [**1938**

"This is a plainly told and interesting account of

our politics, from Jackson's victory at New Orleans in 1815 to the Democratic defeat in 1840. . . . Mr. Peck has sought an original treatment of the period, as a Jackson-Clay 'epoch,' in a separation of the careers and rivalry of the two leaders and of the causes with which they were concerned from the continuity and generality of our history. He has, besides, hit upon the device of an account of public events which shall be more biographical than history and more historical than biography. But the difficulty with this is obvious, that the result must likewise be less historical than history and less biographical than biography. Although it escapes one limitation of each, it does not reach the complete and artistic result of either. . . . Mr. Peck is broad in sympathy and liberal in judgment. He scrupulously sums up the material facts; and if his conclusions need correction, his reader is helped to make it. He sketches Jackson, Clay, Calhoun, Van Buren, and Benton in lifelike fashion; and he generously judges them all." Edward M. Shepard, in *Am. hist. rev.*, 5 : 148.

Perry, Benjamin Franklin. Reminiscences of public men; prefaced by life of the author by H. M. Perry. Phil.: Avil. 1883.
—— Reminiscences of public men, with speeches and addresses. 2d series. Greenville, S. C.: Shannon. 1889. [**1939**

The first series contains notices of fifty public men, mostly southern, originally written for periodicals and newspapers. Mr. Perry for many years edited a newspaper in South Carolina, and was active in public life in that State during the period 1830-70. He was an opponent to nullification, but accepted secession and joined the Confederacy. After the war he was Provisional Governor of South Carolina. There is little new information in regard to the several characters described, but the work as a whole, because of its frankness, and sympathetic interest with the characters described, gives a suggestive picture of the southern gentleman in public life before the war. In addition to the sketches in the second series, there is a history of the nullification movement, pages 199-228. There is also published a speech of July 3, 1865, which created much interest in the North; an account of the provisional governorship of South Carolina in 1865, page 242; and a history of the Philadelphia national union convention in 1866. To the general student, the second series is of more value. Both volumes contain a wealth of anecdote. D. R. D.

Phillips, Wendell. Speeches, lectures and letters. Boston. 1863-91. 2v. Beacon ed.: Lee. 2v. $1.50 ea. pap. 50c. ea. [**1940**

The first series of Phillips' writings was published in 1863, — the collection being made under his supervision. The second series, printed in 1891, after his death, includes not only the most important addresses of his later life but also a few of the earlier period. Among those bearing on the slavery question are the murder of Lovejoy, 1837; the Sims case; opposition to Judge Loring because of the rendition of Burns; John Brown; and the eulogy on Garrison (2d ed.). The second volume is devoted more largely to other reform movements in which Phillips was interested, as Woman's rights, Labor question, Temperance. Here

also are his famous lectures on "The lost arts," and "Daniel O'Connell." As platform utterances effective in the field of agitation, Phillips' speeches are deserving of careful reading by the critical student. The positive information conveyed, however, is not great, nor are his constitutional arguments of much value.
 D. R. D.

—— AUSTIN, GEORGE LOWELL. Life and times of Wendell Phillips. Boston: Lee. 1884. New ed. 1888. $1.50. [**1941**

From the time that Wendell Phillips appeared at the Boston Faneuil Hall meeting after the murder of Lovejoy, in 1837, he occupied a prominent position in the anti-slavery agitation. Of good social position, he originally carried into the radical abolition movement an undoubted force, while his unrivalled eloquence and gifts of oratory commanded, throughout the long struggle, a hearing denied to others. He belonged to the small group who would sacrifice national unity and the constitution to free the North from the responsibilities of slavery. He entered with ardor into other reforms, as in that for Woman's rights in 1850, and after the war showed active sympathy for the labor and greenback movements. This biography is eulogistic and not discriminating. D. R. D.

Pierce, Franklin. HAWTHORNE, NATHANIEL. Life of Franklin Pierce. Boston : Ticknor. 1852.
—— *Same.* (In Hawthorne, N. Sketches and studies. Boston: Houghton. $1.) [**1942**

Hawthorne was a classmate of General Pierce at Bowdoin College, and, when the latter was nominated by the Democratic party for the presidency of the United States in 1852, out of friendship and a sense of justice he wrote this biographical sketch. The characterization of Pierce, as a public man, is more favorable than is now generally accepted by historians. While the sketch is too eulogistic, it is of particular value as an estimate of the personal or more private character of Pierce. D. R. D.

Pike, James Shepherd. First blows of the Civil War. N. Y.: Am. News Co. 1879. [**1943**

A volume of the private correspondence on the politics of the day of Horace Greeley, C. A. Dana, J. S. Pike and their political friends, including Chase, Seward and Sumner. The letters cover the period 1850-1860. Greeley was editor-in-chief, Dana the managing editor, and Pike the Washington correspondent of the *New York tribune*. A most interesting and valuable glimpse behind the scenes of the political struggles which prepared the way for the Civil War.
 E. G. B.

Pillsbury, Parker. Acts of the anti-slavery apostles. Boston: Cupples. 1884. [**1944**

Written by a fanatical Abolitionist and "comeouter," and presents excellently that side of the anti-slavery movement. It is full of information, quoting abolitionist documents and narrating the tempestuous experiences of the writer and his fellows in the abolition crusade in New Hampshire. It bitterly attacks the churches; makes plain the hostility between new school and old school abolitionist, and the impossibility of reaching any compromise with the extremists, men absolutely without judgment, tact, humor or a sense of proportion. The book is very disputatious, with little method and frequent repetitions, and is written in a loose, turgid style.   R. C. H. C.

Polk, James Knox. CHASE, LUCIEN B. History of the Polk administration. N. Y.: Putnam. 1850.   [1945

Chase was a Democratic member of Congress and wrote as the apologist of Polk's administration, especially of the Mexican War measures. He uses documents, but with little judgment, and is extremely partisan, justifying the President's acts throughout. He is fair, however, in his estimate of Polk's character and abilities. The style is abominably rhetorical, and the author's appreciation of American valor in the Mexican War is ludicrously excessive.
R. C. H. C.

Pollard, Edward Albert. Black diamonds gathered in the darkey homes of the South. N. Y.: Rudney. 1859.   [1946

The author, who was editor of the *Richmond examiner* during the Civil War, exhibits the southern view of slavery in the form of a series of letters to a northern friend. The book is of slight moment except for the curious indignation shown by its author over the contempt of some slaves for the poor whites and for his advocacy of the reopening of the slave trade.
F. J. S.

Powell, Aaron M. Personal reminiscences of the anti-slavery and other reforms and reformers. Plainfield, N. J.: Anna Rice Powell. 1899. $2.   [1947

" An unfinished fragment of autobiography, whose chief interest lies in the simple story of the author's enlistment in the abolition cause. . . . His reminiscences add but little to our knowledge of his eminent coadjutors. . . . Numerous portraits and facsimiles further make this volume a useful contribution to anti-slavery literature, as well as a memorial of a most excellent man." *Nation,* 69: 428.

Prentiss, Seargent Smith. SHIELDS, JOSEPH D. Life and times of Seargent Smith Prentiss. Phil.: Lippincott. 1884.   [1948

Mr. Prentiss, a northerner by birth, settled in Mississippi, studied law, and later obtained fame as an unrivalled orator. This biography, written by a friend, is a fairly complete narrative, with copious extracts from many of his speeches and addresses. These it was impossible to report accurately, and, as Prentiss left little manuscript, they are regarded as but inadequate indices of Prentiss' genius. Prentiss took but little part in politics. He earnestly opposed the act of repudiation by Mississippi. He was in Congress a brief period, and made a speech against the sub-treasury system. The style of this biography is characterized in places by exaggerated rhetoric, and as a biography, the narrative is somewhat confused.
D. R. D.

Pro-slavery argument, as maintained by the most distinguished writers of the southern states: containing essays of Chancellor Harper, Governor Hammond, Dr. Simms, and Professor Dew. Phil.: Lippincott. 1853.   [1949

Harper was one of the most distinguished jurists of South Carolina, had been a United States Senator, was twice elected Chancellor of the state, and was prominent in the nullification movement. James Henry Hammond, who made in the United States Senate a speech in which two famous phrases occurred, — one regarding northern " mudsills " and the other declaring " cotton is king," — was governor of South Carolina when he wrote the two letters on slavery in reply to a circular by Thomas Clarkson, the English abolitionist, which here appear. Dr. Simms was William Gilmore Simms, the South Carolina novelist, and his essay on the morals of slavery, here printed in amplified form, appeared originally in the *Southern literary messenger* as a review of Miss Martineau's *Society in America.* Thomas R. Dew was a professor in William and Mary College and afterwards its president. His *Essay in favor of slavery* (1833) " produced an extraordinary effect on the public mind and for a while set at rest the subject of emancipation in Virginia."   F. J. S.

Quitman, *Maj.-Gen.* **John Anthony.** CLAIBORNE, JOHN FRANCIS HAMTRAMCK. Life and correspondence of John A. Quitman. N. Y.: Harper. 1860. 2v.   [1950

The life of a Mississippi disunionist written by a disciple ; containing information upon the nature of slavery in Mississippi ; the development of the opinion that slavery was a " positive good ; " southern plans regarding Texas, Mexico and Cuba ; the growth of the ideas of state sovereignty, nullification, and secession; reveals clearly " the irrepressible conflict." The book is composed largely of original letters, and is written with the utmost frankness, the author being irreconcilably opposed to the North and to all compromise ; his materials are not well digested, the book being original matter rather than a finished product.
R. C. H. C.

Raumer, Friedrich Ludwig Georg von. America and the American people; tr. from the German by Wm. W. Turner. N. Y.: Langley. 1846.   [1951

Written by the great German historian from personal observation and material collected during a visit to the United States. It contains a mass of information on historical, political, social and economic subjects, much of it now without value, though the book is still of service as giving a picture of American life. The author was in sympathy with the country and its people ; possessed insight ; was unprejudiced and thoroughly equipped for his task. The principal criticism of his work is that he depended too much on material furnished by others. Letters written by him while in America are appended, and constitute perhaps the most valuable part of the book. R. C. H. C.

Ross, Alexander Milton. Recollections and experiences of an Abolitionist, 1855–65. Montreal. 1867. Toronto: Rowsell. 1875.
[1952

The author was a Canadian, and in 1856 entered upon the work of freeing slaves. He describes his visit to the United States in order to learn the safest methods of procedure. He frequently visited the South to carry out his projects. He describes several interviews with John Brown, who disclosed some of his plans. Pages 66 to 109 are devoted to Brown's trial. This volume, while very small and brief, is exact in details of the underground railroad. There are brief abstracts from letters of the abolitionists.   D. R. D.

Schmeckebier, Laurence Frederick. History of the Know-Nothing party in Maryland. (Johns Hopkins Univ. studies, ser. 17, nos. 4–5.) Balt. 1899. Pap. 75c.   [**1953**

This is an excellent account of the rise and fall of Know-Nothingism in Maryland. Mr. Schmeckebier has drawn his information from the newspapers of the time, official documents, pamphlets, contemporary letters, and conversations with members of the party who were living when he wrote. His study will form a valuable chapter in that history of the Know-Nothing party in the United States that yet remains to be written.   C. M. A.

Scott, Dred. HOWARD, BENJAMIN CHEW. Report of the decision of the Supreme Court of the U. S. and the opinions of the judges thereof in the case of Dred Scott *vs.* John F. A. Sandford. Dec. term, 1856. From 19th vol. of Howard's reports. Wash. 1857. [**1954**

Text of the opinion of Chief Justice Taney and of the separate opinions of Justices Wayne, Nelson, Grier, Daniel, Campbell, Catron, McLean, and Curtis. The last two dissented from the opinion of the court. Justice Nelson dissented on a single point but expressed no views regarding the Missouri Compromise law. The other six declared that act unconstitutional.   F. J. S.

Seabury, Samuel. American slavery distinguished from the slavery of English theorists and justified by the law of nature. N. Y.: Mason. 1861.   [**1955**

The writer was rector of a church in New York. He admits that slavery may be wrong on economic and legal grounds, but defends it in its moral and religious aspects. The arguments are based largely on the Scriptures. The publication gave offense to many northern readers. See the *North American review*, April, 1861.   E. E. S.

Seaton, William Winston. William Winston Seaton of the National intelligencer : a biographical sketch. Boston : Osgood. 1871.   [**1956**

Mr. Seaton and his brother-in-law, Joseph Gales, were from 1812 until the death of the latter in 1860 the proprietors of the *National intelligencer* of Washington (Mr. Seaton retaining his connection with the paper until 1865), and from 1812 to 1820 they were the exclusive reporters of the debates in Congress. Mr. Seaton was for 12 years from 1840 Mayor of Washington, and, closely associated with many of the leading statesmen from the time of Madison to that of Buchanan, he was especially intimate with Webster. This book, prepared by his daughter, consists chiefly of letters from various hands which, generally of a social and personal rather than a political character, give information about all sorts of celebrities from Lafayette to David Crockett. It has the merit of being as readable as it is discursive.   F. J. S.

Seward, William Henry. Works ; ed. by George E. Baker. N. Y.: Redfield. 1853–61. 4v. New ed. enl. Boston: Houghton. 1883. 5v. $15.   [**1957**

The first three volumes of this work were published in 1853. The first contains a memoir of Seward by the editor. Volume four was added in 1861. It continues the memoir, contains the important speeches which Seward delivered in the Senate between 1853 and 1861, and a brief but helpful biography of De Witt Clinton. Volume five was published after Seward's death and completes the series. In this are found a diary and notes on the war, selections from Seward's diplomatic correspondence, and his later speeches. The gubernatorial addresses in the second volume are of special value to the student of New York politics and furnish helpful material on the development of internal improvements. To the student of national politics, the speeches on the slave question and the beginnings of the Republican party, in the fourth volume, are of special importance. There is an index for each volume. As the work was published at different stages, it lacks a well-digested plan. The editor has added, however, occasional notes of value.   D. R. D.

—— Autobiography, 1801–34 ; with memoir, 1831–46, by Frederick W. Seward. N. Y.: Appleton. 1877.

— SEWARD, FREDERICK W. Seward at Washington, 1846–72. [Suppl. to above.] N. Y.: Derby. 1891. 2v.   [**1958**

The autobiographical portion consists of less than one fourth of the first volume, ending with the year 1834 when Seward was elected Governor of New York at the early age of 33. The narrative of early life, his entrance into and rapid progress in politics is candid and interesting. The memoir by his son begins with the year 1831. A large part of this consists of extracts from Seward's letters, journals and speeches. The letters to his wife were especially frequent and unreserved, so that for considerable periods of Seward's life they serve as a diary. Notes of conversations, anecdotes, political and social gossip are freely included. The editor, Seward's son, was closely associated with his father, being engaged in New York journalism for some years before the Civil War, and after his father's appointment as Secretary of State, made Assistant Secretary. The editor has endeavored to make the work " the story of a life, not the history of a time." The correspondence with Thurlow Weed is particularly noteworthy and includes a considerable number of letters from Weed to Seward.   D. R. D.

— LOTHROP, THORNTON KIRKLAND. William Henry Seward. (American statesmen.) Boston: Houghton. 1896. $1.25.   [**1959**

Seward was Governor of New York 1838–42; United States Senator 1849–61; and Secretary of State during the administrations of Lincoln and Johnson. The most important official incidents during his governorship were the McLeod affair and a controversy with the state of Virginia over the return of fugitive slaves; as Senator he participated in the great debates over the Compromise of 1850, the repeal of the Missouri Compromise, and the Kansas struggle; and as Secretary of State his administration dealt with the delicate questions of diplomacy occasioned by the Civil War. On all these and other minor political events in which Seward, as a public official, was involved, this biography represents a careful and judicious narrative. It is recognized that Seward made mistakes; on the other hand the loftiness of Seward's purpose and the strength of his character are impressed upon the reader. The work is more a partial history of the period covered than a biography. There is little attempt to portray Seward's personality, and in this respect the biography is too colorless and lacks interest.   D. R. D.

Siebert, Wilbur Henry. The underground railroad from slavery to freedom; with an introd. by Albert Bushnell Hart. N. Y.: Macmillan. 1898. $4.   [1960

"No one before Professor Siebert has undertaken to make a survey of the whole field of operations of the philanthropists, southern as well as northern, who made organized efforts to guide and shelter fugitives from slavery. These efforts were necessarily secret, and it was unsafe to keep records. . . . Professor Siebert's work has been to piece together a multitude of independent facts, obtained at the cost of immense labor. It is well he began his task while many are living who were active agents of the underground railroad. . . . He names not only the leaders and heroes of the movement, but humbler devotees to the cause of liberty, to the number of several thousands. In an appendix he gives thirty-five pages of closely printed names of underground railroad operators, arranged alphabetically by states and counties, and this is but one of many examples of his thoroughness which might be given. . . . Professor Hart, of Harvard University, contributes an introduction to this valuable work, in which he calls attention to the points upon which Professor Siebert's immense labor throws new light." Samuel T. Pickard, in *American historical review*, 4: 557.

Smith, Gerrit. FROTHINGHAM, OCTAVIUS BROOKS. Gerrit Smith: a biography. N. Y.: Putnam. 1878.   [1961

Gerrit Smith was a resident of the interior of New York state, devoted during the period 1830–70 to reforms, embracing temperance, land reform, and, especially, the freedom of the negro slave. This account of him, written by a sympathetic friend and radical, is a series of characterizations under the headings of religion, humanity, temperance, slavery, etc., rather than a biographical narrative. Copious extracts are made from Smith's letters, tracts, and speeches. He was an uncompromising abolitionist, and represents on the slavery question, the radical position. The book is of value for its references to the underground

railroad, fugitive slave law, and the John Brown episode.   D. R. D.

Southern literary messenger. Richmond, Aug. 1834–June, 1864. 36 v. (Revived and numbers issued for May, June, July, 1890; from Washington, D. C.)   [1962

This magazine, founded in 1834 by Thomas W. White, was soon put under the editorial management of Edgar Allan Poe, and his remarkable work as a poet, story teller and critic, gave the magazine a national reputation which it maintained with more or less variation during the thirty years of its existence. It became an American magazine and drew both support and contributions from all quarters. All the best writers of the South are represented in its pages. It became the chief depository for the literary output of the South, and as such will bear comparison with other contemporary American magazines. It was devoted principally to literary movements, with history and economic problems as side issues, but in later years became a bold and outspoken advocate of southern institutions and an exponent of southern opinions. Its chief value lies in the fact that it is a great storehouse for the history of southern life and manners.   S. B. W.

Sprague, *Col.* John Titcomb. Origin, progress, and conclusion of the Florida war. N. Y.: Appleton. 1848.   [1963

"The story of the wonderful contests of a savage tribe of less than four thousand, of all ages, in 1822, and less than one thousand in 1845, with the disciplined forces of the United States, for nearly a quarter of a century, is here told with all its minutest relations." T. W. Field, *Indian bibliography*, p. 375.

Still, William. The underground railroad. Phil.: Porter. 1872.

——— Underground railroad records; new rev. ed., with life of author. Phil.: Still. 1883.   [1964

A collection of stories of fugitive slaves related by themselves and compiled by the secretary of the Pennsylvania Anti-Slavery Society, himself a free negro. They concern most largely the fugitives passing through eastern Pennsylvania and show the aid rendered to them by the Friends (Quakers). Sketches of the persons most prominent in this assistance are inserted. The language is frequently complex and difficult to understand. This was the most valuable book on the subject until the appearance of Siebert's *Underground railroad* (sect. 1960).   E. E. S.

Stringfellow, Thornton. Scriptural and statistical views in favor of slavery. 4th ed. Richmond, Va. 1856.   [1965

This is a small work of 150 pages devoted to proving that slavery had the sanction of the Almighty in the patriarchal age; that this institution was incorporated in the only national constitution which ever emanated from God; that its legality was recognized by Jesus Christ; and that it is full of mercy. The statistical view begins with page 109. A comparison is made of six New England states and five old slave states as to the progress of religion, wealth, increase of population, pauperism, etc. The work is of no positive value, save as a reflection of views held fifty years ago. D. R. D.

Stroud, George M. Sketch of the laws relating to slavery in the several states of the United States. Phil. 1827. 2d ed. enl. Phil. 1856. [**1966**

"The state of slavery in this country, so far as it can be ascertained from the laws of the several independent sovereignties which belong to our confederacy, is the subject" of this book, which includes a particular examination of the slave state statutes and a cursory notice of the abolition of slavery in those states in which it had ceased to exist. The final chapter deals with the encroachments induced by slavery on freedom of speech and the press, and the federal laws relating to slavery are treated in the appendix. The author was a lawyer and wrote from an anti-slavery standpoint, though he took pains to say he had never been a member of any anti-slavery society. F. J. S.

Sumner, Charles. Works. Boston: Lee. 1870–83. 15v. $3 per v. [**1967**

Sumner's works are of special importance because of his prominent position in the anti-slavery struggle; but his long experience in political life, and his wide acquaintance, add to the permanent interest of his career. In this collection, orations, addresses and speeches are arranged chronologically, without classification as to subjects. There are useful prefatory notes to the various pieces. W. MacD.

— DAWES, ANNA LAURENS. Charles Sumner. (Makers of America.) N. Y.: Dodd. 1892. $1. [**1968**

An interesting and well written book devoted chiefly to the public career of Sumner, but giving a good portrayal of his personal and social characteristics. Possibly the author may be justly charged with leaning toward stalwart republicanism; but on the whole the work is fair-minded. It furnishes an entertaining narrative of the great slavery contest from the annexation of Texas, 1845, until after the adoption of the fifteenth amendment, 1870. The author is strongly in sympathy with the anti-slavery cause but does not indulge in indiscriminate praise of Sumner.

A. C. McL.

— PIERCE, EDWARD LILLIE. Memoir and letters of Charles Sumner. Boston : Roberts. 1877–93. 4v. Little. 4v. $12. [**1969**

For the rise of the slavery issue, the legislation of the period of Civil War and Reconstruction, and the history of the foreign relations of the United States from 1861 to 1871, this work is almost indispensable. Mr. Pierce was a lifelong friend of Sumner, and has edited his letters with the greatest care. The accompanying memoir is remarkably fair and judicious. The first two volumes are more important for the intellectual and social history of New England than for national history; the fourth volume offers, in many respects, the best general view yet written of the national aspects of Reconstruction. The volumes contain a mass of letters from a large number of distin-

guished foreigners. Additional selections from the letters of John Bright and Richard Cobden to Sumner during the Civil War were published in the *American historical review* for Jan. 1897. E. G. B.

Taney, Roger Brooke. TYLER, SAMUEL. Memoir of Roger Brooke Taney, Chief Justice of the Supreme Court of the United States. Balt.: Murphy. 1872. Rev. ed. 1876. [**1970**

This volume is the work of a friend of the subject and undertaken at his request. The first chapter, treating of the early life of Taney, is an autobiography. The bulk of the book is occupied by comments on Taney's judicial decisions. The author desires to "vindicate" these opinions as well as Taney's action in the bank controversy. The work is scholarly, but strongly biased. One chapter is devoted to the private life of the Chief Justice. The appendix contains the Dred Scott decision and other papers. E. E. S.

Tappan, Arthur. TAPPAN, LEWIS. Life of Arthur Tappan. N. Y.: Hurd. 1870. [**1971**

Tappan was connected with the agitation for the abolition of slavery from its beginning in 1830 to its close; associated with Garrison, Beecher, John Quincy Adams, and Whittier. He became president of the moderate or political wing in the split of 1840. The author is the brother of the subject and writes from personal knowledge. E. E. S.

Trollope, *Mrs.* **Frances Eleanor (Milton).** Domestic manners of the Americans. London : Whittaker. 1832. 2v.

—— *Same;* [with introd. by Harry Thurston Peck.] N. Y.: Dodd. 1894. 2v. $2. [**1972**

Mrs. Trollope came to the United States in 1827 and resided in different parts of the country for about three years and a half. Her observations are concerned chiefly with the manners and customs of the people, which are believed to be the product of the political system of democracy. In her own words, she endeavors "to show how greatly the advantage is on the side of those who are governed by the few instead of the many." The author frankly discloses her dislike for this country, and the work so angered the American people that it stood for a half century as typical of English judgment of American social life. Her travels for the most part were confined to the newer sections of the country. She spent by far the larger part of her time in Cincinnati, then almost a frontier town. The style is excellent and in spite of its prejudiced tone is of value to those who can bear criticism with a calm temper. Moreover, "there are passages of great suggestiveness and power. Such, for instance, is the account of the camp-meeting scene at midnight. Equal in interest are the revival scenes; the description of the religious debate between Alexander Campbell and Robert Dale Owen; the account of the reception of President Jackson in Cincinnati; the writer's impressions of slavery; her picture of the city of Washington in 1830; her view of life in a Philadelphia boarding house; and her survey of contemporary American literature." D. R. D.

"The truth is, that Mrs. Trollope's powers of observation are remarkable. What she sees, she describes with vivacity, and often with accurate skill. . . . Personal disappointment in a pecuniary enterprise vexed her judgment; and, like so many of her nation, she thoroughly disliked the political institutions of the United States, was on the lookout for social anomalies and personal defects." H. T. Tuckerman, *America and her commentators*, p. 225.

United States. *Senate.* [Report of a committee of the Senate on the seizure of Harper's Ferry by John Brown and others.] (36th Cong., 1st sess. Senate rep. no. 278.) 1860.

[**1973**

There is a majority report signed by J. M. Mason, Jefferson Davis, and G. N. Fitch, and a minority report signed by J. Collamer and J. R. Doolittle. The testimony, besides presenting a full report of the events occurring at Harper's Ferry at the time when John Brown seized the armory, including the text of the provisional constitution adopted by Brown and his followers at Chatham, Canada, in 1858, goes largely into the question of the support received by Brown from anti-slavery men in the North and West, and especially into the manner in which he secured his weapons. Among the witnesses whose testimony is printed were John A. Andrew, Joshua R. Giddings, Dr. S. G. Howe, William H. Seward, Henry Wilson, Horace White, and Richard Realf, the last named John Brown's secretary of state under the provisional constitution, though not at Harper's Ferry at the time of the outbreak.   F. J. S.

Van Buren, Martin. BANCROFT, GEORGE. Martin Van Buren. N. Y.: Harper. 1889. $1.50.   [**1974**

The manuscript of this book, written by the eminent historian George Bancroft, was submitted to Van Buren and pronounced by him, " as a record of facts relating to myself, authentic and true." The narrative closes with the retirement of Van Buren from the presidency in 1841. Its tone is warmly laudatory. " A firm reliance on principle, and in the darkest hour, a bright and invigorating hopefulness" are the characteristics attributed to Van Buren as a statesman.   A. D. M.

— MACKENZIE, WILLIAM LYON. Life and times of Martin Van Buren. Boston: Cooke. 1846.   [**1975**

The author led a stormy political career in Canada, culminating in participation in the Canadian insurrection in 1837, for which he was imprisoned a year in the United States. He afterwards obtained a subordinate position in the New York custom house, where he seized the opportunity to copy papers and letters of various politicians, which were on file in that office. His animosity toward Van Buren is marked. The work is scrappy, ill-considered, characterized by violent style, and, save to one well acquainted with the details of New York politics, of little value. Special attention is given to Van Buren's relations to the banks, and his inconsistency on the bank question. There is much curious information in regard to " bankcraft." There is a damaging estimate of Mackenzie's

veracity in a note in Shepard's *Life of Martin Van Buren*, p. 279 [see next title].   D. R. D.

— SHEPARD, EDWARD MORSE. Martin Van Buren. (American statesmen.) Boston : Houghton. 1888. $1.25.   [**1976**

Mr. Shepard places Van Buren upon a distinctively high plane of statesmanship, as the real successor of Jefferson and his associates, — men who had "love for the union, a belief in a simple, economical, and even unheroic government, a jealousy of taking money from the people, and a scrupulous restriction upon the use of public moneys for any but public purposes; a strict limitation of federal powers, a dislike of slavery and an opposition to its extension." "Each of its assertions has been found in other creeds; but the entire creed with all its articles made the peculiar and powerful faith only of the Van Buren men." From this point of view, the biography is an able work. It gives a new interpretation to both national and New York State politics of the period, 1820-50. Of permanent general interest is the chapter on the crisis of 1837. The style is excellent and the volume is one of the best of the Statesmen series, particularly for those seeking a key to New York politics in the first half of the century.   D. R. D.

Van Evrie, John H. Negroes and negro slavery; the first an inferior race; the latter its normal condition. N. Y.: Van Evrie. 1861.

[**1977**

A novel effort to prove from a physiological standpoint that the negro is not a "man" in the usual acceptance of that term. His color, features, brain, affections, and adaptation are considered. The new assertions are unsupported by evidences of scientific investigation. The larger part of the writing consists of truisms which all accept but which prove nothing.   E. E. S.

Wade, Benjamin Franklin. RIDDLE, ALBERT GALLATIN. Life of Benjamin F. Wade. Cleveland: Williams. 1886.   [**1978**

Wade was prominently connected with political life in Ohio and in Washington from 1836 to 1870, especially with the rise of the anti-slavery extension struggle. This is the only biography of him, and it is small, inadequate to the importance of the subject, and contains very few original papers. It seems especially lacking in the reconstruction struggle, where Wade was so prominent. The chapters were originally articles contributed to the *Magazine of western history*, and lack a certain continuity, but are written in an attractive style.   E. E. S.

Webster, Daniel. Works. Boston: Little. 1851. 6v. $18.   [**1979**

Contents. V. 1. Biographical memoir, by Edward Everett, and speeches on various public occasions, 1820-1840. — V. 2. Speeches on various public occasions, 1840-51. — V. 3. Speeches in the convention to amend the constitution of Massachusetts : — Speeches in congress, 1815-34 [Reply to Hayne, p. 270]. — V. 4. Speeches in Congress, 1834-40. — V. 5. Speeches in Congress, 1840-50: — Legal arguments and speeches to the jury. — V. 6. Legal arguments and speeches to the jury: —

Diplomatic and official papers, 1841–51: — Miscellaneous letters.

These volumes are particularly valuable to the student of financial and constitutional questions, Webster possessing more knowledge on these subjects than any other statesman of his day. Specific topics are: — Currency; Banking; the Bank of the United States; Tariff; Sub-Treasury system; the Deposit question; Surplus revenue; Bankruptcy question; Public lands; Nature of the Constitution; Powers of the President; Slavery; and Foreign relations.

R. C. H. C.

—— Private correspondence; ed. by Fletcher Webster. Boston: Little. 1857. 2v. [1980

These volumes contain the materials on which, with additional letters and other supplementary matter, Mr. Curtis founded his *Life of Webster* (see next title). Besides Webster's own letters, they contain his brief autobiography, many personal reminiscences by his friends, especially of his early life, and many letters to him. In many places Mr. Curtis's narrative is merely an abstract from these letters. On the other hand, his volumes include letters that were not available when Fletcher Webster edited the correspondence.

E. G. B.

— CURTIS, GEORGE TICKNOR. Life of Daniel Webster. N. Y.: Appleton. 1870. 2v. $4. [1981

Written from Webster's papers, and the most complete life of that statesman. Discusses also at length the measures in which Webster took part. Unfortunately Mr. Curtis is throughout a special pleader, and always presents his subject in the most favorable light. This fault much reduces the value of an extremely valuable book. The writer is dogmatic and biased, but thoroughly informed and very able. The book is well written; its style is strong and effective.

R. C. H. C.

— HAPGOOD, NORMAN. Daniel Webster. (Beacon biographies.) Boston: Small. 1899. 75c. [1982

See Beacon biographies, in Division 2, beyond.

— HARVEY, PETER. Reminiscences and anecdotes of Daniel Webster. Boston: Little. 1877. $3. [1983

Mr. Harvey was a merchant in Boston, and enjoyed for many years the most intimate confidence of Webster. He asserts that he wishes the world to know Webster's sweetness of temper, kindness of heart, the depth of his friendships, his firm hold upon the facts of the Christian religion, the pathos and humor of his home life. The personal memoirs are supplemented by other memorabilia placed at the author's disposal, and arranged, so far as the material permits, chronologically. The volume is full of anecdotes, many of which, however, are somewhat trite and do not honor Mr. Webster in the sense that the author intended. Mr. Henry Cabot Lodge, in his *Life of Webster* (p. 95), criticises the work as untrustworthy. "There is not a statement in it which can be safely accepted unless supported by other evidence."

D. R. D.

— LANMAN, CHARLES. Private life of Daniel Webster. N. Y.: Harper. 1852. [1984

A gossipy description of Webster's early life, his college days, his residences at Elms Park and at Marshfield, and his death. There are numerous anecdotes and extracts from private letters. The writer was the private secretary of Webster and published this sketch soon after his death. Consequently it embraces much of the eulogistic. E. E. S.

— LODGE, HENRY CABOT. Daniel Webster. (American statesmen.) Boston: Houghton. 1883. $1.25. [1985

An appreciative study written by a well-informed scholar, who has carefully examined the sources. He is no unmeasured panegyrist of the man, pointing out faults as well as merits. The writer considers Hayne to have been nearer right than Webster in respect to the original interpretation of the Constitution. The literary quality of the work is very high.

R. C. H. C.

Weed, Thurlow. [V. 1] Autobiography; ed. by Harriet A. Weed. Boston: Houghton. 1883. [V. 2] Memoir of Thurlow Weed; by Thurlow Weed Barnes. Houghton. 1884. [1986

Vol. 1 covers the years 1809–1880. Unfortunately, the important periods 1842–48 and 1852–60 are only briefly treated. The book is especially useful for the history of the party politics of New York and of the Union, Weed being always a leader of his party, whether Anti-Mason, Whig or Republican. As usual in autobiographies, Weed by no means tells all he knows, excepting in the case of the Morgan mystery, which is discussed at great length. The book is written in a careless, rambling fashion from scattered notes, with excellent temper and in newspaper English.

R. C. H. C.

The second volume is a memoir of Thurlow Weed, written by his grandson, Thurlow Weed Barnes. It contains much matter that will interest and instruct the student of politics; but the tone is always highly eulogistic, and, at times, markedly partisan.

A. D. M.

Weeden, William B. Early African slave trade in New England. See American Antiquarian Society, sect. 237. [1987

Weeks, Stephen Beauregard. Southern Quakers and slavery: a study in institutional history. (Johns Hopkins Univ. studies, extra v. 15.) Balt. 1896. $2. [1988

"In its patient research among original records and rare books, its dispassionate statement of the facts ascertained, and its generally lucid style and orderly arrangement, this forms a valuable contribution to the institutional history of the old states of the South." Howard M. Jenkins, in *Annals of the American Academy*, v. 8. 1896.

"One cannot but acknowledge that Dr. Weeks is a scholar capable of both exhaustive and enthusiastic work. He has laid both a whole religious denomination and a section under obligations to him." Prof. W. P. Trent in *American historical review*, v. 2. 1897.

Wentworth, John. Congressional reminiscences, Adams, Benton, Calhoun, Clay and Webster. (Fergus historical ser., no. 24.) Chicago: Fergus Prtg. Co. 1882. **[1989**

The author, a journalist in Chicago, was a member of Congress, 1843–1851, 1853–1855. This paper is the result of a lecture before the Chicago Historical Society. The reminiscences are frank, and throw light upon the fundamental characteristics of the men named. Although the author entered Congress as a Democrat, his sympathies were broad, and his characterizations are fair. The sketch is naturally brief, and of value only as collateral reading. In the appendix are reprinted several documents of interest to the history of Illinois.   D. R. D.

Wheeler, Henry G. History of Congress, biographical and political. N. Y.: Harper. 1848. 2v. **[1990**

Consists of brief biographies of thirty-two members of Congress, serving about the years 1840 to 1850, and chapters on the House, the Calling of the Roll, and Internal Improvements. The "biographies" are composed largely of the speeches made by the respective subjects. The collection of speeches and statistics under "Internal improvements" is meritorious only because such a compilation has rarely been made. See Lanman's *Dictionary of Congress*, later and better arranged.   E. E. S.

Williams, George Washington. History of the negro race in America, 1619–1880. N. Y.: Putnam. 1833. 2v. 1885. 2v. in 1. [c. 1882.] **[1991**

The only important history of the colored race written by a colored man. Describes the negro in Africa and in the various American colonies, with his share in the war for independence. Treats of slavery extension, anti-slavery organizations, the Civil War and reconstruction period. In the writer's view, hope for the future lies in the education of the negro and his accumulation of property. The work is optimistic, often lacking cohesion and good historic treatment, and replete with faulty rhetoric. Its greatest value to the student lies in certain compilations concerning the negro made from the colonial records.
E. E. S.

Wilson, Henry. History of the rise and fall of the slave power in America. Boston: Osgood. 1872–7. 3v. Houghton. 3v. $9.
[1992

The most extended work on the subject, and one of much value, though corrected in numerous details by the investigations of later scholars. The author was prominent in political life during the more acute phase of the slavery contest, and writes often from personal knowledge. Of especial importance are the summaries of debates in Congress and the accounts of the abolition movement; but the absence of references to authorities is a serious drawback. The author evidently strives after impartiality; but his strong preju-

dices as a northern statesman are not concealed, and slavery is more an evil to be denounced than an institution to be studied and explained.   W. MacD.

Wise, Henry Alexander. Seven decades of the Union. Phil.: Lippincott. 1872.
[1993

Wise was a prominent Virginian politician in Congress during the thirties and Governor, 1855–59. He was of strong personality, at times erratic, forceful, and thoroughly acquainted with the motive forces of politics in his section. He was a special admirer and counsellor of Tyler,—and the sub-title of this volume reads "A memoir of John Tyler with reminiscences of some of his great contemporaries." The style is rhetorical and the material disconnected, so that the reader will be justified in frequent omissions. The work is valuable not only for the numerous anecdotes of prominent statesmen of the Jackson period, but also for the philosophical digressions in regard to the states right doctrine. While accepting the southern interpretation of the Constitution, Wise formulated the doctrine in a less extreme form. The seven decades represent the period, 1790–1860.   D. R. D.

— WISE, BARTON H. Life of Henry A. Wise of Virginia, 1806–76; by his grandson; introd. by John S. Wise. N. Y.: Macmillan. 1899. $3.   **[1994**

"This readable biography of Governor Wise is very largely an index to the history of Virginia during the very important period when a long struggle in the state was ended by the adoption of a modernized constitution, when the greater struggle between state sovereignty and the powers of the federal government came to an issue, and Virginia had to decide her place. . . . General Lee, when about to surrender, gave to Wise, then a Major-General and remembered by northerners as the man who had hung John Brown, an opportunity to leave Virginia, but Wise preferred to surrender, to stay with his people and to help build up his fallen state. His letters and addresses after the war were marked by the same spirit." Jeffrey R. Brackett, in *Am. hist. rev.*, 5: 150.

An extremely well-written biography in its unusual judgment, accuracy, calm impartiality and use of English. There is no attempt to avoid facts militating against Wise, while the man and his principles are clearly presented.   R. C. H. C.

Woodburn, James A. Historical significance of the Missouri compromise. See American Historical Association, sect. 245. **[1995**

Woodbury, Levi. Writings, political, judicial and literary. Boston: Little. 1852. 3v.
[1996

Woodbury's life covered the period of the first half of this century. In 1823 he was made Governor of New Hampshire; 1825, United States Senator; 1831, Secretary of the Navy; 1834, Secretary of the Treasury; 1841, United States Senator; and in 1845 Justice of the Supreme Court of the United States. He thus had a long and varied experience in public affairs. He was specially associated with Jackson's administration, and a supporter of his measures. The first volume

contains speeches; the second, judicial decisions and arguments; the third, "literary" or more general writings. Among the speeches are many devoted to tariff legislation and banking questions, including the removal of deposits from the United States banks. Among the so-called literary papers of the third volume is the valuable report on cotton submitted when Secretary of the Treasury in 1836. Woodbury's speeches are rather ponderous in style but good examples of northern Democratic argument in the period 1830–45.
D. R. D.

Wright, Silas. HAMMOND, JABEZ D. Life and times of Silas Wright. Syracuse : Hall. 1848. [**1997**

A continuation of Hammond's *Political history of New York* (q. v.) and printed as the third volume of that work in the edition of 1852. It is the most trustworthy history of the complicated political situations in the state of New York between 1825 and 1847, and shows the early influence of New York politics on national issues. The treatment is modestly non-partisan, but naturally inclined to favor the Democratic party, of which Silas Wright was a life-long member.
E. E. S.

— JENKINS, JOHN STILLWELL. Life of Silas Wright. Auburn, N. Y.: Alden. 1847. [**1998**

The authority for the political history of the state of New York from 1824 to 1847. It presents the Democratic, strict-construction, anti-tariff side. Especially valuable for information on the canal system of New York, the second bank of the United States, the anti-rent disturbances, and the New York Constitution of 1846. Several of Wright's speeches make up an appendix.
E. E. S.

Yancey, William Lowndes. DUBOSE, JOHN WITHERSPOON. Life and times of William Lowndes Yancey. Birmingham, Ala.: Roberts. 1892. [**1999**

Under this "leader of the southern movement," the author considers Alabama politics from 1840 to 1854 and national politics thereafter to 1863. A most interesting presentation of the southern or states rights side of the great controversy. Treats of nullification, abolition, the compromises, secession, and the southern Confederacy. The descriptions of the acts of secession and the inner history of the Confederacy are the most novel parts.
E. E. S.

THE MEXICAN WAR

Colton, Walter. Three years in California. N. Y.: Barnes. 1850. [**2000**

"Gives an excellent notion of some aspects of the [Mexican] war." J. R. Soley, in *Narrative and critical hist. of Am.*, 7: 444.

Cooke, Philip George. Conquest of New Mexico and California. N. Y.: Putnam. 1878. [**2001**

General Cooke describes many interesting events in which he took part as a young lieutenant-colonel in

1846–7, commanding the so-called Mormon Battalion of 500 dragoons. He opposed Fremont's course in California, and criticises him severely. It is surprising that a volume published more than thirty years after the journey should still perpetuate so many crude and erroneous observations. The author had little or no scientific training in ethnology, botany, geology or natural history. A few curious incidents and much incidental though unconscious light upon the spirit of some of the conquerors towards the Indians, Mexicans and Spaniards they met, constitute the chief value of this desultory book.
C. H. S.

Hughes, *Capt.* **John T.** Doniphan's expedition; containing an account of the conquest of New Mexico. Cin. : James. 1847. [**2002**

A conscientious portrayal of the events attending the expedition of the "Army of the West" during the Mexican War of 1846–7, including the conquest of New Mexico, the treaty with the Navaho Indians, and Doniphan's remarkable invasion and capture of Chihuahua and his triumphant march through Durango and Coahuila with less than 1000 men. Capt. Hughes was "an eye-witness of, and an actor in, many of the scenes which he essays to describe." His account of Kearney's march from New Mexico to California is compiled from other but authentic sources. There is much of historical value in the book not found elsewhere, and it contains in addition a fairly good account of the country traversed at a time when the outer world knew little of it. Its references to the Indians are honest, but not entirely reliable. The Spanish terms are often inaccurate.
F. W. H.

Jay, William. Review of the causes and consequences of the Mexican War. Boston: Mussey. 1849. [**2003**

Written from the Abolitionist point of view. The facts presented are drawn from the sources then available and are incontrovertible. Jay held that the war was merely one act in a conspiracy to secure Mexican territory. He is very severe on the slaveholding politicians and on the policy and management of the war. He possessed an acute intellect and considerable insight into political and social causes and effects. He wrote in a spirited, cutting style, and used the best of English. The story of the Mexican War from this side has never been better told, or more forcibly and logically argued.
R. C. H. C.

Ladd, Horatio Oliver. History of the war with Mexico. N. Y.: Dodd. 1883. $1. [**2004**

This book is suited to young but not the youngest readers, and, says the *Nation*, "ought to be welcomed by a great many persons who have wished to have a compendious account of that important event. It is a great satisfaction to find the cause of the war boldly given as 'the purpose to extend human slavery into free territory.' We are surprised, however, in the account of the early history of Texas, to find no mention of what we have always supposed to be an established fact — the deliberate colonization of that territory by American citizens, with the purpose of detaching it from the Mexican republic." The volume contains a good map. *Nation*, 37: 494.

Livermore, Abiel Abbot. The war with Mexico reviewed. Boston: Am. Peace Soc. 1850. **[2005**

This was the prize essay in a competition opened by the American Peace Society. It describes the expenditures, inhumanities, vices of camps, military executions, and all the horrors of the war. It ascribes the cause of the war to the avarice of the slave owners and the land hunger of the Americans. E. E. S.

Mansfield, Edward Deering. The Mexican War. N. Y.: Barnes. 1848. **[2006**

"In large part composed of official documents; and its narrative is in effect abridged in his *Life of Scott* (sect. 2011)." J. R. Soley, in *Narrative and critical hist. of Am.*, 7: 441.

Mayer, Brantz. History of the war between Mexico and the United States. N. Y. 1848. **[2007**

"Is not without rendering justice to the Mexican arms." Justin Winsor, in *Narrative and critical hist. of Am.*, 7: 441.

Ramsey, Albert C., *tr.* The other side; or Notes for the history of the war between Mexico and the United States, written in Mexico [by R. Alcaraz, *et al.*]; tr. from the Spanish, and ed. with notes. N. Y.: Wiley. 1850. **[2008**

This is apparently a collection of notes on the war, written by fifteen Mexicans. It gives their side of the causes leading to the war, describes their conduct of the campaigns, tells of the sufferings of the soldiers, and closes with the peace. The criticism of General Santa Anna is rather severe. The translator served as a colonel in the American army. E. E. S.

Ripley, *Brig.-Gen.* **Roswell Sabin.** The war with Mexico. N. Y.: Harper. 1849. 2v. **[2009**

"The best military history of the war. . . . Except for a certain tendency to underrate the work of the navy, it is a highly satisfactory book." J. R. Soley, in *Narrative and critical hist. of Am.*, 7: 441.

Scott, *Lt.-Gen.* **Winfield.** Memoirs, written by himself. N. Y.: Sheldon. 1864. 2v. **[2010**

The narrative opens the public life of the writer with the Canadian campaigns of the War of 1812, and carries it through the Black Hawk War, Nullification in South Carolina, removal of the Cherokees, the Mexican War, and the ensuing honors to the victorious general. Six editions were sold during its first month. This autobiography was severely criticised in the *North American review*, January, 1865 and the *Athenæum* (London) of the same month. E. E. S.

— **Mansfield, Edward Deering.** Life of Gen. Winfield Scott. N. Y.: Barnes. 1846. **[2011**

See Mansfield, E. D., *The Mexican War*, sect. 2006, above.

— **Wright,** *Brig. - Gen.* **Marcus Joseph.** General Scott. (Great commanders.) N. Y.: Appleton. 1894. $1.50. **[2012**

"For writing the military life of Scott, Gen. Wright has some peculiar qualifications. As a young soldier following his chief in the greatest of his military enterprises, the invasion of Mexico, he was a devoted subordinate on terms of personal intimacy with Scott. The greater part of the general's career is consequently told with the warm sympathy of a devoted friend and admirer, as it should be. But General Wright has done still better. Although himself a Confederate in our Civil War, he has handled the subject of Scott's consistent loyalty to the Union with an impartial fairness which leaves little to desire." *Nation*, 58: 417.

Taylor, *Maj.-Gen.* **Zachary.** Howard, Oliver Otis. General Taylor. (Great commanders.) N. Y.: Appleton. 1892. $1.50. **[2013**

"General Howard has brought together the available material for a detailed examination of his [General Taylor's] military life, and, by personal visits to the battle-fields of Mexico, has been able to make the history of the battles of Palo Alto, Resaca de la Palma, Monterey, and Buena Vista both interesting and intelligible to the ordinary reader. In this the maps are of great assistance, and the operations on this line in the Mexican contest are put in satisfactory form. The portion of the book which relates to Taylor's Presidency is subordinate, and does not seem to be more than a sketch of public affairs in their relation to his personal life and influence." J. D. Cox, in *Nation*, 56: 18.

United States. *President (Polk).* Message to the two houses of Congress at the commencement of the first session of the 30th Congress. (30th Cong. 1st sess., Sen. ex. doc., no. 1.) Wash. 1847. **[2014**

This bulky volume contains in the first 500 pages a detailed military history of the Mexican War, except the opening operations of 1846. The President's message and the report of the Secretary of War are accompanied by the reports of the officers in the field covering the military operations from the battle of Buena Vista to the capture of the city of Mexico. An appendix of 249 pp. supplies further military reports, chiefly from subordinate officers, received too late to accompany the report of the Secretary of War. The volume includes much matter not relating to the war, and the indices to the military material must be looked for on p. 541 of the main document and p. 234 of the appendix. F. J. S.

Wilcox, *Maj.-Gen.* **Cadmus Marcellus.** History of the Mexican War; ed. by Mary R. Wilcox. Wash.: Church News Pub. Co. 1892. **[2015**

An intensive study of the military operations of the war from an expert standpoint. The writer served as a second lieutenant, and a portion of the description is from personal observation. The book is likely to prove heavy for the non-military reader. The appendix contains among other matters a roster of all the troops in the service.　　　　E. E. S.

WESTWARD EXPANSION, 1828–1860

(See sect. 1754–1826, also, in Part IV.)

Atwater, Caleb. Remarks made on a tour to Prairie du Chien; then to Washington city, in 1829. Columbus, O.: Whiting. 1831.

—— *Same.* [In Writings. Columbus. 1833.]
　　　　　　　　　　　　　　　　　　[**2016**

The author was appointed by President Jackson a member of a commission to negotiate at Prairie du Chien a treaty with the Indians for the cession of the Wisconsin lead region. His account includes historical, topographical, and economic notices of Maysville, Cincinnati, Louisville, and St. Louis. He describes the latter city (then of 7,000 inhabitants) at length. After nineteen days there, he proceeded with others of the commission, up the Mississippi River to Prairie du Chien, stopping *en route* at frontier river posts, studying Indians and the fur trade. Much space is devoted to descriptions of the Indians, their language, oratory, manners and customs, and polity, and the effect upon them of their civilized neighbors. The trip to Washington, to report upon the treaty, was taken partly overland, and partly by the Ohio River. Atwater was a careful observer of men and affairs, with some knowledge of botany and geology; his book is an interesting study of frontier conditions in the Middle West.　　　　R. G. T.

Auger, Edouard. Voyage en Californie. Paris: Hachette. 1854.　　　　[**2017**

The extent and high excellence of the French historical and descriptive books relating to early California is not generally known. Many brilliant writers were seized with the gold-fever, roughed it with Ryan, Marryat and Borthwick, and published their novel experiences on their return to "La Belle France." This little book of M. Auger's is devoted to his observations, made in 1852 and 1853, and often to severe, and notably well-expressed criticisms upon the state of society as he found it at that period.　　　　C. H. S.

Barry, T. A., *and* B. A. Patten. Men and memories of San Francisco in the spring of 1850. San Francisco: A. L. Bancroft. 1873.
　　　　　　　　　　　　　　　　　　[**2018**

A book of reminiscences full of the atmosphere of a forgotten period, hardly anywhere else to be found in greater degree. It contains little history in the ordinary sense, but much of that which enables a historian to make his men and women live and move once more.　　　　C. H. S.

Bartlett, John Russell. Personal narrative of explorations and incidents in Texas, New Mexico, California, Sonora, and Chihuahua. N. Y.: Appleton. 1854. 2v.　　　　[**2019**

The author was commissioner, on the part of the United States, for the survey of the Mexican boundary in 1851–3. A gentleman of scholarly attainments, a skilled journalist, and an excellent observer, appreciative of the needs of students during his operations in a new field of investigation, Bartlett produced a work of lasting importance to science and history. His narrative possesses high literary merit, is exact almost beyond criticism, and altogether is one of the best works devoted to the southwest that has ever appeared.　　　　F. W. H.

Bonneville, *Brig.-Gen.* Benjamin L. E. IRVING, WASHINGTON. The Rocky Mountains: or, Scenes, incidents, and adventures in the far West. Phil.: Carey. 1837. 2v.

—— Adventures of Captain Bonneville; author's rev. ed. N. Y.: Putnam. 1898. $1.50. 75c.　　　　[**2020**

The subtitle states that this book is "digested from the journal of Captain B. L. E. Bonneville, of the Army of the United States, and illustrated from various sources." It is an entertaining narrative of early travel and adventure in the West, but, as might be expected in the digest of an unscientific observer by a literary editor, the geographical features of the region receive scanty attention.　　　　W. M. D.

Brooks, J. Tyrwhitt. Four months among the gold-finders in California. N. Y.: Appleton. 1849.　　　　[**2021**

A rare and very striking pamphlet published as "The result of actual experience" which it doubtless was, being taken from letters sent home by the author. It was very widely circulated in the Atlantic states, in 1849, and has been more or less utilized by all careful students of the period to which it relates.
　　　　　　　　　　　　　　　　　　C. H. S.

Burton, *Sir* Richard Francis. The City of the Saints, and across the Rocky Mountains to California. London: Longmans. 1861. N. Y.: Harper. 1862.　　　　[**2022**

This well known book of travel contains much and valuable material for the historian. It is based upon daily notes written by the author between August 7th and October 19th, 1860, while journeying from St. Joseph, Mo., to Carson City, Nevada, together with several important appendices on emigrant travel and Mormon history, particularly Apostle Taylor's account of the "Martyrdom of Joseph Smith." Captain Burton's studies of Mormon life, doctrine and history preceded those of Hepworth Dixon. No other book of travel of the period gives as complete an account of Mormonism as explained by the Mormons themselves, and the bibliography relating to Mormonism (pp. 203-214) has permanent value. Captain Burton's services to the philology, geography, history and literature of many parts of the world can hardly be overestimated, but he is not quite at his best in the present book, and his somewhat favorable views of the Mormon system are colored by his oriental experiences. Nevertheless, his rare powers of observation and literary genius enabled him to produce a justly famous book.
　　　　　　　　　　　　　　　　　　C. H. S.

Capron, Elisha S. History of California. Boston : Jewett. 1854.   [2023

Only 55 pages are devoted to history, reviewing rapidly, but not from any original sources, the principal events from Cabrillo's discovery, in 1542, to the admission of California, Sept. 9, 1850. The remainder of the book consists of personal observations, notes upon the resources of the region, etc. Mr. Capron's interesting accounts of the miners' courts of justice (pp. 227-236) have often been referred to by later historians. Portions of his book are still readable, and its judicial temper is in the main excellent, though the author knew little about the Spanish-Californians, and was seriously unfair to the mission system. He spent only three months in California (1853) and though both careful and intelligent, could not obtain more than a surface view.   C. H. S.

Coles, Edward. WASHBURNE, ELIHU BENJAMIN. Sketch of Edward Coles, second Governor of Illinois, and of the slavery struggle of 1823-4; prepared for the Chicago Historical Soc. Chicago: Jansen, McClurg. 1882.

     [2024

Edward Coles was a Virginian, and a friend of Jefferson, who made his home in Illinois the year following the admission of the state to the Union. He at once took an active part in public affairs, becoming governor in 1822, and serving to the close of 1826. He died in 1868. The interest of his career, as of the book itself, culminates in the struggle to establish slavery, in which Coles was the leader on the free state side. Mr. Washburne uses all the available material with skill, and his book is a valuable contribution to the history of a struggle on which great issues hung.

     B. A. H.

Connelly, William E. Provisional government of Nebraska territory. Kansas City : for sale by G. D. Fearey, Sec. of Western Hist. Soc. 1898. $4.

—— *Same ;* and the journals of William Walker, Provisional Governor of Nebraska territory. Special publication of the Nebraska State Historical Society. [Proceedings and collections, ser. 2, v. 3.] Lincoln, Neb. 1899.

     [2025

The scope of this work is indicated by the title. It is carefully edited with copious notes and contains many valuable documents. It furnishes an invaluable history of the beginnings of government in the territory.   E. E. S.

Davis, William Watts Hart. El Gringo; or New Mexico and her people. N. Y. : Harper. 1857.   [2026

A record of observation made during two and a half years' official residence in the territory (1853-6). No book treating of New Mexico and its people, at a time when the influence of the United States was so strongly felt, contains so much information pertaining thereto, and few narratives of any period of New Mexico's later history are more interestingly written. The chapter on the early history of the territory formed the basis of the author's *Spanish conquest.*   F. W. H.

Dixon, Susan Bullitt (*Mrs.* **Archibald).** True history of the Missouri Compromise and its repeal. Cin. : Clarke. 1899. $4.   [2027

Certainly not the true history of the Compromise and repeal. Mrs. Dixon uses her husband's papers, and proves that the repealing clause was originally Dixon's, and his alone. In other respects, her work is eminently unsatisfactory. She is not qualified for her task and adopts all through the strict states-rights view and the astonishingly sophistical arguments of Douglas as to the nature of the Compromise and its repeal. The book is too voluminous, and shows little mastery of material, page after page being quotation from the Congressional debates ; its logic is unsound ; its bias pronounced ; its temper marked ; its style diffuse and weak.   R. C. H. C.

Downie, *Maj.* William. Hunting for gold : reminiscences of personal experience in the early days, from Alaska to Panama. San Francisco : California Pub. Co. 1893.   [2028

The author of this book was the founder of the mining camp of Downieville, Sierra Co., California, now a large and flourishing town, and his narrative is of the kind that furnishes many a novelist with his "raw material," so overflowing are his pages with local color and with good frontier stories. It deserves a place among the best of Pacific coast pioneer reminiscences.

     C. H. S.

Dunn, Jacob Piatt. Slavery petitions and papers. (Indiana Hist. Soc. Publications, v. 2, no. 12.) Indianapolis. 1894.   [2029

Petitions to Congress from the Northwest and Indiana territories for the suspension of the article of the Ordinance of 1787 forbidding slavery in the Northwest territory, together with counter petitions, the reports on them, and accompanying papers. The editor has included the report of a committee of the Indiana legislature in 1808 against the admission of slavery.   F. J. S.

Edward, David B. History of Texas ; or The emigrant's, farmer's, and politician's guide to the character, climate, soil and productions of that country. Cin.: James. 1836.   [2030

A sketch covering in a more or less satisfactory way the various subjects included in its title, written by a Texas school-teacher, who belonged to the party opposed, during the earlier stages of the Revolution, to a complete severance from Mexico. The members of this party were called by the radical revolutionists Tories. The style of the book is bad, and the narrative often difficult to follow. Its chief value lies in the insight it gives into the "Tory" view of the Revolution, and in its reprinting entire several rare and important documents.   G. P. G.

Ferguson, Charles D. Experiences of a '49'er during 34 years residence in California and Australia. Cleveland: Williams Pub. Co.

1888. Cleveland: The N. G. Hamilton Pub. Co. $2. [2031

About 200 pages of this book are devoted to experiences " on the plains" and in California. The volume is "edited" by F. T. Wallace, from notes made by Mr. Ferguson "from memory, and from personal interviews." This process has succeeded in almost eliminating the personal equation, and the fine old pioneer has nearly disappeared. His own notes, however illiterate, would have had more historical value. C. H. S.

Foote, Henry Stuart. Texas and the Texans; or Advance of the Anglo-Americans to the south-west; including a history of leading events in Mexico, from the conquest by Fernando Cortes to the termination of the Texan revolution. Phil.: Cowperthwait. 1841. 2v. [2032

A work which the author says he was invited to undertake "by more than twenty of the most conspicuous actors" in the Revolution. It contains many rare documents, and is a valuable authority, but does not always show judicial fairness towards the Mexicans. Vol. 1 gives a brief sketch of Mexican history down to 1824, and a more extended treatment of the history of Texas from the Burr expedition down to the Revolution. Vol. 2 is devoted to the Revolution. A third volume was contemplated, but it never appeared. G. P. G.

Forbes, Alexander (James). California: a history of Upper and Lower California from their first Discovery. London: Smith. 1839. [2033

A rare book. The author was afterwards British Vice-Consul in San Francisco. He published his book under the name of Alexander Forbes, leading later historians to suppose there were two prominent men of the name in California. Forbes's history was the first original work in English on California; it called the attention of Europe to opportunities for settlement and political control, described vast agricultural possibilities, spoke of a future Isthmus canal, etc. A very interesting work, full of information and still worth reading. C. H. S.

Fowler, Jacob. Journal, narrating an adventure from Arkansas through the Indian Territory, Oklahoma, Kansas, Colorado, and New Mexico, to the sources of Rio Grande del Norte, 1821–22; ed. with notes by Elliott Coues. N. Y.: Harper. 1898. $3 net. [2034

This journal "belongs to the rich store of Americana collected by Col. R. T. Durrett of Louisville, Kentucky, the accomplished president of the Filson Club. Major Fowler, born in New York in 1765, came to Kentucky in early life to carry on the profession of a surveyor, . . . and he did much work in this line for the national government. 'His surveying,' says Colonel Durrett, 'extended to the great plains and mountains of the far west, before civilization had reached those distant wilds.' . . . The editor points out the Major's place in

the history of the exploration of the vast region extending from the Missouri to the Rio Grande." *Dial*, 25 : 108.

Frémont, *Maj.-Gen.* **John Charles.** Memoirs of my life. Chicago: Belford. 1887. V. 1. [2035

Only one volume of these memoirs has been published, covering the years to 1847. It is of service for the exploring expeditions of Frémont, and tells the story of his "conquest" of California, though hardly the true story. Sketches of Senator Benton and other public men are scattered through its pages. There are many illustrations, some very good, some very indifferent, and seven maps, on which the same judgment must be passed. The concluding chapter deals with the botany and geology of the territory explored. The literary form is good. R. C. H. C.

—— Report of the exploring expedition to the Rocky Mountains, 1842, and to Oregon and North California, 1843–44. Wash. 1845. Buffalo. 1851. [2036

"The first of the two expeditions, of which we have an account in the volume above referred to, terminated at the summit of the Rocky Mountains, after an examination of the south pass — the lowest depression of the mountains and the present route to Oregon — and an ascent to the summit of Frémont's peak in the Wind River chain, believed to be the highest elevation in the Rocky Mountain range. In the second, by a different route, he reached the same pass, and thence proceeded to the Great Salt Lake and Fort Vancouver; he next went south just to the east of the Cascade range, over an unexplored region, to latitude 38° 44′, where he crossed the snowy heights, and finally after severe trials arrived at San Francisco. From this place he went south, ascending the fine valley of the Joachim, and in latitude 34½° turned northeast across the California semi-desert, to Utah lake. A complete circuit was thus made in eight months, which cost them 3500 miles of travelling; and during this time they were never out of sight of snow. Captain Frémont's journal is written in a graphic style, bearing evidence of literal accuracy in all its statements, and yet in many parts reading like a romance. . . . The work is illustrated by many fine views of scenery, besides five plates of fossils and four of recent plants. There was no retinue of science attached to the expedition, yet by personal exertion, in connection with his other arduous duties, Captain Frémont made valuable geological and botanical collections. Unfortunately, a considerable portion of them were lost by accidents from which our travellers barely escaped with their lives." *American journal of science*, 53: 192.

—— BIGELOW, JOHN. Memoir of the life of John Charles Frémont. N. Y.: Derby. 1856. [2037

"An excellent book, and gives many of the California documents." J. R. Soley, in *Narrative and critical hist. of Am.*, 7 : 445.

Gladstone, Thomas H. The Englishman in Kansas; or Squatter life and border warfare;

with introd. by Frederick Law Olmsted. London : Routledge. 1857. [2038

The work of an English newspaper correspondent. He supplements his own experiences and observations with numerous newspaper extracts, and presents an interesting and valuable picture of Kansas society and Kansas politics in 1856. The book is accurate, well-written and frankly Free-Soil in its sympathies. The introduction deals with the condition of southern slavery. R. C. H. C.

Gray, William Henry. History of Oregon, 1792–1849. Portland, Ore.: Harris & Holman. 1870. [2039

This book, written from the point of view of an intensely partisan Oregon pioneer, reflects to the fullest extent the bitterness of that remarkable conflict between rival commercial companies, different religions and opposing nations and races of men, especially in its erroneous statement that the Whitman massacre was instigated by the Catholic missionaries. No other book so well sets forth pioneer views of the English occupation of Oregon, the acts of the Jesuit fathers, the causes of the failure of the Protestant missions and the difficulties, social, physical and political, that the early settlers had to contend with. It is written with more than ordinary ability and skill in arranging evidence, so that its influence upon later accounts of the founding of Oregon has been much greater than it really deserves. In this book first appears the now disproved story that Dr. Marcus Whitman by his journey to the East in 1842 saved Oregon to the Union, a romantic tale which has passed into many popular histories, but which modern criticism shows to be untrue. The student will find documents of value in Gray, but his statements must always be taken with caution. C. H. S.

See, also, sect. 2075, 3392, 3407, 3425.

Gregg, Josiah. Commerce of the prairies: or The journal of a Santa Fé trader. N. Y.: Langley. 1844. 2v. [2040

The value of the book as an account of the early trading expeditions over the famous Santa Fé trail, of pioneer life in the extreme southwest prior to its acquisition by the United States, of the condition of affairs in New Mexico during the author's nine years' residence as a trader therein, and of the manners and customs of the aborigines of New Mexico and Texas with whom he came in contact, can scarcely be overestimated. The narrative is interesting, truthful almost beyond criticism, and withal is one of the best contributions to southwestern literature that has ever appeared. F. W. H.

Hale, Edward Everett. Kansas and Nebraska. Boston : Phillips. 1854. [2041

The preface bears date of Aug. 21, 1854—less than three months after the passage of the act to organize the territories of Nebraska and Kansas. The book aims to present a concise account of the history and physical conditions of the territories, and assist in the effort of the emigrant aid societies to people the region with free-state settlers. Chap. 8 gives the text of the Kansas-Nebraska act, and Appendix A the constitu-tion of the Worcester Co., Mass., Kansas League. As a contemporary description, with propagandist object, of the Kansas region on the eve of the great struggle for the possession of it, the work still has value. W. MacD.

Harby, *Mrs.* **Lee C.** The earliest Texas. See American Historical Association, sect. 244. [2042

Haskins, Charles W. Argonauts of California: reminiscences of scenes and incidents that occurred in California in early mining days. N. Y.: Fords, Howard & Hurlbert. 1890. $3.25. [2043

A list of about 35,000 pioneers of California occupies 142 pages of this book, constituting its only historical value. The author had interesting experiences in the mines of California, and he tells many curious stories, mingled with a few facts, in a careless, uneducated way, but not without a crude sense of humor and some powers of observation. It cannot be said to have any literary quality whatever. C. H. S.

Helper, Hinton Rowan. Land of gold: reality *vs.* fiction. Balt.: Author. 1855. [2044

A book essential to the understanding of pioneer California, as it gives the strongest possible account of the dark sides of life in 1849. To Mr. Helper the soil was barren, the mines were "played out," society was in a condition of anarchy, the state was bankrupt, and everything had been enormously overrated. He had the courage of his convictions, and thus has preserved much regarding that stormy, many-sided period that cannot be found in the pages of other historians. C. H. S.

Houston, *Gen.* **Samuel.** BRUCE, HENRY. Life of General Houston, 1793–1863. (Makers of America.) N. Y.: Dodd. [c. 1891.] $1. [2045

The author describes himself as "unable or unwilling to undertake the six months' journeying through Tennessee and Texas which would have constituted the ideal preliminary to a life of Houston." Instead, he went to London, and studied in the British Museum. To this course are doubtless due some of the faults of the work. The biography as given by Mr. Bruce is very largely composed of quotations from other biographers and from standard historians, which have been cleverly strung together. In his own contributions, the author is so entirely out of touch with the early career of Houston and with the Texans, that it seems a pity he did not leave the biography to some more sympathetic hand. The style, though bright, is often marred by flippancy. In spite of the defects of the work, however, the extracts given make a graphic story. J. R. F.

— WILLIAMS, ALFRED MASON. Sam Houston and the war of independence in Texas. Boston : Houghton. 1893. $2. [2046

The author was well fitted for the writing of this biography by his sympathy with his hero, by his extensive knowledge of the existing works on the subject, and by his personal acquaintance with Texans who knew Houston. His information is, also, based upon a study of the Texan archives, and upon conversations with Judge Keys, a Cherokee, who knew Houston, while in exile among the Indians. In his estimate of Houston's character and career, the author shows sound judgment and excellent temper. The only departure from this fairness of treatment is at the period of the Civil War, where the author characterizes the southern leaders as a band of conspirators. The style is clear and forcible. The work contains an index, a bibliography, and a map.

J. R. F.

Hubbard, Bela. Memorials of a half-century. N. Y.: Putnam. 1887. [2047

The author of this work, as he tells us, came to Detroit in 1835, when it had fewer than 5,000 inhabitants, and from this point he carried on the studies that furnished the materials which he afterwards worked up into effective literary form. His general field was the old Northwest, but his special field was Michigan. His period for observation was a fortunate one, and he possessed both the faculties of observation and the literary skill to use his opportunities to good advantage. The book is almost wholly a record of personal observation and reflection. Its general divisions are, Scenery and Description, History and Antiquities, Fauna and Flora, and Climatology.

B. A. H.

Huntley, *Sir* **Henry Vere.** California; its gold and its inhabitants. London: Newby. 1856. 2v. [2048

Published without the author's name on the title-page; chiefly compiled from a journal written in 1852 when the author was representing foreign capitalists in the California mines. The author's journeys covered a large part of the state. His observations are generally accurate, extremely outspoken and very English. The state of society he describes was long ago extinct. It is one of the most amusing of the English books on California.

C. H. S.

Hutchings, T. Rosenfield. California magazine. San Francisco. 1856–61. [2049

This magazine began in July, 1856, and ceased publication with the issue for June, 1861. It contained a good deal of history, but devoted more attention to descriptions of California. It was the successor to *Ewer's pioneer magazine* (sect. 2063) and, like that publication, is now difficult to obtain. C. H. S.

Ide, William Brown. IDE, SIMEON. Biographical sketch of the life of William B. Ide, etc. Published "for the subscribers." n. p., n. d. [c. 1880.] [2050

Also titled *Scraps of California history never before published*. Extremely rare. Copy in Library of Univ. of California thought worth $25. Essential to the full understanding of the Bear Flag episode in California, so strenuously discussed by historians. Rambling, illiterate and contradictory, but contains (pp. 100–206) Ide's long letter to Senator Wambough, giving his amended version of the Bear Flag affair. Contains other Ide MSS. not elsewhere published,

some of much interest, from "Colusi," now Colusa, written in 1851. C. H. S.

Irving, Washington. Astoria. Phil.: Carey. 1836. N. Y.: Putnam. $1.50. 75c. [2051

Irving was put in possession of a large number of original manuscripts relating to Astoria by J. J. Astor. In addition he drew largely from other writers on Oregon. The result is a book indispensable to the student of the early history of Oregon, written in the inimitable style of this master of language. Irving's powerful imagination, however, occasionally led him to embellish the facts; he was also ignorant in respect to the geography of the West, and is not infrequently in error as to dates. An edition of the book with critical notes is a desideratum. R. C. H. C.

A writer in the *Nation* (65 : 499. Dec. 23, 1897) attempts to follow the route of the overland Astoria party.

Jones, Anson. Memoranda and official correspondence relating to the republic of Texas, its history and annexation; including a brief autobiography of the author. N. Y.: Appleton. 1859. [2052

Mainly a collection of documents, the nature of which is sufficiently indicated by the title. The author was the last president of the Republic. The work is of special value for the light it throws on the inner history of the time — the personal relations of prominent men of the republic, and especially those between Jones and Houston. G. P. G.

Kennedy, William. Texas: the rise, progress, and prospects of the republic of Texas. London: Hastings. 1841. 2v. [2053

Containing an important map, and being one of the best authorities for the Revolution and the period immediately subsequent. About half of Vol. 1 is devoted to a geographical and physiographical description of Texas, and the remainder of the work to its history and political and social conditions. The author was an Englishman of some literary reputation, who in 1838 had been an official in Lower Canada. In 1839 he visited Texas and gathered materials for his work. It was intended to influence English opinion in favor of the republic, and doubtless did so. Maillard's *History of the republic of Texas*, London, 1842, was written as a reply to it. Mr. Kennedy was subsequently British Consul at Galveston. G. P. G.

Kohl, Johann Georg. Reisen im Nordwesten der Vereinigten Staaten. N. Y.: Appleton. 1857. [2054

Narrative of a journey in the upper Mississippi valley by a studious observer, giving a vivid impression of the earlier conditions in states that are now populous. W. M. D.

Larpenteur, Charles. Forty years a fur trader on the upper Missouri: the personal narrative of Charles Larpenteur, 1833–1872; ed., with many critical notes, by Elliott Coues.

(American explorers, no. 2.). N. Y.: Harper. 1898. 2v. $6 net. [2055

"This book is original matter through and through. From fragments set down now and then and memories of fur-trade as early as 1833, it was written out by its author in 1872. The manuscript was unknown to the editor, Dr. Coues, till 1897. The work embodies the experiences of forty years on the dual Missouri-Mississippi river and its affluents upward from St. Louis." Larpenteur's narrative is a "most entertaining and yet pathetic portrayal of the American fur-trade during the second third of our century. Its true inwardness is turned inside out by a chronicler whose eyes were never opened to see much difference between good and evil, and who so saw nothing to conceal. The fur-trade in beginning, middle, and end meant whiskey." James D. Butler, in *Am. hist. rev.*, 4: 742.

Letts, J. M. California illustrated, including a description of the Panama and Nicaragua routes. N. Y.: Young. 1852. [2056

The first edition, entitled as above, did not contain the author's name. That appeared on the R. T. Young edition (N. Y. 1853). The forty-eight accurate and valuable lithographs from the author's sketches are seldom intact. Letts went to California in 1849, traveled a good deal and worked in the mines. The hundred pages of this book which describe life in California are most faithful notes from personal observation, methodically arranged and excellently expressed. C. H. S.

McCall, *Maj.-Gen.* **George Archibald.** Letters from the frontiers, written during thirty years' service in the army of the United States. Phil.: Lippincott. 1868. [2057

The period covered by this interesting volume is that previous to the Civil War, and it gives valuable reminiscences of the older officers of the army who took different sides in the Rebellion. Its description of the southern and western country are entertaining in themselves, and useful for comparison with the campaigns of the Civil War. It gives the army life, training and field service of that earlier period including the Seminole, Black Hawk and Mexican wars, and is a good introduction to the great war which followed. General McCall commanded the Pennsylvania Reserves in 1861–2. J. D. C.

Manly, W. L. Death Valley in '49. San José, Cal.: Pacific Tree and Vine Co. 1894. [2058

Nearly the whole of this volume is devoted to Mr. Manly's account of adventures during twelve months crossing the plains, and to the desperate experiences of his party in Death Valley. While the author is without literary skill, he tells a plain impressive story, and the entire desert episode deservedly takes a place in Pacific coast history. The pioneer explorers of the Colorado and Mojave deserts narrowly escaped a fate hardly less tragical than that of the Donner party. C. H. S.

Möllhausen, Baldwin. Diary of a journey from the Mississippi to the Pacific, with a

U. S. government expedition; with an introd. by Alexander von Humboldt; tr. by Mrs. Percy Sinnett. London: Longmans. 1858. 2v. [2059

Möllhausen was topographic draftsman and naturalist of a military expedition which, under command of Lieut. A. W. Whipple, explored and surveyed the route for a prospective railroad along the line of the 35th parallel from the Mississippi to the Pacific in 1853–4. [See note on official report, above, sect. 421.] His narrative is a faithful portrayal in popular form of his personal observations; it contains much matter of scientific interest and value, his ethnologic information being as accurately rendered as his limited sojourn among the Indians might be expected to permit. The illustrations are from the author's own drawings. F. W. H.

Nicolay, Charles G. Oregon territory: a geographical and physical account of that country, with outlines of its history. London: Knight. 1846. [2060

Compiled with care and skill from Frémont, Lewis and Clark, Cox of the Northwest Co., Umfraville, Dunn and others of the Hudson Bay Co., and a large number of forgotten explorers. Gives the English side of the Oregon dispute; urges that the northern line of California is the natural boundary between the two countries. C. H. S.

O'Meara, James. Broderick and Gwin: extraordinary contest for a seat in the Senate of the United States: a brief history of early politics in California. San Francisco: Bacon. 1881. 75c. [Sometimes bound under title of History of early politics in California.] [2061

This is a history of the nine eventful years after 1850. The struggle between the North and the South for the control of California was most bitter. Even O'Meara, a trained newspaper man personally acquainted with the public men of the period, cannot be entirely impartial, and shows his sympathies with Judge Terry and the southerners. An able and striking book in a difficult field. C. H. S.

Parkman, Francis. The California and Oregon trail: being sketches of prairie and Rocky Mountain life. N. Y.: Putnam. 1849. —— The Oregon trail; rev. ed. Boston: Little. 1892. $1. [2062

This is one of the classics of western narratives. The journey was undertaken in 1846, "with a view of studying the manners and character of Indians in their primitive state." After going through four editions, a fifth with title, *The Oregon trail: sketches of prairie and Rocky Mountain life*, illustrated by Remington, came out in 1892 (Boston, Little, Brown & Co.). No other book on the West has enjoyed equal popularity. W. M. D.

Pioneer, The; or California monthly magazine. Edited by F. C. Ewer. San Francisco. 1854–5. 4v. [2063

This rare and interesting magazine began in January, 1854, and closed in December, 1855. Its "monthly summary of events" and many other articles have historical interest. The "Shirley letters" on "California in 1851" appeared here.   C. H. S.

Pumpelly, Raphael. Across America and Asia. N. Y.: Leypoldt & Holt. 1870. [2064

The first four chapters give a good picture of rough life in Arizona in 1860–61, when the author was employed there as a mining engineer.   W. M. D.

Remy, Jules. Journey to Great-Salt-Lake City, by Jules Remy and Julius Brenchley; with sketch of the history, religion, and customs of the Mormons, and introd. on the religious movement in the United States. London: Jeffs. 1861. 2v.   [2065

The author was an educated French traveler, and the work was originally published in French. (Paris. 1860.) The first volume contains, besides the philosophical introductory dissertation and a brief account of the journey from Sacramento to Salt Lake in 1855, a fairly complete history of the Mormons from the beginning. The second volume is devoted to the doctrines and customs of the sect and to the return journey. While admitting the imposture of Joseph Smith, the author was favorably impressed by the Mormons and repeatedly expresses his belief in Brigham Young's sincerity. During their stay of a month in Salt Lake the travelers saw a good deal of both Mormon and Gentile leaders, and, perhaps in consequence, the historical sketch is written in a more sympathetic spirit than are most accounts of the sect. There are fine steel portraits of Young and the two Smiths and other plates and a Mormon bibliography.   F. J. S.

Revere, Joseph Warren. Tour of duty in California ; including a description of the gold region, an account of the voyage around Cape Horn, etc. N. Y.: Francis. 1849.   [2066

Lieut. Revere of the U. S. Navy made a well-deserved reputation by this book, and the sketches with which it is illustrated. Something of its charm is due to the careful editing that it received from J. N. Balestier of New York, but Revere evidently had much literary talent. His opportunities for first-hand observations were excellent, and no other book of the period is more accurate in respect to local nomenclature, and topography. The valuable map is copied (with a few changes) from Beechey's *Voyages.*   C. H. S.

Robinson, Alfred. Life in California during a residence of several years in that territory. N. Y.: Wiley. 1846.

—— *Same ;* with an appendix bringing forward the narrative from 1846 to the occupation of the country by the United States. San Francisco: Doxey. 1891. $1.50.   [2067

The last is a partial re-issue of the first edition of Robinson's well-known book (Wiley & Putnam, N. Y., 1846) together with a few pages from the second edition (H. P. Collins, London, 1851), but omitting 112

pages found only in the first edition — Robinson's translation of Father Boscana's important manuscript on the origin, customs and traditions of the Indians of Alta California. Lithographs from drawings by Robinson add much to the value of the first edition. Robinson was one of the best educated observers who published any detailed account of life before the conquest. He was much loved and highly respected among the Californians, and his brief narrative is justly precious to historians. In a sense, it explains, broadens and corrects Dana's admirable *Two years before the mast.* The first edition, long out of print, is much the best.   C. H. S.

Robinson, Charles. The Kansas conflict. N. Y.: Harper. 1892.   [2068

"One would not believe in advance that the story of events so stirring and important could be made so miserably dull. There is no clearness in the narration, and, if one does not know in advance the order of events, to disentangle it from these fragmentary chapters will be no easy matter." *Nation,* 54: 490.

Sabin, Henry *and* **Edwin L.** Making of Iowa. Chicago: Flanagan. [c. 1900.] $1.   [2069

A light sketch of the leading events in the history of the state before the Civil War. Much of the earlier description is occupied by Indian tribes and prominent chiefs. A topical rather than a chronological plan is followed. The style is simple, making the reading easy. This is the chief merit.   E. E. S.

Seyd, Ernest. California and its resources. London : Trübner. 1858.   [2070

The value of this book to the historian lies in two things — (1) the period it covers, which is important, being later than the gold excitement, and earlier than the railroad era ; (2) the business training and carefulness of its author, who writes for merchants, capitalists, and emigrants, and weighs and sifts his evidence. The result is a standard book, always useful for reference in regard to the times and places of which he treats.   C. H. S.

Smet, Pierre Jean de. Oregon missions, and travels over the Rocky Mountains in 1845–6. N. Y. 1847.   [2071

Father De Smet was the Superior of the Indian missions in the region described in this volume, and his opportunities for securing useful notes of the customs, manners, traditions and history of many tribes, were unique. The book necessarily holds a high place among the pioneer missionary records of America. The illustrations from his drawings add greatly to the value of the book.   C. H. S.

Smith, Theodore Clarke. The Liberty and Free Soil parties in the Northwest. (Harvard historical studies, V. 6.) N. Y. : Longmans. 1897. $1.75.   [2072

The result of a painstaking and scholarly investigation of the anti-slavery movement in the Northwest during the twenty years preceding the organization of the Republican party (1854). Newspapers, pamphlets, and manuscript material were carefully examined by the author, and the book has the freshness and spirit that result from a writer's immediate knowledge of the sources. While the pages are crowded with details, tendencies and principles are not altogether neglected. The story is told in strong, vigorous English.   A. C. McL.

Thayer, Eli. History of the Kansas crusade. N. Y.: Harper. 1889. $1.50.   [2073

A work of importance, indispensable to a knowledge of the period with which it deals; but it must be used with care. The author was the promoter of the Massachusetts Emigrant Aid Company, in 1854, and a prominent figure in the movement to people Kansas Territory with northern settlers. He does not always show, however, the part of other agencies than his own in making Kansas a free state ; and he is especially bitter in his criticism of Garrison and the Abolitionists, whom he classes with the enemies of the Union. The book is a compilation, letters and newspaper extracts being freely used.   W. MacD.

Victor, *Mrs.* **Frances Fuller.** The river of the West; life and adventure in the Rocky Mountains and Oregon. Hartford : Columbian Book Co. 1870.   [2074

This book, which has been very widely circulated in various forms, belongs to the class of which *Astoria*, *Bonneville* and *The Oregon trail* are the highest types, and if it had been vigorously condensed, it must have ranked nearer those masterpieces. The narrative is chiefly built about the strong wild figure of " Joe " Meek, the fur-trapper, but Wyeth, Sublette and many other worthies of the northwest move across its pages. The few historical errors of this volume, such as its support of what may be called the Whitman myth, were afterwards corrected by Mrs. Victor in her work for Bancroft's *Oregon*. No writer upon the history of the Northwest has done more careful and conscientious work than Mrs. Victor.   C. H. S.

Whitman, Marcus. Nixon, Oliver W. How Marcus Whitman saved Oregon ; with sketches of life on the plains and mountains in pioneer days. Chicago: Star Pub. Co. 1895.   [2075

The author himself crossed the plains to Oregon in 1850, and, as purser of the first Columbia River steamboat, knew much of the Oregon country pioneers. He attributes to the Washington authorities ignorance of the western region and defends the Whitman legend. A map illustrates Dr. Whitman's famous winter ride in 1842 and his return route. The author's own experience in crossing the continent is illustrative of pioneer hardships. Whitman College and the progress of the Oregon country come in for chapters. Illustrated.   F. J. S.
See, also, sect. 2039, 3392, 3407, 3425.

Wyeth, *Capt.* **Nathaniel Jarvis.** Correspondence and journals, 1831–36 ; ed. by F. G. Young. (Sources of the history of Oregon, V. 1, pt. 3–6.) Portland: Oregon Hist. Soc. 1899.   [2076

" In 1832–33 and 1834–35 some operations of much wider scope and further-reaching effect [than the exploits of Ashley and Bonneville] were conducted by an enterprising person whose name has never yet been popularized, though Irving has much to say of him in *Bonneville*. This is Nathaniel Jarvis Wyeth, whose two expeditions were undertaken in the years last mentioned, both for the purposes of fur trade and for the occupation of Oregon. Wyeth's second expedition was accompanied by the ornithologist J. K. Townsend and the botanist Thomas Nuttall, and a full account of it is given by the former in his *Narrative* (Phil. 1839) ; but of the earlier one our knowledge has hitherto remained very incomplete. Now we have the original documents in the case of both expeditions. . . . This is of prime authenticity and authority, being nothing less than 245 letters written by Wyeth before, during, and after his expeditions, together with his original journal of them both, just as it was jotted down day by day. Nearly all of this is brand-new matter, hidden from the public in manuscript all these years, and no more genuine 'sources' of history of trade, settlement, and adventure in the West will ever be forthcoming. . . . The editor's work is very carefully and thoroughly done." *Nation*, 69 : 447.

Yoakum, Henderson. History of Texas from its first settlement in 1685 to its annexation to the United States in 1846. N. Y.: Redfield. 1856. [c. 1855.] 2v.   [2077

A work evincing a high degree of scholarship and research, and still recognized as one of the prime authorities for the history of Texas, but written without access to much material that has since become available, and therefore to be used with caution. Its treatment of the period of ex-Spanish domination is especially incomplete and unsatisfactory. Each volume contains a rather lengthy appendix filled with important documents.   G. P. G.

---

5. Period of the Civil War : 1860–1865

BIBLIOGRAPHY OF THE CIVIL WAR PERIOD

By General J. D. Cox

[The lamented death of General Cox occurred not long after he had written the last of his contributions to this work. It was good fortune in our undertaking that he lived to assist it, which he did with great interest, and with the conscientiousness of labor that characterized every service he performed in his most useful life. Probably no other prominent survivor of the Civil War, having an experience of its realities equal to his, knew the literature of its history so extensively as he did, and could appraise so much of that literature so judicially, with so accomplished a pen. — *The Editor*.]

The *Official records of the Union and Confederate Armies*, a monumental work published by the Government, is the most important, by far, of all books concerned with the Civil War period. It is divided into four series. The first contains the strictly military reports and correspondence relating to campaigns in the field, with the statistical returns of the armies, both Union and Confederate. The second gives the records and correspondence relating to prisoners of war and prisoners of state so far as the military authorities dealt with them. The third will embody everything relating to calls for national troops, whether militia or volunteers, and the apportionment to the states, the enforcement of drafts, etc. : also the reports, etc., of the administrative bureaus of the War Department, and the correspondence between the national and the state authorities. The fourth will be the compilation of Confederate records similar to those of the third series, so far as they have been preserved. The publication of the first two series is completed and the third is in progress. The first is much the largest and most essential to the study of the period. It is divided into campaigns of separate armies, sieges, detached expeditions, etc. Such as are closely related in theatre of operations and time, usually also in unity of departmental command, are united in one volume, which, however, sometimes runs to four or five parts, each of 1000 to 1500 pages. The total number of serial books reaches 113 in this series, though the formal volumes number only 55. For convenience in reference, each volume is prefaced by a table of contents of preceding volumes. Each has also its separate index of names of officers, and of military organizations. Correspondence is indexed under the names of both writer and person addressed. Calendars of the years are also printed at the beginning of each formal volume to facilitate the change of days of the week, often given in dispatches, into days of the month. [2078

The work of arranging and copying reports, etc., with a view to publication, began before the war had ended, but the lack of money to employ proper clerical help prevented any great progress till Congress took up the work in earnest in 1874. The Loyal Legion, The Grand Army of the Republic and other societies of the veterans of the war had strenuously urged the matter for several years before appropriations of money were made which were at all adequate. A War Records Office was organized under Gen. E. D. Townsend, Adjutant-General, in 1877, and Capt. (afterward Lt.-Colonel) Robert N. Scott, 3d U. S. Artillery,

was put at its head. Under Col. Scott's direction, eighteen volumes (with their parts) had been published and most of the material for eighteen more prepared when he died in 1887. He was succeeded by Lt.-Col. Henry M. Lazelle, 23d U. S. Infantry. Early in 1889 a new law was enacted, providing a Board of Publication, to consist of an officer of the army and two civilian experts. Maj. George B. Davis, Judge Advocate, U. S. A., with Leslie J. Perry and Joseph W. Kirkley were appointed to be this Board. The two civilians had already been responsible assistants in the work. In 1895 Maj. George W. Davis, 11th U. S. Infantry, relieved Maj. G. B. Davis, and continued at the head of the Board till July, 1898. The whole of the first series had now been published and the matter for the others prepared for printing. The supervision of this was transferred to the Pension Office under Gen. F. C. Ainsworth, and the Board dissolved. [2079

An important part of the *Confederate records* were taken south by Mr. Davis, Confederate President, when he left Richmond in April, 1865, and these were at Charlotte, N. C., in charge of Gen. Samuel Cooper, Adjt. and Insp.-Gen., C. S. A. With the devotion of one who fully knew the historical value of these records, Gen. Cooper gave personal attention to them in the confusion of the breaking up of the Confederate Army, remained with them and surrendered them and himself to Gen. Sherman. Other parts of the Confederate archives were separately captured, and preserved by the national government. Col. Scott early began strenuous efforts to supply missing reports and correspondence, and Gen. Marcus J. Wright, late of the Confederate service, was for years engaged in obtaining original documents in private hands, and duplicates which had been preserved by Confederate officers. No pains were spared to make the Confederate records complete, and an astonishing degree of success was attained. [2080

Similar industry was used in obtaining missing papers and dispatches on the national side. Hasty field dispatches were most likely to be lacking, and officers were urged to furnish the Records Office with properly authenticated copies of every such document. Field diaries kept by responsible officers and the staff were also reclaimed. Work done thus with the love of it guided by an educated historical instinct, has made the *Official records* a wonderful collection of historical material, full of personal life as well as of formal documentary evidence. These *Records* are, of course, the original source and ultimate authority for the history of the period. Yet the materials vary in value. National reports need to be compared and checked by the Confederate; the reports of subordinates by the broader summing up of the chiefs, and *vice versâ*. Personal ambitions, interests, vanities, and prejudices often color the statements of officers. In mishaps and defeats reports will be colored by the desire to cover a fault or to shift a responsibility. In success, the participants are tempted to claim an undue share of credit. It is here that the vast mass of testimony gives the patient investigator unprecedented means of eliminating error and establishing the truth. Each important officer's character may be established by a study of his reports in different campaigns, and the comparative clearness of his judgment as well as his candor, his modesty, his cordiality of subordination, or the lack of these qualities, may be learned. His military character is here indelibly written by himself. If precedence in value can be attributed to any portion of such abundant treasures, the field dispatches and daily correspondence would seem to be first. Here we have the very life of passing events. From day to day and from hour to hour the situation is described and interpreted by the actors in it. We read the contemporary dispatches from both camps, and can detect the illusions in either as well as the sagacity with which they infer 'what is behind the hill.' The comparison of these with the campaign reports is often most enlightening: it certainly is fascinating to the real investigator, who has here an apparatus of research undreamt of in other times.   [2081

The *Official records of the Union and Confederate Navies* are upon a plan similar to the army publication, but consist of very few volumes, only three being published up to 1899.   [2082

The *Official medical and surgical history of the war* is a wonderful compilation of facts, scientifically analyzed and commented upon by most able professional editors.   [2083

Of publications made during the war itself, the leading newspapers are, in spite of some serious drawbacks, indispensable to the student of the time. As an index of current opinion, the historical investigator cannot afford to neglect them; but besides this, many of them kept enterprising and able correspondents with

the armies in the field. The letters of these often give fresh views of current campaign history which are most valuable. Unfortunately, there were many just complaints that the relations of writers to officers whose guests they might be warped their statements and made them flatterers or apologists on the one hand, or, on the other, detractors of those who had refused favors. There were among these correspondents some men of highest character and independence. Such generally become known in literature afterward, so that their army work may be identified and appreciated. The work of unknown men must be received with caution. The weekly illustrated press, of which *Harper's weekly* was a prominent type, had artists in the field besides correspondents, and their sketches, though hasty, have often proved of great importance in fixing a situation or solving a disputed question of fact.   [2084

Moore's *Rebellion record*, begun in 1862, was for a long time one of the indispensable aids to the study of the war period. Much of its material is now more authoritatively found in the *Official records*, but it is still a useful repository of semi-official papers, and of facts not easily found elsewhere. Between 1862 and 1868 it reached the ample dimensions of a dozen stout volumes.   [2085

At the close of the war, officers of the national army and navy formed the Military Order of the Loyal Legion, a society similar to the Revolutionary one of The Cincinnati. At the meetings of the State Commanderies the custom was soon introduced of reading papers containing the personal experience of the writer and his observation of campaigns in which he had a part. Though such papers differ in value according to the opportunities and qualities of the writers, it would be hard to overestimate the importance of such a collection of personal testimony to events in which the writers had part and bore positions of responsibility with unusual means of accurate knowledge. Some twelve or fourteen volumes have already been published by the State Commanderies, Ohio leading with four.   [2086

The five series of *Personal narratives* published by the Rhode Island Soldiers' and Sailors' Historical Society are similar in character and in value.   [2087

The Military Historical Society of Massachusetts has since 1876 been one of the most active working organizations of its kind. It is not wholly composed of military men, and one of its most active spirits was the late John C. Ropes, ·the military historian. Its work has not been (like that of the Loyal Legion) confined to the personal knowledge of its members, though the greater number of its papers are of this kind: but its members sometimes present the results of their critical study of the Civil War campaigns in other sources. From their records, this Society has published, in its edited series, three volumes; one on the campaigns in Virginia in 1861–2, one on Gen. Pope's campaign of 1862, and one on 'Some Federal and Confederate commanders.' All are of a very high order of merit, and the more useful because the different papers often have the interest of varying views and acute discussion. [2088

The Southern Historical Society (Richmond) has done similar work for the Confederates, and its published volumes are accepted as original authority by all who are familiar with the Civil War literature. Some of its papers are by men of very high reputation in the southern armies. Similar aids to history are found in southern periodicals like *The bivouac.* [2089

Several societies based on service in particular armies have had a lengthened existence and have published series of proceedings. Of these, the most considerable are of the societies of the armies of the Cumberland, the Tennessee, and the Potomac. Historical papers are not a regular part of these social reunions, but reports on subjects of historical importance are often made, and the addresses are sometimes in the true historical vein, though naturally more often in the lighter one adapted to such a symposium. The same remark will apply to army reunions in general. One held at Chicago in 1868 was so exceptional as to be of itself an historical event. General Grant was there, with nearly every prominent officer of the national armies. The armies of the Tennessee, the Cumberland, the Ohio, and the Georgia were each represented at the public meeting in an address by a selected representative, besides the more general speeches at the banquet. The whole of the proceedings were published in beautiful form.[1] [2090

One's first impression would be that regimental histories, of which there are many, are among the most authentic sources of the war history. It does not turn out so. They are

[1] Chicago: S. C. Griggs & Co. 1869.

almost all devoted to what we may call the domestic side of their experience. The regiment is the most important army unit. It is the largest organization which has permanence enough to make a general acquaintance among its members possible. It is a big family, with its attachments, its exclusiveness, its pride, its jealousy of others, its absorption in its internal affairs and in its own gossip, akin to that of a village. Its line officers have little opportunity to know the larger purposes of the campaign, and both officers and men are influenced by the rumors current in the camp, and have imperfect means of correcting them. For the broader purposes of history, therefore, the regimental view is narrow and full of errors. When the regimental history comes to be written, after the war, it is written for the comrades and only remotely for the public. The memories of their camp life, of their field and company officers, of personal incidents, grave and gay, of their marches and their own part in battles and sieges are the things in demand, including even the prejudices and rivalries they used to cherish. For such local color, these histories are most attractive; but it is among the rarest of things that the writers go beyond this. When they do so, their material is not of personal knowledge or memory, but gathered by subsequent study, as others must gather it. [2091

The histories of brigades, divisions, and corps are, in diminishing degree, subject to the same criticism. By as much as the organization is less than the army in the field, its history is less than the history of the whole campaign. A part is avowedly made the prominent feature, and a well-proportioned treatment of the whole is disclaimed. All such books, therefore, are written for the members of the organizations which are their subjects. We go to them for many matters of interest, but shall be misled if we forget the limitations involved in their professed plan and scope. As the units increase in size and relative importance, their history becomes more necessary as material for the general historian, but it never becomes general history itself. [2092

For the first ten or fifteen years after the close of the Civil War, even the ablest writers who aimed at general history were greatly handicapped by the inability to use original material. The records in the governmental departments were not yet so classified and arranged that the public could have access to them, and the printing of the military archives had not yet begun. Historical work of a permanent character could, as yet, hardly be done. The general thirst for such knowledge made a great demand for such literature; but the ablest of the writers of that time would be the first to admit that their work was provisional, not final. [2093

There was, however, one class of books of inestimable historical importance which could be produced only in that time. The personal memoirs of the great leaders of the period of convulsion must be written then or not at all, for they were rapidly reaching the term of human life and labor. Sherman, Grant, Sheridan, on the National side, Davis, Johnston, Longstreet, on the Confederate, were questioning their memories and giving lasting form to their recollections. Their unassisted memory could give what the world would count as beyond price, but fortunately the documentary material they had preserved, and the possession of the "Open Sesame" to the public records, enabled them to write works worthy of their career. The books have an almost equal value, also, as transparent revelations of the men themselves, their purposes, methods, motives, and the working of their minds and hearts. They were followed by similar personal memoirs by men in varying degrees of close contact with the affairs of the time, civil as well as military; and we are permitted to hope that, as the past few years have seen the bringing to light of many of the most valuable works of this description in the great European period of 1789 to 1815, which have lain among family treasures nearly a century, so the next generation, here, may find its knowledge enriched by similar memorials of a great epoch, deliberately and carefully prepared, and modestly awaiting the fit time for publication. It is impossible to have too much of the testimony of eye-witnesses, and the real investigator will delight in cross-questioning each by the help of the others and of the official record. [2094

About 1880, the government publication of military documents began, and the Records Office was opened to serious students. Enterprising publishers took up the task of furnishing the public with detailed and authentic history of the Civil War. The Century Company brought out Nicolay and Hay's great work on Lincoln and his time, and the *War book* in which

participants on both sides narrated the events they had witnessed. The Scribners issued their *Campaigns of the Civil War*, a series of thirteen volumes, and the *Naval history* in three more, each book by an expert having special knowledge of his own topic, and, with one or two exceptions, official part in the campaigns described. [2095

With these typical examples, the period of formal history of the Civil War based on adequate material may be said to have begun, and every season has borne witness to the industry of investigators, and to the unflagging interest of the reading public. The military records have been supplemented by those of all departments of the civil government. Congressional documents give us the political side of the great struggle, and of the Reconstruction which followed the declaration of peace and amnesty. Monthly magazines gave regular chapters of current events. Annual compilations of political documents, party platforms, and analyses of legislative acts were added to the other sources of history. Statistical almanacs teemed with a wonderful array of tables of everything which could be reduced to numerical statement. None of these aids comes amiss to the student, and what seems at first an overwhelming and confusing mass of material, is by intelligent system in the use reduced to the form of a well-ordered storehouse whose proprietors can lay hand at once upon whatever is wanted. It is the aim of this work to help still further in simplifying and facilitating the use of the accumulated stores of knowledge. [2096

(See, also, in Syllabus of Materials, sect. 22.)

Abbot, Willis John. Battle-fields of '61. N. Y.: Dodd. [c. 1889.] $2.

—— Battle-fields and camp fires. N. Y.: Dodd. [c. 1890.] $2.

—— Battle-fields and victory. N. Y.: Dodd. [c. 1891.] $2. [2097

Spirited and generally accurate popular narratives of the leading campaigns and romantic incidents of the war for the Union. Likely to interest youth and the average adult. G. A. T.

—— Blue jackets of '61. N. Y.: Dodd. 1886. [2098

" While the author has given an animated story, it cannot be said that he has made the most of his opportunity. His battle-scenes are somewhat lurid, and he loses rather than gains in picturesqueness by a turgid style and profuseness of epithet. Occasionally he is guilty of forcing his facts for the sake of effect. Exaggeration of this kind, whether verbal or historical, is not a good thing for his boy readers, and it may be doubted whether it is much to their taste. . . . Many statements are distinctly the reverse of the truth. Thus it is twice said that some of the United States vessels at the beginning of the war were surrendered to the Confederates through the treachery of their officers, when it has always been a source of just pride to the service that, in spite of the temptation, no such case occurred. . . . The effect of each misstatement is increased tenfold by embroidering it with fictitious details. . . . The illustrations show the same faults as the text." *Nation*, 43: 458.

Abbott, John Stevens Cabot. History of the Civil War in America. N. Y.: H. Bill. 1863-5. [c. 1863.] 2v. [2099

Evidently planned in the heat of the war with an eye to the popular demand for literature which should fire the patriotic spirit, these volumes are made up chiefly from the undigested matter of current periodicals, or from contemporary sources in which fact and fancy play a nearly equal part. The style is bombastic, the scenes depicted and battle speeches made are largely arranged for their dramatic effect. Altogether ephemeral history, save in such features as represent the fury of certain of the southern leaders and writers at the outbreak of the secession spirit.
G. A. T.

Allan, *Lt. Col.* **William.** The Army of Northern Virginia in 1862; with an introd. by John C. Ropes. Boston: Houghton. 1892. $3.50. [2100

"Mr. Ropes, with a spirit of broadest liberality, vouches for the ability and the honesty of the southern writer, though the latter combats vigorously some of his own published conclusions. . . . Col. Allan died before his book was published, and, judging by the foot-note references to authorities, he did not have the advantage of some recent books of capital importance in forming a sound historical judgment of the campaigns he describes. . . . We can join heartily in the general praise which Mr. Ropes gives his book. Yet the book is distinctly and manifestly written from the Confederate standpoint, and shows on almost every page the 'bias' peculiar to the author's education and sympathies. . . . The maps, printed in colors, are far above those we ordinarily see." J. D. Cox, in *Nation*, 56: 85.

—— History of the campaign of Gen. T. J. (Stonewall) Jackson in the Shenandoah valley of Virginia, Nov. 4, 1861–June 17, 1862. Phil.: Lippincott. 1880. [2101

Colonel Allan was an officer of Jackson's staff. He wrote with full and accurate information of the Confederate operations which drove back the Union General Banks to the Potomac River and which indirectly served to aid Lee in the defeat of McClellan in the "Seven days' battles." His book is thoroughly impar-

tial, with no partisan heat, and has excellent maps by Captain Hotchkiss, Allan's associate in staff duty.
G. A. T.

Ammen, Daniel. The Atlantic coast. (The navy in the Civil War, 2.) N. Y.: Scribner. 1898. $1. [2102

"Apart from the blockade, the work of the Atlantic squadrons was largely in getting control of the line of sounds or inland seas which skirt the coast south of the Capes; in occupying the important rivers, harbors, and towns along them; and in simplifying the blockade by substituting for it, when possible, a military occupation. This involved many ventures, planned with care and carried out with vigor and daring. . . . All these disconnected expeditions, large and small, are given conscientiously in this book. . . . Throughout the book, Union and Confederate reports of the same occurrences are joined to support or check each other. The work indicates laborious research and straightforward honesty. The tone is fair and manly, and the author's mention of his own service is in excellent taste." *Nation*, 37: 121.

Anderson, *Lt.-Col.* **Thomas M.** Political conspiracies preceding the Rebellion; or The true stories of Sumter and Pickens. N. Y.: Putnam. 1882. [2103

"The writer of this little book vindicates the just fame of his kinsman [Major Anderson, who commanded at Fort Sumter], and retells the story of the fall of Sumter and the rescue of Pickens. There is very little that is new; the letter of General Meigs, giving his version of the curious military expedition which the Secretary of State set on foot without the knowledge of the Secretary of War or of the Navy, being the only original document. Lieut.-Col. Anderson does not accept the conclusions of the writer of the letter. The essay is often diffuse in style, and sometimes lacks dignity; it omits an occasional link of narration, and its story of facts is accompanied by reflections which, although generally just, are frequently commonplace." *Nation*, 35: 316.

Andrew, John Albion. BROWNE, ALBERT GALLATIN, JR. Sketch of the official life of John A. Andrew as Governor of Massachusetts during the Civil War. N. Y.: Hurd. 1868. [2104

A sympathetic and discriminating brief account of the official life of one of the great war governors and statesmen. Written by one closely associated with Governor Andrew as his private secretary, it gives, besides an appreciation of his personal excellences, some of his most notable addresses. G. A. T.

Barnard, *Maj.-Gen.* **John G.** The Peninsular campaign and its antecedents, as developed by the report of Maj.-Gen. McClellan and other published documents. N. Y.: Van Nostrand. 1864. [2105

Gen. Barnard was, during the Civil War, one of the senior officers of the Engineers, having graduated from West Point in 1833. He was Chief Engineer of

the Army of the Potomac during the campaign here discussed, and Gen. McClellan became alienated from him by reason of differences of opinion as to the conduct of the army operations. Gen. Barnard thus became involved in the discussion of the campaign, and later presented his view of it, reviewing McClellan's report. His acknowledged ability, his standing in the army, and his intimate personal knowledge of the events he deals with, combine to make his book an important original contribution to the war history.
J. D. C.

Barnes, David M. Draft riots in New York, 1863 : the metropolitan police, their services. N. Y.: Baker. 1863.   [2106

The " Draft riots " were incited in New York city by the forcible drafting of men for military duty in the Civil War. They raged from July 13 to 20, 1863. This pamphlet gives the part taken by the individual police officers in the different districts. A list of the victims of the riots is added. The pamphlet is of value for the details of the week.   E. E. S.

Bartlett, John Russell. Memoirs of Rhode Island officers in service during the great rebellion. Providence: Rider. 1867. [c. 1866.]
[2107

The volume comprises sketches of 110 officers, with 34 portraits. There is no index or other alphabetical clue to the sketches, the arrangement in the list at the beginning being by rank, and that of the body of the book a still different order. The author's opportunities for securing information were exceptional, Mr. Bartlett having served as secretary of his state during the Civil War. The narratives are told with varying degrees of detail, but nearly all of those no longer living possess a pathetic interest.   W. E. F.

Bartlett, *Maj.-Gen.* William Francis. PALFREY, *Brig.-Gen.* FRANCIS WINTHROP. Memoir of William Francis Bartlett. Boston : Houghton. 1878. $1.50.   [2108

" General Palfrey has used a wise discretion in allowing the story of his old friend and companion in arms, General Bartlett, to tell itself almost entirely in the hero's own words, as set down in his diaries and letters. . . . His character presents itself to the reader almost wholly without critical interpretation or analysis, and without superfluous eulogy. . . . He was an American of such knightly instincts, such heroic courage, such generous ideals of duty united to so much common sense, that among the names made memorable in the great struggle his remains one of the most representative of the highest American soldiership. . . . He never had an opportunity of showing what he might have been as a general officer. . . . In every engagement in which he took part, with the exception of his first at Ball's Bluff, he was wounded within an hour from the time the first gun was fired. . . . What made his life chiefly valuable as a heritage and an example was his character, which in any and all circumstances shone with a marvelous union of strength and sweetness." *Atlantic monthly*, 41: 801.

Battles and leaders of the Civil War : contributions by Union and Confederate officers ;

ed. by Robert Underwood Johnson and Clarence Clough Buel. N. Y. : Century Co. [c. 1887–9.] 4v. $15.   [2109

The war papers originally published in the *Century magazine*, carefully edited, beautifully printed and illustrated, and thoroughly indexed, form an extremely interesting and valuable history of the war.
" As the papers originally appeared, no chronological order was observed ; but in the book form they are so arranged as to make a consecutive history, beginning with the bombardment of Sumter. New papers have been added to the series to supply vacancies and to bind the whole into one narrative, so that a considerable percentage of the volume is new matter. . . . The novel scheme of printing side by side the story of battles and movements as told by men of opposite sides who participated in them, was a delicate experiment, but has proved a great success. Union and Confederate soldiers have told their remembrances in a generous spirit, and the presentation of both sides has never degenerated into controversy or lost its dignity." *Nation*, 46: 30.
" Collected and bound up in four stout quarto volumes, the papers on the American Civil War, . . . which have appeared in the *Century*, form what we venture to call a unique military book. For it is not a body of information and description of great events gathered from various quarters and put together by an enterprising editor. It is the result of a plan to obtain articles from officers on both sides, which succeeded so well among men who, before they were ranged under hostile flags, were old comrades, that the series naturally expanded, and so came to represent the war as seen from both camps. . . . The fruit of this is an instructive mass of information and much admirable writing relating to the whole war, afloat as well as ashore, profusely illustrated by portraits, sketches, maps. . . . It is the all-round, hearty cooperation of the combatants, no matter what their uniform, blue or butternut, and the careful editing, which make this astonishing series such a valuable supplement to the strictly official papers, returns, and reports of both sides." *Spectator*, 63: 51.

Baxter, William. Pea Ridge and Prairie Grove ; or Scenes and incidents of the war in Arkansas. Cin.: Poe. 1864.   [2110

Not an account of battles, but a history of the personal experiences inside the lines of the Confederacy in Arkansas, in the first two years of the war, of an intelligent clergyman and teacher. An effective picture of the cruelty and bitterness of warfare betwixt neighbors, and of the ignorance of respectable people of the South; clear and unpretentious in manner.   G. A. T.

Beath, Robert B. History of the Grand Army of the Republic. N. Y. : Bryan. 1889.
[2111

The author was an early member of the order, was once its commander-in-chief, was for three terms its adjutant-general, besides filling many subordinate offices, and compiled its first manual and its blue book. He gives its history by official administrations, including sketches of officers of the national body, and follows this up with brief accounts of the state departments, with some notice of state legislation regarding veterans, soldiers' homes, monuments, etc. Cuts of Grand Army and army corps badges, the history of other orders growing out of the Civil War and of allied societies, some pension information, and an account of the establishment of Memorial Day will be found.   F. J. S.

Beauregard, *Gen.* **Pierre Gustave Toutant.** ROMAN, *Col.* ALFRED. Military operations of General Beauregard, 1861–65; including his services in the war with Mexico. N. Y.: Harper. 1884. 2v. $7.   [2112

" A considerable part of each volume consists of an appendix, containing official and other documents, many of them of great interest. . . . Colonel Roman has written a careful and exhaustive biography of his chief. Beauregard, in the preface, indorses all his statements and comments, excepting only his eulogiums upon Beauregard himself. The book is, we are obliged to say, unnecessarily loud; there is a good deal of repetition in it, and many episodes, especially those involving the personal differences between General Beauregard and President Davis, are, in our judgment, dwelt upon with needless particularity." *Atlantic monthly*, 53: 551.

" We believe there is not a single superior officer of General Beauregard that is not disparaged in this book, and accused of damaging, at one time or another, the cause of which General Beauregard is represented as the only ever wise and ever unselfish defender. The object of our author's special hostility is Mr. Davis, but the Confederate Secretaries of War, the chiefs of the war bureaus in Richmond, and Generals Cooper, Lee, A. S. Johnson, J. E. Johnston, besides many of lower rank, come in for their share of criticism; a criticism often ill-judged, in most cases partial, and nearly always truculent." *Nation*, 38: 214.

Bigelow, John. France and the Confederate navy. 1862–1868 : an international episode. N. Y.: Harper. 1888. $1.50.   [2113

" Mr. Bigelow's modest little book has a far higher value as history than many more pretentious volumes that bear the name. What he playfully terms an 'international episode' was in truth a diplomatic intrigue of the first magnitude, in respect to the parties concerned in it as well as in the interests at stake. It was nothing less than the attempt of the Confederacy, with the active coöperation of the Emperor Napoleon III., to make France play the same part for the Confederates that she played in 1778 for the Revolutionary colonies." Mr. Bigelow, then Consul-General of the United States at Paris, purchased a series of letters and papers that had passed between the Confederate commissioner Slidell, Captain Bulloch, and others, and promptly exposed the intrigue. With the finding of the Slidell-Benjamin correspondence in the Confederate archives, he became possessed of all the facts of the affair. " In form, his book is primarily a documentary study, three-fourths of its space being taken up by official papers ; but the author's narrative, drawn largely from his personal experience, and enlivened with much caustic observation and incisive comment, connects the docu-

ments and fills out the gaps in the story." J. R. Soley, in *Nation*, 47: 457.

Borcke, Heros von. Memoirs of the Confederate war for independence. Edin.: Blackwood. 1866. 2v.   [2114

The author was a young Prussian who volunteered to serve in the Confederate army in the spring of 1862, and was on the staff of Gen. J. E. B. Stuart, the famous cavalry commander, till the death of the latter in 1864. He could not fail to see many famous men and events, and to have a stirring experience, of all which he gives his recollections. His narration is entertaining, his vanity is *naïve*, and one feels that his own exploits are not diminished in the telling. He is more southern than the Confederates and has few good words for anything northern. His recollections are useful as local pictures of life with Stuart, but he does not properly distinguish between what he saw himself and what he got by hearsay. Tested by the *Official records* they are often inaccurate, and cannot be regarded as historical.   J. D. C.

Botts, John Minor. The great Rebellion. N. Y.: Harper. 1866.   [2115

The author was a southern whig, an earnest supporter of Henry Clay, and a staunch Union man during the Civil War, although he remained in Virginia, where he was twice put under arrest by the Confederate authorities. In this book he charges that secession was long meditated and of set purpose brought about by the Democratic leaders of the South, aided by the northern abolitionists. The repeal of the Missouri Compromise is especially condemned as having been carried through for the sake of reviving the slavery agitation. The book is intended as a vindication of the author's political career, but its value is increased by the light thrown by the appendix on the life of a Union man inside the Confederacy and on the theory of reconstruction, which is discussed at much length. Mr. Botts's views on Lincoln are also of much interest.   F. J. S.

Boynton, Charles Brandon. History of the navy during the Rebellion. N. Y.: Appleton. 1867–8. 2v. $6.   [2116

This book has been sharply criticised, as being written without carefulness of investigation, and with the bias of strong personal and partisan prejudices.

Britton, Wiley. The Civil War on the border. N. Y.: Putnam. 1890–99. 2v. v. 1, $2.50; v. 2, $3.50.   [2117

" We have here a straightforward effort to tell the story of the campaigns in Missouri and the adjacent territory during the first two years of the Civil War. The author served on the national side, and most of what he narrates occurred under his own eye. He is able, therefore, to give more of local color than a mere compiler could give, and estimates the officers and men on both sides according to the impression they made upon those who were in contact with them. . . . The style of the book has, for the most part, the merit of simplicity and directness, though the author occasionally lapses into rhetorical efforts which are not entirely happy. These are not frequent, however.

... It is a valuable addition to the list of special memoirs on the war written by men who took part in what they describe." *Nation*, 51: 38.

Brockett, Linus Pierpont, *and Mrs.* **Mary C. Vaughan.** Woman's work in the Civil War; with introd. by Henry W. Bellows. Boston: Curran. 1867.   [2118

Short biographical sketches of women who in organizations such as the Soldiers' Aid Societies and the branches of the U. S. Sanitary Commission, or in personal services in the hospitals or on the field, devoted their time and money to the aid of the northern soldier.

Brooks, Noah. Washington in Lincoln's time. N. Y.: Century Co. 1895. $1.25.
     [2119

Made up of entertaining articles which appeared originally in the *Century*. "Like all the work from the DeVinne Press, this attractive little volume is easy to read, with its large, clear type, good paper, and press-work. The matter of the book is well worth its permanent form, for it is a vivid and faithful picture of the capital in war-time, as seen by a newspaper correspondent who had more than common facilities for seeing and hearing all that was made public, with occasional peeps behind the scenes. It is, besides, very well and clearly written, in English often terse and vigorous, and has a good many descriptions of persons and things that are worthy of a permanent place in the public gallery of portraits and historical scenes." J. D. Cox, in *Nation*, 61: 312.

Brown, George William. Baltimore and the nineteenth of April, 1861. (Johns Hopkins Univ. studies, extra v. 3.) Balt. 1887. $1.
     [2120

"This is a valuable contribution to the history of the Rebellion, being a clear and candid account of the memorable and shameful attack upon the 6th Regiment of Massachusetts Volunteers by a mob in the streets of Baltimore on the 19th of April, 1861. . . . The author, Judge Brown, was then Mayor of Baltimore, and not only did all in his power to prevent disorder, but, after the attack began, joined the assaulted troops and gallantly marched through the streets to the depot at the head of the column, and saw the regiment embark upon the cars and move out of the city upon the journey to Washington. . . . The author devotes a chapter to showing that the alleged plot to assassinate Mr. Lincoln when he passed through Baltimore in February, 1861, was mere fiction." *Nation*, 44: 412.

Brown, William Wells. The negro in the American Rebellion. Boston: Lee. 1867.
     [2121

Traces the gradual change in the status of the negro from contraband to soldier. Made up largely of newspaper clippings and extracts from official papers, in a chronological order. There are numerous anecdotes, some from the personal observation of the writer. Preliminary chapters treat of the negro in the Revolutionary War and the War of 1812. The book is for the general reader rather than the scholar.
     E. E. S.

Browne, A. K. Story of the Kearsarge and Alabama. San Francisco: Henry Payot. 1868.   [2122

"The author, who has been induced to publish this narrative of the famous combat between the Kearsarge and the Alabama, by the want that existed of a popular, detailed, and yet concise account of the affair, may congratulate himself on having exactly met this want. . . . With no feeble-minded impulses to be dramatic or picturesque, he is graphic in the best way, and brings the whole occurrence before his reader with the simplicity of a sensible man and the quiet power of an artist. We think we could have read even a duller narrative with pleasure in the exquisite print which the publishers have given his little book." *Atlantic monthly*, 22: 640.

Brownlow, William Gannaway. Sketches of the rise, progress, and decline of secession, with a narrative of personal adventures among the rebels. Phil.: Childs. 1862.   [2123

"Fighting Parson" Brownlow was editor of a Knoxville, Tennessee, newspaper. Although favoring slavery, he opposed secession and was imprisoned by the Confederate authorities for refusing to take an oath of allegiance to that government. This volume is a reprint of some of his editorials, correspondence, speeches, and experiences during his eventful life in the South. It was written after Brownlow was transported beyond the northern lines and was lecturing in the northern cities. The book is intensely bitter in tone and interesting chiefly from the author's personality.
     E. E. S.

Buchanan, James. (See in the preceding period, sect. 1846, 1847.)

Bullock, *Capt.* **James D.** Secret service of the Confederate States in Europe; or How the Confederate cruisers were equipped. London: Bentley. 1883. 2v. N. Y.: Putnam. 1883. 2v.   [2124

Easily first in authority upon its subject. Captain Bullock was the naval representative of the Confederacy in Europe and its authoritative agent in building and fitting out the Alabama and other cruisers. Whilst a devoted Confederate officer, his historical purpose is candidly sincere, his store of original knowledge is unequalled, and he has intelligently used collateral sources of information, diplomatic and other. His story is well and naturally told.
     J. D. C.

Burnside, *Maj.-Gen.* **Ambrose Everett.** POORE, BENJAMIN PERLEY. Life and public services of Ambrose E. Burnside; with an introd. by Henry B. Anthony. Providence: Reid. 1882.   [2125

Mr. Poore was for many years a well known journalist at Washington, and intimate with Burnside during the general's senatorship from 1875 to his death. Mr. Anthony was Burnside's colleague from Rhode Island in the Senate. The book is an attractive one in style, beautiful in form, warmly appreciative in tone. It is based on competent research in original materials. Burnside's military prominence began with his very successful military and naval expedition to North Carolina in 1862. His command of the Army of the Potomac in the Fredericksburg campaign brought a temporary eclipse. His East Tennessee Campaign of 1863 again proved solid abilities and a high order of success. His service under Grant in Virginia in 1864 was able and honorable, but controversy as to the Petersburg mine explosion made him retire from the army. His noble personal character was always acknowledged, his disinterested and modest patriotism spoke for itself. J. D. C.

— WOODBURY, AUGUSTUS. Major General Ambrose E. Burnside and the Ninth Army Corps. Providence: Rider. 1867. [2126

Long as this book is, "it is generally readable. It has many merits; but they are more than counterbalanced by one defect which pervades it, and that is its untrustworthiness. . . . Mr. Woodbury was not a soldier of the Ninth Corps, and was not an eye-witness of the scenes which he describes. The third paragraph in his preface makes us doubt his fitness for his task, for he there undertakes to pronounce the following judgment: 'No corps in the army, with the exception of those which made the grand march from Atlanta to the coast and up through the Carolinas, has performed more arduous service, or marched or fought over a wider territory, than the Ninth.' That this corps saw a great deal of the country during the war, is true. That no corps in the army performed more arduous service, is not true. . . . Apart from the defects which are distinctly traceable to the partisanship of the author, Mr. Woodbury's book is as good as could be expected from a man of fair education, much industry, little military knowledge, and a strong tendency to fine writing. . . . It is an interesting book from the necessity of the case. It is most interesting when it treats of operations on a comparatively small scale, which are within the author's grasp. Thus the account of operations in North Carolina, which occupies about the first fifth of the book, is generally excellent, and the chapter on the 'deliverance of East Tennessee' is very good." The Ninth Corps is entitled to honor for its achievements and its admirable *esprit de corps*. It does not need exaggerated praise. *Nation*, 4: 125.

Butler, *Maj.-Gen.* Benjamin Franklin. Autobiography and personal reminiscences: Butler's book. Boston: A. M. Thayer. 1892. [2127

According to the *Nation*, which treats it satirically, the book has no historical value, but is full of egotism, blunders and perversions of the truth. "Among those who could be said to come into rivalry or collision with him, few enough are they who escape the knife that has been long whetted for them. On this point, indeed, he avows his unrepentance, and insists that the 'hard words' which he so freely uses 'are the only ones which ought to be used.'" J. D. Cox, in *Nation*, 54: 195.

— PARTON, JAMES. General Butler in New Orleans. N. Y.: Mason. 1863. Boston: Houghton. 1882. $2.50. [2128

General Butler possessed strong mental and moral characteristics, which brought him severe criticism and drew to him warm friends. The author was one of the latter. After a preliminary history of the subject's career in civil and military life, he devotes the larger part of the book to a defence, with elaborate discussion, of Butler's administration, in his capacity of Department Commander of the city of New Orleans for eight months in 1862. Vivacious, readable, but one-sided and not settling all the charges against its hero. G. A. T.

Caldwell, J. F. J. History of a brigade of South Carolinians, known first as "Gregg's" and subsequently as "McGowan's brigade." Phil.: King. 1866. [2129

This brigade was from 1862 to the end of the war composed of the same five regiments of South-Carolina troops, and was in the Army of Northern Virginia, participating in nearly all its battles. Its service may be properly called typical, and its story is told with candor and honest pride by the author who was one of its officers. He truly calls it "a fair account of the Confederate soldier's life." Its inaccuracies are only such as are incident to personal recollections written before the *Official records* were published. The book is one of the best of the sources of history, for the internal life and experience of one of the minor units of the army under Lee. It is sincerely and earnestly written, free from rancour and from undue boasting. J. D. C.

Callahan, J. M. Diplomatic relations of the Confederate States with England. See American Historical Association, sect. 250. [2130

Campaigns of the Civil War. N. Y.: Scribner. 1881–90. 13v. $1 per v. [2131

Contents: 1. Nicolay, J. G. Outbreak of rebellion. — 2. Force, M. F. From Fort Henry to Corinth. — 3. Webb, A. S. The Peninsula. — 4. Ropes, J. C. Army under Pope. — 5. Palfrey, F. W. Antietam and Fredericksburg. — 6. Doubleday, A. Chancellorsville and Gettysburg. — 7. Cist, H. M. Army of the Cumberland. — 8. Greene, F. V. The Mississippi. — 9. Cox, J. D. Atlanta. — 10. Cox, J. D. March to the sea. — 11. Pond, G. E. Shenandoah valley in 1864. — 12. Humphreys, A. A. Virginia campaign of '64 and '65. — Supplement. Phisterer, F. Statistical record of the armies of the U. S.

For notes, see entry for each volume.

Champlin, John D., Jr. Young folks' history of the war for the Union. N. Y.: Holt. 1881. $2.50. [2132

" Mr. Champlin's *Young folks' history of the war for the Union* is a book that can be heartily recommended, as designed to meet a real want, and meeting it well. Indeed, the book gives a good deal more than it promises, for it is equally well adapted to general readers who are not ' young folks.' It is, in short, a well-written and entertaining history of the War of the Rebellion, very fair and impartial in tone, and aiming rather at incident and graphic narrative than at political and strategic analysis, although these are not neglected; affording, therefore, probably as good an account of these events as most will desire. It is copiously illustrated, as well with maps and plans as with portraits, views, and pictures of special objects of interest (as the Armstrong gun and the barrel torpedo). Few or none of the illustrations are 'made-up' pictures. There is an index." *Nation*, 33 : 419.

Chanal, *Gen.* **François Victor Adolphe de.** The American army in the war of secession; tr. by M. J. O'Brien. Leavenworth, Kansas: Spooner. 1894.   [2133

The author was sent by the French government in 1864, to visit, examine and report upon the U. S. Army engaged in the Civil War. This is his report with some additional matter. It covers the organization, equipment and administration, of both regulars and volunteers, of both line and staff. It includes also the education given at West Point, the methods of raising and officering the volunteers, etc. It is a useful treatise for handy reference, being clear, systematic and impartial.   J. D. C.

Chase, Salmon Portland, *Chief Justice.* HART, ALBERT BUSHNELL. Salmon Portland Chase. (American statesmen.) Boston: Houghton. 1899. $1.25.   [2134

"The author tells us in his preface that it is less the purpose of this book to give a detailed account of Mr. Chase's life than to present him as the central figure in three historic episodes: the western political antislavery movement, the financial measures of the Civil War, and the process of judicial reconstruction. Mr. Hart has therefore followed the historical rather than the biographical method of treatment, and, although the general reader will miss something of the picturesqueness of a more personal narrative, the work is perhaps of greater value as a political study on this account. The entertaining incidents of Chase's early life described in Schucker's biography have been mostly omitted, but the opening chapters of Mr. Hart's book are models of concise and graphic historical style. . . . Mr. Hart, both in his narrative and in his criticism, has displayed in the highest degree his impartiality as well as fidelity to the truth of history. His work will always be an authority." Wm. Dudley Foulke, in *Am. hist. rev.*, 5 : 583.

— SHUCKERS, JACOB WILLIAM. Life and public services of Salmon Portland Chase. N. Y.: Appleton. 1874.   [2135

The only adequate life of Chase. Not unusually well done, but very judiciously. It treats of his public life only. Covers politics in Ohio after 1832; also the growth of the Free Soil and Liberty parties in the northwest, fugitive slave trials, slavery measures in the United States Senate and the execution of the law of 1850 in Ohio. Especially full on the election of 1860, Lincoln's cabinet, the finances of the Civil War, and the imprisonment of Jefferson Davis.   E. E. S.

— WARDEN, ROBERT BRUCE. Account of

the private life and public services of Salmon Portland Chase. Cin.: Wilstach. 1874.   [2136

Treats of life in Ohio and Washington city from 1813 to 1873; of anti-slavery measures, fugitive slave laws, the Republican party, finances during the Civil War, reconstruction, and the Supreme Court after 1864. The author had intimate knowledge of his subject, had access to private journals and papers, but the work is poorly done. The author is constantly in evidence. Gives much more of the personal life of Chase than does Shucker, but lacks his scholarly treatment.   E. E. S.

Cheney, *Mrs.* **C. Emma.** Young folks' history of the Civil War. Boston: Estes. 1884.
—— Popular history of the Civil War. Estes. [c. 1894.] $1.50.   [2137

This is "a book that can be heartily recommended. It improves as the author warms up to her subject. The first few pages strike one as being rather stiff and artificial in style, and altogether there is too great tendency toward digression and 'moralizing.' The story, however, is exceedingly well told, and in a spirit of keen sympathy with the objects and results of the war, if at times a little intolerant in tone. We can afford now to do justice to the aims and motives of the losers in the great contest. The illustrations are not so good as the book deserves." *Nation*, 37 : 508.

Chesney, *Lt.-Col.* **Charles Cornwallis.** Essays in military biography. N. Y.: Holt. 1874. $2.50.   [2138

Four of the ten essays are upon Grant, Lee, Farragut and Porter, and Ulric Dahlgren. These are a notable contribution to the history of our Civil War, because of Col. Chesney's high standing as a military writer and his warm appreciation of the ability and valor shown on both sides. His estimates of the soldiers and seamen named are free from prejudice, unusually clear in comprehension of the new problems involved and of the military insight used in solving them. He was among the first of European soldiers to declare the Civil War a great military lesson for old-world study.   J. D. C.

Chittenden, Lucius E. Report of the debates and proceedings in the secret sessions of the conference convention for proposing amendments to the Constitution of the United States, Washington, Feb., 1861. N. Y.: Appleton. 1864.   [2139

The author was a delegate to the Conference from Vermont, and kept full notes of the proceedings, portions of which were later revised by participants, but without material change. The work is, therefore, of prime importance for the history of the Conference. An appendix contains extracts from the proceedings and debates in Congress on the subject and work of the convention.   W. MacD.

Cist, Henry M. The Army of the Cumberland. (Campaigns of the Civil War, 7.) N. Y.: Scribner. 1882. $1.00.   [2140

"The narrative before us gives a minute account of the various minor incidents, scouts, and skirmishes in Kentucky and Tennessee, as well as of the operations of greater importance; but, owing to the poor maps and plans (reduced from Van Horne's exhaustive work) which accompany the text, it is almost impossible for the reader to get a proper idea of the theatre of war, or the significance of the marches and combinations under consideration. . . . Failing in value to the student of military history, we should naturally expect it to possess such other qualities as would commend it to the approval of the general public; but such is not the case. It is neither brilliant in style nor graphic in its descriptions of marches and battles. The personal qualities of the generals arrayed against each other are quite neglected. . . . Brief touches, . . . a well-placed adjective, are all that we have a right to exact in narratives so condensed. But even these are wanting in the uninspired performance before us." *Nation*, 35: 80.

Coffin, Charles Carleton. Boys of '61; or Four years of fighting. Boston: Estes. 1881. $1.50. [2141

"It is a book which makes evident the very decided difference between fresh news and stale news, for once it was letters from the seat of war. . . . Mr. Coffin does not tell [the story] badly. He was rather above the average of war correspondents in ability and education. And in all parts of the country, from the very outbreak of hostilities to their close, wherever events of most interest were occurring, he was very apt to be within eye-shot. Perhaps his only literary merit is perspicuity." His style is often jerky. *Nation*, 2: 741.

—— Drum-beat of the nation [1861-2]. N. Y.: Harper. 1888. $2. [2142

"The opening chapter, entitled 'Causes which brought about the war,' is rather ambitious in its scope for this grade of historical work. The author's endeavor to focus light from all points on the origin of our civil strife results in confused and hurried passing from topic to topic, even when these are of great importance and demand either much abler handling or to be let alone. . . . Mr. Coffin does his best to enliven the monotony of [battle narrative] with entertaining anecdotes and with graphic touches, which bring near to us thoughts and feelings of those stirring times. . . . All in all, the book is well adapted to interest and instruct the young reader. There are many illustrations." *Nation*, 45: 442.

—— Following the flag. Boston: Ticknor. 1865. Estes. $1.25. [2143

A sketch of the operations of the Army of the Potomac from August, 1861, to November, 1862, under the command of General McClellan. The author was a war correspondent and saw many of the battles here described. The matter is taken from the reports of the generals and from contemporary war books. The book is written in a nervous style. Many legends are incorporated, as in the case of "Barbara Frietchie," rendering the book untrustworthy, although quite readable. There are fanciful illustrations, diagrams of battle-fields, and a roster of the organization of the Army of the Potomac. E. E. S.

—— Freedom triumphant [1864-5]. N. Y.: Harper. 1891. $2. [2144

"Every candid person must think it a good fortune for children that Mr. Coffin has inculcated the true motive of the war — 'the establishment of a government founded on the idea that slavery was a beneficent institution, ordained of God for the best welfare of the human race.' In point of literary style, Mr. Coffin is still open to the charge of an aversion to conjunctions and relative pronouns, and a fondness for staccato." *Nation*, 51: 465.

—— Marching to victory, 1863. N. Y.: Harper. 1889. $2. [2145

"The greater part is necessarily taken up with an account of the military operations; but those civil events, both at home and abroad, directly connected with the war, are also intelligently treated. The author's descriptions of the great battles, especially those of which he was an eye-witness, are exceedingly spirited. He would have given a better idea of each battle as a whole, however, if many of the minor details, such as the movements and fortunes of each separate brigade engaged, had been omitted. Due credit has been given to the valor and patriotism of the Confederates, and, but for a few passages where the author's feelings have got the better of his judgment, the book will give its readers a clear conception of the magnitude of the contest, and at the same time inspire in them a true pride in the men, both North and South, who fought it." *Nation*, 47: 461.

—— My days and nights on the battlefield. Boston. [c. 1865.] Estes. 1887. $1.25. [2146

"'Carleton' ever treats his boy-readers as his intelligent equals, and considers them capable of understanding the common language of books and men. . . . The book is especially valuable as it describes from personal observation the first battles of General Grant. It has no better war-pictures than the taking of Fort Donelson and the Battle of Shiloh or Pittsburg Landing. . . . This battle-book for boys will hold no unimportant place in the war-library of the times. Its style is usually as limpid as the camp-brooks by which much of it was written. In the heat of the contest it becomes a succession of short, sharp sentences, as if the musketry rang in the writer's brain and moulded and winged his thoughts." *Atlantic monthly*, 13: 516.

—— Redeeming the republic, 1864. N. Y.: Harper. 1890. $2. [2147

"It is hardly necessary to say that Mr. Coffin writes in a vigorous manner, and that his account of the scenes of which he was an eye-witness is particularly effective and interesting. He impresses his readers, also, with a sense of his trustworthiness. He shows clearly the bravery and heroic self-sacrifice which characterized multitudes on both sides, and never seeks to heighten the merits of the great Union leaders by belittling or abusing their opponents. He attempts, however, to relate too much, to give far too many details, and the result is very confusing. . . . The spirit which is displayed now and then is not quite so judicious as that of the previous volume, and there are signs of haste in preparation. With all its defects, however, this is, in our opinion, the best long history of the war yet written for young people." *Nation*, 49: 415.

Cox, *Maj.-Gen.* **Jacob Dolson.** Atlanta. (Campaigns of the Civil War, 9.) N. Y.: Scribner. 1882. $1.   [2148

".General Cox has given us a clear and straightforward account of the memorable campaign of Sherman against Atlanta, which terminated in the capture of that city and opened the way for his subsequent 'march to the sea.' The author, himself a distinguished participant in the movements he describes, shows great familiarity with all the details of the campaign, and a minute comprehension of the varied topography of the field of operations. His narrative is careful and painstaking, and his style lucid, though he is likely to become wearisome to other than professional readers, from the particularity with which he describes the positions and movements of the troops. The advantage of this particularity, even to the student of military history, is partially neutralized by the very indifferent maps which accompany the text, and which are, in this, as in some other volumes of this series, unworthy of the books they are intended to illustrate. . . . General Cox's account of the cavalry operations of this campaign is inadequate." *Nation*, 35: 36.

—— Battle of Franklin, Tenn., Nov. 30, 1864. N. Y.: Scribner. 1897. $2.   [2149

Franklin was a critical battle, hard fought and bloody, in a campaign which ended in the destruction of a Confederate army under Hood, and which made clear the wisdom of Sherman in undertaking the march to the sea. The author was a volunteer officer of distinction, an experienced literary worker, especially in the history of the Civil War. In this book he makes an important contribution to our acquaintance with a campaign which has been the subject of much discussion, especially in its bearing upon the respective merits of Sherman and Thomas. A clear and full story of the operations of that period, with some chapters and appendices justifying, against the intemperate assertions of another general, the claim set forth by Gen. Cox in a former book, of having been the authorized and responsible commander of the Union line of battle.   G. A. T.

—— March to the sea; Franklin and Nashville. (Campaigns of the Civil War, 10.) N. Y.: Scribner. 1882. $1.   [2150

"In this volume, the sequel to 'Atlanta,' General Cox has given us a concise but clear narrative of Thomas's defence of Tennessee against Hood in the fall of 1864, and of Sherman's 'March to the sea,' and his subsequent campaign in the Carolinas down to the close of the war. His book is, indeed, a comprehensive sketch of those military operations in Sherman's department during the last six months of the war, which brought speedy and complete disaster to the Confederate cause. The story is simply told. . . . In the statement of comparative numbers, General Cox uniformly uses the 'Present for duty' on the returns as giving the Federal strength, but declines to take the same columns on the Confederate returns for the same purpose. He uses the Confederate 'Present' instead (which included all of the sick, extra-duty men, and those in arrest), under an erroneous impression that the extra-duty men were such as would go into ranks in a fight. As the Confederate conscription placed everybody in military service, all teamsters, etc., had to be detailed, and such constituted in large part the 'extra-duty' men on the returns. This error is the more to be regretted because of the fairness of tone and general accuracy of statement which characterize this valuable contribution to the history of the war." *Nation*, 35: 385.

—— Second battle of Bull Run, as connected with the Fitz-John Porter case. Cin.: P. G. Thomson. 1882.   [2151

"In this little book General Cox has presented some ingenious arguments in opposition to the conclusions arrived at by the Board of Officers (Generals Schofield, Terry, and Getty) who reëxamined the case of General Porter. He seems to have felt it to be his duty to reiterate his belief in Porter's guilt, and he has applied himself diligently to the maintenance of the truth of this position. But we think a careful examination of his work will show that he has approached his task more in the spirit of an advocate than of a judge." J. C. Ropes, in *Nation*, 34: 404.

Crawford, *Maj.-Gen.* **Samuel Wylie.** Genesis of the Civil War: the story of Sumter, 1860–61. N. Y.: Webster. 1887.   [2152

"The story of Sumter is doubtless an important chapter in the genesis of the Civil War, but it is by no means the whole of it; and Gen. Crawford's method of telling the story, full of interesting matter as it is, only makes it more clearly evident how impossible it is to narrate the 'genesis' without writing the full history of the United States during the period immediately preceding the war." General Crawford "took active personal part in the transfer of the little garrison [of Fort Moultrie] to Fort Sumter, and in the defence of the latter fort by Maj. Anderson until it was surrendered to the Confederate army under Beauregard. . . . His part in the historic defence of Sumter led him to collect materials bearing upon all the events connected with it, including not only what public records and printed books and pamphlets would furnish, but what could be procured by private correspondence or conversation with prominent characters on both sides, and from their private papers. . . . The story of Sumter has grown out of all these sources, and is centrally the military history of the forts in and about Charleston harbor, the efforts at relieving them and their reduction by the Confederates, with the political history of the events most closely connected with the fate of the forts and their garrison. In collating the material he has collected, the author has avoided carefully — too carefully, we think — the expression of his own judgment, preferring to let the principal characters speak through their own documents and recorded conversations. The indications of quotation are not in all cases complete." *Nation*, 46: 17.

Dahlgren, *Rear-Admiral* **John Adolphus Bernard.** DAHLGREN, *Mrs.* MADELEINE VIN-

TON. Memoir of John A. Dahlgren, Rear-Admiral, U. S. N. Boston: Osgood. 1882. [2153

"This book upon the whole is good, and throws much light, direct and indirect, upon by-places as well as high places of the Civil War. This is especially true of the naval aspects of that war. An over-fondness of praise, where the statement of the simple fact would have been a more subtle eulogy, may well be pardoned to the wife of a truly grand and heroic man, such as Admiral Dahlgren certainly was. The defensive documents by which his professional position is herein vindicated are rather long and formal, but as material for future history have value. His private journal largely makes up the book, and is the most valuable portion. The life is divided into three periods: 1. The navy of the past; 2. Ordnance record; 3. The Rebellion." *Literary world*, 14: 38.

Dana, Charles Anderson. Recollections of the Civil War: with the leaders at Washington and in the field in the sixties. N. Y.: Appleton. 1898. $2. [2154

Mr. Dana's experiences, first, as confidential reporter to Mr. Stanton upon the situation in the army from Shiloh till Vicksburg, then as Assistant Secretary of War, he has told in this book. "'Recollections' though they are and composed for the most part at the very close of the veteran journalist's life, there was a broad foundation of recorded contemporary impressions upon which to build. There is little in the book for which the authority of dispatches from the field cannot be given. . . . Mr. Dana's position was unique. He lived at army headquarters; he communicated unofficially and freely with all officers, low and high; he made tours of inspection both alone and with the generals; and he was a listener at the councils of war. But he had no responsibility for the success or failure of the plans adopted, and he was not bound by military law to receive commands and obey without question. It was his privilege to stand by and observe and report. . . . His dispatches betray no petty feelings, they are straightforward and significant and he seems to have retained the respect of all with whom he was associated, delicate as his relations with some of them must have been at times. Mr. Dana made mistakes; in exciting emergencies his judgment was sometimes at fault; his own later dispatches often contain corrections of the earlier. . . . His final statement of the matter in hand seldom fails to be convincing. . . . The general reader's interest will be held by the perspicuous descriptions of several great campaigns, by the numerous character-sketches and by many passages of a high order of literary merit." Frederick W. Moore, in *Am. hist. rev.*, 4: 568.

Davis, *Rear-Admiral* **Charles Henry.** DAVIS, *Capt.* CHARLES HENRY. Life of Charles Henry Davis, Rear-Admiral, 1807–1877. Boston: Houghton. 1899. $3. [2155

"The chief claim of this biography to public notice is the light it throws on a number of interesting and important events of the Civil War, in which its subject was a distinguished actor. . . . Captain Davis has

made an interesting addition to naval literature." Roy C. Smith, in *Am. hist. rev.*, 5 : 600.

Davis, Jefferson. Rise and fall of the Confederate government. N. Y.: Appleton. 1881. 2v. Subs. $10. [2156

Largely a history of the military operations of the Civil War, adding few facts to the controversy. Prefaced by excursive essays to prove on historical authority the right of secession. Probably the most scholarly recital of the "states rights" arguments, since it was written by the leader of the movement after mature reflection. Concerning the Confederate states it reveals little inside history; no personal reminiscence; controversial rather than descriptive. Closes with the earlier period of Reconstruction.

E. E. S.

—— Short history of the Confederate States of America. N. Y.: Belford. 1890. [2157

The introductory chapters were written "to prove by historical authority that the states had the reserved power of seceding." The larger portion of the book treats of the southern conduct of the war to show "how thorough was their conviction of the justice of their cause." Contrasts especially the conduct of the northern and southern troops in the treatment of captives and neutrals. The accuracy of the military details has been challenged by certain Confederate generals. The personality of the writer is kept in the background. He closes the narrative with his capture. E. E. S.

— ALFRIEND, FRANK H. Life of Jefferson Davis. Cin.: Caxton. 1868. [2158

Written from a conviction that Davis was not responsible for the failure of the Confederacy. A strong contrast to Pollard. The military conduct of the war is very fully considered as the source of weakness. The volume shows the heat of contemporary writing.

E. E. S.

— CRAVEN, JOHN J. Prison life of Jefferson Davis. N. Y.: Carleton. 1866. [2159

Written by the physician in attendance during the imprisonment in Fortress Monroe from May 25 to December 25, 1865. A kind of diary of the daily life, giving the gist of conversations. Written by a Union man, but sympathetic and forgiving. Unlikely to please the rabid element of either side. E. E. S.

— DAVIS, *Mrs.* VARINA HOWELL. Jefferson Davis, ex-President of the Confederate States : a memoir. N. Y.: Belford. [c. 1890.] 2v. [2160

Mrs. Davis's memoir furnished what her husband's book greatly lacked : the story of the personal and social life in the Confederate executive mansion. His work was severely controversial : hers is an amiable and vivacious presentation of men, women, and events, drawn with insight and full knowledge. It gives us valuable pictures and telling comments, and must always have high rank in its sphere. No doubt it also reflects in considerable measure Mr. Davis's own opinions, softened in the presentation.

J. D. C.

— POLLARD, EDWARD ALBERT. Life of Jefferson Davis, with a secret history of the southern Confederacy. Phil.: National Pub. Co. [c. 1869.]   [2161

Written by the editor of the Richmond (Va.) *Examiner* to place the blame for the failure of the southern Confederacy. A bitter arraignment of Davis, but with little evidence of any secret history. The author accuses him of duplicity, despotism, and cowardice. The evidence submitted rarely substantiates the charge. Many of the accusations were answered, although Pollard is ignored, in the writings of Jefferson Davis (see above, sect. 2156, 2157) and his wife, Varina Howell Davis (see above, sect. 2160).

E. E. S.

Dawes, *Brig.-Gen.* Rufus R. Service with the Sixth Wisconsin Volunteers. Marietta, O.: Alderman. 1890.   [2162

The prime New England stocks of the Putnams, the Cutlers, and the Dawes are mingled in the writer, a child of the Massachusetts colony in Ohio. Recent graduate from college, temporarily lumbering in Wisconsin, he joined the Sixth Wisconsin in 1861. Its service was in the Army of the Potomac and included the Shenandoah campaign of '62, Second Bull Run, Antietam, Fredericksburg, Chancellorsville, Gettysburg, and so on to the muster-out in the Petersburg trenches, August, 1864. A full file of family letters has helped Gen. Dawes to many authentic incidents, and his abilities and unflinching candor make his book weighty evidence of the nature and value of the volunteer service.   J. D. C.

Dicey, Edward. Six months in the federal states. London: Macmillan. 1863. 2v.   [2163

On the publication of this book in 1863, the *Atlantic* praised it for its timeliness, thoughtfulness, and admirable tone. "Mr. Dicey has a manly, English way of accepting the preponderant evidence concerning the crisis he came to study. He seldom gets entangled in trivial events, but knows how to use them as illustrations of great events." He saw the true significance of the slavery struggle and stated his views clearly at a time when the understanding and sympathy of England were greatly needed by the Union. "There is scarcely an offence against good taste or good feeling in Mr. Dicey's volumes. . . . There are small inaccuracies, . . . but . . . the total impression of what Mr. Dicey has written bears honorable testimony to the accuracy of his observation, as well as to his powers of comparison and judgment." *Atlantic monthly*, 12: 395.

Dix, *Maj.-Gen.* John Adams. DIX, MORGAN, *comp.* Memoirs of John Adams Dix. N. Y.: Harper. 1883. 2v. $5.   [2164

"The biography has an individual and personal rather than a historical quality." It does not, "except in a few instances, throw much light on the general history of the time. . . . It might fairly have been expected that we should learn much that was new of the Albany Regency, of which General Dix was a member, and of the inside history of the Democratic party from 1830 to 1860. . . . But Dr. Dix seems to have been so absorbed in the central figure of his biography that he has ventured but little into the wider field of general history. . . . In the last hours of Buchanan's administration, with driveling timidity in the White House and bold treason in the cabinet, General Dix was called upon to take charge of a bankrupt treasury. He restored confidence and raised money; but he did more, far more, than this. . . . Above the confused noises of that miserable winter, the voice of John A. Dix rises clear and strong: 'If any one attempts to haul down the American flag, shoot him on the spot.' . . . He had the good fortune and the inspiration to strike the key-note, to say the one all-embracing word at the very moment of a great conflict. . . . He will always be remembered as the man who, at the crisis of the nation's fate, put into one short sentence the great principle which was at stake, and to which the people rallied and clung for four long years." *Atlantic monthly*, 52: 271.

Dodge, *Col.* Theodore Ayrault. Bird's-eye view of our Civil War. Boston: Osgood. 1883. New ed. rev. Houghton. 1897. $1.   [2165

Of the first edition the *Nation* said: "It has many excellent characteristics: the style is simple and clear, the tone elevated and fair, the conception of military operations comprehensive, and the criticisms upon them judicious. The book is evidently as much the work of an experienced soldier as of a well-informed author. The diagrams that illustrate the text are good for their purpose, and, together with the maps, add greatly to the value of the book. One of the defects grows, perhaps, out of the nature of the undertaking. The attempt to give in a moderate volume a sketch of the Civil War which shall enter as much into particulars as this one does, is apt to result in a *syllabus*, which, if accurate, may be of great use to the historical student, but will hardly serve to give the youthful or uninformed reader a clear and impressive picture. . . . Colonel Dodge's book is in no sense partisan." Colonel Dodge is severely criticised for "the many evidences of haste and inaccuracy." *Nation*, 37: 258.

The preface of the new edition claims that the figures have been carefully revised by the War Department publications and other well-known sources. The facts stated have been compared with the *Official records* by Captain E. B. Robins, long secretary of the Military Historical Society of Massachusetts. New maps have been prepared from the government surveys and charts.

—— Campaign of Chancellorsville. Boston: Osgood. 1881. Houghton. $3.   [2166

"It is sufficient to bespeak for this handsome volume a cordial welcome, which it thoroughly deserves. With the aid of Hotchkiss and Allan from the Confederate side, and of Dodge from the Federal, the interesting campaign of Chancellorsville may be studied with entire satisfaction. . . . The story is not pleasant reading for northern men. The failure at Chancellorsville was not only most discreditable to General Hooker, who then commanded the Army of the Potomac, but it was such a total and extraordinary failure that the story would be incredible if we did not know it to be true. . . . The book is the production of a man with a clear military head, who seems to have possessed himself completely of his subject. The student of military history will find it very valuable, and the general reader will find it interesting in the extreme." *Nation*, 33: 18.

Doubleday, *Maj.-Gen.* **Abner.** Chancellorsville and Gettysburg. (Campaigns of the Civil War, 6.) N. Y.: Scribner. 1882. $1. [2167

" In commenting upon the preceding volumes of this series we have endeavored to call attention to the unbiased and unpartisan spirit in which they have been written, to the manner in which preconceived opinions have been laid aside in the endeavor to form an accurate and impartial historical judgment, and to the fact that the authors have made a careful study of all materials, published or unpublished, in the possession of the War Department ; have used this material in proper proportions, have given full weight to conflicting testimony, and have named their authority for every statement that was likely to be disputed. This historical spirit has permeated each one of the preceding military narratives, and though many people may refuse to accept their conclusions, every one must acknowledge that they have been reached by fair-minded and patient investigation. This uniformity is now sharply broken by a book which is conspicuous for the absence of every one of the good qualities above referred to. The historical spirit is entirely lacking, startling statements are constantly made without any authority being given for them, questions of numbers engaged and losses incurred are quoted at second hand, minor details are dwelt upon at length, while great facts are hastily passed over, and there is a vein of personal animosity running through the book which throws discredit upon everything in it." *Nation*, 34: 257.

—— Gettysburg made plain. N. Y.: Century Co. [c. 1888.] [2168

When Gen. Reynolds fell at the opening of the battle of Gettysburg, Gen. Doubleday took, by seniority, the command of the First Corps. He was active in high command throughout the battle, and had an active part afterward in the discussion of the controversial questions which arose. Doubleday was one of the general officers who asserted that Meade believed Gettysburg an unfit place to fight the battle, and desired to retire to the line of Pipe Creek. His position and means of knowledge make him a weighty factor in the discussion. He also told the story of the campaign at large in his *Chancellorsville and Gettysburg* in the Scribners' *Campaigns of the Civil War*. For his personal career, see his *Reminiscences of Forts Sumter and Moultrie*, the next title. J. D. C.

—— Reminiscences of Forts Sumter and Moultrie in 1860–61. N. Y.: Harper. 1876. $1. [2169

Gen. Doubleday graduated from West Point in 1842, and was a Captain in the 1st U. S. Artillery at Fort Moultrie, under Maj. Anderson's command, in Dec., 1860. The transfer to Sumter was made on the 26th, and Doubleday, with his company, was part of Anderson's force until the surrender in April, '61. His patriotism and loyalty to the Union were earnest and active. He became Maj.-Gen. of Volunteers, Nov. 29,

1862. This career is the best evidence of the value of his memoir upon the dramatic opening of the war in Charleston harbor. He is also a vigorous and interesting writer. J. D. C.

Drake, Samuel Adams. Battle of Gettysburg, 1863. (Decisive events in American history.) Boston : Lee. 1891. 50c. [2170

" Mr. Drake's effort has been to prepare a popular version of the story of the great battle. . . . He makes no reference to authorities, but tells the tale currently, fluently, with well-arranged grouping of incidents and with literary skill. . . . In all the larger elements of the story of Gettysburg, Mr. Drake's narrative is faithful to the accepted facts, and well combines a lively style with adherence to truth. There are some points, however, in which, by accepting a version ill supported, or by incorrect conclusions as to matters of conjecture, he has fallen into error, and, so far, given his assistance to building up mythical features in the history of the battle." J. D. Cox, in *Nation*, 54: 17.

Draper, John William. History of the American Civil War. N. Y.: Harper. 1867–70. 3v. $10.50. [2171

A history of causes and events, with events subordinated, by a member of the school of Buckle. Volume 1 shows how inevitable the war was, as a result of topography and climate, colonization, the introduction and development of negro slavery, economic, social and moral influences, putting extreme stress upon climate ; and comprises a complete survey of American history to the establishment of the Confederacy in 1861. Volumes 2 and 3 give the history of the war, considering it in every aspect, its final effects upon slavery, national life, the government of the Union and the Constitution. Great intellectual power and unusual grasp of the subject are evident ; generalizations abound, sometimes absurd and puerile, sometimes profound. The book is occasionally obscure, lacks proportion, has a northern bias and is inaccurate in military details. The style is strong and brilliant, but lacking in finish. R. C. H. C.

Eggleston, George Cary. A rebel's recollections. N. Y.: Hurd. 1874. 2d ed. Putnam. 1878. $1. [2172

The *Atlantic* deplores the modesty which led the author " to suppress his own feelings and to impersonalize his experiences just where we should like him to be most garrulous about himself." It believes that he has helped northern readers " to understand that those opposed to the Union in the late war were as sincere as its friends, and were moved by a patriotism which differed from ours only in being mistaken. . . . His ideas and observations in regard to the rebel leaders have that certain value which always belongs to the testimony of a keen-sighted eye-witness. . . . Mr. Eggleston's manner is as good as his spirit, and he has given us a book of peculiar interest, one of the pleasures of which is its frank and clear style. One thoroughly likes the author after reading it." *Atlantic monthly*, 35: 237.

Farragut, *Admiral* **David Glasgow.**

BARNES, JAMES. David G. Farragut. (Beacon biographies.) Boston: Small. 1899. 75c. [2173

See Beacon biographies, in Pt. 3, Div. 2 : Comprehensive History, sect. 2491.

— FARRAGUT, LOYALL. Life of David Glasgow Farragut, first Admiral of the United States Navy; by his son. N. Y.: Appleton. 1879. $4. [2174

" With dutiful modesty and with admirable taste the biographer of our great admiral has intruded neither himself nor any attempt at fine writing between the public and his distinguished father. He has depended as far as possible for his narrative upon Farragut's journal and letters and official reports, and upon sketches of toils and battles made by actors and eye-witnesses. The result is a volume which is not so much history as materials for history. So much the better. One could not wish it otherwise with the first life of such a man. The simplicity of the monument is suited to the massive and noble simplicity of the hero. . . . No other such man has plowed the sea since Nelson; perhaps one may also say, no other such man before Nelson; they are, almost without doubt, the two mightiest vikings of all time." *Atlantic monthly*, 45: 688.

The life of Farragut written, at his request, by his only child, " is largely composed of the journal kept by the Admiral himself and of his letters, with an occasional explanatory commentary by the author. There is little that is new after the beginning of the war. The reports had been published before. . . . The latter part is rather tedious with its guide-book descriptions, repeating the voyage of the *Franklin* printed some years ago. But the story of Farragut's early life, the letters to his family, and the revelations of character make the book a marked one in literature. His son has performed his pious duty with excellent taste and modesty, and justified to the world the affection which such a father naturally won." *Nation*, 30: 14.

— MAHAN, *Capt.* ALFRED THAYER. Admiral Farragut. (Great commanders.) N. Y.: Appleton. 1892. $1.50. [2175

1801-1870. This sketch of Farragut is an ideal piece of brief biography. The subject is excellent, the author perfectly adapted in every way to treat it, and the treatment itself well calculated to inspire interest and just admiration for the subject.   E. C. R.

Foote, *Rear-Admiral* Andrew Hull. HOPPIN, JAMES MASON. Life of Andrew Hull Foote. N. Y.: Harper. 1874. $3.50. [2176

A quite detailed yet attractive story of a typical American naval officer of forty years' public service, the latter portion of which was in the organization and command of iron-clad river fleets in the West. Foote was an interesting person, energetic, able, of high principle with a strain of devout sentiment. He bore a large part in the capture of Forts Henry and Donelson early in 1862, and in the opening of the Mississippi. Admiral Foote died in the midst of the war.   G. A. T.

Foote, Henry Stuart. War of the Rebellion : observations upon the causes, course, and consequences, of the late Civil War. N. Y.: Harper. 1866. [2177

Foote, as a Unionist Senator from Mississippi (1847-1852) and Governor of that state (1853) occupied an unfortunate position. Later, he was a member of the Confederate Congress and was opposed to Jefferson Davis. Some of his fellows called him a renegade from the cause. The present book is a rambling dissertation, valuable only for the author's personal experience in the Confederacy. There are also reminiscences of the leaders in Congress, in the Compromise of 1850.   E. E. S.

Forbes, John Murray. Letters and recollections; ed. by his daughter, Sarah Forbes Hughes. Boston: Houghton. 1899. 2v. $5. [2178

" The part played by Mr. Forbes in public affairs, especially during the period of the Civil War, was an important and effective one; but he never held, nor sought, political office. What he did for his country he did as a private citizen, and in the most private way possible. . . . It was as a pioneer and manager of western or middle-western railroads that Mr. Forbes was best known to the American public. . . . He was Governor Andrew's unofficial right-hand man and confidential adviser, taking for a time full charge of the work of moving, feeding, and clothing the [Massachusetts] state troops. He was active in organizing the Sanitary Commission, and in enlisting the colored troops. . . . It is hardly too much to say that he was for a time virtually an unofficial or advisory member of Mr. Lincoln's cabinet." E. G. J. in *Dial* (Chicago), 27: 269.

Force, *Maj. - Gen.* Manning Ferguson. From Fort Henry to Corinth. (Campaigns of the Civil War, 2.) N. Y.: Scribner. 1881. $1. [2179

" Judge Force's volume treats of the early operations in the West, and, though called 'From Fort Henry to Corinth,' its 'preliminary' chapter recounts at wearisome length the movements of Price and Curtis and Van Dorn in Missouri. Though every page bears evidence of careful research — of an earnest desire to adhere strictly to truth, to avoid opinions, and steer clear of controversy — yet it must be confessed that the story is tedious. It lacks animation, and the great events are not sufficiently emphasized to make any impression on the mind. . . . There are not half a dozen pages in the whole book of variation from strict narrative. Nearly half of it is naturally devoted to the battle of Shiloh. . . . No battle of the war has given rise to more bitter jealousies or recriminations. But little suspicion of this, however, meets the reader of this book. . . . Little is said by way of judgment on the battle. . . . With the cautious advance of Halleck on Corinth and the capture of that place the volume ends, and the results of the campaign are summed up." *Nation*, 33: 399.

Forrest, *Brig.-Gen.* Nathan Bedford. WYETH, JOHN ALLAN. Life of General Nathan Bedford Forrest. N. Y.: Harper. 1899. $4. [2180

" Forrest was a picturesque character — few, if any, were more so ; and he has had a correspondingly strong hold on the imagination of all who served with him on the Confederate side during the Civil War. Dr. Wyeth's fine volume is proof that the enthusiasm of southern soldiers for him has hardly waned. . . . A man who was wholly illiterate, and whose business life had been that of a slave-trader, was greatly handicapped in the race for military honors." J. D. Cox, in *Nation*, 69: 394.

Fry, *Maj.-Gen.* **James Barnet.** McDowell and Tyler in the campaign of Bull Run, 1861. N. Y.: Van Nostrand. 1884. [2181

A pamphlet of 63 pages by an officer upon McDowell's staff at Bull Run, vindicating his commander from ill-advised charges of neglect of duty and incompetence, made by Tyler, next in command. Tyler's former official reports are effectively contrasted with his reminiscences printed twenty years after. G. A. T.

—— Military miscellanies. N. Y.: Brentano. 1889. [2182

The author is best known by his able services as Provost-Marshal-General enforcing the draft during the Civil War. His close contact with both civil and military administration gave great opportunities for observation of Lincoln, Stanton, Halleck, and others, and his reproduction of casual essays and reviews is a mine of rich material for personal study of leading men. His earlier service on the staff of General Buell was also an important experience, and his long life as an officer of the regular army gave him the inside view of the character and qualities of prominent soldiers. He writes candidly and clearly from this fulness of knowledge. J. D. C.

—— New York and the conscription of 1863. N. Y.: Putnam. 1885. [2183

The enrolment of troops for the Union army, in the summer of 1863, by a draft, was violently resisted in New York and other large cities, with the loss of many lives and the destruction of much property in New York. The question of the responsibility for these riots is discussed by General Fry, who was the Provost-Marshal-General for the enforcement of the conscription, and who ably defends the officers of the government against charges made by Gov. Seymour, that they had been needlessly precipitate in beginning the draft and unjust and partial in its enforcement. G. A. T.

Gasparin, Agénor Étienne, *comte* de. Uprising of a great people : the United States in 1861; [tr.] by Mary L. Booth. N. Y.: Scribner. 1862. [2184

" De Gasparin's *Uprising of a great people* fell on American hearts, at the darkest hour of the strife, like the clarion note of a reënforcement of the heroes of humanity." H. T. Tuckerman, *America and her commentators*, p. 153.

Gordon, *Maj.-Gen.* **George Henry.** Brook

Farm to Cedar Mountain, 1861–2. Boston: Osgood. 1883. Houghton. 1885. [2185

" General Gordon has done the public a real service in publishing this volume. It is made up of papers written for the annual gatherings of the officers of his regiment. . . . Hence we have as correct a picture of the real life of one of our very best volunteer regiments as it is possible to get. We have the story of its first year's experience, and let us say at once that the story is told very well. General Gordon writes easily ; he passes from one mood to another very naturally ; he has the power of saying strong things ; he has also a nice sense of humor. His narrative is animated ; the details never become tedious." *Nation*, 37 : 169.

—— History of the campaign of the Army of Virginia under John Pope, 1862. Boston: Houghton. 1880. [2186

The book, says the *Nation*, " is one of very considerable interest and of considerable value. The great trouble with General Gordon is that he writes too easily. . . . He does not stop to think over his facts, to digest them, and to marshal them, but collects material from every quarter with active industry, and sends it off, superficially arranged, to the printer. . . . This way of doing things leads to some careless writing, but it leads to some worse things." It leads to intolerable expansion — nearly 500 pages on a campaign of three weeks, on which there is already abundant material in need of being digested. It is to be regretted " that so much good work should be so burdened with superfluities and so disfigured with blemishes. . . . There is real merit in the book. . . . It is thoroughly readable. It is so good that we are vexed that it is not better." *Nation*, 30 : 122.

—— War diary of events in the war of the great Rebellion. 1863–5. Boston: Osgood. 1882. New issue. Houghton. 1885. [2187

The author, a graduate of West Point, organized the 2d Mass. Infantry and commanded it till he was promoted. Preceding volumes (*Brook Farm to Cedar Mountain*, and *The Campaigns of the Army of Virginia under Pope*, see above) dealt with his army experience in 1861-2, and this volume completes his military memoirs. The basis is his diary, and the result is a lively description of his life on the Virginia peninsula, in the blockade of Charleston, in Florida, and on the lower Mississippi. Gen. Gordon was a man of strong prejudices, strong self-assertion, tartly critical of his superiors. With his intelligence and patriotic spirit, his way to greater distinction was open had not the qualities named stood in his way. The book is a valuable one, due allowance being made in the direction intimated, and it covers theatres of operation less familiar than many others. J. D. C.

Goss, Warren Lee. Recollections of a private: a story of the Army of the Potomac. N. Y.: Crowell. [c. 1890.] $1.50. [2188

" The book is interesting as showing what a man experiences as he develops from a recruit to a veteran under the pressure of active service, and is of value in bringing to view the public opinion of the camp concerning the directing forces, intelligent and otherwise, of campaigns. . . . One charming characteristic marks the whole—a simple, sincere, unboastful but genuine patriotism, that leaves no doubt as to the honesty of the author, whether fighting or writing. While deploring the necessity that required force to preserve the Union, he is filled with admiration for the personal gallantry of the men who supported the losing and lost cause. He nowhere scolds, and throughout the book presents an unconscious model of the typical Union volunteer." J. D. Cox, in *Nation*, 51: 510.

Grant, *Gen.* **Ulysses Simpson.** Personal memoirs. N. Y.: Webster. 1885-6. 2v. [New ed. rev] Century Co. 1895. 2v. $5. [2189

These two volumes cover the course of the author's life down to the close of the Civil War. When one considers that the writer was a man of action, altogether without experience in literary work, one is surprised at the remarkable skill with which the narrative is written. The sentences often have the same pithy directness and brevity that marked his despatches from the field of battle. As a general he mastered details but was not overwhelmed by them: so here, he sees the whole field and leads the reader easily along from one principal event to another. The native simplicity and lack of affectation so characteristic of the author are noticeable features of the work. While there is nowhere within the book the faintest strain of self-laudation, he naturally and frankly portrays the military situations as they appeared to him when he was called upon to act, and by disclosing the circumstances and declaring his reasons for action he in reality often takes issue with his critics. A. C. McL.

See sect. 2268 for Col. Carswell McClellan's book criticising these memoirs.

—— Report of the armies of the United States, 1864-5. N. Y.: Appleton. 1865.

[2190

Grant's reports as Lieutenant-General covered the operations of all the national armies, and are among the most succinct and intelligible of historical documents. Their early publication met the popular demand for authentic knowledge of the great closing campaigns of the Civil War, though the separate publication is now superseded by the full *Official records* in which they are found, as well as by the General's *Personal memoirs*, etc. J. D. C.

— BADEAU, *Brig.-Gen.* ADAM. Military history of Ulysses S. Grant, 1861-5. N. Y.: Appleton. 1868-81. 3v. $12. [2191

This book "depends for its interest and its value upon its supply of authentic information, and the supply is so abundant, and so much of the information is original, that it has a great deal of both." The author had access to official papers, both Union and Confederate, and to Grant's correspondence, and was closely associated, for more than three years, with Gen. Grant and his officers. The book is an excellent military history of the war. " It follows the chronological order of events, and it is a good, plain, intelligible, straightforward account. Its effect, as a whole, upon thinking men, can hardly be other than to raise

their estimate of Grant's ability as a soldier. . . . The author's indisposition to make cordial mention of officers outside what may be called the family party, composed of Grant, Sherman, McPherson, and Sheridan, is an unsatisfactory feature of the book." These volumes " are nowhere dull, and it is not too much to say that they are often intensely interesting. The author had a story of the highest dignity to tell, he possessed exceptional opportunities of knowing it thoroughly, and he has told it well; and this is true in spite of the fact that these two volumes are almost an apotheosis of Grant, who is credited with every military virtue and with a large share of the other virtues." The author "writes with clearness and taste, and his methods of arrangement are excellent. . . . We feel a very great distrust of Gen. Badeau's figures, and think that he is uniformly disposed to make the opposing armies less different in numbers than they really were." The maps are good and well placed. J. D. Cox, in *Nation*, 6: 152, 32: 461.

— BROOKS, ELBRIDGE STREETER. True story of General U. S. Grant. (Children's lives of great men.) Boston: Lothrop. [c. 1897.] $1.50. [2192

"Mr. Elbridge S. Brooks furnishes another story of General Grant's life, which he calls the *True story*, and which is published in children's quarto style, with a large page, large print, and plenty of pictures, some of which latter pertain to the text, and others of which might go as well with almost any other book that might be written. . . . The narrative answers its purpose well." *Literary world*, 28: 434.

— CHURCH, *Lt.-Col.* WILLIAM CONANT. Ulysses S. Grant and the period of national preservation and reconstruction. (Heroes of the nations.) N. Y.: Putnam. 1897. $1.50. [2193

" It is a somewhat larger volume than most of the similar series, and the author has used his space judiciously to introduce occasional quotations from others. It takes the strongly eulogistic view of every phase of Grant's life, military and civil, as seems almost a necessity in the conception of such a class of books. Its variation in method from the preceding lives of Grant will, however, give it a distinct and useful place." *Nation*, 65: 241.

— COPPÉE, HENRY. Grant and his campaigns: a military biography. N. Y.: Richardson. 1866. [2194

This was one of the earliest biographies of Gen. Grant, and was based in large measure upon his official reports of his military operations in the Civil War. It was very meagre in his personal history, and though a trustworthy narrative as far as it went, and a warmly appreciative estimate of the man, it was soon superseded by other works based on fuller material. Grant's own *Personal memoirs*, when published, of course eclipsed all preceding biographies.

J. D. C.

— DANA, CHARLES ANDERSON, *and Maj.-Gen.* JAMES H. WILSON. Life of Ulysses S. Grant. Springfield, Mass. 1868. [2195

Written as a "Campaign life" in the presidential election year, this was still a book of more than passing value. Mr. Dana had represented the War Department at Grant's headquarters in most of his campaigns from Vicksburg to Richmond inclusive. General Wilson had been much of the time on his staff. Personal acquaintance, unusual opportunity, intimate knowledge of affairs, and literary ability were all united to make the book. The fuller historical knowledge since opened to us was made up for by the great advantage of close personal association with their subject. J. D. C.

— GARLAND, HAMLIN. Ulysses S. Grant, his life and character. N. Y.: Doubleday. 1898. N. Y.: McClure. $2.50. [2196

"Mr. Garland has not written a military history of Grant nor a political history of the years of his public career, although the latter field is not preoccupied. His book ' is not perhaps everything that is understood by the word biography. . . . It is an attempt at characterization.' The treatment is not analytical, but purely narrative. One after another the scenes of Grant's life are passed in chronological order before the mind of the reader like objects before a sensitive plate. At the end a reflecting reader will find in his mind a composite picture of Grant's character more or less distinct. This method need not be expected to commend itself to all. But some things can be said in its justification." Frederick W. Moore, in American historical review, 4: 377.

— KNOX, THOMAS WALLACE. Boys' life of General Grant. N. Y.: Merriam. [c. 1895.] [2197

"Col. Thomas W. Knox . . . tells the story of our great general's military career in a simple, straightforward way which cannot fail to win the interest of his readers. The narrative shows marks of hasty writing, however, and is too eulogistic to be entirely trustworthy. The illustrations are most of them poor, and one at least, representing the battle of Fredericksburg (p. 287), has no place in the book." Nation, 61: 448.

— PORTER, Brig.-Gen. HORACE. Campaigning with Grant. N. Y.: Century Co. 1897. Subs. $3.50. [2198

"The illustrations are all full-page, on plate paper, and a number of good portraits have been added to the list of engravings. To the presswork of the De Vinne Press add an uncommonly tasteful binding, and we have as handsome a specimen of book-making as one often sees. Speaking to the substance of this work, we cannot rate it highly. Not only is it badly diluted, but there is much more of Porter than of Grant in it. It is a companion-piece to Badeau." J. D. Cox, in Nation, 65: 518.

Greeley, Horace. The American conflict ; its causes, incidents and results. Hartford: Case. 1864-6. 2v. [2199

Greeley's unique relations to men and measures, before and during the war, give a particular value to his book, which is enhanced by the number of documents and quotations from documents included. The first volume is devoted mainly to tracing public opinion on slavery from 1776 to 1861; the second volume, to military events and to the growth of the emancipation movement. The account of the war is necessarily imperfect and inaccurate. Written by a man of unusual frankness, irascible in temper, unbalanced in judgment, and saturated with prejudice, the book is unsparingly hostile to the South. R. C. H. C.

Greene, Francis Vinton. The Mississippi. (Campaigns of the Civil War, 8.) N. Y.: Scribner. 1882. $1.00. [2200

The Vicksburg campaign " is quite plainly described by Lieut. Greene. . . . The maps of this volume are not particularly better than those of its predecessors. Their information is much like that of a wrecked guideboard. As to the text generally, we should say it lacks exactly that which is to be found very frequently, and always most happily, in the author's Army life in Russia — touches of local color, namely, that make the narrative more of a picture and less of a directory. . . . The Mississippi, however, does not profess to be other than a compilation of facts and the interpretation of them. . . . The task in this instance has certainly fallen into careful, and the interpretation into competent hands, and if the description lacks somewhat of the glow of the forge, it is marked by the accuracy of the cabinet." Nation, 35: 558.

Guernsey, Alfred H., and Henry M. Alden. Harper's pictorial history of the great Rebellion. N. Y.: Harper. [c. 1866.] 2v. [2201

During the actual progress of the war, Harper's weekly was the leading illustrated paper in bringing its scenes home in pictorial sketches by artists on the spot. When the war ended, the natural sequel was the collecting, selecting, connecting, and properly editing this war matter, in separate form. This book is the result, and in its way, text and pictures can never be wholly superseded as an authentic current narrative and illustration of the period. J. D. C.

Hale, Edward Everett, ed. Stories of war, told by soldiers. Boston: Roberts. 1879. Little. $1. [2202

This "purports to be a collection of descriptions of battles in the War of Secession, extracted from old newspapers and reports by some boys on a visit to a country house and kept indoors by a northeast storm. It is a pretty good book, nothing more. In the first place, many of the stories are not told by soldiers, but by newspaper correspondents ; others are told by men who have written much but not well on military subjects ; others, again, by self-praising soldiers, and by soldiers whose writings display a bad spirit and a disregard of truth. On the other hand, there are many interesting extracts from the reports of the able and successful soldiers of the war. In the second place, the compiler has admitted into his book much veritable stuff and nonsense. . . . If boys are to begin early to read stories of our war the stories should be told them truly, and the falsities of 1861 and the errors of later dates should not be reproduced for them. Allowance made for these defects, it is to be said that this book is readable, and many boys will probably find it very interesting." Nation, 29: 392.

Hamlin, Augustus Choate. Battle of Chancellorsville. Bangor: Author. 1897. $1. [2203

" In this book the Society of the Officers and Soldiers of the Eleventh Army Corps may be said to have officially challenged the aspersions upon their conduct in the battle of Chancellorsville. By resolution passed at their annual meeting in December, 1895, they adopted the work of Dr. Hamlin as their own, both in its vindication of the soldierly conduct of the corps as a whole and in its arraignment of Generals Hooker, Howard, and Devens. If Dr. Hamlin was not the official historian of the corps, his book would still command attention by the ability with which he has arrayed the evidence which is now made accessible by the publication of the *Official records*, together with the material from private sources which time has brought to light. . . . In one respect Dr. Hamlin might, with a little trouble, have made his book much more valuable. By giving in footnotes the references to the *Official records* which he has analyzed, it would have been easy for us to verify his work. . . . On the other hand, the ample series of maps copied from Col. Michler's official surveys could hardly be improved." J. D. Cox, in *Nation*, 64: 51.

Hamlin, Hannibal. HAMLIN, CHARLES EUGENE. Life and times of Hannibal Hamlin. Cambridge: Author. 1899. $4.50, half mor. [2204

" For a successful ' life and times ' of any one, there are two prerequisites — an important central figure and a skilful writer. Both are lacking in the present case. Persons interested in the political history of Maine during the half-century after 1835 may find compensation for reading this narrative, but, as far as national affairs are concerned, there is surprisingly little that is either new or valuable." *Am. hist. rev.,* 5: 588.

Hancock, *Maj.-Gen.* **Winfield Scott.** WALKER, *Brig.-Gen.* FRANCIS AMASA. General Hancock. (Great commanders.) N. Y.: Appleton. 1894. $1.50. [2205

" Gen. Walker frankly states that the inclusion of Gen. Hancock's name in a list of ' Great commanders ' must be regarded as an enlargement of the natural meaning of the title, since his service was always subordinate, and he was never subjected to the supreme responsibilities of the leader of an independent army in the field." Still, his career " was a model for nearly everything that a brave and patriotic officer would desire to be and to do. . . . The author is also very frank in notifying his readers that, having published a history of the Second Corps, it has been almost a necessity that he should make free use of this material. . . . The habit of dealing with census statistics, and of seeking close logical form for the expression of reasoning in economics, has not deprived the author of the power of making a vivid and most effective narrative, full of color and of deep feeling." J. D. Cox, in *Nation*, 60 : 188.

Harris, Thomas Lake. The Trent affair. Indianapolis: Bowen-Merrill. 1896. $1.50. [2206

A complete survey of the question ; the author being thoroughly informed, and writing from the original sources. The conclusions reached are in all essential particulars favorable to the legal position taken by the English ministry. The author's temper, however, is not equal to his judgment, and he writes with such bitterness that he leaves an impression entirely unjustified by the arguments adduced. R. C. H. C.

Headley, Joel Tyler. The great Rebellion. Hartford: Am. Pub. Co. 1866. 2v. [2207

A reasonably adequate view of the war, for uncritical readers, as seen by one who is in the midst of the northern Union sentiment. The style is simple, and the defects of the narrative are mainly due to inaccessibility of full documentary evidence, such as later compilations now put at the command of all writers.

G. A. T.

Henderson, *Lt.-Col.* **George Francis R.** Campaign of Fredericksburg, Nov.-Dec., 1862 ; by a line officer. London: Paul. 1886. 3d ed. Gale. 1891. [2208

The author is favorably known as a clear and vigorous writer, of excellent reputation as a student of military art and history. He visited and studied the battle-fields of Virginia in preparation for his larger work, the *Life of " Stonewall " Jackson*. He became intimately acquainted with surviving officers of the Confederate army and proclaims his entire sympathy with the Rebellion. This predilection colors his narrative and his judgments, and his knowledge of the Union army, its organization and its characteristics, is much less accurate than of the Confederates. His temper is good, and treating his book as written frankly from the Confederate standpoint as to men and events, it is an able and useful manual for the campaign. As to the men of the national army, the sources from which they were drawn, their organization, appointment of officers, discipline, aptness for military service, etc., his statements need frequent correction. J. D. C.

Higginson, *Col.* **Thomas Wentworth.** Army life in a black regiment. Boston: Fields. 1870. New ed. Lee. 1882. [2209

This " is a series of carefully wrought studies of negro character as a phase of humanity, and of graphically recounted episodes of regimental or personal adventure, all full of the peculiar life and color of southern scenery. A man who took command of the first negro regiment formed during the war, who led it throughout the struggle, and who, having fought the rebels, turned and fought the more disgraceful government for the pay of its true and faithful soldiers, might be expected to write in a spirit of extravagance and even exaggeration; but there is nothing of this kind in Colonel Higginson's records, and nothing is more taking in him than his perfect temperance and reserve. . . . The diction is always clear and bright, with just sufficient movement to have the graces that distinguish good prose from bad rhythm ; and that excellent taste and moderation with which the papers are written is thoroughly imparted to it." *Atlantic monthly*, 24 : 644.

Hodgson, Joseph. Cradle of the Confederacy; or The times of Troup, Quitman and Yancey. Mobile: Register Office. 1877.

[2210

Hodgson writes from facts within his own knowledge and material gathered from newspapers, political reports, speeches, etc. He is of opinion that the southwestern states were driven into secession " by northern enemies, rather than by southern leaders." This thesis he hardly establishes, but he does prove that the Union sentiment in the southwest was exceptionally strong, and he imparts considerable information about the methods of southern secession leaders, particularly Yancey. He is a bitter partisan, intemperate in tone, provincial in his views, and unfair in his deductions, which are made, however, with considerable skill. His style is halting and rough. R. C. H. C.

Hood, *Maj.-Gen.* **John Bell.** Advance and retreat: personal experiences in the United States and Confederate States armies. New Orleans: Hood Orphan Memorial Fund. G. T. Beauregard. 1880. [2211

This book was left in manuscript at Gen. Hood's death. Its few errors " only show that he was writing from memory, and from partial and incomplete data, and that his book must be judged for what it is — a very sincere but controversial defence of his policy as an army commander, and not as a systematic contribution to exact history. It will have a permanent value of its own, and will (as we think it should) modify favorably the judgment of the world upon his last important campaign." J. D. Cox, in *Nation*, 30: 236, 254.

Hosmer, James Kendall. The color-guard: being a corporal's notes of military service in the 19th Army Corps. Boston: Walker. 1864.

[2212

The history of a nine months' regiment, the 52d Massachusetts, from Nov., '62, to July, '63. Its operations were in the department of Louisiana, and the writer, a clergyman of culture, afterwards a college professor and a well-known historian and man of letters, tells with good literary style and with interesting and valuable historical details, of the daily life of the volunteer, as he observed it from the point of view of the man in the ranks. The story includes some account of the siege and capture of Port Hudson.

G. A. T.

Hotchkiss, *Capt.* **Jedediah,** *and Lt.-Col.* **William Allan.** Battle-fields of Virginia: Chancellorsville. N. Y.: Van Nostrand. 1867.

[2213

" A most excellent book has been written by Captain Hotchkiss and Colonel Allan, who were formerly officers of the staff of the Second Corps of the Army of Northern Virginia, in other words, the corps commanded by Stonewall Jackson till his death. . . . It is a monograph . . . and it is . . . thoroughly satisfactory. . . . The story of Chancellorsville is not pleasant reading for northern men *as* northern men. That must be admitted at the outset. All things considered, it was the most glorious battle for the South and the most disgraceful battle for the North that was fought during the war. . . . But . . . it is an intensely interesting story for the student. . . . Captain Hotchkiss and Colonel Allan have done their work so admirably that their account is fascinating. . . . Their moderation and their abstinence from fine writing are eminently creditable, and there is not a word or sentence in the book that even approaches to being offensive. . . . We believe this to be one of the most faithful accounts of a great struggle that was ever written." *Nation*, 4: 410.

Humphreys, *Brig.-Gen.* **Andrew Atkinson.** From Gettysburg to the Rapidan: the Army of the Potomac, July, 1863, to April, 1864. N. Y.: Scribner. 1883. 75c. [2214

" The contents of this book were intended as the opening chapters of General Humphreys's history of the campaign of 1864–5 in Virginia, but because of the length of that work are published separately. Compared with its predecessor, the present volume is very disappointing and unsatisfactory. The simple style, the clear statement of military movements, the absence of criticism found in the larger work are here also. But the narrative is too fragmentary, it assumes too much knowledge on the part of the reader, and there is a singular lack of all full returns of both armies. It is impossible to tell from this book the composition or strength of the forces which for nine months confronted each other in Virginia. . . . The latter part of the book is too much a defence of General Meade's operations in falling back to Centerville, in October, and of his subsequent abortive movement to Mine Run. Here again General Humphreys omits all full statements of numbers. . . . General Humphreys gives a fuller statement of the evidence in regard to the ferocious order of Colonel Dahlgren. Excellent maps accompany the text." *Nation*, 37: 63.

—— Virginia campaign of '64 and '65: the Army of the Potomac and the Army of the James. (Campaigns of the Civil War, 12.) N. Y.: Scribner. 1883. $1. [2215

" General Humphreys brings to his task peculiar advantages. As Chief of Staff to General Meade, his official position rendered him familiar with all the federal movements in the campaign of 1864, while his subsequent career as commander of Hancock's (Second) Corps was not less conspicuous and important. His long and eminent service after the war, in Washington, placed within his easy reach all the official data now extant in regard to the struggle. We are not surprised, then, to find his book a repository of data of the greatest value. The narrative is very clear, concise, and fair in spirit. It is too crowded, and written too much, perhaps, in the style of an official report, to be entertaining to the casual reader; but its interest to the student of the great campaign of 1864–65 can hardly be exaggerated." W. Allan, in *Nation*, 36: 532.

Hyde, *Brig.-Gen.* **Thomas Worcester.** Following the Greek cross: or, Memories of the Sixth Army Corps. Boston: Houghton. 1894. $1.25. [2216

"Colonel Hyde began his military service in 1861 as Major of the Seventh Maine Infantry. He ended it in 1865 as Colonel of the First Maine Veterans and commandant of the brigade in which that regiment was. The whole of his service was in the Army of the Potomac and in the Sixth Corps, of which the 'Greek cross' was the badge. . . . The most interesting and instructive part of his service was that which he spent on the personal staff of General Sedgwick and General Wright at Sixth Corps headquarters. This covers the period from Chancellorsville, at the beginning of Hooker's campaign of 1863, to the defence of Washington against Early in the late summer of 1864. The author expressly disclaims any purpose but that of narrating his own experience, and giving the impressions that men and events made upon him at the time. He has certainly been very successful in doing so. He has a gift for easy narrative, and carries the reader along with him, absorbed in the strong but true picture of the life of the young officer in those bloody campaigns." J. D. Cox, in *Nation*, 59: 450.

Irwin, *Lt.-Col.* **Richard Bache.** History of the Nineteenth Army Corps. N. Y.: Putnam. 1892. $4.50.   [2217

"A more conscientious piece of work was never done. The author spared no pains to be accurate. . . . The tone is one of candor, and the writer's spirit is a judicial one, with as little of prejudice as possible, and a freedom from rancor which is every way admirable. All this is the more noticeable and praiseworthy because the campaigns of the corps have been the subject of much bitter controversy. Some of its regiments were among those which accompanied Butler in the first occupation of New Orleans by the national forces, and most of the others went with Banks to Louisiana in December, 1862. The campaign in the Teche country, the siege of Port Hudson, and the Red River campaign were the chief events in the experience of the corps in the southwest. It was then brought back to the North, and completed its military work in the Shenandoah Valley under Sheridan. . . . In his determination to write a strictly military memoir, Col. Irwin has systematically avoided matters of civil administration of the department." J. D. Cox, in *Nation*, 54: 472.

Isham, *Lt.* **Asa B.**, **Henry M. Davidson**, *and* **Henry B. Furness.** Prisoners of war and military prisons. Cin.: Clarke. 1890. $3.50.
                                           [2218

The fullest compendium of descriptions of southern military prisons and the treatment of the prisoners. The authors were themselves prisoners, one a lieutenant, the others sergeants, and all are men of standing in civil life. Besides personal experience, they have diligently used official documents, and authentic personal narratives by others. The book is an authoritative one. The horrible story is told with calmness and with judgment, discriminating fairly between what is incidental to captivity and what is the result of intentional cruelty and system. It is indispensable to a real study of the subject.   J. D. C.

Jackson, *Lt.-Gen.* **Thomas Jonathan.** COOKE, JOHN ESTEN. Stonewall Jackson: a

military biography. N. Y.: Appleton. 1866. $3.   [2219

"We profess to be unprejudiced by the purely rebel standpoint from which this work was composed, when we attach very little value to it in any particular which would make a real military biography welcome from either side of the late controversy. As regards the hero himself, the author seems qualified to tell us little except a few anecdotes at second-hand, which he subjects to constant repetition. In this way we learn pretty accurately how Jackson looked and dressed; but the analysis given of his character and of his genius for battle is not more intimate than may be fairly deduced from his well-known exploits." *Nation*, 2: 470.

— HENDERSON, *Lt.-Col.* GEORGE FRANCIS R. Stonewall Jackson and the American Civil War. N. Y.: Longmans. 1898. 2v.

—— *Same.* 2d ed.; with an introd. by Field-Marshal Viscount Wolseley. N. Y.: Longmans. 1900. 2v. $4.   [2220

A biography by an English officer, with a distinctly partisan bias. "Turning the pages of the book to learn the author's standpoint, we see an early chapter devoted to the causes of the war. In it we find no mention made of the repeal of the Missouri Compromise . . . nor of the Dred Scott decision. . . . The action of Virginia in seceding the author finds to be 'not only fully justified, but beyond suspicion.' . . . When, in the course of the narrative, he reaches Lincoln's famous emancipation proclamation, he characterizes it as a deliberate violation of the Constitution." *Nation*, 67: 395.

"The first thing that strikes the reader is the author's analysis of Jackson's personal character and mental equipment as bearing upon his military successes; it is most accurate and satisfactory. He seems to have made a study of the man as well as the soldier. . . . There is nothing in Jackson's campaigns which seems to appeal to Col. Henderson's admiration so much as the strategy of them." Hy. Kyd Douglas, in *Am. hist. rev.*, 4: 371.

— JACKSON, *Mrs.* MARY ANNA. Life and letters of General Thomas J. Jackson (Stonewall Jackson); by his wife, with introd. by Henry M. Field. N. Y.: Harper. 1892.
                                           [2221

"Everybody who feels true interest in the history of our Civil War will be thankful to Jackson's widow that she has let us see with so little reserve the character and the life of the great Confederate soldier as it was revealed in the bosom of his family. Mrs. Jackson does not pretend to tell us anything of her husband's campaigns, making only such references to them as are necessary to connect the letters which form the bulk of the volume. . . . In these pages the man stands out as an enthusiast in religion and in the secession cause. . . . Mrs. Jackson's editing is faultlessly done. Having decided to show something of the inner character of her hero, she never slips in taste, in modesty, or in the nice sense of the limits of reasonable disclosure. She indulges in no vituperation, and in no needless laments over the lost cause.

She is partisan only so far as loyalty to her husband and his cause demands." J. D. Cox, in *Nation*, 54: 175.

Johnson, R. U., *and* **C. C. Buel,** *eds.* Battles and leaders of the Civil War.

See sect. 2109.

Johnson, Rossiter. Short history of the war of secession, 1861–1865. Boston: Ticknor. 1888. New ed. Houghton. 1889.

—— *Same ;* Story of a great conflict. N. Y.: Bryan. 1894.

—— *Same, greatly enlarged ;* Camp-fire and battle-field. N. Y.: Knight and Brown. 1894. Subs., full leather. $12.   [2222

"There is need for a convenient single-volume history of the period which in clear statement shall give a popular narrative of its principal events. But the work under consideration is somewhat too narrow in its range of view, too intense in its animus. Our war was unique in its military methods, owing to the immense areas, configuration and character of surface, direction of lines of travel. . . . Even a short popular history should reveal to us some of this why and how. . . . The author is too quick to supply men with questionable motives, and apparently fails to realize that it is easier to criticise a campaign or a policy than to shape and conduct it. While that grand moral hero, Lincoln, is not directly disparaged, there is an unsympathetic treatment of his actions which would mislead one not fully aware of Mr. Lincoln's grandeur of character. The tone throughout is not up to the level of the lofty and noble words of the last three pages." J. J. Halsey, in *Dial* (Chicago), 9: 197.

Johnston, *Gen.* **Albert Sidney.** JOHNSTON, WILLIAM PRESTON. Life of Gen. Albert Sidney Johnston, embracing his services in the armies of the United States, the republic of Texas, and the Confederate States. N. Y.: Appleton. 1879. $5.   [2223

In this eulogy of Gen. Johnston by his son great emphasis is laid upon his services in the Black Hawk war, the Texan war of independence and the Mormon troubles. His death at Shiloh left unsettled the question of his ability for military affairs, for he had never before commanded troops in battle. "The careful array in this book of all that can be said in the affirmative falls a little short of proving the greatest talents for commander. . . . The book abounds with interesting incidents. . . . The story is one which may be wholesome reading for any youth, exhibiting a character which . . . was always true to itself, dignified, uncomplaining, not shifting responsibility for its misfortunes upon others, but nobly bearing its own burdens." The author "fails to see in the origin of the struggle anything more than the fanaticism of abolitionists," and is not above petty display of animosity. "No book issued from the Confederate side has more persistently kept up the false argument based upon garbled returns of opposing armies." J. D. Cox, in *Nation*, 27: 197, 214.

Johnston, *Gen.* **Joseph Eggleston.** Narrative of military operations, directed during the late war between the states, by [him]. N. Y.: Appleton. 1874. $5.   [2224

"Johnston was the only officer of the United States Army of a rank above that of colonel who joined the southern army, and at the beginning he was their ranking officer." He was "the most prominent military actor in both the first and the last scenes of the great conflict, and by common consent stands second, and hardly second, to Lee alone of the Confederate generals. He was intimately acquainted with all the details of the internal history of events within the southern states. He was personally familiar with every leading man in civil or military life in the South. He knew how their armies were formed, officered, recruited, equipped, and fed. No one living can tell us more of all we want to know of these things, or better give us the local color which would bring out the picture with force and vividness. The announcement of this book, therefore, excited no common expectations, and its publication has been followed by no common disappointment. No doubt our expectations were not quite reasonable. . . . General Johnston, it is very evident, has not written a historic memoir to satisfy the demand of the world for information. . . . He has simply written an earnest, almost passionate defence of himself before the southern people from the charge of having caused or contributed to their defeat — charges which it seems President Davis made and reiterated publicly and privately. We have therefore a contribution to controversial polemics rather than to military history, although much light is incidentally thrown upon some important phases of the conflict. . . . In the narrative of strictly military events, Johnston adds very little to our previous knowledge, except to give some interesting details with regard to the parts of his command which actually participated in the engagements he mentions." The statistics of battles are not to be trusted. As is usual with southern writers, he gives the southern forces the smallest estimate possible and exaggerates that of the northern side. J. D. Cox, in *Nation*, 18: 333.

—— HUGHES, ROBERT M. General Johnston. (Great commanders.) N. Y.: Appleton. 1893. $1.50.   [2225

"This memoir of Gen. Joseph E. Johnston by his kinsman . . . is pleasantly written, and its high appreciation of the great Confederate general does not prevent a candid treatment of the portions of his career which have been the subject of more or less controversy. His relations to Jefferson Davis became unfriendly soon after the first battle of Bull Run, when the Confederate President issued commissions as general to the five senior officers of the army with dates which put Johnston fourth on the list instead of first. The general judgment of the southern people has coincided with that of intelligent people elsewhere in awarding to Johnston a place as one of the two greatest commanders whom the Confederate army developed. . . . The controversial part of the biography naturally occupies a considerable space in Mr. Hughes's book ; but his tone is so fair and his advocacy so good-tempered that the interest is rather increased than diminished. . . . The author's treatment of the national commanders is entirely fair and respectful. Their abilities are recognized, and their characteristics are intelligently analyzed. The bias toward the Confederate side is nowhere shown in any exaggerated or offensive form." Like other southern writers Mr. Hughes fails to see that "northern and southern soldiers use the words 'effectives' and 'effective force' with distinctly different meaning," and overestimates the northern and underestimates the southern forces accordingly throughout the book. J. D. Cox, in *Nation*, 57: 475.

— JOHNSON, BRADLEY TYLER, *ed.* Memoir of the life and public service of Joseph E. Johnston. Baltimore: Woodward. 1891.   [2226

"It is hard to find a good reason for the existence of this book. A good memoir of General Joseph E. Johnston would be warmly welcomed. He himself, in his well-known *Narrative*, gave to the world the most full and authentic history of his military career from his own standpoint. Whatever of authentic details of his youth or his private life could be added to this would be useful and interesting as illustrating his individuality of character and opinion. His private and public correspondence must contain much that ought not to be lost, because it would help to an understanding of him and the history of his time. The volume in hand gives us little or no help in either direction. The military part is a not very reliable abridgment of the *Narrative*, untempered and uncorrected by any apparent study of the *Official records*, now easily accessible to everybody who affects authorship on topics connected with the Civil War. A gloss of historical facts from the standpoint of an ultra-partisan in 1865 is certainly an anachronism in 1891." J. D. Cox, in *Nation*, 53: 433.

Joinville, François Ferdinand Philippe Louis Marie d'Orléans, *prince* de. The Army of the Potomac; tr. by William Henry Hurlbert. N. Y.: Randolph. 1862.   [2227
The Prince de Joinville, a son of Louis Philippe, King of the French, accompanied General McClellan in the Peninsular campaign of 1862. His two nephews, the Comte de Paris and Prince Robert d'Orléans were aides-de-camp on the staff with captain's rank. On returning to Europe, de Joinville published a brochure containing his observations on the campaign, and the title above is that of Mr. Hurlbert's translation. The book is dignified, discriminating, and able; personally friendly to McClellan and disposed to support him in most of his differences with the administration, but by no means blind to the lack of decision and aggressive energy in his military leadership. In the discussion of the period the book ranks as one of the milder apologies for McClellan.   J. D. C.

Jones, C. C., Jr. Roster of general officers, heads of departments, senators, representatives, military organizations, etc., in Confederate service during the war between the states. See Southern Historical Society, v. 1, 2, 3, 1876–77.   [2228
Jones, John B. A rebel war clerk's diary

at the Confederate States capital. Phil.: Lippincott. 1866. 2v.
—— A secret rebel diary of the war. Phil.: Lippincott.   [2229
The writer was a southern man, in literary work at the North when the Civil War began. He went South, offered his services to the Davis government while it was still at Montgomery, Ala., and was assigned to a place in the War Department with an apparent understanding that he was to write also for the press. His diary is full of most interesting facts bearing on the internal history of the Confederacy, and picturing life at Richmond during the progressive despondency, poverty and suffering in 1864-5. The value of the book as an index of opinion is diminished by internal evidence of additions interpolated in editing for publication, or at least after the original writing. To eliminate these is an exercise in "higher criticism."

J. D. C.

Kearney, *Maj.-Gen.* Philip. DE PEYSTER, JOHN WATTS. Personal and military history of Philip Kearney, Major-General United States Volunteers. N. Y.: Rice. 1869.   [2230
A highly eulogistic account of the career of a soldier of several wars, by his personal friend. Diffuse and rhetorical, with many excursions into other fields than the Civil War for the Union with which it mainly deals. The author is a well-read military student, and makes many interesting comparisons between the campaigns in the United States and those of European wars.

G. A. T.

Kieffer, Henry Martyn. Recollections of a drummer-boy. Boston: Osgood. 1883. Rev. and enl. Houghton. [c. 1888.] $1.50. [2231
According to the *Nation*, the author of this book has given too much space to practical jokes, camp witticisms, and incidents that might have happened anywhere, and too little to the details of camp life. "When physical comforts were so few their importance was great; and among the most interesting chapters are those giving the different ingenious shifts of which necessity was the mother. . . . The book does not deal at all with strategy, and in the description of battles presents mostly the scenes at the rear, and what might naturally fall under the observation of a drummer-boy. . . . The story of the raising of nine-months' men in a quiet town, and the war fever running through all the young men, seems taken from the life." *Nation*, 37: 423.
The book is intended for boys. It was published first in *St. Nicholas*.

Land we love; ed. by Gen. Daniel Harvey Hill. Charlotte, N. C. 1866–9. 6v. (With April, 1869, incorporated with The new eclectic, of Baltimore.)   [2232
This magazine became the organ of the late C. S. Army and, while announcing itself as devoted to "literature and the arts," was really much broader in scope. It became largely what the *Southern literary messenger* had been before the war; contains many valuable documents, reports and articles, especially of a historical nature, by the best known southern

writers of that period. It was devoted preëminently to the perpetuation of the memory of the heroic deeds of Confederate soldiers and is intensely southern in feeling.　　　　　　　　　　　　　　　　S. B. W.

Lee, *Gen.* **Robert Edward.** COOKE, JOHN ESTEN. Life of Gen. Robert E. Lee. N. Y.: Appleton. 1871. N. Y.: Dillingham. $1.50.　　　　　　　　　　　　　　　　　　　　[2233

Col. Cooke was in such close personal relations to Lee in his closing campaigns, and had such general qualifications for his task, that this *Life*, though one of the earliest published, remains one of the best biographies of Lee. It is an affectionate, reverential estimate of the Confederate chief, full and accurate enough to be a trustworthy guide, and broad enough to command respect. It is thoroughly good from the literary point of view, modest and reticent as to the author's personality. It is strongly Confederate, but free from bitterness.　　　　　　　　　　　J. D. C.

— LEE, *Maj.-Gen.* FITZHUGH. General Lee; by his nephew and cavalry commander. (Great commanders.) N. Y. : Appleton. 1894. $1.50.　　　　　　　　　　　　　　　　　　　　[2234

" Gen. Fitzhugh Lee has told the story of the campaigns in Virginia and Maryland from the Confederate standpoint with clearness and force, and is a model of modesty in hiding his own part in those stirring events. Indeed, it may be thought that he has gone too far in this direction. . . . The fourth chapter is devoted to the causes which led to the Civil War and to Lee's reasons for resigning from the United States Army. To the student of his life this is the crisis. We have the right to ask his biographer that both his words and his conduct shall be here given without gloss or paraphrase. . . . Yet instead of giving Gen. Lee's words and acts in this crisis, the author has given a disquisition of his own on the formation of the Constitution of the United States and on the so-called reserved rights of the states. . . . Such a taking of liberties with Lee's memory is simply astounding. It is done without the quotation of a word from Lee's lips or pen which supports or justifies it. . . . The only letter of Lee's which is quoted in this connection itself contradicts the statement of the text. . . . In the military narrative the sectional standpoint of the writer is most noticeable in the laudatory and friendly treatment of the national officers who did not hurt the Confederacy. . . . Instead of going to the published official records for the numerical forces of Lee's armies and those opposed to him, he uses vague estimates of his own or of others. . . . This mode of writing history cannot satisfy intelligent men of the present generation." J. D. Cox, in *Nation*, 59: 369.

— LONG, ARMISTEAD L. Memoirs of Robert E. Lee, his military and personal history ; together with incidents relating to his private life subsequent to the war, coll. and ed. with the assistance of Marcus J. Wright. N. Y.: Stoddart. 1886.　　　　　　　　　　　　　[2235

The writer, "Gen. Long, as military secretary to Lee at the beginning of his career in the Confederate armies, had some positive advantages in his intimate relations with his chief, and has been able to give many incidents illustrating his personal character and habits of mind which are both interesting and valuable. It is going rather far, however, to claim, as the publishers do, that it is in substance a ' consummation ' of Lee's own purpose to write his autobiography. . . . The greatest value of Gen. Long's book is found in the reminiscences of his personal association with Lee, and in his reports of the conduct and opinions of his chief as they were seen and heard by himself. The narrative of Lee's early life and his service in the army of the United States prior to the Civil War is also more full than usual, and therefore more acceptable." J. D. Cox, in *Nation*, 44 : 321.

— TRENT, WILLIAM PETERFIELD. Robert E. Lee. (Beacon biographies.) Boston: Small. 1899. 75c.　　　　　　　　　　　　　　　　　　　[2236

See Beacon biographies, in Pt. 3, Div. 2: Comprehensive history, sect. 2491.

— WHITE, HENRY ALEXANDER. Robert E. Lee and the southern Confederacy, 1807–1870. (Heroes of the nations.) N. Y.: Putnam. 1897. $1.50.　　　　　　　　　　　　　　　　　　[2237

"Prof. White's life of Gen. Lee has been prepared under circumstances which give it some superiority over previously written biographies of the Confederate leader. The author's relations to Gen. Custis Lee, the president of the same university, who allowed the use of his father's letters and papers, gave the opportunity to quote family letters more fully than others have done, and a most valuable source of knowledge has thus been made available. . . . The work bears evidence in itself that industrious and systematic use has been made of the material at his disposal. . . . A severe taste would have curbed some rhetorical flights and held to a simple style, in keeping with the quiet dignity of Lee himself. . . . The author's studies do not seem to have reached the official statistical returns of the Confederate armies, and he follows the habit of southern writers in preferring the loose expressions of combatants who claim that they always fought one against two or three. Occasionally this involves a puzzling problem, as when the 35,000 with which Lee is said to have fought the battle of Antietam (p. 223) become 72,000 when he had retreated across the Potomac (p. 238)." Dr. White's account of the steps in Lee's service by which he passed from the command of the Virginia forces in April, 1861, to the position of General in the Confederate army is evidently erroneous. J. D. Cox, in *Nation*, 65 : 502.

Lincoln, Abraham. Complete works; ed. by John G. Nicolay and John Hay. N. Y.: Century Co. 1894. 2v. $10.　　　　　　　　　　[2238

The editors of these works have shown great diligence in collecting material from the date of the first document, March 9, 1832, down to the end. The order of arrangement is chronological; the form of mechanical presentation is perfection itself. The "works" are indispensable to all students of our later political history.　　　　　　　　　　　　　　　　B. A. H.

— ARNOLD, ISAAC NEWTON. History of Abraham Lincoln and the overthrow of slavery. Chicago. 1867.

—— —— Life of Abraham Lincoln. Chicago: Jansen. 1885. McClurg. $1.50.   [2239

Although Mr. Arnold was an old and intimate friend of Abraham Lincoln, his *Life*, expanded in 1884 from a *History* more hastily written in 1867, merely duplicates " what may be read in hundreds of others. The portion which deals with Lincoln's personality is, on the other hand, very small, and the new material meagre — hardly more, in fact, than Mr. Arnold's own impression of his friend." *Nation*, 40: 125.

— BROOKS, ELBRIDGE STREETER. True story of Abraham Lincoln, the American, told for boys and girls. Boston: Lothrop. [c. 1896.] $1.50.   [2240

A readable children's narrative of the hardships of Lincoln's early life. Highly colored, if not sometimes extravagant. Grounded on current traditions. Later public life of Lincoln is not so fully treated. The book is of no especial historic value, but it is harmless and entertaining.   E. E. S.

— BROOKS, NOAH. Abraham Lincoln: a biography for young people. (Boys' and girls' lib. of Am. biog.) N. Y.: Putnam. 1888.

—— —— Abraham Lincoln and the downfall of American slavery. (Heroes of the nations.) N. Y.: Putnam. 1894. $1.50.   [2241

A good specimen of the so-called popular style of history, treating its subject in a heroic light rather than as a man. Especially full on the legends of the early life of Lincoln in all its picturesqueness. Partly reminiscent. Readable and easily comprehended by children, although often wandering. Strongly biased against the South and slavery. The pages of the later edition have been renumbered and some of the illustrations changed.   E. E. S.

— CARPENTER, FRANCIS BICKNELL. Six months at the White House with Abraham Lincoln. N. Y.: Hurd. 1866.   [2242

Of all the collections of anecdotes and reminiscences of President Lincoln, this book of 350 pages, though not the largest, is the best. During six months, while painting his large historical picture in one of the rooms of the Executive Mansion, the artist and author had almost constant opportunity to see the daily and familiar life of the White House, and frequent chances to hold brief conversations with the President in his leisure moments. He has recorded many incidents with brevity and fidelity, and made authentic record of stories which he heard from Mr. Lincoln's own lips. To his own recollections he has added many others quoted from newspaper reports of interviews, or what other visitors told him, which are not so trustworthy.   * *

— COFFIN, CHARLES CARLETON. Abraham Lincoln. N. Y.: Harper. 1893. $2. [2243

Mr. Coffin " has of course availed himself of the work of preceding biographers, and he had the advantage of knowing President Lincoln personally from the night following his nomination for the presidency to the fall of Richmond. . . . He presents his work as a sketch rather than as a biography. . . . The strong points of this book are its readableness, its happy selection of matter likely to be of general interest and the very numerous illustrations of places connected with Lincoln's early career and portraits of the leading men in civil and military life during war times." *Literary world*, 23: 477.

— DANA, CHARLES ANDERSON. Lincoln and his cabinet. Cleveland: Lemperly. 1896.   [2244

A lecture before the New Haven Historical Society, 1896. Mr. Dana was employed in the War Department, and his reminiscences concern chiefly Stanton and Lincoln. His estimates of the different men are brief but judicious. He gives many anecdotes of Lincoln.   E. E. S.

— GILMORE, JAMES ROBERTS (EDMUND KIRKE, *pseud.*). Personal recollections of Abraham Lincoln and the Civil War. Boston: Page. 1898. $3.   [2245

" Mr. Gilmore tells us in general that he was in the habit of making notes of his conversations with Mr. Lincoln, and it is to be hoped that the original notes are preserved and may some day be given to the world in their authentic shape. It is a little hard to believe that a young man, as yet quite unknown to fame, lectured Mr. Lincoln upon the mischievous effect of his having Mr. Seward in his cabinet when as yet the cabinet was hardly a month old and Sumter had not fallen. . . . We do not need to conclude that these *Recollections* will have no value to the historian. . . . An expert investigator will judge sagaciously as to the parts which may be antecedently probable. As a direct contribution to history, however, the book will need to be sifted as to every page." J. D. Cox, in *Nation*, 68: 92.

— HAPGOOD, NORMAN. Abraham Lincoln: the man of the people. N. Y.: Macmillan. 1899. $2.   [2246

" So many lives of Lincoln have been written heretofore that for the existence of this one there does not appear to be any good and sufficient reason. . . . Mr. Hapgood's deliberate appeal is to a different judgment and taste than were met and satisfied by Mr. Schurz and by Mr. Morse's volumes in the ' American statesmen' series. We have had *The true George Washington* and *The true Benjamin Franklin*, and we have here, very much in the manner of those doubtful ventures, the True Abraham Lincoln ; the idea being that the true man is the man in his most ungirt and careless moods, the man displaying his seamy side, if he has one, with the least possible reserve." *Nation*, 69: 455.

— HARRIS, *Maj.-Gen.* THOMAS M. Assassination of Lincoln: a history of the great conspiracy. Boston: Am. Citizen Co. [c. 1892.]   [2247

By " a member of the commission which tried the assassins of the martyr-president. General Harris is strongly convinced that President Lincoln was the victim of a conspiracy concocted by Jefferson Davis and the Confederate emissaries in Canada. The charges to this effect which were made on the trial were not proved, according to Nicolay and Hay; but General Harris has no doubts on the subject. He does not impress the hasty reader of his volume with a deep conviction of his very judicial spirit; for our own part, we should much more confidently follow these two writers of the great life of Lincoln." *Literary world*, 23: 374.

— HERNDON, WILLIAM HENRY, *and* JESSE WILLIAM WEIK. Herndon's Lincoln, the true story of a great life. Chicago: Belford. [c. 1889.] 3v.

— — Abraham Lincoln; with introd. by H. White. New ed., rev. and enl. N. Y.: Appleton. 1892. 2v. $3. [2248

This work is the result of Mr. Herndon's memory and suggestions, but Mr. Weik's literary and painstaking industry put it into readable shape. The method on which it is written, however, may be compared to that of an artist undertaking to paint a life-size portrait by using a magnifying glass and camel's hair brush. The narrative continually loses itself in the multitude of its details, the greater portion of which are trivial or commonplace. Most of the contents are taken up with the incidents of Lincoln's youth in Indiana, and early manhood in Illinois. While they somewhat photographically picture the frontier life from which he sprang, they serve in a measure to obscure the individual force of character that lifted him above the prosaic comprehension and judgment of the neighborhood gossips who contributed a large part of the recollections here gathered or copied.　　* *

— KELLEY, WILLIAM DARRAH. Lincoln and Stanton: a study of the War administration of 1861 and 1862, with special consideration of recent statements of Gen. Geo. B. McClellan. (Questions of the day.) N. Y.: Putnam. 1885. [2249

A reply to an article by General McClellan in the *Century magazine*, May, 1885. It is an echo of the difficulty between himself and Lincoln on the conduct of the war. The author of this pamphlet from the war records attempts to disprove the statement that Stanton broke up the confidential intercourse between the President and McClellan. An appendix contains some matter on Lincoln and the Abolitionists.

E. E. S

— LAMON, WARD HILL. Life of Abraham Lincoln, to his inauguration as President. Boston: Osgood. 1872. [2250

This was intended to be the first volume of an extended life of Lincoln, and covers only the period from his birth to his first inauguration as President. Ward H. Lamon was appointed Marshal of the District of Columbia, and as such held close official relations with the President; but his literary ability was not equal to his opportunities for biography. After Mr. Lincoln's death he became law partner of Hon. Jeremiah S. Black, Attorney-General and Secretary of State in Buchanan's cabinet. Filled with an ambition to write Lincoln's life, Lamon purchased from Wm. H. Herndon, Lincoln's former law partner, the material which the latter had gathered for a biography, consisting of "three enormous volumes of MSS.," memoranda of interviews, letters, etc., etc., with and from Lincoln's relatives and acquaintances during his boyhood and early manhood. These were generally people advanced in years, who had led the hard prosaic lives of the frontier, and who gave their recitals the color of their surroundings and personal experiences, subject of course to the inaccuracies which dimness or failure of memory naturally produce. From material thus gathered, and from contemporaries of Lincoln's later years, it is an open secret that not Lamon but another hand wrote the book. Whoever the real author was, while writing perfunctory eulogy, his political bias moved him to infuse into his text an insidious and unfailing undertone of depreciation of Lincoln. So marked was this that the book displeased the public, and no second volume ever appeared.　　* *

— LAMON, WARD HILL. Recollections of Abraham Lincoln. 1847-65; ed. by Dorothy Lamon. Chicago: McClurg. 1895. $1.50. [2251

The daughter of Marshal Ward H. Lamon, who compiled this little volume from newspaper articles and memoranda left by her father, frankly acknowledges in her preface that it is fragmentary and lacking in purpose. It is a miscellaneous collection of alleged anecdotes and reminiscences, some of which are true and some decidedly untrue, notably the one about the Gettysburg address. As one of a growing class of Lincolniana the book has its place, due reservations about authenticity being, however, always kept in mind. Its principal value lies in facsimile reproductions of an autograph memorandum by Mr. Lincoln, and one or two autograph letters.　　* *

— McCLURE, ALEXANDER KELLY. Abraham Lincoln and men of war-times. Phil.: J. W. Keeler. 1892. [2252

This book professes to be, and if the leaves are merely superficially turned it has the appearance of being, a collection of personal reminiscences about the Civil War and its leading actors. Examined more carefully, however, it becomes self-evident that its author has gleaned from other publications nearly every item of general interest or value. This encyclopædic flavor is so strong that it will lead discriminating students to save time and labor by going directly to original sources, some of which are indicated in the preface, instead of accepting made-over statements and views.　　* *

— MORSE, JOHN TORREY, JR. Abraham Lincoln. (American statesmen.) Boston: Houghton. 1893. 2v. $2.50. [2253

The best brief life of Lincoln. Condensed but quite clear. Very careful of facts and inviting confidence. Slightly marred by hero worship. First volume gives a graphic description of Lincoln's early environment, but minimizes his early political struggles. The second volume is devoted entirely to the conduct of the war.

E. E. S.

— NICOLAY, JOHN GEORGE, *and* JOHN HAY. Abraham Lincoln: a history. N. Y.: Century Co. 1890. 10v. $20. [2254

The authors of these volumes were at one time private secretaries of President Lincoln and had unusual opportunities to know him as he was. This familiarity seems to have bred lasting devotion and unwavering admiration. As a biography the work leaves little to be desired. It is exceedingly well written; materials were sought for with patience, examined with care, and woven into the story with skill. As a history it has its defects. The method adopted makes it necessary that men and events should be viewed from Washington, not to say the White House. A desire to present Lincoln's services with clearness and vigor occasionally led the authors unconsciously to underestimate the character and work of other persons. But, withal, the book deserves high praise, and is a signal contribution to the historical literature of the last half century.   A. C. McL.

— PUTNAM, M. LOUISE. Children's life of Abraham Lincoln. Chicago: McClurg. 1892. $1.25.   [2254 a

The author "disclaims any expectation of amusing the children for whom she has written. She hopes to interest them and instruct them, and we think she will succeed. But the children who will enjoy the chapters dealing with Lincoln's maturity must be older than those who will enjoy the first chapters. The book improves as it goes on, and there is some danger that those who would delight in the later chapters will be discouraged by the earlier. These are a little sentimental, and they give a decidedly rose-colored account of Lincoln's parents, while the sordid misery of his childhood and early youth would hardly be guessed from what is written. Consequently, no adequate sense is conveyed of that innate nobility which triumphed over the most unfavorable environment. A good feature of the book is its brief expositions here and there of the forms of government. . . . The best feature of the book is the copious extracts from Lincoln's speeches and addresses. They will prove the most comprehensible parts of the story." *Nation*, 55: 357.

— RAYMOND, HENRY JARVIS. Life and public services of Abraham Lincoln; with anecdotes and personal reminiscences by Frank B. Carpenter. N. Y.: Derby. 1865.   [2255

The first edition of this book was written by the accomplished editor of the *New York times* before the Civil War was ended, and the second and greatly enlarged edition immediately after its close. At the time it was published it was one of the best condensed reviews of the public administration of President Lincoln. Unfortunately the numerous official documents printed in it were so carelessly gathered by the mere process of newspaper clipping, and underwent such slovenly proof-reading, that their many omissions and errors render the volume untrustworthy as a book of reference.   * *

— RICE, ALLEN THORNDIKE, *ed.* Reminiscences of Abraham Lincoln, by distinguished men of his time. N. Y.: North American Pub. Co. 1886.   [2256

The thirty-three able and distinguished men who contributed the reminiscences which form this volume were nearly all prominent and official actors in the civil and military service of the government during the War of the Rebellion and the administration of President Lincoln. While this gives the book unusual strength of authority, its weakness lies in the fact that it was written about thirty years after the events narrated in it, when the sharpness of memory had so far faded out that incidents and anecdotes are generally repetitions of what had been often printed, and that the bulk of the text is mere generalization of personal character and the spirit of the time it deals with, rather than concise and definite historical statement with date and detail of action.   * *

— SCHURZ, CARL. Abraham Lincoln: an essay. Boston: Houghton. 1891. $1.
— *Same;* Gettysburg address, etc. (Riverside literature series.) Houghton. Net 15c.
                                         [2257

One of the most noteworthy essays on a biographical subject to be found in American literature. The writer makes no pretence of giving minute historical knowledge, and he happily avoids all effort at psychical analysis; but he is able to do much more than analyze his subject; he comprehends the man, appreciates the real meaning of his work and tells in a simple but graphic way the wonderful story of his life.
                                    A. C. McL.
This essay appeared first in the *Atlantic monthly*, 67: 721.

— TARBELL, IDA M. Life of Abraham Lincoln; drawn from original sources and containing many speeches, letters, and telegrams hitherto unpublished. N. Y.: Doubleday & McClure; McClure, Phillips. 1900. 2v. $5.
                                         [2258

One of the best of the anecdotal lives of Lincoln. It is based on original search for new material pertaining to the early life of the President, made for *McClure's magazine*, with great labor and much coöperative assistance. A second series included similar work on the presidential career of Lincoln. Finally the whole was enlarged to a complete life by compilations from published sources. The work is well done in its kind, is free from sensationalism, is sympathetic with the noble elements of the character. Its fault is that of the class, — overlaying the important elements with a mass of trivial details which tend to belittling the subject, and which have no claim to preservation.
                                       J. D. C.

— WELLES, GIDEON. Lincoln and Seward. N. Y.: Sheldon. 1874.   [2259

Vigorously written by President Lincoln's Secretary of the Navy, this volume is authentic, historical, and successful in refuting the aspersion of Hon. Charles Francis Adams that Seward was the real President.

Lincoln, *Mrs.* **Nancy (Hanks).** HITCHCOCK, *Mrs.* CAROLINE (HANKS). Nancy Hanks: the story of Abraham Lincoln's mother. N. Y.: Doubleday & McClure; Doubleday, Page. 1899. Net 50c.   [2260

An attempt to correct the "injustice" done by various biographers of Lincoln. The little book contains facsimiles of a will and a marriage bond to prove the legitimacy of Nancy Hanks and her claims to a better descent than that sometimes ascribed.

E. E. S.

Livermore, *Mrs.* **Mary Ashton.** My story of the war. Hartford : Worthington. 1888. [2261

Commencing with the first gun at Sumter, Mrs. Livermore "outlines the progress of events to the assassination of Lincoln, dwelling upon the work of the Sanitary Commission as it came under her notice during a close acquaintanceship with the horrors of war. Seldom does one meet with so rich an experience of human nature. The reader must be made of stern or indifferent stuff who can peruse this book without having his heart deeply stirred. If an American heart, it must throb with pride at this fresh revelation of heroism — the heroism of the forlorn hope in the face of lingering disease and horrible mutilation. A marked feature of the work of the Sanitary Commission, in the light of Mrs. Livermore's story, was the wonderful executive ability of many of its gentle representatives in the field. Duties pertaining to half-a-dozen of the great administrative departments of the army were performed with a mingled intelligence, tact, and force that was simply irresistible. Before this new power, red-tape, custom of service, bad roads, want of transportation, as obstacles to prompt succor of the sick and wounded, were promptly brushed aside. . . . The practical workings of the system of voluntary aid in war-time are thoroughly illustrated by a series of anecdotes." *Nation,* 48: 471.

Logan, *Maj.-Gen.* **John Alexander.** The great conspiracy. N. Y.: Hart. 1886. [2262

In eight preliminary chapters the author sketches the growth of the contest between the Union and the States, and in seventeen chapters the history of the War of the Rebellion. The author keeps himself entirely in the background and mingles the civic with the military conduct of the war. The book is too partisan and bitter against the Confederates to rank as history. The matter is derived from Congressional speeches and reports, but with few references. The appendix contains a summary of the Lincoln-Douglas debates, and the report of Judge-Advocate Holt on conspiracies against the government during the war.

E. E. S.

Longstreet, *Lt.-Gen.* **James.** From Manassas to Appomattox. Phil.: Lippincott. 1896. Net $4, subs. [2263

"While . . . General Longstreet's memoirs cover the whole period of his military career, we find, as we might expect, that his vindication from aspersion becomes the most stimulating part of his book. . . . As the criticisms upon Longstreet impugn the value of his services to his chief, it was natural that he should give the evidence of Lee's confidence in him as a soldier and his trust in him as a faithful comrade and friend. The frank and free correspondence between them seems to establish this beyond reasonable controversy. . . . The memoir is a work without which the literature of the

war would be incomplete. The personal views of so prominent a character are part of the evidence which cannot be spared. The revelations of his own character are a great help in judging of every event in which he had a part. His methods of action and of thought, his canons of military judgment, his influence upon officers and men, are all worthy of careful study. . . . Blunt, careless, sometimes even egotistic," the author "'says his say' with a kind of defiant earnestness which commands attention and rouses sympathy. The references in footnotes to the *Official records* are made under the name of 'Rebellion record,' which is somewhat misleading. . . . The author's intention is to refer to the *Official records of the Union and Confederate armies* published by the Government." J. D. Cox, in *Nation,* 62: 146.

Lossing, Benson John. Pictorial history of the Civil War. Phil.: Childs. Hartford : Belknap. 1866–9. 3v. [Some eds. called "Pictorial field-book."]
—— *Same.* 3v. Phil.: McKay. $7.50. [2264

Of the first volume the *Nation* said that it "possesses substantial claims to remembrance in the lively pictures it presents, both with pen and pencil, of the actors in our great drama of Civil War, and particularly of those who were instrumental in raising the standard of rebellion. Mr. Lossing has for the most part permitted the latter to tell their own story, drawing liberally for that purpose upon newspapers, speeches, letters, and every available source of authentic information. . . . In no history of the war which has yet appeared do we remember to have seen the infatuation under which the southern people rushed into rebellion more clearly or copiously set forth than in his pages. This constitutes the chief merit of the work, which will compare favorably with the author's well-known *Field-book of the Revolution.* . . . Written in a popular style, and in the main complete and accurate, it reflects too fully the earnest Union feeling of the author to be classed among the works which will hereafter be universally referred to for information concerning the war. Mr. Lossing is a good hater, and scruples not to call things by their right names. . . . The pictorial illustrations are numerous and of unequal merit." Of the second volume the *Nation* said : " To the labor of compilation necessary in the preparation of this as of the first volume the author has added that of visiting in person the battle-fields of the South, and the result is a record — for more than this his history does not pretend to be — that will take a very high, if not the first, rank among similar chronicles of the rebellion. All things considered, we incline to give the preference to *Harper's pictorial history,* although in point of fulness, so far as we have compared the two, Lossing's seems to be superior." *Nation,* 2 : 789 and 7: 55.

Lyon, *Brig.-Gen.* **Nathaniel.** Peckham, *Lt.-Col.* James. General Nathaniel Lyon and Missouri in 1861. N. Y.: Am. News Co. 1866. [2265

A contribution to the history of the effectual efforts of the Union supporters of St. Louis to prevent the secession of Missouri, with details of the important part to that end performed by Capt., afterwards Gen.

Lyon. The book contains valuable material, mostly of current public and newspaper opinion, but with official documents of the first few months of the war, and has the strong convictions of Union partisanship.

G. A. T.

— WOODWARD, ASHBEL. Life of General Nathaniel Lyon. Hartford. 1862.   [2266

The leading incidents of the public services of a capable and brave officer of the regular army, who was killed in the first year of the War for the Union, at the head of a hastily organized army of volunteers. The story is told by a friend resident in the state of Lyon's birth, Connecticut, and covers the officer's career in Indian and the Mexican wars, as well as in his preparations at St. Louis for resisting movements for the secession of Missouri. Straightforward and simple in style, and trustworthy as to its statements of fact.   G. A. T.

McCarthy, Carlton. Detailed minutiæ of soldier life in the Army of Northern Virginia, 1861–5. Richmond: McCarthy. 1882. [2267

A very lively series of sketches of life in the ranks of the Confederate army in Virginia. The characters and scenes selected are the amusing and humorous, mostly; but they have the ring of true experience, from the enthusiastic enlistment, through the disillusion of hard campaigning, to the despair and surrender at Appomattox. Without pretending to be historical narration, the book is so full of the spirit of the camp and the battle-field, that it may be trusted as a presentation of the personal side of the southern soldier's life in the field, done with no little literary skill.   J. D. C.

McClellan, Carswell. The Personal memoirs and Military history of U. S. Grant, *versus* the Record of the Army of the Potomac. Boston: Houghton. 1887. $1.75.   [2268

"Colonel McClellan's book purports to compare the statements of both Grant and Badeau with the *Record of the Army of the Potomac*, but at the outset of his task he declares his purpose 'to use, with very little other reference, the work of General Humphreys [*Virginia campaign of 1864 and 1865*, sect. 2215], as embodying substantially the established record, as far as it shall be necessary to examine it.' Indeed, throughout the book, when the *Record* is referred to, it will be found that a textual quotation from Humphreys is made, whether the usual marks of quotation are inserted or not. What is in fact given is therefore a series of quotations from Grant and Badeau, compared with others from Humphreys, connected by a running comment, in which the proof of error in the first two books is supposed to be complete when their disagreement with the last is exhibited." J. D. Cox, in *Nation*, 47: 276.

McClellan, *Maj.-Gen.* George Brinton. McClellan's own story. N. Y.: Webster. 1887. [2269

This is in substance a revised edition of the *Report on the Army of the Potomac* [see next title], "with considerable additions, a few omissions. . . . The change in the present edition which is most noticeable

is the attribution to the administration of Mr. Lincoln, and to the leaders of the Union party (as it was then called), of a conscious purpose to sacrifice the Army of the Potomac in order to diminish the personal and political importance of the general in command. This he speaks of as a 'treasonable conspiracy,' and says that it was to be carried out, 'first, by endeavoring to force me into premature movements, knowing that a failure would probably end my military career; afterwards, by withholding the means necessary to achieve success." Gen. McClellan ignores the facts that have been made known in regard to his own and the Confederate forces, and he brings nothing new in his own defence against the judgment of competent military critics. "Perhaps the most painful thing in this volume, to those who once made Gen. McClellan their idol, is to see the revelation of blinding self-esteem which it exhibits. The country is ruled by rogues and incapables. . . . He has no word of recognition for the military achievements of Grant or Sherman or Sheridan. Yet the army was devoted to him. . . . For twenty years friend and foe have alike challenged the first commander of that army to justify his assertion that his enemy was multifold his superior in force. He has answered, and his answer is the silence on this point which is confession." J. D. Cox, in *Nation*, 44: 57, 79.

——— Report on the organization of the Army of the Potomac, and of its campaigns in Virginia and Maryland under the command of Major-General George B. McClellan, from July 26, 1861, to November 7, 1862. Wash.: Govt. Printing Office. 1864.

——— *Same:* Complete report; with last revision. N. Y.: Sheldon. 1864.   [2270

"The volume before us . . . has much more the air of being addressed to a jury than to the War Department at Washington. It is, in short, a letter to the people of the United States, under cover to the Secretary of War. . . . He has omitted many documents essential to the formation of a just opinion; and it is only when we have read these also, in the *Report* of the Committee on the Conduct of the War, that we feel the full weight of the cumulative evidence going to show the hearty support in men and confidence that he received from the administration, and, when there were no more men to be sent, and confidence began to yield before irresistible facts, the prolonged forbearance with which he was still favored. . . . He was an accomplished soldier, but lacked that downright common sense which is only another name for genius with its coat off for actual work in hand. . . . The *Report* is a political manifesto, and not only that, but an attack on the administration which appointed him to the command, supported him with all its resources, and whose only fault it was not sooner to discover his incapacity to conduct aggressive movements." James Russell Lowell, in his *Political essays*.

— SWINTON, WILLIAM. McClellan's military career reviewed and exposed: the military policy of the administration set forth and vindicated. Wash. 1864.   [2271

Mr. Swinton was War correspondent of the *N. Y.*

Times, and this work in ten chapters is a revision of articles published in February, March and April, 1864. It was used as a campaign document for the Union Congressional Committee in the reëlection of Mr. Lincoln. It is an able and very damaging review of McClellan's military career, and a defence of the administration in its relations to him. Its permanent significance, besides, is its curious contrast to the treatment of the same subject in his *Campaigns of the Army of the Potomac* (1866 and 1882) [sect. 2342]. Substantially contradictory conclusions are supported in the two works. Their comparison makes an instructive study on the relation of conscience to historical writing. Grant and Burnside both charged Mr. Swinton with dishonorable conduct as a newspaper correspondent with the army. (*Personal memoirs* of Grant, 2: 145.) J. D. C.

See, also, sect. 2365.

McPherson, Edward. Political history of the United States during the great Rebellion. Wash.: Philip and Solomons. 1864. [2272

An ill-arranged but invaluable compilation of material illustrative of the history of the United States during the Civil War. In it will be found summary accounts of the progress of secession in the several rebellious states; the proceedings of Congress, with the votes of each House, on all important questions relating to the Rebellion; messages, proclamations, addresses, and other papers of Buchanan and Lincoln; some important diplomatic correspondence; letters and papers from members of the cabinet, opinions of the Attorney-General, and decisions of the courts; many orders of commanding generals; legislation of the Confederate States, etc. There is a fair index. The compiler was for a number of years clerk of the House of Representatives, and does not conceal his strong Union sympathies; but his presentation of facts is unbiased. W. MacD.

Mahan, *Capt.* **Alfred Thayer.** The Gulf and inland waters. (The navy in the Civil War, 3.) N. Y.: Scribner. 1883. $1. [2273

The *Nation,* in a long review, speaks of "the fulness and accuracy that characterize the book." *Nation,* 37: 232.

Mahan, Asa. Critical history of the late American war. N. Y.: Barnes. 1877. [2274

The author was an American clergyman of distinction, an early President of Oberlin College, later connected with the Wesleyan Methodists of England and editor of their organ in London. He was author of books on psychology and ethics. His history of the Civil War is a sketch for general readers, with criticisms of campaigns, often acute, but also often without access to the full information necessary for clear judgment. He claimed to have anticipated Sherman's plan of the "March to the sea," as other civilian writers have done, but it was without accurate comprehension of the problem before that general and the essential character of his solution of it. The interest in the book is for study of current contemporaneous criticism of our great struggle by various classes of active minds. J. D. C.

Marshall, John A. American Bastile; a

history of the illegal arrests and imprisonment of American citizens during the late Civil War. Phil.: Hartley. 1869. [New ed.] 1883.
[2275

A subscription book, "written by order of a Convention of the prisoners of state," and one which had a large sale. Its purpose is manifest from the title. The experiences of one hundred prisoners are told, each separately, and descriptions given of the leading places of detention. The most prominent of Secretary Stanton's orders for the arrest of disaffected persons are given in the appendix. E. E. S.

Massachusetts, Military Historical Society of. Papers, v. 1: Peninsular campaign of General McClellan in 1862. Boston. 1881.

—— *Same* [New ed.]: Campaigns in Virginia, 1861–1862. Boston: Houghton. 1895. $2. [2276

Of the first volume the *Nation* says: "The nature of this book is to some extent peculiar. It consists of papers of unequal length and unequal merit, prepared either by committees or by single members of the Society, and read before it at various times between 1876 and 1880. Taken together, they make up a somewhat fragmentary history or criticism of the entire campaign to which they refer. The first paper, which is by far the most valuable of the series, was prepared by a committee consisting of Mr. John C. Ropes, Gen. F. W. Palfrey, and Capt. W. E. Perkins. It discusses the general subject of McClellan's plans: What were his plans? what were their advantages and defects? what authority had he to execute them? and how much was he interfered with in their execution? These are fundamental questions which have been much debated and written upon, but we do not remember to have ever seen in print so concise, so closely reasoned, carefully worded, and thoroughly conclusive a statement of the subject as is given in the twenty-five pages here devoted to it. . . . The second paper treats of the siege of Yorktown, and is written by Gen. John C. Palfrey, who was an officer of engineers. It criticises the unnecessary slowness of McClellan's movements, but does not add much to our previous knowledge of the subject. . . . The third, fourth, and fifth papers treat of the battles of the campaign from Williamsburg to Malvern Hill; they are written by Gen. F. W. Palfrey, or by committees of which he was chairman. They are analytical rather than descriptive, and to a very large extent are taken up with quotations from official reports in the vain attempt to reconcile hopelessly conflicting statements." *Nation,* 33: 200.

—— Papers, v. 2. The Virginia campaign of General Pope in 1862. Boston: Houghton. 1886. $2. [2277

Of the second volume, the same journal remarks: "The ability, the research, the calm historical tone which characterize these papers, are most admirable. They treat briefly and clearly the Union side of the campaign, and the controversies which grew out of it in regard to the conduct of Porter, McClellan and Halleck. . . . Two of the best papers in the volume are those of Gen. Walcott on Chantilly, . . . and they constitute perhaps the most important contributions to the volume." The maps are excellent. *Nation*, 43: 422.

—— Papers, v. 10: Critical sketches of some of the Federal and Confederate commanders; ed. by Theodore F. Dwight. Boston: Houghton. 1896. $2.   [2278

The *Nation* says that all the papers "are worthy to be thus collected in a permanent volume. Great freedom is allowed the writers, who strongly but candidly make their estimates, each from his own standpoint, sometimes with strong contrasts of view and of conclusion." *Nation*, 61: 63.

Matthews, Franklin. Our navy in time, of war, 1861–98. (Appleton's home reading-books, division 3, history.) N. Y.: Appleton. 1899. 75c.   [2279

A book for young people. Well adapted to its purpose. Concise and interesting. Devoted mainly to the combats of the Civil War.   E. C.

Maury, *Brig.-Gen.* Dabney Herndon. Recollections of a Virginian in the Mexican, Indian and Civil Wars. N. Y.: Scribner. 1894. $1.50.   [2280

"General Maury's *Recollections* are even broader than his title-page indicates, for some of his pleasantest chapters, showing a natural gift for narrative, are those which tell of his boyhood and his education at West Point. The sketches of old Virginia plantation homes in the vicinity of Fredericksburg are admirably done, and make a valuable addition to our material for the social history of the South in ante-bellum times. He has drawn with delicate touch and genial spirit pen-portraits of comrades in the cadet corps who became historical characters afterwards. . . . The book is a pleasing one if we look at it simply as a narrative of the author's varied and adventurous experience; but it has a much higher and more permanent value in helping us to a personal acquaintance with a considerable group of men who made reputations on either side in the great Civil War. To know them first as boys at school, and to see them develop into brave soldiers, daring Indian fighters, adventurous hunters of 'big game,' and finally into commanders of armies, is to give history a real life and power which the pages of the more systematic historian must lack." J. D. Cox, in *Nation*, 58: 415.

Meade, *Maj.-Gen.* George Gordon. BACHE, RICHARD MEADE. Life of General George Gordon Meade. Phil.: Coates. 1897. $3.   [2281

" The intimate history of Meade is limited to a dozen pages at the beginning and a score at the end of the volume. We cannot even say that the comments on the several campaigns represent Meade's views; for he is rarely quoted, and the author informs us in the preface that he does not remember ' ever having asked him a question about the war, or his ever having volunteered to speak of it, or having spoken of it to me.' . . . We find the standpoint of the writer to be that of a group of the younger officers who surrounded Gen. Meade, who, starting with the intensest preju-

dices against the men who succeeded McClellan, transferred the dislike with equal hostility to Grant and Sheridan, when Meade was superseded." *Am. hist. rev.*, 3: 573.

Memminger, Christopher G. CAPERS, HENRY D. Life and times of C. G. Memminger. Richmond, Va.: E. Waddey Co. 1893.   [2282

Memminger was a resident of South Carolina, opposed to Calhoun's nullification movement, for many years in the state legislature, secession commissioner to Virginia in 1860, and three years secretary of the Confederate treasury. There are interesting details of the Confederate cabinet and local reconstruction. The author was chief clerk in the Confederate treasury, and in the appendix has given many valuable documents and accounts connected with the finances of the Confederacy.   E. E. S.

Mitchel, *Maj.-Gen.* Ormsby MacKnight. MITCHEL, FREDERICK AUGUSTUS. Ormsby MacKnight Mitchel, astronomer and general; by his son. Boston: Houghton. 1887. $2.   [2283

" Ormsby Mitchel's life . . . is an attractive story from his infancy onward. . . . He graduated [from West Point] in the class of 1829 with Robert E. Lee and Joseph E. Johnston, with good standing, and was retained at the Academy for two years as Assistant Professor of Mathematics. . . . In 1836 he was made Professor of Mathematics and Civil Engineering in the Cincinnati College, then newly organized. . . . Gen. Mitchel's military career was a great disappointment to him and to those who were close to him." J. D. Cox, in *Nation*, 46: 55.

Moore, Frank, *ed.* Rebellion record. N. Y.: Putnam; Van Nostrand. 1862–8. 12v. [2284

A miscellaneous collection of state papers, military and naval despatches, and official documents relating to the Civil War, together with a great number of illustrative anecdotes and poems. The arrangement is chronological, and a day-by-day summary of events introduces each volume. Until the publication of the *Official records* of the war of the Rebellion by the United States, this collection was much relied upon ; and although no longer authoritative, it is still useful.   W. MacD.

Morton, Oliver Perry. FOULKE, WILLIAM DUDLEY. Life of Oliver P. Morton, including his speeches. Indianapolis : Bowen-Merrill. 1899. 2v. $6.   [2285

"In any list of a dozen men most prominent in civil life during the Civil War period, Oliver P. Morton's name would pretty surely be found. . . . Whether he were an able demagogue or a statesman was and is the question. His biographer has given us a book which will help the historian, for it is a fair presentation of the acts and events of Morton's life, without overstraining to force them into consistency or to justify them." *American hist. rev.*, 4: 570.

Moss, Lemuel. Annals of the United States

Christian Commission. Phil.: Lippincott. 1868. [2286

The author, in his preface, states that the work was prepared at the request and under the superintendence of the Commission ; and that no attempt is made to discuss the causes or consequences of the movement, but merely to relate the events which occurred in the course of the Commission's operations. This Commission was organized by a convention of the Y. M. C. A. of the loyal states "to promote the spiritual and temporal welfare of the men of the army and navy." Pp. 602–638 contain a list of delegates.

Navy in the Civil War. N. Y.: Scribner. 1883. 3 v. $1 ea. Contents: 1. Soley, J. R. The blockade and the cruisers. — 2. Ammen, D. The Atlantic coast. — 3. Mahan, A. T. The Gulf and inland waters. [2287

"In the three volumes on the *Navy in the Civil War* the division of the subject is not clearly defined. 'The Blockade' was on the 'Atlantic coast' and also on the 'Gulf' and the 'Inland waters' connected with the sea on both sides of the Florida Keys. This ambiguity leads to repetition, and the same events sometimes appear in two of the volumes." *Nation*, 37: 121.

For individual notes, see entry for each volume, sect. 2328, 2102, 2274.

Nichols, *Maj.* **George Ward.** Story of the great march. N. Y.: Harper. 1865. $1.50. [2288

Major Nichols joined General Sherman at Atlanta and was at once placed upon his staff. The *Nation* says that "the volume which he now presents to the public is compiled from notes taken on the spot, and has, therefore, freshness, raciness and vigor. There is included in it an appendix containing the official reports of the campaigns of Georgia and the Carolinas, the letters pertaining to the famous conference, Sherman's testimony before the Committee on the War, and much other matter necessary for the complete illustration of the subject. Altogether it is a valuable addition to our war literature. . . . If the reader hopes for revelations . . . he will be disappointed. . . . Nevertheless, the book is full of interest. Military movements . . . are made intelligible to the uninitiated." In style the sentences of the writer "are photographic of the march. They have a dash of national music in them ; but the instruments sometimes get dust-clogged." *Nation*, 1: 250.

Nicolay, John George. The outbreak of Rebellion. (Campaigns of the Civil War, 1.) N. Y.: Scribner. 1881. $1. [2289

Mr. Nicolay tells how the southern states left the Union ; how the national flag was fired upon ; how the North responded ; how both sides skirmished on the border, and, finally, came into pitched battle at Bull Run. He tells it — as it appears in his mind — admirably well. That is to say, he narrates those events, and those only, which are worth remembering ; his style is never dull, often brilliant, always clear and concise ; he speaks directly and to the point; and whether we agree with his opinions or not, he gains and holds our undivided attention. The manner in which Mr. Nicolay discusses the causes of Rebellion will necessarily give rise to much controversy. . . . We think that Mr. Nicolay gives undue prominence to the acts of the southern leaders, intolerant, overbearing, scheming and unscrupulous as they undoubtedly were ; and he overestimates the force of southern sentiment in favor of the Union ; and that he entirely fails to bring into sufficient prominence the underlying causes which had been gathering force for many years, and but for the existence of which no conspiracy could have succeeded in creating the mighty conflict of 1861–1865." *Nation*, 33: 398.

Our living and our dead; ed. by Stephen D. Pool. Raleigh, N. C., Sept., 1873–March, 1876. 17 nos. in 4v. [2290

This magazine, which appeared from Sept., 1873, to August, 1874, in newspaper form, was the official organ of the North Carolina branch of the Southern Historical Society, and undertook to do for the history of North Carolina in the Civil War what the parent society undertook for the Confederacy. It prints many official reports and many sketches prepared for its pages by surviving members of the various commands. It did not confine its attention to the Civil War, but printed numerous articles on the past history of the state, on education, etc. Its chief value lies in its official reports and historical sketches of separate commands.　　　　　　　　　　　　S. B. W.

Palfrey, *Brig. - Gen.* **Francis Winthrop.** The Antietam and Fredericksburg. (Campaigns of the Civil War, 5.) N. Y.: Scribner. 1882. $1. [2291

"Two features are distinctly noticeable in the book which General Palfrey has here given us: first, there is a certain flavor of the time itself, which could only be recalled by an actor in it ; second, there is abundant evidence of historical qualifications in the author — conscientious study of all the data available, good judgment in digesting and reconciling these data, clear and straightforward expression of well-founded opinions. The story is one of great interest. . . . Its manner of treatment and its literary execution are admirable. One battle being a dismal failure, and the other little more than a half-success, the narration of them must involve any author in constant criticism. General Palfrey has not been sparing of this, but we believe his strictures are in general abundantly justified by the facts. Of McClellan the author holds substantially the same opinion that has been expressed by General Webb and Mr. Ropes in the preceding numbers of this series." *Nation*, 34: 172.

Paris, Louis Philippe Albert d'Orléans, *comte* **de.** Battle of Gettysburg. Phil.: Porter. [c. 1886.] Coates. $1.50. [2292

"It is . . . especially fortunate that among the many accounts of this great battle which have been published, there is one to which the reader can turn with confidence that its author is free from partiality or any desire to do more than truthfully tell his story, and, knowing that he has devoted years of study to his subject and carefully consulted all authorities, feel sure that he has given an account of Gettysburg which is the fairest and most graphic story of that battle that has yet been or probably ever will be written. This author is the Count of Paris, author of the *History of the Civil War in America* [see next title], who has devoted three chapters to the Gettysburg campaign, which, with his authority, are now issued in a volume by themselves, edited by Col. John P. Nicholson, himself an enthusiastic student of the great Rebellion. . . . The volume is well printed, and seems, with a very few slips here and there, to be exceedingly well translated. There are three well-executed maps, besides interesting addenda containing a very full itinerary of the Army of the Potomac during the months of June and July, 1863, and showing the organization of that army and the returns of casualties on both sides." Wm. Eliot Furness, in *Dial* (Chicago), 7 : 126.

—— History of the Civil War in America ; tr. from the French.   Phil. : Porter & Coates. 1875–88.   Coates.   4v. $3.50 ea.   [2293

"No other historian of the Civil War can compare with him in grasp of the subject as a whole, and in judicious proportioning of the parts." J. D. Cox, in *Nation*, 47 : 379.

"The Count's history is so animated, so vigorously written, so fair, so full of just and generous appreciation of the military virtues of the contesting armies and their leaders, that it is a great gift to the people of this country. . . . As a military history the Count's work leaves, it is true, much to be desired. He does not, for instance, give sufficient space to stating the military problems, to explaining them in such a way that they can be apprehended by the non-professional reader. Nor does he as a rule sum up the results of military criticism on the different campaigns in such a way as to afford the student the advantage of his superior military knowledge and judgment. But as a narrator of military events the Count has few superiors. He is sufficiently clear, — or at least would be, if his publishers furnished more maps, — his style is always animated and often brilliant, and his evident familiarity with and earnest interest in the great events which he brings before the reader's mind carry his audience with him." His narrative is just and careful in the extreme. The volumes need an index. John C. Ropes, in *Dial*, 9 : 33.

Patterson, *Maj.-Gen* **Robert.** Narrative of the campaign in the valley of the Shenandoah, in 1861.   Phil.   1865.   [2294

This is General Patterson's vindication of himself in his conduct of operations collateral to the Bull Run battle, for which he was much criticised. A question of responsibility between him and General Scott was involved. Patterson's services in the Mexican War and his very high standing as a citizen added interest to the historical discussion. *Per contra*, the paper on the same campaign in Mass. Mil. Hist. Soc. *Papers* (v. 1, no. 3), by Colonel J. L. Livermore, should be read. The two make an excellent example of military discussion in admirable temper, tone and thoroughness.
                                        J. D. C.

Phisterer, *Capt.* **Frederick.** Statistical record of the armies of the United States. (Campaigns of the Civil War, supplementary vol.) N. Y. : Scribner.   1883. $1.   [2295

"This volume is a supplement to the collection of monographs on the *Campaigns of the Civil War*, . . . and completes the work. As an addition, it is valuable ; as the completing supplement, it is very inadequate. As the title shows, it is only a record of the Union armies, the statistics of the Confederate armies being almost totally ignored. It is all but wholly compiled with regard to military organizations, as if intended only to satisfy the special historical interest of members of such organizations. . . . Its Part 1, embracing 80 pages, specifies President Lincoln's 'Calls for troops,' the 'Organizations mustered into the service of the United States,' the 'Military divisions, departments and districts of the United States,' the 'Military division of the United States forces,' the 'Principal armies,' the 'Army corps,' the 'Strength of the army at various dates,' the 'Honors' conferred by Congress for special merits, the 'Losses' sustained by the army collectively, and the 'National cemeteries.' Part 3 — upward of 90 pages — contains only lists of 'General officers of the United States' (according to rank, and with dates of appointment, promotion, death, or mustering out), of 'General officers of states entering service in April, 1861,' and of 'General officers deceased while in the service.' Part 2 is the main portion of the volume, presenting, in 160 pages, a full 'Chronological record of engagements, battles, etc.,' — no fewer than 2,261, — with a partial list of losses, and an alphabetical index ; but this division, too, gives only scanty information, and mostly information of no general interest." *Nation*, 36 : 475.

Piatt, Donn. Memories of the men who saved the Union.   N. Y. : Belford.   1887.
                                        [2296

The author was a young Ohio Democrat who had been Secretary of Legation with Mr. Mason at Paris before the war. He served in the national army in the great conflict, chiefly on the staff of General Schenck. Afterward he was known as a witty, slashing journalist, "on his own hand." He had a large acquaintance with men in public life, and hit them off in a brilliant way, often with amusing shrewdness, never with judicial estimate. This book is a series of such essays on Lincoln, Stanton, Chase, Seward and General Thomas. When he indulges in hero-worship, his devotion has no bounds. When he dislikes, he is equally without measure. In either case he is entertaining, and, for those who form their judgments on wider reading, his "hits" often help to give life to the sketch of a character.   J. D. C.

Pickett, *Brig. - Gen.* **George Edward.** PICKETT, *Mrs.* LASALLE CORBELL. Pickett and his men.   Atlanta, Ga. : Foote.   1899. $2.   [2297

"In this handsome volume the widow of the Confederate General who led his division in the historic and desperate charge at Gettysburg relates the facts of his military career. She does more : she tells parts of the romantic story of her own married life in the closing year of the Civil War, and the strange experiences of the interval between the wreck of the Confederacy and the full establishment of peace, when the survivors of the southern army could settle themselves to industrious bread-winning with assurance of unmolested safety. These passages have a value that no other chapters of the book can possess. Her outline of her hero's life is authentic, and her praise of him and his devoted followers is eloquent, yet this deals with history that others could write, if not in such glowing terms. But her personal experience is unique and all her own. . . . She was in Richmond when it fell into our hands, half destroyed by the fires set by the retreating Confederates. . . . With dramatic instinct the story is begun here." J. D. Cox, in *Nation*, 69: 303.

Pittenger, William. Daring and suffering. Phil.: Daughaday. 1863.

—— *Same*, 2d ed. : Capturing a locomotive. Phil.: Lippincott. 1882.

—— *Same*, 3d ed. [rewritten and enl.]: Daring and suffering. N. Y.: War Pub. Co. 1887.

—— *Same*, 4th ed. : The great locomotive chase. N. Y.: Alden. [c. 1893.] Phil.: Penn Pub. Co. $1.25. [2298

"This story is founded upon what was unquestionably one of the most remarkable of the minor incidents of the war. About the time of the battle of Shiloh, Mitchel's division of Buell's army was detached to advance from Nashville toward the railroad connecting Memphis with Chattanooga and Richmond. It was then planned to destroy the bridges on the railroad from Chattanooga to Atlanta. . . . If Mitchel could fortify and hold his position until reinforced, the connection between the eastern and western armies of the rebels would be completely broken. The destruction of the railroad was entrusted to twenty-four men, under the leadership of J. J. Andrews. . . . These men penetrated the southern lines, in disguise, almost to Atlanta." They seized a part of a train and started toward Chattanooga, the conductor and engineer in pursuit. Owing to various delays Andrews was unable to destroy the bridges behind him. His pursuers gained on him ; his engine broke down ten miles from Chattanooga, and the men scattered, but all were captured. Eight were hanged. The others were imprisoned and treated with frightful cruelty. Some escaped after six months, and the others were exchanged five months later. "The author (one of the survivors) has himself told the story once before, in a book entitled *Daring and suffering ; or The great railroad adventure*, . . . published in 1863. . . . In rewriting it the author has . . . enlarged and amplified the story, and has told it much better than he did twenty years ago." *Nation*, 34: 43.

In a later notice of a new edition [1887] of Mr. Pittenger's narrative again rewritten and published under its early title, *Daring and suffering*, the *Nation* warns readers " that the unquestionable reliance which may be placed upon his account of what he saw must not be taken as a reason for receiving with the same confidence his opinions upon the campaign plans of Buell or of Mitchel." *Nation*, 45: 358.

Plum, William Rattle. The military telegraph during the Civil War. Chicago: Jansen. 1882. 2v. [2299

"This is a curious medley of trivial personal anec-

dotes about telegraph operators, glimpses of hazardous war service, an interesting chapter on military cryptographs, a little valuable history, and, as expressed in the title, a running account of the war." *Nation*, 35: 228.

Polk, *Lt.-Gen.* **Leonidas.** POLK, WILLIAM MECKLENBURG. Leonidas Polk, bishop and general. N. Y.: Longmans. 1893. 2v. $4. [2300

This work, by the son of Lieut.-Gen. Polk, treats both his ecclesiastical and military career. The work is based largely on family correspondence and official documents, a number of which are reproduced. To a large extent the story is told in the words of its actors. The history of the celebrated quarrel with Bragg is given in a calm and dignified way and with no bitterness of spirit. General Polk was high in command in the army of the West, and the carefulness, temperate judgment and literary skill shown in the book will commend it as of especial value for the history of domestic life in the South and of the Civil War in Kentucky and Tennessee.   S. B. W.

Pollard, Edward Albert. The lost cause. N. Y. : Treat. 1866. [2301

A book struck off at a white heat by a Richmond editor of the most uncompromising secessionist principles, who was utterly unappreciative of northern character and sentiment. Valuable for the southern side of the slavery controversy and the Civil War, though necessarily untrustworthy because of the writer's temper, lack of judgment and inability to get complete information. Pollard is savagely hostile to President Davis. The book is written in an interesting, but turgid and oratorical style.   R. C. H. C.

Pond, George E. The Shenandoah valley in 1864. (Campaigns of the Civil War, 11.) N. Y.: Scribner. 1883. $1. [2302

"This book deals with one of the most exciting and interesting of the subordinate campaigns of the war. It is written with unusual clearness ; the arrangement is lucid, the style good, the description simple and straightforward. The book is as interesting as a novel. The maps are better than in many of the series. From an historical standpoint, however, the merits of Mr. Pond's book are more doubtful. There is nothing intemperate in it, and the author has evidently aimed at fairness. He is probably unconscious that his field of view is so filled with the deeds of the Federal army and its leaders as to leave space for only a distant, imperfect and sometimes incorrect view of the Confederates." *Nation*, 36: 218.

Porter, *Admiral* **David Dixon.** Incidents and anecdotes of the Civil War. N. Y. : Appleton. 1885. $2. [2303

Nobody in the navy saw more of the Civil War than Admiral Porter, and few equalled him in " spinning yarns." He has made a most racy and entertaining book, full of the spirit and the incidents of the time, and of the local color of passing events. Like most purely personal recollections unchecked by careful comparison with contemporary records, it must be used for historical purposes with caution. A comparison, for instance, of the Admiral's story of the occupation of Richmond by General Weitzel in April, 1865, with the correspondence and documents in the *Official records* will emphasize this caution.

J. D. C.

—— Naval history of the Civil War. N. Y. : Sherman Pub. Co. 1889. [2304

Admiral Porter's accuracy of statement has been seriously impeached. His report of conversations and proceedings during President Lincoln's visit to Richmond (the Admiral being present) is said to be untrue to a degree which cannot easily be accounted for.

Powell, *Lt.-Col.* **William Henry.** The Fifth Army Corps, Army of the Potomac. N. Y. : Putnam. 1896. $7.50. [2305

This is "a book sure to be very attractive to the veterans of the Civil War who were members of that corps organization in the Army of the Potomac. For the general reader, who naturally thinks that in a stout octavo he should find a complete history of the campaigns mentioned, it has the defect of being limited to the standpoint of a minor fraction of the army in Virginia. A more serious fault is that the author, in his laudation of McClellan as a commander, pays no attention to the definite criticisms of that general's campaigns which are based on the fuller knowledge gained since 1862, and especially upon the established fact that his army was greatly superior in numbers and equipment to the Confederates. He also shows a confusion of ideas with regard to the relations of the President, the Cabinet, and Congress to the army which is simply astonishing." J. D. Cox, in *Nation*, 62 : 158.

Reed, Samuel Rockwell. The Vicksburg campaign and the battles about Chattanooga under the command of Gen. U. S. Grant in 1862–63. Cin. : Clarke. 1882. $1. [2306

Mr. Reed was a brilliant editorial writer on the *Cincinnati Gazette*, whose style was clear and forcible, and whose rôle was that of *advocatus diaboli*, challenging the admission of a great reputation to the list of the immortals. His criticism of Grant (and incidentally of Sherman) is acute, ingenious, and sophistical ; bitterly hostile, unrelenting and armed by whatever a very industrious study of the records could discover. Utterly misleading to the casual reader, it will prove suggestive, and a spur in the investigation of new points to the thorough student.

J. D. C.

Riddle, Albert Gallatin. Recollections of war times. N. Y. : Putnam. 1895. $2.50.

[2307

The author was a member of Congress from 1861 to 1863 and was almost continuously in Washington thereafter. He writes from a Republican standpoint of the war measures, early reconstruction, the election of 1864, ·and of Lincoln's death. The retreat from the first battle of Bull Run is graphically described. The personal comments and gossip about contemporaries give the work a peculiar value. In the appendix are addresses on Stanton and on John Brown. E. E. S.

Ropes, John Codman. The army under

Pope. (Campaigns of the Civil War, 4.) N. Y. : Scribner. 1881. $1. [2308

"The author says of Pope roundly in the outset that ' he was a brave and zealous officer, but destitute of military judgment.' Mr. Ropes's story, we think, does not fully sustain the latter clause. . . . [The] book is not quite so tender toward the Confederates as Webb's. Some severe criticism is bestowed on Jackson for his risky movement clear around Pope's extreme right and rear to Manassas. . . . Mr. Ropes has here and there shown the good conduct and fair generalship of McDowell. . . . The accounts of the battles of Groveton, Second Bull Bun or Manassas, and Chantilly show a careful sifting of the reports, and with the maps give any reader a clear and brief compendium of those important combats." *Literary world*, 13 : 204.

—— Story of the Civil War. N. Y. : Putnam. 1894–8. Pt. 1–2. Pt. 1, $1.50. Pt. 2, with case of maps, $2.50. [2309

The second volume of this interesting work "makes good the promise of the first. It is incontestably the most intelligent as well as the most complete and impartial analysis of the campaigns and battles of the great Rebellion, so far given to the world." Mr. Ropes's narrative " is remarkably free from prejudice, and is nowhere marred by the bias of personal friendship or personal enmity. On the other hand, his desire to appear impartial perhaps causes him to praise Lee and Jackson excessively, and to condemn Halleck and Pope more than they deserve. It may be maintained, also, that he is unduly severe at times on the alleged ignorance of Lincoln and Stanton in military affairs. . . . We regret to say, in conclusion, that the maps accompanying this excellent work are far inferior in merit to the text. . . . Since the foregoing was written the distinguished author has died, leaving his work, like that of the Count of Paris, only a little more than half finished. This is a profound loss to history and to the country." James H. Wilson, in *Am. hist. rev.*, 5: 592.

At his death, in 1899, the publishers said: "We shall plan to have the narrative completed by some other historian who will be interested in the general points of view taken by Mr. Ropes, and whose narrative will be made to harmonize as nearly as practicable with that of the original author."

Rusling, James F. Men and things I saw in Civil War days. N. Y. : Eaton ; Methodist Bk. Concern. 1899. $2.50. [2310

"The author served through the war and rose from first lieutenant to brigadier-general of volunteers. The men who are written about are: Lincoln, Andrew Johnson, McClellan, Burnside, Hooker, Meade, Thomas, Sherman, Sheridan, Grant and Lee. There are chapters also on: Campaigning and soldiering; A great quartermaster; The angel of the Third Corps and some army letters. Index." *Publisher's weekly*, 56: 25.

Russell, William Howard. My diary, north and south. London: Bradbury. 1862. 2v. N. Y.: Harper. 1863. [2311

The author was the well-known war correspondent of

the *London times*, a man of intellect, of great energy and enterprise, practised in observation. In our Civil War, especially its earlier part, and in the period immediately before it, he visited both sections for the purpose of gathering information bearing upon our affairs. Some of his earlier letters greatly exasperated our people, but, with due allowance for the unfriendly attitude of the great journal he wrote for, his collection of experiences and observations has great historical value. He was a very effective writer, a leader in the class of war correspondents, and recognized in other departments of literature and learning.   J. D. C.

Schalk, Emil. Campaigns of 1862 and 1863. Phil.: Lippincott. 1863.   [2312

The author was a European officer, and his books (this and an earlier one, *Summary of the art of war*) were among the few manuals in English available for our soldiers during the Civil War. They were written with clearness, applied acknowledged principles of strategy to the actual situation, and criticised with discrimination. The maps were good, and the army, as well as the public, was benefited by the intelligent analysis of the earlier campaigns and suggestive comment on them. The books remain as interesting evidence of what conclusions were reached by contemporaneous criticism, though they are superseded by works based on much fuller knowledge of facts than was then possible.   J. D. C.

Scharf, John Thomas. History of the Confederate States Navy. N. Y.: Rogers. 1887. 2d ed. Albany: McDonough. 1894. $1.50.
          [2313

"Having been himself one of the pupils of the Naval Academy at Richmond, and having borne a creditable part in some of the famous exploits of his service," Mr. Scharf "has exceptional advantages for his task of authorship. He has shown evident diligence in accumulating materials, and his book includes a valuable collection of *mémoires pour servir*. A more careful revision would have saved him from many little inaccuracies in names and dates, and from occasional lapses in the use of his mother tongue. In many chapters his materials have been loosely thrown together, with little regard to style or to structural arrangement. In these respects the book is seriously defective. The most extraordinary feature, however, of Mr. Scharf's otherwise useful book is the undercurrent of political animosity and bitterness which penetrates all his references to the causes of the war and the conduct and motives of the Union leaders. In holding that secession was a constitutional right, he only expresses the sincere conviction of the majority of southern men before the war; but he goes far beyond this, and appears to think that no other view was possible to men of sincerity and average intelligence." J. R. Soley, in *Nation*, 45 : 115.

Schmucker, Samuel Mosheim. History of the Civil War in the United States, 1863, v. 1; rev. and completed by L. P. Brockett. Phil. [c. 1865.]   [2314

Dr. Schmucker was an industrious compiler of historical books in many different fields. His death hav-

ing left this work incomplete, it was finished by another voluminous compiler of miscellaneous books. It is undiscriminating, and is marred by a newspaper-like rhetoric, and it was written too early for the authors to know what was going on behind the scenes, especially on the Confederate side. But it presents the story of the conflict as it was read in the newspapers of the period and in a reasonably compact form.
          F. J. S.

Schofield, *Gen.* **John McAllister.** Forty-six years in the army. N. Y.: Century Co. 1897. $3.   [2315

"The book is not a connected narrative of the author's life. It is rather a collection of notes and comments on events that he had part in. The first two or three chapters are most closely biographical, dealing with his boyhood and education at West Point and his service prior to the outbreak of the great Rebellion. The campaigns of 1861 and 1863 in Missouri are then briefly but lucidly treated. Next follows a series of comments upon Sherman's generalship in the campaigns of Atlanta and the Carolinas, written in 1875, upon the publication of the first edition of Sherman's memoirs. These are followed by a discussion of the campaign of Franklin and Nashville in the autumn of 1864, and of the author's relations to Gen. George H. Thomas in that important crisis. This will no doubt be considered as the most important part of the book. Further comment on Sherman's March to the Sea, its purpose, and its strategy, with the final campaign which resulted in Johnston's surrender, close the treatment of the war period. Entertaining and instructive chapters are given to the French intervention in Mexico, to reconstruction in the South, to army administration in time of peace, and to some of the lessons of the war, military and financial." The author has done his duty to posterity in giving us "his frank and full judgment upon the events in which he bore so important and honorable a part." J. D. Cox, in *Nation*, 66 : 328.

Semmes, *Admiral* **Raphael.** Memoirs of service afloat during the war between the states. Balt.: Kelly. 1869.
—— Service afloat. Balt.: Balt. Pub. Co. 1887. N. Y.: P. J. Kenedy. 1900. $3. [2316

An interesting story of the *Sumter* and the *Alabama*, Confederate cruisers, their construction, and their exploits. The cruise of the *Alabama* in foreign parts is well told. The author commanded each vessel and writes from personal experience. There are a few preliminary chapters justifying the South in trying to secede from the Union.   E. E. S.

Seward, William Henry. (See in the preceding Period, sect. 1957–1959.)

Sheridan, *Lt.-Gen.* **Philip Henry.** Personal memoirs. N. Y.: Webster. 1888. 2v. [2317

"As a book for general reading, Sheridan's *Memoirs* have attractive features that will insure success. . . . For purposes of permanent history, one could wish that the aim had been less popular and more critical; but a long narrative by so distinguished an officer in a great war cannot lack value, even when the narrative is cursory and superficial. . . . The fact that so eminent a soldier could compose so long a memoir without anything approaching a critical or comprehensive judgment of a campaign must be in itself a curious revelation of his military character. . . . The episode of Sheridan's service in reconstruction in Louisiana contains new matter. . . . He claims to have been the real cause of the downfall of Maximilian in Mexico by forcing the hand of our national administration." His story of his observations of the campaigns of Gravelotte and Sedan is interesting, but without instructive criticism. But the book is "a splendid record, which makes a few blemishes only seem a foil for a brilliant career." J. D. Cox, in *Nation*, 48: 100.

— DAVIES, HENRY EUGENE. General Sheridan. (Great commanders.) N. Y.: Appleton. 1895. $1.50.   [2318

Of his book, the author "frankly says that it is a compilation more than a composition, for the basis is necessarily the autobiography of Sheridan, aided by other memoirs of campaigns written by comrades and friends of Davies. The result is a warm eulogy, faithful 'to the leading historical facts, and earnestly espousing the hero's side whenever a question arises between him and any other." J. D. Cox, in *Nation*, 60 : 461.

— NEWHALL, *Col.* FRED. C. With General Sheridan in Lee's last campaign. By a staff officer. Phil.: Lippincott. 1866.   [2319

" A capital book on a capital subject. Of all that has been said and written about ' Cavalry Sheridan,' there is little that gives a fair idea of the man or of his merit. Here we have the story, told in good plain English, full of strong phrases, smacking of the camp and of the field, showing an understanding of the subject that could be got only by real experience, yet not a word of self, not even the author's name. There is a hearty tone, a running, bubbling vein of fun, a style that is made by the subject, and not for it ; now and then a little doubtful English." *Nation*, 3 : 494.

Sherman, John. (See sect. 2323, and in the Period next following, sect. 2412.)

Sherman, *Gen.* William Tecumseh. Memoirs, by himself. N. Y.: Appleton. 1875. 2v.

—— *Same ;* with an appendix bringing his life down to its closing scenes. 4th ed. N. Y.: Webster. 1896. 2v. Appleton. 2v. $5. [2320

" His book is such as our knowledge of him prepared us to expect, and it is a treat. . . . His style is characteristic of the man. It makes no pretensions to grace, finish, or dignity, other than the dignity of simplicity. It is absolutely free from rhetorical ornament, and it does not hesitate to be colloquial in the extreme, but it is admirable in its clearness and directness. . . . He abounds in anecdotes, well told and often humorous, and sometimes he paints a picture in a few phrases, as when he sketches his last view of Atlanta and the battle-fields around it. . . . If it be added that he never in a single instance yields to the temptation to be sentimental, enough has been said about the manner of the book. . . . His blame falls freely upon the

living, but there is not a trace of malice in the book, so far as we can see, and he never goes out of his way to find fault, and never, or very rarely, imputes unworthy motives for the actions which he disapproves. . . . The free use he makes of his letters, orders, and reports gives a very great interest and value to his book. He is never dull, and he contrives to break up and enliven even the accounts of the movement of troops so that the attention never seriously flags. . . . His memoirs close with the great review in Washington, but he appends a concluding chapter on the military lessons of the war, which is full of knowledge, wisdom, and sound sense. His book is one which every true American ought to read, and one which no such man can read without pride and pleasure." *Atlantic monthly*, 36 : 245.

"This new [2d] edition of Sherman's memoirs is enlarged by preliminary and supplementary chapters, and by an appendix made up in the main of letters from officers who served under the General, containing corroboration or criticism of the opinions expressed in the first edition of the book. . . . The ten years which have passed since General Sherman published these memoirs have not diminished the authority of the book or of the author. The correspondence in the appendix to the present edition is good proof that the criticisms to be fairly made upon it are neither very numerous nor important. . . . In some instances he has softened the form while preserving the substance ; in others he has supplied omissions ; in a few he has corrected errors. It may safely be said that, for purposes of military instruction and for giving a clear and fair view of the events described, it takes, and probably will continue to take, the first rank among the personal memoirs of the war period." J. D. Cox, in *Nation*, 42 : 473.

— BOWMAN, *Col.* SAMUEL M., *and Lt.-Col.* RICHARD B. IRWIN. Sherman and his campaigns. N. Y.: Richardson. 1865.   [2321

Although among the earliest of the lives of Sherman, this was among the most authentic. It was written by officers who served with Sherman, and were given access to his papers. They also had the coöperation of leading generals and others who had part in the events narrated. The book is well and clearly written, but is of course subject to the drawback that the *Official records* were not then available, and many important topics were not fully understood. It was, however, a leading authority till Sherman published his own memoirs ten years later.

J. D. C.

— FORCE, *Brig.-Gen.* MANNING FERGUSON. General Sherman. (Great commanders.) N. Y.: Appleton. 1899. $1.50. [2322

This volume " was begun with love, by Gen. Force, a soldier of honorable service in the campaigns which he undertook to describe; but growing disease . . . compelled him to turn over his unfinished task to his friend Gen. Jacob D. Cox, who is, therefore, responsible for the latter (and, measured by the significance of its attempt to fix Sherman's fame among soldiers of genius, the more important) part of the biography. The completion of the work could not have fallen to better hands. . . . The early portions of the book are of unequal satisfactoriness as a specific biography of the man. . . . The movement of the narrative, after Sherman's appearance at the relief of Chattanooga, in October of 1863, leaves nothing for criticism. Especially interesting are the accounts of Sherman's relations towards his peers, like Grant and Thomas." *Nation*, 69: 37.

Sherman, *Gen.* **William Tecumseh** *and* **John.** The Sherman letters. N. Y.: Scribner. 1894. New ed. $2.   [**2323**]

These letters of two brothers to each other cover a period from 1837 to 1891. The editor, Mrs. Thorndike, daughter of General Sherman, connects the correspondence by a series of brief notes, and also exercises the right to cut freely. The letters by General Sherman are the more numerous, possibly due to the fact that the time has not arrived for the publication of many of the letters of Senator Sherman. The letters are not only an interesting illustration of the constant affection of two strong and famous men, widely different in character, but add many lines to the portraiture of contemporary character. They also assist in the proper interpretation of critical events of the Civil War period. General Sherman's letters are particularly frank and energetically express his antagonism to politicians and political methods.

                                        D. R. D.

Smith, Goldwin. The Civil War in America: an address, 1866. London: Simpkin. 1866.   [**2324**]

" It is something more than this title would seem to indicate; it really is a brief account of the people of the free states, of the spirit of their political system, of their social theories and practice, by a philosophic student of history, his defence of all these against the attacks commonly made on them by the friends of absolutism and aristocracy, and his exposition of their virtues and defects. The literary merits of the work are such as by themselves make it worthy the perusal of most readers and the study of most writers." *Nation*, 2: 726.

Smith, *Maj.-Gen.* **Gustavus Woodson.** Battle of Seven Pines. N. Y.: Crawford. 1891.   [**2325**]

General Smith succeeded to the command of the Confederate Army in front of Richmond during the battle of Seven Pines (or Fair Oaks), when General Johnston was disabled by a cannon-shell. Controversy subsequently arose as to the parts of President Davis, and Generals Lee, Johnston, Smith, Longstreet and Huger on the field. General Smith's views are here presented. At the outbreak of the war he was universally regarded as one of the best qualified of the southern officers, a northern man by birth. Ill health prevented him from great activity later, and his career culminated in the battle he here discusses. His contribution to the discussion is, of course, essential to it.   J. D. C.

Smith, *Maj.-Gen.* **Thomas Kilby.** SMITH, WALTER GEORGE. Life and letters of Thomas Kilby Smith, Brevet Major-General United States Volunteers, 1820–1887; by his son. N. Y.: Putnam. 1898. $2.50.   [**2326**]

"During the campaign of Shiloh, the attack on Chickasaw Bluff, the capture of Arkansas Post, the siege of Vicksburg, and the Red River campaign, we have a full current account of the experiences of the writer, his comments on what he saw, his opinions of the men about him and over him, and his transcript of the émotions which stirred him. It would be hard to imagine a more unreserved disclosure. . . . The letters of such a brave gentleman and good soldier, holding the mirror up to his daily life with its adventures, to his own heart with its hopes and fears, its aspirations and its disappointments, must needs be a typical study, which students of the period would not willingly lose." J. D. Cox, in *Nation*, 66: 212.

Snead, Thomas Lowndes. The fight for Missouri, from the election of Lincoln to the death of Lyon. N. Y.: Scribner. 1886. $1.50.   [**2327**]

" This is a lively narrative of the efforts made by the Secessionists of Missouri to carry that state into the southern Confederacy, and of the bold and successful efforts made to resist it by the Union men under the leadership of Frank P. Blair and General Lyon. It bears evidence of the sincerity with which it is written on every page. The writer, who both saw and took an active part in all that he relates, has tried to tell the story with as complete impartiality as is possible to one whose feelings and interests were deeply involved in the struggle. . . . Sterling Price is evidently the author's hero, and the picture presents him as an estimable and able man. . . . This narrative stops with the battle of Wilson's Creek, but enough is told to make it easy to understand why General Price had the confidence of his neighbors and the devotion of his soldiers." J. D. Cox, in *Nation*, 42: 325.

Soley, James Russell. The blockade and the cruisers. (The navy in the Civil War, 1.) N. Y.: Scribner. 1883. $1.   [**2328**]

" The claim of our government was that the blockade was simply a domestic embargo; that subjects of the Confederacy were rebels, and its ships-of-war pirates; and this view was for some time adhered to and asserted on paper. But a blockade is essentially an act of war. The size of the Rebellion, its completely organized government, and the certainty of reprisals, made our position untenable in practice, and almost from the beginning the laws of war were observed as in a foreign war. This subject is discussed with some fulness by Professor Soley, and, with the admirable justice which characterizes his book, he shows that the unfriendliness of England was shown more by her haste to recognize the Confederacy as a belligerent than by the recognition itself. The experiences of the blockading squadrons are given in detail. . . . The career of the Confederate cruisers included some of the most stirring episodes of the war, and is told in some detail. It is customary at the North to refer to it as wanton and wicked. This is natural to the victims of it, but not justified by the facts. It does not appear that their course in the main was without law, or that their acts were different from those of all hostile men-of-war. . . . This book is well arranged, written clearly, without technical terms, and shows great familiarity with the subject. It is marked by thoroughness of preparation, sound judgment and admirable impartiality." J. G. Palfrey, in *Nation*, 36: 387.

—— Sailor boys of '61. Boston: Estes and Lauriat. 1888. $1.50.   [2329

"This clear, spirited and authoritative narrative is indeed quite within the comprehension of children, but it is not at all 'written down' to them or with any special reference to them. It can therefore be read with interest by adults, and we know of no better brief picture of the naval features of our Civil War. The spirit in which Prof. Soley writes is admirable, and southerners can read his pages from beginning to end without offence. So good a text merited better illustrations." *Nation*, 47: 504.

Southern Historical Society. Richmond, Va. Organized in 1869. From 1876 to 1898 it has published 26 volumes of *Papers*.   [2330

Among its other publications is a Roster of general officers, heads of departments, senators, representatives, military organizations, etc., in Confederate service during the war between the states, by C. C. Jones, Jr.

Speed, *Capt.* **Thomas,** *Col.* **R. M. Kelly,** *and Maj.* **Alfred Pirtle.** The Union regiments of Kentucky ; published under the auspices of the Union Soldiers' and Sailors' Monument Assoc. Louisville : Courier-Journal. 1897. $2.   [2331

As many Kentuckians served on either side in the great Rebellion, the history of the Union regiments, of the men who led in organizing them, who held Kentucky in the Union and who won distinction in the field, is an important part of the national struggle in a broader sense than that of some other states. The work has been well done by the collaboration of the three authors. Capt. Speed (Clerk of U. S. Courts) has written the regimental histories and sketches of campaigns, much the greater part of the book ; Colonel Kelly writes the chapter on the political conditions of the state during the war ; and Maj. Pirtle contributes the biographical sketches of general officers and others appointed by the President. The authors all served with distinction, were peculiarly qualified for their task, and their tone and treatment are excellent.
                                                        J. D. C.

Stanton, Edwin McMasters. GORHAM, GEORGE C. Life and public services of Edwin M. Stanton. Boston: Houghton. 1899. 2v. $6.   [2332

"As a defence of Stanton the work is a great success, but there seems to be room to doubt if it will make Stanton popular. . . . If the author would condense these octavo volumes into one and would give more space to a consideration of Stanton's peculiarities, he would spread the fame of his hero and win the popularity that he himself has already earned by his serious undertaking. Stanton deserves to be very prominent among a score of the greatest of our national heroes." Frederic Bancroft, in *Am. hist. rev.*, 4: 745.

"The true view of Mr. Stanton's character seems to be, that, with great intellectual abilities and high ideals, his impulsive nature made him exceptionally liable to the mistakes of intense partisanship. So long as he was under the influence of Lincoln's calmly practical and eminently sane judgment, his honesty and his great powers made him one of the most useful of public officers ; but when left without that leadership, his eccentricities led him into many and great errors. The two large volumes of this biography come short of being historically valuable because they do not get beyond the limits of the thought and action of the period of political storm and stress, and give us no help in correcting the misjudgments inseparable from such a time." J. D. Cox, in *Nation*, 68 : 497.

— WILSON, HENRY, *and* J. S. BLACK. A contribution to history : Edwin M. Stanton, on the eve of the Rebellion. Easton, Pa. 1871.
          [2333

A pamphlet reprint of a magazine controversy about the services of Stanton in President Buchanan's cabinet. Valuable for inside political history of the latter part of Buchanan's administration and the first part of its successor. Covers Buchanan's actions, relief of Sumter, suspected secret societies of Indiana, the abolitionism of Stanton, and the retirement of Cameron from Lincoln's cabinet.   E. E. S.

Stephens, Alexander Hamilton. CLEVELAND, HENRY. Alexander H. Stephens in public and private, with letters and speeches. Phil.: National Pub. Co. 1866.   [2334

The writer deals with Stephens' life to 1866, and appends a number of his letters and speeches. The biography is written in the vein of an admirer, but the delineation of Stephens' character is fair and judicious, and the facts are plainly and accurately stated. It is, however, not a complete biography even for the period covered. The speeches and letters are valuable.
                                                        R. C. H. C.

— JOHNSTON, RICHARD MALCOLM, *and* WILLIAM HAND BROWNE. Life of Alexander H. Stephens. Phil.: Lippincott. 1878. New ed. 1883.   [2335

"This biography does not differ in construction or mode of treatment from other books of the same sort, the subjects of which have been dead for ten or twenty years. The material used is of the kind common in such works, and is drawn from public documents and private letters. The latter, however, indulge in the most intimate personal detail to an extent which seems most extraordinary when it is remembered that the subject of it all is still alive [in 1878, when the book was first published ; Mr. Stephens died 1883], and is a prominent actor upon the stage of public affairs. Apparently Mr. Stephens desires to become an historical character during his own lifetime, and listen to the criticism which is usually withheld while a man is still before the world. The freak seems a strange one, and is not perhaps in the best taste ; but if Mr. Stephens enjoys it there is nothing more to be said. Mr. Stephens's biographers have performed their portion of the work very creditably. They have kept themselves in the background and allowed their hero to tell his own story in his own way. . . . The style is simple and unpretentious, but it is disfigured by the constant use of the present tense in narrating past events." *Nation*, 27: 241.

Stevens, Thaddeus. CALLENDER, EDWARD B. Thaddeus Stevens, commoner. Boston: Williams. 1882. [2336

This work is in no sense a biography, but consists of sketches of the more important incidents in the life of Stevens. It does not merit much consideration, since the publication of the biography by McCall. Stevens did not enter Congress until 1849, when he was 57 years old. During the Civil War he was Chairman of the Committee on Ways and Means. He represented the type of uncompromising hostility to the leaders of the southern rebellion during the early period of reconstruction. D. R. D.

— McCALL, SAMUEL W. Thaddeus Stevens. (American statesmen.) Boston: Houghton. 1899. $1.25. [2337

"Thaddeus Stevens is one of those parliamentary leaders who are peculiarly identified with the policy and the legislation of a critical time. We talk of the President's policy and the policy of Congress as distinctly marked in the political handling of our Civil War, and should not be far wrong in saying that, within the Union party, it was Lincoln's choice of measures against the theories of Stevens which were in debate. . . . Mr. McCall's limitations in space have made a current sketch of this history all that was possible for him; but he has given it with fair accuracy of drawing, very properly making it his task to present the personality of Mr. Stevens rather than a full discussion of measures, or an estimate of the men with whom he acted and the reasons for his leadership. The little volume will satisfy the popular demand for a short story of the life of a man so prominent in the politics of the 'war period,' while it will be useful to the student as an outline." J. D. Cox, in *Nation*, 69: 190.

Stevenson, Alexander F. Battle of Stone's River, near Murfreesboro', Tenn., 1862–3. Boston: Osgood. 1884. [2338

This book was written by one who had part in the battle, and who was moved to prepare a critical narration of it by his conviction that contradictions, grave errors and omissions occurred in the reports then before the public. It is a serious, intelligent and honest contribution to the history of the battle. Some points made were and are matters of controversy; but the book is an able effort to bring truth to light, and should be read by any one who seeks to understand the battle thoroughly and to judge of its effect upon reputations of officers engaged. J. D. C.

Stillé, Charles Janeway. History of the United States Sanitary Commission. Phil.: Lippincott. 1866. [2339

"It is in reality a most important and valuable contribution to American history; more important, we venture to assert, at the risk of appearing guilty of exaggeration, than anything that can be dug out of

the archives of the War Department or found in the *Congressional globe*. For, we are satisfied it will be admitted, and perhaps more readily a hundred years hence than now, that the Sanitary Commission, from the very first hour of its conception, represented the American people more fully and fairly in its best and noblest mood — in its intelligence, its purity of purpose, its far-sightedness, its humanity, its patriotism — than either the Government or the politicians. . . . Mr. Stillé is entitled to the credit of having furnished a calm, well-written, and dignified memorial of the very noblest episode in our history." *Nation*, 3: 367.

Stine, James H. History of the Army of the Potomac. Phil.: Rodgers Prtg. Co. 1892. Wash.: Stine. 1893. [2340

This book grew out of the appointment of the author by the Association of the First Army Corps, to be the historian of that Corps of the Army of the Potomac. It has many of the characteristics of an historical address to such a body of men, such as eulogies of men not widely known, anecdotes of individual bravery, and the opinions of officers of various ranks upon the Union and the Confederate side concerning battles. It is therefore material for the more methodical historian rather than a sifted discussion of the rise and conduct of an army. G. A. T.

Stuart, *Maj.-Gen.* James Ewell Brown. McCLELLAN, *Maj.* HENRY BRAINERD. Life and campaigns of Major-General J. E. B. Stuart, commander of the cavalry of the Army of Northern Virginia. Boston: Houghton. 1885. $4. [2341

Written by a chief of staff of the Confederate army and largely reminiscent. Covers the capture of John Brown, battle of Manassas Junction, and subsequent military history on the Confederate side to the Wilderness campaign. Authentic records and sources seem to have been used. A roll of the second Regiment of Virginia Cavalry is appended. E. E. S.

Sumner, Charles. (See in the preceding Period, sect. 1967–1969.)

Swinton, William. Campaigns of the Army of the Potomac: a critical history. N. Y.: 1866. New ed., rev. N. Y.: Scribner. 1882. $3. [2342

On the appearance of the new edition in 1882 the *Nation* said: "We have here a very old and valued friend in a new and attractive dress. The reputation of Mr. Swinton's *Army of the Potomac* is so well established that we need do no more than to say here, once for all, that it is a work well-nigh indispensable to the student of the war. The general correctness of the narrative, the spirit of fairness with which praise and blame are awarded, the perspicuity of the style, have always been admitted. Still, written as the book was, a year only after the war was over, many topics were more or less imperfectly treated, and a revision which should have embodied all that has been since ascertained would have been a very great boon. This we do not find in the present edition, nor, in fact, does Mr. Swinton pretend to give it to us. All that he has done is to correct some trifling errors in the first issue, and to add twenty pages of notes in an appendix. These notes are, however, valuable." *Nation*, 35: 429. See end of note, sect. 2271.

—— Twelve decisive battles of the war. N. Y. : Dick & Fitzgerald. [c. 1867.] $3.50.   [2343

The twelve battles which the author has selected as decisive are Bull Run, Donelson, Shiloh, Antietam, Murfreesboro, The Monitor and Merrimac, Vicksburg, Gettysburg, Wilderness, Atlanta, Nashville and Five Forks. The *Nation* says of the book that "though it has many defects of style, it is in many parts a book of intense and absorbing interest. The preface declares that the book is designed more for popular than professional instruction. . . . The tone of the book is satisfactory. The writer appears to have been in a much better humor when he wrote it than while he was at work upon the *Campaigns of the Army of the Potomac*. His treatment of prominent officers is more impartial and more just. . . . The author's plan of dividing each sketch into three sections, which he calls the prelude, the battle, and the results is excellent. . . . He collects his material with industry and uses it with skill. He has been much with the army, which in itself gives him great advantages for writing of it, and he seems to have a good theoretical knowledge of the art of war. He is a clear, forcible and dramatic writer. Unfortunately we do not know just how much confidence to repose in his accuracy. We give him the credit of taking pains to be correct ; but he is certainly sometimes inaccurate, sometimes careless, and he sometimes exaggerates excessively." *Nation*, 5: 27.

Taylor, *Lt.-Gen.* **Richard.** Destruction and reconstruction. N. Y. : Appleton. 1879. $2.   [2344

The military recollections of a lieutenant-general in the Confederate army, especially in the Louisiana campaign of 1863 and 1864. Of some value to persons interested in this subject. The last few chapters are valuable to a student of the reconstruction period. They set forth the author's futile attempts to assist the governments of President Johnson and his despair for the South under negro suffrage and the governments inaugurated by Congress. Hopeless for the future. Written in a sarcastic and not unattractive style.   E. E. S.

Temple, Oliver Perry. East Tennessee and the Civil War. Cin. : Clarke. 1899. $3.50.   [2345

Judge Temple is one of the few survivors of the men who had a distinguished part in the events which made East Tennessee the home of national loyalty when the Civil War began, and who became supporters of Emancipation (himself a slaveholder) when the fate of slavery and of secession became one. No one had more original knowledge of the history of the mountain region in the great struggle, or was better fitted by acquirements and judicial mind to tell it. The book is a leading authority upon its subject, and interesting as a history reaching back to the first settlements of the Holston valley.   J. D. C.

Tenney, William Jewett. Military and

naval history of the Rebellion in the United States; with biographical sketches of deceased officers. N. Y. : Appleton. 1866.   [2346

The author was the editor of the *Annual cyclopœdia*, and the book is a painstaking and very full history of the Civil War, covering not only the principal battles by land and sea, but also important skirmishes, and including most official documents, besides describing with diagrams the hospital and ambulance service and elucidating the manner of organizing and equipping troops, methods of fortification, treatment of prisoners, and political and civil affairs incidental to the war. The biographical sketches cover officers of both armies who died between May 24, 1861, and June 23, 1865, regardless of rank, provided their names were in any way brought before the public. The narrative is, however, colorless and has the aridity of an encyclopædia, being far better for reference than for continued reading. It was compiled too early for the author to command all the sources of information enjoyed by later writers.   F. J. S.

Thayer, William Makepeace. A youth's history of the Rebellion. Boston : Walker. 1865. 4v. N. Y. : Miller. 1879. 4v.   [2347

Narratives in conversational style, written during the progress or close upon the end of the war by a clergyman whose books of similar character have had a wide circulation. They reflect the warm feeling and prejudices of the North, and freely use the epithets current towards the supporters of the Confederacy. Some religious moralizings have an eye to Sunday-school purposes. The books are chiefly valuable as memorials of the spirit of the time.   G. A. T.

Thomas, *Maj.-Gen.* **George Henry.** Coppée, Henry General Thomas. (Great commanders series.) N. Y. : Appleton. 1893. $1.50.   [2348

"The tone of Professor Coppée's life of Gen. Thomas is in refreshing contrast to some other publications on the same subject. He has found it easy to eulogize his hero without vilifying others. . . . The author's characterizations of Gen. Thomas are happy, both in the development of the man in the earlier chapters, and in the summary near the end of the book. The military preëminence which is attributed to him over all his contemporaries will not be accepted as the final verdict. . . . In one respect, however, we had the right to expect from the author another sort of workmanship than that which he has given us. It certainly would not be asking too much to demand that a résumé of campaigns should be accurate and intelligible. The errors in the present one are so numerous and so serious that it is not going too far to say that the more familiar the reader may be with the military operations of 1864, the more he will be puzzled in reading these pages. . . . The combat of New Hope Church is said to have been (p. 209) 'one of the most terrible battles of the war,' but the description which follows is that of the affair at Pickett's Mill, which occurred at another time and place." Many such errors are noted. J. D. Cox, in *Nation*, 58: 125.

—— Piatt, Donn. General George H. Thomas : a critical biography ; with concluding chapters

by Henry V. Boynton.   Cin. : Clarke.   1893.
$3.   [2349

" The title of this book is a misnomer. The name
of Gen. Thomas is only a stalking-horse for coarse
abuse of Gens. Grant, Sherman, Sheridan and other
prominent officers in our Civil War. It is not confined
to events or campaigns in which Thomas had a part.
As much space is given to campaigns in Virginia or
on the Mississippi as to those in Kentucky or Tennessee. The object seems to be simply to make occasion
to pronounce everything done by Grant and Sherman,
especially, to be stupid and wicked, and themselves
destitute of character as soldiers or as men." The
extravagance of the book " defeats itself, and it will
pass into literature as railing and not criticism."
J. D. Cox, in *Nation*, 57 : 333, 351.

— VAN HORNE, THOMAS BUDD. Life of
Major-General George H. Thomas.   N. Y.:
Scribner.   1882. $3.   [2350

The author has probably injured General Thomas,
rather than honored him, by his ill-advised attempt
to clear him of the charge of slowness at Nashville.
He has unfortunately revived an unpleasant discussion. He has not carefully analyzed the situation, but
has gathered a formidable number of criticisms and
suspicions and has failed to refute them. Instead of
disproving them, he has contented himself with sweeping assertions, with condemning the military plans of
every officer to whom Thomas was subordinate, and
with depreciating the services of other commanders.
" The biography is nowhere a critical examination of
the campaigns touched upon." J. D. Cox, in *Nation*,
35 : 335.

Toombs, Robert. STOVALL, PLEASANT A.
Robert Toombs, statesman, speaker, soldier,
sage.   N. Y.: Cassell.   1892.   [2351

Toombs was a resident of Georgia, and for many
years a member of the national House of Representatives and Senate. Although a southern states-rights
Whig, and devoted to the political fortunes of Webster,
he was an intense defender of slavery, and is typically
regarded as a " southern fire-eater." He was talked
of for the presidency of the southern confederacy,
and his differences with Jefferson Davis are here presented. Toombs opposed the firing on Sumter. The
biographer writes in a moderate spirit, though with
warm affection for Toombs. The biography, however,
is incomplete, several important episodes in Toombs'
life are omitted ; and throughout, there is missing
much that would be interesting in the life of such an
energetic personality. There is an account of Toombs'
lecture in Boston on slavery.   D. R. D.

An eulogistic memoir, rather than a biography, but
more judicious than the title would indicate. The
treatment of political questions is fairer than in most
writings of this class. Candid and unreserved in criticisms of South as well as North. Valuable for all public issues after the annexation of Texas, and especially
on the organization of the Confederacy and its later
internal difficulties.   E. E. S.

Townsend, *Maj. - Gen.* Edward Davis.
Anecdotes of the Civil War. N. Y. : Appleton.
1884. $1.25.   [2352

Gen. Townsend was on the personal staff of Gen.
Scott in 1861, was transferred to the Adjutant-General's office as Chief Assistant, and was closest of
all our officers of rank to the War Department and
Army Headquarters during the Civil War. He was
among the most able administrative officers, clear in
intellect, perfect in temper, the soul of system, honor
and conscience. No one had closer contact with military affairs at Washington. His modest title of *Anecdotes* for his book does not do justice to the capital
importance of many things he relates, though he mingles interesting matter of varying degrees of weight.
No writer of personal recollections can claim greater
authority for what he tells. We can only wish he had
told more. His style is simple and direct, relying
wholly on clearness in presenting facts.   J. D. C.

Trobriand, *Maj. - Gen.* Régis de. Four
years with the Army of the Potomac ; tr. by
George K. Dauchy. Boston: Ticknor.   1889.
Houghton. $3.   [2353

The author was a French resident of New York and
Colonel of the 55th N. Y. Vol. Infantry, taking the field
in Sept., 1861. His record was an honorable one. His
book was written in French and first published in
France. It is well translated. Its special merit is its
transparent candor and its intelligent judgment of
men and events. Those most familiar, personally,
with the Army of the Potomac will rate it highest.
Its personal descriptions and characterizations of officers are of great value. It is among the best of the
memoirs of the period.   J. D. C.

Trumbull, Henry Clay. War memories of
an army chaplain. N. Y. : Scribner.   1898.
$2.   [2354

" Mr. Trumbull has given us a book upon the Civil
War which is in some respects unique." His " position in his regiment was exceptionally free from irk-
some conditions. He had a cordial understanding
with the commandant, who took uncommon pains to
give dignity and official recognition to the chaplain's
work. . . . He was recognized by the officers as a useful supporter of discipline and an aid to good relations
with the rank and file, and by the latter as a friend in
need and a hearty sympathizer in suffering or in sick-
ness." J. D. Cox, in *Nation*, 67 : 316.

Turchin, *Brig.-Gen.* John Basil. Chicka-
mauga. (Noted battles for the Union during
the Civil War.) Chicago: Fergus Printing
Co.   1888.   [2355

" This book is so good it is a thousand pities it is not
better, for it is so disfigured by minor and petty errors
and omissions that a reader familiar with the subject
is . . . much annoyed. . . . Very few if any better accounts of a campaign culminating in a battle during
our Civil War have been written. . . . General Turchin, a Russian by birth and education, is a thorough
American in feeling and conviction. He writes, therefore, from a standpoint impossible to one born and
educated among us. His work on this account alone
has a distinct importance of its own." It " is admirably printed and fully illustrated with maps, besides
containing an invaluable index." *Literary world*,
20 : 142.

United States. *Congress.* Fort-Pillow massacre : report from the joint select committee on the conduct of the war. (38th Cong. 1st sess., House report, 65.) Wash. 1869. [2356

Here is the testimony taken by Messrs. Wade and Gooch as a sub-committee of the joint select committee on the conduct of the war, together with its report, which was adopted as that of the full committee. The testimony was taken chiefly at the Mound City, Ill., hospital, most of the witnesses being wounded survivors of the Fort-Pillow affair, which occurred April 12, 1864. The operations of Gen. Forrest against Union City, Tenn., and Paducah, Ky., just before the capture of Fort Pillow, are also touched upon.

F. J. S.

United States. *State Department.* Correspondence concerning claims against Great Britain [the so-called Alabama claims]. (41st Cong. 1st sess., Sen. ex. doc. 11.) Wash. 1869-70. 5v.

—— Papers relating to the treaty of Washington. Geneva arbitration. (42d Cong. 3d sess., House ex. doc. 1, part 1.) Wash. 1872-3. 4v.

—— The case of Great Britain as laid before the Tribunal of arbitration convened at Geneva. (42d Cong. 2d sess., House ex. doc. 282.) Wash. 1872. 3v.

—— The counter case of Great Britain as laid before the Tribunal of arbitration convened at Geneva. (42d Cong., 2d sess., House ex. doc. 324.) Wash. 1872.

—— Argument at Geneva : a complete collection of the forensic discussions on the part of the United States and of Great Britain before the Tribunal of arbitration under the treaty of Washington. N. Y.: Appleton. 1873.

—— Official correspondence on the claims of the United States in respect to the Alabama. London : Longmans. 1867. [2357

Of the five volumes of *Correspondence concerning claims against Great Britain* three consist chiefly of communications passing between Secretary Seward and Minister Adams and other representatives of the United States abroad during the Civil War, the other two containing appendices in the form of newspaper extracts, judicial and parliamentary reports, and miscellaneous papers bearing on the American grievances against England. The four volumes of *Papers relating to the treaty of Washington* contain the American and British cases and counter cases as laid before the Geneva tribunal, argument of counsel on both sides, report of the United States agent, award of the tribunal, opinions of the arbitrators, and opinions of European statesmen and journals on the construction of the treaty ; but the British case as given here lacks the appendices containing additional documents, correspondence, and evidence which cause it to fill four volumes published separately. The *Official correspondence* published by the Longmans in 1867 is that between Minister Adams and Earls Russell and Clarendon regarding the Alabama and Shenandoah, and it includes documents regarding the former use made of North American ports by vessels sailing under the flags of the revolting South American colonies. The Appleton volume of *Argument* is identical with v. 3 of the *Papers relating to the treaty.* Others of this series of papers are to be found elsewhere in the government documents, but not in every case in the same form.

F. J. S.

United States Sanitary Commission. Narrative of privations and sufferings of United States officers and soldiers while prisoners of war in the hands of the rebel authorities. Phil. 1864. [2358

Dr. Valentine Mott was chairman of this commission to take evidence, which relates for the most part to the treatment of federal prisoners in Libby prison and at Belle Isle and, in contradistinction thereto, to the treatment of Confederate prisoners at Fort Delaware, David's Island and Johnson's Island. The report, which summarizes the evidence, is followed by the evidence itself, taken at Annapolis and Baltimore hospitals and elsewhere. There is furthermore testimony by Confederate prisoners as to the clothing and food issued to them while in the Confederate military service, taken for the sake of showing that there was no necessity for subjecting the federal prisoners to neglect. A brief supplement to the report takes up the treatment of the Andersonville prisoners and includes a letter from Gen. Butler to Col. Ould on the exchange of prisoners, the two being the commissioners of exchange for their respective governments.

F. J. S.

—— The U. S. Sanitary Commission in the valley of the Mississippi, 1861-6 : final report of Dr. J. S. Newberry, Secretary, western department. Cleveland : Fairbanks. 1871.

[2359

The official report and record of the western department of the Sanitary Commission is indispensable in the study of the noble work of private philanthropic aid to the Government in the hospitals and in the field, in supplying nurses, clothing, surgical appliances, varied diet for sick and wounded, etc. Dr. Newberry, since celebrated as one of the foremost geologists of the country, was at the head of the Commission in the West. His report was made in 1866, but the publication was delayed. It is a work of a high order, both in substance and in form. J. D. C.

Vallandigham, Clement Laird. VALLANDIGHAM, JAMES L. Life of Clement L. Vallandigham. Balt.: Turnbull. 1872. [2360

Made up largely of newspaper articles and extracts from speeches, addresses and public documents. It contains few explanations and no deductions, but it is one of the few biographies in which a reader may study the situation of a northern Democrat, opposed to Lincoln's conduct of the war, and suffering the penalties imposed by the application of military law to non-combatants. It also affords material for a study of organizations opposed to the war, such as the Knights of the Golden Circle and Sons of Liberty.

E. E. S.

Van Horne, Thomas Budd. History of the Army of the Cumberland, its organization, campaigns, and battles; written at the request of Major-General George H. Thomas, chiefly from his private military journal and official and other documents furnished by him, . . . maps comp. by Edward Ruger. Cin.: Clarke. 1875. 2v. and atlas. $5. [2361

"A glance at the array of reports, despatches, orders, and letters referred to as authorities and quoted, shows that a long continued and methodical collection of material had been made by Gen. Thomas or some one under his eye, and that the author has thus been furnished with exceptional facilities for his work. The maps . . . were prepared by the superintendent of the Topographical Engineers Office of the Department of the Cumberland, who had supervision of the official surveys of the battle-fields and lines of works upon a large part of the theatre of war in which took place the operations narrated in the history. No pains have been spared to make the work as nearly as possible exhaustive in its special province, and when we add to this that it is brought out by the publishers in thoroughly good style, it is clear that it must become the principal authority with all the members of the organization known as the Army of the Cumberland for its campaigns, marches and engagements. . . . The author's part of the work is creditable to him. . . . Mr. Van Horne does not profess to give us much general criticism of campaigns, wisely limiting himself, in the main, to the narration of events as they passed. In the nature of the case, his work is strongly eulogistic. . . . This could not well be otherwise, and we note it, not to condemn it, but to draw the line sharply between historical works of this class and the true history, in which the . . . historian shall take the larger view of events, and judge generals and armies from a standpoint which enables him to combine reasons of state with those of military necessity, and fully comprehend the relation of each army to the great common purpose." J. D. Cox, in *Nation*, 21 : 404.

Victor, Orville James. History, civil, political and military, of the southern Rebellion. N. Y.: J. D. Torrey. [1861–8, c. 1861.] 4v. [2362

A fragmentary collection of materials for a story which is carried only to the beginning of 1862. An extended abstract of the political documents and debates during 1861, including messages of southern and Union Presidents, occupies the larger part of both volumes, military affairs taking a secondary place. The intention of the author was to write accurate and impartial history, but the matter needs sifting and digestion. G. A. T.

Walker, *Brig.-Gen.* Francis Amasa. History of the Second Army Corps in the Army of the Potomac. N. Y.: Scribner. 1886. $2. [2363

"Of the many well-written books on the Civil War which have issued from the press of recent years, we have seen none more interesting than this excellent piece of work by Gen. Walker. The narrative is clear, the style vivid, the account of military movements simple, straightforward, and free from the dulness that too often makes narratives of campaigns but a wearisome labor to the general reader. The book is one that could have been written by no other than an accomplished soldier. . . . There may be things omitted that ought to have been included, there may be some errors, but there is not an obscure page, there is not a tiresome chapter, in the book. Gen. Walker writes, too, *con amore*. . . . A few of the maps in Gen. Walker's book are good, but the majority are poor." J. D. Cox, in *Nation*, 44 : 149.

Watson, William. Adventures of a blockade runner. (Adventure series.) London: Unwin. 1892. N. Y.: Macmillan. 1892. Pop. ed. Phil.: Lippincott. 1898. [2364

"Mr. Watson was forced to engage in the dangerous traffic that forms the burden of his story, by stress of conditions brought about by the war; and he saw enough of the service, chiefly in small-craft traffic in the Gulf towards the close of hostilities, to give a fairly satisfactory first-hand view of this not unimportant phase of the 'late unpleasantness.' . . . The story is told in a modest, straightforward way that speaks for its veracity." *Dial*, 13 : 280.

Webb, *Brig.-Gen.* Alexander Stewart. The Peninsula: McClellan's campaign of 1862. (Campaigns of the Civil War, 3.) N. Y.: Scribner. 1881. $1. [2365

"None can doubt that General Webb, himself an actor in the scenes which he records, seeing now the falsity of the impressions with which he was then heartily in accord, justly claims to be doing but the work of an honest historian in 'recording the sad tale of the want of unity, the want of confidence, the want of coöperation, between the administration and the general commanding the army.' . . . Of the value of the services which he [McClellan] contributed to the national cause, and of his eminent fitness for command up to the moment when, in the writer's expressive phrase, the armies had 'locked horns,' none can speak in higher terms than does our author. . . . The final chapter is devoted to an able and clear review of the campaign, in which one cannot well avoid reading between the lines General Webb's opinion that for the distrust with which he was regarded at Washington General McClellan had himself to thank, having never properly appreciated his true relations with the President and commander-in-chief. . . . It is charitable to suppose, with our author, that an unwillingness to sacrifice, even for the good of the whole, any portion of the troops by whom he was thus idolized was the cause of many a failure. Postponing action until he could secure his army from every possible chance of failure, the golden moment of opportunity was missed." S. M. Quincy, in *Atlantic monthly*, 49: 412.

Werner, Edgar A., *comp.* Historical sketch of the War of the Rebellion. Albany: Weed. 1890. [2366

A compendium of the campaigns, engagements, losses, proclamations, etc., making up a skeleton of the official history of the war. In the same manner the reconstruction of the Union is given. Presumably taken from the official records. A kind of *multum in parvo* for such information.   E. E. S.

Wherry, W. M. The campaign in Missouri and the battle of Wilson's Creek. See Missouri Historical Society, Publications, No. 1. [2367

Wilkeson, Frank. Recollections of a private soldier in the Army of the Potomac. N. Y.: Putnam. 1887. $1. [2368

The grim, sordid prose of war as seen by a man in the ranks. An effective picture of the daily life of the Army of the Potomac in Grant's campaign of 1864, representing rather more of the shadows than the brighter aspects of camp and field, and somewhat bitter in its comments upon general officers. The writer's account of the "bounty jumpers," and of the other dregs of the army, is authentic, and his explanation of the demoralization of the Union troops towards the end of the siege of Petersburg accords with many of the observations of other witnesses. The style is simple narrative, clear and interesting.   G. A. T.

Williams, George Forrester. Bullet and shell. N. Y.: Fords. 1883. $1.50. [2369

This "is a slight and superficial narrative of the career of an officer through the war, in the lively and florid style of a newspaper report. He is made to share in several of the largest Virginia battles, and takes his turn at almost every kind of special duty. Plenty of adventure falls to his lot. . . . The humor, which is of the thinnest, is supplied by an Irish corporal whose brogue is given with tiresome phonetics. Some of the loathsome horrors of war are dwelt on with a minuteness which is unnecessary, and most of the description gives a much better idea of the general appearance of army life as seen by a spectator than of the real experiences of the rank and file. . . . The illustrations are numerous, and much above the ordinary. . . . Together with the good paper and type, they make the book a handsome and attractive one." *Nation,* 36: 261.

Williams, Lt.-Col. George Washington. History of the negro troops in the war of the Rebellion, 1861–5, preceded by a review of the military services of negroes in ancient and modern times. N. Y.: Harper. 1888. $1.75. [2370

The *Nation* says that the book shows honest intention and praiseworthy diligence. It claims to be the result of much labor in archives and in personal intercourse. Its author served with colored troops and had had some literary experience. But it shows a want of method, and an inability to command materials, so that the reader is interested but is left with imperfect comprehension. To begin with, there is no distinct and systematic account of the origin and service of the pioneer colored regiments. Much information in regard to them is given, but it is widely scattered. *Nation,* 46 : 180.

Williamson, James J. Mosby's Rangers: a record of the operations of the forty-third battalion Virginia cavalry, with personal reminiscences, etc. N. Y.: R. B. Kenyon. 1896. [2371

"It is a pity that the author of *Mosby's Rangers* had not given at least a chapter to a frank history of the law under which they were organized, and to their actual practice of scattering after a raid and pretending to be peaceful farmers till called together again by preconcerted signal. He protests against calling them guerrillas, but something more than a protest is needed when the law shows that they were irregular, and practically irresponsible, not on the pay-roll nor acting under definite orders, authorized to plunder and to keep the profits of their raids. What all this leads to, the history of war plainly tells. On the representation of the higher military officers the Confederate Government, at the beginning of 1864, disbanded all such organizations but Mosby's, and Virginia would doubtless have suffered less if his also had been suppressed." J. D. Cox, in *Nation,* 62 : 323.

Wirz, Henry. The demon of Andersonville; or The trial of Wirz for the cruel treatment and brutal murder of helpless Union prisoners in his hands. Phil.: Barclay. [c. 1865.] [2372

This pamphlet contains a running and newspaper-like — not a verbatim — account of the trial of Henry Wirz, commandant of the interior of Andersonville prison, before a special military commission on charges of conspiracy and murder, in connection with the treatment of Union prisoners. The general effect of the imperfectly reported evidence is that Wirz was the passionate and irritable tool of a superior, Gen. Winder, who was worse than himself. The full text of the charges, specifications, findings and death sentence is given, and a brief sketch of Wirz's life and of his execution, Nov. 10, 1865, is appended.

F. J. S.

Wise, John Sergeant. The end of an era. Boston: Houghton. 1899. $2. [2373

"The 'Era' is that of slavery in the United States, and the end of it was the Civil War, which Mr. Wise saw as a boy of only eighteen when it closed. . . . The book is meant to give the conditions of life on the Virginia plantation of the author's family from his earliest recollections of childhood in Accomack. Similar life on the larger and more luxurious plantations of the rich landowners of the most cultivated class in the valley of the James is described. . . . He describes his own gradual growth in a time of ferment, and the beginning of some intelligence as to the real meaning of slavery and of the political agitation based upon it. . . . The annals of the great rebellion are enriched by such a book as Mr. Wise has given us, preserving as it does the personal note of his own youthful memories, which we may easily believe seem to him of 'the stuff that dreams are made of,' as if belonging to another world, hardly related to this. The temper and spirit of it all could not be bettered, and he has shown that, like his father, he not only accepted the results of the war as the act of God, but learned very soon to see that it was best for the world and for his country that the old era should have an end." J. D. Cox, in *Nation*, 69 : 379.

Wormeley, Katharine Prescott. The other side of war with the Army of the Potomac : letters from the headquarters of the United States Sanitary Commission during the Peninsular campaign in Virginia in 1862. Boston : Ticknor. 1888.

—— The cruel side of war with the Army of the Potomac. Boston : Roberts. 1898. Little. $1.25.   [2374

"It is a bright sketch of a sad subject, comprising a brief but clear account of the origin and development of the great auxiliary to the Medical Department of the Army, followed by a bundle of letters full of the spirit of the time when McClellan was the idol, and the Army of the Potomac the most completely appointed of the land forces. Miss Wormeley's letters are cheerful in tone, sparkling with clever descriptions of persons and places, and showing an appreciation of the romantic as well as the prosaic side of war. Between the lines, however, it is not difficult to catch glimpses of the mountain of misery which the Sanitary Commission did so much to alleviate and reduce." *Nation*, 48 : 472.

6. Period of Reconstruction, and after : 1865–1899

America and Europe : a study of international relations. (Questions of the day.) N. Y. : Putnam. 1896. 75c.   [2375

Contents : Wells, David A. The United States and Great Britain. — Phelps, Edward J. The Monroe doctrine. — Schurz, Carl. Arbitration in international disputes. These three essays were prompted by President Cleveland's Venezuelan message in 1896. Mr. Wells' essay, which constitutes more than half of the volume, is an argument to show that there was no reason at that time for prejudice and ill feeling, as expressed by so many, against England, on the ground that she represented a colonial policy of selfishness. Mr. Phelps takes the ground that the United States had no right to meddle in the question of the Venezuelan boundary line. Mr. Schurz urges arbitration, asserts its practicability, deplores the war spirit, and believes in the peace mission of the United States.

D. R. D.

American annual cyclopædia and register of important events, 1861–74. N. Y. : Appleton. 1862–75. V. 1–14. Since 1874 continued as Appleton's annual cyclopædia, 1875-. N. Y. : Appleton. 1876-. V. 15+. [Two or three of later vols. are still (1901) in print. $5.25 ea.]

—— Index, 1861–75, 1876–87. 2v. $5 ea.

[2376

This contains regularly a survey of the world's progress, historical, religious, scientific and literary, arranged in dictionary form. The various nations and the states of the U. S., the various religious denominations and the different sciences have separate articles, and other standard sections of importance and value are Obituaries, Literature, Finance and Congress. Besides the standard subjects treated from year to year, the special topics which have attracted attention during a year, such as Klondike, Tin-plate manufacture, the Expositions of the year, etc., etc., are included. It is comprehensive and up to date, with an excellent corps of contributors and well edited, the best of its class, far surpassing the English *Annual register*, and indispensable to every collection for the study of contemporary history.   E. C. R.

Andrews, Elisha Benjamin. History of the last quarter-century in the United States, 1870–95. N. Y. : Scribner. 1896. 2v. $6.

[2377

"This history, although, as President Andrews tells us in his preface, it has been revised and enlarged, is still in substance the series of magazine articles which, with their rich abundance of pictorial illustrations, lately appeared in *Scribner's magazine*. The author has sought to seize upon the more striking events which lend themselves most readily to description, by both pen and pencil, and to give us a telling series of tableaux. . . . It is something like teaching by the stereopticon, with the slightest thread of lecture to connect the views. When we know the class of entertainment to which we are invited we shall have no cause for complaint that it is not something else. . . . The book, as a whole, will aid the young to understand the wonderful growth of the country since the great Civil War. It will help the middle-aged to recall with profit the connection and meaning of all that has passed under their own eye. It may even serve the systematic historian in fixing his own scale of treatment." J. D. Cox, in *Nation*, 63 : 458.

Barnes, William Horatio. History of the Thirty-ninth Congress. N. Y. : Harper. 1868.

[2378

"The substance [of the book] consists of extracts, abridged but not condensed, from long speeches delivered in Congress by members of the two great parties ; its only personal sketches, huddled together at the end of the volume, consist of the baldest outline of the birth, education, and official career of each member, and as much space is given to the obscurest as to the most distinguished. Out of the 576 pages which form the body of the work less than 66 consist of original matter." But the author's "preliminary sketch of the memorable organization of the first Congress after the war is well done. . . . Notwithstanding all faults and shortcomings, . . . the book under review is a valuable contribution to our current political literature. It gives a clear account of the origin of the civil rights bill, the Freedmen's Bureau bill, the constitutional amendment fixing the basis of representation, the tenure-of-office bill, the bill to provide for the more efficient government of the rebel states (commonly called the 'military bill'), and the other measures for which the Thirty-ninth Congress will be remembered in history. It also commemorates the ten vetoes which met, but failed wholly to overcome, these measures." *Nation*, 6 : 414.

Blaine, James Gillespie. Twenty years of Congress, from Lincoln to Garfield; with a review of the events which led to the political revolution of 1860. Norwich, Conn. : H. Bill Pub. Co. 1884–6. 2v. N. Y. : Funk. $3.75 ea. [2379

One of the best works on the later period of American history. The preliminary sketch to 1860 is written with a national, loose-construction bias, but the especially valuable account of subsequent events contemporaneous with the author is very generous. The share of the author in the scenes described is almost wholly eliminated. No analyses of characters is attempted. Many present-day questions, such as the tariff and foreign relations, are treated. The writer shows a pro-tariff sympathy.   E. E. S.

— DODGE, MARY ABIGAIL (GAIL HAMILTON, *pseud.*). Biography of James G. Blaine. Norwich, Conn. : H. Bill Pub. Co. 1895. N. Y. : Funk. $2.75. [2380

"This is not in reality a biography at all: it is the history of a family, written by a kinswoman who was practically an inmate of the household ; it is a volume of letters, few of which bear upon public affairs, or even on the public life of James G. Blaine, set in a framework of the rhetorical and antithetical statement in which the author was so skilful. More than half the thick volume is given up to details about others than Mr. Blaine himself, with many accounts of children's sayings and neighbors' gossip ; it does not invite the criticism of a serious biography. Considering the eminence of Mr. Blaine and his influence on the national government, it is unfortunate that the plan of the book should be so unscientific, and its contribution to our knowledge of the man so scanty. No authorities are anywhere mentioned or cited. . . . The letters are printed in a haphazard manner, so' that writer and recipient are not to be distinguished, or are hidden under initials. There is neither an index nor a list of papers ; and one feels timid about accepting any historical statement from the author after learning (p. 64) that Gallatin was Washington's Secretary of the Treasury. . . . Without the presidency, Mr. Blaine had one opportunity to make a great reputation as a statesman, his service as Secretary of State in 1881. On this period, and this alone, does Miss Dodge's biography render a substantial service to American history. In pages 490 to 503 appears a most intimate and confidential correspondence between President-elect Garfield and his future Secretary of State. . . . Here we have the key of the aggressive policy of Garfield's short administration: the Republican party was to be consolidated within, and the country aroused by a vigorous foreign attitude." Albert Bushnell Hart, in *American historical review*, 2: 181.

Brackett, Jeffrey R. Notes on the progress of the colored people of Maryland since the war. (Johns Hopkins Univ. studies, ser. 8, nos. 7–9.) Balt. 1890. Pap. $1. [2381

These *Notes* " are an extremely interesting supplement to the same writer's careful volume, *The negro in Maryland*, ' a study of the institution of slavery ' in that state, viewed historically. The four chapters after the introduction treat of Indians and white servants, slaves, manumission, and the free negro. They combine to form a calm, dispassionate, historical view of slavery, as it existed in a border state—such a view as we may now take to our mental and moral profit. Dr. Brackett's contribution to the sober history of the institution outweighs libraries of denunciation and advocacy." *Literary world*, 21 : 291.

Cable, George Washington. The negro question. N. Y. : Scribner. 1890. 75c.

—— The silent South. N. Y. : Scribner. 1885. New ed., rev. and enl. 1889. $1. [2382

Essays calling the attention of the country to the equities and ethics of the southern treatment of the negro problem, and impassioned pleas for awarding to the negro his full rights, as accorded by the Constitution. Enforced with arguments drawn from statistics and incidents that came within the author's own experience ; they are well worth reading as papers of that period in the history of the United States when the enfranchised negro confronted his old master as a political rival.   G. K.

Chadsey, Charles Ernest. The struggle between President Johnson and Congress over reconstruction. (Columbia Univ. studies in history, etc., v. 8, no. 1.) N. Y.: Macmillan. 1896. Pap. net $1. [2383

Covers the time from the July resolutions of 1861 to the end of the impeachment trial, and presents the leading facts in a well-arranged outline. Unbiased. References rather sparse. Valuable as a guide for students and investigators.   E. E. S.

Cleveland, Grover. Writings and speeches ; selected and ed. by George F. Parker. N. Y. : Cassell. [c. 1892.] [2384

Contains well-classified speeches and writings and extracts from writings, giving a good survey of Mr. Cleveland's opinions and public utterances during the whole period of his public life up to 1892. It contains a biographical and critical introduction by the editor, and a good index. The writings themselves are always clear, forcible and instructive, and, as a compact source for the history of the development of the ideas which shaped Mr. Cleveland's public policy, the work is invaluable.   E. C. R.

— DORSHEIMER, WILLIAM, *and* W. U. HENSEL. Life and public services of Grover Cleveland. Phil. : Edgewood Pub. Co. [c. 1892.] [2385

This is a campaign life, and is not to be regarded in any way as a critical or scholarly work ; but it is reasonably full, has the advantage of having been several times worked over and improved, and cannot quite be dismissed as worthless. It is not, however, in the same class with such a book as Whittle's *Cleveland*.   E. C. R.

— WHITTLE, JAMES LOWRY. Grover Cleveland. (Public men of to-day.) N. Y. : Warne. [1896.] $1.25.　　　　　　　　　[2386

"This sketch, by an Englishman, was written before the presidential election of last year [1896]. It is, the author says, a study of 'Mr. Cleveland's attempt to apply the original teaching of Jefferson and his followers to the republic of to-day.' Brought within a small compass, and told with considerable skill, the story is very different from the dreary record some readers might expect from this definition. It is full of the most dramatic interest, for it gives us the picture of a great struggle. . . . Of the man in private station we get no sort of glimpse. . . . We see him here solely in his relation to the people. . . . The evident haste with which the book has been compiled has marred its accuracy, and consequently its effectiveness." *Nation*, 64: 151.

Cox, Samuel Sullivan. Three decades of federal legislation, 1855–85. Providence, R. I. : Reid. 1885.　　　　　　　　　[2387

Cox was a war Democrat, and his book has the merits and the defects of a history written by an acute politician who took part in many of the events narrated. The last decade is very inadequately discussed; the value of the book is principally in that portion devoted to the events of the reconstruction period. It is written in a controversial spirit and colored throughout by the writer's political sympathies; is rambling and discursive, and clothed in rough and choppy English.　　　　　　　　　R. C. H. C.

Curtis, George William. CARY, EDWARD. George William Curtis. (American men of letters.) Boston : Houghton. 1894. $1.25.　　　　　　　　　[2388

A straightforward and satisfactory, brief biography by one who knew Curtis well. The author's training qualifies him to speak particularly of Curtis as editor, politician and reformer; but the earlier years of literary life are treated with equal skill.　W. MacD.

Cushing, Caleb. Treaty of Washington. N. Y.: Harper. 1873.　　　　　　　　　[2389

The author has had unusual opportunities of becoming familiar with the foreign state relations of our government. He might have produced a valuable book, by giving a clear account of matters not generally understood. But this has not been his purpose. He has thrown no light on the great diplomatic controversy. "The book was written with a single object: it was designed and executed as a means of attack and retaliation upon Sir Alexander Cockburn, the British arbitrator. Undoubtedly the provocation was great. . . . But there is in this book rather a personal attack upon the Chief-Justice as a man than a searching and severe analysis of his official work ; and unfortunately, in some respects, the charges which it contains are not based upon a foundation of fact. . . . Finally, Mr. Cushing conveys the impression that the British Government itself has repudiated Sir Alexander Cockburn's opinion and conduct at Geneva as unnecessary and mischievous. This is a grave error of fact." J. N. Pomeroy, in *Nation*, 16: 303.

Custer, *Maj. - Gen.* **George Armstrong.**

WHITTAKER, *Capt.* FREDERICK. Complete life of General George A. Custer. N. Y.: Sheldon. 1876.　　　　　　　　　[2390

Capt. Whittaker " has written a very good book, but it is repellently large and heavy. A solid octavo of 650 pages is a serious matter to take in hand in these busy days. . . . The book . . . is well written, without possessing any positive charm of style. Much of it reads like ' Charles O'Malley.' The author quotes Custer freely, and does not always draw with sufficient clearness the line between what Custer says and what he says himself. He is extremely partial to Custer, and his partiality is the great drawback to the satisfaction with which we read." *Nation*, 24: 179.

Dabney, Robert Lewis. Defence of Virginia in recent and pending contests against sectional party. N. Y.: Hale. 1867.　　[2391

Presents the Old Testament, New Testament, ethical, and economic justification of slavery. Very little new material, but interesting for new conditions under which the essays were composed. Written in the heat of the close of the war. Takes almost a hopeless view of the future.　　　　　　　　　E. E. S.

Garfield, *Maj.-Gen.* **James Abram.** Works: ed. by B. A. Hinsdale. Boston: Osgood. 1882. 2v.　　　　　　　　　[2392

A collection of speeches and addresses, edited by a sympathetic friend and competent scholar, President of Hiram College, where Garfield was formerly a teacher. None of Garfield's writings before 1863 are included, and subsequent to that date only those which had been previously published. Nor are the speeches delivered between his nomination for president and inauguration included. The chronological order is followed, and the editor's introductory notes are excellent.

— RIDPATH, JOHN CLARK. Life and work of James A. Garfield. Cin.: Jones. [c. 1881.]　　　　　　　　　[2393

A subscription book, written immediately after the death of Garfield. The first part is made up quite largely of his speeches and writings; the latter gives all the particulars of his assassination, death and public funeral. No especial merit is apparent.　　　　　　　　　E. E. S.

Gibson, A. M. A political crime: the history of the great fraud. N. Y.: Wm. S. Gottsberger. 1885.　　　　　　　　　[2394

" We have a solid volume of 400 pages of vigorous campaign-newspaper denunciation of the counting in of President Hayes in 1877. On the other side, so far as we can learn, all was fair and lovely. . . . Whether Hayes was elected or not unimpassioned history will decide; but the whole affair was iniquitous on both sides to the extent of their several abilities, and it will require a much less heated, one-sided, and partisan book than the one before us to give the true history of the transaction." *Literary world*, 17: 12.

Grady, Henry Woodfin. The new South ;

with character sketch by Oliver Dyer. N. Y.: Bonner. 1890. $1. [2395

An interesting little volume by the late Henry W. Grady, a brilliant journalist and orator of Georgia. One half of the book consists of an excellent sketch of the author, with copious extracts from his orations. The remainder of the volume consists of letters, which Grady originally published in the *New York ledger*. They present an accurate picture of the growth of the South since the Civil War in manufactures and agriculture, concluding with a temperate discussion of the race problem from the southern standpoint. The statistics are attractively presented, being interspersed with anecdotes. The style is clear and sparkling. J. R. F.

Harrell, John M. The Brooks and Baxter war: a history of the reconstruction period in Arkansas. St. Louis: Slawson. 1893. [2396

Refers to a contest for the governorship of Arkansas in 1872-4, growing out of Congressional reconstruction in that state. Of local value only. Avowedly in favor of Baxter. Of service in appreciating the effort required to restore the rebellious states to harmonious relations with the general government. E. E. S.

Herbert, Hilary A., *et al.* Why the Solid South ? or Reconstruction and its results. Balt.: R. H. Woodward. 1890. [2397

A series of sketches of the abuses of the reconstruction governments in the South from 1865 to 1876, written to set forth the historical reasons why the southern people feel that political security can be obtained only through a solid adherence to the Democratic party. Although strongly partisan in temper and purpose, these sketches are substantially trustworthy. This history is for the most part still unwritten, and this is the only book which deals with the actual working of the reconstruction governments in all the southern states. Special stress is laid on the pecuniary corruption and financial extravagance of the negro governments which, while they lasted, made impossible the recovery of those communities from the losses of the war. E. G. B.

Johnson, Andrew. Ross, Edmund G. History of the impeachment of Andrew Johnson. Santa Fé, N. M., and N. Y.: H. B. Philbrook. 1896. [2398

The author was one of the seven Republican Senators whose votes acquitted President Johnson. The first five chapters are devoted to demonstrating that Johnson's reconstruction policy was in line with that of Lincoln and that Lincoln and Johnson were elected as Union men rather than as Republicans, and to the passage of the tenure-of-office law. The remainder of the book is a condensed account of the formal trial proceedings, almost nothing being said of occurrences outside the Senate chamber. F. J. S.

Kennaway, Sir John Henry. On Sherman's track; or The South after the war. London: Seeley. 1867. [2399

"Mr. Kennaway is an Oxford man and a practising barrister, who spent a hundred and twenty-eight days

of 1865 in making a hasty tour of the southern states. His work is, upon the whole, an agreeable disappointment. . . . It is generally uncommonly sensible, manly and gentlemanly. . . . We think its author has tried, and tried successfully, to be impartial as between the South and North, and between the North and England, and if he tells not very much about us, what he does tell is true. He is by no means what one would call an ardent admirer of this country. . . . But his beliefs do not run into prejudices, and, as we have said, we think him extremely fair, and it is difficult to find fault with him, whether he is discussing President Johnson and his policy ; Mr. Seward, the Alabama, and the Fenian raid ; the treatment of prisoners of war in rebel and Federal military prisons, or the causes of the Rebellion and the attitude of the English government throughout the war." *Nation*, 4 : 48.

King, Edward. The southern states of North America. London: Blackie. 1875.

—— The great South. Hartford: Amer. Pub. Co. 1875. $6. [2400

A large volume, well illustrated, revised from a series of articles published in *Scribner's magazine* to describe the condition of the southern states after the abolition of slavery. It is of value in portraying conditions that were prevalent at the beginning of the revival of industries in later years. W. M. D.

Lamar, Lucius Quintus Cincinnatus. Mayes, Edward. Lucius Q. C. Lamar, his life, times, and speeches, 1825-93. Nashville, Tenn.: M. E. Pub. House. 1896. $3. [2401

Begins with the Kansas-Nebraska bill and closes with 1892. As a Mississippian, Lamar was connected with slavery, secession, the Confederacy, reconstruction, and the new South. Especially valuable for local reconstruction in Mississippi. As a member of the Supreme Court in his later years he was the great pacificator. The author's attitude is calm and reasonable. He was chosen as the biographer by Lamar's family and had access to all papers. E. E. S.

McCulloch, Hugh. Men and measures of half a century. N. Y. : Scribner. 1888. $2.50. [2402

This book is one of the most valuable of reminiscent contributions on American political and social life for the half century, 1830-1880. The first chapters give a picture of the professions of the law and the church in New England in the first part of the century, and discuss changes which have taken place since then. About 1833 the author settled in Indiana, and from that time until 1860 the recollections deal chiefly with western men and pioneer life. Of special value is the discussion in regard to state banking. McCulloch settled in Washington in 1863, and his account of his administration of the Treasury Department, 1866-69, forms one of the original sources of American financial history. His acquaintance was large, and his judgments are freely though kindly expressed. He is sympathetic in his judgments toward the South. Six years of his later life were spent in England, and give to his opinions a different point of view, particularly on the tariff, from that of many of his party contemporaries. The book throughout is thoroughly enjoyable, and there is very little padding by reprinting of lectures, speeches, etc.   D. R. D.

McDonald, John. Secrets of the great whiskey ring, containing a complete exposure of the illicit whiskey frauds culminating in 1875. Chicago: Belford. 1880.   [2403

"It is difficult to classify this book. It was meant for a campaign document, in the confident expectation that the third term would triumph at Chicago, and that abuse of General Grant would then be in order. To save it from going to waste, it was turned into a high moral arraignment of General Garfield, which, as the author is an ex-convict, placed it at once in the *bouffe* category. Historically it breaks down in the attempt to implicate General Grant in the whiskey conspiracy of 1871-75." *Nation*, 31: 313.

McPherson, Edward. Political history of the United States of America during the period of reconstruction, 1865-70. Wash.: Solomons. 1871.   [2404

The title is misleading, as the work is not a narrative history, but, like its predecessor, *Political history of the great rebellion*, is rather a reference book and an invaluable collection of documents. It is a revised reprint of the annual *Political manuals* issued 1866-1870. It contains a classified compilation of Presidential messages and proclamations, diplomatic papers, documents of cabinet secretaries, court decisions, Congressional votes, and state constitutional amendments. This is a work for the teacher and special student.   D. R. D.

Nordhoff, Charles. The cotton states in the spring and summer of 1875. N. Y.: Appleton. 1876.   [2405

This book deals with political and economic conditions in Arkansas, Louisiana, Mississippi, Alabama, North Carolina and Georgia, as seen from March to July, 1875. The author states that he is a northern man, an opponent of slavery and a Republican, but his book is a scathing review of the methods used during reconstruction times to whip the negroes into line for party purposes. He is independent and fearless, and gave satisfaction to neither side, for the whole reconstruction system, the conduct of both parties, the issue of fraudulent bonds, stealing and corruption, ballot box stuffing and proscription, are reviewed and bitterly denounced. The material advance made by the negro was pronounced satisfactory; the necessity of the ballot for his full development and the belief that his vote would be gradually divided between the contending parties are reiterated. The author says in substance, and more fairly, in this book, what leading southern men said in 1890, in *Why the Solid South? or Reconstruction and its results* (sect. 2397).   S. B. W.

Paris. *Tribunal of arbitration for the determination of questions concerning the jurisdictional rights of the United States in the waters of Bering Sea.* Proceedings. (53d Cong., 2d sess., Sen. ex. doc. 177.) Wash. 1895. 16v.   [2406

The first volume contains the gist of the matter — a brief history of the tribunal's proceedings (Feb. 23 to Aug. 15, 1893) in the form of the final report of the United States agent, Mr. Foster; the protocols, the award and attending declarations; and the opinions of the two United States arbitrators, Judge Harlan and Senator Morgan, that of the former including a 22-page statement of the merits of the case. Of the remaining volumes 14 are occupied with the cases and counter cases of the two governments, the arguments of counsel, etc. The final volume contains simply facsimiles of Russian documents in the Alaskan archives. The second and third volumes supply much information in regard to seal habits and the sealing industry, and are furnished with many photographs, diagrams, and maps.   F. J. S.

Pike, James Shepherd. The prostrate state; or South Carolina under negro government. N. Y.: Appleton. 1874.   [2407

A most vivid contemporary picture of South Carolina in 1872 under negro rule. Especially noteworthy as the testimony of a Republican, long prominent before the war as the Washington correspondent of the *N. Y. tribune*, and later U. S. Minister to the Netherlands. Particular attention is given to the enormous financial corruption prevalent under the reconstruction government.   E. G. B.

Pollard, Edward Albert. The lost cause regained. N. Y.: Carleton. 1868.   [2408

Brought out by the 14th and 15th amendments to the Constitution. It treats of reconstruction and the negro problem, seeing the only hope for the South in the maintenance of white supremacy. In a much more optimistic tone than the author's *Lost cause* (sect. 2301), to which it is a kind of supplement. Valuable as a southern view of a phase of reconstruction.   E. E. S.

Schurz, Carl. Report on the states of South Carolina, Georgia, Alabama, Mississippi and Louisiana. (39th Cong., 1st sess., Sen. ex. doc. 2.) Wash. 1865.   [2409

Mr. Schurz had been commissioned by President Johnson to make a trip through the South to gather information that should guide his policy of reconstruction. The report is to the effect that the loyalty of the South consisted only in submission to necessity, and that anarchy could be prevented only by continuing the control of the federal government until free labor by the negroes was firmly established. It is accompanied by confirmatory letters from military officers in the South and other documents, and by a two-page letter from Gen. Grant, in which, however, he takes a more favorable view of the situation, though admitting the necessity of retaining a military force in that region.   F. J. S.

Scott, Eben Greenough. Reconstruction during the Civil War in the United States. Boston: Houghton. 1896. $2.   [2410

The book consists largely of an introduction which presents the rights of the states against the encroachments of the Federal Union, the lack of coercive power in the latter, and the just demand of the seceding states for restoration unimpaired. Hence true reconstruction history is treated very briefly and largely by extracts from speeches of the radical Republicans in Congress. Marked by vigorous style. Valuable as an essay on the rise and progress of political parties in the United States.   E. E. S.

Shaler, Nathaniel Southgate, *ed.* The United States of America. N. Y. : Appleton. 1894. 2v. Subs. $10.   [2411

Excepting a brief historical introduction, this is a description of the United States in 1890–94. It is written by different hands. The chapters are very unequal in merit, and the work, on the whole, is disappointing. Among the valuable chapters are those on Physiography by the editor, the Tariff by Prof. F. W. Taussig, Political organization by Prof. J. B. McMaster, Productive industry by Edward Atkinson.   E. C.

Sherman, John. Recollections of forty years in the House, Senate and cabinet : an autobiography. Chicago : Werner. 1895. 2v. Subs. $7.50.   [2412

The book ends with the convening of Congress, Dec., 1894. It is a very frank self-revelation. The long public career of the author-subject (began 1854) and especially his identification with the financial history of the U. S. during and since the Civil War, make his book a history of American politics for the period. It is, however, the work of a strong party man, and is also written largely from recollections without sufficient verifications. The book is unequal, the interest continuous. It may also be especially consulted for the political history of Ohio. Though written entertainingly, it makes no effort at literary finish.
    V. L. C.
"The value of these volumes is chiefly in their relation to financial history. There is elsewhere a want of fulness and clearness of statement even as to events in which the author took part, a want of research where his knowledge is only at second hand, and a passing over of important transactions on which he might have thrown light." Edward L. Pierce, in *American hist. rev.*, 1 : 553.

Strong, Josiah. Our country, its possible future and its present crisis. N. Y.: Baker & T. 1885. Rev. ed. 1891. 60c.   [2413

Not historical either in conception or execution. An alarmist presentation of statistics to prove that the church is in danger of losing "the West," unless the Home Missionary Society is provided with funds. Sees perils in immigration, Romanism, the Mormons, intemperance, etc. Pessimistic for a purpose.
    E. E. S.

Tilden, Samuel Jones. Writings and speeches; ed. by John Bigelow. N. Y.: Harper. 1885. 2v. $6.   [2414

"Mr. Bigelow has done his work as editor ... very thoroughly. Each document or speech (the series begins as early as 1833, when Jeffersonian Democracy was a living creed ...) is introduced by a short note showing the circumstances which led to its composition or delivery; and thus the papers with the notes make a

tolerably connected history of the life and times of the subject. The collection will probably become more and more valuable as time goes on. ... Mr. Bigelow's zeal has run away with him a little, and led him to speak of Mr. Tilden in a vein of prefatory laudation which is inappropriate." *Nation*, 41 : 406.

— BIGELOW, JOHN. Life of Samuel J. Tilden. N. Y.: Harper. 1895. 2v. $6.   [2415
"Every student of politics or political history, every one who believes that political ideals and institutions practically and enormously affect the welfare of men, will find these volumes interesting. ... Adverse testimony, perhaps naturally enough, is not set very fully and frankly before the reader ; but the material is sufficiently given for a tolerably just estimate of a political career of high rank. ... If the book be read with judicious skipping ... the narrative will be found as lively as it is valuable and instructive. ... Mr. Bigelow was a most intimate friend. ... He argues, therefore, like an advocate. ... The editing or proof-reading of [the] work is imperfect. ... Long documents are thrust bodily into the narrative instead of their substance being made a part of it. ... Names are occasionally disguised. ... Dates are misprinted. ... Some of the disparagements of Tilden's political associates seem quite out of place. ... They apparently represent rather the personal dislikes of the biographer than the opinions of his subject. ... More striking illustration of this fault is seen in the elaborate indictment of Mr. Cleveland, to which its latter part is dedicated." Mr. Tilden's life and his gallant struggle against political corruption, in spite of lifelong invalidism, is profoundly interesting. His biographer has not always been happy in the tone of his narrative. Edward M. Shepard, in *American hist. rev.*, 1 : 174.

United States. *Congress.* Report of the joint committee on reconstruction at the 1st session, 39th Congress. Wash. 1866.   [2416

This committee of six Senators, with W. P. Fessenden at their head, and nine Representatives, with Thaddeus Stevens at their head, was appointed in December, 1865, "to inquire into the condition of the states which formed the so-called Confederate States of America, and report whether they, or any of them, are entitled to be represented in either house of Congress." April 30, 1866, the committee reported a proposed amendment to the Constitution which in a changed form was passed in June and duly became the 14th amendment. With it were reported two bills, designed to carry out its provisions, one "to provide for restoring to the states lately in insurrection their full political rights," and the other "declaring certain persons ineligible to office under the government of the United States." The report of the committee reviews the situation in 15 pages and concludes "that the so-called Confederate States are not at present entitled to representation in the Congress of the United States." The remainder of the bulky document consists of the testimony on which the conclusions of the committee were founded, and which was taken by several sub-committees, being the evidence of southern unionists, freedmen's bureau officials, men of northern origin domiciled in the South, and negroes. The part of the report relating to Tennessee includes a documentary history of the Union movement in that state from 1862, when Andrew Johnson was appointed its military governor.   F. J. S.

—— Report of the joint select committee to inquire into the condition of affairs in the late insurrectionary states. (42d Cong., 2d sess., Sen. rept. 41.) Wash. 1872. 13v.

—— *Same.* (42d Cong., 2d sess., House rept. 22. 13v.)   [2417

This is the Ku-Klux report. Early in 1871 a committee of seven Senators and 14 Representatives was appointed "to inquire into the condition of the late insurrectionary states, so far as regards the execution of the laws and the safety of the lives and property of the citizens of the United States." The committee extended its inquiries beyond the existence and acts of organized bands of disguised men known as Ku-Klux so as to include the maladministration of justice, bad legislation, and official incompetency and corruption, which had been assigned as accounting for these outrages. The majority report of the committee occupies 100 pages of the first volume and is followed by the elaborate report of a sub-committee on the debts and election laws of the insurrectionary states. Then comes a 300 page report of the Democratic minority of the committee. The evidence taken by sub-committees and the reports of trials in federal courts in the South fill the remaining 12 volumes, as follows: v. 2, North Carolina; v. 3, 4, 5, South Carolina; v. 6, 7, Georgia; v. 8, 9, 10, Alabama; v. 11, 12, Mississippi; v. 13, Florida and miscellaneous testimony and documents. There are separate indexes at the beginning of each series of volumes.   F. J. S.

United States. *House of Representatives.* Report of the select Committee on the New Orleans riots. (39th Cong., 2d sess., House report, 16.) Wash. 1867.   [2418

These riots occurred July 30, 1866, on the reassembling of the convention which had adopted the constitution of 1864 for the purpose of amending that instrument. The two Republican members of the committee, Messrs. Eliot and Shellabarger, after reviewing the circumstances of the outbreak, which they declare to have been premeditated, report that the existing civil government of Louisiana should be superseded by act of Congress, and that a provisional government should be established and maintained by military power. The Democratic member, Mr. Boyer, presents a minority report holding that the reassembling of the convention was unlawful, that the riot was provoked by incendiary speeches, and that it would be unjust to the people of the state to overthrow their government on account of a riot confined to a small portion of New Orleans.   F. J. S.

United States. *Senate.* Trial of Andrew Johnson, President of the United States, before the Senate on impeachment by the House of Representatives, for high crimes and misdemeanors. Wash. 1868. 3v.   [2419

This is a phonographic report of the trial made by the regular stenographers of the Senate for the use of that body, but the preliminary proceedings of Congress are abridged into four pages for the House and six pages for the Senate, four of which are occupied by the articles of impeachment. The first volume contains the opening argument of the managers and the evidence, the second the argument in general of the managers and of the counsel for the President, and the third the opinions filed by the individual Senators and, in an appendix, the debate on the right of Senator Wade to sit as a member of the court. Each volume contains an index of the whole.   F. J. S.

United States. *State Department.* Correspondence in relation to the boundary controversy between Great Britain and Venezuela; a reprint of Senate ex. doc. 226, 50th Cong., 1st sess., and Senate doc. 31, 54th Cong., 1st sess. Wash. 1896.

—— Report and accompanying papers of the commission appointed by the President of the United States "to investigate and report upon the true divisional line between the republic of Venezuela and British Guiana." Wash. 1897. 3v.

—— Maps of the Orinoco-Essequibo region, South America, compiled for the commission, etc. Wash. 1897.   [2420

The correspondence runs back to 1876, but the greater part of it passed during the years 1882–8 between the State Department and the American ministers at Caracas and London and the State Department and the Venezuelan Minister at Washington. Included in this is certain correspondence between the British and Venezuelan governments, and added to it are President Cleveland's special message of Dec. 17, 1895, Secretary Olney's instructions to Minister Bayard of July 20, 1895, and Lord Salisbury's instructions of Nov. 26 to Sir Julian Pauncefote in reply. The subjects covered by the report of the commission are the Spanish and Dutch settlements prior to 1648, the meaning of articles 5 and 6 of the treaty of Muenster, the territorial rights of the Dutch West India Company, and the evidence of the Dutch archives as to European occupation in western Guiana. Accompanying are a volume of extracts from the Dutch archives and a volume of reports and notes upon the 76 maps of the disputed territory which are of various dates from 1534 down to 1897, and which form the fourth volume of the report.   F. J. S.

Warner, Charles Dudley. Studies in the South and West, with comments on Canada. N. Y.: Harper. 1889. $1.75.   [2421

Most of these papers were originally published in *Harper's monthly.* They are all written in Mr. Warner's peculiarly happy style, and embody the results of very careful study and observation. Mr. Warner did not attempt to give a history of the portion of the country he visited, but to describe certain representative developments, tendencies, and dispositions. Mr. Warner's *Studies* probably describes the transition period of the South — or the ten years from 1880 to 1890 — better than any other book, and his facts are usually substantiated, his conclusions fair and reasonable. He is remarkably well-meaning, honest, and balanced, and his book did a great deal to convince the North that the South was in sympathy with the Union, that it had decided to bury the past, and that the "bloody shirt" was merely the scarecrow of politicians.

B. J. R.

THE SPANISH–AMERICAN WAR : 1898

Bigelow, *Capt.* John, Jr. Reminiscences of the Santiago campaign. N. Y.: Harper. 1899. $1.25. [2422

"Captain Bigelow gives as the scope of his book 'a narration of what an officer participating in that campaign saw, felt and thought, with such explanations and suggestions as his observations and reflections prompted.' He is a witness, not a prosecutor or an advocate. . . . The author disclaims any purpose to draw conclusions." He states what the facts were, "seen from the inside of the army by an officer who had given public evidence of his zeal and capacity in the study of his profession. Capt. Bigelow has not only told a most interesting tale, but he has contributed valuable material for the comprehension and solution of the problems involved." *Nation*, 69: 248.

Brooks, Elbridge Streeter. Story of our war with Spain. Boston: Lothrop. [c. 1899.] $1.50. [2423

"Mr. Elbridge S. Brooks has placed the young people, for whom he has written so much, under still further obligation by this timely volume. Of course it contains nothing new; but from the vast mass of material with which our country has been flooded since one year ago this time, he has prepared a continuous, condensed, and comprehensive narrative of events, from the day when the Maine steamed into Havana harbor to the ratification of the treaty. He does not obtrude his own opinions, but he shows that his personal attitude is both patriotic and optimistic. The 'story' is supplemented by a chronology which will be found of much use, taken from the *Boston Transcript*." *Literary world*, 30: 155.

Cervera y Topete, *Rear Admiral* **Pascual**, *ed.* Spanish-American war : a collection of documents relating to the squadron operations in the West Indies; tr. from the Spanish. (U. S. office of naval intelligence. Information from abroad. War notes, no. 7.) Wash. 1899. [2424

Admiral Cervera obtained permission, for his own vindication, to publish these documents, which consist chiefly of communications between himself, the Spanish minister of marine, and the captain-general of Cuba. They cover a period from November, 1897, to the Admiral's return to Spain, and afford a pretty complete history of Spanish naval operations in the West Indies. They show that Cervera protested vigorously against taking his fleet thither, expected nothing but disaster from its feebleness and ill-equipped condition, and sailed out of Santiago harbor only because expressly so ordered by his superior, Captain-General Blanco. The appendix contains the instructions for Camara's "squadron of reserve," which never got any further than Port Said.   F. J. S.

Davis, Oscar King. Our conquests in the Pacific. N. Y.: Stokes. [c. 1899.] $1.25. [2425

"Mr. Oscar King Davis, the special correspondent of the New York *Sun* at Manila from May to December, 1898, has reprinted his letters to that journal, describing scenes and events during the American occupation. These letters justly acquired a high reputation for the light which they cast on new and untried conditions. Half-tone illustrations accompany the text." *Rev. of reviews*, 20: 247.

Davis, Richard Harding. Cuban and Porto Rican campaigns. N. Y. : Scribner. 1898. $1.50. [2426

"Mr. Davis's book ought to be entitled, '*What I saw of the Cuban and Porto Rican campaigns.*' Chatty and entertaining, it is a sort of picture-book (of which the hearsay is the least interesting), full of individual acts of bravery, and with enough blood-spots to suit the lover of terrible war. The latest act of bravery is always the greatest. But it does not add to the effectiveness of a battle-tale to exaggerate the hotness of the fire or the heroism of the combatants." Theodore Ayrault Dodge, *Am. hist. rev.*, 4: 752.

Dewey, *Admiral* **George.** BARRETT, JOHN. Admiral George Dewey : a sketch of the man. N. Y. : Harper. 1899. $1.25. [2427

"Ex-Minister John Barrett's *Admiral George Dewey* has been put together so hastily that the biography proper stands last, and the opening sounds like an apologia of the author himself. Mr. Barrett . . . [was] employed as a syndicate press correspondent at Manila. A fellow-Vermonter, he saw Dewey often and familiarly for the better part of a year, and with much verbiage and repetition conveys, no doubt, a just idea of the Admiral's character, now tolerably familiar. . . . Numerous portraits and views lend value to the book." *Nation*, 69 : 296.

Doubleday, Russell. A gunner aboard the Yankee ; ed. by H. H. Lewis. N. Y. : Doubleday & McClure ; Doubleday, Page. 1898. $1.50. [2428

"This book, which carries with it an introduction by Rear Admiral Sampson, is the result of the experience of a member of the New York Naval Reserve in the war just closed, and is based upon the personal diary of the . . . author, who is known on the title-page as No. 5 of the 'after-port (5-in.) gun.'" The commander of the Yankee was "one of the best all-round officers in the regular service. The story will be found to be of interest, and is told with a sprightliness and humor that should give it many readers." *Nation*, 68 : 114.

Draper, Andrew Sloan. Rescue of Cuba. N. Y. : Silver. 1899. $1. [2429

Dr. Draper extols the war with Spain as a precedent in favor of liberty, humanity and justice, and is a fervent champion of extreme imperialistic views.

Goode, William Athelstane Meredith. With Sampson through the war: being an account of the naval operations of the North Atlantic squadron during the Spanish-American war of 1898; with contributed chapters by Rear Admiral Sampson, Capt. Robley D. Evans, Commander C. C. Todd. N. Y.: Doubleday & McClure; Doubleday, Page. 1899. $2.50.

[2430

"Admiral Sampson possesses a staunch champion in Mr. Goode, who, as correspondent of the Associated Press, was aboard the flagship New York, and gives us numberless details about the daily life on our battleships. . . . Considerable space is devoted to the unfortunate journalistic Sampson-Schley controversy. . . . The chapter by Admiral Sampson himself is noteworthy as showing how completely outclassed Cervera was. . . . Captain Evans, in an equally interesting chapter, sums up the lessons of the war." Theodore Ayrault Dodge, *Am. hist. rev.*, 4: 756.

Hall, Tom. Fun and fighting of the Rough Riders. N. Y.: Stokes. [c. 1899.] 50c. [2431

"Tom Hall, well known to the readers of the lighter magazines as a frequent contributor in both prose and verse, was adjutant of the First United States Volunteer Cavalry during the Cuban war. . . . He bears witness to the mass of inaccurate writing which has overwhelmed the history of the Santiago campaign. . . . El Caney he calls 'a useless victory, won at an awful cost;' and the siege of Santiago and the previous fighting are summarized in a pregnant sentence: 'A siege without siege guns was the logical climax of a battle without tactics and a campaign without strategy.'" *Dial* (Chicago), 27: 364.

Harper's pictorial history of the war with Spain; with introd. by Nelson A. Miles. N. Y.: Harper. 1899. 32 pts. [2v.] Subs. pap. 25c. per pt. [2432

"It was hoped by some that photography would play a much more important part in illustrating battles of the war with Spain than it did in the Civil War. Such hopes, however, were not destined to fruition. With very few exceptions, photography was found impracticable in illustrating actual battle scenes. The man with the pencil was as much in demand as ever. The corps of able and brilliant artists employed by the Harpers produced a remarkable series of drawings." *Rev. of reviews*, 19: 630.

Hemment, John C. Cannon and camera: sea and land battles of the Spanish-American war in Cuba; introd. by W. I. Lincoln Adams. N. Y.: Appleton. 1898. $2. [2433

This "merits a place among the authentic records of the war for Cuba. The author is a man of courage and of feeling, and, having been a National Guardsman, he could judge fairly the military operations which fell under his eye. He was making photographs in Havana before and after the blowing up of the Maine; he witnessed the advance on Santiago; he saw Cervera's fleet destroyed; he was at Camp Wikoff. His numerous views illustrate these various phases of the campaign. His unaffected narrative shows the horrid side of war as well as the brilliant

and fame-making. Mr. Hemment concludes with some hints to amateur and professional photographers in like circumstances." *Nation*, 67: 466.

Hobson, Richard Pearson. Sinking of the Merrimac. N. Y.: Century Co. 1899. $1.50.

[2434

A good piece of literary work, "in spite of his lack of reserve in describing the actual submergence of the vessel. But he dwells too long upon the minor matters of his imprisonment, making an anti-climax in spite of the thrilling scenes attending his return to his own flag. Had there been judicious suppression in the account of his detention by Spain, the book would be nearly perfect; even as it is, it deserves wide circulation." *Dial*, 26: 272.

Johnston, William A. History up to date: a concise account of the war of 1898 between the United States and Spain, its causes, and the treaty of Paris. N. Y.: Barnes. 1899. $1.50. [2435

"Mr. William A. Johnston, who is an editorial writer for the New York *Herald*, begins his *History up to date* with the statement that 'This book is a concise account of the birth of a new era in the United States. It is a record of the dying moments of the Monroe doctrine, the spirit that for more than one hundred years inspired the civic body born in the Revolution of the American Colonies of Great Britain near the end of the last century.'" Wallace Rice, *Dial* (Chicago), 27: 100.

Kennan, George. Campaigning in Cuba. N. Y.: Century Co. 1899. $1.50. [2436

"In a number of chapters which are easy, agreeable reading, Mr. Kennan gives a much-needed account of the doings of the Red Cross, and his personal adventures when quarantined in Santiago lend a crisp idea of what manner of city it then was. . . . We owe much to Mr. Kennan for his interesting work, . . . but he will pardon us if we refrain from taking his criticism of the Santiago campaign too seriously. Overmuch of it is hearsay." T. A. Dodge, *Am. hist. rev.*, 4: 755.

King, W. Nephew, Jr. Story of the war of 1898; [introd.] for the army, [by] O. O. Howard, for the navy, [by] Robley D. Evans. N. Y.: P. F. Collier. 1899. Subs. $15.

[2437

"In mere luxury of edition" Lieut. King's book "leaves nothing to be desired. It is a great oblong folio, printed in large type on heavy paper, and overflowing with illustrations, mostly half-tones from nature. The author is a naval officer, and has secured Capt. Robley D. Evans to write an introduction for the navy, while Gen. O. O. Howard supplies one for the army. Capt. Evans's summary review is a criticism of Congress for forcing the navy to do its thorough work with such poor tools. Gen. Howard opens his with a praise of the preparation of the navy of late years, 'as if in anticipation of a conflict.' . . . The 'story' proper need not be examined. It is not meant to be read in such a shape as this, being but a sort of obligato to the illustrations. These are mostly of a high degree of excellence, if more or less familiar. The lurid colored plates could well have been dispensed with." *Nation*, 68: 90.

Lodge, Henry Cabot. The war with Spain. N. Y.: Harper. 1899. $2.50.   [2438

" Mr. Henry Cabot Lodge's account of *The War with Spain* exhibits him as an ardent partisan and a good hater, with but little of the historian's patience in research or capacity for impartiality." Wallace Rice, in *Dial*, 27: 363.

Mahan, *Capt.* **Alfred Thayer.** Lessons of the war with Spain, and other articles. Boston: Little. 1899. $2.   [2439

"Consists of five articles which appeared in *McClure's magazine* from Dec., 1898, to April, 1899, dealing especially with the navy and coast defence : The peace conference and the moral aspect of war, in *North American review ;* Relations of United States to their new dependencies, in *Engineering magazine ;* Distinguishing qualities of ships of war, in Scripps Rae Newspaper League; Current fallacies upon naval subjects, in *Harper's magazine.* The chief lesson reads, ' In time of peace prepare for war.' " *Publishers' weekly*, 56: 1268.

Marshall, Edward. Story of the Rough Riders, 1st U. S. Volunteer Cavalry. N. Y.: Dillingham. 1899. $1.50.   [2440

" Mr. Marshall, though not a soldier, is one of the heroes of our war. In the discharge of his duty, as arduous and dangerous as that of the men whose heroism he so well describes, he received a wound that won for him the sympathy of thousands. . . . This book is a complete record of the military manœuvres of the war in Cuba. . . . But it is rather the personal element of the narrative that gives it its value. It deals with incidents that the historian will not consider worth chronicling." *Critic*, 35 : 765.

Miley, *Lt.-Col.* **John D.** In Cuba with Shafter. N. Y.: Scribner. 1899. $1.50.   [2441

" The military student turns with pleasure and profit to the even-handed, keen statement of facts by Colonel Miley of the headquarters staff, whose soldierly leaven gives authority to every page. Writing as an advocate, Colonel Miley would have made a less good case ; General Shafter is happy in his historian. The maps supply a marked need, as the accentuation of the ground and the movements are carefully set down. No space is devoted to personal details. The facts are clearly and conservatively given." Theodore Ayrault Dodge, in *American hist. rev.*, 4: 754.

Millet, Francis Davis. Expedition to the Philippines. N. Y.: Harper. 1899. $2.50.   [2442

" Mr. Millet was already favorably known by his career as an artist and war correspondent . . . and his employment as correspondent of the London *Times* gave him, in the Philippines, exceptional advantages. . . . His narrative . . . covers the original expedition of the army, the short campaign against the Spaniards, and the establishment by the insurgents of the invest-

ing lines about Manila, which was practically a siege as before, the garrison being changed from Spanish to American. For this period he seems to be a competent and candid guide. Both directly and incidentally, Mr. Millet gives us much interesting and useful knowledge of Luzon and its people." *Nation*, 70 : 14.

Morris, Charles. The war with Spain. Phil.: Lippincott. 1899. $1.50.   [2443

" No history of contemporary events can be final. Mr. Morris's book gives a useful sketch of their sequence in the Spanish War, illustrated rather by pictures than by military charts. Skeleton histories are fast filling up with stories of personal experiences, and meanwhile Mr. Morris gives us a crisp narrative, breathing full-chested patriotism, and naturally exaggerating both the dangers and the exploits of what, after all is said, remains a hyper-lucky war." Theodore Ayrault Dodge, in *American hist. rev.*, 4: 751.

Müller y Tejeiro, *Lt.* **José.** Battles and capitulation of Santiago de Cuba ; tr. from the Spanish. (U. S. office of naval intelligence. Information from abroad.) Wash. 1898.

—— *Same* [completed]. Wash. 1899. [2444

The first edition published by the United States Navy Department of this account of the war from the Spanish side was incomplete, but the second contains all but the first three chapters. One of the chapters added in the second edition describes the march of Gen. Escario's column from Manzanillo to Santiago, and shows the effectiveness of the aid given the United States by the Cubans. Although the account of the field operations of the two armies is rather scant, there is a day by day record of events in Santiago, and the author was an eye-witness of most that he has put down. He appears to be perfectly trustworthy and free from bias, and had no delusions as to the inevitable result of the war. He, however, heartily praises the conduct of both the Spanish fleet and army.

F. J. S.

Musgrave, George Clarke. Under three flags in Cuba: a personal account of the Cuban insurrection and Spanish-American war. Boston: Little. 1899. $2.   [2445

" Mr. Musgrave was an Englishman holding Spain in high favor when he went to the island as a correspondent for a British journal, and the knowledge gained on the ground saw him within a few months fighting in the insurgent ranks. He bears the testimony of an eye-witness to the disinterested valor of the Cuban patriots, but he makes little prophecy for the future." *Dial*, 28 : 160.

Roosevelt, *Col.* **Theodore.** Rough Riders. N. Y.: Scribner. 1899. $2.   [2446

" It is a minute account of the doings of his regiment, and suffers from having been anticipated by the newspapers. It is impossible to escape the conclusion that he has avoided printing much that would have lent interest to his narrative. For instance, his account of the proceedings which led to the recall of the regiment from Cuba is extremely tame; we almost get the impression that ' round robins ' to generals, and letters from officers in the field demanding the recall of troops, are commonplace matters, such as are constantly met with in military literature from Cæsar to Jomini." *Nation*, 68 : 439.

Severance, Frank Hayward, *and* **Brayton L. Nichols.** Illustrated Buffalo Express souvenir history of the war with Spain. Buffalo, N. Y.: The Express, Matthews. 1898. [2447

A compilation, from official and other sources deemed trustworthy. The causes and incidents of the war, on sea and land, are narrated with fulness adequate to the demands of the average reader. In no wise a political or philosophical history, it well achieves the end aimed at — to supply with newspaper-like promptness a straightforward story of the war, so carefully and attractively written that it has permanent value.

Sigsbee, *Capt.* **Charles Dwight.** The Maine: an account of her destruction in Havana harbor : personal narrative. N. Y.: Century Co. 1899. $1.50. [2448

" There is in this work . . . an assumption of Spanish guilt which is not justified by the facts which have so far come to light, however strongly it may be inferred ; and there is a notable lack of information from that side, though it was at hand and available. But the story of the sinking of the great battleship has much merit as a bit of literary work." John J. Culver, in *Dial* (Chicago), 26 : 272.

Spanish-American war : the events of the war described by eye-witnesses. Chicago : Stone. 1899. $1.50. [2449

This book consists of " chapters from the war correspondence of leading American journals. The narrative shifts from the East to the West Indies in a carefully prepared chronological sequence, the date being given in the running-title. For this reason, and because of the illustrations, the compilation will be found convenient to refer to." *Nation*, 68 : 295.

Spears, John Randolph. Our navy in the war with Spain. N. Y.: Scribner. 1898. $2. [2450

" This is a decided acquisition to the history of the United States Navy, and but for the occasional violations of the canons of good taste the book would receive our hearty approval. The object of the author was to give a truthful account of the part taken by the navy in the war with Spain. This he has done. We wish some other matters had been left undone." *Critic*, 34 : 361.

See, also, sect. 2614.

United States. *Congress.* Affairs in Cuba : message of the president on the relations of the United States to Spain ; and report of the committee on foreign relations, Senate, relative to affairs in Cuba. Wash. 1898. [2451

The message briefly reviews the Cuban situation since 1896 and is accompanied by the correspondence between the government and its representatives in Cuba between Nov. 17, 1897, and Feb. 28, 1898. The Senate committee's report includes a great mass of documentary matter of every sort regarding Cuban affairs since 1875 down to and including testimony

taken on the Maine explosion. While the greater part of the report is devoted to the illustration of Spanish misgovernment, the evidence before the Spanish commission in Havana regarding the Maine catastrophe is included, as are photographs and diagrams exhibiting that disaster. F. J. S.

United States. *Naval court convened to inquire into the loss of the battle ship Maine, Feb. 15, 1898.* Report. (55th Cong., 2d sess., Sen. doc. 207.) Wash. 1898. [2452

The court, of which Capt. Sampson was president, held its sessions in February and March, 1898, partly on board a lighthouse tender in Havana harbor and partly at Key West. The witnesses were officers and men of the Maine and divers who examined the wreck. The finding explains briefly the reasons why the court held that the catastrophe could have been produced only by the explosion of a submarine mine. There are diagrams and photographs illustrating the appearance of the wreck, and the *Report* is introduced by a message from President McKinley transmitting it to Congress. F. J. S.

Vivian, Thomas J. Fall of Santiago. N. Y.: Fenno. 1898. $1 50. [2453

" The first of the war histories . . . pays the penalty of its timeliness by cumulative evidences of haste in letter-press, illustrations, and proof-reading. It also appears to be rather the raw material of history than history itself." Wallace Rice, *Dial*, 25 : 258.

Wheeler, *Maj.-Gen.* **Joseph.** Santiago campaign, 1898. Boston : Lamson. 1898. Phil.: Biddle. 1899. $2.50. [2454

General Wheeler's book, " including as it does some pages of a diary, a number of personal letters, and reports and orders galore, . . . rather suggests the soldier's note-book. The general himself appears in but a third of it. While the padding is interesting as a record, we could have wished for a fuller representation of the ingenuous soldier. That part which is General Wheeler's was written at Montauk Point in August, 1898, and is full of the freshness of the recent operations. General Wheeler has no special point to make, his pages are purely narrative." T. A. Dodge, *Am. hist. rev.*, 5 : 376.

Wilcox, Marrion. Short history of the war with Spain. N. Y.: Stokes. [c. 1898.] $1.25. [2455

" An agreeable disappointment, being fair, comprehensive, succinct, and, considering the material at hand, when it was put forth, accurate." John J. Culver, *Dial* (Chicago) 26 : 274.

THE NEW POSSESSIONS AND THE EXPANSION POLICY OF THE UNITED STATES

American Academy of Political and Social Science. Foreign policy of the United States, political and commercial : addresses and discussion, April 7-8, 1899. Phil. 1899. $1.50. [2456

Addresses by Theodore S. Woolsey, A. Lawrence Lowell, W. Alleyne Ireland, Carl Schurz, W. C. Ford, Robert T. Hill, John Bassett Moore, and His Excellency, Wu Ting Fan; with a report of the discussion that followed each address. The arguments for and against the policy of imperial expansion are strongly presented.

Bancroft, Hubert Howe. The new Pacific. San Francisco : Bancroft Co. 1900. $2.50.

[2457

" Presents the Pacific Ocean, shores, and islands in their entirety, their resources and climate, history and romance, with the events culminating in the present active development. Important chapters are: Interoceanic communication; Resources of the Pacific; Mines and manufactures; Commerce on the Pacific; Hawaii; Race problems, etc., etc. The condition of the Chinese in the United States is fully treated." *Publishers' weekly*, 56: 896.

Blackman, William Fremont. Making of Hawaii: a study in social evolution. N. Y.: Macmillan. 1899. $2.

[2458

" Much that the ordinary history includes he has omitted, to give, instead, an admirable exposition of the social development from the early barbarous period, through the period of conquest, down to the present day. The volume supplies precisely the kind of information concerning the people, the social organization, the industries and commerce, the land tenure, and the possibilities for the white man in the tropics that Americans now greatly need." *Literary world*, 30: 266.

Carpenter, Edmund Janes. America in Hawaii : a history of United States influence in the Hawaiian Islands. Boston : Small. 1899. $1.50.

[2459

" In the first half of the present century Boston was the centre of activity in the religious and commercial enterprises which the American people directed toward the Hawaiian Islands. In Boston and from official sources Mr. E. J. Carpenter has gathered the material for an opportune and very interesting history . . . of the growth of American influence in our new territory, from the landing of the little shipload of missionaries from Boston in 1819 to the culmination in the annexation ceremonies of August 12, 1898." *Dial*, 26: 248.

Copeland, Thomas Campbell. American colonial handbook. N. Y.: Funk. 1899. 50c.

[2460

" ' A ready reference-book of facts and figures, historical, geographical and commercial, about Cuba, Puerto Rico, the Philippines, Hawaii and Guam,' is the self-definition, well justified, of the *American colonial handbook*. . . . It is in the form of a catechism, preceded by a synopsis of the treaty of peace, and in the case of each division by an historical sketch. Authorities are duly marshalled at the end. Each section has a map. A parallel index binds all together. The little volume, with rounded corners, slips easily into the pocket." *Nation*, 68: 295.

Davis, Oscar King. Our conquests in the Pacific. N. Y.: Stokes. [c. 1899.] $1.25.

[2461

" A reprint in book form of the letters sent to the New York *Sun* from May to December, 1898, by its correspondent in the Philippines. . . . Reflecting as a matter of course the pronounced attitude toward the war which his paper identified itself with, Mr. Davis still gives estimates of the Filipino patriots which are highly encouraging to those advocating local self-government." *Dial*, 27: 364.

Dinwiddie, William. Puerto Rico, its conditions and possibilities. N. Y.: Harper. 1899. $2.50.

[2462

" Calm, dispassionate, and statistical, Mr. William Dinwiddie still depends largely upon profuse illustration to make his work on Porto Rico attractive. The fourth or fifth of recent works treating of this island, it is by much the most inclusive. . . . The action of the American authorities is subjected to searching criticism." *Dial* (Chicago), 27: 364.

Foreman, John. The Philippine Islands · a political, geographical, ethnographical, social and commercial history of the Philippine archipelago and its political dependencies. [1st ed. London. 1890.] 2d ed. rev. and enlarged. N. Y.: Scribner. 1899. $5.

[2463

" The beginning of wisdom, historically, politically, geographically and commercially, about the Philippine Islands had been (before Dewey's exploit) the work of John Foreman, F. R. G. S. In his own language, it ' is not a history, nor a geography, nor an account of travels, in the strict sense of the word ; it is a concise review of all that may interest the reader who seeks for a general idea of the condition of affairs in this colony in the past and in the present.' His authority caused his services to be availed of by the American Peace Commission, and he gladly joined in what he took to be ' the noble efforts of a free people to raise the weight of monastic oppression from millions of their fellow creatures.' His minutely descriptive and statistical chapters, already bulky, have now been swelled by about one fourth, taking up the parable at the Tagálog rebellion of 1896–98, and bringing the narrative of a change of oppressors down to date, with a map of the revolted province of Cavité and another of Dewey's engagement." *Nation*, 68: 396.

Griffis, William Elliot. America in the east: a glance at our history, prospects, problems and duties in the Pacific Ocean. N. Y.: Barnes. 1899. $1.50.

[2464

" Doctor Griffis's *America in the east* is an intelligent but not too accurate summary of what the United States has stood for in China, Japan, Hawaii, overlaid with much special pleading for the conquest of the Philippines." *Dial*, 27: 365.

Hamm, Margherita Arlina. Porto Rico and the West Indies. N. Y.: Neely. 1899. $1.25.

[2465

Like her book on the Philippines, this " is also the result of visits to the scene of observation, and possesses a like interest, conveyed (with the aid of many illustrations) in the same newspaper English. To make a thick volume, she has had to resort to historical compilation, and is most to be trusted in matters obviously within the range of her observation — climate, manners and customs, the status of women, cookery, products, trade and transportation, and the like. . . . Miss Hamm has a wholesome dread of ' the adventurer and the carpet-bagger.' " *Nation*, 68: 295.

Jordan, David Starr. Imperial democracy. N. Y.: Appleton. 1899. $1.50. [2466

"Eight addresses bearing on the policy of the United States, especially concerning the war with Spain and its results. The author, who is President of Leland Stanford, Jr., University, is an opponent of colonial expansion. The addresses are entitled: Lest we forget ; Colonial expansion ; A blind man's holiday ; The colonial lessons of Alaska ; The lessons of the Paris Tribunal of Arbitration ; A continuing city ; The captain sleeps ; The last of the Puritans." *Publishers' weekly*, 55: 972.

Krout, Mary H. Hawaii and a revolution. N. Y.: Dodd. 1898. $2. [2467

The author " is happy in describing people, places and institutions which came to her notice, and her anecdotes and personal incidents give a strong local color to the book. Politically, [she] is frankly on the side of the party which successfully carried through the revolution, though she acknowledges that she went to the Islands with strong sympathy for the natives as a people who had been unjustly defrauded of their rights." *Dial*, 25: 228.

Laist, Alexander, *comp.* Handbook of the Philippine Islands ; tr. from the *Compendio de Geografia* of P. Francisco X. Baranera ; with a historical sketch by Alex. Laist. Manila : W. Partier. 1899. [Butte City, Montana. J. F. Davies, Silver Bow Block.] 75c. [2468

" Contains in condensed form the information that the average person desires about the Philippines. Mr. Laist compiled the book when a private in the 1st Montana Volunteers on duty in the islands. Mr. J. F. Davies, formerly Librarian of the Butte Free Public Library, Montana, has agreed to sell the work for him in the United States." *Publishers' weekly*, 56: 1298.

Lala, Ramon Reyes. Philippine Islands. N. Y.: Continental Pub. Co. 1899. $2.50. [2469

" A rather novel contribution to the literature of ' our new possessions ' is given us in this book by Ramon Reyes Lala, a native of Manila, and at the same time a citizen of the United States. Mr. Lala was educated in Europe. . . After his return to his home he began his work by a study of the colonial archives ; and when, in 1887, he was banished by the Spanish government, he brought with him to America a large portion of the material necessary for his book. . . . Mr. Lala discusses the islands from the point of view of early history, their varied religions, their

commercial and agricultural possibilities and achievements. . . . In his preface Mr. Lala speaks warmly of ' the manifold advantages and benefits incident to American occupation,' and is evidently a warm friend of the United States." *Literary world*, 30: 71.

Mahan, *Capt.* **Alfred Thayer.** Interest of America in sea power, present and future. Boston : Little. 1897. [c. 1890–7.] $2. [2470

" Under the title given above, Capt. Mahan has republished a series of eight papers which he has contributed to magazines during the last six or eight years, and in all of which he has industriously advocated making the United States a great naval power among the nations of the world. . . . The spirit of the book is so plain that he that runs may read. Military glory and far-reaching domination are the great ends of man's aspiration. To give opportunity for these, the United States must have numerous distant, outlying possessions." J. D. Cox, *Nation*, 67: 34.

Morris, Charles. Our island empire: a hand-book of Cuba, Porto Rico, Hawaii and the Philippine Islands. Phil.: Lippincott. 1899. $1.50. [2471

" The author has compiled useful material regarding each of these on such points as (1) history, (2) physical conditions, (3) natural productions, (4) civil and political relations, (5) centres of population, (6) manners and customs, (7) agricultural productions, (8) manufactures and commerce. A very good small map and an index accompany the volume — making it a kind of vade-mecum. Its information is not, as that of many new works on special islands, first-hand, but collated from many sources." Ira M. Price, *Dial* (Chicago), 26: 395.

Musick, John Roy. Hawaii, our new possessions : travels and adventure, scenery, customs and manners, mythology and history of Hawaii : and the treaty of annexation to the United States. N. Y.: Funk. 1898. $2.75. [2472

" Problems which lie at the root of the question of annexation are airily ignored, in order to tell us what wicked plots the British tried to put up but failed to carry out, to oust the hated Americans, and what a bloodthirsty woman Queen Liliuokalani would have been, if she had succeeded in suppressing the ' missionary ' element. This is all the more to be regretted because Mr. Musick has written a readable though very diffuse account of his visit to the Hawaiian Islands." *Critic*, 32: 38.

Ober, Frederick Albion. Puerto Rico and its resources. N. Y.: Appleton. 1899. $1.50. [2473

" Mr. Frederick A. Ober is an old West Indian traveller, and his book . . . is therefore not an extemporized affair. Mr. Ober also knows his Spanish authorities and how to make good use of them." He gives " an orderly and intelligent account of the island, with full details as to the climate, agricultural products, cities and towns, routes of travel, government and people, etc. A series of illustrations add value to a book which, for being both timely and trustworthy, should be much in demand." *Nation*, 68: 67.

Robinson, Albert Gardner. Porto Rico of to-day: pen pictures of the people and the country. N. Y.: Scribner. 1899. $1.50. [2474

" The work is based upon a series of letters furnished the N. Y. *Evening Post* during the past year, which have been revised and amplified. As a correspondent for that paper the writer accompanied one of the first detachments of the army of invasion to Porto Rico, and remained on the island until after the conclusion of the campaign by the raising of the American flag over the city of San Juan on October 18, 1898." *Annual Am. catalog*, 1899.

Vivian, Thomas J., *and* **Ruel P. Smith.** Everything about our new possessions: being a handy book on Cuba, Porto Rico, Hawaii and the Philippines. N. Y.: Fenno. 1899. 60c. [2475

" A compilation, much of it in statistical form, of some things only, rather than everything, about our new possessions. It contains many valuable facts gleaned from many sources, but lack of discrimination in the use of material, lack of harmony in matter taken from different sources, lack of any map or chart or table of contents, and a poor index, rather hastily decide the fate of this little book." Ira M. Price, in *Dial* (Chicago), 26: 395.

Whitney, Caspar. Hawaiian America: something of its history, resources and prospects. N. Y.: Harper. 1899. $2.50. [2476

" A good general account of the Hawaii of to-day, with some notice of the Hawaii of yesterday. Mr. Whitney regards Hawaii as the only one of our possessions ' likely to become an American community.' . . . The work is fully illustrated from photographs, and is well provided with maps, making a very useful sketch of the islands." H. M. Stanley, in *Dial* (Chicago), 27: 318.

Woolsey, Theodore Salisbury. America's foreign policy. N. Y.: Century Co. 1898. $1.25. [2477

" Mr. Woolsey is professor of international law in the Yale Law School. This book consists of a number of essays and addresses, many of them reprinted from magazines and reviews, and most of them called out by public events during the past four years. Taken together, they give a good idea of the foreign policy of the United States from a thoroughly practical point of view. On several subjects of great importance, such as the Monroe Doctrine, the Nicaragua Canal, and the Philippines, they deal with questions of policy. Questions of policy are, however, involved with questions of international law, especially in this country, and the book discusses so many recent questions of international law that, for the last few years, it serves very well as a popular guide in that study." *Nation*, 67: 433.

Worcester, Dean Conant. Philippine Islands and their people: a record of personal observation and experience; with a short summary of the more important facts in the history of the archipelago. N. Y.: Macmillan. 1898. $4. [2478

" The author has drawn his historical facts from Foreman. He is evidently well acquainted also with the good books which have been written concerning this part of the world. The first three chapters are valuable for their solid information, but the delightful part of the book begins with the author's story of his own adventures, of which he had many." *Critic*, 34: 79.

Young, Lucien. The "Boston" at Hawaii. Wash. 1898.

—— *Same, rev. and enl.* The real Hawaii, its history and present condition. N. Y.: Doubleday & McClure; Doubleday, Page. 1899. $1.50. [2479

" A history of Hawaiian politics, with a full account of present industrial and social conditions. During a period of seven months before and seven months after the overthrow of the Hawaiian monarchy in 1892–93, Lieutenant Young was stationed at Honolulu on the *Boston*. He knew the inner history of the revolution, and was on terms of intimacy with many of the leading men of all parties." *Review of reviews*, 20: 120.

Younghusband, George John. The Philippines and round about. N. Y.: Macmillan. 1899. Net $2.50. [2480

This is " a free-and-easy description of the Philippine Islands, Aguinaldo, Iloilo, Manila, Dewey's naval battle, the fall of Manila, Admiral Dewey, the American soldier, the career of Rizal, the future of the Philippines, Saigon, Java, etc. The value of his work lies in the fact that it gives the impressions of a widely travelled, wide-awake, and straightforward Englishman. . . . The author attributes to Aguinaldo great credit for the manner in which he maintains his hold upon his people, and the determination which he exhibits to fight for complete independence. His criticisms of the American army are free and outspoken." Ira M. Price, in *Dial* (Chicago), 26: 394.

DIVISION 2: COMPREHENSIVE HISTORY

Abbott, Jacob. American history. N. Y.: Sheldon. [c. 1860–5.] 8v. [2481

1. Aboriginal America.—2. Discovery of America.— 3. Southern colonies.—4. Northern colonies.—5. Wars of the colonies.—6. Revolt of the colonies.—7. War of the Revolution.—8. Life of Washington.

A set of juvenile histories by the author of the " Rollo " books. The narration is simple but tedious, and unenlivened by any personality. The books find very little use now. E. E. S.

Allen, John Gamaliel. Topical studies in American history. Rochester: Scranton. 1886. New ed. rev. N. Y.: Macmillan. 1899. Net 40c. [2482

"This little book is, . . . as the name implies, an outline of American history, arranged by topics, rather than in strictly chronological order. An introduction gives suggestions as to methods of teaching, and this is followed by ten pages of *Memory lessons*, comprising an outline of American history from the early explorers to the present time, which is to be committed to memory. . . . The *General topical outline* of the history of the United States covers 68 pages, and includes a synopsis of the government under the heads, Legislature, Executive, Post Office, and Judiciary. A Chronological conspectus follows. . . . Marginal references to secondary authorities and to works of fiction are given with some fulness. A few collections of source-material are quoted." *Am. hist. rev.*, 5 : 398.

American Historical Association. *Historical Manuscripts Commission.* Annual reports, 1896–. Wash. : Gov. Prtg. Off. 1897–.
—— *Same.* (In American Historical Association. Annual reports.)   [2483

"The second report of the Historical Manuscripts Commission comprises a continuation of the correspondence of Phineas Bond, British Consul at Philadelphia, through the years 1790–1794, the Florida side of the French intrigues to get possession of Florida and Louisiana, and a very useful check-list of colonial Assemblies and their journals to the year 1800. . . . This second report of the Manuscripts Commission is edited with the same scholarly fidelity as the first, and for this service we are indebted to the chairman, Professor Jameson, and, for the Mangourit papers, to Professor Turner." Edward G. Bourne, in *Am. hist. rev.*, 4 : 738.

American state papers: documents, legislative and executive. Wash. : Gales & Seaton. 1832–61. 38v.   [2484

Commerce and navigation, 1789–1823. 2v.— Finance, 1789–1828. 5v.— Foreign relations, 1789–1859. 6v.— Indian affairs, 1789–1827. 2v.— Military affairs, 1789–1838. 7v.— Miscellaneous, 1789–1823. 2v.— Naval affairs, 1789–1836. 4v.— Post Office Department, 1789–1833.— Public lands, 1789–1837. 8v.

"Of the volumes on military affairs, the first contains considerable material relating to the War of 1812, especially the campaign of the northern army in 1813 and the capture of Washington. It also comprises all the documents relating to the first Seminole war. A vast quantity of papers on the second Seminole war will be found in volumes 6 and 7. The other volumes relate almost wholly to administrative matters. . . . The four volumes on naval affairs are also chiefly useful as a history of naval administration. Much space is given to the record of unimportant courts-martial. . . . The first volume contains Fulton's scarce pamphlet on the torpedo. The Pirate's war is partly covered in vols. 1 and 2. . . . Many papers referring to the war-history will be found in the early volumes of the series on foreign relations, which throw light on the subject of French spoliations and the hostilities of 1798, difficulties with the Barbary powers, and the negotiations which preceded and terminated the War of 1812." J. R. Soley, in *Narrative and critical hist. of Am.*, 7 : 413.

Ammen, *Rear-Admiral* **Daniel.** Old navy

and the new : memoirs ; with personal letters from Gen. Grant. Phil. : Lippincott. 1891.   [2485

"This volume, dedicated 'to the officers and men of the old navy, who had to learn their profession as best they could,' comprises the reminiscences and experiences of Rear-Admiral Ammen during a naval career embracing now a period of nearly fifty-five years. . . . The first chapters of the book, devoted to the early naval life of the Admiral as midshipman and lieutenant, have a decided sea flavor, like Marryat's tales, and often seem to have been written for the benefit of the younger officers of the service, to whom they should be both interesting and instructive. . . . Owing to his absence upon the China station, then vastly more remote than now, the author took no part in the Mexican War, seeing his first actual war service in the Civil War. . . . As chief of the Bureau of Navigation during the administration of Grant, Ammen embraced every feasible opportunity to extend the work of the navy in time of peace. . . . One of the final chapters of the book is devoted to the question of the Interoceanic Canal, and no one person, in or out of the service, is entitled to speak more positively and intelligently upon this subject than the author. For more than twenty-five years he had advocated its practicability and desirability, directed surveys for its location, weighed the advantages of the various routes." C. H. Stockton, in *Nation*, 52 : 463.

Andrews, Elisha Benjamin. History of the United States. N. Y. : Scribner. 1894. 2v. $4.   [2486

"A book of this scope, written in good style, giving cleverly an outline of facts for the four centuries in which America has been known, has long been needed. . . . President Andrews has endeavored to satisfy the need of such a work. The disagreeable task of recording his failure is thrust upon the reviewer. . . . The chapter on 'American manhood in the Revolution' is well written, but space might have been found for the statement that all of the Americans were not Whigs — for we are loth to attribute to any reason save want of space the fact that the Loyalists are not mentioned. Of course this leaves the impression that the American Revolution was a vast national uprising, in which every one entered heart and soul. Space, it seems, might also have been given, if only a line or two, to an admission that we did not always whip the British frigates and schooners in the War of 1812. . . . One would like to be able to say that, in spite of occasional errors in fact, the generalizations and final judgments of these volumes are sound and trustworthy, and that the narrative is so arranged that the reader is led to a judicious and sensible comprehension of the drift and scope of our history. But it is impossible to reach that decision. The book has been written in the utmost haste, at a reckless rate of speed, and the indications are apparent on almost every page." A. C. McLaughlin, in *Dial*, 18 : 111.

"A somewhat monotonous and unimpressive style, a lack of individuality and freshness in its conception of men and events, and a total absence of references keep it out of the category of high-class literary work. It fails, too, somewhat in the matter of proportion." J. A. Doyle, in *English hist. rev.*, 10 : 604.

Appleton's cyclopædia of American biography; ed. by James Grant Wilson and John Fiske. N. Y.: Appleton. 1886–9. 6v. Rev. ed. 1898. 6v. V. 7 [supplement]. 1900. 7v. $5 ea. **[2487**

The best cyclopædia of American names, containing over 20,000 short biographies of people prominent in history. Persons of foreign birth connected with America are included. Although embracing chiefly citizens of the United States, other parts of both Americas are represented. Bibliographies are attached to the biographies. Discrimination is occasionally apparent in the laudation of Federalist names. The work is as trustworthy as is likely to be produced on so large a scale. E. E. S.

Appleton's home reading books; ed. by W. T. Harris : History.

—— AUSTIN, OSCAR PHELPS. Uncle Sam's soldiers. N. Y.: Appleton. 1899. 75c.

—— HALE, E. E. Historic Boston and its neighborhood. N. Y.: Appleton. 1898. 50c.

—— MATTHEWS, FRANKLIN. Our navy in time of war, 1861–98. N. Y.: Appleton. 1899. 75c. **[2488**

These are intended for the use of children in connection with their school work. Dr. Hale's book is a sort of guide for an historical pilgrimage of seven days about Boston, Cambridge, etc., and its author's name is a certificate of its readableness. Mr. Matthews's is a history of the navy during the Civil and Spanish-American wars. Mr. Austin's book, while in the form of a story covering the events of the Spanish-American war, is really a description of military life and modern warfare, the details of which are explained by means of diagrams. All the volumes are profusely illustrated. F. J. S.

Bancroft, George. History of the United States [to 1782]. Boston : Little. 1834–74. 10v.

—— *Same* [to 1789]; author's last revision. N. Y.: Appleton. 1883–5. 6v. $15. **[2489**

The latest edition of Mr. Bancroft's famous and really monumental work, to which reference is here made, combines his *History of the United States to the close of the Revolution* and his *History of the formation of the Constitution*, though the appendices, which greatly increased the value of the latter work as originally issued, have been omitted. It also contains the many improvements which have resulted from the author's frequent and laborious revisions. A comparison of it with any of the earlier editions will reveal the fact, that many somewhat irrelevant passages — sometimes almost entire chapters — have been omitted, and that innumerable minor changes have been made. The language and tone have been to an extent chastened, errors of statement or emphasis corrected, a better proportion given to the whole. Yet the fundamental views of the author remained unchanged, and he could with truthfulness reproduce in 1882 the introductory sentences which in 1834 ushered the book upon its career of popularity.

Mr. Bancroft's work, as contained in this edition, falls into three parts:— the history of the colonies to 1748, the history of the Revolution, the history of the formation of the Constitution. Of these the second part is by far the most important and valuable. It was to this that he mainly devoted his energy, and in securing access to the material for writing its history he was fortunate beyond all others. The result is that two thirds of the entire work is devoted to the period between 1748 and 1783. In the main he concerns himself throughout with external political events, during the time of war with military and diplomatic history. His strict adherence in narration to the chronological order of events is often a source of weariness and perplexity to the reader. He also uses quotations to an excess. Mr. Bancroft's accuracy, so far as the statement of facts and the description of external events are concerned, has never been successfully impeached. The record of these, so far as he has gone, will probably stand much as he has left it. He was at great pains to be accurate. But when it comes to his opinions about men and events, critics would probably not agree. Like all writers, he shared in the ideas and predispositions of his times ; in his case these were the exultant Americanism and the enthusiasm for democracy which were characteristic of the middle of the 19th century. While his book is invaluable as a statement of the American side of questions, one will look there in vain for an adequate treatment of the British side of the same questions. No thorough or satisfactory estimate of Mr. Bancroft as an historian has yet appeared. The best, though brief, is contained in Prof. Jameson's *History of historical writing in America*. (Boston: Houghton. $1.25.) A few valuable statements concerning his work may be found in Winsor's *Narrative and critical history*, 8: 475 *et seq.* H. L. O.

"An interesting though far from pleasing episode in the history of Bancroft's labors was the chapter of controversies with critics. . . . The historian was so much superior to his critics in knowledge and skill, that in most cases he seemed to come off victorious from the encounter. But the careful reader of this mass of controversial literature will probably feel that a good number of the criticisms made were just, especially as concerned Bancroft's use of quotations, which he sometimes so excises and transposes as strangely to pervert their meaning." J. F. Jameson, *Hist. of historical writing in Am.*, p. 109.

Barnes, Mary Sheldon *and* **Earl.** Studies in American history. Boston : Heath. 1891. $1.12. **[2490**

Not a narrative text-book, but a collection of well-chosen illustrative extracts, with brief connecting passages of comment and explanation. It is designed for use as a text-book, but demands, for success, an accompanying narrative account, a good reference library, and a teacher of rare ability. There is a "manual for teachers" (Heath. 60c.) to accompany the work. W. MacD.

Barnes' popular history of the United States. See Steele, J. D. *and* Mrs. E. B. (sect. 2620).

Beacon biographies; ed. by M. A. De Wolfe Howe. Boston: Small. 1899. 75c. ea. **[2491**

"The little books are very pretty, and each one contains a good photogravure of its subject. In each the narrative is preceded by a chronological summary of the events of the life, and followed by a brief select bibliography. . . . Mr. James Barnes writes of David Farragut, in a popular style; Professor William P. Trent of Robert E. Lee, presenting the view of one who is an intense admirer of that noble man without greatly admiring the school of politics in whose cause he fought. . . . Mr. Norman Hapgood deals with Daniel Webster. The books are pleasant reading, but by no means masterpieces. Their chief interest is that they present their subjects from the point of view of a generation younger than that which has hitherto written of these great men." *Am. hist. rev.*, 5: 169.

Benton, Thomas Hart. Abridgment of the debates of Congress, 1789–1856. N. Y.: Appleton. 1857–61. 16v.   [2492

A notable piece of condensation, invaluable where the *Annals of Congress, Register of debates*, and *Congressional globe* cannot be had. The selection covers all the important topics in the period, and the abridgment is skilful and impartial.   W. MacD.

Bicknell, Edward. Territorial acquisitions of the United States: an historical review. Boston: Small. 1899. 50c.   [2493

"Those who are looking for an account of the enlargement of American territory, told in a brief and plain way, will find what they want. . . . The general reader and the teacher of the history of the United States in the common schools should find the little book useful, and will no doubt do so. The ground covered is from Louisiana to Hawaii." *Dial* (Chicago), 28: 24.

Bigelow, *Capt.* **John, Jr.** Principles of strategy, illustrated mainly from American campaigns. N. Y.: Putnam. 1891. 2d ed., enl. Phil.: Lippincott. 1894.   [2494

"The method pursued is to state a principle or rule of strategic movement in technical form, explain and illustrate it by geometric diagram when possible, and then briefly refer to some example of its application in the history of American wars. The execution of the task is creditable to the author, and cannot fail to be of great service to his brother officers. . . . Whether the conflict be with the aborigines or between civilized communities, the character of the country makes it necessary to modify all accepted rules when they are to be applied in circumstances every way different from those of old, compact, and densely populated states. To point out these differences, to show the inventions and new methods which they have occasioned, and thus to give American military art the flexibility and the progressive character which belong to it, are noteworthy and valuable features of Mr. Bigelow's book. . . . There are rather more typographical and other minor errors than should be in such a book." *Nation*, 53: 341.

Bonner, John. Child's history of the United States. N. Y.: Harper. 1855–76. 3v. $3.   [2495

The history of the United States is narrated in a style easily apprehended by children, at considerable length, in a work covering three volumes. It is interesting, but defective in the division of space given to the several periods of history. The first volume treats of colonial settlement down to 1776; the second, 1776 to 1860; and the third is devoted simply to the Civil War. A child may also derive from these volumes an exaggerated idea of the hostility of the mother country England to this country, and to conclude generally that England and other European countries are naturally predisposed to meanness. The author's judgments of statesmen and generals engaged in the Civil War are in many instances erroneous according to the latest revisions of historical students. By far too much space is given to military history. The work is defective in not being supplied with maps.

D. R. D.

Breck, Samuel. Recollections, with passages from his note-books (1771–1862); ed. by H. E. Scudder. Phil.: Porter. 1877. Coates. $2.   [2496

"Mr. Scudder is quite right in his estimate of the value and interest of Mr. Breck's *Recollections*. It is one of those contemporary pictures which one is always glad to meet with, by whomsoever sketched; but Mr. Breck was not a commonplace man, and had no ordinary opportunities. He was rich and well connected, occupied a high social position, and had some political prominence; lived both in Boston and Philadelphia, and travelled more than once in Europe; his reminiscences are of personages as far removed in every way from one another as Mirabeau and Marryat, including a large proportion of the most prominent public men of this country during the first half-century of the republic. . . . Enough examples are given of corruption, nepotism, and inefficiency in the government to show that we are not very much worse than our fathers. . . . What were then abuses are now recognized practices." *Nation*, 25: 31.

Brooks, Elbridge Streeter. Historic Americans. N. Y.: Crowell. [c. 1899.] $1.50.   [2497

"Beginning with John Winthrop and ending with U. S. Grant, Mr. Brooks includes Franklin, Washington, Samuel Adams, John and John Quincy Adams, Patrick Henry, Jefferson, Hamilton, Robert Morris, Jay, Marshall, Madison, Monroe, Eli Whitney, Jackson, Webster, Irving, Clay, Calhoun, Morse, Horace Mann, Lincoln, and Longfellow." *Publishers' weekly*, 56: 384.

—— Story of the American sailor. Boston: Lothrop. [c. 1888.] $1.50.   [2498

This book is not "intentionally adapted for the juvenile understanding, though offered to young and old. It begins with the prehistoric canoeist and ends with the yachtsman, and manages to suggest the naval history of the United States without being closely bound in its selection or proportionate treatment of topics." *Nation*, 47: 504.

—— Story of the United States. Boston: Lothrop. 1891.

—— *Same;* True story of the United States. Rev. and enl. Lothrop. [c. 1897, '98.] $1.50.
[2499

From Columbus to the Spanish-American war. A sketch or outline along old lines. Embraces more of the real historical than is usually found in children's histories, but the language is adapted to mature children only. The illustrations are of some educational value although not always germane to the text. E. E. S.

Brooks, Noah. Short studies in party politics. N. Y.: Scribner. 1895. $1.25. [2500

This small volume is a collection of four papers previously published in *Scribner's magazine,*—the first three of which, taken together, make a concise review of party politics from 1789 until 1884. It is especially serviceable to those already acquainted in a measure with American political history, who wish to review. The points of emphasis are on the whole well placed. The fourth paper is a bare epitome of party platforms for sixty years. D. R. D.

Brown, John Howard. American naval heroes, 1775-1812-1861-1898 ; with the editorial assistance of Gertrude Battles Lane. Boston : Brown & Co. 1899. Subs. $3. [2501

These are lively accounts of nearly all the men whose names have become famous in American naval history, from Esek Hopkins and Paul Jones down to Hobson and Worth Bagley. The author has in some cases accepted doubtful tradition as fact. The proof-reading is so bad as sometimes to obscure the meaning. The book is intended for boys and will stir their blood. F. J. S.

Bryant, William Cullen, *and* **Sydney Howard Gay.** Popular history of the United States. N. Y.: Scribner. 1878-81. 4v.

—— *Same, enlarged :* Scribner's popular history of the United States. [Supplementary matter and revision by Noah Brooks.] N. Y.: Scribner. 1896. 5v. Scribner-History Club. $20. [2502

Called Bryant's *Popular history,* but Bryant wrote only the introduction. The work was really written by Gay and Brooks. It covers the whole period, but is badly proportioned. There is only one volume for the whole constitutional period to 1861. Based largely on research and generally readable. Profusely illustrated—often with "fancy" pictures. E. C.

Butterworth, Hezekiah. Young folks' history of America. Boston : Estes. 1881. Rev. and enl. Chicago: Werner. 1895.

—— *Same,* rev. and enl.: Story of America. N. Y.: Werner. [c. 1898.] $1.50. [2503

A series of stories and poems arranged in chronological order but not consecutive history. Taken from old histories and including improbable traditions. Important events often condensed into a few lines to connect the stories. Style too heavy for young readers. Latter part a jumble of attempts to bring the book to date at various times. E. E. S.

Callahan, James Morton. Neutrality of the American lakes and Anglo-American relations. (Johns Hopkins Univ. studies, ser. 16, nos. 1-4.) Balt. 1898. Pap. $1.50. [2504

"A study of the diplomacy through which the neutrality of the Great Lakes was secured, in chapters entitled: The northern lake boundary of a new American nation ; The struggle for the control of the lakes, 1783-1815 ; The agreement of 1817 ; The Canadian rebellion and boundary questions, 1837-1861 ; Agitation of lake defences during the American Civil War; After the storm, 1861-1896. Index." *Annual Am. catalog.* 1898.

Champion, *Mrs.* **Sarah E.** Our flag, its history and changes, 1620-1896. 2d ed. New Haven: Tuttle. 1896. 75c. [2505

A short essay describing the evolution of the American flag from the flag of England. The known facts bearing on the many changes are succinctly told, the various conjectures stated, and the reader left to draw his conclusions. There are no references. A short biography of Betsey Ross and a tradition on the origin of the term " Old Glory " are added. Fourteen large colored plates illustrate the descriptions in the text. E. E. S.

Channing, Edward. Students' history of the United States. New ed. enl. N. Y.: Macmillan. 1898. Net $1.40. [2506

" Professor Channing's book, decidedly the best one-volume American history yet published, is admirably fitted for use as a text-book with advanced secondary classes. In the preface the author has explained that his purpose . . . is to provide a text-book suited to the needs of the senior class in high schools and academies. . . . The book is not adapted to the use of young pupils. . . . It is full of suggestions for both teachers and pupils. Miss Anna Boynton Thompson of Thayer Academy has written a chapter entitled *Suggestions to teachers* in which she has described her own methods of teaching. These suggestions will be very helpful to the teacher if he accepts them as 'suggestions' and not as rules. . . . Especially valuable and useful are the marginal references on every page to standard works which contain a fuller account of each topic. Each chapter is headed by a list of books, special accounts, sources and bibliography, maps and illustrative material. . . . Everything is done to stimulate and aid a more thorough investigation by the student. . . . Of the 600 pages 450 are given to the period since 1760. Considerable space is devoted to constitutional and industrial history not found in more elementary text-books. : . . The author displays a judicial and impartial spirit in relation to all controverted questions. . . . The maps are not numerous but sufficient, while there is a gratifying absence of cheap illustrations. The volume contains many excellent portraits." A. A. Freeman, *Am. hist. rev.,* 3: 544.

—— United States of America, 1765-1865. (Cambridge historical series.) N. Y.: Macmillan. 1896. $1.50. [2507

"The aim of this little book," says the author, " is

to trace the steps by which the American people and its peculiar type of federal state have developed out of such heterogeneous and unpromising materials for nation-building as were to be found in the English-American colonies in 1760." Within the space allotted the work has been excellently done. It is an accurate, well balanced and readable book, written in a scholarly, catholic spirit, and furnishing an acceptable outline of the subject.　　　　　　　　　H. L. O.

Channing, Edward, and Albert Bushnell Hart. Guide to the study of American history. Boston: Ginn. 1896. $2.　　[2508

A most useful manual for readers, students, and teachers of American history; compiled as the result of years of experience in college and university instruction. It contains hints on the reading and teaching of history, a selected bibliography of American history, and a long and well-arranged series of topics on colonial and United States history. The book is also elaborately indexed. It will be especially helpful for those engaged in private reading or who are without the guidance of a teacher.　　　H. L. O.

Cluskey, Michael W. Political text-book, or Encyclopædia. Wash. 1857. 2d ed. Phil. 1858. 13th ed. Phil.: Smith. 1860.　　[2509

This volume of 800 pages presents, in a condensed form, a history of public measures of the United States government. It is designed, not only for the politician, but also for the citizen. The topics are arranged alphabetically under titles, and there is also an index. The scope of the work may be illustrated as follows: Abolitionist petitions, includes extracts from such petitions between 1790 and 1857, pages 5–16; on the Dred Scott case there are 60 pages, including judicial decisions; Madison's letters in defence of the American party are given 30 pages; Nebraska and Kansas, 110 pages; squatter sovereignty, 20 pages. Throughout there are many extracts from letters, speeches, and resolves of abolitionists. The appendix covers the period 1858–1860. The work is useful at the present time as a ready collection of documentary literature.　　　　　　　　　D. R. D.

Cooper, James Fenimore. History of the navy of the United States. Phil.: Lea. 1839. 2v.

—— *Same;* continued to 1853. N. Y.: Putnam. 1853.　　　　　　　　　　　[2510

"In some respects, relating to the War of 1812, Cooper's views have been called in question; but his story of the Revolutionary navy is the result of investigations that have not, on the whole, been improved upon. Cooper gives a list of the Continental cruisers, with the fate of each." J. Winsor, in *Narrative and critical hist. of Am.*, 6: 589.

—— Lives of distinguished American naval officers. Auburn, N. Y.: Derby. 1846. 2v.
　　　　　　　　　　　　　　　　　[2511

Contains lives of Bainbridge, Somers, Shaw, Shubrick, Paul Jones, Preble, Woolsey, Perry, and Dale. Originally printed in *Graham's magazine*. Biographies founded on best material available at the time of writing. Style admirable.　　　　　E. C.

Cooper, Thomas V., and Hector T. Fenton, comp. American politics (non-partisan) from the beginning to date. Phil.: Fireside Pub. Co. 1882. Rev. ed. Chicago: Baird. 1884.　　　　　　　　　　　　[2512

Seems to have been compiled mainly by Cooper. Contains a sketch of the history of political parties since 1774 (304 pp.); party platforms (79 pp.); great speeches (251 pp.); parliamentary practices (55 pp.), existing political laws (106 pp.); information as to offices, salaries, etc. (112 pp.), and a mass of historical tables (114 pp.). All bound together in one stout vol. — each part having its own pagination. An excellent book of reference — but now somewhat out of date.
　　　　　　　　　　　　　　　　　E. C.

Davidson, Hannah A. Reference history of the United States, for high schools and academies. Boston: Ginn. 1892. 80c.　[2513

A topical outline, with references for collateral reading, and occasional explanatory notes. The references, especially well-chosen, are to works suitable for high-school pupils. As a manual for use under the so-called "library method," this is one of the best.
　　　　　　　　　　　　　　　W. MacD.

Dawson, Henry Barton. Battles of the United States, by sea and land; with important official documents. N. Y.: Johnson. [c. 1858.] 2v.　　　　　　　　　[2514

Vol. I is given to the Revolutionary War; the greater part of Vol. II is devoted to the War of 1812, including the naval combats. The account of the Mexican War is very brief. There is no index. The illustrations are "fancy pictures," and there are no maps or plans. The value of the book consists in the documents printed at the close of the chapters — especially of those relating to the Revolutionary War.
　　　　　　　　　　　　　　　　　E. C.

Dodge, Nathaniel Shatswell. Stories of a grandfather about American history. Boston. 1874.

—— *Same;* Stories of American history. Boston: Lee. $1.　　　　　　　　　　[2515

A child's book, containing twenty-two stories, beginning with Columbus and closing with the end of the Revolutionary War. They are written in a simple style. Historical accuracy is wanting in many statements.　　　　　　　　　　E. E. S.

Doyle, John Andrew. History of the United States. (Freeman's Historical course for schools.) London: Macmillan. 1875. N. Y.: Holt. 1876. $1.　　　　　　　　[2516

A compact and readable narrative, by one of the most scholarly of English writers on American history. As a text-book, it has never found much favor in the United States, while its disproportionate treatment of the period before 1789 makes its account of the constitutional period slight; but its accuracy and impartiality make it one of the best of single-volume manuals.　　　　　　　　W. MacD.

Eggleston, Edward. First book in American history. N. Y.: Appleton. 1889. N. Y.: Am. Book Co. [c. 1889.] 60c. [2517

This is an exceptionally good introductory book in American history for children seven to nine years of age. The author dwells upon the important periods as represented in the lives of great men. Biography is regarded as " the natural door into history for children." " Primary education should be presented along the line of the least resistance. Nothing, moreover, is more important to the young American than an acquaintance with the careers of the great men of his country." The men thus chosen are Columbus, Cabot, John Smith, Hudson, Standish, Penn, King Philip, Bacon, Franklin, Washington, Jefferson, Boone, Fulton, Harrison, Jackson, Morse and Lincoln. There is an abundance of personal anecdotes. The volume abounds in illustrations, many beautifully executed, and generally well selected as to subjects. There are numerous small picture maps or bird's-eye views which will be of great help to the young reader. D. R. D.

—— History of the United States and its people, for the use of schools. N. Y.: Appleton. 1888. $2.50. [2518

The author lays special stress upon correctness of statements, clearness, and topical rather than chronological arrangement. Emphasis is laid upon the presentation of democratic and social life. It is strictly a text-book with questions, skeleton outlines, reviews, suggestions for blackboard illustrations, diagrams, etc. A special merit lies in the illustrations, which represent an exceptional artistic selection and execution for this class of publications. As the text is so broken by inserts, notes, and illustrations, its value for consecutive reading for children is lessened.
D. R. D.

Eliot, Samuel. Manual of United States history, 1492–1550. Boston: 1856.

—— *Same:* History of the United States, 1492–1872. Boston: Brewer. 1874. [2519

A manual for the use of advanced classes in high schools and academies. Large amount of space devoted to the earlier period. Topics treated are mainly military and political, but some attention is given to social progress. Not illustrated. The best of the earlier text-books. E. C.

Ellis, Edward Sylvester. History of the United States. Phil.: Syndicate Pub. Co. [c. 1899.] 6v. $16. [2520

Written to be sold by subscription, the subject-matter is quite secondary to the illustrations. The perspective is bad, nearly three of the six volumes being given to the Civil War and one to the Spanish-American War. The political and social evolution of the people is scarcely touched. Old tradition, rather than modern investigation, has furnished much of the material. Several editions seem to be published under the same date, but bearing different imprints.
E. E. S.

—— Young people's history of our country. Boston: Lee. 1898. Boston: T. R. Shewell & Co. $1. [2521

This is a condensation of the author's larger *History of the United States*, containing many of the same illustrations. Biographical notes on the presidents and prominent men have been added. The wars occupy a large portion of the space. E. E. S.

Elson, Henry William. Side lights on American history. N. Y.: Macmillan. 1899–1900. 2v. 75c. ea. [2522

Not a connected history, but two series of short essays on various topics connected with American history, chronologically arranged. Begins with the Declaration of Independence and ends with the Spanish-American war. The style is pleasing and the attitude strictly non-partisan. Not much new matter, but mainly old material attractively presented. E. E. S.

First century of the republic: a review of American progress; by Theodore D. Woolsey, *et al.* N. Y.: Harper. 1876. [2523

" This compact volume is one of the best contributions to our Centennial literature, being a collection of the interesting papers which have appeared in *Harper's magazine*, each of which treats of American progress in some branch of literature, political and social science, mechanics, agriculture, and art. Written by the most competent authorities in each department, selected with care by these skillful publishers, and thoroughly classified and indexed, it will be found a valuable text and reference book." *Magazine of Am. hist.*, 1: 62.

Fiske, John. History of the United States, for schools; with topical analysis, suggestive questions and directions for teachers by Frank Alpine Hill. Boston: Houghton. 1894. $1.
[2524

In the main this volume deserves the high rank which it has taken as a school text-book. Maps are abundant in it, the illustrations are excellent, the topics and questions which are appended to each chapter are helpful both for teacher and pupil, references are frequently made to the best literature. The arrangement of subjects and chapters is natural and suggestive. The book was written by a master of clear and forcible English. It seems to me very free from errors of statement, and the few which may be noted are generally not important. The weakest point in the work, as in all current text-books and histories, is the failure to set forth correctly the nature and objects of the old colonial system. If text-book writers would make it plain that the social system of England, and in the main that of the colonies, in the 18th century was aristocratic, and that the methods and ideals of their governments were necessarily of that type also, the spirit in which the history of that period is set before the young would be seriously modified. Mr. Fiske in this volume has sinned less against the relativity of history than have many of his predecessors, and hence the spirit, as well as the form, of his book is, on the whole, to be commended. H. L. O.

Flanders, Henry. Lives and times of the Chief Justices of the Supreme Court. Phil.: Lippincott. 1855–8. 2v. Phil.: Johnson. 1881. 2v. [2525

The first volume or series contains biographies of Jay and Rutledge ; the second of Cushing, Ellsworth and Marshall. They form a standard work, although not brought down to include the later Chief Justices.

E. E. S.

Foster, William Eaton. References to the history of presidential administrations, 1789–1885. (Economic tracts, no. 17.) N. Y.: Soc. for Political Education. 1885. [2526

Ends with the administration of Arthur. It is based upon the same author's *Monthly reference lists.* In its present form, it is the best brief reference handbook in its field. Authorities are judiciously chosen, and their value or significance indicated. W. MacD.

Franklin, *Rear-Admiral* **Samuel Rhoads.** Memories of a Rear-Admiral. N. Y.: Harper. 1898. $3. [2527

" The admiral entered the navy as a midshipman in 1841, then being in his sixteenth year. His memories or reminiscences, therefore, cover a period of fifty-seven years. . . . The book is replete with incidents and anecdotes of service life, and descriptive of his acquaintance and association with many distinguished men and women in all parts of the world." George E. Belknap, *Am. hist. rev.*, 4: 378.

Gilman, Arthur. Historical readers: 1. Discovery and exploration of America. 2. Colonization of America. 3. Making of the American nation. Chicago: Interstate Pub. Co. [c. 1887.] 3v. Boston: Lothrop. 3v. V. 1, 45c. V. 2, 60c. V. 3, 75c. [2528

An excellent series for children of grammar school age. Written from a thorough knowledge of the subject, but comprehensible to the mind of a child. Replaces stories, commonly constituting this class of writing, by simple statements of historic facts. The scope of the various volumes is indicated in the titles. No illustrations. E. E. S.

—— History of the American people. Boston: Lothrop. [1883.] $1.50. [2529

This compendium is larger than the school histories of the United States and yet small for a one-volume detailed history. There is no express statement that it is prepared for youth, though that is undoubtedly its special field. It is an interesting narrative ; " special passages have been devoted to the manners and habits of the past, and the work has been illustrated throughout with extracts from letters, diaries, newspapers, and other contemporary writings." On page *viii* of the preface the author gives a list of points which have been selected for special consideration. Less attention has been paid to the wars of the nation. The work closes with the assassination of Garfield.

D. R. D.

Goldsborough, Charles W. United States naval chronicle. Wash.: Wilson. 1824. v. 1 [no more published]. [2530

" Although entirely devoid of literary construction, [it] is the most useful book of reference on the navy

during the period of the first four presidential terms." J. R. Soley, in *Narrative and critical hist. of Am.*, 7: 416.

Goodrich, Samuel Griswold. American child's pictorial history of the United States. Phil.: Butler. 1866. [2531

Appeared in 1831 as *A first book of history*, by the author of Peter Parley's tales. Over thirty editions were brought out before this one appeared. The history since Washington's inauguration occupies but one fifth of the book. It is of value only as a curiosity. E. E. S.

Gordy, John P. History of political parties in the United States. Columbus, O.: Ohio Pub. Co. 1895. 3v. [2532

Written primarily for the use of teachers in preparing themselves to teach American history. It begins with the difficulties under the Articles of Confederation. The debates of Congress and public papers are followed quite closely, but supplemented by extracts from letters. The studious aim to exclude everything " merely episodical " has given a certain heaviness to so prolonged a story. The proof-reading is unfortunate. E. E. S.

Gordy, Wilbur Fiske. History of the United States for schools. N. Y.: Scribner. 1898. Net $1. [2533

A helpful history for young students, keeping always in sight the object of making them think on historical subjects. Much space is given to social and economic history. Excellent maps, summaries and full chronological tables are included. There are too many illustrations, some good, some very bad. In statement of facts, one notes a few inaccuracies ; otherwise the work is satisfactory ; written in clear but rather dry English. R. C. H. C.

Gordy, Wilbur Fiske, *and* **Willis I. Twitchell.** Pathfinder in American history. Boston: Lee. 1893. $1.20. [2534

A handbook for teachers, containing topical outlines, lists of readings mainly from secondary sources, and suggestions as to methods of teaching. The style and treatment are adapted to the needs of elementary classes. W. MacD.

Greg, Percy. History of the United States from the foundation of Virginia to the reconstruction of the Union. London: W. H. Allen. 1887. 2v. Richmond: West. 1893. [2535

This is a singularly one-sided history written by an English author who achieved considerable note as a journalist and essayist. It is a large and comprehensive two-volume history, scholarly in its proportions and style. The knowledge of American history is regarded as an essential element in the education of an Englishman. The Revolution, Constitution, and Civil War are considered the three central events of American history. In the first part, down to 1783, the author declares that his history follows in the main Bancroft and Palfrey. In the treatment of the Civil War and the questions that led up to that, the author, however, writes in full accord with the southern State Rights political philosophy of a past generation, and presents this philosophy in its extremest form. Abolition is asserted to have been treason. In the account of the Civil War attention is repeatedly called to the inferiority of the northern soldiery during the last half century. There has been a continuous degeneration in American politics. The work is so biased that it is absolutely unsafe for the elementary student.

D. R. D.

Hale, Edward Everett. History of the United States; written for the Chautauqua reading circles. N. Y.: Chautauqua Press. 1887. [2536

Begins with the voyages of the Northmen and ends with 1813. Clearness rather than literary style has been sought. It is a good general account of the period which it covers, and fully satisfies the purpose for which it was written. V. L. C.

Hamilton, Schuyler. History of the national flag of the United States of America. Phil.: Lippincott. 1852. [2537

This is a brief and unpretentious sketch of the selection of the United States flag, beginning with an account of the flags used by the colonists. Special attention is given to the part which Gen. Washington bore in the selection. The volume is practically superseded by the larger and more recent work of Preble.

D. R. D.

Hart, Albert Bushnell. Epoch maps illustrating American history. [14 maps.] N. Y.: Longmans. 1893. 50c. [2538

The maps here gathered into a small atlas also appear in the volumes of the *Epochs of American history.* (N. Y.: Longmans, 3v. $1.25 ea.) They show the territorial extent of the European colonies in North America at different periods, and illustrate the territorial expansion of the United States. Two excellent maps will prove helpful to the student of the slavery controversies. All the work is done with a careful regard for historical accuracy. A. C. McL.

—— *ed.* American history told by contemporaries. N. Y.: Macmillan. 1897. v. 1+. $2 ea. [2539

The object of these volumes is to furnish a collection of sources for the study of American history. The purpose is to cover the field from the age of discovery to the present time in four volumes. Few public documents are given, but rather extracts from diaries and contemporary narratives. The editor believes that by means of such material the reader will get a knowledge of the real life of the past and catch its true spirit. The selections will be of great service in furnishing illustrative material for teachers or for students who are reading modern authors. Each selection is preceded by a very short statement concerning the life of the author. A. C. McL.

—— *ed.* Source-book of American history; ed. for schools and readers, with practical introductions. N. Y.: Macmillan. 1899. 60c. [2540

"The purpose of this book is to make illustrative material in American history accessible to secondary schools. Such a book, to supplement the work of the text, has long been a desideratum. . . . The general plan . . . is the same as that of the editor's *American history told by contemporaries.* It has elaborate introductions, giving many helpful suggestions to teachers on the use of sources. . . . There are also long lists of carefully selected subjects for topical study from sources, brief bibliographies, and on each page marginal explanatory notes. The book contains 145 selections, of which 75 relate to the period since the organization of the national government. Very few of these are documents. They are mostly letters, extracts from books, pamphlets and periodicals, extending from the time of Columbus to the war with Spain, and reproduced in the typography and spelling of the original editions. They are well-chosen and make a most useful and interesting book." John William Perrin, *Am. hist. rev.,* 5: 397.

Hart, Albert Bushnell, *and* **Edward Channing,** *eds.* American history leaflets : colonial and constitutional. N. Y. : A. Lovell. 1892–. No 1+. Pap. 10c. ea. [2541

A collection of original documents and extracts from important state papers, contemporary narratives and like material, intended to offer the historical student an opportunity to study some of the more important sources in American history. The selections have been wisely made. A short historical introduction and references to good secondary histories are given in each leaflet and add to its value. Thirty-one numbers have so far been published. A. C. McL.

Hawthorne, Julian. History of the United States, from the landing of Columbus to the signing of the peace protocol with Spain. N. Y. : P. F. Collier. 1898. 3v. Subs. $5.

[2542

Written upon the assumption "that the American nation is the embodiment and vehicle of a Divine purpose to emancipate and enlighten the human race." Vol. I from Columbus to the beginnings of the Revolution ; vol. II to the Seminole War ; vol. III to the end of the Spanish War. The style is that of a series of essays, verbose, dramatic, often lacking chronological order, and presupposing no little familiarity with the general facts. Represents the extreme "popular" historical writing which aims to be readable rather than scholarly. A maximum of military and a minimum of political and social history. Stock illustrations and entirely imaginary. Volumes divided into equal number of pages instead of by chapters. No references. E. E. S.

Higginson, Thomas Wentworth. Larger history of the United States, to the close of Jackson's administration. N. Y. : Harper. 1886. $2. [2543

This was written in 1882, subsequent to the author's *Young folks' history,* as the result of requests "to tell the story of the nation over again upon a much larger scale." From the standpoint of interest there is no falling off. There is, however, a lack of continuity essential to a well-prepared history, nor is the work so large as might be inferred from the title. The volume rather represents a series of historical essays, which together form a suggestive and helpful survey to the close of Jackson's administration. As in the smaller work, the author devotes considerable space to the pre-Columbian and discovery periods. Attention should be directed to the portraits illustrating the volume.

D. R. D.

—— Young folks' history of the United States. Boston: Lee. 1875–86. N. Y.: Longmans. $1. [2544

This history, first published in 1875, has deservedly met with much favor. It is essentially a book for reading which will arouse an interest in the reading of other histories. There has been no sacrifice of scholarship, nor has the use of a special juvenile dialect been attempted. It may well engage the attention of adults as well as youth, for the subject-matter has not been unduly condensed. " Less space than usual is given to the events of war." There are " two plain rules,— to omit all names and dates not really needful, and to make liberal use of the familiar traits and incidents of every day."

D. R. D.

Hildreth, Richard. History of the United States [to 1821]. N. Y.: Harper. 1849–52. 6v. New ed. 6v. $12. [2545

Three volumes are devoted to the period before 1783. An annalistic work. Often poorly arranged. Often very dry. It is, however, very accurate as to names and dates, and this gives it its place. The volumes dealing with period from 1783 to 1821 are written from the federalist point of view, and are intensely hostile to Jefferson and his supporters. The work was written before 1850.

E. C.

Hinsdale, Burke Aaron. How to study and teach history, with particular reference to the history of the United States. (International education series.) N. Y.: Appleton. 1894. $1.50. [2546

This volume belongs to the *International education series*, edited by William T. Harris. As the title indicates, it treats of the subject of history in general, with special reference to the United States. To this topic belong chapters 14 to 22, on the Historical geography of the old world; North America in outline; the Colonization of North America; the Struggle between France and England in North America; the American Revolution; the War of 1812; the Territorial growth of the United States; Phases of industrial and political development; and Slave power. These chapters are narrative in character, prefaced by bibliographical references. The aim has been to emphasize fundamental forces and relationship in history, and to present material which is generally omitted in the more condensed histories and which will be of special value to a teacher in presenting the subject in the classroom. The aim is " to state the uses of history, to define in a general way its field, to present and to illustrate criteria or the choice of facts, to emphasize the organization of facts with reference to the three principles of association, to indicate sources of infor-

mation, to describe the qualification of the teacher, and finally to illustrate causation and the grouping of facts by drawing the outline of some important chapters of American history." From a bibliographical point of view the work is deficient, considering the large amount of material to which both teacher and student need a guide.

D. R. D.

Holst, Hermann von. Constitutional and political history of the United States. Chicago: Callaghan. 1877–92. 8v. $25. [2547

See notes in division 3, — *Constitutional history*, sect. 2749, 2750.

Houghton, Walter R. History of American politics. Indianapolis. 1883. Chicago. 1884. [2548

Slight attention paid to colonial politics. Arranged chronologically by administrations. Really a large one-volume history of the federal administration from 1789 to 1882. Style dull and monotonous. Not well arranged for reference.

E. C.

Jameson, John Franklin. Dictionary of United States history, 1492–1894. Boston: Puritan Pub. Co. [c. 1894.] Phil.: Century Manufacturing Co. 1901. 2v. $6. [2549

A useful reference work, supplying, under an alphabetical arrangement of topics, a large amount of information about the states, public men, treaties, statutes, etc., as well as political events of importance. The statements are brief and comprehensive, and aim to meet the needs of the general reader; but the range of topics is wide.

W. MacD.

—— Introduction to the study of the constitutional and political history of the states. (Johns Hopkins University studies in hist. and pol. science, ser. 4, no. 5.) Balt. 1886. Pap. 50c. [2550

Three short suggestive papers in which the author pleads for a broader conception of the value and scope of state history and for a more thorough and intelligent study of that neglected field. The work should be done, not to indulge mere local pride, or to satisfy antiquarian curiosity, but for the purpose of making substantial contributions to the political and constitutional history of the United States, which can be understood only after an examination of local forms and forces.

A. C. McL.

Johns Hopkins University. Studies in historical and political science. Balt. 1882–. No. 1+. [2551

A collection of monographs, in 17 annual series and 21 extra volumes, on historical, political, administrative, and economic subjects, mainly the work of past or present members of the Johns Hopkins University. The range is wide, but local and municipal institutions, and the history of the southern states, receive special attention. The papers are of unequal merit, and some are not important; but the series as a whole has marked value for special study.

W. MacD.

The more important of these *Studies* are entered elsewhere, according to subject, and separately estimated.

Editor.

Johnston, Alexander. History of American politics. N. Y.: Holt. 1877. 4th ed. rev. and enl. 1898. 80c. [2552

The best brief presentation of the narrowly political phases of American history. A chapter is devoted to each presidential administration, with important events in each grouped by Congress and session. While the methodical arrangement robs the book of literary importance, and the statements of fact are not inerrant, the work has high value either as a text-book, a reference manual, or a guide for private study. A useful appendix gives a list of cabinet officers, with their terms of service. W. MacD.

—— History of the United States, for schools ; with an introductory history of the discovery and English colonization of North America. N. Y.: Holt. 1885.

—— Same ; rev. and continued by Winthrop More Daniels. N. Y.: Holt. 1897. $1. [2553

The best school history of the United States at the time of its publication and still among the best. It shows a profound sense for the really vital events in the life of the nation, and is the work of a scientific historian of exceptional ability and unusual judgment. R. C. H. C.

"Professor Johnston's book strikes us as preëminently manly — for that matter, womanly, too ; it is not the childish article which would apparently suit some 'eminent educationists' who think a teacher's business is to amuse the little ones, and keep them amused up to the time when they have children of their own. Where all is good it is hard to specify ; but we would particularly select the development of the southern colonies, the land operations of the War of 1812, the political movements from 1838 to 1848, and the comparative exhibition of the campaigns of the Civil War, as especially indicative of impartiality and due proportion in the writer's mind." *Nation,* 42: 17.

—— United States ; its history and constitution. N. Y.: Scribner. 1889. $1. [2554

First prepared for the ninth edition of the *Encyclopædia Britannica.* It is probable that a better history of its size has never been written. It treats the periods of exploration and colonization with unusual brevity, and gives the proper attention to social and economic facts. Johnston was particularly happy in presenting clearly causes and effects. He wrote from the sources, was accurate, fair, possessed excellent judgment and the command of a clear, direct style. R. C. H. C.

—— ed. Representative American orations, to illustrate American political history. N. Y.: Putnam. 1884. 3v.

—— Same : American orations ; reëdited with notes by James Albert Woodburn. 1896–7. N. Y.: Putnam. 4v. $1.25 ea. [2555

By a master in American history. Designed to show the spirit and motives of the leading men of America from the Revolutionary era to the present. The series are : — 1. Colonialism, 1775–1789 ; — 2. Con-

stitutional government, to 1801 ; — 3. Rise of democracy, to 1815 ; — 4. Rise of nationality, to 1840 ; — 5. Slavery struggle, to 1860 ; — 6. Secession and reconstruction, to 1876 ; — 7. Free trade and protection. An historical essay introductory to each series furnishes a valuable commentary on the vital measures discussed in the orations. The revised edition adds a number of orations and a section on finance and civil service reform, besides supplying helpful biographical and illustrative notes. R. C. H. C.

Johonnot, James, comp. Stories of our country. N. Y.: Appleton. [c. 1887.] American Bk. Co. 40c. [2556

This is part of an historical series of readers for young pupils in schools. It is not designed as a complete narrative history, but includes interesting tales and episodes to which no great space can be given in the historical compendiums. There are in all thirty-six stories, only four of which deal with the period since the Revolution. The stories are in part compiled by the editor, and in part taken from the works of Lossing, Abbott, Coffin, and Hawthorne. The purpose of the work is good, but it is a question whether the editor might not have made a better choice in his extracts, selecting more passages associated with the greater names of literature. The illustrations are rude ; the type, however, is excellent. D. R. D.

Judson, Harry Pratt. Growth of the American nation. (Chautauqua reading circle literature.) Meadville : Flood. 1895. N. Y.: Macmillan. 1899. Net $1. [2557

A plain and simple narration of the leading events of United States history. Nothing novel. Very fair and unbiased. Treats slavery and disunion from the standpoint of commercial reconstruction. Written in an easy and rather terse style ; a valuable manual. E. E. S.

Knapp, Samuel Lorenzo, ed. Library of American history : a reprint of standard works connected by editorial remarks, with notes, biographical sketches, [etc.] N. Y. 1837. 2v. [2558

The works reprinted are Jeremy Belknap's biographies of the early discoverers, and William Robertson's *History of South America,* James Grahame's *History of North America,* David Ramsay's *Revolutionary War,* President Stiles's *Account of the regicides* (Dixwell, Whalley and Goffe), William Hubbard's *Narrative of the Indian Wars in New England,* and Benjamin Church's *King Philip's War.* The editor pieces out Ramsay at the beginning and end without indicating in any way the change to another author, and does not hesitate to make unimportant verbal changes in his text. F. J. S.

Leeds, Josiah W. Smaller history of the United States. Phil.: Lippincott. 1882. [2559

This is a beginners' text-book written for "intermediate schools and for home students." The spirit animating the book is excellent. The author deprecates the undue amount of space given in many histories to war; consequently in this volume military affairs are treated as interruptions to the normal arts of peace. For the same reason the author eliminates pictures of battle scenes. The American Revolution occupies but fifteen pages and the Civil War but twenty in a total of 260. It is unfortunate that the author attempts to compress too many facts into the volume. The author wrote a larger *History of the United States* (Phil. 1877). D. R. D.

Lodge, Henry Cabot, *and* **Theodore Roosevelt.** Hero tales from American history. N. Y.: Century Co. 1895. $1.50. [2560

This is a series of narrative sketches of the more dramatic scenes of American history, including accounts of Gen. Boone, George Rogers Clark and the conquest of the Northwest, the battle of Trenton, the storming of Stony Point, the Cruise of the Wasp, "Remember the Alamo," the charge at Gettysburg, Lieut. Cushing and the ram Albemarle, etc. The scenes are generally those of war, and the heroes are martial rather than industrial. From the standpoint of the worshipper of heroes of war, the tone of the work is healthy and manly. The authors have about evenly divided the preparation of the volume.
D. R. D.

Logan, *Maj.-Gen.* **John Alexander.** The volunteer soldier of America. Chicago : Peale. 1888. [2561

General Logan was one of the most brilliant leaders of troops in battle in the Civil War, from a regiment to an army corps. His book supports the theme that our existing system of military education for the regular army does not produce any satisfactory proportion of great soldiers. He advocates a general system of militia organization, with tests of aptitude for higher military work and competitive selection for permanent service. He has brought together a great body of laws, regulations, tables and records, bearing upon the subject, and argues from the history of our wars, judged in the light of his own experience. His book is of real importance in the study of the subject. He is a trenchant debater, an ardent and eloquent advocate of his opinions. J. D. C.

Lossing, Benson John. Harpers' popular cyclopædia of United States history, from the aboriginal period to 1876. N. Y.: Harper. 1881. 2v.

—— Family history of the United States. Hartford : Belknap. 1883.

—— Common-school history of the United States. N. Y.: Sheldon. 1864. N. Y.: Butler. $1.28. [2562

Under the first title about five thousand topics in American history, within the limits prescribed in the text, are given, with descriptions varying from a few lines to several pages, according to their importance. They are as a whole well chosen and clearly written. The volumes are likely to prove useful as a short cut to information, but are inadequate to the needs of the scholar, and give no references for further information.

The second is a popular subscription book along old lines. The later events are grouped under administrations. It closes with the death of Garfield. There is no especial feature of merit aside from the profuse illustration.

The third is an antiquated text-book. It forms the intermediate volume in a series of three school texts on American history. Five of the six chapters are devoted to colonial and Revolutionary history. E. E. S.

—— Story of the United States navy, for boys. N. Y.: Harper. 1881. $1.75. [2563

"This instructive and entertaining volume . . . was prepared at the suggestion of Captain Luce, the intelligent captain of the training-ship Minnesota. Its correctness was assured by submission to the authorities of the Navy Department, and its nautical terms have been corrected by an officer in the service." *Magazine of Am. hist.*, 7: 472.

Lyman, Theodore, Jr. Diplomacy of the United States. Boston : Wells. 1826. [2564

An early attempt at a history of American diplomacy. It begins with the sending of American agents to France in 1776, and extends through the treaty of Ghent which ended the War of 1812. The work was never brought down to a later period. Superseded to some extent by Sparks's *Diplomatic correspondence of the Revolution* (sect. 1504), by Wharton's volumes bearing the same title, and by the official *Treaties and conventions* of the United States (sect. 2633).
E. E. S.

Mabie, Hamilton Wright. Popular history of the United States; with special chapters by John Sherman and others. Phil.: J. C. Winston Co. [c. 1897.] $3. [2565

This is a large one-volume history of over 800 pages in excellent type. There are many illustrations. Of these a considerable number are fanciful, and some are exceedingly sensational. The work is advertised on the title-page as prepared by Hamilton Wright Mabie, but the introduction is signed also by Marshal H. Bright, indicating a divided responsibility. There are also inserted chapters written by specialists, among which may be mentioned Struggle for liberty and government by Francis N. Thorpe, the Indian of the nineteenth century by Henry L. Dawes, National currency by J. K. Upton, School, college and university by T. S. Doolittle, The Northwest by Albert Shaw, Old south and new by W. C. P. Breckinridge, Women in America by Frances E. Willard, and the American church by Bishop Vincent. A history prepared in this fashion is naturally of uneven merit. The narrative is fairly complete down to this century, but from the close of the War of 1812 it would be difficult for a reader to derive a clear idea of the sequence of events. There are many omissions. The confusion in the order of events may also be illustrated by noting that the chapter on Difficulties with foreign powers follows the treatment of the Civil War. In the topical method here presented, however, there is a freshness of treatment which makes the work of service for supplementary reading. D. R. D.

McCarthy, Justin. History of our own times, from the accession of Queen Victoria to the Berlin Congress. London: Chatto. 1879-

80. 4v. N. Y.: Harper. 1880. 2v. $2.50. Supplementary vol. [1880–97]. Lond. : Chatto. 1897. N. Y.: Harper. 1897. $1.75.   [2566

This book includes a survey of English literature during the reign, and gives much space to social details, but is devoted principally to the spectacular side of history. It is, of necessity, based mainly upon secondary sources, though the writer's experience furnishes something. McCarthy touches American history only as it relates to English affairs, and in a superficial manner, though with evident sympathy for the American point of view.   R. C. H. C.

McCarthy, Justin Huntly. Short history of the United States. Chicago: Stone. 1899. $1.50.   [2567

" It is hard to account for Mr. Justin Huntly Mc-Carthy's *Short history of the United States* except as an unusually desperate case of cram and potboiling. It is superficially conceived and crudely executed. . . . A more inadequate and misjudged sketch of the Civil War, for example, we do not remember to have seen. There is not even a coherent outline, and men and movements are jumbled together in an altogether hopeless muddle. All the disasters of the North in the first two years of the war are laid in a bundle upon the shoulders of one man — McClellan. There is not a mention of Pope and his rout (the name is not even in the index) ; Burnside and Fredericksburg receive a single line, and Chancellorsville is to this historian apparently unknown. . . . The reading of a single book written by his fellow countryman, Colonel Henderson, might have saved Mr. McCarthy from blunders such as these." *Dial*, 26: 280.

MacCoun, Townsend. Historical charts of the United States : territorial growth. N. Y.: Silver. 1889. $15.   [2568

A set of twenty-eight mounted maps, 24 by 36 inches, printed in colors to denote divisions of territory. They are progressive from 1755 to 1861. They are not always exact, but this is due partly to the many disputed points in American cartography. They are used in many schoolrooms. A reduced size for desk work was printed in 1888 (Silver. 90c.).   E. E. S.

Macdonald, William, *ed.* Select documents illustrative of the history of the United States [v. 1], 1776–1861 ; with notes. N. Y.: Macmillan. 1898. $2.25.   [2569

Relate mainly to constitutional development, foreign relations and banking. Most notable omissions are documents relating to tariff history and judicial decisions. It is a useful compilation for college classes in its restricted field.   E. C.

McLaughlin, Andrew Cunningham. History of the American nation. (Twentieth century series.) N. Y.: Appleton. 1899. Net $1.40.   [2570

" A new high-school book, . . . from Professor Mc-Laughlin, is a notable event ; and its appearance just now derives added significance from the author's services as chairman of the Committee of seven on the study of history in schools. . . . The work will appeal

also to an audience outside the schoolroom as a welcome addition to our one-volume histories. . . . The author's interest centres, and rightly, in the national period. . . . Here we have 300 pages, compact of sound scholarship and accurate statement, that make a distinct addition to our briefer historical narratives. . . . Many current misapprehensions and prejudices are quietly corrected. . . . Generous tribute is paid the honesty and heroism of the South, and the contradictory phases of reconstruction are set forth with admirable lucidity and fairness. I know no brief account of that intricate period so satisfactory. And this sturdy impartiality is characteristic of the book. No page is marred by slur or epithet, and foreign nations are treated with justice and generosity — all without abatement of virile Americanism. In colonial history we have no right to expect the same easy mastery." W. M. West, in *Am. hist. rev.*, 5: 351.

Maclay, Edgar Stanton. History of American privateers. N. Y.: Appleton. 1899. $3.50.   [2571

Mr. Maclay has " divided his subject into two parts : ' The War of the Revolution ' and ' The War of 1812.' From forgotten monographs, the records of historical societies, from unpublished log-books, and from descendants of noted privateersmen, he has obtained intimate and vivid accounts of the fitting out of the vessels, the incidents of their voyages, and the thrilling adventures of the brave sailors who manned them. His work is accompanied by reproductions of contemporary pictures, portraits and documents, and also by illustrations by George Gibbs." *Publishers' weekly*, 56: 1327.

—— History of the United States navy, 1775–1901. N. Y.: Appleton. 1894. 2v. New ed. rev. and enl. 1898–1901. 3v. $9.   [2572

" Mr. Maclay has had the advantage, which he has partly used, of the revival in American historical research, and has had opportunities afforded him of personal investigation in the library of the British Museum and also in the archives of the French Ministry of Marine in Paris. Besides this he has gathered information bearing upon the War of 1812 from private sources in Great Britain. The result is a narrative much more full and interesting than Cooper, as well as more accurate. This is especially the case in the account given of the quasi-French war, as may be supposed, and also the wars with the Barbary States." There is a want of proportion and perspective. There are many errors, and the author glides over controverted topics. C. H. Stockton, in *Nation*, 58: 455. 60: 35.

The new edition " consists of a rearrangement and enlargement of the previous one rather than a revision. . . . The additional matter in the second volume brings it down, by the aid of newspaper accounts, to the battle of Manila Bay." Some matters before omitted are included in this issue. " Taken as a whole, this history of the navy . . . is the best in print, but the perspective needs correction." *Nation*, 66: 499.

—— Reminiscences of the old navy ; from the journals and private papers of Captain Edward Trenchard and Rear-Admiral Stephen

Decatur Trenchard. N. Y.: Putnam. 1898. $2.50. [Ed. limited to 750 copies.] [2573

"There are many acts of heroism, many thrilling episodes, and many romances wrapped up in the private lives of our officers which have not been made public, and are known only to a few of their most intimate messmates. The records left by the two Trenchards, covering eighty years of service in the United States navy, are singularly rich in romance and in details of historic interest. It is, in truth, an 'inside history' of the navy for the period covered." *Preface.*

McMaster, John Bach. History of the people of the United States from the Revolution to the Civil War. N. Y.: Appleton. 1883–1900. V. 1–5. $2.50 ea. [To be 7v.] [2574

In its special devotion to social and economic conditions, this work suggests Green's *Short history of the English people*, but on a vastly enlarged scale. The style is attractive, and the author has industriously searched contemporary records, especially newspapers, journals and books of travel, for his material. The promise of the first volume, however, has not been fulfilled. Beginning with vol. II, the mass of relatively unimportant details overshadows broad political movements, and the work becomes a succession of essays rather than a connected and conclusive exposition. Within its field it has no equal, and is not likely soon to have a successor so pretentious ; but it gives, at best, only a partial view of the course and significance of American history. W. MacD.

—— School history of the United States. N. Y.: American Book Co. [c. 1897.] $1.
[2575

The 476 pages of this text-book are packed full of material on American history from the beginning of the discoveries to the year 1897. For the most part it is well selected and is stated with simplicity and force. Of special interest and novelty are the chapters on the social conditions existing in the country at successive periods. The book is well supplied with maps, illustrations and summaries. The accumulation of details and the adoption of a uniform narrative style must tend to limit the independence of the teacher and tempt the pupil to learn by rote. Though this is the form in which text-books in this country are usually written, it is believed that something more resembling the syllabus would produce better results. Errors or loose statements occasionally appear, especially in the early part of the book. H. L. O.

—— With the fathers: studies in the history of the United States. N. Y.: Appleton. 1896. $1.50. [2576

This is a collection of thirteen essays previously published in magazines or daily newspapers. Several were prompted by important crises in contemporary politics. In this group is The Monroe doctrine, occasioned by the discussion over the Venezuelan message. Of similar character is The third term tradition; The riotous career of the Know-Nothings ; and A century's struggle for silver. Other essays are simply historical narratives. The style is clear and interesting.
D. R. D.

Magazine of American history. N. Y. 1877–93. 30v. [2577

Somewhat unevenly edited and quasi-popular in character, but containing a great number of original documents and articles more or less monographic in character and often of considerable excellence. The portraits, maps, plans, pictures of old mansions, etc., are numerous and valuable. E. C. R.

Mahan, *Capt.* **Alfred Thayer.** Interest of America in sea power, present and future. Boston: Little. 1897. $2. [2578

Collected essays from various periodicals written between 1890 and 1897, discussing the American naval problem and the relation to it of Hawaii, the Isthmus, the Caribbean Sea and the Gulf of Mexico, and the problem of an Anglo-American reunion. Much of what was prophecy in these essays has become history in 1899, and given further force to the remarkable authority of the author, already easily first among the world's naval writers. E. C. R.
See, also, sect. 2470.

Moireau, Auguste. Histoire des Etats-Unis de l'Amérique du nord. Paris: Hachette. 1892–. v. 1–2. 20 fr. [2579

Of the two volumes of this work that have appeared, the first covers the period from the discoveries to the Declaration of Independence, and the second the next twenty-five years to the election of Jefferson. The author has produced an accurate, well-proportioned and discriminating narrative, founded on the best sources. Select lists of sources and the best books are supplied with each group of chapters. His work is judicial in temper and infused with the historic spirit. When completed it will be one of our best general histories. E. G. B.

Monroe, *Mrs.* **Adeline F.** Story of our country. Boston: Lockwood. 1876. Lee. 50c.
[2580

The history of the United States down to the close of the Revolution is told by a mother to her two children in the form of a dialogue. There is no attempt to make the narrative comprehensive. The style is adapted to children, although in places the remarks are slightly pedantic or over-naïve for the present generation. The conflicts of history are not treated critically but entirely from an American standpoint, and the child is easily led to positive convictions of antagonism toward other countries. The illustrations are crude and unsatisfactory. D. R. D.

Montgomery, David Henry. Beginner's American history. Boston: Ginn. 1892. New ed. 1899. 60c. [2581

This book follows the plan of the larger volumes by the same author in a lighter and much more attractive style. E. E. S.

—— Leading facts of American history. Boston: Ginn. 1890. 1899. $1. [2582

A popular text-book for intermediate schools, describing the chief events from the discovery by Columbus to 1894. There is no attempt at elaboration of the bare facts. The topical system is employed.

Various tables, lists of dates, and a bibliography are added. E. E. S.

—— Student's American history. Boston : Ginn. 1897. $1.40. [2583

An acceptable text-book for high schools. It is refined down to concise statements along the lines and in the proportions of older texts. E. E. S.

Moore, John Bassett. History and digest of the international arbitrations to which the United States has been a party, with the treaties relating to such arbitrations and historical and legal notes on other international arbitrations, ancient and modern. (53d Cong., 2d sess., House misc. doc. 212.) Wash. 1898. 6v. [2584

The first two volumes cover with great fulness the boundary and other disputes which have been referred to arbitration, the third and fourth give the procedure, legal principles, etc., which rule in such matters, the fifth recites the history of international claims which have been settled by domestic commissions, and the sixth consists exclusively of maps, other maps being placed with the text in the first two volumes. We have, therefore, a history of most American claims against foreign nations. The table of contents for the whole and lists of cases reported and cited and of authorities are in the first volume. F. J. S.

Moore, Joseph West. The American Congress, 1774–1895. N. Y. : Harper. 1895. $3. [2585

A compendium of the sessions, debates, leading measures, prominent members and political trend of the Congress of the United States. An introductory chapter leads to the Continental Congress and it, in turn, through the Constitutional convention to the Federal Congress in the eighth chapter. The remaining twenty-six chapters are devoted to the various sessions, ending with the third of the fifty-third Congress, March 4, 1895. The book is not likely to prove attractive to general readers, but may be useful to students who have not access to originals. The nonpartisan attitude assumed is fairly well carried out. The usual public papers together with lists of congressional sessions and presidents pro tempore of the Senate are added. E. E. S.

Morris, Charles. History of the United States of America, its people, and its institutions. Phil. : Lippincott. 1898. $1.50. School ed. $1. [2586

Mr. Morris is a veteran compiler. The present work is a text-book on American history neither better nor worse than many others of its kind. It is without special merits or serious defects ; repeats stock anecdotes and contains illustrations that are merely imaginative. It displays neither originality nor a knowledge of modern methods of instruction. There are at the end lists of questions and a meagre bibliography, but no other aids for either teacher or student. C. M. A.

—— The nation's navy. Phil. : Lippincott. 1898. $1.50. [2587

"It is to be regretted that the book under consideration, owing to its inaccuracies, falls short of being the useful hand-book of the United States navy which it might otherwise have been. . . . The book, after a thorough revision, may claim a place among works of reference, but until then its careless compilation seriously affects its utility." *Nation*, 67 : 246.

Mowry, William Augustus *and* **Arthur M.** History of the United States for schools. N. Y. : Silver. 1896. $1. [2588

Designed as a text-book for the senior classes in grammar schools. The story is pleasantly told, with stress upon personal and military incidents rather than political and governmental questions, and with no great effort to show the development of issues. W. MacD.

Oliveira Lima, Manoel da. Nos Estados Unidos : impressoes politicas e sociaes. Leipzig : Brockhaus. 1899. [2589

" Mr. Oliveira records his impressions and reflections under the following titles : The negro problem ; Effects of immigration ; Characteristics of the people ; Influence of woman ; Society ; The political fashion-plate ; Catholicism and education ; American authors ; Foreign policy ; Relations of Brazil with the United States ; Colonial policy. . . . The good and the bad sides of our politics are set forth with a poise of judgment and a scientific detachment that remind one of Bryce and Tocqueville. That like both of these great publicists, so careful a student and observer from South America as Mr. Oliveira proves himself to be should feel and show a sincere admiration for the United States is a legitimate cause for gratification. A translation of this book into English would be welcomed here, but a translation of it into Spanish would render a great service to the cause of Inter-American comity and friendly understanding." E. G. Bourne, in *Am. hist. rev.*, 5 : 605.

Parmele, *Mrs.* **Mary Platt.** Evolution of an empire : a brief historical sketch of the United States. N. Y. : W. B. Harison. 1896.

—— *Same :* Short history of the United States. N. Y. : Scribner. 1898. Net 60c. [2590

A text-book written to demonstrate a theory that the study of history should be " acquired first in its utmost brevity, then enlarged, and enlarged again and again." Dates and battles are made subordinate. The result is a simple narrative, well proportioned, extending from the discovery of America to the administration of Cleveland. The departure from the old style of writing is sufficient to nullify the virtues of that method, while the new treatment along old lines lacks sufficient interest to give it special merit. E. E. S.

Parton, James. Famous Americans of recent times. Boston : Ticknor. 1867. Houghton. $2.50. [2591

Sketches of Clay, Webster, Calhoun, Randolph, Girard, J. J. Astor, Theodosia Burr, J. G. Bennett, Charles Goodyear, Beecher and Cornelius Vanderbilt. The sketch of Clay is the most accurate and the best ; that of Webster is overdone and unduly severe ; that of Calhoun unjust and mistaken throughout. The usual deficiencies of Parton are present. He generalizes on insufficient evidence, is superficial, partial and dogmatic. There is considerable research evident, and the essays are very entertainingly written.

R. C. H. C.

Patton, Jacob Harris. Concise history of the American people. N. Y.: Fords. 1883. 2v.

—— Same: Four hundred years of American history. N. Y.: Fords. [c. 1892.] 2v. $5.

[2592

A history for general readers on the old lines of division and treatment. The first volume is devoted to the colonial foundations and conflicts and to the Revolutionary War. The second volume treats of the leading political events by administrations of Presidents, including that of Benjamin Harrison. In one chapter is a comparison of the nation in 1789 and in 1889, and in another an explanation of the system of national government. The usual documents, such as the Constitution and the Declaration of Independence, are added. The style is plain and the viewpoint strictly national or Hamiltonian. The social development of the people is entirely omitted. The references are meagre and indefinite. The ninety-eight portraits are omitted in the reprint. E. E. S.

Poore, Benjamin Perley. Perley's reminiscences of sixty years in the national metropolis. Phil.: Hubbard. [c. 1886.] 2v. [2593

A peculiar running comment on incidents connected with life at the national capital from 1827 to 1867. The author was for many years compiler of the Congressional directory and came into the possession of numerous stories concerning the prominent men of Washington. He treats of public characters, the inauguration of the Presidents, the foreign embassies, and the city during war times. The book is quite interesting, although far from infallible and without any official basis. E. E. S.

Powell, Edward Payson. Nullification and secession in the United States. N. Y.: Putnam. 1897. $2. [2594

A keen, but strongly biased and not very thorough study of nullification and secession, as exemplified in the Kentucky and Virginia resolutions of 1798-99, the plan for a northern confederacy in 1803-4, Burr's conspiracy, 1806-7, New England opposition to the War of 1812, South Carolina nullification in 1832, and the secession of the southern states in 1861. The author has been industrious in gleaning facts favorable to his purpose ; and has succeeded in showing, as others before him had done, that "political righteousness has not been the exclusive property of any one part of the United States." As an offset to blind hero-worship, the book may be useful; but its extreme and partisan judgments deny it permanent value. The style is loose, though often incisive and vigorous.

W. MacD.

Pratt, Mara L. American history stories. Boston: Educational Pub. Co. 1888–91. 4v. 50c. ea. [2595

We know from observation that these book; interest young children. The poems and songs which are introduced add to their attractiveness. The exceedingly high key of patriotism to which the text is pitched is naturally attractive to the youthful American ear. The illustrations, though not very good, add something to the general interest. The series presents a more or less continuous, though not always a well-arranged, account of American history. Children under twelve will of course ask few questions about style, arrangement or accuracy, and if they are satisfied, why should others complain? Still, in reading these books one sometimes wonders which part of their contents should be taken the more seriously, the history or the stories. We know that some of the history contained in them is mythical and that some of the stories are historical. That indeed is more than can be said of Mr. Lang's fairy books. But in all seriousness, should not accuracy of statement be the first requisite in the preparation of a book for children ? Is it not even more important in such books, which give the first impressions, than in books which are to be used wholly by adults? If such be true — and we believe it is — this series, notwithstanding its power to interest, comes far short of what it might and should be. It has been very carelessly written, and apparently has been subjected to no criticism or correction that is worth the name. H. L. O.

Preble, *Rear-Admiral* **George Henry.** Our flag. Albany: Munsell. 1872.

—— Same: 2d ed. rev.: History of the flag of the United States. Boston: Williams. 1880. New rev. ed. Houghton. 1893. $5. [2596

This is a large work of 800 pages, well illustrated, covering an extensive field, including accounts of navy and yacht-club signals, seals and arms, and principal national songs of the United States, with a "chronicle of the symbols, standards, banners and flags of ancient and modern nations." The first edition was published in 1872, — the second much revised in 1880. There are ten colored plates, 206 woodcuts, and numerous autographs. The work is valuable for the reference shelf. D. R. D.

Ratzel, Friedrich. Die Vereinigten Staaten von Nord-Amerika. Munich. 1878–80. 2v. V. 2, new ed. Munich. 1893. M. 29 (for 2 vols.). [2597

Volume 1 deals with physical geography, topography and natural resources. Abounds with good charts. The second edition of v. 2 is practically a new book. It treats such topics as slavery, immigration, industries and religion. The book as a whole is the result of the study of good material, and is replete with usable information. E. C.

Reddaway, W. F. Monroe doctrine. N. Y.: Macmillan. 1898. $1.25. [2598

In this essay the author attempts to trace historically the origin of the Monroe doctrine, and to determine its political and international value. The work is a profound analysis of an intricate historical problem, and should be compared with the equally able work of Dr. de Beaumarchais on the same subject published in the same year. The author's attitude is impartial and judicial, a fact that is the more remarkable in that the essay was written at the time of the Venezuelan controversy. C. M. A.

Rhodes, James Ford. History of the United States, from the compromise of 1850. N. Y.: Harper. 1893–9. 4v. Macmillan. 4v. Net $2.50 ea. [2599

The four volumes of this work thus far published cover the period from 1850 to Lincoln's second election. The author's narrative is based on a critical study of the sources, and is characterized by a high degree of impartiality and independence of judgment. In the third and fourth volumes, which deal with the Civil War, military matters so far as possible are subordinated to the political and social history of the time, and especial attention is devoted to the fluctuations of public opinion — North and South, in England and on the Continent — on the issues of the great struggle. No previous writer has so thoroughly studied this phase of the Civil War history, so important in the life of a people whose government rests on public opinion. The author's fairness of mind, poise of judgment, historic sympathy and thoroughness of research place him in the front rank of American historians. E. G. B.

Richardson, Abby Sage. History of our country. Boston: Houghton. [c. 1875.] $4.50. [2600

This is a history from the discovery of America by Columbus down to the celebration of the centennial in 1876. It is a fairly large one-volume history for popular use. The style is conversational, direct, and interesting, and the book is generously illustrated. It shares in the defects of so many of the compendiums, in giving much space relatively to colonial settlement and later wars and not enough to industrial and social movements. D. R. D.

Ridpath, John Clark. Popular history of the United States. N. Y. [c. 1876.] 2v. Rev. and enl. N. Y.: Hunt. [c. 1891.]
—— *Same:* United States history. Columbian ed. Boston and N. Y.: U. S. Hist. Co. [c. 1891.] [2601

A fair specimen of a book made to be sold by solicited subscriptions. Aims to give leading facts in a simple manner and to " discuss the philosophy of history " as fully as space will allow. Divides the narrative into five periods : The aborigines, discovery, colonies, Revolution, and the later events by administrations of Presidents. The resulting perspective is bad. The real making of the Union is condensed, and social factors almost wholly omitted. Sixty pages of the last edition are devoted to the Centennial Exposition of 1876. There are many imaginary illustrations and some chronological charts. E. E. S.

Rodenbough, *Col.* **Theophilus Francis,** *and* **William L. Haskin,** *eds.* Army of the United States : historical sketches of staff and line. N. Y.: Maynard. 1896. $5. [2602

The history of each staff-corps and regiment of the

line is told by its chosen historian, the regimental sketches varying in length from two to 20 pages. The publication was undertaken by the Military Service Institution, and the material was originally published in its journal. F. J. S.

Rosengarten, Joseph George. German soldier in the wars of the United States. Phil.: Lippincott. 1886. 2d ed. rev. and enl. 1890. [2603

A well-compiled manual of German-born officers of distinction in the armies of the United States, of those of German descent, and of the German organizations (regiments, batteries, etc.), from the Revolution to the Civil War. Perhaps the author goes too far in including the second generation of German immigrants, and graduates of West Point, etc. All the matter, however, is valuable and interesting, and shows the great importance of the German element in our present citizenship, with its share in our military history. The book is a labor of love in memory of Major A. G. Rosengarten, an officer of the Civil War who fell at Stone's River, Tenn. J. D. C.

Schouler, James. Historical briefs ; with a biography. N. Y.: Dodd. 1896. $2. [2604

" His new book . . . contains the chips from his workshop, as well as a curious biography written by some unknown third person, but rendered authoritative by a large admixture of contributions in the first person. The several papers on President Polk (reprinted from this magazine), Lafayette's Tour in 1824, and Monroe and the Rhea letter are minor studies in American history, but the volume has its chief interest and value through the paper on Francis Parkman, and the group dealing with subjects bearing directly upon the historian and his task. This group and the biography, which occupies nearly half the work, form the real excuse for the publication, and they have the curious value which attaches to an author's reflection on his own career, his methods of work, his aims and his ideals." *Atlantic monthly*, 79: 566.

—— History of the United States of America under the Constitution. V. 1–4. Wash. 1880–89. V. 5–6. N. Y.: Dodd. [c. 1891–9.] Rev. ed. Dodd. 1899. 6v. $13.50. [2605

Undoubtedly the best balanced and most serviceable large work dealing with the whole of the constitutional period to 1865. It is distinctly a narrative history, and not, like Von Holst's great work, a political disquisition. The story is closely packed with facts, but avoids the excessive incident and detail which encumber McMaster's pages. Vol. 6, on the Civil War, is probably the best account of that period in equal compass. The limitation of the work is its literary style, which is never easy, and often awkward and ungainly. W. MacD.

Schuyler, Eugene. American diplomacy and the furtherance of commerce. N. Y.: Scribner. 1886. $2.50. [2606

The first part of this work is an account of the administrative elements of the United States government which deal with foreign affairs, — involving a description of the Department of State, the diplomatic service, and the consular system. The remainder — the larger half — is historical, treating particularly of important diplomatic relations which have affected American commerce. The titles of these chapters are: Piratical Barbary powers, Right of search and the slave trade, Free navigation of rivers and seas (with special divisions on the Mississippi, St. Lawrence, North Pacific Ocean, Sound dues, Bosphorus and Dardanelles, River Plate, Amazon, Congo and Niger), Neutral rights, Fisheries and commercial treaties. The volume had its origin in courses of lectures previously delivered at Johns Hopkins University and Cornell University. The author had been in the consular and diplomatic service of the United States during a period of seventeen years, beginning with 1867. The style is good, and for the field covered there is no better book. D. R. D.

Scudder, Horace Elisha. History of the United States for the use of schools and academies. Phil.: Butler. 1884. N. Y.: Butler, Sheldon & Co. 1897. $1. [2607

At the time this work was written, it ranked as one of the best of the school text-books. The author placed emphasis upon clearness and attractiveness. There are abundant maps, colored, and illustrations of more than usual merit. The author does not isolate the United States, but attempts to connect the history of this country with the contemporary changes taking place in Europe. The relationship, therefore, of America and Europe is dwelt upon. The style is excellent. In the appendix there are questions for examination, with bibliographical references for special reading, including titles of historical novels. D. R. D.

—— Short history of the United States for beginners. N. Y.: Taintor. [c. 1890.] N. Y.: Butler, Sheldon & Co. 60c. [2608

An attractive text-book for children, written in simple style. The wars are reduced to a minimum. Careful comparisons are drawn of the different sections and their manner of life. Undue proportion is given to colonial history. The latter fourth of the book is devoted to the states and to local and national forms of government. E. E. S.

Smith, Goldwin. The United States: an outline of political history, 1492–1871. N. Y.: Macmillan. 1893. $2. [2609

A brilliantly written sketch, well proportioned and marvellously condensed. The author's standpoint, while critical, is distinctly sympathetic. The work is too compact to admit of novelty in the treatment of details; but the recognition of slavery, as almost from the beginning a moulding force, is to be specially noted as giving emphasis and continuity to the exposition. W. MacD.

Snow, Freeman, *comp.* Treaties and topics in American diplomacy. Boston: Boston Bk. Co. 1894. $2. [2610

Contains extracts bearing on the American colonies from European treaties prior to 1783, and in full all treaties constructed by the United States with foreign nations to 1893. They are arranged in chronological order, under the different countries concerned. A résumé in each paragraph is a time-saving device. Matters of especial interest, such as the Monroe doctrine, Inter-oceanic canal, Samoa, etc., are described under separate topics. This compilation will prove a handy substitute for the more bulky *Treaties and conventions of the United States* (sect. 2633).
E. E. S.

Soley, James Russell. Boys of 1812, and other naval heroes. Boston: Estes. [c. 1887.] $2. [2611

A juvenile book, describing in vivid style the principal operations of the navy of the United States in the Revolutionary and Algerian Wars, the War of 1812 and the Mexican War. It is profusely illustrated. E. E. S.

Sparks, Edwin Erle. Topical reference lists in American history with introductory lists in English constitutional history. Columbus, O.: Smythe. 1893. [2612

A slight topical bibliography. Begins practically with the Revolution. References selected with care. A good small guide to the study of American history. E. C.

Sparks, Jared, *ed.* Library of American biography. Series 1. Boston: Hilliard, Gray & Co. 1834–8. 10v. Series 2. Boston: Little. 1844–8. 15v. N. Y.: Harper. 10v. $1.25 ea. [2613

V. 1. Stark, John; by Edward Everett.—Brown, Charles Brockden; by Wm. H. Prescott. — Montgomery, Richard; by John Armstrong. — Allen, Ethan; by Jared Sparks.
2. Wilson, Alexander; by Wm. B. O. Peabody. — Smith, Captain John; by George S. Hillard.
3. Arnold, Benedict; by Jared Sparks.
4. Wayne, Anthony; by John Armstrong. — Vane, Sir Henry; by Charles Wentworth Upham.
5. Eliot, John; by Convers Francis.
6. Pinkney, Wm.; by Henry Wheaton. — Ellery, Wm.; by Edward T. Channing. — Mather, Cotton; by Wm. B. O. Peabody.
7. Phips, Sir William; by Francis Bowen. — Putnam, Israel; by Oliver W. B. Peabody. — Davidson, Lucretia Maria; by Catharine Maria Sedgwick. — Rittenhouse, David; by James Renwick.
8. Edwards, Jonathan; by Samuel Miller. — Brainerd, David; by Wm. B. O. Peabody.
9. Steuben, Baron; by Francis Bowen. — Cabot, Sebastian; by Charles Hayward, Jr. — Eaton, Wm.; by Cornelius C. Felton.
10. Fulton, Robert; by James Renwick. — Warren, Joseph; by Alexander H. Everett. — Hudson, Henry; by Henry R. Cleveland. — Marquette, Father; by Jared Sparks.
Series 2, v. 1. La Salle, Robert Cavelier de; by Jared Sparks. — Henry, Patrick; by Alexander H. Everett.
2. Otis, James; by Francis Bowen. — Oglethorpe, James; by Wm. B. O. Peabody.
3. Sullivan, John; by Oliver W. B. Peabody. — Leisley, Jacob; by Charles F. Hoffman. — Bacon, Nathaniel; by Wm. Ware. — Mason, John; by George E. Ellis.

4. Williams, Roger; by Wm. Gammell. — Dwight, Timothy; by Wm. B. Sprague. — Pulaski, Count Casimir; by Jared Sparks.

5. Rumford, Count; by James Renwick. — Pike, Zebulon Montgomery; by Henry Whiting. — Gorton, Samuel; by John M. Mackie.

6. Stiles, Ezra; by James L. Kingsley. — Fitch, John; by Charles Whittlesey. — Hutchinson, Anne; by George E. Ellis.

7. Ribault, John; by Jared Sparks. — Rale, Sebastian; by Convers Francis. — Palfrey, Wm.; by John Gorham Palfrey.

8. Lee, Charles; by Jared Sparks. — Reed, Joseph; by Henry Reed.

9. Calvert, Leonard; by George W. Burnap. — Ward, Samuel; by Wm. Gammell. — Posey, Thomas; by James Hall.

10. Greene, Nathanael; by George W. Greene.

11. Decatur, Stephen; by Alexander Slidell Mackenzie.

12. Preble, Edward; by Lorenzo Sabine. — Penn, Wm.; by George E. Ellis.

13. Boone, Daniel; by John M. Peck. — Lincoln, Benjamin; by Francis Bowen.

14. Ledyard, John; by Jared Sparks.

15. Davie, Wm. Richardson; by Fordyce M. Hubbard. — Kirkland, Samuel; by Samuel K. Lothrop.

This series of biographical essays is still of great interest. Whatever may be said of Sparks's method as an editor of text, he remains one of the greatest of our historical scholars, and this series is edited to as high a level of excellence as such a series in his time could be. E. C. R.

Spears, John Randolph. History of our navy, 1775–1897. N. Y.: Scribner. 1897. 4v. $8. [With later volume] 5v. $10. [2614]

"There is a great lack of proportion in devoting only 599 pages, out of over 1850, to the Civil War. In order to compress the latter within the dimensions thus assigned to it, details of interest have to be ruthlessly cut off. . . . To the American Revolution ,302 pages are given. The amount is not excessive. . . . In this beginning of his work, the author shows little evidence of the haste so painfully perceptible towards the close. . . . Where economy of space for better objects was so much needed, some of the easy-tongued abuse of Great Britain's action during the Revolution could be spared. . . . But the author shows a considerable amount of philosophic appreciation of the bearing of events, which causes regret that he did not exert his powers more adequately upon the later period of the Civil War. . . . The War of the Revolution and the War of the Rebellion are the two great military, as well as political, crises of the history of the United States. In the popular appreciation of Americans, however, the War of 1812 is the great naval epic. . . . Mr. Spears evidently shares this prevalent sentiment, for to this theme he gives 725 pages — a volume and a half — of his total space. . . . The fact that there were no better officers nor braver men, the world over, than those who then took our frigates and sloops to sea, should never be allowed to obscure the lesson that our statesmen had so pitiful an appreciation of the necessity of a navy, that they brought the country to war practically powerless upon the ocean. . . . The portion of the work not touched upon so far gives an account of the wars with the Barbary States and with Mexico, of the putting down of piracy in the West Indies, and of the slave trade on the coast of Africa; with incidental mention of other naval matters of interest. These occupy the latter half of Volume III. Thirty pages at the end of the work are very properly devoted to a description of the present navy." A. T. Mahan, *Am. hist. review*, 3: 747.

See sect. 2450.

Stanwood, Edward. History of presidential elections. Boston: Osgood. 1884.

—— *Same:* History of the presidency. Boston: Houghton. 1898. $2.50. [2615]

An enlarged and entirely rewritten edition of the author's *History of presidential elections*, brought down through 1896. A political history of the United States in the form of detailed studies of the presidential campaigns and of the issues on which the elections have turned. The author gives an account of the nominating conventions, the relative strength of candidates, the text of platforms, the striking incidents of the campaign and the tabulated results of the election. The work is impartial and accurate, and a very serviceable manual for reference for the external details of party struggles. E. G. B.

Staples, Hamilton B. Origin of the names of the states of the Union. See American Antiquarian Society, sect. 233. [2616]

Statesman's manual, 1789–1849; comp. by Edwin Williams. N. Y.: Walker. 1849. 4v.

—— *Same;* continued by B. J. Lossing. 1789–1858; enl. ed. N. Y. [1858.] 4v. [2617]

Williams gives the addresses and messages of the Presidents to 1849, with concise, accurate biographical notices, and sketches of the events of their administrations. These sketches and notices contain the facts almost without comment. In the fourth volume are a number of useful appendices, containing the names of the delegates to the congresses at Albany (1754), and New York (1765), of the signers of the Declaration of Independence; of United States Senators and Representatives to 1849; of acts passed; vetoes; electoral votes; members of the Supreme Court and of the cabinet; foreign ministers; Speakers of the House; presidents pro tempore of the Senate, and synopses of the constitutions of the states. R. C. H. C.

Stedman, Edmund Clarence, *and* **Ellen M. Hutchinson,** *eds.* Library of American literature, from the earliest settlement to the present time. N. Y.: Webster. 1887–90. 11v. N. Y.: Wm. Evarts Benjamin. 11v. $30. [2618]

This is an anthology, not a history. The arrangement is in general chronological. Throughout the work the dates of birth and death of author are prefixed to the selection, and in the final volume there is given a brief biographical dictionary of authors represented, together with a general index of the whole work. It is illustrated with numerous portraits. It is an ably edited and extremely useful anthology. E. C. R.

Steele, Joel Dorman *and Mrs.* **Esther B.**
Brief history of the United States. N. Y.:
Barnes. [1885.] Am. Bk. Co. $1.25. [**2619**

Strictly a text-book of facts for schools. The history
of the United States is arbitrarily divided into six
epochs, and the work is provided with chronological
summaries, blackboard analyses, and other mnemonic
aids. Care is taken not to express any positive convictions or generalizations on disputed points of political policy. The narrative is clear, and as a record
of annals may give satisfaction.　　　　D. R. D.

—— Centenary history of the United States.
N. Y.: Barnes. 1876.

—— *Same :* Popular history of the United
States. N. Y.: Barnes. 1899. $3.50. [**2620**

This work is intended to provide a more detailed
treatment of the history of the United States from its
discovery until 1896 in one volume than can be given
in the ordinary school or college compendium. A
work of such proportions is highly desirable, but this
cannot be recommended as entirely satisfactory. The
first part of the work treating of settlement and colonial life is better than the long chapters on the wars
and later political administrations. Particularly in
the last part of the book there is not sufficient generalization, and topics are treated indiscriminately without due regard to their importance or perspective.
There are a great many illustrations, but many of
them are badly executed, and the subjects of a considerable number are sensational, and for youth distinctively unhealthy.　　　　D. R. D.

**Talleyrand - Périgord, Charles Maurice
Camille,** *marquis* de. 1776–1876: étude sur
la république des États - Unis d'Amérique.
N. Y. : Hurd. 1876. [**2621**

Author was an "Attaché à la Commission Française
de l'Exposition de Philadelphie." The book is a comparison of what he had read as to the period before
1789 with what he saw in 1876. Begins with Columbus
and surveys the history of the thirteen colonies and
Canada. Then follows a discussion of the causes of
the Revolution and the text of the Constitution in
French. The concluding chapter is entitled Parallèle
entre l'Amérique de 1776 et l'Amérique de 1876. It
contains a few pages of interesting comment on modern conditions. Otherwise the book is of little value.
　　　　E. C.

Thomas, Allen C. History of the United
States. Boston: Heath. 1897. Rev. ed. $1.
[**2622**

One of the best of recent text-books for high schools
and academies. The literary interest is not great, but
facts are judiciously chosen and clearly presented, the
maps are superior to those found in most similar works,
and there are discriminating and helpful indications
for collateral reading. The revised edition of 1897
brings the narrative to the close of 1896. W. MacD.

Thompson, Richard Wigginton. Recollections of sixteen Presidents, from Washington to Lincoln. Indianapolis: Bowen-Merrill.
1894. 2v. $6. [**2623**

By an Indiana lawyer, Whig member of Congress,
1841-3 and 1847-9, and a member of the Hayes Cabinet.
These "recollections" are arranged by administrations of Presidents, and consist of judicious comments
on national political history. They are strongly Hamiltonian or Unionist in their attitude. They make a
series of essays, but have little value from the personality of the author. The illustrations are portraits of
the Presidents.　　　　E. E. S.

Towle, George Makepeace. The nation in
a nutshell; a rapid outline of American history.
Boston: Lee. 1887. • 50c. [**2624**

A condensed description of the factors entering into
the history of the United States, beginning with the
Indian antiquities and ending with the close of the
Civil War. Political, social and economic aspects well
balanced. Follows the picturesque traditions of the
past and makes no use of later investigations. Contains several supplementary chapters on the Presidents, the literary and scientific progress of the nation, and the political changes of a century. Might
be useful as a pocket book for ready reading.
　　　　E. E. S.

Townsend, Malcolm, *comp.* U. S., an index to the United States of America, historical, geographical and political : a handbook of
reference combining the "curious" in U. S.
history. Boston : Lothrop. [c. 1890.] $2.
[**2625**

A review in the *Nation* (v. 52: 18) states that the
facts in this scrapbook are in most cases correct, few
loose statements and but one positive misstatement
having been noticed. The book is rich in documents,
in addition to the Constitution and Declaration containing the Confederate Constitution, with a joint index to both papers. It contains such miscellaneous
information as the history of geographical names,
nicknames, elections and cabinets, coins, etc. The
index is inadequate but well made as far as it goes.

Tribune almanac, 1838–68 : comprehend-
ing The politician's register and The Whig almanac ; containing annual election returns by
states and counties ; lists of Presidents, cabinets, judges of the Supreme Court, foreign ministers, etc. ; summaries of acts of Congress and
other political statistics ; political essays, addresses, party platforms, etc. N. Y. : New
York Tribune. 1868. 2v. [**2626**

The information here given is accurate. There are,
in addition to the summaries noted above, statistics
of value on railroads, the army and navy, population
and national finance, besides a mass of information
on less important topics. The *Almanac* has a strong
Whig bias, and its political addresses and essays are
not impartial.　　　　R. C. H. C.

Trumbull, Benjamin. General history of the
United States of America, 1492–1792. Boston.
1810. V. 1: 1492–1765. [**2627**

This is the first of three proposed volumes which
would extend to Washington's second administration,

but the series was never completed. It aims to point out the especial interpositions of Providence in behalf of the United States. The work is faithfully but very tediously done as compared with modern historical writing. E. E. S.

Tucker, George. History of the United States, to end of the 26th Congress in 1841. Phil. : Lippincott. 1856–8. 4v. [2628

Vol. I to the end of Washington's administration ; vol. II to the end of Madison's first term; vol. III to the close of J. Q. Adams' administration ; vol. IV to the election of Gen. W. H. Harrison. The author practiced law in Virginia and was for twenty years a professor in the University of Virginia. The treatment of the colonial and Revolutionary periods differs from the general line by giving more space to the southern and middle colonies than to New England. After the appearance of political parties the treatment inclines strongly to the Jeffersonian or states-rights school. No references are given. Official documents form the larger share of materials used. The narrative is confined to political aspects ; no social. A final chapter presents the southern view of the early slavery contest. E. E. S.

Tucker, George Fox. Monroe doctrine. Boston : Reed. 1885. [2629

This is a clear and readable account of the application of the Monroe doctrine, from the time of its original statement to 1885. It embraces chapters on the Panama Congress, Clayton-Bulwer treaty, French intervention in Mexico, and other minor applications of the theory. The attitude of the author is fair, and the arguments for and against the retention of the doctrine are impartially presented. The reader, however, should remember that there has been much history added to this doctrine since 1885. D. R. D.

Tuckerman, Henry Theodore. America and her commentators ; with a critical sketch of travel in the United States. N. Y.: Scribner. 1864. [2630

A useful and entertaining guide to the literature of description and criticism of the United States. Extensive extracts are given from some of the less accessible sources. Three chapters are given to the French and English travellers, respectively, and one each to the Germans and Swedish, the Italian and American travellers. Of especial value to librarians and to students of social history. E. G. B.

United States. *Presidents.* Compilation of the messages and papers of the Presidents, 1789–1897 ; published by authority of Congress, by James D. Richardson. Wash. : Govt. Prtg. Off. 1896–9. 10v. [2631

" Mr. James D. Richardson's *Compilation of the messages and papers of the Presidents, 1789–1897*, published by authority of Congress, is now completed by the issue of the tenth volume of 677 pages. Indeed, it is much more than completed, for more than half of the volume is mere padding, which has no proper place in the compilation, and ought not to be here printed with government money. . . . There is no suf-

ficient excuse for swelling the index to more than four hundred pages, by thrusting into it ' a large number of encyclopedic articles ; ' . . . still less ' short accounts of several hundred battles in which the armies of the United States have been engaged,' whether mentioned in presidential documents or not; still less ' descriptions of all the states of the Union and of many foreign countries,' — all prepared by the editor's son. Of course Mr. Richardson had the consent of the committee on printing, but the result is a most extraordinary farrago. . . . It is unfortunate that so useful, and in the main well executed a series should have so lame a conclusion. The index itself, when one penetrates to the items, is not constructed according to modern methods." *Am. hist. rev.*, 5: 170.

The manner in which the compiler got possession of the copyright and published for his own benefit a work paid for by the government has been the subject of much criticism. F. J. S.

United States. *State department.* Bulletin of the Bureau of Rolls and Library of the Department of State. Wash. 1893–7, Nos. 1–9. [2632

These are indexes of documents in the possession of the government, each volume containing a list of the subjects covered in all those which precede it. There are calendars of the correspondence of Monroe, Madison, and Jefferson showing the purport of each letter, a series of partial indexes of the Continental Congress manuscripts, and catalogues showing the arrangement of the Washington, Hamilton, Franklin, and other papers. The bulletins purport to contain also a documentary history of the Constitution in three parts, which is properly a distinct work with different title-pages, though coming from the same source. This is a literal reprint of the documents in the bureau relating to the formation of the Constitution as adopted, amended, and now in force. F. J. S.

—— Treaties and conventions concluded between the United States and other powers since July 4, 1776 ; containing notes, a chronological list of treaties, and an analytical index. (48th Cong., 2d sess., Sen. ex. doc. 47.) Wash. 1889. [2633

The preface contains a history of former compilations of treaties. The treaties are arranged alphabetically by countries, and are followed by the nearly 200 pages of notes in the form of a connected narrative of the correspondence with each country giving a history of the negotiation of the several treaties. The notes are those of J. C. Bancroft Davis, prepared for a similar compilation in 1873, with additions in brackets, and are preceded by a list of the official publications respecting foreign relations. Postal conventions were excepted in the resolution calling for the publication of this volume. F. J. S.

Van Buren, Martin. Inquiry into the origin and course of political parties in the United States. N. Y. : Hurd. 1867. [2634

This historical and philosophical disquisition on the origin and development of the Federalist, Anti-Federalist, and the first Republican parties, was written after

Van Buren retired from the presidency in 1841, with the understanding that it should not be published until after his death. The manuscript was edited by the author's sons and printed in 1867. It is a valuable commentary on the political creeds of the early statesmen, Washington, Hamilton, Jefferson and Adams. Less detailed attention is given to the Jacksonian period. In particular the political lives of the four statesmen above named are subjected to an exhaustive analysis. The work is characterized by a dignity of style and sobriety of statement characteristic of state documents, and full credit is given to the honesty of purpose of Hamilton and Adams. There is considerable repetition, and for many students the first half of the book may be sufficient. The work illustrates Van Buren's political convictions, as accepted by his biographer, Shepard (sect. 1976). It is enlivened by an occasional anecdote, drawn from the author's long experience in politics. D. R. D.

Walton, William, *et al., eds.* Army and navy of the United States. Phil.: Barrie. [c. 1889–1900.] 25 pts. Pap. $1 ea. [2635

"To be illustrated by 300 pictures in the text and 50 full-plate photogravures of the uniforms worn by soldiers and sailors of famous ships in service, from the Revolution to the present day. There are to be 25 parts of 16 pages each. This work was originally undertaken by the Government, whose aid and official approval the present publishers have received. The reading-matter is intended to be absolutely trustworthy, historically, and the supplement is to contain over two hundred thousand names of all officers in active service from Bunker Hill to Santiago and Manila. Paper and printing are both of the best." *Nation,* 67: 311.

Wharton, Francis, *ed.* Digest of the international law of the United States, taken from documents issued by Presidents and Secretaries of State, and from decisions of federal courts and opinions of Attorneys-General. Wash.: Govt. Prtg. Off. 1886. 3v. [2636

Not a formal treatise, but a collection, under a topical classification, of official declarations of the United States on points of international law. Extracts from judicial decisions, opinions of Attorneys-General, and leading text-books are also included. An appendix to vol. 3 gives important extracts from the Stevens collection of Franklin papers relative to the treaty of peace, 1783, between Great Britain and the United States. The work is an authoritative manual of American doctrine and precedent in its field. W. MacD.

Willard, *Mrs.* **Emma (Hart).** History of the United States. N. Y. 1828. New ed. enl. N. Y.: Barnes. 1854. [2637

This was one of the first of the text-books on United States history prepared for schools, and has much information of the period covered, but lacks style and generalization. It is now out of date, and is of interest only to the historian of educational methods. An abridged edition was published in 1843 with mnemonic aids and questions. D. R. D.

Wilson, James Grant, *ed.* Presidents of the United States, 1789–1894; by John Fiske, Carl Schurz and others. N. Y.: Appleton. 1894. [c. 1886.] $3.50. [2638

This is a collection of biographical sketches, several of which are revisions of contributions previously made to Appleton's *Encyclopædia of biography.* The biographies of John Adams, Madison, Jackson and Tyler are treated by John Fiske; that of Lincoln by John Hay; Polk by George Bancroft, and that of Hayes by Carl Schurz. There is a set of portraits and voluminous letters written by several Presidents. The editor adds brief biographical notes. The work is reliable and makes a good reference book. D. R. D.

Wilson, Woodrow. Division and reunion, 1829–89. (Epochs of Am. history.) N. Y.: Longmans. 1893. $1.25. [2639

As a southerner of the generation since the war who has lived most of his adult life in the North, Prof. Wilson is in an especially favorable position for understanding the temper of the North and the South, and for writing the history of this momentous period with an exceptional degree of fairness and sympathy. As a text-book, it is well supplied with maps and bibliographies, but its literary quality raises it above the ordinary text-book, and makes it at once the best and most readable general history of these sixty years. E. G. B.

Wright, Henrietta Christian. Children's stories in American history. N. Y.: Scribner. 1885. $1.25. [2640

Attractive stories, largely biographical, of the American aborigines, discoverers and explorers, and of the settlement of the country. Belongs to the early period of American history. Does not attempt much instruction. Profitable reading for children. E. E. S.

—— Children's stories of American progress. N. Y.: Scribner. 1886. $1.25. [2641

A series of sketches under such topics as Western settlement, the First steamboat, the Battle of Tippecanoe, the Story of slavery, the Rebellion, etc. The style is simple, but there is no personality to give interest. Traditions are freely used. E. E. S.

DIVISION 3:
CONSTITUTIONAL AND INSTITUTIONAL HISTORY AND EXPOSITION

Teutonic and English Origins

Adams, Herbert Baxter. Germanic origin of New England towns. (Johns Hopkins Univ. studies, v. 1, no. 2.) Balt. 1882. Pap. 50c. [2642

This paper, which was prepared about 1880, was intended as an incitement to the comparative study of early American and European local institutions. Its author was strongly influenced by the writings of Von

Maurer, Laveleye, Maine, Freeman and others, who had then turned attention toward the study of primitive society, and had developed a theory which lays great stress on the claim that communal property generally preceded private property in the order of development. Prof. Adams attempted to indicate that New Plymouth was a village community, and was established in much the same way as those which are supposed to have existed in various parts of Teutonic Europe. Its settlement was regarded as a natural return to primitive social forms consequent on the founding of colonies in a new country. In other papers relating to common lands about Cape Anne the same idea was enforced, as it was on a much more ambitious scale in Prof. Howard's *Local constitutional history of the United States,* published in the same series. But it is safe to say that Prof. Adams did not prove that his theory was necessary to the explanation of the origin of communal institutions in New Plymouth. Meantime such a thorough comparative study of towns within and outside of New England as would conclusively settle the question has not yet been undertaken. Prof. Adams's hypothesis, suggestive and stimulating though it has been, remains an hypothesis still.   H. L. O.

—— Norman constables in America. (Johns Hopkins Univ. studies, v. 1, no. 8.) Balt. 1883. Pap. 50c.   [2643

Reprinted from the *New England historical and genealogical register* for April, 1882. This paper, which the author meant to be a contribution to the origin of local institutions in New England, was written for the purpose of presenting the petty constable as a connecting link between the old English parish and the New England town. The subject is treated in a popular and entertaining way, but the author errs in one of his most important theses, — that is, that the constable is the successor of the Anglo Saxon hundred-man and tithing-man ; for no such connection is even probable. In fact, all that Prof. Adams says of Anglo-Saxon institutions must be received with caution. The second part of the essay, which deals with the constable in America, is full of interesting extracts from the colonial records.   C. M. A.

—— Saxon tithing-men in America. (Johns Hopkins Univ. studies, v. 1, no. 4.) Balt. 1883. Pap. 50c.   [2644

This is a semi-popular essay upon the tithing-man in England and America. It does not attempt to follow out in any consecutive way the history of the tithing-man, but deals with scattered evidence drawn from the Anglo-Saxon laws, mediæval English writings, and New England town and colony records. The essay is very happy in calling attention to the continuity of English institutions in America, but beyond that has little scientific value.   C. M. A.

Bagehot, Walter. The English constitution, and other political essays. London : Chapman. 1867. Rev. ed. N. Y.: Appleton. 1876. $2.   [2645

The *English constitution* is one of the most brilliant pieces of modern political writing, and one of the best known of its author's works. It is not a detailed account of the facts of English political organization and work, but a keen and philosophical exposition of the principles on which the English political system rests, and in accordance with which its operations are carried on in practice. The great merit of Bagehot is the clearness with which he expounds the difference between the nominal and the actual English constitution, and the practical working relations of the Crown, the Cabinet, the House of Commons, and the House of Lords. The essays in the volume are on Brougham and Peel.   W. MacD.

This book is both scientific politics and good literature. No other writer has presented in a single volume so adequately what is most essential in the forms and spirit of the English constitution. Of especial interest to the American student is the comparison of Parliamentary with Presidential government.

                        A. D. M.

Barrington, Boyd Cummings. The Magna Charta and other great charters of England ; with an historical treatise and copious explanatory notes. Phil.: Wm. J. Campbell. 1900 [1899]. $3.   [2646

" No more worthless book was ever published. The historical treatise reads like a sophomoric essay, and is full of inaccuracies, ridiculous statements, and bad grammar, while the notes to *Magna Charta* are simply antiquarian rubbish. . . . Where has Mr. Barrington buried himself for the past quarter of a century, that for him Stubbs, Freeman, Norgate, Bigelow, Brunner, Liebermann, Bémont, Round, Pollock, and Maitland, not to mention Digny, Taswell-Langmead, and Medley, have done their work in vain ? " *Am. hist. rev.,* 5 : 387.

Borgeaud, Charles. Rise of modern democracy in Old and New England , tr. by Mrs. Birkbeck Hill. (Social science series.) London : Sonnenschein. 1894. N. Y.: Scribner, 1894. $1.   [2647

A most interesting and suggestive study of the beginnings of democratic agitation in the Puritan Revolution of the 17th century. The exact nature of the contribution of the Calvinistic thinkers to the growth of democratic ideas is perhaps as well set forth here as anywhere. Dr. Borgeaud, by studying the movements in Old and New England together, illustrates very effectively the truth, sometimes neglected, that the early history of New England cannot be studied understandingly without a careful investigation of the contemporary history of English Puritanism.   E. G. B.

Bowen, Francis, *comp.* Documents of the constitutions of England and America, from Magna Charta to the federal Constitution of 1789. Comp. and ed. with notes. Cambridge: John Bartlett. 1854.   [2648

This manual is one of the earliest collections of sources made in this country for class use. It was compiled by Prof. Bowen of Harvard for his classes in constitutional history and law. The volume contains Magna Charta, Confirmatio Cartorum, the Statute of Treason, the Petition of Right, the Habeas Corpus Act, the Bill of Rights, the Massachusetts Body of Liberties, the Confederacy of the New England Colonies, Franklin's Plan of Union, the Declaration of Independence, the Virginia Bill of Rights, the Articles of Confederation, the Massachusetts Declaration of Rights, and the Constitution of the United States. The notes to Magna Charta are of but little value, but the introduction is suggestive and good.   C. M. A.

Campbell, Douglas. The Puritan in Holland, England, and America. N. Y.: Harper. 1892. 2v. $5. [2649

One of the most pretentious, but least substantial, of all the works ever written on early American history. The reader may find the gist of the writer's argument in his preface and in vol. II, p. 410 *et seq.* The book was written for the purpose of showing that certain important American institutions — as written constitutions, the organization of the Senate, free public schools, freedom of religion and of the press, the township system, the system of recording deeds and mortgages, the division of land among all the children of the deceased parent, the independence of the judiciary, the written ballot, reformed judicial procedure and penal and prison systems — are of Dutch rather than of English or native origin. That the author has rendered a service by calling the attention of students to the possibility that some of these institutions may have owed their origin among us to suggestions derived from the Continent, no competent critic will deny. But the evidence adduced by the author in proof of his claims is altogether too flimsy to outweigh the positive documentary evidence in favor of the English origin or the native American growth of our institutions in general. He relies wholly on second, third and fourth rate authorities for his material, and he uses it, when it is obtained, in a most unscientific way. The book is brilliantly written, and, in spite of poor arrangement and frequent digressions, is interesting to the reader. But it abounds in loose statements of fact, as well as in bad reasoning. In the note to the fourth edition the statement is made that the book had then been reviewed in about 200 magazines and papers, and it was a source of gratification to the writer to find that the critics had pointed out no essential error in his narrative, and only a few had differed from his conclusions. If that be true, no better evidence of the superficiality of the great mass of current reviews could be adduced.   H. L. O.

See sect. 2681, 2722.

Coffin, Charles Carleton. Story of liberty. N. Y.: Harper. 1879. [2650

The qualities that made Mr. Coffin successful as a war correspondent lend a kind of attraction also to this volume, which, however, as a historic narrative is thoroughly misleading and harmful. While the Catholic Church can justly be called to account for many shortcomings, it is not the only imperfect institution which the world has seen. Though often the foe of liberty, the Catholic Church has not been the only foe. Of Protestant sins against liberty there is in Mr. Coffin's book little or no mention ! Nor is there any mention of such palliations of the guilt of the church as the fact that the Catholics of Maryland were tolerant while their Protestant neighbors were trying to thrust down men and ideas out of square with their strict measure. The effectiveness of the book for creating a wrong impression is increased by its illustrations. In the hands of the young for whom it is intended it is certain to be an instrument of harm.

J. K. H.

Colby, Charles William, *ed.* Selections from the sources of English history : being a supplement to text-books of English history, B. C. 55–A. D. 1832. London and N. Y. : Longmans. 1899. $1.50. [2651

" Professor Colby's excellent little book contains 117 selections, which, when the original is not English, are presented in English translations. They are remarkably well chosen, and illustrate English history in varied ways. Some of them set forth important or striking events. . . . A larger number illustrate more generally the characteristics of political and social life in each age. . . . Narratives and descriptive pieces are used, as a rule, rather than documents ; and as a whole the collection is an unusually interesting and even entertaining one. . . . The book is prefaced by a long introduction on the use of original sources, and each piece by an explanatory paragraph. All these are well executed." *Am. hist. rev.*, 5: 161.

Curtis, George William. Orations and addresses; ed. by C. E. Norton. N. Y.: Harper. 1894. 3v. $3.50 ea. [2652

Vol. 1 contains addresses " on the principles and character of American institutions, and the duties of American citizens ; " Vol. 2, addresses on the civil service ; Vol. 3, historical and memorial addresses. Curtis touched no subject to which he did not make a contribution of value ; and the collection admirably illustrates the wide range of his interests, the strength and soberness of his convictions, his keen sense of political honor, and his hopeful public spirit.

W. MacD.

Forsyth, William. History of trial by jury. London : Parker. 1852.

—— *Same ;* ed. by J. A. Morgan. N. Y. 1875. [2653

This is one of the earliest and most noteworthy attempts to discover the origin and to write the history of trial by jury. As regards the origin of this institution Mr. Forsyth's conclusions are largely negative ; for he denies that the jury system came from either Germany or Scandinavia, or was derived from Anglo-Saxon institutions. He further declares that the modern jury procedure did not originate before the time of Henry II, and takes high ground in asserting that section 39 of Magna Charta had nothing to do with jury trial. His work is exceptionally able considering the time when it was written, but it has been superseded by the writings of Brunner, Pollock and Maitland, and Thayer. The final chapters, which contain a comparative study of the jury systems of Scotland, Germany, France, America, and other countries, are still of value.   C. M. A.

Freeman, Edward Augustus. The English people in its three homes. (In his Lectures to American audiences.) Phil.: Porter. [c. 1882.] Coates. $1.75. [2654

The great historian who occupied himself with so many lands and races always put more heart into his work when his theme was his own stock; and probably never wrote a book into which more of his heart went than this. The three homes of the English are, 1st, the German land from which came the fore-fathers; 2d, the island, which has become the mother-country of so vast an empire; 3d, America, in which for three hundred years the race has been developing. Scouting the nomenclature "Anglo-Saxon" and "English-speaking" as clumsy and inadequate, Freeman will admit only "English" as properly descriptive of his masterful folk. The style is marked by simplicity, honesty and warm sympathy, — with monosyllabic Saxon ruggedness. With the artlessness of one grown gray in the teacher's chair, he will take nothing for granted as regards the knowledge of his readers, but repeats and elucidates as if they were children. J. K. H.

—— Growth of the English constitution. London. 1872. N. Y.: Macmillan. 1884. $1.75. [2655

"What the reader has here," says the author, "is a somewhat extended form of two lectures given at Leeds and Bradford." The latter part of the second lecture was expanded so as to make a third chapter, and notes and references were added preparatory to the issue of the whole in book form. In this volume, within a brief compass, the reader will find set forth Mr. Freeman's leading ideas concerning English constitutional development; its predominantly popular and democratic character, its Teutonic origin, its steady and continuous growth as a result of which it had by the time of Edward I attained the form which essentially it was to retain throughout. The place of the executive in history is largely ignored or deprecated. The age of feudalism and of the strong monarchy is treated as a time during which there was a questionable departure, if not a degeneracy, from the original model, while the advent of the modern democratic régimes is regarded as in many respects a return to the good old ways. This is the view of a modern Radical, whose mind was steeped in antiquarian lore, and who frequently dealt in superficial resemblances and remote analogies. H. L. O.

—— History of the Norman conquest of England. London: Macmillan. 1872-79. 6v. N. Y.: Macmillan. 1876. V. 1-5. N. Y.: Oxford Univ. Press. 1880. V. 1-2, o. p. V. 3-5, $5.25 ea. V. 6, $2.75. [2656

In this work the origin of Teutonic civilization in England and its development till the reign of Edward the Confessor are reviewed; the history of the reigns of Edward the Confessor, Harold, and William I is given in great detail; the political and social results of the Norman Conquest are fully discussed, and the history of the nation, so far as it tended to show the results of that Conquest, is sketched till the reign of Edward I. The view that the author took of the great transitional event which he set himself the task of portraying was, that it did not break the continuity of English history. Freeman is among English historians the Prince of Teutonists. The material which he used was chiefly the chronicles, and he deals more with the external facts of history than with social and legal development. It is a work of vast learning and great originality. It is written in a vigorous, at times lofty, style. The author was a man of ardent temperament, and his likes and dislikes appear prominently in his work. Its faults and errors are found to have proceeded largely from that source. So earnestly did he insist upon the Teutonic, the national, and the democratic elements in early English history, that he laid himself fairly open to the charge of exaggeration. Still, the *History of the Norman conquest* will always be one of the great and inspiring works on mediæval England. Mr. Bryce sums up Freeman's merits as an historian under the following six points: "love of truth, love of justice, industry, common sense, breadth of view, the power of vividly realizing the past." H. L. O.

Gardiner, Samuel Rawson. History of England from the accession of James I to the civil war, 1603-42. London: Longmans. 1883-4. 10v. New ed. N. Y.: Longmans. 1899. 10v. $20.

—— History of the great civil war, 1642-9. London: Longmans. 1886-92. 3v. New ed. London and N. Y.: Longmans. 1893. 4v. $8.

—— History of the Commonwealth and Protectorate, 1649-60. London and N. Y.: Longmans. 1894-. V. 1+. $7 per v. [2657

The history of the age of the Stuarts and of Cromwell has occupied Mr. Gardiner's attention for thirty-eight years, and in 1900, when the latest volume appeared, had been brought to the year 1656. The first series of volumes were revised and in part rewritten in 1883-4 and issued as a History of England in ten volumes. Mr. Gardiner has devoted little attention to picturesque narrative or brilliant word-painting, but as a laborious and conscientious investigator, who has pursued a systematic course of inquiry into the history of a definite period, he has given the first full, critical and unbiassed narrative of the important years from 1603 to 1656. The great merit of his work lies in its thoroughness and impartiality; for Mr. Gardiner is not a great analyst or a philosophical interpreter. His subjects are mainly political and military, little space being given to the consideration of social and economic questions. C. M. A.

—— *ed.* Constitutional documents of the Puritan revolution, 1628-60. N. Y.: Oxford Univ. Press. 1890. 2d ed. 1899. $2.60. [2658

A study of this collection of documents will give the student of American history a clear conception of the political aims and aspirations of the Puritan party in England. Several of the pieces are here printed for the first time. In these documents will be found in the germ political methods which were brought to full development in America, and which have come to be regarded as peculiarly American, such as a written Constitution, representation according to population, short term legislative bodies, etc. E. G. B.

Gneist, Rudolph. History of the English constitution, trans. by Philip A. Ashworth.

London : Clowes. 1886. N. Y. : Putnam. 1886. 2v. New ed. rev. and enl. 1889. 2v. $8. 2v. in 1. $4.50. [2659

Rudolf Gneist was primarily a jurist, but his writings on English constitutional history rank high. He undertook the researches which led to their publication, to obtain knowledge with the help of which to better reform the system of Prussian local government. His *History of the English constitution* is the outgrowth of two larger works, one on the system of English administrative law and the other on self-government in England. It covers, at least in outline, the whole subject. Gneist was chiefly interested in tracing the development of the machinery of government, of the crown and its councils, the central courts, the exchequer, the church, and in explaining the way in which the connection between these and the local courts in the shires and hundreds was slowly evolved. The combination of the two resulted in the English system of self-government, through which all classes were brought to coöperate in the daily duties of public life. His treatment of the subject is more incisive and systematic than that of Stubbs, and the two works can be used together with great profit. Gneist's treatment of the subject from the accession of the Stuarts to the present time is sketchy and inadequate. A valuable review of these works and résumé of Gneist's ideas, by G. W. Prothero, is in the *English hist. rev.* for Jan., 1888. H. L. O.

—— Student's history of the English Parliament in its transformations through a thousand years ; new Eng. ed., rewritten, with a complete index by A. H. Keane. N. Y.: Putnam. 1887. $3. [2660

This book is mostly a repetition of those parts of the author's *Constitutional history* which concern the history of Parliament. The new parts of the book are the introduction, and the sections at the close which relate to the development of Parliament in the present century. The introduction is especially valuable, because it sets forth in convenient form the author's view of the relations between society and the state, and of the general conditions of historical development. The translation here referred to is the best. A translation of inferior merit by R. J. Shee was issued in 1886. H. L. O.

Gooch, George Peabody. History of English democratic ideas in the 17th century. Cambridge: Univ. Press. 1898. N. Y.: Macmillan. 1899. $1.50. [2661

The origin of the modern democratic idea appears in the mind of the author to lie wholly in the sixteenth century, and in the Reformation. It is difficult to accept this statement in its entirety, as it excludes all prior influences such as the rise of free cities, and, especially, all economic factors. On the whole, the book is a valuable addition to English historical writing, although it contains several portions that ought to be critically examined before their conclusions are accepted, and although it leaves economic considerations entirely out of view. It is stimulating to thought and the style is, on the whole, clear and spirited. The notes are short but abundant, point the way to a great

mass of material, and form one of the best features of the book. Frank Strong, in *Am. hist. rev.*, 4: 148.

Grand remonstrance, 1641. See Old South Work, sect. 368. [2662

Gross, Charles. Bibliography of British municipal history. See Harvard University, sect. 269. [2663

Hallam, Henry. Constitutional history of England, from the accession of Henry VII. to the death of George II. London. 1827. 2v. Murray. 1871. 3v. 30s. N. Y.: Harper. 1899. 1v. $2.

—— *Same ;* ed. by Wm. Smith. (Student's ed.) N. Y.: American Book Co. 1899. $1.25. [2664

Written from original sources for the use of the student in English constitutional history. Still valuable, though, in the light of later research, much of the information needs correction, particularly that relating to the Stuart period. Written with insight, sound judgment and impartiality ; but has a Whig bias and is too dogmatic in expressing opinions founded on insufficient evidence. The style is elaborate and involved. Supplementary chapters on the history of Scotland and Ireland contain valuable information. R. C. H. C.

Hosmer, James Kendall. Short history of Anglo-Saxon freedom. N. Y.: Scribner. 1890. $2. [2665

The theme of this book is the essential unity in political development of the English and American peoples. Its practical object is, by calling attention to this fact, to promote harmony and sympathy between them. The author reproduces Freeman's view of early English history. He brings into undue prominence the democratic side both of English and of early American history. H. L. O.

Jenks, Edward. Constitutional experiments of the Commonwealth : a study of the years 1649–60. Cambridge: Univ. Press. 1890. N. Y.: Macmillan. 1890. [2666

The constitutional experiments of the Commonwealth have been either ignored or very inadequately treated by writers on the English constitution, because they have been viewed as temporary aberrations from the logical development of the English system. Prof. Jenks' little volume thus fills an important gap in the works of Hallam, Taswell-Langmead, etc. To the student of American history and of democracy the political thinking of the Commonwealth period is of the first importance. E. G. B.

Kemble, John Mitchell. The Saxons in England. London. 1848. 2v.

—— *Same ;* new ed., rev. by Walter De Gray Birch. London: Quaritch. 1876. 2v. [2667

This in its day was an epoch-making work. Kemble had edited a great collection of Anglo-Saxon charters, and was led by that to a first-hand study of the sources of that period of English history. He was the earliest to affirm the Teutonic character of English institutions, and he set forth his views in this work. It is not a history, but a series of original studies of early English institutions — the mark, folkland and bocland, social classes, the king, the witan, officials, the clergy, etc. It is by a study of institutions rather than by an attempt to trace the history of the English conquest of Britain that Kemble sought to establish his view. Errors and exaggerations of his have been corrected by later writers, but the best among them have gladly acknowledged their obligations to him, and have built on the foundation which he laid. Kemble was the first to affirm the intimate connection between landholding and the development of institutions.   H. L. O.

Langmead, Thomas Pitt Taswell-. English constitutional history. London: Stevens. 1875. 5th ed. rev., with notes by Philip A. Ashworth. 1896. Boston: Houghton. 1896. $6.   [2668

This book covers the entire period of English constitutional history, and is the best single volume on the subject. The work is based mostly on secondary authorities. The author writes from a legal point of view, and is too much influenced by legal traditions and prejudices, hence needs occasional correction. His judgment is, on the whole, sound, his temper even and fair; his work is carefully written in a pleasant though rather dry style.   R. C. H. C.

Macy, Jesse. The English constitution. N. Y.: Macmillan. 1897. $2.   [2669

The purpose of this book is to teach the American reader the ever-changing character of his own constitution, by comparing and contrasting it with the history and latest development of the English constitution. Though it may be a question whether Prof. Macy has chosen the best method of accomplishing his purpose, there can be no doubt that he has written one of the best accounts in existence of the organization and operation of parliamentary government in England. The historical portion, on the other hand, is not satisfactory. The earlier chapters are not abreast of the subject; the later chapters presuppose too much knowledge; while the point of view being always that of the present, obscures the fundamental idea of growth, upon which Prof. Macy lays so much stress.   C. M. A.
"Written in the first instance for American readers, the book may be studied by Englishmen with no small advantage. Professor Macy is neither an Anglophobe nor an Anglomaniac. He sees our merits and our defects with the same keenness of insight, and he is not blindly prejudiced in favour of the American method of government. Criticism, it will be understood, is not his object, though it incidentally becomes necessary. He describes and compares."
The Spectator, (London), Mar. 5, 1898.

Maitland, Frederic William. Domesday book and beyond: three essays in the early history of England. Cambridge: Univ. Press. 1897. Boston: Little. 1897. Net $4.50.
                                              [2670

The three essays contained in this volume are upon Domesday book, England before the Conquest, and The Hide. They relate to the organization of society at the time the Domesday survey was taken, to the territorial system of the early English, and to early land measurements. Taken together, they constitute the most original and profound study of the origin of English institutions — mainly on their territorial side — which has appeared since Kemble wrote. To a certain extent the book is controversial, for it is a reply to Seebohm's *English village community.* In it Prof. Maitland argues that the original condition of the English was one of relative freedom, and that the manor was not a survival from Roman times. His wide knowledge of the origin and history of law has been brought to bear on every subject he touches with illuminating effect. His discussion of the vill, the manor, the various social classes, the varieties of Anglo-Saxon land tenure, are very profound and suggestive. In temper he is catholic, while his style possesses a grace which in works of this character has perhaps never been equalled. In a small work, entitled *Township and borough* (sect. 2671), Prof. Maitland has illustrated some of his views by a detailed study of Cambridge and its common fields. This he puts forth as an example of the kind of detailed local work which should be done.   H. L. O.

—— Township and borough. Cambridge: Univ. Press. 1898. N. Y.: Macmillan. 1898. Net $2.50.   [2671

This volume contains a series of six lectures which were delivered by Prof. Maitland at the University of Oxford in 1897, and an appendix of notes relating to the history of the town of Cambridge. The lectures deal with the development of property, ownership, and corporate unity in one borough of England, Cambridge; and incidentally treat of the origin of the borough and its differentiation from the township. These subjects are brilliantly and luminously presented. The appendix contains not only comments and elucidations illustrating the text, but also documents relating to the open fields and town life of Cambridge, which are here printed for the first time.   C. M. A.

May, *Sir* Thomas Erskine. Constitutional history of England since the accession of George III., 1760-1860. London: Longmans. 1861-2. 2v. 3d ed. enl. Longmans. 1871. 3v. N. Y.: Armstrong. 1895. 2v. $2.50.   [2672

The work of May differs from that of Hallam, of which it is, in a sense, a continuation, in that it deals with the subject topically and not chronologically. Each special topic is taken up in turn and its history followed consecutively for a century. The work is therefore not so much a constitutional history as a series of essays upon aspects of the English constitution, historically considered. This method of treatment lays the work open to criticism, for it neglects the mutual interdependence of the different parts of the constitutional system, and renders the work difficult for students to use. In other respects, however, May's treatment is admirable.   C. M. A.

Medley, Dudley Julius. Student's manual

of English constitutional history. London : Simpkin. 1894. 2d ed. enl. London : Simpkin. 1898. 10s. 6d. [2673

Treats the constitutional history of England by topics. More space given to the period since the accession of Henry VII than is usual in works of this class. Supplied with marginal references to standard works. Appendix of brief synopses of some important cases in English constitutional law. An eminently usable and accurate manual.   E. C.

Petition of rights, 1628. See Old South Work, sect. 368. [2674

Pollock, *Sir* **Frederick,** *and* **Frederic William Maitland.** History of English law before the time of Edward I. Cambridge : Univ. Press. 1895. 2v. Boston : Little. 1899. 2v. Net $9. [2675

" Two legal historians, who long ago gave notable proofs of capacity, have at once brought the history of English law, for the period from 1154 to 1272, up to the full height of modern scientific research. With a style that is always dignified and often captivating, it has what I regard as the highest excellence in legal-historical writing : it is thought out, all through, in an eminently realistic spirit." Heinrich Brunner, in *Political science quarterly,* 11 : 534.

Sir Frederick Pollock gives to Professor Maitland the credit for producing most of the work. " In Mr. Maitland we have the learning and the intimacy, with the *fontes* of Brunner ; shall we add, that we have further what we find in Sohm . . . the gift which men call genius ? We must be temperate ; but there are chapters and parts of chapters in this work in which there is penetration not found in ordinary books of history. The chapter on Roman and Canon Law is masterly ; so is the one on the age of Bracton. . . . In style the book is fresh, ready, almost conversational. . . . The work is divided, unequally in point of bulk, into two books, preceded by a short introduction, itself a good piece of work. Book I is entitled ' Sketch of early English legal history ; ' Book II ' The doctrines of English law in the early Middle Ages.' . . . The central feature of the whole work is, roughly speaking, the Angevin period, or from the middle of the twelfth to the last quarter of the thirteenth century — from Henry II to Edward I. . . . How has the plan of the work been wrought out ? In one word, thoroughly." Melville M. Bigelow, in *Am. hist. rev.,* 1 : 112.

Prothero, George Walter, *ed.* Select statutes and other constitutional documents illustrative of the reigns of Elizabeth and James I. London : Frowde. 1894. 2d ed. N. Y.: Oxford Univ. Press. Net $2.60. [2676

Professor Prothero's Introduction is the most satisfactory account known to the writer of the English constitution as a working system in the time of Elizabeth and James. The documents selected illustrate all the phases of governmental activity, and form an almost indispensable supplement to the formal constitutional histories of the Elizabethan and early Stuart period.   E. G. B.

Ranke, Leopold von. History of England, principally in the 17th century ; tr. from the German. Oxford : Clar. Press. 1875. 6v. N. Y.: Oxford Univ. Press. 6v. $16. [2677

" The translators . . . are of opinion that Von Ranke's History of England ' may well be regarded as the concluding portion of the author's cycle of works on the international relations of the Continental States.' Although it is a history ' principally of the 17th century,' the writer does not confine himself to that period ; but, *more Germanico,* traces the development of the elements that moulded the national character and story from the commencement. The studies of the epochs in English history which are thus introductory to the main work of the historian are among the most valuable portions of his volumes, and bring into clear light the identity of the political and religious forces through whose action and counteraction the problems presented in England's career as a nation were at length resolved." *British quart. rev.,* 61 : 514.

Rose, John Holland. Rise of democracy. (Victorian era series.) London : Blackie. 1897. Chicago : Stone. 1898. $1.25. [2678

Beginning with the early years of the reign of George III, Mr. Rose traces the growth of the democratic movement in England to the close of the 19th century. The treatment throughout is characterized by insight, sympathy and candor. The book is scholarly and well written ; the student of American democracy will find it greatly useful.   A. D. M.

Smith, George Barnett. History of the English Parliament. London : Ward, Lock. 1894. 2v. 12s. [2679

Relates at length the events in which Parliament was an immediate actor instead of discussing the nature and development of Parliament itself. There is little information that cannot be secured from other works. The writer has consulted original sources, though using mostly secondary ones, is accurate enough and tells his story pleasantly ; but is too discursive, and shows little judgment and no depth of thought. Sketches of the Scotch and Irish Parliaments are included, and useful addenda comprise great constitutional acts, parliamentary procedure, and lists of ministers and chancellors.   R. C. H. C.

Smith, Goldwin. The United Kingdom : a political history. N. Y.: Macmillan. 1899. 2v. $4. [2680

In this greatly condensed political history of the United Kingdom, Mr. Goldwin Smith gives to the entire period before the Norman Conquest only fifteen pages. The history proper begins, therefore, with the advent of the Normans in 1066 ; and closes with the retirement of the Whigs from office in 1841. To the history is appended a chapter entitled "The Empire," which contains a brief but admirable summary of the history of Canada since the Seven Years' War, and of the British conquests and rule in India. The book is not in any way a contribution to the fund of historic material ; throughout it is simply an interpretation of facts generally accepted ; and as such it deserves high rank.

The style is clear, terse and forceful; every page is interesting. Mr. Smith is not an optimist. In praise he is temperate and discriminating, but in the exposure of defects of character and errors of policy, unsparing. Of modern books there are but few so well calculated to deepen in citizen and statesman the sense of public responsibility. A. D. M.

Stevens, Charles Ellis. Sources of the Constitution of the United States considered in relation to colonial and English history. London and N. Y.: Macmillan. 1894. $2. [**2681**

Seeks to trace the origin of American institutions directly to England. Written largely to refute Douglas Campbell's claim for a Dutch origin (sect. 2649). Author not familiar with colonial history, and does not give due prominence to institutional development of colonial times. Nevertheless, the book is stimulating and useful as attracting attention to an important field of study. E. C.

Stubbs, William. Constitutional history of England. N. Y.: Oxford Univ. Press. 1874-8. 3v. (demi 8vo.) $12. 3v. (crown 8vo.) $2.60 ea. [**2682**

In this work the highest reach of scholarship is attained. In depth and thoroughness of research, keenness of insight, soundness of judgment, the author of these volumes has been equalled by few and surpassed by none. For an indefinite period to come it will be the standard work on the subject of which it treats. Corrections here and there have been necessitated by the researches of younger scholars, but they in no respect impeach the supreme authoritativeness of Bishop Stubbs' views. The book is not easy reading; the material is not in all respects well arranged; repetitions are not infrequent. There are many dry details, but there are also many passages and chapters of great power, written in the most finished style. H. L. O.

—— *ed.* Select charters and other illustrations of English constitutional history, from the earliest times to the reign of Edward I. N. Y.: Oxford Univ. Press. 1870. $2.10. [**2683**

When the Yorkshire boy William Stubbs, at length a man, working his way forward to the highest positions in university and church, had fairly within his grasp the development of the English polity, he prepared the way for his *magnum opus*, the *Constitutional History*, by an edition of the great documents, the landmarks in the long course from the earliest times down to the date at which the polity becomes settled. The book opens with a sketch, expanded a few years later into the important three volumed work. It is a book for scholars ; for, while the Anglo-Saxon and Norman text is translated, the Latin of most of the documents is not. This memorable series of instruments, the foundation upon which America no less than England rests, is here conveniently set forth and lucidly explained. J. K. H.

Taylor, Hannis. Origin and growth of the English constitution. Boston : Houghton. 1889-98. 2v. $4.50. [**2684**

The book also attempts to show the growth out of

the English system "of the Federal Republic of the United States." It is made up entirely from second-hand sources, which the author has thoroughly read, but uses with too little discrimination. He shows no ability at original thinking, no skill in analysis, but has written with care and accuracy a book useful as giving a sketch of English constitutional history for elementary students. R. C. H. C.

Todd, Alpheus. Parliamentary government in England: its origin, development and practical operation. London : Longmans. 1867-9. 2v.

—— *Same ;* abrgd. and rev. by Spencer Walpole. London : Low. 1893. 2v. 15s. [**2685**

This is the most elaborate treatise in existence on the modern constitution of England, and it holds a deservedly prominent place among the standard works on the subject. Its contents — filling nearly 2000 pages — relate exclusively to the constitution as it has been under the aristocratic and democratic systems which have prevailed since 1689. A review of the events in the earlier history of England which tend to explain the origin of the modern constitution is given at the outset. This is followed by a summary of the constitutional history of the successive administrations since 1782. The position of the crown, with its prerogatives, is then described, and the control which may be exercised by the two houses over the royal administrative affairs. The organization and powers of the Privy Council are next outlined at length, the duties of the cabinet and the political functions of the members who compose it. Finally the duties devolving on the ministers in the conduct of public business in parliament are explained, and the organization of the departments of state and the relations of the judges to the crown and to parliament are described. Upon all points of importance treated in the work the statements of the text are confirmed and illustrated by ample citations of precedents and of the opinions of leading statesmen as found in their speeches and writings. The work is written from the standpoint of a moderate liberal. H. L. O.

—— Parliamentary government in the British colonies. Boston : Little. 1880.

—— *Same.* 2d ed.; edited by his son. London and N. Y.: Longmans. 1894. Net $10. [**2686**

"Whilst it is apparently intended to be a *vade mecum* for British colonial governors, giving them the application of both principle and precedent to the work of conducting their administrations, it is really a constitutional history, in no inadequate sense, of colonial government. ... It would be hard to find anywhere better evidence of the practical sense, the steady, tempered patience which can afford to wait, the rooted confidence in the ultimate judgment of the people, which distinctively mark the English race, than is shown in Mr. Todd's compendium of precedents established by the recent history of the British colonies. One may point to them confidently as exhibiting with the greatest clearness the fundamental reasons why the Anglo-Saxon race has made constant progress in civil liberty and in representative government." J. D. Cox, *Nation*, 30: 371.

American Development

Adams, John. Defence of the Constitution of government of the United States against the attack of M. Turgot. London. 1787–8. 3v. New ed. 1794. 3v. [2687

John Adams, it is safe to say, bestowed more thought on the nature of government, and exerted more influence in determining the character of the constitutions adopted during the Revolution by most of the original states, than any one of his contemporaries. When, therefore, Turgot attacked these constitutions because of "an unreasonable imitation of the usages of England," and because of a want of centralization, it was natural that Adams should come forward as their champion. The *Defence* was written in 1786 and 1787 during the ministry of Mr. Adams at the Court of St. James. It is a work marked by insight, breadth of views, conviction, courage, and — we may venture to add — much wisdom. The book is not well written ; evidences of haste and carelessness abound ; there is considerable repetition and a great excess of historical illustration. The first volume was published in time to be consulted by the members of the Convention of 1787 ; and the work, when completed, was widely read. The opponents of Mr. Adams made great use of it to support the accusation of a predilection for aristocracy and monarchy. A. D. M.

Aldrich, P. Emory. Origin of New England towns, their powers and duties. See American Antiquarian Society, sect. 242. [2688

Ames, Herman V. Proposed amendments to the Constitution of the U. S. during the first century of its existence. See American Historical Association, sect. 248. [2689

Andrews, C. M. Origin of Connecticut towns. See American Academy of Political and Social Science, sect. 226. [2690

Bancroft, George. History of the formation of the Constitution. N. Y.: Appleton. 1882. 2v. $5. 1v. $2.50. [2691

The text of these volumes is identical with vol. 6 of the latest edition of Bancroft's *History of the United States*. It is also published separately in one volume. The distinctive feature of this original edition is the most interesting collection of transcripts from unpublished *Letters and papers illustrating the formation of the Federal Constitution*, filling in all about 350 pages. The narrative is devoted mainly to showing the need of a more effective union and to the debates on the formation of the Constitution and its ratification by the states. This material Mr. Bancroft summarized and wove together with masterly skill. Although written in a more restrained style than his earlier volumes, this work presents a somewhat idealized picture of men and things in our "critical period." E. G. B.

Barlow, Joel. Political writings. New ed., cor. N. Y. 1796. [2692

Interesting as setting forth the views of an American radical, writing under the influence of the French Revolution. Contains no direct reference to American affairs or experience. E. C.

Bishop, Cortlandt F. History of elections in the American colonies. (Columbia Univ. studies in history, etc., v. 3, no. 1.) N. Y. Macmillan. 1893. $1.50. [2693

The only detailed study of the technical data on which a knowledge of the subject depends. A sketch of the history of elections in each colony is followed by a discussion of the conditions of the suffrage, the management of elections, and the machinery of local elections. An appendix gives forms of writs, returns, and oaths, and the texts of some hitherto unpublished statutes relating to elections. W. MacD.

Blodgett, James H. Free burghs in the United States. See American Historical Association, sect. 247. [2694

Boutwell, George Sewell. Constitution of the United States at the end of the first century. Boston : Heath. 1895. $2.50. [2695

Described as an attempt "to set forth in a concise form the substance of the leading decisions of the Supreme Court, in which the several articles, sections, and clauses of the Constitution of the United States have been examined, explained, and interpreted." A third of the book is taken up with the texts of the Declaration of Independence, the Articles of Confederation, the Ordinance of 1787, and the Constitution, together with an elaborate index to the latter, all reproduced, apparently, from the *Revised statutes of the United States* (ed. 1878), which the author edited. The clauses of the Constitution are then taken up in order, and a few important decisions under them summarized. The precise purpose which the volume is intended to serve is not clear, but its digests of cases have a superficial usefulness. W. MacD.

Boyd, Carl Evans, *ed.* Cases on American constitutional law. Chicago: Callaghan. 1898. $3. [2696

A thorough understanding of our constitutional history requires a knowledge of the leading decisions of the courts in which fundamental principles have been declared. In this volume sixty-three of the most important cases are given in condensed form. The selection is on the whole judiciously made, and opinions are condensed with care and discretion. A. C. McL.

Bradford, Gamaliel. Congress and the cabinet. See American Academy of Political and Social Science, sect. 226. [2697

—— Lesson of popular government. N. Y.: Macmillan. 1899. 2v. $4. [2698

"For more than thirty years Mr. Bradford has been an earnest student of our democratic institutions, both in themselves and in comparison with other examples of popular government. Seeing clearly the shortcomings and abuses incident to freedom, he has not lost faith in the people, but has found his conviction ripening that a republic is, after all, the form of government which has secured the greatest average happiness for a community. . . . The thesis of this important work is, he says, 'that so far as popular government has failed, the main cause has been in defective machinery, so that public opinion is brought to bear either not at all, or so imperfectly that what is assumed to be the will of the people is, in fact, only that of a comparatively small number of political managers, more or less dishonest, who avail themselves of the forms of government to carry out their private schemes and purposes, by virtue of a nominal expression of the popular will' (1: 38). Looking into the defects of the machinery, he finds the chief in the absorption of governmental power by the Legislature. . . . Mr. Bradford concludes that 'the ideal constitution of the executive is a single head, surrounded by a staff of his own selection, appointed and removed at his pleasure, one man being at the head of each department' (1: 46). . . . Whether we wholly follow Mr. Bradford's reasoning or not, we must bear witness that he has given us a most valuable book, inspired by a noble faith in the capacity of man for self-government, and by a pure and disinterested patriotism devoting a lifetime of laborious investigation to the task of smoothing our pathway towards a pure and successful republicanism." J. D. Cox, in *Nation*, 68: 335, 361.

Brooks, Elbridge Streeter. Century book for young Americans. N. Y.: Century Co. [c. 1894.] $1.50. [**2699**

Under the guise of a tour to Washington City by a party of boys and girls, the author describes the actual workings of the national government in its various departments. Additional chapters are given to the capital city and the resources of the United States. This book was prepared at the request of the Sons of the American Revolution for educational purposes. With its photographic illustrations it is a valuable book for children. E. E. S.

Brooks, Noah. How the republic is governed. N. Y.: Scribner. 1895. 75c. [**2700**

Very brief definitions of the functions of each division of the national government. Gives names of officers and their duties, and explains provisions for naturalization, patents, etc. Contains the Constitution and Declaration of Independence. Gives no concrete illustrations of the workings of the government, and is not likely to prove interesting. E. E. S.

Brownson, Orestes Augustus. The American republic, its constitution, tendencies and destiny. N. Y.: O'Shea. 1866. [**2701**

"In a volume which might well be compressed into one fourth its present size, he covers a great deal of ground, and has pungent suggestions on both sides of a great many questions. Even in the preface he announces his abandonment of the doctrine of state sovereignty, after holding it for thirty-three years, and at once proceeds to explain how, in a profounder sense, he holds it more thoroughly than ever. In the chapter on 'Secession,' which is the best in the book, he indorses Charles Sumner's theory of state suicide; holds that the southern states are now 'under the Union, not of it,' and seems quite inclined to pardon

Mr. Lincoln for abolishing slavery by proclamation. On the other hand, he scouts the theory that the rebels committed treason, in any moral sense, and proclaims that we are all 'willing and proud to be their countrymen, fellow-citizens, and friends.' . . . Of a standing army Mr. Brownson thinks well, and wishes it to number a hundred thousand; but his reason for the faith that is in him is a little unexpected. He thinks it useful because 'it creates honorable places for gentlemen or the sons of gentlemen without wealth.' . . . He sees danger in the horizon, and frankly avows it. . . . It is, that, if matters go on as now, foreign observers will never clearly understand whether it was the 'territorial democracy' or the 'humanitarian democracy' which really triumphed in the late contest ! . . . It is needless to say that its author is the same Mr. Brownson whom the American people long since tried and found wanting as a safe or wise counsellor; the same of whom the Roman Catholic Church one day assumed the responsibility, and found the task more onerous than had been expected." *Atlantic*, 17: 523.

Bryce, James. The American commonwealth. London and N. Y.: Macmillan. 1888. 2v. 3d ed., rev., with additional chapters. 1893–5. 2v. $4.

—— *Same;* abridged for colleges and high schools. N. Y.: Macmillan. 1896. $1.75. [**2702**

A work of rare philosophical power and insight, easily first among descriptions and criticisms of American political and social institutions. It is based upon extensive personal knowledge of the United States as well as thorough study of its history. The work falls into six parts. Part I treats of the organization and work of the national government, and Part II of state and local government. Part III is a detailed study of the party system. Part IV discusses the nature, action, and influence of public opinion, while Part V, "illustrations and reflections," groups a few topics, such as the Tammany ring, Kearneyism, woman suffrage, etc., not falling properly within other divisions, together with observations on the strength and weakness of American democracy. Part VI treats of social institutions, including under this head the bar, the universities, the church, etc. Constitutional history, as such, is outside the author's sphere, and is touched upon only in so far as is necessary to elucidate the governmental system. The exposition of the relations between the federal government and the states, political methods, and the working of public opinion, is especially notable. Incidentally the book serves as a corrective of the theories of De Tocqueville and other European observers.

The abridgment contains the greater part of vol. 1 of the original work, and a few chapters from vol. 2, but abridged mainly by omitting most of the references to English institutions, and cutting down the longer passages of comment. The resulting condensation is dry, and devoid of both the literary and philosophic charm and the expository power of the original. W. MacD.

—— Predictions of Hamilton and De Tocqueville. (Johns Hopkins Univ. studies, ser. 5, no. 9.) Balt. 1887. Pap. 25c. [**2703**

In the pages of this little pamphlet, the author of the *American commonwealth* discusses the predictions of Hamilton in the Federalist and of De Tocqueville in his Democracy in America. No one is better qualified than Mr. Bryce to test such prophecies by the actualities of the present. The volume is written in the interesting and suggestive way characteristic of all the author's work.   A. C. McL.

Burgess, John William. Political science and comparative constitutional law. Boston: Ginn. 1890. 2v. $5.   [2704

An elaborate and learned comparison of the constitutional systems of the United States, Great Britain, France, and Germany, from the point of view of an abstruse theoretical discussion of the nature of government, state, and nation. German authorities seem mainly to have been relied upon. The literary interest is small, and the personal views of the author are strongly emphasized; the descriptive portions, however, have marked value and usefulness. An appendix to vol. 1 gives the texts, in the original, of the constitutions of Prussia and the German Empire, and of the " constitutional laws " of France.
          W. MacD.

Caldwell, Joshua W. Studies in the constitutional history of Tennessee. Cin. : Clarke. 1895. $2.   [2705

Based upon a series of newspaper articles written in 1895 in aid of an effort for a constitutional convention. The work makes no pretension to being a history of the state, but treats historically six important periods or phases, viz., the Watauga association, 1772–1777, the State of Cumberland, 1780–1783, the State of Franklin, 1784–1788, and the constitutions of 1796, 1834, and 1870. The book shows first-hand research, and has historical value.   W. MacD.

Chambrun, Adolphe de. Le pouvoir executif aux États-Unis. Paris. 1876.
—— The executive power in the United States; tr. by Madeleine Vinta Dahlgren. Lancaster, Pa. 1874.   [2706

This foreign commentator on one phase of the government of the United States comes chronologically between De Tocqueville and Bryce, but possesses the peculiar perceptive and analytic power of neither of these writers. His work consists chiefly in tracing the various functions of the executive as conceived in the Constitutional Convention, and showing how custom has made them otherwise. There are practical chapters on the administrations of Lincoln and of Johnson.   E. E. S.

Channing, Edward. Town and county government in the English colonies of North America. (Johns Hopkins Univ. studies, ser. 2, no. 10.) Baltimore. 1884. Pap. 50c.   [2707

This study, which received the Tappan prize at Harvard University, was one of the first fruits of the interest aroused by Professor H. B. Adams in the local institutions of the colonies. But, as Professor Channing was strictly limited to such printed material as the Harvard University Library contained, his study

is inevitably imperfect. Notwithstanding the fact that some of his conclusions must be revised in view of the new material that has been utilized for both regions since 1884, he still gives perhaps the best comparative study of the local institutions of New England and Virginia. The history of the origin of the New England town has yet to be written, while such works as Bruce's *Economic history of Virginia* throw great light upon the conditions in that colony. But considering the time and the material, the essay is one of unusual excellence.   C. M. A.

Clark, Charles C. P. The " machine " abolished and the people restored to power, by the organization of all the people on the lines of party organization. N. Y. : Putnam. 1900. $1.   [2708

This is a new and considerably re-written edition of a remarkably suggestive book, first published in 1878, under the title of *The commonwealth reconstructed*. It is a penetrating study of the conditions under which parties and party nominations have fallen under the control of the " bosses " of political " machines." In the writer's view, which many are coming to share, this deadly paralyzing of the popular will is an inevitable consequence of the arrangement of constituencies, for the representation of the people, on geographical lines. He proposes to substitute a formation of constituencies by lot, with periodical drawings, to make a frequent change. The book is fascinating in thought and admirably clear in style. It deserves more attention than it has received.

Cooley, Thomas McIntyre. General principles of constitutional law in the United States of America. Boston : Little. 1880.
—— *Same*, 3d ed.; [revised] by Andrew C. McLaughlin. Little. 1898. $2.50.   [2709

One of the well-known *Students' series* of elementary law text-books, and the work of an authority of the first rank. It is by far the best brief manual of constitutional law. The arrangement is systematic, the style simple and clear, and the exposition admirable. The edition of 1898, besides revision of the text, adds a chapter on the formation and construction of state constitutions, mainly extracted from the same author's *Constitutional limitations*.   W. MacD.

—— Treatise on the constitutional limitations which rest upon the legislative power of the states of the American union. Boston : Little. 1868.
—— *Same :* 6th ed.; with additions by A. C. Angell. Little. 1890. $6.   [2710

An elaborate legal treatise, and one of the best known of its author's works. The several chapters discuss, with the usual extensive citation and comparison of cases, such topics as the formation, amendment, and construction of state constitutions, legislative powers and the enactment of laws, constitutional protection of persons and property, liberty of speech and of the press, religious liberty, taxation, the police power, and the expression of the popular will through elections.   W. MacD.

Cooley, Thomas McIntyre, *et al.* Constitutional history of the United States as seen in the development of American law. N. Y.: Putnam. 1889. $2. [2711

This book, made up of five lectures by as many eminent jurists, seeks to mark out the course of the constitutional development of the United States, as that development appears in the decisions of the courts. Important cases are discussed ; decisions are chronologically arranged, and it is shown how one important principle followed upon another. In this way the main steps in constitutional development, as far as that depends on judicial action and construction, are declared. All of the lectures are able ; but the most valuable are " The Supreme Court, its place in the American constitutional system," and " Constitutional development in the United States as influenced by Chief Justice Marshall." A. C. McL.

Cooper, Thomas V., *and* **Hector T. Fenton,** *eds.* American politics. Phil.: Fireside Pub. Co. 1882. [2712

Contents: History of the political parties. — Political platforms. — Great speeches on great issues. — Parliamentary practice. — Existing political laws. — Federal blue book. — Tabulated history of politics.

Curry, Jabez Lamar Monroe. Southern states of the American Union considered in their relations to the Constitution of the United States. N. Y.: Putnam. 1894. Richmond : Johnson. $1. [2713

A historical argument for the southern view of the Constitution written by one prominently identified with the southern Confederacy and aimed " to reconstruct ideas and opinions adverse to the South, in so far as they are founded on ignorance and prejudice." While mainly *ex parte,* and not always dispassionate, the presentation is manly and, on the whole, fair and strong. Its explanation of the attitude of the South will be found well worth reading by those who have studied only the other side of the question.

G. P. G.

Curtis, George Ticknor. Constitutional history of the United States. N. Y.: Harper. 1889–96. 2v. $6. [2714

Vol. 1 is a revised edition of the same author's *History of the constitution of the United States,* 2 vols., 1854. The high legal standing of Curtis, his judicial temper, and the clearness of his style, gave his original work great favor, especially with lawyers, and caused it to be often quoted by the courts as an authority. Of the two volumes, the first, covering the period of the Revolution and the Confederation, is the better. The vol. 2 of the revised edition (1896) contains thirteen chapters left unfinished at the author's death, and published under the supervision of J. C. Clayton. The special merits of vol. 2 are not considerable, and the account of the period covered by it (1789-1876) is slight. Curtis's fundamental political views were those of Webster, whose friend and biographer he was ; but his opinions on the constitutional aspects of the slavery controversy, shown in his *Life of Buchanan,*

are not altered here. The latter half of vol. 2 comprises documents and miscellaneous papers.

W. MacD.

Cushing, H. A. History of the transition from provincial to commonwealth government in Massachusetts. See Columbia University, sect. 259. [2715

Dallinger, Frederick William. Nominations for elective office in the United States. (Harvard historical studies, 4.) N. Y.: Longmans. 1897. $1.50. [2716

An interesting discussion, given additional weight by the practical experience of the author as a member of the Massachusetts Legislature. A brief history of the caucus and nominating convention in the United States is followed by a description of the present nominating system ; the remainder of the book treats of remedies for existing evils. The remedies relied upon by the author are: (1) a reduction of the number of elective offices ; (2) separation of local elections from state and national ; (3) abolition of the spoils system. W. MacD.

Dawes, Anna Laurens. How we are governed ; an explanation of the Constitution and government of the United States. Boston : Lothrop. [c. 1885.] Boston : Ginn. $1. [2717

Varies little from the old line of text-books on " civil government," but expressed in simple language. Not likely to fulfill the promise in the title, but of some service to the searcher for general information. Comments are arranged under the general divisions of the Constitution. Gives minute descriptions of the practical working of the Federal government, but is meagre on state governments, and lacking on local self-government. Purely theoretical in treatment of questions of reform. Optimistic.

E. E. S.

Douglas, Stephen Arnold. CUTTS, JAMES MADISON. Brief treatise upon constitutional and party questions and the history of political parties, as I received it orally from the late Stephen A. Douglas. N. Y.: Appleton. 1866. [2718

In the summer of 1859, the author had a series of " interviews " with Mr. Douglas on the questions named in the title of this book. The replies of Mr. Douglas " were taken down in writing, verbally, at the time," says Mr. Cutts, " Mr. Douglas always pausing long enough to enable me to obtain his exact language." The result is a valuable, though fragmentary and meagre " confession of political faith " from the lips of the man who during the eventful six years between 1854 and 1860 was the leader of the northern section of the Democratic party. The book is one which every student of that period should read.

A. D. M.

Dunning, William Archibald. Essays on the Civil War and reconstruction, and related topics. N. Y.: Macmillan. 1898. $2. [2719

Seven essays, on The Constitution in Civil War, The Constitution in reconstruction, Military government during reconstruction, Process of reconstruction, Impeachment and trial of President Johnson, Are the states equal under the Constitution?, and American political philosophy. All except the fourth first appeared in periodicals. The last is unimportant: the others are constitutional and legal studies of high value, written with judicial temper and in an interesting style. W. MacD.

Federalist, The: a commentary on the Constitution of the United States; reprinted from the original text [1788] of Alexander Hamilton, John Jay, and James Madison; ed. by H. C. Lodge. N. Y.: Putnam. 1888. $1.50. —— *Same;* ed. by Paul Leicester Ford. N. Y.: Holt. 1898. $1.75. [2720

A collection of essays designed to convince the people of New York that the Articles of Confederation were hopelessly defective as a national constitution, that a more effective system was indispensable for the prosperity of the country, and that the Constitution framed by the Philadelphia convention promised a remedy for the existing evils, and an energetic administration without imperilling liberty. The second part of the *Federalist* is a detailed explanation of the provisions of the Constitution and of the general plan of government proposed. Of the many editions, those by Lodge and Ford are to be preferred. H. B. Dawson's edition of 1863, which is now out of print, has a very learned introduction on the bibliography and authorship of the essays. Both Mr. Lodge and Mr. Ford are somewhat biassed in favor of Hamilton in their discussion of the authorship, and their treatment of the question cannot be considered as final or satisfactory. The distinctive features of Ford's edition are the indication of place and date of the first publication of each essay, the suggestive running commentary on portions of the text and the ample index, far more complete than is possessed by any other edition. E. G. B. See next title.

Federalist, The, and other constitutional papers, by Hamilton, Jay, Madison, and other statesmen; ed. by E. H. Scott. Chicago: Scott. 1895. 2v. $5. [2721

A cheap but well-printed text of *The Federalist* based upon the edition of 1818 and the index of 1831. It lacks the valuable suggestions made in Dawson's revision and the annotation of Lodge's edition. To the text are added twenty-two of the best essays and pamphlets on the Constitution taken from Ford's collections. E. E. S.

Fisher, Sydney George. Evolution of the Constitution of the United States. Phil.: Lippincott. 1897. $1.50. [2722

An attempt to show how the Constitution developed from the colonial charters and plans of union, as well as from English practice. In addition to a general sketch of the development of the charters, and an account of the first state constitutions, the various provisions of the Constitution in detail are compared with corresponding provisions in the earlier documents, the texts of the passages in question being printed in full. A final chapter criticises adversely the theory of Dutch influence upon American history and institutions, set forth in Douglas Campbell's *The Puritan in Holland, England, and America* (sect. 2649). W. MacD.

Fiske, John. American political ideas viewed from the standpoint of universal history. N. Y.: Harper. 1885. $1. [2723

This book comprises a course of three lectures, the Town meeting, Federal union, and Manifest destiny, originally delivered at the Royal Institution of Great Britain in 1880. Mr. Fiske confutes the notion that centralization is needed for very large nations; contends that the stability of a great political aggregate, like the United States, can be maintained only through the combination of local self-government and federal union; and sees a great future for federation in the history of mankind. The lectures are popular in character, but very suggestive, and are marked by a strong American spirit. B. A. H.

—— Civil government in the United States, considered with some reference to its origins. Boston: Houghton. 1890. Net $1. [2724

An attractively written elementary account, descriptive and historical, of American political institutions, with special reference to the origin and historical development of existing forms. More than usual attention is paid to local and state government. The book is intended for use as a text-book, but purposely avoids arbitrary arrangement and didactic presentation. An apparatus of questions and topics has been provided by F. A. Hill. W. MacD.

Follett, Mary Parker. The Speaker of the House of Representatives. N. Y.: Longmans. 1896. $1.75. [2725

An admirable historical examination of the speakership, and the duties and responsibilities of the office. English and colonial precedents are only briefly touched upon, but the whole course of development under the Constitution is minutely traced. The results of the inquiry go to show that "the whole history of the House of Representatives, from an institutional point of view, has been the history of the concentration of legislative power in the hands of the Speaker of the House;" but the author writes as an historian, and without a theory to prove. W. MacD.

Ford, Henry Jones. Rise and growth of American politics: a sketch of constitutional development. N. Y.: Macmillan. 1898. $1.50. [2726

"Mr. Ford . . . starts out with the proposition that American political conditions can be understood only in the light of English political conditions in the eighteenth century, of which American political conditions are the natural outgrowth." He "shows, in a most interesting and instructive manner, that in both countries the necessary harmony between the executive and the legislature was attained in the same way — through the establishment of strong national parties. In both countries these parties secured their existence and perpetuated their power by the employment of means which we can hardly fail to regard as corrupt. . . . The great difference between the two countries lies in the fact that England has progressed further than the United States. England has practically solved the problem, through the establishment of the cabinet system with the prime minister at its head. . . . The only questionable part of this invaluable book is the suggestion made at the close — a suggestion upon which considerable emphasis is laid — that we can solve the problem in the same way in which England has already solved it : namely, by the admission of the members of the President's cabinet to the floor of Congress. . . . Mr. Ford has written the best book that has appeared for a long time on American politics. . . . It treats of the details of our political development and present conditions with a thoroughness which has nowhere been excelled." Frank J. Goodnow, in *Political science quarterly*, 14: 155.

Ford, Paul Leicester. Bibliography of the adoption of the Constitution of the United States. See Historical Printing Club, sect. 272. **[2727**

—— *ed.* Essays on the Constitution of the United States, published during its discussion by the people, 1787–88. Brooklyn : Historical Printing Club. 1892. **[2728**

An invaluable collection for the special student who would know the arguments used for and against the adoption of the Constitution. The essays originally appeared in the newspapers, as did the similar articles that make up *The Federalist*. Among the writers represented are Oliver Ellsworth, Alexander Hamilton, Robert Yates, Charles Pinckney and others who were well-known and influential persons of the time.
A. C. McL.

—— *ed.* Pamphlets on the Constitution of the United States, published during its discussion by the people, 1787–88; with notes and a bibliography. Brooklyn : Ford. 1888. **[2729**

What is said of the *Essays* mentioned above is applicable in large measure to these pamphlets, which disclose very clearly the main outline of the great controversy over the Constitution. The editor has rendered the student of American history good service by gathering these pamphlets from many sources, determining their authorship and publishing them in convenient form. Written by men like Gerry, Jay, Wilson, Dickinson and others hardly less famous, they are essential and valuable portions of our historical literature.
A. C. McL.

Ford, Worthington Chauncey, *ed.* American citizen's manual. (Questions of the day.) N. Y.: Putnam. 1882–3. 2v. **[2730**

Part I is a brief description of the organization and work of government, national, state, and local, in the United States, with chapters on the electoral system and the civil service. Part II discusses elementary principles of constitutional law, particularly such as relate to taxation and expenditure, the regulation of commerce and industry (the author is opposed to protection) and the care of the poor and defective classes. The work as a whole has been superseded, but its tone of critical reflection still gives it worth.
W. MacD.

Foster, Roger. Commentaries on the Constitution of the United States. Boston : Boston Book Co. 1895–. V. 1+. V. 1, $4.50. **[2731**

The most pretentious recent treatise, aiming, apparently, to rival Story's famous *Commentaries*. The plan contemplates extended comment on the clauses of the Constitution in their order, and not under a topical classification. Vol. 1 (all published), with the subtitle, ' Preamble to impeachment,' deals with the preamble, and so much of Art. I as relates to the organization of the Senate and House of Representatives. Incidentally, the author goes, sometimes at great length, into the discussion of historical and political questions more or less related to the topic in hand. Chap. XIII, on impeachment, and the appendix on state impeachment trials. together form the best recent account of that subject available ; but, with that exception, the work offers nothing for the lawyer, and little that the historical student or non-professional reader will not find better stated elsewhere. The style is loose, and the tone often unjudicial. W. MacD.

Foster, William Eaton. References to the Constitution of the United States. (Economic tracts, no. 29.) N. Y. : Soc. for Political Education. 1890. **[2732**

Relatively much more elaborate than the same author's *References to the history of Presidential administrations*, and invaluable as a guide to the historical study of the Constitution. The strictly legal side of constitutional history and interpretation seems to have been beyond the author's purpose, although an appendix gives significant extracts from a few leading decisions.
W. MacD.

Freeman, Edward Augustus. Introduction to American institutional history. (Johns Hopkins Univ. studies, ser. 1, no. 1.) Balt. 1882. Pap. 25c. **[2733**

The introduction to institutional history covers only six pages, but it is supplemented by extracts from the writer's *Impressions of America*. Most of the matter is now fruitless and not very interesting. The suggestions concerning the value and true historic character and origin of American local institutions, though perhaps not altogether to be relied upon, have been productive of good in encouraging a thoughtful and profound study of local government.
A. C. McL.

Frothingham, Richard. Rise of the republic of the United States. Boston : Little. 1872. 6th ed. 1895. $3.50. **[2734**

This book is not so much a relation of events as a discussion of their causes, having for its object the tracing of the development of the two ideas of local self-government and union to their culmination in the Constitution, and covering the period from early colonial times to 1790. This work, based upon original sources and the fruit of diligent research and unusual industry, is an authority upon the subject; the choice of facts and arguments is made with great skill and judgment; and the book is carefully written. An appendix contains Governor Hutchinson's plan of union (1754), and a letter of John Adams on the discussion of independence in the colonial congress. R. C. H. C.

Godkin, Edwin Lawrence. Problems of modern democracy: essays. N. Y.: Scribner. 1897. $2. [2735

One can find nowhere else abler discussions or keener analyses of problems presented by the political and social life of America. The book is made up of a number of essays that have appeared at different times as magazine articles, and one or two are in a measure occasional only. All of them, however, are clever efforts to detect the actual basis of important problems. Perhaps the most suggestive essay in the collection is the one entitled *The real problems of democracy*, which is a comment on W. E. H. Lecky's *Democracy and liberty;* but of almost equal value is the one called *Popular government*, a review of Sir Henry Maine's book bearing that title. The style is simple, but direct, keen, effective. A. C. McL.

—— Unforeseen tendencies of democracy. Boston: Houghton. 1898. $2. [2736

A trenchant and suggestive discussion of "some of the departures" which democracy has made "from the ways which its earlier promoters expected it to follow." Of the difficulties which democracy has encountered, the author draws particular attention to two—political corruption accompanying the scramble for wealth, and the necessity of governing the large masses of population in cities. The essays bear titles as follows : Former democracies; Equality; The nominating system; The decline of legislatures; Peculiarities of American municipal government; The growth and expression of public opinion; The Australian democracy. The author is a keen and exacting critic, but here no pessimist. The literary style is that long familiar in the editorial writing of the *Nation* and the New York *Evening Post* — clear, simple, incisive, and abounding in apt illustration.

W. MacD.

Each of the seven essays is a thoughtful and instructive study of the important subject to which it relates. The writer is a keen and intelligent, but always friendly critic of democracy. A. D. M.

Goodnow, Frank Johnson. Comparative administrative law: an analysis of the administrative systems, national and local, of the United States, England, France, and Germany. N. Y.: Putnam. 1893. 2v. $5. [2737

The only scholarly work in English, as yet, which seeks to give a concise comparative view of the administrative, as distinguished from the constitutional, law of the countries named. It is based upon a first-hand study of the essential material, but is written with a view to the needs of students rather than of mature scholars. It thus supplements Burgess's *Political science and comparative constitutional law* (sect. 2704), on the one side, and Lowell's *Governments and parties in continental Europe*, on the other.

Vol. 1 treats of the organization of government, and central and local administration; Vol. 2, of legal relations, particularly the law of public officers, and the control over the administration. The point of view is not seldom European, especially where the American system shows defects; and the style occasionally suggests German influence. A consolidated index accompanies each volume. W. MacD.

Guthrie, William Dameron. Lectures on the fourteenth article of amendment to the Constitution of the U. S.; delivered before the Dwight Alumni Association, N. Y. April–May, 1898. Boston: Little. 1898. Net $2.50. [2738

"The most interesting constitutional questions which now come before the United States Supreme Court are those connected with the interpretation of the fourteenth amendment. . . . At a single term (October term, 1896), the amendment was discussed in twenty-one cases, fifteen of which turned upon its interpretation. At the following term a most important decision was made. The opening clause defining citizenship was applied to the case of a child born in the United States of Chinese parents, and the child was held to be a citizen even though his parents cannot be naturalized. . . . It is altogether too early to expect any elaborate and well-rounded treatise upon this the newest branch of our constitutional law. The decisions are numerous and many of them conflicting. But in the meantime discussions of decisions rendered and of the principles underlying them will form an important part of our legal literature. Such a work is [this] volume. . . . An ample table of cases, a well-annotated copy of the Constitution, and an analytical index add greatly to the value of the volume. The circumstances under which the lectures were prepared are perhaps a sufficient excuse for their numerous shortcomings in the selection of matter and the form of its arrangement. The author promises a more elaborate work on the same subject." Carl Evans Boyd, in *Annals of the Am. Academy of Political and Social Science,* 14: 88.

Harding, Samuel Bannister. Contest over the ratification of the federal Constitution in the state of Massachusetts. (Harvard historical studies, 2.) N. Y.: Longmans. 1896. $1.25. [2739

The title is an accurate indication of the scope of the volume. The author writes from the belief that it is through a study of state politics, during and immediately after the Revolution, that later political and party struggles over the Constitution can best be understood; and his work, a detailed study of primary sources, is an important contribution to that end. An appendix reprints some contemporary newspaper letters, and adds a bibliographical note on the sources.

W. MacD.

Hare, John Innes Clark. American constitutional law. Boston : Little. 1889. 2v. $12. [2740

This is the longest and most thorough work as yet published on this subject, if Story's *Commentaries,* the first edition of which appeared over sixty years ago, be not taken into account. In the first volume some space is devoted to a consideration of the early constitutional history of the United States, and to a comparison of the English and American systems of government. The reader will find these portions of the book interesting as well as instructive. The strictly legal parts are also well written. Possibly the work shows a tendency to diffuseness, and occasionally one may feel that there is a lack of thorough organization as well as compactness. But such criticisms are not serious. The book is a learned and scholarly treatise. A. C. McL.

Harrison, Benjamin. This country of ours. N. Y.: Scribner. 1897. $1.50. [2741

Chiefly remarkable as being the work of an ex-President, and written, accordingly, from personal knowledge. It is an agreeable surface description of the practical workings of the national government, mainly with reference to the executive departments. Chap. X gives an interesting view of the daily life of a President. The treatment of the legislative and judicial departments is scanty. W. MacD.

Hart, Albert Bushnell. Introduction to the study of federal government. (Harvard historical monographs, no. 2.) Boston: Ginn. 1891. [2742

A very useful reference handbook, which will be found helpful in the study of constitutional history and especially in the comparative study of constitutions. It is composed of two distinct parts. The first is a short outline history of all the important confederations and federal states that have ever existed. The second presents a conspectus of the four leading federal constitutions, arranged for easy comparison. Copious bibliographies add to the value of the volume. A. C. McL.

—— Practical essays on American government. N. Y.: Longmans. 1893. $1.50. [2743

The author has not sought to discuss American government as a whole, or work out the characteristics of American politics, but simply to treat isolated or detached topics. He is especially interested, not in theory or reform, but in the actual working of governmental machinery. Some of the essays are strictly historical in character, while all are the results of investigation, not of mere speculation. They are written in a simple, effective style and are interesting as well as valuable to the student of American institutions. A. C. McL.

Hinsdale, Burke Aaron. American government, national and state. Ann Arbor: Register Pub. Co. 1893. Rev. ed. Chicago: Werner. 1895. $1.25. [2744

Designed as a text-book for high schools and colleges. The book does not attempt to rival Bryce's *American commonwealth* either in scope or in philosophic character; but the mass of facts is large and the material systematically arranged. Within its field, it is perhaps the best concise treatment of the subject. The operations of the national government naturally hold chief place, but the government of states and local communities is better attended to than is usual in works of this character. The earlier chapters trace at considerable length the history of the colonies and states, with special reference to the preparation for the Constitution. W. MacD.

Hinsdale, Burke Aaron *and* **Mary L.** History and civil government of Pennsylvania, and the government of the United States. Chicago: Werner. 1899. $1. [2745

A plain, straightforward account of the history of Pennsylvania from the days of the Dutch and the Swedes, followed by similar accounts of the governments of the state and of the United States.

—— History and civil government of Ohio, and the government of the United States. Chicago: Werner. 1896. $1. [2746

This forms the second volume of a "State government series," the idea of which is so good that it should be carried out to the full extent of the Union of American states. No more than a sketch is given of the history of Ohio, in Part I, and of the organization of its government, in Part II; but the essential facts are simply and clearly set forth. Part III, similarly treating the government of the United States, is an excellent piece of condensed exposition, but not necessary to the object of the book.

Hitchcock, Henry. American state constitutions: a study of their growth. (Questions of the day, 37.) N. Y.: Putnam. 1887. 75c. [2747

This address was delivered by Mr. Hitchcock to the New York State Bar Association at its tenth annual meeting at Albany, January 18, 1887. In it the author, accepting Sir Henry Maine's axiom that social necessities and social opinions are always more or less in advance of law conventions, endeavors to interpret the various state constitutions to 1887 in this light. He gives important facts and, drawing his evidence from these constitutions, reaches important conclusions. The final portions of the work deal with amendments, the system of checks and balances, and the changes that have been made in the constitutions during the last forty or fifty years. The entire address is extremely suggestive and valuable. C. M. A.

Hoar, George F. Government in Canada and the U. S. compared. See American Antiquarian Society, sect. 239. [2748

Holst, Hermann Edouard von. Constitutional and political history of the United States; tr. by John J. Lalor, *et al.* Chicago: Callaghan. 1877-92. 8v. New ed. 1899. 8v. Net $12. [2749

This great work, the most valuable contribution of any foreign author to American history, is really a history of the slavery question in American politics, and was intended to depict the workings of democracy in handling a great moral and social question under the restraints imposed by the federal Constitution. It covers the period from the formation of the Union to the Civil War, but more than half of the entire work is devoted to the decade 1850–1860. As it was a pioneer work over a good deal of the field, the labor of gathering materials was enormous; but the author blinked no difficulties. His narrative is pervaded by a tone of intense moral earnestness. His sympathies are strongly with the anti-slavery cause. Impressed with the greatness of the moral issues at stake, he is so unsparing in his criticism of time-serving measures and time-serving politicians that he has been censured unjustly, for lack of sympathy with American institutions and a lack of insight into the inevitable conditions of popular government. E. G. B.

—— Constitutional law of the United States of America; authorized ed., tr. by A. B. Mason. Chicago : Callaghan. 1887. $2. [2750

Originally written to form a part of Marquardsen's *Handbuch des offentlichen Rechts;* designed, therefore, primarily for European readers. It is a brief and meritorious sketch, similar in scope to Cooley's *Principles of constitutional law,* but inferior to the latter in orderliness, simplicity and expository power. Parts I and II, on the Genesis of the Constitution and the Federal Constitution, have useful bibliographical notes prefixed. The author's style, at its best on the larger field of his *Constitutional and political history,* suffers here from compression, and does not become smooth even in translation. W. MacD.

Houston, D. F. Critical study of nullification in South Carolina. See Harvard University, sect. 267. [2751

Howard, George Elliott. Introduction to the local constitutional history of the United States. (Johns Hopkins Univ. studies, extra v. 4.) Balt. 1889. V. 1. $3. [2752

Imbued with the theory of the Germanic origin of English and American local institutions, the author has traced, with wide research and in great detail, the development, particularly in the United States, of the township, hundred, and shire from the earliest appearance of these or similar forms of government, to the present time. Primary authorities have been mainly relied upon, and the citations are profuse. The author's theory of institutional origins, essentially the same as that of Freeman, is not generally accepted in its extreme form; but the work is of the highest importance, and unquestionably one of the foremost products of American historical scholarship. W. MacD.

Hunt, Rockwell Denis. Genesis of California's first constitution, 1846–49. (Johns Hopkins Univ. studies, ser. 13, no. 8.) Balt. 1895. Pap. 50c. [2753

This is an excellent account of the circumstances that led to the adoption of the first constitution of California. The purpose of the author has been to analyze popular sentiment in California, and to show its influence in shaping the form of the constitution; and, at the same time, he has had in mind the national significance of this event in California's history. Mr. Hunt has written a readable monograph, and has succeeded in showing that California's first constitution, which was modelled largely on those of Iowa and New York, is remarkable when one considers the circumstances under which it was produced. C. M. A.

Hyslop, James Hervey. Democracy : a study of government. N. Y.: Scribner. 1899. $1.50. [2754

"The practical reformer, as well as the student of political philosophy, will find Professor James H. Hyslop's pungent and venturesome little study of *Democracy* decidedly interesting. Unlike Mr. Lecky and most recent critics of democracy, Professor Hyslop does not content himself with fault-finding. . . . He grapples boldly with the much more difficult task of proposing specific remedies for the most crying defects. He offers for debate a set of apparently feasible remedial devices which go to form ' a complete system of government which is neither a reaction toward monarchy, nor an acceptance of the *status quo.*' . . . Broadly stated, the direction of political reforms should be, Professor Hyslop thinks, that of specializing the functions of government, simplifying those of the citizen, and of increasing the powers of the executive." *Dial* (Chicago), 26: 278.

Ingle, Edward. Parish institutions of Maryland. (Johns Hopkins Univ. studies, ser. 1, no. 6.) Balt. 1883. 40c.

—— Local institutions of Virginia. (Johns Hopkins Univ. studies, ser. 3, no. 2–3.) Balt. 1885. 75c. [2755

Commended by Justin Winsor in *Narrative and critical hist. of Am.,* 5: 271 and 281.

Iredell, James. McREE, GRIFFITH JOHN. Life and correspondence of James Iredell, one of the associate justices of the Supreme Court of the United States. N. Y.: Appleton. 1857–58. 2v. [2756

" We find in the second volume a correspondence of interest in disclosing the Federal side of the interpretation of the Constitution, and also various charges to juries (1790–1798), in which judicial opinions are set forth with more warmth and partisanship than we would countenance in these days." Justin Winsor, in *Narrative and critical hist. of Am.,* 7: 313.

James, E. J. First appointment of federal representatives in the U. S. See American Academy of Political and Social Science, sect. 226. [2757

Jameson, John Alexander. The constitutional convention; its history, powers, and modes of proceeding. N. Y.: Scribner. 1866.

—— *Same :* Treatise on the constitutional convention ; 4th ed. enl. Chicago : Callaghan. 1887. $5. [2758

The only comprehensive treatise on this subject. It treats of the essential character and functions of the constitutional convention and the methods of making and altering constitutions. A large portion of the book is historical, tracing the development of the convention and showing how it has come to occupy the place it now holds in our constitutional system. The legal rules as now established and some of the more important judicial decisions are also given. The material is carefully analyzed, the method and style are good, and the whole book is the product of accurate and painstaking scholarship.   A. C. McL.

Jameson, John Franklin, *ed.* Essays in the constitutional history of the United States in the formative period, 1775–89; by graduates and former members of the Johns Hopkins University. Boston: Houghton. 1889. [2759

This volume contains five essays dealing with constitutional topics of the "formative period." They are the results of careful and scholarly investigation, are written in a good style, and, while they will appeal to the specialist in American history, will prove not uninteresting to the general reader. Of chief interest are the essays on The predecessor of the Supreme Court, The movement towards a second constitutional convention, and The development of executive departments.   A. C. McL.

Jennings, Louis John. Eighty years of republican government in the United States. London: Murray. 1868. N. Y.: Scribner. 1868. [2760

The author's object is to explain the original plan of the American Constitution, to review the changes which have been made, and to describe its present mode of working. He asserts that he has no theory to enforce. The work is clearly written, and shows research. It is brief and succinct. It fails, however, in a lack of knowledge of actual conditions, both of the life and the thought of the masses in the United States. The author, an Englishman, for some years a journalist in New York, frequently errs in relying upon isolated examples. He is particularly weak in his use of the judicial interpretations of the Constitution. His work was the more difficult because of attempting to write on constitutional changes in 1868, a transition period after the Civil War.   D. R. D.

Kent, James. Commentaries on American law. N. Y.: Halsted. 1826–30. 4v.
—— *Same ;* 12th ed. by O. W. Holmes, Jr. Boston. 1873. 4v.
—— *Same ;* 14th ed. by J. M. Gould. Boston: Little. 1896. 4v. Net $14. $3.50 ea. [2761

The first edition of this great work appeared seventy years ago. From that day to this it has remained an authoritative treatise, and the opinions of the writer have had great weight with courts and lawyers, and influenced the development of American law. The work is marked by a firm grasp of essentials, by explicit statement of fundamental principles, and by a clear, unaffected, straightforward style, which avoids any pedantic exhibition of learning. The four volumes cover in a general way nearly all the main divisions of the law, including international law and constitutional law. The last edition mentioned above contains full notes, prepared with the purpose of showing the growth in recent years of the chief doctrines or topics discussed in the main body of the work.   A. C. McL.

—— **Kent, William.** Memoirs and letters of James Kent, late Chancellor of the state of New York. Boston: Little. 1898. $2.50. [2762

Compiled from material left by Chancellor Kent and from family papers. Valuable as the record of a scholar's life. The editor's work well done. An admirable portrait of the Chancellor opens the volume. It is an interesting and valuable work.   E. C.

Lalor, John Joseph, *ed.* Cyclopædia of political science, political economy, and of the political history of the United States. Chicago: Rand, McNally; M. B. Cary. 1881–4. 3v. N. Y.: Maynard. 3v. $15. [2763

For the student of American history the most valuable parts of this work are the articles by the late Alexander Johnston, which amount in bulk to about one fifth of the whole. They deal with almost every phase of our national history and political life in a singularly dispassionate, thorough, and accurate manner, and constitute by far the most important work of this admirable scholar. The articles on foreign history, institutions, and many of those on political economy, are translated from the best French and German cyclopædias. In addition, there are a large number of original articles on economic subjects relating to Great Britain, Canada and the United States, from the hands of thoroughly competent writers, and in some cases from the most eminent specialists in the subjects concerned.   E. G. B.

Lamphere, George N. United States government, its organization and practical workings. Phil.: Lippincott. 1880. [2764

An outline of the organization and functions of the three divisions of government, and especially of the principal executive departments. Being an epitome of the workings of the national government, the offices, salaries, and duties, it forms a valuable handbook of information on the practical workings of the government. Such a publication needs frequent revision. Much of the matter here presented is now antiquated.   E. E. S.

Landon, Judson Stuart. Constitutional history and government of the United States. Boston: Houghton. 1889. $3. [2765

A book made up of a series of lectures delivered to college students. They discuss the chief events in the constitutional history of the United States during the one hundred years after the close of the Revolution. In addition to the historical narrative, an exposition of the main principles of constitutional law is given, as well as a treatment of some important political problems. The work is on the whole carefully and judiciously written, and it may be doubted whether any other single volume covers so successfully the facts of constitutional history, although some other books giving side views of social and industrial progress are more entertaining.   A. C. McL.

Lawton, George W. American caucus system, its origin, purpose and utility. (Questions of the day, no. 25.) N. Y.: Putnam. 1885. $1. Pap. 50c. [2766

A series of eight chapters on the origin, authority, growth and methods of the political meeting known as the " caucus." They are without method or results; a collection of ill-digested facts and anecdotes of no particular value to the student.   E. E. S.

Libby, Orin Grant. Geographical distribution of the vote of the thirteen states on the federal Constitution, 1787-8. (Univ. of Wisconsin. Bulletin. Economics, v. 1, no. 1.) Madison. 1894. [2767

This is an excellent study of an interesting portion of the important subject of geographical politics, throwing new light, not merely upon the adoption of the national Constitution, but also upon the social, political and intellectual condition of the country in 1787, 1789.   B. A. H.

Lieber, Francis. Contributions to political science. (Miscellaneous writings, v. 2. Phil.: Lippincott. 1881. $3.) [2768

The contents of this book include discussions of the origin and nature of the Constitution of the United States, such as, — Rise of our Constitution and its national features : — What is our Constitution — league, pact, or government? (written in 1860 and 1861, at the outbreak of the Civil War): — Contributions to military law, among which is found Instructions for armies in the field (prepared at the request of President Lincoln and promulgated in 1863 as General order, 100) : — On prisoners of war: — Contributions to international law which treat of Plebiscites, The Latin race, International arbitration, and International copyright. Other papers relate to Anglican and Gallican liberty, Penal law, Amendments proposed for the constitution of New York (1867), Nationalism and internationalism, and Religious instruction in colleges. These titles indicate the practical nature and wide range of the subject matter ; the treatment discloses the great qualities of the author as publicist, thinker and citizen. Lieber's style, though not brilliant, is good; some of the papers which were written as lectures appear without revision, and one or two are fragments ; but these defects are of minor importance.   A. D. M.

—— Miscellaneous writings; ed. by D. C. Gilman. Phil.: Lippincott. 1881. 2v. $6. [2769

The essays and addresses are on subjects in economics, political science, constitutional law, international law and military law. Among these papers is Brief code of military law, which Lieber prepared for the use of the federal army during the Civil War (General order, 100), and which he thought his most valuable contribution to public law. According to Pres. Woolsey, Lieber " influenced political thought more than any one of his contemporaries in the United States," and is to be regarded as " the founder of this [i. e. political] science in this country."   E. G. B. See sect. 2768.

—— On civil liberty and self-government. Phil. 1853. 2v.

—— *Same.* New ed. ; ed. by Theodore D. Woolsey. Phil. : Lippincott. 1874. New ed. $3.15. [2770

A historical and comparative study of the institutions of self-government as they have been developed in England and transplanted to America or the Continent. Somewhat diffuse in style, but full of suggestion and infused with an enthusiasm for English free institutions. The last third of the volume consists mainly of the great constitutional documents of English and American liberty, including a translation of Magna Charta, and four French constitutions in translation.   E. G. B.

Loring, Caleb William. Nullification, secession: Webster's argument, and the Kentucky and Virginia resolutions, considered in reference to the Constitution and historically. N. Y.: Putnam. 1893. $1. [2771

" In a short monograph, as well conceived as it is close compacted with historical facts and authorities," Mr. Loring " has subjected to a new discussion the perennial question whether, under the Constitution, a permanent national union or a dissoluble league was established by the United States. . . . The author has been incited to this reinvestigation by an intimation of Mr. Cabot Lodge, in his *Life of Webster*, to the effect that Hayne, in his famous controversy with the Massachusetts statesman, had the better of the argument, however much he may have.been worsted in the trial of oratory. Mr. Lodge, it will be remembered, adventures the bold statement that ' when the Constitution was adopted, it is safe to say that there was not a man in the country, from Washington and Hamilton on the one side to George Clinton and George Mason on the other, who regarded the new system as anything but an experiment entered upon by the states, and from which each and every state had the right peaceably to withdraw — a right which was very likely to be exercised.' Mr. Loring does not find it difficult to explode this astonishing assertion." *Nation*, 56: 237.

McConachie, Lauros Grant. Congressional committees: a study of the origin and development of our national and local legislative methods. (Library of economics and politics.) N. Y.: Crowell. [c. 1898.] $1.75. [2772

A product of extended research, and the most thorough study of the subject yet made. The origin and development of the Congressional committee system, as a legislative method, are traced with much detail. Appendices give lists of committees, with their history, and the rules of the House of Representatives in the 55th Congress. The style lacks distinction, and the discussion is occasionally marred by the injection of debatable theories as to the origin of American political institutions, and speculations as to their future. For completeness, Follett's *Speaker* (sect. 2725) should be read in connection.   W. MacD.

McMaster, John Bach, *and* **Frederick D. Stone,** *eds.* Pennsylvania and the federal Constitution, 1787-8. Phil.: Historical Soc. of Pennsylvania. 1888. [2773

A volume of nearly eight hundred pages in which is gathered together a large amount of material showing the circumstances under which the federal Constitution was adopted in Pennsylvania. No complete report of the debates of the convention is in existence; but this book contains much more than is obtainable elsewhere. It includes important essays, speeches and like material bearing on the adoption of the Constitution, most of them taken from the newspapers of the day. The editorial work has been done by thorough and competent scholars. A. C. McL.

Macy, Jesse. Institutional beginnings in a western state [Iowa]. (Johns Hopkins Univ. studies, ser. 2, no. 7.) Balt. 1884. Pap. 25c. [2774

The real local institutions of the early settlers of a western state cannot be understood from a study of the statute book. Much that was done was not formulated in law; much that was law was never made actual in fact. The value of this interesting little pamphlet consists in the fact that the author has in some measure brought to view the situation of sixty years ago, by gathering various sorts of contemporary testimony, the oral and written recollections of old residents of the state of Iowa. A. C. McL.

—— Our government. Boston: Ginn. 1886. Rev. ed. [c. 1890.] 75c. [2775

A deservedly popular school-book, tracing clearly the derivation of the various factors in self-government and setting forth its local and national activities, with constant references to illustrative cases. It is a vast improvement on the old style "civil government," but needs intelligent illustration by the teacher to avoid a wearisomeness threatened by its condensed style. E. E. S.

Madison, James. Journal of the federal convention; ed. by E. H. Scott. Chicago: Albert. 1893. Scott, Foresman & Co. $2.50. [2776

A good clear reprint in 800 pages of the edition of 1840 with an elaborate index especially prepared. No notes or references. Of service as a text only. Not the official journal, but Madison's private notes or journal. E. E. S.

Marshall, John. Writings upon the federal Constitution. Boston: Munroe. 1839. [2777

The title may be misleading. The volume contains reprints of the official opinions on constitutional questions rendered by Marshall while he was Chief Justice of the United States. An appendix contains a few important constitutional decisions rendered by other judges before 1839. The collection is a useful one, but probably not so useful for the student or reader as a more complete set of leading cases, such as the one edited by J. B. Thayer (sect. 2803). A. C. McL.

Mason, Edward Campbell. Veto power in the United States. See Harvard University, sect. 263. [2778

Meigs, William Montgomery. Growth of the Constitution in the federal convention of 1787. Phil.: Lippincott. 1900 [1899]. $2.50. [2779

"Instead of simply paraphrasing and condensing Madison's *Notes*, Mr. Meigs has carefully traced the development of each clause, with a brief summary of the discussions of it, from the earliest suggestions through all its transformations until it takes its place at last in the completed Constitution. Or, in other words, he has arranged our records of the debates in the order of the topics in the text of the Constitution and compressed them to perhaps one third their present length mainly by the omission of unessentials. It is now possible to read in two or three minutes the outline of the history in the convention of any provision in the Constitution, and, with the help of the dates, to follow the details of the discussion in Madison's *Notes* with almost equal readiness. So far as I have tested the work, it seems to have been done very thoroughly and accurately. Mr. Meigs, however, has not merely rendered old material doubly available for our instruction by a fresh analysis and a rearrangement of it, but he has identified an important missing link in the records of the convention and so has, in effect, brought new material to light. . . . In 1887, or thereabout, Mr. Moncure D. Conway found among the papers of George Mason a draft of a constitution in Randolph's writing, of which he published an account with extracts in *Scribner's magazine* in September, 1887, and also in his *Edmund Randolph* (sect. 1684). . . . In a critical appendix Mr. Meigs proves beyond a doubt that this document is an outline draft prepared by Randolph *on the basis* of the twenty-three resolutions for the Committee of detail to use as foundation of their draft." E. G. Bourne, in *Am. hist. rev.*, 5: 582.

Morey, W. C. First state constitutions. See American Academy of Political and Social Science, sect. 226. [2780

—— Sources of American federalism. See American Academy of Political and Social Science, sect. 226. [2781

Mulford, Elisha. The nation. N. Y.: Hurd. 1870. Boston: Houghton. $2.50. [2782

A theory of the state from the standpoint of the Hegelian philosophy and the Christian religion. Learned, able and valuable. The work is substantial and scholarly, rather than of popular interest. E. C. R.

A book which "grew out of the enthusiasm for the nation enkindled by the Civil War. It is a profound study of speculative politics, with the main ideas borrowed from Bluntschli and Hegel." P. Schaff, in *Church and state in the U. S.*, p. 53.

Nordhoff, Charles. Politics for young Americans. N. Y.: Harper. 1875. Rev. ed. for schools. N. Y.: Am. Book Co. [c. 1899.] 75c. [2783

This is one of the first attempts to break away from the old plan of dissecting the Constitution to make a text on civics. The author treats, in a familiar style, such topics as the suffrage, taxes, money, the duties of citizenship, etc. Some critics think the author too communistic in his views.   E. E. S.

Ohio. Constitution, 1851. See Old South Work, no. 14, sect. 368.   [2784

Poore, Benjamin Perley, *comp.* Federal and state constitutions, colonial charters, and other organic laws of the United States; comp. under an order of the U. S. Senate. Wash.: Govt. Prtg. Off. 1877. 2v.   [2785

An official compilation, and the standard collection of charters and state constitutions. The arrangement is alphabetical by states, and chronological under each state. The two volumes are paged continuously. Brief historical notes accompany most of the documents. As the sources of the texts are not indicated, the verbal accuracy of the reprint cannot be affirmed. A revision and continuation of the work is much to be desired.   W. MacD.

Porter, Luther Henry. Outlines of the constitutional history of the United States. N. Y.: Holt. 1883. $1.20.   [2786

This work is adequately described in its preface as a "beginning book for students or general readers, who desire to learn something of the character and history of the constitution of the United States." Its chief merit lies in the many constitutional documents which are here printed in full; its chief defect in its want of any aids to a further study of the subject. It differs from other collections of "sources" in containing a running commentary that connects the different documents. Though all these documents are readily accessible elsewhere, Mr. Porter's book may still serve a useful purpose as a compact and handy manual on the constitutional history of the United States from 1606 to 1865.   C. M. A.

Prentice, E. Parmalee, *and* **John G. Egan.** Commerce clause of the federal Constitution. Chicago: Callaghan. 1898. $5.   [2787

"Since Marshall wrote his famous decision in the case of Gibbons *v.* Ogden seventy-five years ago, constitutional law relating to interstate and foreign commerce has had a large development; yet it would doubtless surprise most persons to find that a volume on 'the commerce clause of the federal constitution' could contain references to nearly 1,800 cases. This, however, is the number of cases cited in the scholarly volume by Mr. Prentice and Mr. Egan; and the authors have studied these cases and the numerous statutes cited in their work with assiduity and discretion. The result of their study is a comprehensive and systematic treatise that makes a substantial addition to the literature of commercial law. . . . Possibly the admirable survey of the decisions and statutes concerning the power of Congress and the states to tax commerce will be appreciated more than any other chapter of the book," Emory R. Johnson, in *Annals of the Am. academy of political and social science*, 14: 87.

Preston, Howard Willis, *ed.* Documents illustrative of American history, 1606–1863. N. Y.: Putnam. 1886. 1899. $1.50. [2788

A serviceable selection of somewhat over thirty constitutional documents of which two thirds are colonial charters or constitutions. About two thirds of the colonies are represented in the collection. Brief introductions exhibit the historical setting of the documents and provide references to the general histories. The editor has neglected, however, to direct his readers to where the authentic texts of his documents are to be found.   E. G. B.

Salmon, Lucy Maynard. History of the appointing power of the President. (Am. Hist. Assoc. Papers, v. 1, no. 5.) N. Y.: Putnam. 1886.   [2789

Miss Salmon's historical exposition of the clause in the Constitution conferring the appointing power upon the President, instead of upon Congress, is not merely statistical, but displays real insight into the character of constitutional development and an ability to draw sound conclusions of importance to every student of constitutional history. The study may well be called a history of civil service reform. Probably the most important portion is that which deals with the "spoils" period from 1820 to 1861. The work is based upon printed sources, and an excellent final chapter sums up the author's conclusions.   C. M. A.

Schouler, James. Constitutional studies, state and federal. N. Y.: Dodd. 1897. $1.50.   [2790

Based upon lectures given by the author at Johns Hopkins University. The book is a surface description of American political institutions, with glances at their historical development. As a law book, it does not compare with Cooley's *Principles of constitutional law* (sect. 2709); as a descriptive account, it is surpassed by Hinsdale's *American government* (sect. 2744). The best chapters are those of Part I., on Early charters and constitutions; but the author's style, everywhere uneasy and angular, is here especially difficult. Considered as a contribution to the subject, the book must be pronounced superfluous.   W. MacD.

Compared with Mr. Harrison's *This country of ours* (sect. 2741), Mr. Schouler's is "a little more national, both in principle and conclusion, . . . a little sounder, a little truer to a correct understanding of our history and a little more harmonious with present conditions and relations." John W. Burgess, *Political science quarterly*, 13: 190.

Scott, Eben Greenough. Development of constitutional liberty in the English colonies of America. N. Y.: Putnam. 1882. $2.50.   [2791

A thoughtful and suggestive but somewhat imaginative piece of historical work, philosophical in tone, seeking to disclose the moving spirit and dominant ideals of colonial life. It does not contain, as its name might imply, a careful and systematic unfolding of the constitutional forms and principles or the governmental methods of the colonies; but it treats of the sentiments, the social and industrial characteristics of the times. A tendency to over-generalization and to throw a bright light upon all phases of colonial life detracts somewhat from the value of a very helpful and stimulating book. A. C. McL.

Scott, John. The republic as a form of government; or The evolution of democracy in America. London: Chapman. 1889. 7s. 6d. [2792

A series of well-written essays to prove that since the Civil War the United States is a republic by force instead of by consent; that democracy does not exist in America. Reviews the many points of the old contest between the North and the South and touches incidentally on the southern confederacy. Also considers at length the electoral commission. An interesting presentation of theory as opposed to existing conditions. E. E. S.

Shinn, Charles Howard. Mining camps: a study in American frontier government. N. Y.: Scribner. 1885. $2. [2793

"Mr. Shinn modestly and justly calls his book *A study in American frontier government;* it is exactly that — a 'study;' and, so regarded, it is one of the best of the class of books to which we have just referred. The free, instinctive methods which the early Californian miners followed are illustrated by graphic accounts of their proceedings; and they are connected with the mining usages of earlier times by a thread of information which, although slight, is enough to make these later usages significant, and to stimulate the reader's curiosity to know more." *Nation,* 40: 406.

Small, Albion Woodbury. Beginnings of American nationality: the constitutional relations between the Continental Congress and the colonies and states, 1774–89. (Johns Hopkins Univ. studies, ser. 8, nos. 1–2.) Balt. 1890. Pap. $1. [2794

A study of the relations between the states and the United States from 1774 to 1789, based upon an examination of the journals of Congress and the state archives. The work is a fragment, the published portion extending only through the first session of the Continental Congress of 1775. The purpose of the author is to show that "the colonial authorities looked to the Continental Congress not for sanctions, in the legal sense, but for signs;" and the facts adduced are significant in that direction. W. MacD.

Speer, Emory. Lectures on the Constitution of the United States. Macon, Ga.: Burke. 1897. $1.25. [2795

Five short lectures, supplemented by a fourth-of-July oration. In no sense a treatise on constitutional law, but a popular narrative of the events of the Revolutionary period and of the adoption of the Constitution, with a brief statement of a few legal principles. A. C. McL.

Stanwood, Edward. History of presidential elections. Boston: Osgood. 1884.

—— *Same:* A history of the presidency. Boston: Houghton. 1898. $2.50. [2796

See sect. 2615.

Stephens, Alexander Hamilton. Constitutional view of the late war between the states. Phil: National Pub. Co. [c. 1868–1870.] 2v. [2797

These volumes by the Vice-President of the southern Confederacy are not in any proper sense a history of the war of secession. The first volume is a long argument in support of the proposition that the war was neither a rebellion nor a civil conflict, but a war between sovereign states. Its purpose is by presentation of historical material and by processes of logic to demonstrate that the doctrine of state sovereignty was sound and secession a legal right. The second volume contains some account of military movements, but is chiefly a consideration of constitutional questions. The work constitutes the best published defence of the southern position. A. C. McL.

—— The reviewers reviewed: a supplement to The war between the states, etc. N. Y.: Appleton. 1872. $1.50. [2798

The title indicates the purpose and character of the book. It is a further defence of the positions taken in the *Constitutional view of the late war between the states.* It is largely composed of articles written for the newspapers in answer to criticisms. Some of the original criticisms are also given. The volume does not add much to the force of the author's main argument. A. C. McL.

Sterne, Simon. Constitutional history and political development of the United States. N. Y.: Cassell. 1882. 4th rev. ed. 1883. Putnam. 1888. $1.25. [2799

"Mr. Sterne has attempted to give a sketch of the Constitution as it stands, accompanied by a history of the political controversies which resulted in its formation and in the changes which it has undergone, together with a presentation of the actual present condition of politics and of questions demanding the attention of parties. The work is of a popular character. . . . It can hardly supplant the constitutional text-books used in schools and colleges now. In his chapter on Current questions Mr. Sterne takes up civil service reform, the silver question, the transportation problem, revenue reform, and, indeed, most of the questions of the day, and discusses them briefly. Mr. Sterne does not hesitate to tell his readers how they ought to be disposed of, and, in the main, his 'soundness' cannot be questioned. We only complain here of a certain looseness of treatment." *Nation,* 35: 317.

Story, Joseph. Commentaries on the Constitution of the United States. Boston: Hilliard. 1833. 3v.

—— *Same.* 4th ed., rev. by T. M. Cooley. Boston: Little. 1873. 2v.

—— *Same.* 5th ed., by M. M. Bigelow. Boston: Little. 1891. 2v. $12. [2800

The great classic commentary on the Constitution, written by Judge Story after twenty years of service as a member of the Supreme Court. Although much of the work was done nearly sixty years ago, it continues to be valuable, because of the great learning of the author, and because the author was a contemporary of Marshall and a judge of the court during the period in which it was establishing its authority and giving out the fundamental decisions on which the fabric of our constitutional law has been reared.

A. C. McL.

—— Familiar exposition of the Constitution. Boston. 1842. N. Y.: Am. Bk. Co. 1899. 90c. [2801

This is an epitome of the author's large *Commentaries on the Constitution*. It was intended for a text-book and passed through several editions. Each paragraph of the Constitution is taken in regular order and its workings explained. A number of documents form an appendix. The treatment is entirely abstract and the style heavy. It is superseded by modern texts. E. E. S.

Straus, Oscar Solomon. Origin of republican form of government in the United States of America. N. Y.: Putnam. 1885. [2802

In considering the influences which led first to a provisional, and, secondly, to a permanent form, the author "reviews briefly the history of other revolutions, the bearing of the petitions to the crown, the other negotiations which preceded the Declaration of Independence, the moral influence exerted by the first settlers in the different colonies, and the early acts of the colonial assemblies. The religious and political causes which led to the revolt are considered at length. . . . His conclusion is that religious convictions and associations were mainly instrumental in shaping the purposes of our first legislators. The convictions of all of them, consciously or not, were, he thinks, modeled by the divinely given constitution of the Israelitish commonwealth, and he holds that our existing institutions are based upon the teachings given from Sinai." *Magazine of Am. hist.*, 15: 104.

Thayer, James Bradley. Cases on constitutional law, with notes. Cambridge, Mass.: C. W. Sever. 1894–95. 2v. Net $12. [2803

A working collection of cases, designed primarily for class-room use under the "case system" of instruction, but equally valuable for private study, or in connection with a text-book or systematic treatise. Most of the cases are abridged, many appear in significant extracts only. The work is the best in its field, and, like all books similarly constructed, has permanent value. The author is professor of law in Harvard University, and a recognized authority.

W. MacD.

Thorpe, Francis Newton. Constitutional history of the American people, 1776–1850. N. Y.: Harper. 1898. 2v. $5. [2804

"An examination of his volumes shows that the chief emphasis throughout is laid upon two or three subjects only, those, namely, of citizenship, suffrage, and eligibility for office. . . . Two fifths of the entire space . . . is devoted to an account of constitutional conventions in four states. . . . Mr. Thorpe's conception of constitutional history, if we may gather it from

this his latest work, is that of a history of the formation of state constitutions ; and it is this that he has given us in his book. . . . His pages show abundant evidences of knowledge, industry, and zeal. Yet we can but think that his work is, after all, hardly more than an elaborate monograph, a valuable section of a possible larger whole, but wanting in the broad conception of the subject which his title implies. . . . It nevertheless makes important additions to our knowledge of American history." *Nation*, 68: 208.

—— Recent constitution-making in the U. S. See American Academy of Political and Social Science, sect. 226. [2805

Tiedeman, Christopher Gustavus. Unwritten constitution of the United States. N. Y.: Putnam. 1890. $1. [2806

"Professor Tiedeman's thesis seems to have been written to illustrate an American 'unwritten constitution' in the British sense of the term, — that 'unwritten constitution whose flexible rules reflect all the changes in public opinion.' It is true, he expects to find that 'unwritten constitution' in 'the decisions of the courts and acts of the legislature which are published and enacted in the enforcement of the written constitution,'—a development, as it were, out of the latter. But what he there finds, he characterizes as 'constantly changing with the demands of the popular will,' and thus he imputes to it the same characteristics as those of the unwritten constitution of Great Britain." James O. Pierce, in *Dial*, 13: 18.

Tocqueville, Alexis Charles Henri Clérel de. Democracy in America [1st Eng. ed. 1835] ; translation by Henry Reeve, as rev. and annotated from the author's last ed. by Francis Bowen, with an introd. by Daniel C. Gilman. N. Y. : Century Co. 1898. 2v. $5. [2807

"For two generations the treatise of De Tocqueville has held its own as a discriminating criticism of republican institutions. During this long period it has been frequently quoted in Europe and in the United States by the highest political authorities; it has been read as a text-book in schools and universities, and it is quite sure to be found on the book-shelves of editors, lawyers, and statesmen. Though it contained no sailing directions, it has been a sort of chart, by which the pilot of the ship might be informed of rocks and shoals, lighthouses, and harbors of refuge. It remains the best philosophical discussion of democracy, illustrated by the experience of the United States, up to the time when it was written, which can be found in any language. More than this is true. Notwithstanding the changes which have occurred in the material and social circumstances of the United States during the last sixty years, the consequent elimination of certain factors in the civilization of this country, and the introduction of new and unforeseen problems, — notwithstanding all this, the student of modern popular government must revert to Tocqueville. James Bryce is a good illustration of this statement. So is Lecky, whose admirable study of *Democracy and liberty* shows his use of the French memoir. More noteworthy, perhaps, more recent certainly, are the careful and suggestive studies of France by J. E. C. Bodley, an English writer long resident in the country he describes. . . . His study of France since the Revolution is a serviceable commentary on De Tocqueville's instructions and apprehensions. Henri Michel, a Professor in the Lycée Henri IV of Paris, may likewise be cited. Democracy, he says, was revealed to De Tocqueville in America. When his work appeared, democracy was to some an 'ideal,' a 'brilliant dream;' to others, 'ruin, anarchy, robbery, murder.' De Tocqueville wished to lessen the fears of the latter, the ardor of the former class. He treats Democracy as a fact." Daniel C. Gilman (Introduction to *Democracy in America*, by A. de Tocqueville).

Tucker, John Randolph. The Constitution of the United States; a critical discussion of its genesis, development and interpretation; ed. by Henry St. George Tucker. Chicago: Callaghan. 1899. 2v. $7. [2808

"The author of these volumes was born in Virginia in 1823, and died in 1897. . . . He was at one time Attorney-General of Virginia, for twelve years a Representative in Congress and for some years before his death a Professor in Washington and Lee University. The manuscript of this work, left unfinished by the author, was edited by his son. . . . The work has many faults, some of which, probably the majority, are attributable to the fact that the author seems not to have revised his manuscript, and that the editor has not corrected even palpable and obvious errors. . . . It is a very difficult task to appraise the work in general terms. There are a few serious blunders, there is a tendency to theorize when a clear statement of well-established principles is desirable, and there is occasional evidence of a bias which seems to militate against the trustworthiness of some of his conclusions. But withal the matter is forcibly handled, and no small portion is written with exceptional clearness and strength. On the whole, one is left with a feeling of disappointment that the author could not have finished his undertaking, made his final corrections and published the work himself." Andrew C. McLaughlin, in *American hist. rev.*, 5 : 367.

Tyler, Lyon Gardiner. Parties and patronage in the United States. (Questions of the day.) N. Y. : Putnam. 1891. $1. [2809

The author, president of William and Mary College, and biographer of his father, President Tyler, takes the ground that the spoils system in politics is the legitimate result of the enlargement of governmental administration through protective tariffs, and of the broad construction of the Constitution which has led to a blending of private and public interests. Such a conviction prompts an historical survey of party action from 1789 until the present, from which it is concluded that the early Federal administrations, 1789-1801, with the subsequent broad construction given to the Constitution by the Supreme Court, is responsible for the evils of party patronage. Jackson's removals are simply an episode in the evolution. The exaggerated tone makes the book unsafe for beginners, but for more advanced readers it provides useful suggestions, both in text and notes, for critical use.

D. R. D.

United States. *Bureau of Rolls.* Documentary history of the Constitution of the United States of America, 1787-1870 ; derived from the records, manuscripts and rolls deposited in the Bureau of Rolls and Library of the Dept. of State. Wash. 1894-. v. 1-. [2810

A literal reprint, but not a facsimile reproduction, of the documents in the Bureau that relate to the formation, adoption or amendment of the federal Constitution. The first volume contains the proceedings of the Annapolis convention, the official journal of the Philadelphia convention, and other important material ; the second gives the material relating to the passage and adoption of the fifteen amendments; the third is taken up with Madison's journal of the Philadelphia convention so far as the manuscript is preserved in the Bureau. A. C. McL.

United States. *Congress.* Civil service: report from the joint select committee on retrenchment, made to the House of Representatives, May 14, 1868. (40th Cong., 2d sess., House rept. 47.) Wash. 1868. [2811

This important report, which formed the basis of all subsequent legislation for the reformation of the United States civil service, begins with a brief history of that branch of the government, which it follows with a striking chapter from Parton's *Life of Jackson*. The answers sent by over 450 officers of the civil service to a series of 37 questions regarding the administration of their duties propounded by the committee, the testimony of former Presidents and of the press upon the scramble for office and on the proposed remedy, and explanations of the systems of China, Prussia, England, and France make up the bulk of the report. To these are appended extracts from a former report (39th Cong., 2d sess., House rept. 8), including the text of the proposed bill. The copy of the report before the writer has also annexed to it two speeches on the bill delivered in the house by Mr. Jenckes in 1867 and 1868. F. J. S.

United States. *Constitutional Convention,* 1787. Our knowledge of the proceedings of the Constitutional Convention depends mainly on the following sources mentioned in the order of publication : —

Martin, Luther. Genuine information. Phil. 1788.

Journal of the Constitutional Convention. 1818.

Yates, Robert. Secret proceedings and debates of the Convention, 1787. Albany. 1821.

Madison, James. Debates on the adoption of the federal Constitution. (v. 5 of Elliot, J. Debates.) Wash. 1845.

Pierce, William. Notes on the federal Convention of 1787. (Am. hist. rev., 3: 310.) [2812

Luther Martin's *Genuine information* is a general summary of the course of the debates, with a running criticism on the provisions of the Constitution, and was delivered orally as a report to the legislature of Maryland. It has been frequently reprinted, especially with Yates's *Debates*. The *Journal* is a formal record of proceedings of the Convention. Yates's notes on the debates are brief summaries of the discussions between May 25 and July 5, at which date Yates withdrew, owing to his hostility to the plan favored by the majority. They were first edited by Genét, the former French minister. Madison criticised them severely for inaccuracy. Cf. Madison's *Writings*, III. 226, 229. IV. 9–12, 16, 17, 288, 310. Madison's *Debates* are by far the fullest and most trustworthy report of the Convention. He was present at every session and took careful notes, which he wrote out at the close of each session. Toward the end of his life (beginning 1821, see *Writings*, III. 229) he digested this material into the form in which it appeared in Gilpin's *Madison papers*. All the above material is contained in Elliot's *Debates*, which also includes the reports of the debates in the state conventions and a number of important constitutional documents. Pierce's *Notes* are brief, and chiefly interesting for the brief pen portraits of the speakers. They were first printed in the *Savannah Georgian* in 1828, but became generally accessible only in 1898, when they appeared in the Jan. no. of the *Am. historical review*. Madison's *Debates* were reprinted in a separate vol. ed. by E. H. Scott in 1893 (sect. 2776).　　E. G. B.

Warfield, Ethelbert Dudley. The Kentucky Resolutions of 1798; an historical study. N. Y.: Putnam. 1887. 2d ed. $1.25.　[**2813**

"Mr. Warfield has mainly worked from the newspapers and correspondence of the day, and particularly from the papers of John Breckinridge, the mover of the resolutions in the assembly. Warfield contends that Breckinridge's authorship of the resolutions was not questioned before the publication of John Taylor's *Inquiries into the principles and policy of the government of the U. S.* (Fredericksburg, 1814, p. 174), where they are credited to Jefferson." Justin Winsor, in *Narrative and critical hist. of Am.*, 7: 320.

Washburn, Emory. Sketches of the judicial history of Massachusetts from 1630 to 1775. Boston: Little. 1840.　[**2814**

Really an essay on the constitutional history of Massachusetts with notices of the more eminent judges and lawyers of the colonial era. Author was a Massachusetts judge and a close student of history. The book is written from original sources; but contains few bibliographical references. A creditable work when published, but now antiquated.　　E. C.

Webster, W. C. State constitutions of the American Revolution. See American Academy of Political and Social Science, sect. 226.　[**2815**

Weeks, Stephen Beauregard. History of negro suffrage in the South. Boston: Ginn. 1894.　[**2816**

Presented originally to the World's Congress Auxiliary on Government, in Chicago, August, 1893, and reprinted from the *Political science quarterly*. The history of negro suffrage before the war, its evolution after that event, and the efforts to limit its influence by centralization, taxes, registration laws, and education, are traced.

Whiting, William. War powers under the Constitution of the United States. Boston. 10th ed. 1864. 43d ed. Lee. 1871. $3.50.　[**2817**

The author was for three years during the Civil War solicitor of the War Department. His book advocates the theories he put forth at the time, that the Constitution gave sufficient power for the confiscation and emancipation of the slaves. There are chapters on reconstruction, and a collection of war cases decided in the federal courts, with valuable notes throughout the book.　　E. E. S.

Willoughby, Westel Woodbury. The Supreme Court of the United States, its history and influence in our constitutional system. (Johns Hopkins Univ. studies, extra v. 7.) Balt. 1890. $1.25.　[**2818**

"The inception of this high court—or, rather, the ideas which suggested and developed into it—being noted, the essayist then illustrates the relations of the court to the coördinate branches of the government and to general politics. The two chapters which treat of its power and authority over legislative acts which contravene the Constitution are of especial interest, and are the kernel of the essay." James O. Pierce, *Dial* (Chicago), 12: 323.

Wilson, James. Works; [ed. by] Bird Wilson. Phil.: Bronson. 1884. 3v.

—— *Same;* ed. [with notes] by James De Witt Andrews. Chicago: Callaghan. 1896. 2v. $7.　[**2819**

The works here given consist almost entirely of law lectures on the organization of society, frames of government, the judiciary, crimes, etc. They have been extensively used by law students. Four speeches are added, including the appeal for the adoption of the Constitution in the Pennsylvania convention and an oration delivered at the celebration of its adoption. The first editor made no explanations or annotations.　　E. E. S.

Wilson, Woodrow. Congressional government. Boston: Houghton. 1885. $1.25.　[**2820**

A treatise on the congressional machinery of the American government, directed particularly to the system of government by committee, describing the working of that system in detail; the power of the Speaker as appointing the committees; the relations of the executive to Congress; the bad effects of the system upon financial legislation, and the impossibility of holding any one responsible for its acts. The author is adequately informed, gifted with excellent judgment and keen logical powers, and has done his work carefully and thoroughly. The literary merit of the book is of a high order.　　. R. C. H. C.

—— The state and federal governments of the United States. Boston: Heath. Rev. ed. 1898. $2. [2821

A reprint of the chapters on the United States contained in the same author's *The state* (Boston: Heath. 1889). The reprint is from the edition of 1889. In its present form, the book makes a serviceable manual for school use. W. MacD.

DIVISION 4: ECONOMIC HISTORY

Adams, Charles Francis, Jr., *and* **Henry.** Chapters of Erie, and other essays. Boston: Osgood. 1871. N. Y.: Holt. 1886. $1.75. [2822

In this collection of eight narrative and critical essays, six deal with American history. Three by Charles F. Adams treat of different phases of railway development as follows: A chapter of Erie, An Erie raid, and The railroad system. They are substantially reprints of essays published 1868-71 in the *North American review*. The first of the essays relates to the efforts of Cornelius Vanderbilt to wrest the Erie Railway from the control of Daniel Drew, and illustrates the ease with which laws, directors' meetings, and records of the courts were manipulated for financial schemes in the period immediately following the Civil War. The second essay illustrates the same defects in New York political life with a change of characters to Jay Gould and James Fisk, Jr. These essays, while incisive and entertainingly sarcastic, lack a judicial tone. The essay on the railway system discusses the origin of railways in this country, railway charges, consolidation, stock watering, and the relation of the government to railroad corporations. The essay on the New York gold conspiracy by Henry Adams tells the story of the effort of Jay Gould to corner the gold market in 1869, culminating in the disaster of Black Friday, September 23. The Legal-tender act by Francis A. Walker and Henry Adams is an adverse criticism of Spaulding's *History of the Legal-tender act*, as well as the government policy of issuing treasury notes instead of borrowing in the early years of the Civil War. D. R. D.

Adams, Henry Carter. Taxation in the United States, 1789-1816. (Johns Hopkins Univ. studies, ser. 2, nos. 5-6.) Balt. 1884. Pap. 50c. [2823

This is a brief but clear monograph of 80 pages written by the author while a graduate student at Johns Hopkins University. Its aim is naturally scholarly accuracy rather than popular interest. At the same time it is more attractive in style and presentation than most studies of this character. It is especially full and suggestive in the discussion of the political origin of protection. It is shown that protection has been a product of evolution. A second chapter deals with the early internal revenue duties; and a third with criticisms upon revenue legislation. This essay may be safely commended as a thoughtful

and interesting introductory chapter of a detailed study of the revenue history of the United States. D. R. D.

American almanac and repository of useful knowledge, 1830-62. Boston. 1830-62. 33v. [2824

This contained each year considerable carefully edited statistical information concerning the country at large and each state, such as names of officials, tables of imports and exports, statements of expenditures of the several departments, average quarterly prices of leading articles, mileage of railroads and canals in each state, etc. It was not unlike the present newspaper almanacs, but contained more information regarding the several commonwealths. F. J. S.

American almanac and treasury of facts, statistical, financial, and political, 1878-89; ed. by A. R. Spofford. N. Y.: Am. News Co. 1878-89. [2825

It was the aim of the editor "to glean the most important and practically useful facts out of the multitudinous reports concerning the public lands, finances, post-office system, tariff and internal revenue, currency, patent office, pension bureau, commerce and navigation, army and navy, reports of the commissioner of education, and statistics of the census." Beginning with 1880 there were two editions of each issue, one containing 100 additional pages. F. J. S.

Bagnall, William R. Textile industries of the United States, including sketches and notices of cotton, woollen, silk and linen manufacture in the colonial period. V. 1: 1639-1810. Boston: W. B. Clarke. 1893. [2826

This is a detailed history in which the author has endeavored to verify all statements by personal examination of contemporaneous documents, newspapers, etc. He visited many offices of record and libraries. The work represents years of labor. It is not only an industrial history, but it also furnishes minute biographical data in regard to early manufacturers. It is of the same general detailed character as Bishop's history of manufactures (sect. 2831), but much more carefully digested and arranged. It is also limited to textile industries. There is no index, but there are fourteen pages of topical contents. There are twenty-four portraits of leading manufacturers of the early period. D. R. D.

Bancroft, Hubert Howe. Book of the Fair: an historical and descriptive presentation of the world's science, art, and industry, as viewed through the Columbian Exposition at Chicago in 1893. Chicago: Bancroft Co. 1893-4. 25 pts. Pap. $1 ea. [2827

"It ranges, in its account of the Columbian Exposition of 1893, from previous world's fairs to the Midwinter California Exposition. We are shown pictorially the great buildings in process of erection, and their ruins after fire has begun its devastation of them. The naval review in New York is fitly embraced in the list of ceremonial observances connected with the continental celebration. The auxiliary congresses are also taken note of. It would be idle to criticise the text for accuracy or fulness, since only a part could be told, and errors there must be in the most summary record of this nature. . . . The typography is excellent, and the vast array of illustrations well chosen where choice was free — as in all the external aspects of the Fair. The treatment is systematic and orderly, and there is an index sufficient for its purpose." *Nation*, 59: 463.

Batchelder, Samuel. Introduction and early progress of the cotton manufacture in the U. S. Boston: Little. 1863.   **[2828**

The author, as early as 1808, was interested in cotton manufacture in New England, and retained an active interest in the industry throughout the first half of the century. This little book is practically nothing more than a collection of notes of reading, and of miscellaneous information in regard to cotton manufacture. As such it has value for a special few.
         D. R. D.

Bayley, Rafael A. History of the national loans of the United States, July 4, 1776–June 30, 1880. (In U. S. Census, 1880. Report on valuation, taxation, etc., pp. 295–486. Wash. 1881.)   **[2829**

The author — an officer in the Treasury Department — contributes a careful and precise account of the national loans, showing the issues and redemptions of the several loans for each year, together with a brief historical résumé, with the causes that led to their negotiation. The work is carefully done, and is based upon authoritative histories and public documents. It is specially full on the early loans during the Revolutionary period. Careful references are given to the public statutes. The work is of value to every student of finance who wishes clear and accurate statement.   D. R. D.

Beer, G. L. Commercial policy of England toward the American colonies. See Columbia University, sect. 255.   **[2830**

Bishop, James Leander. History of American manufactures, 1608–1860. Phil.: Young. 1864. 2v. 3d ed. enl. and rev. 3v. Phil. 1867.   **[2831**

Vol. 1: Colonial period; 2: 1789–1867; 3: Description of American industries in 1867, prepared by others than Bishop, and distinctly inferior to the preceding volumes. The work constitutes a valuable storehouse of facts, especially for the industries of New England and the Middle States. It includes numerous statistical tables collected from the Census Reports and other sources; also sketches of prominent manufacturers and inventors. Bishop wrote from the point of view of a warm advocate of a protective tariff.   R. C. H. C.

Bolles, Albert Sidney. Financial history of the United States. N. Y.: Appleton. 1879–85. 3v. V. 1, $2.50; v. 2–3, $3.50 ea. **[2832**

This is practically the only single work which cov-

ers the financial history of the United States from the period of national independence to a recent date, and as such it must be relied upon for help and guidance. It is an unsatisfactory work to characterize. The first volume embraces the period 1774–1789; the second, 1789–1860; and the third, 1861–1885. It shows much research and, on the whole, temperate judgment. The style, however, is overwrought, and the arrangement is confusing. The work contains abundant, and for the most part apt, quotations from speeches and extracts from documents. It is also an attempt to trace the causes and consequences of legislation; but in this the author is not successful. There is sympathy throughout for protection, and in the last volume pronounced advocacy of the national banking system. In the second period there is relatively but little space given to banking history. Of special utility throughout this work are the chapters on appropriations and government accounting, subjects on which it is difficult to find treatment elsewhere.   D. R. D.

—— Industrial history of the United States; with a description of Canadian industries. Norwich, Conn.: H. Bill. 1878. N. Y.: Funk. $4.25.   **[2833**

The seven books treat of agriculture and horticulture, pp. 1–184; manufactures, 185–568; shipping and railroads, 569–666; mines, and mining, and oil, 667–782; banking, insurance, and commerce, 783–880; trade unions and the eight-hour movement, 881–906; industries of Canada, 907–936. The scope of this work may be further indicated by the titles of the chapters under I: agricultural implements, cotton, wheat, corn, sugar and molasses, tobacco, grass and hay, minor crops, neat cattle, butter and cheese, the horse, sheep, swine, horticulture, minerals, and fruit raising. While the work is out of date, it is a useful reference book for the historical period covered. The work shows considerable research. It is abundantly illustrated.
        D. R. D.

Bourne, Edward Gaylord. History of surplus revenue of 1837. (Questions of the day.) N. Y.: Putnam. 1885. $1.25. **[2834**

This is a work for students and those interested in government finance. It is a scholar's contribution to an important incident in the financial history of the United States. The study was published in 1885 when the question of a Treasury surplus was again attracting attention. It covers the proposals of distribution of surplus revenue made by statesmen in the early part of the century; the growth and distribution of the surplus in 1837; a résumé of opinion in regard to the measure; and then, in careful detail, the action of the several states in disposing of their respective portions. This part is a distinctly original study. There are many notes from newspapers, reports, and documents of the period. Exact references are given and a bibliography is added. As some of the states appropriated a considerable part of the funds thus distributed to school-funds, the work throws light upon the history of governmental support of education.
        D. R. D.

Breck, Samuel. Historical sketch of continental paper money. Phil.: Clark. 1843.
        [2835

The author endeavors to trace briefly the origin, rapid increase, and downfall of continental paper money, the cause of its depreciation, the honest intention of Congress to repeal it, and " incidentally shows its powerful, if not indispensable, agency in gaining our independence." Owing to the gradual depreciation of the notes, their non-retirement is regarded as nothing more than a moderate tax. The essay is not primarily a historical research, but an apologetic essay. It contains some slight inaccuracies. (See Phillips' *Historical sketches of the paper currency of the American colonies*, Vol. I, p. iii.) On page 14 is given a list of the mottoes printed on the several denominations of continental bills. D. R. D.

Bristed, John. Resources of the United States. N. Y.: Eastburn. 1818. [2836

While this work for most purposes is out of date, yet it will furnish valuable suggestions for the student who wishes to receive contemporary impressions. The first chapter treats of the territory, agriculture, population, and navigable capacity of the United States; the second, commerce of the United States; third, manufacturing ; fourth, finance ; fifth, government policy and laws; sixth, literature; and seventh, habits, manners and character of the people. The author makes frequent reference to other works, so that the book is of some value from a bibliographical point of view. The author regards public questions from the Federalist standpoint, and generally believes in a vigorous policy. He is quick to note the absurd statements which have been made by foreign writers. He had previously written a work on the resources of the British Empire, and consequently makes frequent comparison with the condition of other countries. The style lacks simplicity, clearness and directness.
D. R. D.

Bromwell, William J. History of immigration to the United States. N. Y.: Redfield. 1856. [2837

The author, an official in the Department of State, presents a compilation from official documents of facts in regard to the number, sex, age, occupation, and country of birth of immigrants for the period 1819 to 1855. Statistical tables relating to these facts take up pages 21 to 185. This is prefaced by a few introductory pages on the extent of immigration prior to 1819 ; and in the appendix is a reprint of the naturalization and passenger laws of the U. S., as well as of some of the state laws pertaining to immigration. The book has but slight value at the present time, save for reference to particular statistical data. There is no discussion of immigration from the sociological or industrial standpoint. D. R. D.

Bronson, Henry. Historical account of Connecticut currency, continental money, and the finances of the Revolution. (In New Haven Colony Hist. Soc. Papers, v. 1. New Haven. 1865.) [2838

This is more than a local study. In writing a history of Connecticut currency the author was drawn into a general review of the currency of America and then of the continental paper money policy, and the financial measures of the Revolutionary War. " That the historical truths presented might be duly appreciated, I have occasionally paused to set forth some of the principles of financial science — to explain briefly the nature and uses of money." The author is severe in his criticism of the state and continental issues during the war of the Revolution. He does not agree with historians who argue that the issues were a necessity. Chapter 12 treats of the cost of the Revolution ; chapter 13, of coinage ; and chapter 14, of funding the debt. The essay is scholarly and the style vigorous. D. R. D.

Bruce, Philip Alexander. Economic history of Virginia in the 17th century. N. Y.: Macmillan. 1896. 2v. $6. [2839

One of the best historical works on early Virginia, and without equal in its special field. On nearly every phase of the economic life of the colony the information offered is full, and always first-hand ; while the general presentation is balanced, and the literary merit considerable. The author is perhaps too trustful of early contemporary writers, and somewhat lavish of incident ; and his views regarding the profitableness of slave labor are not those now generally held. W. MacD.

Bullock, Charles Jesse. Finances of the United States, 1775–89, with especial reference to the budget. (Univ. of Wisconsin. Bulletin, economics, etc., v. 1, no. 2.) Madison. 1895. Pap. 75c. [2840

The various revenues and expenditures of the government in its formative state are considered in order, including continental paper money loans, taxes, and miscellaneous receipts. Part II deals with the administration of the finances and the organization of the budget. Each chapter is prefaced by a serviceable bibliography, and at the end of the work there is a general bibliography of eight pages. There is no index, but a well-constructed topical table of contents forms a helpful substitute. The foot-notes are abundant and precise. The monograph is that of an investigator, academic in character. The treatment is a continued narrative of fact, often statistical. At the same time occasional independent judgments of interest are given. The monograph is not a finished essay and will not attract the general reader. It is of value to the advanced student, who will find his labors lightened by the careful research. D. R. D.

Channing, Edward. Navigation laws. See American Antiquarian Society, sect. 238.
[2841

Clarke, Matthew St. Clair, *and* **David A. Hall,** *comp.* Legislative and documentary history of the Bank of the United States, including the original Bank of North America. Washington : Gales. 1832. [2842

The design of the work is to collect the various bills and projects for a national bank which had been brought forward down to the date of publication, 1832. It is especially concerned, therefore, with the history of the first and second United States Banks. It is almost entirely a documentary history, including reports of committees and public officials, and debates in Congress. For the proceedings and debates of Congress in Committee of the Whole the files of the *National intelligencer* have been used. The original plan was to stop with the year 1816, and after that date the record of proceedings is not so full. The history of the final attack on the United States Bank and its dissolution is not included. It is a volume of over 800 pages. It contains the important decision of the Supreme Court, McCulloch *vs.* State of Maryland, delivered in 1819, on the power of Congress to incorporate a bank. **,**   D. R. D.

Codman, John Thomas. Brook Farm: historic and personal memoirs. Boston: Arena Pub. Co.   1894.   [2843

Brook Farm is one of the most noted experiments of community life in the United States. The association was organized in 1842, and settled on a farm in West Roxbury, Mass., nine miles from Boston. Its history has been made famous because of its association with Emerson, Hawthorne, Margaret Fuller, Charles A. Dana, William H. Channing, and its manager, Dr. Ripley. It lasted until 1847. It passed through two stages: the first termed by some the Transcendental; the later, which came more definitely under the influence of Fourierism, industrial. The author of this book, when a youth, with his parents joined the association in 1843, at the beginning of the second stage. His book is composed of recollections, anecdotes, extracts from letters, documents, and journals published, — the *Dial* and the *Harbinger*. In the appendix are letters to Dr. Ripley from inquirers and others, and his replies. The work is rambling and the style diffuse. It gives, however, a frank and intimate account of the impressions and experiences of a sympathetic participant, in the enthusiasm of youth. There is an extremely unfavorable criticism of this book by Rev. John W. Chadwick in the *Nation*, 60: 207.   D. R. D.

Coxe, Tench. View of the United States of America. Phil.: Hall. 1794. London. 1795.   [2844

"As Commissioner of the Revenue, Tench Coxe, of Philadelphia, investigated and wrote upon several economical interests of the country, and, in 1794, published his *View of the United States of America*, in a series of papers written in 1787-94. There is much statistical information in regard to trade and manufactures during the period indicated. The progress of the country at that time is authentically described, and the resources of Pennsylvania exhibited." H. T. Tuckerman, *America and her commentators*, p. 393.

De Bow, James Dunwoody Brownson. Industrial resources, etc., of the southern and western states. New Orleans. 1852-3. 3v.   [2845

This work is encyclopædic in character, made up of separate articles on a great variety of topics relating to commerce, agriculture, manufactures, internal improvements, slave and free labor, sketches of states and cities, and census returns. The author was professor of political economy in the University of Louisiana and editor of *De Bow's Review*. He was assisted by competent collaborators. The work is useful for reference.   D. R. D.

De Bow's review. New Orleans; Charleston; Wash. 1846-64. 34v. N. Y. 1866-70. 8v.   [2846

This review was to commerce, manufactures, agriculture, internal improvements, and industrial activity in any line, what the *Southern literary messenger* was to literature, while in history they met on common ground. Its field was the south, west and southwest; it undertook to defend their rights, develop their resources, collect and preserve their statistics, and, during much of its existence, made these objects superior to the questions of national politics. Its greatest value is that it is, together with the *Industrial resources of the southern and western states*, which was compiled from it (sect. 2845), a great repository of material bearing on the economic life of the section.
                                S. B. W.

Depew, Chauncey Mitchell, *ed.* One hundred years of American commerce. N. Y.: D. O. Haynes. 1896. 2v.   [2847

This work consists of one hundred chapters, written by as many men, representing the trades and industries which have been specialized in recent years. The writers selected, on the whole, are men closely identified with the trade or business of which they treated, and to that extent the papers may be regarded as authoritative. American labor, for example, is treated by Carroll D. Wright; merchant marine by E. T. Chamberlain; an investigation of life insurance by Sheppard Homans; the telegraph by Thomas T. Eckert, President of the Western Union Telegraph Co., and sugar by J. R. Searles, President of the American Sugar Refining Co. The individual papers are from five to fifteen pages in length, and are both descriptive and scientific. Naturally there is a great difference of style. The paper and typography are especially good. The work is useful as a reference book, but unfortunately there is no index.   D. R. D.

Douglas, C. H. J. Financial history of Massachusetts. See Columbia University, sect. 254.   [2848

Elliot, Jonathan. Funding system of the United States and of Great Britain, with tabular facts of other nations touching the same subject. Wash.: Blair & Rives. 1845.

—— *Same.* (In U. S. 28th Cong., 1st sess. House ex. doc. v. 2.)   [2849

The author, a journalist in Washington, in the early part of the century, and editor of *The debates on the Constitution* and other public documents, brought together in this volume a mass of extracts from reports and statements of the Treasury Department, sinking fund commissioners, Congressional committees, etc., which were concerned with the public debt. The collection treats of the creation of the Revolutionary debt of 1775, the assumption and funding by the federal government of this debt, the new debt of the Louisiana purchase, loans of the War of 1812, the extinction of the debt in 1835, and the new loans down to 1843. The volume closes with a series of papers, pp. 1103-86, showing the rates of exchange, price of specie and bank paper, fluctuations growing out of the suspension of specie by banks, etc. This report constituted document no. 15, House of Representatives, 28th Cong., First session, and was transmitted to Congress December 16, 1843. In the few notes which are included, the author discloses his federalist sympathies and admiration for Hamilton. There is a serviceable index of eighteen pages. D. R. D.

Elliott, Orrin Leslie. Tariff controversy in the United States, 1789–1833; with a summary of the period before the adoption of the Constitution. (Leland Stanford, Jr., Univ. monographs, hist. and economics, no. 1.) Palo Alto, Cal. 1892. Pap. $1. [2850

The several chapters treat of the colonial period, the tariff of 1789, Hamilton's report on manufactures, manufactures vs. commerce, the American system, and the nullification act in its relation to the tariff. This is an academic research based upon contemporary documents. Special attention is given to the character of the arguments rather than to American history of industries affected, nor is much space given to legislative action beyond that of debate. The treatment is, on the whole, impartial. For the general reader the work is altogether too detailed, but for the advanced student it will be of special service, not only for the author's interpretation but for the scholarly references and foot-notes appended. There is an index. D. R. D.

Ely, Richard Theodore. Labor movement in America. N. Y.: Crowell. [c. 1886.] $1.50. [2851

Although this is not a thorough or complete narrative of the history of labor in the U. S., it furnishes some historical material on the development of organized labor and the industrial reform movement associated with communism, socialism and co-operation in the U. S. The arrangement is not clear, and unless the reader has some previous acquaintance with American social history and is skilled in relating cause and effect, he may go astray. The author's sympathies for the efforts and methods of organized labor are marked. The appendix contains several trade union documents and manifestoes of reform parties. D. R. D.

Fearon, Henry Bradshaw. Sketches of America: narrative of a journey of 5000 miles through the eastern and western states. London: Longmans. 1818. [2852

Fearon came to America on a tour of inspection in the interest of some English farmers who contemplated settling in Illinois. His narrative is interesting and, as he observes with especial care everything of importance to intending settlers, it is especially instructive to the student of social and economic history. The price and quality of land, the conditions of trade, the competition between English and domestic goods, the cost and conditions of travel by sea and over land, types of settlers, and phases of public opinion are the features of the United States to which Fearon devoted most of his attention. For a knowledge of the years just following the War of 1812 Fearon's book is an important source. E. G. B.

Field, Henry Martyn. History of the Atlantic telegraph. N. Y.: Scribner. 1866.
—— *Same :* Story of the Atlantic telegraph ; rev. ed. N. Y.: Scribner. 1893. $1.50. [2853

Dr. Field, the former editor of the *Evangelist*, writes in an interesting way of the long struggle to lay the cable between Newfoundland and Ireland. A brother of Cyrus Field, by whose persistent efforts success was finally achieved, he was put in possession of all the facts and documents relating to the enterprise. It may therefore be regarded as an authentic account. D. R. D.

French, Benjamin Franklin. History of the rise and progress of the iron trade of the United States, 1621–1857. N. Y.: Wiley. 1858. [2854

This work is largely statistical in character, showing the production, imports and exports, and cost of manufacture. It is annalistic rather than critical. There is little, if any, literary form. It will be of special service to the special student of industrial development and of tariff history. For the latter purpose the tables scattered through the volume will be of help. The report on iron of the convention of the Friends of domestic industry, held in 1831, is reprinted, pp. 33–54; also the memorial of iron masters of Philadelphia in 1849, pp. 77–100; and remarks submitted at the same time by Mr. Stephen Cowell, pp. 105–117. D. R. D.

Gannett, Henry. Building of a nation: growth, present condition and resources of the United States. N. Y.: Thomas. 1895. $2.50. [2855

This book is largely made up of statistics, either run into text, or in tabular form, with many maps and charts. The author was chief geographer of the last two censuses, and the statistics are reliable as far as official authority can justify. It is not a book to read through. It would, however, be of assistance to a school teacher of United States history, furnishing illustrations and suggestions for special work by young students in fields of study, frequently escaping attention, such as the elements of the population, immigration, voters, illiteracy, religions, mortality and transportation. The statistics include census returns of 1890: for some topics these are out of date and should be supplemented by the last *Statistical abstract of the United States.* D. R. D.

Gibbons, James Sloan. Banks of New York, their dealers, the clearing house, and the panic of 1857, with a financial chart. N. Y. 1858. N. Y.: Appleton. 1870. [2856

This is an extremely interesting and entertaining account of the organization of New York banks and the duties of the various officers, and description of the clearing-house system. Anecdotal conversations are introduced, and the illustrations are amusingly instructive. The historical portion is to be found in the history of the panic of 1857, which is intelligently discussed, pp. 343–99. The author was a well-known merchant of New York City. D. R. D.

Goss, J. D. History of tariff administration in the U. S. See Columbia University, sect. 254. [2857

Gouge, William M. Fiscal history of Texas, 1834–52. Phil.: Lippincott. 1852. [2858

Covering the period 1835–52. Mr. Gouge had gained considerable reputation from *A short history of paper-money and banking in the United States*, published in 1833. The *Fiscal history* is pervaded by a tone of rasping criticism. It condemns Texas severely for its alleged failure to keep faith with its creditors. The sources of the book were the official records, and it is valuable for its collection and arrangement of facts, not only to students of Texas finance, but to those of the science in general. It should not, however, be regarded as a fair historical presentation of the subject. G. P. G.

—— Short history of paper money and banking in the United States, including an account of provincial and continental paper money. Phil. 1833. [2859

The first part of this work, 140 pages, is a general essay on banking ; the remainder, 240 pages, is one of the original sources of American banking history for the colonial and revolutionary periods. The author relies largely upon standard writers, such as Hutchinson and Pelatiah Webster. The latter period came within his own observation. The work is badly arranged, and the author is indiscriminating in denunciation of all banking systems. Nevertheless the last of the volume is of importance to students of economic history. D. R. D.

Great Britain. *Privy Council.* Report of a committee on the trade of Great Britain with the U. S. Jan., 1791. See Historical Printing Club, sect. 273. [2860

Hall, James. Statistics of the West. Cin.: James. 1836. [2861

Treats of the topography, productiveness of the soil, the native animals, and the extent and administration of the public domain. Contains trade statistics of New Orleans and a valuable list of 588 river steamboats, with place and time of building, etc. Useful for appreciation of the environment and life in the trans-Alleghenian region. E. E. S.

Halle, Ernst von. Trusts ; or Industrial combinations and coalitions in the United States. N. Y.: Macmillan. 1895. $1.25. [2862

This is a scholarly and interesting sketch of the growth, character, and effect of industrial combinations of capital. The author, a German, studied the question in the United States from personal observation, and was fortunate in securing facts at first-hand from trust officials. More than half of the work, pp. 153–350, is an appendix containing trust deeds, by-laws of corporations, anti-trust statutes, rebate vouchers, reorganization proceedings, lists of combinations, and a bibliography. There is no index. As there is but little scholarly literature on this subject in book form,

the work at the present date (1899) may be regarded as indispensable. The author states that the manuscript was read by Prof. Ashley, of Harvard University. D. R. D.

Hammond, M. B. Cotton industry. (Am. Economic Assoc. Publications.) N. Y.: Macmillan. 1897. Pt. 1. Pap. $1.50. [2863

This work (part I) treats of cotton culture and the cotton trade in the U. S. from colonial times to 1897. Part II, not yet published, is to treat of the manufacture of cotton. The author, who is a special student of economics, had access to the best authorities, which he cites in the foot-notes, and has, also, made a trip through the South to study the economic conditions. His information is accurate and varied. Though writing from a northern standpoint on the subject of slave labor, he is generally fair in his statements and sound in judgment. The work contains valuable statistics, a bibliography, and an index. The style is excellent. It is a book of extraordinary merit. J. R. F.

Hilgard, Eugene Woldemar. Report on the cotton production in the United States. (U. S. Census, 1880.) Wash. 1884. 2v. [2864

This is an exhaustive account of the agricultural and physico-geographical character of the several cotton states and of California. The author, professor of agriculture at the University of California, was formerly professor at the University of Mississippi, as well as state geologist. The work contains a large amount of local descriptions of the cotton lands of the South. It is not elaborated on the side of cotton-growing industry. As a contribution to botany and physiography, for the section of the country concerned, the work may be of great value. Interesting maps are included. D. R. D.

Hill, Charles S. History of American shipping. N. Y.: Amer. News Co. 1883. [2865

This book is made up of scraps, illustrations, and extracts from political documents in regard to the shipping industry. It has no literary value whatever, but may be of some service to a student who is endeavoring to secure facts in regard to the history of shipping legislation and, more especially, shipping conditions. D. R. D.

Hill, William. First stages of the tariff policy of the United States. (Am. Economic Assoc. Publications, v. 8, no. 6.) Balt. 1893. Pap. $1. [2866

This is an excellent study of the tariffs of the American colonies and the tariff legislation from independence until 1789, including the consideration of the first tariff act. Under the colonial tariffs space is given to the tonnage duties, tobacco tax, slave duty and tariff schedules. Clear summaries are presented of the opinions of leading statesmen of the Revolutionary period on the subject of restrictive duties. In the appendix are twenty pages of reprints from resolutions, tariff acts, and legislative reports. The essay is carefully annotated with references. The author shows clearly how English restrictive legislation affected the development of the tariff policy of the new republic. D. R. D.

Hinds, William Alfred. American communities. Oneida, N. Y. : American Socialist. 1878. [2867

This work consists of brief sketches of Economy, Zoar, Bethel, Aurora, Amana, Icaria, the Shakers, Oneida, Wallingford, and the Brotherhood of the New Life. The author made a tour of most of the communities mentioned above in the summer of 1876. He endeavors to give in smaller space the material treated by Nordhoff and Noyes in their works on communities (sect. 2880) and American socialisms (sect. 2882). The author was a believer in community life, but does not commend any one of the above as a model. He writes in an interesting style, selects his material with good judgment. In the appendix are the covenants and articles of association of some of the communities.
D. R. D.

Hughson, Shirley Carter. Carolina pirates and colonial commerce, 1670–1740. (Johns Hopkins Univ. studies, ser. 12, nos. 5–7.) Balt. 1894. Pap. $1. [2868

This is a helpful monograph upon a greatly neglected subject, but it throws less light than might have been expected upon the subject of colonial commerce. It is, in fact, a treatise upon the attitude of the government of South Carolina towards pirates and piracy, and contains excellent and full accounts of the careers of Thatch, Bonnet, Moody, Worley, and other well-known colonial characters. It is based largely on printed and unprinted material accessible in South Carolina, and contains information not elsewhere given ; but it presents nothing that is new regarding the commerce of South Carolina. C. M. A.

Kearney, John Watts. Sketch of American finances, 1789–1835. N. Y. : Putnam. 1887. $1. [2869

This brief sketch of 150 pages was written at a time when the national debt was being rapidly paid off, and the question of readjustment of taxation and treatment of annual surplus pressed upon public attention. The essay is divided into four chapters : Settlement of the Revolutionary War debt ; Revenue, Expenditure, and the Sinking fund ; the War of 1812, Increase of the public debt, Financial embarrassment, Peace with Great Britain, the Protective tariff ; Extinguishment of the public debt. The essay is specially devoted to the funding of the debt, its maturity, rate of interest, sinking fund, etc. Less attention is given to taxation. It is exceedingly clear, and is a valuable piece of work. The style is excellent, and the narrative is well connected. D. R. D.

Keyes, Emerson Willard. History of savings banks in the United States, 1816–74. N. Y. : Bradford Rhodes. 1876–78. 2v. [2870

The author, a lawyer, was for many years an official of the state banking system of New York. The work is a careful and detailed history, which is likely to remain standard and authoritative for the period named. The first volume includes New England and in part New York ; the second, New York, Middle States and

Western States. The last chapter contains a general review with comprehensive statistical tables, discussion of failures, savings banks in panics, and as a force in social economy. Savings banks are viewed, as a whole, from the legislative and institutional side rather than from the social. D. R. D.

Kinley, David. History, organization and influence of the independent treasury of the United States. N. Y.: Crowell. [c. 1893.] $1.50. [2871

Prof. Kinley's book is the only scholarly and complete work on the methods followed by the Treasury Department in the care of its funds which daily pour in from revenue and other sources. The first part is historical. The last and larger part is a discussion of various financial and commercial problems which arise under the working of the finally developed system, such as the management of government loans, its influence on business, its relation to crises. The author began his work with a prejudice in favor of the sub-treasury system, but was forced to change his opinion, concluding that the system is injurious to the business interests of the people. He consequently recommends the development of the national banking system to replace the independent treasury. In spite of the author's conviction, the tone is fair. In the appendix there are reprints of several Treasury circulars. D. R. D.

Knox, John Jay. United States notes : a history of the various issues of paper money by the government of the United States. N.Y. : Scribner. 1884. 3d ed. rev. 1892. $1.50. [2872

Mr. Knox was comptroller of the currency from 1872 until 1884. Previous to the former date he had been in the service of the Treasury Department of the United States since 1862. During this long period he devoted much inquiry to the history of paper money. This, in portions, found a printed record in the comptroller's reports of 1875 and 1876, in papers read at various associations, such as the Bankers' Association, and in articles in Lalor's *Encyclopædia of political science.* The work, therefore, is the product of long investigation and reflection. Especial emphasis is given to the development of the doctrine of the constitutionality of government paper money. The work bears the marks of fairness and accuracy, and is historical rather than controversial. It is a compact narrative, easily read, and for the topics considered, while not exhaustive, an adequate and interesting authority. In the appendix are opinions given by the Supreme Court in 1884 on the constitutionality of the issue of United States notes in times of peace.
D. R. D.

Laughlin, James Laurence. History of bimetallism in the United States. N. Y. : Appleton. 1885. 4th ed., with new appendices. 1897. $2.25. [2873

Prof. Laughlin is a pronounced monometallist. His work is more than a history ; it includes a discussion of economic principles in the hope that this, with the lessons of American experience, may help to suppress some of the theoretical vagaries of the day. The historical portions which will be of assistance in tracing the course of financial history in the U. S. are chap. 2, describing the adoption of bimetallism in 1792; chaps. 4–7, on the legislation of 1834, 1853, and 1873 ; chaps. 14 and 15 on the silver legislation in 1878 ; chap. 16, act of 1890; and chap. 17, cessation of silver purchases, 1893. The work contains much statistical matter and many extracts of speeches. Much has since been written on this subject, but this volume remains on the whole the most serviceable historical compendium, if the reader will bear in mind that the author is writing with a purpose to persuade.   D. R. D.

Lewis, Lawrence, Jr. History of the Bank of North America. Phil.: Lippincott. 1882.   [2874

This well-printed volume was prepared at the request of the officers of the Bank of North America to commemorate the centennial anniversary of the founding of the first bank chartered in the United States. This bank is of more than local interest, inasmuch as it was founded through the efforts of Robert Morris and other Philadelphia patriots, to assist the financial operations of the government during the Revolutionary period. There are eight portraits and three pages of facsimiles of bank-notes.   D. R. D.

Linderman, Henry Richard. Money and legal tender in the United States. N. Y.: Putnam. 1877.   [2875

The author of this book was for many years Director of the Mint. While the character of the money question has naturally changed greatly since 1877, this little work has present value for the clear and concise definitions of technical terms and processes. It presents in a brief form the laws relating to coinage, legal tender, and money standards. The author was opposed to the further coinage of silver, and although the book is not argumentative, it is clear in its adverse criticism.   D. R. D.

Lord, Eleanor Louisa. Industrial experiments in the British colonies of North America. (Johns Hopkins Univ. studies, extra v. 17.) Balt. 1898. $1.25.   [2876

"This volume contains a somewhat detailed study of one phase of the British commercial system in the eighteenth century, viz., the policy which that government followed for the purpose of procuring from the colonies a supply of naval stores. Attention is mainly directed to the New England colonies, as they were the chief source of supply of that kind. Occasional reference, however, is made to the production of stores in the Carolinas and Pennsylvania, while an account is given of the experiment with the Palatines in New York. The concluding chapter deals summarily with a cognate subject, the rise of manufactures in the plantations. In appendices two price-lists of naval stores, principally tar, pitch, hemp and masts, are given. . . . For the material of this monograph the author has gone to the original documents in the British public record office. Her references are almost exclusively to these, and she has apparently examined everything bearing on the subject which is to be found in the New England papers. This is the only proper

course to follow." Herbert L. Osgood, in *Am. hist. review*, 4: 365.

Macgregor, John. Progress of America. London: Whittaker. 1847. 2v.   [2877

This large work of nearly three thousand pages was the result of many years of preparation by the Secretary of the English Board of Trade. Mr. Macgregor was a voluminous author on commercial and economic subjects, and afterwards a member of Parliament. His work is an account of the origin, growth, and condition of settlements on the American continent. It is not intended as a complete narrative, but as an exposition from the mistaken standpoint that the "history of navigation and commerce is the history of civilization." The author made independent researches and used at first-hand Spanish, Portuguese, Dutch, Italian, and English authors. The first volume is historical and statistical ; the second geographical and statistical. The several states of our country are reconsidered, followed by chapters on the economic sources and institutions of the country. The work is not well digested, but contains a valuable mass of reliable economic and financial information. Unfortunately there is no index.   D. R. D.

Mason, David Hastings. Short tariff history of the United States : part 1, 1783–89. Chicago: Author. 1884. New ed. 1886. Chicago: Kerr. 1896. 25c.   [2878

The author, an ardent advocate of protection of American industries, writes to convince the popular mind. There are no qualifications in the author's philosophy. All prosperity has been under the reign of protective principles. There is little indication of reading beyond standard histories and Congressional debates. As an illustration of protective argument the essay has interest, but in no sense can be called history. Only the first part of what was designed to be a complete history was published.   D. R. D.

Morris, Robert. SUMNER, WILLIAM GRAHAM. The financier and the finances of the American Revolution. N. Y.: Dodd. 1891. 2v. $5.   [2879

This work will not be serviceable to the general reader, but is invaluable to the special and advanced student. It is badly arranged, with little regard to chronological sequence, and is consequently confusing. Many chapters appear to be simply a string of notes gathered by wide reading ; other chapters are detached studies on revolutionary taxation, embargoes, specific supplies, paper currency, etc., and successive episodes in the life of Morris, without any binding generalization or helpful perspective. The work is an original study, and is based in a considerable degree upon material not yet printed. The author, however, was not able to secure the use of Morris' diary. The authorities are given with painstaking care, and there is an excellent index. As compared with the first volume of Bolles' *Financial history of the United States*, this is the more scholarly, but, as a book to read, compares unfavorably.   D. R. D.

Nordhoff, Charles. Communistic societies

of the United States. N. Y.: Harper. 1875. $4. [2880

This is one of the best works on the subject, prepared by a trained journalist. It is a valuable account, from personal visits and observations in a large number of communistic societies in the United States, especially of the Economists, Zoarites, Shakers, the Oneida Community, and Icarian Society. The author writes sympathetically of the efforts of these communities to solve industrial evils, although he recognizes the underlying obstacles to final success. In the concluding chapter he endeavors to compare the customs of the different communities. The illustrations are interesting. There is an index. D. R. D.

Noyes, Alexander Dana. Thirty years of American finance, 1865-96. N. Y.: Putnam. 1898. $1.25. [2881

" Mr. Noyes's book should be welcome both to general readers and to students. His selection of topics, the admirable perspective of his treatment, the clearness and forcibleness of his style, and the fair-mindedness which he displays in the treatment of political parties should commend it to the former; while his grasp of the principles involved, his thorough mastery of the facts, his constant reference to original sources of information, and his skill in unraveling and interpreting the complex phenomena of the period should give him the admiration and confidence of the latter. . . . Mr. Noyes has succeeded in making very clear the relations between our currency experiments, the tariff laws, the foreign rates of exchange, the speculation on the stock markets and produce exchanges, and the vicissitudes of trade and industry during the period, on the one hand, and the financial problems of the government, on the other. Especially noteworthy are his analysis and interpretation of the period since 1890. . . . Critics of this book must aim their shafts at the author's interpretations of men and events. Here there is frequently opportunity for differences of opinion; and in many cases Mr. Noyes has not presented a sufficiently comprehensive array of facts to justify completely his conclusions. . . . But he has performed a very difficult task in an eminently satisfactory manner." Wm. A. Scott, in *Political science quarterly*, 13: 558..

The author is financial editor of the *Evening post*, New York. He wrote *The Evening post's free coinage catechism*, 1896, a pamphlet which had a circulation of nearly two millions.

Noyes, John Humphrey. History of American socialisms. Phil.: Lippincott. 1870. [2882

The author, educated at Dartmouth, Andover, and Yale, became an advocate of Perfectionism, and finally the founder of a community, in 1848, at Oneida, N. Y. A man of education and force, he developed this community to considerable success. He was interested in all forms of community life in this country, and consequently came into possession of a body of notes collected by J. Macdonald, who spent 1842 to 1854 visiting the various communities throughout the United States. His book combines this valuable mass of original material with the critical judgments of the author. Two important movements are noted: the Owen which culminated in 1826 and the Fourier movement in 1843.

In the latter part of the work the history is given of Oneida with an exposition of the real doctrines of the members. The author's fundamental principle is that communities to be successful must be religious and exercise control over the sexual relation. D. R. D.

Patton, Jacob Harris. Natural resources of the United States. N. Y.: Appleton. 1888. Rev. ed. [enl.] 1894. $3. [2883

This work is not a narrative history; but, in showing the development of the economic resources of the nation, is suggestive and helpful to the proper interpretation of social and political history. In the volume of about 500 pages nearly one fifth is devoted to a description of the coal fields; successive chapters deal with oil, iron, precious metals, mercury, copper, lead, zinc, tin, precious stones, clays and building stones, salt and mineral springs. This leads to the consideration of health resorts, climate, and rainfall, pp. 366-395. Lastly the subject of food supply is considered. The work is based upon official documents, federal and state. Naturally, much of the statistical material is now out of date. D. R. D.

Phillips, Henry, Jr. Historical sketches of the paper currency of the American colonies prior to the adoption of the federal constitution. Roxbury, Mass. 1865-6. 2v. [2884

The first volume includes sketches of the paper money of Pennsylvania, New Jersey, Rhode Island, Virginia and Vermont; the second of continental money. The papers represent a careful and antiquarian research with readable text, and furnish a guide to collectors of paper currency. This study is the most detailed account of the continental paper money in print. There are generous extracts from contemporaneous documents, and as far as possible light is thrown upon the causes of depreciation. The preface of vol. 1 contains a brief notice of the chief publications on the subject published before 1865. The appendices give catalogue of issues, reprints and colonial documents, and in the second volume there is a collection of poetry, epigrams, etc., relating to continental money. The edition of these two volumes was limited. D. R. D.

Powderly, Terence Vincent. Thirty years of labor, 1859-89. Columbus, O.: Excelsior Pub. House. 1889. Rev. ed. Phil. 1890. [2885

The author, for many years a prominent leader of the Knights of Labor, attempts to trace, in a popular form, the transition of industrial life to the factory system, and the agitation for labor organization which accompanied this change. His book is valuable as a record, by a labor leader, of many events which would otherwise have no chronicler. Early efforts at national organization, the adoption of an eight-hour day, the relation of labor organizations to questions of currency, land, religion, immigration, coöperation, and temperance are discussed. Inasmuch as there are few books on the history of American labor movements, this volume deserves special recognition. The style, however, is diffuse, and it will be difficult for the reader to obtain a clear idea of the sequence of events. D. R. D.

Ringwalt, John Luther. Development of transportation systems in the United States. Phil.: Railway World Office. 1888. [2886

The author, editor of the *Railway world*, describes the changes in methods of conveyance, roads, canals, railways, furnishes cost of transportation at various periods, and the financiering, engineering, mechanical, and governmental questions involved. The work is scrappy and not well digested, but contains a large mass of material. Many tables of statistics are included. There are nearly fifty pages of interesting illustrations. The work is suitable for reference rather than for general reading. D. R. D.

Ripley, W. Z. Financial history of Virginia, 1609–1776. See Columbia University, sect. 256. [2887

Sato, Shosuke. History of the land question in the United States. (Johns Hopkins Univ. studies, ser. 4, nos. 7–9.) Balt. 1886. Pap. $1. [2888

The author, a graduate student at the Johns Hopkins University, was commissioned by the Japanese government to investigate the land question of the U. S. The essay is a scholarly monograph, based upon original records and careful research. The historical portion treats of the formation of the public domain. Part II of the administration of the public domain, and Part III describes the land system under topics of bounties, methods of sale, credits, pre-emption, educational land grants, etc. The author is quick to note the abuses which have occurred in the administration of the federal domain by the government. The essay is designed for the special student rather than for the general reader. D. R. D.

Schuckers, Jacob William. Brief account of the finances and paper money of the Revolutionary War. Phil.: John Campbell. 1874. [2889

This is a sketch of the finances of the Continental Congress and the Confederacy down to 1790 when the debt was funded. A description of the bills of credit, both continental and state, loans domestic and foreign, the allotment of taxes, and other sources of revenue, including lotteries, confiscation, etc., is given. A few pages are devoted to the penal laws recommended by Congress against those who refused to take the bills. The style is somewhat rhetorical, and while the writer, on the whole, has chosen sound authorities, his reading does not indicate a very wide research. The essay is a readable account within a moderate space. D. R. D.

Scott, William Amasa. Repudiation of state debts: a study in the financial history of Mississippi, Florida, Alabama, N. Carolina, S. Carolina, Georgia, Louisiana, Arkansas, Tennessee, Minnesota, Michigan and Virginia. N. Y.: Crowell. [c. 1893.] $1.50. [2890

Only a portion of this work, chapters 2 to 6, is historical. These chapters describe with some detail the history of the various acts of repudiation passed by the twelve states named in the title. By repudiation is meant cases of scaling of debts and of refusals to pay bonds. In tracing the pretext for repudiation, valuable information is thrown upon the careless and reckless aid given by states to internal improvements and public works in the second quarter of the century, upon the disastrous results of the panic of 1837, the corruption of state officials in some states, and the financial distress which existed in some of the southern states during the reconstruction period subsequent to the Civil War. The historical portion is confined strictly to the subject treated. It is written from the standpoint of the publicist rather than that of the historian. There is an exhaustive list of the sources of information and a good index. The volume belongs to the *Library of economics and politics* edited by Dr. R. T. Ely. D. R. D.

Smith, Richmond Mayo. Emigration and immigration. N. Y.: Scribner. 1890. $1.50. [2891

The author has contributed the most important and judicial investigation yet made of the history and effects, — political, economic, and social, — of immigration to the United States. There is an analytic table of contents which will enable the reader to inform himself quickly on special points. The book is a good illustration of statistical method combined with interesting text. It was published in 1890, and consequently the student must supply from elsewhere the statistics of the later movements of population, and the facts in regard to the recent persistent agitation for restriction. The question of restriction of immigration is discussed in chapters 12 and 13, and the author concludes that the evils of indiscriminate immigration demand legislation. To the citizen endeavoring to think and act wisely on this important question now debated, this volume will be very suggestive. A bibliography is added. D. R. D.

Smith, William Prescott. Book of the great railway celebrations of 1857. N. Y.: Appleton. 1858. [2892

This is an account of the opening of the Ohio and Memphis and other railroads making a through line between Baltimore and St. Louis, in connection with the Baltimore & Ohio R. R. The occasion of the opening of the first road was celebrated by an excursion, to which leading men from the eastern states were invited. The author writes of this excursion in detail, giving accounts of the construction of the road, the scenes through which it passes, and the towns along the line. The work is of value as throwing light upon the history of railroads and the economic conditions of the sections spoken of. D. R. D.

Spaulding, Elbridge Gerry. History of the legal tender paper money issued during the great Rebellion. Buffalo. 1869. [2893

Mr. Spaulding was the chairman of the sub-committee of the Ways and Means committee which framed the legal tender act of 1862. Naturally he possessed much material which would throw light on the causes leading to the adoption of a legal tender currency. The book is not a critical history, but is a collation of documents, speeches, and letters relating to the subject. The author was an ardent defender of the legal tender measure. A full synopsis of Congressional debates is given, with the votes. Somewhat fuller extracts are given in favor of the act, but on the whole the book is a useful compendium for opinion on either side. There is also some space devoted to a few of the other finance measures during the Rebellion.

D. R. D.

Sumner, William Graham. History of American currency. N. Y.: Holt. 1874. New ed. 1876. $3. [**2894**

This book consists of sketches in the rough of the principal episodes in the development of the different kinds of currency used in the United States. There is no attempt to connect the several topics, the character of the work being somewhat similar to that of an encyclopædia. But little space is given to the Civil War period. The volume is the product of wide reading in original sources at a time when but little scholarly investigation had been made, and for many years it remained one of the few helpful books in American finance. As students have worked this field more fruitfully in the past quarter of a century, the book does not have the immediate value that it did formerly; but to the careful student of the details of American history, the volume is a most useful guide. There is, however, no table of contents or index, defects which occasion considerable inconvenience. The latter part of the volume, pp. 229-333, treats of the English bank restrictions and Austrian paper money, and in the appendix is a reprint of *The bullion report.*

D. R. D.

—— History of banking in the United States. (Vol. 1 of History of banking in all the leading nations; compiled by thirteen authors. N. Y.: Journal of Commerce. 1896. 4v.) [**2895**

This is a handsome well-made volume both as to type and paper, of nearly 800 pages. The author divides the subject into six monetary periods: 1630-1780; 1780-1812; 1812-1829; 1829-1845; 1845-1863; 1863-. In each chronological period the subject is treated topically, and the subdivisions are so arranged that the reader can easily trace the banking history of each state separately. There is a fairly good index. The author has worked from first sources; for the states north and east of Maryland secondary authorities have been used more liberally. Prof. Sumner is severe in his criticism of early banking methods. He is diligent in the collection of extracts and material, but the work is at times defective in lack of recognition of social and political conditions of the period to which the material belongs. The reader may therefore derive a pessimistic opinion of commercial practice and business intelligence of previous generations. The work practically stops with 1863, for there are only a dozen pages on the last period covering the national banking system. In spite of these deficiencies the volume is by all odds the best collection of material, and is especially serviceable for the reference library. D. R. D.

—— Lectures on the history of protection in the United States. N. Y.: Putnam, for N. Y. Free Trade Club. 1877. 75c. [**2896**

These lectures were delivered before the International Free Trade Alliance in New York in 1876. The author endeavors to show the history of American tariff legislation, attributing to it "weakness, ignorance, confusion, and oscillation," and secondly discusses the arguments for and against free trade as they have presented themselves in the industrial and legislative history of the country. From the standpoint of the author, who writes with a definite purpose to convince others, the work is suggestive. It is not safe, however, to be used as a judicial presentation. The style is characteristically clear and incisive.

D. R. D.

Swank, James Moore. History of the manufacture of iron in all ages, and particularly in the United States, 1585-1885. Phil.: Author. 1884. 2d ed. rev. and enl. Am. Iron and Steel Assoc. 1892. [**2897**

This work is the outgrowth of notes collected over many years and in considerable part derived from information given by manufacturers actively engaged in building up the industry. The author was in charge of the iron and steel statistics for the Census of 1880, and for many years has been Secretary of the American Iron and Steel Association. The volume is a complete history of the American industry and does not emphasize the technical side. Successive chapters, beginning with p. 6, treat of the manufacture in the several states. The work is crowded with detail and is annalistic in character, but lacks style. There is a personal index. D. R. D.

Taussig, Frank William. Tariff history of the United States. (Questions of the day.) N. Y.: Putnam. 1888. 4th ed. rev. 1898. $1.25. [**2898**

This book is made up of a series of separate essays published at various times between 1882 and 1897, by the author, now Professor of political economy at Harvard University. Although the papers are revised, there is a lack of the unity and completeness that the title of the book would properly call for. Nevertheless it is by far the best book on the subject, and for the general student is sufficiently full. The several parts treat of: Protection to young industries as applied in the United States; Early protection movement and the tariff of 1828; History of the existing tariff, 1860-1890; including chapters on the tariff acts of 1894 and 1897, and Some aspects of the tariff question. Although the writer shows his adherence clearly to the free-trade doctrine, there is an entire absence of impatient criticism or denunciation of protectionist thought. The author recognizes that there are social and political elements as well as fiscal in the problem of protection. The book is more than a narrative of legislation; it includes inquiries into the conditions and development of important businesses whose interests have been protected, and presents much of general industrial value. Throughout there is displayed a strong power of analysis and generalization. D. R. D.

—— ed. State papers and speeches on the tariff. Cambridge: Harvard Univ. 1892. N. Y.: Holt. $1. [**2899**

This includes Hamilton's *Report on manufactures,* 1791 ; Gallatin's *Memorial of the free trade convention,* 1831 ; Walker's *Treasury report,* 1845 ; and Clay's and Webster's speeches on the tariff, 1824. These make a convenient collection for those who wish to read the earlier arguments for and against protection as presented by party leaders. The anti-protectionist position is represented by Gallatin's *Memorial,* Walker's *Report,* and Webster's speech. It is to be noted that Webster changed his opinion after 1824. The editor's part is limited to the selection and an introduction of four pages. D. R. D.

United States. *Bureau of Statistics.* Immigration into the United States, 1782–1890. Wash. 1891. [2900

There were no records kept of the arrival of foreigners up to 1820, and from 1820 to 1856 immigrants were not distinguished from other alien passengers. From 1856 to 1868 the immigrants were recorded separately from transient passengers, and from 1868 the number of immigrants of each nationality has been recorded. This volume gives the most complete information afforded by the records of the nationality, sex, age, and occupation of the aliens and immigrants received. The tables containing it are followed by a statement of the principal acts, including the immigration treaty with China, and treasury regulations regarding passengers and immigrants promulgated from 1881 to 1891. F. J. S.

United States. *Public Land Commission.* The public domain; prepared by Thomas Donaldson. Wash. 1881. Rev. 1884. [2901

An extremely useful compilation, but too ill-digested to be used with entire reliance. Almost every matter connected with the territorial history of the United States — colonial grants, state claims and boundaries, national accessions, the various systems of survey, classification, sale and distribution, grants for wagon roads, railroads, canals, etc., and the financial management of the public land system — will be found treated at more or less length. As is usual in such works, there is extended inclusion of statutes, official instructions, diagrams and maps, blank forms, etc. W. MacD.

Walker, F. Double taxation in the U. S. See Columbia University, sect. 257. [2902

Watson, David K. History of American coinage. N. Y.: Putnam. 1899. 2d ed. rev. and enl. $1.50. [2903

This is an interesting narrative of the history of gold and silver coinage in the United States beginning with the colonial mint of Massachusetts, established in 1652. It is a history of legislation and legislative opinion, rather than an account of the more technical details of the art of minting. The history of the Acts of 1873, 1890, and 1893 are given quite fully, including amendments, conference reports, votes, etc. The author quotes freely from acts of Congress, reports of committees and public documents, and is precise in his references. The work is not an exhaustive monograph, but, as far as it goes, scholarly in form and spirit. It is of special merit in throwing light upon the question of bimetallism and the position of

the American silver dollar in the American coinage system. The author is opposed to the free coinage of silver. In the appendix is a reprint of the reports made by the Board of Treasury to Congress April 8, 1786, with a letter, etc., of the Board. There is a good index. The first edition does not give as much attention to the acts of 1834 and 1853. D. R. D.

Webster, Pelatiah. Political essays on the nature and operation of money, public finance, and other subjects. Phil.: Cruikshank. 1791. [2904

This work in no sense belongs to narrative history, but presents the reasoning which governed the states in their fluctuating finance from 1776 to the adoption of the Constitution. The author is a very severe critic of the issue of paper money, although he admits that some of the disastrous consequences which he anticipated were not realized. He covers the topics of taxation and paper money. Pages 128 to 138 contain strictures on the tender acts ; pp. 198 to 221 are devoted to the nature of the political union of the thirteen states; pp. 376 to 402 discuss the establishment of the national capital in which the author favors Philadelphia ; pp. 403 to 406 argue in favor of the adoption of the constitution ; pp. 444 to 464 give a short history of the Bank of North America. The last essay treats of the extent and value of the western unlocated lands. In the appendix are given four scales of appreciation of Continental money by months for the years 1777 to 1781, the scales representing those of Congress, the Assembly of Pennsylvania, and merchants' books in Philadelphia and Virginia. D. R. D.

Weeden, William Babcock. Economic and social history of New England, 1620–1789. Boston: Houghton. 1890. 2v. $4.50. [2905

The best book yet written from which to obtain an idea of the life in colonial and provincial New England, the work of an industrious antiquarian fully equipped through patient study in the historical libraries, of sufficient judgment to avoid being overwhelmed by the weight of his materials, possessed also of a faculty of presentment, so that the story is set forth entertainingly. In the foreground are such topics as the intercourse of Indians and colonists, the tenure and management of lands, the merging of the early barter into larger commerce, the development under many embarrassments of manufactures, manners and morals, survivals of ancient and mediæval usages, finance, schools, ideas as to charities and corrections, dress, indentured servants, religion. It is a vast array of topics with the statements well fortified by citation of patiently sought authorities. Among matters of special interest, as subjects here for the first time well presented, or subjects bearing in important ways on great events, or as subjects especially capable of picturesque treatment, may be mentioned the economic and symbolic use of wampum, the slavetrade, the whale-fishery, currency problems, and piracy. Interspersed are sketches of persons, hardly to be reckoned as historic figures, but interesting and instructive as types, — such as John Hull, Peter Faneuil, and Haskett Derby. J. K. H.

White, Horace. Money and banking illustrated by American history. Boston : Ginn. 1895. $1.50. [2906

Only a portion of this volume belongs strictly to American history. Beginning with page 120 there is a narrative account and discussion of colonial paper money, continental money, greenbacks, confederate currency, the gold reserve, the silver dollar and its demonetization. In book ii, p. 248, there is a detailed sketch of colonial banking, the First and Second Banks of the U. S., the Suffolk banking system, safety fund system, free bank system, and national banks. There is an excellent bibliography of nine pages and an index. The author has pronounced opinions as to the advisability of the cancellation of greenbacks and the abandonment of the banking business by the U. S. government, and writes to convince his readers of the evils which have come from legal-tender powers granted to paper money and also from silver coinage. The work has a wealth of interesting material, is written in an entertaining and scholarly style, and easily stands as one of the best books on the money question in the United States. D. R. D.

The author is editor of the *Evening post*, New York. An enlarged edition of *Money and banking*, revised to date, is to be issued early in 1902.

Whitney, Josiah Dwight. The United States : facts and figures illustrating the physical geography of the country and its material resources. Boston : Little. 1889.

—— Supplement 1 : Population, immigration, irrigation. Boston : Little. 1894. Net $2. [2907

Originally written as the article on *United States* in the Encyclopædia Britannica, edition 1888, and so printed, but with certain condensations and changes. Now published in full with corrections and a supplement, giving results of various investigations by the federal government on population, irrigation, reforestation, etc. Valuable as a repository of information on resources of the United States. E. E. S.

Wright, Carroll Davidson. Report on the factory system of the United States. (In U. S. Census, 1880. Reports on manufactures.) Wash. 1883. [2908

The author, at the time Chief of the Bureau of Statistics of Labor of Massachusetts, was a special agent of the U. S. census. He reports on the history of the factory system not only in the U. S., but also as to its origin and growth in Great Britain. He considers the results, benefits and disadvantages of the system, drawn from personal observations in the principal factory towns of Europe in a visit made in 1881. But a small portion — pp. 5-16 — of this belongs strictly to the history of the United States. The essay is not only statistical in its character, but also embraces a philosophical discussion of the new system of industry. Various chapters are devoted to the influences of the factory system, upon wages, prices, and production, factory legislation in Europe, homes of factory operatives, and the future of the factory system. There are several plates of the houses of operatives, and a bibliography. D. R. D.

Young, Andrew W. National economy : history of the American protective system. N. Y. 1860. [2909

Gives summaries of congressional debates.

DIVISION 5 : EDUCATIONAL HISTORY

(Excepting one or two notes that are otherwise signed, the selection and appraisal of books in this division are by the late Professor B. A. Hinsdale, of the University of Michigan, whose death followed the completion of this task after no long interval.)

Adams, Herbert Baxter. College of William and Mary. (U. S. Bur. of Education. Circ. of information, 1887, no. 1.) Wash. 1887. [2910

This is No. 1 of the valuable series of monographs edited by Dr. Adams for the United States Bureau of Education. It gives in outline the history of the second college planted in the United States, and, all things ·considered, the most influential one ever planted south of Mason and Dixon's line. Incidentally much light is thrown upon the history of culture in Virginia and the states farther to the southward.

—— Thomas Jefferson and the University of Virginia. With authorized sketches of Hampden-Sidney, Randolph-Macon, Emory-Henry, Roanoke, and Richmond colleges, Washington and Lee University, and Virginia Military Institute. (U. S. Bur. of education. Circ. of information, 1888, no. 1.) Wash. 1888. [2911

No. 2 of the *Series of monographs* edited by Dr. Adams for the national Bureau of Education, entitled *Contributions to American educational history.* The monograph is an excellent account of the origin and history of the first real university planted in the United States, and an important contribution to the general history of culture in Virginia and the old South. The authorized sketches of other institutions of learning in the state add materially to its value.

Alexander, Archibald. Biographical sketches of the founder and principal alumni of the Log college. Princeton. 1845. Phil.: Presbyterian Bd. of Pub. [c. 1851.] [2912

An interesting picture of the first of that primitive type of educational institutions, the log colleges, that came to be so prominent and so useful in certain parts of the country. Founded by Rev. William Tennant at Neshaminy, Pa., about 1726. The book also throws light upon the great religious revivals of the last century, including the work of George Whitefield.

American Historical Association. *Committee of seven.* Study of history in schools : report by Andrew C. McLaughlin, Herbert B. Adams. George L. Fox, Albert Bushnell Hart,

Charles H. Haskins, Lucy M. Salmon, H. Morse Stephens. N. Y.: Macmillan. 1899. 50c.

—— *Same.* (In Report of the Association, 1898.) [2913

The report of a committee of teachers of history appointed by the American Historical Association to consider the subject of history in the secondary schools and to draw up a scheme of college entrance requirements in history. It recommends at least a four years' course of four periods each. These are fully described. A list of valuable books and maps relating to the subject is added.   E. E. S.

Ballantine, W. G., *ed.* Oberlin jubilee, 1833–83. Oberlin : Goodrich. 1883. [2914

For note, see under Fairchild, James H., below, sect. 2927.

Barnard, Frederick Augustus Porter. FULTON, JOHN. Memoirs of Frederick A. P. Barnard, tenth president of Columbia College. N. Y.: pub. for Columbia Univ. press, by Macmillan. 1896. Net $4. [2915

This work has a double interest. It is in form a biography of a distinguished scholar and educator, but the story is so told as to include a part of the history of several important educational institutions. Dr. Barnard studied and taught as a tutor in Yale College, served as a professor in the University of Alabama, was also a professor in, and afterwards president of, the University of Mississippi, and finally rounded out his life as president of Columbia College, 1864–1888. However, the author does not attempt a full history of Columbia for the period of Dr. Barnard's administration. The work is carefully prepared, mainly from Barnard's papers, and is a contribution of decided value to the educational history of the times.

Barnard, Henry, *ed.* Educational biography: memoirs of teachers, educators and promoters and benefactors of education, literature and science. N. Y.: Brownell. 1859. V. 1. [2916

This is a series of thirty admirable memoirs, nearly all of men who were active in the great educational revival that marked the first half of the present century in the United States, reprinted from the *American journal of education.* Some of the articles were written by the editor of that journal, Dr. Henry Barnard, and the others by writers selected by him. The title is misleading ; it is limited to teachers and educators, the volume that was to include benefactors, etc., never having been published.

Blackmar, Frank Wilson. History of federal and state aid to higher education in the United States. (U. S. Bur. of Education. Circ. of information, 1890, no. 1.) Wash. 1890.

[2917

No. 9 of Contributions to *American educational history.* The monograph contains a great amount of important information, well arranged and presented.

While professing to deal with only a single phase of a specific subject, it really presents a much wider view, and is one of the most valuable of the series to which it belongs.

Boone, Richard G. Education in the United States ; its history. (International education ser.) N. Y.: Appleton. 1889. $1.50.

[2918

The value of the book lies in its encyclopædic character ; it is an inventory, tolerably complete, of valuable facts pertaining to the general history of education in the United States. It is more valuable for the period following the Revolutionary War than for the colonial period. Contains an introduction by Dr. W. T. Harris.

—— History of education in Indiana. N. Y.: Appleton. 1892. [2919

This book presents an outline view of the growth and conditions of education, particularly state education, in Indiana, from the organization of the territory northwest of the River Ohio, and is a valuable compilation of facts.

Bourne, William Oland. History of the Public School Society of the city of New York. N. Y.: Wood. 1870. [2920

An exhaustive history of public elementary education in the metropolis, from the birth of the Public School Society in 1805 to its union with the Board of Education in 1853. One of the characteristic features of the work is the full account of the unsuccessful effort made by the Roman Catholic Church, led by Archbishop Hughes, to secure a portion of the public school funds for the support of the Catholic parochial schools. The book is rich in documents, a veritable mine of information, but not inviting to any but specialists.

Boynton, *Capt.* **Edward Carlisle.** History of West Point and its military importance during the Am. Revolution ; and origin and progress of the United States military academy. N. Y.: Van Nostrand. 1863. [2921

The contents of this book are about equally divided between the two topics named in the title. In the second part the author, who was a captain in the United States army and adjutant of the military academy, presents a general view of the school from its organization in 1794 to the date of publication. The work was subjected to the revision of competent authorities at the academy, and was published with their approbation and encouragement.

Chase, Frederick. History of Dartmouth College and the town of Hanover, N. H.: ed. by J. K. Lord. Cambridge : J. Wilson, Univ. Press. 1891. [V. 2 not published.] [2922

This work traces the life of Dr. Eleazar Wheelock from birth to his founding of Dartmouth College, in 1770, then follows the broader history till his death in 1779, and last relates the later story of the College down to 1815. The book shows indefatigable research, and it is hard for the critic to believe that the author left anything of value to be discovered. The story is one of unique interest, but it is marred, save for those immediately interested, by its minuteness and detail. The characteristic of early Dartmouth was its dedication to the cause of Indian education.

Cleveland, Nehemiah. History of Bowdoin College, with biog. sketches of graduates, 1806–79 ; ed. and completed by A. S. Packard. Boston: Osgood. 1882. [2923

The principal value of this heavy volume lies in its carefully prepared biographies of trustees and professors, and especially alumni of the College. The historical matter properly so-called, while well prepared, is slight. The book is keyed to the sentence quoted from President Quincy in the preface. "No duty is more incumbent upon seminaries of learning than the commemoration of the virtues and labors which have contributed to their existence and prosperity."

Clews, Elsie W. Educational legislation and administration of the colonial governments. (Columbia Univ. Contributions to philosophy, etc., v. 6, nos. 1–4.) N. Y.: Macmillan. 1899. Net $2. [2924

A thesis submitted to the faculty of philosophy of Columbia University, in partial fulfillment of the requirements for the degree of Ph. D. It is a painstaking compilation and a useful addition to the literature of colonial education.

Cornell, Ezra. CORNELL, ALONZO BARTON. Biography of Ezra Cornell, founder of the Cornell University. N. Y.: Barnes. 1884. [2925

This volume presents an adequate history of a career remarkable both in business and in philanthropy. Scholars and students of educational history will find the centre of interest in the three chapters that deal with the great institution of learning that bears Mr. Cornell's name. Here will be found a comprehensive but clear account of the institution from its inception to its complete establishment. Two other chapters deal with the Cornell library, an earlier foundation, which was, in a sense, the forerunner of the university.

Demmon, I. N., *et al.* Semi-centennial celebration of the organization of the University of Michigan, June 26–30, 1887. Ann Arbor: pub. by the Univ. 1888. [2926

Besides the introductory sketch, this volume consists of the addresses and speeches made at the commemoration named in the title, together with congratulatory letters, programmes, etc. The most valuable of the addresses are Professor Frieze's *Relations of the state university to religion*, Mr. Justice S. F. Miller's *The Supreme Court of the United States*, and President James B. Angell's *Commemoration oration*. The book is an indispensable part of the University's history.

Fairchild, James H. Oberlin, the colony and the college, 1833–83. Oberlin, O.: Goodrich. 1883.

—— BALLANTINE, W. G., *ed.* The Oberlin jubilee, 1833–83. Oberlin, O.: Goodrich. 1883. [2927

Together these two works, which are really companions, present a full view of Oberlin history for its first half century. The first one presents the colony and the college in their mutual relations particularly, while the jubilee addresses deal almost wholly with prominent phases of college work and influence. The books are strongly marked by Oberlin thought and feeling.

Fay, Edwin Whitfield. History of education in Louisiana. (U. S. Bur. of Education, Circ. of information, 1898, no. 1.) Wash. 1898. [2928

This well-prepared monograph gives a full outline view of the history of education in a community that has a peculiarly composite character and changeful history. Perhaps the most curious section is the account of the old University of Orleans, somewhat resembling the University of France ; created, on paper, three years before that famous organization was put in motion, but unlike in proving a total failure.

Four American universities. N. Y.: Harper. 1895. $3.50. [2929

This volume comprises sketches of four leading universities from the hands of representatives at their own faculties at the time they were written : Harvard, Charles Eliot Norton ; Yale, Arthur T. Hadley ; Princeton, William N. Sloane ; Columbia, Brander Matthews. These names guarantee the excellence of the letterpress, which is well set off by the illustrations. The writers do not attempt formal histories, but rather sketches, at once scholarly and popular. Of the kind, no better accounts of the four institutions have been written.

Germann, George B. National legislation concerning education, its influence and effect in the public land states east of the Mississippi River, admitted prior to 1820. N. Y. : Author. 1899. $1. [2930

This study was submitted to the faculty of philosophy, Columbia University, as a thesis in partial fulfillment of the requirements for the degree of Doctor of Philosophy. It is a careful piece of work, dealing with the national legislation concerning education of a general character previous to the admission of any of the public land states, and then with Ohio, Tennessee, Indiana, Mississippi, Illinois, and Alabama. State legislation has been introduced only for the purpose of interpreting and binding together the acts of Congress.

Goode, George Brown. Origin of the national, scientific and educational institutions of the United States. (In Am. Hist. Assoc. Annual rept., 1889.) Wash.: Govt. Prtg. Off. 1890. [2931

An admirable presentation of the subject, revised and corrected to July, 1890. Numerous documents, as

Joel Barlow's Prospectus of a national institution to be established in the United States, 1806, and a still earlier plan of a Federal University, are included.

—— *ed.* Smithsonian Institution, 1846-96. Wash. 1897.   [2932

This work is divided into two main parts. First comes, following the preface and introduction, a series of fifteen chapters, dealing with the more important historical phases of the Smithsonian Institution, as the life of Smithson, the founding of the institution, the establishment of the board of regents, etc., and then a series of appreciations of its work in various departments, as physics, mathematics, and astronomy, also fifteen in number. Both series of chapters are from the pens of recognized specialists and experts. The work is of the highest authority, and a very valuable contribution to the history of science in America.

Gordy, J. P. Rise and growth of the normal school idea in the United States. (U. S. Bur. of Education. Circ. of information, 1891, no. 8.) Wash. 1891.   [2933

The author presents a clear outline of his subject from a time anterior to the appearance of the normal school idea until its final incorporation in the American common school system. Then he sketches certain typical schools, in which, as he judges, the idea has attained to its best development. Brief chapters are devoted to several debatable topics, as to chairs of pedagogy in universities and colleges, for example.

Guild, Reuben Aldridge. History of Brown University, with illustrative documents. Providence, R. I. 1867.

—— Life, times, and correspondence of James Manning, and early history of Brown University. Boston: Gould. 1864.   [2934

These two works present, with some overlapping, the history of the institution that was first called Rhode Island College, afterwards Brown University, from its small beginning just before the Revolutionary War to the dates of publication. Mr. Guild was not only a Brown University man, but for many years its librarian, and wrote from large personal knowledge and active personal sympathy. His two books are essential to the student of the history of their subject.

Hinsdale, Burke Aaron, *comp.* Documents illustrative of American educational history. (Reprint from U. S. Commissioner of Education. Rept., 1892-3, v. 2, pp. 1225-1414.) Wash. 1895.   [2935

The subjects to which these documents relate are Massachusetts, Plymouth, Connecticut, and Pennsylvania school legislation; the Connecticut school fund; Congressional land grants for common schools and universities; Colleges of agriculture and mechanical arts; Bureau of Education; a national university, and educational provisions of the state constitutions. The documents are annotated, and the publication is a contribution to the raw material of educational history.

Knight, George W. History and management of land grants for education in the northwest territory. (American Historical Assoc. Papers, v. 1, no. 3.) N. Y.: Putnam. 1885.   [2936

A good piece of original investigation, and indispensable to students of the educational history of the country. The book deals with the origin, so far as endowments are concerned, of the western state universities, as well as the common schools, of the old Northwest.

Lewis, Samuel. LEWIS, WILLIAM G. W. Biography of Samuel Lewis, first Superintendent of common schools for the state of Ohio. Cin. 1857.   [2937

Mr. Lewis, a resident of Ohio from 1812 to his death in 1854, was bred to the bar, but he was more prominent in politics and reformatory movements than in his profession. He was a leader of the anti-slavery interests in the state, and one of the most active and useful of the men who established the public school system, over which he presided as the first Superintendent, antedating by a few months even Horace Mann in Massachusetts. This carefully prepared biography is a valuable contribution to the antislavery and particularly to the educational literature of the time.

McLaughlin, Andrew Cunningham. History of higher education in Michigan. (U. S. Bur. of Education. Circ. of information, 1891, no. 4.) Wash. 1891.   [2938

No. 11 of Contributions to American educational history, published by the U. S. Bureau of Education. The book contains a full account of the University of Michigan by the present Professor of American history in that institution, and of the other institutions of higher learning in the state by responsible writers. The principal value of the monograph consists in the fact that it sets forth the origin and character of the Michigan system of public instruction.

Maclean, John. History of the College of New Jersey, to 1854. Phil.: Lippincott. 1877. 2v.   [2939

Written by its tenth President at the request of the governing authorities, this work may be termed an official history of the College of New Jersey, now Princeton University, down to the year 1854. It is particularly full and satisfactory for the earlier period. The author denies the truth of the common account that the College of New Jersey was an outgrowth of the Log College at Meshaminy, Pa.

Mann, Horace. HINSDALE, BURKE AARON. Horace Mann and the common school revival in the United States. (Great educators.) N. Y.: Scribner. 1898. Net $1.   [2940

" Aside from the practical importance of the work and permanent influence of Horace Mann, his uncommon moral and mental traits, the pathetic incidents of his private life, and the dramatic events of his public career, leading up to the tragic catastrophe at

Antioch College, are fascinating in the extreme. Prof. Hinsdale has succeeded admirably in giving in comprehensive, compact, and, withal, very readable form, all the essentials of the life and main work of the great educator." *Nation*, 66: 148.

Martin, George H. Evolution of the Massachusetts public school system. (International education ser.) N. Y.: Appleton. 1894. $1.50. [2941

The book well fulfills its title: it is a well-written historical sketch of the Massachusetts system of public schools from the Puritan fathers down. The author is an experienced educator, possesses literary gifts, and shows throughout a warm appreciation of the educational work of Massachusetts. The book contains a characteristic preface by the editor of the series to which it belongs, Dr. W. T. Harris.

Meriwether, Colyer. History of higher education in South Carolina ; with a sketch of the free school system. (U. S. Bur. of Education. Circ. of information, 1888, no. 3.) Wash. 1889. [2942

No. 4 of Contributions to American educational history. It is a comprehensive view of the subject. One of the most valuable features of the book is Appendix II, pp. 211–235, *Education in South Carolina prior to and during the Revolution*, by Edward McCready, Jr., in refutation of certain statements made by Professor McMaster in his *History of the people of the United States.*

Merriam, Lucius Salisbury. Higher education in Tennessee. (U. S. Bur. of Education. Circ. of information, 1893, no. 5.) Wash. 1893. [2943

The student of our educational history will find the chief significance of this book in the development of higher education in a new state, the second to be organized west of the Allegheny Mountains. The work is carefully done, only the few pages devoted to the public school system should have been more in number, and should have been put at the beginning rather than at the end.

New England's first fruits in respect to the progress of learning at Cambridge, 1643. See Massachusetts Historical Society, sect. 286.
[2944

Peabody, George. CURRY, J. L. M. Brief sketch of George Peabody, and a history of the Peabody Education Fund. Cambridge: Univ. Press. 1898. [2945

No man is more competent to deal historically with the Peabody Educational Fund than the present Secretary of the Board of Trustees. The book is comprehensive but luminous, and culminates in the history of the normal school carried on on the foundation of the University of Nashville. A feature of the book is the series of "appreciations" of the notable men connected with the trust whose terms of service had expired by death or otherwise in the period covered.

Occasionally the author's southern feeling crops out, but is generally held under restraint. The volume presents, also, a general view of Mr. Peabody's life and character.

Peter, Robert *and* **Johanna.** Transylvania University; its origin, rise, decline, and fall. (Filson Club. Publications, no. 11.) Louisville, Ky.: Morton. 1896. [2946

A fitting memorial, in the handsome style of the Filson Club, of the first institution of higher learning founded west of the Allegheny Mountains, and the first to confer the degrees of Bachelor of Arts and Doctor of Medicine. Dr. Peter was long an active member of the University Faculty, and writes from an intimate personal knowledge of his subject. His story, at least in part, relieves the apparent extravagance of the statement of the Secretary of the Filson Club, who declares in his preface that if the original policy had been persisted in, Transylvania would to-day be one of the leading universities of the country and the world, but was doomed, he says, upon the altar of denominational antagonism. The book is also valuable for the light that it throws upon the early history of culture in the Ohio valley.

Pierce, John. Notes on Harvard commencements. See Massachusetts Historical Society, sect. 342. [2947

Quincy, Josiah. History of Harvard University. Cambridge: Owen. 1840. 2v. 2d ed. Boston: Crosby. 1860. [2948

This work, written by the President and published with the sanction of the corporation of Harvard University, has the rank and dignity of an official history. The author disclaims that character, but his book is the standard authority on the subject for the first two centuries of Harvard history. It originated with the celebration of the second centennial, 1836. The history is marked by the weighty matter and grave style so characteristic of President Quincy. Documentary and statistical material filling more than 400 pages is found in the appendices.

Randall, Samuel Sidwell. History of the common school system of the state of New York. N. Y.: Ivison. 1871. [2949

The author was at one time Deputy State Superintendent of common schools, and afterwards Superintendent of public schools of the city of New York. His book contains little of value relating to the colonial period, but is satisfactory for the period it is intended to cover. The numerous quotations from public documents add value to the work, but, together with the author's habitual style, tend to make it heavy reading. The accounts of religious controversies in the state and city of New York are marked by fairness and impartiality, a note of the book throughout.

Rupp, G. P., *ed.* Twenty-eighth annual report of the Board of Directors of city trusts of the city of Philadelphia for 1897. Phil. 1898. [2950

The interest of this volume is suggested by the alternative title, "Report of the proceedings in connection with the semi-centennial anniversary of the opening of Girard College, January 3, 1898." The story of this unique institution, and of the celebration of its fiftieth anniversary, is well told in the addresses, historical statements, and documents presented.

Shearman, Francis W. System of public instruction and primary school law of Michigan. Lansing. 1852. [2951

A very useful compilation, consisting of laws, reports, extracts from official documents, etc., bearing on education in the state, with sufficient narrative and explanatory matter to bind the documents together and to make them intelligible. Here will be found a complete presentation of the rise and development down to 1852 of the Michigan system of public instruction.

Stearns, John William, *ed.* Columbian history of education in Wisconsin. Pub. under authority and by direction of the state committee on educational exhibit for Wisconsin. Milwaukee. 1893. [2952

This volume of sketches and accounts, with a few general chapters, deals with the institutional features of education in the state from territorial days to 1893. The work was done on the coöperative plan, and is of great value as a book of educational information. It contains numerous brief biographies of prominent educators in the history of the state, and is illustrated with portraits.

Steiner, Bernard Christian. History of education in Connecticut. (U. S. Bur. of Education. Circ. of information, 1893, no. 2.) Wash. 1893. [2953

The history of education in Connecticut is of peculiar interest, from the day that New Haven, under the guidance of Davenport and Eaton, resolved " to train up youth that, through God's blessing, they may be fitted for public service either in church or common weal." This interesting subject is well handled by the writer, and the monograph is one of·the most interesting of the series.

—— History of education in Maryland. (U. S. Bur. of Education. Circ. of information, 1894, no. 2.) Wash. 1894. [2954

This monograph presents an interesting account of education in Maryland from the early colonial days. Different parts of the work are written by different authors, that on Johns Hopkins University by President Gilman. The history of the " dead colleges " contains an account of Cokesbury College, the first attempt made by the Methodists to found an institution of higher education.

Sturtevant, Julian Monson. An autobiography. N. Y.: Revell. 1897. [2955

This book offers to the student of educational history two interesting pictures, one of an Ohio boy resorting to Yale College early in the century in quest of an education ; the other of the same boy, grown to be a man, engaged in building up a new college in the

West (Illinois College). The book also gives views of many phases of pioneer life, and sheds light upon the efforts put forth in the East to promote education and religion in the West.

Ten Brook, Andrew. American state universities, their origin and progress: a history of congressional university land-grants. Cinc.: Clarke. 1875. $1.50. [2956

The interest of this work is found in the general account of the western state universities, and in the particular account of the first of these institutions to attract national attention, that is, the University of Michigan. For these purposes, it possesses considerable value. The author was at one time a professor in the University of Michigan, and he wrote with a full knowledge of its history from the beginning.

Thorpe, Francis Newton, *ed.* Benjamin Franklin and the University of Pennsylvania. (U. S. Bur. of Education. Circ. of information, 1892, no. 2.) Wash. 1893. [2957

This valuable monograph renders Franklin and the University of Pennsylvania more interesting, for the writer's purpose, by the fact of their being coupled together. The opening chapters, devoted to Franklin's self-education, and his ideas of education as seen in his writings, pp. 9–205, form a fitting introduction to the history of the University, and give, no doubt, the best account of the educational side of the philosopher's mind and life that is accessible in any single work.

Tolman, William Howe. History of higher education in Rhode Island. (U. S. Bur. of Education. Circ. of information, 1894, no. 1.) Wash. 1894. [2958

The history of higher education in Rhode Island is unique in this, that it is wholly the history of Brown University. Nor was there any system of public schools until a comparatively late date. The author has, however, prefixed to his history of Brown University accounts of elementary education previous to the establishment of the present system, and of various academies, preparatory schools, and ladies' seminaries that existed in the earlier period.

Tyler, William S. History of Amherst College during the administrations of its first five presidents, 1821–91. N. Y.: Hitchcock. 1895. [2959

This abridgment of the author's larger work, *History of Amherst College during its first half century* (Springfield, Mass.: Clark W. Bryan & Co. 1873), traces the history of the institution from its feeble beginning through seventy years of growth. The author was long connected with the college as a student and professor, and writes *con amore*. His book may be called a " warm " book, glowing, as it does, with interest in and devotion to the college. The religious life of Amherst, which has always been remarkable, is fully recognized.

Venable, William Henry. Beginnings of

literary culture in the Ohio valley. Cinc.:
Clarke. 1891. Net $3. [2960

An important contribution to the history of western
civilization, showing research and literary skill. The
book takes a wide view of the subject, embracing
schools and education, newspapers, literary periodicals and books, societies of various kinds, science
and the professions, publishing enterprises, the pulpit
and the bar, political oratory and orators, annalists,
travellers and missionaries, teachers and men of letters. The numerous sketches of men and women
abound in fact, incident, and anecdote.

White, Emerson Elbridge, *and* **T. W.
Harvey,** *eds.* History of education in the
state of Ohio : a centennial volume ; pub. by
authority of the General Assembly. Columbus. 1876. [2961

This work was prepared on the coöperative plan
under the direction of the Centennial Committee
of the Ohio Teachers' Association as a part of the
representation of the educational interests of the
state at the Centennial Exhibition at Philadelphia.
With the exception of female seminaries, it deals
with all the principal features of education that had
been developed previous to 1876. While marked by
the usual defects of books prepared on the same plan,
such as overlapping and lack of coördination, the
work was still prepared with care by some of the foremost educators of the state and is of permanent
value.

Wickersham, James Pyle. History of
education in Pennsylvania. Lancaster, Penn.:
Author. 1886. [2962

The best state history of education yet produced in
this country. A competent scholar, the author of valuable educational works, for years State Superintendent
of public instruction and editor of the *Pennsylvania
school journal,* and a student of much diligence and
fairness of mind, the author possessed unusual qualifications for the preparation of such a work. Bred a
Quaker, he naturally took much interest in setting
forth the educational views of the fathers of the
Society of Friends, and such of their religious views
as he deemed favorable to education. The interest of
the books culminates in the development of the free
school system in the state.

Wood, George B. History of the University of Pennsylvania to 1827. See Pennsylvania, Historical Society of, sect. 372. [2963

DIVISION 6: CHURCH
HISTORY

(Except as otherwise signed or credited, the notes in this
Division have been prepared by Professor Samuel Macauley
Jackson, Professor of Church History, New York Univer-
sity, who has also supplied the introductory note on the
"Sources of American Church history." — See, also, in Part
I : Sources, sect. 39.)

SOURCES OF AMERICAN CHURCH HISTORY

American church history is virgin soil, which
under cultivation will yield much fruit and a
few flowers ! Up to the present time the surface has been only scratched, mainly over the
graves of the Puritan ancestors. The explanation is two-fold: the cultivators of American
history in general have naturally been New
Englanders, proud of their descent from those
who exiled themselves for opinion's sake, and
they have felt little drawn away from home;
while those springing from the newer parts of
the country have made history rather than
written it. So it has come about that, except
in what relates to the Congregationalists of
New England, there is little that is satisfactory. [2964

It must be confessed that, generally speaking, American church history is not, as hitherto
written, specially interesting, much less fascinating. The subject has too many subdivisions
and the human material among the emigrants
is for the most part too commonplace. The
Pilgrim Fathers look well in the mellow light
of the Mayflower's cabin ; but, alas, so many
of the other early emigrants were unattractive
that the sects they started or perpetuated, carrying over into the new world the feuds of the
old, are narrow, appeal to emotional rather
than to educated audiences, and set up a code
of conduct based on the example of John the
Baptist rather than of Jesus himself. Again,
the religious history of our country does not
centre around any one individual. Each sect
or section has its particular star, but there
is no central sun around which they all re-
volve. Consequently our interest is distracted,
and we find ourselves studying temporary
movements of very minor consequence. Still,
as American general history has been relieved
of the charge of dulness by the skilful treatment it has received, perhaps American religious history will be, also. But, at present,
heavy vapors hang about the subject. [2965

A professor of American history once complained that the church history of America consisted of the lives of clergymen ! True, it does ;
but the clergymen were the leaders, and all
history is made up of the doings of the leaders.
The remark suggests the further one that the
study of religious biography is of primary importance, for biography is raw material for history. [2966

The sources of American church history are varied and scattered. Nor is there any great centre for collections of them. Broadly speaking, they may be divided into the unprinted and the printed. The former are again the written and the unwritten. Such sources are everywhere to be discovered, either collected or not. They consist of letters, annotations, sermons, family trees, inscriptions, and the like; also monuments, such as churches and tombstones, and historic scenes, legends — whatever has to do with man which has not found its way into print. The unprinted sources are in private hands, in public libraries, and in the open air. They have not been utilized to any extent. [2967

The printed sources are also very miscellaneous. They may be divided into the biographic, including the genealogical, and the general, denominational or local historical — such as sermons, orations and formal treatises. As a rule they are not literature. They appeal, and that only feebly, to a limited, frequently to a very prejudiced, audience. Those that proceed from denominational publishing houses make no pretense of interesting those not of the denomination, and commonly they do not. Many such books do not get into the currents of the book trade at all. Few of them, however, sent into the world, ever sell more than a single edition, if they do that. In the list which follows, and as I did not draw it up but only revised and slightly enlarged it I feel the freer to commend it as fairly representative, those books which give bibliographies are specially mentioned in the annotations. Some of them also indicate where denominational sources have been collected in considerable number. [2968

Putting together the information acquired from them and other sources, the following is a list of a few of the libraries particularly rich in literature, both printed and in MS., to which the student of American church history should be directed, classed by denominations, alphabetically arranged: —

BAPTISTS: American Historical Society, Philadelphia, Pa.; Colgate historical collection, Hamilton, N. Y.

CONGREGATIONALISTS: Congregational Library, Boston, Mass.; Theological Seminary, Hartford, Conn.; Yale University, New Haven, Conn.; American Antiquarian Society, Worcester, Mass.

FRIENDS: London Yearly Meeting, 12 Bishopsgate Street Without, London, England.

LUTHERANS: Lutheran Historical Society, Gettysburg, Pa.; University of Pennsylvania (Beckstein collection), Philadelphia, Pa.; Lutheran Theological Seminary, Mount Airy, Philadelphia, Pa.; St. Matthew's German Church, Manhattan, New York City.

METHODISTS: Methodist Book Concern, Manhattan, New York City; Drew Theological Seminary, Madison, N. J.

MORAVIANS: Moravian Church Archives, Bethlehem, Pa.

PRESBYTERIANS: Presbyterian Historical Society, Philadelphia, Pa.; Theological Seminary, Princeton, N. J.; Union Theological Seminary (Gillett collection), Manhattan, New York City.

PROTESTANT EPISCOPALIANS: General Theological Seminary, Manhattan, New York City.

REFORMED (DUTCH): Theological Seminary, New Brunswick, N. J.

REFORMED (GERMAN): Theological department of Ursinus College, Philadelphia, Pa.; Theological Seminary of the Reformed Church, Lancaster, Pa.

ROMAN CATHOLICS: The American Catholic Historical Society, Philadelphia, Pa.; The United States Catholic Society, Manhattan, New York City.

UNITARIANS: Harvard University, Cambridge, Mass.; Public Library, Boston, Mass.

UNITED BRETHREN: Historical Society of the Church of the United Brethren, Dayton, Ohio.

UNIVERSALISTS: Universalist Historical Society, Tufts College, Medford, Mass.; St. Lawrence University, Canton, N. Y. [2969

Adams, C. F., *ed.* Antinomianism in the colony of Massachusetts Bay. See Prince Society, sect. 387. [2970

Alexander, Gross. History of the Methodist Episcopal Church, South. (In Am. church history series, v. 11, pp. 1–142. N. Y.: Christian Lit. Co. 1894. Scribner. Net $2.) [2971

This occupies pages 1-142 of v. 11 of the *American church history* series; also separately issued. The author is professor of Greek exegesis in Vanderbilt University, and an enthusiastic student of his denominational history, while at the same time inclined to deal fairly with northern Methodism. The style is rather exuberant. After one page of bibliography and two pages of preface the author presents his history, treating it according to its development as exhibited by the successive general conferences and quoting liberally from the sources. The matter is separately indexed.

Allen, Joseph Henry. Historical sketch of the Unitarian movement since the reformation. (In Am. church history series, v. 10, p. 249. N. Y.: Christian Lit. Co. 1894. Scribner. $2.) [2972

The first part of Vol. X of the *American church history* series, but also separately issued. As the title indicates, it is not so much the history of a denomination as of a movement. Accordingly seven of its ten chapters are devoted to this movement in Europe from its origin in Italy prior to the Reformation to its modern English development. The chapters on the movement in the United States during the 19th century are very largely derived from and rendered authoritative by the author's personal acquaintance with its initiators and principal leaders. There is no formal bibliography, but ample marginal references. At the end is an important letter from James Martineau. The whole is separately indexed.

American Baptist Historical Society. Philadelphia, Pa. This society was organized in 1853, and has published *Annual reports* from 1865, and other publications relating to the history of the Baptist church in the U. S. [2973

American Catholic Historical Society. Philadelphia. This society was organized in 1884, and has published *Records*, 12 volumes from 1884 to 1901, and a quarterly *Bulletin*, the only volume of which appeared in 1892. [2974

American Society of Church History. New York City. This society was organized in 1888, and from 1893 to 1897 published a series of histories of American churches, under the general title, *American church history* series, the several volumes of which are separately noticed under this division. In the volumes of papers on church history published by the Society, only a few relate to American subjects. On Dec. 31, 1896, the society was amalgamated with the American Historical Association, which formed a church history section. [2975

Anderson, James Stuart Murray. History of the Church of England in the colonies and foreign dependencies of the British Empire. London: Rivington. 1845–55. 3v. 2d ed. [rev.]. 1856. 3v. [2976

The second edition is an improvement on the first, through the incorporation of new matter and the correction of errors. This is an interesting, scholarly and comprehensive work. In vol. 1 is a map of the world showing the spread of the Church of England.

The history of English colonization begins with 1496, but is not carried beyond 1784, and embraces Bermuda, the West Indies, North America outside of the United States, and India, as well as the colonies which became parts of the United States down to 1776. The author discusses the condition of the Mother Church in the successive periods. Of special interest to Americans is the following appendix matter, Vol. 1: Daily prayer to be said in the Court of guard (Virginia); Royal instructions to the governor of Newfoundland. Vol. 3: Address of the General convention, held at Christ Church, Philadelphia, October 5, 1785, to the Most Reverend and Right Reverend the Archbishops of Canterbury and York, and the Bishops of the Church of England; the Answer from them, 1786; the text of the Act to empower the Archbishop of Canterbury, or the Archbishop of York, for the time being, to consecrate to the office of bishop, persons being subjects or citizens of countries out of His Majesty's dominions; Directions to Catechists for instructing Indians, Negroes, etc.; Charter of the Society for the Propagation of the Gospel in Foreign Parts; the first report (1703) of this Society. The volumes are fully indexed and analyzed in the tables of contents. This is one of the foundation books in the American church history student's library.

Backus, Isaac. History of New England, with particular reference to the denomination of Christians called Baptists. Boston; Providence. 1777–96. 2v. Newton, Mass.: Backus Hist. Soc. 1871. 2v. $2. [2977

"A wider interest than that of theological record attaches to a book which all students of New England history have united in thinking valuable. This is the work of Isaac Backus, a Baptist minister in Middleborough, Mass., who published at Boston in 1777 a first volume, which was called [as above]. This volume brought the story down to 1690 only, but an appendix summarized subsequent history down to the date of the book. In the second volume, which appeared at Providence in 1784, the title was changed to *A church history of New England, vol. ii, extending from 1690 to 1784*. The same title was preserved in the third volume, which was published in Boston in 1796, bringing the narrative down to that date. . . . The whole work has been reprinted under the title of the original first volume, with notes by David Weston"—as entered above. Justin Winsor, in *Narrative and critical hist. of Am.*, 5: 159.

Bacon, Leonard. Genesis of the New England churches. N. Y.: Harper. 1874. $2.50. [2978

A virile study from second-hand sources of the English origins of New England church organization and life. Clear distinction marked between "Pilgrim" and "Puritan," and the triumph of the former with its genius for voluntary religious worship in emancipation from secular power. The larger part of the book deals with affairs in England and Holland. The last six out of twenty chapters show how the problem was worked out in America. H. W. H.

Bacon, Leonard Woolsey. History of American Christianity. (Am. church history series, v. 13.) N. Y.: Christian Lit. Co. 1897. Scribner. $2. [**2979**

Also republished by Clarke, London, 1899, with a preface by Rt. Hon. James Bryce. This is not a mere unscholarly compilation, but a genuine history, by a man who has style, convictions, independence, ample knowledge and a sense of humor. The book is thoroughly readable and for the most part entirely reliable, and will long remain the standard brief history in its field. It contains many novel views and telling statements. The author criticises freely but in good temper. The proportions are admirably preserved. Altogether the book is worthy of the subject and displays first class literary workmanship. There are occasional marginal references and an adequate index.

Baird, Robert. View of religion in the United States. Glasgow: Blackie. 1843.
—— *Same ; rev. and enl.:* Religion in America. N. Y.: Harper. 1856. [**2980**

This famous book, which has been translated into Danish, Dutch, French, German, Italian and Swedish, is in the nature of a church history of the United States. The author was the secretary of the American and Foreign Christian Union and as such prominent before the protestant communions of America and Europe. The book was written in response to the request of his numerous prominent foreign friends for reliable information on religious affairs in the United States ; and answers it very satisfactorily. Of course it is in statistics and in many other respects hopelessly behind the times. But it is so well written, with such ample resources at command, that it will never be entirely superseded.

Barclay, Robert. Inner life of the religious societies of the Commonwealth. London: Hodder. 1877. [**2981**

"The author . . . makes an elaborate effort to trace to its sources and in its course the development of religious opinion in England previous to 1640. He marks the rise of Barrowism, Brownism, of the Johnsonists, the Separatists, the early Independents, the two parties of Baptists, and the Friends, or Quakers." G. E. Ellis, in *Narrative and critical hist. of Am.*, 3: 251.

Beardsley, Eben Edwards. History of the Episcopal Church in Connecticut. N. Y.: Hurd. 1865–8. 2v. 4th ed. Boston: Houghton. 1883. [**2982**

The volumes are separately indexed. At the end of vol. I is a list of the works used. Each volume has an appendix of documentary material. There are few footnotes or references. The style is good and the matter is well arranged. It is indeed one of the standard works. Being confined to a single colony and spread over two volumes, it goes into much detail, but as the detail is derived from prolonged researches into the official and other sources, it carries its own stamp of authenticity.

Benedict, David. General history of the Baptist denomination in America, and other

parts of the world. Boston. 1813. 2v. N. Y.: Colby. 1848. [**2983**

The author frankly confesses that he gave too much "space [363 out of 945 pp. exclusive of tables and index] to foreign Baptists, Baptist authors, and the baptismal controversy." The value of the book for the student begins with chapter vii on American Baptists, where its readability ends, for the remainder of the book is taken up with sketches of individual churches and associations arranged under states, and consists largely of mere names. There are two indexes — to foreign Baptists, Baptist authors and the baptismal controversy, and to American Baptists. The book can safely be neglected by the general reader.

Berger, Daniel. History of the church of the United Brethren in Christ. (In Am. church history series, v. 12, pp. 309–382.) N. Y.: Christian Lit. Co. 1897. Scribner. $2. [**2984**

There is a 5 page bibliography, properly divided, and the matter is separately indexed. The author, who is one of the church editors, is in a position to know its history from the inside, has wisely devoted most of his space to the origins, and touches lightly and impartially upon the split in the denomination which occurred in 1889.

—— History of the church of the United Brethren in Christ. Dayton, O.: United Brethren Pub. House. 1897. $2.50. [**2985**

This is the official and full history of the denomination in 4 parts. Part I: General history, is divided into 6 periods which carry the story down to 1897. Part II: Departments of church work, is made up of sketches of the church's activity in publication, education, missions, etc. Part III: Annual conferences, gives the outline history of each. Part IV: Historical and statistical tables. Then comes a bibliography of 4 pages. The volume is carefully prepared, fully indexed and appropriately illustrated.

Bernheim, Gotthardt Dellmann. History of the German settlements and of the Lutheran Church in North and South Carolina [to 1850]. Phil. 1872. [**2986**

"The best modern summary of these Swiss and German immigrations." Justin Winsor, in *Narrative and critical hist. of Am.*, 5: 345.

Besse, Joseph. Collection of the sufferings of the people called Quakers, 1650–89; from original records and other authentic accounts. London: Hinde. 1753. 2v. [**2987**

This book is of the highest value in the history of the Quakers and thoroughly trustworthy. In vol. 2 the New World comes under treatment, chap. V being on New England ; VI–IX on the West Indies, X on Maryland, and XI on Jamaica. There is a very full index of persons, whose names are collected under geographical heads. At Manchester, Eng., in 1841 there appeared a small volume of extracts from the book presenting some of the martyrdoms which took place at Boston, Mass., and further matter relating to New England.

Blaikie, Alexander. History of Presbyterianism in New England. Boston: Moore. 1881. 2v. in 1. [2988

The author was for 33 years pastor of the First Presbyterian Church in Boston. His loneliness, denominationally, probably accounts for his defiant denominationalism. The occasion of the researches which are here embodied was an act of injustice towards his church. The chapters are fully analyzed and there is an index. He traces organized Presbyterianism of different forms in New England from 1704 to 1881, dealing in a minute way with churches and their pastors. Much of the matter is therefore annalistic, authentic and very dry. Vol. 1 goes to 1793; vol. 2 from 1793 to 1881.

Boardman, George Nye. History of New England theology. N. Y.: Randolph. 1899. $1.50. [2989

The author was professor of systematic theology in the Congregational theological seminary in Chicago and his lectures upon the subject have been expanded into this volume. The aim of the present work is to trace the " New Divinity," formerly so called, in its development through the century between 1730 and 1830, through its Berkshire and Hopkinsian eras, to its final form in New England theology. Chapter I is historical. The book really overlaps its announced boundaries, as it takes in Bushnell's moral influence theory of the Atonement, the Oberlin theology and even later developments. The treatment is sympathetic, scholarly and interesting. There are many references to the sources and a sufficient index. Pp. 305–309 present a table which brings together and sets in chronological order the important events in the development of the New England theology.

Bowden, James. History of the Society of Friends in America. London: Bennett. 1861. 2v. [2990

" The most important of late works. . . . Its author enjoyed great advantages in preparing it, having the MSS. deposited in Devonshire House at his command. In it many original documents of the greatest interest are printed for the first time. . . . The work is spirited and readable. . . . The second volume . . . is the best Quaker history of Pennsylvania that has appeared." F. D. Stone, in *Narrative and critical hist. of Am.*, 3: 505 and 508.

Bradford, Amory Howe. The Pilgrim in old England : a review of the history, present condition, and outlook of the independent (Congregational) churches in England. (Andover lectures on Congregationalism.) N. Y.: Fords. 1893. $1.25. [2991

This is a very able exposition of Congregational history and polity as exemplified in the career of the Congregational churches in England. The eight chapters are as follows: 1. Life and form; 2. Beginning and growth; 3. Church and state; 4. The present condition; 5. Creeds; 6. Doctrinal condition of church membership; 7. The pulpit; 8. The outlook. The second chapter belongs to the history of the Pilgrims in America as well as in England, and the fifth chapter deals with the creeds of Congregationalism as a whole; otherwise the work relates exclusively to the Pilgrims who remained in England and does not concern American history. C. M. A.

Brainerd, David. EDWARDS, JONATHAN. Memoirs of David Brainerd, missionary to the North American Indians; new and complete edition on the basis of Sereno E. Dwight's (1822) ; ed. by James M. Sherwood with notes and introd. by editor, and essay on God's hand in missions by A. T. Pierson. N. Y.: Funk. 1885. $1.50. [2992

The edition here noted is the edition to buy of this religious classic, originally written by Jonathan Edwards and reissued by Sereno Edwards Dwight. Brainerd's life was very short (1718–1747), and his missionary activity extended over only 4 years, but his memory is imperishable, thanks to the fact that Jonathan Edwards wrote his memoir, and no student of American church history can pass his life by.

Briggs, Charles Augustus. American Presbyterianism ; its origin and early history. N. Y. : Scribner. 1885. $3. [2993

This is the best history of the Presbyterian Church in America for the period it covers, which is from about 1700 to 1788. The author has chosen Orientalia for his continuous study, but this book is evidence that he might have attained equal eminence as a historian. He has not followed precedent but struck a new path. Every page shows his independent and fruitful labors. He is remarkably familiar with the confessional sources and with the writings of those who produced them. He quotes from both with telling effect. Of his nine chapters he devotes two to Presbyterianism on the Continent and in Great Britain. Then he traces American Presbyterianism from its feeble and sporadic beginnings down to the time when peace after the Revolution enabled it to address itself to the needs of the growing population. The appendix contains much documentary matter, which he discovered, and reprints of denominational literary monuments of various kinds. The index is adequate. No student of American church history can afford to neglect this volume. No other denomination has its superior.

Brown, John. Pilgrim Fathers of New England and their Puritan successors. N. Y.: Revell. 1896. [c. 1895.] New ed. 1897. $1.50. [2994

The author of this book is the pastor of the Bunyan Meeting, Bedford, England, author of the best biography of Bunyan, Yale lecturer in 1899 upon the Puritan preachers, and has been a life-long student of Nonconformist history. He has gone to the sources, well digested his material, writes with sympathy and even admiration for the men whose fortunes he records. His matter is good, his spirit is gentle and his tone has the authority of genuine learning. The illustrations are very interesting and, being made on the spot by an artist, have a charm beyond that of photography. There is a list of works quoted or otherwise referred to, and also a general index. The book is introduced to the American public by Rev. Dr. A. E. Dunning.

Brumbaugh, Martin Grove. History of the German Baptist Brethren in Europe and America. 3d ed. rev. Mt. Morris, Ill.: Brethren Pub. House. 1900. $2.   [**2994 a**

The accepted history of this denomination, better known as Dunkards.

Buckley, James Monroe. History of Methodists in the United States. (Am. church history series, v. 5.) N. Y.: Christian Lit. Co. 1897. 2v. Scribner. $2.   [**2995**

Now published by Charles Scribner's Sons, New York City. The author is the editor of the *Christian advocate*, and one of the foremost men in Methodism. His volume covers all periods and branches of its subject. This of course necessitated sketches rather than elaborate studies of many features. The temper is genial; the effort is plainly to do all parties justice, and as the author can speak from inside knowledge of the last 40 years, and from personal acquaintance with the leaders of the preceding times, he is a reliable guide. He presents a brief bibliography, an appendix of historical documents, and a full index. Harper & Brothers brought out an edition of the work in 2 vols. with portraits, 1898, $5.

Burrage, Henry Sweetser. History of the Baptists in New England. Phil.: Am. Baptist Pub. Soc. 1894. $1.25.   [**2996**

This is a good specimen of a concise denominational local history. The author is a New England man, editor of a leading Baptist paper, a practised historical student of wide denominational range, an ardent admirer of his denomination, and of good temper. He quotes at first-hand from the rich collection of sources he mentions in his preface, and comes down to 1893. In his appendix he presents tables showing the amount contributed to several objects by the Baptist churches in New England, what they gave and the annual growth of the denomination from 1800 to 1893. The volume is indexed. It is one of a series upon the history of the Baptists in this country, which includes volumes by A. H. Newman, B. F. Riley, J. H. Smith and H. C. Vedder mentioned below.

Caldwell, David. CARUTHERS, E. W. Sketch of the life and character of Rev. David Caldwell. Greensboro, N. C.: Swaim. 1842.   [**2997**

While this work is nominally a biography of Rev. David Caldwell (1725–1824), a Presbyterian preacher and teacher, it is in reality a history of the Regulation War and of ecclesiastical and Revolutionary affairs in central and western North Carolina in which Dr. Caldwell was an actor. It is based on conversations and traditions of people acquainted with the subject, on papers furnished by members of his family, on church records and to a limited extent on printed authorities. The arrangement is bad, for there are no chapters, no table of contents and practically no index. It is also prejudiced in favor of the

Presbyterians and the Regulators, but is of considerable value and has become, to a limited extent, a source for the period covered.   S. B. W.

Carroll, Henry King. Religious forces of the United States enumerated, classified, and described on the basis of the census of 1890; with introd. on the condition and character of American Christianity. (Am. church history series, v. 1.) N. Y.: Christian Lit. Co. 1893.
—— *Same;* new ed. rev. Jan. 1, 1896, with additional tables of statistics for the five years since the census of 1890. Scribner. 1896. Net $2.   [**2998**

The author was religious editor of *The Independent*, New York City, and had charge of the division of churches in the eleventh census. No better selection could have been made, as he had an extraordinary knowledge of American sectarian history. In this volume, after a general introduction in which he discusses and analyzes the religious population, he gives a brief historical and interesting sketch, derived from first-hand information, of each sect in the United States, in alphabetical order, as a preface to its statistics. He follows the statistics with general statistical summaries, in different combinations. In the revised edition these are followed by the statistics by denomination for 1895, summaries, net gains for 5 years, the figures of the twelve largest denominations, and denominational families; various ingenious diagrams. An admirable, laborious, satisfactory work, with an index.

Chase, Philander. Reminiscences: an autobiography. N. Y. 1844. 2v. 2d ed. [continued to 1847]. Boston: Dow. 1848. 2v.   [**2999**

The value of these volumes centres in the account given of the formation and early history of the Episcopal dioceses of Ohio and Illinois, of both of which the author was the first bishop, and especially of the founding of Kenyon College. They also give, from an important point of view, a picture of pioneer life in the west. The work is colored by the strong personality of Bishop Chase.   B. A. H.

Checkley, John. John Checkley; or Evolution of religious tolerance in Massachusetts Bay. See Prince Society, sect. 387.   [**3000**

Coleman, Leighton. The Church in America. London: Wells Gardner, Darton & Co. N. Y.: Pott. 1895. $2.50.   [**3000 a**

By "The Church" is meant the Protestant Episcopal Church of the United States. The book reprints a diocesan map, a United States list of "authorities," and an index. It is well written and very churchly in tone.

Corwin, Edward Tanjore. History of the Reformed Church, Dutch. (In Am. church history series, v. 8, pp. 1–212. N. Y: Christian Lit. Co. 1895. Scribner. $2.)   [**3001**

The author as the recognized historian of his denomination, has presented in compendious form and with greater completeness much matter previously published in his *Manual*. He includes "the Christian Reformed Church." The treatment throughout is careful, documentary and in good temper. There is a bibliography of 5 pages which includes books on the foreign missions of the denomination and a separate index.

—— Manual of the Reformed [Protestant Dutch] Church in America. N. Y.: Ref. Ch. Bd. Pub. 1859. 3d ed. 1879. [3002

This is an exhaustive treatise; complete as far as it goes but now needing much addition. Part 1 is a general history of the denomination; Part 2 is in substance a biographical dictionary of its ministry living and dead, and of the ministry of the German Reformed Church while under the Classis of Amsterdam, i. e. till 1792; Part 3 treats historically of the churches in alphabetical order, and of the Board of Education. The appendix is on the Widows' Fund; then follow chronological lists of ministers and churches in the Reformed Church in America from 1628–1878; and list of missionaries from 1819–1878.

Davis, George Lynn-Lachlan. Day-star of American freedom; or The birth and early growth of toleration in the province of Maryland. N. Y.: Scribner. 1855. [3003

To Mr. Davis " is due the credit of having settled the vexed question of the religious faith of the legislators who passed the Toleration Act of 1649." W. T. Brantly, in *Narrative and critical hist. of Am.*, 3: 560.

Dexter, Henry Martyn. Congregationalism of the last 300 years, as seen in its literature. N. Y.: Harper. 1880. [3004

"This elaborate work . . . takes its flavor from the past. Its abounding extracts from the quaint writings, and its portraitures and relations of the experiences, of the old-time worthies, transfer us to their presence, make us sharers of their buffeted fortunes and listeners to their living speech. . . . The text is elaborately illustrated by notes, with references and extracts. . . . The writer is careful to authenticate all his statements from prime authorities." The bibliography (Collections toward a bibliography of Congregationalism) contains " 7250 titles of publications, from folios down to a few leaves, dating between the years 1546 and 1879." G. E. Ellis, in *Narrative and critical hist. of Am.*, 3: 246.

Dorchester, Daniel. Christianity in the United States. N. Y.: Methodist Book Concern. 1888. rev. ed. 1895. $3.50. [3004 a

An industrious and intelligent compilation, extending to 1894 and blazing the way for later students of the subject. It contains a number of ingenious and helpful charts and diagrams and much statistical matter.

Doyle, John T. Some account of the pious fund of California, and the litigation to recover it. San Francisco: Bosqui. 1880. [3005

Exceedingly rare; compiled by Mr. Doyle from historical material in his possession, bearing on this very remarkable lawsuit, for the prosecution of which he received a fee of $500,000. The contents and pagination are as follows (in perfect copies): Introductory pp. 5; memorial (of claim), pp. 14; brief history of claim, pp. 20; extracts from *Noticia de la California* (and other books), pp. 68; American and Mexican joint commission (various papers presented), pp. 8, 40, 12, 32, 7, 32, 38, 19, and 7, the last being the decision of Edward Thornton, the final umpire chosen. No other American book gives so clear and complete an account of the relations of the Marquis of Villapuente to the Catholic missions in California, Mexico and other parts of the world in the first part of the 18th century. The historical and literary portions of this book are written with all the ability of one of the most brilliant and highly educated lawyers of California. C. H. S.

Dubbs, Joseph Henry. History of the Reformed Church, German. (In Am. church history series, v. 8, pp. 213–423. N. Y.: Christian Lit. Co. 1895. Scribner. $2.) [3006

The author is Professor in Ursinus College, Collegeville, Pa., and a recognized authority upon denominational affairs. The book is well proportioned and brings the history down to date. Like the other volumes of the series and in accordance with the instructions of the editorial committee, it presents the European roots of the denomination. It has a prefatory bibliography of 7 pages, arranged under appropriate headings, and a separate index.

Dunning, Albert Elijah. Congregationalists in America. N. Y.: Hill. [c. 1894.] Boston: Pilgrim Press. 1897. $2. [3007

This is a popular book, in the better sense of that term, with a clerical introduction by Rev. Dr. Richard S. Storrs, a lay introduction by Major-General O. O. Howard and chapters on special subjects by several other writers. The book is fully illustrated with portraits and views of buildings. It has no references or footnotes and the list of authorities is not in proper form, but there is a good index, both personal and general, and a valuable " chronological table of important events in Congregational history." The style is flowing and rather discursive, but its treatment of other denominations is courteous and of its own not unduly laudatory.

Eddy, Richard. History of Universalism. (In Am. church history series, v. 10, pp. 251–493. N. Y.: Christian Lit. Co. 1894. Scribner. $2.) [3008

The second part of Vol. 10 of the American church history series. The author, who is the recognized historian of his denomination, traces the course of the movement from the ante-Nicene age to the present day, claiming among its leaders many who are not usually reckoned Universalist. When he gets down to the 19th century he is upon much firmer ground, and from then on writes with authority. The last three of his ten brief chapters present the polity, missions, literature, hymnology, educational institutions and Sunday-schools of the denomination in the United

States. There is a 2 pp. bibliography, and a separate index.

—— Universalism in America: a history. Boston: Universalist Pub. House. 1884–6. 2v. ea. $1.50. [3009

These volumes are an authoritative and exhaustive history of the denomination. The first goes from 1636 to 1800, the second from 1801 to 1886. In the bibliography are 2278 titles. Bibliographical and general indexes to the entire work cover 35 pp.

Engelhardt, *Fr.* **Zephyrin.** Franciscans in California. Printed and published "cum permissu superiorum," at the Holy Childhood Indian School, Harbor Springs, Michigan. 1897. Net $1.50. [3010

This book is very interesting, and embodies the result of much, though narrow, historical research. Its point of view is of course that of a Franciscan friar, and it criticises many statements of the early American observers of Spanish-Californian life. The defense made of Padre Junipero Serra and other pioneer priests against Bancroft, his principal authority quoted, is striking. A supplementary part, "modern history," brings the story of the Franciscans in California to February, 1897. C. H. S.

Felt, Joseph Barlow. Ecclesiastical history of New England. Boston: Congregational Library Assoc. 1855–62. 2v. [3011

Each volume is separately indexed, and at the end of vol. 1 is a closely printed page of errata. The author was an eminent antiquarian, and so has arranged his history in annalistic form under the separate colonies. Documents and sources of all kinds are textually quoted. But as trivial events and biographical notices, extracts from letters and from diaries, from court records and printed volumes, follow in an endless stream, and the annals go from colony to colony, the reader gives up in despair. Yet for the student they are very valuable. The matter is divided into chapters, though why is not plain. The double index is a sufficient key. The period covered is 1517–1678.

Foote, William Henry. Sketches of North Carolina, historical and biographical. N. Y.: Carter. 1846. [3012

This work is a history of the Presbyterian Church in North Carolina. It shows "the influence of Presbyterian doctrines, habits, and population upon the past and present generations of citizens of the North State, and in some degree also upon the population of those states which owe much to emigration from Carolina." It traces that history from the first appearance of Presbyterianism in the state until the date of publication. It is based largely on original sources, on traditions collected from the survivors of the Revolutionary period, on private correspondence and church records. It is well arranged, shows evidence of the most thorough and conscientious preparation, is not sectarian, and is altogether one of the most valuable books on the history of the state. S. B. W.

—— Sketches of Virginia, historical and bio-

graphical. Phil.: Martien. 1850. 2d series. Lippincott. 1855. [3013

A vast collection of historic material relating to the Presbyterian Church in Virginia from the earliest times to about 1850. Includes sketches of prominent clergymen, histories of parishes and churches, sermons, histories of colleges, and incidentally the growth of other religious sects. Mingled with these are stories of Indian wars and the experiences of white captives. Shows a good historic basis for most of the statements. Lacks orderly arrangement and index.
E. E. S.

Ford, David Barnes. New England's struggles for religious liberty. Phil.: Am. Baptist Pub. Soc. 1896. $1. [3014

Not the work of a first-class scholar, still a useful and interesting compilation of easily accessible material upon the sufferings of Baptists and Quakers in early New England, and upon the efforts to separate church and state, which in Massachusetts succeeded in 1833. The many quotations of documents are not usually located at all, but there is an index.

Foster, Robert Verrell. Sketch of the history of the Cumberland Presbyterian Church. (In Am. church history series, v. 11, pp. 257–309. N. Y.: Christian Lit. Co. 1894. Scribner. $2.) [3015

The author is Professor in the theological school of his denomination at Lebanon, Tenn. While modestly called a "sketch" and only covering 50 pp., it yet meets sufficiently the wants of other than special students. It is prefaced by a one-page bibliography, and closes with a statement of the distinctive doctrinal position of the denomination. It is based throughout upon the sources, and is separately indexed.

Frothingham, Octavius Brooks. Transcendentalism in New England: a history. N. Y.: Putnam. 1876. $1.75. [3016

The author's portrait is inserted. He was for years the leading representative of the radical wing of Unitarianism and an eloquent preacher. He did not choose the task, but he writes with full knowledge, as he had been a Transcendentalist himself; finds the beginnings of the movement in Germany in the *Critique of pure reason* of Immanuel Kant (1781); shows how it spread thence to France and Great Britain, and came to New England. He speaks from personal acquaintance of Emerson, Alcott, Margaret Fuller, Theodore Parker, George Ripley and others who were its exponents. The book is indexed and must remain an authority on the subject.

Funk, John F. Mennonite Church and her accusers: a vindication. Elkhart, Ind.: Mennonite Pub. Co. 1878. [3017

A statement of the position of the Old Mennonite Church, over against the so-called Reformed Mennonite Church as represented in a book by Bp. Daniel Musser of that body issued in 1873; originally published as a series of articles in *The herald of truth.* The style is polemical, but incidentally the book furnishes much information. It has a table of contents and a brief index — both in the back.

Garfield, James A. Manuscript of Solomon Spaulding and the Book of Mormon. See Western Reserve Historical Society, sect. 3387. [3018

Gillett, Ezra Hall. History of the Presbyterian Church in the United States. Phil.: Presb. Pub. Com. [c. 1864.] 2v. Rev. ed. 1875. 2v. [3019

These volumes are very laboriously and faithfully compiled. But it is their great misfortune that they were the work of a commission of the New School body of the Presbyterian Church and then revised to meet the requirements of the Old School! Of course no one will expect from volumes thus produced any independence of treatment. Still they are useful as records, and as interesting in style as the conditions allow. Only 42 pp. are given to the period 1837-1875. There is an index.

Good, James Isaac. History of the Reformed Church in the United States, 1725-1792. Reading, Pa.: Daniel Miller. 1899. $1.75. [3019 a

This is the standard history of the (German) Reformed Church as far as it goes, as the author is the recognized historian of his denomination. It contains illustrations and an index.

Gregory, James. Puritanism in the old world and the new, from its inception in the reign of Elizabeth to the establishment of the Puritan theocracy in New England ; introd. by Amory H. Bradford. N. Y.: Revell. 1896. $2. [3020

The author was pastor of the leading Congregational church in Edinburgh. He has written, not a history of English Puritanism, but a philosophico-historical sketch, based upon perfectly accessible material, but cleverly arranged, of Puritanism in England and New England, down to about the middle of the 17th century. He accepts Douglas Campbell's theory of the influence of the Dutch in producing Puritanism. The book is provided with references, notes and an index.

Hallowell, Richard Price. Quaker invasion of Massachusetts. Boston: Houghton. 1883. New ed. rev. 1887. $1.25.
—— The pioneer Quakers. Boston: Houghton. 1887. $1. [3021

The second book to some extent repeats the first, and both are written by a Quaker " to correct popular fallacies and to assign to the Quakers their true place in the early history of Massachusetts." The first goes to 1677 and the second to 1724. Much new material is presented and utilized. In the first the appendix is particularly noteworthy and is nearly half the book. Each is indexed.

Hamilton, John Taylor. History of the

Unitas Fratrum, or Moravian Church, in the United States. (In Am. church history series, v. 8, pp. 425-508. N. Y.: Christian Lit. Co. 1895. Scribner. $2.) [3022

The concluding part of vol. 8 of the American church history series. The author is professor of church history in the Moravian theological seminary at Bethlehem, Pa., and editor of *The Moravian.* He had only limited space at his disposal, but since he was master of the subject he was able to present the essential facts. He gives 3 pp. to the bibliography. It is a careful and satisfactory piece of work.

—— A history of the Church known as the Moravian Church, or the Unitas Fratrum, or the Unity of the Brethren, during the eighteenth and nineteenth centuries. Bethlehem, Pa. : Times Pub. Co. 1900. Net $2.50. [3022 a

This is the full story, carefully written, and is the authentic history of the Church to 1890. 4 pp. Bibliography and full index.

Harsha, William Justin. Story of Iowa. Omaha: Cen. West. Co. 1890. [3023

Not a history of the state of Iowa, but a history of Presbyterianism in that state. It shows the beginnings of the church and its gradual growth. From the historian's standpoint, there is some local matter of value concerning missionary work among the Indians and the foreign immigrants. This consists largely of extracts from old letters. But the mass is valuable only as a summing up of missionary labor in the state. E. E. S.

Hawks, Francis Lister. Contributions to the ecclesiastical history of the United States. N. Y.: Harper. 1836-9. 2v. [3024

V. 1. The Protestant Episcopal Church in Virginia. V. 2. The Protestant Episcopal Church in Maryland. These volumes are not indexed. In v. 1 the journals of the conventions of the Protestant Episcopal Church in the diocese of Virginia, from 1785-1835, are printed in full (pp. 1-332). These volumes are justly considered of prime importance. They came so early that they record at first-hand almost the beginnings of the Episcopal Church. The author was a devoted student of his church's history and its official historiographer.

Hawks, Francis Lister, *and* **William Stevens Perry,** *eds.* Documentary history of the Protestant Episcopal Church in the United States of America, containing numerous hitherto unpublished documents concerning the Church in Connecticut. N. Y.: Pott. 1863-4. 2v. [3025

For notes on this, see sect. 3065.

Hays, George Price. Presbyterians : a popular narrative of their origin, progress, doctrines, and achievements ; with special chapters by Rev. W. J. Reid, *et al.*; introds. by John Hall and William E. Moore. N. Y.: Hill. 1892. [3026

The title-page sufficiently explains the object of this book and enables one to judge of its quality. It makes no pretence, or should make none, to scholarly handling of the subject. But as the numerous authors are competent in their respective fields, the result of their coöperation is a comprehensive and in the main accurate treatment of denominational affairs in all branches of American Presbyterianism. It is the kind of book which one should read first in a denomination study, as it will give him a view of the body from the inside as it appears to those who are its enthusiastic friends. The volume is fully illustrated with inartistic but presumably accurate cuts of various kinds. It is not always easy to see why the illustrations were selected. The book is indexed.

Hazard, Caroline. Narragansett Friends' meeting in the XVIII century, with a chapter on Quaker beginnings in Rhode Island. Boston: Houghton. 1899. $1.50. [3027

"The book is chiefly drawn from eight folio volumes of records belonging to the men's meeting, with three volumes treating of the doings of the women, who were certainly an important constituent in the Friends' system of living. . . . Besides this matter and the preliminary essay on early Rhode Island Quakerism, there is an interesting reprint of the *Quaker's sea journal, being a true relation of a voyage to New England, performed by Robert Fowler of the town of Burlington in Yorkshire, anno 1659*. . . . The Narragansett meeting extended its outposts over the whole south county, and even to Stonington in Connecticut. Miss Hazard tells its story in seven topical chapters. . . . We may regret that these records yield no more matter of direct historical interest. The accomplished author [President of Wellesley College] has drawn out the best. It is mostly an account of narrow domestic life and petty discipline." W. B. W., in *Am. hist. review*, 5: 361.

Hazelius, Ernest Lewis. History of the American Lutheran Church, 1685–1842. Zanesville, O.: Church. 1846. [3028

No index. Appendix no. 1, "Ministerial regulations of the German Evangelical Lutheran congregations in Pennsylvania and the adjacent states," and no. 2, "Constitution of the General Synod," are still of value and interest, but otherwise the volume, although drawn from good sources and a useful publication, is superseded by Jacobs' history, sect. 3043.

Heckewelder, John Gottlieb Ernestus. RONDTHALER, EDWARD. Life of John Heckewelder. Ed. by B. H. Coates. Phil.: T. Ward. 1847. [3029

Heckewelder was a Moravian missionary, an authority upon the Delawares, and assistant of Zeisberger's. This life is based on original records, but is unpretentious in style. Dr. Coates' edition contains W. Rawle's *Vindication of Mr. Heckewelder's History of the Indian nations* (Phila. 1818. Lippincott. 1876).

Higginson, Francis. HIGGINSON, THOMAS WENTWORTH. Life of Francis Higginson, first minister in the Massachusetts Bay colony. (Makers of America.) N. Y.: Dodd. [c. 1891.] $1. [3030

Mr. Higginson gives a scholarly and interesting sketch, based upon first-hand study of the sources, which are copiously quoted. The references are abundant and the index is adequate.

Hodge, Charles. Constitutional history of the Presbyterian Church in the United States [1705–88]. Phil.: Martien. 1839–40. 2v. Phil.: Presbyterian Board of Pub. 1v. $1.25. [3031

For the period it covers this history is the highest authority. It originated in a desire to defend the Old School body, but it is not partisan. The author has gone to the sources and examined the beginnings of Presbyterianism in this country in a masterly manner. His work should be supplemented. It cannot be supplanted, as it is drawn from official and contemporary records by one who was a master of statement and eminently fair. The book has no index.

Holmes, John. Historical sketches of the missions of the United Brethren. Dublin: Napper. 1818. 2d ed. Lond. 1827.

—— History of the Protestant church of the United Brethren. London: Author. 1825–30. 2v. [3032

These standard works supplement one another. They are written from the inside, in sober but interesting style, and are indexed. The narrative goes down to 1818.

Hooker, Thomas. WALKER, GEORGE LEON. Thomas Hooker, preacher, founder, democrat. (Makers of America.) N. Y.: Dodd. 1891. $1. [3033

This scholarly and interesting volume upon the founder of Hartford, Conn., and pastor of the First Congregational Church there, is abundantly supplied with references and fully indexed.

Hopkins, Samuel. Puritans; or The church, court, and Parliament of England, during the reigns of Edward VI. and Queen Elizabeth. Boston: Gould. 1859–61. 3v. 2d ed. N. Y.: Randolph. 1875. [3034

In the first volume the author indulges in some imaginary conversations, but his general style is sober. The history is very elaborate, as his notes and the list of his authorities (Vol. 1, v–viii and preface to vol. 3) show, but not of the first rank. There is no independent search for materials, but diligent use of what was already in print and accessible. There is an index.

Hotchkin, James Harvey. History of the purchase and settlement of western New York, and of the Presbyterian Church in that section. N. Y.. M. W. Dodd. 1848. [3035

This is a good specimen of a sectional and denominational history. The author came to western New York in 1801 and knew personally every important Presbyterian Church, if not every important person in his region. But not trusting to such knowledge, he sought diligently for information from every source. He sketches persons, churches, presbyteries, missionary operations, and Auburn Theological Seminary. The book has no index, a defect partly made up by full chapter analyses.

Howard, *Maj.-Gen.* **Oliver Otis.** Fighting for humanity; or Camp and quarter-deck. N. Y.: Neely. 1898. $1.25. [3036

General Howard "confines himself to the means taken for the Christianization of American soldiers and sailors, and his book is of religious rather than warlike interest. It will supply some interesting paragraphs to the future historian." John J. Culver, *Dial* (Chicago), 26: 274.

Howells, William Dean. Three villages. Boston: Osgood. 1884. [3037

This little volume of three essays treats of the three villages of Lexington, Shirley, and Gnadenhütten. In the first essay Mr. Howells describes in a light and, at times, gossipy manner the typical New England town of Lexington; in the second he gives an appreciative account of the Shakers of Shirley; and in the third reviews historically the causes that led to the Moravian settlement at Gnadenhütten, giving at the same time an account of the government and life of the village. All the essays are accurate historically, and their author is peculiarly successful in reproducing the atmosphere of the places he describes, and in making seem very real the varied experiences of the Shakers and the Moravians. C. M. A.

Huguenot Society of America. Collections. N. Y.: the Society. 1886. V. 1.
—— Registers of the births, marriages and deaths of the "Église Française à la Nouvelle York" from 1688 to 1804, edited by the Rev. Alfred V. Wittmeyer, Rector of the French Church du Saint-Esprit, and historical documents relating to the French Protestants in New York during the same period.
—— Proceedings. 1884-. V. 1+.
—— Tercentenary celebration of the promulgation of the Edict of Nantes, April 13, 1598; with portraits, facsimile of the first and last pages of the edict and other illustrative matter. N. Y. 1900. [3038

The last named volumes contain papers upon the Huguenots in South Carolina, Virginia, New Rochelle, New York and New Jersey.

Hunter, Joseph. Collections concerning the church or congregation of Protestant separatists formed at Scrooby in North Nottinghamshire in the time of James I: the founders of New Plymouth. London: Smith. 1849. [3039

This appeared first in a tract, in 1849; reissued, in 1852, in the Mass. Hist. Soc. coll. v. 31. "The author's careful examination of local records made plain the position of the Brewsters in Scrooby, and of the Bradfords in Austerfield (with the entry of Governor Bradford's baptism), and traced their families, as well as the families of other early members of the Scrooby flock, in the neighboring parishes." F. B. Dexter, in *Narrative and critical hist. of Am.,* 3: 284.

Hurst, John Fletcher. Literature of theology. A classified bibliography of theological and general religious literature. N. Y.: Meth. Bk. Concern. 1896. $4. [3040

This book is here mentioned for its rich contents under American church history. It has been very carefully and laboriously compiled, and is a literary tool of great value.

—— Short history of the church in the United States. N. Y.: Chau. Press. 1890.
—— *Same, enl.:* Short history of the Christian church. N. Y.: Harper. 1893. $3.
—— *Same, enl.:* History of the Christian church. N. Y.: Meth. Bk. Concern. 1897–1900. 2v. $5 ea. [3040 a

In this work the author has reissued with considerable enlargement and improvements the matter previously published. The bibliographical section heading is well done, and indicates the sources and guides to further study. It is a very useful sketch, readable and accurate.

Hutchinson, Anne. ELLIS, GEORGE E. Life of Anne Hutchinson, with a sketch of the antinomian controversy in Massachusetts. (Sparks, J., *ed.* Library of Am. biography, ser. 2, v. 6, pp. 167–376. Boston: Little. 1845.) [3041

A carefully written account with judicious use of authorities at hand. Unbiased. H. W. H.

Jackson, Samuel Macauley, *comp.* Bibliography of American church history, 1820–93. (In Am. church history series, v. 12, pp. 441–513. N. Y.: Christian Lit. Co. 1894. Scribner. $2.) [3042

It is the first separately issued bibliography of American church history, but is not by any means exhaustive, and users are recommended to consult Hurst's *Literature of theology* (sect. 3040). It is declaredly derived from Roorbach and Kelly and the *American catalogue,* compared with the British Museum catalogue; hence does not mention numerous books which are not recorded in those lists. The compiler was unable to index his titles as he wished and to present the long list of American ecclesiastical biography which he had gathered. He was also compelled to issue it before the series was completed, and so could not avail himself of the special bibliographies which appear in the later volumes. It is a pity that the smaller denominational publishing houses do not take more pains to report their publications regularly in the trade journals, because their neglect prevents the librarians and cataloguers from hearing of them, oftentimes to their mutual loss.

Jacobs, Henry Eyster. History of the Evangelical Lutheran Church in the United States. (Am. church history series, v. 4. N. Y.: Christian Lit. Co. 1893. Scribner. $2.) [3043

The author is Professor of systematic theology in the Lutheran Theological Seminary in Philadelphia, and has written several other historical works, including a life of Luther in the *Heroes of the Reformation* series. He belongs to the General Council, the conservative party among the Lutherans, but has dealt fairly with all factions and divisions of the Lutheran body. He presents a selected bibliography under these heads: I. The Lutheran Church and its doctrine, history, organization, and worship in general. II. MS. collections of historical material (a note stating where they are found). III. Printed collections. 1. Bibliography. 2. Statistics. 3. Minutes of synods and diets. 4. Histories of synods. 5. Histories of institutions. 6. Histories of congregations. 7. Collection of biographies. 8. Legal trials and decisions. IV. European and denominational relations. 1. Holland. 2. Sweden. 3. Pietism and its London adherents. 4. The Salzburg persecution. 5. The Moravian factor. V. Reports of the founders and their contemporaries. 1. The Swedes. 2. Salzburg colony. 3. Pennsylvania Lutherans. 4. North Carolinians. VI. Histories. 1. General. 2. Of particular periods and localities. VII. Biographies. VIII. Doctrinal, symbolical and controversial. The bibliography demonstrates his fitness to turn out a sober, connected, orderly, correct narrative of Lutheranism in the United States. And such he gives. Beginning with the European centres whence the Lutherans came, he traces their history from 1624 when the first of the mighty host entered the New World, down to 1893. The index is sufficient, and supplements the chapter analyses.

Janney, Samuel Macpherson. History of the religious society of Friends, to 1828. Phil.: Hayes. 1860–7. 4v. [3044

"The author was a follower of Elias Hicks, and his work contains a history of the separation of the meetings caused by the doctrines preached by the latter." F. D. Stone, in *Narrative and critical hist. of Am.*, 3: 504.

Johnson, Thomas Cary. History of the southern Presbyterian Church. (In Am. church history series, v. 11, pp. 313–479. N. Y.: Christian Lit. Co. 1894. Scribner. $2.) [3045

The volume is very belligerent against northern Presbyterianism; yet is derived from the sources, which are carefully quoted. The author is Professor of church history in Union Theological Seminary, Richmond, Va., and had access to reliable information. The treatise is preceded by a two-page bibliography, and is separately indexed.

Kane, Thomas S. The Mormons. See Pennsylvania, Historical Society of, sect. 385. [3046

Kip, William Ingraham. Early days of my episcopate. N. Y.: Thomas Whittaker. 1892. $1.50. [3047

An account of church work in California, 1854–1860, including much that is illustrative of the social life of the times, often in the form of extracts from the author's journal. While largely personal and so far only interesting to the author's friends and relatives, a good deal of Bishop Kip's dignified narrative illustrates the building of the commonwealth and helps the historian to understand local problems.

C. H. S.

—— *comp.* Early Jesuit missions in North America; comp. and tr. from the letters of the French Jesuits, with notes. N. Y.: Wiley. 1846. Albany: Munsell. 1873. N. Y.: Randolph. 1875. [3048

Opposite the title-page is a copy of a map published by the Jesuits in 1664, which relates to that part of New York state where the Five Nations lived and where the Jesuit missions were carried on. It is very curious. The book itself consists of translations, not arranged chronologically and but meagerly annotated, of eleven of the "Lettres edifiantes et curieuses écrites des missions étrangères," relating Jesuit missionary heroism from 1656–1750. The author performed a useful service. He carefully guards his readers against the inference that the Jesuit missionaries absorbed all the zeal there was. The book has no index. For the story of these Jesuit missions fully and much better presented see *The Jesuit relations*, edited by R. G. Thwaites, which gives both the French or Latin text and an English translation.

Krehbiel, Henry Peter. History of the general conference of the Mennonites of North America. Canton, Ohio: Author. 1898. $1.85. [3049

The book has an introduction by Rev. A. B. Shelly, a prominent worker in the Conference almost from the beginning, and for 24 years president of the organization. It covers the coöperative unification movement among the Mennonites from its inception to the present time, and is based on independent study of the sources, and is the first and only work on the subject. It has received the endorsement of the denomination. The book is indexed.

Landis, George B. Society of separatists of Zoar, Ohio. See American Historical Association, sect. 250. [3050

Loskiel, Georg Heinrich. History of the mission of the United Brethren among the Indians in North America; tr. from the German by Christian Ignatius La Trobe. London. 1794. [3051

Part I is entirely taken up with an account of the Indians themselves; the other parts with the missionary operations of the United Brethren, i. e. the Moravians. The story which goes down to 1787 is minute and manifestly painstaking and derived from the narratives of the workers, as the preface claims. The impress of honesty and veracity is on every page. The translation is well done. The appendix gives the stated rules of the society of the United Brethren, for propagating the gospel among the heathen. There is an index of 21 pages.

McConnell, Samuel David. History of the American Episcopal Church. N. Y.: Whittaker, 1890. 8th ed. 1899. $2. [3052

A book of this character, which has passed through seven editions in as many years, is one which has received the approval of the great body to which it is addressed. And it is worthy of it. The author is a frank admirer of his own communion, but is by no means blind to its faults. He writes out of fullness of knowledge, in a pleasantly enthusiastic style, with occasional humor. The eighth edition differs from the seventh only in the fact that it has a few illustrations. The story is carried down to 1895, but since the Civil War only in a very sketchy way. The book is indexed.

Marsden, John Burton. History of the early Puritans, from the Reformation to the opening of the Civil War in 1642. London: Hamilton. 1853.

—— History of the later Puritans, from the opening of the Civil War in 1642 to the ejection of the Nonconforming clergy in 1662. London: Hamilton. 1852. [3053

Neither volume has an index, but the chapters are fully analyzed by both section and page. There are a few notes and references. The style is sober. But the author is not a genius. In the first volume he pays some attention to the American Puritans.

Mather, Cotton. Magnalia Christi Americana; or The ecclesiastical history of New-England. 1620–98. London. 1702.

—— *Same;* with introd. and notes by Thomas Robbins. Hartford. 1853. 2v. [3054

"The *Magnalia* has great merits; it has, also, fatal defects. In its mighty chaos of fables and blunders and misrepresentations are, of course, lodged many single facts of the utmost value — personal reminiscences, social gossip, snatches of conversation, touches of description, traits of character and life — that can be found nowhere else, and that help us to paint for ourselves some living picture of the great men and the great days of early New England; yet herein, also, history and fiction are so jumbled and shuffled together that it is never possible to tell, without other help than the author's, just where the fiction ends and the history begins. On no disputed question of fact is the unaided testimony of Cotton Mather of much weight." Moses Coit Tyler, in *History of American literature,* v. 2, p. 83.

The best and most usable edition of this extraordinary book is that published in 1853; but it has no index. Mather knew a great deal of the history he here essays, and most of the persons whose biographies he writes, and where he does not know he pads it out. He inserts documents of all sorts, and the most miscellaneous information. But he is eminently readable and enjoyable, and in the edition cited all his many quotations in foreign languages are translated.

Maury, Ann. Memoirs of a Huguenot family; tr. and comp. from the original autobiography of the Rev. James Fontaine, and other family manuscripts; comprising an original journal of travels in Virginia, New York, etc., 1715–16. N. Y.: Putnam. 1853. New ed. 1872. [3055

Portions of this volume originally appeared under the auspices of the Rev. Dr. F. L. Hawks; but the translation is here complete. The appendix renders accessible important documents not elsewhere translate l. The subject was a Huguenot refugee. The journal of John Fontaine, a sermon by Rev. Peter Fontaine, and various letters from the 18th century make up a very interesting and important volume upon one who was the ancestor of many prominent Virginians. It shows the stuff of which the Huguenot emigrants were made.

Meade, William. Old churches, ministers and families of Virginia. Phil.: Lippincott. 1857. 2v. Enl. ed. 1861. 2v. [Subsequent editions without change.] $5. [3056

The author was P. E. Bishop of Virginia, and collected the materials for this work through a long lifetime by means of personal investigations and searches especially made for him in this country and in England. He was able to recover much that was supposed to have been hopelessly lost, and here presents a rich mine of information which has been explored by succeeding generations of students. The work contains numerous woodcuts of churches and other buildings, etc. No clue to the mazes of its contents, aside from chapter headings, was furnished by the Bishop, but the late J. M. Toner, M. D., of Washington, D. C., made an index for his own use, and this was discovered after his death, revised by Hugh A. Morrison, and published by the Southern History Association, Washington, D. C. 1898. $1.

Milton, John. MASSON, DAVID. Life of John Milton, narrated in connection with the political, ecclesiastical and literary history of his time. London: Macmillan. 1858–80. 6v. N. Y.: Macmillan. 6v. V. 1, 2, 3, 6, $6 ea., v. 4, 5, $10 ea. Index vol. 1894. $4.50. [3057

This is one of the monumental works of English literature. Each volume has a very full table of contents, but the index is in a separate and supplemental volume. In connection with Milton's life according to the very discursive plan of the author, there are many references bearing upon the history of Puritanism and Independency in this country.

Moravian Historical Society. Nazareth, Pa. [3058

This society was organized in 1857, and, beginning in 1858, has published occasional volumes of *Transactions,* the sixth appearing in 1900, relating to the history of the Moravians in Pennsylvania.

Murray, John O'Kane. Catholic pioneers of America. N. Y.: Kenedy. 1882.

—— Popular history of the Catholic Church in the United States. N. Y.: Sadlier. 1876. 9th ed. rev. and enl. 1888. [3059

The second work was written for the centennial year. The author dedicates it to the Virgin Mary. He is very enthusiastic, and has made a lively book. He inserts numerous biographical sketches, and there are several portraits. This is not the sort of book one quotes as an authority, but it is the kind one reads. The index is inadequate.

Neal, Daniel. History of the Puritans, or Protestant non-conformists. London : Hett. 1732–38. 4v.

—— Same ; rev., cor. and enl. by Joshua Toulmin. London. 1822. 5v.

—— Same ; ed. by John O. Choules. N. Y. 1848. 2v. [3060

" Mr. Neal, born in London in 1678, was a Dissenting minister in that city, and died in 1743. His history was published in portions between 1731 and 1738. The editions of it now in general circulation are those edited with valuable notes by Dr. Toulmin, the first of which appeared in London in 1793, and the last in 1837. The editor continued the history after the English Revolution. Mr. Neal made diligent research, in order to verify his statements from all the original sources which were open to him. . . . Mosheim accepted Neal's work as of the highest authority." G. E. Ellis, in *Narrative and critical hist. of Am.*, 3 : 250.

Newman, Albert Henry. History of the Baptist churches in the United States. (Am. church history series, v. 2. N. Y.: Christian Lit. Co. 1894. Scribner. $2.) [3061

The author is Professor of church history in McMaster University, Toronto, but an American by birth and training and in close touch with American affairs. He divides his material into four parts : — historical introduction upon continental and English antipedobaptists, the progenitors of the American ; period 1, from Roger Williams and the first Baptist church in America (1639) to the Great Awakening (1740); period 2, Great Awakening (1740) to the organization of the Triennial convention (1814); period 3, to 1894. He shows study, thought and care, and while a strong denominationalist is no partisan. He gives a select bibliography, under the heads English Baptist history; English and American Baptist history; American Baptist history. The volume is trustworthy throughout, and the style is good. Full index. Also separately issued by the American Baptist Publication Society, Philadelphia ($1.75), as part of the series of Baptist histories. See H. L. Burrage, sect. 2996.

O'Gorman, Thomas. History of the Roman Catholic Church in the United States. (Am. church history series, v. 9. N. Y.: Christian Lit. Co. 1897. Scribner. $2.) [3062

At the time he wrote the book the author was Professor of church history in the Catholic University of America in Washington, D. C., but in 1896 became Bishop of Sioux Falls, the diocese comprising the state of South Dakota. The book is based upon study at first-hand of the sources of Roman Catholic history in this country, and while, of course, making out a good case, is not offensively partisan. After 8 pages of bibliography and a brief introduction the author presents: Book I, The mission period, Spanish, French and English, — many well-written sketches of events unknown to most Protestants ; Book II, The Organized church — part 1, Beginning of the hierarchy to the first provincial council of Baltimore (1790–1829) ; part 2, to the first plenary council (1852) ; part 3, to the second plenary council (1866); part 4, to the establishment of the apostolic delegation (1893). The last part is mostly names. Pp. 486–487 present in tabular form the general summary, which brings out many striking facts. The volume is adequately indexed.

Penn, William. Select works. London. 1771. 3d ed. London: Phillips. 1782. 5v. 4th ed. 1825. 3v. [3063

No index. To the first volume is prefixed the author's life, pp. 1–115. This set answers the purpose of those who would read the more noteworthy of the productions of the founder of Pennsylvania.

Perry, William Stevens, *ed.* History of the American Episcopal Church, 1587–1883. Boston : Osgood. 1885. 2v. [3064

This valuable work was " projected by Clarence F. Jewett," so the title-page states. It is made up of consecutive historical chapters written by Bishop Perry, supplemented by *Illustrative monographs* by a number of writers. It is also fully illustrated with portraits, maps, views and autographs. Written upon a large plan and unstinted space, it goes into detail ; but this only makes it more satisfactory to those who have leisure or whose business it is to study our religious history. Our confidence in the authority of the narrative is increased by the number of documents inserted. There is a general index. Compare F. L. Hawks, sect. 3024.

—— *comp.* Historical collections relating to the American colonial church. [Hartford.] 1870–8. 5v.

—— Same : Papers relating to the history of the church in Virginia, etc. [Privately printed.] 1870. 5v. [3065

Contents: V. 1. Virginia. — V. 2. Pennsylvania. — V. 3. Massachusetts. — V. 4. Maryland. — V. 5. Delaware.

" The great collection of church documents is that of Bishop Perry, consisting of 2 octavo volumes for Connecticut (sect. 3025), and 5 quarto volumes, 1 each for Virginia, Pennsylvania, Massachusetts, Maryland, and Delaware. These volumes contain largely letters and reports, mostly signed, but some anonymous, from missionaries and others of the Society [for the Propagation of the Gospel], which was chartered in 1701 and continued the pay of its missionaries until 1785. In the same volumes are also to be found letters written from the colonies to the Archbishop of Canterbury and the Bishop of London. Unfortunately Bishop

Perry did not print all the documents in full, and the volumes are to a considerable extent made up of extracts. This fact will send the careful student back to the collection from which Bishop Perry got his material. This collection, consisting of 18 large folio volumes of manuscripts, is that brought to America by Dr. F. B. Hawks in 1836, and at present in the possession of the registrar of the Protestant Episcopal Church in New York. But the copies contained in these volumes are not complete." Charles M. Andrews, *American colonial history*, in *Annual rept.*, Am. Hist. Assoc., 1898, p. 59.

Powers, Laura Bride. Story of the old missions of California. San Francisco: Doxey. 1893.

—— *Same:* Missions of California. N. Y.: Doxey. 1897. $1.25. [3066

An unpretentious and interesting little book of mission sketches, lacking, however, in broad, general conceptions of the life of the time, and hardly in any real sense a history. It is written in an earnest spirit, not often carelessly, and with considerable literary expression. C. H. S.

Presbyterian Historical Society. Philadelphia, Pa. [3067

This society was organized in 1852. Among its more important publications is, History of the Presbyterian church in America until 1760, by R. Webster ($1).

Prime, Nathaniel Scudder. History of Long Island. N. Y.: Carter. 1845. [3068

"More particularly concerned with its ecclesiastical history." Justin Winsor, in *Narrative and critical hist. of Am.*, 4: 441.

Punchard, George. History of Congregationalism from about A. D. 250 to the present time, in continuation of the account of the origin and earliest history of this system of church polity contained in *A view of Congregationalism*. Salem, Mass. 1841. 2d ed., rewritten and greatly enl. N. Y.: Hurd. 1865-7. 3v. V. 4: Congregationalism in America. Boston: Congregational Pub. Soc. 1880. [3069

The last two chapters of v. 3 and all of v. 4 are devoted to America. V. 4 was finished by the author before his death, but issued posthumously. The title-page promises, and so does the literary executor's preface, another volume which was left ready to be printed, but it never appeared. The index was reserved probably for this closing volume, and so as the work now stands it has none. With the exception of sections upon Congregationalism outside of the United States and a few extremely unsatisfactory pages in the last chapter, the history is not carried beyond 1783. The volume has the good qualities of the previous ones in the series, being based upon long-continued study of the sources and written in a sober but interesting style.

Reichel, William Cornelius, *ed.* Memorials of the Moravian Church. Phil.: Lippincott. 1870. [3070

On the title-page appear the words "Volume I," but they relate to the series, for the book covers the ground assigned to it, viz. the early history of the Moravian Church in this country. Most of it is about Zinzendorf. It only goes down to 1757. Many pages (pp. 189-366) are taken up with the Account of the United Brethren at Bethlehem with the commissioners of the province of Pennsylvania during the Indian war of 1755, '56, and '57. No index, nor adequate analysis of contents.

See, also, sect. 3022.

Riley, Benjamin Franklin. A History of the Baptists in the Southern States east of the Mississippi. Phila. : Am. Bap. Pub. Soc. 1898. $1.25. [3070 a

The volume belongs to the same series as that by J. A. Smith mentioned below, sect. 3086.

Robinson, Charles Edson. Concise history of the United Society of Believers called Shakers. East Canterbury, N. H. [c. 1893.] 50c. [3071

The author is not a Shaker, but his sketches, written originally for *The Manufacturer and builder*, New York, found such acceptance with them that the directors of the community at East Canterbury, N. H., requested their publication in book form. They are very readable, describe the different communities, and are drawn from such authorized publications as *The Shaker compendium* by Elder F. W. Evans (New Lebanon, N. Y. 1859) and *Plain talks concerning the Shakers* by G. A. Lomas (Watervliet, N. Y. 1883), together with personal recollections. But still more authentic as well as much better arranged matter is given in an article on the Shakers in the *Schaff-Herzog encyclopædia of religious knowledge*, vol. iv. 2168-2170.

Sachse, Julius Friedrich. German Pietists of provincial Pennsylvania, 1694-1708. Phil.: Author. 1895. Subs. $5. [Ed. limited to 500 copies.]

—— German Sectarians of Pennsylvania, 1708-1800: a critical and legendary history of the Ephrata Cloister and the Dunkers. Phil.: Author. 1899-1901. 2v. Subs. $5 ea. [Ed. limited to 350 copies.] [3072

The author is a learned antiquary, and his numerous publications upon the Pennsylvania Germans are justly highly esteemed. Both works here named are fully indexed and based upon mastery of the sources.

Schaff, Philip. America; a sketch of the political, social and religious character of the United States, in two lectures; tr. from the German. N. Y.: Scribner. 1855. [3073

One of Dr. Schaff's most useful works. His honest love for his adopted country finds here ardent expression. He wrote it in Germany and Switzerland, and for those countries; apart from libraries but probably from memoranda; at all events out of a full mind. He gives a valuable précis of American church history in the year 1854. No index.

—— Church and state in the United States; or The American idea of religious liberty and its practical effects; with official documents. N. Y.: Putnam. 1888. Scribner. $1.50.   [3074

This treatise upon the First amendment to the Constitution is unique and very valuable. It is in the interesting style of its learned and genial author and fairly glows with its ardent patriotism. The different branches of the subject are suggestively treated, and the progress of religious freedom in Europe is noted by countries. Various official documents are given in the appendix. In the same volume is a brief account of the inauguration of Dr. Schaff as Professor of church history in Union Theological Seminary, on which occasion he delivered an address on the same subject which he here presents in expanded form, reprinted from the *Papers* of the American Historical Association, II, 4. There is no index.

Schmucker, Samuel Simon. American Lutheran Church, historically, doctrinally, and practically delineated, in several discourses. Springfield, O. 1851. 5th ed. Phil.: Miller. 1852.   [3075

The first discourse is a sketch of Lutheranism in the United States down to 1841; the third of the "patriarchs of American Lutheranism." The second deals with the body in Germany, the last three with its doctrinal peculiarities. The whole is fully indexed. The author's portrait faces the title-page. Though prepared so long ago, the volume is still readable and valuable.

Schroeder, Gustavus W. History of the Swedish Baptists in Sweden and America; being an account of the origin, progress and results of that missionary work during the last half of the nineteenth century. N. Y.: Author. 1898. $1.   [3075 a

The author was a sailor before the mast when converted in 1845, but since has been a strong Baptist and the means of starting Baptist missionary operations in Sweden. His book is partly autobiographical, contains little information as to Swedish Baptists in America, but much about the Baptists in Sweden, and still more irrelevant matter. It has no index, only a personal register. Its faults are easily pardoned, as the author is not a literary man and does not pretend to be.

Schweinitz, Edmund Alexander de. History of the church known as the Unitas Fratrum, or The unity of the Brethren, founded by the followers of John Hus, the Bohemian reformer and martyr. Bethlehem, Pa.: Moravian Pub. Off. 1885.   [3076

A history of the old Moravian Church extending to 1722. It begins with a history of Bohemia and Moravia (451–1369); next comes an account of the life and times of John Hus (1369–1415); next the history of the Hussites (1415–1457) and then the Moravian Church history proper. It is drawn from the best sources, German,

Polish and Bohemian, some recent, has footnotes, references and a full index. There are seven portraits. The author was the principal literary man among the Moravians and wrote this book to make the history of the progenitors of the present Church better known. But for the later and especially the American history of the Brethren see the volume by J. T. Hamilton, sect. 3022.

Scouller, James Brown. History of the United Presbyterian Church of North America. (In Am. church history series, v. 11, pp. 145–255. N. Y.: Christian Lit. Co. 1894. Scribner. $2.)   [3077

The author was the accepted historian of his denomination, and wrote in full mastery of its rather complicated history, doing justice to its sects in Scotland and to the previous history of the components. He stated frankly their peculiar tenets. There is no bibliography, but a separate index.

—— Manual of the United Presbyterian Church of North America, 1751–1881. Harrisburg, Pa.: Patriot Pub. Co. 1881.   [3078

This volume is intended primarily for the communion named, and is written by its most prominent historian. It contains the histories of its component parts and of its present unity; historical records of its present and past presbyteries and synods; list of existing congregations; biographical sketches of the entire ministry, past and presen⁺: sketches of the church boards, theological seminaries, colleges, and periodicals. The table of contents is called the index and put at the end! So there is no index. The work was a labor of love and the serious student of American church history will value it highly. It were well if the denomination should bring the records down to date.

Semple, Robert Baylor. History of the rise and progress of the Baptists in Virginia. Richmond: Author. 1810.

—— *Same;* rev. and enl. by G. W. Beale. Richmond: Randolph. 1894.   [3079

The original edition appeared in one small volume in 1810. It is considered an invaluable history, as it conserves so much material regarding individual churches, and so it merited the revision and enlargement it has here received.

Sewel, William. History of the rise, increase and progress of the christian people called Quakers; tr. from the original Low Dutch. London. 1722. [Various later eds.] N. Y.: Chapman. 1844. 2v. in 1.   [3080

"Possesses great value, not only on account of its freedom from error, but because it was written at an early period in the history of the Society of Friends." F. D. Stone, in *Narrative and critical hist. of Am.,* 3: 503.

Shea, John Gilmary. History of the Catholic Church in the United States. N. Y.: Shea. 1886–9. 4v.   [3081

V. 1: The Catholic Church in colonial days, 1521-1763. V. 2: Life and times of the Most Rev. John Carroll, Bishop and first Archbishop of Baltimore; embracing the history of the Catholic Church in the United States, 1763-1815. V. 3: History of the Catholic Church in the United States from the division of the diocese of Baltimore, 1808, and death of Archbishop Carroll, 1815, to the fifth Provincial Council of Baltimore, 1843. V. 4: [the same] to the Second Plenary Council of Baltimore, 1866. Each volume is separately indexed, and is illustrated. The author devoted his life to the subject and is justly considered the historian of his Church in this country.

—— History of the Catholic missions among the Indian tribes of the United States, 1529-1854. N. Y.: Dunigan. 1857. Kenedy. 1882. $2.50. [3082

Opposite the title-page are portraits of John Bapst, missionary to the Abnakis, and Catharine Tehgah-kwita, an Algonquin saint, while in the volume are those of Anthony Peyri, founder of the California mission of San Luis Rey; John de Brebeuf, founder of the Huron mission, and Isaac Jorgues, founder of the Iroquois mission. In the appendix is a list of missionaries, and also of the authorities used in the compilation of the work, which is the standard on the subject, drawn from the sources by a practised literary hand, and covers the ground in scholarly fashion. There is an adequate index.

Simpson, Matthew. A hundred years of Methodism. N. Y.: Methodist Book Concern. 1876. $1.35. [3083

This is a glowing sketch of Methodism, derived from Tyerman and Stevens, without footnotes, references, bibliography or index. The matter is, however, divided into paragraphs and chronologically arranged. It fulfils its purpose to increase the interest of the Centennial year.

Smith, Joseph. GREGG, THOMAS. The prophet of Palmyra. N. Y.: Alden. 1890. [3084

The title further describes this book as "Mormonism reviewed and examined in the life, character, and career of its founder, from 'Cumorah Hill' to Carthage jail and the desert, together with a complete history of the Mormon era in Illinois, and an exhaustive investigation of the 'Spalding manuscript' theory of the book of Mormon." The author was especially familiar with the Nauvoo part of the story, and this and the earliest incidents are well covered, the Missouri persecution being very inadequately treated. An important feature is a letter from Judge Harding of Indiana, who in his boyhood knew the Smith family. The book contains many original documents, but is marred by an unskilful arrangement of the material and by a strong animus against the Mormons.   F. J. S.

—— TULLIDGE, EDWARD WHEELOCK. Life of Joseph the prophet. Plano, Ill.: Bd. Pub. Latter-Day Saints. 2d ed. enl. 1880. [3085

This volume gives the autobiography, the biography and many of the prophetic utterances of Joseph Smith, Jr., the founder of Mormonism; the history of

the body which rejected the Brigham Young type of Mormonism, and the biography of the present Joseph Smith, the head of the church which claims to be the true Mormondom. The author belongs to it. The publishers have inserted steel portraits of Joseph Smith, Jr., his wife Emma, his son Joseph, and of his brother Hyrum, but no index.

Smith, Justin Almerin. History of the Baptists in the western states east of the Mississippi. Phil.: Am. Bap. Pub. Soc. 1896. $1.25. [3086

This volume belongs to the same series ([American] Baptist history series) to which the books here noted by H. S. Burrage, A. H. Newman, B. F. Riley and H. C. Vedder belong. It is to be followed by a volume on the Baptists in the trans-Mississippi states by Lemuel Moss. Each volume is a 12mo, of about 320 pp., is indexed, and retails at $1.25.

Sprague, William Buell. Annals of the American pulpit; or Commemorative notices of distinguished American clergymen of various denominations. N. Y.: Carter. 1856–68. 10v. New ed. 1865–1873. 9v. [3087

This is a monumental work in denominational ministerial biography carried out upon a uniform plan. The author lists the ministers he proposes to commemorate in chronological order, writes a brief notice of each from the best sources available and with much help from competent persons, and then supplements it with letters from those acquainted with the subject. At the end of the volume which concludes his treatment of the denomination he gives an alphabetical index of the names of the subjects, of those who have furnished original letters, and of names incidentally introduced into the text or notes. If there were an adequate index, one to the contents of the volumes, their extraordinary value and interest would be better appreciated. They have rescued many a name from undeserved oblivion and present a rich variety of instructive and entertaining matter. There is an unpublished volume upon several minor sects. Nothing was prepared upon the Roman Catholics. The list is as follows: vols. 1, 2, Trinitarian Congregationalists. — 3, 4, Presbyterians. — 5, Episcopalians. — 6, Baptists. — 7, Methodists. — 8, Unitarians. — 9, Lutherans, Reformed Dutch. — 10, American Associate, Associate Reformed, Reformed Presbyterians.

Spreng, Samuel P. History of the Evangelical association. (In Am. church history series, v. 12, pp. 383–439.) N. Y.: Christian Lit. Co. 1894. Scribner. $2. [3088

The author is editor of the denominational organ, and entirely competent to present its brief history. There is a one page bibliography and the matter is separately indexed.

Stapleton, Ammon. Annals of the Evangelical Association of North America and history of the United Evangelical Churches. Harrisburg, Pa.: Pub. Ho. Un. Evan. Ch. 1900. $3. [3088 a

This valuable volume is in three parts: I. "The early days;" a detailed account derived largely at first-hand of the origin of the Church under Rev. Jacob Albright and his co-laborers, and making much out of the laymen whose homes were the first meeting-houses, and who shared the persecutions of the beginnings. — II. "Conference records:" a documentary history of the Church to 1887, largely a matter of names, closing with statistical tables. — III. Biographies of the prominent ministers of the Church. — IV. The United Evangelical Church: embracing an account of the division of the Evangelical Association, the causes which led thereto, and the organization of the United Evangelical Church; also a continuation of the annals of the annual conferences adhering thereto, and brief abstracts of general conference proceedings, church organizations, literary institutions, statistics, etc. The volume contains several interesting photographs and is indexed. It must have cost much labor to prepare and will remain a standard work.

Steiner, Bernard C. Protestant revolution in Maryland. See American Historical Association, sect. 249. [3089

Stephens, J. V. Causes leading to the organization of the Cumberland Presbyterian Church. Nashville, Tenn.: Cumberland Pres. Pub. House. 1898. 40c. [3090

An authoritative defense of the Church's position. The author is Professor of ecclesiastical history in Cumberland University. He prefaces his little book with nine pages of bibliography, but provides no index. He quotes many volumes and endeavors to be impartial, while of course he is strongly denominational.

Stevens, Abel. History of the Methodist Episcopal Church in the United States. N. Y.: Meth. Bk. Concern. [c. 1864–7.] 4v. $6. [3091

V. 1: Planting of American Methodism. V. 2: Planting and training of American Methodism. V. 3: [1792–1804]. V. 4: [to 1820]. Portraits are of Thomas Rankin, Rev. Thomas Vasey, Rev. William McKendree, Bishop Whatcoat. This is the standard history of the denomination for the period it covers. The contents are indexed in the 4th volume.

—— *Same, abridged :* Compendious history of American Methodism. N. Y.: Meth. Bk. Concern. 1867. $2.50. [3092

The narrative is brought down to 1866. It meets the wants of those who desire a succinct account, and is characterized by the same qualities as the larger work, of which it is an abridgment.

—— History of the religious movement of the 18th century, called Methodism. N. Y.: Meth. Bk. Concern. [c. 1858–61.] 3v. $4.50. [3093

V. 1: From the origin of Methodism to the death of Whitefield. V. 2: From the death of Whitefield to the death of Wesley. V. 3 : From the death of Wesley to the Centenary jubilee of Methodism [1839]. In v. 3 is the index to the entire work, which is the standard American work on the subject. It contains much matter relating to America. But to that subject the author devoted the volumes mentioned above and below (sect. 3091–2, 3094). The portraits are of John Wesley, Charles Wesley and Jabez Bunting.

—— Supplementary history of American Methodism : a continuation of the author's abridged history of American Methodism. N. Y.: Methodist Book Concern. [c. 1899.] $1.50. [3094

This volume was finished only a short time before the author's death. It goes from 1866 to 1890, but upon a different plan, being a series of studies rather than a chronological arrangement of data, and affected more or less consciously by the knowledge that many of the persons mentioned were still living and many of the events still passing. Portraits are given of 14 bishops, including Simpson, Janes, Gilbert Haven and John P. Newman. There is no index.

Thomas, Allen Clapp *and* **Richard Henry.** History of the Society of Friends in America. (In Am. church history series, v. 12, pp. 163–308. N. Y.: Christian Lit. Co. 1894. Scribner. $2.) [3095

The authors are brothers. The first is a Professor in Haverford College, the second was the editor of the *Friends' review*. Their joint labor is a fine specimen of literature. The story they have to tell might well be tame, but as told by them it becomes fascinating, since they know its sources and its past and present, and are so deeply in love with their once suffering and now unmolested friends. They give, in seven pages, a well-divided bibliography ; and the work is indexed.

Thompson, Robert Ellis. History of the Presbyterian churches in the United States. (Am. church history series, v. 6.) N. Y.: Christian Lit. Co. 1895. Scribner. $2. [3096

On the whole the best book on the subject. Yet it would have been better if the author had not been pressed for time and had not attempted to cover so much space. The preceding bibliography is full, and arranged under detailed heads.

Thornton, John Wingate, *ed.* The pulpit of the American Revolution ; or The political sermons of the period of 1776 ; with hist. introd., notes and illustrations. Boston: Gould. 1860. 2d ed. Boston: Lothrop. 1876. [3097

A collection of nine discourses, ranging from Dr. Mayhew's (Jan. 30, 1750) to Dr. Stiles' Election sermon, 1783, to prove that "to the Puritan pulpit we owe the moral force which won our independence." The general introduction and the nine prefatory notes are careful. Judicious notes are interspersed. A good edition of characteristically stirring discourses which have occasionally an astonishingly modern ring to them. **H. W. H.**

Tiffany, Charles Comfort. History of the Protestant Episcopal Church in the United States of America. (Am. church history series, v. 7.) N. Y.: Christian Lit. Co. 1895. Scribner. $2. [3098

This is a most admirable volume. The author has style and the historic sense. His position as Archdeacon of New York testifies to his churchmanship, but so judicial is his mind and so impartial his statements that none could decide from this volume to what party in the church he belongs. He is master of his materials and has produced a well-proportioned volume, setting forth in 17 chapters the colonial church and the Protestant Episcopal Church. The story is uniformly well told, although the early part is largely the story of an unpopular exotic; and the middle part of "suspended animation and feeble growth." He presents a bibliography under the heads: I. General history; II. Church history, 1. General. 2. Special histories. 3. Local histories. III. Biography. IV. Prayer-book. V. Constitution and canons. VI. Miscellaneous. The volume is adequately indexed, and is in all respects a model of what a denominational history should be.

Tulloch, John. English Puritanism and its leaders: Cromwell, Milton, Baxter, Bunyan. Edin.: Blackwood. 1861. [3099

Biographical essays by one of the great leaders of Scotch liberalism.

Tyler, Benjamin Bushrod. History of the Disciples of Christ. (In Am. church history series, v. 12, pp. 1–162. N. Y.: Christian Lit. Co. 1894. Scribner. $2.) [3100

The author is well qualified for his task, as he is a recognized leader among his brethren; and his work here is based on thorough acquaintance with the sources. It is, however, discursive and too much like a denominational tract. There is a one page bibliography and a separate index.

Uhden, Hermann Ferdinand. The New England theocracy: a history of the Congregationalists in New England to the revivals of 1740. Tr. from the 2d German ed. [Berlin, 1857] by H. C. Conant. Boston. 1859. [3101

The theme of the volume is the relation of church and state in New England down to the Great Awakening under Edwards and Whitefield. The author, though a German and working in Germany, had access to good materials and wrote under the guidance of the great historian Neander. In the appendix are Robinson's letter to the Leyden emigrants, July 27, 1620; an annotated list of the books used in the work, and a chronological view of New England history to 1740. The book is indexed. The translator bestowed much labor upon its verification.

United States Catholic Historical Society. New York City. This society was organized in 1884, and from 1887 to 1890 published the *United States Catholic historical magazine*, 3v. [3102

Vedder, Henry C. History of the Baptists in the middle states. Phil.: Am. Baptist Pub. Soc. 1898. $1.25. [3103

The preface is in two parts, one before and one after the body of the book! The author has very assiduously cultivated the virgin soil of his denominational history, quotes documents and gives occasional references, and has produced a trustworthy volume, with an index. One of the series of Baptist history. See J. A. Smith, sect. 3086.

Walker, Williston. Creeds and platforms of Congregationalism. N. Y.: Scribner. 1893. $3.50. [3104

He who would really understand American church history must read its documentary sources. Nothing could be more satisfactory than the way Prof. Walker, of Hartford Theological Seminary, now of Yale Divinity School, upon whom the mantle of Henry Martyn Dexter has fallen, presents these sources for Congregational history in our country, and in the mother country as well. Here we have the famous confessions of the London-Amsterdam church, the Mayflower compact, the Cambridge (Mass.) platform, the Savoy (London) declaration, and many others, all accurately reprinted in well-nigh facsimile, and prefaced with special introductions and carefully annotated. The volume is elaborately indexed, beautifully printed, and in every way a delight to the scholarly eye.

—— History of the Congregationalist churches in the United States. (Am. church history series, v. 3.) N. Y.: Christian Lit. Co. 1894. Scribner. $2. [3104 a

Prefaced by a careful bibliography. This is by far the best account of the Congregationalist denomination in America. Dr. Walker writes in clear style, with a thorough information and with a directness which wins the reader. He gives a hundred pages to the antecedents of the body on the other side of the Atlantic and another hundred to the early developments in New England. He is particularly strong in his analyses of platforms of belief and the development of theological schools. H. W. H.

—— Ten New England leaders. N. Y.. Silver. 1901. $2. [3104 b

The Southworth lectures of 1898-9 in Andover Theological Seminary. The leaders are: William Bradford, John Cotton, Richard Mather, John Eliot, Increase Mather, Jonathan Edwards, Charles Chauncy, Samuel Hopkins, Leonard Woods, Leonard Bacon. A masterly volume.

Weeks, Stephen Beauregard. The religious development in the province of North Carolina. (Johns Hopkins Univ. studies, ser. 10, no. 5–6.) Balt. 1892. 50c. [3105

The purpose of Dr. Weeks's study is two-fold. "First, it seeks to show that the earliest settlers in North Carolina were not religious refugees, that they came to the province not from religious but economic motives; second, it traces the struggle for an establishment, and shows that religious freedom, like political freedom, was a growth."

—— Church and state in North Carolina. (Johns Hopkins Univ. studies, ser. 11, no. 5–6.) Balt. 1893. 50c. [3106

A continuation of the study begun in *The religious development*, tracing the relations between church and state until their final separation.

Weiss, Charles. History of the French Protestant refugees, from the revocation of the Edict of Nantes to our own days; tr. from the French by Henry William Herbert. N. Y.: Stringer. 1854. 2v. [3107

The appendix, in the second volume, is upon the Huguenots in America; the author is anonymous, — probably Mr. Herbert himself. The book is a standard one. It has no index.

White, D. A. New England Congregationalism. See Essex Institute, sect. 3143. [3108

White, William. Memoirs of the Protestant Episcopal Church in the United States of America. Phil. 1820.

—— *Same;* ed. with notes and a sketch of the origin and progress of the colonial church by the Rev. B. F. DeCosta. N. Y.: Dutton. 1881. $4. [3109

This is the best edition of the work which must always remain one of the chief sources of American church history. It is indexed. •

—— WARD, JULIUS HAMMOND. Life and times of Bishop White. (Makers of America.) N. Y.: Dodd. 1892. $1. [3110

It belongs to the *Makers of America* series, with the biographies of Higginson and Hooker elsewhere mentioned (sect. 3030, 3033), and has the same excellent features. It is indexed, and has a portrait of Bishop White as its frontispiece.

Whitefield, George. Journal of a voyage from London to Savannah [1737–8]. 5th ed. London. 1739. [3111

The experiences of Whitefield on his voyages to and from the American colonies and as an itinerant preacher there went through many editions as *Journals* and as *Continuation of journals*, which were afterward placed in his *Life* and *A short account of Whitefield*, etc. He traveled several times from Georgia as far north as New York, preaching and collecting money for his orphan house. His journals are composed largely of prayers, exhortations, and Scriptural quotation, but interspersed with accounts of his daily life. Much information may be gathered concerning the means of travel, colonial life, the race elements of the different colonies, and the state of religion in America. E. E. S.

Whittemore, Thomas. Modern history of Universalism: from the Reformation to the present time. Boston: Author. 1830. New ed. Boston: Tompkins. 1860. V. 1. [3112

Unfortunately no more than the first volume of the new edition was published, and that relates exclusively to non-American matters. It has value for the student of American church history because it sets forth in an authoritative way the claim of the denomination to an inheritance in the past; but for the later and American history see Eddy (sect. 3008).

Wilberforce, Samuel. History of the Protestant Episcopal Church in America. London: Burns. 1844. New ed. Rivington. 1856. N. Y.: Stanford. 1849. Pott. 1856. [3113

Opposite the title-page in the American edition is an "ecclesiastical map of America," i. e., of the dioceses of the church in Canada and the United States, and in the work is a diocesan conspectus of the United States. The American editor was Evan M. Johnson. The author was at the time the archdeacon of Surrey, and afterwards the famous bishop of Oxford. He never visited this land, but used diligently the sources at his command in England, which were ample for the pre-Revolutionary part of his history, and so that part is well done. He speaks out his mind freely upon persons and things, and is particularly severe, as might be expected of a son of William Wilberforce, upon the attitude of the church toward slavery. This caused his book to be much criticised in some quarters. There is no index.

Williams, Roger. NARRAGANSETT CLUB. Publications. Providence. 1866–74. 6v. [3114

1. Biographical introduction to the writings of Roger Williams, by Reuben Aldridge Guild; with Roger Williams's Key to the Indian language, and Cotton's Letter to Roger Williams, and his reply, ed. by James Hammond Trumbull and Reuben Aldridge Guild. 1866.
2. Master John Cotton's answer to Master Roger Williams, etc.; ed. by J. Lewis Diman and Reuben Aldridge Guild. 1867.
3. The bloody tenant of persecution; ed. by Samuel L. Caldwell.
4. The bloody tenant yet more bloody; ed. by Samuel L. Caldwell. 1870.
5. George Fox digg'd out of his burrowes; ed. by J. Lewis Diman. 1872.
6. Letters of Roger Williams; ed. by John Russell Bartlett. 1874.

The Narragansett Club was formed in 1865 for the purpose of republishing all the known writings of Roger Williams. The six volumes of its publications are "edited by well-known historical scholars, and are a valuable contribution to the personal history of Roger Williams and to the history of the controversy on religious liberty of which he was the great advocate." C. Deane, in *Narrative and critical hist. of Am.*, 3: 377.

See, also, sect. 1034–1037.

Zeisberger, David. Diary of David Zeisberger, a Moravian missionary among the Indians of Ohio; tr. from the German MS. and ed. by Eugene F. Bliss. Cin.: Clarke. 1885. 2v. $6. [3115

This is a satisfactory translation and edition of one of the noblest lives in American history. It is fully indexed. The biographical sketch is taken from De Schweinitz' biography. The diary goes from 1781-1798, and by it we come into daily contact with a great soul.

— SCHWEINITZ, EDMUND DE. Life and times of David Zeisberger. Phil.: Lippincott. 1870.

[3116

The standard and unsupersedable life of the great Moravian missionary who spent 62 years among the Indians in Georgia, Pennsylvania, New York, New England, Ohio, Michigan, and Canada, told from the original MSS. preserved in the archives of Moravian churches, including Zeisberger's diary and from printed sources by the most illustrious of modern American Moravians. The author has made his book a thesaurus of information about the American Indians and their relations, peaceful and hostile, with the colonists. It has a geographical glossary of forts, Indian villages and other settlements mentioned in it, and a full index.

PART IV. THE UNITED STATES BY SECTIONS

Griffin, Appleton Prentiss Clark. Index of articles upon American local history in the historical collections in the Boston Public Library. Boston. 1889. (Boston Public Library. Bibliographies of special subjects, no. 3.) [3117

A note states that the publication of this index was begun in the Bulletin of the Library, April, 1883. The index is intended to serve as a guide to historical and descriptive sketches, which relate to localities, contained in historical publications — including periodicals devoted to history, official publications, collections and proceedings of historical societies, and in state and county histories. Of these last only those are taken where a town, city, or county receives independent treatment. Independent works are not included. The arrangement is alphabetical under place.

Perkins, Frederic Beecher, *comp.* Check list for American local history, reprinted with additions from the Bulletins of the Boston Public Library. Boston: Rockwell. 1876. [3118

The compiler states that this list is a memorandum to promote the completion of the historical department of the Boston Public Library. The list is confined to towns, counties and regions less than states, and titles of works reprinted in collections are not included. Titles of public documents, publications and histories of local institutions are not generally included, except in the case of Massachusetts. Arrangement is alphabetical under place. Titles are much condensed and abbreviated ; those of books not in the library have not been verified. Includes independent works only. Gives date of publication but not place.

NEW ENGLAND

(*Comprehensive history, covering all or several periods. For Colonial history, see Part III, sect. 891–1048. See, also, Part I : Sources.*)

Adams, Charles Francis. Massachusetts: its historians and its history. Boston: Houghton. 1893. $1. [3119

A brief discussion, originally delivered as lectures, of the place of Massachusetts in the general history of the world's civilization. The fundamental idea of the book is derived from Buckle. It is a strong and brilliant protest against the narrow, provincial views which are usually found in histories of the American colonies, and a plea for the adoption of such a view as shall show the connection of their history with that of the world at large. The feature of Massachusetts history on which the author specially dwells is religious intolerance, which checked intellectual and moral growth, and caused a " theologico-glacial period," lasting from the middle of the 17th till the beginning of the 19th century. A very suggestive book.   H. L. O.

Adams, Charles Francis, *et al.* Genesis of New England towns. See Massachusetts Historical Society, sect. 344. [3120

Aldrich, P. Emory. Massachusetts and Maine, their union and separation See American Antiquarian Society, sect. 242. [3121

Allen, Ira. Natural and political history of the state of Vermont. London. 1798.

—— *Same.* (In Vermont Hist. Soc. collections, v. 1. Montpelier. 1870.) [3122

Treats the period from 1764 to 1791. Written by a leader in the contest between the Vermonters and the people of New York and in the conflicts of the Revolutionary War. Written from memory and from information derived from other participants. Prejudiced, uncritical and dull. The foundation of all other histories of Vermont so far as this period is concerned.   E. C.

Arnold, Samuel Greene. History of the state of Rhode Island and Providence Plantations, 1636–1790. N. Y.: Appleton. 1859–60. 2v. 4th ed. Providence: Preston. 1894. 2v. net $7.50. [3123

The standard history of Rhode Island, and one of the best of our state histories. The period covered by this work closes at 1790. From it one may obtain the distinctively Rhode Island view of New England history. It should be used thus as a valuable corrective to the exaggerations of many historians of Massachusetts. Events are treated pretty strictly in chronological order, but great pains were taken by the author to secure fulness and accuracy of detail. The work is solid rather than interesting.   H. L. O.

Austin, George Lowell. History of Massachusetts. Boston : Estes. 1876. [3124

This is one of the abundant crop of " histories " to which the centennial of national independence gave birth. The compiler states in his preface that he found " the researches of earlier historians have been such as to render almost unnecessary any special investigation on the part of those who follow after them." This last statement, together with the admission that he had " generally followed the arrangement adopted by Barry," indicates the character of the book. If the reader will follow the hint thus given, he will find that the book, so far as events prior to 1820 are concerned, is a mere outline or epitome of Barry's *History of Massachusetts*. Austin's *History of Massachusetts*, in short, belongs to the company of masqueraders which appear before the public in clothing that was not made for them, and of their right to which they can apparently give no clear account.

H. L. O.

Bacon, Edwin Monroe. Historic pilgrimages in New England. Boston : Silver. [c. 1898.] Net $1.50. [3125

"One of a rapidly increasing class of books, given to details of the homes and customs of Americans. The familiar plan of answering the questions of a bright young companion is adopted, and much that is valuable information is thus set forth. There are many illustrations, some of them uncommon, some very familiar; and the book will serve to while away more than one hour with the fathers of New England." *Dial* (Chicago), 26 : 162.

Barber, John Warner. Connecticut historical collections, relating to the history and antiquities of every town in Connecticut. New Haven : Durrie. 1836. 2d ed. 1846.

[3126

The text and illustrations of the first and second editions are the same — the latter contains descriptions of new towns and statistics, in the form of an appendix. The work contains nearly 200 illustrations — mostly from woodcuts, but of considerable historical interest. The text is valuable, especially on account of extracts from records and newspapers scattered through the volume. One of the best works of its kind. E. C.

Bartlett, John Russell. Bibliography of Rhode Island, with notes, historical, biographical and critical. Providence. 1864. [3127

"Rhode Island has been fortunate in its bibliographer." Justin Winsor, in *Narrative and critical hist. of Am.*, 3 : 380.

Belknap, Jeremy. History of New Hampshire. V. 1, Phil. 1784. V. 2, Boston : Thomas. 1792. V. 3, Boston : Belknap. 1792. 2d ed. [enl.] Boston : Bradford. 1813. 3v. [3128

Volumes 1 and 2 of this work contain the history of New Hampshire from the discovery of the river Piscataqua to the adoption of the Federal Constitution. Volume 3 is a treatise on the geography, natural history, productions, society, laws and government of that Commonwealth at the time the author wrote. The first two volumes are the most valuable. The author was one of the most refined and scholarly men of his time, and his excellencies are reflected in his writings. His work has always held the highest rank among the older state histories. Said De Tocqueville, "The reader of Belknap will find more general ideas and more strength of thought, than are to be met with in other American historians, even to the present day." H. L. O.

Boston. *Record Commission*. Reports. See Syllabus of materials, sect. 118. [3129

Bostonian Society. Boston, Mass. This society, organized in 1881, publishes *Annual proceedings* beginning with 1883, and has issued three volumes of *Collections*, 1886–88 ; among its occasional publications is *Old Boston taverns and tavern clubs*, by S. A. Drake.

[3130

Bowen, Clarence Winthrop. Boundary disputes of Connecticut. Boston : Osgood. 1882. [3131

Covers the whole subject from the beginning to 1880. Arranged topically. Admirably illustrated with facsimiles of old maps and plans. A sound, scholarly work. Written entirely from the sources and supplied with bibliographical notes. E. C.

Bradford, Alden. History of Massachusetts. Boston. 1822–29. 3v. [3132

In the first of these volumes the history of Massachusetts is traced from 1764 to 1775 ; in the second the period from 1775 to 1789 is treated ; in the third the period from 1790 to 1820. The author was one of the most thorough and systematic of the earlier students of Massachusetts history. His style was clear and forcible, but without ornament. His sympathies were strong in favor of the colonial course in the Revolution. Much of the documentary material used in the preparation of the first volume is in the *Massachusetts state papers*, which had previously been edited by Mr. Bradford. These volumes are of importance to the investigator and are a credit to the scholarship of their time. H. L. O.

—— History of Massachusetts, 1620–1820. Boston : Hilliard. 1835. [3133

This book of some 400 pages was written for the purpose of supplying the people of Massachusetts with "a full but condensed narrative" of their history. At the time when it was published it fulfilled well the purpose for which it was prepared. For the period of the Revolution it contains the substance of the author's larger works, though with the omission of much of the purely political history. The outline of the earlier history of the colony and province, and the later history of the state, is clearly and effectively presented. H. L. O.

Brooks, Elbridge Streeter. Stories of the old Bay state. N. Y. : Am. Book Co. 1899. 60c. [3134

This is a history of Massachusetts colony and state "written down" to suit children of from ten to fourteen years of age. Mr. Brooks is a veteran story-teller and has done his work well. The stories, which centre largely in the lives of individuals and touch politics, religion, literature, inventions, and dramatic events of any kind, are interesting and accurate. The illustrations, unfortunately, are idealized and poor.

C. M. A.

Colburn, Jeremiah. Bibliography of the

local history of Massachusetts. Boston: Lunt. 1871. [3135

"A volume of 119 pages; deserves a place in every New England library." C. Deane, in *Narrative and critical hist. of Am.*, 3: 363.

Connecticut. Records and documents. See in Syllabus of materials, sect. 151–156. [3136

Connecticut Historical Society. Hartford, Conn. Organized in 1825, this society has published 7 volumes of *Collections*, 1860–99. Vol. 8 in press, Oct. 1901. [3137

Among their contents are: V. 1: Roger Wolcott's journal at the siege of Louisbourg, 1745: — Connecticut officers at Louisbourg: — The Ticonderoga expedition, 1775.
V. 2: Correspondence of Silas Deane, delegate to the congress of Philadelphia, 1774–76.
V. 4–5: The Talcott papers; correspondence and documents during Joseph Talcott's governorship of Connecticut, 1724–41.
V. 7: Orderly book and journals kept by Connecticut men while taking part in the American Revolution.
Among their other publications are: Indian names of places, etc., in and on the border of Connecticut, by J. H. Trumbull; and History of the Indians of Connecticut to 1850, by John W. De Forest.

Deane, Charles. Connection of Massachusetts with slavery and the slave trade. See American Antiquarian Society, sect. 236. [3138

Dexter, Franklin B. History of Connecticut, as illustrated by the names of her towns. See American Antiquarian Society, sect. 235. [3139

Drake, Samuel Adams. Around the Hub: a boy's book about Boston. Boston: Roberts. 1881. Little. $1.25. [3140

Tells the story of Boston in an attractive way for boys. Well illustrated with facsimiles and drawings of real things. E. C.

—— Historic fields and mansions of Middlesex. Boston: Osgood. 1874.

—— Old landmarks and historic fields of Middlesex. Boston: Roberts. 1876. [c. 1873.]

—— Historic mansions and highways around Boston; new and rev. ed. Boston: Little. 1899. $2.50. [3141

With the exception of a few pages of ch. xix, the text of these three editions is substantially identical. The illustrations of the 1874 edition are decidedly superior to those in the other volumes. A few errors are corrected in the later editions. This work contains the facts and traditions of the most interesting portion of Massachusetts outside of Boston and Plymouth. The book is valuable, although no attempt has been made to separate the true from the fictitious. E. C.

—— Old Boston taverns and tavern clubs. See Bostonian Society, above, sect. 3130. [3142

Essex Institute, Salem, Mass. The Essex Historical Society was organized in 1821; the name was changed to the present form and the institute incorporated in 1848. Between 1848 and 1870, 6 volumes of *Proceedings* (discontinued) were published, which were supplemented through 1898 by 30 volumes of *Bulletins*. This latter publication, in the form of a quarterly periodical, has ceased, but monographs will be printed from time to time in continuation. From 1859 to 1898, 34 volumes of *Historical collections* have been issued. [3143

These are devoted largely to local history and genealogy. Among the occasional publications of the Institute are: New England Congregationalism in its origin and purity, by D. A. White: — Historical sketch of Salem, 1626–1879, by C. S. Osgood and H. M. Batchelder: — Journal of Dr. Caleb Rea in the expedition against Ticonderoga, 1758: — Diaries of Lemuel Wood of Boxford, in the Canadian expedition of 1759–60: — Reminiscences of the Revolution, prison letters and sea journal of Caleb Foote. Compiled by his grandson, Caleb Foote.

Farmer, John, *and* **Jacob Bailey Moore,** *comps.* Collections, topographical, historical, and biographical, relating principally to New Hampshire. Concord: Hill. 1822. Reprinted 1831. [3144

Two volumes entitled *Collections, historical and miscellaneous, and monthly literary journal*, Concord, 1823–24, are generally regarded as vols. 2 and 3 of the above. The work as a whole contains many useful documents — often printed elsewhere — and a mass of miscellaneous information, poetry, anecdotes, and biographical sketches now of slight service to the student. E. C.

Gilman, Arthur. Story of Boston. (Great cities of the republic.) N. Y.: Putnam. 1889. $1.75. [3145

A well-written account of many of the famous personages who have lived in Boston and of the events with which they have been connected. Occasional references to social life and manners. In no sense a history of the town or the municipality, but rather the events dwelt on are those of special significance in the history of the colony. Shows considerable acquaintance with original authorities, and is a good popular treatment of the subject. H. L. O.

Greene, George Washington. Short history of Rhode Island. Providence: Reid. 1877. [3146

"An excellent compendium, much needed. It is compiled largely from Mr. Arnold's work" (sect. 3123). C. Deane, in *Narrative and critical hist. of Am.*, 3: 376.

Griffin, Appleton Prentiss Clark. Bibliography of the historical publications issued by the New England states. (Reprinted from the Publications of the Colonial Society of Massachusetts, v. 3.) Cambridge : University Press. 1895. [3147

"The purpose of this paper is to give a bibliographical accóunt of the collections of printed archives of the New England states, with descriptive analyses of their contents. . . . It has been no part of my plan to include reprints of the bodies of laws, such as Whitmore's . . . or Goodell's editions." *Introd.*

Hale, Edward Everett. Historic Boston and its neighborhood : an historical pilgrimage personally conducted; arranged for seven days. (Appletons' home reading books.) N. Y.: Appleton. 1898. 50c. [3148

Historic Boston is one of a series of home reading books edited by Dr. W. T. Harris. The title explains the character of the book, but it does not disclose the delightfully chatty and informal manner in which Dr. Hale conducts his party, or the excellent illustrations which the book contains. The visitor to Boston will find this an admirable supplement to his Baedeker.
C. M. A.

—— Story of Massachusetts. (Story of the states.) Boston : Lothrop. 1891. $1.50. [3149

In this book, which was prepared for young people, the writer has selected certain episodes in the history of Massachusetts as representative of the whole, and has dwelt upon these at considerable length. This method is to be particularly commended in books of this class, and the author has used it judiciously. His selection of topics has been such as to bring into relief many of the chief features of Massachusetts history. Occasionally the narrative is thrown into the form of a story, or is further illustrated by a poem, both of which increase its interest, but are not used to such excess as to seriously impair the truthfulness of the history. The vigorous and natural style for which the author is well known is used with good effect to increase the attractiveness of the book. But Dr. Hale assumes throughout an extremely patriotic tone, which the facts will scarcely justify, and occasionally expresses his dislike of historic characters in needlessly offensive terms. He is habitually guilty of the error of identifying the navigation act with the acts of trade. Such errors as the statement that the stamp act was to go into force the first Tuesday in October, 1765, and that the Grenville ministry ordered troops to be transferred from Castle Island into Boston, unnecessarily impair the usefulness of an otherwise good book.
H. L. O.

Hall, Hiland. History of Vermont from its discovery to its admission into the Union in 1791. Albany : Munsell. 1868. [3150

Usually cited from binder's title as Hall's *Early history of Vermont.* Written from the original documents and from personal descriptions, such as Ira Allen's *Vermont.* The volume also contains very many documents. It gives the Vermont view of the

contest with New York. The standard history of Vermont before 1791. Style and make-up of the book dull.
E. C.

Hawthorne, Nathaniel. Whole history of grandfather's chair; or True stories from New England history, 1620–1803. (Riverside literature series.) Boston: Houghton. [c. 1850–96.] Net 70c. (Children's favorite classics.) Crowell. 1898. 75c. [3151

Hawthorne, taking a carved oaken chair made in England of wood grown in the park of the Earl of Lincoln, supposes it to have been brought to America by the Lady Arbella Johnson, at the founding of Boston. From the Lady Arbella it descends to Roger Williams, and from him to Harry Vane. Later the chief worthies of Massachusetts, as the generations pass, become owners of the chair, until from Samuel Adams, at his death in 1803, it falls to "Grandfather," who, seated in it, tells to his grandchildren its story, thus unfolding the chronicles of New England. It is a book of absorbing interest as the work of the "prentice-hand" which presently with master-power was to write the *Gentle boy, Howe's masquerade,* and *Lady Eleanor's mantle;* and a little later *The scarlet letter* and *The marble faun.* To children, indeed to their parents, this book offers such an introduction to the New England history as perhaps can never be surpassed.
J. K. H.

Heaton, John L. Story of Vermont. (Story of the states.) Boston: Lothrop. [c. 1889.] $1.50. [3152

Written from the sources with a liberal sprinkling of traditional anecdote. Covers the history of the state from the coming of Champlain to 1880. Considerable attention given to industrial history and to the "life of the people." Well written and attractively printed. Illustrated with "fancy pictures." E. C.

Holland, Josiah Gilbert. History of western Massachusetts. Springfield : S. Bowles. 1855. 2v. [3153

A valuable local history, which originally appeared in unrevised form in the *Springfield Republican.* The author later greatly improved and enlarged it, and issued it in permanent form. Its subject is the history of that part of Massachusetts which lies west of Worcester County. It consists of three parts, 1, an outline of the history of the region ; 2, essays on the geology, agriculture and leading interests of the region ; 3, a history of the towns of western Massachusetts. The third part occupies all of the second volume. In its preparation the author had the aid of many correspondents, who copied records, gathered statistics, and corrected errors. A great array of facts and the greatest accuracy possible at the time were thus secured. In the first part the settlement of Springfield, Northampton and Hadley, the Indian wars, and Shays's Rebellion are treated with special fulness.
H. L. O.

Hollister, Gideon Hiram. History of Connecticut, to the adoption of the present constitution. New Haven : Durrie. 1855. 2v. 2d ed., enl. and improved. Hartford: Case. 1857. 2v. Belknap. $5.   [3154

Different pagination in the two editions. The second edition is the one usually cited. This is a narrative of Connecticut's history to 1815, with supplementary chapters on the present (1857) constitution of Connecticut, early jurisprudence, episcopacy, schools, etc. An old style book founded largely on secondary materials, without adequate foot-notes or sufficient index. Dull to the last degree. Still the only large history of Connecticut which brings the story down through the Revolution.   E. C.

Hudson, Charles. History of the town of Lexington. Boston: Wiggin. 1868.   [3155

Gives very minutely the history of the town to 1783 and leading events thereafter. Special chapters on church, educational, military and municipal affairs. Quite valuable for data connected with the battle of Lexington. The latter half of the volume contains a genealogical register of Lexington families.   E. E. S.

Johnston, Alexander. Genesis of a New England state (Connecticut). (Johns Hopkins Univ. studies, ser. 1, no. 11.) Baltimore. 1883.
—— Connecticut: a study of a commonwealth-democracy. (American commonwealths.) Boston: Houghton. 1887. $1.25.   [3156

The book last named was an outgrowth from the author's *Genesis of a New England state*, which is a slight essay. Both are studies of Connecticut's history and not formal narrative of history. They were written to prove a thesis, and are often uncritical.   E. C.
This is one of the best works in the "American commonwealth series." It is written in a genial style, with a thorough knowledge of the subject and sympathy with the people of whom the author wrote. The writer's theory that Connecticut was formed by a federation of towns is fanciful and is not sustained by the documents. But that does not seriously detract from the essential value of the book.   H. L. O.

Levermore, Charles H. The republic of New Haven : a history of municipal evolution. (Johns Hopkins Univ. studies, extra v. 1.) Balt. 1886. $2.   [3157

This is an important and learned study of the history and institutions of the town and colony of New Haven from its settlement to the present time. The work is done in a thorough and scholarly manner, and is based throughout on a study of the original records of the town, colony and city of New Haven, the greater number of which are still in manuscript. The most valuable portion of the work is that which deals with the history of New Haven after its union with Connecticut. For the history of New Haven as an independent colony Atwater's *History of the colony of New Haven* is more useful to the student. Dr. Levermore's style is marred by a levity that is not always pleasing to the reader.   C. M. A.

Lodge, Henry Cabot. Boston. (Historic towns.) N. Y.: Longmans. 1891. $1.25.
    [3158

The greater part of this well written and scholarly account of the city of Boston treats of the period extending from the settlement of Massachusetts Bay colony to the year 1820. The early history of Boston, which is inevitably the history of the Massachusetts Bay colony, is successfully narrated, but the last chapter, which deals with the period from 1820 to the present time, is wholly inadequate. The conclusions are in the main just, but the work as a whole contains nothing that is either new or original. The author displays unmistakable sympathy for New England in general and for Massachusetts Bay in particular, and his attitude is throughout strenuously American.   C. M. A.

Loomis, Dwight, *and* **J. Gilbert Calhoun.** Judicial and civil history of Connecticut. Boston: Boston Hist. Co. 1895.   [3159

Contains, in 90 pages, a sketch of the history of Connecticut from the beginning to date of publication. Next comes a description of the legal system and government of the state, including a detailed account of the judicial system. Pages 199 to 622 form a biographical register of the bench and bar. Most of the articles are short and most of the persons noticed have only a local reputation. The historical matter is compiled from easily accessible material. On the whole the volume has only a local interest.   E. C.

Loring, James Spear. The hundred Boston orators. Boston : Jewett. 1852.   [3160

Beginning with specimens of the eloquence of Warren, Hancock, Lovell, and other Revolutionary worthies, by which we are put in touch with contemporary thought and manner of public speaking, the collection includes public addresses, chiefly Fourth of July orations, by men of national fame, like J. Q. Adams, Josiah Quincy, Fisher Ames, Webster, Everett, and Choate. Its references to the opening events of the Revolution, with its excellent biographical notices, put this book in the class of historical literature. The title is misleading.   S. A. D.

McClintock, John N. History of New Hampshire. Boston: Russell. 1889.   [3161

Covers the history of New Hampshire from 1623 to 1888. Compiled from the sources and from secondary material, as Belknap's *New Hampshire*. Treats of such topics as canals and railroads, as well as the mere annals. Style rather dull, but suitable to a work of reference. The standard complete history of New Hampshire.   E. C.
See sect. 3172.

Maine. Records, documents and bibliography. See in Syllabus of materials, sect. 121-123.   [3162

Maine Historical Society. See sect. 275.
    [3163

Massachusetts. Records, documents, and bibliography. See in Syllabus of materials, sect. 134-143.   [3164

Massachusetts Historical Society. See sect. 284.   [3165

Massachusetts, History of the Connecticut valley in; with illustrations and biographical sketches. Phil.: Everts. 1879. 2v. [**3166**

Contains a history of the settlement of the Connecticut valley within the limits of Massachusetts, from the beginning of colonization to the close of the Civil War, with accounts of the civil organization of Hampshire, Franklin and Hampden counties, and a mass of minor biographical matter. The publisher writes the preface. The *History of the valley* is written by N. B. Sylvester, but the names of the authors of the other portions of the volumes are not given. Illustrations poor. E. C.

Merriam, J. McK. Concord, [Mass.]. See American Antiquarian Society, sect. 241.
[**3167**

Narragansett Club. Providence, R. I. The Narragansett Club, organized in 1865, has published 6 volumes of *Publications*, as follows: — [**3168**

V. 1. Biographical introduction to the writings of Roger Williams, by Reuben A. Guild: — V. 2. Master John Cotton's answer to Master Roger Williams, etc.; ed. by Rev. J. Lewis Diman and Reuben Aldridge: — V. 3. The bloudy tenant of persecution, and V. 4. The bloudy tenant yet more bloudy, ed. by Rev. Samuel L. Caldwell: — V. 5. George Fox digged out of his burrowes ; ed. by Rev. J. Lewis Diman: — V. 6. Letters of Roger Williams: ed. by John Russell Bartlett.

See, also, sect. 3114.

New England Historic Genealogical Society. Boston. This Society, organized in 1844, renders invaluable service in its chosen field by the publication of the *New England historical and genealogical register*, which, beginning in 1847, completed its 54th volume in 1900. [**3169**

New England state and town records. See in Syllabus of materials, sect. 107–120. Also, see Griffin, Appleton P. C., sect. 3117.
[**3170**

New Hampshire. Records, documents and bibliography. See in Syllabus of materials, sect. 124–128. [**3171**

New Hampshire Historical Society. Concord, N. H. This society was organized in 1823; from 1824 to 1893 it published 10 volumes of *Collections*, and in 1884 began a series of *Proceedings*, of which part 1 of v. 3 was issued in 1897. [**3172**

Both series furnish valuable material on the history of New Hampshire. The most important contents are: Records of the N. H. Committee of Safety, 1775–1784, in v. 7, and Province records and court papers from 1680 to 1692, in v. 8.

New Haven Colony Historical Society. New Haven, Conn. Organized in 1862, this society had published, down to 1894, 5 volumes of *Papers*, chiefly on subjects of local history.
[**3173**

Parker, Joel. Origin of the towns of New England. See Massachusetts Historical Society, sect. 327. [**3174**

Powell, Lyman Pierson, *ed.* Historic towns of New England. (American historic towns.) N. Y.: Putnam. 1898. $3.50. [**3175**

"This book . . . is partly the product of a tour undertaken by a party starting from Philadelphia at the close of the University extension summer meeting in 1894, for 'a ten days' pilgrimage in the footsteps of George Washington.' . . . About one half of the book consists apparently of the addresses made to the travelling party at the places actually visited ; and the other half includes valuable descriptions, by different authors, of other towns, which have been added in order to give a larger representation of what New England has been in history." Mr. Powell "has prevailed upon fifteen writers — each of them well known and abundantly qualified — to furnish the contents of the book ; and we may well thank any man who has the enterprise to secure such a staff, and give permanent form to such excellent materials for our local and municipal history. . . . The illustrations are numerous and unusually good." *American historical review,* 4: 575.

Providence. Early records. See in Syllabus of materials, sect. 118. [**3176**

Quincy, Josiah. Municipal history of Boston to 1830. Boston: Little. 1852. [**3177**

An authoritative and detailed history of the establishment of municipal government in Boston in 1822 and of its growth from that time till 1830. During six years of that period the author was mayor, and was more influential than any other man in securing the many reforms which were then instituted. Mayor Quincy was a firm believer in the advantages of uniting large authority with responsibility in the hands of the mayor, and calls attention to the success of his own administrations as evidence of it. The first two chapters of the book contain a brief and inadequate account of two centuries of town government in Boston. H. L. O.

Rhode Island. Records, documents and bibliography. See in Syllabus of materials, sect. 144–150. [**3178**

Rhode Island Historical Society. Providence, R. I. Organized in 1822, the publications of this society include 9 volumes of *Collections*, issued at various dates from 1827 to 1897, *Proceedings* in 21 nos. from 1872 to 1892, and 8 volumes of *Publications*, 1893–1901.
[**3179**

The important articles in the *Collections* are the following: — V. 1, 1827, 163 pp., is a reprint of Roger Williams' Key to the language of America, the best guide we have to the speech and manners of the Narragansett Indians: — V. 2, 1835, 278 pp., is a reprint of Samuel Gorton's Simplicity's defence against seven-headed policy, edited by W. R. Staples, a curious exposition of the author's religious and political views : — V. 3, 1835, 315 pp. (republished with additional notes 1886, 423 pp.), is Elisha R. Potter's Early history of Narragansett, a mass of facts concerning that county, chronologically arranged: — V. 4, 1838, 270 pp., is a reprint of John Callender's Historical discourse on the colony of Rhode Island, edited with biography and notes by Romeo Elton. The discourse covers from 1638 to the close of the 17th century : — V. 5, 1843, 670 pp., is W. R. Staples' Annals of the town of Providence, covering as far down as 1832, and containing reprints of many documents : —V. 6, 1867, 380 pp., contains (1) Captain Simeon Thayer's Journal of the invasion of Canada, 1775, edited by E. M. Stone; (2) R. I. Revolutionary correspondence from 1775 to 1782 ; (3) Morgan Edwards' History of the Baptists in Rhode Island: — V. 7, 1885, 380 pp., contains (1) Early attempts at Rhode Island history, edited by W. E. Foster ; (2) The Narragansetts, by H. C. Dorr; (3) Early votaries of natural science in Rhode Island, by C. W. Parsons; (4) The first commencement of Rhode Island College, by R. A. Guild; (5) The British fleet in Rhode Island, by G. C. Mason ; (6) Nicholas Easton vs. The City of Newport, by G. C. Mason: — V. 8, 1893, 132 pp., contains The diary of John Comer, edited by C. E. Barrows, covering a residence in Rhode Island and Massachusetts from 1704 to 1734 : — V. 9, 1897, 141 pp., is Henry C. Dorr's Proprietors of Providence and their controversies with the freeholders.

The *Proceedings*, published in annual numbers, contain original papers, reprints of documents, notes on local history, necrologies of members, and a detailed account of the transactions of the Society during the period.

The *Publications*, issued quarterly, contain matter similar to that which appeared in the *Proceedings*, but in a much more enlarged form. The contributed papers, particularly in the early volumes, have considerable value. Volume 7 contains The diary of Enos Hitchcock, a Revolutionary chaplain, edited by W. B. Weeden.   C. S. B.

Rhode Island historical tracts. Providence : S. S. Rider. 1877–84. Nos. 1–20. Ser. 2, 1889-. No. 1+.   [3180

The publication of the first series of these tracts falls between the dates given above. A second series is now in progress, of the same character as its predecessor. The object of the editor in their issue is to preserve papers, addresses, monographs on Rhode Island history, which otherwise would never pass beyond the pamphlet form, and hence soon become scarce or be lost wholly to view. The series possesses great value for students of Rhode Island annals. Potter and Rider's account of Bills of credit ; Foster's Stephen Hopkins, a Rhode Island statesman ; Brayton's Defence of Samuel Gorton ; Dorr's Planting and growth of Providence, are some of the most important monographs which have found a place in these volumes. Through them is accomplished to an extent for Rhode Island history the work which the Prince Society is doing for northern New England.   H. L. O.

Robinson, Rowland Evans. Vermont.

(American commonwealths.) Boston : Houghton. 1892. $1.25.   [3181

This is a reliable and well-written history of Vermont from the time of its settlement until its admission into the Union ; while in a few of the later chapters its development is sketched till times subsequent to the Civil War. The author has used with fidelity the printed records of the state and of New York, and all the standard histories which bear upon the subject. The most important chapters are those which treat of the controversy with New York, the negotiations with the British toward the close of the Revolution, and the dealings with Congress which resulted in the admission of Vermont as a state. All these, though done in outline, are satisfactory. Descriptions of natural scenery, when they occur in the book, suggest the influence of Parkman.   H. L. O.

Sanford, Elias Benjamin. History of Connecticut. Hartford : Scranton. 1888. Subs. $2.   [3182

Based on secondary materials and on tradition. Large amount of space given to colonial period and to wars, especially the French and Indian wars. Style unattractive.   E. C.

Smith, Philip Henry. The Green Mountain boys : or Vermont and the New York land-jobbers. Pawling, N. Y.: Author. 1885.   [3183

One hundred and twenty-five small pages in good type. Contains the meat of Ira Allen's *History*. Makes no pretence to historical accuracy. Written in a dull and turgid manner.   E. C.

Smyth, Egbert C. French Canadians in New England. See American Antiquarian Society, sect. 239.   [3184

Sullivan, James. History of the district of Maine. Boston. 1795.   [3185

"Judge Sullivan was too busy a man to write so complicated a history as that of Maine ; and he fell into some errors, and came short of what would be expected of a writer at the present day." C. Deane, in *Narrative and critical hist. of Am.*, 3 : 364.

Trumbull, James Hammond, *ed.* Memorial history of Hartford County, Conn., 1633–1884. Boston. 1886. 2v.   [3186

This is a large " co-operative work." It covers nearly every side of the history of Hartford County: the Indians, the colonial period, Hartford in literature, freemasonry, insurance ; Hartford, town and city ; the second volume is devoted to the towns in the county outside Hartford. The chapters are naturally of unequal interest and value. Illustrations better than in most histories of its class. A good example of a county history.   E. C.

Underwood, Francis Henry. Quabbin : the story of a small country town ; with outlooks upon Puritan life. Boston : Lee. 1893. $1.75.   [3187

The author had an ambition to write the story of life in a small New England country town, as he knew it sixty odd years ago. Every phase of that life, moral, social, and civil, is sharply brought out, even to the most minute detail. As Quabbin is described as being a very dull place, its people narrow-minded, bigoted and unsocial, the story, well written though it is, lacks sustained interest and vitality. It is undoubtedly a faithful picture, not only of this, but of many other Quabbins, yet its perusal leaves no strong impression. Mr. Underwood often drops his story to indulge in polemical discussion. He ascribes much of the low state of society and manners in Quabbin to provincial isolation, but more to the influence of Puritan teachings and training still dominant, austere and unyielding.   S. A. D.

Vermont. Records, documents and bibliography. See Syllabus of materials, sect. 129–133.   [3188

Vermont Historical Society. Montpelier, Vt. This society was organized in 1838, and has issued a number of pamphlets on subjects of Vermont history. In 1870 and 1871 two volumes of *Collections* and in 1898 one volume of *Proceedings* were published.   [3189

These are devoted chiefly to the history of Vermont during the Revolution and the period immediately following, and to the controversy with New York over the boundaries of that state and the " New Hampshire grants." Volume 2 contains selections from the Haldimand papers relating to Vermont. The latest publication of the society is a volume of *Proceedings*, most of the contents of which relate to Ethan Allen. Several documents from the facsimiles of Mr. B. F. Stevens are so badly misprinted in the appendix to this volume, and such editorial liberties are taken with one of them, that their historical value is destroyed. A communication in the *Nation*, Sept. 27, 1900, points out the flagrant maltreatment which these papers have received.

Whittier, John Greenleaf. Supernaturalism of New England. London. 1840. N. Y.: Wiley. 1847.   [3190

Some articles contributed to the old *New England Magazine* formed the groundwork for this thin volume. Not all of them, however, are to be found in it. Evidently the venerated author was willing that these earlier efforts of his should be forgotten, and in this respect his later judgment is to be commended, so far as literary quality is concerned ; but so far as the book goes to establish the status of superstition in Mr. Whittier's day, it has some historical value to students of folk-lore, and is an interesting clew to the motive of much that he has written.   S. A. D.

Williamson, Joseph. Slavery in Maine. See Maine Historical Society, sect. 278. [3191

Williamson, William Durkee. History of the state of Maine. Hallowell: Glazier. 1832. 2v.   [3192

The work begins with a dissertation of 182 pp. on the geography and flora and fauna of Maine. The author then proceeds with the history of the colony and state, beginning with discovery and ending with the separation of Maine from Massachusetts in 1820. The book throughout is a sober, compact recital of facts, without ornament and with no display of partisan zeal. Citations of authorities are abundant. In diligence Williamson was the equal of Belknap, but in style and grasp of the larger relations of the subject far his inferior.   H. L. O.

Winsor, Justin, *ed.* Memorial history of Boston, 1630–1880. Boston: Osgood. 1880–82. 4v.   [3193

A sumptuous and exhaustive work, in which, after a description of the geology and natural history of the region, the story is given in great detail from the landing of Winthrop to the moment of the book's appearance. The function of Mr. Winsor is for the most part editorial, each one of the four massive volumes being made up of chapters written by the best obtainable expert in the field considered. Dividing the account into three periods, the colonial, the provincial, and the post-revolutionary, the development of the city is considered from every side, social, political, economic, religious, educational, etc. While the body of information is vast, the method pursued makes necessary a considerable sacrifice. There is no consecutive narrative, but simply a mass of fragments. For continuous reading the breaks are incessant and embarrassing. For reference, however, chapter by chapter, the book is very satisfactory. The eye of the laborious editor has been everywhere : each line has had the benefit of his revision, and the work of his great corps of writers is constantly supplemented by his own notes. Several of the most important chapters are by Mr. Winsor himself. The cartography, and autograph and pictorial illustrations, are attended to with great taste and accuracy. Probably no American historian possessed so vast a fund of learning as Justin Winsor, and he lavished of his abundance in preparing this record of the city which in so many ways has been the leader of America.   J. K. H.

THE OLD "MIDDLE STATES"

(*Comprehensive history, covering all or several periods. For Colonial history, see Part III, Division 1, sect. 1049–1118. See, also, Part I: Sources.*)

Barber, John W., *and* **Henry Howe.** Historical collections of the state of New York. N. Y.: Author. 1841. Improved ed. 1851.
                                            [3194

This is one of several state gazetteers which were issued about the middle of this century by Barber and Howe. Howe shared in the preparation of the first edition of this work. It contains an outline of the history of the state from its settlement to approximately the time of publication. In the case of New York this outline is very meagre, and not a few errors appear. By far the larger part of the volume is filled with an account of the various counties of the state, giving such common facts concerning their history, topography, population, towns and industries as usually appear in gazetteers. Numerous woodcuts are given. The work is crudely done. Lapse of time has taken from it nearly all the value it may once have possessed.   H. L. O.

Benton, Nathaniel S. History of Herkimer County, including the upper Mohawk valley. Albany: Munsell. 1856.   [3195

This ranks among the best of the older county histories. It was prepared with care by one who had long been a resident of the region and conversant with its affairs. He made thorough use of existing materials, both in print and in manuscript, while he drew largely on his personal information and the knowledge of others. As Herkimer County was one of the first erected in the state after the Revolution, not a little of the history of western New York is involved in its annals. The volume in fact is more truly a history of the region in general than it is of the administrative district known as Herkimer County. The volume closes with the presentation of a considerable amount of genealogical material relating to the families of the district. The book in the miscellaneous character of its contents and their discursiveness is typical of its class.   H. L. O.

Booth, Mary L. History of the city of New York. N. Y.: Clark. 1865. New ed. N. Y.: Dutton. 1880.   [3196

This book was expressly prepared for the benefit of the general reader, and contains the most common and easily accessible facts which relate to the history of New York City from the earliest times to the opening of the Civil War. The style of writing is agreeable, and it is generally accurate. It contains illustrations of some value, and a limited amount of additional matter in an appendix. But the reader will not find in this volume, or in any others in existence on the same subject, a genuine history of New York City. Instead — save in the case of Valentine's *History* — he will find an outline of the history of the Province of New Netherland, and later of that of New York, with an account of some of the external events of the Revolution in this vicinity, and a very meagre collection of facts relating to the growth of the city in the present century. Some account he will also find of local topography, of public buildings, of private residences, of modern structures erected for business or other purposes. But in general the writers have failed to recognize the distinction between the municipality and the province and state, and so have written histories of the latter with only occasional reference to the former.   H. L. O.

Brodhead, John Romeyn. History of the state of New York [1609-91]. N. Y.: Harper. 1853-71. 2v. V. 1, rev. ed. [c. 1871.] [3197

" An excellent and scholarly work, though occasionally disfigured by a proneness to ascribe unworthy motives to New York's neighbours." John Fiske, *The Dutch and Quaker colonies*, v. 2, p. 146, note.
" It is to be regretted that death prevented the completion of the work, which does not go farther than 1691 ; but what Mr. Brodhead has given us must, for its completeness and accuracy of research, and for the general acumen displayed in it, rank as a standard

work and a classical authority on the subject." B. Fernow, in *Narrative and critical hist. of Am.*, 4: 432.

Brooks, Elbridge Streeter. Story of New York. (Story of the states.) Boston: Lothrop. [c. 1888.] $1.50.   [3198

" Mr. Brooks's volume opens as if designed for youthful readers, but one quickly finds that the serious preface is a truer indication of the author's intention. A philosophical treatment has seemed to him at once best and within his grasp, and to it he sacrifices freely the details which distinguish and enliven Mr. Todd's annals. . . . Mr. Brooks asserts, with quite as much positiveness as the evidence warrants, a Spanish occupation or exploration a century before Hudson's arrival. With equal positiveness he finds a Spanish etymology for the name Manhattan. . . . Mr. Brooks makes up for his generalizations by appending ' the story of New York told in chronological epitome,' in a very handy form. He gives, too, the Constitution of the state of New York, and a bibliography." *Nation*, 47: 39.

Buffalo Historical Society. Buffalo, N.Y. This society was organized in 1862, and has published *Annual reports* from 1885 to 1898, and 4 volumes of *Collections* (v. 3 entitled *Transactions*) relating chiefly to local history, taking in the Niagara frontier and considerable parts of western New York.   [3199

Cayuga County Historical Society. Auburn, N. Y. This society was organized in 1876, and from 1879 to 1894 published 11 volumes of *Collections*. Volume 1 is the Journal of Lieut. J. L. Hardenbergh, in Sullivan's expedition, May 1–Oct. 3, 1779.   [3200

Cheyney, Edward P. Anti-rent agitation in the state of New York, 1839-46. (Univ. of Penn. Publications, no. 2.) Phil. 1887. [3201

This pamphlet is No. 2 of the Publications of the University of Pennsylvania, political economy and public law series. It is a brief, but clear and impartial, study of the origin of the large grants of land made in the province and state of New York, of the forms of tenure which existed within them, and of the agitation, followed by resistance, against the collection of rents on the Van Rensselaer manor, which began in 1839. Little space is devoted to the part played by this movement as a political issue, but an outline is given of the collision between the state authority and the agitators, and of the legislation and decisions of the courts which resulted finally in the disappearance of the old leasehold system. A list of authorities used is given at the close.   H. L. O.

Clark, Joshua V. H. Onondaga; with notes on the several towns in the county, and Oswego. Syracuse : Stoddard. 1849. 2v.   [3202

" Mr. Clark has evidently examined almost every source of information regarding the Six Nations, we possess in the English, French, and Spanish languages, and accordingly the first seventy-eight pages are occupied with a résumé of what he thus gleaned. But it is in chapter v, pp. 79 to 125, that he adds entirely new material to their history in his *Biographical sketches of distinguished chiefs of the Onondaga tribe.* This valuable work was principally derived from chiefs or pioneers then living. . . . The first volume of this work is in fact a history of the Onondaga tribe of the Six Nations, and holds the highest rank among the treatises on aboriginal affairs for original and valuable information." T. W. Field, in *Indian bibliography,* p. 77.

Clinton, De Witt. Life and writings of De Witt Clinton; by William W. Campbell. N. Y.: Baker. 1849. [3203

This contains very brief introductory sketches of the lives of Col. Charles Clinton and Gen. James Clinton, and about fifteen pages on De Witt Clinton. These are followed by several addresses. The most important portion of the book is the Private canal journey, 1810, which is a diary of a journey through New York between Schenectady and Buffalo, and contains considerable historic and economic information, gathered while the country was still in a primitive state. Helpful data will here be found in regard to wages, prices, value of land and local products. Clinton was afterwards an ardent supporter of the construction of the Erie Canal. The book is inadequate as a biography, and must be regarded simply as a contribution to the history of New York state in the first quarter of the century. D. R. D.

— **Hosack, David.** Memoir of De Witt Clinton. N. Y. 1829. [3204

This is a memorial discourse delivered by the author before the Literary and Philosophical Society and the citizens of New York City in 1828 in honor of Mr. Clinton, who had recently died. The life and character of the deceased statesman are reviewed at considerable length. Not only is his official and political career outlined, but the decisions he rendered while on the bench, the services he performed for popular education in New York, for higher education, for charities, his character as a speaker and writer, are reviewed. Above all is his work as an originator of the Erie Canal detailed. In that connection a valuable sketch is given of the origin of the idea of canals or a canal system in the state of New York, and the suggestions of public men from Cadwallader Colden down. The chief credit is claimed for Mr. Clinton. The tone of the book is of course eulogistic, but it is not extravagantly so. An elaborate appendix occupies more than two thirds of the volume. Of special interest are the contributions it contains toward the documentary history of the Erie Canal project. H. L. O.

Dayton, Abram C. Last days of knickerbocker life in New York. N. Y.: Harlan. 1882. Putnam. 1897. $2.50. [3205

This is a volume of personal reminiscences of life as it was in the middle and higher circles of New York society about 1840. The author, says the editor, "was witness to the scenes described, and contemporary with the events detailed." With the development of the railway and steam navigation, and the beginning

of foreign immigration on a large scale, the provincial period of New York City life closed and its metropolitan period began. Prior to that change the old characteristics of a Dutch and English town of moderate size had been retained. These in the last stage of their existence, as he witnessed and shared in them, the author has here delineated with truthfulness and in considerable detail. He has selected as typical of the whole, the observance of the Sabbath; the home with its furnishings, its internal economy and social life, its relations to the world outside; the city hotel, with the boon companions who permanently resided there; the shopkeepers and caterers; the business habits of the merchant and lawyer; the dress, manners and sports of fashionable society; the places of fashionable resort, as the Vauxhall Gardens and the theatres. The book has the limitations which are characteristic of personal memoirs, viz., it deals exclusively with the social classes among which the author moved, while the material is presented without regard to logical order or to completeness in itself. H. L. O.

De Costa, Benjamin Franklin. Notes on the history of Fort George during the colonial and revolutionary periods. N. Y.: Sabin. 1871. [3206

The Fort George here referred to was a fort planned and partly completed under the orders of Gen. Amherst during the French and Indian War, and was located near the head of Lake George. The material used in this *brochure* consists of letters, extracts from documents, journals, etc., showing the origin and location of the fort, and the fortunes of the successive garrisons which held it during the period in question. The documentary material is interspersed with brief explanatory comment. H. L. O.

Eastman, F. S. History of the state of New York. N. Y.: Bliss. 1828. [3207

See note under Lambrechtsen's *New Netherland,* sect. 1078.

Egle, William Henry. Illustrated history of the commonwealth of Pennsylvania. Harrisburg. 1877. 2d ed. rev. Phil.: Gardner. 1880. [3208

The most comprehensive local history of Pennsylvania, comprising histories of the individual counties, prepared by different writers. Very minute in detail and trustworthy. Extracts are given from many documents. The illustrations are largely of historic import. E. E. S.

Fisher, Sydney George. The making of Pennsylvania. Phil.: Lippincott. 1896. $1.50. [3209

A study of the various nationalities and religions which formed elements in the population of early Pennsylvania, with special reference to their dispersion, and to their influence upon the history of the colony and state. To this are added chapters on the early development of science and the mechanic arts, the Wyoming controversy, and the boundary dispute with Maryland. The style is popular, and at times flippant, but the facts have been industriously accumulated, and the book may be read with profit. The work is properly an introduction to the same author's *Pennsylvania, colony and commonwealth.*

W. MacD.

—— Pennsylvania, colony and commonwealth. Phil.: Coates. 1897. $1.50. [3210

Follows the same author's *Making of Pennsylvania.* The larger part of the volume is given to an entertaining sketch of the history of Pennsylvania to the close of the Revolution, with additional chapters on the Whiskey insurrection, Fries's rebellion, the Civil War, and the "preëminence of Philadelphia." The style and treatment are of a piece with the *Making of Pennsylvania.* W. MacD.

Furman, Gabriel. Antiquities of Long Island, ed. by Frank Moore. N. Y.: Bouton. 1875. [3211

As stated in its introduction, this volume contains the notes of Gabriel Furman on the antiquities of Long Island and on the manners and customs of its inhabitants; also his historical notes on Brooklyn, and a bibliography of Long Island which was prepared by Henry Onderdonk, Jr. The manuscript from which the *Antiquities* is printed is said to be fragmentary, "and seems to have been put together at odd times during the period embraced within the years 1824 and 1838." It is printed in this volume for the first time. The notes relating to Brooklyn are here reprinted from an edition of 1824, and they contain some slight repetitions of the material to be found in the *Antiquities.* The book has no special unity. The material is derived from tradition and the personal knowledge of the writer and his acquaintances. The book is authoritative, is valuable as a collection of undigested material, and has often been used as a source by later writers. H. L. O.

Goodwin, *Mrs.* **Maud Wilder,** *et al., eds.* Historic New York: being the Half moon papers. N. Y.: Putnam. 1897–8. 2v. $2.50 ea. [3212

"These monographs, upon topics relating to the history of New York City, were originally intended to meet the demands of students in classes organized by the City History Club. The first series, edited by Maud Wilder Goodwin, Alice Carrington Royce, and Ruth Putnam, was the most successful effort ever made to popularize the history of colonial New York. The second series, which has the services of a fourth editorial associate, Eva Palmer Brownell, shows no diminution in any essential excellence. The present [second] volume contains twelve monographs, each with an appropriate bibliography, and there is an index to the whole work which seems to be adequate. . . . The volume, like its predecessor, is finely illustrated and beautifully printed. In view of its professed purposes it has one serious defect. That is the limitation of each monograph by the attempt to crowd twelve of them into one issue." *Am. hist. rev.* 4: 547.

Hammond, Jabez D. History of political parties in the state of New York. Albany: Van Benthuysen. 1842. 2v. [3213

This work covers the first fifty years of the political life of New York State, touching also upon the more important national issues of that period. The rise of political parties on the adoption of the Federal Constitution in 1787–8 is detailed, as are also the fluctuations of parties shown in every election thereafter till 1840. Though the author was a Republican and stood in close relations with leaders and members of that party, he preserved throughout his work an attitude of remarkable candor and impartiality. His book justifies the statement made in the preface, that he had written it with the same regard to truth which he would have if testifying in a court of justice. The material of the work was derived from the author's own knowledge, from witnesses of events, from letters, contemporary newspapers and pamphlets, and from official sources. Justly, therefore, to the work has always been attributed high authority, and it has been regarded as one of the most valuable of American political histories. The style in which it is written is clear and interesting, tracing effectively the origin of political movements and the causes of crises in the life both of individuals and parties. An edition with notes by Gen. Erastus Root was published in 1842. Also in 1849 a continuation of the "History" to 1847 was published, the added material taking the form of a life of Silas Wright and a study of his connection with political parties subsequent to 1840 (Syracuse, N. Y.: Hall and Dickson. 1848). H. L. O.

Hemstreet, Charles. Nooks and corners of old New York. N. Y.: Scribner. 1899. $2. [3214

"The object of the writer was . . . not to produce an exhaustive history of the island, or even a scholarly monograph, but to accompany the reader in a series of interesting strolls. It cannot be said that he has satisfactorily accomplished this purpose. There is little of literary charm, and in many places the list of house-sites reads like a catalogue of the ships. In fact, the strict adherence to the topographical plan and the hurried succession of short notices render the book a species of Baedeker." Edmund K. Alden. *Am. hist. rev.,* 5: 617.

Hendrick, Welland. Brief history of the Empire state. Syracuse: Bardeen. 1890. 75c. [3215

This is a text-book, intended for the use of pupils in the grammar grades. It is furnished with some illustrations, a few sketch maps, abundant summaries and review questions, and is clearly printed. A brief and simple outline of the political history of the province and state is presented, with paragraphs and chapters on social conditions. The book is generally accurate, while its style and topical arrangement is well adapted for a brief and elementary course on the history of the state. H. L. O.

Holland Society of New York. New York City. The Holland Society, organized in 1885, has published, beginning 1886, an annual *Yearbook,* and from 1891 to 1896, 3 volumes of *Collections,* containing records of the Dutch in New Netherland. These records are published, 1896–1901, in the *Yearbooks.* [3216

Jenkins, John S. History of political parties in the state of New York. Auburn: Alden. 1846. [3217

This book possesses no independent value whatever; it is simply a reproduction of Hammond's *History of political parties in New York*, without any credit whatever being given to the author of the original work. It is surprising that a plagiarism so gross as this should have been issued and sold so soon after the publication of the work of which it is a reduced copy (sect. 3213). H. L. O.

Ketchum, William. Authentic and comprehensive history of Buffalo, with historic notices of the Six Nations or Iroquois Indians. Buffalo. 1864–5. 2v. [3218

The first volume embraces the period from the first records of white man's intercourse with the Iroquois, down to the breaking up of their Confederacy, consequent on the American Revolution. The second volume ends with the burning of Buffalo, 1813. The work as a whole is scarcely to be called a history of Buffalo; it deals with western New York prior to settlement; is largely based on documentary sources, and despite a tendency to diffuseness and prolixity, testifies to much painstaking research. Of especial value to the student of the Six Nations Indians in their relation to the whites. F. H. S.

Lamb, *Mrs.* **Martha Joan Reade (Nash).** History of the city of New York. N. Y.: Barnes. 1877–81. 2v. Net $16.

—— *Supplement:* Externals of modern New York, by Mrs. Burton Harrison. N. Y.: Barnes. 1896. Net $3.

—— *Same,* new ed. [containing supplement]. 3v. Net $15. [3219

Mrs. Lamb's history is the result of careful investigation. The first volume gives a faithful and picturesque account of the colony. The later history is "too large and diversified to be treated otherwise than as a series of sketches. . . . There is one thread, however, running through this progress and woven in with all its ramifications — perhaps the only continuous one — which Mrs. Lamb has taken as a clue in tracing the changes of the past century." The struggle of one group of houses, crushed at the Revolution, to regain confiscated estates, "colored the politics of the state for a generation. The names and the leadership of the early settlers of New York thus reappear throughout her annals, and the author uses their connection with all marked events in her history to give coherence as well as personal interest to the narrative. . . . The treatment of the subjects touched in the latter part of the second volume is . . . necessarily only fragmentary, and the impression left a broken one. During the last half-century of the city's history the subject has expanded to such dimensions and with such diversity that no outline can embrace it all." Mrs. Lamb occasionally errs in matters of genealogy. The volumes are well printed and well illustrated. *Nation*, 32: 117. 26: 296.

Mrs. Harrison continues the story from 1880, giving a succinct and lively description of events. "To read her book is to gain a pretty clear notion of the salient externals of the Gotham of to-day. With the deeper moral, religious, social, and political issues that suggest themselves to the philosophical observer of New York's civilization, Mrs. Harrison does not pretend to deal." *Dial* (Chicago), 21: 335.

Latrobe, John H. B. History of Mason and Dixon's line. See Pennsylvania, Historical Society of, sect. 385. [3220

Long Island Historical Society. Brooklyn, N. Y. This society was organized in 1863 and has published the following: [3221

Journal of a voyage to New York and a tour in several of the American colonies, by Jasper Dankers and Peter Sluyter; tr. by H. C. Murphy: — Battle of Long Island, by Thomas W. Field: — Campaign of 1776 around New York and Brooklyn, by H. P. Johnston: — George Washington and Mount Vernon, a collection of George Washington's unpublished agricultural and personal letters; by M. D. Conway.

Lossing, Benson John. The Empire state. Hartford: Am. Pub. Co. 1888. Subs. ed. N. Y.: Funk. 1887. $5. [3222

In 576 pages of text the author has reviewed the history of the state of New York to the close of 1875. About one half of the space is devoted to the Colonial period and the Revolution; nearly four fifths is occupied with the history prior to the close of the War of 1812. The book is written in an agreeable style, and it contains such matter as the ordinary reader finds interesting. But the material is derived almost wholly from the ordinary standard sources, and not the slightest originality of view or method is exhibited. Loose statements also are not infrequent. A large amount of general history, with which New York had no special concern, is introduced. The book is illustrated with many portraits. For the larger and higher purposes of history the work is without significance. H. L. O.

—— History of New York City. N. Y.: Perine. 1885. 2v. *Same,* 1v. [3223

"Mr. Lossing is a chronicler and an antiquarian, rather than an historian, and his narrative is formless and scrappy to the last degree. We are not surprised that no table of contents is provided; it would have implied a scheme of orderly arrangement of which there is very little beyond the chronological division. . . . We should be glad if we could vouch for Mr. Lossing's punctiliousness in such information as he chooses to give, but we cannot." *Nation*, 47: 39.

Macauley, James. Natural, statistical and civil history of the state of New-York. N. Y.: Gould. 1829. 3v. [3224

See note under Lambrechtsen's *New Netherlands*, sect. 1078.

Mellick, Andrew D., Jr. Story of an old farm. Somerville, N. J.: Unionist gazette. 1889. [3225

The sub-title, *Life in New Jersey in the eighteenth century*, describes the work. On an almost imperceptible thread of Mellick family history is strung a wealth of information on early German immigration, and New Jersey history, especially during the Revolution. It is followed by a genealogy of the Mellicks and is well indexed. E. C. R.

Miner, Charles. History of Wyoming [valley]. Phil.: Crissy. 1845. [3226

Miner was a local antiquarian, who gathered his materials from the people of the Valley, from printed sources and from original documents in state and English archives. His work is especially valuable for its accounts of the controversy between Connecticut and Pennsylvania, and the Wyoming massacre, on which subjects it is accurate and very full. It ends with the settlement of the controversy. It contains two rare maps, one showing the Connecticut claims, the other the projected state of Westmoreland in northeastern Pennsylvania; also Colonel Adam Hubley's journal of Sullivan's expedition against the Indians in 1799. There is much space given to social details and much worthless gossip. The style is rhetorical and very faulty. R. C. H. C.

Miner, Lewis H. The valley of Wyoming: the romance of its history and its poetry. N. Y.: R. H. Johnston. 1866. [3227

Mr. Miner truly says that his book "has not the slightest claim" to be "a history;" and it is nearly valueless as a handbook of the valley, its intended purpose. Two thirds of the contents are given to Campbell's *Gertrude of Wyoming*, local poems, and specimens of Indian eloquence. The historical portions are compiled from the histories of Chapman, Charles Miner and Stone. R. C. H. C.

Munsell, Joel, *comp.* Annals of Albany. Albany : Munsell. 1850-9. 10v. [3228

This is a miscellaneous collection of records, newspaper extracts, biographical notices, reprints of documents and relations, quotations from standard histories, lists of the names of resident freeholders, maps, charts and other material relating to the history of Albany. It concerns indifferently all periods of the history of the city from its settlement to the middle of the nineteenth century. Though uncritical in form and arrangement, it is a monument to the local pride and antiquarian zeal of its compiler and publisher. It was issued as an annual to subscribers for ten years, and then was discontinued owing to lack of financial support. Unlike Valentine's *Manual of New York City*, after the first volume it ceased to have the character of a city directory and became wholly an historical series. The material contained in the collection is of very unequal value. Of greatest importance for historical purposes are the reprints and outlines of the records of the common council of the city from 1686 to 1753. Each volume has an index. H. L. O.

—— Collections on the history of Albany, from its discovery to the present time. Albany : Munsell. 1865-71. 4v. [3229

These volumes form a continuation of the *Annals of Albany*. The *Collections* contains much less heterogeneous and useless material than does the *Annals;* its contents are more solid and valuable, and it shows

an improvement on the part of its editor in the art of compilation. Its most valuable feature, however, is a reprint of that part of the records of Albany county which had been translated by Professor Jonathan Pearson, and published by Munsell in 1869 under the title of *Early records of the county and city of Albany.* Those records appear on pp. 1-224 of Vol. III, and pp. 225-510 of Vol. IV of this collection. The records of the city of Albany which, for the period 1686 to 1753, were printed nearly in full in the *Annals*, are published in the *Collections* in full for the years from 1753 to 1788. They will be found in Vol. I, pp. 81-355 and Vol. II, pp. 236-323. The publication of notes from newspapers, which was continued through the *Annals*, is resumed in this series. They are taken from the Albany papers, and cover the decade 1859-1869. Under the above heads the larger part of the material contained in the *Collections* is included. Some 63 shorter articles appear, among which the reprint (with translation) of the Deacon's Account book of the first Dutch church of Albany for 1665, with synopsis of its contents from 1666 to 1715, is worthy of mention; as is also the account of the origin of the Ticonderoga patent, the material which is presented on the genealogy of inhabitants of Albany and on the history of its churches, and the reprint of a part of the *Journals of Jasper Dankers and Peter Sluyter.* H. L. O.

Murray, David. The anti-rent episode in the state of New York. See American Historical Association, sect. 248. [3230

New Jersey. Records, documents and bibliography. See in Syllabus of materials, sect. 167-170. [3231

New Jersey Historical Society. Newark, N. J. This society was organized in 1845. Between 1846 and 1872, it issued 7 volumes of *Collections;* its *Proceedings* have been published since 1845, the first series of 10 volumes being completed in 1867. The 2nd series, from 1867 to 1895, contains 13 volumes, and v. 1 of the 3rd series appeared in 1899. These are devoted almost exclusively to New Jersey history, and contain much excellent material. *Documents relating to the colonial history of the state of New Jersey* are in process of publication, the 1st volume having been issued in 1880, the 19th in 1897. These are made up of official documents covering the history of the government of New Jersey from 1631 to 1775. Volumes 11, 12, and 19 contain newspaper extracts relating to New Jersey from 1704-55. [3232

The most important contents of the *Collections* are the following: v. 1. East Jersey under the proprietary governments, by W. A. Whitehead, containing The model of the government of East Jersey, in America, by George Scot:— v. 2. The life of William Alexander, Earl of Stirling:—v. 3. The provincial courts of New Jersey, by R. S. Field:—v. 4. The papers of Lewis Morris, governor of the province of New Jersey, from 1738 to 1746: — v. 5. Analytical index to the colonial documents of New Jersey, in the state paper offices of England, comp. by H. Stevens.

New York City. Records of New Amsterdam. See in Syllabus of materials, sect. 119. [3233

New York State. Records, documents and bibliography. See in Syllabus of materials, sect. 157–166. [3234

—— *Regents' Boundary Commission.* Report upon the New York and Pennsylvania boundary. Albany: Weed. 1886. [3235

This Commission was appointed under a New York act of 1880 to coöperate with one from Pennsylvania for the purpose of locating the boundary line between the two states, as originally established. This its Report contains: 1. A history of the "parallel boundary," or east and west line between New York and Pennsylvania; 2. The history of the "meridian line," or north and south line, extending from Lake Erie southward to the northwest corner of Pennsylvania, together with the final adjustment and setting of its monuments; 3. The appendix to the Report contains a variety of material relating to the surveys of these lines, also references to many old New York maps, and the sketch maps in sections of the boundaries in question. Extracts are printed from the survey books of the Holland Land Company, and from the papers of Geo. Palmer, a deputy surveyor of the province and commonwealth of Pennsylvania.   H. L. O.

—— *Regents of the University.* Report on the boundaries of the state of New York. Albany. 1874–84. 2v. [3236

The matter contained in these volumes is documentary, and relates to the boundaries of New York on the north and east, and to that part of its south line which separates it from New Jersey. The most important part of the material necessary for a documentary history of the establishment of the boundary between Canada and New York, of the controversies of New York with Massachusetts, Connecticut and New Jersey over their limits is collected here. The act for determining the boundary toward Vermont is given, but comparatively little space is devoted to the earlier question of the New Hampshire Grants. The first volume contains material of a more general nature. The original territorial extent of the province of New Netherland, and later of New York, is traced, and the successive steps are shown by which New York was reduced to its present limits. An index adds to the value of the compilation as a work of reference.   H. L. O.

New York Genealogical and Biographical Society. New York City. This Society was organized in 1869, and began the next year the publication of the *New York genealogical and biographical record*, which is still issued quarterly and completed its 29th volume in 1899. It contains much excellent material relating to New York families and history. [3237

New-York Historical Society. See sect. 351. [3238

Oneida Historical Society. Utica, N. Y. This Society was organized in 1876. The 1st volume of its *Transactions* was issued in 1881, the 8th in 1898. The series is continued at irregular intervals. Their contents relate chiefly to the history of Oneida County and the Mohawk valley. [3239

Peck, George. Wyoming [valley]; its history, stirring incidents, and romantic adventures. N. Y.: Harper. 1858. [3240

" The author was familiar with the scenes, as well as many of the actors in the Wyoming tragedy, for a period of forty years commencing with 1820. He was thus enabled to glean many particulars regarding the Indians, the pioneers and their bloody skirmishes, which had escaped the eager inquiries of Chapman, Miner, and Stone." T. W. Field, *Indian bibliography*, p. 304.

Pennsylvania. Records, documents and bibliography. See in Syllabus of materials, sect. 171–179. [3241

Pennsylvania German Society. Reading, Pa. This Society was organized in 1891, and from that year to 1898 published 8 volumes of *Proceedings and addresses.* Volumes 7 and 8 contain an account of the history of Pennsylvania as developed under German influence. [3242

Pennsylvania, Historical Society of. See sect. 369. [3243

Pennypacker, Samuel Whitaker. Historical and biographical sketches. Phil.: Tripple. 1883. [3244

This volume is composed, for the most part, of careful studies in Pennsylvania history, the most valuable of them relating to the German element in the population of the state, and their contributions to its civilization and culture. The longest study, and one of the most valuable, is entitled Christopher Dock, the pious schoolmaster of the Skippack and his works. This paper contains a translation of the major part of Dock's *School ordering*, or *School management*, published in Germantown, in 1770, the first book on the subject of education that appeared in the United States.   B. A. H.

Philadelphia. *Common Council.* Minutes, 1704–76. See in Syllabus of materials, sect. 120. [3245

Powell, Lyman Pierson, *ed.* Historic towns of the Middle States. (American historic towns, v. 2.) N. Y.: Putnam. 1899. $3.50. [3246

" This volume presents monographs on Albany, Saratoga, Schenectady, Newburgh, Tarrytown, Brooklyn, New York, Buffalo, Pittsburgh, Philadelphia, Princeton, Wilmington. The general introduction is by Dr. Albert Shaw, who points out some interesting special facts in the early history and colonization of the Middle states, notably the mixed and cosmopolitan character of their original population, whch served to differentiate them pretty sharply from the other two sections, and to make them, as it were, a useful buffer between the morally and socially rather antagonistic groups of New England states and southern states." *Dial* (Chicago), 27: 431.

Price, Eli K. History of the consolidation of the city of Philadelphia. See Pennsylvania, Historical Society of, sect. 385.   [3247

Randall, Samuel S. History of the state of New York. N. Y.: Ford. 1870.   [3248

This is a well-written and generally accurate textbook on the history of the state of New York from its settlement by the Dutch till the close of the Civil War. Some errors appear, but they are not numerous. The material also is well selected and presented with a due regard to proportion. Not an undue amount of space is devoted to general history. The development of the state constitutions receives considerable attention. The standard works were used in the preparation of the book.   H. L. O.

Raum, John Otto. History of New Jersey. Phil.: Potter. [c. 1877.] 2v. Phil.: McVey. 2v. $5.   [3249

The larger part of the first volume of this work is an impudent plagiarism. It is for the most part a *verbatim* reproduction of Smith's *History of New Jersey* (sect. 1108, 3255), without, so far as I have noticed, the slightest acknowledgment until, on page 240, Smith is credited with being the authority for a minor detail of local history. It is an impudent plagiarism, because, in a solemn preface, the compiler repeatedly states that he has spared no labor or expense to obtain accurate information, has not neglected to consult any work of value that was within his reach, and in cases of doubt has compared and sifted conflicting accounts, so as to lay before the reader the nearest approximation to the truth which can be attained. The cool effrontery of this preface should entitle the book to a place among the curiosities of literature. The second volume, and that part of the first volume which was prepared without the silent coöperation of Smith, is a hotchpotch of history and statistics and local details, which, if they were well put together, might make a respectable gazetteer of New Jersey. But the character of the first part of the work throws doubt on all the statements made in the latter part.   H. L. O.

Repplier, Agnes. Philadelphia, the place and the people. N. Y.: Macmillan. 1898. $2.50.   [3250

" Miss Repplier, whose success as an essayist is well known, has made for us an extended essay — not a study — upon the experiences and qualities of those people who lived, or who persist in living, on the site selected by Penn's Commissioners in 1681 for his city on the Delaware. Her purpose, well fulfilled, is to make a readable volume, and she has applied a light and graceful touch — sometimes disclosing the firmness beneath — to her work. . . . There are some good illustrations in the book, by E. C. Peixoto, and some that are so exceedingly 'sketchy' as to be of no service in such a work." Howard M. Jenkins, in *Am. hist. rev.*, 4: 551.

Roberts, Ellis Henry. New York. (American commonwealths.) Boston: Houghton. 1887. 2v. $2.50.   [3251

The most considerable work which has yet appeared in the Commonwealth series. The entire history of New York is reviewed in it, from its discovery and settlement to the present time. The style is agreeable and the author possesses a good general knowledge of the subject. The volumes are not free from errors; in many points they fail, of course, to give adequate treatment to the subject; occasionally the arrangement is confused. Still, for a work of this kind and extent, a commendable degree of accuracy has been attained. The amount of space devoted to the successive periods of the history is also well apportioned. The tone of the work is impartial. Social, as well as political, development receives attention. The reader will find in the book a well-balanced general history of New York, from which no important feature of her development has been wholly omitted.   H. L. O.

Roosevelt, Theodore. New York. (Historic towns series.) N. Y.: Longmans. 1891. $1.25.   [3252

The story of New York, as Mr. Roosevelt tells it, "and as we fear it must be told, is not inspiring. The record is almost bare of glorious deeds, of lofty ideals, of elevating thoughts. The city was sordid when it was small, and sordid when it became great. No glamour of romance can be made to surround it. From a very early time it has been a mart, a place to buy and sell and get gain ; and in this respect its past has been great and its future will be greater. But in civic life, . . . New York has always been deficient. . . . The causes of this lack are clearly shown by Mr. Roosevelt. The city did not develop: it simply grew. Development was swamped by wave after wave of immigration, and, after it had been populated by those who came to it as a place for money-getting, it fell a victim to their parasites. . . . The chief merit of Mr. Roosevelt's sketch, so far as it relates to the history of the city of New York — for we think his digressions the best part of it — is the clearness with which he brings out the mongrel character of its population, and it is surprising that he should give so little consideration to the natural consequences of this feature. The purely narrative portions of the history are very agreeably written, and leave the reader with the single regret that they are necessarily so much abbreviated. . . . The subject is really too large for the prescribed limits." *Nation*, 52 : 406.

Scharf, John Thomas, *and* **Thompson Westcott.** History of Philadelphia. Phil.: Everts. 1884. 3v.   [3253

The standard history of Philadelphia. Characterized by good arrangement, legitimate purpose, and the subordination of the reminiscent to order and to fact. The first volume gives a chronological sketch of the rise and progress of the city generally ; the remaining volumes treat of specific characteristics, such as government, art, education, etc. The illustrations possess historic value. E. E. S.

Severance, Frank Hayward. Old trails on the Niagara frontier. Buffalo: Author. 1899. [3254

A series of carefully studied and admirably written papers touching episodes in the history of the Niagara frontier. The cross bearers (Jesuit and Recollet missionaries); With Bolton at Fort Niagara; What befell David Ogden; Journals and journeys of an early Buffalo merchant; Misadventures of Robert Marsh; Underground trails,—are among the titles. "Mr. Severance is well known as an authority upon the history of this section of the country, and he has made himself familiar with the material to be found in the archives of Canada and of the different states, so that his statements of fact may be trusted." University of Toronto, *Review of historical publications relating to Canada,* 1899.

Sheafer, P. W., *et al.* Historical map of Pennsylvania. See Pennsylvania, Historical Society of, sect. 385. [3254 a

Smith, Samuel. History of the colony of Nova-Cæsaria or New Jersey to the year 1721. Burlington, N. J. 1765. Reprinted. Trenton. 1877. [3255

This book is one of the most valuable original sources of New Jersey history. The text is brief and inadequate, but the documents which are printed in the text and in the appendix are of great value. Some of them are still inaccessible elsewhere. The book is especially important as a contribution to the history of West Jersey. It is still the main source of information which we have concerning the early history of that part of the province. The book contains much material which illustrates the relations between New York and New Jersey. To the reprint is prefixed a sketch of the author. H. L. O.

See, also, sect. 1108.

Stiles, Henry Reed. History of the city of Brooklyn. Albany: Munsell. 1867–70. 3v. [3256

"No merely book-making enterprise, even with superior publishing facilities, could have made this work what it is. It has evidently been a labor of love on the part of its author and editor, who has not only harvested but gleaned in every field of available information touching Brooklyn history with an industry and ability deserving signal acknowledgment. And Mr. Stiles's work is of more than merely local interest. . . . One half of Mr. Stiles's first volume is filled with early colonial sketches; the remainder of the volume is mainly devoted to an admirable account of the battle of Long Island, the movements of the American and British armies, the British prison-ships of Wallabout, and other incidents of the Revolutionary period, and brings down the history of Brooklyn to the close of the War of 1812. The second volume gives the history of Brooklyn . . . to 1869, besides interesting biographies of early settlers. The third volume is devoted to the institutions of the city. . . . All these volumes are profusely illustrated with views,

maps, plans, autographs, portraits, and other illustrations, all well selected and admirably executed. Few cities are so fortunate in a historian as Brooklyn." *Nation,* 11: 110.

Stockton, Francis Richard. Stories of New Jersey. N. Y.: Am. Bk. Co. 1896. 60c.

—— *Same:* New Jersey. (Stories from Am. history.) N. Y.: Appleton. $1.50. [3257

The reputation of the author of this little book is a sufficient guarantee of its literary quality. Not a little historical truth is also set forth in its pages, with such a mingling of tradition and fancy as to make it attractive to a child of ten or twelve. The incidents chosen are in substance historical and, for the purpose of the book, a legitimate use has been made of literary art in setting them forth. The events dwelt upon in the stories occurred mostly in the colonial and revolutionary periods. On p. 27 a gross error appears concerning the grant of Virginia to Raleigh, and also concerning the extent of Virginia at the time when the Duke of York granted New Jersey to Berkeley and Carteret. In general, however, the book is fairly accurate. H. L. O.

Stone, William Leete, Jr. History of New York city. N. Y.: Virtue. 1872. [3258

Mr. Stone's *History of New York city* differs in no important respect from the type of the ordinary popular history. It is more truly an account of events which occurred in the city, than a history of the city itself; a large proportion of these events, however, really belong to the history of the province. Mr. Stone's treatment of the present century constitutes the most valuable part of his book. But in that he dwells on the popular, spectacular and superficial aspects of the subject rather than on the essentials of municipal history. He has presented many facts of interest. Noteworthy among these are the accounts of the riots, especially of the Draft riots of 1863; of the fires by which the city has been visited; and of the overthrow of the Tweed Ring in 1872. H. L. O.

Thompson, Benjamin Franklin. History of Long Island. N. Y. 1839. 2d ed. rev. and enl. N. Y. 1843. 2v. [3259

"The most comprehensive of the accounts of that island." Justin Winsor, in *Narrative and critical hist. of Am.,* 4: 441.

Tilden, Samuel Jones. The New York city "Ring;" discussed in a reply to the New York Times. N. Y.: Polhemus. 1873. [3260

"The title of this pamphlet shows what its chief subject is, to wit: a summary account of the real means by which the 'Ring' was assaulted and beaten. Mr. Tilden shows that as chairman of the Democratic State Committee of New York, he had already been fighting with the 'Ring' for a long time when the *Times* joined in the attack." F. B. Perkins, in *Old and new,* 7: 613.

Todd, Charles Burr. Story of the city of New York. N. Y.: Putnam. 1889. $1.75. [3261

Mr. Todd " ends his history where Mr. Lossing begins his, *i. e.*, with the year 1830. . . . Mr. Todd's narrative is agreeable and thoroughly readable. More might have been told in the same compass, but he has, we presume consciously, disregarded proportion in favor of picturesqueness." *Nation*, 47: 39.

Turner, Orsamus. History of the pioneer settlement of Phelps and Gorham's purchase, and Morris' reserve. Rochester. 1851. [3262

Traces the records of the Genesee Valley through the periods of warfare, exploration and settlement. Too diffuse and disconnected for an adequate history, it is an invaluable repository for a vast quantity of pioneer reminiscences, much of which no doubt would have been lost but for the zeal of the author, himself the son of a pioneer of western New York. F. H. S.

—— Pioneer history of the Holland purchase of western New York ; including reminiscences of the War of 1812 ; the origin, progress and completion of the Erie Canal, etc. Buffalo. 1850. [3263

Although the best existing " history " of the Holland Purchase, it is a disorderly encyclopædia of data on every phase of pioneer settlement and early development of the region. A valuable repository of information, it falls far short of being an adequate narrative, and utterly fails to show its particular subject as related to the general history of the United States. F. H. S.

Valentine, David Thomas, *comp.* Manual of the corporation of the city of New York. N. Y. 1842–70.
—— Historical index to Manuals, 1841–70. N. Y.: F. P. Harper. 1900. Net $2.50. [3264

This serial was begun as an enlargement of the *City Hall directory*. Under the title of *Manual* it appeared first in 1841, the issue for that year being compiled by S. T. Willis. In 1842 it passed under the editorship of David T. Valentine, clerk of the Common Council. Annually thereafter till Mr. Valentine's death in 1866 it was issued under his management, he continuing for that period to hold the office of Clerk of the Council. No volume was issued in 1867. In 1868 the publication of a new series was begun, but this proved to be much less valuable from an historical standpoint than the volumes edited by Valentine. The series is first of all a manual of the city, official and statistical. As time passed and the city grew, not only did information of this kind increase in amount, but it became more detailed. Valentine's *Manual*, however, from 1850 on, contained in its successive issues a large amount of purely historical material, which was selected and compiled by its editor. This has given a value and individuality to the series such as few similar publications have. The historical matter consists of extracts from the early records of the city, Dutch and English, extracts from old newspapers, abstracts of conveyances of property in early times and the location of Dutch and early English grants on Manhattan Island, biographical sketches of magistrates and public men of the city, a digest

of city ordinances during the colonial period, accounts of public improvements and of the growth of the city and its people in very many of its phases. Another most valuable feature of the series is the large number of maps and plans of the city which are reproduced in it. Valentine's *Manual* has been one of the chief storehouses whence recent historians and topographers have drawn their material. Its value has been so much greater than that of any other printed collection of sources relating to the locality that its contents may be said to have given a certain character to the writing of New York city history. An index of the series has recently been issued in one volume. H. L. O.

See, also, in Syllabus of materials, sect. 119.

Van Pelt, Daniel. Leslie's history of the Greater New York. N. Y.: Arkell Pub. Co. 1899. Subs. $25. [3265

This book " disposes of New York proper in one volume and of the outlying boroughs in another. The work is frankly a popular compilation, not a philosophical history in any sense. For example, the career of Tweed and his gang is rehearsed justly and in proper reprobation, but the continuity between Tweed and Croker, or between the ring system and the boss system, is not even suggested. In fact, Croker's name does not, we believe, appear in these pages — but there is no index." *Nation*, 68: 110.

Watson, John Fanning. Annals and occurrences of New York city and state in the olden time. Phil. 1846. [3266

This book was compiled by the author of the more widely known *Annals of Philadelphia*, and is of the same general character as that work, though less valuable. It is a collection of miscellaneous facts relating to the settlement of the state and city and to their history till the time the compilation was made. Some valuable and interesting notices of Dutch and early English life in New York City and Albany appear here, also life-like portrayals of the experiences of pioneers in western New York. Many details as to dress, furniture, marriage customs, also many extracts from advertisements in old newspapers are given. The material was drawn from a variety of sources, oral and written, and may be regarded as generally authentic ; it is of a nature which relates especially to culture-history. But it is in no sense scientifically selected or arranged. The reader of the present day will find the book worthless, except for an occasional fact which he may need to complete some picture of the life and personalities of a past time. H. L. O.

Wilson, James Grant, *ed.* Memorial history of the city of New-York. N. Y.: New York History Co. 1891–3. 4v. Subs. $7.50 ea. [3267

This work was undertaken, in imitation of a similar enterprise in Boston, with the purpose of presenting in popular form and from the pens of various writers a detailed history of New York City. It is copiously illustrated and is made up in such a way as to recommend itself to purchasers. The material contained in its pages is abundant, and, on the whole, it is agreeably presented. Among the corps of writers appear the names of several specialists whose reputation guarantees thoroughness of preparation and general reliability of statement. There are, therefore, some excellent chapters in the work. But the information which has been included concerning the city itself is largely of a topographical, social, or statistical character. In fact the last volume of the series relates most strictly to New York City, but that is more truly a gazetteer than a history of its development during the present century. The writers have made practically no use of the municipal records, but have confined themselves to accessible printed authorities and to the newspapers. The work is not in any true sense a municipal history, while it throws little new light on the relations between New York City and the state or the nation. It can be best used as a cyclopedia wherein one can find a large amount of miscellaneous information concerning the city, the state, and some periods even of national history.   H. L. O.

Wyoming Historical and Genealogical Society. Wilkes - Barré, Pa. Organized in 1858.   [3268

Among its publications are: Massacre of Wyoming; — Acts of Congress for the defence of the Wyoming valley, Pa., 1776-1778, with introductory chapter by H. E. Hayden; — The Palatine or German emigrants to New York and Pennsylvania.

THE OLD "BORDER" AND "SOUTHERN" STATES

(*Comprehensive history, covering all or several periods. For colonial and pioneer history, see Part III, Division I, sect. 1119–1171, 1754–1826, 2016–2077.*)

Alabama. Records, documents and bibliography. See in Syllabus of materials, sect. 205, 206.   [3269

Alabama Historical Society. Tuscaloosa, Ala. Organized in 1850, and reorganized in 1898.   [3270

Among the publications of the Society are papers on the expedition of De Soto, and on the Creek Indians, both by R. A. Hardaway.

Avery, Isaac Wheeler. History of the state of Georgia, 1850–81. N. Y.: Brown. [c. 1881.]   [3271

This book is in reality a biography of Joseph E. Brown, the war Governor of Georgia, whose "public career for a quarter of a century has been the history of his state." It embraces the period of transition from the old to the new South, and is divided into three parts: The decade before the war, the war, and the period of reconstruction. The decided influence of Georgia upon questions like slavery, secession, and reconstruction is carefully traced and duly emphasized. The style is florid, colloquial and fulsome, with no reference to authorities. The appendix has a list of Georgia officers in the Civil War.   S. B. W.

Brewer, W. Alabama; her history, resources, war record and public men. Montgomery, Ala. 1872.   [3272

" This volume is a collection of such facts in relation to the present and past of Alabama as best deserve preservation." The work is introduced by a historical sketch; then come lists of officers, and histories, political and economic, of the separate counties. Under these are placed authoritative sketches of all who have been prominent in the state. The whole shows remarkable industry, is well arranged and forms one of the most important and accurate books of its kind. It is a valuable supplement to Pickett (sect. 3321).   S. B. W.

Brinton, Daniel Garrison. Notes on the Floridian peninsula. Phil.: Sabin. 1859.   [3273

One of the favored volumes in historical writing that makes a friend of its reader. It would indeed be difficult to find one more admirable in conception and execution, one better adapted to give profit and pleasure. The interest holds to the last line. While each division — The literary history of Florida, Indian tribes of the 16th century, and later Spanish missions and conquests — is complete for the general reader, the generous provision of footnotes, bibliography, cartography, and an appendix give the student the means for making his own all the sources of information possessed by the author.   G. K.

Browne, William Hand. Maryland. (American commonwealths.) Boston: Houghton. 1884. $1.25.   [3274

A well-written and reliable outline of the history of Maryland. It begins with the colonizing experiment of Lord Baltimore in Newfoundland, and closes with the downfall of proprietary government in Maryland during the Revolution. Its author is not only thoroughly acquainted with the subject, but has shown good judgment. The account of events in the 18th century is very brief.   H. L. O.

Burk, John Daly. History of Virginia. Petersburg, Va.: Author. 1804-5. 3v. [3275

The title of this work is misleading, for the author lived only to carry it to 1776. It was dedicated to Jefferson, and written by an ardent disciple of his. The strong democratic bias of the author is evident throughout. Burk wrote in a highly rhetorical style, moralized not a little, and, therefore, consumed much space in the effort to convey a little information. But he had access to records, some of which are now lost, and valuable appendices are to be found in his volumes. These by the modern reader will often be found more useful than the text. The material for the first volume was derived largely from Smith, the Records of the London Company, and from Stith. It is, on the whole, the most solid volume of the three. The treatment of the period of the Commonwealth is fair. A full and not unfair account of Bacon's Rebellion is given, but the reader will need to correct and supplement it by the use of later works.   H. L. O.

—— History of Virginia, continued by Skelton Jones and Louis H. Girardin, 1775–81. Petersburg, Va. 1816. [3276

Burk had planned to continue his *History* to a period contemporary with his own life. After his death his plan was in part completed by the issue of this volume, which is often bound as the fourth volume of Burk's *History*. It seems to have been written by Girardin, and the share which Jones had in its preparation is not made clear by the preface. The subject of the volume is the history of Virginia during the Revolution. The events which preceded the outbreak of war are reviewed in great detail. Many documents are printed which bear on the controversy with Gov. Dunmore. The formation of the state constitution and the proceedings of the early legislatures are traced; but after the beginning of war much more space is devoted to that than to state affairs. The style is excellent, and the tone usually moderate.

H. L. O.

Butler, Mann. History of the commonwealth of Kentucky. Louisville: Wilcox. 1834. [3277

From the Indian occupation of the country to the middle of the War of 1812. The author was long a resident of the state, and in writing this little book had access to the George Rogers Clark and other papers. The early land disputes, the difficulty between Virginia and Kentucky, and the navigation of the Mississippi question are especially well treated. The book ranks among the better class of work of its day, although now antiquated. E. E. S.

Cable, George Washington. Creoles of Louisiana. N. Y.: Scribner. 1884. $2.50. [3278

The Creoles of Louisiana, presented from the historical point of view, by the same hand that has made them a study in the romantic, cannot fail to interest; nor do they, even though (as in his Creoles of fiction) the author sacrifices his tale to his lesson, and makes history subservient to a moral, rather too vigilant for opportunities of application. The hereditary sources of the Crèoles, their tastes, habits, religion, politics; their foibles and virtues, their fortunes and misfortunes; their mispronunciation of the English; their city of New Orſeans, — are laid bare in an uncomplimentary if not unsympathetic light. G. K.

See sect. 2382 for Cable's *Negro question, and Silent South.*

Carr, Lucien. Missouri, a bone of contention. (American commonwealths.) Boston: Houghton. 1888. $1.25. [3279

" Of 371 pages, 138 are devoted to the ante-commonwealth stage, of which much is padding. Of the remainder of the book, 24 pages contain an account of the struggle over the admission of Missouri, the Mexican War takes up 31, the Civil War 96, and the years from 1865 to 1888 only 8 pages. The author says nothing about the constitutional law of the Commonwealth; he does not even mention the three constitutions, with their respective modifications. . . . Mr. Carr has forgotten a great many things, but he has learnt nothing of the interpretation put on the Constitution of the United States by the late war. He clings

to the doctrine of Cass and Douglas, once so popular in the southwest. He regards slavery as a domestic institution, beyond the jurisdiction of the United States, even in the territories. . . . The struggle in Missouri in 1861 was precipitated by General Lyon, F. P. Blair and the loyalists, according to Mr. Carr." Robert Weil, *Political science quarterly,* 3: 525.

Charleston, S. C. City year books. Charleston. [3280

See in Syllabus of materials, sect. 120.

Claiborne, John Francis Hamtramck. Mississippi, as a province, territory and state. Jackson, Miss.: Power. 1880. v. 1. [3281

The MS. of Vol. 2 was accidentally burned, and the death of the author prevented rewriting. Vol. 1 extends to the Civil War. For the early period the author relies partly on Gayarré, and partly on original documents. He gives an excellent account of the Natchez War (1730). For the 19th century the author relies on valuable documents left by his father, Gen. Claiborne, and his uncle, Governor Claiborne, and on his own knowledge of men and matters. His account of the customs of Indian tribes in Mississippi and of events leading to the Civil War is of special importance. The tone of the work is strongly southern. With a few exceptions the statements are accurate, but the materials are not treated in proper proportion, nor is the arrangement good. The work will be used by future historians as a storehouse to draw upon. Unfortunately it has no index. J. R. F.

Collins, Lewis. History of Kentucky; rev., enlarged, and brought down to 1874, by his son, Richard H. Collins. Louisville, Ky.: Collins. 1874. 2v. $10. [3282

It would, perhaps, be easier to state what this book does not, than what it does, contain. Among the topics treated are prehistoric facts, annals for 331 years (1529–1860), history in outline and by counties, statistics, antiquities and natural curiosities, geographical and geological descriptions, sketches of the court of appeals, the churches, freemasonry, odd-fellowship, internal improvements, incidents of pioneer life, and nearly 500 biographical sketches of distinguished pioneers, soldiers, statesmen, etc.; with 70 engravings, 84 portraits, and a map of Kentucky. There is a full index to each volume. Three hundred and fifty pages belong to the old edition prepared by Judge Collins; the remainder were prepared by his son Richard, with the exception of some of the historical and biographical sketches, which were written by special contributors. The annals contain a great mass of facts, some of which are important, and many of which are trivial. The outline history of Kentucky, written partly by John A. McClung and partly by George B. Hodge, is well condensed and interesting. It is evident that strenuous effort has been made to obtain accuracy of detail. This monumental work is a storehouse of information about Kentucky rather than a well-digested history of the state. J. R. F.

"This remarkable work embodies as much patient labor as has ever been given to the history of any American state, but the multitude and variety of the facts brought together make it rather a store-nouse

of information than a feast that invites the reader."
N. S. Shaler, *Kentucky*, p. vi.

Connelly, Emma M. Story of Kentucky. Boston: Lothrop. [c. 1889.] $1.50.   [3283

A running commentary on the chief events of the history of the state as illustrated in the development of a Kentucky family. The narrative extends from the early settlement to 1890. It is a peculiar composition, and not likely to prove interesting as a sketch or valuable as history. A chronological epitome, abridgment of the state Constitution of 1850, and a bibliography make up an appendix.   E. E. S.

Cooke, John Esten. Virginia. (American commonwealths.) Boston: Houghton. 1883. $1.25.   [3284

In this work the author has undertaken to present in a running narrative a history of the Virginia people. More than three fifths of his space is taken up with the seventeenth century, while the nineteenth receives but slight notice. The chief value of the work lies in its successful appeal to the popular mind through its attractive literary style.   S. B. W.

Davis, *Mrs*. Mary Evelyn Moore. Under six flags: the story of Texas. Boston: Ginn. 1897. 50c.   [3285

The author is a distinguished southern writer in prose and poetry. Though now living in New Orleans, Mrs. Davis was reared in Texas, and possesses an intimate knowledge of the history of that state. The book was written primarily for young people, but it is delightful reading for older folks as well. The story is not closely woven. Only the most striking and romantic events in the history of the state are given; but the author has succeeded "in presenting the salient points of the drama of two centuries as a consistent whole." The book is based on the best authorities, and the temper of the work throughout is most praiseworthy. The work is cleverly illustrated, and it has a series of maps and an index.   J. R. F.

Delaware. Records and documents. See in Syllabus of materials, sect. 180, 181.   [3286

Delaware, Historical Society of. Wilmington, Del. This society was organized in 1864, and has published 22 numbers of *Papers*, 1879-98.   [3287

Among them are: no. 3. Some account of William Usselinx and Peter Minuit, by Joseph J. Mickley:—no. 6. Minutes of the council of the Delaware state from 1776 to 1792:—no. 15. Journal of the southern expedition, 1780-1783, by William Seymour.

Fairbanks, George R. History of Florida, 1512-1842. Phil.: Lippincott. Jacksonville: Drew. 1871.

—— *Same:* Florida; its history and its romance, 1497-1898. [New ed.] Jacksonville: Drew. 1898. $1.50.   [3288

Mr. Fairbanks is one of the best authorities on the early history of Florida, where he has resided for many years. He writes in a strong, terse style, but his book is badly proportioned. Like many other early southern historians, he seems unable to get beyond the early colonial period. The book is one of value, however, and contains a luminous description of Florida during the American Revolution. The period from the acquisition of Florida by the United States to the present time Mr. Fairbanks does not cover as thoroughly as he might have done, although there is a somewhat detailed account of the Seminole War. In the first edition the narrative is brought down to the year 1843; the second, to 1898. The second edition contains several illustrations, but no maps. On the whole the work is the best on the subject.   B. J. R.

Filson Club. Louisville, Ky. This Club was organized in 1884, and has issued 14 volumes of *Publications*.   [3289

The most important are the following: V. 1. Life and writings of John Filson, by R. T. Durrett:—V. 2. The wilderness road, by Capt. T. Speed:—V. 6. Political beginnings of Kentucky, by Col. J. Mason Brown:—V. 11. History of Transylvania University, by Robert Peter and Miss Johanna Peter:—V. 13. The first explorations of Kentucky, by Col. J. Stoddard Johnston:—V. 14. The Battle of Tippecanoe, by Captain Alfred Pirtle. The *Nation* (July 11, 1898) says of the Filson Club publications that they are "simply indispensable to students of Kentucky history."

Florida. Records, documents and bibliography. See in Syllabus of materials, sect. 202-204.   [3290

Fortier, François Alcée. Louisiana studies. New Orleans: Hansell. 1894. $1.50.   [3291

The topics embraced in these studies are literature, customs, dialects, history and education. Literature and education are treated in rapid sketches from the colonial period down to the present time (1894); the customs and dialects described are those of the 19th century. As the author's ancestors—French Creoles—have lived in Louisiana for more than a century, he has been able to gather a great deal of information about the past history of the state that is not to be found in books. Perhaps the most valuable portion of this work, however, is the study of the existing Creole, Acadian, and Isleños dialects in Louisiana. As Professor of Romance languages in Tulane University, New Orleans, the author was specially qualified to make these researches.   J. R. F.

French, Benjamin Franklin, *comp.* Historical collections of Louisiana. V. 1. N. Y.: Wiley & Putnam. (Other volumes, various publishers.) 1846-53. 5v.

—— Historical collections of Louisiana and Florida. N.Y.: Sabin. 1869-75. 2v.   [3292

This is the most valuable collection of documents concerning the early history of Louisiana and Florida that exists in the English language. The historical collections of Pierre Margry (sect. 1182) in the French language give the originals of many of Mr. French's documents, and as Mr. French is not a careful translator, they should be consulted by the student.

The more important contents are as follows : —
First Series: Vol. 1, Series of papers describing the
voyages of La Salle down the Mississippi and to Texas ;
Tonty's Account of the route from the Illinois to the
Gulf. Vol. 2, Account of the Louisiana Historical Society; Discourse on Judge F. X. Martin; translation
of an original letter by De Soto on the conquest of
Florida: the journal of Biedener and the narrative of
a Gentleman of Elvas, describing the expedition of De
Soto; Coxe's description of Carolana (not complete) ;
Marquette and Joliet's account of their voyage, etc.
Vol. 3, Translation of La Harpe's journal; of Charlevoix's journal ; also Sauvole's journal (in French);
and a mémoire (also in French) of the first Natchez
war by Richebourg, etc. Vol. 4, Discovery and exploration of the Mississippi valley, with the original
narratives of Marquette, Allouez, Membré, Hennepin,
and Douay, by John Gilmary Shea. Mr. French had
no hand in this volume ; it was wholly the work of
the distinguished scholar Mr. Shea. Mr. French, it is
said, bore the expense of publication. Vol. 5, Memoirs of Louisiana, from the first settlement of the
colony to the departure of O'Reilly in 1770. These
memoirs include a translation of Dumont's and of
Champigny's Mémoires ; an appendix, containing treaties of peace and other historical documents. *Second
Series:* Vol. 1, Translations of De Remonville's Memoir, of D'Iberville's Narrative, of Penicaut's Annals
of Louisiana ; also the history of Jean Ribault's First
voyage to Florida, by R. Laudonnière (trans. by Hakluyt). Vol. 2, Translation from a copy of the original
MS. in the Marine department, Paris, of a memoir by
La Salle. Journal of Iberville's expedition to Louisiana (printed for the first time) ; a letter of Jacques
Gravier, etc. For the history of Florida, there is a
letter of Columbus, a proclamation of Narvaez, a narrative of Ribault's first voyage ; a memoir of Menen-
dez's expedition ; and an appendix containing historical documents in French and in Spanish. Mr. French
was a pioneer in the publication of historical documents, which he generally translated into English, and
to which he added biographical and critical notes.
Some of his materials were drawn from his own fine
library ; others from the archives of France. While
Mr. French's works have been of invaluable aid to historians, they can hardly be commended for accuracy.
Not only does he omit in his translations portions of
the originals without calling attention to the fact, but
he adds critical notes which are not free from errors.
The style is clear and simple.   J. R. F.
"It is to be regretted that French sometimes
abridges the documents which he copies, without indicating such method, — as in the case of Charlevoix and
Dumont." Justin Winsor, in *Narrative and critical
hist. of Am.,* 5 : 73.

Galveston, Historical Society of. Galves-
ton, Texas. Organized in 1871. In 1876 published *Reminiscences of the Texas Republic,* by
Ashbel Smith. In 1894, the Society was reorganized as the Texas Historical Society.
[3293

Gayarré, Charles Étienne Arthur. His-
tory of Louisiana. N. Y. 1854–66. 4v. 3d
ed. enl. New Orleans : Hawkins. 1885. 4v.
[3294

V. 1, 2, French domination. V. 3, Spanish domination. V. 4, American domination.
"Charles Gayarré is the author of two distinct
works which must not be confounded. *Louisiana,
its colonial history and romance* is a history of colonial romance rather than a history of the colony. The
Histoire de la Louisiane is an essentially different
book. It is mainly composed of transcripts from
original documents, woven together with a slender
thread of narrative. . . . His final work (reprinted in
1885) was in English, and was continued [from 1770,
at which date the *Histoire* was ended] to 1861." A.
McF. Davis, in *Narrative and critical hist. of Am.,*
5: 65.
Louisiana, its colonial history and romance, published in N. Y. in 1851, also forms the first part of
History of Louisiana: French domination.

Georgia Historical Society. Savannah,
Ga. Organized in 1839. From 1840 to 1878
the Society published 4 volumes of *Collections,*
which are made up of important contemporary
accounts, by B. Martyn and others, of the early
settlement and progress of Georgia.   [3295

Among its other publications are: History of Georgia,
by William Bacon Stevens, in two volumes, 1847–59.
Siege of Savannah in 1779 as described in two contemporaneous journals of French officers in the fleet of
Count d'Estaing ; ed. by C. C. Jones, Jr.

Gould, E. W. Fifty years on the Missis-
sippi; or Gould's History of river navigation.
St. Louis : Nixon-Jones. 1889.   [3296

Interesting chapters concerning the days when river
navigation was more important than now, by an
experienced river-man, with accounts of floods, ice-
dams, river improvements, along with much historical
material not otherwise accessible.   W. M. D.

Hamilton, Peter J. Colonial Mobile ; an
historical study of the Alabama-Tombigbee
basin, 1519–1821. Boston: Houghton. 1897.
Net $3.   [3297

The author, a lawyer of Mobile, has made a special
study of the church records and other archives of old
Mobile. His legal training qualifies him to understand, and, for the most part, to use them wisely in
reconstructing the colonial history. In parts, however, the information given is dry and statistical ;
and the work would be improved by omissions. The
temper of the author is judicial, and his style clear,
concise and vigorous.   J. R. F.

Harris, Joel Chandler. Georgia, from the
invasion of De Soto to recent times. N. Y. :
Appleton. 1896. $1.50.
—— *Same :* Stories of Georgia. N. Y. : Am.
Book Co. 1896. 60c.   [3298

This work, by the well-known author of *Uncle Re-
mus,* was not intended to be a connected history of
Georgia, but rather a series of sketches, picturing the
most striking persons and events in the history of
the state. The author handles the difficult subjects
of Slavery and Reconstruction without partisanship,

and the temper of the work is for the most part excellent. The wit and humor of the state would perhaps have ranked higher, if the chapter with that title had been omitted. Some of the matter is trivial, but as a whole the work commands the attention of the reader, and from it may be drawn a fairly good idea of the progress of the state in recent times.

J. R. F.

Haywood, John. Civil and political history of Tennessee. Knoxville. 1823. Nashville: Haywood. 1891.   [3299

This is the original work for the history of Tennessee and the one on which later books are to a greater or less extent based. The author lived near enough to the pioneers to receive reports and memories from them. He was also a student and a sound political thinker and is the chief authority for accounts of the Indians; but as he rested his work mainly on the narratives of the pioneers in their old age he has fallen into many blunders.   S. B. W.

Howison, Robert R. History of Virginia. V. 1, Phil.: Carey. 1846. V. 2, Richmond: Drinker. 1848.   [3300

" The most comprehensive history of Virginia is that of Robert R. Howison, vol. 1 coming down to 1763 . . . and vol. 2 ending in 1847. . . . He is a pleasing writer, but sacrifices fact to rhetoric." R. A. Brock, in *Narrative and critical hist. of Am.*, 3: 166.

Hutchins, Thomas. Historical, narrative and topographical description of Louisiana and West Florida. Phil. 1784.   [3301

An historical sketch of Louisiana and West Florida (as Spanish possessions west of the Rio Perdido were called), followed by a topographical description of the Mississippi, its principal branches, the climate, the soil, the products of the country, the settlements, with minute directions for navigating the Mississippi and other water-ways into the interior. Written and published during Spain's possession of New Orleans and of the mouth of the Mississippi, the volume not only gives interesting information in an interesting way, it furnishes also important testimony as to the state of affairs existing and portending, that brought on the political agitation which was only settled by American ownership of the mouth of the Mississippi.

G. K.

Jones, Charles Colcock, Jr. History of Georgia. Boston: Houghton. 1883. 2v.

[3302

One of the very best of the state histories. The author is the leading authority upon the subject, and has devoted great care to the collection of materials. The treatment is full, and in the text will be found many valuable documents. The style is smooth and agreeable. The first volume is devoted mainly to the history of Georgia under the Trustees. Oglethorpe, the Wesleys and Whitefield are the central figures in it. The history of Georgia as a royal province, which follows, leads presently into the Revolution. To the share which Georgia bore therein nearly all of the second volume is devoted. The history closes with the achievement of independence.   H. L. O.

Lanier, Sidney. Florida: its scenery, climate, and history. Phil.: Lippincott. 1877.

[3303

The historical portion is neither full nor complete, but it is pleasantly written, and will suffice for the ordinary traveller. The author was a distinguished southern poet, who spent a year in Florida (1874–5), seeking relief from consumption. This work was written with special reference to the fitness of Florida as a home for invalids. The most valuable portion is the description of climate and localities.

J. R. F.

Louisiana. Records, documents and bibliography. See in Syllabus of materials, sect. 207, 208.   [3304

Louisiana Historical Society. New Orleans, La. This Society was organized in 1836 and reorganized in 1895. Since the reorganization it has issued *Publications*, v. 1 in 4 parts, and parts 1–4 of v. 2.   [3305

Lowndes family. CHASE, GEORGE BIGELOW. Lowndes of South Carolina: an historical and genealogical memoir. Boston: Williams. 1876.   [3306

A little book containing a genealogy of the Lowndes family, and brief, accurate, judicious and well-written sketches of such members of that family as played considerable parts in the history of South Carolina and the nation, particularly of the celebrated William Lowndes. A number of letters is appended containing valuable information about the " early settlement and administration of South Carolina " (1726–1752).   R. C. H. C.

Lowry, Robert, *and* **William Henry McCardle.** History of Mississippi. New ed. N. Y.: University Pub. Co. 1893. $1. [3307

This is a history of Mississippi from the earliest times to the present. The only portion of the work possessing originality is that which treats of the period immediately preceding and following the Civil War. Mr. Lowry has been twice Governor of the state, and both he and Colonel McCardle are well informed as to its more recent political history. The remainder of the work is largely based on an uncritical study of Gayarré and Claiborne. The matter is often ill-digested, and there is little attempt at historical perspective. The style, while generally clear, is neither accurate nor graceful. There is no index.

J. R. F.

McCall, *Maj.* **Hugh.** History of Georgia. Savannah: Seymour. 1811–16. 2v.   [3308

Written by a contemporary from the Georgia standpoint. The foundation of much of our present knowledge of Georgia history.   E. C.

McSherry, James. History of Maryland. Balt.: Murphy. 1849.   [3309

This book is written in a smooth, interesting style, and in its day was useful as a popular presentation of the subject. The author wrote from the moderate

Catholic standpoint, and made use of Bozman, Mc-Mahon, and other accessible printed authorities. The book is especially slight after the guidance of Bozman is lost. Subsequent to the outbreak of the Revolution, general history occupies a much more prominent place in it than does the history of the state proper. The book is not inaccurate, but inadequate; and the facts which it sets forth can now be found better and more authoritatively stated elsewhere.

H. L. O.

Marshall, Humphrey. History of Kentucky. Frankfort. 1824. 2v. [3310

" This is an excellent history in many respects, but is extremely Federalistic in tone, and exceedingly unjust to those who differed from the author in politics." N. S. Shaler, *Kentucky*, p. vii.

Martin, Francois Xavier. History of Louisiana. New Orleans: Gresham. 1882. [3311

This work is a valuable compilation of facts relating to the origin and progress of Louisiana, embracing valuable statistical tables, but shows no trace of the historian's art. In this edition the original work is accompanied by a memoir of the author, and the annals of Louisiana from the close of that work, 1815, to the commencement of the Civil War, by John F. Condon.

B. A. H.

—— History of North Carolina. New Orleans : Penniman. 1829. 2v. [3312

These volumes are a dull compilation, mostly from printed sources ; they are arranged largely in the form of annals, and contain much that is either entirely irrelevant or of little importance. The compiler was indifferent to the collection of facts, even when his opportunities were of the best and they concerned his own profession. His work has clearness and precision, but there is no effort to set forth events in the relation of cause and effect, nor even to state them in such a way that this will be obvious. It comes no later than 1776 and is of little value.

S. B. W.

Maryland. Records, documents and materials. See in Syllabus of materials, sect. 182–188. [3313

Maryland Historical Society. Baltimore, Md. This Society was organized in 1844, and has published two editions of the *Journal of Charles Carroll of Carrollton, during his visit to Canada in 1776 as one of the commissioners of Congress;* a series of *Fund publications*, of which 34 numbers were issued from 1869 to 1894 ; and the *Archives of Maryland*, published under the authority of the state, 15 volumes being issued between 1883 and 1896. [3314

Among the *Fund publications* are the following: Nos. 5 and 6. A lost chapter in the history of the steamboat, and First steamboat voyage on the western waters, by J. H. Latrobe : — No. 7. Relatio itineris in Marylandiam (narrative of a voyage to Baltimore), by Father Andrew White, S. J., with translation by J. H. Converse, and Supplement, Excerpta ex diversis

literis missionariorum, 1638 ad 1677 : — No. 9. Papers relating to the early history of Maryland, by S. F. Streeter : — No. 11. Maryland's influence in founding a national commonwealth, by Herbert B. Adams : — Nos. 28 and 34. The Calvert papers, nos. 1 and 2.

Mills, Robert. Statistics of South Carolina. Charleston : Hurlbut. 1826. [3315

This work is intended as an appendix to his *Atlas of South Carolina*, published in 1826. It carries out the plan suggested by Ramsay as a possible continuation of his work, and treats the natural, civil and military history of the province and state as a whole. This general historical survey is followed by a series of chapters treating with much detail the civil, economic and natural history of the counties, with many statistics. His historical sections are not as correct as his statistics and atlas. These are unquestioned. They supply a want in the state and must remain the basis of any subsequent work of the kind.

S. B. W.

Missouri Historical Society. St. Louis, Mo. This Society was organized in 1866. From 1880 to 1897, it published 15 numbers of *Publications*, which together form volume 1 of its *Collections*. [3316

Among the most important articles are : The campaign in Missouri and the battle of Wilson's Creek, by W. M. Wherry. — The American Revolution and the acquisition of the valley of the Mississippi, by C. F. Robertson.

Moore, John Wheeler. History of North Carolina. Raleigh : A. Williams. 1880. 2v. [3317

Mr. Moore does not reprint original documents, as Hawks, nor lists of names, as Wheeler. There is no pretense to original research, nor is there use of materials inaccessible to earlier writers. In the matter of secession, the standpoint is a vigorous defense of state sovereignty ; and the account given of the part of North Carolina in the Civil War is the fullest that has yet appeared. But the colonial period, written on the basis of the old works, and with them alone as an authority, is teeming with errors. It is not a history of the people nor of their development, but of the politicians. It has no literary style and the arrangement is poor, yet it is the latest, most complete, and most accessible history of the state, and for the whole of the period covered by the second volume (1825-1880) there is no other available work. S. B. W.

North Carolina. Records, documents and bibliography. See in Syllabus of materials, sect. 194–196. [3318

Page, Thomas Nelson. The old South : essays, social and political. N. Y.: Scribner. 1892. $1.25. [3319

This is a collection of pictures of southern life from the colonial period to the Civil War. The last essay discusses the race problem in the present and the past, prophesying that the negro will gradually disappear. The book owes its significance to the fact that the author is descended from a distinguished Virginia family, and has had special opportunities to absorb the traditions of southern life. Moreover, he has made a careful study of old records — some unpublished. While he recognizes the faults of the old régime, the author generally presents only the brighter side. Incidentally a strong defence is made of the much-maligned civilization of the South. Mr. Page writes in the best of tempers, and his style is generally marked by the same fine literary touch that is found in his stories. Occasionally he admits so many details as to mar the perspective of his pictures.

J. R. F.

Phelan, James. History of Tennessee. Boston: Houghton. 1888. $2. [3320

This is the first attempt to write a history of Tennessee covering a later period than the early settlement of the state, and hence only a small space is devoted to the Indian wars which occupy such a disproportionate amount in the earlier books. Political history is not expanded to the exclusion of all other subjects, as is so usual in state histories, but the making of the state in all its phases is traced, and its development told in vigorous English, which has called to its aid all the arts of the trained historical investigator. It is beyond question the best history of a southern state with which I am familiar. It stops with the outbreak of the Civil War. S. B. W.

Pickett, Albert James. History of Alabama and incidentally of Georgia and Mississippi from the earliest period. Charleston: Walker. 1851. (3 editions that year.) 2v. 5th ed. enl. Birmingham, Ala. : Webb Book Co. 1900. 2v. $2.50. [3321

Pickett's work is founded in part on original printed authorities and in part on the interviews of the author with Indian chiefs and white pioneers during the first half of the 19th century. It is far above the average state history in the author's grasp of his subject ; has been accepted as an authority on the subjects of which it treats and is invaluable to students, but it comes no later than the admission of the state to the Union in 1819 and is filled with many details of small historical importance. A fourth edition was published in 1896 (Sheffield, Ala.) and a fifth in 1900 (Birmingham) which has been greatly increased in value by the addition of the *Annals of Alabama, 1819-1900*, by Thomas M. Owen, a brief general history of the state during that time, with additional chapters on literary history, bibliography and state officers and an index which is wanting in all previous editions. S. B. W.

Ramsay, David. History of South-Carolina. Charleston : Longworth. 1809. 2v. Newberry, S. C. 1858. [3322

This was long the acknowledged authority for South Carolina history. It does not trace that history in a chronological order, but according to subjects. It treats in detail the Proprietary period, the Revolution of 1719, military history and the Revolution, to which more than half of the first volume is devoted. For the period of the Proprietary and Royal governments the author draws very largely from Hewatt, apparently trusting to him exclusively. The second volume, which is of more value as an original source, deals

with ecclesiastical, medical, legal, constitutional, fiscal, agricultural and commercial, natural and literary history, and that of the arts. There are also a number of biographical sketches. Dr. Ramsay was a zealous investigator, and had been a participant in many of the events narrated from the time of the Revolution. S. B. W.

Scharf, John Thomas. History of Maryland. Balt. 1879. 3v. [3323

" Mr. Scharf has had one advantage over all his predecessors in this field. Mr. George Peabody, among his many liberalities to his adopted state, had abstracts made of over seventeen hundred original documents in the State Paper office, London, relating to the history of Maryland between the years 1626-1780, and presented them to the Maryland Historical Society. By their assistance Mr. Scharf has been able to procure official transcripts of documents whose existence was unknown to previous workers in this field. . . . The whole work is encumbered with copies of unimportant papers, citations, often pages in length, from easily accessible books, long lists of names and copious extracts from newspapers. The typography, especially of the last volume, is very defective, while as for the index, it is best passed over in charitable silence." Had Mr. Scharf " more thoroughly digested the material he has collected so laboriously, and condensed his three volumes into two, his history would have been none the worse book to refer to, and much the better book to read." W. H. Browne, in *Nation*, 30 : 217.

" More than one half of the material used in the first volume of this history is taken from papers in the possession of the Maryland Historical Society. These valuable papers were copied by the office boys of the historian and were not compared with the originals. . . . The general reader will be deterred from reading this history of Maryland from its size, and the student will fail to derive much benefit from it on account of its defective arrangement." Eugene L. Didier, in *Magazine of Am. hist.*, 4 : 314.

Shaler, Nathaniel Southgate. Kentucky (American commonwealths.) Boston : Houghton. 1885. $1.25. [3324

The author, a well-known geologist, was qualified by a long personal knowledge of men and events in Kentucky, to write the history of the state. He fought in the Civil War on the Union side, and presents a vivid picture of the events that marked the great conflict, as well as of the period of " reconstruction." Naturally, also, there is a good description of the geology of the state. Outside of his personal knowledge and the information gleaned from friends, the author acknowledges his great debt to Collins' monumental *History of Kentucky*, " without which his book could not have been written." The author's judgment seems to be occasionally biassed by excessive state pride; but he shows an earnest effort to be fair towards those who thought differently from him in the Civil War. The style is clear and vigorous. The work has a map, a bibliography, and an index. J. R. F.

Simms, William Gilmore. History of South Carolina. Charleston: Babcock. 1840. New and rev. ed. N. Y.: Redfield. 1860. [3325

This history is based on printed authorities and was intended for school use. It is devoted mainly to the Colonial and Revolutionary periods. The story of political development and military campaigns is told with spirited and graphic power. A supplementary chapter brings the subsequent history of the state down to the date of publication; but this is by no means as well done as the colonial period. The whole work shows intense local patriotism and is rich in arguments for secession.　　　　　S. B. W.

South Carolina. Records, documents and bibliography. See in Syllabus of materials, sect. 197–201.　　　　　[3326

South Carolina Historical Society. Charleston, S. C. This Society was organized in 1856. It has published 5 volumes of *Collections*, 1857–97, and *Documents connected with the history of South Carolina*, ed. by P. C. J. Weston.
[3327

Southern History Association. Washington, D. C. This Association issues its *Publications* at regular intervals beginning 1897, the fifth volume starting with a number for January, 1901.　　　　　[3328

Among their contents are John Brown's raid, by Andrew Hunter, and a Journal of the siege of Savannah in 1779, by General Prevost, both in volume 1. The first number was welcomed by the *American historical review* with praise of its contents. "The new journal is well printed and carefully edited. Its possibilities are manifest to any one who thoughtfully surveys the southern field. . . . A scientific intention and spirit on the part of its chief promoters is, at any rate, already evident." *Am. hist. review*, 2: 755.

Stevens, William Bacon. History of Georgia. V. 1. N. Y.: Appleton. 1847. V. 2. Phil.: Butler. 1859.　　　　　[3329

These volumes constitute the standard history of Georgia from its discovery to the adoption of the revised constitution of the state in 1798. The work is based almost entirely upon original sources, and is a model of excellence. The first volume sketches the early history of the French and Spanish explorations and gives valuable data concerning the southern Indians. It also contains an interesting account of the London debtors and the persecuted Protestants of Salzburg who found a home in Georgia after Oglethorpe had obtained his patent. The second volume continues the narrative through the Revolutionary period. There are several good illustrations and a valuable index. The latter was prepared by the Rev. William Stevens Perry.　　　　　B. J. R.

Tennessee. Records and documents. See in Syllabus of materials, sect. 209, 210. [3330

Texas. See sect. 3293.

Thompson, Maurice. Story of Louisiana. (Story of the states.) Boston: Lothrop. [c. 1888.] $1.50.　　　　　[3331

This is a history of Louisiana from the earliest times to the present; but, within the compass of such a

work, the author has naturally been compelled to omit a great deal that belongs to the history of the state. He seems to have followed Gayarré and other standard historians, rather than the old records. Mr. Thompson is to be commended for the excellent judgment he shows in his discussion of the relations of the Creoles with the Americans. Unfortunately the book seems to have been hastily written, and some errors have crept in. The style shows the practiced literary nand. To the general reader the book will be extremely attractive.　　　　　J. R. F.

Trent, William Peterfield. Southern statesmen of the old régime. N. Y.: Crowell. 1897. $2.　　　　　[3332

Biographical and critical essays on Washington, Jefferson, John Randolph, Calhoun, Alex. H. Stephens, Robert Toombs, and Jefferson Davis. They are pleasantly written, and useful as popular accounts; those on Washington and Jefferson, however, are least important, and none have primary value. The author writes as "an American who is at the same time a southerner," but his work is free from bias or sectional partisanship.　　　　　W. MacD.

Tyler, Lyon Gardiner. Letters and times of the Tylers. Richmond: Whittet & Shepperson. 1884–5. 2v. V. 3 [with additional letters]. Williamsburg, Va. 1896. (For sale by author at Williamsburg, Va. 3v. $7.)　　　[3333

A most valuable collection of letters with a large body of narrative, throwing much light on Virginia history from the beginning of the Revolution, and on the history of the nation from the close of the War of 1812 to the end of the Civil War. The narrative is written in a tone of devoted loyalty to the position of Virginia in the crises of American history and to the old Virginia Republicanism of which the Tylers were eminent exponents. One of the ablest presentations of the southern view of American history for the period which is covered.　　　　　E. G. B.

Virginia. Records and documents. See in Syllabus of materials, sect. 189–193. [3334

Virginia Historical Society. Richmond, Va. Organized in 1832. Among its publications are H. A. Washington's *Virginia constitution of 1776*, and a series of *Virginia historical collections*, of which 11 volumes were issued from 1882 to 1892.　　　　　[3335

The contents of the latter include the following: V. 1 and 2. Official letters of Alexander Spotswood, Lt.-Gov. of Virginia, 1710–1722. — V. 3 and 4. Official records of Robert Dinwiddie, Lt.-Gov. of Virginia, 1751–1758. — V. 5. Documents relating to the Huguenot settlements in Virginia. — V. 7 and 8. Abstract of the proceedings of the Virginia Company, 1619–25. — V. 9 and 10. History of the Virginia Federal convention of 1788, by Hugh Blair Grissby.

Waring, George Edwin, Jr., *and* **George W. Cable.** History and present condition of New Orleans. (U. S. Census, 1880: Social statistics of cities.) Wash. 1881.　　　　　[3336

A full yet concise report including all the essential interests concerning the New Orleans of 1880. A sketch of the city's past history is contributed by G. W. Cable. A series of maps illustrates the various stages of its growth and development, and the statistics are minute and complete. G. K.

Weeks, Stephen Beauregard. Bibliography of the historical literature of North Carolina. Cambridge, Mass. 1895. Balt.: Hopkins. $1. [3337

A list of books, pamphlets, magazine and other articles relating to North Carolina with notes.

Wheeler, John Hill. Historical sketches of North Carolina, 1584–1851. Phil.: Lippincott. 1851. 2v. in 1. [3338

This work, two volumes in one, is the first product of a native historian. Volume 1 traces the history of the colony and state in a rapid sketch, with chapters on the press, literary institutions, internal improvements, resources, and public officers. Volume 2 gives a history of each county, with sketches of many leading citizens. The author had better opportunities than any previous writer, as he worked from official documents and made extracts from the British records. He was industrious and faithful, but his work is "a jumble of ill-digested material," is partisan in character, and, because of a fatal carelessness which marks all that he does, any statement he may make, unsupported by other evidence, is of little authority. S. B. W.

—— Reminiscences and memoirs of North Carolina and eminent North Carolinians. Columbus, O.: Columbus Prtg. Works. 1884. [3339

This work is a revision and expansion of the biographical part of the author's *Historical sketches of North Carolina*, and, like it, is arranged by counties. It is full of errors of omission and of commission, but is of importance as the fullest attempt towards a biographical history of the state, and is the basis of most subsequent compilations. S. B. W.

White, George, *comp.* Historical collections of Georgia. N. Y. 1854. 3d ed. 1855. [3340

About one third of this work is devoted to a collection of documents dealing with the Colonial and Revolutionary periods. This is followed by a series of biographies, including all the governors. The remainder is devoted to a topographical history of the counties. This includes many traditions, statistics and sketches of local worthies. An appendix gives the principal statistics of the whole state from the census of 1850. There are many illustrations, and the whole volume forms a compilation of the greatest value, extensively used by subsequent writers. S. B. W.

Wilhelm, Lewis Webb. Local institutions of Maryland. (Johns Hopkins Univ. studies, ser. 3, no. 5–7.) Balt. 1885. $1. [3341

"Covers a history of the land system, the hundreds, the counties and towns of the province." Justin Winsor, in *Narrative and critical hist. of Am.*, 5: 261.

Wooten, Dudley G., *ed.* Comprehensive history of Texas. Dallas: Scarff. 1899. 2v. [3342

A reprint of Yoakum's *History of Texas* without the documentary matter in the appendixes, but with notes relating almost entirely to the Revolution and made up mainly from F. W. Johnson's manuscript *History of Texas*, together with a series of monographs on various aspects of the life of the republic and the state, bringing the history up to 1895. The chapters concerning the Austins and their work in colonizing Texas are especially rich in documents previously unpublished. G. P. G.

THE MIDDLE WEST AND NORTHWEST

(Comprehensive history, covering all or several periods. For pioneer history, see Part III, sect. 1754–1826, 2016–2077.)

Andreas, A. T. History of Chicago. Chicago: Author. 1884–6. 3v. [3343

The largest history of Chicago and probably the best, but rendered unwieldy by many "biographies," selected with small regard for merit. Divisions: vol. 1, from 1670 through the panic of 1857; vol. 2, through the fire of 1872; vol. 3, through 1884. Various topics, such as commerce, press, bench, education, etc., are treated according to these periods, marring continuity and engendering bad arrangement. The preliminary sketch of the early history of the city is fairly accurate and accompanied by reproductions of many valuable maps. Indexes are very inadequate save for the "biographies." E. E. S.

Atwater, Caleb. History of the state of Ohio, natural and civil. Cin.: Glezen. [c. 1838.]. [3344

Save Chief Justice Chase's earlier sketch, this was the first history of Ohio to be published. The author was prominent in the early history of the state, and wrote his book largely from personal knowledge. He devoted much time to the collection and arrangement of material. His book shows no literary art, but is a rich miscellany of information of varying degrees of value. It is a ready source of knowledge concerning such subjects as the origin of the canal system, the educational system, and the taxation system of the state. B. A. H.

Barrett, Jay Amos. Nebraska and the nation. 2d ed. [rev. and enl.]. Chicago: Ainsworth. 1898. 75c. [3345

"A revised edition of *History and government of Nebraska*, published in 1892. The principal addition is a systematic 'Study of the United States government.' The author is librarian of the Nebraska State Historical Society." *Publishers' weekly*, 55: 368.

Black, Alexander. Story of Ohio. (Story of the states.) Boston: Lothrop. [c. 1888.] $1.50. [3346

This book well fills out the ideal of the State series, a graphic narrative descriptive of the rise and development of the state. For his purpose, the writer selects his facts with care, and weaves them into an effective story. The book is wholly popular in character, and has no value as a contribution to history.

B. A. H.

Blanchard, Rufus. History of Illinois, to accompany an historical map of the state. Chicago: National School Furnishing Co. 1883. [3347

An outline history of the state, with chapters by different hands, summarizing its political and commercial history and statistics, and giving the origin of Illinois geographical names, a description of the Indian tribes of Illinois, a sketch of early settlement, and notes explaining the map. This is 27½ × 42½ inches in size, well printed, and shows, with dates, the principal Indian trails, routes of exploring and military expeditions, early stage roads, historic sites, and dates of settlement of the principal towns. A chronological table borders the chart. A useful work, but the text has slight literary merit. It fairly represents historical knowledge at the time of publication; but later investigations have naturally wrought the need for revision. R. G. T.

Brown, Henry. History of Illinois. N. Y.: Winchester. 1844. [3348

Commencing with the discovery of Columbus, and rambling through the early Spanish, French, and English settlements in North America, it is long before our author gets down to Illinois history; and when he does, it is a discursive, often incoherent and flippant, and frequently inaccurate narrative, without perspective or sense of proportion. The book is valueless, save as a curious example of one type of early western histories. R. G. T.

Campbell, James Valentine. Outlines of the political history of Michigan. Detroit: Schober. 1876. [3349

This book is well described by its title: it presents in full outline the political history of Michigan from the earliest times to the centennial year, 1876. Other topics and materials are used only in so far as they serve to illustrate the long series of political facts. Michigan is, therefore, seen under French, British, and American jurisdiction, and under American in three territorial forms before it finally became a state. The author was long a member of the state Supreme Court, and much of the history of the later period fell under his own observation. The book is a solid contribution to the history of Michigan and of the old Northwest. B. A. H.

Caxton Club. Chicago, Ill. The Caxton Club was organized in 1895, and has published three pamphlets, one of them being: Joutel's *Journal of La Salle's last voyage.* [3350

Chicago Historical Society. Chicago, Ill. This Society was organized in 1856. A number of addresses, delivered before the Society, have been printed separately and others are included in the *Proceedings* which have been published since 1888 in pamphlet form with continuous paging. Between 1882 and 1890 were published 4 volumes of *Collections.* [3351

V. 3 contained *The Edwards papers,* — portions of the letters, papers and manuscripts of Ninian Edwards.

Among the occasional publications of the Society are: Historical sketch of the early movement in Illinois for the legalization of slavery, by Wm. H. Brown: — History of Illinois from 1778 to 1833, and Life and times of Ninian Edwards, by Ninian W. Edwards: — Last of the Illinois and sketch of the Pottowatomies, by J. D. Caton.

Colbert, Elias, *and* **Everett Chamberlin.** Chicago and the great conflagration. Cin.: Vent. 1872. [3352

The first part is devoted to a history of Chicago, its inception and growth. Statistics of the city in 1870 show its condition prior to the fire. The latter half of the book gives an account of the conflagration of 1872, made up largely of the descriptions of eye-witnesses and from newspaper reports. The story of the relief sent to the city widens the interest of the book, although the whole has now become an incident.

E. E. S.

Cooley, Thomas McIntyre. Michigan: a history of governments. (Am. commonwealths.) Boston: Houghton. 1885. $1.25. [3353

The distinguished author of this book claims that the changes of sovereignty, as well as of subordinate jurisdiction, have been greater in Michigan than in any other part of the American Union; also that the circumstances attending its admission to the Union made its history at that period quite unique. Both claims are well founded, and the first one gives character to the book as the explanatory title suggests. It is a volume in every way worthy of the subject and of the series. B. A. H.

Davidson, Alexander, *and* **Bernard Stuvé.** Complete history of Illinois, 1673–1873; embracing the physical features of the country; its early explorations; aboriginal inhabitants; French and British occupation; conquest by Virginia; territorial condition and the subsequent civil, military, and political events of the state. Springfield, Ill.: Illinois Journal Co. 1874. [3354

The first serious attempt at a history of the state. The title sufficiently describes the scope. The authors are hero-worshippers, and display old-fashioned prejudices against Indians and British; naturally, considering the time, they are weak in ethnology and archæology; and are amateurish in style. The type is solid, the pages uninteresting in appearance, and there is no index. Despite these drawbacks, the book is of considerable merit, and deserves careful attention from the historical student. R. G. T.

Drake, Samuel Adams. Making of the great West, 1512–1883. N. Y.: Scribner. 1887. $1.50. [3355

The author " has succeeded in his task — easy so far as relates to the collection of the historical materials, difficult in making them into a connected and lively story — very well, both in his arrangement and manner of narration. Young persons who may find the earlier chapters somewhat dry reading cannot fail to be interested in those describing the events of the past eighty years. . . . The book would have been more valuable had there been two general maps of the region treated, the one so shaded as to show the original possessions of the Spaniards, French, and English ; the other showing the present political divisions. Some of the numerous illustrations are very good, but others . . . are simply execrable. There is an excellent index." *Nation*, 45: 422.

Edwards, Ninian Wirt. History of Illinois, 1778–1833 ; and life and times of Ninian Edwards. Springfield, Ill. : Illinois State Journal Co. 1870. [3356

This is a life of Edwards primarily, a history of Illinois incidentally. Speeches and letters compose more than three fourths of the volume. These are mainly by Edwards, though there is a considerable number of letters written by Wirt, John McLean, Calhoun, and other prominent men. Hence the book furnishes much valuable material for historical purposes. Slavery in Illinois is thoroughly discussed, the " A. B. Plot " exhaustively. A memoir of Daniel P. Cook is also given. The author is accurate, careful and temperate in tone, but has not mastered his materials, and so has produced an unsystematic, amorphous book, written in a bald and prolix style.
R. C. H. C.

Farmer, Silas. History of Detroit and Michigan ; or The metropolis illustrated ; including the annals of Wayne County. Detroit : Farmer. 1884. Rev. and enl. 1890. 2v. $15. [3357

A magazine of historical materials relating to Michigan, but more especially to Detroit ; a " cyclopædia of the past and present," as it is termed on the title-page. The notes of the work are thoroughness of research and fullness of detail, not skill in the organization of material or literary art. It is rather the materials of history than history. The second volume, entitled *Biographical edition*, contains more than 200 biographical sketches of well-known men. B. A. H.

Fire lands pioneer. Norwalk, Ohio. 1858–78. 13v. New ser. 1882–91. V. 1–6. [3358

A quarterly publication of the Fire Lands Society, an organization of residents within the district set apart by Congress in northern Ohio for the sufferers from British depredations during the Revolutionary War. The volumes consist largely of local biographies and minor reminiscence, beginning about 1808. Occasionally there is a good article on some such subject as the Moravian missionaries, the Connecticut Reserve, or early politics in Ohio. Much space is consumed by the record of the " proceedings " of the Society.
E. E. S.

Ford, Thomas. History of Illinois. Chicago : Griggs. 1854. [3359

Covers the years 1818–1847. Gives a valuable account of banking operations ; of internal improvements ; of the Black Hawk War, and especially of Mormonism in Illinois. Ford was active in state affairs during the entire period, being Governor from 1842 to 1846. His history is based on his own experience and facts drawn from original sources. He was a man of moderate temper and moderate intellect, of strict integrity and positive opinions. Writing from the democratic point of view, he is not impartial or always just ; against individuals he is frequently unduly severe. His style is uncouth, though at times forcible and direct. R. C. H. C.

Hinsdale, Burke Aaron. The old Northwest, with a view of the thirteen colonies as constituted by the royal charters. N. Y.: T. MacCoun. 1888. 2d ed. rev. N. Y.: Silver. 1899. $2.50. [3360

A series of essays rather than a continuous narrative. The old Northwest includes Ohio, Indiana, Illinois, Michigan, Wisconsin, Minnesota east of the Mississippi, and the Erie purchase in Pennsylvania. The story of this territory is told to the time of the admission of the separate states. Eleven maps are included. A closing chapter illustrates the development of the Northwest, up to 1880. A creditable piece of work, mostly based upon secondary sources. R. C. H. C.

Howells, William Dean. Stories of Ohio. N. Y.: Am. Book Co. 1897. 60c. [3361

This book is a successful attempt to present an outline view of the history of Ohio from the earliest times, in the form of stories drawn from the annals of the state. The stories are true to the essential facts of history, and are told in Mr. Howells's well-known style. As a matter of course, it is much fuller in the pioneer period than in the later period, and throws far more light upon what may be called the strictly social side of life than upon the political and civic side. The book is intended for young readers, especially pupils in the public schools. B. A. H.

Indiana Historical Society. Indianapolis. This Society was organized in 1830, and in 1895 issued a volume of *Publications*, the parts of which had previously appeared as *Pamphlets* 1–5, and *Publications* 6–12. Among its contents is the *Acquisition of Louisiana*, by T. M. Cooley. [3362

Iowa State Historical Society. Iowa City. This Society was organized in 1857, and from 1863 to 1874 published the 1st series of the *Annals of Iowa*, 12 volumes. The 2d series of 3 volumes, 1882 to 1884, was published by Samuel Storrs Howe, who, as Librarian of the Society, had edited the first numbers of the series. The Historical department of Iowa began a 3rd series in 1894, and in 1899 had issued 4 volumes. In 1885, the Society began the publication of the *Iowa historical record*, which completed its 15th volume in 1899. *Documentary material relating to the history of Iowa* is edited by B. F. Shambaugh, and published in numbers by the Society, the first number having been issued in 1895, the 24th in 1901. Numbers 1 to 8 form volume 1, numbers 9–16 volume 2, numbers 17–24 volume 3. Several monographs have also been issued. [3363

Johnson, Harrison. History of Nebraska. Omaha: Gibson. 1880. [3364

The first fourth of the book is occupied by a topical history of the state, arranged under such heads as Indians, Minerals, Public Lands, Railroads, Climate, Churches, Immigration, etc. A description of each county follows, arranged in alphabetical order. In each county a systematic order is followed: water courses, timber, fruit, crops, etc. A historical sketch of the county is added. The work gives a vast amount of information concerning the state, and bears the marks of investigation. It is rather a gazetteer than a history. E. E. S.

Kansas State Historical Society. Topeka. Organized in 1875. Publishes occasional volumes of *Transactions*, six having appeared between 1881 and 1896. [3365

King, Rufus. Ohio, first fruits of the Ordinance of 1787. (Am. commonwealths.) Boston: Houghton. 1888. $1.25. [3366

A book that well fulfils the ideal of the series to which it belongs, viz.: volumes narrating the history of " the states of the Union that have exerted a positive influence in the shaping of the national government or have a striking political, social, or economical history." The special significance of the book is seen in the explanatory title. While admirably qualified for his task, the writer maintains some opinions that, to say the least, are doubtful, as that the Old Congress insisted upon its jurisdiction over the Old Northwest. He minimizes, too, the legal value of the Ordinance of 1787. B. A. H.

Michigan Pioneer and Historical Society. Lansing. Organized in 1874, and from 1877 to 1900 published 29 volumes of *Pioneer and historical collections*, a series which is still continued. [3367

Volumes 15, 16, 19, 20, and 23 are made up of copies of papers in the Dominion archives at Ottawa; vols. 15 and 16 contain papers concerning the relations of the British government with the U. S. during the War of 1812; v. 20 contains transcripts from the Haldimand papers, 1782–1789; in volume 21 there is a paper of

value on the Patriot War, by Robert B. Ross, and one on the siege of Detroit, by J. T. Headley.

Minnesota Historical Society. St. Paul. This Society was organized in 1849, and publishes occasional volumes of *Collections*, relating chiefly to the history and biography of Minnesota. From 1860 to 1898 eight volumes have appeared. Volume 2 contains *Early French forts and footprints in the valley of the upper Mississippi*, by E. D. Neill. [3368

Moses, John. Illinois, historical and statistical. Chicago: Fergus. 1889–93. 2v. [3369

The author had lived in Illinois fifty years, and had served the state in numerous public capacities before writing this work. Moreover, he was at the time secretary and librarian of the Chicago Historical Society. These facts point to a large personal knowledge of the state and real historical interest. He undertook to connect the older and fragmentary accounts, to correct and modify many previous statements in the light of later information, and to present new facts and later events, all in a form accessible to persons in every field of labor; and success may be accorded to him in the undertaking. He covered the ground from aboriginal times to the date of publication. The book contains a vast amount of information, much of it in documentary and statistical form. B. A. H.

Nebraska State Historical Society. Lincoln, Neb. This Society was organized in 1878: from 1885 to 1893 it published 5 volumes of *Transactions and reports*, and in 1894 began the publication of a series entitled *Proceedings and collections*, of which the third volume was issued in 1899. Both series are devoted to the history of Nebraska. [3370

Neill, Edward Duffield. History of Minnesota. Phil.: Lippincott. 1858. [3371

The design of this history, in the words of the preface, was " to show where Minnesota is, its characteristics and adaptations for a dense and robust population, and then to consider the past and present dwellers on the soil." The more practical of these purposes the book no doubt well accomplished. For the rest, it contains a large amount of information pieced together from many authorities, making more the appearance of a historical scrap-book than a history. B. A. H.

" The principal and sufficient account of the state's history . . . which in 1883 reached an improved fifth edition, and is supplemented by his [Mr. Neill's] *Minnesota explorers and pioneers, 1659–1858*, published in 1881." Justin Winsor, in *Narrative and critical hist. of Am.*, 4: 199.

Ohio. Records, documents and bibliography. See in Syllabus of materials, sect. 211, 212. [3372

Ohio Archæological and Historical Soci-

ety. Publications. Columbus. 1887–. V. 1+. V. 1–3, 6+, quarterly. V. 4, 5, annual. Republished. 1891–. [3373

With much that is of only local or temporary interest, these publications contain a large amount of matter that is of general and permanent value. Mention may be made of the numerous contributions to Ohio archæology, and papers or reports dealing with state boundaries and centennial celebrations.

B. A. H.

Ohio, Historical and Philosophical Society of. Cincinnati. This Society was incorporated in 1831. [3374

Its more important publications are the following: Notes on the early settlement of the northwestern territory, by Jacob Burnet. Pioneer history, and biographical and historical memoirs of the early pioneer settlers of Ohio, by S. P. Hildreth. Journal and letters of Col. John May, of Boston, relative to two journeys to the Ohio country in 1788 and 1789. Some early notices of the Indians of Ohio, by M. F. Force. Diary of David Zeisberger, translated and edited by E. F. Bliss, 2v.

Oliphant, Laurence. Minnesota and the far West. Edin. and London : Blackwood. 1855. [3375

The author had been superintendent-general of Indian affairs, in Canada, and a wide traveler. Part I. is devoted to a description of the tour from Portland, Me., through the White Mountains, to Quebec; later to Toronto, and westward to Lake Simcoe and Georgian Bay. Part II. is concerned with a trip to Lake Superior, as far west as Grand Portage, and a visit to Superior, to investigate Wisconsin as a field for emigration. Part III. gives an account of his journey by way of St. Louis River and Sandy Lake to the headwaters of the Mississippi, and a descent by canoe to St. Paul, thence by steamboat (with frequent stops) to Dubuque; from there the author took wagon across the Illinois prairie until he reached a railway which took him to Chicago, whence he soon found his way to Canada by way of Detroit. Mr. Oliphant was a keen observer of men and nature, with a well-developed sense of humor, and quite graphically describes the polity, habits, and personal aspects of Indians, trappers, traders, and frontiersmen generally, over a wide extent of territory which included a large variety of types. R. G. T.

Parkman Club. Milwaukee, Wis. The Parkman Club was organized in 1895, and between that year and 1897 issued 18 *Publications.* [3376

The most important are the following: Eleazer Williams, his forerunners, himself, by W. W. Wight. — George Rogers Clark and his Illinois campaign, by D. B. Starkey.

Pratt, Mara L. The great West. Boston: Educational Pub. Co. [c. 1890.] 50c. [3377

A small volume designed to be used as "supplementary reading" for about the fourth grade of the public schools. It well serves as an introduction to the later study of United States history, being arranged chronologically from the mound builders and Indians through the stories of Texas and California to the building of the Union Pacific railroad. Well written and easily comprehended by children. E. E. S.

Reynolds, John. My own times. Chicago: Fergus. 1879. [3378

An expansion of a little volume, *My own times,* by the same author, printed at Belleville, Illinois, in 1854–5. It covers the settlement of the Illinois country from 1800 to 1853, but is largely reminiscent and local. It contains valuable information, buried under idle gossip and "old settler" stories. Rambling and extremely verbose. Some local light is given on the public land system in Illinois, on internal improvements, on the visit of Lafayette, Lovejoy riots, Black Hawk war, the Nauvoo Mormons, and the Icarian community. E. E. S.

Smith, William Rudolph. History of Wisconsin, historical, documentary, and descriptive. V. 1 : Historical. V. 3 : Documentary. Madison : State Printing Office. 1854. [3379

Smith was President of the State Historical Society; the state undertook the publication. Vols. I and III were alone issued; the MS. of Vol. II was prepared in part, but owing to the withdrawal of official patronage, remains unpublished. Vol. I, commencing with the early history of the Mississippi valley, and dealing quite fully with the French régime, takes the story of Wisconsin down to the organization of the territory (1836) ; there are numerous and copious notes on details, chiefly documentary. Vol. III is a compilation of documents, beginning with translations from those portions of the *Jesuit relations* touching on Wisconsin history, and closing with a history of the Milwaukee and Rock River canal (1836–53). Smith was a lawyer of much ability and learning ; and while his history is to-day seldom cited, having in many matters been outdated by modern research, it deserves serious consideration from students. R. G. T.

Spring, Leverett Wilson. Kansas. (American commonwealths.) Boston : Houghton. 1885. $1.25. [3380

A work of considerable literary charm, and the most readable history of Kansas. Most of the book is devoted to the period before the Civil War. The author has drawn his material from primary sources ; the shortcoming of the work, however, is the fact that its point of view is that of Gov. Charles Robinson, himself the leader of a faction in the early days of the Territory. The volume cannot, accordingly, be accepted as final by those who do not accept the author's judgment as to the value of Robinson's services. W. MacD.

Thompson, Maurice. Stories of Indiana. N. Y.: Am. Book Co. 1898. 60c. [3381

This book is one of a series designed to present outlines of state history in the form of stories, by well-known writers. Young persons, and particularly pupils in the public schools, are the readers held especially in view. Still older and better informed people may draw from them both instruction and diversion. Mr. Thompson has chosen his subjects with excellent judgment, and has told his tales with commendable skill.   B. A. H.

Thomson, Peter G. Bibliography of Ohio : a catalogue of books and pamphlets relating to the state. Cin.: Author. 1880.   [3382

This is a painstaking piece of work, done by a thoroughly competent hand; a bibliography of the highest authority, and of great value as a contribution to the history of the state.   B. A. H.

Thwaites, Reuben Gold. Historic waterways : canoeing down the Rock, Fox, and Wisconsin Rivers. Chicago: McClurg. 1888. $1.25.   [3383

This book is composed of accounts or descriptions of three summer vacation tours on the rivers named, made by canoe. To this sort of an outing, the author adds a faculty for observation and a wealth of local historical information that helps to make him what he is in his own field, easily the first historical specialist of the time. The accounts are written in a clear, pleasant style that combines qualities of the diary, the personal letter, natural description, and historical narrative.   B. A. H.

—— Story of Wisconsin. (Story of the states.) Boston: Lothrop. 1889. Rev. ed. $1.50.   [3384

A popular, racy and scientific account of a picturesque section of history, by a master hand. One of the very best books in the useful *Story of the states*, edited by Elbridge S. Brooks. Especially rich in its handling of the period under French and English domination. Appendix comprises Story of Wisconsin, told in chronological epitome, and The people's covenant as embodied in the constitution of the state of Wisconsin.   H. W. H.

Turner, Frederick J. The West as a field for historical study. See American Historical Association, sect. 248.   [3385

Tuttle, Charles Richard, *comp.* General history of the state of Michigan ; with biographical sketches. Detroit : Tyler. 1873. [3386

This book is a popular account of Michigan, compiled exclusively from secondary sources. The author tells his story in a fluent and readable style, but the book moves on the level of cheap woodcut illustrations.   B. A. H.

Western Reserve Historical Society. Cleveland, Ohio. Organized in 1867, and rechartered in 1892. In 1877 the Society began the publication of a series of numbered *Tracts*, of which the 89th was issued in 1899.   [3387

The most important are the following : War of 1812. Papers of Elisha Whittlesey and of Maj. George Tod, and Biography and correspondence of the War of 1812. Col. Bradstreet's expedition, 1764: — North West territory, discovery and ownership, by Hon. James A.

Garfield : — Discovery of the Ohio River, by Robert Cavalier de la Salle, 1669–70, by Chas. Whittlesey: — Manuscript of Solomon Spaulding and the Book of Mormon, by Hon. James A. Garfield: — The underground railroad, by James H. Fairchild: — Journal of Capt. William Trent, from Logstown to Pickawillany, 1752 ; ed. by A. T. Goodman: — Journal of Capt. Jonathan Heart, Sept. 7–Oct. 12, 1785. Archæology of Ohio, by M. C. Read: — Brulé's discoveries and explorations, by C. W. Butterfield.

Wilder, Daniel Webster. Annals of Kansas. Topeka: Martin. 1875. Topeka: Thacher. 1886.   [3388

A compilation of facts concerning the state of Kansas, arranged in chronological order from 1542 to 1874. It includes the platforms and organizations of the parties in the sectional struggle for Kansas, the various constitutions, names of state officials, military organization in the Civil War, together with countless incidents connected with the social and economic development of the state. There is no surplus matter. The work appears to be trustworthy.   E. E. S.

Wisconsin University. See sect. 389.   [3389

Wisconsin, State Historical Society of. Madison, Wis. Collections. V. 1–10 ; ed. by Lyman C. Draper; v. 11–15 ; ed. by Reuben G. Thwaites. Madison. 1885–. v. 1+.   [3390

The publications of this Society are the principal source for the original study of early Wisconsin history. They are of varied character, consisting of monographs, interviews, reminiscences, and documents, chiefly bearing upon the pre-Territorial and Territorial periods. The following is the range of subjects: General history of Wisconsin, prehistoric, Indians and Indian wars, French régime, fur trade, missions, education, lead mining, military history, foreign groups (an important series), political and economic studies, narratives and documents, and local history. Since 1893, the tendency has been to restrict monographs to the *Proceedings* of the Society, and narratives and documents to the *Collections*. Each of the volumes is indexed, v. 10 containing a general index to the first ten.   R. G. T.

The publications of the Society include *Annual reports* from 1875 to 1886, followed by *Proceedings* with reports, 1887 to 1899. 15 volumes of *Collections* were issued at various dates from 1885 to 1900 ; they are now issued biennially. Among their important contents are the following: V. 3. The Cass MSS., consisting of translations of New France material from 1723–26, bearing especially upon the Wisconsin and Michigan region, and transcribed from the French archives by Lewis Cass ; and Seventy-two years' recollections of Wisconsin, by Augustin Grignon. — V. 5 contains Canadian documents relating to Wisconsin history from 1690–1730 ; and The Winnebago war of 1827, by Col. Thomas L. McKenney. — V. 6. Capt. Jonathan Carver and " Carver's grant," by Daniel S. Durrie. — V. 10. Early French forts in western Wisconsin, by Lyman C. Draper. — V. 11. Jean Nicolet, 1618–1642, by Henri Jouan, tr. by Grace Clark ; Radisson and Grosseilliers in Wisconsin ; The boundaries of Wisconsin, by Reuben Gold Thwaites. — V. 11 and

12 contain selections from the Haldimand papers. The important articles in v. 12 include also: Robert Dickson, the Indian trader, by E. A. Cruikshank; Story of the Black Hawk War, by Reuben Gold Thwaites; How Wisconsin came by its large German element, by Kate Asaphine Everest; and The Wisconsin Winnebagoes, by Moses Paquette. — V. 13. The Bulger papers regarding the British occupation of Prairie du Chien, 1812–15; the Papers of James Duane Doty, his Official journal, 1820, and his Documents on territorial organization. — V. 14. The most notable articles are Story of Mackinac, by R. G. Thwaites; and Abraham Lincoln in the Black Hawk War, by Alfred Augustus Jackson.

In the *Proceedings* the following articles are chiefly important: The character and influence of the fur trade in Wisconsin, by Frederick J. Turner, in 35th annual meeting: — The significance of the frontier in American history, by Frederick J. Turner, in 41st meeting: — The Free Soil Party in Wisconsin, by Theodore C. Smith, in 42d meeting: — Radisson's Journal, its value in history, by Henry C. Campbell, in 43rd meeting: — Available material for the study of the institutional history of the Old Northwest, by Isaac S. Bradley, in 44th meeting: — Allouez, and his relations to La Salle, by Joseph Stephen La Boule, in 46th meeting.

The Society also issues occasional *Bulletins of information* upon various phases of its work.

MIDCONTINENTAL AND PACIFIC REGIONS

(Comprehensive history, covering all or several periods. For Early history, under Spanish domination, see Part VI: Mexico, and Part III, Division I, Period I: Spanish (sect. 1190–1199). For Early history as part of the United States, see Part III, Division I, 4th Period: Westward Expansion (sect. 2016–2077). On Documentary collections, official records, etc., see in Part I: Sources.)

Bancroft, Hubert Howe. History of the Pacific states of North America. San Francisco: Bancroft. 1882–90. 21v. [3391

Mr. Bancroft's history has been severely criticised by some and condemned by others — principally those who had become accustomed to the superior methods of such historians as Parkman, Winsor and Bandelier. The compiler amassed the most extensive and complete collection of books and manuscripts bearing on his chosen field that had ever been brought together, and these formed the basis of his voluminous history. As might be expected of a work of its scope, prepared within such a comparatively limited period of time, the accuracy of statement and soundness of judgment do not always attain the standard demanded by historical students of the present day. Nevertheless, by reason of the unusual library facilities which the compiler enjoyed, the volumes contain a vast body of valuable data not found elsewhere. F. W. H.

See, also, Jameson's *History of historical writing in America*, pp. 152–156.

Barrows, William. Oregon: the struggle for possession. (Am. commonwealths.) Boston: Houghton. 1884. $1.25. [3392

This book is utterly unreliable as a history of the Oregon question. It is based on the fictitious accounts of the efforts of Marcus Whitman to save Oregon which were first published in 1865 by the Rev. H. H. Spalding in the "Pacific" newspaper of San Francisco and later in *Senate Ex. Doc. 37, 41st Cong., 3rd Sess.* (1871). In the effort to show how Whitman saved Oregon almost every phase of the history is thrown out of proportion and much of it is grotesquely distorted. Besides its large fictitious element and its perversions of facts, Mr. Barrows's book is bewildering in its repetitions and digressions. For a critical discussion of the widely diffused story of Marcus Whitman, see The legend of Marcus Whitman, by the writer [Prof. E. G. Bourne], in the *Am. hist. review*, Jan. 1901, or in his *Essays in historical criticism*, N. Y.: Macmillan. 1901. $2. E. G. B.

See, also, sect. 2039, 3407, 3425.

Beadle, John Hanson. The undeveloped West; or Five years in the territories. Phil.: National Pub. Co. 1873. [3393

A badly written, careless, pretentious book, seemingly compiled from the author's hasty newspaper letters upon Arizona, California, Oregon, Colorado and other parts of the region west of the Mississippi. C. H. S.

Bell, William Abraham. New tracks in North America: a journal of travel, 1867–8. London: Chapman. 1869. 2v. [3394

Dr. Bell served as the photographer of a surveying expedition organized by the Kansas Pacific Railway Co. to determine the best route for a railroad to the Pacific coast through Kansas, Colorado, New Mexico, Arizona, and southern California. He was a good observer, possessed the power of presenting his narrative in a highly interesting way, and succeeded in embodying much information of both general and scientific interest. He falls into the usual errors prevalent at the time concerning the Indians, and many terms of Spanish origin are sadly misspelled. An excellent map, many good illustrations, and a number of tables of distances, etc., lend the work additional worth. F. W. H.

Browne, John Ross. Adventures in the Apache country. N. Y.: Harper. 1869. [3395

Some account of natural features is included among many adventures and personal details: one of the more interesting books of its numerous class. W. M. D.

Bruce, Miner W. Alaska: its history and resources, gold fields, routes, and scenery. Seattle: Lowman. 1895. New ed. 1897.

—— *Same;* 2d ed. rev. and enl. N. Y.: Putnam. 1899. $2.50. [3396

"Mr. Miner Bruce's book on Alaska is a hand-book to the territory from the point of view of the practical man. It contains instructive chapters on the history, animals, inhabitants, and minerals of Alaska, with special directions to prospectors. Illustrations and maps are satisfactory." H. M. Stanley, *Dial* (Chicago), 27: 73.

"The author writes in good faith and soberly, from six years' experience, supplies a large number of excellent illustrations, and a map of the Territory." *Nation*, 65: 129.

California Historical Society. San Francisco. This Society was organized in 1852, and in 1887 published two volumes of *Papers.* Among its other publications is: *Noticias de la Nueva California*, por el Rev. Padre Fr. Francisco Palou. [3397

Custer, *Mrs.* **Elizabeth Bacon.** Tenting on the plains. N. Y.: Webster. 1888. New issue. 1893. N. Y.: Harper. $1.50. [3398

"Mrs. Custer has broken open and lavishly exposed her memories of military life in Texas and Kansas during the two years immediately following Lee's surrender. Again, as in *Boots and saddles*, we are taken directly into her home, and share her daily hopes and fears. . . . The book is as open as the sky. . . . But the book is not meant to be a mere chronicle of the small beer of domestic pleasures and trouble and nothing more. . . . Its public value consists in its presentation of the constant trials and privations, as well as of more heroic adventures, that befell the troops when 'there was no wild clamor of war to enable them to forget the absence of the commonest necessities of existence.'" *Nation*, 46: 455.

Custer, *Maj.-Gen.* **George Armstrong.** My life on the plains; or Personal experiences with Indians. N. Y.: Sheldon. 1874. [3399

These papers, which were originally printed in the *Galaxy* magazine during 1872 and 1873, recount the writer's adventures while campaigning against the southern Cheyennes and other Indians in the region between the Missouri River and the Rocky Mountains. The period covered begins with Gen. Hancock's Kansas expedition in the spring of 1867 and ends with the defeat of Black Kettle's band by Gen. Custer himself at the rather important engagement on the Washita River in the Indian Territory, Nov. 27, 1868. The dangerous character of the service and the military view of Indian questions are strongly brought out, and frontiersman, scout and Indian are vigorously depicted. F. J. S.

Davis, William Heath. Sixty years in California: events and life in California under the Mexican régime; during the quasi-military government by the United States, and after the admission of the state into the Union. San Francisco: A. J. Leary. 1889. [3400

The author of this book is still living (Sept. 1901), and is revising his book for a second edition. He saw much of California life, and records many interesting incidents that would otherwise have been lost; but the really valuable portions of his book are overloaded with minor details. The resulting picture of old Spanish days in California is, therefore, often less distinct than that given by Robinson, Dana and others. Nevertheless, the work is an important addition to the short list of books on the period written by eye-witnesses. C. H. S.

Dimsdale, Thomas J. Vigilantes of Montana. Virginia City: Montana Post Press. 1866. [3401

Very rare; gives the first complete account ever printed of the infamous group of desperadoes known in 1862 as "Henry Plummer's Road Agent Band." This book is one of the chief sources from which many writers of novels, short stories and sketches of pioneer life in the Rocky Mountains have drawn their information. C. H. S.

Dodge, *Lt.-Col.* **Richard Irving.** The plains of the great West, and their inhabitants. N.Y.: Putnam. 1877. [3402

Half of this entertaining book is devoted to the Indians, the remainder to game and to a description of the Plains. From the latter one derives a good idea of a portion of the country on which few travellers now stop on their way further west, and to which even the government surveys have given subordinate attention. W. M. D.

Dunn, Jacob Piatt, Jr. Massacres of the mountains: a history of the Indian wars of the far West. N. Y.: Harper. 1886. $3.75. [3403

An excellent portrayal of the causes and results of the various Indian uprisings in the West during comparatively recent years. It is compiled from the best sources, including many official records. The entire story is related in a straightforward, entertaining manner. The introduction is worthy the attention of all students of the Indian question, and indeed of Indian history in general. F. W. H.

Dwinelle, John W. Colonial history of the city of San Francisco. San Francisco. 1864. 3d ed. enl. San Francisco: Towne & Bacon. 1866. [3404

The first and second editions were mere law-briefs with some addenda, the whole relating to the history of the Pueblo of San Francisco. The second was somewhat enlarged from the first; the third, still further enlarged, constitutes the valuable one and will always remain a book of prime historical importance. Dwinelle's narrative argument, in 140 sections (pp. 1–106), is a legal masterpiece, and the 171 documents arranged as addenda include copies (with translations) of Spanish laws, decrees and other papers hardly elsewhere accessible. C. H. S.

Elliott, Henry Wood. Our Arctic province. N. Y.: Scribner. 1886. $2.50. [3405

"The author is well known among those interested in Alaskan affairs, as once assistant agent of the Government on the Seal Islands, subsequently a Commissioner to investigate the sealing operations of the Alaska Commercial Company, and latterly as a representative in Washington before Congressional committees of the aforesaid Company. He possesses a facile pencil, and his book contains many characteristic and well-executed sketches. . . . For the Aleutian region and the Seal Islands, barring unintentional inaccuracies, the account given by the author is, for general reading, a very good one. . . . In regard to the rest of the country, a great deal of information is given, but as most of this is untrodden ground to Mr. Elliott, his narrative is defective. . . . The writer's style is bad. . . . Proper and geographical names are very generally inaccurately spelled. The maps of the Seal Islands are given as they resulted from the imperfect tape-line-and-pocket-compass survey made by Mr. Elliott, but it is ten years since the general outlines were corrected and mapped by the Coast Survey. The general map of Alaska is dated 1886," but important discoveries from 1869 to 1884 are not shown. "To complete our fault-finding, this large and handsome volume, crammed with unsystematized information, has a very imperfect index." *Nation*, 43: 507.

"We have rarely read so engaging a book about a country which even in this exploring age few men would wish to see or would be much the better for seeing. . . . Mr. Elliott's chapters on animal life equal or surpass in interest his accounts of Eskimos, Innuits, Sitkans, and Ingaleeks. Indeed every part of his book is the work of a hardy and educated pioneer and naturalist, and not of a traveller for pleasure." *Saturday review*, 63: 27.

Frost, John. History of the state of California, from the conquest by Spain to her occupation by the United States; also, a brief account of the formation of the government and constitution of the state. Auburn, N. Y.: Derby & Miller. 1853. **[3406**

A hasty compilation made in New York by Dr. Frost, who had never visited California. No maps; illustrations often more Mexican than Californian. Quotes from some now rare newspapers and other sources of information. Contains in appendix Halleck's *Report on Lower California*. On the whole a poor piece of hack-work and one of the least creditable of Dr. Frost's writings.   C. H. S.

Gray, W. H. History of Oregon, 1792–1849. Drawn from personal observation and authentic information. Portland, Oregon: Author. 1870. **[3407**

The author was a man of little education who went as mechanic and helper with Whitman and Spalding in 1836 to start the Oregon mission of the American Board of Commissioners for Foreign Missions. His violent personal and religious prejudices are thoroughly ventilated in these recollections. The narrative is highly unreliable and the author personally vouches for events that did not take place. This was the first general historical work to give currency to the Whitman legend. The earlier and diplomatic history of Oregon will be found best in Greenhow's *History* and the colonization and development in Bancroft's *Oregon*.   E. G. B.

See, also, sect. 2039, 3425.

Heilprin, Angelo. Alaska and the Klondike; with hints to the traveller and observations on the physical history and geology of the gold regions, the condition of and methods of working the Klondike placers, and the laws governing and regulating mining in the North-

west Territory of Canada. N. Y.: Appleton. 1899. $1.75. **[3408**

"*Alaska and the Klondike*, by Professor Angelo Heilprin, the distinguished geologist, is written from the scientific point of view, describing the journey to Dawson as made in 1898 by way of the White Pass and out by the Chilkoot. The author made a stay of some weeks in Dawson, which he quite fully describes, and he found the summer weather and scenery superb. . . . Professor Heilprin examined the Klondike gold fields and reports on their geology and on the methods of working. The style of the book is at times diffuse, strained and affected. Maps and illustrations are good." H. M. Stanley, *Dial* (Chicago), 27: 72.

Hinton, *Col.* Richard Josiah. Hand-book to Arizona: its resources, history, towns, mines, ruins, and scenery. San Francisco: Payot. N. Y.: Am. News Co. 1878. **[3409**

An excellent guide in its day, and still of importance as a record of the conditions existing in the territory during the author's sojourn therein. It contains much valuable information bearing on the natural (particularly the mineral) resources of Arizona. The accounts of the early Spanish explorations and missionary labors have been superseded by the writings of Bandelier, Bancroft, Winship, Coues, and others, although the book still contains much important historical information relating to the present century, and a (probably inaccurate) copy of a rare manuscript map made by Pedro Font in 1777, not before published. The sections on archæology and ethnology contain but little accurate information not compiled from other works. Many misprints of Spanish and Indian names occur throughout. F. W. H.

Hittell, Theodore Henry. History of California. San Francisco: Stone. 1886–97. 4v. **[3410**

"It is evident that Mr. Hittell has done much and faithful work for many years upon his book, which probably represents the largest result yet obtained by any one man's unaided work in historical writing about California. . . . Mr. Hittell's peculiar virtues, which show to better advantage in the later than in the earlier volumes of his book, will probably attract more readers than Bancroft's, and will make at least his later volumes indispensable to the historian. Briefly, these virtues are those of a trained lawyer, unusually well versed in land-matters and legislative proceedings. His accounts of mission secularization and of Spanish and Mexican land-grants constitute some of the most valuable portions of his two earlier volumes. So, also, in the last two, whatever touches upon law or the administration of law is told in a quiet, careful, deliberate, and wholly convincing way." *Nation*, 68: 15.

Inman, Henry. Old Santa Fé trail. N. Y.: Macmillan. 1897. $3.50. **[3411**

"This book is dedicated to and prefaced by 'Buffalo Bill' (W. F. Cody), but the author introduces it to us with some of the wildest statements we have ever heard concerning early Spanish explorers. . . . Nowhere in the book is what historians and geographers know as the Santa Fé caravan route traced in its entirety, as surely we had a right to expect. It is touched upon only here and there, in places known to the author personally, with precision and particularity. It is true that Col. Inman gives us a map of the Trail, but this is too small and slight to convey much more than what everybody knew before. . . . The map, moreover, does not always coincide with the text, nor the text with itself. . . . Where Col. Inman is not obviously wrong he needs confirmation to convince us he is right. . . . Our criticism of Col. Inman as historian and geographer is so serious that we are glad to end it. . . . He has written a most readable and entertaining book, full of incident." *Nation*, 65: 463.

Inman, Henry, *and* **William F. Cody.** The Great Salt Lake trail. N. Y.: Macmillan. 1898. $3.50. [3412

"Col. W. F. Cody, popularly known as 'Buffalo Bill,' is joint author of the volume, and his quota has at least the distinctive merit of being drawn mainly from its narrator's own experience. . . . Most interesting, perhaps, of . . . pioneering adventurers were the Mormons; and to the trials of these sectaries during their arduous march Col. Inman devotes some interesting, let us add charitable, pages. The Salt Lake Trail was also the route followed by the expeditions of Fremont, Stansbury, and Lander, and by the famous Pony Express, with its lumbering colleague, the Overland Stage. It is to the annals of the Trail in this its romantic period, long before a railway through the wilderness of sage-brush and alkali dust was thought possible, that Col. Inman's story is devoted. . . . The work has little claim to literary style; it is essentially history in the rough. . . . The *Great Salt Lake trail* is a book that Young America, especially, will relish and profit by. . . . A map of the Trail is of course included." *Dial* (Chicago), 25: 460.

Ladd, Horatio Oliver. Story of New Mexico. (Story of the states.) Boston: Lothrop. 1892. $1.50. [3413

"Story is a modest title for a book which, in fact, is the most accurate 'history' of that territory that has ever been published. . . . Mr. Ladd's book has the advantage of being based upon information of a documentary character more detailed and more special even than that at Mr. Bancroft's command, touching the obscure periods in New Mexico's history that intervened between 1608 and 1680. The author enjoys, furthermore, the advantage of having resided in the country. . . . On the whole, Mr. Ladd's book is a gratifying step in the direction of fairness in history and independent judgment, unaffected by the stereotyped clamor against Spain in the New World." *Nation*, 54: 237.

Ludlow, Fitz Hugh. The heart of the continent: a record of travel across the plains and in Oregon. N. Y.: Hurd. 1870. [3414

One of the better books of western travel, entertaining but unscientific. The Mormon problem receives much attention. W. M. D.

Lummis, Charles Fletcher. The land of poco tiempo. N. Y.: Scribner. 1893. $2.50.

——Some strange corners of our country; the wonderland of the southwest. N. Y.: Century Co. 1892. $1.50. [3415

The Land of "Pretty soon" was the home of the author for several years, and there are few who know its out-of-the-way places so well. A keen observer; familiar with the natives, both brown and white; a lover of nature, with an insatiable desire to see all that was to be seen, and possessed of rare power to tell the story in a charming way, the author has given us the best popular books on the most interesting physiographic and ethnologic features of New Mexico and Arizona that have appeared. F. W. H.

Marcy, *Maj.-Gen.* **Randolph Barnes.** Thirty years of army life on the border: comprising descriptions of the Indian nomads of the plains; explorations of new territory; trip across the Rocky Mts. in winter; descriptions of the habits of different animals found in the west, methods of hunting them, etc. N. Y.: Harper. 1866. [3416

"Colonel Marcy's volume is the result of a lifetime of frontier experience, during which period almost everything which he describes has changed or passed away, except the natural features of the country. No writer has had more intimate communication with the warlike tribes of the plains, and his official relation gives authenticity to his statements." T. W. Field, *Indian bibliography*, p. 260.

Mowry, Sylvester. Arizona and Sonora; geography, history and resources of the silver region. 3d ed. rev. N. Y.: Harper. 1866. [3417

Within its limited range, this book is important to students of the Southwest, and more particularly Arizona between 1859 and 1864. The present edition is enlarged from two earlier ones, published by A. Roman & Co., San Francisco. Mowry, a West Point graduate and a member of the Boundary Commission, was one of the most noted pioneer miners of his time, and his views of the relation of the government to mining interests, of the southern railroad route across the continent, and of various Indian outbreaks, are still interesting. Much of the descriptive portion of the book is purely local, and for that reason it must always remain a classic of early Arizona, preserving valuable letters and glimpses of pioneer mining camps that would otherwise be forgotten. He writes of little with which he is not familiar, and he usually mentions the sources of his information. The book decidedly lacks literary quality. But Arizonians should hold in high regard this passionately earnest appeal for Arizona made at a time when the region seemed utterly neglected. C. H. S.

Norman, Lucia. Youth's history of California. San Francisco: Roman. 1867.

——*Same:* Popular history of California. 2d ed. rev. and enl. 1883. [3418

The second edition of this book appeared in 1883 (same publisher), enlarged to 216 pp. chiefly by addition of four chapters. Dull, untrustworthy in matters of fact, and justly neglected in recent years.

C. H. S.

Overland monthly. San Francisco : Roman. 1868–. v. 1+. [3419

The first issue of this famous Pacific coast magazine appeared in July, 1868, with A. Roman & Co., San Francisco, as publishers, and F. Bret Harte as editor. The last issue of this series was that for December, 1875. Many of the old friends and contributors to the *Overland* a few years later assisted Charles H. Phelps and others to establish the *Californian* (January, 1880–December, 1882). The *Californian* passed into the hands of M. W. Shinn and others who, securing the copyrights and material of the *Overland*, began in January, 1883, "The *Overland monthly*, Second series," with Samuel Carson as publisher, and M. W. Shinn as editor. After several changes of ownership, this series still continues (1901) in its 36th volume. During its long and varied career, the *Overland monthly* has brought out many excellent writers. It has been especially notable for its descriptive and historical articles, which are indispensable to every student of the Pacific Coast. The first series of 15 volumes contains upwards of 120 such historical articles and the second series contains nearly 300. A general index to the 53 volumes is greatly needed. Many volumes are now out of print, are very hard to obtain and are rapidly increasing in value. C. H. S.

Parkman, Francis. The Oregon trail. Boston: Little, Brown & Co. 1900. Author's ed. $1. [3419 a

Appears as a volume in the various editions of Parkman's works issued by Little, Brown & Co. For note, see sect. 2062.

Prince, Le Baron Bradford. Historical sketches of New Mexico. N. Y.: Leggat. 1883. [3420

"A useful and in the main a trustworthy compendium." H. W. Haynes, in *Narrative and critical hist. of Am.*, 2 : 503.

Royce, Josiah. California : a study of American character. (American commonwealths.) Boston : Houghton. 1886. $1.25. [3421

"Professor Royce, in view of the peculiar circumstances attending the settlement of California by Americans, has sought to make his work a study of character." He "has discovered that the Americans in California were, on the whole, a pretty poor lot, with little ambition in life beyond plundering the Spanish settlers of their land, and hoisting the American flag on every conceivable occasion. . . . Individuals have fared no better than classes under the survey of the social philosopher. Fremont, Stockton, and the other celebrities of the conquest of California, are compelled to shoulder heavy responsibility for wrong-doing. . . . About the only characters in California's early history that come with any sort of credit through the critic's examination are the Spanish natives. They appear as a simple, harmless people,

whose idyllic life is rudely interrupted by despicable interlopers from the United States. If only the excellence of the author's literary style were at all proportionate to the captiousness of his criticism, his book would easily take rank as a classic. An unfortunate devotion to disagreeable mannerisms, however, seems likely to render such a consummation doubtful." Wm. A. Dunning, *Political science quarterly*, 1: 491.

Rusling, Brig.-Gen. James F. Across America ; or The great West and the Pacific coast. N. Y.: Sheldon. 1874.

—— *Same :* The great West and Pacific coast. New ed. [1877.] [3422

Gen. Rusling was sent by the War Department on a tour of inspection to the Pacific coast just after the Civil War, and, besides his reports that appeared as public documents, prepared a general narrative of his travels. It is of interest from giving a picture of the far West at the time of its most rapid awakening.

W. M. D.

Smalley, Eugene V. History of the Northern Pacific Railroad. N. Y.: Putnam. 1883. [3423

The work of a trained newspaper man, with abundant facilities, and much knowledge of the development of the Northwest. It is highly readable, and is certainly more than merely an account of the efforts of railroad builders and capitalists to open a way across the continent. The spirit of national growth westward from the Great Lakes to Puget Sound is excellently expressed by Mr. Smalley, whose book cannot but have a value for thoughtful readers for years to come. C. H. S.

Tuthill, Franklin. History of California. San Francisco: H. H. Bancroft. 1866. [3424

Mr. Tuthill was long editor of the San Francisco *Bulletin.* His account of events that led to the formation of the famous Vigilance committees and his views of California life between 1850 and 1865 are of permanent value. His treatment of the earlier period, 1542-1848, is less successful, from lack of original documents open to later historians. The style is that of a well-trained newspaper man accustomed to exactness and condensation. C. H. S.

Whitman, Marcus. Nixon, Oliver W. How Marcus Whitman saved Oregon, etc. Chicago: Star Publishing Co. 1895. [3425

This work like those of Barrows (sect. 3392) and Gray (sect. 3407), incorporates the Spalding fiction of the saving of Oregon by Marcus Whitman. As noted under Barrows this is entirely unhistorical. Nixon gives in addition some interesting contemporary material illustrative of Whitman's life. Jesse Applegate's interesting narrative, *A day with the cow column*, is given on pp. 146-163. On Whitman see *Am. hist. rev.*, Jan. 1901, or Bourne's *Essays in historical criticism*, N. Y.: Macmillan. 1901. $2. E. G. B.

See, also, sect. 2075.

Willey, S. H. Thirty years in California. San Francisco: A. E. Bancroft. 1879. [3426

A preliminary review (22 pp.) contains original material collected from the late General John Bidwell, General Vallejo and others. The remainder of the book details personal observations from 1849 to 1879 in California, founding churches and the College of California which later developed into the University of California. Essential to every student of the beginnings of social organization in California. The full story of the College of California appears in Willey's history of that institution (papers Calif. Hist. Soc., vol. I, part 2, 1887). C. H. S.

Wright, William (Dan De Quille, *pseud.*). History of the Big Bonanza: discovery, history and working of the Comstock silver lode of Nevada, etc. Hartford: Am. Pub. Soc. 1876. [3427

The author of this book was for many years a reporter on the Virginia City *Enterprise*. His opportunities for knowing the life of the period were equalled only by those of his fellow-reporter, Mark Twain. His book, a unique account of early Nevada, is alive with fact and fancy, a storehouse of literary material for careful investigators of the early mining period. It is, however, a book of rambling chronicles and romances, grave and gay, with hardly more real history than Mark Twain's *Roughing it*, but filled, nevertheless, with the true atmosphere of the period. Wright was one of the three or four men who thoroughly understood Nevada and the mining men of Bonanza days. C. H. S.

PART V. CANADA

(*Most of the titles in this part have been se-lected, and the notes, unless otherwise signed, prepared by William McLennan, F. R. S. C., Montreal.*)

A GENERAL NOTE ON THE CANADIAN SECTION

By William McLennan

A difficulty in the preparation of an ade-quate list of titles and documents relating to the history of Canada meets the compiler at the outset; namely, the inclusion, in the earlier records, of territory which has long ceased to be regarded as Canadian, and on which infor-mation must be sought in collections purely "American" — using the term in its native and restricted sense.   [3428

The story of LaSalle's final expeditions and the tragedy of his death reaches to the confines of Mexico, that of d'Iberville, Bienville, Ju-chereau de St. Denis, and many other Canadi-ans is centred in Louisiana, of LaMothe Ca-dillac in Michigan, of Tonti and Laforest in the Illinois — while that of Hennepin, LaHon-tan, Dulhut, Nicolet, and LeSueur stretches far beyond the Mississippi into the West.   [3429

In consequence the student of the earlier ef-forts and ambitions of the makers of New France must not confine his search to this or any list of purely "Canadian" material, but must ever remember that there is not an his-torical society, not a church record, not a col-lection of archives or documents of any con-siderable age in all the vast territory between New York, Wisconsin and New Orleans, and even as far as Mexico itself, which may not contain matter as vital to his subject as any to be found within the confines of Canada as it now exists. The *Bibliography of American historical societies*, edited by Appleton Prentiss Clark Griffin, which was published by the government at Washington, 1896, has made much of this important matter available. [3430

The *Annual reports* of Douglas Brymner, the Dominion Archivist (which may be had on application to the Department of Agricul-ture, Archives, Ottawa, Ont.) contain anno-tated lists of the important Haldimand and Bouquet collections, of the state papers, and other important original documents. The re-cords and maps of the War Office in London are but little known, and much unpublished material of value still remains in Paris and in the archives of some of the seaports of France. Every year sees the publication of private and official manuscripts, both here and abroad, and no doubt there still exist unpublished manu-scripts of importance in the keeping of fam-ilies in Canada.   [3431

A wealth of material peculiar to the Pro-vince of Quebec is to be found in the *greffes* (collections of original deeds) of notaries, now in the custody of the Prothonotary of each judicial district. These go back to the begin-nings of the colony, and besides much material for purely historical and biographical purposes, no surer or more authentic information can be had on the material condition of every class of society. How valuable these records may be in competent hands is well shown in the *Histoire de la colonie française en Canada*, by the Abbé Faillon, and in the *Histoire de la Seigneurie de Lauzon*, by J. Edmond Roy. The Abbé Tan-guay's immense *Dictionnaire généalogique* was rendered possible by the completeness of the church records, which are also in the same keeping. Both these sources are accessible to the student.   [3432

Owing to the limited space for the Canadian section, it has been impossible to include an adequate list of the blue-books and publica-tions of the Dominion and Provincial govern-ments. This material is of such extent and so important that it has been decided to leave it untouched rather than present a partial and haphazard list. Here it is that the student must look for matter on the little known period between 1791 and 1837.   [3433

The following note, furnished by a corre-spondent, will serve for a general idea of the government publications since Confederation, 1867.

"The publications of the Canadian government consist chiefly of the reports put forth annually by the several executive departments, for sale by the King's Printer, Ottawa. Booksellers are allowed a trade discount.

Department of Justice. — Report on Penitentiaries.

Department of Customs. — Trade and navigation returns monthly and yearly : imports and exports, movements of ocean and lake shipping.

Department of Trade and Commerce deals with the same figures in a more general way: issues monthly bulletins and annual reports, giving changes in foreign tariffs and general commercial information.

Department of Inland Revenue. — Excise returns, Reports on adulteration of food, Inspection of weights and measures, etc.

Department of Finance. — Public accounts, Bank returns, Insurance returns.

Department of Public Works. — Reports on Harbor improvements, Government telegraphs.

Department of Railways and Canals. — Report on government railways and canals, and expenditure of railway subsidies.

Department of the Post Office. — Report on the Post Office and Official postal guide.

Department of Militia and Defence. — Report on the militia of Canada.

Department of the Interior. — Reports on Dominion lands, Dominion surveys, Irrigation, Geodetical work and boundary determinations, Immigration, etc., also report of the Geographical Board.

Geological Survey. — Report on surveys.

Department of Indian Affairs. — Report on Indian tribes and expenditure of grant.

Department of the Auditor-General. — Report on the expenditure of parliamentary appropriations.

Department of Marine and Fisheries. — Report on state of fisheries, Expenditure of bounty moneys, Light-house service, Shipping registration, etc.

Department of Secretary of State. — Report of civil service examiners. List of Charters.

Department of Agriculture and Statistics. — Reports on experimental farms, Patents and copyrights, Quarantine and public health, and on the Archives, also Census returns and Statistical abstract and Record (Year book). This Year book compiled by the Dominion Statistician contains a large amount of well-arranged information respecting the natural resources, trade and manufactures, and general condition and progess of the Dominion. Issues Criminal Statistics.

Department of Labour. — Monthly labour gazette. Annual report.   [3434

Certain publications of purely administrative interest have been omitted from the above list. The departmental reports occasionally embrace some report of special interest and value. Amongst these may be counted the late Sir William Logan's *Report* (1863) of the progress made in the previous twenty years in the Geological Survey of the Dominion, the Survey as a Department having been established in 1843 ; also the reports made by the late Dr. G. M. Dawson, C. M. G. (1886), on a geological exploration of Vancouver Island and the adjacent coasts, and on an exploration in the Yukon District (1887).   [3435

The Canadian government has from time to time issued Commissions to inquire into specially important questions, and the reports thus called forth have frequently contained matter of much interest. Some of the principal of these may be mentioned.

Commission on Chinese Immigration. Report of the Honorable Judge Gray, published in one volume in 1885.

Commission on the Labour Question in Canada. Report of Commissioners in 6 vols., published in 1889, with additional volume on the Economic Section of the Universal Exhibition held in Paris in that year.

Commission on the Liquor Question. Report in 6 vols., published in 1895.

Commission on the Civil Service. Report in 1 vol., published in 1892.   [3436

Of special interest also are the Reports of the Militia Department (1886) on the Suppression of the rebellion in the North West in 1885, as well as the Report published in 1870 on the troubles of the previous year arising out of the objection of a portion of the inhabitants of the Red River country to being incorporated in the Dominion of Canada without a previous settlement of terms. Quite recently (1901) the same Department has published an exhaustive report on the sending of Canadian troops to South Africa and their operations there.   [3437

Much interesting matter in regard to interprovincial trade is contained in the Report published in 1894 on the proceedings of the Intercolonial Conference held from June 28 to July 9 of that year.   [3438

Certain subjects in which Canada is largely interested, such as fur sealing in Alaskan waters, have been dealt with by the Home Government, and the official reports of the Commissioners have been published by that government and, separately, by the government of the United States.   [3439

Mention may perhaps here be made of a work which, though not brought out under official auspices, has largely an official character, namely, a collection of *Documents illustrative of the Canadian Constitution* made by William Houston, M. A., Librarian of the Legislative Assembly of Ontario, and published in 1891 (Toronto: Carswell and Co.). The documents selected go back to the Treaty of Utrecht, 1713, and take in the British North America Act (Confederation Act) of 1867 and the several subsequent acts by which the powers of the Canadian Parliament are further defined. They also embrace the instructions given by the Home Government to successive Governors-General of Canada.   [3440

There is no Dominion bureau of education. Annual reports on education are published by the several Provincial Governments." [3440 a

For more than a hundred years past there has been a laudable ambition for the establishment of a good Canadian magazine, and many attempts, both in French and English, have been made to this end. Although the aim in each case has been distinctly literary, much of historic value has appeared in this ephemeral form ; but as such publications are practically inaccessible, no attempt has been made at a catalogue.   [3441

The publication of newspapers began with the Halifax *Gazette*, 1752, followed by the Quebec *Gazette*, 1763, and the Montreal *Gazette*, 1785. These early sheets contain little save official announcements and European news. But the papers from 1825 to 1840, of which many files are preserved in the libraries throughout the Dominion, contain many valuable data.   [3442

If omissions of even well-known works be noticed, we must plead lack of space, and the desire to retain only the more important titles; but many apparent omissions are included and appraised in the "American" section. On account of our poverty in published material, many local studies, which often fall far below the dignity of history, as well as many of the

older books of travel, are included on account of important historic detail unnoticed elsewhere ; this is also the justification for the mention of certain biographies of a distinctly religious character, notably those by the Abbé Faillon.   [3443

As publishers appear and disappear with puzzling rapidity, especially in the Province of Quebec, it may be useful to mention that a fair selection of the more recent Canadiana (French) may generally be found at Granger Frères, 1699 Notre Dame St., Montreal (catalogue); Pruneau & Kirouac, Fabrique St., Quebec; Congdon & Britnell, 11 West Richmond Street, Toronto, have the largest selection of older work (regular catalogue). [3444

DIVISION I: MATERIALS FOR HISTORY

Cartography and Bibliography

Harrisse gives full descriptions and notes of all important maps up to 1700 (sect. 3453). There were comparatively few maps published between that date and the Seven Years' War ; the more important of these are mentioned in *Narrative and critical history of America*, vol. V, pp. 79, 472, 483, et seq. There was much detailed work done by English engineers in and about Quebec during and after the siege, much of which is still unpublished.   [3445

Both Holland and Bouchette published some fine maps during the first quarter of the 19th century, and a map of the Hudson's Bay Territory, showing the sites of the old French forts, by Thomas Devine, published by the government of Ontario, Toronto, 1857, cannot be passed over by the student. A standard map of Canada is now in course of preparation by the Government. Many special maps have been published by the Geological Survey. A list of which, 1898, with prices, may be had on application to the Director, Sussex Street, Ottawa, Ont.   [3446

Bibaud, Maximilien. Dictionnaire historique des hommes illustrés du Canada et de l'Amérique. Montreal. 1857.

—— Le Panthéon canadien, choix de biographies, dans lequel on a introduit les hommes les plus célèbres des autres colonies britanniques. Montreal. 1858.   [3447

Both of these are useful especially for a past generation of French Canadian celebrities.

—— Bibliothèque canadienne, ou annales bibliographiques. Montreal. 1859.　　[3448

This pamphlet of 52 pages, though of value in its day, is now superseded by Morgan and Gagnon (sect. 3458 and 3451).

Bibliotheca Americana ; or, A chronological catalogue of the most curious and interesting books, pamphlets, state papers, etc., upon the subject of North and South America, from the earliest period to the present, in print and manuscript ; for which research has been made in the British Museum, and the most celebrated public and private libraries, reviews, catalogues, etc., with an introductory discourse on the present state of literature in those countries. London : Debrett. 1789.　　[3448 a

There is no certainty as to the authorship of this curious collection. It contains some sixteen hundred titles, but no uniform plan was followed in their transcription, some being given in full, but many are so shortened as to be almost useless ; however, the price and the publisher are generally stated, and many of the pamphlets on Canada are of great interest and rarity.

Biggar, H. P. See his Early trading companies of New France, sect. 3603, for valuable bibliography and list of documents up to 1632.
　　[3449

Faribault, George Barthélemi. Catalogue d'ouvrages sur l'histoire de l'Amérique et en particulier sur celle du Canada et de la Louisiane, de l'Acadie et autres lieux ci-devant connus sous le nom de Nouvelle France ; avec des notes bibliographiques, critiques, et litteraires. Quebec. 1837.　　[3450

The first and in many respects the best Canadian bibliography published ; its range is large and the notes are full ; the book is now rare and commands a high price. The catalogue of maps at end of volume though incomplete is of importance.

Gagnon, Philéas. Essai de bibliographie canadienne. Quebec : Author. 1895. $4.
　　[3451

M. Gagnon has long been a collector of Canadiana, and this is the catalogue of his library. It includes autographs and other MSS. as well as books, pamphlets, newspapers, etc. It is, however, only the inventory of a single library, and many well-known titles are omitted. A supplement is announced.

G. M. W.
The titles in facsimile and the notes make this a valuable work despite its somewhat mixed character and incompleteness. It is especially rich in material on the early history of the Province of Quebec. The list of maps and plans contains some valuable detail.

Griffin, Appleton Prentiss Clark. Bibliography of American historical societies (The

United States and Dominion of Canada). American Historical Assoc. Washington : Government Printing Office. 1896.　　[3452

Includes lists of proceedings, transactions and publications of historical and allied associations throughout British North America.

Harrisse, Henry. Notes pour servir à l'histoire, à la bibliographie, et à la cartographie de la Nouvelle France et des pays adjacents, 1545–1700. Paris. 1872.　　[3453

This admirable piece of work is as nearly complete as is possible up to 1700, and in addition to the bibliography contains a detailed list of maps published and in the original, with full descriptions and historical notes. The preface is valuable in indicating the sources of the material with some history of the archives, and in the *Notes historiques* many documents are transcribed and noted.

Historical publications relating to Canada, Review of. Edited by George M. Wrong and H. H. Langton. 1896–. Toronto: Univ. Library. 1897–. v. 1+. $1.50 ea.　　[3454

This is an annual critical review, published at the beginning of each year (the first volume appeared in 1897), of all the historical matter relating to Canada appearing in the previous year. History is interpreted in a wide sense and includes economics, archæology, folk-lore, etc. Pamphlets and magazine articles are noticed as well as books. The contributors are usually specialists in the departments assigned to them, and their criticism is frank and impartial. Perhaps the most valuable feature of the *Review* consists in its being a complete bibliography of current historical literature relating to Canada.

Kingsford, William. Canadian archæology: an essay. Montreal : Drysdale. 1886. 75c.

—— Early bibliography of the Province of Ontario. Toronto: Rowsell & Hutchison. Montreal: Picken. 1892. $1.　　[3455

An attempt at the bibliography of Ontario—material was difficult of access, but Dr. Kingsford largely remedied the defects of the first by his later essay.

Lucas, Fred W. See under French Régime, sect. 3654.　　[3456

Important bibliography and cartography for period 1750–1760.

Marcel, Gabriel. Reproductions de cartes et de globes relatifs à la découverte de l'Amérique du XVI au XVIII siècle. Paris. 1894.
　　[3457

Besides maps of North America this collection contains Quebec, 1722 ; Montreal, about the same date ; Discoveries of Joliet ; Lake Superior ; The Great Lakes ; Discoveries of La Verenderye ; Lake Champlain, The Mississippi, etc. These maps are all reproduced by photography and are in consequence exact. For the most part they are well selected and are of much greater value to the student than are the notes which are included in a separate volume.

Morgan, Henry J. Bibliotheca Canadensis, or a manual of Canadian literature. Ottawa. 1867.   [3458

Especially valuable for English works; complements in this respect Faribault and Gagnon.

Morin, P. L. Le vieux Montréal, 1611–1803. Montreal. 1884.   [3459

A collection of thirteen old plans and maps of Montreal and various public buildings. The collection is interesting, but is not exact in detail, especially in the historical and personal notes.

Ethnology

Ethnological Survey of Canada. The Committee on an Ethnological Survey of Canada was organized at the Toronto meeting of the British Association for the Advancement of Science, 1897, with fourteen resident members, and three members of the Committee for the Ethnographical Survey of the United Kingdom. It was designed that the work should be carried out on lines corresponding with those already followed by the latter Committee in Great Britain, and that it should continue, so far as possible, the work already carried on since the Montreal meeting in 1884, by the Committee on the North-Western Tribes of Canada. The Committee's work is carried on under a grant from the British Association, and it is hoped that a certain measure of permanence may be secured through the coöperation of local societies and governments. The officers are Prof. D. P. Penhallow, Chairman, McGill University, Montreal, Que., and Mr. C. Hill-Tout, Secretary, Vancouver, British Columbia. The publications are as follows: —   [3460

An ethnological survey of Canada. Brit. Assn. Adv. Sc. 1897, p. 440; 1898, p. 497; 1899, p. 696; 1900, p. 468.

Hill-Tout, C. Haida stories and beliefs. Rept. Brit. Assn. 1898, p. 500.

— Notes on the N'tlaka' pamuq, a branch of the great Salish stock of North America. Brit. Assn. 1899, p. 700.

— Notes on the Sk·q̇o'mic of British Columbia, a branch of the great Salish stock of North America. Brit. Assn. 1900, p. 472.

Sulte, Benjamin. Customs and habits of the earliest settlers of Canada. Brit. Assn. 1898, p. 499.

— Origin of the French Canadians. Brit. Assn. 1897, p. 449 ; 1899, p. 709 ; 1900, p. 470.

Boas, Dr. Franz. Growth of Toronto children. Brit. Assn. 1897, p. 443.

Gérin, Léon. Hurons of Lorette. Brit. Assn. 1900, p. 549.

Committee on North-West Tribes of Canada, Report of. Brit. Assn. 1885, p. 696 ; 1887, p. 173 ; 1888, p. 233; 1889, p. 797 ; 1890, p. 553 ; 1891, p. 407 ; 1892, p. 545 ; 1893, p. 653 ; 1894, p. 453 ; 1895, p. 522; 1896, p. 569.

Hale, Horatio. Report on the Blackfeet tribes. Brit. Assn. 1885, p. 696 ; 1887, p. 197.

— Notes on the Indians of British Columbia. Brit. Assn. 1888, p. 233.

— North American ethnology. Brit. Assn. 1889, p. 797.

— Ethnology of British Columbia. Brit. Assn. 1890, p. 553.

— Remarks on linguistic ethnology. Brit. Assn. 1892, p. 545.

Wilson, Rev. E. F. Report on the Blackfeet tribes. Brit. Assn. 1887, p. 183.

Boas, Dr. Franz. Report on the Indians of British Columbia. Brit. Assn. 1889, p. 801.

— Notes on the Indians of British Columbia. Brit. Assn. 1888, p. 236.

— Indians of British Columbia. Brit. Assn. 1891, p. 408.

— Indian tribes of the lower Fraser River. Brit. Assn. 1894, p. 454.

— Report on the Indians of British Columbia. Brit. Assn. 1895, p. 522 ; 1896, p. 569.

Chamberlain, A. F. Report on the Kootenay Indians of S. E. British Columbia. Brit. Assn. 1892, p. 549.

Lawson, George. On the food plants used by the North American Indians. Brit. Assn. 1886, p. 918.

Tylor, E. B. Canadian ethnology. Presidential address. Brit. Assn. 1886, p. 899.   [3461

The Minister of Education, Toronto, has published valuable ethnological information, dealing with Indian tribes in Ontario, in his annual reports. These may be had on application.

[3461 a

Collections of Documents, Proceedings of Societies, etc.

Archives. Reports on Canadian archives. Edited by Douglas Brymner. Ottawa. [3462

Under the efficient direction of the Dominion Archivist, Douglas Brymner, a large number of documents relating to Canada have been copied at the Record Office in London, and in other European collections. Great care has been taken to secure verbal accuracy, and the copies now accumulated at Ottawa can be used with the same confidence as their originals. The Archivist's Reports began in 1873, but remained till 1884 of a preliminary character. Since the latter date they have possessed decided value for historians, both American and Canadian. As an instance of their bearing upon the United States the case of the Haldimand Papers may be cited. In 1884 a calendar of these important sources began to appear in Mr. Brymner's reports, and for the Revolutionary War they are indispensable. Nowhere else can the attempt to disconnect Vermont from the colonial cause be so clearly traced.   C. W. C.

[3463

The documents reprinted in these volumes are so important that a complete list is given : —

1882. Reports of vessels arriving at and clearing from Quebec, 1780 and 1791.   [3464

1883. Letter, Elliot to Taylor. Political. 1835. — Letter, Morin to Hincks. Political. 1841. — Transactions between England and France relating to Hudson's Bay, 1687.   [3465

1884. Description of Nova Scotia. Lieut.-Col. Morse. 1784. — Letter, Charles I to Sir Chas. Wake, Ambassador to France. Reddition of Quebec and Acadia, 1631. — Martyrdom of Brebœuf and L'Allemant, by Christophe Regnault, 1678.   [3466

1885. Register of Anglican Parish of Montreal, 1776-87. — Col. Gother Mann. Boundaries with U. S. 1802. — Letter, Dudouyt to Mgr. Laval. Liquor traffic. 1677. — Letters between Sir Guy Carleton and Lord Germaine. 1777. — Sketch of petition. Roubaud.
                                               [3467

1886. Proposal for reduction of Louisburg. Samuel Waldo. 1758. — Proposal for settling Nova Scotia. Samuel Waldo. — Journal of Jacques Repentigny Legardeur de St. Pierre. 1750-2. — Sir Guy Carleton to Lord Shelburne. On western trade. 1768. — Embarkation of French officers and officials. Quebec and Montreal, 1759-60. — Letter book of Capt. Miles Macdonell. Selkirk settlement, 1811-12.   [3468

1887. Capture of Fort McKay, Prairie du Chien, 1814.   [3469

1888. The Walker outrage, 1864. — General Murray's recall. — French noblesse in Canada after 1760. (In connection with this, see article by Judge Baby in Canadian antiquarian, Montreal, July-October, 1899.) — Pierre du Calvet. (See also article in Canadian antiquarian, 8: 64.) — North-west trade, 1780-4. — French royalists in Upper Canada, 1798.   [3470

1889. North-west exploration, 1738-90. — Vermont negotiations, 1791. — Before and after the Battle of Edge Hill, 1762-3.   [3471

1890. Constitutional act of 1791. — North-west explorations, 1785. — Internal communications, 1783. — Relations with the United States after peace of 1783.
                                               [3472

1891. Settlements and surveys, 1793. — Division of Upper Canada. Chief Justice Elmsley on act of 1798. — War with France, 1793. — French Republican designs on Canada, 1793. — Marriage law in Upper Canada. Richard Cartwright, Jan. 1792.   [3473

1892. Settlements and surveys, 1788. — Lower Canada in 1800. — Ecclesiastical affairs in Lower Canada, 1803. — Political state of Upper Canada, 1806-7. — Courts of justice for Indian country. Lieut.-Gov. Miles to Lord Hobart, 1802.   [3474

1895. Relations des voyages de Pierre Esprit Radisson, 1682-4. Sable Island.   [3475

1896. Indian lands on the Grand River. Sir Peregrine Maitland to Earl Bathurst, 1821. — Anticipation of War of 1812. — Roman Catholic Church in Upper Canada, 1784, etc.   [3476

1897. Proposed union between Upper and Lower Canada, 1822. — Claim for losses, 1812-15. — Internal communications, 1818, etc. — North-West disputes, 1819, etc. — Cabot map. Memorandum by S. E. Dawson, with legends in Latin and Spanish, and translated in English.   [3477

1898. Siege of Quebec, 1759. — Land companies of Canada. — Naturalization question.   [3478

1899. Clergy reserves, 1820, etc. — Education, 1818, etc. — Report of civil and other establishments of Upper Canada, 1831, with supplement containing valuable reports on Paris archives by Edouard Richard.
                                               [3479

1900. Education, 1832. — Emigration, 1832.   [3480

Bouchette, Joseph. Topographical description of the province of Lower Canada. London. 1815.   [3481

An important review of the seigniories, townships and counties of Lower Canada, as they were when the author filled the post of Surveyor-General to the Province. With a knowledge derived from personal inspection of the regions described, Bouchette sketches the physical character of each, and indicates the stage of material progress which has been reached. He is inclined to be optimistic, but his essay is an unusually good contribution to economic geography. It was issued six or seven weeks before the battle of Waterloo. Seventeen years later Bouchette published in London (Longmans) a more ambitious work in two volumes, *The British dominions in North America*. In scope and fulness this goes beyond the *Topographical description*, which, nevertheless, it by no means supersedes.   C. W. C.

—— Topographical description of the province of Lower Canada. London. 1832.
                                               [3482

This work is more categorical and methodical than the first bearing the same title, and greatly exceeds it in scope and statistical information, but on the other hand it is entirely lacking in the descriptive interest of the first.

—— British dominions in North America. London: Longmans. 1832. 2v.   [3483

Full of valuable detail, statistical and geographical ; the maps and plates are excellent. Bouchette (1774-1841) was Surveyor-General ; he came of a family holding various offices under government and was always a strong upholder of imperial rule — traces of this throughout his works gave offence at the time, but apart from this defect all his work is authoritative and valuable.

Bulletin de recherches historiques. Pierre-Georges Roy, 9 Wolfe St., Lévis, Quebec. Issued monthly, began December, 1895. $2 per annum.   [3484

Important for minute detail, chiefly confined to Province of Quebec.

Canada Français. Revue publiée sous la direction d'un Comité de professeurs de l'Université Laval, Québec.   [3485

1888-91. 4 vols., with a supplementary volume (see below).

Among the historical articles we note the following : —

Vol. 1. Gosselin, L'Abbé A. H. Rôle politique de Mgr. de Laval. — Chapais, Thos. La Bataille de Carillon. — Casgrain, L'Abbé H. R. L'Acadie. — Poisson, Adolphe. La population française dans les Cantons de l'Est. — Gérin-Lajoie, A. Dix ans au Canada, 1840-

1850. Continued through Vols. ii, iii, iv. — Beaudoin, L'Abbé J. D. Cabot. [3486

Vol. 2. Sulte, Benjamin. Le pays des Grands Lacs au xvii siècle. — Casgrain, L'Abbé H. R. Montcalm peint par lui-même. — Dionne, N. E. Miscou. — Roy, Jos. Edmond. Du notariat, etc.; au Canada avant 1663. [3487

Vol. 3. Lusignan, Alphonse. L'affaire de St. Denis. — McLennan, William. Anciens Montréalais. Basset, notaire, 1639–1699. — Dionne, N. E. La Traite des pelleteries sous Champlain. — Roy, Jos. Edmond. Notes sur le greffre, etc., de Québec. [3488

Vol. 4. Actes du frère Didace. First Canadian Recollet. [3489

—— SUPPLEMENTARY VOLUME. Documents inédits sur l'Acadie, selected by M. l'Abbé H. R. Casgrain. 1710–1815. [3490

Canadian antiquarian and numismatic journal. Montreal. 1872–. (Now issued irregularly by various printers for the Society.) $3 per annum. [3491

Contains a great variety of matter, but chiefly of value to the local antiquary; the earlier volumes are out of print. 3d Series, vol. iii, 1901, contains the interesting Journal of Thomas de Vercheres, 1803 to 1819.

Canadiana, edited by W. J. White. Montreal. Began Jan. 1889, discontinued December, 1890. [3492

Contains some articles of value, e. g., Canadian histories, John Reade: — Battle of Stony Creek, Douglas Brymner: — Indians in War of 1812, Henry Mott: — Sir Wm. Alexander, W. W. L. Chipman : — Scene of de Maisonneuve's fight, Wm. McLennan: — Cruises of a Nova Scotian privateer, Ernest Cruikshank: — St. Regis, W. J. White: — 1812-15, J. P. Edwards: — Colonial privateers, 1812, Ernest Cruikshank: — DeLiancourt and Simcoe, James Bain, Jr.: — Reminiscences of Col. Claus, Ernest Cruikshank: — The literary movement in Canada up to 1841, Blanche L. Macdonell: — Early interpreters, John Reade: — Le Père Marquette, J. T. Lespérance.

Canadian Institute. Toronto, Canada. The Canadian Institute was organized in 1849. It was originally intended to confine its papers to science and the arts, but many valuable historical and archæological papers have been included, especially those of Sir Daniel Wilson, Prof. John Campbell, Father A. G. Morice, and E. Cruikshank. [3493

Its publications are as follows : — 1st Series, 1852–1855, 3 vols. entitled The Canadian journal, a repertory of industry, science and art. — 2nd Series, 1856–1878, 15 vols., entitled The Canadian journal of science, literature, and history. — 3rd Series, 1879–1890, 7 vols., Proceedings of the Canadian Institute. — 4th Series, commenced in 1890 and continued under the title, Transactions of the Canadian Institute, of which No. 1, vol. 7, was published in 1901. In February, 1897, a series was commenced, entitled Proceedings of the Canadian Institute, intended for short papers and

abridgments of which part 4, vol. 2, was published in January, 1901. The Institute has also published separately, An appeal to the Canadian Institute on the rectification of Parliament, by Sir Sanford Fleming. 1892. — Essays received in response to an appeal by the Canadian Institute on the rectification of Parliament, 1893. — Catalogue of the Library of the Canadian Institute, 1858. — Annual report of the Canadian Institute on the Archæology of Ontario, 1886-7, now continued as the Appendix to the Report of the Minister of Education of Ontario.

Conseil Souverain, Jugements et délibérations du ——, de la Nouvelle France, 1663–1704, et du Conseil Supérieur, 1705–1716, 6 vols. Québec: published by Government. 1885–. [3494

Although containing only the judgments of these two courts without annotations or explanation, these volumes are of the highest importance. Judgments on every crime and misdemeanor from high treason to family jars may here be found. Magic, blasphemy, duels, scandal, abduction, breach of promise, questions of ceremony, of precedence, piracy, wreckage, *Te Deums* for victories in all quarters of the globe, mischievous regulations of trade and labor, permits to travel, to trade, to go into the woods, investigation of character, enregistration of grants, edicts and ordonnances form the subject of some of the cases. There is no more instructive collection for a study of the social and official conditions of the period, but unfortunately its value is seriously impaired by the want of an index; a chronological list of cases at the end of each volume of 1000 pages is of very trifling assistance to the student.

Desaulniers, F. L. Les vieilles familles d'Yamachiche, dix généalogies. Montreal: C. O. Beauchemin & Fils. 1898. 2v. $1.50. [3495

Compiled on the plan of the Abbé Tanguay's *Dictionnaire généalogique*, but only of local interest.

Ferland, *Rev.* J. B. A. Notes sur les Registres de Notre Dame de Québec. Québec: Coté. 1854. [3496

An interesting series of well-chosen memoranda from 1621 to 1651 of the same character as the Abbé Tanguay's *A travers les registres*, but without index.

Hay, George Upham. Canadian history readings; edited and published by George Upham Hay. V. 1. St. John, N. B. 1900. $1. [3496 a

A series of twelve monthly pamphlets dealing in great part with the early periods of discovery and conquest of eastern Canada. The following titles will give an idea of the scope of this publication : —

Bourinot, Sir John George. Siege of Louisbourg, 1758.

Cruikshank, Ernest. Mackinac, 1812, 1814.

Fronsac, F. G. Forsaith de. Canadian nobility of French epoch.

Ganong, Wm. F. On the study of ancient maps.

— Suggestions for the investigation of local history.

Hannay, James. Lady Latour: responsible government.

Hay, George U. Champlain at St. Croix, etc.

Jack, I. Allan. General Coffin.

Paltsits, Victor Hugo. A scheme for the conquest of Canada, 1746.

Raymond, Rev. Wm. O. Notes on Madawaska.

Silver, Arthur P. The maroons of Nova Scotia.

Thatcher, George E. The Acadian land in Louisiana.

Vroom, James. The Pennfield colony.

Levis documents. Collection des manuscrits du Maréchal de Lévis. Publié sous la direction de l'Abbé H. R. Casgrain. Quebec. 1889–1895. 8v. [3497

V. 1. Journal du Chevalier de Lévis.— V. 2. Lettres du Chevalier de Lévis.— V. 3. Lettres de la Cour de Versailles.— V. 4. Pièces militaires.— V. 5. Lettres de M. de Bourlamaque.— V. 6. Lettres du Mgr. de Montcalm.— V. 7. Journal du Marquis de Montcalm.— V. 8. Lettres du Marquis de Vaudreuil.— V. 9. Lettres de l'Intendant Bigot.— V. 10. Lettres de divers particuliers.— V. 11. Relations et journaux, 1775–1760. The series is completed by an excellent Table analytique.

On March 15, 1888, Count Raimond de Nicolay, great-grandson of the Chevalier (afterwards Maréchal and Duc) de Lévis, wrote to the Abbé H. R. Casgrain, of Laval University, Quebec, offering through him to the Government of the Province of Quebec permission to publish the whole of the invaluable collection of manuscripts made by the Chevalier and inherited by him from his uncle the last Duc de Lévis (branch Lévis-Léran), subject to the following conditions: "I shall have an authentic copy of the papers of the Maréchal de Lévis concerning Canada made under my direction, and I shall offer this to the Province of Quebec on condition that the Premier shall officially oblige himself towards me to have them printed literally and in entirety, and shall reserve the exclusive right in such publications. At the beginning shall be placed a sketch of the Maréchal de Lévis, of his family and of my relationship, explaining the uninterrupted and hereditary transmission of the manuscripts."

This generous offer was accepted by the Government, and thanks to the zeal and recognized position of the Abbé Casgrain, we are now in possession of a series of documents the importance of which can hardly be exaggerated.

Lundy's Lane Historical Society. Niagara Falls South, Ontario. See Griffin's *Am. historical societies*, p. 1152, for list; material is all local. [3498

Cruikshank, E. Battle of Lundy's Lane, 1814. Welland. 1888.— Curzon, Sarah Anne. Laura Secord. Toronto. 1891.

See, also, sect. 1722.

McCord, Fred. A. Handbook of Canadian dates. Montreal: Dawson Brothers. 1888. [3499

This little book is so accurate and so useful to the student and writer that we have no hesitation in including it as material for history.

Manitoba Historical and Scientific Society, Winnipeg. Transactions and proceedings from 1879. [3500

The following is a selection of the historical titles. See Griffin's *Am. historical societies* for complete list.

1882. McArthur, A. Red River rising.— Panton, J. H. Arctic regions and Hudson Bay route.

1883. Bryce, Geo. Winnipeg country. Discovery, etc.— Dennis, W. Sources of North-West history.

1885. Bell, C. N. Some historic names and places of the North-West.— Bryce, Geo. Old settlers of the Red River.

1887. Bryce, Geo. The Souris country.— Drummond, L. The French element in the Canadian North-West. — McArthur, A. The fate of Thomas Simpson.— Bell, C. N. Red River settlement.

1888. Bryce, Geo. John Tanner, a famous Manitoba scout.— Bell, C. N. Henry's journal.— McMicken, Geo. Fenian raid on Manitoba.

1889. Bryce, Geo., and C. N. Bell. Original letters regarding the Selkirk settlement.

1890. Bryce, Geo. The first recorder of Rupert's Land.

1892. "Seven Oaks."

1893. MacBeth, John. Early days in Red River settlement, etc.

1894. Schultz, John. The old Crow Wing trail.— Bryce, Geo. Early days in Winnipeg.— Schultz, John. A forgotten northern fortress.

Margry, Pierre. Découvertes et établissements des Français dans l'ouest et dans le sud de l'Amérique septentrionale, 1614–17. Paris. 1879. 6v. [3501

A storehouse of documents throwing light on the history of LaSalle, d'Iberville, Bienville, Juchereau de St. Denis, Le Sueur, Hennepin, LaMothe Cadillac, Dulhut, and other explorers of the 17th and 18th centuries. For extended notice, see sect. 1182.

Mingan Seigniory. Legal documents submitted in the appeal to the Privy Council. 2 vols. and a sup. vol. maps. 1884–88. [3502

May be consulted, McGill Univ. Library, Montreal.

This record of proceedings in the suit of the Crown vs. the Labrador Company contains a large amount of historical material. The action was commenced by the Provincial Government of Quebec, which claimed that the Labrador Company was wrongfully in possession of territory belonging to the Province. The Mingan Islands extend along the north shore of the St. Lawrence at its mouth and the mainland of Mingan, as held by the Company, was four hundred miles in length by six in depth. The defence of the Company was that it had been in possession since 1661, when the Company of New France gave title to François Bissot. The case after coming before the Superior Court and the Court of Appeal was finally carried to the Judicial Committee of the Privy Council. The record of proceedings, which fills two volumes of text and one of maps, embraces a large number of valuable documents relating to seigniorial tenure, besides the pleadings and judgments. C. W. C.

Minnesota Historical Society. St. Paul, Minn. [3503

The following titles are chosen from the collections: —

V. 1. French voyageurs to Minnesota during the 17th century. — Letter of Mesnard, 1654. — Memoir of Jean Nicollet. — Louis Hennepin. — DuLuth ; Le Sueur ; D'Iberville.

V. 2 (part 3). The geography of Perrot.

V. 3. Relation of M. Penicaut.

V. 6 (part 1). The sources of the Mississippi, their discoverers real and pretended. — (part 2.) The Hennepin bicentenary.

Montréal, Société Historique de. Mémoires et documents relatifs à l'histoire du Canada publiés par la Société Historique de Montréal. 9v. Montréal. 1859–1880. [3504

A most valuable collection, but unfortunately difficult to procure. Amongst the publications are : — De l'esclavage en Canada. Jacques Viger et Sir Louis Hypolite Lafontaine. — Ordonnances de M. de Maisonneuve. — Guerre de 1812–15. Sir Etienne P. Taché. — Histoire du Montréal. Dollier de Casson. — Règne militaire en Canada, 1760–64. Verreau. — Voyage de Kalm (Extraits traduits par L. W. Marchand). — Les véritables motifs de Messieurs et Dames de la Société de Notre Dame de Montréal, etc.

Morgan, Henry J. Sketches of celebrated Canadians and persons connected with Canada. Quebec : Hunter Rose & Co. London : Trübner & Co. 1862. [3505

The selection of subjects is not made on any regular plan and the articles vary greatly in value, but despite its evident defects the work is important.

—— Canadian men and women of the time. Toronto : Briggs. 1898. $3. [3506

A careful compilation, but extended to undue length by the introduction of hundreds of subjects of little or no importance.

New York, Documentary history of the state of. Edited by E. B. O'Callaghan. 4v. Albany. 1849–1851. [3507

Vols. I and III contain much information touching Canadian affairs, particularly the raids and intercourse between the two neighbours during the 17th and 18th centuries. Contains some good maps.

New York, Documents relative to the colonial history of the state of, procured in Holland, England, and France by John Romeyn Brodhead. Edited by E. B. O'Callaghan. 10v. Albany. 1856–1858. Index. Albany. 1861. [3508

The most complete and valuable collection in existence. Canadian affairs occur throughout ; Vols. IX and X are from the French Archives and largely devoted to Canada ; the translations and biographical notes are admirably done ; the index is so complete that this immense collection of material is perfectly available for the student.

Nouvelle France, Collection de documents relatifs à l'histoire de la. 4v. Quebec. 1883–5. [3509

There is much material of value in this collection, but unfortunately it appears to have been edited "with discretion," and charges of errors and omissions have seriously damaged its value as an authority.

Nouvelle France. Documents historiques, correspondance échangée entre les autorités françaises et les Gouverneurs et Intendants. Vol. I (1620–1685). Published by the Government. Quebec. 1893. [3510

Nova Scotia Historical Society. Halifax, N. S. [3511

The following titles are selected from the list of contents published in Griffin, pp. 1156–7, of nine volumes of *Transactions.*

V. 1. Nicholson's Journal of the capture of Annapolis, 1710. — Thomas' Diary of expedition against Acadians, 1755.

V. 2. Journal of Witherspoon. — Memoir of James Murdoch, 1767–1799. — Memoir Sir Alexander Cook. — Acadian French.

V. 3. Winslow's Journal of expulsion of Acadians, 1755.

V. 4. Notice of Samuel Vetch, 1710–13. — Winslow's Journal.

V. 5. Expulsion of Acadians, Sir Adams Archibald. — Gordon's Journal of siege of Quebec, 1758.

V. 6. Acadian boundary disputes.

V. 7. Deportation of negroes to Sierra Leone.

V. 8. History of Halifax by Thomas B. Akins.

V. 9. Voyages of Cabots by Moses Harvey. — Ships of war lost on coast of Nova Scotia and Sable Island in 18th century. — Louisbourg by J. P. Edwards.

Quebec Literary and Historical Society. Historical documents published under the auspices of the Society. Quebec. 1868 .

—— Transactions. Quebec. 1829–. [3512

The publications of this Society from 1829–77 are divisible into two classes : the *Transactions,* which comprise papers and addresses of various kinds ; and the *Historical documents,* which have been printed under its direction from manuscripts or from books so rare that they are virtually inaccessible. While the essays read by members between 1829 and 1866 are a proof of intellectual vitality in Quebec, the documents mentioned are of more permanent historical value. They extend through five series, and comprise numerous works or brochures which students of Canadian history must consult ; e. g., *Mémoires sur les affaires du Canada, depuis 1749 jusqu'à 1760 ; Mémoires du Sieur de Ramezay :* and Dollier de Casson's *Histoire du Montréal.* C. W. C.

See, also, in Syllabus of materials, sect. 81.

The *Historical documents* are so important that the list is given in full.

First Series.

1838. Mémoires sur le Canada, depuis 1749 jusqu'à 1760. Good maps. Reprinted 1873.

1840. (1) Mémoire sur l'état présent du Canada, attribué à M. Talon. (2) Mémoire sur le Canada, 1736, attribué à M. Hocquart.

(3) Considérations sur l'état présent du Canada, 1758. (4) Histoire du Canada par M. l'Abbé de Belmont. (5) Relation du siége de Québec en 1759, par une religieuse de l'Hôpital Générale de Québec. (6) Jugement impartial sur les opérations militaires de la compagne en Canada, en 1759. (7) Réflexions sommaires sur le commerce qui s'est fait en Canada. (8) Histoire de l'eau de vie en Canada. Quebec, 1840.

1843. Voyages de découvertes au Canada entre les années 1534 et 1542 par Jacques Cartier, le Sieur de Roberval, Jean Alphonse de Xaintonge, etc. ; suivis de la description de Québec et de ses environs en 1608, et de divers extraits relativement au lieu de l'hivernement de Jacques Cartier en 1535–6, etc. Facsimile engravings.

1861. Mémoire du Sieur de Ramezay, commandant à Québec, au sujet de la reddition de cette ville le 18 Septembre, 1759, etc. [3513

Second Series : — 1868.

1. Extract from a manuscript journal relating to the siege of Quebec in 1759, kept by Colonel Malcolm Fraser.

2. Journal du siége de Québec en 1759 par M. Jean Claude Panet.

3. The campaign of Louisbourg, 1750–58.

4. A dialogue in Hades, a parallel of military errors of which the French and English armies were guilty during the campaign of 1759 in Canada.

5. The campaign of 1760 in Canada. These three pamphlets (3, 4 and 5) are attributed to the Chevalier Johnstone.

6. The invasion of Canada in 1775. Letter attributed to Major Henry Caldwell.

7. A journal of the expedition up the River St. Lawrence, republished from the New York *Mercury*, December 31, 1759. [3514

Third Series : — 1871.

1. Histoire du Montréal, 1640–1672 ; et Abrégé de la Mission de Kenté. Ouvrage attribué à M. François Dollier de Casson, Prêtre.

2. Journal des opérations de l'armée Américaine lors de l'invasion du Canada en 1775–6, par M. J. B. Badeaux. Badeaux was a notary at Three Rivers at this time.

3. Recueil de ce qui s'est passé en Canada au sujet de la guerre, tant des Anglais que des Iroquois, depuis l'année 1682. Covers period from 1682 to 1713. Probably by Gedéon de

Catalogne, engineer at Montreal. Published with variations of text in Vol. 1 of *Documents relatifs à l'histoire de la Nouvelle France.* See sect. 3509.

4. Voyage d'Iberville, 1698. See, also, Margry, vol. 4, sect. 3501.

5. Journal of the siege of Quebec, 1759–60, by General James Murray. [3515

Fourth Series : — 1875.

1. A journal of the expedition up the River St. Lawrence, 1759.

2. General orders in Wolfe's army during the expedition up the River St. Lawrence, 1759.

3. Journal du siége de Québec en 1759 par Jean Claude Panet, témoin oculaire.

4. Journal of the siege and blockade of Quebec by the American rebels in autumn 1775 and winter 1776, attributed to Hugh Finlay. [3516

Fifth Series : — 1877.

Documents relating to the War of 1812.
[3517

A complete index of the proceedings and publications of this Society was compiled by F. C. Wurtele, its librarian, in 1891, and this may be had as well as many of the publications on application to the Secretary, Quebec. [3518

The following are a selection from the *Proceedings* which may serve as an indication of the historical value of the work done. A full list may be found in Griffin, pp. 1147–51.

Anderson, Dr. W. J. On Canadian history and biography. 1867.
— Military operations Quebec, winter, 1759–60. 1870.
— Siege of Quebec, 1775. 1872.
— Archives of Canada. 1872. [3519
Casgrain, P. B. Les Plaines d'Abraham, 1759–1760. 1898–1900. [3520
Cochrane, Hon. A. W. Acadia ; LaTour and D'Aulnais families. 1835. [3521
Coffin, W. F. Quebec, siege, 1775. 1873. [3522
Demazières. Notes sur Jacques Cartier. 1862. [3523
Langton, John. Early French settlements in America. 1873. [3524
Lemoine, Sir J. M. Quebec, siege, 1775. 1877.
— Quebec, 1749–1759. 1880.
— The Scot in New France, 1535–1880. 1881. [3525
McGee, T. D'Arcy. A lately discovered manuscript of Champlain. 1863. [3526
Miles, H. H. Canadian archives. 1871. [3527
Riddell, H. S. H. Red River expedition of 1850. 1871. [3528
Stevenson, James. Currency card money of French régime. 1875.
— Currency after the capitulation. 1877.

— Causes of War of 1812. 1880. See special notice under English régime, sect. 3775-3777. [3529

Strange, T. B. Notes on defence of 1775. 1877. [3530

Royal Society of Canada. Ottawa. Proceedings and Transactions. 1882-1893. 1st series, 12v. 1895-1900. 2nd series, 6v. [3531

The following titles are selected from the *Transactions*: — [O. S. indicates 1st ser., N. S. 2d ser.]

Archibald, Sir Adam. First siege and capture of Louisbourg, 1745. V. 5. [3532

Audet, M. F. J. Protestant clergy in Lower Canada from 1760-1800. V. 6, N. S. [3533

Bourinot, Sir John George. Local government in Canada. V. 4. — Some memorials of Dundurn, etc. V. 6, N. S. [3534

Bryce, George. The five forts of Winnipeg. V. 3. — Outlines of famous journeys in Rupert's Land. V. 4. — The Assiniboine River and its forts. V. 10. — A further history of Radisson. V. 4, N. S. [3535

Brymner, Douglas. The Jamaican maroons and Nova Scotia. V. 1, N. S. — Death of Sir Humphrey Gilbert. V. 2, N. S. [3536

Dawson, Samuel Edward. Voyages of the Cabots in 1497-98. V. 12, O. S. ; 2, 3, N. S. — Line of demarcation of Pope Alexander VI. V. 5, N. S. [3537

Decazes, Paul. Four voyages of Jacques Cartier. V. 2. — Dubious points in the voyages of Jacques Cartier. V. 8. — Ile de Sable. V. 10. [3538

Decelles, A. D. Constitutions of Canada. V. 6, N. S. [3539

Dionne, N. E. Chouart and Radisson. V. 11, 12. — Roberval. V. 5, N. S. [3540

Doughty, Arthur G. Probable site of the battle of the Plains of Abraham. V. 5, N. S. [3541

Ganong, W. F. Jacques Cartier's first voyage. V. 5. — Cartography of the St. Lawrence from Cartier to Champlain. V. 7. — The Cabot legends. V. 3, N. S. [3542

Garry, Nicolas. Diary of Nicolas Garry, 1822-35. V. 6, N. S. [3543

Gerin, Léon. The French gentilhomme and the colonization of Canada. V. 2, N. S. — The habitant of St. Justin. A most important study of the French-Canadian farmer. No other such scientific work has ever been attempted in Canada. V. 4, N. S. — The Seigniory of Sillery and the Hurons of Lorette. V. 6, N. S. [3544

Gosselin, L'*Abbé* Auguste. The founder of Ogdensburg. V. 12. — Quebec in 1730. V. 5, N. S. — The Canadian clergy and the declaration of 1732. V. 6, N. S. [3545

Harrisse, Henry. The Cabots. V. 4, N. S. [3546

Howley, *Right Rev.* Michael F., Roman Catholic Bishop of Newfoundland. Cartier's course. V. 12. — Vinland vindicated. V. 4, N. S. [3547

Legendre, Napoléon. Frontenac. V. 4, N. S. [3548

O'Brien, *Most Rev.* Cornelius. Cabot's landfall and chart. V. 5, N. S. [3549

Patterson, *Rev.* George. The Portuguese on the northeast coast of America. V. 8. — Sir William Alexander. V. 10. — Sable Island. V. 12. — Last years of Charles de Biencourt. V. 2, N. S. — Sir Humphrey Gilbert. V. 3, N. S. [3550

Reade, John. The half-breed. V. 3. — The Basques in North America. V. 5. [3551

Rogers, Walter. Rogers, ranger and loyalist. V. 6, N. S. [3552

Roy, Joseph-Edmond. Bissot de la Rivière. V. 10. — La Hontan. V. 12. — La Potherie. V. 3, N. S. [3553

Sulte, Benjamin. The first seigniors of Canada. V. 1. — The de Callières family. V. 8. — The Tonty. V. 11. — Morel de la Durantaye. V. 1, N. S. — Pierre Boucher and his work. V. 2, N. S. — Military organization, 1636-1648. V. 2, N. S. — The death of LaSalle. V. 4, N. S. [3554

Thatcher, John Boyd. The Cabotian discovery. V. 3, N. S. [3555

Verreau, L'*Abbé* Hospice. Founders of Montreal. V. 1 & 5. — Jacques Cartier. V. 8, 9, O. S. ; 3, N. S. — Champlain. V. 5, N. S. [3556

Wilson, *Sir* Daniel. The Vinland of the Northman. V. 8, O. S. [3557

Sulte, Benjamin. Histoire des Canadiens-Français. See under French Régime, sect. 3685. [3558

Tanguay, *l'Abbé* Cyprien. Dictionnaire généalogique des familles canadiennes. Montreal: Senecal. 1871-90. 7v. (For sale by Modern Printing Co., 20 St. Vincent St., Montreal. Pap. $14. Cl. $17.50.) [3559

The great genealogical thesaurus of the French Canadian race. It begins with the founding of the colony and comes down in complete form to 1763. The author's original design was that it should reach his own day, but though he is still living at an advanced age, it is unlikely that this purpose will be fulfilled. Even in its present state the *Dictionnaire généalogique* is a veritable *opus*, representing 25 years of steady labour, 1,226,230 entries, and an enormous amount of travel. No other undertaking of a similar kind has ever been attempted in Canada on at all the same scale, nor is it probable that the ancestry of any nation has been more thoroughly investigated than that of the French Canadians. C. W. C.

—— A travers les registres. Notes recueillies. Montreal. 1886. [3560

A common-place book kept by the Abbé during his many years' work on his *Dictionnaire généalogique*, containing historical notes of great interest.

Taylor, Fennings. Portraits of British Americans, by W. Notman, with biographical sketches. Montreal: Notman. 1865. 3v. [3561

The selection of subjects is good, and the notices are well and carefully written. The portraits are photographs.

Trade under French régime. See Martin, Horace T. ; Biggar, H. P. ; Colonial Documents State of New York. [3562

Wisconsin, State Historical Society of. Collections. Madison, Wis. [3563

See Vols. 10, 11 for Nicolet, Lingeris, Radisson, and DesGroseliers, also, sect. 3390.

DIV. II. CONSTITUTIONAL AND INSTITUTIONAL HISTORY

Barthe, J. G. Souvenirs d'un demi-siècle ou mémoires pour servir à l'histoire contemporaine. Montreal : Chapleau & Fils. 1885. $1. [3564

An extreme partisan review of events from 1811–1837, but necessary for an understanding of the point of view of the ultra-liberal party.

Bourinot, *Sir* **John G.** Canada under British rule, 1760–1900. Toronto : Copp, Clark Co. 1901. $1. (Cambridge historical series.) Cambridge : Univ. Press. N. Y. : Macmillan. $1.50. [3565

A "short history" which is satisfactory for the periods treated, but lacks the sequence of a continuous narrative.

—— Federal Government in Canada. Baltimore : Johns Hopkins University Studies. 1889–98. $1. [3565 a

—— How Canada is governed. 3d ed. Toronto : Copp, Clark Co. 1897. $1. [3566

This is an elementary text-book in citizenship. It outlines the functions of the crown, the federal parliament, the provincial legislatures, the government of the territories, the school systems, etc. Bibliographies are appended to each chapter. It is the best short manual on the institutions of Canada. G. M. W.

—— Manual of the constitutional history of Canada. Rev. and enl. ed. Toronto : Copp, Clark Co. 1901. $1.25. [3567

The author, who is clerk of the House of Commons of Canada, is the author of a larger work on *Parliamentary practice and procedure*, and this *Manual* is chiefly a revised issue of some chapters of the earlier work. It is a useful summary of the principal points in the evolution of the federal system in Canada. The French régime is passed over briefly, and chief attention is given to the act known as The British North American Act, which forms the constitution of the Dominion. The author's meaning is always expressed in lucid terms. G. M. W.

—— Parliamentary procedure and government in Canada. New ed. of Parliamentary procedure and practice. Toronto : Copp, Clark Co. 1901. $8. [3568

The author's most important work, and one dealing with a subject upon which he is the acknowledged Canadian authority. It is mentioned here less on account of its current parliamentary value than because it embraces a long and useful preliminary chapter on parliamentary institutions in Canada. This begins with the French régime and reaches 1883. Moreover, a great many significant features in the political history of Canada since Confederation are touched upon and elucidated in the body of the text. C. W. C.

Clergy reserves. LINDSEY, CHARLES.

Their history and present position, showing the systematic attempts that have been made to establish in connection with the state a dominant church in Canada. With a full account of the rectories. Also an Appendix, containing Dr. Rolph's speech on the clergy reserves, delivered in 1836. Toronto. 1851. [3569

See sect. 3479 above.

Constitutional Act of 1791. [3570

See sect. 3472. Important correspondence and reports, pp. 10–48.

Douglas, James. Canadian independence, annexation and British imperial federation. N. Y. : Putnam. 1894. 75c. [3571

This is a volume in the "Questions of the day" series. Its chief purpose is to state the political alternatives which lie before the Dominion of Canada, and to examine the relations of that country with the United States. Imperial federation is treated less as an independent subject than as an ideal which affects American problems. Mr. Douglas has a wide knowledge of the two countries with whose future he deals, and is zealous for the advantage of both. His summing-up is strongly against the utility of annexation. "Whether the question be looked at from the point of view of an American or a Canadian, most impartial minds will come to one conclusion, that it would be better for the two great communities to live in closest commercial and social intercourse, but in separate houses." The essay besides being conceived in an admirable spirit of candor is written with much force and clearness. It omits few of the arguments that can be urged against the absorption of Canada by the United States, and furnishes a fine example of the temper which should be observed in such discussions. C. W. C.

Houston, William, *ed.* Documents illustrative of the Canadian constitution ; with notes. Toronto : Carswell. 1891. $2. [3572

"This volume is the result of an attempt to bring together in a single collection the documents which contain the constitution of the Dominion of Canada and illustrate its historical development." Believing that the true line of development runs back, not to the French régime but to the colonial governments of the United States, the editor has included no French documents except the Quebec and Montreal articles of capitulation. Those portions of Great Britain's foreign treaties which affected Canada are given, as well as a part of Lord Durham's famous report of 1839. F. J. S.

Lefroy, A. H. F. Law of legislative power in Canada. Toronto : Canada Law-Book Co. 1897–8. $9. [3573

"Mr. Lefroy's aim in publishing this acute and valuable constitutional treatise is fully explained by him in his preface. His object is to present a comprehensive view of the actual working of the scheme of government established in Canada thirty years since, and of the division of legislative powers between the Dominion and the various provincial parliaments, extracting all that is pertinent from the judicial decisions, and citing other authorities where necessary." *Nation*, June 30, 1898.

Masères, Francis, *Baron.* Account of the proceedings of the British and other Protestant inhabitants of the Province of Quebec in North America in order to obtain an House of Assembly in that Province. London. 1775.

—— Additional papers concerning the Province of Quebec. London. 1776. (An appendix to the book entitled An account of the proceedings, etc.)

—— Canadian freeholder ; in two dialogues between an Englishman and a Frenchman settled in Canada. London. 1777–79. 3v. (Titles of vols. II and III read " in three dialogues.") [3574

The Canadian Freeholder is ascribed to F. Masères, an Englishman of Huguenot descent, who held an official legal post in Canada shortly after the British conquest. His purpose is to effect a reconciliation between Great Britain and her revolted colonies. The Quebec Act of 1771 is described as mischievous and its repeal urged. Lord Mansfield's judgment of 1774 in favor of the King's sole authority in conquered countries, without the consent of Parliament, is combated, and the guarantee to the English colonies of the permanency of their charters is urged.

G. M. W.

When this book was written the author was Attorney-General of the Province of Quebec, and he afterwards became agent in London for the Protestant settlers in Canada. His opinions, therefore, may be taken to represent the views of the extreme English and Protestant party in that province. He was a learned and able lawyer, and this huge pamphlet is a skilful and well-reasoned argument for making timely concessions to the colonies. Masères is prejudiced and narrow in many respects, but his work is ably written and will repay careful examination. E. Cr.

—— Collection of commissions, public instruments and other papers relating to the Province of Quebec, from 1760. London. 1772.

—— Considerations on the expediency of admitting representatives from the American colonies into British House of Commons. London. 1770.

—— Mémoire à la défense d'un plan d'acte de Parlement pour l'établissement des loix de la Province de Quebec, . . . contre les objections de F. J. Cugnet. London. 1773.

—— Occasional essays on various topics, chiefly political and historical. London. 1809.

—— Answer to an introduction to observations made by the Court of Common Pleas upon the testimony adduced upon investigation into past administration of justice. London. 1790.

[3574 a

The last title mentioned has been frequently attributed to Masères.

François Masères, born 1731, died 1824, was appointed Attorney-General at Quebec from 1766 to 1769, and on his return to England was made Cursitor Baron of the Exchequer. He was a writer of high talent, and his tastes extended from politics to the higher mathematics. Although tolerant in his *personal* relations, he was in principle and practice a life-long opponent of the Church of Rome ; he headed the extreme English and Protestant party in Quebec against that led by François Joseph Cugnet. His works were all published anonymously, and though somewhat difficult reading and narrow in tone are of the utmost value for any understanding of the earlier years of English rule in Canada.

For further notice see Morgan's *Celebrated Canadians*, Gagnon's *Bibliographie*, and *Dominion illustrated*, 31 Oct., 1891.

Munro, Joseph E. C. Constitution of Canada. Cambridge: Univ. Press. 1889. [3575

An essay in political anatomy. It does not deal with active physiological functions, i. e., with the practical working of the constitution, but restricts itself narrowly to structure. It comprehends provincial legislative institutions as well as federal. Within the limits defined it is a useful text, and should appeal not only to those who have its precise subject in view, but also to students of constitutional forms in their comparative aspect. C. W. C.

Munro, W. Bennet. The droit de banalité during the French régime in Canada. (From the Annual Report of the American Historical Association for 1899, vol. I, pp. 207–228.) Washington. 1900. [3576

This study may be called the first fruits of a long investigation which Dr. Munro has made regarding the seigniorial system in Canada. Although dealing minutely with a special subject, it involves the whole question of feudal tenure, which it regards from the historical rather than from the strictly legal standpoint. The conclusion reached is that while Louis XIV governed New France even worse than he did the mother country, the *droit de banalité* was more tolerable in Canada than at home. C. W. C.

In connection with this subject: *Pièces et documents relatifs à la tenure seigneuriale*, Quebec, 1852, 2 vols., containing titles of the different seigneuries ; and *Lower Canada reports; seigniorial questions*, Quebec, 1856, 2 vols., containing the Act and proceedings of the special court, should be consulted.

Quebec act : Debates of the House of Commons in the year 1774 on the bill for making more effectual provision for the government of the Province of Quebec, drawn up from the notes of the Rt. Hon. Sir Henry Cavendish, Bart., and now first published by J. Wright. London. 1839. [3576 a

The adoption by the British Parliament of the Quebec act was one of the chief grievances of the American colonists, and it forms the subject of a clause in the Declaration of Independence. In these debates, the report of which is compiled from the shorthand notes of a member, the friends of the colonists strenuously opposed the passage of the act as an extension of arbitrary government, and intimated that it squinted toward the suppression of popular government in that part of America which it did not directly affect. The report includes the testimony of several persons who were familiar with Canada as to the conditions prevailing there. F. J. S.

Smith, Goldwin. Canada and the Canadian question. N. Y.: Macmillan. 1891. $2. [3577

A sketch which embodies the writer's well-known views on the present condition of Canada and her manifest future. It discusses in essay form the outstanding features of Canadian political development both French and English; next considers Confederation together with its fruits, and finally reaches the conclusion that Canada should be politically allied with the United States — not by "annexation," which is a term implying inferiority, but by a union similar to that between England and Scotland. The reader should not expect, then, from this treatise, a colourless outline of events, but such a use of historical fact as contemplates purposes of political demonstration. In literary style it far surpasses the common quality of writing on Canadian topics. C. W. C.

Todd, Alpheus. Practice and privileges of the two Houses of Parliament. Toronto. 1840. [3578

This first manual of parliamentary procedure in Canada, although written when Mr. Todd was only nineteen, held its place until superseded by May's *Usage of Parliament.* Mr. Todd's importance as a writer on constitutional subjects was established by the high esteem of his standard work *On Parliamentary Government in England* (sect. 2685). See, also, his *Brief suggestions in regard to the formation of local governments for Upper and Lower Canada, in connection with a Federal Union of the British North American provinces.* Ottawa, 1866, and *On the position of a constitutional governor under responsible government.* Ottawa. 1878.

Watson, Samuel James. Constitutional history of Canada. Toronto. 1874. [3579

This first volume (the second never was published) comes down to the union of the Provinces, and was long the only comprehensive study on the subject.

DIVISION III. COMPREHENSIVE HISTORIES

Archer, Andrew. Canada : short history of the Dominion of Canada. St. John, N. B.: McMillan. 1884. [3580

This is a school-book, dwelling with especial fullness upon the Maritime provinces. No original research has been involved. The style is pleasing and the tone impartial. G. M. W.

Bourinot, *Sir* **John George.** Canada and the United States. See American Academy of Political and Social Science, sect. 226. [3581

—— Story of Canada. (Story of the nations.) London: T. Fisher Unwin. 5s. N. Y.: Putnam. 1896. $1.50. Toronto: Copp, Clark Co. $1.25. [3582

A popular sketch of Canadian history from John Cabot's first voyage to 1891. Sir John Bourinot has enjoyed remarkable advantages for investigating his subject: viz. proximity to the Canadian archives, a long acquaintance with administrative life, and a personal position which places him half-way between French and English. The present work is largely conditioned by its connection with a uniform series. Its temper is fair, its statements of fact careful; and its style — if not unexceptionable — is ordinarily clear and correct. The illustrations are very good, both as regards selection and reproduction. C. W. C.

Bryce, George. Short history of the Canadian people. London : Low. 1887. 7s. 6d. [3583

A comprehensive and well-proportioned sketch of Canadian history from the legendary period to 1886. Each chapter is furnished with a brief bibliographical introduction, and thus possesses a feature which is usually lacking in Canadian text-books of this sort. The author's spirit is temperate, and though he writes avowedly from the federal standpoint, he cannot be accused of political heresy on that ground. One's chief item of adverse criticism is that the style of the work would be more attractive if its pages were less crowded with facts. C. W. C.

Clement, William Henry Pope. History of the Dominion of Canada. Toronto : Briggs. 1897. 50c. [3584

This work received the prize offered by a committee representing the provincial governments of Canada for the best school text-book. It is now in use in many of the schools of Canada. The sources of information are generally secondary. The author, a barrister, is especially alert upon constitutional questions. He is accurate, and is impartial to the point of being colorless. Perhaps because the work was subjected to revision by a committee, the style has little vigor and individuality. G. M. W.

Dawson, Samuel Edward. Canada and Newfoundland : with maps and illustrations. London : Stanford. 1897. 16s. [3585

This is volume 1 of the North American section of Stanford's *Compendium of geography and travel,* and covers all British America. (Vol. 2 relates to the United States.) This volume contains historical sketches of all the provinces and notices of the progress of discovery and settlement, besides being a geography of the northern part of the continent. The geology, productions, climatology, statistics and trade of British America are fully treated.

From the London *Times:* — "Carefully prepared and full of interesting matter, Dr. Dawson's volume does not suffer from the drawbacks of some numbers of the series — it is readable as well as instructive; there is not a surfeit of statistical and geological information, and we hear much of the people as well as the physical contour and products of the country."

Ferland, J. B. A. Cours d'histoire du Canada. Quebec: Coté. 1861–7. 2v. Montreal: Granger Frères. $2. [3586

The *chef d'œuvre* of one of the most eminent among French Canadian historians. It bears signs of being written by a priest and a patriot, but cannot be accused of wanting sincerity. It represents solid learning, and is composed with a view to literary effect. Ferland dying before the second volume was issued, the Abbé Laverdière acted as his literary executor in preparing his manuscript for the press, and in continuing it to the conquest. C. W. C.

Garneau, François Xavier. Histoire du Canada. Quebec; Montreal. 1845–52. 4v. 4e éd. Montreal: C. O. Beauchemin & Fils. 1882–3. 4v. Pap., $6. Half morocco, $8.

—— History of Canada, till 1840–1; tr. [and ed.] by Andrew Bell. Montreal. 1860. 2v. 3d ed. Toronto: Belford. 1876. 2v. [3587

A work of much force and spirit, besides being well grounded in knowledge. The French Canadians consider it their most distinctively "national" history, and though readers of scientific temper may find it at times too "patriotic," it contains the best general sketch of New France which has appeared from a Canadian pen during the present century. Its chronological limits are 1492–1840. In the fourth edition, which is recommended, the text occupies three volumes; while the fourth volume is of a memorial character, containing tributes to Garneau by his friends. C. W. C.

Greswell, William Parr. History of the Dominion of Canada. Oxford: Univ. Press. 1890. 7s. 6d. N. Y.: Oxford Univ. Press. $2. [3588

A sketch of Canadian history which was published under the auspices of the Royal Colonial Institute. The author has, apparently, no very wide knowledge of Canadian affairs, except in so far as he has informed himself from books. Nevertheless, the work possesses a distinct value. Besides being well written, it is, on the whole, well proportioned and presents the European affiliations of Canada in a lucid manner. It is particularly adapted to the needs of the beginner. C. W. C.

Hopkins, John Castell, *ed.* Canada: an encyclopædia of the country. Toronto: Linscott. [c. 1898–1900.] 6v. $30. [3589

This large work has been produced hastily to be sold by subscription. It is not an orderly arranged encyclopædia; but a collection of articles of unequal merit upon Canadian history, commerce, education, and other important topics. There is much padding, and what is of value is obscured by the mere bulk of the work. The defective arrangement of the matter makes easy use difficult. A copious index to each volume atones in some degree for this fault. Many of the articles are by writers of recognized authority in their chosen subjects. There are many inaccuracies. G. M. W.

Kennedy, Howard Angus. Story of Canada. (Story of the empire series.) London: Marshall. 1897. N. Y.: M. F. Mansfield. 50c. [3590

The author, though not a dweller, has seen service in Canada. This is a readable short narrative based upon secondary sources. It is accurate, and, while enthusiastic about Canada, is on the whole discriminating. The style is good. G. M. W.

Kingsford, William. History of Canada. Toronto: Briggs. 1887–98. 10v. $3 ea. London: Paul. 1888–98. 10v. 15s. ea. [3591

This is a composition of such dimensions and such diverse qualities that it cannot be adequately estimated in a short notice. It begins at "the earliest date of French rule," and reaches the union of the provinces "as carried out by Lord Sydenham in 1841." Though Kingsford possessed uncommon diligence, and had ready access to the materials collected by Brymner, he has not produced anything like a final history of Canada. He finished his volumes so rapidly that the style has suffered, and he is guilty of many inaccuracies. A statement of this kind is necessary because his achievements have usually been overpraised. On the other hand, one must commend him for having brought together much new information, and especially with having done a good deal for the English side of Canadian history. His work, while falling short of the first class, will long remain a useful magazine of political facts. C. W. C.

McIlwraith, Jane N. Canada. London: T. Fisher Unwin. 1899. 2s. 6d. [3592

One of "The children's study" series, written in an easy narrative style with excellent judgment as to the selection of material.

McMullen, John. History of Canada. Brockville. 1868.

—— 2d ed. rev. London: Low. Phil.: Lippincott. 1869.

—— 3d ed. rev. and enl. Brockville, Ont.: McMullen. 1891–2. 2v. $5. London: Low. 1893. 2v. 25s. [3593

The first edition, published in 1856, left much to be desired both in accuracy and fulness; the second, 1868, is an improvement upon it, but does not reach the level of mature scholarship. The third edition marks a still further advance, yet even in final form it is a work which approximates the class of annals more closely than that of modern critical history. C. W. C.

Miles, Henry H. Child's history of Canada, prepared for the use of elementary schools. Montreal: Dawson Brothers. 30c. [3594

Written in an easy and familiar style for young children. Sanctioned by the Council of Public Instruction for use in Protestant and Catholic schools throughout Quebec. Many editions have been published and there is a French translation (which is also authorized) published at 25c.

—— School history of Canada, prepared for use in the elementary and model schools. Montreal: Dawson Brothers. 7th ed. 1888. 60c.   [3595

This book was sanctioned by the Council of Public Instruction of the Province of Quebec for use in the Protestant and Catholic schools.

Parkin, George R. The great Dominion; studies of Canada: with maps. London and N. Y.: Macmillan. 1895. $1.75.   [3596

The chapters of this book were first published, with some abbreviation, as a series of letters to the London *Times*. Together they form an important sketch of Canada and its population at a recent date, 1894. The author's design is above all things to " leave upon the mind of the reader a true impression." It is a short book and, with a view to clearness, only the most important subjects are chosen: — the condition of the different provinces, economic resources, the Canadian Pacific Railway, labour and education. But though his aim is chiefly descriptive, Dr. Parkin has no wish to avoid the discussion of political questions. His tone throughout is frankly imperialistic, while chapters such as those on trade policy and political tendencies are a strong counterblast to Prof. Goldwin Smith. The concluding sentences furnish an epitome of the main views which the work expounds. " That it is the highest interest of Canada and the prevailing wish of her people to maintain connection with the Empire is one of the conclusions to which my study of the country had led me. That she cannot be separated from the Empire without results incalculably hazardous to the maintenance of the national position of the British people is another." The author is principal of Upper Canada College, Toronto.
                                                      C. W. C.

Roberts, Charles George Douglas. History of Canada. Boston: Lamson. 1897.
                                                      [3597

This book, though nowhere called a manual by its author, is of elementary character. It is comprehensive in survey and of moderate bulk. While not based on original sources, it represents intelligent compilation, and is written with conscious regard to literary form. The temper displayed is " patriotic," and at times the style degenerates into bombast. These lapses, however, are relatively rare, and do not form serious blemishes on a work which is much less arid than the ordinary text-book.   C. W. C.

Smith, William. History of Canada; from its first discovery to the peace of 1763. Vol. 1. Quebec: John Neilson. 1815.

—— History of Canada; from its first discovery to the year 1791. Vol. 2. Quebec: John Neilson. 1815.   [3598

The Hon. William Smith, son of the Chief Justice of the same name, was born in New York in 1770; educated in England, and came to Canada in 1786; he was Clerk of Parliament and Master in Chancery in Quebec, and wrote this, the first English history of Canada. " This narrative (it does not deserve the

name of a history) I intended only for my private use," he says in his introduction; and so much material has been edited since his day that the earlier portion serves merely as an approximately correct introduction to the events of the Seven Years' War. From this point the narrative grows in interest; the author undoubtedly knew many who were personally engaged in the events described. Valuable documents are transcribed at length in the notes and addenda, particularly in regard to the sieges of 1759 and 1775. The book was completed in 1812, the date on the title-page is 1815, it was not issued till 1826; the reason being the caution of the publisher, who probably looked upon Mr. Smith as a better historian than man of business. Bibaud mentions a third volume bringing the work down to 1815, but this is certainly unknown to the general public.

Withrow, William H. Popular history of the Dominion of Canada. Toronto: Briggs. [c. 1886.] 1899. $3.   [3599

This book, which has been frequently reissued, with additions, has the qualities that its title, as a popular history, implies. Its author, a Canadian, writes in a fair spirit; he is usually accurate, and, while he has not made any complete study of original materials, he has yet consulted some of them and his information is adequate. The style is agreeable.   G. M. W.

DIVISION IV.   FRENCH RE-GIME, INCLUDING ENGLISH CONQUEST

(*For accounts of French exploration and settlement in the Ohio and Mississippi valleys and in the north-west of the United States, see sect. 1172–1189, 1754–1826.*)

Baugy, Louis Henry, *Chevalier* de. Journal d'une expédition contre les Iroquois au Canada, en 1687, etc. Paris: Ernest Leroux. 1883.   [3600

This journal of the expedition of the Marquis de Denonville, to whom Baugy acted as aide-de-camp, occupies only 78 pages, and is a creditable piece of writing for the young officer. There is an excellent introduction and the notes are good throughout, but the real value of the book lies in the letters written to his brother, Eugène de Baugy. They have an unusual charm for letters of that time, when letter-writing had not as yet become an art, but was encumbered by form so rigid that it crushed out all life and nature. Apart from their charm these letters are important as the Chevalier is perfectly open in his criticism of the country, its officials and inhabitants, both men and women, and he reiterates Lahontan's statement as to les filles du roi.

Beaubien, *Rev.* **Charles P.** Le Sault-au-Récollet; ses rapports avec les premiers temps de la colonie. Mission-Paroisse-Montréal: C. O. Beauchemin & Fils. 1898. $1.   [3601

A creditable local history. It goes back to 1610, and the author has grouped round his parish many names of personal interest; — Viel, the first Canadian martyr, Sagard-Theodat, the chronicler, Dr. Kalm, the Swedish naturalist, and others ; he tells the story of the English captives (accidentally falling foul of Miss Alice Baker therein) with much of the lives and material condition of the early settlers ; so that this has a somewhat wider range than most books of its class.

Bibaud, Michel. Histoire du Canada sous la domination française. Montreal. 1837. 2e éd., rev., corrigée, et augmentée. Montreal : Lovell. 1843. [3602

See note on same author under English Régime, sect. 3694.

Biggar, H. P. Early trading companies of New France. Toronto : University of Toronto Library. 1901. $4. Boston : Boston Book Co. $4. [3603

A careful and detailed study which deals chiefly with the period of Champlain, although its dates are 1497-1632. It was presented for a "research degree" at Oxford, and is in many respects a university thesis of the higher type. Nearly one half of the space is assigned to bibliographical lists and notes which will be found useful both by historical students and readers at large. Mr. Biggar has not only accumulated a mass of facts, but has shown how they explain the failure of France to build up a profitable trade with Canada. Good index and map. C. W. C.

Boucher, Pierre. Histoire véritable et naturelle des mœurs et productions de la Nouvelle France, vulgairement dite le Canada. Paris. 1664.

—— *Same* (In Album du Canadien, pp. 9 to 73. Montréal. 1849).

—— *Same*, edited by G. Coffin. Montreal. 1882.

—— True and genuine description of New France, commonly called Canada, and of the manners and customs of that country. Translated by Edward Louis Montizambert. Montreal : Desbarats. 1883. [3604

Pierre Boucher had been Governor of Three Rivers and was the proprietor of the important seigniory of Boucherville. He had made a voyage to France to represent the needs of the country, and this book was the result. The annual reports of the Jesuits, with a pardonable inclination to emphasize the difficulties of their task, dwelt rather on the dangers and hardships of the life, the truculence of the savage, the rigor of the winter and the loneliness of the unbroken forest, than on the growth of Quebec, Three Rivers, and Montreal, and the ever-strengthening line of habitations binding them together, with the St. Lawrence a natural barrier between them and their enemies to the south. One is tempted to believe that they would rather have kept Canada as a close preserve for Indian converts than have encouraged immigration and settlement. But — " it is a good country," Pierre Boucher

says in his opening sentence, and there he strikes the key-note of his *True history.*

For biographical detail see *Transactions* Roy. Soc., Sulte (sect. 3554), under Material, and also Boucherville, by R. P. L. Lalande, S. J., next title.

Boucherville. LALANDE, *R. P. L., S. J.* Une vieille Seignieurie, Boucherville. Montreal : Cadieux & Derome. 1890. 50c. [3605

Contains details of the Boucher family, including Pierre Boucher its founder and author of the *Histoire véritable et naturelle de la Nouvelle France.*

Bougainville, Louis Antoine de. KERALLAIN, RENÉ DE. Les Français au Canada : la jeunesse de Bougainville et la guerre de sept ans. Paris. 1896. [Privately printed.] [3606

A sprightly and, in certain respects, a brilliant work. Its subject is the Canadian experiences of Louis-Antoine de Bougainville, one of Montcalm's staff officers and afterwards the first French circumnavigator. M. Kerallain is one of Bougainville's descendants and his monograph is frankly polemical. It seeks in general to justify the dislike which the French regular troops entertained towards Canada; and in particular to damage the Abbé Casgrain, who as editor and author, M. de Kerallain charges with having garbled the Bougainville family papers. Apart from the controversial points involved, this essay deserves attention for its conspicuous cleverness. It is not easily procurable through book dealers, but will be found in the chief libraries. C. W. C.

Bourgeoys, Marguerite. FAILLON, E. M., *l'Abbé.* Vie de la Sœur — fondatrice de la Congrégation de Notre Dame de Villemarie en Canada, etc. [3607

This forms vols. 1, 2 of the *Mémoires particuliers pour servir à l'histoire de l'Église de l'Amérique du Nord.* Paris. 1853. By the Abbé Faillon. The life of Mlle. Mance (sect. 3657) forms vols. 3, 4. Much valuable historical material is necessarily included in these purely religious biographies, but they are of little interest to the general reader.

Bradley, Arthur G. Fight with France for North America. New York : Dutton. 1901. $5. [3608

This history of the Seven Years' War in America not only holds the reader's interest from the beginning, but the narrative is so consecutive, so little encumbered with unimportant detail, that the whole remains clear and distinct. Mr. Bradley's treatment of all parties, English, French, and even Colonists, is impartial, and he has a knowledge of conditions and localities which saves him happily from those misconceptions and errors irritating to the susceptibilities of those who have inherited the land and its traditions. The work deserves the highest commendation.

—— Vie de la Vénérable 'Sœur Marguerite Bourgeois, dite du Saint Sacrement, etc. A Villemarie : Wm. Gray. 1818. [3609

Attributed to M. Mongolfier, SS., to M. de Ransonnet, SS., and M. Jean-Henri-Auguste Roux, SS. Rare, but superseded by the Abbé Faillon's biography.

Brulé, Stephen. BUTTERFIELD, CONSUL WILLSHIRE. History of Brulé's discoveries and explorations, 1610–1626: being a narrative of the discovery by Stephen Brulé of Lakes Huron, Ontario and Superior; with biographical notice. Cleveland: Helman-Taylor Co. 1898. $2. [3610

The incidents of his life—"matters of common knowledge to readers of Parkman, Winsor, etc.—are the warp and woof of Mr. Butterfield's work. They hardly demand or warrant a two-dollar volume of well-nigh two hundred pages. . . . The contention of Mr. Butterfield is that he has proved what has always been admitted to be possible, indeed probable, that Brulé was in some sense a four-fold Columbus—first to go down the Susquehanna, and first to discover Lakes Ontario, Huron and Superior, and by a sort of anti-climax, first to shoot Lachine rapids. . . . His geographical details are helpful in identifying localities. His keen exposures of many a minor error will be accepted with thanks by a score of victims humbly kissing the rod. . . . But Brulé's champion brings forward no new authorities, no newly discovered fact, to thicken the old proofs that did demonstrate thinly." James D. Butler, *Am. hist. review*, 4: 543.

Cabot. See sect. 800–810, also, Transactions Royal Society; Dawson, Harrisse, O'Brien, Thatcher, sect. 3537, 3546, 3549, 3555. — Le Canada français. — Beaudoin, vol. 1. — Archives, Canada. 1897. Memorandum by S. E. Dawson on Cabot map, with legends in Latin and Spanish, and translations in English. — Consult, also, index to this bibliography. [3611

Carhiel, *Le révérend père* **Etienne de,** *S. J.* Par le R. P. Orhand, S. J. Paris: Retaux Bray. Lille: Ducoulombier. [3612

Important for Huron Missions, Michilimackinac and Detroit, 1668-1726.

Cartier, Jacques.

A complete list of the original editions with explanatory notes may be found in Harrisse's *Notes pour servir etc.* (sect. 3459). See, also, Faribault and Winsor. These early editions are all extremely rare and costly, but new editions have been published in France, and in 1890 Hiram P. Stevens published (Montreal: Drysdale. $3) an essay with a translation of the narrative of the four voyages. See, also, *Transactions* Royal Society of Canada; Decaze, Ganong, Verreau, sect. 3538, 3542, 3556. [3613

Casgrain, H. Raymond, *l'Abbé.* Montcalm et Lévis. Quebec: Demers. 1891. 2v. Tours: Alfred Mame. 1898. Fr. 5.50. [3614

Based largely on the Lévis manuscripts (which the author edited from originals belonging to the Comte de Nicolay), and intended as a supplement or counterblast to Parkman's *Montcalm and Wolfe*. Despite the fact that Abbé Casgrain is deeply versed in the history of French Canada, one misses in this, his principal work, the historical virtues which depend upon viewing the past through a medium of "dry light." In other words, his predilections in favor of the French Canadians are so marked that they bias his attitude in cases of conflict between them and the regular officers who are sent out from the mother country. The work, however, is one of importance. C. W. C.

" The Abbé had the use of much material unknown to Parkman. The peculiar value of his narrative is that it admits us to the inmost details of the French campaign, and some of the verdicts of history regarding the chief actors must be revised. The Abbé is convinced that Lévis, Montcalm's second in command, is the real hero of the war in Canada." University of Toronto, *Review of hist. publications relating to Canada, 1898.*

See, also, sect. 3497.

Champlain, Samuel de. Œuvres de Champlain; publiées sous le patronage de l'Université Laval, par l'Abbé C.-H. Laverdière. Quebec: Desbarats. 1870. 6v. Montreal: Granger Frères. $16.

—— Voyages; ed. C.-H. Laverdière. 2e éd. Quebec. 1870. 2v.

—— Voyages; tr. by Chas. P. Otis [ed.] with memoir by Edmund F. Slafter. Boston: Prince Soc. 1878–82. 3v. [3615

The narratives of Champlain's explorations are a source of the first importance for the early history of Canada, and for the life and manners of the Indians in Canada, New York and New England. He was the first to explore carefully and to describe with accuracy the New England coast as far south as Buzzard's Bay, the upper St. Lawrence, Lake Champlain, the Ottawa, Georgian Bay, the Muskoka Lakes region, Lake Ontario and part of Central New York. The original editions of his voyages are very rare and expensive. Laverdière's collected edition is an accurate reproduction of the early texts. The Prince Society edition of the *Voyages* gives a careful and readable translation of the voyages of 1603, and of the *Voyage* pub. in 1613 and 1619 with full annotations. Mr. Slafter's memoir is extended, and is written with sympathy and admiration. It summarizes the voyages after 1619. Mr. Slafter puts Champlain "at the head of the long list of explorers and navigators, who early visited this part of the continent of North America." E. G. B.

The commission of Geographer which was given Champlain by Henry IV, in 1603, led him to keep full notes of his voyages and travels. These journals, which were published from time to time during his life, are invaluable records of his own experiences, of the fortune which befell his expeditions, and of the early intercourse between French and natives. The dates of their appearance were 1604, 1613, 1619 and 1632. Between 1878–82 the Prince Society published an English translation of the first three voyages by Prof. C. P. Otis. The best French edition of the text is that of the Abbé C.-H. Laverdière. Quebec: Desbarats. 1870. C. W. C.

—— GRAVIER, GABRIEL. Vie de Samuel

Champlain, fondateur de la Nouvelle France (1567–1635). Paris : Maisonneuve. 1900. 20fr. [3616

The latest and most important study on Champlain.

Charlevoix, Pierre François Xavier de. Histoire et description générale de la Nouvelle France. Paris. 1744. 3v.

—— History and general description of New France ; tr. with notes by J. G. Shea. N. Y. 1866–72. 6v.

—— *Same,* new ed. N. Y.: F. P. Harper. 6v. $18. [3617

The author, a Jesuit, reached Canada in 1720 with a special charge to inspect the missions of the country, and was the first who wrote a general history of consequence. His standpoint is naturally that of a churchman and a Jesuit, but Parkman (though often finding him careless) advises students who would regard the Old Régime from the French side to consult his work. He had command of invaluable sources and shows undoubted cleverness. Among his limitations is a prejudice against Montreal which is revealed, among other ways, by his silence concerning Dollard's magnificent exploit at the Long Sault. C. W. C.
" The extent and value of Dr. Shea's work in annotating his translation of this history can only be appreciated by careful study. Through this means the translation is more valuable for many purposes of research than the original work." A. McF. Davis, in *Narrative and critical hist. of Am.*, 5: 63.
The 4to edition of 1744 above described is much more expensive than the 8vo edition of the same year in 6 vols.

Crespel, *le R. P.* **Emmanuel** (*Récollet*). Voiages dans le Canada et son naufrage en revenant en France, mis au jour par le Sr. Louis Crespel son frère à Frankfort sur le Meyn 1742. Reimpression. Quebec: Côté. 1884. $1. [3618

" Pray for those who died in this shipwreck and the book will have been of some effect," said the modest Récollet in reference to his recital of the loss of " La Renommée" on Anticosti in 1736. This pitiful story of suffering and death is included here because it is well to realize that the sea was an ever present danger to be faced by those who would try their fortunes in New France. Many of the sufferers were Canadians, M. de Freneuse the Captain, Jacques Hypolite Le Ber de Senneville, and others. It was translated into English and published by Sampson Low, London, 1797; the original was reproduced by A. Côté et Cie., Quebec, 1884, with a short notice of le Père Crespel. A pendant to this will be found in the *Journal du voyage de M. Saint-Luc de la Corne, dans le navire L'Auguste en l'an 1761*, reprinted by A. Côté et Cie., Quebec, 1863.

DeLingeris' expedition against the Foxes. See Collections State Hist. Doc. Wisconsin. Vol. 10. [3619

Desandrouins, Gabriel, *l'Abbé.* Le maréchal de camp Desandrouins, 1729–1792. Verdun (France) : Renvé-Lallemant. 1887. [3620

A military biography of services in Canada from 1756–1760, in Malta and in America, with the French troops, 1780–1783. The journal is not given in entirety.

D'Iberville. See under Hudson's Bay and North-West (sect. 3843). [3621

Dollier de Casson, François. Histoire du Montréal, 1640–1672; annotated by Jacques Viger and Pierre Margry. Société Historique de Montréal, 1868 ; also published in 3d series Historical documents, Literary and Historical Society, Quebec, 1871. [3622

Dollier de Casson was a gentleman of family and a soldier by profession ; when he became a priest he preserved the traditions of his birth and much of the vivacity of his days in camp and field. He dedicates his history " to the invalids of the Seminary of St. Sulpice," and it surely lightened many a heavy hour with its quaint humor and honest story-telling. The first Curé of Montreal troubles not his head nor his book with policy nor politics of church or state; he has not written history, but he has told his tale well, and one feels throughout that he never loses sight of those " Invalids," for whose pleasure it was chiefly written. It forms the most important document we possess on the beginnings of Montreal.

Donohoe, Thomas. Iroquois and the Jesuits ; the story of the labors of Catholic missionaries among these Indians. Buffalo, N. Y.: Buffalo Catholic Pub. Co. 1895. $1.25. [3623

A survey of Jesuit missions, especially among the Indians of central and western New York, 1635–1709 ; with chapters on the work of other religious orders, subsequent to 1615, among the aborigines from Quebec to Lake Huron. The data were drawn from the *Relations* (before these were made accessible to the English reader by the admirable translation edited by Reuben Gold Thwaites) and other trustworthy sources. Of particular value is the map of Sulpician and Jesuit missions among the Iroquois from 1656 to 1684, as located by Gen. John S. Clark. Narrated from the view-point of a scholarly Catholic, who glories in the labors, often seemingly barren, of the apostles of his faith ; but devout ardor has not impaired the accuracy of the chronicle. F. H. S.

Doughty, Arthur George. The siege of Quebec and the battle of the Plains of Abraham by — in collaboration with George W. Parmelee. Quebec : Dussault & Proulx. 1901. 6v. $40. [3623 a

In the *Transactions* of the Royal Society of Canada for 1899 will be found a paper on " The probable site of the battle of the Plains of Abraham," by Arthur G. Doughty (sect. 3541). This, in conjunction with the rumored sale of property popularly accepted as the battlefield, aroused much discussion, criticism, and, finally, sufficient enthusiasm to result in the purchase of the property in question by the Government, for its preservation as a public park. Mr. Doughty's paper has resulted in the production of this exhaustive work, in collaboration with Mr. Parmelee. The Abbé Laverdière's edition of Champlain printed by George E. Desbarats, who was an enthusiast in his art (Quebec, 1870), is, perhaps, finer as regards typography, but no other Canadian publication can compare with this, especially in the rarity of the plans and the beauty of the prints, the greater number of which are unknown even to the local antiquarian. The edition is limited, and only a certain number of copies thereof will be issued to the public.

As the work is at present (Nov. 1901) in press no just appreciation can be given of the text, but through the courtesy of Mr. Doughty we are furnished with the following information of its scope : — V. 1. Life of Wolfe; Life of Montcalm. — V. 2. Siege of Quebec, June–Sept., 1759. — V. 3. Battle of the Plains, etc. — V. 4. Letters of Bougainville ; Journal of Foligné ; Journal of Joannes ; Extracts of despatches of Russian Ambassadors in London and Paris to Catherine II. ; Other letters and journals. — V. 5. Journals of Moncrief, of Sergeant-Major Hopson, of Q. M. Sergeant Johnson, of Townsend, of an Aide-de-Camp ; A MS. relation of the siege ; The Galway papers ; Letters of various English officers and others. — V. 6. Letters of Wolfe, Pitt, Saunders, and others; Secret instructions of the King ; Bibliography of siege ; Index.

The portraits hitherto unpublished include those of Wolfe, Montcalm, M. de Bougainville, Miss Lowther and others. Hitherto unpublished plans and deeds, Wolfe's will, articles of capitulation and the original deed of the Plains, form interesting features of the work.

Druillettes, Gabriel. Journal of his embassy from Canada to New England in 1650. See New-York Historical Society, sect. 353.

[3624

Faillon, Etienne Marcel, *l'Abbé.* Histoire de la colonie française en Canada. Villemarie. 1865–6. 3v. Montreal: Granger Frères. $10.   [3625

The author was a member of the Sulpician order which has, ever since 1657, been closely identified with Montreal, and he devotes his special attention to the origin and early years of that city. Although three quartos were published, the narrative does not descend below 1675. Faillon's merits are an untiring zeal for his subject, and a rare command of the literature relating to it. His shortcomings as a historian spring from excessive devotion to his society, and from lack of historical perspective. He is a fine type of the antiquary. Following the Sulpician custom, his name does not appear on the title-page.

C. W. C.

The Abbé Faillon collected an immense amount of material for this history which still remains unedited in the library of the Seminary of St. Sulpice, Montreal. His skill in reviving the dead bones of "authentic" documents is marvellous. He was born in Tarascon in 1799, and his earlier studies were pursued in Avignon ; when he decided to enter the Church he pursued his education at Aix and afterwards at Paris, entering St. Sulpice about 1820. He came to Canada in 1849 when he had already gained standing as an author, his principal work being a life of M. Olier,

founder of St. Sulpice, and an edition of his works in 10 volumes. He paid three different visits to America, and while there wrote or edited : Vie de Mlle. Bourgeois. 2v. — Vie de Mlle. Mance. 2v. — Vie de Mme. d'Youville. — Vie de Mlle. LeBer. — Histoire de la colonie française, 3v. (1865-6), his most important work for Canada. — Nouvelle histoire de M. Olier, 3v. Also other works of a purely ecclesiastical interest. M. Desmazures, his biographer (M. Faillon, sa vie et ses œuvres. Montreal. 1882), notices unpublished material for a history of the colonies of Montreal. He finished a life of extraordinary activity in 1870, and his last words to a fellow priest were, " I am seventy-one and now the night comes."

Franquet, *Le Sieur.* Voyages et mémoires sur le Canada en 1752, publiés par l'Institut Canadien de Québec. Québec. 1889.   [3626

Franquet was an engineer, and in addition to the strictly professional part of his memoir he gives entertaining glimpses of the fashionable Canadian society before the Conquest ; the work is used effectively by Parkman.

Frontenac, Louis de Buade, *comte* de. Lo-RIN, HENRI. Le comte de Frontenac. Paris: Colin. 1895. 10 fr.   [3627

Frontenac, the ablest of the rulers of New France, was governor from 1672 to 1682, and from 1689 to his death in 1698. M. Lorin, who is a Frenchman, has studied exhaustively the French archives, and has, besides, travelled in Canada. His work is a history of the period to which it relates, rather than a biography of Frontenac. The rivalries of the French and English for supremacy in North America occupy an important place. These, and the disputes between the ecclesiastical and civil authorities, are treated impartially. There are a few minor errors. The style, while not picturesque, is lucid, and the matter well arranged. It is the most adequate study of the period yet made.

G. M. W.

Gagnon, Ernest. Le fort et le château de St. Louis (Quebec). Quebec: Brosseau. 1893.

[3628

An antiquarian and historic study covering both régimes, and of much wider scope than its title would indicate.

Gardner, Richard. Memoirs of the siege of Quebec, and of the retreat of Monsieur DeBoulamarque from Carillon to the Isle aux Noix in Lake Champlain ; from the journal of a French officer, on board the Chezine frigate, taken by His Majesty's ship the Ripon : compared with the accounts transmitted home by Major-General Wolfe and Admiral Saunders ; with occasional remarks. London : Dodsley. 1762.   [3629

Garneau. See under Comprehensive Histories, sect. 3587.   [3630

Girouard, Désiré. Lake St. Louis old and new, and Cavalier de La Salle. Montreal: Poirier, Bessette & Co. 1893. $5.   [3631

Of value for local detail and the establishment of historic sites.

Hart, Gerald E. Fall of New France, 1755–60. Montreal: Drysdale. Pap. $3. N. Y.: Putnam. 1888. [3632

This is the work of a man who, though greatly interested in his subject, was unable to devote the time necessary for original research or even for a careful examination of printed authorities — and in consequence it is unreliable. The prints are excellent and many of them rare.

Hennepin, *R. P.* Louis. Déscription de la Louisiane nouvellement découverte au sudouest de la Nouvelle France, avec carte du pays, les mœurs et la manière de vivre des sauvages. Paris. 1683.

—— Nouvelle découverte d'un très grand pays, situé dans l'Amérique, entre le Nouveau Mexique et la mer glaciale, etc. Utrecht. 1697.

—— Nouveau voyage dans un pays plus grand que l'Europe, etc. Utrecht. 1698. [3633

This wonderful Récollet rivalled Lahontan in the popularity of his works, and more than outdid him in exaggeration and dishonesty. He boldly claimed the discovery of the Mississippi to its mouth against La Salle ; to support which assertion he stole facts from Father Membré's journey with La Salle included in Le Clerc's *Établissement de la foi.* Of this theft Parkman says, " the records of literary piracy may be searched in vain for an act of depredation more recklessly impudent " (La Salle, p. 247). He is grossly ungrateful to Dulhut, who rescued him from captivity and brought him safely back to friends by the generous abandonment of an expedition on which he had staked much. He is utterly unreliable in regard to his personal narrative, and yet his works are of great importance, as he was a keen observer with a nice humor for what is picturesque and important. His works were written in French and translated into Italian, Dutch, German, English and Spanish; the different editions cover a period from 1683 to 1880 and their end is not yet. They are in three parts: " Déscription de la Louisiane," " Nouvelle découverte d'un très grand pays," and "Nouveau voyage d'un pays plus grand que l'Europe."

Jefferys, Thomas. Natural and civil history of the French dominions in North and South America, etc. London: Jefferys. 1760. [3634

This compilation was made during the war which resulted in the destruction of the French power in North America. Jefferys was a map-maker, and his plans of Quebec, Montreal, Louisbourg, New Orleans, etc. were at the time especially significant and are still valuable. The first part of the work deals with Canada and Louisiana, and contains much information, not always critical, about the Indians, the natural features and the history of the regions concerned. This is " collected from the best authorities " who are not named. There are some original letters from Wolfe and other contemporaries. The second part deals, in a similar manner, chiefly with the French West Indies.   G. M. W.

Jesuit Relations, and allied documents, 1610–1791: the original French, Latin, and Italian texts, with English translations and notes ; ed. by Reuben Gold Thwaites. Cleveland: Burrows Bros. 1896–1901. 73v. Net $3.50 ea. [3635

" The sources of information concerning the early Jesuits of New France are very copious. During a period of forty years the Superior of the mission sent, every summer, long and detailed reports embodying or accompanied by the reports of his subordinates to the Provincial of the Order at Paris, where they were annually published in duodecimo volumes, forming the remarkable series known as the Jesuit *Relations.* Though the productions of men of scholastic training, they are simple and often crude in style, as might be expected of narratives hastily written in Indian lodges or rude mission-houses in the forest, amid annoyances and interruptions of all kinds. In respect to the value of their contents, they are exceedingly unequal. Modest records of marvellous adventures and sacrifices, and vivid pictures of forest-life, alternate with prolix and monotonous details of the conversion of individual savages, and the praiseworthy deportment of some exemplary neophyte. With regard to the condition and character of the primitive inhabitants of North America, it is impossible to exaggerate their value as an authority. I should add, that the closest examination has left me no doubt that these missionaries wrote in perfect good faith, and that the *Relations* hold a high place as authentic and trustworthy historical documents. They are very scarce, and no complete collection of them exists in America. The entire series was, however, republished, in 1858, by the Canadian government, in three large octavo volumes." Francis Parkman, *Jesuits in North America, preface.*

Little need be said concerning former efforts to bring together the Jesuit documents, since they have been superseded, for practical working purposes, by Mr. Thwaites's edition. Much new material is included. The original text — whether Latin, French or Italian — is given on the left-hand, and its translation on the right-hand, page. In addition to notes a bibliographical apparatus is furnished. As typography and editing are alike excellent, a noble series is at last rendered accessible in worthy form.

C. W. C.

For an extended review by Prof. C. W. Colby, see *Am. historical review,* 7: 1.

Johnstone, James, *Chevalier* de. Memoirs of the Rebellion of 1745 and 1746, translated from a French MS. Third edition. London: Longmans. 1822.

—— Journal in Louisbourg, 1750–58. See Vol. 3, p. 465, of Collection des documents relatifs à la Nouvelle France (sect. 3509).

—— Journal of occurrences, Quebec, 1759, 1760, ibid. Vol. 4, pp. 231 et seq. and pp. 245 et seq.

—— A Dialogue in Hades between Wolfe and Montcalm. The French text may be found in *Le Marquis de Montcalm*, par R. P. Félix Martin, S. J., *Un vieux missionaire*, p. 237 (sect. 3663), and the English text in the *Historical documents* of the Literary and Historical Soc., Quebec, second series (The Louisbourg Journal, 1750–58 and the Quebec Journal for 1760 are also included in this series).

—— Memoirs. Translated from the original French MS. of the Chevalier by Charles Winchester, advocate. Aberdeen, 1870–71. 3v. [3636

No more interesting or instructive memoirs on the period from 1750 to 1760 in Canada exist than these of the Chevalier Johnstone, one of the many Jacobite officers in the service of France. They were written long after the events, and as the Chevalier had a lively imagination and is always inclined to exaggerate his own importance, it is well to verify statements which conduce to this end. But this very tendency to romance has its value; for example, no part of these memoirs is so suggestive as the *Dialogue in Hades between Wolfe and Montcalm*, no picture so real as that walk and conversation of Montcalm, Pouliariez, and Johnstone, under the midnight stars at Beauport until the dawn of the fatal thirteenth of September. It is probable that there was another memoir from the time of his appointment as aide-de-camp to Lévis in the summer of 1759 until the battle of the Plains. In order to form some estimate of Johnstone's character, his memoir for 1745-6 should be read as well as those on Canada; throughout we feel the pride, the constant humiliation and the consciousness of superiority of the unfortunate Jacobite adventurer forced by stern poverty into a struggle with the natural claimants for any employment which would not derogate from his gentility. The edition of 1870 is badly translated.

Kalm, Peter. Voyages en Amérique; traduit par L. W. Marchand. Mémoires de la Société Historique de Montréal. Nos. 7 and 8. Montreal: Berthiaume. 1880. [3637

The translator gives but an analysis of the first and second volumes, the third, which is of special importance to Canada, is given in full. This painstaking journal of the Swedish naturalist is of special value, as we have few works on Canada of the date of his journey, 1748-9. A short, but interesting note with details of the cost of Kalm's entertainment at Quebec may be found in a pamphlet by J. Edmond Roy, *Voyage de Kalm au Canada* (Lévis: Revue du Notariat. 1900, 25c.).

Kip, William Ingraham. Early Jesuit missions in North America; comp. and tr. from the letters of the French Jesuits. N. Y.: Wiley. 1846. Albany: Munsell. 1873. [3638

Mr. Kip has attempted to make literal translations of letters from the Jesuits in our country, contained in *Lettres édifiantes et curieuses, écrites des missions étrangères*.

"To avoid repetition, he has made certain abridgments. Some of the material thus left out has value to the student of the early history of Illinois." A. McF. Davis, in *Narrative and critical hist. of Am.*, 5: 68.

Kirke, Henry. The first English conquest of Canada; with some account of the earliest settlements in Nova Scotia and Newfoundland. London: Bemrose. 1871. [3639

" Deals mainly with the lives of Sir David Kirke and his brothers, and its chief value is biographical; but it comprises some hitherto unpublished documents from the Record Office, and throws considerable light on obscure portions of the early history of Canada and Acadia." Charles C. Smith, in *Narrative and critical hist. of Am.*, 4: 158.

Knox, John. Historical journal of the campaigns in North America, for the years 1757–58–59 and 60, containing the most remarkable occurrences of that period; particularly two sieges of Quebec, under the orders of the Admirals, and General Officers; description of the countries where the author has served, with their forts and garrisons, their climate, soil, and a regular diary of the weather; also several manifestos, a mandate of the Bishop of Canada, and the French order and dispositions for the defence of that colony. London. 1769. 2v. [3640

This exceedingly rare and valuable journal includes the whole campaign, and is rich not only in statistics but in personal detail and graphic incidents. It is indispensable for any serious study of the struggle for the possession of Canada.

Lafiteau, Le R. P., Jean François, S. J. Mœurs des sauvages américains comparées aux mœurs des premiers temps. Paris. 1724. 2v. [3641

Charlevoix and Parkman hold him as a high authority, especially on the Iroquois.

La Hontan, *Baron* de. Nouveaux voyages dans l'Amérique septentrionale, qui contiennent une relation des différens peuples qui y habitent. La Haye. 1703. 2v.

—— New voyages to North-America, containing an account of the several nations of that vast continent. London. 1703. 2v. 2nd ed. London: Osborn. 1735. 2v. [3642

When Louis Armand de Lom d'Arce, Baron de Lahontan et d' Erlèche was wintering at Michilimackinac in 1688, he passed many a long winter's evening listening to the interminable stories of the coureurs de bois, and there probably heard the foundation of his fatal Rivière longue. When he returned to Europe without money, and without credit at Court, he took refuge in Holland, and in 1703 published at Amsterdam his travels in which he announced his discovery of this wonderful river, — "a pure fiction, as fabulous as the Isle of Bataria," says Charlevoix a few years later.

His book had an immense vogue, rivalled only by that of Hennepin, but his reputation was so damaged by this futile dishonesty that he has long been refused the credit which his otherwise remarkable work deserves. It will not serve as a text-book nor a historic guide, but is of much value as a clear and fearless picture of Canada, and the Canadians of his day. His book has that charm which brings one back to it again and again, he has a light caustic humor, one feels the life of the man, and despite his faults he claims a sympathy withheld from many a worthier writer. For spirit and brightness there is nothing in Canadian literature which approaches it, save some of the earlier letters of Lamothe Cadillac. As to his value from a historic standpoint, Parkman sums it up thus: — " La Hontan attempted to impose on his readers a marvellous story of pretended discoveries beyond the Mississippi; and his ill-repute in the matter of veracity is due chiefly to this fabrication. On the other hand, his account of what he saw in the colony is commonly in accord with the best contemporary evidence " [Frontenac, p. 110, note]. The first volume consists of familiar letters, the second of a more serious memoir, and the third of descriptions of Indian life and customs and speculations as to their origin. The editions of 1703-4 are the best. See an important monograph on La Hontan by Joseph Edmond Roy. Trans. Royal Society, Vol. 12, Old Series (sect. 3553).

La Potherie, Claude-Charles LeRoy de, *and* **Bacqueville de la Potherie.** Histoire de l'Amérique septentrionale, etc. Paris. 1722. 4v. [3643

A narrative rather than a history, contains, in vol. 1, a detailed history of D'Iberville's expedition against Hudson's Bay in 1687. An exhaustive monograph on La Potherie by Joseph Edmond Roy is published in Trans. Royal Society; see sect. 3553.

LaSalle, René Robert Cavalier, *Sieur* **de.** We have no personal memoir of LaSalle, but fortunately there exist many contemporary records. The first three volumes of Margry (*Découvertes et établissements des français*, sect. 3501) contain the most valuable collection of documents, letters, and memoirs of LaSalle, Tonti, Joutel, and others. [3644

— HARRISSE, H. Notes pour servir à l'histoire de la Nouvelle France, sect. 3453. [3644 a

— GRAVIER, GABRIEL. Découvertes et établissements de Cavalier de la Salle, etc. Paris. 1870. 15 fr. [3644 b

— JOUTEL. Journal historique du dernier voyage que feu M. de LaSalle fit dans le Golfe de Mexique etc. Paris. 1713. [3645

The record of this faithful and honest friend of the great explorer is the most valuable contemporary record.

— PARKMAN, FRANCIS. LaSalle and the discovery of the great West. Sect. 3672. [3645 a

— TONTI, HENRI DE. Derniers découvertes dans l'Amérique septentrionale de M. de la Salle, etc. Paris. 1697. —— Relation de la Louisiane. Amsterdam. 1720. [3646

Although grave doubts exist as to the alleged authorship of this *Relation* (see Charlevoix, vol. 6, p. 413, and Harrisse, *Notes pour servir*, pp. 169–172), it is important, well-written, and gives many details not mentioned elsewhere.

Laval. LA TOUR, BERTRAND, *l'Abbé* DE. Mémoire sur la vie de M. de Laval, premier évêque de Quebec. Cologne: Motiens. 1761. 2v.

— LANGEVIN, EDMOND, *l'Abbé.* 1674–1874. Deuxième centenaire: notice bibliographique. Montreal. 1874. [3647

Of value on account of the documents reproduced.

—— Vie de Mgr. de Laval, premier évêque de Québec, et apôtre du Canada. Québec. 1890. 2v. [3648

A careful and important study of historic as well as biographical interest.

Le Ber, Jeanne. FAILLON, *l'Abbé.* L'héroine chrétienne du Canada ou Vie de Mlle. Le Ber. Villemarie. 1860. [3649

The *Notice sur la famille Le Ber*, pp. 301–383, allied to the LeMoyne family is important for the early history of Montreal.

LeBlond de Brumath, A. Histoire populaire de Montréal, depuis son origine jusqu' à nos jours. Montréal: Granger Frères. 1890. $1. [3650

A satisfactory compilation, well arranged.

Le Clercq, Chrétien. First establishment of the faith in New France; tr. with notes by John Gilmary Shea. N. Y.: Translator. 1881. 2v. [3651

The original work, also in 2 vols., was published at Paris in 1691, and is now rare. This is its first appearance in English, the translator having added numerous notes and a lucid biographical sketch of the author. The Recollets, a now extinct branch of the Franciscans, were the first missionaries in New France, being soon overshadowed by the more vigorous Jesuit order. The Jesuits have left behind a large body of printed and MS. material; but the literary remains of the Franciscans are relatively slight, consisting in the main of Sagard's *Histoire du Canada* and *Pays des Hurons*, Hennepin's *Description of Louisiana*, and this work of Le Clercq. Sagard is useful for studying in detail the earliest North American missions of the Recollets; Le Clercq, less garrulous, covers the entire range of their annals, but is strongest in the later years. While all of the work is ostensibly from Le Clercq's pen, it is now generally agreed that his MS. forms but a part: his simple annals having been edited by others, probably Frontenac among them, and made the medium for a violent attack on the Jesuits, whose published *Relations* are treated as of doubtful authenticity. Mr. Shea has carefully traced the extent and animus of these emendations; his notes and biographical sketches have greatly increased the value of the work to historical students.

　　　　　　　　　　　　　　　　　R. G. T.

Le Gardeur de St. Pierre, Jacques Repentigny. Journal of expedition of 1750–2. [3652

See Archives for year 1886 (sect. 3468).

Lemoine, Sir James Macpherson. Maple leaves — 4 series.

—— Quebec past and present. Quebec: Coté. 1876.

—— Picturesque Quebec. Montreal: Dawson. 1882. [3653

Sir James has been an indefatigable worker and has preserved much of value. His *Maple leaves* are now rare and out of print. His *Quebec past and present* and *Picturesque Quebec* form an entertaining if rather loosely woven account of Quebec's history from the foundation of the settlement in 1608 to 1876. It is a narrative of external events, not a municipal study with which one is familiar in the case of leading European towns. Such readers as are unable to approach the original French authorities will find this the best general story of the place which has appeared in English.　　　　　　　　　　　　　C. W. C.

Separate studies on historical subjects may be found in the *Transactions* of the Royal Society of Canada, sect. 3531 et seq.

Lucas, Fred W. Appendiculæ historicæ: or, Shreds of history hung on a horn. London: Henry Stevens & Son. 1891. [3654

Despite the somewhat fanciful title suggested by a map of the route between New York and Montreal carved on a powder horn (c. 1760), this work contains a concise view of the war 1755–1760, a good bibliography and cartography, with much important topographical detail. The varying names of the posts, forts, rivers are given in detail.

Maisonneuve, Paul de Chomedey, *Sieur* **de.** ROUSSEAU, P. Histoire de la vie de — fondateur et premier gouverneur de Villemarie, 1640–1676. Montreal: Cadieux & Derome. 1885. [3655

M. Rousseau has carefully compiled the few existing traces of Maisonneuve's personal life, but has written rather a history of Montreal than a biography. He treats his subject from the standpoint of a priest of St. Sulpice.

Malartic, Anne Joseph Hippolyte Marrès, *Comte* **de.** Journal des compagnes au Canada de 1755 à 1760; pub. par le Comte Gabriel de Maurès de Malartic et par Paul Gaffarel. Paris: Plon. 1890. 8fr. [3656

Although this is the dryest of military journals, it is of importance for the period; Malartic records his daily work and observations and throws light on the

important characters, perhaps all the more valuable that it is done in his business-like matter-of-fact manner, without any attempt at fine writing. The maps are excellent.

Mance, Jeanne. FAILLON, *l'Abbé*. La vie de Mademoiselle Mance et histoire de l'Hôtel-Dieu de Villemarie en Canada. Paris: 1854. 2v. [3657

Important for the early history of Montreal.

Marie de l'Incarnation. Lettres de la vénérable mère Marie de l'Incarnation première supérieure des Ursulines de la Nouvelle France. Paris. 1681. [3657 a

The personal portion of these letters of Marie Guyard gives a curious and ingenuous relation of the life and thoughts of the mystic of her day. The second part contains the historical letters beginning with her departure for Canada with Madame de la Peltrie in 1639. That these letters contain much that is miraculous goes without saying; the author was at the head of a religious foundation surrounded by devoted women in a colony which was held to be under the direct protection of the Almighty, where trial and danger were the lot of all and the belief in a personal and special Providence universal. Due allowance being made for this, the letters are not only of interest but of the utmost importance as the daily record of a woman of strong intelligence and good position during the most critical period in the life of the struggling colony. Marie Guyard was born in Tours, 1599, married M. Martin, entered her convent life, a widow, in 1631, died at Quebec, 1672.

For biography see: — La vie de la vénérable mère Marie de l'Incarnation. (Paris. 1677.) This is by her son Dom Claude Martin. — Vie (Paris. 1724) by Charlevoix. — Life by a religious of the Ursuline Community, Blackrock, Cork (c. 1880). — Vie by the Abbé H. R. Casgrain. See vol. III of his collected works. Montreal: C. O. Beauchemin & Fils. 1886. 4v. $6.

Martin, Horace T. Castorologia, history of the Canadian beaver. See under Hudson's Bay (sect. 3853). [3658

Mason, Edward G. Chapters from Illinois history. Chicago: H. S. Stone. 1900. $2.50. [3659

These essays by a well-known lawyer of Chicago were, with some exceptions, read or printed during the author's lifetime, and have since then been collected in this volume. The first and largest section of the book is entitled "The land of the Illinois." The four chapters which are ranged under this heading — "Discovery," "Exploration," "Occupation," and "Settlement" — really belong to the literature of Canadian history, inasmuch as they centre about the explorers of New France from Nicolet to LaSalle. Mr. Mason had read widely and wrote well. When describing the career of LaSalle, his chief character, it is not too much to say that his views were coloured by Margry, but in his own right he had the merits of a good local historian.　　　　　　　　C. W. C.

Miles, Henry H. History of Canada under French régime, 1535-1763. Montreal: Dawson Brothers. 1881. $3. [3660

A book which represents a creditable amount of research, but is deficient in breadth of historical outlook, and follows too slavishly the chronological sequence of events. Though written without animation and not very suggestive, it forms a convenient manual of reference for the period which it covers.
C. W. C.

Montcalm de Saint-Veran, Louis Joseph, *Marquis* de. GUÉNIN, EUGÈNE. Montcalm; préface de Gabriel Bonvalot. (Les hommes d'action.) Paris: Challamel. 1898. 75 centimes. [3661

"M. Guénin's work is carefully done. He gives no references to authorities, but it is not apparent that he has done more than consult the more obvious ones." University of Toronto, *Review of hist. publications relating to Canada, 1899.*

— LE MOINE, J. M., *comp.* La mémoire de Montcalm vengée, ou Le massacre au Fort George; documents historiques. Quebec. 1864. [3662

"The details of this frightful massacre by the Indians under Montcalm are given by an eye-witness, and go far to prove him innocent of conniving at it. The principal portion of this defense is a journal of the events of the siege, surrender, and massacre, written by a French missionary." T. W. Field, *Indian bibliography*, p. 232.

— MARTIN, FÉLIX, *S. J.* Le marquis de Montcalm et les dernières années de la colonie française au Canada, 1756-60. 4e éd. Paris: Tequi. 1898. 2fr. Granger Frères: Montreal. 75c. [3663

This work first appeared anonymously in 1867 as by "an Old Missionary," and under the title *De Montcalm en Canada.* It has gone through several editions. The author, a Jesuit priest, long resident in Canada, used the chief original authorities accessible in his day. His work is impartial and accurate. Later works have in some degree superseded it; but it is still of value. The tone is critical and the style good.
G. M. W.

— BONNECHOSE, CHARLES DE. Montcalm et le Canada français. Paris: Hachette. 1877. 85 centimes. [3664

This little book is based upon printed, and in large part secondary, material. The author, a Frenchman, has keen sympathy for the French in conquered Canada, but writes impartially. He gives a vivid outline of the events of the Seven Years' War in Canada.
G. M. W.

See Lévis documents, for letters and journals of Montcalm (sect. 3497). [3665

Montreal. For local histories, guides, etc., see under English Régime. [3666

Montreal, Société de Notre-Dame de. Les véritables motifs pour la conversion des sauvages de la Nouvelle France. [3667

Printed originally in Paris, 1643, republished by the Société Historique de Montréal in 1880 with Preface and Notes by the Abbé Verreau. Important for the local historian.

Myrand, Ernest. Une fête de Noël sous Jacques Cartier. 2me éd. Quebec: Demers & Frère. 1890. [3668

M. Myrand has chosen to present his work under the guise of a phantasy, but it is none the less of value to the serious reader.

—— Sir William Phipps devant Québec. Quebec: Demers & Frère. 1893. $1. [3669

A careful study of this episode with valuable personal and topographical detail.

Nicolet, Jean. History of the discovery of the North-West by — in 1634 with a sketch of his life by C. W. Butterfield. Cincinnati: R. Clarke & Co. 1881. $1. [3670

See, also, State Hist. Society of Wisconsin. Collections, v. 10, Jean Nicolet, by Garneau and Ferland. — V. 11. Jean Nicolet, 1618-1642, by Henri Jouan. — Bibliography of Nicolet, by C. W. Butterfield.

Olier, Jean-Jacques. FAILLON, *l'Abbé.* Vie de M. Olier, fondateur du Séminaire de Saint-Sulpice. 4me éd. Paris. 1873. 3v. [3671

An important work for the beginnings of Montreal, civil and ecclesiastical.

Parkman, Francis. Works. Boston: Little, Brown & Co. 1898. Popular ed. 12v. $1.50 ea. New library ed. With portraits of Parkman, 24 plates from historical portraits, original drawings and paintings. 12v. $2 ea. [3672

The "new library edition" is the latest and best. The volumes should be read in the following order: —Pioneers of France in the new world: —Jesuits in North America: —LaSalle and the history of the great West: —The old régime in Canada: —Frontenac: —A half century of conflict: —Montcalm and Wolfe:—The conspiracy of Pontiac. (The Oregon trail; the twelfth volume, forms no part of the Canadian series.) Although these volumes form a fairly connected narrative of the French Régime in Canada, it must be borne in mind that they were written as separate studies, and have all the merits and shortcomings of historical work in such form. There is greater detail and development of incident than could have found place in a longer narrative; the writer was freer from conventional restraints, and was enabled to relieve and lighten his work with description unsuited to a more pretentious history; on the other hand there is the repetition unavoidable with the introduction of each new subject, which, though admirably managed, would not be necessary in a history planned for continuous writing; again, the *Half century of conflict*, the link necessary to bind together Frontenac and Montcalm, is the least interesting of the series. But these objections once stated, no serious disparagement can be made of Mr. Parkman's work.

No man ever came to his calling more perfectly equipped. He knew the Indian at first hand, he had made a personal study of his ground, his literary acquaintance included the best men on his subject, his means were sufficient to enable him to pay for research and command rarities in print and manuscript, his judgment was rarely at fault, difficult as were many of the cases he passed upon in the course of his studies. The one thing he lacked for his undertaking was health : this failed him at the very beginning, but he was wise in his economy of what was left him ; he laid aside work and turned gardener, cultivating his roses for many years at Jamaica Plain. When he worked he did so with a full regard of what was before him, rising above pain and serious physical disability, and, when he put his pen away, his lifework was accomplished. He threw open to the world the doors of a storehouse of unexpected romance ; he delighted the French-Canadian with his brilliant studies of a history but little known, and did much to enlighten the mind and clear away the prejudice of Canadians of English blood. He was in no sense a partisan ; no man ever wrote with a greater desire to deal out justice with an even hand. The story of French Canada will never have a more favorable telling by an outsider, for, apart from his command of the subject, Mr. Parkman's sympathies were rather with the sentiment of "Church and King" than of "Liberty, Equality, Fraternity." No one who has not prosecuted some original research on the same lines can have an idea of the extreme care with which he worked, or of the almost petty detail which he was at pains to master, not to use necessarily, but simply to inform himself thoroughly of the circumstance or the man. The ordinary reader sees nothing of this as he is carried along by the flow of the narrative; but it is there, underneath, an honest, firm foundation which will enable his work to stand for all time, complete, in the fashion in which it was originally planned.

— FARNHAM, CHARLES HAIGHT. Life of Francis Parkman. Boston: Little, Brown & Co. 1900. Toronto: Morang. 1900. $2.   [3673

Perrot, Nicolas. Mémoire sur les mœurs, coustumes et religion des sauvages de l'Amérique septentrionale. Publié pour la première fois par le R. P. J. Tailhan, S. J. Leipzig et Paris. 1864.   [3674

This manuscript, well known to Charlevoix and other early historians, is of great importance as it throws much light on Indian trade, the coureurs de bois, etc. Perrot was a fur trader, interpreter, and guide in the West for many years, but had his headquarters in Montreal and Three Rivers. See, also, a pamphlet by Gardner P. Stickney, published by the Parkman Club, Milwaukee, 1895, for personal detail.

Radisson, Pierre Esprit, *and* Médard Chouart des Groseilliers. See sect. 3860, 3540, and Collections State Hist. Soc. of Wisconsin. Vol. 11.   [3675

Reveillaud, Eugène. Histoire du Canada et des Canadiens français. Paris: Grassart. 1884. fr. 7.50.   [3676

The author, a Frenchman, has consulted a few documentary and the chief secondary sources and has apparently also visited Canada. His view is confined to the French race in Canada and chiefly to what is now the Province of Quebec. Unlike most of those who have written in French about Canada he is anti-clerical. There are many small errors, but the book is carefully written, cosmopolitan in tone and moderate. The author hopes to see a French republic established in North America.   G. M. W.

Rochemonteix, Le P. Camille de, *S. J.* Les Jésuites et la Nouvelle-France au XVIIe siècle, d'après beaucoup de documents inédits. Paris. 1895. 3v. 22.50fr.   [3677

An elaborate and spirited defence of the Jesuit missionaries. To say that it is written in justification of the society to which the author belongs is not to imply that it shows unfairness in the use of materials. Father de Rochemonteix is a powerful antagonist because he has mastered the subject and employs only such arguments as are warranted by a legitimate use of historical evidence. The enemies of the Jesuits whom he seeks to refute are partly authors of the seventeenth century, like Arnauld, Le Clercq, and Le Hontan, and partly moderns like Faillon and Sulte. As compared with other historians, Father de Rochemonteix has had the advantage of being able to consult sources which the Society of Jesus has not yet thrown open to the public. His discussion of the causes which account for the sudden discontinuance of the *Relations* is an example of his persuasive, and often convincing, style. In brief the work is indispensable.   C. W. C.

Roy, J. Edmond. Histoire de la seigneurie de Lauzon. Levis, Quebec: Mercier & Cie. 1896. 5v. $3.   [3678

This is a detailed study of a district in Canada under the feudalism established by France in the New World. The author has used copious MS. material preserved locally. Much of the work is not of general interest. It is, however, valuable as a study of a community in America under feudal tenure. Some side-lights are thrown on Wolfe's campaign against Quebec in 1759. The style is clear.   G. M. W.

M. Roy's training as a notary, and his constant historical investigations, have resulted in a rare appreciation of the value and application of official documents; in consequence his study of Lauzon is by far the most important local history yet published in Quebec and may be relied on as authoritative. The third volume carries the history up to 1812, the fourth volume (1812–1845) will be published in May or June, 1902, and will be followed by a fifth bringing the story down to date.

—— Lahontan (in Royal Soc. Trans., v. 12, O. S.). See sect. 3553.   [3679

—— La Potherie (in Royal Soc. Trans., v. 3 N. S.). See sect. 3553.   [3680

Sagard-Theodat, Gabriel. Histoire du

Canada. Paris. 1636. Nouvelle éd. Paris: Tross. 1865–6. 4v. [3681

Largely concerned with missionary attempts. Sagard belonged to the Récollets, a reformed branch of the Franciscans, who preceded the Jesuits in the Huron country. Historically his report derives its chief consequence from the copious details of Indian manners, beliefs and language which it furnishes. Copies of the first edition are not easily secured outside the leading libraries, but the Tross reprint (Paris. 1865) can still be found. Sagard should be read in conjunction with the more famous Jesuit *Relations.* C. W. C.

St. Luc de la Corne. Journal du voyage de M. St. Luc de La Corne, dans le navire l'Auguste, en 1761; avec le détail des circonstances de son naufrage, des routes difficiles qu'il a tennues pour se rendre en sa patrie (Canada) et des peines et traverses qu'il a essuyées dans cette catastrophe affligeante. Montreal: F. Mesplet. 1778. Reprinted. Quebec: Côté. 1863. [3682

This little pamphlet tells a story of shipwreck equalled only in its tragedy by that of the Père Crespel. The passengers were chiefly French and Canadian officers and troops returning to France after the fall of Canada.

St. Vallier, *Mgr.* **de.** St. Félix, *Sœur* (*née* O'Reilly). Mgr. de St. Vallier et l'Hôpital Général de Québec. Quebec: Darveau. 1882. [3683

There is much of historical interest in this somewhat formidable volume. Admiral Walker's expedition, Famine of 1743, War of 1758–60, Invasion of 1775, etc.

Sheldon, Electra M. Early history of Michigan from the first settlement to 1815. N. Y. and Chicago: A. S. Barnes & Co. 1856. [3683 a

This well-written local history contains the best material for the character of Lamothe-Cadillac, which the student should supplement by Margry, vols. V and VI. Mrs. Sheldon had an excellent choice of documents, which are adequately translated.

Stevenson, James. Currency; with reference to card money in Canada during the French régime. [3684

As this article includes the settlement between the French and British governments, for note and subsequent articles see under Stevenson in English Régime, sect. 3775–3777.

Sulte, Benjamin. Histoire des Canadiens-français, 1608–1880. Montreal: Wilson. 1882–4. 8v. Montreal: Granger Frères. 40 parts, paper. $10. 4v., cl. $12. [3685

This history is essentially "popular," and contains a suggestion of journalistic methods, nevertheless it

has distinct merit. Among its useful features may be mentioned such a width of scope as includes social institutions and usage. Concerning the copious illustrations, it may be said that while the plates are not very well done, the choice of subjects is good.
C. W. C.

—— Pages d'histoire du Canada. Montreal: Granger Frères. 1891. 75c. [3686

Contains, inter alia, Les histoires du Canada; Le Golfe Saint Laurent; Les interprèts de Champlain; Expédition de 1666; Lachine; La Vérenderie; Juifs et Chrétiens. All of value as well as interest.

—— Histoire de la ville de Trois-Rivières et ses environs. Montreal. 1870. [3687

Only one volume published, bringing the story down to 1637.

Warburton, *Maj.* **George D.** Conquest of Canada. (Edited by Eliot Warburton.) London. 1849. 2v. N. Y. 1850. 2v. [3688

Major Warburton, R. A., with his brother Eliot, made the first complete English study on this important period. It is an admirable piece of work, and, despite the scanty resources then available, still holds honourable position with the studies of Parkman, Kingsford and Casgrain.

Winsor, Justin. Cartier to Frontenac; with full cartographical illustrations from contemporary sources. Boston: Houghton. 1894. $4. [3689

The second title of this work is admirably descriptive, — *Geographical discovery in the interior of North America in its historical relations, 1534–1700.* Neither the cartographical nor the historical side of the study is slighted and, without parade of learning, the results of a profound though special erudition are given in each chapter. Equally interesting and thorough, it is a standard of what such writing should be. The illustrations are also a strong feature of the book. It abounds with excellent reproductions of plans, portraits and early maps. C. W. C.

Wolfe, *Maj.-Gen.* **James.** Wright, Robert. Life of Major-General James Wolfe. London: Chapman. 1864. [3690

The standard biography of Wolfe. It is founded on excellent sources, is written in good taste, and reveals the character of its hero with unmistakable clearness. C. W. C.

See, also, Knox (sect. 3640).

Youville, Marie-Marguerite Dufrost de la Jemmerais Ve. d'. Faillon, *l'Abbé.* Vie de Mme. d'Youville, fondatrice des Sœurs de la Charité de Villemarie. Villemarie. 1852. [3691

Apart from the biographical and local value there are interesting details of the end of the French and the beginnings of the English rule.

DIVISION V: ENGLISH REGIME

Anbury, Thomas. Travels through the interior parts of America. In a series of letters. By an Officer. London. 1789. 2v. With author's name, 1792. In French with notes, Paris, 1790; in German, Berlin, 1792. [**3692**

This is from the English journal of Thomas Anbury, an officer in Burgoyne's Army, 1776–1781. The first eight months spent in and about Quebec and Montreal give good detail on the conditions and sentiment in Canada.

Argenteuil *and* **Prescott.** THOMAS, CYRUS. History of the Counties of Argenteuil and Prescott. Montreal. 1896. [**3693**

Good local history with sketches of early settlers.

Bibaud, Michel. Histoire du Canada sous la domination anglaise. Montreal. 1837–1844–1878. 3v. [**3694**

A careful and unpretentious work; it is lucid and direct, generally moderate and reliable in statement, and singularly free from national or political prejudice. Later writers have not wholly succeeded in superseding its usefulness as a handy book of reference. E. Cr.

Bonnycastle, *Sir* **Richard Henry.** Canadians in 1841. London: Colburn. 1842. 2v. [**3695**

The author, a British officer long resident in Canada, travelled extensively, sometimes in the train of the Governor of the day. His observations include points so widely separated as Lake Superior, New Brunswick and Labrador. He was a good observer. The notes about the Indians, climate, prices, the state of society, canals, highways, etc., are discursive but interesting. He had a share in the events of the rebellion of 1837, and denounces the insurgents in a polemical spirit. Notwithstanding slight inaccuracies, the book is a valuable picture of conditions in Canada before the introduction of the railway and when British regular soldiers occupied the centres of population. G. M. W.

—— Canada and the Canadians in 1846. London: Colburn. 1846. 2v. [**3696**

These volumes have the same qualities as the preceding. The author writes in a tone of considerable alarm lest the U. S. should attempt to annex Canada, while convinced that such a plan could not succeed. The notes relate almost wholly to what is now the Province of Ontario. He predicts great mineral development, and gives anecdotal pictures of society in a pleasant style. G. M. W.

Bosworth, Newton. Hochelaga depicta: the early history and present state of the city and island of Montreal. Montreal: Wm. Greig. 1839. Reprinted in facsimile. Toronto: Congdon & Britnell, 1901. $3. [**3697**

The historical chapters are of little value, as the author failed to consult those archives of which the Abbé Faillon afterwards made such admirable use, but the sketch of the rebellions of 1837–8, though very brief, has the value of a contemporary narrative. The descriptive portions of the book are written with great exactitude, the illustrations are excellent for the day and there are two good maps.

Bourinot, *Sir* **John G.** Canada under British rule. See under Constitutional History, sect. 3565. [**3698**

Campbell, *Rev.* **Robert.** History of the Scotch Presbyterian Church, St. Gabriel Street, Montreal. Montreal: Drysdale. 1887. $3. [**3699**

As the history of this congregation begins in 1782, and the author has performed his task with great care and accuracy, the biographical sketches of the English inhabitants of Montreal at the beginning of the 19th century are of importance for local study.

Canniff, William. History of the province of Ontario. Toronto: Hovey. 1872. [**3700**

The author is descended from loyalist or "Tory" refugees from the United States who settled in Upper Canada. His book, based upon original material, contains much information about the early history of these people. While it is principally of local interest, the descriptions of manners, of mission work among the Indians, of abuses connected with the Crown's grants of lands, of the conditions of trade, etc., at the end of the 18th century give it permanent value. The tone is anti-American, and the style without distinction. G. M. W.

Christie, Robert. History of the late province of Lower Canada. Quebec, Montreal. 1848–55. 6v. [**3701**

Christie was an active politician in a stormy period, yet his *History of Lower Canada* is less blameworthy on the score of partisanship than for its uncouth style and faulty arrangement. It contains quite enough data to equip a good book, and notwithstanding much incoherence should still be used by those who would master the sequence of events in Lower Canada between 1791 and 1841. It comprises the text of numerous documents either in partial or complete form. C. W. C.

Codman, John, 2nd. Arnold's expedition to Quebec. N. Y.: Macmillan. 1901. $2.25. [**3702**

This book, which was published four years after the author's death, gives a minute and animated description of Arnold's march through the wilderness, besides a full narrative of the operations before Quebec. In comparison with its predecessors it can claim superiority on the two following grounds. Mr. Codman studied the topography of the expedition step by step. He went through the woods on foot or by canoe, following the route of the army. Secondly, he discovered and used a large amount of new data, in which are included passages from contemporary journals. While

Arnold's courage is duly recognized, this work is in no sense a piece of biography, still less of apology.

C. W. C.

Coffin, Victor. Province of Quebec and the early American Revolution. (Univ. of Wisconsin. Bulletin: economics, etc., v. 1, no. 3.) Madison. 1896. 75c. [3703

The most distinctive feature of this monograph is its author's attitude towards the Quebec Act, 1774. The view has long been accepted that it was judicious and humane. Mr. Coffin defends the thesis that it was "one of the most unwise and disastrous measures in English colonial history." We cannot say that he has decisively established this point, because, when individual opinion hinges on considerations of general expediency, absolute demonstration is difficult. But at least he furnishes ground for the belief that the Act "was founded on the misconceptions and false information of the Provincial officials." The quality of Mr. Coffin's style hardly equals that of his ideas or of his erudition. C. W. C.

Confederation. Parliamentary debates on the subject of the confederation of the British North American provinces; printed by order of the Legislature. Quebec. 1865. [3704

As a practical measure the Confederation of the British North American Provinces dates from the Conference of Thirty-three, which was held at Quebec in the autumn of 1864. Resolutions favouring federal union on certain terms were then adopted by the most eminent public men of the various provinces, but the issue was not decisively settled in all its details. The debates on this question which were held in the Legislature of the Two Canadas during February and March, 1865, throw much light on contemporary feeling, and are indispensable to a proper knowledge of the question. Among the leading speakers were George Brown, G. E. Cartier, A. T. Galt, L. H. Holton, J. A. Macdonald, J. S. Macdonald, T. D'Arcy McGee, Christopher Dunkin, and Sir E. P. Taché. C. W. C.

David, L. O. Les patriotes de 1837-1838. Montreal: Senecal. 1884. $1. [3705

A strongly partisan series of sketches of the leaders of the rebellion in Lower Canada, but with useful biographical notes.

—— L'union des deux Canadas. Montreal: Senecal. 1898. [3706

Instructive for the "Liberal" French-Canadian view of the union.

Davidson, J. Growth of the French Canadian race in America. See American Academy of Political and Social Science, sect. 226. [3707

Dawson, Samuel Edward. Old colonial currencies. In Canadian monthly, April, 1872; Canadian antiquarian, July, 1872; Bankers' magazine (N. Y.), Feb., 1874. [3708

The question is treated in relation to all the Ameri-

can colonies of Great Britain. Comparative values, etc. See sect. 3775-3777. See, also, under Montreal, sect. 3752, also, Comprehensive History, sect. 3585.

Dent, John Charles. Story of the Upper Canadian rebellion. Toronto: Robinson. 1885. 2v. [3709

An actively polemical version of the events which attended the rising of 1837-38 in Upper Canada. Its object is to vindicate Dr. Rolph at the expense of William Lyon Mackenzie, and also to tell the story of their plots in vivid, picturesque fashion. While more energetic and readable than any other account of this episode, its *ex parte* character is very glaring, and it can only be used with caution. C. W. C.

—— The last forty years: Canada since the union of 1841. Toronto: Virtue. 1881. 2v. [3710

Almost wholly an abstract of political occurrences. The second volume contains a concluding chapter on *Literature and journalism*, but the social and economic development of the country is quite neglected. One noticeable feature of the book is the biographical element which pervades it. Numerous character sketches of public men are interspersed through the text, and the attempt to make each chapter an entertaining essay is very apparent. The illustrations which accompany it are poorly executed. C. W. C.

Dufferin, Earl of. STEWART, GEORGE, JR. Canada under the administration of the Earl of Dufferin. London. 1878. Toronto: Rose-Belford Co. 1878. [3711

The volume consists mainly of the speeches of Lord Dufferin while Governor-General (1872-78). During his term of office important public questions arose—such as charges of corruption in connection with the building of the Canadian Pacific Railway, the right of a Canadian province to withdraw from the confederation and the limits of the authority of Lieutenant-Governors of Provinces. The speeches and correspondence relating to these issues are of value; the other portions of the volume are of only transient interest. G. M. W.

Durham, John George Lambton, *1st earl of.* Report on the affairs of British North America. London. 1839.

—— *Same:* Report and despatches. London. 1839. New ed. London: Methuen. 1901. 7s. 6d. [3712

As a result of the rebellion in the Canadas in 1837-38, the author was sent out from England as High Commissioner and Governor-General of all the provinces of British North America including Newfoundland. He enquired into their affairs with great energy, but soon exceeded his powers, was censured and resigned. His official position gave him every advantage in regard to sources of information. He dissects with skill the causes of discontent in Canada and urges a union of all the provinces that should involve the supremacy of the English over the French. The *Report*, with its copious appendices, shows great care and labor, and is the most striking document in the colonial history of the nineteenth century. The style is admirable.

G. M. W.

The most important state paper relating to Canada which appeared between 1791 and 1867, and one which had a deep effect on public opinion. It was called forth by the disturbances of 1837 and among other salient recommendations it suggested a closer union of the British North American Provinces. It also emphasizes very strongly the mutual animosity which existed at the time in Lower Canada between the French and English races. Though issued under Lord Durham's name, it was almost wholly written by Charles Buller. Gibbon Wakefield collaborated with Buller, but in comparison his contribution is of minor moment.

C. W. C.

See, also, Haliburton, under Maritime Provinces sect. 3803.

Edgar; Matilda, *Lady*. See Ridout, sect. 3770. [3713]

Faucher de St. Maurice, N. H. E. De Tribord à Babord : trois croisières dans le Golfe Saint-Laurent. Montreal. 1877. [3714]

A vivid relation of a voyage down the Gulf, with admirable descriptions of Anticosti, the Magdalen Islands, Gaspé, etc., the expedition of Admiral Sir Hovenden Walker, 1711, legends and folk-lore. The best book of travel in Canada by a Canadian.

Fenian invasion. Correspondence relating to the Fenian invasion and the rebellion of the southern states. Ottawa. 1869. [3715]

This is the correspondence between Canadian officials, and between the Canadian government and the governments of Great Britain and the United States, relative to recruiting in Canada for the United States army ; to violations of neutrality by Confederate agents in Canada ; to the attempt to release the Confederate prisoners confined on Johnson's Island in Lake Erie ; to the manufacture of "Greek fire" in Canada for use in United States cities ; to the charge that vessels were being fitted out in Canadian ports with hostile designs against this country ; to the raid upon St. Albans, Vt., etc. It is followed by the correspondence regarding the Fenian invasion of Canada from Buffalo in June, 1866 ; and a table shows the amount of injury suffered by the inhabitants of Fort Erie on that occasion. The correspondence is indexed.

F. J. S.

Ferland, *l'Abbé* J. B. A. La Gaspésie. Nouvelle éd. Quebec: Côté. 1877. 50c. [3716]

This pleasant description of a trip to Gaspé in 1836 describes the condition of the people, white and red, preserves their legends and notes much of historic interest.

Gailly de Taurines, Charles. La nation canadienne : étude historique sur les populations françaises du nord de l'Amérique. Paris : Plon. 1894. fr. 3.50. [3717]

A flattering appreciation of the French Canadians by a modern Frenchman. It reviews briefly the history of French Canada, considers existing political arrangements, and concludes with a criticism of the national culture and destiny. Whether or not M. de Taurines' admiration of the French in America be considered excessive, must rest a matter of individual opinion. At least it may be said that he writes vigorously, and with an intelligence which is proportionate to his warmth of sympathy.

C. W. C.

Gaspé, Philippe Aubert de. Les anciens Canadiens. Quebec. 1863. Montreal : Granger Frères. $1.

—— Mémoires. Quebec. 1866. Montreal : Granger Frères. $1. [3718]

M. de Gaspé, descendant of a long line of Canadian seigniurs, wrote these two works when upwards of seventy years of age. Apart from the charm of style as pictures of the social conditions in the early years of the English régime they will always hold high place.

Gérin-Lajoie, Antoine. Dix ans au Canada, 1840–1850. See Le Canada francais, Vols. 1, 2, 3, 4. [3719]

An important political study.

Glengarry. MACDONELL, J. A. Sketches illustrating the early settlement and history of Glengarry in Canada. By J. A. Macdonell, of Greenfield. Montreal : W. Foster Brown. 1893. $2.50. [3720]

This is in reality a history of the Macdonell family in Canada ; much interesting detail has been gathered, but there is no consecutive narrative, and the lack of an index and even a table of contents demands too much of the ordinary reader.

Globensky, Charles Auguste Maximilien. La rébellion de 1837 à Saint-Eustache. Précédé d'un exposé de la situation politique du Bas Canada depuis la cession. Québec : Côté. 1883. $1. [3721]

Contains much local and personal detail, and is of value as one of the few French accounts favorable to the Government ; it is in effect a defence of the memory of the author's father.

Greenough, William Parker. Canadian folk-life and folk-lore. N. Y.: Richmond. 1897. N. Y. : Taylor. $1.50. [3722]

An interesting series of sketches by one whom business relations brought into close contact with the French Canadians. The element of "folk-lore" is slight, amounting only to a chapter on the habitant "contes ;" but many characteristics of the rural population in Quebec are truthfully delineated. The author's style, though somewhat colloquial, bears a just relation to his manner of treatment. It is by anecdote and from personal observation that he illustrates the topics which he has selected. English-speaking travelers in the lower St. Lawrence valley will gain from this book much serviceable information, conveyed in a form which enables it to be quickly seized.

C. W. C.

Haight, Canniff. Country life in Canada fifty years ago. Toronto : Hunter. 1885.

[3723

" A very agreeable account of the reminiscences of a sexagenarian, who was a grandson, on both sides, of refugees from New York after the peace. They settled in the first of the settlements in Upper Canada, near the Bay of Quinte, with other exiles, scattered over a wide wilderness. The writer faithfully portrays their hardships, not without an inheritance of grievances against the new republic for its harsh course towards the loyal subjects of the king ; but, happily, his pages are more full of the triumphs of the industry and the virtues of the exiles in securing great prosperity for their descendants." G. E. Ellis, in *Narrative and critical hist. of Am.*, 7: 213.

Hawkins, Alfred. Picture of Quebec ; with historical recollections. Quebec: Neilson. 1834.

[3724

An important and highly interesting work for the local history of Quebec compiled by Hawkins, Andrew Stuart, Solicitor-General, and Judge Andrew Thom, at a time when there were still survivors of the events under Wolfe and of the siege of 1775 ; in consequence many of the " recollections " are of value.

Head, *Sir* **Francis Bond.** A narrative. London. 1839.

[3725

A defence and justification of his policy as Lieutenant-Governor of Upper Canada 1835-8. Cleverly written and contains many important official documents. Specially valuable for the curious insight it affords into the hasty and indiscreet character of the author and the light thrown upon his opinions and the motives of his conduct. Accuracy and impartiality cannot be expected in a book that is avowedly a piece of special pleading from first to last; no statement of fact in it should be unreservedly accepted without corroboration from an independent source.

E. Cr.

No diatribe of a political opponent exposes to the world the causes of his failure so clearly as the words of his own *Narrative*. At the same time this book has the literary interest which springs from a lively and unfaltering aggressiveness. C. W. C.

Henry, John Joseph. Account of Arnold's campaign against Quebec and of the hardships and sufferings of that band of heroes who traversed the wilderness of Maine from Cambridge to the St. Lawrence in the autumn of 1775. Albany. 1877.

[3726

This is the reprint of the rare original published in Lancaster, Pa., 1812. It is the best and most interesting account published from the American side; it contains only such errors as are inevitable to a narrative written many years after the events.

See, also, Codman, sect. 3702.

Heriot, George. Travels through the Canadas ; to which is subjoined a comparative view of the manners and customs of several of the Indian nations of North and South America. London. 1807.

[3727

The author's position as Deputy Postmaster-General for Canada in 1805-6 gave him exceptional opportunities for personal observation of the topographical features, economic conditions and social life of Lower Canada and of the new settlements on the north shore of the St. Lawrence and Great Lakes. Of the interior of the country he knows nothing. The illustrations are specially valuable. The nine chapters on the Indians are compiled from second and third rate authorities. J. B.

Hincks, *Sir* **Francis.** Reminiscences of his public life. Montreal: Drysdale. 1884. $4.

[3728

The author took an active part in public life in Canada between 1836 and 1855 — the period in which, after much controversy, responsible government was won. His book consists mainly of long extracts from his own and other speeches and from official correspondence. These give it its chief value. There is a chapter on the labor question in the West Indies, where the author was a governor for some time after 1855. The book is without literary merit. G. M. W.

Huntingdon. SELLAR, ROBERT. History of the county of Huntingdon, and seigniories of Chateauguay and Beauharnois, to 1838. Huntingdon, Que.: Canadian Gleaner. 1888. $2.

[3729

Sellar's *History of Huntingdon*, besides furnishing the best descriptive account which exists of any English county in the Province of Quebec, has real intrinsic merits. Huntingdon was involved in the War of 1812 and also in the events of 1838, so that, apart from interesting stories of the early settlement, its annalist has considerable material upon which to depend. This sketch was written without any view to financial results, and proves that the English of Quebec are not altogether lacking in antiquarian curiosity. C. W. C.

Jodoin *and* **Vincent.** See Longueuil, sect. 3742.

[3730

Kirby, William. Annals of Niagara. Welland, Ont., 1897. Lundy's Lane Hist. Soc., Niagara Falls South, Ont. $1.

[3731

A history of the old town of Niagara, Ont., and a review of events on the Canadian side of the Niagara from the middle of the 17th century ; by one long a resident of the region, who should be well equipped as local annalist. He makes some contribution to the history of the region from MS. sources ; but his pages abound in error, both of fact and grammar, and give frequent evidence of intense anti-American prejudice. F. H. S.

Lambert, John. Travels through Canada and the United States of North America in the years 1806, 7, and 8, etc. London. 1810. 2v.

[3732

The sketches of society in Quebec and Montreal are written with much humor ; the descriptive portions are well done, and much important information is given on trade, ship-building and manufactures.

Landmann, *Col.* Adventures and recollections. London. 1852. 2v. [3733

A little known but amusing account of a young officer's life in the fashionable circles of Quebec and Montreal during the closing years of the eighteenth century.

Laterrière, Pierre de Sale. Mémoires de . . . et de ses traverses. Quebec. 1873. [3734

These memoirs of a typical country gentleman, Seignieur of Les Eboulements, were not only privately printed, but special care was taken that they should not reach the general public. Being written with a happy indiscretion, they contain intimate and valuable detail on matters both social and political (period of Sir Frederick Haldimand).

Leavitt, T. W. H. See Leeds and Grenville, sect. 3737. [3735

Leblond de Brumath. See sect. 3650. [3736

Leeds *and* **Grenville.** LEAVITT, T. W. H. History, 1749–1879. Brockville, Ont. 1879. [3737

Of local interest only.

Lemoine, *Sir* **J. M.** See sect. 3653. [3738

Lizars, Robina, *and* **Kathleen Macfarlane.** In the days of the Canada Company, 1825–50. Toronto: Briggs. 1896. $2. [3739

The Canada Company, founded in London by John Galt the novelist, in 1824, for colonizing Canada, purchased a large district in what is now western Ontario. This book is not a history of that powerful corporation which still exists; but rather an anecdotal account of the experiences of the settlers, mostly Scots, from some of whom the authors are descended. They have had access to private papers, and have, besides, collected oral traditions. The volume is thus an original contribution to the knowledge of the period. For the purposes of systematic history the narrative is obscured by the abundance of sometimes trivial detail, not always treated with critical insight. There is no orderly account of the progress of colonization. The style is agreeable.   G. M. W.

—— Humours of '37; grave, gay and grim. Toronto: Briggs. $1.25. [3740

The note to the preceding work of the Misses Lizars will apply to this in regard to its general scope and character.

Long, John. Voyages and travels of an Indian interpreter and trader, describing the manners and customs of the North American Indians ; with vocabulary of the Chippeway language, list of words in the Iroquois, Mohegan, Shawanee, and Esquimeaux, etc. London. 1791. [3741

This rather rare book contains much reliable information respecting the condition of the settlements, military stations and trading-posts in Upper Canada in 1789–90, mainly derived from the personal observations of the author, whose style is simple and direct. As an interpreter in the British Indian department during the Revolutionary War he had become intimately acquainted with the languages and customs of the principal Indian tribes, and made excellent use of his opportunities.   E. Cr.

Costs from $16 to $20.

Longueuil. JODOIN, ALEXANDRE, *and* J. L. VINCENT. Histoire de Longueuil et de la famille de Longueuil. Montreal: Gebhardt-Berthiaume. 1889. $1.50. [3742

Unfortunately the authors left Margry, the one informed guide for D'Iberville and Bienville, to follow men who were ignorant of his sources of information. Neither is Gayarré consulted. The statements on the earlier history of the LeMoyne family must not be accepted without verification. Apart from this the book has its value as a history of the seigniory and parish. In connection with this Miss Grace King's *Jean Baptiste LeMoyne, Sieur de Bienville,* New York: Dodd, Mead & Co., 1898, $1.00; and her sketch of D'Iberville in *Harper's magazine,* October, 1894, are of importance.

Macdonald, *Sir* **John Alexander.** MACPHERSON, J. PENNINGTON. Life of the Right Hon. Sir John A. Macdonald. St. John, N. B.: Earle Co. 1891. 1v. $4.25. 2v. $6. [3743

This book is written by a relative of the late Prime Minister of Canada. It however shows no particular insight into his character, and is devoted wholly to his public career. All his opinions are endorsed and defended. The long extracts, extending to many pages, from debates in Parliament, newspaper articles, petitions, etc., prevent any literary unity. The volumes are without style, but the collection of some otherwise fugitive material gives the work a certain though not great value.   G. M. W.

—— POPE, JOSEPH. Memoirs of Sir John Alexander Macdonald. Ottawa, Ont.: Durie. 1894. Ottawa: James Hope & Sons. 2v. $5. London: Arnold. 1894. 2v. 32s. [3744

The authorized life of Sir John Macdonald. Mr. Pope was for many years his private secretary and a confidant in whose judgment he placed great trust. Lady Macdonald states that her husband designated his biographer before his death, giving as a reason for the selection of Mr. Pope: "He knows more about me than any one else." Papers which Sir John Macdonald had accumulated with a view to writing an autobiographical sketch were thus handed "unreservedly" to the writer of his choice, and have been discreetly used. While somewhat lacking in lightness of touch, this biography is an authority of the highest class.   C. W. C.

Macdonell. See Glengarry, sect. 3720.

Mackenzie, William Lyon. LINDSEY, CHARLES. Life and times of Wm. Lyon Mackenzie. Toronto: Randall. 1862. 2v. [3745

The name of William Lyon Mackenzie is inseparably connected with the Rebellion of 1837–38 in Upper Canada. Lindsey, his chief biographer, was also his son-in-

law, and one to whom he was in the habit of expressing his opinions with perfect frankness, though they differed fundamentally on political questions. Lindsey claims credit for impartiality on the ground that he only knew Mackenzie during the last twelve years of the latter's life, and was himself unconnected with the events of 1837. This profession has been challenged with some force by J. C. Dent in his *Story of the Upper Canadian Rebellion*, but in many respects Lindsey deserves praise. He has pictured clearly a Scotch radical bred in the bone: violent and impracticable, but sincere and beyond suspicion of venality.
C. W. C.

Maclean, J. P. An historical account of the settlements of Scotch Highlanders in America prior to the peace of 1783. Cleveland: Helman-Taylor Co. 1900. $5. Glasgow: John Mackay. 1900. 21s. [3746
Contains much of interest in regard to Highland emigration, but badly arranged and without index. Chapters 8, on the Mohawk settlement, Sir William Johnson; 9, Prince Edward Island; 10, Nova Scotia, are of special interest regarding Canada. See, also, Macdonell's *Glengarry*, sect. 3720; and consult military history of the Highland regiments in Brown's *History of the Highlands*, v. 4.

Maude, John. Visit to the Falls of Niagara. London: Longmans. 1826. [3747
This charmingly intimate record of travel in 1800 by an Englishman of quick sympathies, keen appreciation, and intelligent observation, is unfortunately rare, but will well repay the difficulties of the search. His pictures of Montreal society are of biographical value, and he had enough humor to record incidents in an entertaining manner.

Montreal. Local histories, sketches, and articles of importance.
— ANGLICAN PARISH REGISTER. 1766–87. See Archives, 1885, sect. 3467. [3748
— BOSWORTH, *Rev.* NEWTON. Hochelaga depicta, see sect. 3697. [3749
— BORTHWICK, *Rev.* J. DOUGLAS. History of Montreal prison, 1784–1886, etc. Montreal. 1886. [3750
— CAMPBELL, *Rev.* ROBERT. History of the Scotch Presbyterian Church, St. Gabriel St., see sect. 3699. [3751
— DAWSON, SAMUEL EDWARD. Montreal, 1842–1892. In semi-centennial report, Board of Trade. Montreal: Gazette. 1893. [3752
A sketch of commercial growth.
— DOLLIER DE CASSON. Histoire du Montréal, sect. 3622. [3753
— LE BLOND DE BRUMATH, A. Histoire populaire de Montréal, sect. 3650. [3753 a
— LIGHTHALL, WM. DOUW. Montreal after two hundred and fifty years. Montreal: Grafton. 1899. $1.50. [3754

— MAISONNEUVE. Ordonnances. Trans. Société Historique de Montréal.
— —— Vie de Maisonneuve, see sect. 3655. [3755
— McLENNAN, WILLIAM. Montreal, 1642–1842. Semi-centennial report, Board of Trade. Montreal: Gazette. 1893. [3756
— —— Montreal and some of the makers thereof. Montreal Board of Trade, Memorial vol. 1893. Montreal: Sabiston Co. 1893. [3757
A series of biographical and historical sketches. Important maps.
— —— Anciens Montréalais. Benigne Basset, notaire royale, 1639–1699. [3758
See Canada-Français, 1890, sect. 3488.
— SANDHAM, ALFRED. Villemarie, or Sketches of Montreal past and present. Montreal: Bishop. 1870. [3759
Out of print. Copies may be had of W. Foster Brown, Montreal. $2.50.

Moodie, *Mrs.* **Susanna (Strickland).** Roughing it in the bush; or Forest life in Canada. London. 1852. 2v. Rev. ed., with introductory chapter. Toronto: Hunter. 1871. [3760
Written by a sister of Agnes Strickland, who married a half-pay officer and emigrated to Upper Canada in 1832. She was destitute of any special training which could fit her for life in the wilderness, but succeeded in adapting herself to the trials of her new existence. Her book is a loose narrative, founded on personal experience and largely interspersed with dialogue. It contains a sprightly picture of the life led by English settlers in Canada during the first half of the century, and in this sense is of distinct historical value.
C. W. C.

Prescott. See Argenteuil and Prescott, sect. 3693. [3761
Quebec. Special works on history, topography, etc. : —
— HAWKINS, ALFRED. Picture of Quebec, sect. 3724. [3762
— LEMOINE. Quebec past and present, sect. 3653. [3763
— —— Picturesque Quebec, sect. 3653. [3764
— —— Historical notes on Quebec and its environs. Quebec. 1887. [3765
Read, David B. The Canadian rebellion of 1837. Toronto: Briggs. 1896. $2. [3766
Narrates the events of the outbreaks in Lower Canada led by Papineau, in Upper Canada by Mackenzie. The facts are drawn from other works, though a few documents have been newly levied upon. Not wholly free from error or prejudice, it is the least par-

tisan and most comprehensive work on the subject, dispassionate in temper, unadorned in style.

F. H. S.

Rebellion 1837. *Commissioners appointed to inquire into the grievances complained of in Lower Canada.* Reports. London. 1837. [3767

The appointment in 1835 by the British government of these commissioners, who were the Earl of Gosford, — also appointed Governor of Lower Canada, — Sir Charles Edward Grey, and Sir James Gipps, was made in the hope of settling the long continued complaints of the French Canadians ; but, according to D. B. Read (*Canadian rebellion of 1837*, sect. 3766), the commissioners were restrained from the start from reporting against the chief grievance, which was the existence of the legislative council. This bulky volume contains five preliminary reports, chiefly on crown revenues, feudal tenures, and ecclesiastical rights, a general report of 50 pages covering political, land, and educational questions, and an appendix of 160 pages of statistics and evidence. While Sir Charles Grey did not agree fully with his colleagues, the report was strongly adverse to the French Canadian demands. It was debated in the House of Commons in March, 1837, and approved by a large majority. F. J. S.

—— Report of a select committee on the political state of the provinces of Upper and Lower Canada. Toronto. 1838. [3768

This report to the Legislature of Upper Canada presents the extreme Conservative view of the causes that led to the 1837 outbreak, with suggestions as to the future government of the two provinces. But, while extravagant in its expressions of loyalty to the home government, it recommends the control of colonial affairs by a board composed in part of colonists and the admission to Parliament of representatives of the leading colonies. F. J. S.

Règne militaire en Canada ou Administration militaire de ce pays par les Anglais du 8 Septembre 1760 au 10 Août 1764. Mémoire de la Société Historique de Montréal. Montreal. 1872. [3769

An important study and collection of orders, proclamations, ordonnances, etc., with notes by the Abbé Verreau and others.

Ridout, Thomas, *et al.* Ten years of Upper Canada in peace and war, 1805–15: being the Ridout letters, with annotations by Matilda Edgar; also narrative of captivity among the Shawanese Indians, in 1788, of Thos. Ridout, and vocabulary of the Shawanese language. London: Unwin. 1891. 10s. 6d. Toronto: Briggs. $1.50. [3770

A fairly important collection of letters chiefly written by members of the Ridout family from various parts of Upper Canada, many of which relate to the War of 1812. The connecting narrative is slight and often inaccurate. E. Cr.

Rousseau, P. See Maisonneuve, Vie, sect. 3655. [3771

Roy, J. Edmond. Histoire de la seignieurie de Lauzon. See under French Régime, sect. 3678. [3772

Sellar, Robert. See Huntingdon, sect. 3729. [3773

Silliman, Benjamin. Remarks made on a short tour between Hartford and Quebec in the autumn of 1819. New Haven. 1820. [3773 a

This autumn vacation of a man of science is delightful reading and one feels throughout that its composition was a pleasure to the author. He was the first Anglo-Saxon who presented the French Canadian in a fair light to the outside world. Apart from his sympathetic treatment of his subject, his presentation of historic pictures and events is vivid and unusually correct.

Smith, Michael. Geographical view of the province of Upper Canada, and promiscuous remarks on the government. Hartford. 1813. Enl. and rev. ed. N. Y., Phil., Trenton. 1813.

—— Geographical view of the British possessions in North America; with an appendix containing a history of the war in Canada to date. Balt. 1814.

—— Complete history of the late American war with Great Britain; [with] narrative of the author's sufferings in Canada and journey to Virginia and Kentucky. Lexington, Ky. 1816. [3774

The preface to the first edition or series of Michael Smith's publications states that it was principally written before the war between the United States and Great Britain had begun, with the approval of Lieut.-Governor Gore. In December, 1812, or January, 1813, the author was deported to the United States for refusing to take the oath of allegiance. These books contain the most complete and accurate description of Upper Canada at the beginning of the War of 1812 in print, and throw much curious light on the feelings of the inhabitants. They are slip-shod and ungrammatical in diction, but studiously candid and moderate in tone. E. Cr.

Stevenson, James. Currency : with reference to card money in Canada during the French régime.

—— Convention for liquidation of Canada paper money belonging to the subjects of Great Britain between the King of Great Britain and the most Christian King, 29 March, 1766. [3775

The above are found in Journals of the Lit. and Hist. Soc. of Canada, v. 2, 1875.

—— The currency of Canada after the capitulation. Lit. and Hist. Soc. of Canada Journals, v. 12. 1877. [3776

—— The War of 1812 in connection with the Army bill act. Montreal: W. Foster Brown. 1892. [3777

Mr. Stevenson was not only a successful banker of great experience, but a thorough student of the theory and history of his calling as well; this combination of personal qualifications makes these brief monographs of distinct value. The history of the card money begins in 1685 when Demeulles, the Intendant, at his wit's end for money to pay the troops, cut up a pack of ordinary playing cards, and with a few strokes of the pen turned them into Government bonds. It was so simple! And the story is traced for us from its first success through all the depressing chapters of imperial extravagance, distress and depreciation down to the final repudiation and dishonor. Some excellent photographs of the money are given.

The history of the currency after the capitulation does not offer as interesting a subject, but it is of importance for a clear understanding of the commercial development of the country. Dr. Samuel E. Dawson's study on old colonial currencies, sect. 3708, should be read in connection with this of Mr. Stevenson.

The story of the effort of the Government to provide for the financial support of the War of 1812 is an important and unusual study.

Strachan, J. A visit to the Province of Upper Canada in 1819. Aberdeen. 1820. [3778

Strickland, Lt.-Col. Samuel. Twenty-seven years in Canada West; ed. by Agnes Strickland. London: Bentley. 1853. 2v. [3779

The author emigrated from England in 1825 to the county of Peterborough, residing near his relations, Mrs. Moodie and Mrs. Trail. His book much resembles theirs, in being an interesting account of the experiences of an English settler in the bush, but is inferior in interest and style. His after connection with the Canada Company enables him to throw some light on that institution. J. B.

Sydenham, Charles Edward Poulett Thomson, baron. SCROPE, GEORGE JULIUS DUNCOMBE POULETT. Memoir of the life of the Rt. Hon. Charles, Lord Sydenham. London: Murray. 1843. [3780

The distinguished geologist, George Julius Scrope, was an elder brother of Lord Sydenham, and his memoir is based largely on family correspondence. Lord Sydenham was a firm and able Governor-General of Canada at a critical moment, — viz., in the years immediately following the rebellion of 1837 and the drafting of Lord Durham's Report. It was during his term of office that Upper and Lower Canada were united, and the work which he accomplished has an unmistakable bearing on the confederation of 1867. By reason both of author and subject this sketch takes a high place in Canadian biography. C. W. C.

Talbot, Edward Allen. Five years' residence in the Canadas. London: Longmans. 1824. 2v. [3781

Mr. Talbot was a young Irishman who accompanied his father and a party of emigrants in 1818 to the Talbot settlement in Upper Canada, and remained with them until 1823. His accounts of the new settlements in the, then, extreme west of the Province are among the earliest. His book is full of extravagant statements and ridiculous errors, interlarded with disquisitions on the natural history of the country. It is of little practical value, beyond giving occasional glimpses of a form of life which existed only for a few years. J. B.

Theller, Edward Alexander. Canada in 1837–38. Phil. 1841. 2v. [3782

The author, an Irish-American, joined a raid from the United States into Canada in support of the rebellion of 1837–38. He was taken prisoner and condemned to death on the doubtful charge of treason, but ultimately escaped to the United States. His narrative describes vividly the scenes of the rebellion in some of which he was an actor. Often exaggerated and permeated with hatred of England, it yet is valuable as reflecting the passions of the time. G. M. W.

Thomas, C. See Argenteuil and Prescott, sect. 3693. [3783

Toronto. SCADDING, Rev. HENRY. Toronto of old; collections and recollections illustrative of the early settlement and social life of the capital of Ontario. Toronto: Willing & Williamson. 1878. [3784

This large history of a city, only about 100 years old, is mainly a description, street by street, of changes of which the author had personal knowledge. The style is scholarly and agreeable, but the book does not contain any systematic study of social conditions. G. M. W.

—— SCADDING, Rev. HENRY, and JOHN CHARLES DENT. Toronto, past and present. Toronto: Hunter, Rose & Co. 1884. [3784 a

Prepared as a memorial volume for the semi-centennial of the city in 1884, it is the most complete history of its rise and progress. The period from 1792–1834 is by Dr. Scadding, and that from 1834–1884 by Mr. Dent. Dr. Scadding's *Toronto of old* treats in detail of houses and their inmates in a series of reminiscences, while this treats Toronto as a corporate whole with a municipal history. J. B.

Veritas, pseud. The letters of Veritas, republished from the *Montreal Herald*, containing a succinct narrative of the military administration of Sir George Prevost during his command in the Canadas, whereby it will appear manifest that the merit of preserving them from conquest belongs not to him. Montreal. 1815. [3785

The author is supposed to have been Hon. John Richardson, an influential Montreal merchant and a member of the Legislative Council of Lower Canada belonging to the extreme English party. His book is a bitter and biased criticism of the conduct of Sir George Prevost as Governor-General of Canada from 1811 to 1815. It is controversial and undisguisedly prejudiced in tone, and although valuable as an index of the sentiments of a powerful faction, few of the statements can be accepted without close examination. The style is commonplace and labored, besides being strongly colored by party feeling and possibly personal animosity.   E. Cr.

Verreau. See Règne Militaire, sect. 3769.
[3786

Wait, Benjamin. Letters from Van Diemen's Land during four years' imprisonment for political offences in Upper Canada; also letters descriptive of personal appeals in behalf of her husband by Mrs. B. Wait. Buffalo. 1843. [3787

The author was captured during a raid into Upper Canada in the "patriot's war" of 1837, and condemned to death, being saved from this fate by the devotion of his wife. While his story gives almost no history of the outbreak, his account of his journey to Quebec and thence to England, of his life aboard the hulks, and of his voyage to Van Diemen's Land on a convict ship, and his wife's history of her successful efforts in Canada and England to secure first the commutation of his sentence and then his pardon, are interesting and present a view of the times that it would be difficult to obtain elsewhere.   F. J. S.

Warburton, *Maj.* **George D.** Hochelaga; or England in the New World; ed. by Eliot Warburton. London. 1846. 2v. N. Y.: Putnam. 1846. 2v. London: Routledge. 1854. [3788

One of the best of the many works on American travel published in England during the third, fourth and fifth decades of the nineteenth century. The author's first volume is devoted to Canada, where he arrived in the early autumn of 1844. Entering by the St. Lawrence route, he describes Newfoundland and Quebec, and later Montreal and Niagara, by which latter path he entered the United States; he visited Buffalo, Saratoga, New York, Philadelphia, Baltimore, Washington, Boston and Plymouth, and returned to Canada by way of Vermont. Maj. Warburton faithfully kept up his diary, was a shrewd observer, and describes scenery and manners, and reports conversations and public opinion with a pleasant spice. Although his remarks upon American men and manners were doubtless not relished here at the time of publication, they are well meant and kindly, and are interesting and instructive. Valuable for the study of American social conditions.   R. G. T.

Weld, Isaac. Travels through the states of North America and the provinces of Upper and Lower Canada during the years 1795–7. London. 1799. [3789

A book which well deserved its popularity; the description is excellent and exact. There were several editions in English, of which the first is the best; the work was equally successful in its French version.

DIVISION VI: MARITIME PROVINCES, INCLUDING NEWFOUNDLAND

Bourinot, Sir John George. Cape Breton and its memorials of the French régime. Montreal: Dawson. 1892. 2d ed. Toronto: Copp, Clark Co. 1896. [3790

This volume, first issued in the *Transactions* of the Royal Society of Canada, for 1891, is the most authoritative account of the island that has yet appeared. The author, long resident in Cape Breton, has consulted the printed sources, and the bibliographical notes are valuable. The style is interesting.
         G. M. W.

—— Builders of Nova Scotia. Toronto: Copp, Clark Co. 1900. $1.50. [3791

One of the most valuable of Sir John Bourinot's contributions to Canadian history. Excellent plates.

Brown, Richard. History of the island of Cape Breton. London: Low. 1869. 15s.
[3792

The author, long resident in the island, addressed this work "to the youth of Cape Breton" after he had retired to England. He consulted the chief printed material besides the MS. collections in the British Museum and the Public Record Office. Abundant local knowledge and a judicial spirit give the work permanent value. The account of the two sieges of Louisbourg is very full, and the contemporary history of Nova Scotia and of Canada receive some attention. The style is plain but dignified, and hardly suited to what the volume professes to be, — "familiar letters."
         G. M. W.

Calnek, William Arthur. History of the county of Annapolis, including old Port Royal and Acadia, with memoirs of its representatives in the provincial parliament, and of its early English settlers; ed. and completed by A. W. Savary. Toronto: Wm. Briggs. 1897. $3.25.
[3793

"The early annals (1604–1605) are contained in the first eight chapters. The ninth is a defence of the Acadians, by the editor, against the charge, made by Mr. Parkman among others, that 'they would neither leave the country nor take the oath.' He certainly makes a strong case against Governor Lawrence, the chief agent in their removal. . . . The second half of the volume contains biographical memoirs of members of the provincial parliament for the county, and biographical and genealogical sketches of the early settlers and grantees." *Nation*, 65: 246.

Casgrain, *L'abbé* **H.-Raymond.** Un pèlerinage au pays d'Evangéline. Paris: Cerf. 1886. 4e éd. 1890. fr. 3.50. [3794

A brief in favor of the Acadians and their conduct at the period of deportation. Parkman made the mistake (which at the same time was a perfectly natural one) of relying on materials published by the Province of Nova Scotia— *Selections from the public documents of the Province of Nova Scotia*. These were badly garbled, as Casgrain from his researches in the British Museum and the Record Office has been able to show. But it does not, therefore, follow that the case against the Acadians falls to the ground. For a comparatively recent statement on the English side the reader should consult Sir Adams Archibald's *Expulsion of the Acadians*, Collections of the Nova Scotia Historical Society. Vol. V. Halifax. 1887. **C. W. C.**

—— Les Sulpiciens et les prêtres des missions-étrangères en Acadie, 1676–1762. Québec: Pruneau & Kirouac. 1897.

—— Mémoires sur les missions de la Nouvelle-Ecosse, du Cap Breton, et de l'Ile du Prince Edouard de 1760–1870. Québec: Darveau. 1895.

—— Documents inédits sur l'Acadie, 1710–1815. See sect. 3490. [3795

The Abbé Raymond Casgrain stands in the first rank of Canadian historians, and his conclusions must always be received with respect. As a French-Canadian and a cleric they will naturally differ from those of English and lay writers; and while full allowance may be necessary for his natural point of view, the same credit must always be given to his ripe scholarship and the untiring energy which has triumphed over failing sight to the completion of his many invaluable studies. He takes strong grounds on all points touching the Acadians, and no view of the subject can be complete without full consideration of his pleading in their behalf.

Confederation. Addresses from the two houses of Parliament of Canada, praying for admission of the colony of Newfoundland into the Dominion of Canada. London. 1869. [3796

Dawson, Samuel Edward. Canada and Newfoundland. See sect. 3585. [3796 a

Denis, Nicolas. Déscription géographique et historique des côtes de l'Amérique-Septentrionale, avec l'histoire naturelle de ce pays. Paris: Billaime. 1672. 2v. [3797

Charlevoix accords high praise to this work; it is the result of actual observation, but has little historic value.

Diéreville. Relation du voyage du Port Royal de l'Acadie ou de la Nouvelle France. Rouen. 1708. Amsterdam. 1710. [3798

A reprint of this curious work, with an introduction and notes by L. U. Fontaine, was published in Quebec, 1885, $1.

DuBoscq de Beaumont, Gaston. Les derniers jours de l'Acadie, 1748–1758 : correspondances et mémoires extraits du portefeuille de M. Le Courtois de Surlaville. Paris: Lechevalier. 1899. 6fr. [3799

Both the material and the notes of the editor are good.

Field, Rt. Rev. Edward. Journal of the Bishop's visitation of the missions on the western and southern coast. Aug. and Sept., 1845. London. 1846. [3800

Guénin, Eugène. Histoire de la colonisation française: La Nouvelle-France. Paris: Fourneau. 1896–8. 2v. fr. 3.50 ea. [3801

This work is published under the patronage of the Comité Dupleix, a society for promoting the revived colonization interests of France. Besides the work of France in Canada, it covers the efforts in the more southerly parts of America. The authorities used are mainly secondary, and few if any of them are in English, though the period of British rule in Canada is included. The tone is impartial, with an occasional display of strong national feeling. There are too many long quotations from other writers; but the narrative is accurate and clear in style. **G. M. W.**

Haliburton, Thomas Chandler. Historical and statistical account of Nova-Scotia. Halifax: Howe. 1829. 2v. [3802

"A work of conscientious and faithful labor, but in its preparation the author was under serious disadvantages from his inability to consult many of the books on which such a history must be based; and as he was not able to correct the proofs, his volumes are disfigured by the grossest typographical blunders. No one without some previous familiarity with the subject can safely read it; but such a reader will find in it much of value." Charles C. Smith, in *Narrative and critical hist. of Am.*, 4: 155.

—— Reply to the Report of the Earl of Durham. Halifax. 1839.

—— Rule and misrule of the English in America. Halifax: 1843. 2v. [3803

Judge Haliburton, like his friend the Rev. Richard Harris Barham, is better known by his pseudonym than by his own name. "Sam Slick" and "Ingoldsby" are household names the English world over, but many would be puzzled to say for whom they stand. Sam Slick is popularly believed to be a Yankee humourist who was "something in clocks," and but few connect the ridiculous name with that of the Hon. Thomas Chandler Haliburton, the able jurist, pamphleteer, and historian of Nova Scotia. He long discharged the somewhat unpleasant duties of a disturbing conscience to his quiet-going, overly-contented fellow-countrymen who would neither see nor seize the natural and political opportunities offered them. Much of his work was necessarily ephemeral, but the two titles above quoted will always be of value to the student of Nova Scotian history. Judge Haliburton was born at Windsor, N. S., in 1796, and died at Gordon House, Ilesworth, near London, England, in 1865.

A careful notice of Haliburton may be found in Morgan's *Bibliotheca Canadensis*, sect. 3458, see also the *Dictionary of national biography*, London, 1890, vol. 5, p. 24.

Hannay, James. History of Acadia. St. John, N. B. : McMillan. 1879. London: Low. 1880. [3804

A serviceable narrative of events in Acadia from the time of John Cabot till 1763, when the province was finally surrendered by France. While the product of care and research, it manifestly proceeds from an amateur rather than from a trained historian. In the specification and criticism of sources it is deficient.
C. W. C.

Harper, John. History of the maritime provinces of Canada. St. John, N. B. : McMillan. 1876. 40c. [3805

This is a well-arranged school-book. The author has adequate local knowledge and has read the best authorities. He gives a view of Newfoundland and of Nova Scotia, ₁New Brunswick, and Prince Edward Island, whose history is usually treated either separately or in connection with the history of Canada as a whole. It is a convenience to have them united as they are here.
G. M. W.

Hatton, Joseph, and **M. Harvey.** Newfoundland : its history, its present condition and its prospects in the future ; reprinted from Eng. ed., rev. and enl. Boston : Doyle. 1883. [3806

So far as can be made out from preface and contents, this book was prepared with the design of conveying a great deal of general information. It is not a history of Newfoundland in any true sense, for the historical part of the work is confined to 131 pages — hardly more than one fourth of the total space. Apart, too, from their limited extent, the historical chapters are not very satisfactory. On the other hand the descriptive portion contains much that is still valuable. Dr. Harvey, the principal contributor, also wrote a readable short sketch entitled, "Newfoundland in 1897," which was published on the occasion of Queen Victoria's Diamond Jubilee.
C. W. C.

Lescarbot, Marc. Histoire de la Nouvelle-France. Paris: Millot. 1609. 2v. Paris: Tross. 1866. 3v. [3807

Lescarbot's authority relates chiefly to the affairs of Port Royal in Acadia. A lawyer by profession and a Huguenot by faith, he connected himself with De Monts in the hope that he might help lay the foundation of a Protestant colony. He is an admirable writer, and infuses into his pages that sense of freshness and novelty which the pioneers felt. He reached Acadia in 1606, and his history was published at Paris three years later.
C. W. C.

Louisbourg. Lettre d'un habitant, etc. Repr. University of Toronto. Toronto. 1897. 75c. [3808

The extremely rare account of the first siege, 1745, is well reproduced and adequately translated by Professor George M. Wrong, of Toronto University. It is an essential document for any study of the history of this fortress.

McGregor, John. Historical and descriptive sketches of the maritime colonies of British America. London: Longmans. 1828. [3809

Moreau, M. Histoire de l'Acadie française de 1598–1755. Paris. 1873. [3810

Murdoch, Beamish. History of Nova Scotia. Halifax : Barnes. 1865–7. 3v. [3811

Not a history but a chronological digest, 1604–1827, which contains much excellent raw material. A skilful writer could easily transmute it into an admirable account of Nova Scotian affairs. Actually it is a very rough diamond.
C. W. C.

Pedley, Rev. **Charles.** History of Newfoundland from the earliest time. London. 1863. [3812

Good map. Superseded by Prowse. See next title.

Prowse, Daniel Woodley. History of Newfoundland from the English, colonial, and foreign records. London: Macmillan. 1895. 21s. [3813

The standard work on its subject and a historical sketch of considerable importance. Judge Prowse has gone beyond his predecessors in the matter of research, even culling unprinted documents from private collections in England, as well as from the British Museum and the Record Office. His own experiences enable him to speak with special authority on the relations existing between Newfoundland and the French colonies of St. Pierre and Miquelon. The treatise is comprehensive, extending from the earliest settlement to the date of publication. The type and plates of the first edition (1895) are of notable excellence.
C. W. C.

Rameau de Saint-Père, E. Une colonie féodale en l'Amérique ; l'Acadie, 1604–1881. Montreal: Granger Frères. 1889. 2v. $2. [3814

A valuable and interesting work, the most complete history of the period. The Acadian question is treated from the French point of view.

Reeves, John. Governors of Newfoundland : history of the Government of Newfoundland. London. 1793. [3815

Of sufficient note in its day to be translated into French during the year of publication and is still of value.

Richard, Edouard. Acadia ; missing links of a lost chapter in American history, by an Acadian. N. Y. : Home Book Co. [c. 1895.] 2v. Montreal: Granger Frères. 1895. $2. [3816

A labored and unconvincing attempt to refute Parkman's justification of the removal of the Acadians. It is involved and tedious in style, controversial and intemperate in tone, sometimes lapsing into personal invective. The partisan character of the book is evident on every page. The author gives few references, and shows little discrimination in appraising the value of documents. Although he writes English with facility, it is apparent that French is his mother tongue.

E. Cr.

Smith, Philip H. Acadia, a lost chapter in American history. N. Y.: Nash. 1884. [**3817**

The author travelled in Nova Scotia, and was impressed by the pathos of the story of the deportation of the Acadians in 1755. His work covers not only this event, but the whole period of the struggle between the French and English. In an appendix are some interesting French-Canadian legends. The book, crudely illustrated and printed by the author himself, is avowedly based upon "upwards of fifty" authorities, who are not named, but are apparently included in the more obvious printed sources. In his desire to do justice to an oppressed people the author sometimes forgets the calm impartiality of the historian. His theme, too, has been less neglected than he imagines. The book is throughout amateurish in both substance and style.   G. M. W.

Taché, Joseph Charles. Les Sablons (Ile de Sable). Montreal: Cadieux & Derome. 1885. 75c.   [**3818**

So little has been written on Sable Island that this modest description and history is worth mention. See, also, separate studies in Transactions of Royal Society, "Materials," sect. 3538, 3550.

Trade. Reports from the Committee on the state of trade to Newfoundland — March, April, June, 1793. London. n. d.   [**3819**

Gagnon notes this as important.

Willson, Henry Beckles. The Tenth Island; being some account of Newfoundland, its people, its politics, its problems and its peculiarities. London: Grant Richards. 1897. 3s. 6d. N. Y.: Mansfield. $1.50.   [**3820**

The Right Hon. Sir William Whiteway, Lord Charles Beresford, and Mr. Rudyard Kipling all stand as sponsors for Mr. Willson's book. Its defects in taste and style are obvious, but on the other hand many points are stated with the incisiveness of the practiced journalist. Its historical value is slight.

DIVISION VII: HUDSON'S BAY, NORTH-WEST AND LABRADOR

General Note

The modern history of the Canadian North-West begins with the foundation of the North-West Company in 1784. The Hudson's Bay Company claimed all the territory by a hundred years' priority of title, but their establishments in and about Hudson's Bay were cut off by a country so bare of game, and so difficult of travel, that they had never even tapped the West. Their shareholders and partners were English, and their entire intercourse was with Great Britain. Prior to the conquest their posts had been captured and destroyed by Canadians, but after that date there was no contact whatever with Canada. On the other hand, the North-West Company was distinctively Canadian, and formed perhaps the most important factor in the growth of Montreal from 1760 to 1800. Their headquarters were at Montreal, where lived the partners who built themselves handsome country-houses and entertained their friends and all accredited comers with a lavish hospitality, their ships sailed thence and returned every year, they founded the Beaver Club in 1785, and these keen-witted Scotchmen soon perceived the value of the French Canadian as a voyageur and an intermediary with the Indian. Their ranks were soon filled with the most adventurous youth of the country, and in this way the North-West Company probably took the first steps towards a practical reconciliation of the two races. Every trace of the North-West Company is so important that the travels of Mackenzie and of later explorers have been included in this section of the North-West without special notes.

[**3821**

Adam, Græme Mercer. The Canadian North-West : its history and its troubles. Toronto : Rose Pub. Co. 1885.   [**3822**

A book obviously suggested by the Riel rising of 1885, for a sketch of which it is chiefly valuable. However, it also touches on the era of exploration and colonization. It is not in any sense a work of erudition, but is calculated to arouse the interest of the "general reader" in the western regions of Canada.

C. W. C.

Back, *Capt.*, *Sir* **George.** Journal of the Arctic land expedition to the mouth of the Great Fish River, and along the shores of the Arctic Ocean, in the years 1833, 1834 and 1835. London : Murray. Paris : Gagliani. 1836. 1v.

—— Voyage aux régions arctiques à la recherche du Capitaine Ross, en 1834, et 1835; par le Capitaine Back. Paris: Bertrand. 1836. 2v.   [**3823**

Ballantyne, Robert Michael. Hudson's Bay ; or Every-day life in the wilds of North America, during six years' residence in the territories of the Hon. Hudson's Bay Company. Edin.: Nelson. 1848. Boston. 1859. [**3824**

"Among the considerable number of writers who have served that Company, none have produced a more complete, interesting and evidently faithful narration of the various phases of a fur trader's life among the Indians, than Mr. Ballantyne." T. W. Field, *Indian bibliography*, p. 17.

Ballantyne, who for an earlier generation held the place of Henty in this, wrote the book out of the fulness of his knowledge of the place and its people, for which reason it will always be of value.

Begg, Alexander. *1825–*. History of British Columbia. Toronto : Briggs. 1894. $3. London: Low. 1896. 12s. 6d.   **[3825**

This volume contains a mass of interesting information concerning the Pacific slope of British North America, which is digested in chronological order ; but it can hardly be called a symmetrical history. Still it is the best general account of British Columbian origins and progress which at present exists, and possesses the merit of clearness. It begins with Capt. Cook's third voyage in 1776, and is brought down to 1894. The material is topically arranged under paragraphs, each of which bears a separate title. One distinct shortcoming which may be mentioned is the lack of an index.   C. W. C.

Begg, Alexander. *1840–1897*. History of the North-West. Toronto: Hunter. 1894–5. 3v. (For sale by Raymond Finchamp, Dundas, Ont. Half leather, $6; cl., $5.)   **[3826**

An extensive, well-compiled account of European settlement and progress in the region which was originally granted to the Hudson Bay Company. It thus includes within its survey both the Province of Manitoba and the Northwest territories in their present political sense. While deriving little assistance from graces of style, this book is written by one who has a sound knowledge of the country described, and has brought great zeal to the examination of its past. Each volume contains a useful appendix of documents.   C. W. C.

Bryce, *Rev.* **George.** Manitoba : its infancy, growth and present condition. London: Sampson Low. 1882.   **[3827**

—— The remarkable history of the Hudson's Bay Company, including that of the French traders of North-Western Canada and of the North-West, X. Y., and Astor Fur Companies. London : Sampson Low. N. Y.: Scribner. 1900. $4.   **[3828**

The best history of this great monopoly. Mr. Bryce had the great advantage of knowing his ground personally, and much of his information of the later days he received from the lips of survivors of the days when the " H. B. C." owned the land as well as the inhabitants thereof.

Cartwright, George. Journal of transactions and events during a residence of nearly sixteen years on the coast of Labrador. Newark. 1792. 3v.   **[3829**

Coues, Elliott. New light on the history of the greater North-West. See Alexander Henry the Younger, sect. 3838.   **[3830**

Cox, Ross. Adventures on the Columbia River, including a narrative of six years' resi-

dence on the western side of the Rocky Mountains, together with a journey across the American continent. London. 1831. N. Y.: Harper. 1832.   **[3830 a**

An important and well-known book.

Dobbs, Arthur. Account of the countries adjoining Hudson's Bay. London. 1744. **[3831**

An exceedingly important work on the early history and struggle for the possession of Hudson's Bay, with valuable addenda containing charter, exports and profits of the Company, vocabularies of Indian languages, etc.

Dugas, *l' Abbé* **G.** Légendes du Nord-Ouest. Montréal: C. O. Beauchemin and Fils. n. d. 25c.   **[3832**

Folk-lore and historical legend.

—— Un voyageur des pays d'en haut. Montreal: C. O. Beauchemin and Fils. n. d. Paper, 60c.   **[3833**

Both these small books contain much good detail on early days. See, also, Provencher, sect. 3859.

Ellis, Henry. Voyage for the discovery of a north-west passage by Hudson's Straits to the western and southern ocean of America in the years 1746 and 1747. London. 1748. 2v.   **[3834**

The best French translation is that by Sellius. Paris. 1750.

Gunn, Donald, *and* **C. R. Tuttle.** History of Manitoba, from the earliest settlement to 1835, by the late Hon. Donald Gunn; and from 1835 to the admission of the province into the Dominion, by Charles R. Tuttle. Ottawa, Ont.: Printed by MacLean, Roger & Co. 1880.   **[3835**

Hearne, Samuel. Journey from Prince of Wales Fort in Hudson's Bay to the northern ocean, etc., 1769–1772. London. 1795. **[3836**

The account of the first overland journey to the Arctic Ocean. Much attention is given to the natural history of the region traversed. Fine maps.

Henry, Alexander. Travels and adventures in Canada and the Indian territories between the years 1760 and 1776 : in two parts. N. Y. 1809. New ed., edited by James Bain. Toronto: G. N. Morang & Co. 1901. $3.50. Boston: Little, Brown & Co. $4.   **[3837**

The original edition has been a rare book as far back as 1839. Mr. Bain has added to his handsome work excellent notes containing much additional information. This simple narrative of the first English fur-trader beyond the Ottawa is well told ; it is filled with stirring adventure, and is the best account of the opening of the English fur-trade in the North-West.

Henry, Alexander, *the Younger.* Manuscript journals of a fur-trader in the North-West Company, and of David Thompson, official geographer and explorer of the same Company, 1799–1814. Edited by Elliott Coues. Index and Maps. N. Y. : Francis P. Harper. 1897. 3v. $20. [3838

No work on the North-West has been so ably edited ; the numerous biographical notes are a monument of patient research. The text is full of most important detail on Indian customs, and incidentally the methods of trading are given without reserve. Dr. Coues entitled the work " New light on the early history of the greater North-West," and it well deserves the description. Henry was a nephew of the elder Alexander Henry, see sect. 3837.

Hind, Henry Youle. North-West Territory. Toronto. 1859.

—— Narrative of the Canadian Red River exploring expedition of 1857. London. 1860. 2v.

—— Sketch of the overland route to British Columbia. Toronto. 1862. [3839

Hinsdale, B. A. The old North-West. N. Y. 1888. [3840

Contains information as to exploration and occupation by the French. For notice, see sect. 3360.

Hudson's Bay. Committee appointed to inquire into the state and conditions of the countries adjoining to Hudson's Bay, and of the trade carried on there.

—— Papers presented to committee. London. 1754. Report from the committee ; together with an appendix. Reported by Lord Strange, 24th April, 1749. 2v. [3841

. An important collection of extracts from official letters and journals relating to the explorations and trade carried on by the Hudson's Bay Company's agents between 1676 and 1748. It contains the journal of Henry Kelsey's exploring expedition from York Fort in 1691-2 ; the narrative of Joseph La France ; many letters from Richard Norton, factor at Prince of Wales's Fort from 1724 to 1740 ; the evidence of witnesses examined, besides statistics of exports and imports, from 1738 to 1748, with accounts of sales of furs and the standard of trade used in dealing with the Indians. E. Cr.

—— Transactions between England and France relating to Hudson's Bay, 1687. See Archives "Materials," sect. 3465, for year 1883. [3842

Important.

Iberville, Pierre le Moyne d'. Desmazures, Charles, l'Abbé. Histoire. Montréal : J. M. Valois. 1890. $1.50. [3843

This monograph, though containing little that is new, is carefully written and illustrated with good maps. See, also, sect. 3742.

Jeremie, M., Gouverneur du Fort Bourbon. Relation du Detroit et de la Baie Hudson. (In Charlevoix's Voyages au nord, v. 5.) [3844

Charlevoix said: "I knew the author, who was a most honorable man and an experienced traveller. It was he who, after the Peace of Utrecht, gave up Fort Bourbon or Port Nelson in Hudson's Bay, where he had commanded for six years, to the English. His journal is instructive and written with judgment."

Long, John. See under English Régime, sect. 3741. [3845

MacBeth, Roderick George. Making of the Canadian west. Toronto : Briggs. 1898. $1. [3846

The author, born in the Canadian west when it was still ruled under the charter of the Hudson's Bay Co., describes the isolation of the settlers, and their suspicions when the government of the new Dominion of Canada assumed authority. He remembers and describes scenes in the first rebellion under Louis Riel, crushed by Lord Wolseley in 1870, and he took an active part against the second one in 1885. The book, which is written in good literary style, is mainly confined to personal reminiscence, and is thus not a complete history. It is the most attractive volume dealing with the subject that has yet appeared.
G. M. W.

—— The Selkirk Settlers in real life : with an introduction by Lord Strathcona. Toronto : Briggs. 75c. [3847

*A short but useful addition to the history of the Selkirk experiment. See Selkirk Settlement, sect. 3863-3874.

Macdonald, Duncan George Forbes. British Columbia and Vancouver's Island ; comprising a description of these dependencies : their physical character, climate, capabilities, population, trade, natural history, geology, ethnology, gold-fields and future prospects : also an account of the manners and customs of the native Indians. London: Longmans. 1862. [3848

MacFie, Matthew. Vancouver Island and British Columbia : their history, resources and prospects. London: Longmans. 1865. [3849

The author, a geologist of mark, resided in British Columbia five years.

Mackenzie, Sir **Alexander.** Voyages from Montreal, through the continent of North America, 1789 and 1793. London : Cadell. 1801. Phil.: Morgan. 1802. [3850

The work of an undaunted and successful explorer. Mackenzie's expeditions were undertaken on behalf of the North-West Fur Co. (which towards the close of the 18th century was attempting to break through the Hudson's Bay Company's monopoly), and were attended by many dangers both from nature and man. His main point of departure was Fort Chipewayan on Lake Athabasca — then called Lake of the Hills — whence he set out in 1789 for the Arctic Sea, and in 1792 for the Pacific. In both cases he reached his goal, surmounting constant and most obstinate difficulties. In this region he was the pioneer among Europeans, and his book is a classic. Prefaced to the narrative of his own discoveries is a general history of the fur trade.   C. W. C.

Maclean, John. Native tribes of the Dominion. Toronto: Briggs. 1900. $2.50. [3851
The most important work discussing the origin, traditions, and history of Canadian Indians of late years.

Martin, Archer. The Hudson's Bay Company's land tenures and the occupation of Assiniboia by Lord Selkirk's settlers, with a list of the grantees under the Earl and the Company. London: Wm. Clowes & Son. 1898. 15s.   [3852
Though interested in a highly technical argument as to legality of titles, Mr. Martin has found and preserved much valuable material with good notes and maps.

Martin, Horace T. Castorologia; or, The history and traditions of the Canadian beaver. Montreal: W. Drysdale & Co. $2. London: Edward Stanford. 1892. 10s. 6d.   [3853
Much information on the fur trade. Good maps, illustrations, and titles in facsimile. Includes natural history, important details of fur trade, values, qualities of beaver, manufactures, folk-lore, etc.

Masson, Louis François Rodrigue. Les bourgeois de la compagnie du Nord-Ouest : récits de voyages, lettres, et rapports inédits relatifs au Nord-Ouest canadien ; publiés avec une esquisse historique et des annotations. Quebec. 1889–90. Ser. 1–2. 2v. (For sale by Granger Brothers. Montreal. $4.)   [3854
A careful historical sketch of the North-West Fur Company of Montreal, followed by journals, confidential reports, and letters written by F. W. Wentzel, Simon Fraser, François Victoire, John MacDonell, F. A. Larocque, Charles Mackenzie, George Keith, John Johnston, S. H. Wilcocke, Duncan Cameron, Peter Grant, and James Mackenzie, partners in or agents of the Company. The historical essay, a very good piece of work, is in French, and the documents (with a single exception) and the notes are in English. An invaluable storehouse of materials for the history of the exploration of the Canadian North-West and the fur trade, and also of cardinal importance from an ethnological standpoint. It is a matter of regret that all the documents were not published entire.
                                        E. Cr.

Mayne, *Commander* **R. C.** Four years in British Columbia and Vancouver Island: an account of their forests, rivers, coasts, goldfields and resources for colonization. London: John Murray. 1862.   [3855
Milton, William Wentworth Fitzwilliam,

viscount, and **W. B. Cheadle.** The north-west passage by land: being the narrative of an expedition from the Atlantic to the Pacific. London: Cassell. 1865. Cheaper ed. 1867.
                                        [3856
Packard, Alpheus Spring. The Labrador coast : a journal of two summer cruises to that region : with notes on its early discovery, on the Eskimo, on its physical geography, geology, and natural history. N. Y.: N. D. C. Hodges. London: Kegan Paul. 1891. [3857
Proulx, *Rev.* **J. B.** A la Baie d'Hudson ou récit de la première visite pastorale de Mgr. N. Z. Lorrain, Evêque de Cythère, etc. Montreal: Cadieux et Derome. 1886.   [3858
A series of well-written letters from June to August, 1884, describing the canoe route by Abbitibi to Moose and Albany, together with historical sketches of the early missionaries and d'Iberville's exploits in Hudson's Bay.

Provencher, *Mgr.* **Joseph Norbert.** Monseigneur Provencher et les missions de la Rivière Rouge. Montreal : Beauchemin. 1889.
                                        [3859
Contains interesting detail on the conditions of the North-West during the earlier part of the 19th century.

Radisson, Pierre Esprit, *and* **Médard Chouart,** *Sieur* **des Groseilliers.** Voyages. See Prince Society, sect. 387; Transactions Royal Society of Canada under Bryce, Dionne, sect. 3535, 3540 ; Archives of Canada 1895, sect. 3475 ; State Hist. Soc. Wisconsin Collections, sect. 3390.   [3860
Riel's Rebellion. BOULTON, *Major* CHARLES A. Reminiscences of the North-West rebellions. Toronto. 1886.   [3861
— CANADA. *Department of Militia and Defence.* Report upon the suppression of the rebellion in the North-West, and matters in connection therewith, in 1885. Ottawa. 1886.
                                        [3862
A minute official account of the military operations which resulted in the suppression of Louis Riel's rebellion fills the first 75 pages, and is accompanied by plans and views illustrating several engagements. The remainder of the book is devoted to war claims and reports of the surgical staff.   F. J. S.

Selkirk, *Earl of.* A sketch of the British fur trade in North America ; with observations relative to the North-West Company of Montreal. 2d ed. London : James Ridgway. 1816.
                                        [3863
—— Narrative of occurrences in the Indian countries of North America since the connexion of the Rt. Hon. the Earl of Selkirk with

the Hudson's Bay Company, and his attempt to establish a colony in the Red River; with a detailed account of His Lordship's military expedition to, and subsequent proceedings at Fort William, in Upper Canada. London. 1817. [3864

—— Sketch of the British fur trade in North America; with observations relative to the North-West Company of Montreal. London and N. Y. 1818. [3865

—— Statement respecting the Earl of Selkirk's settlement upon the Red River in North America, its destruction in 1815 and 1816, and the massacre of Gov. Semple and his party: with observations upon a recent publication, entitled "A narrative of occurrences in the Indian countries." 1817. [3866

—— Trials of the Earl of Selkirk, vs. the North-West Company in 1818. Montreal. 1819. [3867

Selkirk Settlement. Amos, A. Report of trials in the courts of Canada, relative to the destruction of the east of Selkirk's Settlement on the Red River, with observations. London: John Murray. 1820. [3868

— Gale, Samuel. Notices of the claims of the Hudson's Bay Company, and the conduct of its adversaries. Montreal: Printed by William Gray. 1817. [3869

— MacBeth, R. G. Selkirk settlers in real life. See sect. 3847. [3870

— MacDonald, Archibald. Reply to letter lately addressed to the Right Honorable the Earl of Selkirk, by the Hon. and Rev. John Strachan, D. D., Rector of York, in Upper Canada; being four letters (reprinted from the Montreal Herald) ; containing a statement of facts concerning the settlement on Red River, in the District of Assiniboia, territory of the Hon. Hudson's Bay Company, properly called Rupert's Land. Montreal: Gray. 1816. [3871

— "Mercator." The communications of Mercator, upon the contest between the Earl of Selkirk, and the Hudson's Bay Company, on one side, and the North-West Company on the other: republished from the Montreal Herald. Montreal: Printed by William Gray. 1816. [3872

— Proceedings at a Court of Oyer and Terminer appointed for the investigation of cases from the Indian territories ; held by adjournment at Quebec in Lower Canada, 21st October, 1819; at which the following gentle-

men, partners of, and connected with, the North-West Company, viz.: Arch. N. McLeod, Simon Fraser, James Leith, Alex. Macdonnell, Hugh McGillis, Arch. McLellan, and John Siveright, who were under accusation by the Earl of Selkirk, as private prosecutor, for great crimes and offences, alleged to have been by them committed, made their appearance, in pursuance of official notices given to both parties, and demanded their trials, which they could not obtain because the private prosecutor was not ready: with the speeches of counsel, the arguments held on the occasion, and the decision given thereon, from minutes taken in Court. Montreal: Gray. 1819. [3873

— Proceedings connected with the disputes between the Earl of Selkirk and the North-West Company, at the assizes, held at York, in Upper Canada, October, 1818; from minutes taken in Court. Montreal: Printed by James Lane and Nahan Mower. 1819. [3874

Simpson, Sir George. Narrative of a journey round the world, 1841–2. London. 1847. Philadelphia. 1847. [3875

Interesting account of Canadian North-West. Sir George was Governor of Hudson's Bay Company.

Simpson, Thomas. Life and travels, by his brother Alexander. London. 1845. [3876

Thomas Simpson was secretary to Sir George Simpson. He was believed to have been murdered by the Indians near Red River. This record runs from 1829–40.

Tassé, Joseph. Les Canadiens de l'ouest. Montreal. 1878. 2e éd. 2v. Montreal: Granger Frères. $3. [3877

Short biographies of Charles de Langlade, J. B. Cadot, Charles Reaume, Jacques Porlier, Joseph Rolette, Salamon Juneau, Julien Dubuque, Antoine Leclerc, Jacques Duperon Baby, Joseph Rainville, Louis Provençal, J. B. Faribault, J. B. Lefebvre, J. B. Perrault, J. M. Ducharme, Vital Guerin, Joseph Rolette, fils, J. B. Mallet, François Ménard, J. B. Beaubien, Noel Levasseur, Joseph Robidou, J. B. L. Roy, L. V. Baugy, Jacques Fournier, M. B. Ménard, F. X. Aubry, Antoine Leroux, Prudent Beaudry, Gabriel Franchère, P. C. Pambrun, Joseph Larocque, Pierre Falcon, and Louis Riel, père. These volumes contain much important information as to the participation of French Canadians in the exploration, commerce, and settlement of the American and Canadian North-West since the conquest of Canada. Journalistic and slightly exaggerated in tone, but fairly accurate in statement and indicating much research.   E. Cr.

Thompson, David. Geographer of North-West Company. See Alexander Henry the Younger, sect. 3838. [3878

Umfreville, Edward. The present state of Hudson's Bay; containing a full description of that settlement, and the adjacent country; and likewise of the fur trade, with hints for its improvement, etc.: to which are added remarks and observations made in the inland parts during a residence of nearly four years; a specimen of five Indian languages; and a journal of a journey from Montreal to New York. London. 1790. [3879

Willson, Henry Beckles. The Great Company: merchant adventurers trading in Hudson's Bay. Toronto: Copp. 1899. $3. New and enl. ed. London: Smith, Elder & Co. 2v. 18s. [3880

" It is to be regretted that Mr. Willson has not done better justice to the importance and interest of a subject that he so well understands. He shows commendable diligence and application in the accumulation and presentation of material that is at once interesting and valuable, but he does not show literary art, or even a good book-maker's skill. . . . Sometimes he seems to miss the connection of events, and his narrative becomes confused and vexing to the reader. . . . Sometimes the sources of the narrative are given, and sometimes they are not. . . . We do not say that his narrative is always heavy and slow; but it does seem a pity that he should not have made a more effective use of the picturesque and romantic elements of his story. . . . Still the author is entitled to the praise of having brought together in an accessible and readable form a vast amount of important information relative to a great subject." B. A. Hinsdale, in *Dial*, 28: 197.

DIVISION VIII: EDUCATION

Archives, Canadian. Education in the Canadas, 1818–1831. Report for 1899, see pp. 49 to 67. Sect. 3479.

—— Sessional paper with documents, etc. Report for 1900. See pp. 1 to 49, 1832–1835. Sect. 3480. [3881

Includes Provinces of Quebec and Ontario.

Chauveau, Pierre J. O. L'instruction publique au Canada: précis historique et statistique. Québec: Côté. 1876. [3882

This summary by an ex-Minister of Public Instruction is devoted to the existing state of education in the provinces taken in detail. It contains no general historical view.

Dawson, Sir John William. Fifty years' work in Canada, scientific and educational. Edited by Rankine Dawson, M. D. London: Ballantyne Hanson & Co. 1901. $1.50. [3883

In great part compiled from Sir William's own notes. Whatever difference of opinion there may have been as to the position taken by Sir William Dawson in scientific subjects, there has been unanimous recognition of the high value of his long service to Canada as a leader in education, especially in his position of Principal of McGill University.

Hodgins, J. George. Documentary history of education in Upper Canada, 1791–1876. Vols. 1–6 now ready. Toronto: Department of Education. 1894–9. [3883 a

A reprint in detail of all parliamentary proceedings, orders in council, correspondence and official documents relating to the introduction and maintenance of education in Ontario prior to confederation (1867).

J. B.

Manitoba school question. When Rupert's Land and the North-West Territory were admitted into the Dominion of Canada as the Province of Manitoba, it was enacted in section 22 of the "Manitoba Act," in relation to education: (1) that existing denominational schools shall not be prejudicially affected; (2) that an appeal shall lie to the Governor-General-in-Council from any act affecting the rights of the Protestant or Roman Catholic minority; and (3) in the event of any law not being passed to carry out these provisions or that any appeal hereunder is not made efficient, that the Parliament of Canada is empowered to make remedial laws to meet the case. [3884

At that time, 1870, the minority was Protestant, but twenty years later, in 1890, conditions had changed and the minority was Roman Catholic. The provisions of the Manitoba Act were faithfully carried out in the beginning, but in 1888, the agitation over the Jesuits' estates, in Quebec, led to the formation of the Equal Rights Association in Ontario, and undoubtedly to the cry in Manitoba of "No dual language, no separate schools!" [3885

The history of the Manitoba school question may be thus traced:—

Many papers at first published separately by the Queen's Printer, Ottawa, can only be found now in the bound vols. of Sessional Papers, 1891–6. Every vol. has a table of contents by subjects for its year. The Manitoba school question was first formally raised in two suits in Manitoba, Barrett *vs.* City of Winnipeg and Logan *vs.* City of Winnipeg. These passed through all the courts until final decision was reached in the Imperial Privy Council. Then followed the attempt to apply a remedy by legislation. [3886

— EWART, J. S. Manitoba school question. Toronto: Copp, Clark Co. 1894. $1.75. [3887

— WADE, F. C. The Manitoba school question. Winnipeg: Manitoba Institution for the Deaf and Dumb. 1895. [3888

— EWART, JOHN S. The Manitoba school question. A reply to Mr. Wade. Winnipeg: Manitoba Free Press Co. 1895. [3889

— FISHER, JAMES, *M. P. P.* The Manitoba school question. Winnipeg. 1895. [3890

— "Is Manitoba right?" A review of the Manitoba school question published by the Winnipeg Tribune. 1895. 15c. [3891

— TUPPER, *Sir* CHARLES HIBBERT, *K. C. M. G.* The Manitoba school question. *National review*, May, 1896. London and N. Y.: Edward Arnold. Other articles on same theme by T. C. Down, *Nineteenth century*, 40: 117; Clifford Sifton, *Review of reviews*, N. Y., 12: 452; Goldwin Smith, *Forum*, 21: 65. [3892

— The Manitoba school case. People's almanac, 1896, "The Gazette," Montreal. [3893

— The Ontario Legislature : debate on Mr. Crawford's motion regarding remedial legislation, March 4, 1896. (Supplement to "The Week," Toronto, March 6, 1896.) [3894

— POWER, *Senator*. The remedial bill from the point of view of a Catholic member. Ottawa : Thoburn & Co., Printers. 1896. [3895

— The remedial act. (Manitoba.) Hon. Arthur Rupert Dickey. Ottawa: Queen's Printer. 1896. Debate in House of Commons. Part I. From rev. ed. Hansard. Ottawa. 1896. Part II. Proceedings subsequent to second reading. Ottawa: Queen's Printer, 1896. [3896

Part I. is much the more important.

— Articles in "Montreal Daily Witness," May 18, 1896, and "A political review," April 15, 1896. [3897

— Papal Encyclical. In Le Propagateur, 15 Janvier, 1898, bulletin bi-mensuel du clergé et des familles. Montréal : Cadieux & Derome. [3898

Meilleur, Jean Baptiste. Mémorial de l'éducation du bas-Canada. Montréal. 1860. 2e éd. Québec. 1876. [3899

Dr. Meilleur, first Superintendent of Education for Lower Canada, was peculiarly fitted by his training for the requirements of his position. He had studied law, took his degree as M. D. in 1825, was a member of Parliament and a student and writer on natural science. His memorial is of the highest importance for the history of primary and higher education in Canada, with special reference to the Province of Quebec. It is wide in scope and thorough in detail, and is handled throughout with that authority which arises from an acknowledged mastery of his subject.

New Brunswick school law, Manual. Rev. ed. Fredericton, N. B. 1901. (To be had on application to the Chief Superintendent of Education, Fredericton, N. B.) [3900

A leading educator of the province says: "The Act set forth in this manual provides for a free non-sectarian education for every child in New Brunswick, without any privileges to one denomination more than to another. By tacit consent, however, of the Provincial Board of Education, local boards of trustees may give permission to Roman Catholic teachers to instruct the children of Roman Catholics in religion after school hours. This is general in the larger towns and cities of the province, the use of the school-rooms being granted for the purpose."

Ontario, Educational system of. MILLAR, JOHN. Toronto : Department of Education. 1893. [3900 a

An official description of the kindergartens, public schools, high schools, collegiate institutes and colleges. Details are also given as to the requirements of teachers, their training and examinations. Lists of text-books are included. J. B.

Perrault, Joseph François. CASGRAIN, P. B. Biographie. Quebec. 1898.

— CASGRAIN, H. R., *l'Abbé*. Vie. Quebec: Darveau. 1899.

— BENDER, P. Old and new Canada; historic scenes and social pictures, or, The life of Joseph François Perrault, 1753–1844. Montreal. 1882. $3. [3901

Joseph François Perrault was Prothonotary at Quebec. After an adventurous youth among the Indians of the Ohio valley, he devoted his energies to the foundation and encouragement of primary and agricultural education in the Province of Quebec. In 1821 he organized an Educational Association, and under its auspices the first free Roman Catholic school in Quebec was founded. He not only gave liberally of time and money, but wrote many primary text-books himself; he was the father of lay education in the Province. When he died, in 1844, at the great age of 91, he had the satisfaction of seeing much of his long effort crowned with success.

Quebec, Province of, School law; with notes of numerous judicial decisions thereon, and the regulations of the Protestant and Roman Catholic Committees of the Council of Public Instruction: compiled by G. W. Parmelee, secretary of the Department of Public Instruction. Quebec. 1899. [3902

In the Province of Quebec the children of Roman Catholics attend schools under Roman Catholic direction, the children of Protestants attend schools under Protestant control.

Ryerson, *Rev.* **Adolphus Egerton.** Report on a system of public elementary instruction for Upper Canada. Montreal. 1846–7.

—— Correspondence on subject of separate schools. Toronto. 1855.   [3902 a

Dr. Ryerson was for many years Superintendent of Education for the Province of Ontario, and during a long life issued many pamphlets and works on education. He was eminently a controversialist.

Universities of Canada, their history and organization, with an outline of British and American systems. Appendix to the Report of the Minister of Education, Ontario. Toronto. 1896.   [3902 b

An official report upon the history and present condition of Canadian Universities by the Minister of Education for Ontario. It is the best authority for a knowledge of these institutions.   J. B.

PART VI: SPANISH AND PORTUGUESE AMERICA AND THE WEST INDIES

(*Most of the titles of books in this list on Mexico, Central and South America, and the West Indies, have been selected, and the notes, unless otherwise signed, prepared, by Mr. George Parker Winship, of the John Carter Brown Library in Providence, R. I.*)

GENERAL NOTE ON THE LITERATURE OF SPANISH-AMERICAN HISTORY

By G. P. Winship.

THE study of Spanish-American history in English is not an easy task. The professional student of history, working at the larger libraries, finds an abundance of books and ample documentary material, all relating to certain limited periods in the annals of South America. If his interest takes him beyond the limits of these periods, he finds few books, of very unsatisfactory quality, and almost nothing which will enable him to investigate the actual course of events or the development of the social and political characteristics of the people. Aside from a few episodes chiefly made up of marching and fighting and shooting, almost no good work has yet been done towards elucidating the course of Spanish-American history.   [3903

The episodes which have attracted writers, either because of the opportunities for dramatic narrative or on account of temporary popular interest, have been made the subject of many books. In several cases the best of these books were written in English, although it is unfortunately true that very often the books which enjoy the widest reputation are not those upon whose accuracy and fairness the reader can rely most safely. It is a comparatively easy task to acquaint one's self with the course and the causes of events in Mexico in 1520 or 1865, or in Peru in 1525 or 1880, despite the fact that the casual reader is likely to find considerable difficulty in reconciling the statements and the explanations in any two books about the same episode. With a little

persistence, also, much information of very uncertain value can be secured in regard to the revolutionary period during which the South American republics established their independence from Spain. It is, however, very far from easy to find out what happened in Central or South America between 1550 and 1810, or to secure any satisfactory explanation of events in general since 1825. There are a few books which offer everything except the information most desired, in regard to these periods, but there is nothing which can fairly claim to describe the historical development of any of the southern republics. One or two of the Mexican historians have collected large quantities of details concerning the political changes in their country, but no satisfactory narrative of the course of events has yet been written.   [3904

It might be possible to secure accurate information about certain episodes in Spanish-American history without a knowledge of the Spanish language. It is utterly impossible to comprehend that history without an intimate appreciation of the Spanish national characteristics — of the habits of thought and action of the Spanish-American race. Such an understanding of the way in which the men who took part in that history regarded words and actions — of the effect produced by proclamations and enactments, by victories, truces and executions — can only be secured by most persons by prolonged residence among these peoples and by continued observation of their habits of living and thinking, of their social and political customs. Such a preparation will be impossible for most North Americans who will read about South American history. This consideration explains why a number of books of travel and recollections of residence in the Spanish-American countries have been included in the following bibliography. Most of these books contain chapters devoted to historical narrative. In the majority of cases, these

441

chapters possess only the slightest value, from the standpoint of technical history. But these volumes contain also the record of personal, individual experiences, and every such record of human experiences is valuable. Not only are these books more interesting in themselves, to the majority of readers, but they are also of vastly more practical value than the formal historical narratives for giving the reader an idea of what real history is like. In any event, a preliminary course of reading in books of this sort is of almost imperative importance if the ordinary North American reader is to understand the significance of historical events in Central and South America.   [3905

Readers who wish to understand the history of the native Americans in the central and southern portions of this hemisphere, or who wish to secure a clear conception of the kind of civilization which the Spanish conquerors found in the New World, should examine the collections of American antiquities which are to be found in most public museums. Nowhere, except at the ruins themselves, scattered about in several widely separated countries, can so good an idea of what that civilization really amounted to be secured, as in some of the larger eastern museums. There are a number of these collections which give a very good representation of the original remains and of casts taken from buildings still standing or from noteworthy specimens in other museums. These provide ample opportunities for a comparative study of the relative development of the earlier inhabitants of Mexico, Honduras, Peru, and their neighboring countries. The American Antiquarian Society at Worcester, Mass., and the Peabody Museum, now a part of Harvard University, were among the first to recognize the importance of gathering together specimens of the aboriginal handiwork from Central and South America, at the time when interest in these matters was stirred up by the publications of Brantz Mayer, Squier, Catherwood, and Stephens, late in the first half of the nineteenth century. The museum at Cambridge has fortunately been enabled to maintain an uninterrupted interest in the collection of Central American antiquities, and by its expeditions equipped through the liberality of the Hon. Stephen Salisbury, Mr. Charles P. Bowditch, and a few others, it has secured specimens which, when added to its casts secured by exchange with other museums, make this

probably the best collection for the general uses of students in this country. The American Museum of Natural History in New York is rapidly acquiring a very valuable collection, which is especially notable for its Peruvian antiquities secured by Mr. A. F. Bandelier, who was sent to South America several years ago for this purpose by the late Henry Villard. It also contains much important data secured in Mexico, through the liberality of the Duke of Loubat, by Mr. M. H. Saville, who has described many of his acquisitions in the publications of the museum. In Chicago the Field Columbian Museum contains the nucleus of a most valuable collection, especially rich in aboriginal gold work, and its published memoirs describing its specimens, by Messrs. Mason, Dorsey, and others, have greatly increased the serviceableness of the museum. The National Museum at Washington also has an extremely useful collection of casts and specimens from Mexico and the southern countries. At each of these museums the curious visitor will find abundant opportunity to secure a realizing sense of the surprising ruins at Mitla, Copan, and hundreds of other less known places, where the ruins of buildings bear convincing witness to the capacity and the advancement of the more highly developed of the aboriginal Americans. Most of these ruins have now been carefully surveyed, photographed, and copied by means of casts. The descriptions, plans, and illustrations may be found scattered through the publications of the museums and learned societies of Europe and America. The more important of the works published for the general reader, descriptive of these ruins, are noted in the following lists.   [3906

GENERAL WORKS

Acosta, Joseph de. Natural and moral history of the Indies, reprinted from the translated ed. of Edward Grimston, London, 1604, and ed. by Clements R. Markham. London: Hakluyt Soc. 1880. 2v.   [3907

A philosophical historical work, by a brilliant graduate from the Jesuit schools. It shows much learning, and a wide acquaintance with the New World. It is, altogether, the most satisfactory of the earlier general works (first Spanish edition, 1590). It contains an account of the cosmography of the New World, of the religion and government of the natives of Peru and Mexico, together with a brief recital of their conquest by the Spaniards.

Bonnycastle, *Sir* **Richard Henry.** Spanish America. London. 1818. 2v.   [**3908**

Captain Bonnycastle compiled his work with considerable care from the writings of Humboldt, and from the standard early Spanish books upon the American colonies. His volumes present a very useful summary of the condition of Spanish America at the time when the several colonies began their career as independent states.

Brackenridge, Henry M. Voyage to South America, performed by order of the American government, 1817–18. Balt.: Author. 1819. 2v. London. 1820. 2v.   [**3909**

Mr. Brackenridge was secretary of the commission despatched by President Monroe to investigate the condition and prospects of the revolted colonies of Spain. Long familiar with Spanish American life from his residence in Louisiana and conversant with the Spanish language, he was an exceptionally well-equipped observer. His observations were for the most part confined to the River Plate region and the eastern coast of Brazil. Alexander von Humboldt is quoted by Allibone as having characterized this work as containing "an extraordinary mass of information, replete with philosophic views." It is especially valuable for the insight it gives into the causes and character of the Spanish-American revolution.

E. G. B.

Brownell, Henry. North and South America; illustrated. Hartford. 1863. 2v.   [**3910**

The account of the South American republics in volume 1 possesses the characteristics of untrustworthy inaccuracy which are usually associated with the narratives prepared by hack writers for books designed to be sold by subscription in the rural districts. It is a readable summary of the picturesque details taken from the more available works of earlier date.

Butterworth, Hezekiah. South America: a popular illustrated history of the struggle for liberty in the Andean republics and Cuba. N. Y.: Doubleday & McClure; Doubleday, Page. 1898. $2.   [**3911**

A summary of extensive reading inspired by travel. A readable narrative of events, based upon the most reliable available books, compiled with conscientious skill.

Curtis, William Eleroy. Capitals of Spanish America. N. Y.: Harper. 1888. $3.50.   [**3912**

An interesting narrative, describing the impressions of an intelligent American visiting the South American countries as the authorized representative of the United States. It repeats many of the stories of history which are inevitably retailed to travellers in strange and foreign climes.

Deberle, Alfred. Histoire de l'Amérique du sud depuis la conquête jusqu'à nos jours. 3e éd. revue par Albert Milhaud. Paris: Alcan. 1897. fr. 3.50.   [**3913**

An excellent work, first published in 1876. One of the very best short outlines of the general history of the southern continent.

—— History of South America from its discovery to the present time, compiled from the works of the best authors and from authentic documents, many hitherto unpublished, in various archives and public and private libraries in America and Spain; by an American; tr. from the Spanish by Adnah D. Jones. London: Sonnenschein. N. Y.: Macmillan. 1899. Net $3.   [**3914**

" This ostentatious title masks a fraud. The anonymous author of the *Historia de la America del Sur, desde su descubrimiento hasta nuestros dias, etc., etc., por un Americano* (Barcelona. 1878), which a confiding translator has now given to the English public, solved the perplexities of research and original composition by lifting bodily the work of Alfred Deberle, *Histoire de l'Amérique du sud, depuis la conquête jusqu'à nos jours* (2e éd. Paris. 1876). Occasionally a paragraph is added, here and there a page ; of more considerable additions there are two: the earlier pages of Chapter IV on colonization are excerpted from Robertson's *America* without any indication of the fact, and pp. 312–330 are not in Deberle. . . . Mr. Jones has given us a faithful rendering of his Spanish text. One cannot but lament, however, that his labor should have been thus expended, when the same effort would have enabled him to make accessible to English readers the new edition of Deberle which has been revised and brought down to date by Alfred Milhaud (Paris. 1897). . . . My eye has not fallen on any glaring errors in Deberle's chapters on the history of the South American states, and this part of his work will be found to contain a clear and concise account of their political life during the first two generations of their independence. In view of the facts in the case, Mr. Jones and his publishers can hardly do less, in justice to Deberle and to the public, than to change the title-page so that the book will seem to be what it is, a translation of Deberle with slight additions. Would it, however, be too much to ask of Mr. Jones that he revise and extend his text so as to conform to Milhaud's improved edition? He would then give the public something for which it can be more sincerely grateful than for this version of a Spanish translation of an antiquated original." Edward G. Bourne. *American hist. rev.,* 4: 756.

Helps, *Sir* **Arthur.** The Spanish conquest in America. London: Parker. 1855–61. 4v. N. Y.: Harper. 4v.   [**3915**

A standard work, written in a vein of philanthropic philosophy, not intended as a narrative of the annals of the conquest, but rather as a study of the causes and the results of the course of events. The author's underlying intention was to make a contribution to the history of slavery. The method of treatment adopted resulted naturally in the production of a series of biographical essays which are joined together to make the completed work. Each of these essays has been abstracted by the author and reprinted separately, with additions and modifications suggested by later study and criticism, as the lives of Columbus, Cortez, Pizarro and Las Casas. (See sect. 4102.)

Humboldt, Friedrich Heinrich Alexander von, *and* **Aimé Bonpland.** Voyage aux régions équinoxiales du nouveau continent, 1799–1804. Paris. 1807–17. 29 v.   [3916

Under this general title, Humboldt published the results of his explorations and observations in America. These results fall naturally into several subject groups, most of which have been translated and reprinted independently. The more important of these, for historical purposes, are the *Researches concerning the ancient inhabitants, Political essay on New Spain,* and *The island of Cuba.*

At the end of the nineteenth century, as at its beginning, the writings of Humboldt provide the best introductory reading preparatory to any effort to understand the history and the characteristics of Spanish America. His works are still the most instructive, the most intelligent, the most suggestive books about Mexico. In accuracy of observation and of information, in clearness of insight into the real significance of events and of conditions, and in broadness of appreciation and of conception, Alexander von Humboldt has had few superiors in any field, and no superior among those who have written about Spanish America.

International American Conference, Washington, 1889–90. Minutes [text in Spanish and English]. Wash. 1890.

—— Reports and recommendations. Wash. 1890.

—— Reports of committees and discussions thereon; excursion appendix; historical appendix. Wash. 1890. 4 v.   [3917

The five volumes of minutes and reports of committees, etc., contain a detailed report of the Pan-American Conference held in Washington under the act of May, 1888, including in the last a documentary history of the congress of 1826 at Panama, and of the several other attempts to hold such conferences down to 1888. The excursion appendix is a report, prepared from the newspapers, of the delegates' tour through the United States. The volume of reports and recommendations is chiefly taken up with accounts of the railways, existing and projected, in Mexico and Central and South America, with some information regarding the proposed intercontinental railway, a list of maps and books on Spanish America, a table of distances, etc. Many railway maps are included. Other subjects of reports are a customs union, improved postal communication and sanitary regulations, and a uniform code of international law.

F. J. S.

Moses, Bernard. Establishment of Spanish rule in America. N. Y.: Putnam. 1898. $1.25.   [3918

By far the best brief work in English upon Spanish-American history. Its faults — occasional indefiniteness of facts and uncertainty as to their meaning, the failure of the text to meet the promises of the chapter headings, and the introduction of detail to which

no significance is assigned — are the faults of the books from which Professor Moses has been obliged to draw his material. These very faults illustrate what is most distinctly needed in the way of intelligent study of Spanish-American history. Professor Moses' book contains an admirable outline of the formal, legal position of the Spanish-American colonial governments. It affords a starting-point from which the thoughtful reader will proceed to remark how constantly the actual situation and the conduct of affairs differed from what the requirements of the laws would seem to imply.

Raynal, Guillaume Thomas François, *l'abbé.* Philosophical and political history of the settlements and trade of the Europeans in the East and West Indies; tr. by J. O. Justamond. London. 1776. 5 v.   [3919

A very popular work, of which many editions were printed in the original French and also in several translations. A work of distinct merit, especially for its suggestive value, although the author's fondness for philosophic discussion and interpretation often affects his account of events which he desires to use for the purposes of his argument. Everything in turn is affected by his clearly recognized intention of writing a book which should influence the course of contemporary history and throw light upon the existing conditions in France and elsewhere in Europe.

Stanford's compendium of geography and travel: Central America, the West Indies, and South America; ed. by H. W. Bates. London: Stanford. 1878. 3d ed. 1885. 21s.   [3920

Like every other contemporary survey of a country or continent, the successive editions of *Stanford's compendium of geography and travel* rapidly acquire historical value as being a view of what the land and people were like, at the date at which the respective volumes appeared. Mr. Bates' volume, in the Stanford series, is the most trustworthy and the most comprehensive single account of modern South America.

Stevens, Henry, *and* **Fred W. Lucas,** *eds.* New laws of the Indies. London: privately printed. 1893.   [3921

A reprint of a series of laws promulgated in 1542–43 by Charles V, for the good treatment and preservation of the American natives. The volume is especially valuable for its presentation of the conditions which developed naturally and inevitably into the later conditions which resulted in the decadence and eventual disruption of the American colonies of Spain.

United States. *Bureau of the American Republics.* Bulletins, no. 1–67. Wash. 1893. 6 v. in 9.   [3922

These nine books are made up of the earlier bulletins of the Bureau, which were numbered up to 67. While devoted chiefly to the commercial conditions of Latin-America — the three parts of v. 5 being confined to tariffs and v. 6 to commercial directories — there will be found scattered through them brief historical sketches of most of the countries, with a fund of information concerning their geography and their mining, land, and immigration laws, etc. There are fair maps and a few illustrations. Since October, 1893, the bulletins have been published monthly. That for June, 1898, contains a sketch of the origin and objects of the Bureau.   F. J. S.

— *Same.* Handbook of the American republics. Eds. of Jan., 1891, Feb., 1891, Jan., 1893.   [3923

These are bulletins nos. 1, 2, and 50, and contain chiefly condensed commercial information about the several countries, with some facts as to their government, travellers' and postal guides, lists of rivers and mountains, etc. No. 1 has the recommendations of the International American Conference and a list of existing autographs of Columbus.   F. J. S.

Watson, Robert Grant. Spanish and Portuguese South America during the colonial period. London: Trübner. 1884. 2v. [3924

The best compendium in English of the history of South America viewed as a whole. It covers the entire field of the colonial period very intelligently.

MEXICO

Abbott, Gorham Dummer. Mexico and the United States. N. Y.: Putnam. 1869.   [3925

A useful guide to the constitutional history, especially for the period from 1824 to 1859.

Alaman, Lúcas. Historia de Méjico. Mexico. 1849–52. 5v.   [3926

Still a standard work, of considerable suggestive value, on the history of Mexico and on the significance of events.

Bancroft, Hubert Howe. History of the Pacific states : Mexico, 1516–1887. San Francisco : Bancroft Hist. Co. 1883–8. 6v. [3927

Useful as a compendium and abstract of the sources of information on Mexican history. A valuable work for professional students of history, who are accustomed to judge the critical value of statements. The extended references to the literature of the subject are extremely valuable. For the general reader, it is a hodge-podge of information, put together without much appreciation of perspective or historical proportion, but useful as a chronological summary of the sources.

— Popular history of the Mexican people. San Francisco. 1887.   [3928

An abstract from the larger work, possessing almost none of the qualities which give some value to those volumes.

Bandelier, Adolphe François Alphonse. On the art of war and mode of warfare of the ancient Mexicans. (In Peabody Museum. 10th annual report. Cambridge, Mass. 1877.)

— On the distribution and tenure of lands, and the customs with respect to inheritance, among the ancient Mexicans. (In Peabody Museum. 11th annual report. Cambridge. 1878.)

—— On the social organization and mode of government of the ancient Mexicans. (In Peabody Museum. 12th annual report. Cambridge. 1880.)   [3929

These three papers contain by far the best exposition yet written of the conditions under which the natives conquered by the Spaniards were living before their contact with Europeans.

Baqueiro, Serapio. Ensayo historico sobre las revoluciones de Yucatan, desde 1840, hasta 1864. Mérida de Yucatan. 1865–71. 2v.   [3930

An important work, containing a very large number of significant documents. The narrative treats the course of events with considerable historical insight.

Bibesco, *Le prince* **Georges.** Au Mexique 1862 : combats et retrait des six mille. Paris: Plon. 1887. 20fr.   [3931

The standard French account of this campaign, which signified so much to Mexican nationality.

Brasseur de Bourbourg, *l'abbé* **Étienne Charles.** Collection de documents dans les langues indigènes. Paris. 1861–8. 4v.   [3932

These four volumes contain translations of the *Popul Vuh*, or *Sacred book of Guatemala*, a Quichua grammar, Landa's *Yucatan relation*, and four letters on the material for the study of native Mexican history. The comment of an early reviewer, "so thoughtful, but so doubtful," is the best characterization of the Abbé's suggestive introductory essays and annotations.

Bullock, William. Six months' residence and travels in Mexico. London. 1824. 2d ed. 1825. 2v.   [3933

An entertaining account of observations and of information picked up in the course of a trip in search of curiosities for exhibition in England. The work appears to have had considerable influence in forming the current English ideas respecting Mexico.

Butler, William. Mexico in transition. N. Y.: Hunt. 1892. 3d ed. rev. 1893. $2.   [3934

A conscientious effort to set forth the motives and the facts of the military and civil struggle by which the Mexican liberals relieved their country from the domination of the church party. Written by a missionary who has been uncommonly successful in appreciating the point of view of the masses of the people among whom he is working.

Calderon de la Barca, *Madame* **Frances Erskine Ingles.** Life in Mexico. Boston: Little. 1843. 2v.   [3935

An entertaining collection of letters, describing the experiences of a foreign lady resident in Mexico during a period of much political uncertainty. They throw considerable light upon the actual condition of the country at the time.

Campos, Sebastian I. Recuerdos históricos de la ciudad de Veracruz y costa de Sotavento durante las campañas de "Tres años," la "Yntervención" y el "Imperio." Mexico. 1895. [3936

An interesting narrative of the struggle against the French armies, from the Mexican point of view.

Chavero, Alfredo. Obras históricas de Don Fernando de Alva Ixtlilxôchitl. Mexico: Secret. de Fomento. 1891–2. 2v.

—— Historia de Tlaxcala por Diego Muñoz Camaro. Mexico: Secret. de Fomento. 1892. [3937

The standard editions, published by the Mexican government, of two of the most important works upon the native history of Mexico and the early relations between the aborigines and their Spanish conquerors.

Chevalier, Michel. Mexico, ancient and modern; tr. by Thomas Alpass. London: Maxwell. 1864. 2v. [3938

A well-proportioned work, untrustworthy in details. Written from a strong anti-Romish point of view.

Chynoweth, W. Harris. Fall of Maximilian, late emperor of Mexico; with an historical introd. London: Author. 1872. [3939

A well-balanced account of the events which made Maximilian's execution necessary, and of the brilliant legal efforts to save him from the effect of events which had been in large measure entirely beyond his control. Inspired by a desire to remove the inevitable stigma left by the execution upon the character of the Mexican people, by one who knew them intimately, and who desired no less to place on record the many fine qualities of the emperor.

Clavigero, Francisco Saverio. History of Mexico, collected from Spanish and Mexican historians, from MSS. and ancient paintings of the Indians; tr. from the Italian by Charles Cullen. London. 1787. 2v. [3940

An important and valuable compendium from many sources of native information which were only within the reach of the friars who labored among the Indians. Written by one of the most learned of the Jesuits who were expelled from the Spanish possessions. Trustworthy, if used with care and intelligence.

Cortes, Hernando. Dispatches to Charles V.; tr. with introd. and notes by George Folsom. N. Y.: Putnam. 1843. [3941

A good, and at present the only, English version of the letters in which Cortes described to the Emperor Charles V the conquest of Mexico. These letters, written during the progress of the conquest, are the basis for almost all that is known about the actual happenings of these years. They reveal the excitement and the misconceptions inevitable in the presence of new, strange and incomprehensible peoples and customs, but they are probably a trustworthy, honest account of things as they seemed to the conqueror.

—— Fifth letter; tr. by Don Pascual de Gayangos. London: Hakluyt Soc. 1868. [3942

This dispatch contains the account of Cortes' expedition to Honduras. A new edition, with added matter, is in course of preparation for the Hakluyt Society by Mr. A. P. Maudslay.

Cubas, Antonio Garcia. The republic of Mexico in 1876; tr. by George F. Henderson. Mexico: "La Enseñanza." 1876. [3943

A semi-official publication, designed to remove misapprehensions in regard to the advantages of Mexico.

Diaz del Castillo, Bernal. Memoirs, containing a true and full account of the discovery and conquest of Mexico; tr. from the Spanish by John Ingram Lockhart. London: Hatchard. 1844. 2v. [3944

A fascinating, soldier-like narrative by one of the companions of Cortes, who felt that he and his fellows had not received their due share of credit from their leader in his account of the conquest, as represented by his published dispatches.

A new edition, edited by Vice-Admiral Lindesay Brine, is in preparation for the Hakluyt Society.

Elton, *Capt.* James Frederick. With the French in Mexico. London: Chapman. 1867. Phil.: Lippincott. 1867. [3945

A pleasant, unpretentious narrative of the author's travels in Mexico, during an interesting period in the history of the country. Of no especial value.

Fancourt, Charles St. John. History of Yucatan from its discovery to the close of the 17th century. London: Murray. 1854. [3946

A very useful summary in English of the references to Yucatan in the early Spanish histories. The author possessed a thorough and intimate acquaintance with the country and with its peoples.

Flint, Henry Martyn. Mexico under Maximilian. Phil.: National Pub. Co. 1867. [3947

An untrustworthy, ex parte statement of the imperial cause, designed to weaken popular support for the efforts of the United States government to secure the withdrawal of the French forces.

Gage, Thomas. Survey of the West Indies. 4th ed. London. 1711. [3948

First issued as *The English-American, his travail by sea and land;* or, *A new survey of the West India's,* London, 1648, and frequently reprinted during the next hundred years, in several of the European languages. A curious work, by a Catholic turned Anglican clergyman, containing much information about Mexico which is interesting when true, as a large part of it probably is. The author's account of his travels is founded on fact.

Gaulot, Paul. La vérité sur l'expédition du Mexique: rêve d'empire; l'empire de Maximilien; fin d'empire. Paris: P. Ollendorff. 1889–90. 3v. Fr. 10.50. [3949

Based upon the papers of the chief paymaster in the French expeditionary forces. These supply many significant details of material value for a correct understanding of the course of events.

Gooch, *Mrs.* Fanny Chambers. Face to face with the Mexicans: the Mexican people as seen and studied by an American woman during seven years of intercourse with them. N. Y.: Fords. 1888. $2.50. [3950

A faithful account of what the author saw. The historical chapters are derived from Brantz Mayer, Prescott, and the talk of the drawing-rooms.

Hale, Susan. Story of Mexico. (Story of the nations.) N. Y.: Putnam. 1889. $1.50. [3951

A readable volume, written in a style of entertaining familiarity, and with a thoughtless disregard for exact accuracy in the statements of facts.

Hall, Frederic. Life of Maximilian I, late emperor of Mexico, with a sketch of the Empress Carlotta. N. Y.: Miller. 1868. [3952

A combination of gossipy details descriptive of the Emperor's private life with documentary and legal data relating to his trial and execution. A lawyer's attack, written by one of his Majesty's legal advisers, upon the position and arguments of his opponents, prepared after the success of the latter.

Hall, William Henry Bullock. Across Mexico in 1864–5. N. Y.: Macmillan. 1865. London: Macmillan. 1866. [3953

An entertaining book of travel, useful as portraying the impressions received by a stranger to the land and the people, travelling under very favorable auspices, but possessing no particular sympathy or insight into the significance of what he saw.

Haven, Gilbert. Our next-door neighbor: a winter in Mexico. N. Y.: Harper. 1875. [3954

A useless and provoking book, but perhaps as good a volume as could have been produced by a militant Protestant divine while occupied in touring through the country for a few weeks, investigating fields for future missionary labors.

Humboldt, Friedrich Heinrich Alexander von, *Baron.* Political essay on the kingdom of New Spain; tr. by John Black. London: Longmans. 1811. 2v. N. Y. 1811. 2v.

—— Researches concerning the institutions and monuments of the ancient inhabitants of America; tr. by H. M. Williams. London: Longmans. 1814. 2v. [3955

These two important works are characterized among the *General works*, sect. 3916.

—— Selections from the works of the Baron de Humboldt relating to Mexico; with notes by John Taylor. London: Longmans. 1824. [3956

The selections are chiefly such as would interest prospective investors in Mexican mines.

Icazbalceta, Joaquin Garcia. Bibliografía Mexicana del siglo xvi. Mexico: Andrade y Morales. 1886. $10. [3957

A descriptive list of books printed in Mexico between 1539 and 1600; a model of what such a list should be. The essays appended to many of the titles contain a great deal of invaluable information in regard to the early history of printing in America, the lives and surroundings of the most important figures in sixteenth century Mexico, and the agricultural, financial and social conditions of the country.

—— Obras. Mexico: V. Agüeros. 1896–8. 8v. $1.50 ea. [3958

These volumes contain nearly all of the historical and biographical essays written by Sr. Icazbalceta for the various works which he edited. Taken together, these constitute the most valuable contribution yet made by any student to the understanding of the first century of Spanish-American history. They relate for the most part to the social, economic and industrial phases of the early contact between Europeans and the native Americans.

The most important of the volumes edited by Sr. Icazbalceta are noted below. Most of them were issued in limited editions, and copies are not now easily secured. All are especially valuable for the documentary sources which they contain, and for the intelligent and learned elucidations by the editor.

Coleccion de documentos para la historia de Mexico. Mexico. 1858–1866. 2v.

Nueva coleccion de documentos. 1886–1892. 5v.

Historia eclesiástica Indiana, por Fr. Jerónimo de Mendieta, escrita en 1596. Mexico. 1870.

Mexico en 1554. Mexico. 1875.

Noticias de Mexico recogidos por D. Francisco Sedano, 1756–1800. Mexico. 1880. 2v.

Juarez, Benito. BURKE, ULICK RALPH. Life of Benito Juarez, constitutional president of Mexico. London: Remington. 1894. $1.25. [3959

A fair, well-balanced biography, containing a useful account of the more significant events, derived from the best of the books written by the contemporaries of Juarez. The opinions as to his work and personal character contributed by those who, as partisans of Maximilian, were opposed to him during the period of intervention, are especially interesting.

Kendall, John Jennings. Mexico under Maximilian. London : Newby. 1871. [3960

This volume contains a few interesting historical data, which are of value when they relate to events which came under the personal observation of Captain Kendall during his service in the imperial army.

Kingsborough, Edward King, *viscount.* Antiquities of Mexico: comprising facsimiles of ancient Mexican paintings and hieroglyphics, with monuments of New Spain, by Dupaix ; illustrated by many valuable inedited MSS. London: Bohn. 1831-48. 9v. [3961

This superb monumental work, the publication of which virtually ruined Lord Kingsborough, has been to a considerable extent superseded by facsimiles of most of the important codices and other documents which it reproduced, made by the more accurate modern photographic processes.

Lefèvre, Eugène. Documents officiels recueillis dans la secrétairerie privée de Maximilien ; histoire de l'intervention française au Mexique. Bruxelles. 1869. 2v. [3962

This work throws considerable light upon the real causes and the international complications of the intervention.

Le Plongeon, Augustus. Queen Móo and the Egyptian sphinx. N. Y.: Author. 1896. N. Y.: Alliance Pub. Co. $6. [3963

A work which has enjoyed considerable popularity among those who believe that Central American culture is directly connected with that of Egypt. Serious scientific students for the most part regard it as a work absolutely lacking in merit of any sort. It is interesting as an illustration of the extent to which pseudo-historical theorizing can be carried, when it is applied to sources of information which are dependent for their safe elucidation upon keen and discriminating judgment, sound common sense, and wide and accurate knowledge.

Lester, Charles Edwards. The Mexican republic. N. Y.: Am. News Co. 1878. [3964

A very good essay, showing close familiarity with the actual state of affairs in Mexico at the time when Diaz secured his final mastery of the country.

Loiseau, Claude Joseph Desiré. Notes militaire sur le Mexique en 1864-7. Bruxelles: Merzbach. 1872. [3965

A useful account of French military movements during the intervention, interspersed with descriptions of the country.

Lummis, Charles Fletcher. The awakening of a nation; Mexico of to-day. N. Y.: Harper. 1898. $2.50. [3966

An enthusiastic account by the man who, more than any one else, is thoroughly conversant with the actual condition of all parts of the Mexican republic. A

brilliant presentation of the bright side of existing conditions, with frequent references to the historical events which have made the present progressive state of the country possible.

Maximilian I, *emperor of Mexico.* [3967

See the books entered under Bibesco, Campos, Chynoweth, Elton, Flint, Gaulot, Hall, Kendall, Lefèvre, Loiseau, Salm-Salm, Schroeder, Smissen, Stevenson.

Besides the books referred to above, there are a considerable number of other documentary narratives, prepared for the most part by French officers who served in the army sent to Mexico by Napoleon III. All of these have a certain value as a presentation of the arguments which influenced the French in undertaking the intervention, and which have since been advanced by them to explain the outcome of events.

Mayer, Brantz. Mexico as it was and as it is. N. Y.: Winchester. 1844. [3968

An interesting and typical specimen of the sort of writing which found favor with the American public at the middle of the nineteenth century. The widespread interest in Mexico at that time gave this volume a large circulation, so that it had a considerable influence in shaping the popular conception of Mexico. It is an honest record, but the author, despite his official position, apparently neither saw nor understood much of the people or the true state of the country. The historical chapters are untrustworthy.

—— Mexico, Aztec, Spanish and republican. Hartford : Drake. 1852. 2v. [3969

As good a book of its size as could have been written without considerable labor fifty years ago. The many statistical tables are as accurate as most Mexican work of this sort at that period. The book is still occasionally useful to students sufficiently well informed to recognize its errors.

Mexico. Constitution ; tr. by B. Moses. See American Academy of Political and Social Science, sect. 226. [3970

Mill, Nicholas. History of Mexico from the Spanish conquest. London. 1824. [3971

A description of the country intended for English investors in Mexican mining stocks. Based in part upon conversations with informants who seem to have been more anxious to dispose of mining property than to provide precise and accurate statements. The narrative of recent political history gives a fairly trustworthy résumé of events from 1810 to 1820.

Noll, Arthur Howard. Short history of Mexico. Chic.: McClurg. 1890. $1. [3972

A good, convenient summary of Mexican history, as it was gleaned by the author during his brief residence in Mexico, from the more accessible standard authorities.

Ober, Frederick Albion. Travels in Mexico. Boston : Estes. 1884. Rev. ed. $1. [3973

A popular work, in which the author endeavors to

suggest to the reader some of the fascination which the country exercises over almost all who visit it without prejudice. Written with a ready pen, neither deep nor scholarly, but distinctly interesting. The historical illustrations are not designed to challenge critical examination.

Obregon, Luis Gonzalez. Mexico viejo. Mexico. 1894. [3974

A book of solid merit on early Mexican history.

Orozco y Berra, Manuel. Historia antigua y de la conquista de Mexico. Mexico. 1880. 4v. [3975

The standard Mexican treatise on the period anterior to the conquest. A compendium, prepared with considerable skill, of the native chroniclers.

Prescott, William Hickling. History of the conquest of Mexico; with a preliminary view of the ancient Mexican civilization, and the life of the conqueror, Hernando Cortéz. N. Y.: Harper. 1843. 3v.
—— *Same;* ed. by John Foster Kirk. Phil.: Lippincott. 3v. Universal ed. $1.50. Popular ed. $3. [3976

The later editions, edited by Mr. Prescott's secretary, contain corrections and notes from Ramirez and other Mexican historians.

Prescott's history is a masterpiece of clear, well-arranged historical narration, based upon careful and diligent study of all available sources of information. The chapters which relate the history of Mexico previous to the Spanish conquest contain little more than a skilful adaptation of Clavigero. For a safe appreciation of the account of the conquest, the reader must bear constantly in mind the fact that Prescott, perhaps unwittingly, was a devoted hero-worshipper. He desired, most sincerely, to describe events and characters as they really were, but he found it impossible to believe statements which contradicted those made by Cortés, or to credit opinions disparaging to the heroic figure whose great achievement had fascinated him. The unfairness of many of Prescott's critical comments, and the frequent injustice of his attitude towards the natives who were opposed to Cortés, are alike directly traceable to this concentration of his imagination on the figure of the conqueror.

Robinson, Fayette. Mexico and her military chieftains. Phil. 1847. [3977

A popular work of no great reliability, but containing some biographical information not easily found elsewhere.

Robinson, William Davis. Memoirs of the Mexican revolution, including a narrative of the expedition of General Xavier Mina. Phil.: Author. 1820. [3978

Based on the journal of Mina's English commissary general, and upon the personal experiences of the author, whose mercantile visits to Mexico were ended by his imprisonment and deportation to Spain under circumstances which perhaps explain his severe strictures upon the acts of those who were trying to put down the revolution.

Romero, Matias. Geographical and statistical notes on Mexico. N. Y.: Putnam. 1898. $2. [3979

An advance issue, under an admirably descriptive title, of the first three hundred pages of Sr. Romero's very poorly named *Mexico and the United States*, in which these pages are inserted without note or comment. An exceedingly valuable compendium upon the country of Mexico, as it was known to the Mexican minister to the United States.

—— Mexico and the United States; preceded by geographical and statistical notes on Mexico. N. Y.: Putnam. 1898. $4.50. [3980

The historical portion of this bulky volume consists of revisions and enlargements of articles originally printed in magazines. Although frequently characterized by the sophistry of logic which assumes the truth of stated premises, this volume is probably as good a work as exists in English on the significance of the history of nineteenth century Mexico.

Salm-Salm, Felix, *prince.* My diary in Mexico in 1867, including the last days of the Emperor Maximilian. London: Bentley. 1868. 2v. [3981

This is one of the most substantial sources of information in English on the French intervention.

Schroeder, Seaton. Fall of Maximilian's empire, as seen from a United States gun-boat. N. Y.: Putnam. 1887. [3982

An interesting narrative of events on the outskirts of the struggle. Useful as an index to the spirit of the country and the combatants.

Smissen, Alfred Louis Adolphe Graves, *baron van der.* Souvenirs du Mexique. 1864–67. Bruxelles: Lebègue. 1892. 5fr. [3983

A soldierly, documentary review of events, as recalled a quarter of a century afterwards, by the commander of the French forces during the retreat from Mexico.

Solis y Rivadeneyra, Antonio de. History of the conquest of Mexico by the Spaniards; [tr.] by Thomas Townsend. London. 1724. 1738. 2v. [3984

A work, first printed in Spanish in 1684, whose many editions and frequent translations afford conclusive testimony to the charm exercised over the reading public by a thoroughly unreliable work, through the elegance and purity of its literary style. Its virtues are those of a prose epic; superficial and panegyrical. This was the precursor of those histories of Mexico which contain nothing except the story of the conquest by Cortes.

Stevenson, Sara Yorke. Maximilian in Mexico. N. Y.: Century Co. 1899. $2.50. [3985

An entertaining narrative of personal experience, describing intimately the social, unofficial life of the French officers in Mexico. Much light is thrown upon the apparent reasons for the course taken by events, as they appeared to a clever woman watching things happening day by day. The book is useful as a commentary upon works written with the purpose of showing the philosophic causes of these same events.

Thompson, Waddy. Recollections of Mexico. N. Y.: Wiley. 1846. [3986

These impressions of the country, as seen by the United States minister, make no pretensions to scholarly accuracy or to critical insight. A well-written work, in which distinct traces are visible in the existing notions held by the people of the United States in regard to Mexico.

Tylor, Edward Burnett. Anahuac; or Mexico and the Mexicans, ancient and modern. London: Longmans. 1861. [3987

An interesting narrative of travel and scientific observation.

United States. *State Department.* Report regarding the present condition of Mexico. (37th Cong., 2d sess., House ex. doc. no. 100.) Wash. 1862. [3988

This document consists chiefly of the correspondence between the State Department and Minister Corwin in Mexico and Minister Adams in England during 1861 and a part of 1862, including papers relating to Mexico which were laid before Parliament in 1862. The disorganized condition of Mexico, the grievances of England, the unwillingness of the latter country to interfere with Mexican internal affairs, and the earnestness of the United States in seeking to prevent the establishment of a European government on this continent are brought out. F. J. S.

Ward, *Sir* **Henry George.** Mexico in 1827. London. 1828. 2v. 2d ed. enl. 1829. 2v. [3989

An extremely valuable account of the then-existing mining and commercial conditions, and of the political and social conditions prevailing in Mexico and elsewhere in Spanish America during the preceding century. This is one of the very few satisfactory accounts of the course of events which led up to, and rendered inevitable, the wars of independence and the separation from Spain.

Wilson, Robert Anderson. Mexico, its peasants and its priests. N. Y.: Harper. 1855. New ed., rev. 1856. [3990

A useful, but somewhat too vigorously expressed account of Santa Anna and of the events cotemporaneous with his career, combined with an effort to show the fabulous character of the account of the conquest written by Cortes.

—— New history of the conquest of Mexico, in which Las Casas' denunciations of the popular historians of that war are fully vindicated. Phil.: Challen. 1859. [3991

A useful offset to Prescott. The valuable chapters, in which the author analyzes with a lawyer's insight the untrustworthy portions of the contemporary histories of the conquest, are hard to separate from his amateurish efforts to discover an origin for aboriginal American culture in Phoenicia.

Winship, George Parker. The Coronado expedition, 1540–42. (*In* United States Bureau of Ethnology, 14th annual report, pt. 1. Wash. 1896.) [3992

The most valuable contribution to the history of the most noteworthy exploring expedition that ever journeyed witnin the limits of the United States. Coronado set out from the City of Mexico with an enormous retinue, exploring the region as far as eastern Kansas, conquering the "Seven Cities of Cibola" occupied by the Zuñis, visiting Tusayan or the Moki country, the Grand Cañon of the Colorado, the Pueblos of the Rio Grande, and the vast buffalo plains. Winship's account includes all the known documents bearing on the expedition, printed in Spanish and English, with copious historical and ethnological notes, a bibliography, and an historical introduction that displays the author's great knowledge of the expedition and its causes and results. Reproductions in facsimile of many early maps of the region covered, as well as a number of plates illustrating ethnologic subjects, illumine the text. The original documents had not hitherto appeared in English. F. W. H.

Wright, *Mrs.* **Marie Robinson.** Picturesque Mexico. Phil.: Lippincott. [c. 1897.] [3993

An account of a trip undertaken on behalf of "the most notable feature of modern journalism," a special edition of the *New York World.* A description of the country as seen by two enthusiastic women, travelling under official guidance, with every facility for seeing the country at its best.

Young, Philip. History of Mexico. Cin. 1847. [3994

Uncritical. Made up chiefly of the annals of the War of Independence, and of the civil wars which followed.

Zaragoza, Justo. Noticias históricas de la Nueva España. Madrid. 1878. [3995

An edition, with valuable notes, of an important sixteenth century treatise upon the early Spanish dominion in Mexico, by Suarez de Peralta. Especially useful for the second half-century following the conquest.

Zumarraga, Juan de. ICAZBALCETA, JOAQUIN GARCIA. Don Fray Juan de Zumarraga, primer obispo y arzobispo de Mexico. Mexico: Andrade y Morales. 1881. $5. [3996

Distinctly the ablest work that has yet been written upon Spanish American history. A thorough and masterly study, a contribution to historical literature as well as to the facts of history, of the leading figure in the first quarter century of the Spanish domination of Mexico. Reprinted in the Agüeros edition of the *Obras* of Icazbalceta, sect. 3958.

CENTRAL AMERICA AND NORTHERN SOUTH AMERICA

Bancroft, Hubert Howe. History of the Pacific states: Central America. San Francisco. 1882–7. 3v. [3997

Like the other volumes in the monumental work of Mr. Bancroft, these books contain a mass of valuable information collected from a very wide range of manuscript and printed sources, put together in a fairly consecutive chronological arrangement, without critical judgment or any appreciation of the significance of historical fact or historical philosophy.

Bandelier, Adolf Francis Alphonse. The gilded man (El Dorado) and other pictures of the Spanish occupancy of America. N. Y.: Appleton. 1893. $1.50. [3998

A collection of popular essays, suggestive and interesting, but less reliable than Mr. Bandelier's other writings, because of their hasty preparation and the entrusting of the proof-reading to other hands. Four of the chapters relate to the exploration of the Orinoco region, one to the conquest of Mexico, and the remainder to the southwestern United States.

—— Notes on the bibliography of Yucatan and Central America. See American Antiquarian Society, sect. 233. [3999

Biggs, James. History of Don Francisco de Miranda's attempt to effect a revolution in South America. London. 1809. [4000

A revised, corrected and enlarged edition of a series of letters from an officer in the service of Miranda to a friend in the United States, printed in Boston in 1808. A good summary of events, written while they were in progress, and the standard source of information in English regarding this important episode in the struggle for the liberation of the Spanish-American colonies.

Bolivar y Ponte, Simon. DUCOUDRAY HOLSTEIN, *Gen.* H. L. VILLAUME. Memoirs of Simon Bolivar, president, liberator of the republic of Colombia, and of his principal generals. Boston: Goodrich. 1830. London: Colburn. 1830. 2v. [4001

A useful outline of military operations, in which the author at times acted as Chief of staff to Bolivar. The writer fell out with his chief, and in this work undertakes to show the vanity and the mediocrity of mind of Bolivar. Its main value is as a counterbalance to the works by Bolivar's admirers.

Colombia. Constitution; tr. by B. Moses. See American Academy of Political and Social Science, sect. 226. [4002

Curtis, William Eleroy. Venezuela, a land where it's always summer. N. Y.: Harper. 1896. $1.25. [4003

A description of the country, interspersed with more or less history of the popular sort.

Dalton, Henry G. History of British Guiana. London: Longmans. 1855. 2v. [4004

An intelligent compendium from the standard works, by one who was very familiar with the life and the traditions of the colony.

Davis, Richard Harding. Three gringos in Venezuela and Central America. N. Y.: Harper. 1896. $1.50. [4005

A delightful narrative, which has done much to establish, beyond the reach of historical correction, the popular conception in the United States of the people and the institutions of Spanish America.

Flinter, *Maj.* George D. History of the revolution of Caracas. London. 1819. [4006

An especially useful work, as it gives the arguments and the point of view of those who supported the side of Spain in the revolution. The author, an English officer, enjoyed many opportunities for intercourse with the people who were driven out of Venezuela by the revolutionists, and he seems to have transmitted their stories without much effort to verify the truth or probability of the narratives.

Gibbs, Archibald Robertson. British Honduras, an historical and descriptive account of the colony from its settlement, 1670. London: Low. 1883. 7s. 6d. [4007

A readable and apparently trustworthy sketch of events.

Hall, *Col.* Francis. Present state of Colombia, containing an account of the principal events of its revolutionary war; by an officer late in the Colombian service. London: Baldwin. 1824. Phil. 1825. [4008

An intelligent account, by one who enjoyed his experiences.

Juarros, Domingo. Statistical and commercial history of the kingdom of Guatemala; tr. by J. Baily. London. 1823. [4009

A good English version of what was for a long time the standard Spanish work on Guatemala, and one which contains much valuable material relating to the condition of the country towards the end of the Spanish domination.

Keasbey, L. M. Nicaragua canal and the Monroe doctrine. See American Academy of Political and Social Science, sect. 226. [4010

Maudslay, Anne Cary, *and* Alfred Percival. A glimpse at Guatemala, and some notes on the ancient monuments of Central America. Maps, illust. London: Murray. 1899. Net 84s. [4011

An elaborate and beautiful book, hardly answering to Mr. Maudslay's original design of preparing a comparatively inexpensive account of his travels in Guatemala and of the extremely important archæological and historical work which he has done there. The complete results of his seven expeditions are published in the costly *Biologia Centrali-Americana.* In the present volume, which is popular as well as scientific, Mrs. Maudslay, with her husband's help, describes the country and the people, and explains what has been accomplished by the scientific investigations. The volume combines the freshness and enthusiasm in observation of one who was visiting the country for the first time, with the accurate appreciation and understanding of the meaning of things as seen by the trained scientist, thoroughly equipped student and careful scholar who has mastered the historical and archæological puzzles of Central America more satisfactorily than any of his predecessors. This volume is easily worth all the other books which have appeared or are likely to be published for many years, as a guide to the things which make Central America of general world interest.

Pereira, Ricardo S. Les états-unis de Colombie : précis d'histoire et de géographie. Paris : Marpon. 1883.   [4012

A very valuable work prepared by the secretary of the Colombian legation in Paris. The historical summary is thoroughly trustworthy, and the geographical descriptions and maps are prepared with great care.

Pons, François-Raimond-Joseph de. Voyage to the eastern part of Terra Firma or the Spanish Main in South America, 1801–4 ; tr. by an American gentleman [Washington Irving ?]. N. Y.: 1806. 3v.

—— *Same :* Travels in South America. London. 1807. 2v.   [4013

A detailed description of the old Captain-Generalcy of Caraccas by the French government agent. One of the most complete and satisfactory pictures of a part of Spanish America just before the collapse of Spanish authority. Especially interesting for the light that it throws on the Spanish colonial administration, the religious system and the state of commerce. The processes employed in the production of sugar, cotton and tobacco receive much attention. E. G. B.

—— Recollections of a service of three years during the war of extermination in the republics of Venezuela and Colombia ; by an officer of the Colombian navy. London : Hunt. 1828. 2v.   [4014

A narrative of experiences and observation, by a typical English adventurer. Valuable for its sketches of the characteristic traits and dispositions of the native leaders in the struggle.

Several similar narratives were written by English officers who served with the revolutionary forces. Each of these has the value which always belongs to any account of personal participation in historical events. The bias of each writer is usually sufficiently obvious to enable the attentive reader to determine quickly what degree of reliance may safely be placed upon his statements.

Robinson, J. H. Journal of an expedition 1400 miles up the Orinoco and 300 up the Arauca. London : Black. 1822.   [4015

The experiences of an English officer enlisted as surgeon in the Venezuelan patriot army, who became much disgusted with the country and its people. Some important light is thrown upon the war operations and upon the motives of various participants, from the unprejudiced standpoint of one who became definitely attached to no especial leader.

Rodney, Cæsar Augustus, *and* **John Graham.** Reports on the present state of the United Provinces of South America. London. 1819.   [4016

An intelligently edited reprint of a Congressional report presented by two commissioners sent by the United States government to investigate the commercial and political situation and resources of the revolted Spanish colonies. The appendices contain much valuable material on the state of the country during and at the end of the revolutionary period.

Rodway, James. History of British Guiana, from 1668. Georgetown, Demerara : Thomson. 1891–4. 3v.   [4017

A good summary of the available works of historical reference. Uncritical.

Spence, James Mudié. Land of Bolivar. London: Low. 1878. 2v.   [4018

An historical appendix supplements the information, not always trustworthy, which occasionally appears in the course of the author's narrative of his adventures while trying to secure a mining concession from the Venezuelan government.

Squier, Ephraim George. Honduras, descriptive, historical, and statistical. London: Trübner. 1870.

—— Nicaragua : its people, scenery, monuments. N. Y.: Appleton. 1852. 2v.

—— Notes on Central America. N. Y.: Harper. 1855.

—— States of Central America. N. Y.: Harper. 1858.   [4019

Mr. Squier's Nicaragua volumes were supplemented by the *Notes*, which relate mainly to Honduras and San Salvador. These in turn were completed by the *States*, of 1858, which is a substantial compendium of all the available information, giving a complete view of the actual social, economic and political conditions of the Central American republics at that time. Mr. Squier made most admirable use of his exceptional opportunities for gathering extended and reliable data, during his long career in the United States diplomatic service to these countries.

Stephens, John Lloyd. Incidents of travel in Central America, Chiapas, and Yucatan. N. Y.: Harper. 1841. 2v.

—— Incidents of travel in Yucatan. N. Y.: Harper. 1843. 2v.   [4020

These volumes, recording the adventures and impressions of Mr. Stephens and Mr. Catherwood, are of especial interest, apart from their value as an intelligent record of the country as these travellers found it, because to them is due in large measure the awakening of scientific scholarly interest in the countries and in the ruins of Central America.

Thompson, Edward H. Yucatan at the time of its discovery. See American Antiquarian Society, sect. 240.   [4021

United States. *Congress.* Documents relative to Central American affairs and the enlistment question. Wash.: Govt. Prtg. Off. · 1856.   [4022

A collection of "sources" in which there are a few grains of historical wheat for the student of Central American diplomatic annals.

United States. *President.* Message transmitting information in relation to the proposed congress to be held at Panama. (19th Cong., 1st. sess., House ex. doc. 129.) Wash. 1826.   [4023

The President's message urges reasons for the acceptance of the invitation to be represented at the proposed congress and reaffirms the Monroe doctrine. The accompanying documents begin with a letter from J. Q. Adams as Secretary of State in 1823 to our minister at Colombia on the subject of the independence of the South American countries and the negotiation of commercial treaties with them. Letters from the ministers of Colombia, Mexico and Central America in 1825 formally invite the United States to take part in the congress and state the subjects to be discussed, and Secretary Clay urges the abandonment of a contemplated attack by Colombia upon Cuba and Porto Rico. There is also correspondence between the State Department and certain of our ministers in Europe in regard to the independence of the South American states.   F. J. S.

United States. *Venezuelan Boundary Commission.* Report and accompanying papers of the Commission appointed by the President of the United States "to investigate and report upon the true divisional line between the Republic of Venezuela and British Guiana." Washington. 1897. 7v. Atlas, folio.   [4024

These volumes embody an extremely significant example of the application of trained historical skill and learning to the elucidation of a problem of practical international politics. The accompanying papers, each of which possesses distinct historical value, were the result for the most part of independent studies in the Dutch archives. They include: —

Report on Spanish and Dutch settlements prior to 1648, by Professor J. Franklin Jameson.

Report as to the meaning of Articles V and VI of the treaty of Münster, by George Lincoln Burr. Except as noted, the following reports are also by Professor Burr.

Report as to the territorial rights of the Dutch West India Company.

Report on the evidence of the Dutch archives as to European occupation and claims in western Guiana. With the documents, in Dutch and an English translation.

Reports on the maps covering the region in dispute,

by Justin Winsor, Severo Mallet-Prevost, Marcus Baker and Professor Burr. Facsimiles of all the significant maps are given in the accompanying atlas.

The commission also issued the *Official history*, a brief and accompanying document submitted by the Venezuelan counsel, and likewise the Blue book containing the British case.

Van Heuvel, Jacob A. El Dorado : a narrative of the circumstances which gave rise to reports in the 16th century of the existence of a rich and splendid city in South America. N. Y. [c. 1844.]   [4025

"It was left for Humboldt to set the seal of disbelief firmly upon the story [of El Dorado]. . . . Nevertheless, as late as 1844, Jacob A. Van Heuvel, in his *Eldorado* . . . published in New York, clung to the idea." Justin Winsor, in *Narrative and critical hist. of Am.*, 2: 589.

Walker, *Gen.* **William.** The war in Nicaragua. Mobile. 1860.   [4026

A statement of the case for the Filibusters.

Wells, William V. Explorations and adventures in Honduras, and a review of the history and general resources of Central America. N. Y.: Harper. 1857.   [4027

The historical chapters contain a useful introduction to Central American events of the first half of the nineteenth century.

THE PACIFIC STATES OF SOUTH AMERICA

Barros Arana, Diego. Histoire de la guerre du Pacifique, 1879–80. Paris : Baudoin. 1881.   [4028

An important work, by one of the leading Chilean historians. It is especially valuable for its account of the course of the events which resulted in the outbreak of war.

Sr. Barros Arana is the author of a number of valuable essays upon South American history. He has also edited several important documents and narratives which relate to the beginnings of Spanish domination on the Pacific coast.

Boyd, R. Nelson. Chili: sketches of Chili and the Chilians during the war, 1879–80. London : Allen. 1881.   [4029

A collection of notes made by an intelligent and observant on-looker.

Child, Theodore. The Spanish-American republics. N. Y.: Harper. 1891. $3.50.   [4030

An account of Chile, Peru, the Argentine, Paraguay and Uruguay as they appeared in 1890 to an active and well-equipped traveller from the United States, but one who failed to appreciate the point of view and the reason for the characteristics of peoples with different ancestry and natural surroundings.

Hancock, Anson Uriel. History of Chile. (Latin-American republics.) Chicago: Sergel. 1893.   [4031

A useful work, based upon the best native histories and the standard reference-books.

Hassaurek, Friedrich. Four years among Spanish-Americans. N. Y.: Hurd. 1868. Cin.: Clarke. $1.50.   [4032

A lively account, first published in 1867, of social and political conditions in Colombia, Ecuador, Peru and Bolivia, with which the author acquired considerable familiarity.

Hervey, Maurice H. Dark days in Chile: an account of the revolution of 1891. N. Y.: Macmillan. 1891.   [4033

A readable narrative by the London *Times* special correspondent. An excellent example of responsible, reliable, unprejudiced newspaper work.

Hutchinson, Thomas J. Two years in Peru, with exploration of its antiquities. London: Low. 1874. 2v.   [4034

Written for the purpose of destroying the popular traditions in regard to Inca civilization, and of restoring to the predecessors of the Incas some of their due glory. Useful as an offset to the standard works of traditional history. Written by one who fell under the spell of the charms of Peru and the Peruvians, while the country was in the full flush of prosperity.

Jiménez de la Espada, Márcos. Relaciones geográficas de Indias. Madrid. 1881, 1885, 1897. 3v.

—— Tres relaciones de antigüedades Peruanas. Madrid. 1879.   [4035

Sr. Márcos Jiménez de la Espada has done more than any one else to render accessible to students the original sources of Peruvian history. Besides the four volumes mentioned above, which were published by the Spanish government, from the office of the Secretaria de Fomento, for presentation to the International Congress of Americanists, Sr. Jiménez de la Espada has edited, with much care:

Tercero libro de las guerras civiles del Perú, por Pedro de Cieza de Leon. Madrid. 1877.   [4036

Segunda parte de la Crónica del Perú, por Cieza de Leon. Madrid. 1880.   [4037

Suma y narracion de los Incas, por Juan de Betánzos. Madrid. 1880.   [4038

These three volumes are published in the Biblioteca Hispano-ultramarina.

Varias relaciones del Perú y Chile y conquista de la isla de Santa Catalina. 1535 á 1658. Madrid. 1879.   [4039

Historia del Nuevo Mundo, por Bernabé Cobo. Seville. 1890-1895. 3 volumes, published by the Sociedad de bibliofilos Andaluces.   [4040

Memorias antiguas historiales y políticas del Perú, por Fernando Montesinos. Madrid. 1882. A French version was published by Ternaux-Compans. Paris. 1840.   [4041

Juan y Santacilia, Jorge, *and* **Antonio de Ulloa.** Voyage to South America; [tr. by John Adams.] London. 1758. 2v.   [4042

First printed in Spanish in 1748, 4 volumes folio. The English version, which is seriously abridged, has been frequently reprinted. This is an extremely valuable report of a scientific expedition, to which these two Spanish naval officers were assigned with special instructions to observe all things that would interest the Spanish government. These volumes contain their published report. Their secret report, which is full of important information in regard to the actual working of the internal administration of the colonies on the Pacific coast, was first published with the title *Noticias secretas de America,* Londres: Taylor. 1826.

Lummis, Charles Fletcher. The Spanish pioneers. Chicago: McClurg. 1893. $1.50.

                                                [4043

A most successful effort to present to English readers the heroic and the human side of the Spanish conquerors, to write their history from the same point of view in which most of the accepted history of Anglo-America has been written. The spirit suggests that of the New England "filio-pietistic" school, but there is careful faithfulness to the facts of history as they appear in the early chronicles.

Markham, *Sir* Clements Robert. History of Peru. Chic.: Sergel. 1892. $2.50. [4044

An admirably clear and well-balanced narrative, in which the successive periods of Peruvian history are portrayed in their due proportion and relation to past and future. A considerable residence in Peru, while many of the heroes of the struggles which won independence were still alive, a continued intercourse with friends closely allied with the best interests of the country, and a diligent study of the literature in which is contained the history of the aboriginal rulers of the land, alike contribute to make Sir Clements Markham the leading authority upon Peruvian history, and almost the only competent English student of Spanish-American history since the conquest. In his treatment of the native civilization, he is handicapped by the characteristic fault of every preceding historian of these aborigines, the inevitable temptation to rely upon the written records of the early travellers, to the neglect of acquaintance with and careful study of the living descendants of the natives, and with the visible remains of their handiwork prior to European contact.

The President of the Royal Geographical Society and of the Hakluyt Society has made it possible, by means of his admirable translations from the more important sources which relate to the earliest contact between the Spaniards and the aborigines in Peru, for the reader unacquainted with the Spanish language to examine these sources for himself, and thus to study the history of native Peru more satisfactorily and more thoroughly than is possible with any other portion of aboriginal America south of the United States. These translations, which were, except as noted, published by the Hakluyt Society, include:—

Expeditions into the valley of the Amazons, 1539, 1540, 1639. London. 1859.   [4045

Expedition of Pedro de Ursua and Lope de Aguirre

in search of El Dorado and Omagua in 1560-1. London. 1861.   [4046

Life and acts of Don Alonzo Enriquez de Guzman, 1518 to 1543. London. 1862.   [4047

Travels of Pedro de Cieza de Leon, 1532-50. London. 1864.   [4048

Second part of the chronicle of Peru by Pedro de Cieza de Leon. London. 1883. The introduction discusses the ancient Ynca drama.   [4049

Ollanta; ancient Ynca drama. London: Trübner. 1871. This translation should be compared with the French version by Gavino Pacheco Zegarra, published in the *Collection linguistique Américaine*, vol. iv. Paris: Maisonneuve. 1878.   [4050

Narrative of the proceedings of Pedrarias Davila, in the provinces of Tierra Firme, and of the discovery of the South sea and the coasts of Peru and Nicaragua, by Pascual de Andagoya. London. 1865.   [4051

First part of the royal commentaries of the Yncas by Garcilaso de la Vega. London. 1869-71. 2v.   [4052

Reports on the discovery of Peru. London. 1872. Comprises four important early narratives.   [4053

Narratives of the rites and laws of the Yncas. London. 1873. Four valuable accounts of the natives.   [4054

Natural and moral history of the Indies by Joseph de Acosta. London. 1880. 2v.   [4055

—— The war between Peru and Chile, 1879-82. London: Low. 1882. 10s. 6d. N. Y.: R. Worthington. 1882.   [4056

Although based, of necessity, almost entirely upon the documents and narratives published by Chileans, Sir Clements Markham presents in strong light the unwarrantable nature of the Chilean aggressions, and the utterly unjustified barbarity with which the Chileans pursued their designs to the bitter end. Compare the note under Vicuña Mackenna (sect. 4070).

Mason, *Lt.* Theodorus B. M. The war on the Pacific coast of South America between Chile and the allied republics of Peru and Bolivia, 1879-81. (U. S. Office of Naval Intelligence. Information from abroad: war series, no. 2.) Wash. 1883.   [4057

—— *Same.* (48th Cong., 2d sess., House misc. doc., v. 7, no. 30.)

A convenient summary of the struggle, with details of the naval engagements based upon the observation of United States officials stationed off the coast.

Miers, John. Travels in Chile and La Plata. London. 1826. 2v.   [4058

An important work of permanent value, embodying the observations and notes of several years' residence in South America by a trained engineer in government employ.

Miller, *Gen.* William. MILLER, JOHN. Memoirs of General Miller in the service of the republic of Peru. London. 1828. 2v. 2d ed. 1829. 2v.   [4059

An effort, based upon the private papers, letters, and recollections of General Miller, to paint in their true colors "the merit, the valor, the constancy and the natural benevolence of the Peruvian, Chileno, and Argentine peasantry and soldiers, who possess these good qualities in spite of many evils resulting from Spanish contagion and misrule." The second edition contains a translation from the interesting preface to the Spanish version, which presents the Spanish view of the colonial system, making the best defence possible of eighteenth century conditions.

Molina, Giovanni Ignazio. Geographical, natural and civil history of Chili; tr. from the Italian. London: Longmans. 1809. 2v. Middletown, Conn. 1808. 2v.   [4060

A standard work, frequently translated into most of the European languages. Its chief historical interest now results from the information which the author derived from the friends and fellow-countrymen whom he met in Italy. These recollections are often suggestive, but in most cases they are thoroughly unreliable if taken literally. The descriptions of the country possess considerable value.

Narrative of the events which led to the declaration of war by Chile against Bolivia and Peru. London. 1879.   [4061

The official Chilean version of the negotiations preliminary to the war. Published by the Chilean minister to England, for the purpose of influencing British opinion.

Prescott, William Hickling. History of the conquest of Peru, with a preliminary view of the civilization of the Incas. London: Bentley. 1847. 2v.

—— *Same;* ed. by John Foster Kirk. Phil.: Lippincott. 1874. Universal ed. 2v. $1. Popular ed. 2v. $2.   [4062

This work is, to a greater extent than Prescott's *History of Mexico*, based upon the standard original authorities, whose opinions are adapted, with their facts, to the requirements of a master of historical narrative. It is a less entertaining work than its predecessor, just in proportion as Pizarro's character proved less fascinating than that of Cortés.

Reiss, Wilhelm, *and* Alphonse Stübel. Necropolis of Ancon in Peru. Berlin. 1880-7. Agent, N. Y.: Dodd. [3v.] 14 pts., each pt. net $7.50.   [4063

An English version, edited with much care and intelligence by A. H. Keane, of an elaborate German scientific work. One of the principal printed authorities on the aboriginal Peruvians, and on the history of the country prior to the conquest. There are a number of other works, in German, prepared by Messrs. Reiss and Stübel, containing elaborate reports of the results of their Peruvian investigations. All are important helps for the student who is compelled to rely upon published works for his knowledge of Peruvian antiquities.

Rivero y Ustariz, Mariano Eduardo de, *and* Johann Jakob von Tschudi. Peruvian antiquities ; tr. by Francis L. Hawkes. N. Y.: Putnam. 1853. Barnes. 1864. [4064

A good version of the text of the standard work on the subject, but without the 58 large plates which render the original Spanish edition very expensive.

Squier, Ephraim George. Peru : incidents of travel and exploration in the land of the Incas. N. Y.: Harper. 1877. N. Y.: Holt. $5. [4065

A standard work, and probably the best book on Peru in English, although far from satisfactory in many lines. A pioneer work which made possible the more accurate details of later investigation. Useful alike for its careful investigation into the ancient remains and for the intelligent description of the people and the country through which the author travelled.

Stevenson, W. B. Historical and descriptive narrative of twenty years' residence in South America. London. 1825. 3v. [4066

An invaluable storehouse of information and observations noted during the author's travels in Chile, Peru and Colombia, between 1804 and 1825. He was placed for the larger part of this time in positions of confidential association with several persons of high official station in the colonies previous to the revolution, and after the outbreak of hostilities he took an active part in the naval struggle for independence.

Sutcliffe, Thomas. Sixteen years in Chile and Peru, 1822–39, by the retired governor of Juan Fernandez. London. 1841. [4067

A very useful account of events on the Pacific coast of South America during these years, from the point of view of a friend of the British volunteers in the various struggles.

United States. *State Department.* Papers relating to the war in South America. Wash. 1882. [4068

This volume provides an available source of official information regarding the course of events, as reported through the various diplomatic channels.

Vicuña Mackenna, Benjamin. Francisco Moyen ; or, The Inquisition as it was in South America ; tr. by James W. Duffy. London : Sotheran. 1869. [4069

An excellent translation of an important work, based upon official documents of the Inquisition which detail the treatment to which a young man accused of frivolous but heretical utterances was actually subjected. The courageous independence and fearless insistence upon historic truth, in the face of intense popular religious prejudice, which characterized the publication of this volume, rivals that of Sr. Garcia Icazbalceta of Mexico in the preparation of his letter on the image of Our Lady of Guadalupe.

—— Historia de la independencia del Perú. Santiago de Chile. 1860.

—— Historia de los diez años de la administracion de Don Manuel Montt. Santiago de Chile. 1862. 3v.

—— La guerra á muerte : memoria sobre las últimes campañas de la independencia de Chile, 1819–21. Santiago de Chile. 1868. [4070

These three works give the best connected account of events upon the western coast of South America during the first half of the nineteenth century. As Sir Clements Markham has so well said : "The author's powers of description, of delineating character, and of critical analysis are of a very high order. His industry in collecting materials is extraordinary, and it is equalled by his ability in arranging them. Vicuña Mackenna is above all things a historical biographer. He could not, if he would, omit a trait or an incident, however much their mention might tell against the view he advocates. His love of historical truth amounts to a passion." The justness of this characterization is best seen in the vigorous and uncompromising manner in which this Chilean statesman and author denounces the manner in which his countrymen conducted their war of conquest against Peru.

—— Juan Fernandez : historia verdadera de la islá de Robinson Crusoe. Santiago de Chile : Jover. 1883. [4071

An admirable historical monograph, giving a comprehensive account of the actual happenings upon the island which must ever be a shrine for all who have come under the spell of *Robinson Crusoe.*

THE ATLANTIC STATES OF SOUTH AMERICA

Armitage, John. History of Brazil, 1808–31. London : Smith. 1836. 2v. [4072

A conscientious detailed narrative of events succeeding the arrival of the Braganza family from Portugal, the point where Southey stops. The appendix contains considerable documentary material.

Burton, *Capt. Sir* Richard Francis. Letters from the battle-fields of Paraguay. London : Tinsley. 1870. [4073

A most successful effort, by one to whom nature granted uncommon capacity for understanding the out-of-the-way world in which most of his life was passed, to explain the actual situation so as to enable Englishmen to understand what had been and was taking place in Paraguay during its period of storm and stress.

Captivity of Hans Stade of Hesse, in 1547–55, among the wild tribes of eastern Brazil ; tr. by A. Tootal ; annotated by R. F. Burton. London : Hakluyt Soc. 1874.

Conquest of the river Plate, 1535–55 : 1. Voyage of Ulrich Schmidt to the rivers La Plata and Paraguai ; 2. Commentaries of Alvar Nuñez Cabeza de Vaca. London: Hakluyt Soc. 1891. [4074

These narratives are by eye-witnesses and participants in the early exploration and colonization of the La Plata region. They cover respectively the years 1534–54, 1541–44, and 1547–1554. Schmidt's narrative received a wide circulation in the collections of voyages in the 16th and 17th centuries. His name became early transformed to Schmidel. His story is a simple narrative of experiences and observations and contains a good deal about the natives. He was the agent of a mercantile house. The narrative of Nuñez Cabeza de Vaca's career there presents a somewhat different view of the same external history. The editor has supplied important geographical identifications and other notes. Stade was a gunner on Spanish and Portuguese vessels. As Stade and Schmidt were unlettered men, Dominguez, the editor of Schmidt's voyage, utters a word of caution against relying too much on their narratives, which are probably of the nature of recollections rather than of notes taken at the time. E. G. B.

Fletcher, James Cooley, *and* **Daniel Parrish Kidder.** Brazil and the Brazilians. Phil. 1857. 9th ed. Boston: Little. 1879. [4075

A carefully revised and enlarged edition of an earlier work by the Rev. Mr. Kidder. An intelligent and sensible account of the country and of the people among whom the authors were engaged in missionary labors. Portions of this volume were reprinted by the London Religious Tract Society, as —
Brazil, its history, people, etc. London. 1860.

Henderson, James. History of the Brazil. London: Longmans. 1821. [4076

An abridged version of an extended native work on Brazil, prepared with special reference to geographical, commercial, and statistical details, as supplementing the more strictly historical treatment by Southey. Contains much useful information, which needs to be used with some discrimination.

Herndon, William Lewis, *and* **Lardner Gibbon.** Exploration of the valley of the Amazon under direction of the Navy Department. (33d Congress, 1st sess., Ho. ex. doc. 53.) Wash. 1854. 2v. [4077

A valuable report describing a part of the country which possesses some commercial importance.

Hutchinson, Thomas Joseph. The Paraná; with incidents of the Paraguayan war, and South American recollections, 1861–8. London: Stanford. 1868. [4078

Chiefly valuable as a contemporary record of opinions and events during the important years of the author's residence as British Consul in the Argentine Confederacy. The volume contains a summary of the early history of the Argentine region, with some suggestive notes on Spanish-American conditions during the first half of the 19th century and the period preceding the revolt from Spain.

King, *Col.* **John Anthony.** Twenty-four years in the Argentine Republic. N. Y.: Appleton. 1846. [4079

An effort to show forth in their true light the actual motives and achievements of the revolutionary partisans in the Argentine region, and the consequent justification for English interference.

Mitre, Bartolomé. Emancipation of South America: a condensed translation by Wm. Pilling of the *History of San Martin.* London: Chapman. 1893. 12s. [4080

The translator has condensed Mitre's *Historia de San Martin*; preserving the narrative of the national struggle and omitting the details of personal controversy.

—— Historia de Belgrano y de la independencia Argentina. Buenos Ayres. 1887. [1st ed. 1857.] 3v. [4081

A work of great merit, by one of the most eminent of Argentine's publicists. Of permanent historical value, ranking among the noteworthy contributions to the historical literature of the 19th century.

Mulhall, Michael George. The English in South America. Buenos Ayres. London: Stanford. [1878.] [4082

The unpleasant first impression caused by the Buenos Ayres printing and paper in this volume gives a wholly untrue idea of the very considerable merits of this intelligent outline of the history of the eastern coast of South America, and especially of the various Englishmen who have played an important part in its development.

Page, Thomas Jefferson. La Plata, the Argentine confederation, Paraguay. N. Y.: Harper. 1859. New ed. enl. 1860. [4083

A useful narrative of explorations and observations made during 1853–56 by order of the United States government.

Parish, *Sir* **Woodbine.** Account, historical, political and statistical, of the united provinces of Rio de la Plata. London. 1825. [4084

A semi-official publication, containing an authoritative account of the existing state of affairs in the Argentine country, and also a letter written at the request of Woodbine Parish by Sr. D. Ygnacio Nuñez of Buenos Ayres, for the information of the British ministry while it was considering the advisability of recognizing the independence of that republic. Both parts are supported by documentary appendices.

—— Buenos Ayres and the provinces of the Rio de la Plata. London: Murray. 1838. 2d ed. enl. 1852. [4085

The second edition is much superior to the first edition, London, 1838. An admirable work, usually trustworthy, both in the statement of facts and in the judgments passed upon them.

Rengger, Johann Rudolph. Reign of Dr. Joseph Gaspard Roderick de Francia in Paraguay : an account of a residence by Messrs. Rengger and Longchamps. London. 1827.

[4086

This narrative of six years' residence by two trained European scientists is one of the important sources of information concerning this very curious episode in South American history.

Robertson, John Parish *and* **William Parish.** Francia's reign of terror. London: Murray. 1839.

—— Letters on Paraguay : four years' residence. London: Murray. 1838. 2v.

—— Letters on South America. London: Murray. 1845. 3v. [4087

These three works are based upon twenty-five years' residence and travel in the regions drained by the Paraguay and the Rio de la Plata. Their historical value is not great, although they contain some striking descriptions of the state of the country and of the curious events which were then taking place. They were popular works in their day, and left a strong impress upon popular opinion.

Sarmiento, Domingo Faustino. Life in the Argentine republic in the days of the tyrants: tr. by Mrs. Horace Mann. N. Y.: Hurd. 1868. [4088

Written in the style of historical fiction so popular with the Spanish-American public, by one of the most intelligent and well-informed among the leaders in Argentine affairs during his generation. The book seems to give a very fair idea of the period of the Tyrants.

Southey, Robert. History of Brazil. London: Longmans. 1810-19. 3v. [4089

The standard work, of considerable solid merit as an historical narrative.

Thompson, George. The war in Paraguay, with historical sketch of the country and its people. London: Longmans. 1869. [4090

A straightforward and apparently unprejudiced account of events, in many of which the author took an active part as a military engineer.

Washburn, Charles Ames. History of Paraguay, with notes of personal observations. Boston: Lee. 1871. 2v. [4091

A scholarly work. The active participation of Minister Washburn in local affairs during the Lopez struggles renders it impossible to accept with entire confidence his interpretation of events, although the frank and straightforward narrative tells strongly in favor of his positions. These volumes form one of the main sources for an understanding of this turbulent period.

Wilcocke, Samuel Hull. History of the vice-royalty of Buenos Ayres. London. 1807.

[4092

A compilation of no critical value, except when the statements are based upon information derived through personal observation or experience by the author, whose extensive mercantile pursuits gave him a considerable familiarity with the country.

Zeballos, Estanislao S. Argument for the Argentine Republic upon the question with Brazil in regard to the territory of Misiones. Wash. 1894. [4093

A good ex-parte discussion of historical and geographical data, illustrated by facsimiles of a number of interesting maps, of early and later dates, showing the region in dispute.

THE WEST INDIES

Abbot, Abiel. Letters written in the interior of Cuba in 1828. Boston. 1829. [4094

A very valuable account of what was noticed by an observant traveller who visited the country before it had begun to outgrow its earlier colonial conditions.

Ballou, Maturin Murray. History of Cuba. Boston : Phillips. 1854. [4095

The first of the series of desultory but delightful records of traveller's gossip written by Mr. Ballou.

Beckford, William. Descriptive account of the island of Jamaica. London. 1790. 2v. [4096

The standard work on the earlier state of the colony.

Bonsal, Stephen. The real condition of Cuba to-day. N. Y.: Harper. 1897. Pap. 60c. [4097

A picture of western Cuba in the spring of 1897 under the " Concentration " system established by Gen. Weyler. The diplomatic experience of the author in Spain and his work as a correspondent in Macedonia and in the Bulgarian-Servian war gave him some special qualifications for observing the conditions in Cuba. His sympathy for the Cubans is marked.　　　　　　　　　　　　E. G. B.

Bridges, George Wilson. Annals of Jamaica. London : Murray. 1827-8. 2v.

[4098

A charming work, in the best style of the older school of historical writers, who knew that literary merit and ideas were not inconsistent with an honest and intelligent narration of historical facts.

Burney, James. Buccaneers of America. London : Payne and Foss. 1816. [4099

A detailed account, prepared with considerable care from sources of information, a large proportion of which existed only in contemporary gossip and which have since disappeared.

Cabrera, Raimundo. Cuba and the Cubans ; tr. by Laura Guiteras, rev. and ed. by Louis

Edward Levy. Phil.: Levytype Co. 1896. $1.50. [4100

A work, frequently reprinted in the original Spanish, which is said to have been accepted by Spanish public opinion as a fair presentation of the liberal ideas current among the more intelligent Cubans of property and social standing twenty years ago, representing the ideas of those who organized the Autonomist Party.

Callahan, James Morton. Cuba and international relations : a historical study in American diplomacy. (Johns Hopkins Univ. studies, extra v. 21.) Balt. 1899. $3. [4101

" Carefully threading his way between the devious diplomacy of Spain and the confused partisan politics of the United States, [Dr. Callahan] fairly exhausts his subject within the compass of 500 octavo pages. It is safe to conclude that no future historian of Spain, Cuba, or the United States can afford to neglect Dr. Callahan in any of his statements or conclusions, which appear to be as well considered as his researches have been thorough." *Dial*, 28 : 160.

Casas, Bartolomé de las. HELPS, *Sir* ARTHUR. Life of Las Casas, the Apostle of the Indies. London. 1868. Phil.: Lippincott. 1868. New ed. London: Bell. 1896. 3s. 6d. (Bohn) N. Y. : Macmillan. $1. [4102

This sympathetic and warmly appreciative sketch is made up of the chapters in the author's *Spanish conquest of America* which are devoted to the career of Las Casas. The sources for the life of Las Casas are mainly his own writings, in particular his *Historia general de las Indias*. Of this Helps had a MS. copy (it was first printed in 1875). He also had access to a MS. of Las Casas, *Historia apologetica*, a description of the culture of the Indians of the New World. The Indian policy of Spain and the work of Las Casas is critically studied by Henry C. Lea in the *Yale review*, Aug. 1899. E. G. B.

Clark, William J. Commercial Cuba : a book for business men ; with an introd. by E. Sherman Gould. N. Y.: Scribner. 1898. $4. [4103

The author " has investigated the island with direct reference to its promise as an opening for business enterprises from the United States. The book contains much important statistical information, and a pretty full gazetteer of the Cuban cities and towns. One who proposes entering Cuba for business, agricultural, mining, or commercial purposes will find that Mr. Clark has foreseen and answered many of the questions which would naturally arise." Selim H. Peabody. *Dial* (Chicago), 27 : 129.

Dallas, Robert Charles. History of the maroons, and the state of the island of Jamaica. London : Longmans. 1803. 2v. [4104

A popular work, which serves very well as a supplement to Bryan Edwards' *West Indies* (sect. 4107).

Davey, Richard. Cuba : past and present. N. Y. : Scribner. 1898. [4105

"A well-written and interesting history. . . . The writer understands his work well, and has the faculty of making it interesting even to those who have realized Cuba least. . . . Mr. Davey, though his sympathies, on the whole, are clear, deserves from his book a high reputation for impartiality. No special pleader in the cause, he gives us the means of thinking for ourselves as we go on." *The Spectator* (London), Oct. 1, 1898.

Eden, Charles Henry. The West Indies. London: Low. 1880. 3s. 6d. [4106

A convenient but not always trustworthy summary of other works on the history of the West Indies, with especial reference to the colonies under the British flag.

Edwards, Bryan. History, civil and commercial, of the British colonies in the West Indies. London. 1793–1801. 3v. 5th ed. London. 1819. 5v. [4107

The fifth is the best edition of this most deservedly popular work. In charm of style, in historical grasp of facts and movements, and in accurate presentation of actual conditions, this work still holds its place at the head of the literature of the West Indies.

Fiske, Amos Kidder. The West Indies. (Story of the nations.) N. Y.: Putnam. 1899. $1.50. [4108

A skilful compilation from the best works on the separate islands, prepared with much discrimination. An admirable brief account of the West Indies as a whole.

Flannigan, *Mrs.* Antigua and the Antiguans. London. 1844. 2v. [4109

A well-informed work, covering every phase of the actual and the traditional history of the colony.

Flint, Grover. Marching with Gomez ; with an historical introd. by John Fiske. Boston : Lamson. 1898. Houghton. $1.50. [4110

A vivid picture of the aspects of the Cuban insurrection that appeared to a war correspondent in the spring of 1896, who was with Gomez for four months. The author's previous service in the regular army of the United States gave him special qualifications for comment on military matters. E. G. B.

Flinter, *Col.* **George Dawson.** Account of the present state of the island of Puerto Rico. London. 1834. [4111

A valuable work, by a British officer long resident in the West Indies, and thoroughly familiar with the affairs and the characteristics of the islands. Written with a design to influence English opinion in favor of the emancipation of the slaves in the British colonies. The author brings out clearly the theoretical and technical points of superiority of the Spanish colonial legal system. See the note under Moses, among the general works (sect. 3918).

Froude, James Anthony. The English in the West Indies. N. Y. : Scribner. 1888. $1.50. [4112

Pictures of travel in the British West Indies, with glimpses of Hayti and Cuba. Jamaica receives the most attention. The book contains much suggestive comment on the government, the present conditions, and future prospects of the West Indies. Mr. Froude's habitual inaccuracy makes it necessary for one to exercise caution in relying upon his statements. His sympathies in politics were conservative and in some respects reactionary.   E. G. B.

The reader may compare *Froudacity: West Indian fables, by J. A. Froude: explained by J. J. Thomas.* London: Unwin. 1889.   E. G. B.

Gallenga, Antonio (L. Mariotti, *pseud.*). The pearl of the Antilles. London: Chapman. 1873.   [4113

A description of Cuba in the midst of the ten years' insurrection, 1868–1878, by a famous correspondent of the London *Times*, whose residence in Spain, England, the United States, and travels in South America specially fitted him for a broad and enlightening discussion of the Cuban question. This is one of the most satisfactory and trustworthy of the books on Cuba.   E. G. B.

Godet, Theodore L. Bermuda, its history, geology, climate, etc. London : Smith, Elder. 1860.   [4114

A work of moderate merit, giving a fairly intelligent account of the islands.

Halstead, Murat. Story of Cuba. Chicago: Werner. 1896. New ed. rev. 1898. $2.
                                          [4115

A voluminous work, extensively read during the war with Spain by the uncritical public. The author, a successful war correspondent, gratefully records his indebtedness, for the body of his work, to books " that are authoritative, or that excel in picturesqueness; but above all other writings, to the New York *Journal, Herald, World, Sun,* and *Mail and Express.*" The work is up to the level of these sources.

Hassam, John T. Bahama Islands. See Massachusetts Historical Society, sect. 350.
                                          [4116

Hazard, Samuel. Santo Domingo, past and present, with a glance at Hayti. N. Y.: Harper. 1873. $3.50.   [4117

A popular, sketchy work.

Hill, Robert Thomas. Cuba and Porto Rico, with the other islands of the West Indies. N. Y.: Century Co. 1898. Rev. and enl. 1899. $3.   [4118

" This book is strongest on the side of its author's special studies. The geological formation and relations of the West Indies are set forth with ample knowledge, and with no little skill in untechnical exposition. . . . On the side of the natural history of the islands, too, their flora and fauna, minerals and climate, Mr. Hill presents a great deal of valuable information. About one-quarter of the volume is devoted to Cuba, one-tenth to Porto Rico. Jamaica and Santo

Domingo come next in space assigned, and each of the remaining islands has its chapter or page, according to its prominence. The historical and political matter is frankly compiled, and not from very extensive sources. Spanish authorities for Cuba shine by their absence. But, except here and there a wrong date, which may be a misprint, we have detected no inaccuracies of moment in Mr. Hill's narrative, which is necessarily very general. He takes a higher view of the native Cuban than is popular in this country just now." *Nation,* 67 : 435.

Humboldt, Alexander von. The island of Cuba; tr. by J. S. Trasher. N. Y.: Derby. 1856.   [4119

A translation, with valuable annotations, of a work which Humboldt had intended to make a companion treatise to his masterly *Political essay on New Spain,* or Mexico, but which he never completed. The work of which this formed a portion is characterized among the *General works* (sect. 3916).

Kimball, Richard Burleigh. Cuba and the Cubans. N. Y.: Hueston. 1850.   [4120

A typical predecessor of the would-be historical works of which so many were made up to meet the popular demand during the war time of 1898.

Latané, John H. Diplomacy of U. S. with regard to Cuba. See American Historical Association, sect. 249.   [4121

Lefroy, *Sir* John Henry. Memorials of the discovery and early settlement of the Bermudas or Somers Islands, 1511–1687. London : Longmans. 1877–9. 2v.   [4122

An exhaustive work, compiled with most admirable skill, and containing all the important early narratives which relate to the islands, with editorial notes and connecting narrative.

Long, Edward. History of Jamaica. London. 1774. 3v.   [4123

A work of great merit, and of permanent value, on the early state of the colony.

Louverture, François Dominique Toussaint. REDPATH, JAMES. Toussaint L'Ouverture. Boston: Redpath. 1863.   [4124

A reprint of the Rev. John R. Beard's biography, together with Toussaint's autobiographical memoirs, and other illustrative material. Published to meet the demand for something which might assist in solving the problem as to the advisability of employing negro troops in the North American Civil War.

Lucas, Charles Prestwood. Historical geography of the British colonies. Oxford: Clar. Press. N. Y.: Macmillan. 1888–1897. 4v. V. 1, $1.25. V. 2, $1.90. V. 3, $2. V. 4, $2.40. V. 2: West Indies. 1890. $1.90.
                                          [4125

Few works have ever fulfilled more satisfactorily the author's design, which was to give " a connected account of the colonies, of the geographical and historical reasons for their belonging to England, and of the special place which each colony holds in the empire." The materials have been gathered with great care, and they are presented with the literary skill which is apt to make the reader forget the amount of painstaking condensation and verification which must have been employed.

Madden, Richard Robert. The island of Cuba; its resources, progress, and prospects. London: Partridge. 1849.   [4126

Exactly described by the author as "memoranda made in the Island of Cuba in the years 1836-7-8-9, respecting slavery and the slave trade, the state of society, commerce, religion, and education." The most useful book in English for that period of Cuban history. The author's official position gave him special opportunities for the collection of material, and he presents much statistical information not else easily to be found as well as a first-hand picture of Spanish colonial administration. The details on the slave trade are especially valuable.   E. G. B.

Matthews, Franklin. New - born Cuba. N. Y.: Harper. 1899. $2.50.   [4127

This is "largely the work of a newspaper man who is reporting the condition of the island during the first sixty days of American occupation as seen through the eyes of the officials in charge of its new destinies. . . . Deriving his impressions from the military men in charge of Cuba, his report is exceedingly favorable to the work they have done, which, indeed, appears to have been excellently well done for the most part. He bears ample testimony to the fact that there is no disorder throughout the extent of Cuba at this time, and is frank enough to report those American generals correctly who believe in withdrawing now, and leaving its inhabitants to work out their own salvation like the rest of Latin America." *Dial* (Chicago), 27: 364.

Noa, Frederic M. The pearl of the Antilles: a view of the past and a glance at the future. N. Y.: [Putnam, for author.] 1898. 75c.   [4128

"Mr. Noa's little book . . . is a brief, concise statement of some of the Spanish movements which aroused and justified the Cuban struggle for independence. His access to sources and state papers not mentioned by other writers gives his book a kind of permanent value to students of Cuban history." Ira M. Price. *Dial* (Chicago), 26: 395.

Oliver, Vere Langford. History of the Island of Antigua. London: Mitchell. 1894-99. 3v. £12.   [4129

An expensive "patriotic-hereditary" work, containing valuable historical documents and narrative text interlarded with pedigrees. The author has endeavored to extract everything of importance from all the earlier works which refer to the island.

Pepper, Charles Melville. To-morrow in Cuba. N. Y.: Harper. 1899. $2.   [4130

"Of the various American essays on the subject, Mr. Pepper's is easily the first. While his book has

admittedly cost him but a couple of years, he has none the less brought to its composition an impartiality, industry, and sympathy that are most creditable. He appends a small and well-selected bibliography of recent Cuban history, political and economic, which is by itself evidence of the extent of his reading. . . . He puts his finger on the three features of the Autonomist constitution of 1897 that proved it a sham: the autocratic power still reserved to the Governor-General; the creation of life-appointees of the Crown, one less in number than a majority of the Council; and the limitation of the powers of the Insular Parliament to voting the local budget (*Gastos Domésticos*), after first having granted the national tribute (*Gastos de Soberania*), which was about 85 per cent. of the total revenues of the island. In this last abuse—the exploitation of Cuba by aliens—lay the secret of all her revolutions. Refusal to remedy it made the offer of such 'autonomy' a mockery. . . . As to American occupation, Mr. Pepper thinks its best work is in setting up a standard of official honor, administering well while it does at all, and ending as soon as it can. . . . A second edition would be improved by an index and a revision of the proof-reading, which is very bad." *Nation*, 69: 473.

Perkins, Samuel G. Narrative of the insurrection in San Domingo, 1793. See Massachusetts Historical Society, sect. 338.   [4131

Pinckard, George. Notes on the West Indies. London. 1806. 3v.   [4132

A very readable and useful description of Barbadoes, Guiana, and the West Indian islands visited by General Abercromby during his expedition.

Porter, Robert Percival. Industrial Cuba: being a study of present commercial and industrial conditions, with suggestions as to the opportunities presented in the island for American capital, enterprise, and labour. N. Y.: Putnam. 1899. $3.50.   [4133

The author is "well known as a publicist and as the Commissioner of the United States Census of 1890. Soon after the signing of the protocol of peace between the United States and Spain, August 12, 1898, Mr. Porter was sent to Cuba by President McKinley as a special commissioner to observe and report upon the conditions of the island, industrial, commercial, and financial. In the prosecution of his mission Mr. Porter visited all the provinces and most of the cities and principal towns of Cuba, examined many witnesses, and collected a vast amount of evidence, personal and documentary. This volume, if not his report in exact form as made to the President, may be accepted as his report to the American people." Selim H. Peabody, *Dial* (Chicago), 27: 129.

Poyer, John. History of Barbados, 1605-1801. London. 1808.   [4134

A substantial work, by a typical historian of the old school, who relied mainly upon what had been published by his predecessors. A defence of the islands against those who were attacking the slave-holding colonies; of no special merit.

Pyle, Howard, *ed.* Buccaneers and marooners of America. N. Y.: Macmillan. 1891. Phil.: Lippincott. 1897.   [4135

A new edition, abridged and turned into modern English, of Esquemelin's and Johnson's narratives of the doings of the most noted sea rovers and pirates.

Rainsford, Marcus. Historical account of the black empire of Hayti. London. 1805.
[4136

A work of permanent value on the beginnings of the Haytian republic.

Roche, James Jeffrey. Story of the Filibusters. London: Unwin. 1891. 3s. 6d. N. Y.: Macmillan.   [4137

An interesting narrative of considerable historical merit.

Rodway, James. The West Indies and the Spanish Main. N. Y.: Putnam. 1896. $1.75.
[4138

A condensed summary of the standard works on the history of the West Indies.

Rowan, Andrew Summers, and **Marathon Montrose Ramsey.** The island of Cuba. N. Y.: Holt. 1896. $1.25.   [4139

A very useful introduction to the study of Cuba, treating of its geography, history, political condition, and resources. The historical sketch is slight in texture and not free from errors. It is brought down to March, 1896. A valuable feature of the geographical section is a brief gazetteer of the provinces and towns of the island. An appendix contains some of the diplomatic correspondence of the U. S. relative to the insurrection of 1868–78. Another appendix supplies a bibliography of about 100 titles of works on Cuba (mainly in Spanish), a finding list of *U. S. Executive documents on Cuba*, and page references to articles on Cuba in the *Consular reports* of May, 1893 — April, 1896.   E. G. B.

Sagra, Ramon de la. Histoire physique, politique et naturelle de l'île de Cuba. Traduction de Berthelot. Paris. 1842. 2v.
[4140

These two volumes contain the historical portions of the standard work, comprising twelve volumes in the original Spanish edition, on the natural and physical features of the island. It is a work of very solid merit, which has been extensively used by succeeding writers about Cuba.

St. John, *Sir* **Spenser.** Hayti; or The black republic. London: Smith, Elder. 1884. New rev. ed. N. Y.: Scribner. 1890.
[4141

An important and interesting work, by one who was located on the island during the twenty years in which its decadence from the more civilized times of the middle century was beginning to be increasingly noticeable. The bitter hostility which continues to be expressed by native Haytians whenever the author or his book is mentioned furnishes excellent proof of the accuracy of his observations and the justness of his opinions.

Schomburgk, *Sir* **Robert Hermann.** History of Barbados. London: Longmans. 1848.
[4142

An extremely valuable work, showing a thoroughly intelligent familiarity with actual and antecedent conditions in the islands.

Sturge, Joseph, and **Thomas Harvey.** Visit to the West Indies in 1837. London: Hamilton. 1837. 2d ed. 1838.   [4143

This work, of which there were two editions within six months, contains the journal of a visit by two Quakers to Antigua, Montserrat, Dominica, St. Lucia, Barbados and Jamaica, undertaken for the purpose of ascertaining the actual condition of the negro population of those islands. It is a very valuable contribution to the literature relating to the abolition of slavery.

Thornbury, George Walter. The buccaneers; or, The monarchs of the main. London: Hurst. 1855. 3v. Abrgd. ed. Routledge. 1857.   [4144

A popular work, but one compiled with considerable historical skill from the most trustworthy of the earlier works — none of which can be considered as very reliable — on the buccaneers and other pirates of the West Indies.

Turnbull, David. The British West Indies. London: Longmans. 1840.

—— Travels in the west: Cuba, with notices of Porto Rico and the slave trade. London: Longmans. 1840.

—— St. Domingo, the French and Danish West Indies. London: Longmans. 1840.
[4145

These volumes describe the West Indies as they appeared to a well-equipped traveller enjoying exceptional facilities for examining existing conditions under official guidance.

APPENDIX

SELECTED TITLES FOR STUDENTS AND READERS

By Edward Channing, Professor of History in Harvard University

HISTORY at best is an inexact science. The materials for reaching a decision are widespread and voluminous; the liability of error from human prejudice is great and probable; the very canons of historical criticism vary from generation to generation. There is, therefore, no absolute standard of excellence and no fixity in decision, so far as it may be reached. Books that enjoy great reputation in one half century are regarded in the next half century as literature or as lumber, — in any case they are not history. In spite of these disadvantages in its subject-matter and in its treatment, the study and reading of history will always be one of the most frequent and profitable pursuits of man; for it is the study of one's fellow men, — not the doings of the body only, but the growth of the mind, the development of the soul. A knowledge of the history of the founding and development of the United States is of peculiar value to the American people. In the first place this acquaintance with the nation's past will enable those having the decision in present day affairs to avoid the blunders of the earlier time. In the second place it will give the people power to detect the mistaken sentiments which politicians sometimes ascribe to the great men of the past as a justification of their own designs. Every school and library, supported by public money, should place where they may be freely used a well-selected collection of books on American history. In the following lists the best books for such select libraries are indicated.

There is no one work on American history which can be recommended to any student or reader to the exclusion of other works. The study of history in itself demands the use of more than one book. Given the same mass of facts, two writers will seldom draw the same conclusions from them, — and two writers rarely if ever have before them the same set of facts. Every student or reader, therefore, should use at least two books on every part of the field.

In general there are two distinct ways of studying history. One of these is to take some large comprehensive work, read it through, and correct the impression derived from it by readings in more accurate works on small portions of the whole field. Unfortunately, the scholar whose master mind and tireless hand could tell our story, as Gibbon told that of the fall of Rome, has not yet appeared. Probably he never will appear, as the intricacy of our American narrative is baffling and the material to be consulted monumental. It is necessary, therefore, to study American history by the second of these two methods, — the topical method.

This method consists in gaining first of all a knowledge of the whole field from some comprehensive manual. That done, the serious study may follow by reading on isolated topics which will readily fall into their appointed places in the mind's "conspectus of American history." In making this topical study one's inclination and opportunities may be consulted. With the skeleton of fact in one's mind, it does not greatly matter in what order the topics are taken up. Many persons find an interest in biography; for them there is no better way to study American history than to peruse the lives of its five or six greatest men. In general an effort should be made to study some one topic deeply enough to gain an insight into the way history is written; but only the professional historian can hope to study any considerable portion of American history in the original documents.

It is well to have an "original source" always near at hand. The most accessible of famous sources are Franklin's *Autobiography* and Bradford's *History of Plymouth Plantation*. These are classics. One of them is the story of his own life by the greatest mental prodigy America has produced; the other is the modest, admirable narrative of the doings of the Pilgrim Fathers, from the pen of the leading man among them. Any one who will read the first half of these two works will obtain a firmer view of the mainsprings of the success of the American people than he can gain by reading ten times the number of pages in collections of extracts. The perusal of sources is usually tedious; it is always dangerous except to the skilled student. The reading of one journal, or one letter, or one report gives the student a one-sided view. The author of an important historical work on the same field has read five, ten, or even twenty pieces of evidence on that one point. Sources, to the ordinary student and reader, therefore, are useful only for purposes of illustration. In using them it is well, if possible, to read enough in one author to get into the spirit of his life or story. If no book of this kind is available, the next best thing is to read a collection of sources on one topic.

To sum up, the first thing to be done in the acquisition of any valuable information on American history is to get a concise view of the whole field. Next to take up selected topics or the lives of great men. Finally, to do enough work in the "sources" to see for one's self how history is written.

[The section numbers which follow most of the titles here given refer to notes in the main body of this book. —Ed.]

I. A Good School Library

COMPREHENSIVE WORKS

Two manuals: — A. C. McLaughlin. *History of the American nation.* (Twentieth century series.) N. Y.: Appleton. 1899. $1.40. (Sect. 2570.) Edward Channing. *Students' history of the United States.* N. Y.: Macmillan. 1898. $1.40. The "Lists of books' prefixed to each chapter and the specific topical references on the margins of this work are frequently revised. (Sect. 2506.)

Four topical works: — G. P. Fisher. *Colonial era.* N. Y.: Scribner. $1.25. (Sect. 846.) A. B. Hart. *Formation of the Union.* N. Y.: Longmans. $1.25. F. A. Walker. *Making of the nation.* N. Y.: Scribner. $1.25. Wood-

row Wilson. *Division and reunion.* N. Y.: Longmans. $1.25. (Sect. 2639.)

WORKS ON SPECIAL FIELDS

C. F. Lummis. *Spanish pioneers.* Chicago: McClurg. 1893. $1.50. (Sect. 1194.) Francis Parkman. *Pioneers of France.* Boston: Little. $1.50. (Sect. 3672.) John Fiske. *Beginnings of New England* ($2). (Sect. 937.) *American revolution* (2 vols. $4). (Sect. 1315.) *Critical period of American history* ($2). Boston: Houghton. (Sect. 1616.)

T. A. Dodge. *Bird's-eye view of our Civil War.* Boston: Houghton. $1. (Sect. 2165.)

BRIEF BIOGRAPHIES

C. R. Markham. *Christopher Columbus.* London. 1892. (Sect. 780.)

Horace Scudder. *George Washington.* (Riverside literature series, no. 75, 40c. Riverside library for young people, no. 2, 75c. Riverside school library, 60c.) Boston: Houghton. (Sect. 1565.)

American statesmen series. Boston: Houghton. $1.25 per vol. H. C. Lodge. *George Washington* (2 vols.) (sect. 1560), and *Daniel Webster* (sect. 1985); John T. Morse. *John Quincy Adams* (sect. 1584), and *Abraham Lincoln* (2 vols.). (Sect. 2253.)

Makers of America series. New York: Dodd, Mead, & Co. $1 per vol. W. G. Sumner. *Robert Morris* and *Alexander Hamilton.* (sect. 1629); James Schouler. *Thomas Jefferson.* (Sect. 1381.)

W. G. Brown. *Andrew Jackson* (Riverside biographical series). Boston: Houghton. 75c.

SOURCES

Benjamin Franklin. *Autobiography.* Innumerable editions have been published. The best for school use is that in the "Riverside literature series." Boston: Houghton. 40c. (Sect. 1323.)

American history leaflets. New York: A. Lovell. 10c. ea. (Numbers especially suited to school use: 1. Letter of Columbus; 3. Extracts from the Sagas; 9. Voyage of John Cabot; 18 and 26. Lincoln's state papers; 27. John Smith's *True relation ;* 29. Extracts from Bradford's *Plymouth;* 31. Extracts from Winthrop's *New England ;* 33. Otis on writs of assistance.)

A. B. Hart. *Source book of American his-*

tory. New York: Macmillan. 60c. (Sect. 397, 2540.)

T. W. Higginson. *Young folks' book of American explorers.* New York: Longmans. $1.20. (Sect. 721.)

Old South leaflets. Boston: Directors of Old South Work. 122 nos. Pap. 5c. ea. Nos. 1–100 bd. in 4 vols. $1.50 ea. (Sect. 367, 368.)

Histories of the town and state in which the school is situated, and whatever can be obtained in the shape of biographies of local celebrities, local records, traditions having local color, books of travel describing the state.

II. A Collection for a Town Library

The books already mentioned and the following works:—

COMPREHENSIVE WORKS

Justin Winsor. *Narrative and critical history of America* (8 vols. $44), and his *Memorial history of Boston* (4 vols.). Boston: Houghton. These two works are in a manner supplementary, as the "Boston" is really a history of Massachusetts and many of the bibliographies in it are not repeated in the "America." (Sect. 404, 3193.)

Scribner's popular history of the United States (5 vols.). New York: Scribner-History Club. $20. The first four volumes originally appeared as Bryant and Gay's *Popular history.* N. Y. 1878–81. A set of the original edition will serve most purposes. (Sect. 2502.)

James Schouler. *History of the United States* (6 vols.). New York: Dodd. $13.50. (Sect. 2605.)

SOURCES AND COLLECTIONS

William Bradford. *History of Plymouth Plantation.* Boston: issued by the state of Massachusetts. (Sect. 903.)

Stedman and Hutchinson. *Library of American literature* (11 vols.). New York: Wm. E. Benjamin. $30. (Sect. 2618.)

J. N. Larned. *History for ready reference.* Springfield, Mass.: Nichols. 6v. $30. (Sect. 399, 399 a.)

A. B. Hart. *American history told by contemporaries* (4v.). New York: Macmillan. $2 ea. (Sect. 2539.)

William MacDonald. *Select charters and other documents, 1606–1775* ($2), and his *Select documents, 1776–1861* ($2.25). New York: Macmillan. (Sect. 864, 2569.)

WORKS ON SPECIAL FIELDS, TOPICS, OR PERIODS

John Fiske. *Discovery of America* (2v. $4) (sect. 714), *Old Virginia and her neighbours* ($4) (sect. 1131), *The Dutch and Quaker colonies* (2v. $4) (sect. 1066), and *The War of Independence* (Riverside library for young people, no. 1. 75c.). (Sect. 1316.) Boston: Houghton. Fiske's *New England, Revolution,* and *Critical period* have already been enumerated under I.

Francis Parkman. *Half-century of conflict* (2v. $3), *Montcalm and Wolfe* (2v. $3), and *Conspiracy of Pontiac* (2v. $3). Boston: Little. Parkman's *Pioneers* has been noted under I. (Sect. 3672.)

Richard Frothingham. *Rise of the Republic.* Boston: Little. $3.50. (Sect. 2734.)

G. O. Trevelyan. *American Revolution*, pt. 1. N. Y.: Longmans. $3. (Sect. 1527.)

Theodore Roosevelt. *Winning of the West.* (4v.) New York: Putnam. $10. (Sect. 1812.)

H. B. Carrington. *Battles of the Revolution.* New York: Barnes. $5, or his *Washington the soldier.* Boston: Lamson. 1898. (Sect. 1255, 1548.)

Henry Adams. *Administrations of Jefferson and Madison* (9v.). New York: Scribner. $18. (Sect. 1580.)

J. B. McMaster. *History of the people of the United States* (5v.). New York: Appleton. $2.50 ea. (Sect. 2574.)

J. F. Rhodes. *History of the United States since 1850* (4v.). New York: Macmillan. $2.50 ea. (Sect. 2599.)

J. C. Ropes. *Story of the Civil War* (2v.). New York: Putnam. $4. (Sect. 2309.)

H. von Holst. *Constitutional and political history of the United States* (8v.). Chicago: Callaghan. $12. (Sect. 2749.)

BIOGRAPHY

Twelve volumes of the *American statesmen series* (Boston: Houghton. $1.25 per vol.): J. T. Morse. *Thomas Jefferson* (sect. 1377), *John Quincy Adams* (sect. 1584), and *Abraham Lincoln* (2v.) (sect. 2253); H. C. Lodge. *George Washington* (2v.) (sect. 1560), and *Daniel Webster* (sect. 1985); W. G. Sumner. *Andrew Jackson* (sect. 1905); Carl Schurz. *Henry Clay* (2v.) (sect. 1865); A. B. Hart.

Salmon P. Chase (sect. 2134) ; Moorfield Storey. *Charles Sumner.*

Four volumes of the *Makers of America series* (New York : Dodd. $1 per vol.) : Barrett Wendell. *Cotton Mather;* W. G. Sumner. *Robert Morris* and *Alexander Hamilton* (sect. 1629) ; James Schouler. *Thomas Jefferson.* (Sect. 1381.)

Four "studies" in biography : Carl Schurz. *Abraham Lincoln.* Boston : Houghton. $1. (Sect. 2257.)

P. L. Ford. *The true George Washington.* Philadelphia : Lippincott. $2. (Sect. 1551.)

Norman Hapgood. *Abraham Lincoln.* New York : Macmillan. $2. (Sect. 2246.)

Owen Wister. *Ulysses S. Grant.* Boston : Small. 75c.

Five large biographies : James Parton. *Thomas Jefferson* ($2.50) (sect. 1378), and his *Andrew Jackson* (3v. $7.50). (Sect. 1904.) Boston : Houghton.

William Tudor. *James Otis.* Boston. 1823. (Sect. 1451.)

S. M. Janney. *William Penn.* Philadelphia. 1852. (Sect. 1095.)

Frederic Bancroft. *William H. Seward.* N. Y. : Harper. 2v. $5.

RECOLLECTIONS AND MEMOIRS

James F. Clarke. *Anti-slavery days.* New York. 1884. (Sect. 1863.)

L. E. Chittenden. *Personal reminiscences, 1840–1890.* N. Y. : Dodd. $2.

Hugh McCullough. *Men and measures of half a century.* New York : Scribner. $2.50. (Sect. 2402.)

Josiah Quincy. *Figures of the past.* Boston : Little. $1.50. (Sect. 1683.)

Noah Brooks. *Washington in Lincoln's time.* New York : Century Co. $1.25. (Sect. 2119.)

U. S. Grant. *Personal memoirs* (2v.). New York : Century Co. $5. (Sect. 2189.)

W. T. Sherman. *Memoirs* (2v.). New York : Appleton. $5. (Sect. 2320.)

P. H. Sheridan. *Personal memoirs* (2v.). New York. 1888. (Sect. 2317.)

G. B. McClellan. *McClellan's own story.* New York. 1887. (Sect. 2269.)

ILLUSTRATIVE MATERIAL

B. J. Lossing. *Pictorial field-book of the Revolution* (N. Y. : Harper. 2v. $7) (sect. 1420), and his *Pictorial history of the Civil*

War (3v.). Phil. : McKay. $7.50. (Sect. 2264.)

Guernsay and Alden. *Harper's pictorial history of the great Rebellion.* New York : Harper. 1866–68. 2 pts. (Sect. 2201.)

Johnson and Buel. *Battles and leaders of the Civil War.* New York : Century Co. 4v. $15. (Sect. 2109.)

Only one of these illustrated histories of the Civil War is recommended. "Harper's" is the most graphic, "Lossing's" will probably give the most truthful picture, and "Battles and leaders" is the most recent and the easiest to procure.

James Thacher. *Military journal during the Revolution.* Boston. 1823. (Sect. 1524.)

G. C. Eggleston. *A Rebel's recollections.* N. Y. : Putnam. $1. (Sect. 2172.) For this may be substituted J. B. Jones. *A Rebel war clerk's diary.* 2v. Phil. 1866. (Sect. 2229.)

Local histories, records, biographies, books of travel or description, portraits of local celebrities, and, in general, any material which will arouse an interest in the town, county, and state in which the library is situated.

MAPS

A. B. Hart. *Epoch maps.* N. Y. : Longmans. 50c. (sect. 2538); Townsend MacCoun. *Historical geography of the United States.* N. Y. : Silver. $1 (sect. 524) ; B. A. Hinsdale. *Old Northwest.* N. Y. : Silver. $2.50 (sect. 3360) ; the latest *Statistical atlas* published by the Census Bureau.

The *Land Office map of the United States,* latest issue, can be obtained by sending eighty-seven cents to the "Financial Clerk of the Interior Department." It is the best large wall map for a school or library.

III. A Good Working Library

The "collection" last noted will serve the purpose of the general reader and the ordinary student. He who desires to gain a thorough knowledge of the history of the United States or of any portion thereof must have access to more and better records, to larger biographical and autobiographical works and memoirs, and to more books on special fields and topics. The following list contains the most available and most usable works. It is too large to place on "reserve shelves." A good plan would be to have a special printed catalogue of these books, noting in each case the library shelf-mark.

COMPREHENSIVE WORKS AND MANUALS

A. B. Hart. *Epochs of American history* (3 vols.). New York: Longmans. $1.25 ea. (Sect. 884, 1633, 2639.)

Scribner. *American history series* (5 vols.). New York: Scribner. $7.50. (Sect. 846, 1500, 1533, 1850.)

Richard Hildreth. *History of the United States* (6 vols.). New York: Harper. $12. (Sect. 2545.)

George Bancroft. *History of the United States* [to 1789 only]. New York: Appleton. 6v. $15. The original edition (Boston. 1834–66. 8v.) is by far the best. For most libraries the reprint of the latest volumes will suffice. It is entitled: *History of the formation of the Constitution* (New York: Appleton. 2v. $5). The abridged editions of Bancroft's book are not recommended. (Sect. 2489, 2691.)

Justin Winsor. *Narrative and critical history of America* (Boston: Houghton. 8v. $5.50 ea.), and *Memorial history of Boston* (Boston. 1880–82. 4v.). The two sets form together a tolerably complete history of the Colonial and Revolutionary periods with some reference to later times. (Sect. 404, 3193.)

John Fiske's historical writings: *Discovery of America* (2v. $4) (sect. 714), *Virginia* (2v. $4) (sect. 1131), *New England* ($2) (sect. 937), *Dutch and Quaker colonies* (2v. $4) (sect. 1066); *American Revolution* (2v. $4) (sect. 1315), *Critical period* ($2) (sect. 1616), *Mississippi valley in the Civil War* ($2). Boston: Houghton.

Francis Parkman. *Works*. Boston: Little. 13v. $26. (Sect. 3672.)

Scribner. *Popular history* (5 vols.). New York: Scribner - History Club. $20. (Sect. 2502.) Or Bryant and Gay. *Popular history* (4v.). New York. 1878–81. (Sect. 2502.)

James Schouler. *History of the United States* (6v.). New York: Dodd. $13.50. (Sect. 2605.)

J. B. McMaster. *History of the people of the United States* (5v.). New York: Appleton. $2.50 ea. (Sect. 2574.)

Henry Adams. *Administrations of Jefferson and Madison* (9v.). New York: Scribner. $18. (Sect. 1580.)

J. F. Rhodes. *History of the United States*

since 1850 (4v.). New York: Macmillan. $2.50 ea. (Sect. 2599.)

H. von Holst. *Constitutional and political history of the United States* (8v.). Chicago: Callaghan. $12. (Sect. 2749.)

A. C. McLaughlin. *History of the American Nation* (Twentieth century series). New York: Appleton. $1.40. (Sect. 2570.)

Edward Channing. *Students' history of the United States*. New York: Macmillan. $1.40. The bibliographies and marginal references in this work are revised from time to time. (Sect. 2506.)

Channing and Hart. *Guide to the study of American history*. Boston: Ginn. $2.15. A small select bibliography arranged by classes of books and by topics. (Sect. 2508.)

WORKS ON SPECIAL FIELDS AND PERIODS

C. F. Adams. *Three episodes of Massachusetts history* (2v.). Boston: Houghton. $4. (Sect. 892.)

J. A. Doyle. *English colonies in America* (3v.). New York: Holt. $10.50. (Sect. 840, 918.)

Richard Frothingham. *Rise of the Republic* ($3.50) (sect. 2734), and *Siege of Boston* ($3.50). Boston: Little. (Sect. 1334.)

J. A. Woodburn, ed. *Lecky's American Revolution*. New York: Appleton. $1.25 (sect. 1406); or vols. 3 and 4 of

W. E. H. Lecky. *History of England in the 18th century*. New York: Appleton. 8v. $20. (Sect. 1407.)

G. O. Trevelyan. *American Revolution*, part 1. N. Y.: Longmans. $3. (Sect. 1527.)

H. B. Carrington. *Battles of the Revolution*. N. Y.: Barnes. $5 (sect. 1255); or his *Washington the soldier*. Boston. 1898. (Sect. 1548.)

G. W. Greene. *Historical view of the American Revolution*. Boston: Houghton. $1.50. (Sect. 1345.)

B. J. Lossing. *Field-book of the Revolution*. New York: Harper. 2v. $7. (Sect. 1420.)

G. T. Curtis. *Constitutional history*. New York: Harper. 2v. $6. (Sect. 2714.)

Theodore Roosevelt. *Winning of the West* (4v.). New York: Putnam. $10. (Sect. 1812.)

J. F. Cooper. *History of the United States Navy* (3v.). N. Y. 1856. (Sect. 2510.)

E. S. Maclay's *History of the United States Navy* (3v.). New York: Appleton. $9. (Sect. 2572.)

Theodore Roosevelt. *Naval War of 1812.* N. Y. : Putnam. $2.50. (Sect. 1750.)

George Coggeshall. *American privateers.* N. Y. 1856. (Sect. 1720.)

B. J. Lossing. *Field-book of the War of 1812.* New York : Harper. $3.50. (Sect. 1741.)

Horace Greeley. *American conflict* (2v.). Hartford. 1864–66 (sect. 2199) ; and his *Slavery extension.* N. Y. 1856. (Sect. 1893.)

H. R. Helper. *Impending crisis.* N. Y. 1857. Many editions. (Sect. 1897.)

Jefferson Davis. *Rise and fall of the Confederate States* (2v.). New York: Appleton. $10. (Sect. 2156.)

Scribner. *Campaigns of the Civil War* (13v. $12.50) (sect. 2131), and *Navy in the Civil War* (3v. $3). (Sect. 2287.)

Henry Wilson. *Rise and fall of the slave power* (3v.). Boston : Houghton. $9. (Sect. 1992.)

B. J. Lossing. *Pictorial history of the Civil War* (3v.). Phil. : McKay. $7.50. (Sect. 2264.)

Guernsay and Alden. *Harper's pictorial history of the great Rebellion* (1866–68. 2v.) (Sect. 2201.)

Johnson and Buel. *Battles and leaders of the Civil War* (4v.). New York : Century Co. $15. (Sect. 2109.)

Edward McPherson. *Political history of the United States during the great Rebellion.* Washington. 1864. (Sect. 2272.)

J. G. Blaine. *Twenty years of Congress* (2v.). N. Y.: Funk. $7.50. (Sect. 2379.)

Edward McPherson. *Political history of the United States, 1865–70.* Wash. 1880. (Sect. 2404.)

Noah Brooks. *Washington in Lincoln's time.* New York: Century Co. $1.25. (Sect. 2119.)

Frank Moore. *Rebellion record* (11v.). New York. 1861. (Sect. 2284.)

C. A. Dana. *Recollections of the Civil War.* N. Y. : Appleton. $2. (Sect. 2154.)

G. C. Eggleston. *A Rebel's recollections.* N. Y.: Putnam. $1. (Sect. 2172.)

J. B. Jones. *A Rebel war clerk's diary* (2v.). Phil. 1866. (Sect. 2229.)

WORKS ON SPECIAL TOPICS

C. F. Lummis. *Spanish pioneers.* Chicago: McClurg. 1893. $1.50. (Sect. 1194.)

G. P. Winship. *The Coronado expedition.* (Bureau of Ethnology. 14th ann. report, pt. 1. 1896.) (Sect. 3992.)

Morton Dexter. *Story of the Pilgrims.* Boston: Pilgrim Press. 75c. (Sect. 917.)

E. Arber. *Story of the Pilgrim Fathers.* Boston: Houghton. $2. (Sect. 896.)

Peleg Chandler. *American criminal trials* (2v.). Boston. 1841–44.

E. A. Freeman. *English people in its three homes.* Phil. : Coates. $1.75. (Sect. 2654.)

C. Borgeaud. *Rise of modern democracy in Old and New England.* N. Y.: Scribner. $1. (Sect. 2647.)

J. R. Seeley. *Expansion of England.* Boston: Little. $1.75. (Sect. 878.)

James Bryce. *American Commonwealth* (2v. $4.). N. Y.: Macmillan. The abridged edition in 1v. ($1.75) will serve the needs of most students. (Sect. 2702.)

John Fiske. *American political ideas.* N. Y.: Harper. $1. (Sect. 2723.)

Edward Stanwood. *History of the presidency.* Boston: Houghton. $2.50. The same author's earlier work entitled, *History of presidential elections* (Boston. 1896), can take the place of this book. (Sect. 2615.)

Martin Van Buren. *Origin and course of political parties.* New York. 1867. (Sect. 2634.)

F. W. Taussig. *Tariff history.* New York: Putnam. $1.25. (Sect. 2898.)

Philip A. Bruce. *Economic history of Virginia in the seventeenth century.* New York : Macmillan. 2v. $6. (Sect. 2839.)

W. B. Weeden. *Economic history of New England.* Boston: Houghton. 2v. $4.50. (Sect. 2905.)

J. L. Bishop. *History of American manufactures* (2v.). Philadelphia. 1861–64. (Sect. 2831.)

Ann Maury. *Memoirs of a Huguenot family.* N. Y. 1853. (Sect. 3055.)

Timothy Dwight. *Travels in New England and New York* (4v.). New Haven. 1821–2. (Sect. 1615.)

Alexander Johnston. *History of American politics.* New York : Holt. 80c. (Sect. 2552.)

J. S. Landon. *Constitutional history and government.* Boston : Houghton. $3. (Sect. 2765.)

Simon Sterne. *Constitutional history.* New York: Putnam. $1.25. (Sect. 2799.)

J. B. Thayer. *Cases on constitutional law.* Cambridge: C. W. Sever. 2v. $12. (Sect. 2803.)

Francis Wharton. *Digest of the international law of the United States* (3v.). Washington. 1886. (Sect. 2636.)

STANDARD STATE AND LOCAL HISTORIES

J. G. Palfrey. *New England.* Boston : Little. 5v. $20. Boston : Houghton. 4v. $6. Either edition will do. (Sect. 1000, 1001, 1002.)

Thomas Hutchinson. *Massachusetts* (3v.). London and Boston. 1795–1828. (Sect. 961.)

J. R. Brodhead. *New York* (2v.). New York. 1853–71. (Sect. 3197.)

J. G. Wilson. *Memorial history of New York* (4v.). New York : New York History Co. $7.50. (Sect. 3267.) (Sect. 1105.)

Robert Proud. *Pennsylvania* (2v.). Philadelphia. 1797–98. (Sect. 1098.)

Isaac Sharpless. *Quaker government in Pennsylvania* (2v.). Philadelphia: Leach. 1898–99. $1.50 ea. (Sect. 1105.)

J. L. Bozman. *Maryland* (2v.). Baltimore. 1837. (Sect. 1122.)

Charles Campbell. *Virginia.* Richmond. 1847. (Sect. 1126, 1127.)

Thomas Jefferson. *Notes on Virginia.* London. 1787. Many editions. (Sect. 1374.)

J. D. Burk. *Virginia* (4v.). Petersburg, Va. 1804. (Sect. 3275, 3276.)

Edward McCrady. *South Carolina* (3v.). New York : Macmillan. $7.50. (Sect. 1142.)

C. C. Jones. *Georgia* (2v.). Boston : Houghton. 1883. (Sect. 3302.)

A. J. Pickett. *Alabama* (2v.). Charleston. 1851. (Sect. 1806, 3321.)

H. H. Bancroft. *History of the Pacific states* (34v.). San Francisco. 1883–90. (Sect. 3391, 3927, 3997.)

J. P. Dunn. *Indiana.* Boston : Houghton. $1.25. (Sect. 1775.)

L. W. Spring. *Kansas.* Boston : Houghton. $1.25. (Sect. 3380.)

Charles Gayarré. *Louisiana* (4v.). New York. 1852. (Sect. 3294.)

J. W. Monette. *Valley of the Mississippi* (2v.). New York. 1846. (Sect. 1183.)

E. D. Neill. *Minnesota.* Minneapolis. 1887. (Sect. 3371.)

B. A. Hinsdale. *Old Northwest.* New York. 1888. (Sect. 3360.)

BIOGRAPHIES, AUTOBIOGRAPHIES AND MEMOIRS

(*Arranged alphabetically by subjects*)

American statesmen series. Boston: Houghton. 31v. $38.75.

J. Q. and C. F. Adams. *John Adams* (2v.). Philadelphia: Lippincott. $3. (Sect. 1203.)

John Quincy Adams. *Memoirs* (including his "Diary," 12v.). Philadelphia. 1874–77. (Sect. 1588.)

W. V. Wells. *Samuel Adams* (3v.). Boston. 1865. (Sect. 1208.)

I. N. Arnold. *Benedict Arnold.* Chicago. $2.50. (Sect. 1228.)

T. H. Benton. *Thirty years' view* (2v.). New York: Appleton. $6. (Sect. 1832.)

William Birney. *James G. Birney.* New York. 1890. (Sect. 1835.)

J. G. Blaine. *Twenty years of Congress* (2v.). New York : Funk. $7.50. (Sect. 2379.)

F. B. Sanborn. *John Brown.* Boston: Little. $2. (Sect. 1845.)

J. C. Calhoun. *Works* (6v.). New York : Appleton. $15. (Sect. 1853.)

J. F. Clarke. *Anti-slavery days.* New York. 1884. (Sect. 1863.)

Henry Clay. *Works* (6v.). New York. 1857. (Sect. 1864.)

C. R. Markham. *Columbus.* London : Philip. 4s. 6d. (Sect. 780.)

Justin Winsor. *Columbus.* Boston : Houghton. $4. (Sect. 783.)

C. F. Adams. *Richard H. Dana* (2v.). Boston: Houghton. $4.

Frederick Douglass. *Life and times.* Hartford. 1883. (Sect. 1881.)

J. E. Cabot. *R. W. Emerson* (2v.). Boston: Houghton. $3.50.

Benjamin Franklin. *Autobiography.* Many editions, also in the several editions of his *Works.* Boston: Houghton. Riverside literature series, nos. 19, 20. 15c. ea. (Sect. 1322 a, 1323.)

James Parton. *Benjamin Franklin* (2v.). Boston : Houghton. $5. (Sect. 1331.)

P. L. Ford. *The many-sided Franklin.* N. Y. : Century Co. $3. (Sect. 1327.)

John Bigelow, *ed. Franklin's complete works* (10v.). New York. 1887–89. There are many other editions of Franklin's *Works.* Any one of them will serve the purposes of most students and readers. (Sect. 1322.)

F. J. and W. P. Garrison. *William Lloyd Garrison* (4v.). Boston: Houghton. $8. (Sect. 1889.)

S. G. Goodrich. *Recollections* (2v.). New York. 1856. (Sect. 1622.)

U. S. Grant. *Personal memoirs* (2v.). New York : Century Co. $5. (Sect. 2189.)

Owen Wister. *Ulysses S. Grant.* Boston: Small. 75c.

F. V. Greene. *General Greene.* New York: Appleton. $1.50. (Sect. 1346.)

J. T. Morse. *Alexander Hamilton* (2v.). Boston: Little. $4.50. (Sect. 1628.)

W. G. Sumner. *Alexander Hamilton.* New York: Dodd. $1. (Sect. 1629.)

H. C. Lodge, *ed. Works of Alexander Hamilton* (9v.). New York: Putnam. $45; or J. C. Hamilton's edition in 7v. N. Y. 1851. (Sect. 1624.)

W. W. Henry. *Patrick Henry* (3v.). New York: Scribner. $12. (Sect. 1361.)

W. E. Foster. *Stephen Hopkins* (R. I. historical tracts, no. 19). Providence, R. I. 1884. (Sect. 1365.)

James Parton. *Andrew Jackson.* New York: Appleton. $1.50. (Sect. 1904.)

W. G. Brown. *Andrew Jackson* (Riverside biographical series). Boston: Houghton. 75c.

William Jay. *John Jay.* New York. 1833. (Sect. 1639.)

H. S. Randall. *Thomas Jefferson* (3v.). New York. 1858. (Sect. 1379.)

James Parton. *Thomas Jefferson.* Boston: Houghton. $2.50. (Sect. 1378.)

James Schouler. *Thomas Jefferson.* New York: Dodd. $1. (Sect. 1381.)

P. L. Ford, *ed. Jefferson's writings* (10v.). New York: Putnam. $50. This is the best edition; but any other edition will serve the purpose of any but the closest student. (Sect. 1373.)

Amos Kendall. *Autobiography.* Boston: Lee. $3. (Sect. 1911.)

Charlemagne Tower. *Marquis de La Fayette* (2v.). Philadelphia: Lippincott. $8. (Sect. 1402.)

J. E. Cooke. *R. E. Lee.* New York. 1871. (Sect. 2233.)

R. H. Lee. *Richard Henry Lee* (2v.). Philadelphia. 1825. (Sect. 1416.)

Nicolay and Hay. *Abraham Lincoln* (10v.). New York: Century Co. $20. (Sect. 2254.)

Carl Schurz. *Abraham Lincoln.* Boston: Houghton. $1. (Sect. 2257.)

Norman Hapgood. *Abraham Lincoln.* New York: Macmillan. $2. (Sect. 2246.)

Nicolay and Hay, *eds. Complete works of Abraham Lincoln* (2v.). New York: Century Co. $10. (Sect. 2238.)

William Maclay. *Journal.* New York: Appleton. 1890. $2.25. (Sect. 1650.)

G. B. McClellan. *McClellan's own story.* New York. 1887. (Sect. 2269.)

Hugh McCullough. *Men and measures of half a century.* New York: Scribner. $2.50. (Sect. 2402.)

W. C. Rives. *James Madison* (3v.). Boston. 1859. (Sect. 1655.)

James Madison. *Papers* (3v.). Washington. 1840; and his *Letters and other writings* (4v.). Philadelphia. 1865. (Sect. 1652.)

Mrs. Dorothy Madison. *Memoirs and letters of Dolly Madison.* Boston: Houghton. $1.25. (Sect. 1651.)

John Marshall. *Writings upon the Federal Constitution.* Boston. 1838. (Sect. 2777.)

K. M. Rowland. *George Mason* (2v.). New York: Putnam. $8. (Sect. 1658.)

Jared Sparks. *Gouverneur Morris* (3v.). Boston. 1832. (Sect. 1665.)

Gouverneur Morris. *Diary and letters* (2v.). New York: Scribner. $7.50. (Sect. 1663.)

Barrett Wendell. *Cotton Mather.* New York: Dodd. $1.

W. G. Sumner. *Robert Morris.* (New York: Dodd. $1; or his *Financier of the Revolution* (2v.). New York: Dodd. $5. (Sect. 2879.)

William Tudor. *James Otis.* Boston. 1823. (Sect. 1451.)

M. D. Conway. *Thomas Paine* (2v.). New York: Putnam. $5. (Sect. 1454.)

T. N. Page. *The old South.* New York: Scribner. $1.25. (Sect. 3319.)

Thomas Clarkson. *William Penn* (2v.). Philadelphia. 1813. (Sect. 1092.)

S. G. Fisher. *The true William Penn.* Philadelphia: Lippincott. $2. (Sect. 1094.)

Octavius Pickering. *Timothy Pickering* (4v.). Boston. 1867–73. (Sect. 1671.)

Josiah Quincy. *Figures of the past.* Boston: Little. $1.50. (Sect. 1683.)

Madame de Riedesel. *Letters and memoirs.* Albany. 1867. (Sect. 1477.)

Richard Rush. *Memoranda of a residence at London.* Philadelphia. 1833. (Sect. 1688.)

Samuel Sewall. *Diary* (3v.). In Mass. Hist. Soc. Collections. 5th series, v. 5–7. (Sect. 1013.)

Frederick Bancroft. *William H. Seward* (2v.). N. Y.: Harper. $5.

Philip H. Sheridan. *Personal memoirs.* N. Y. 1888. 2v. (Sect. 2317.)

John Sherman. *Recollections.* Chicago: Werner. 2v. $7.50. (Sect. 2412.)

W. T. Sherman. *Memoirs* (2v.). New York: Appleton. $5. (Sect. 2320.)

William Sullivan. *Familiar letters.* Boston. 1834. (Sect. 1695.)

E. L. Pierce. *Memoir and letters of Charles Sumner* (4v.). Boston: Little. $12. (Sect. 1969.)

Richard Frothingham. *Joseph Warren.* Boston. 1865. (Sect. 1536.)

P. L. Ford. *The true George Washington.* Phil. Lippincott. $2. (Sect. 1551.)

John Marshall. *George Washington* (5v.). Philadelphia. 1804. (Sect. 1561.)

Washington Irving. *George Washington* (5v.). New York: Putnam. $3.75. Also a one volume abridgment by John Fiske. Boston: Ginn. 85c. (Sect. 1555, 1556.)

Woodrow Wilson. *George Washington.* N. Y.: Harper. $3. (Sect. 1567.)

W. C. Ford, *ed. Washington's writings* (14v. N. Y.: Putnam. $70); or Jared Sparks's edition of *Washington's writings* (12v.). Boston. 1837. (Sect. 1538, 1539.)

Daniel Webster. *Works* (6v.). Boston. 1851. (Sect. 1979.)

RECORDS OF THE UNITED STATES

Peter Force. *American archives* (1774–1783. 9v.; all ever published). Washington. (Sect. 1220.)

Journals of Congress (1774–88. 13v.). Phil. and N. Y. 1777–89. Several reprints. (Sect. 86.)

Secret journals (1775–88. 4v.). Boston. 1821. (Sect. 86.)

Annals of Congress (1789–1824. 42v.). Washington. 1834–56.

Congressional debates (1825–37. 29v.). Washington. 1825–37. (Sect. 90.)

Congressional globe (1833–73. 108v.). Washington. 1834–73. (Sect. 91.)

Congressional record (1873–. 34v.+). Washington. 1873–1901. (Sect. 91.)

The statutes-at-large (31v. to 1901). Boston and Washington. 1860–1901. (Sect. 92.)

Treaties and conventions between the United States and other powers. Washington. 1889. (Sect. 2633.)

Charters and constitutions of the United States (2v.; various editions). Washington. 1877. (Sect. 2785.)

Messages and papers of the Presidents (53d Cong., 2d sess., House misc. doc. v. 37). Washington. 1896–99. 10v. (Sect. 2631.)

COLONIAL AND STATE RECORDS

Only the largest libraries can have complete sets of colonial records and constitutional conventions. The following sets are representative, and will be found useful by careful students.

Massachusetts colony records (5v.). Boston. 1853–54; and *Plymouth colony records* (12v.). Boston. 1855–61. The two sets can be purchased for about fifty dollars. (Sect. 134.)

Documents relative to the colonial history of the State of New York (15v.). Albany. 1856–87. (Sect. 157, 1086.)

W. W. Hening. *Statutes-at-large of Virginia*, 1619–1792. (13v. — the earlier vols. are the most important and the least expensive.) Philadelphia, New York and Richmond. 1819–23. (Sect. 190.)

William Bradford. *Plymouth Plantation.* (The best edition for the student is Charles Deane's annotated edition in the Mass. Hist. Soc. *Collections*, 4th series, vol. 3; the most easily obtained is that issued by the State of Massachusetts.) (Sect. 903.)

John Winthrop. *History of New England* (2v.). Boston. 1825-6. (Sect. 1041.)

Alexander Brown. *Genesis of the United States* (2v.). Boston: Houghton. $15. (Sect. 1124.)

James Madison. *Notes of debates in the Federal convention* (various editions). Chicago: Scott. $2.50. (Sect. 2776.)

J. Elliot. *Debates on the adoption of the Constitution* (5v.). Phil. 1861. (Sect. 20.)

Journals and *Debates* of the state in which the Library is situated and all of its printed records — if obtainable at reasonable cost. See, also, note on local material under II., p. 466, second column.

LIST OF PUBLISHERS

OF BOOKS IN PRINT, JANUARY, 1902

Abbatt. Abbatt, William, 281 Fourth Ave., New York.

Agüeros. Agüeros, V., Mexico, Mexico.

Alcan. Alcan, Félix, 108 Boulevard Saint-Germain, Paris.

Alliance. Alliance Pub. Co., 569 Fifth Ave., New York.

American Academy. American Academy of Political and Social Science, Philadelphia.

American Antiquarian Office. American Antiquarian Office, 5827 Madison Ave., Chicago.

American Antiquarian Society. American Antiquarian Society, Worcester, Mass.

American Baptist. American Baptist Publication Society, 1420 Chestnut St., Philadelphia.

American Book. American Book Co., 100 Washington Sq., E., New York.

American Economic. American Economic Association, Baltimore, Md.

American Historical. American Historical Association, Washington, D. C.

American Publishing. American Publishing Co., 424 Asylum St., Hartford Conn.

American Unitarian. American Unitarian Association, 25 Beacon St., Boston.

Anderson, W. H. Anderson, W. H., & Co., 524 Main St., Cincinnati, Ohio.

Andrade. Andrade y Morales, Mexico, Mexico.

Appleton. Appleton, D., & Co., 72 Fifth Ave., New York.

Arkell. Arkell Publishing Co., 110 Fifth Ave., New York.

Armstrong. Armstrong, A. C., & Son, 3–5 E. 18th St., New York.

Arnold. Arnold, Edward, 37 Bedford St., Strand, London.

Backus Hist. Backus Historical Society, Newton, Mass.

Bacon. Bacon & Co., 508 Clay St., San Francisco, Cal.

Baker. Baker, Charlotte Alice [author], Cambridge, Mass.

Baker & T. Baker & Taylor Co., 33 E. 17th St., New York.

Bancroft-W. Bancroft-Whitney Co., 438 Montgomery St., San Francisco, Cal.

Bardeen. Bardeen, C. W., 406 S. Franklin St., Syracuse, N. Y.

Barnes. Barnes, A. S., & Co., 156 Fifth Ave., New York.

Barrie. Barrie, George, & Son, 1313 Walnut St., Philadelphia.

Beauchemin, Beauchemin, C. O., & Fils, 256 St. Paul St., Montreal, Canada.

Belknap. Belknap & Warfield, 77–79 Asylum St., Hartford, Ct.

Bell. Bell, Geo., & Sons, 4, 5, 6 York St., Covent Garden, W. C., London.

Benjamin. Benjamin, Williams Evarts, 22 W. 33d St., New York.

Biddle. Biddle, Drexel, 228 S. 4th St., Philadelphia.

Bonner's. Bonner's, Robert, Sons, 182 William St., New York.

Boston Bk. Boston Book Co., 83 Francis St., Back Bay, Boston.

Bouton. Bouton, James W., 10 W. 28th St., New York.

Bowen-M. Bowen-Merrill Co., 9 W. Washington St., Indianapolis, Ind.

Brethren. Brethren Pub. House, Mt. Morris, Ill.

Briggs. Briggs, Wm., 29 Richmond St. West, Toronto, Canada.

Brown. Brown, Wm. Foster, & Co., 2323 St. Catherine St., Montreal, Canada.

Brownson. Brownson, H. T., Detroit, Mich.

Buffalo Catholic. Buffalo Catholic Club, Erie and Franklin Sts., Buffalo, N. Y.

Burke. Burke, T. J. W., & Co., Macon, Ga.

Burnett. Burnett Publishing Co., 11 Broadway, New York.

Burrows. Burrows Bros. Co., 133 Euclid Ave., Cleveland, O.

Butler. Butler, Sheldon & Co., 45 E. 12th St., New York.

Cadieux. Cadieux & Dérome, Montreal, Canada.

Callaghan. Callaghan & Co., 114 Monroe St., Chicago.

Campbell W. J. Campbell, William J., 1218 Walnut St., Philadelphia.

Canada Law-Book Co. Canada Law Book Co., Toronto, Canada.

Canadian Gleaner. Canadian Gleaner, Huntingdon, P. Q., Canada.

Carlon. Carlon & Hollenbeck, Circle & Meridian Sts., Indianapolis, Ind.

Carswell. Carswell Co., 28 Adelaide St. East, Toronto, Canada.

Century Co. Century Co., 33 E. 17th St., New York.

Century Manuf. Century Manufacturing Co., 1336 Cherry St., Philadelphia.

Cerf. Cerf, L., 12 Rue Sainte-Anne, Paris.

Challamel. Challamel, Augustin, 17 Rue Jacob, Paris.

Chapleau. Chapleau & Fils, Montreal, Canada.

Chapman. Chapman & Hall, 11 Henrietta St., Covent Garden, London.

Christian. Christian Literature Co., New York. [Sold to Scribner.]

Clarke. Clarke, Robert, Co., 31–35 E. 4th St., Cincinnati.

Clowes. Clowes, William, & Son, 27 Fleet St. & 13 Charing Cross, S. W., London.

Coates. Coates, Henry T., & Co., 1222 Chestnut St., Philadelphia.

Colin. Colin, Armand, 5 Rue de Mézières, Paris.

Collier. Collier, P. F., & Son, 203 Broadway, New York.

Columbia. Columbia University, New York City.

Columbian Corr. Coll. Columbian Correspondence College, Washington, D. C.

Congdon. Congdon & Britnell, 11 Richmond St. West, Toronto, Canada.

Continental Pub. Continental Publishing Co., 24 Murray St., New York.

Copp. Copp, Clark Co., 64 Front St. West, Toronto, Canada.

Courier Journ. Courier Journal Co., Office of, Louisville, Ky.

Crowell. Crowell, Thomas Y., & Co., 426 W. Broadway, New York.

Cumberland Press. Cumberland Press, Nashville, Tenn.

Damrell. Damrell & Upham, 283 Washington St., Boston.

Davies. Davies, F. F., Silver Bow Block, Butte City, Montana.

Dawson. Dawson Brothers, 16 De Bresoles St., Montreal, Canada.

Demers. Demers & Frère, Quebec, Canada.

De Wolfe. De Wolfe, Fiske & Co., 361–365 Washington St., Boston.

Dick. Dick & Fitzgerald, 18 Ann St., New York.

Dillingham, G. W. Dillingham, George W., Co., 119 W. 23d St., New York.

Dodd. Dodd, Mead & Co., 372 Fifth Ave., New York.

Doubleday, P. Doubleday, Page & Co., 34 Union Square, E., New York.

Doxey. Doxey, Wm., San Francisco. [Now Doxey's, New York.]

Doxey's. Doxey's, 15 E. 17th St., New York.

Drallop. Drallop Publishing Co., 166 Sixth Ave., New York.

Drew. Drew, H. & W. B., Co., Jacksonville, Fla.

Drysdale. Drysdale, Wm., & Co., 2478 St. Catherine St., Montreal, Canada.

Dussault. Dussault & Proulx, Quebec, Canada.

Dutton. Dutton, E. P., & Co., 31 W. 23d St., New York.

Earle. Earle Publishing & Mercantile Co., 45 Princess St., St. John, New Brunswick, Canada.

Eaton. Eaton & Mains, 150 Fifth Ave., New York.

Editor. Editor Publishing Co., 327 Pike Bldg., Cincinnati, O.

Educ. Pub. Educational Publishing Co., 50 Bromfield St., Boston.

Estes. Estes, Dana, & Co., 208–218 Summer St., Boston.

Farmer. Farmer, Silas, & Co., 31 Monroe Ave., Detroit, Mich.

Fearey. Fearey, George D., 614 Delaware St., Kansas City, Mo.

Fenno. Fenno, R. F., & Co., 11 E. 16th St., New York.

Ferris. Ferris, Alfred J., 29 N. 7th St., Philadelphia.

Finchamp. Finchamp, Raymond, Dundas, Ont., Canada.

Finerty. Finerty, John Frederick, 69 Dearborn St., Chicago.

Flanagan. Flanagan, A., Co., 268 Wabash Ave., Chicago.

Foote. Foote & Davies Co., 65 E. Alabama St., Atlanta, Ga.

Fords. Fords, Howard & Hulbert, 47 E. 10th St., New York.

Frowde. Frowde, H., Clarendon Press, Amen Corner, E. C., London. Branch, 93 Fifth Ave., New York.

Funk. Funk & Wagnalls Co., 30 Lafayette Pl., New York.

Gagnon. Gagnon, Philéas, 67 du Pont St., St. Roch du Quebec, Canada.

Ginn. Ginn & Co., 29 Beacon St., Boston.

Goodrich. Goodrich, E. J., Oberlin, O.

Grafton. Grafton, F. E., & Sons, Montreal, Canada.

Granger. Granger Frères, 1699 Notre Dame St., Montreal, Canada.

Guillaumin. Guillaumin et Cie., 14 Rue de Richelieu, Paris.

Hachette. Hachette & Cie., 79 Boulevard Saint-Germain, Paris.

Hamilton. Hamilton, N. G., Pub. Co., 504–506 The Arcade, Cleveland, O.

Hamlin, A. C. Hamlin, Augustus Choate, Bangor, Me.

Hamlin, C. E. Hamlin, Charles Eugene, Cambridge, Mass.

Hammett. Hammett, J. L., & Co., 116 to 120 Summer St., Boston.

Hansell. Hansell, F. F., & Bro., 714 Canal St., New Orleans, La.

Harper. Harper & Bros., Franklin Sq., New York.

Harper, F P. Harper, Francis P, 14 W. 22d St., New York.

Harvard. Harvard University, Cambridge, Mass.

Hay. Hay, Geo. Upham, St. John, New Brunswick, Canada.

Heath. Heath, D. C., & Co., 110 Boylston St., Boston.

Helman-T. Helman-Taylor Co., 23–27 Euclid Ave., Cleveland, O.

Holt. Holt, Henry, & Co., 29 W. 23d St., New York.

Holy Childhood. Holy Childhood Indian School, Harbor Springs, Michigan.

Hope. Hope, James, & Sons, 49 Sparks St., Ottawa, Ontario, Canada.

Houghton. Houghton, Mifflin & Co., 4 Park St., Boston.

Humphrey. Humphrey, Geo. P., 25 Exchange St., Rochester, N. Y.

Johns Hopkins. Johns Hopkins Press, Baltimore, Md.

Johnson. Johnson, B. F., Pub. Co., 1013 Main St., Richmond, Va.

Judd, E. P. Judd, Edward P., Co., P. O. Box 405, New Haven, Ct.

Kenedy. Kenedy, P. J., 5 Barclay St., New York.

Kerr. Kerr, Charles H., & Co., 56 Fifth Ave., Chicago.

Knight. Knight & Brown, 150 Fifth Ave., New York.

Krehbiel. Krehbiel, Henry Peter, Canton, O.

Kuhl. Kuhl, W. H., 73 Jager Strasse, Berlin.

Leach. Leach, T. S., 29 N. 7th St., Philadelphia.

Lebègue. Lebègue et Cie., Bruxelles.

Lechevalier. Lechevalier, E., 39 Quai des Grands-Augustins, Paris.

Lee & S. Lee & Shepard, 202 Devonshire St., Boston.

Leland. Leland Stanford, Jr., University, Palo Alto, Cal.

Leroux. Leroux, E., 28 Rue Bonaparte, Paris.

Levytype. Levytype Co., 628 Chestnut St., Philadelphia.

Lindsay. Lindsay, Robert M., 11th & Walnut Sts., Philadelphia.

Linscott. Linscott Publishing Co., 157 Bay St., Toronto, Canada.

Lippincott. Lippincott, J. B., Co., Washington Sq., Philadelphia.

Little. Little, Brown & Co., 254 Washington St., Boston.

Longmans. Longmans, Green & Co., 91–93 Fifth Ave., New York; 38 Paternoster Row, London.

Lothrop. Lothrop Pub. Co., 530 Atlantic Ave., Boston.

Lovell, A. Lovell, A., & Co., 3 E. 14th St., New York.

Low. Low (Sampson), Marston & Co., St. Dunstan's House, Fetter Lane, London.

Lowdermilk. Lowdermilk, W. H., & Co., 1424–26 F. St., Washington, D. C.

Lundy's. Lundy's Lane Historical Society, Niagara Falls South, Ontario, Canada.

Lyon. Lyon, Gardiner Tyler, Williamsburg, Va.

McBride. McBride, D. H., & Co., 733 Dearborn St., Chicago.

McClure, P. McClure, Phillips & Co., 141–155 E. 25th St., New York.

McClurg. McClurg, A. C., & Co., 215–221 Wabash Ave., Chicago.

McDonough. McDonough, Joseph, 41 Columbia St., Albany, N. Y.

McKay. McKay, David, 1022 Market St., Philadelphia.

Mackay, J. Mackay, John, 1 Blythswood Drive, Glasgow, Scotland.

Macmillan. Macmillan Co., 66 Fifth Ave., New York; St. Martin's St., Leicester Square, W. C., London.

McMillan, I. & A. McMillan, I. and A., 78 Prince William St., St. John, New Brunswick, Canada.

McMullen. McMullen & Co., Brockville, Ontario, Canada.

McVey. McVey, Jos. J., 31 N. 13th St., Philadelphia.

Maine Hist. Maine Historical Society, Portland, Me.

Maisonneuve. Maisonneuve, J., 6 rue de Mézières, Paris.

Mame. Mame et fils, Tours, France.

Mansfield. Mansfield, M. F., & Co., 14 W. 22d St., New York.

Mass. Hist. Massachusetts Historical Society, Cor. Boylston St. & the Fenway, Boston.

Maynard. Maynard, Merrill & Co., 29–33 E. 19th St., New York.

Mercier. Mercier & Cie., Lévis, P. Q., Canada.

Methodist. Methodist Episcopal Pub. House, Nashville, Tenn.

Methodist Book. Methodist Book Concern, 150 Fifth Ave., New York.

Meyers. Meyers, Herman B., 138 Washington St., Chicago.

Miller. Miller, Daniel, Reading, Pa.

Mitchell. Mitchell & Hughes, 140 Wardour St., W., London.

Modern Printing Co. Modern Printing Co., 20 St. Vincent St., Montreal, Canada.

Morang. Morang, G. N., & Co., 90 Wellington St. West, Toronto, Canada.

Morton. Morton, John P., & Co., 440–446 W. Main St., Louisville, Ky.

Munsell. Munsell's, Joel, Sons, 82 State St., Albany, N. Y.

Murray. Murray, C., 11 Ludgate Square, E. C., London.

Narragansett. Narragansett Club, Providence, R. I.

Neely. Neely, F. T., Co., 114 Fifth Ave., New York.

Nelson. Nelson, Thomas, & Sons, 37–41 E. 18th St., New York; Parkside Works, Dalkeith Road, Edinburgh, Scotland.

New Amsterdam. New Amsterdam Book Co., 156 Fifth Ave., New York.

New York Hist. New York Historical Society, 170 Second Ave., New York.

New York History. New York History Co., 114 Fifth Ave., New York.

Nichols. Nichols, C. A., Co., 33 Lyman St., Springfield, Mass.

Norstedt. Norstedt, P. A., & Sons, 165 Washington St., Chicago.

Old South. Old South Work, Directors of, Old South Meeting House, Boston.

Ollendorff. Ollendorff, Paul, 50 Chaussée d'Antin, Paris.

Oxford Univ. Oxford University Press (Am. Branch), 91–93 Fifth Ave., New York.

Page, L. C. Page, L. C., & Co., 200 Summer St., Boston.

Partridge. Partridge, S. W., & Co., 8–9 Paternoster Row, E. C., London.

Paul. Paul (Kegan), Trench, Trübner & Co., Paternoster House, Charing Cross Rd., W. C., London.

Penn., Hist. Pennsylvania, Historical Society of, 1300 Locust St., Philadelphia.

Penn. Pub. Co. Pennsylvania Publishing Co., 923 Arch St., Philadelphia.

Philip. Philip, Geo., & Son, 32 Fleet St., E. C., London.

Picken. Picken, Eben, 33 Beaver Hall Hill, Montreal, Canada.

Pilgrim Press. Pilgrim Press, 14 Beacon St., Boston.

Plon. Plon-Nourrit et Cie., 8 Rue Garancière, Paris.

Poirier. Poirier, Bessette, & Co., Montreal, Canada.

Porter. Porter, Peter Augustus, Niagara Falls, N. Y.

Pott. Pott, James, & Co., 119 W. 23d St., New York.

Powell. Powell, Anna Rice, Plainfield, N. J.

Presbyterian. Presbyterian Board of Publishers, 1319 Walnut St., Philadelphia.

Preston. Preston & Rounds Co., 98 Westminster St., Providence, R. I.

Prince. Prince Society, 12 Bosworth St., Boston, Mass.

Putnam. Putnam's, G. P., Sons, 29 W. 23d St., New York.

Quaritch. Quaritch, Bernard, 15 Piccadilly, London.

Randolph. Randolph, A. D. F., 63 West 87th St., New York.

Revell. Revell, Fleming H., Co., 156 Fifth Ave., New York.

Richards. Richards, Grant, 9 Henrietta St., Covent Garden, W. C., London.

Rousseau. Rousseau, A., 23 Rue d'Aboukir, Paris.

Roy. Roy, Pierre-Georges, 9 Wolfe St., Lévis, Quebec, Canada.

Sachse. Sachse, Julius Friedrich, 4428 Pine St., Philadelphia.

Schroeder. Schroeder, Gustavus W., 393½ 14th St., Brooklyn, N. Y.

Scotch Irish. Scotch Irish Society of America, Drexel Building, Philadelphia.

Scott, F. & Co. Scott, Foresman & Co., 378–388 Wabash Ave., Chicago.

Scranton. Scranton, S. S., Co., 281 Asylum St., Hartford, Ct.

Scribner. Scribner's, Charles, Sons, 153–157 Fifth Ave., New York.

Scribner History Club. Care of Chas. Scribner's Sons, 153 Fifth Ave., New York.

Senecal. Senecal, Eusebe & Co., 73 St. James St., Montreal, Canada.

Sergel. Sergel, Charles H., Co., 358 Dearborn St., Chicago.

Sever. Sever, C. W., & Co., Cambridge, Mass.

Shewell. Shewell, T. R., & Co., 68 Chauncy St., Boston.

Silver. Silver, Burdett & Co., 29–33 E. 19th St., New York.

Simpkin. Simpkin, Marshall, Hamilton, Kent & Co., 4 Stationer's Hall Court, E. C., London.

Small. Small, Maynard & Co., Pierce Bldg., Copley Sq., Boston.

Smith. Smith, Elder & Co., 15 Waterloo Place, S. W., London.

Sower. Sower, Christopher, Co., 614 Arch St., Philadelphia.

Stanford. Stanford, Edward, 12 Long Acre, W. C., London.

Steiger. Steiger, E., & Co., 25 Park Place, New York.

Stevens, B. F. Stevens, B. F., & Brown, 4 Trafalgar Sq., London.

Stevens, H. Stevens, Henry, & Son, 39 Great Russell St., W. C., London.

Stokes. Stokes, Frederick A., Co., 5–7 E. 16th St., New York.

Stone, H. S. Stone, Herbert S., & Co., 11 Eldridge Place, Chicago.

Syndicate. Syndicate Pub. Co., 234 S. 8th St., Philadelphia.

Taylor. Taylor, J. F., & Co., 5 & 7 East 16th St., New York.

Times. Times Pub. Co., Bethlehem, Pa.

Tribune. Tribune Printing Co., South Bend, Ind.

Tuttle, M. & T. Tuttle, Morehouse & Taylor Co., New Haven, Ct.

United. United Brethren Pub. House, Dayton, O.

Universalist. Universalist Pub. House, 30 West St., Boston.

University. University Pub. Co., 43–47 E. 10th St., New York.

University of Toronto. Toronto, Canada.

University of Wis. University of Wisconsin, Madison, Wis.

Unwin. Unwin, Thomas Fisher, 11 Paternoster Buildings, London.

Utley. Utley, Herbert D., 153 State St., New London, Ct.

Valois. Valois, J. M., 726a Sanguinet St., Montreal, Canada.

Ward. Ward, Lock & Co., Salisbury Sq., E. C., London.
Warne. Warne, Frederick, & Co., 36 E. 22d St., New York.
Way. Way, W. Irving, 203 Michigan Ave., Chicago.
Webb. Webb & Owings, 2003 Second Ave., Birmingham, Ala.
Webster. Webster, Franklin, 120 Liberty St., New York.
Weeks. Weeks, Stephen Beauregard, Santa Fé, N. M.

Welter. Welter, H., 4 Rue Bernard-Palissy, Paris.
Werner. Werner, E. S., Pub. and Supply Co., 43 E. 19th St., New York.
Werner Sch.-Bk. Werner School-Book Co., 378–388 Wabash Ave., Chicago.
Whittaker. Whittaker, Thomas, 3 Bible House, New York.
Williams. Williams & Norgate, 14 Henrietta St., Covent Garden, London.
Winnipeg Tribune. Winnipeg Tribune, Winnipeg, Manitoba, Canada.
Winston. Winston, John C., Co., 45–51 7th St., Philadelphia.

Young Churchman. Young Churchman Co., 412 Milwaukee St., Milwaukee, Wis.

INDEX

NOTE. — Entries are arranged in numerical order, by section numbers; except that, in the case of a book with two or more section numbers, the number of the full annotated entry is given first; and that in some cases related entries have been brought together, without regard to section numbers.

Names of forts are entered only under the word fort; lakes appear under name of lake, and rivers under name of river.

Abbreviations used are usually self-explanatory. Among those used are the following : —

acct. = account.	exped. = expedition.	polit. = political.
admin. = administration.	finan. = financial.	proc. = proceedings.
bibliog. = bibliography.	govt. = government, govern-	pubs. = publications.
biog. = biography.	mental.	rel. = relating, relative.
cat. = catalogue.	hist. = history, historical.	Rev. = Revolution.
coll. = collection, college.	illus. = illustrated, illustrative.	rpt. = report.
conc. = concerning.	inst. = institute.	ser. = series.
cong. = congressional.	lib. = library.	soc. = society.
corr. = correspondence.	lit. = literature.	terr. = territory.
desc. = description, descriptive.	L. C. = Lower Canada.	trans. = transactions.
disc. = discovery.	milit. = military.	Univ. = University.
doc. = document, documentary.	narr. = narrative.	U. C. = Upper Canada.

Buckingham, J. S., Am. (1837-38), 1848; Slave states of Am., 1849.

Buckley, J. M., Hist. of Methodists in the U. S., 2995.

Buddhists, disc. of Am. by Chinese, Leland, 747; disc. of Am. by Afghanistan, Vining, 756.

Buel, C. C., *ed.* *See* Battles and leaders of the Civil War, 2109.

Buena Vista, battle of. *See* Taylor, 2013.

Buenos Ayres, and the provinces of the Rio de la Plata, Parish, 4085; hist. of the vice-royalty of, Wilcocke, 4092.

Buffalo (N. Y.), desc. of [about 1840-45], *see* Nichols, 1931; hist., Buffalo Hist. Soc., 3199; authentic and comprehensive hist., Ketchum, 3218; monograph on, *see* Powell, 3246; journals and journeys of an early merchant, *see* Severance, 3254; invasion of Can. from, *see* Fenian invasion, 3715; visit to (1844-5), *see* Warburton, 3788.

Buffalo Historical Society, pubs., 3199.

Builders of Great Britain series: Cabots, *see* Beazley, 800, Raleigh, *see* Hume, 1155.

Building of a nation, Gannett, 2855.

Building the nation, Coffin, 1611.

Bulger papers, regarding the British occupation of Prairie du Chien (1812-15), *see* Wis. State Hist. Soc., 3390, coll., v. 13.

Buller, C. *See* Durham, 3712.

Bullet and shell, Williams, 2369.

Bulletin de recherches historiques, 3484.

Bullock, C. J., Finances of the U. S. (1775-89), 2840, *see also* Wis. Univ., 390.

Bullock, *Capt.* J. D., Secret service of the Confederate states in Europe, 2124.

Bullock, W., Six months' residence and travels in Mex., 3933.

Bull Run (also known as battle of Manassas), second battle of, Cox, 2151, *see also* Ropes, 2308; McDowell and Tyler in, Fry, 2181; first battle of, *see* Riddle, 2307; battle of, *see* Stuart, 2341, Swinton, 2343.

Bunker Hill, letters of Brit. officers from battlefield, Drake, 1302; battle of, Ellis, 1311, Frothingham, 1334, *see also* Heath, 1358, Putnam, 1466.

Bunyan, John, biog. essay on. *See* Tulloch, 3099.

Bureau of American Ethnology. *See* Smithsonian Institution.

Bureau of Education. *See* United States Bureau of Education.

Burgess, J. W., Middle period (1817-58), 1850; Polit. sci. and comparative constitutional law, 2704.

Burgess, Tristam, Battle of Lake Erie, 1717; memoir of, Bowen, 1596.

Burgher rights in New Amsterdam. *See* N. Y. Hist. Soc., 1054.

Burgoyne, *Lt.-Gen.* John, A state of the exped. from Can., 1248; and the Convention of Saratoga, Deane, *see* Am. Antiquarian Soc., 242; polit. and milit. episodes, from life and corr. of, Fonblanque, 1250; invasion of 1777, Drake, 1300; journal of campaign, Hadden, 1351, Pausch, 1459; prisoners after surrender of, *see* Heath, 1358; march, capture, and experiences of prisoners, *see* Lowell, 1423; acct. of campaign, Neilson, 1445; corr. respecting operations against, *see* Sparks, 1503; campaign of, Stone, 1515, *see also* Johnson, 1383, Riedesel, 1477, 1478; ballads and poems rel. to campaign, Stone, 1516; *see also* Morgan, 1425.

Burial customs, *see* Jones, 575; Aleut, *see* Dall, 566.

Burk, J. D., Hist. of Va., 3275; Hist. of Va., continued by Jones and Girardin (1775-81), 3276.

Burke, Edmund, writings for *Annual register*, 392; Acct. of European settlements in Am., 832; speech on conciliation with the colonies, 1251; services as agent of Province of N. Y., Stebbins, *see* Am. Antiquarian Soc., 241; studies of, Morley, 1252.

Burke, U. R., Life of Benito Juarez, 3959.

Burke (N. C.), Revolutionary War in. *See* Hunter, 1370.

Burnaby, Andrew, Travels through the middle settlements of N. Am. (1759-60), 833; travels of, *see* Pinkerton, 731.

Burnap, G. W., Leonard Calvert. *See* Sparks, 2613, ser. 2, v. 9.

Burnet, J., Notes on the early settlement of the northwestern terr., 1766, *see also* O. Hist. and Philosoph. Soc., 3374.

Burney, J., Buccaneers of Am., 4099.

Burns, Anthony. *See* Parker, 1935.

Burnside, *Maj.-Gen.* Ambrose E., life and public services, Poore, 2125; and the Ninth Army Corps, Woodbury, 2126.

Burr, Aaron, letters, *see* Biddle, 1593, journal, 1597; relations to Jefferson, *see* Morse, 1377; partisanship of, *see* Adams, 1582; memoirs of, Davis, 1598; life, Knapp, 1599, Merwin, 1600, Parton, 1601; conspiracy, *see* Wilkinson, 1706, Blennerhassett, 1762, Powell, 2594; trial, *see* Wirt, 1707; exped., *see* Hall, 1786, connexion with Wilkinson, Clark, 1824; *see also* Martineau, 1925.

Burr, G. L., Rpt. on treaty of Münster, *see* U. S. Venezuelan Boundary Commission, 4024; Rpts. on maps, 4024.

Burrage, H. S., Hist. of the Baptists in New Eng., 2996.

Burton, *Capt. Sir* R. F., City of the Saints, 2022; Letters from the battle-fields of Paraguay, 4073; *annotator, see* Conquest of the river Plate, 4074.

Bury, W. C. K., Exodus of the western nations, 834.

Bushnell, Horace, theory of atonement. *See* Boardman, 2989.

Butler, *Maj.-Gen.* Benjamin F., autobiog., 2127, letter on exchange of prisoners, *see* U. S. Sanitary Commission, 2358; in New Orleans, Parton, 2128.

Butler, M., Hist. of the commonwealth of Ky., 3277.

Butler, N. M., Effect of the War of 1812 upon the consolidation of the Union, 1718.

Butler, W., Mex. in transition, 3934.

Butterfield, C. W., Hist. of the disc. of the Northwest by John Nicolet, 1184, 3670; Hist. of the Girtys, 1338; Brulé's discoveries and explorations (1610-1626), 3610, *see also* Western Reserve Hist. Soc., 3387; Bibliog. of Nicolet, *see* 3670; *ed., see* Washington-Crawford letters, 1542.

Butterworth, H., Young folks' hist. of Am., 2503; Story of Am., 2503; S. Am., 3911.

Byfield, Nathaniel, Acct. of the late rev. in New Eng. *See* Force, 848.

Byington, E. H., Puritan as a colonist and reformer, 908.

Byrd, William, Westover MSS., 1125; Hist. of the dividing line, 1125.

Byrdsall, E., Hist. of the Loco-foco or Equal Rights party, 1851.

Cabal, Conway. *See* Conway cabal.

Cabeça de Vaca. *See* Nuñez Cabeça de Vaca.

Cable, G. W., Negro question, 2382; Silent South, 2382; Creoles of La., 3278; *see also* Waring, 3336.

Cable, Atlantic, hist., Field, 2853.

Cabot, George, life, Lodge, 1602.

Cabot, John *and* Sebastian, Beazley, 800, Tarducci, 809, Beaudoin, *see* Can. Français, 3486, Harrisse, *see* R. Soc. of Can., 3546, *see also* Eggleston, 2517; letters patent of Henry VII to, *see* Hakluyt, 716; voyages of, Dawson, 802, 3537, Deane, 803, d'Avezac, *see* Kohl, 820, Harvey, *see* N. S. Hist. Soc., 3511, v. 9, *see also* Old South Work, 368 (37), Bost. Pub. Lib., 712, Higginson, 721; Cabot's disc. of N. Am., Weare, 810; legends of, Ganong, *see* R. Soc. of Can., 3542; landfall and chart, O'Brien, *see* R. Soc. of Can., 3549; Cabotian disc., Thacher, *see* R. Soc. of Can., 3555; Cabot map, Dawson, *see* Archives, 3477, *see also* Mass. Hist. Soc., 343; crit. essay on John, Bellenio, *see* Raccolta colombiana, 699; Voyages of John, Markham, 788; Disc. of Am. by John, Harrisse, 805; John, discoverer of Am., Harrisse, 806; Memoir of Sebastian, Biddle, 801; life of Sebastian, Nichols, 808, Hayward, *see* Sparks, 2613, ser. 1, v. 9, *see also* Peschel, 730.

Cabot, J. E., Ralph W. Emerson, app., p. 469.

Cabrera, R., Cuba and the Cubans, 4100.

Cada Mosto, A. da, Navigatione, 697, *see also* Raccolta colombiana, 699, Kerr, 726, Henry, Prince, 743, 744.

Cadillac, Antoine de la Mothe, story of, centred in Mich., 3429; *see also* Sheldon, 1817, 3683 a, Margry, 3501.

Cahokia, life of habitans in. *See* Clark, 1269.

Cairnes, J. E., Slave power, 1852.

Calderon de la Barca, *Mme.*, F. E. I., Life in Mexico, 3935.

Caldwell, David, life, Caruthers, 2997.

Caldwell, *Maj.* H., Invasion of Canada, 1775. *See* Quebec Lit. and Hist. Soc., 3514 (6).

Caldwell, J. F. J., Hist. of a brigade of South Carolinians, 2129.

Caldwell, J. W., Studies in constitutional hist. of Tenn., 2705.